THE COMPLETE
MENTAL
HEALTH
RESOURCE GUIDE

THE COMPLETE
MENTAL
HEALTH
RESOURCE GUIDE

2022/2023
THIRTEENTH EDITION

GREY HOUSE PUBLISHING

PUBLISHER:	Leslie Mackenzie
EDITORIAL DIRECTOR:	Stuart Paterson
EDITORIAL ASSISTANTS:	Olivia Parsonson & Margarita Vachenkova
MARKETING DIRECTOR:	Jessica Moody

Grey House Publishing, Inc.
4919 Route 22
Amenia, NY 12501
518.789.8700
Fax: 518.789.0545
www.greyhouse.com
books@greyhouse.com

Publisher's Cataloging-In-Publication Data
(Prepared by The Donohue Group, Inc.)

Names: Gottlieb, Richard (Richard Harris), editor. | Grey House Publishing, Inc., publisher.
Title: The complete mental health resource guide : a comprehensive source book for professionals and
    individuals / [editor: Richard Gottlieb].
Description: Amenia, NY : Grey House Publishing, 2018- | "A Sedgwick Press Book." | Includes indexes.
Subjects: LCSH: Mental health services--United States--Directories. | LCGFT: Directories.
Classification: LCC RA790.6 .C625 | DDC 362.20973--dc23

ISBN: 978-1-63700-144-8

Table of Contents

SECTION ONE: Disorders

Each chapter includes detailed description and the following categories as available:
Associations & Agencies; Periodicals & Pamphlets; Research Centers;
Support Groups & Hot Lines; Video & Audio; Web Sites.

SECTION TWO: Associations & Organizations

SECTION THREE: Government Agencies

SECTION FOUR: Professional & Support Services

Introduction

This thirteenth edition of *The Complete Mental Health Resource Guide* provides comprehensive coverage of 22 major mental health disorder categories, from ADHD to Trauma and Stressor-Related Disorders, with over 100 subcategories and specific disorders.

The major categories are organized to reflect current scholarship and changes regarding mental health, including:

- Separate entries for Bipolar and Related Disorders; Depressive Disorders; Obsessive Compulsive Disorders; and Trauma and Stressor-Related Disorders;

- Updated names for Neurocognitive Disorders; Neurodevelopmental Disorders; Feeding and Eating Disorders; Sleep-Wake Disorders and Disruptive, Impulse-Control and Conduct Disorders;

- Incorporating Paraphilias into Sexual Disorders.

All chapter introductions have also been reviewed for accuracy and currency.

A repeat winner of the *National Health Information Awards* by the Health Information Resource Center, *The Complete Mental Health Resource Guide* provides relevant, useful information or patients and their support network.

Praise for previous edition:

> *"... useful to libraries providing consumer health information and [to] medical libraries...valuable to professionals and patients..."*
>
> Cheryl A. Capitani, Chief Librarian, Harrisburg Hospital

> *"...the introductory essay's...thoughtful...comments...open many topics to discussion and searches for further information. Recommended. All levels."*
>
> Choice Magazine

> *"...array of materials...helpful addition to public, academic, medical libraries."*
>
> 4-Star, Doody's Review Service

Front Matter

This edition includes the following expanded front matter:

- The State of Mental Health in America 2022 is a colorful, 36-page report that combines narrative and charts, including many topics that are compared by states;

- State Legislation Report: Trends in State Mental Health Policy is a 64-page report by the National Alliance on Mental Illness (NAMI), examining the latest state-level policies affecting mental health;

- Navigating a Mental Health Crisis is a 31-page resource prepared by NAMI, for individuals experiencing a mental health emergency;

- A number of single-page info-graphics from NAMI with content on warning signs of mental illness, why your mental health matters, and ripple effects of mental health;

- Emergent Crisis of COVID-19 Pandemic: Mental Health Challenges and Opportunities is a scholarly, yet accessible, article on the pandemic's negative impact on the economy and mental health worldwide;

- Mental Disorders by Diagnostic Category educates patient and professional about categorical diagnoses, symptoms and treatments

Content

The Complete Mental Health Resource Guide has been streamlined to include nearly 3,000 crucial listings, and continues to cover more than 100 disorder categories. Chapters include clear, concise descriptions of current diagnoses and treatment methods, and a variety of disorder-specific resources, including Associations, Periodicals, Research Centers, and Support Groups, Professional Services, Publishers, Facilities, Clinical Management and Pharmaceutical Companies.

Section One: Disorders

This section consists of 22 chapters dealing with broad categories of mental health issues from Adjustment Disorders to Trauma and Stressor-Related Disorders. Each chapter begins with a description, written in clear, accessible language and includes symptoms, prevalence and treatment options.

These descriptions include information on specific syndromes within a general category, such as Agoraphobia, Social Anxiety, Selective Mutism and Separation Anxiety within the Anxiety Disorders chapter, and Delirium, Dementia and Anmestic Disorders within the Neurocognitive Disorders chapter.

Following the descriptions are specific resources relevant to the disorder, including Associations, Government Agencies, Periodicals, Support Groups, Hot Lines, Resource Centers, Audio & Video resources, and Web Sites.

Sections Two & Three: Associations, Organizations, Government Agencies

More than 1,000 National Associations, and Federal and State Agencies are profiled in these sections that offer general mental health services and support for patients and their families.

Section Four: Professional Support & Services

This section provides resources that support the many different professionals in the mental health field. Included are specific chapters on Accreditation and Quality Assurance, Associations, Conferences and Meetings, Periodicals, Training and Recruitment, Audio & Video resources, and Web Sites.

Section Five: Publishers

This section lists major publishers of books and magazines that focus on health care or mental health issues. This material is suitable for both professionals in the mental health industry as well as patients and their network community.

Section Six: Facilities

This section lists major facilities and hospitals, arranged by state, which provide treatment for persons with mental health disorders.

Section Seven: Clinical Management

Here you will find products and services that support the Clinical Management aspect of the mental health industry, including Directories and Databases, Management Companies, and Information Services, which provide patient and medical data, as well as marketing information.

Section Eight: Pharmaceutical Companies

This section offers current information on the pharmaceutical companies that manufacture drugs to treat mental health disorders. This data is presented alphabetically by company name, including address, phone, fax, and web site.

Three Indexes

- Disorder Index lists entries by disorders and disorder categories.

- Entry Index is an alphabetical list of all entries.

- Geographic Index lists entries by state.

- Drugs A-Z presents drugs used to treat mental health conditions alphabetically by brand name of drug, with its generic name, the disorder/s it is typically prescribed for, and its manufacturers.

For even easier access, *The Complete Mental Health Resource Guide* is available on our online database platform, http://gold.greyhouse.com. Subscribers have access to all of this health information, and can search by geographic area, disorder, contacts, keyword and so much more. With this online database, locating mental health resources has never been faster or easier.

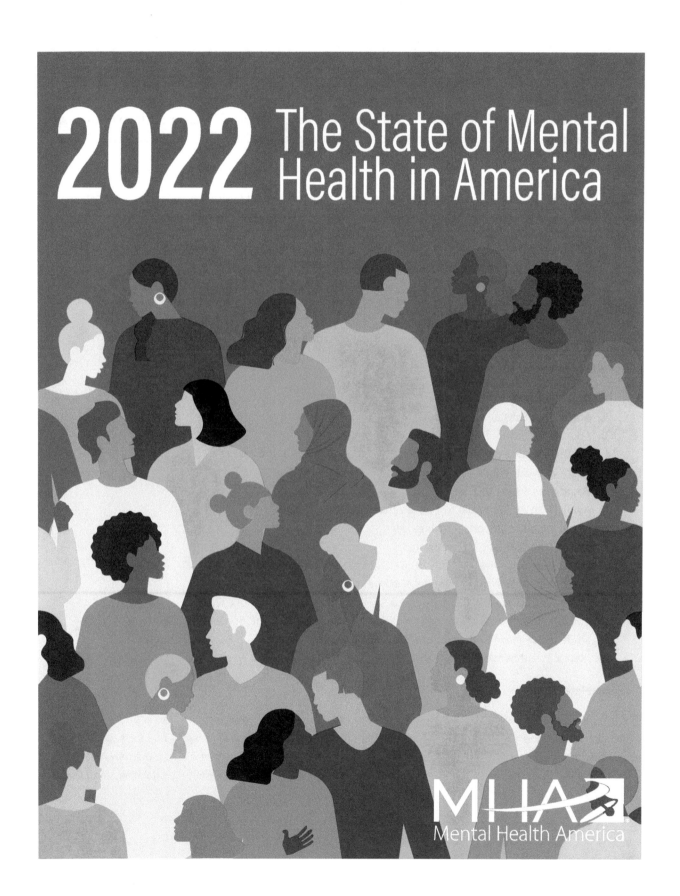

2022 The State of Mental Health in America

MHA
Mental Health America

Ranking Overview and Guidelines

This chart book presents a collection of data that provides a baseline for answering some questions about how many people in America need and have access to mental health services. This report is a companion to the online interactive data on the MHA website (https://www.mhanational.org/issues/state-mental-health-america). The data and tables include state and national data and sharable infographics.

MHA Guidelines

Given the variability of data, MHA developed guidelines to identify mental health measures that are most appropriate for inclusion in our ranking. Indicators were chosen that met the following guidelines:

- Data that are publicly available and as current as possible to provide up-to-date results.
- Data that are available for all 50 states and the District of Columbia.
- Data for both adults and youth.
- Data that captures information regardless of varying utilization of the private and public mental health system.
- Data that could be collected over time to allow for analysis of future changes and trends.

Our 2022 Measures

1. Adults With Any Mental Illness (AMI)
2. Adults With Substance Use Disorder in the Past Year
3. Adults With Serious Thoughts of Suicide
4. Youth With At Least One Major Depressive Episode (MDE) in the Past Year
5. Youth With Substance Use Disorder in the Past Year
6. Youth With Severe MDE
7. Adults With AMI Who Did Not Receive Treatment
8. Adults With AMI Reporting Unmet Need
9. Adults With AMI Who Are Uninsured
10. Adults With Cognitive Disability Who Could Not See a Doctor Due to Costs
11. Youth With MDE Who Did Not Receive Mental Health Services
12. Youth With Severe MDE Who Received Some Consistent Treatment
13. Children With Private Insurance That Did Not Cover Mental or Emotional Problems
14. Students Identified With Emotional Disturbance for an Individualized Education Program
15. Mental Health Workforce Availability

A Complete Picture

While the above 15 measures are not a complete picture of the mental health system, they do provide a strong foundation for understanding the prevalence of mental health concerns, as well as issues of access to insurance and treatment, particularly as that access varies among the states. MHA will continue to explore new measures that allow us to capture more accurately and comprehensively the needs of those with mental illness and their access to care.

Ranking

To better understand the rankings, it is important to compare similar states.

Factors to consider include geography and size. For example, California and New York are similar. Both are large states with densely populated cities. They are less comparable to less populous states like South Dakota, North Dakota, Alabama, or Wyoming. Keep in mind that the size of states and populations matter, both New York City and Los Angeles alone have more residents than North Dakota, South Dakota, Alabama, and Wyoming combined.

The rankings are based on the percentages, or rates, for each state collected from the most recently available data. For most indicators, the data represent data collected up to 2019. States with positive outcomes are ranked higher (closer to one) than states with poorer outcomes. The overall, adult, youth, prevalence, and access rankings were analyzed by calculating a standardized score (Z score) for each measure and ranking the sum of the standardized scores. For most measures, lower percentages equated to more positive outcomes (e.g., lower rates of substance use or those who are uninsured). There are two measures where high percentages equate to better outcomes. These include "Youth With Severe MDE (Major Depressive Episode) Who Received Some Consistent Treatment" and "Students Identified With Emotional Disturbance for an Individualized Education Program." Here, the calculated standardized score was multiplied by -1 to obtain a reverse Z score that was used in the sum. All measures were considered equally important, and no weights were given to any measure in the rankings.

Along with calculated rankings, each measure is ranked individually with an accompanying chart and table. The table provides the percentage and estimated population for each ranking. The estimated population number is weighted and calculated by the agency conducting the applicable federal survey. The ranking is based on the Z scores. Data are presented with two decimal places when available.

The measure "Adults With Disability Who Could Not See a Doctor Due to Costs" was previously calculated using the Behavioral Risk Factor Surveillance System (BRFSS) question: "Are you limited in any way in any activities because of physical, mental, or emotional problems?" (QLACTLM2). The QLACTLM2 question was removed from the BRFSS questionnaire after 2016, and therefore could not be calculated using 2019 BRFSS data. For this report, the indicator was amended to "Adults With Cognitive Disability Who Could Not See a Doctor Due to Costs," using the BRFSS question: "Because of a physical, mental, or emotional condition, do you have serious difficulty concentrating, remembering, or making decisions?" (DECIDE). This indicator likely serves as a better measure for individuals who experience disability tied to mental, cognitive, or emotional problems, as it is less likely to include people who experience limitations due to a physical disability and is therefore a more sensitive measure for the population we are attempting to count.

For the measure "Students Identified With Emotional Disturbance for an Individualized Education Program," due to data suppression because of quality, the 2016-2019 figures for Wisconsin were not available. This report notes the 2015 figure for Wisconsin. The 2019 figure for Iowa was also not available because Iowa no longer captures disability category data, and therefore the number of students identified with emotional disturbance could not be determined. This report notes the 2018 figure for Iowa.

Survey Limitations

Each survey has its own strengths and limitations. For example, strengths of both SAMHSA's *National Survey of Drug Use and Health* (NSDUH) and the CDC's *Behavioral Risk Factor Surveillance System* (BRFSS) are that they include national survey data with large sample sizes and utilize statistical modeling to provide weighted estimates of each state population. This means that the data is more representative of the general population. An example limitation of particular importance to the mental health community is that the NSDUH does not collect information from persons who are experiencing homelessness and who do not stay at shelters, are active-duty military personnel, or are institutionalized (i.e., in jails or hospitals). This limitation means that those individuals who have a mental illness who are also experiencing homelessness or are incarcerated are not represented in the data presented by the NSDUH. If the data did include individuals who were experiencing homelessness and/or incarcerated, we would possibly see prevalence of behavioral health issues increase and access to treatment rates worsen. It is MHA's goal to continue to search for the best possible data in future reports. Additional information on the methodology and limitations of the surveys can be found online as outlined in the glossary.

In addition, these data were gathered through 2019. This means that they are the most current data reported by the states and available to the public. They are most useful in providing some comparative baselines in the states for the needs and systems that were in place prior to the COVID-19 pandemic, as data reflective of the COVID-19 pandemic will not be made available until next year. MHA regularly reports on its real-time data gathered from more than 11 million completed mental health screenings (through September 2021). Based on these screening results from a help-seeking population, and both U.S. Census Bureau 2020-2021 Pulse Survey data, which included brief depression and anxiety screening questions, and survey data reported by the Centers for Disease Control and Prevention (CDC), it appears that (1) the data in this report likely under-reports the current prevalence of mental illnesses in the population, both among children and adults, (2) higher-ranked states may have been better prepared to deal with the mental health effects of the pandemic at its start, and (3) because of its nationwide effect, nothing in the pandemic by itself would suggest that the relative rankings of the states would have changed solely because of the pandemic.

Spotlight 2022

The two spotlights within this report provide a deeper dive into two of Mental Health America's policy priorities in 2021-2022: suicide prevention and access to crisis care and prevention and early intervention for children, youth, and young adults. The first spotlight, "Suicidal Ideation and 988 Implementation," discusses the need for states to pass legislation to support a continuum of crisis services. With the passage of the new 988 number for suicide prevention and mental health crises, there is an opportunity to create a continuum of crisis care with adequate funding that ensures mental health responses to mental health crises and prioritizes equity, particularly for BIPOC individuals. The second spotlight, "Disparities in Mental Health Treatment for Youth of Color," examines data from SAMHSA's 2018-2019 National Survey on Drug Use and Health (NSDUH), to examine disparities in the kinds of care youth with depression are able to receive and where they receive it. Students of color disproportionally access their mental health care at school, often because they don't have access to specialty mental health services. Given this data, increasing access to school-based mental health services can promote equity and reduce disparities in access to care.

NEARLY 50 M OR 19.86% OF AMERICAN ADULTS EXPERIENCED A MENTAL ILLNESS IN 2019.

4.58% OF ADULTS REPORT HAVING SERIOUS THOUGHTS OF SUICIDE. THIS HAS INCREASED EVERY YEAR SINCE 2011-2012.

15.08% OF YOUTH EXPERIENCED A MAJOR DEPRESSIVE EPISODE IN THE PAST YEAR.

24.7% OF ADULTS WITH A MENTAL ILLNESS REPORT AN UNMET NEED FOR TREATMENT. THIS NUMBER HAS NOT DECLINED SINCE 2011.

OVER **60%** OF YOUTH WITH MAJOR DEPRESSION DO NOT RECEIVE ANY MENTAL HEALTH TREATMENT. EVEN IN STATES WITH THE GREATEST ACCESS, NEARLY **1 IN 3** ARE GOING WITHOUT TREATMENT.

MORE THAN HALF OF ADULTS WITH A MENTAL ILLNESS DO NOT RECEIVE TREATMENT, TOTALING OVER 27 MILLION U.S. ADULTS.

10.6% OR OVER 2.5 MILLION YOUTH IN THE U.S. HAVE SEVERE MAJOR DEPRESSION. THIS RATE WAS HIGHEST AMONG YOUTH WHO IDENTIFY AS MORE THAN ONE RACE, AT **14.5%**

EVEN AMONG YOUTH WITH SEVERE DEPRESSION WHO RECEIVE SOME TREATMENT, ONLY **27%** RECEIVE CONSISTENT CARE. IN STATES WITH THE LEAST ACCESS, ONLY **12%** RECEIVE CONSISTENT CARE.

11.1% OF AMERICANS WITH A MENTAL ILLNESS ARE UNINSURED, THE SECOND YEAR IN A ROW THAT THIS INDICATOR INCREASED SINCE THE PASSAGE OF THE AFFORDABLE CARE ACT (ACA).

8.1% OF CHILDREN HAD PRIVATE INSURANCE THAT DID NOT COVER MENTAL HEALTH SERVICES, TOTALING 950,000 YOUTH.

Overall Ranking

An overall ranking 1-13 indicates lower prevalence of mental illness and higher rates of access to care. An overall ranking 39-51 indicates higher prevalence of mental illness and lower rates of access to care. The combined scores of all 15 measures make up the overall ranking. The overall ranking includes both adult and youth measures as well as prevalence and access to care measures.

The 15 measures that make up the overall ranking include:

1. Adults With Any Mental Illness (AMI)
2. Adults With Substance Use Disorder in the Past Year
3. Adults With Serious Thoughts of Suicide
4. Youth with At Least One Major Depressive Episode (MDE) in the Past Year
5. Youth With Substance Use Disorder in the Past Year
6. Youth With Severe MDE
7. Adults With AMI Who Did Not Receive Treatment
8. Adults With AMI Reporting Unmet Need
9. Adults With AMI Who Are Uninsured
10. Adults With Cognitive Disability Who Could Not See a Doctor Due to Costs
11. Youth With MDE Who Did Not Receive Mental Health Services
12. Youth With Severe MDE Who Received Some Consistent Treatment
13. Children With Private Insurance That Did Not Cover Mental or Emotional Problems
14. Students Identified With Emotional Disturbance for an Individualized Education Program
15. Mental Health Workforce Availability

The chart is a visual representation of the sum of the scores for each state. It provides an opportunity to see the difference between ranked states. For example, Massachusetts (ranked one) has a score that is higher than Illinois (ranked 12). Virginia (ranked 20) has a score that is closest to the average.

State	Rank
Massachusetts	1
New Jersey	2
Pennsylvania	3
Connecticut	4
Vermont	5
New York	6
Wisconsin	7
Maine	8
Maryland	9
Minnesota	10
Rhode Island	11
Illinois	12
New Hampshire	13
Hawaii	14
Kentucky	15
District of Columbia	16
South Dakota	17
Michigan	18
Louisiana	19
Virginia	20
Montana	21
Delaware	22
Iowa	23
California	24
Ohio	25
Nebraska	26
Georgia	27
Florida	28
North Dakota	29
South Carolina	30
North Carolina	31
Washington	32
Oklahoma	33
Tennessee	34
New Mexico	35
Mississippi	36
Colorado	37
West Virginia	38
Arkansas	39
Missouri	40
Kansas	41
Indiana	42
Utah	43
Texas	44
Alabama	45
Oregon	46
Alaska	47
Wyoming	48
Arizona	49
Idaho	50
Nevada	51

15.00   10.00   5.00   0.00   -5.00   -10.00

Largest Changes in Overall Ranking

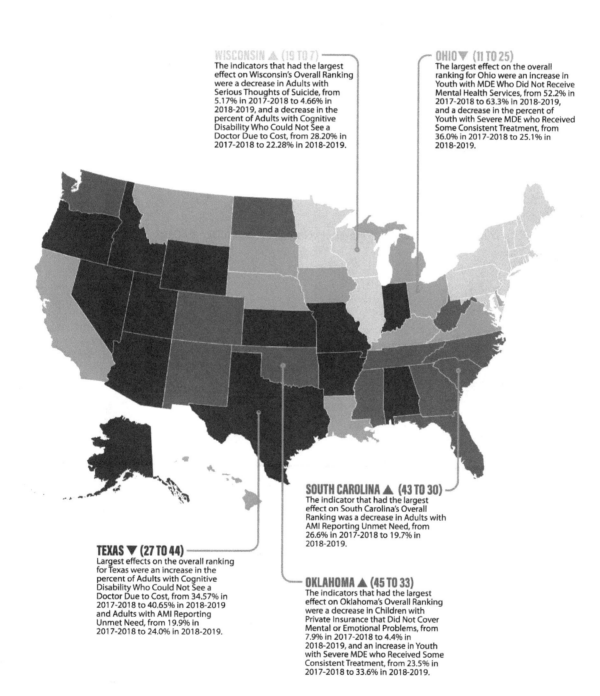

WISCONSIN ▲ (19 TO 7)
The indicators that had the largest effect on Wisconsin's Overall Ranking were a decrease in Adults with Serious Thoughts of Suicide, from 5.17% in 2017-2018 to 4.66% in 2018-2019, and a decrease in the percent of Adults with Cognitive Disability Who Could Not See a Doctor Due to Cost, from 28.20% in 2017-2018 to 22.28% in 2018-2019.

OHIO ▼ (11 TO 25)
The largest effect on the overall ranking for Ohio were an increase in Youth with MDE Who Did Not Receive Mental Health Services, from 52.2% in 2017-2018 to 63.3% in 2018-2019, and a decrease in the percent of Youth with Severe MDE who Received Some Consistent Treatment, from 36.0% in 2017-2018 to 25.1% in 2018-2019.

SOUTH CAROLINA ▲ (43 TO 30)
The indicator that had the largest effect on South Carolina's Overall Ranking was a decrease in Adults with AMI Reporting Unmet Need, from 26.6% in 2017-2018 to 19.7% in 2018-2019.

TEXAS ▼ (27 TO 44)
Largest effects on the overall ranking for Texas were an increase in the percent of Adults with Cognitive Disability Who Could Not See a Doctor Due to Cost, from 34.57% in 2017-2018 to 40.65% in 2018-2019 and Adults with AMI Reporting Unmet Need, from 19.9% in 2017-2018 to 24.0% in 2018-2019.

OKLAHOMA ▲ (45 TO 33)
The indicators that had the largest effect on Oklahoma's Overall Ranking were a decrease in Children with Private Insurance that Did Not Cover Mental or Emotional Problems, from 7.9% in 2017-2018 to 4.4% in 2018-2019, and an increase in Youth with Severe MDE who Received Some Consistent Treatment, from 23.5% in 2017-2018 to 33.6% in 2018-2019.

Adult Rankings

States that are ranked 1-13 have a lower prevalence of mental illness and higher rates of access to care for adults. States that are ranked 39-51 indicate that adults have a higher prevalence of mental illness and lower rates of access to care.

The seven measures that make up the Adult Ranking include:

1. Adults With Any Mental Illness (AMI)
2. Adults With Substance Use Disorder in the Past Year
3. Adults With Serious Thoughts of Suicide
4. Adults With AMI Who Did Not Receive Treatment
5. Adults With AMI Reporting Unmet Need
6. Adults With AMI Who Are Uninsured
7. Adults With Cognitive Disability Who Could Not See a Doctor Due to Costs

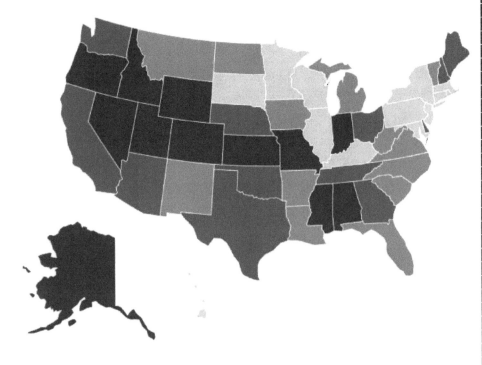

Rank	State
1	New Jersey
2	Wisconsin
3	Massachusetts
4	Connecticut
5	New York
6	Minnesota
7	Hawaii
8	Pennsylvania
9	Maryland
10	Illinois
11	Rhode Island
12	South Dakota
13	Kentucky
14	Iowa
15	New Mexico
16	Arkansas
17	Montana
18	Michigan
19	Vermont
20	Virginia
21	North Carolina
22	South Carolina
23	West Virginia
24	North Dakota
25	Florida
26	Louisiana
27	Nebraska
28	California
29	Tennessee
30	New Hampshire
31	Georgia
32	Washington
33	Texas
34	Delaware
35	Arizona
36	Ohio
37	Maine
38	Oklahoma
39	Idaho
40	Nevada
41	Mississippi
42	Kansas
43	Indiana
44	Missouri
45	District of Columbia
46	Alaska
47	Alabama
48	Utah
49	Oregon
50	Wyoming
51	Colorado

Youth Rankings

States with rankings 1-13 have a lower prevalence of mental illness and higher rates of access to care for youth. States with rankings 39-51 indicate that youth have a higher prevalence of mental illness and lower rates of access to care.

The seven measures that make up the Youth Ranking include:

1. Youth With At Least One Major Depressive Episode (MDE) in the Past Year
2. Youth With Substance Use Disorder in the Past Year
3. Youth With Severe MDE
4. Youth With MDE Who Did Not Receive Mental Health Services
5. Youth With Severe MDE Who Received Some Consistent Treatment
6. Children With Private Insurance That Did Not Cover Mental or Emotional Problems
7. Students Identified With Emotional Disturbance for an Individualized Education Program

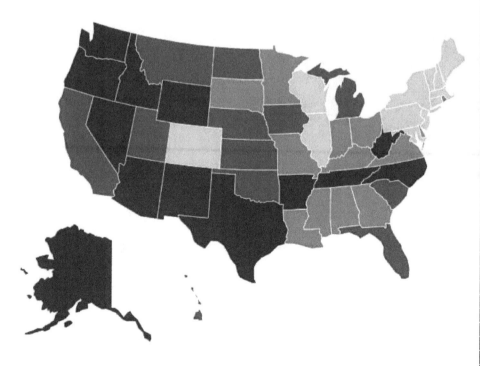

Rank	State
1	Pennsylvania
2	Maine
3	District of Columbia
4	Vermont
5	Massachusetts
6	New Hampshire
7	New Jersey
8	Connecticut
9	New York
10	Maryland
11	Wisconsin
12	Illinois
13	Colorado
14	Minnesota
15	Rhode Island
16	Mississippi
17	Georgia
18	Delaware
19	Ohio
20	Alabama
21	Virginia
22	Missouri
23	South Dakota
24	Kentucky
25	Louisiana
26	Indiana
27	Michigan
28	Oklahoma
29	Hawaii
30	Florida
31	Iowa
32	Utah
33	Kansas
34	North Dakota
35	South Carolina
36	California
37	Nebraska
38	Montana
39	Washington
40	Tennessee
41	Texas
42	North Carolina
43	Wyoming
44	West Virginia
45	Oregon
46	Alaska
47	New Mexico
48	Arkansas
49	Arizona
50	Idaho
51	Nevada

Prevalence of Mental Illness

The scores for the six prevalence measures make up the Prevalence Ranking.

The six measures that make up the Prevalence Ranking include:

1. Adults With Any Mental Illness (AMI)
2. Adult With Substance Use Disorder in the Past Year
3. Adults With Serious Thoughts of Suicide
4. Youth With At Least One Major Depressive Episode (MDE) in the Past Year
5. Youth With Substance Use Disorder in the Past Year
6. Youth With Severe MDE

A ranking of 1-13 for Prevalence indicates a lower prevalence of mental health and substance use issues compared to states that ranked 39-51.

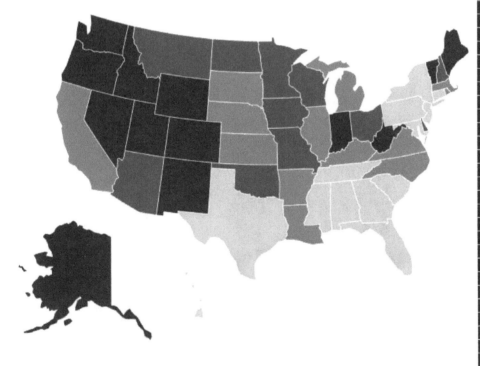

Rank	State
1	New Jersey
2	Florida
3	Georgia
4	Texas
5	New York
6	Pennsylvania
7	Mississippi
8	Hawaii
9	Connecticut
10	South Carolina
11	Maryland
12	Alabama
13	Tennessee
14	Louisiana
15	Virginia
16	Illinois
17	North Carolina
18	South Dakota
19	Kentucky
20	California
21	Michigan
22	Nebraska
23	Rhode Island
24	Kansas
25	Arkansas
26	Massachusetts
27	Minnesota
28	Missouri
29	Wisconsin
30	District of Columbia
31	New Hampshire
32	Arizona
33	North Dakota
34	Ohio
35	Delaware
36	Iowa
37	Oklahoma
38	Montana
39	West Virginia
40	Maine
41	Idaho
42	Indiana
43	New Mexico
44	Washington
45	Colorado
46	Nevada
47	Utah
48	Wyoming
49	Alaska
50	Vermont
51	Oregon

Access to Care Rankings

The Access Ranking indicates how much access to mental health care exists within a state. The access measures include access to insurance, access to treatment, quality and cost of insurance, access to special education, and mental health workforce availability. A high Access Ranking (1-13) indicates that a state provides relatively more access to insurance and mental health treatment.

The nine measures that make up the Access Ranking include:

1. Adults With AMI Who Did Not Receive Treatment
2. Adults With AMI Reporting Unmet Need
3. Adults With AMI Who Are Uninsured
4. Adults With Cognitive Disability Who Could Not See a Doctor Due to Costs
5. Youth With MDE Who Did Not Receive Mental Health Services
6. Youth With Severe MDE who Received Some Consistent Treatment
7. Children with Private Insurance that Did Not Cover Mental or Emotional Problems
8. Students Identified with Emotional Disturbance for an Individualized Education Program
9. Mental Health Workforce Availability

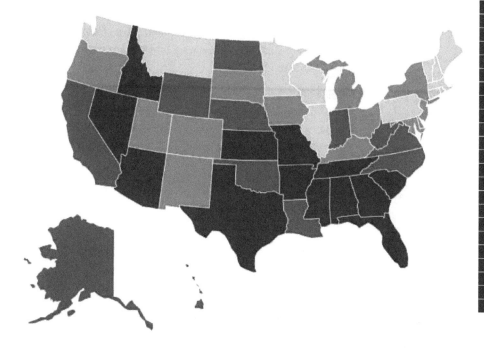

Rank	State
1	Vermont
2	Massachusetts
3	Maine
4	Wisconsin
5	Minnesota
6	New Hampshire
7	Rhode Island
8	Pennsylvania
9	Connecticut
10	District of Columbia
11	Washington
12	Montana
13	Illinois
14	Maryland
15	New York
16	Kentucky
17	Delaware
18	Iowa
19	Oregon
20	New Mexico
21	Colorado
22	Ohio
23	South Dakota
24	New Jersey
25	Michigan
26	Utah
27	North Dakota
28	Oklahoma
29	West Virginia
30	California
31	Hawaii
32	Indiana
33	Nebraska
34	Alaska
35	Louisiana
36	Wyoming
37	Virginia
38	North Carolina
39	Nevada
40	Arkansas
41	Missouri
42	Idaho
43	South Carolina
44	Kansas
45	Tennessee
46	Arizona
47	Mississippi
48	Georgia
49	Florida
50	Alabama
51	Texas

Largest Changes in Adult Rankings: State of Mental Health in America 2021-2022

Largest Improvements in Ranking:

Wisconsin (24 to 2): In Wisconsin, the percentage of Adults With Serious Thoughts of Suicide decreased from 5.17% in 2017-2018 to 4.66% in 2018-2019.

Montana (34 to 17): Montana's percentage of Adults With Serious Thoughts of Suicide decreased from 5.21% in 2017-2018 to 4.63% in 2018-2019, and the percentage of Adults With AMI Reporting Unmet Need decreased from 24.6% in 2017-2018 to 21.5% in 2018-2019.

Rhode Island (26 to 11): In Rhode Island, the percentage of Adults With Cognitive Disability Who Could Not See a Doctor Due to Cost decreased from 25.71% in 2017-2018 to 18.48% in 2018-2019, and the percentage of Adults With AMI Reporting Unmet Need decreased from 27.9% in 2017-2018 to 25.4% in 2018-2019.

Largest Declines in Ranking:

Ohio (14 to 36): In Ohio, the percentage of Adults With Serious Thoughts of Suicide increased from 5.18% in 2017-2018 to 6.09% in 2018-2019.

Delaware (13 to 34): Delaware's rate of Adults With AMI Who Did Not Receive Treatment increased from 49.7% in 2017-2018 to 54.2% in 2018-2019 and the rate of Adults With AMI Reporting Unmet Need increased from 23.0% in 2017-2018 to 28.1% in 2018-2019.

Arizona (17 to 35): In Arizona, the percentage of Adults With AMI Who Did Not Receive Treatment increased from 52.7% in 2017-2018 to 57.0% in 2018-2019.

Texas (15 to 33): Texas' percentage of Adults With Cognitive Disability Who Could Not See a Doctor Due to Cost increased from 34.57% in 2017-2018 to 40.65% in 2018-2019, a reversal from the improvement in last year's report.

Largest Changes in Youth Rankings: State of Mental Health in America 2021-2022

Largest Improvements in Ranking:

Colorado (42 to 13): Colorado's percentage of Youth With Past Year MDE Who Did Not Receive Treatment decreased from 60.4% in 2017-2018 to 39.3% in 2018-2019.

Illinois (36 to 12): In Illinois, the percentage of Youth With Severe MDE Who Received Some Consistent Treatment increased from 25.0% in 2017-2018 to 38.3% in 2018-2019.

Oklahoma (46 to 28): Oklahoma had an increase in insurance coverage and access to care for youth. The percentage of Children With Private Insurance That Did Not Cover Mental or Emotional Problems decreased in Oklahoma from 7.9% in 2017-2018 to 4.4% in 2018-2019, and the percentage of Youth With Severe MDE Who Received Some Consistent Treatment increased from 23.5% in 2017-2018 to 33.6% in 2018-2019.

Largest Declines in Ranking:

Nebraska (21 to 37): In Nebraska, the percentage of Youth With Severe MDE increased from 9.0% in 2017-2018 to 12.4% in 2018-2019 and the percentage of Youth With Severe MDE Who Received Some Consistent Treatment decreased from 35.9% in 2017-2018 to 27.8% in 2018-2019.

Texas (30 to 41): Texas' percentage of Children With Private Insurance That Did Not Cover Mental or Emotional Problems increased from 11.5% in 2017-2018 to 13.8% in 2018-2019.

Delaware (8 to 18): In Delaware, the percentage of Youth With Severe MDE increased from 9.3% in 2017-2018 to 12.8% in 2018-2019.

South Dakota (13 to 23): South Dakota's percentage of Youth With Severe MDE increased from 8.0% in 2017-2018 to 12.0% in 2018-2019 and the percentage of Youth With Past Year MDE Who Did Not Receive Treatment increased from 49.7% in 2017-2018 to 59.6% in 2018-2019.

Largest Changes in Need/Prevalence Rankings: State of Mental Health in America 2021-2022

Largest Improvements in Ranking:

Connecticut (20 to 9): Connecticut's percentage of Youth With Severe MDE decreased from 9.0% in 2017-2018 to 7.8% in 2018-2019.

Wisconsin (39 to 29): In Wisconsin, the percentage of Adults With Serious Thoughts of Suicide decreased from 5.17% in 2017-2018 to 4.66% in 2018-2019.

Idaho (49 to 41): In Idaho, the percentage of Adults With Any Mental Illness decreased from 24.46% in 2017-2018 to 22.48% in 2018-2019, and the percentage of Adults With Serious Thoughts of Suicide decreased from 5.45% in 2017-2018 to 5.30% in 2018-2019.

Largest Declines in Ranking:

Wyoming (35 to 48): In Wyoming, the percentage of Adults With Serious Thoughts of Suicide increased from 5.04% in 2017-2018 to 5.74% in 2018-2019 and the percentage of Youth With Past Year MDE increased from 14.91% in 2017-2018 to 17.59% in 2018-2019.

Minnesota (16 to 27): Minnesota's percentage of Youth With Substance Use Disorder in the Past Year increased from 3.86% in 2017-2018 to 4.62% in 2018-2019.

Delaware (25 to 35): In Delaware, the percentage of Youth With Severe MDE increased from 9.3% in 2017-2018 to 12.8% in 2018-2019.

Nebraska (13 to 22): In Nebraska, the percentage of Youth With Severe MDE increased from 9.0% in 2017-2018 to 12.4% in 2018-2019.

Largest Changes in Access to Care Rankings: State of Mental Health in America 2021-2022

Largest Improvements in Ranking:

Illinois (28 to 13): Illinois' largest improvements in Access to Care were for youth. In Illinois, the percentage of Youth With Severe MDE Who Received Some Consistent Treatment increased from 25.0% in 2017-2018 to 38.3% in 2018-2019 and the percentage of Youth With MDE Who Did Not Receive Mental Health Services decreased from 62.1% in 2017-2018 to 55.2% in 2018-2019.

Colorado (31 to 21): In Colorado, the largest effects on the Access to Care Ranking were also for youth. The percentage of Youth With Past Year MDE Who Did Not Receive Treatment decreased from 60.4% in 2017-2018 to 39.3% in 2018-2019 and the percentage of Youth With Severe MDE Who Received Some Consistent Treatment increased from 21.5% in 2017-2018 to 43.1% in 2018-2019.

Nevada (46 to 39): In Nevada, the percentage of Children With Private Insurance That Did Not Cover Mental or Emotional Problems decreased from 12.6% in 2017-2018 to 7.1% in 2018-2019.

Largest Declines in Ranking:

Hawaii (14 to 31): In Hawaii, the percentage of Youth With MDE Who Did Not Receive Mental Health Services increased from 56.2% in 2017-2018 to 71.0% in 2018-2019 and the percentage of Youth With Severe MDE Who Received Some Consistent Treatment decreased from 28.3% in 2017-2018 to 13.3% in 2018-2019.

Ohio (9 to 22): Ohio's percentage of Youth With MDE Who Did Not Receive Mental Health Services increased from 52.2% in 2017-2018 to 63.3% in 2018-2019.

Delaware (5 to 17): In Delaware, the percentage of Adults With AMI Who Did Not Receive Treatment increased from 49.7% in 2017-2018 to 54.2% in 2018-2019.

Changes in Overall Ranking: State of Mental Health in America 2021-2022

State	Overall Ranking (2021)*	Overall Ranking (2022)*
Alabama	36	45
Alaska	49	47
Arizona	40	49
Arkansas	42	39
California	25	24
Colorado	47	37
Connecticut	13	4
Delaware	10	22
District of Columbia	9	16
Florida	35	28
Georgia	37	27
Hawaii	8	14
Idaho	50	50
Illinois	22	12
Indiana	33	42
Iowa	23	23
Kansas	29	41
Kentucky	17	15
Louisiana	21	19
Maine	14	8
Maryland	4	9
Massachusetts	3	1
Michigan	15	18
Minnesota	7	10
Mississippi	32	36
Missouri	38	40

State	Overall Ranking (2021)*	Overall Ranking (2022)*
Montana	30	21
Nebraska	20	26
Nevada	51	51
New Hampshire	18	13
New Jersey	5	2
New Mexico	34	35
New York	6	6
North Carolina	41	31
North Dakota	24	29
Ohio	11	25
Oklahoma	45	33
Oregon	48	46
Pennsylvania	2	3
Rhode Island	12	11
South Carolina	43	30
South Dakota	16	17
Tennessee	28	34
Texas	27	44
Utah	46	43
Vermont	1	5
Virginia	26	20
Washington	31	32
West Virginia	39	38
Wisconsin	19	7
Wyoming	44	48

■ **Ranking Worsened**　　■ **Ranking Remained the Same**　　■ **Ranking Improved**

*2021 Overall Ranking is taken from The State of Mental Health in America 2021 Report, based on data from 2017-2018. 2022 Overall Ranking is taken from this report, based on data from 2018-2019.

Adult Prevalence of Mental Illness
Adults With Any Mental Illness (AMI)

19.86% of adults are experiencing a mental illness.

Equivalent to nearly 50 million Americans.

4.91% are experiencing a *severe* mental illness.

The states with the largest increases in Adults With Any Mental Illness (AMI) were Ohio (2.24%), Nebraska (2.22%), Wyoming (2.22%), and Oklahoma (2.11%).

The state prevalence of adult mental illness ranges from:

16.37% (NJ)
Ranked 1-13

26.86 % (UT)
Ranked 39-51

Rank	State	%	#
1	New Jersey	16.37	1,122,000
2	Texas	17.17	3,602,000
3	Florida	17.23	2,903,000
4	Hawaii	17.45	185,000
5	Maryland	17.57	810,000
6	Georgia	17.88	1,406,000
7	South Dakota	18.26	118,000
8	Iowa	18.50	441,000
9	Virginia	18.58	1,199,000
10	Connecticut	18.85	526,000
11	Illinois	19.18	1,858,000
12	North Carolina	19.31	1,532,000
13	Tennessee	19.40	1,006,000
14	South Carolina	19.43	760,000
15	California	19.49	5,864,000
16	New York	19.52	2,972,000
17	Pennsylvania	19.70	1,963,000
18	Arizona	20.06	1,099,000
19	Mississippi	20.16	446,000
20	Wisconsin	20.19	904,000
21	Nebraska	20.30	290,000
22	Michigan	20.32	1,571,000
23	Arkansas	20.34	460,000
24	North Dakota	20.50	116,000
25	Minnesota	20.53	876,000
26	Kansas	20.56	442,000
27	Montana	20.81	171,000
28	Delaware	20.92	157,000
29	Massachusetts	21.15	1,157,000
30	Louisiana	21.21	734,000
31	Alabama	21.29	794,000
32	New Mexico	21.39	338,000
33	Alaska	21.47	113,000
34	Nevada	21.97	512,000
35	Maine	22.10	238,000
36	Vermont	22.25	112,000
37	Indiana	22.29	1,125,000
38	New Hampshire	22.37	243,000
39	Rhode Island	22.38	187,000
40	Idaho	22.48	293,000
41	Oklahoma	22.54	657,000
42	Kentucky	22.54	762,000
43	Wyoming	22.56	98,000
44	Missouri	22.71	1,056,000
45	District of Columbia	22.83	129,000
46	Colorado	23.20	1,014,000
47	Washington	23.43	1,360,000
48	Ohio	23.64	2,112,000
49	Oregon	23.75	783,000
50	West Virginia	24.62	347,000
51	Utah	26.86	599,000
	National	19.86	49,564,000

According to SAMHSA, "Any Mental Illness (AMI) is defined as having a diagnosable mental, behavioral, or emotional disorder, other than a developmental or substance use disorder, assessed by the Mental Health Surveillance Study (MHSS) Structured Clinical Interview for the Diagnostic and Statistical Manual of Mental Disorders—Fourth Edition—Research Version—Axis I Disorders (MHSS-SCID), which is based on the 4th edition of the Diagnostic and Statistical Manual of Mental Disorders (DSM-IV)."

Adults With Substance Use Disorder in the Past Year

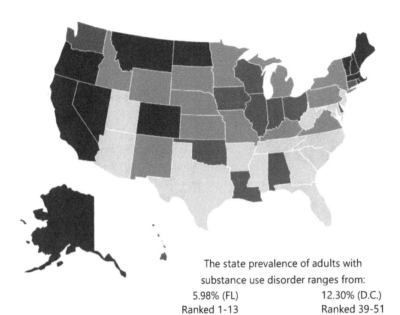

7.74% of adults in America reported having a substance use disorder in the past year.

2.97% of adults in America had an illicit drug use disorder in the past year.

5.71% of adults in America had an alcohol use disorder in the past year.

The largest increases in the prevalence of adults with substance use disorder were in Hawaii (1.32%) and California (1.11%). The largest decreases were in South Dakota (1.48%) and Iowa (1.08%).

The state prevalence of adults with substance use disorder ranges from:

5.98% (FL)   12.30% (D.C.)
Ranked 1-13   Ranked 39-51

Rank	State	%	#
1	Florida	5.98	1,007,000
2	West Virginia	6.29	89,000
3	Texas	6.48	1,360,000
4	Utah	6.56	146,000
5	Georgia	6.60	519,000
6	New Jersey	6.71	459,000
7	South Carolina	6.73	263,000
8	Maryland	7.01	323,000
9	Arizona	7.11	390,000
10	Mississippi	7.15	158,000
11	Arkansas	7.16	162,000
12	Tennessee	7.22	375,000
13	North Carolina	7.26	576,000
14	Kansas	7.29	157,000
15	Pennsylvania	7.31	728,000
16	Virginia	7.33	473,000
17	New York	7.43	1,131,000
18	Michigan	7.56	585,000
19	Minnesota	7.62	325,000
20	Idaho	7.67	100,000
21	South Dakota	7.69	50,000
22	New Mexico	7.70	122,000
23	Missouri	7.71	358,000
24	Nebraska	7.71	110,000
25	Wyoming	7.84	34,000
26	Kentucky	7.87	266,000

Rank	State	%	#
27	Alabama	7.89	294,000
28	Ohio	7.94	709,000
29	Wisconsin	7.98	358,000
30	Oklahoma	8.01	234,000
31	Illinois	8.02	777,000
32	Iowa	8.05	192,000
33	Louisiana	8.06	279,000
34	Indiana	8.42	425,000
35	Connecticut	8.43	235,000
36	Hawaii	8.45	90,000
37	Washington	8.62	500,000
38	Delaware	8.79	66,000
39	Massachusetts	8.83	483,000
40	New Hampshire	8.84	96,000
41	North Dakota	8.88	50,000
42	Maine	8.89	96,000
43	Rhode Island	8.95	75,000
44	California	9.23	2,778,000
45	Nevada	9.32	217,000
46	Oregon	9.78	322,000
47	Montana	10.04	83,000
48	Vermont	10.10	51,000
49	Alaska	10.23	54,000
50	Colorado	11.75	514,000
51	District of Columbia	12.30	70,000
	National	7.74	19,314,000

Adults With Serious Thoughts of Suicide

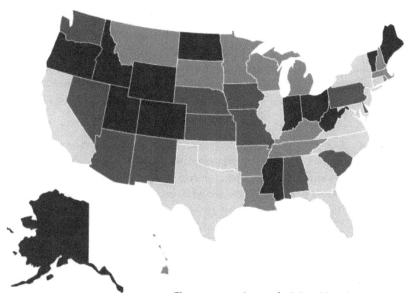

The percentage of adults reporting serious thoughts of suicide is 4.58%. The estimated number of adults with serious suicidal thoughts is over 11.4 million—**an increase of 664,000 people from last year's data set.**

The national rate of adults experiencing suicidal ideation has increased every year since 2011-2012.

States with the highest increases in suicidal ideation were Ohio (0.92%), Wyoming (0.70%), and Pennsylvania (0.66%).

Utah has had the highest rate of suicidal ideation among adults every year since 2012-2013.

The state prevalence of adults with serious thoughts of suicide ranges from:

3.79% (NJ)　　　　　6.19% (UT)
Ranked 1-13　　　　Ranked 39-51

Rank	State	%	#
1	New Jersey	3.79	260,000
2	Georgia	3.85	303,000
3	Texas	3.86	812,000
4	North Carolina	3.87	307,000
5	Illinois	4.00	388,000
6	Florida	4.04	682,000
7	New York	4.21	642,000
8	Virginia	4.22	272,000
9	Maryland	4.34	200,000
10	District of Columbia	4.43	25,000
11	Connecticut	4.46	125,000
12	California	4.55	1,370,000
13	Oklahoma	4.58	134,000
14	Rhode Island	4.59	38,000
15	Michigan	4.61	357,000
16	South Dakota	4.62	30,000
17	Montana	4.63	38,000
18	Wisconsin	4.66	209,000
19	Tennessee	4.68	243,000
20	Kentucky	4.68	158,000
21	New Hampshire	4.68	51,000
22	Arkansas	4.71	107,000
23	Louisiana	4.72	163,000
24	Minnesota	4.74	202,000
25	Hawaii	4.74	50,000
26	Massachusetts	4.77	261,000

Rank	State	%	#
27	New Mexico	4.81	76,000
28	Pennsylvania	4.83	482,000
29	Alabama	4.83	180,000
30	Nebraska	4.88	70,000
31	South Carolina	4.89	191,000
32	Washington	4.92	286,000
33	Iowa	4.94	118,000
34	Nevada	4.94	115,000
35	Kansas	4.96	107,000
36	Arizona	5.01	275,000
37	Missouri	5.05	235,000
38	Delaware	5.18	39,000
39	North Dakota	5.28	30,000
40	Idaho	5.30	69,000
41	Mississippi	5.31	118,000
42	West Virginia	5.44	77,000
43	Maine	5.44	59,000
44	Colorado	5.54	242,000
45	Indiana	5.62	284,000
46	Oregon	5.65	187,000
47	Vermont	5.66	29,000
48	Wyoming	5.74	25,000
49	Ohio	6.09	545,000
50	Alaska	6.11	32,000
51	Utah	6.19	138,000
	National	4.58	11,434,000

Spotlight: Suicidal Ideation and 988 Implementation

In July 2020, the Federal Communications Commission (FCC) designated 988 as the new three-digit number for the National Suicide Prevention Lifeline. This three-digit phone number was created to increase access to immediate crisis supports and provide a nationwide, easy-to-remember alternative to calling 911 for mental health crises. Traditionally, when an in-person crisis response was necessary, law enforcement was dispatched to provide support. Mental health crisis calls may result in potentially dangerous and traumatizing outcomes when police are called, especially in historically marginalized communities. According to a 2015 study, people with untreated mental illness are 16 times more likely to be killed in a police encounter than other civilians.[1] Implementing 988 ensures that mental health crises can be met with a mental health response while resulting in substantial cost-savings and allowing for law enforcement resources to be saved for non-mental health-related emergencies.

By July of 2022, all telecommunications companies will have to make the necessary changes so calls to 988 will be directed to the current National Suicide Prevention Lifeline call centers. However, full implementation of 988 requires each state to submit its own legislation to fund and implement 988 infrastructure. The current National Suicide Prevention Lifeline serves about 4 million callers each year. According to Vibrant Emotional Health, the administrator of the Lifeline, even in a low scenario with a minimal growth rate, it is estimated that 988 will be serving 13 million callers by the fifth year following implementation.[2] Additional resources for 988 are necessary to scale supports to meet that projected call volume with a reliable and timely response, as well as to develop a better system of crisis care. A comprehensive 988 crisis system necessitates: training call staff to provide empowering, linguistically, and culturally appropriate supports to callers, ensuring the inclusion of appropriate care for subpopulations like LGBTQ+ individuals, making appropriate and accessible referrals, creating a system of mobile crisis teams that can be deployed to respond to individuals in crisis in place of law enforcement, and offering crisis stabilization programs that connect people to a continuum of care when it is needed most.

In October 2020, Congress passed the National Suicide Hotline Designation Act, which allows states to administer small user fees to pay for: the efficient and effective routing of calls, personnel, and the provision of acute mental health crisis outreach and stabilization services. Each state must pass individual legislation to generate the funding necessary for 988 to be implemented effectively such that every call from a person in crisis can be answered and callers can be connected to appropriate and available mental health care when needed.

The designation of 988 as the new suicide prevention and mental health crisis hotline created an opportunity for an equitable health care response to mental health crises with better outcomes as people receive the services and supports they need to remain in their communities and thrive.

However, of the 13 states (ranked 39-51) with the highest rates of suicidal ideation, only four have successfully passed state legislation for 988 implementation: Utah, Oregon, Indiana, and Colorado.

Of these, only one currently includes user fees.

[1] Fuller, DA, Lamb, HR, Biasotti, M & Snook J. (2015). Overlooked in the Undercounted: The Role of Mental Illness in Fata Law Enforcement Encounters. *Treatment Advocacy Center.* https://www.treatmentadvocacycenter.org/overlooked-in-the-undercounted
[2] Vibrant Emotional Health (2020). 988 Serviceable Populations and Contact Volume Projections. https://www.vibrant.org/wp-content/uploads/2020/12/Vibrant-988-Projections-Report.pdf?_ga=2.62739180.1718066263.1611784352-1951259024.1604696443

Policy Implications for 988 Implementation

While it is imperative to build out a system to respond to individuals in a mental health crisis, we should not wait until people reach crisis before providing them with mental health care. The following are a list of policy recommendations for consideration as part of any 988 implementation:

- The 988 system should be built as a continuum of crisis care that includes resources for the prevention of mental health conditions.
- Data should be collected on why people get into a crisis and continual planning and analysis should identify ways to avoid crises.
- Peer teams for unhoused people and others at high risk of crisis and police involvement must be added to conduct outreach and connect individuals to services before they experience mental health crises.
- Data collected through 988 can be used to identify individuals at high risk of mental health crisis and proactive peer supports and other community-based resources should be deployed to coordinate with 988 and prevent crises.
- Supportive housing, supportive education, Assertive Community Treatment (ACT) teams, and early psychosis programs may also be helpful in avoiding crises and can be employed in continuous care following interaction with the mental health crisis system.

Youth Prevalence of Mental Illness

Youth With At Least One Major Depressive Episode (MDE) in the Past Year

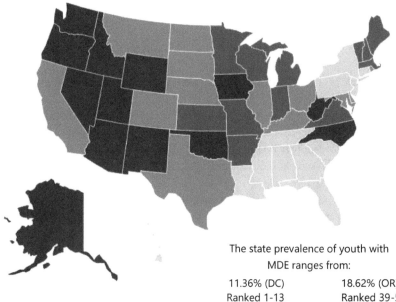

15.08% of youth (age 12-17) report suffering from at least one major depressive episode (MDE) in the past year.

Childhood depression is more likely to persist into adulthood if gone untreated, but only half of children with pediatric major depression are diagnosed before adulthood.[1]

The number of youths experiencing MDE increased by 306,000 (1.24 percent) from last year's dataset.

The state prevalence of youth with MDE ranges from:

11.36% (DC) 18.62% (OR)
Ranked 1-13 Ranked 39-51

Rank	State	%	#
1	District of Columbia	11.36	4,000
2	Mississippi	12.64	31,000
3	New Jersey	12.71	86,000
4	Pennsylvania	12.88	117,000
5	Florida	13.25	191,000
6	New York	13.29	179,000
7	Tennessee	13.72	70,000
8	Georgia	13.75	119,000
9	South Carolina	13.82	52,000
10	Louisiana	14.14	51,000
11	Hawaii	14.16	13,000
12	Connecticut	14.41	39,000
13	Alabama	14.51	54,000
14	Texas	14.60	363,000
15	Rhode Island	14.64	11,000
16	Ohio	14.73	131,000
17	Maryland	14.93	67,000
18	Colorado	15.02	65,000
19	North Dakota	15.07	8,000
20	Montana	15.11	12,000
21	Kentucky	15.15	51,000
22	Illinois	15.15	149,000
23	California	15.22	459,000
24	South Dakota	15.41	11,000
25	Delaware	15.48	11,000
26	Nebraska	15.50	24,000
27	Missouri	15.54	72,000
28	Virginia	15.57	98,000
29	Maine	15.60	14,000
30	Massachusetts	15.61	75,000
31	New Hampshire	15.85	15,000
32	Minnesota	15.94	70,000
33	Wisconsin	15.99	71,000
34	Arkansas	16.27	39,000
35	Vermont	16.36	7,000
36	Kansas	16.53	39,000
37	Michigan	16.55	125,000
38	Indiana	16.61	89,000
39	West Virginia	16.62	21,000
40	North Carolina	16.68	132,000
41	Iowa	16.69	41,000
42	Oklahoma	17.01	54,000
43	Arizona	17.41	98,000
44	Idaho	17.44	27,000
45	Wyoming	17.59	8,000
46	Utah	17.77	56,000
47	Nevada	17.93	42,000
48	Alaska	17.93	10,000
49	Washington	18.22	99,000
50	New Mexico	18.60	31,000
51	Oregon	18.62	55,000
	National	15.08	3,755,000

[1] Mullen, S. (2018). Major depressive disorder in children and adolescents. *The Mental Health Clinician*, 8(6):275-283. Doi: 10.9740/mhc.2018.11.275

Youth With Substance Use Disorder in the Past Year

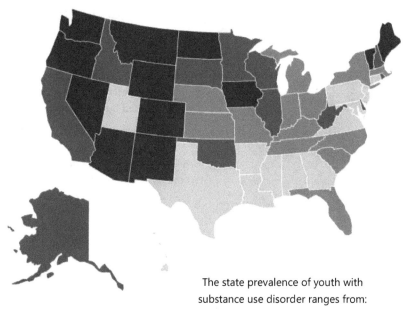

4.08% of youth in the U.S. reported a substance use disorder in the past year.

1.64% had an alcohol use disorder in the past year, while 3.16% had an illicit drug use disorder.

The rate of youth with substance use disorder increased 0.26% from last year's dataset. The largest decreases were in Arkansas (0.48%), Florida (0.48%), and Alabama (0.44%).

The largest increases were in Oregon (1.12%) and Iowa (0.87%).

The state prevalence of youth with substance use disorder ranges from:

3.19% (AL)
Ranked 1-13

5.77% (OR)
Ranked 39-51

Rank	State	%	#
1	Alabama	3.19	12,000
2	Louisiana	3.29	12,000
3	Mississippi	3.32	8,000
4	New Jersey	3.33	22,000
5	Georgia	3.45	30,000
6	Texas	3.49	87,000
7	Pennsylvania	3.52	32,000
8	Arkansas	3.63	9,000
9	Maryland	3.70	17,000
10	Virginia	3.71	23,000
11	Connecticut	3.74	10,000
12	Hawaii	3.75	4,000
13	Utah	3.77	12,000
14	Florida	3.86	56,000
15	New York	3.87	52,000
16	North Carolina	3.91	31,000
17	Nebraska	3.94	6,000
18	South Carolina	3.95	15,000
19	Michigan	3.98	30,000
20	Tennessee	4.00	21,000
21	Kansas	4.02	10,000
22	Missouri	4.04	19,000
23	Kentucky	4.10	14,000
24	Massachusetts	4.10	20,000
25	Indiana	4.20	23,000
26	Ohio	4.23	38,000

Rank	State	%	#
27	Illinois	4.25	42,000
28	Delaware	4.31	3,000
29	Wisconsin	4.34	19,000
30	Oklahoma	4.36	14,000
31	West Virginia	4.44	6,000
32	Idaho	4.47	7,000
33	California	4.55	137,000
34	New Hampshire	4.57	4,000
35	Rhode Island	4.58	3,000
36	South Dakota	4.60	3,000
37	Minnesota	4.62	20,000
38	Alaska	4.63	3,000
39	Maine	4.67	4,000
40	Arizona	4.83	27,000
41	Washington	4.84	26,000
42	Iowa	5.07	12,000
43	North Dakota	5.08	3,000
44	Wyoming	5.22	2,000
45	New Mexico	5.43	9,000
46	Colorado	5.44	24,000
47	Vermont	5.50	2,000
48	District of Columbia	5.57	2,000
49	Nevada	5.59	13,000
50	Montana	5.68	4,000
51	Oregon	5.77	17,000
	National	4.08	1,017,000

Youth With Severe Major Depressive Episode

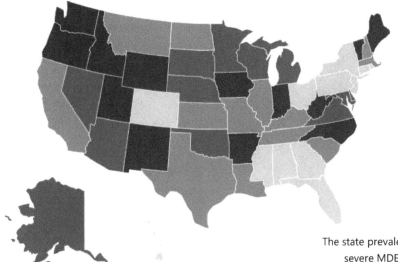

10.6% of youth (over 2.5 million youth) cope with severe major depression.

The number of youths experiencing severe MDE increased by 197,000 from last year's dataset.

Rates of a severe major depressive episode were highest among youth who identified as more than one race, **at 14.5%** (about 119,000 youth).

The state prevalence of youth with severe MDE ranges from:

7.3% (DC)
Ranked 1-13

14.8% (WY)
Ranked 39-51

Rank	State	%	#
1	District of Columbia	7.3	2,000
2	Alabama	7.5	27,000
3	Connecticut	7.8	20,000
4	Mississippi	8.0	19,000
5	Pennsylvania	8.2	73,000
6	New York	8.3	109,000
7	Rhode Island	8.3	6,000
8	Hawaii	8.4	8,000
9	New Jersey	8.4	55,000
10	Colorado	9.0	38,000
11	Florida	9.0	124,000
12	Ohio	9.0	78,000
13	Georgia	9.1	76,000
14	South Carolina	9.1	33,000
15	Texas	9.7	234,000
16	California	9.8	284,000
17	Kentucky	9.9	32,000
18	Louisiana	10.2	36,000
19	New Hampshire	10.2	9,000
20	North Dakota	10.3	5,000
21	Tennessee	10.3	51,000
22	Missouri	10.4	47,000
23	Massachusetts	10.5	48,000
24	Illinois	11.0	104,000
25	Kansas	11.2	26,000
26	Montana	11.4	8,000

Rank	State	%	#
27	Minnesota	11.6	49,000
28	Arizona	11.9	64,000
29	Michigan	11.9	87,000
30	South Dakota	12.0	8,000
31	Alaska	12.1	7,000
32	Maryland	12.3	54,000
33	Nebraska	12.4	19,000
34	Wisconsin	12.7	55,000
35	Delaware	12.8	9,000
36	Oklahoma	12.8	39,000
37	Virginia	13.0	79,000
38	Nevada	13.2	29,000
39	West Virginia	13.3	16,000
40	Iowa	13.5	32,000
41	Washington	13.5	69,000
42	Maine	13.6	12,000
43	Vermont	13.7	5,000
44	New Mexico	13.8	22,000
45	Oregon	14.1	40,000
46	North Carolina	14.2	110,000
47	Arkansas	14.3	33,000
48	Indiana	14.5	76,000
49	Utah	14.5	45,000
50	Idaho	14.7	22,000
51	Wyoming	14.8	6,000
	National	10.6	2,540,000

According to SAMHSA, youth who experience a Major Depressive Episode (MDE) in the last year with severe role impairment (Youth With Severe MDE) reported the maximum level of interference over four role domains including: chores at home, school or work, family relationships, and social life.

Adult Access to Care
Adults With AMI Who Did Not Receive Treatment

Over half (56%) of adults with a mental illness receive no treatment.

Over 27 million individuals experiencing a mental illness are going untreated.

Although adults who did not have insurance coverage were significantly less likely to receive treatment than those who did, 54% of people covered by health insurance still did not receive mental health treatment, indicating that ensuring coverage is not the same as ensuring access to mental health care.

The state prevalence of untreated adults with mental illness ranges from:

42.6% (VT) Ranked 1-13

67.1% (HI) Ranked 39-51

Rank	State	%	#
1	Vermont	42.6	49,000
2	Iowa	44.2	181,000
3	Massachusetts	44.7	526,000
4	Wisconsin	44.8	400,000
5	Minnesota	46.1	401,000
6	Maine	47.7	117,000
7	Nebraska	48.8	134,000
8	Arkansas	49.6	228,000
9	Utah	49.7	307,000
10	North Dakota	50.1	56,000
11	Ohio	50.3	1,088,000
12	Rhode Island	51.0	99,000
13	Montana	51.1	89,000
14	Kansas	51.2	229,000
15	North Carolina	51.6	801,000
16	West Virginia	51.7	191,000
17	Pennsylvania	51.9	1,012,000
18	New Hampshire	52.3	131,000
19	South Dakota	52.3	56,000
20	Illinois	52.6	958,000
21	Missouri	53.3	575,000
22	Idaho	53.4	161,000
23	Kentucky	53.5	420,000
24	Tennessee	53.5	514,000
25	Colorado	53.6	558,000
26	Connecticut	54.0	276,000
27	Delaware	54.2	86,000
28	New Mexico	54.2	185,000
29	Washington	54.3	778,000
30	Oregon	54.5	439,000
31	Virginia	54.7	645,000
32	District of Columbia	55.2	74,000
33	Michigan	55.4	866,000
34	South Carolina	56.1	427,000
35	Oklahoma	56.6	376,000
36	Indiana	56.7	643,000
37	Arizona	57.0	619,000
38	New Jersey	57.1	627,000
39	Alabama	57.3	454,000
40	Maryland	58.0	452,000
41	Nevada	58.0	305,000
42	New York	58.3	1,690,000
43	Alaska	58.7	66,000
44	Mississippi	59.3	265,000
45	Louisiana	59.6	453,000
46	Texas	60.7	2,148,000
47	Wyoming	61.7	64,000
48	California	61.8	3,617,000
49	Florida	63.5	1,823,000
50	Georgia	63.5	860,000
51	Hawaii	67.1	127,000
	National	55.9	27,646,000

Adults With AMI Reporting Unmet Need

Almost a quarter (24.7%) of all adults with a mental illness reported that they were not able to receive the treatment they needed. **This number has not declined since 2011.**

Individuals reporting unmet need are those seeking treatment and facing barriers to getting the help they need, including:

1) No insurance or limited coverage of services.
2) Shortfall in psychiatrists and an overall undersized mental health workforce.
3) Lack of available treatment types (inpatient treatment, individual therapy, intensive community services).
4) Disconnect between primary care systems and behavioral health systems.
5) Insufficient finances to cover costs – including copays, uncovered treatment types, or when providers do not take insurance.

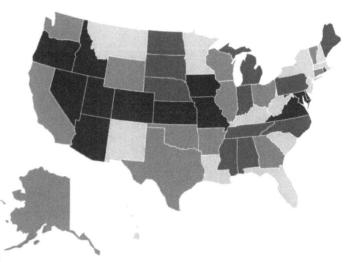

The state prevalence of adults with AMI reporting unmet treatment needs ranges from:

14.9% (HI)	37.1% (DC)
Ranked 1-13	Ranked 39-51

Rank	State	%	#
1	Hawaii	14.9	28,000
2	Louisiana	18.4	139,000
3	South Carolina	19.7	150,000
4	Montana	21.5	37,000
5	Minnesota	21.6	187,000
6	New Jersey	21.6	238,000
7	Massachusetts	21.7	255,000
8	New York	21.7	628,000
9	West Virginia	22.2	82,000
10	Florida	22.4	643,000
11	New Hampshire	22.4	56,000
12	New Mexico	22.7	78,000
13	Kentucky	22.9	181,000
14	Oklahoma	22.9	152,000
15	Wisconsin	22.9	204,000
16	Illinois	23.2	422,000
17	California	23.5	1,379,000
18	Connecticut	23.5	120,000
19	Texas	24.0	845,000
20	Washington	24.0	341,000
21	Georgia	24.1	326,000
22	Alaska	24.4	28,000
23	Wyoming	24.5	25,000
24	Arkansas	24.7	114,000
25	Ohio	24.8	540,000
26	Vermont	25.2	29,000

Rank	State	%	#
27	Mississippi	25.3	113,000
28	South Dakota	25.3	27,000
29	Rhode Island	25.4	50,000
30	North Dakota	25.6	29,000
31	Pennsylvania	25.7	499,000
32	Tennessee	25.7	249,000
33	Maine	25.9	63,000
34	Alabama	26.7	212,000
35	Indiana	26.8	306,000
36	Michigan	26.8	419,000
37	North Carolina	27.2	423,000
38	Nebraska	27.6	76,000
39	Virginia	27.7	326,000
40	Utah	27.9	172,000
41	Delaware	28.1	45,000
42	Arizona	28.4	306,000
43	Oregon	28.8	231,000
44	Idaho	29.1	88,000
45	Nevada	29.3	154,000
46	Missouri	30.1	325,000
47	Maryland	30.2	236,000
48	Colorado	31.8	331,000
49	Kansas	32.6	145,000
50	Iowa	32.9	134,000
51	District of Columbia	37.1	50,000
	National	24.7	12,236,000

Adults With AMI Who Are Uninsured

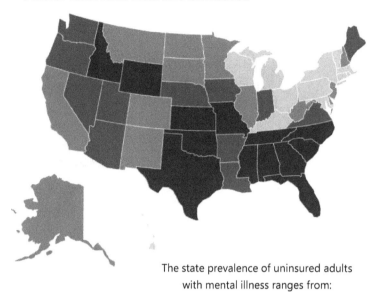

The state prevalence of uninsured adults
with mental illness ranges from:

3.8% (MA)	21.5% (TX)
Ranked 1-13	Ranked 39-51

Rank	State	Rate	#
1	Massachusetts	3.8	45,000
2	Kentucky	4.2	33,000
3	Rhode Island	4.4	9,000
4	District of Columbia	4.7	6,000
5	Hawaii	4.7	9,000
6	Vermont	5.1	6,000
7	New York	5.2	151,000
8	Connecticut	5.4	28,000
9	Maryland	5.6	43,000
10	Pennsylvania	5.9	115,000
11	Wisconsin	6.3	56,000
12	Michigan	6.9	108,000
13	Ohio	6.9	150,000
14	Illinois	7.1	130,000
15	Delaware	7.3	12,000
16	California	7.4	434,000
17	Minnesota	8.0	69,000
18	New Mexico	8.1	28,000
19	New Hampshire	8.8	22,000
20	Alaska	9.7	11,000
21	North Dakota	9.8	11,000
22	South Dakota	9.8	10,000
23	Montana	10.0	17,000
24	West Virginia	10.1	37,000
25	New Jersey	10.6	116,000
26	Colorado	10.8	113,000
27	Arkansas	11.3	52,000
28	Iowa	11.3	46,000
29	Utah	11.3	70,000
30	Nevada	11.5	61,000
31	Arizona	11.6	127,000
32	Nebraska	11.6	32,000
33	Washington	11.6	165,000
34	Oregon	11.8	95,000
35	Louisiana	12.4	95,000
36	Virginia	12.4	147,000
37	Maine	12.6	31,000
38	Indiana	13.4	153,000
39	Idaho	14.0	42,000
40	Kansas	14.0	63,000
41	Georgia	15.2	207,000
42	Tennessee	15.3	148,000
43	North Carolina	15.4	240,000
44	South Carolina	15.6	119,000
45	Oklahoma	17.6	117,000
46	Florida	17.8	512,000
47	Wyoming	18.0	19,000
48	Mississippi	18.2	81,000
49	Alabama	19.3	154,000
50	Missouri	19.3	209,000
51	Texas	21.5	759,000
	National	11.1	5,514,000

11.1% (over 5.5 million) of adults with a mental illness are uninsured.

The rankings for this indicator used data from the 2018-2019 NSDUH. There was a 0.3 percent **increase** from last year's dataset, the second year in a row that this indicator increased since the passage of the Affordable Care Act (ACA).

Data from the U.S. Census Bureau found that the percentage of Americans with Medicaid coverage decreased from 20.5% in 2018 to 19.8% in 2019.[1] Medicaid is the largest payer for mental health services in the U.S. Studies have shown that Medicaid expansion is associated with a significant reduction in the percentage of adults with depression who are uninsured, and in delaying mental health care because of cost.[2] Medicaid expansion is also an issue of mental health equity, as expansion has been found to reduce racial disparities in health coverage.[3]

Every state ranked 39-51 on this indicator is a state that had not expanded Medicaid by 2018-2019. Idaho implemented Medicaid expansion in 2020, and both Oklahoma and Missouri implemented Medicaid expansion in 2021, which may lead to a large change in coverage in future reports.

[1] Keisler-Starkey, K. & Bunch, L.N. (September 2020). Health Insurance Coverage in the United States: 2019. *U.S. Census Bureau Current Population Reports, P60-271..* Available at https://www.census.gov/library/publications/2020/demo/p60-271.html

[2] Fry, C.E. & Sommers, B.D. (August 2018). Effect of Medicaid Expansion on Health Insurance Coverage and Access to Care Among Adults with Depression. *Psychiatric Services, 69(11): 1146-1152.* https://doi.org/10.1176/appi.ps.201800181
[3] Guth, M., Artiga, S., & Pham, O. (September 2020). Effects of the ACA Medicaid Expansion on Racial Disparities in Health and Health Care. *Kaiser Family Foundation,* https://www.kff.org/medicaid/issue-brief/effects-of-the-aca-medicaid-expansion-on-racial-disparities-in-health-and-health-care/

Adults With Cognitive Disability Who Could Not See a Doctor Due to Costs

29.67% of adults with a cognitive disability were not able to see a doctor due to costs.

Cognitive disability is defined as having serious difficulty concentrating, remembering, or making decisions because of a physical, mental, or emotional disability.

According to the Centers for Disease Control (CDC), 12% of people in the U.S. had a cognitive disability in 2019, even when adjusted for age. The percentage of people with cognitive disability ranged from 8.9 percent in some states to 19.6 percent.[1]

A 2017 study found that compared to working-age adults without disabilities, those with disabilities are more likely to report problems of affordability and access to care, including problems or inability to pay medical bills and delaying medical care due to cost. While implementation of the ACA reduced some issues of access, adults with disabilities were still over three times more likely to report an access problem.[2]

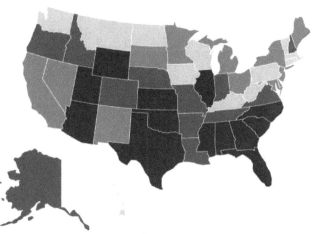

The prevalence of adults with cognitive disability who could not see an M.D. due to cost ranges from:

18.48% (RI)   40.65% (TX)
Ranked 1-13   Ranked 39-51

Rank	State	%	#
1	Rhode Island	18.48	18,204
2	Vermont	20.33	9,346
3	Connecticut	20.59	52,774
4	Iowa	21.22	47,967
5	Massachusetts	21.68	122,701
6	North Dakota	22.25	12,879
7	Wisconsin	22.28	94,587
8	Hawaii	22.90	24,832
9	Kentucky	23.34	132,541
10	West Virginia	23.35	63,123
11	Washington	23.45	129,850
12	Montana	23.68	24,375
13	Pennsylvania	23.77	269,121
14	Maryland	23.87	102,734
15	Nevada	24.31	72,956
16	New York	24.53	351,676
17	District of Columbia	24.59	13,849
18	New Jersey	25.19	*
19	California	25.54	798,630
20	South Dakota	26.14	17,659
21	New Mexico	26.15	54,176
22	Minnesota	26.19	102,491
23	Ohio	26.99	290,259
24	Maine	27.34	39,967
25	Michigan	27.50	281,553
26	Delaware	27.59	21,424

Rank	State	%	#
27	Louisiana	27.79	155,929
28	Idaho	28.05	43,386
29	Colorado	28.69	111,500
30	Nebraska	29.48	37,445
31	Alaska	29.49	17,492
32	Tennessee	29.93	224,845
33	New Hampshire	30.40	35,528
34	Arkansas	30.53	117,147
35	Indiana	30.53	191,026
36	Oregon	30.67	118,469
37	Virginia	30.71	198,169
38	Missouri	30.88	192,461
39	Arizona	31.35	203,838
40	Oklahoma	31.52	138,679
41	South Carolina	31.70	161,528
42	Illinois	32.25	306,123
43	North Carolina	32.94	356,776
44	Wyoming	32.94	14,280
45	Utah	33.31	81,119
46	Mississippi	33.37	121,330
47	Florida	34.90	733,738
48	Alabama	38.35	233,440
49	Kansas	38.74	97,643
50	Georgia	39.18	370,081
51	Texas	40.65	954,935
	National	29.67	8,496,389

[1] Centers for Disease Control and Prevention, National Center on Birth Defects and Developmental Disabilities, Division of Human Development and Disability. Disability and Health Data System (DHDS) Data [online]. (2019). Available at https://dhds.cdc.gov
[2] Kennedy, J., Geneva Wood, E. & Frieden, L. (2017). Disparities in insurance coverage, health services use, and access following implementation of the Affordable Care Act: A comparison of disabled and nondisabled working-age adults. *Inquiry*, 54. Available at https://www.ncbi.nlm.nih.gov/pmc/articles/PMC5798675/

Youth Access to Care

Youth With MDE Who Did Not Receive Mental Health Services

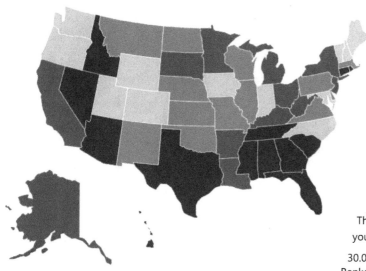

60.3% of youth with major depression do not receive any mental health treatment.

Youth experiencing MDE continue to go untreated. Even among the states with greatest access for youth, one in three youth are still not receiving the mental health services they need.

In Texas (ranked 51), nearly **three-quarters** of youth with major depression did not receive mental health treatment, nearly two-and-a-half times the rate in Maine (ranked one).

The state prevalence of untreated youth with depression ranges from:

30.0% (ME)   73.1% (TX)
Ranked 1-13   Ranked 39-51

Rank	State	%	#
1	Maine	30.0	4,000
2	Colorado	39.3	20,000
3	District of Columbia	41.0	1,000
4	Vermont	42.6	3,000
5	Maryland	44.7	32,000
6	Wyoming	44.9	4,000
7	Utah	45.4	25,000
8	New Hampshire	46.6	7,000
9	Iowa	49.3	21,000
10	Oregon	49.7	29,000
11	Washington	49.8	50,000
12	Indiana	51.5	50,000
13	North Carolina	51.9	74,000
14	Delaware	52.3	6,000
15	Nebraska	52.6	12,000
16	Montana	53.5	6,000
17	Kansas	54.5	21,000
18	North Dakota	54.6	4,000
19	Wisconsin	55.1	36,000
20	Illinois	55.2	77,000
21	Pennsylvania	55.2	57,000
22	Virginia	55.2	58,000
23	New Mexico	55.9	18,000
24	Oklahoma	56.0	30,000
25	Massachusetts	56.8	44,000
26	Missouri	57.3	37,000
27	Minnesota	58.3	42,000
28	Arkansas	58.9	23,000
29	New Jersey	58.9	42,000
30	Kentucky	59.3	27,000
31	South Dakota	59.6	6,000
32	Michigan	59.7	74,000
33	New York	60.9	103,000
34	Louisiana	62.5	32,000
35	Ohio	63.3	76,000
36	Alaska	63.4	6,000
37	West Virginia	63.9	13,000
38	California	64.5	278,000
39	Rhode Island	64.9	6,000
40	Nevada	65.2	28,000
41	Connecticut	65.6	24,000
42	Tennessee	66.5	40,000
43	Alabama	66.8	34,000
44	Idaho	67.1	19,000
45	Florida	67.3	117,000
46	South Carolina	67.6	34,000
47	Georgia	67.8	75,000
48	Arizona	70.1	67,000
49	Hawaii	71.0	7,000
50	Mississippi	71.7	20,000
51	Texas	73.1	255,000
	National	60.3	2,173,000

Youth With Severe MDE Who Received Some Consistent Treatment

Nationally, **only 27.2% of youth** with severe depression receive some consistent treatment (7-25+ visits in a year).

Consistent treatment is determined if a youth visits a specialty outpatient mental health service, including a day treatment facility, mental health clinic, private therapist, or in-home therapist, more than seven times in the previous year.

It does not consider the quality of the care – for example, whether the mental health service was specialized toward youth, whether the provider was representative of the youth being served, what the outcomes of treatment were, or whether the child was offered a continuum of supports.

Even with simply measuring the number of visits, fewer than one in three youth with severe depression meet this determination of

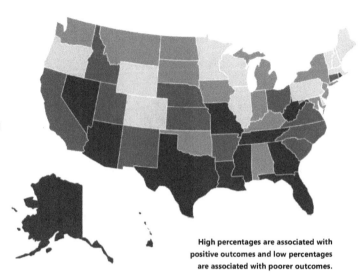

High percentages are associated with positive outcomes and low percentages are associated with poorer outcomes.

The state prevalence of youth with severe depression who received some outpatient treatment ranges from:

65.6% (ME)	12.2% (TN)
Ranked 1-13	Ranked 39-51

Rank	State	%	#
1	Maine	65.6	7,000
2	Vermont	49.7	3,000
3	New Hampshire	47.6	4,000
4	Wyoming	45.6	3,000
5	Colorado	43.1	16,000
6	Massachusetts	42.2	19,000
7	Pennsylvania	39.9	28,000
8	Illinois	38.3	38,000
9	Oregon	36.6	14,000
10	Wisconsin	36.4	19,000
11	Delaware	36.3	3,000
12	Minnesota	35.9	17,000
13	District of Columbia	35.8	1,000
14	Washington	35.7	24,000
15	Montana	35.5	3,000
16	Maryland	34.5	18,000
17	Oklahoma	33.6	12,000
18	North Dakota	33.0	2,000
19	Indiana	32.9	23,000
20	Alabama	31.3	8,000
21	Michigan	30.4	26,000
22	Iowa	29.5	9,000
23	South Dakota	29.3	2,000
24	Kentucky	28.6	9,000
25	New Jersey	28.4	14,000
26	New York	28.3	29,000

Rank	State	%	#
27	Nebraska	27.8	5,000
28	Idaho	27.7	6,000
29	Utah	27.3	11,000
30	California	26.1	72,000
31	Ohio	25.1	19,000
32	Virginia	25.0	19,000
33	North Carolina	24.9	27,000
34	South Carolina	24.2	8,000
35	Connecticut	23.6	5,000
36	Arkansas	22.7	7,000
37	Kansas	22.7	6,000
38	New Mexico	22.5	5,000
39	Louisiana	21.1	7,000
40	West Virginia	20.9	3,000
41	Rhode Island	20.4	1,000
42	Alaska	20.2	1,000
43	Georgia	20.1	14,000
44	Texas	19.2	44,000
45	Nevada	18.7	5,000
46	Florida	17.0	20,000
47	Arizona	16.1	10,000
48	Mississippi	13.5	2,000
49	Hawaii	13.3	1,000
50	Missouri	12.6	5,000
51	Tennessee	12.2	6,000
	National	27.2	661,000

Children With Private Insurance That
Did Not Cover Mental or Emotional Problems

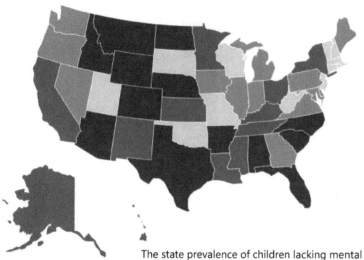

The state prevalence of children lacking mental health coverage ranges from:

1.9% (MA)	17.7% (AR)
Ranked 1-13	Ranked 39-51

The Mental Health Parity and Addiction Equity Act (MHPAEA) was enacted in 2008 and promised the equal coverage of mental health and substance use services. However, despite increasing pressure and parity enforcement action from the Department of Labor, the rate of children with private insurance that does not cover mental or emotional problems increased 0.3 percent from last year's dataset, and there are still 950,000 youth without coverage for their behavioral health.

In 2019, a Milliman research report[1] found large disparities between behavioral health and medical/surgical services, including that patients saw out-of-network behavioral health providers at much higher rates than physical health providers. It also found that these disparities were worse for children. In 2017, a behavioral health visit for a child was over 10 times more likely to be out-of-network than a primary care office visit. This was over two times the disparity shown for adults.

Ensuring that mental health care is covered by insurance is a baseline and does not mean that an individual can access care. In the lowest ranked states, over 15% of children do not have that baseline of insurance coverage for mental health services. This indicator does not account for whether those with coverage have a provider in their area, or for the network adequacy of the insurance they have.

Rank	State	%	#
1	Massachusetts	1.9	5,000
2	Vermont	2.1	0
3	Connecticut	3.5	5,000
4	Rhode Island	3.8	1,000
5	Missouri	4.2	9,000
6	New Hampshire	4.3	2,000
7	Oklahoma	4.4	6,000
8	District of Columbia	4.5	1,000
9	West Virginia	4.5	2,000
10	Wisconsin	4.5	12,000
11	South Dakota	4.7	2,000
12	Utah	4.7	10,000
13	New Jersey	5.0	18,000
14	Washington	5.2	15,000
15	Maine	5.4	3,000
16	Michigan	6.1	27,000
17	Virginia	6.4	22,000
18	Maryland	6.5	15,000
19	Illinois	6.6	33,000
20	Oregon	6.6	10,000
21	Pennsylvania	6.8	32,000
22	Delaware	7.0	3,000
23	Georgia	7.0	25,000
24	Nevada	7.1	8,000
25	Indiana	7.4	22,000
26	Iowa	7.4	10,000
27	Ohio	7.4	33,000
28	Alaska	7.5	2,000
29	New York	7.7	48,000
30	New Mexico	7.8	5,000
31	Kansas	7.9	8,000
32	Minnesota	8.0	20,000
33	California	8.2	111,000
34	Mississippi	8.2	6,000
35	Hawaii	8.3	3,000
36	Tennessee	8.8	19,000
37	Louisiana	9.0	11,000
38	Kentucky	9.3	15,000
39	Montana	9.5	3,000
40	Colorado	9.6	22,000
41	North Carolina	10.0	34,000
42	Arizona	10.2	27,000
43	Florida	11.7	65,000
44	Idaho	12.2	11,000
45	South Carolina	12.4	19,000
46	Alabama	12.5	16,000
47	Wyoming	12.7	3,000
48	Texas	13.8	135,000
49	Nebraska	15.4	13,000
50	North Dakota	15.6	5,000
51	Arkansas	17.7	17,000
	National	8.1	950,000

[1] Melek, S., Davenport, S. & Gray, T.J. (November 19, 2019). Addiction and mental health vs. physical health: Widening disparities in network use and provider reimbursement. *Milliman Research Report*. Available at https://us.milliman.com/en/insight/worldwide-insight

Students Identified With Emotional Disturbance for an Individualized Education Program

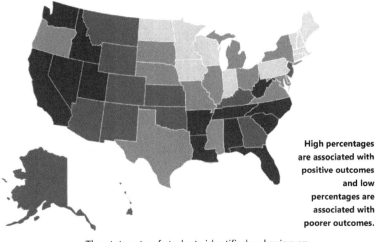

High percentages are associated with positive outcomes and low percentages are associated with poorer outcomes.

The state rate of students identified as having an Emotional Disturbance (ED) for an Individual Education Program (IEP) ranges from:

32.23% (VT)	2.13% (AL)
Ranked 1-13	Ranked 39-51

Only .759 percent* of students are identified as having an ED for IEP.

Early identification for IEPs is critical. IEPs provide the services, accommodations, and support students with ED need to receive a quality education. For purposes of an IEP, the term "Emotional Disturbance" is used to define youth with a mental illness that is affecting their ability to succeed in school. In 2018-2019, 10.6% of youth had severe MDE, reporting the maximum level of interference over four role domains including school, yet less than 1% were identified for an IEP under ED.

In addition to ensuring that students in need of accommodations and supports in school receive them through an IEP, we must work toward prevention of mental health problems that may necessitate an Emotional Disturbance IEP. Youth identified with ED were more likely to live in households below the poverty line, with multiple risk factors that may affect their mental health.[1] It is imperative that we continue to work toward prevention of mental health conditions by improving the social safety net for families and addressing the social determinants of mental health that may contribute to the emergence of mental health problems.

The rate for this measure is shown as a rate per 1,000 students. The calculation was made this way for ease of reading. Unfortunately, doing so hides the fact that the percentages are significantly lower. If states were doing a better job of identifying whether youth had emotional difficulties that could be better supported through an IEP – the rates would be closer to .8 percent.

Rank*	State	Rate	#
1	Vermont	32.23	2326
2	Minnesota	21.20	17016
3	Massachusetts	20.22	17455
4	Pennsylvania	16.33	26105
5	Wisconsin	16.18	*
6	Maine	15.32	2468
7	Indiana	13.36	12712
8	Iowa	13.31	*
9	New Hampshire	13.24	2132
10	Connecticut	12.43	5824
11	Rhode Island	12.34	1610
12	North Dakota	11.99	1240
13	District of Columbia	11.54	802
14	Illinois	10.59	18381
15	Oregon	10.30	5568
16	South Dakota	10.04	1251
17	Ohio	10.03	15281
18	Nebraska	9.98	2861
19	Delaware	9.47	1211
20	New York	9.10	22063
21	Missouri	8.87	7188
22	Michigan	8.52	11314
23	Virginia	8.47	9913
24	Maryland	7.61	6180
25	Mississippi	7.53	3193
26	Texas	7.41	35851
27	Arizona	7.39	7756
28	Kentucky	7.39	4501
29	Colorado	6.98	5687
30	Wyoming	6.80	589
31	Montana	6.68	906
32	Oklahoma	6.66	4057
33	Alaska	6.48	765
34	Georgia	6.35	10124
35	New Mexico	6.15	1830
36	New Jersey	5.84	7313
37	Hawaii	5.80	959
38	Kansas	5.60	2459
39	Washington	5.49	5633
40	Florida	5.43	14062
41	Idaho	4.95	1412
42	Nevada	4.64	2085
43	California	4.51	25424
44	West Virginia	4.45	1025
45	Tennessee	3.84	3470
46	North Carolina	3.65	5187
47	Utah	3.12	1933
48	South Carolina	3.05	2143
49	Louisiana	2.74	1727
50	Arkansas	2.54	1123
51	Alabama	2.13	1420
	National	**7.59**	345,160

[1] Wagner, M., Kutash, K., Duchnowski, A.J., Epstein, M.H. & Sumi, W.C. (2005). The Children and Youth We Serve: A National Picture of the Characteristics of Students with Emotional Disturbances Receiving Special Education. *Journal of Emotional and Behavioral Disorders,* 13(2): 79-96. Retrieved from https://journals.sagepub.com/doi/abs/10.1177/10634266050130020201?journalCode=ebxa

Spotlight: Disparities in Mental Health Treatment for Youth of Color

The following analyses are based on data from the 2018-2019 Substance Use and Mental Health Services Administration's (SAMHSA's) National Survey on Drug Use and Health (NSDUH).[3]

While rates of mental health treatment are low for all youth with major depression, youth of color are significantly less likely to receive depression treatment than white youth. Asian youth were least likely to have seen a health professional or received medication for their depression (8.30%), followed by Black or African American youth (9.40%) and Hispanic youth (9.50%).

Of Youth With MDE: Did you see a Health Professional or Receive Medication for Depression in the Past Year?		Asian	Black or African American (non-Hispanic)	Hispanic	More than one race	White (non-Hispanic)	Native American or Alaska Native	Native Hawaiian or Other Pacific Islander
Yes	Percentage	8.30%	9.40%	9.50%	15.60%	22.00%	15.20%	*
	Count	16,000	33,000	89,000	25,000	424,000	4,000	*
No	Percentage	91.70%	90.60%	90.50%	84.40%	78.00%	84.80%	*
	Count	175,000	316,000	849,000	133,000	1,503,000	21,000	*

*Data suppressed due to small sample size.

These analyses not only reflect disparities in who gets to receive mental health treatment, but what kinds of services they are able to receive and where they can access care. Youth of color with major depression were less likely to receive specialty mental health care than white youth. Specialty mental health treatment is defined as staying overnight in a hospital, staying in a residential treatment facility, spending time in a day treatment facility, receiving treatment from a mental health clinic, receiving treatment from a private therapist, or receiving treatment from an in-home therapist. Asian youth with a past year major depressive episode were least likely to have received specialty mental health care (71% did not receive care), followed by Native American or Alaska Native youth (68%), and Black or African American Youth (68%). White youth with MDE were most likely to receive specialty mental health care, but still over half of white youth with a past year major depressive episode did not receive treatment (54%).

---

[3] U.S. Department of Health and Human Services, Substance Abuse and mental Health Services Administration (SAMHSA), Center for Behavioral Health Statistics and Quality. (2018-2019). *National Survey on Drug Use and Health 2018-2019*. Retrieved from https://rdas.samhsa.gov/

Of Youth With MDE: Did You Receive Specialty Mental Health Care in the Past Year?		Asian	Black or African American (non-Hispanic)	Hispanic	More than one race	White (non-Hispanic)	Native American or Alaska Native	Native Hawaiian or Other Pacific Islander	Total
Yes	Percentage	29.00%	32.00%	32.40%	40.50%	45.80%	31.90%	36.90%	**39.70%**
	Count	55,000	111,000	306,000	63,000	883,000	8,000	6,000	**1,432,000**
No	Percentage	71.00%	68.00%	67.60%	59.50%	54.20%	68.10%	63.10%	**60.30%**
	Count	135,000	235,000	638,000	93,000	1,045,000	17,000	10,000	**2,173,000**

Native American, Black, and multiracial youth were all more likely to receive non-specialty mental health care than white youth. Non-specialty mental health care is defined as receiving services from a school social worker, school psychologist, or school counselor; special school or program within a regular school for students with emotional or behavioral problems; pediatrician or other family doctor; juvenile detention center, prison, or jail; or foster care or therapeutic foster care.

Native American or Alaska Native youth with major depression were most likely to receive non-specialty mental health care (43%), followed by youth identifying with more than one race (39%), and Black or African American youth (39%).

Of Youth With MDE: Did You Receive Non-Specialty Mental Health Care in the Past Year?		Asian	Black or African American (non-Hispanic)	Hispanic	More than one race	White (non-Hispanic)	Native American or Alaska Native	Native Hawaiian or Other Pacific Islander	Total
Yes	Percentage	24.40%	38.80%	32.10%	39.00%	35.70%	43.30%	10.70%	**34.60%**
	Count	46,000	135,000	299,000	61,000	687,000	11,000	2,000	**1,241,000**
No	Percentage	75.60%	61.20%	67.90%	61.00%	64.30%	56.70%	89.30%	**65.40%**
	Count	144,000	213,000	632,000	96,000	1,238,000	14,000	13,000	**2,350,000**

Of the 18.1% of youth who received non-specialty mental health services in 2019, most (15.4%) received those services in school. Despite the fact that youth of color comprise less than half of the total population of youth with MDE, 52% of youth with MDE who only received care in educational settings were youth of color.[4] Of youth with MDE, Black youth were most likely to receive school mental health services (37%), followed by Native American or Alaska Native youth (35%), and multiracial youth (34%).

---

[4] Ali, M. M., West, K., Teich, J. L., Lynch, S., Mutter, R., & Dubenitz, J. (2019). Utilization of Mental Health Services in Educational Setting by Adolescents in the United States. The Journal of school health, 89(5), 393–401. https://doi.org/10.1111/josh.12753

Among Youth With MDE Who Received Non-Specialty Mental Health Services:

Did You Receive Mental Health Services From Education Sources?		Asian	Black or African American (non-Hispanic)	Hispanic	More than one race	White (non-Hispanic)	Native American or Alaska Native	Native Hawaiian or Other Pacific Islander
Yes	Percentage	20.30%	37.30%	26.80%	34.30%	29.00%	34.70%	*
	Count	39,000	130,000	250,000	54,000	558,000	9,000	*
No	Percentage	79.70%	62.70%	73.20%	65.70%	71.00%	65.30%	*
	Count	152,000	219,000	682,000	103,000	1,367,000	16,000	*

*Data was suppressed due to small sample size

Students of color disproportionally access their mental health care at school, often because they don't have access to specialty mental health services. Given this data, increasing access to school-based mental health services can promote equity and reduce disparities in access to care. However, there is not sufficient federal funding for local education agencies to meet the mental health needs of students. To create healthier communities and to better serve students of color who may only receive mental health services in educational settings, schools need long-term financial support to build up sustained and sufficient school infrastructure. This infrastructure should include, at minimum, implementing comprehensive mental health education, increasing the number of mental health providers in schools, creating connections and coordinating with community-based mental health services, identifying processes and supports for screening and treating students, and reducing the gap in care when students transition from school to college and college to the workforce.

Although some states have adopted innovative practices to improve mental health education and access to mental health services and supports in schools, no state has fully enacted a set of laws and policies to improve youth mental health. MHA has compiled a report on innovative state policies and recommendations for future state legislative work geared toward serving the mental health needs of students and advancing equitable access to supports in schools.

Mental Health Workforce Availability

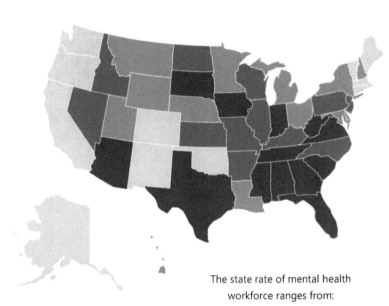

The state rate of mental health workforce ranges from:

150:1 (MA)
Ranked 1-13

920:1 (AL)
Ranked 39-51

Rank	State	#
1	Massachusetts	150:1
2	Oregon	180:1
3	District of Columbia	190:1
4	Alaska	200:1
5	Maine	200:1
6	Vermont	210:1
7	Connecticut	240:1
8	Oklahoma	240:1
9	Rhode Island	240:1
10	New Mexico	250:1
11	Washington	250:1
12	California	270:1
13	Colorado	270:1
14	Utah	290:1
15	Wyoming	290:1
16	New Hampshire	310:1
17	Montana	320:1
18	Louisiana	330:1
19	New York	330:1
20	Delaware	350:1
21	Maryland	360:1
22	Michigan	360:1
23	Nebraska	360:1
24	Minnesota	370:1
25	Hawaii	380:1
26	Ohio	380:1
27	North Carolina	390:1
28	Illinois	410:1
29	Arkansas	420:1
30	Kentucky	420:1
31	New Jersey	420:1
32	Pennsylvania	450:1
33	Idaho	460:1
34	Nevada	460:1
35	Wisconsin	470:1
36	Kansas	490:1
37	Missouri	490:1
38	North Dakota	510:1
39	South Dakota	530:1
40	Virginia	530:1
41	South Carolina	550:1
42	Florida	590:1
43	Indiana	590:1
44	Mississippi	590:1
45	Iowa	610:1
46	Tennessee	630:1
47	Georgia	690:1
48	Arizona	710:1
49	West Virginia	730:1
50	Texas	830:1
51	Alabama	920:1

The term "mental health provider" includes psychiatrists, psychologists, licensed clinical social workers, counselors, marriage and family therapists, and advanced practice nurses specializing in mental health care, but not yet certified peer specialists (because peer specialists are primarily covered only by Medicaid, and qualifications for them vary by state).

The rate of mental health providers has improved in nearly every state since last year's report. However, the need for mental health care is greatly outpacing these additions to the workforce. The mental health workforce shortage affects more people than primary care and dental workforce shortages combined, according to data from the Health Resources and Services Administration, with only 27% of mental health need being met in health professional shortage areas.[1]

One of the primary barriers to establishing a robust, diverse mental health workforce is low provider reimbursement. Payment affects the diversity of the workforce, especially in a field that requires high levels of education and certification. Provider reimbursement should take into account workforce shortages and promote equity in access. This could be accomplished at the level of individual health insurers and states through assessments of network adequacy and offering additional incentives when providers practice in areas with few appropriate providers taking new clients. This could also be accomplished more systemically by including an additional incentive in payment fee schedules based on shortages to incentivize growth in the mental health provider pipeline.

[1] Health Resources and Services Administration (HRSA) Bureau of Health Workforce (June 2021). Third Quarter of Fiscal Year 2021 Designated Health Professional Shortage Area Quarterly Summary. Retrieved from https://data.hrsa.gov/topics/health-workforce/shortage-areas

STATE LEGISLATION REPORT

Trends in State Mental Health Policy

2019
LEGISLATIVE
REVIEW

Introduction

NAMI State Organizations bring the voice of people with lived experience of mental illness and their family members to the policymaking process to create positive and systemic change.

Overview

In 2019, an extensive number of mental health-related bills were introduced and passed in state legislatures across the country, indicating that policymakers may be reaching a turning point in their awareness of mental illness, which affects one in five adults and one in six adolescents each year.

Yet, awareness alone does not equal access to mental health services and supports that individuals and families affected by mental health conditions need to thrive. The mental health community still faces many challenges. In fact, **well over half of the people who need mental health treatment do not receive it in any given year.**

Formed in 1979 by a small group of families of adult children with serious mental illness, NAMI has grown into a nationwide grassroots network. With more than 600 state and local affiliates, NAMI is dedicated to improving the lives of individuals and families affected by mental health conditions. A pillar of NAMI's mission is advocating for public policies that ensure individuals and families can get help early, get the best possible care, and be diverted from criminal justice system involvement.

Many mental health policy decisions are made at the state level. Historically, care for people with mental illness was considered the responsibility of the state government, and even now states have tremendous control over the design and funding level of their state mental health systems. NAMI State Organizations bring the voice of people with lived experience of mental illness and their family members to the policymaking process to create positive and systemic change.

This report is a showcase of significant state mental health legislation that was enacted (or nearly enacted) in calendar year 2019. The report explains key trends in mental health policy and offers lessons from NAMI State Organization leaders who played an important role in shaping some of these policies.

The report is intended to offer policy options for state policymakers, NAMI State Organizations, and other mental health advocates to pursue in order to improve the lives of individuals living with mental health conditions and their families.

Structure of Report

The report is divided into three main sections based on the pillars of the NAMI 2020–2025 Strategic Plan:

- **Section 1 "People Get Help Early"**
- Section 2 "People Get the Best Possible Care"
- **Section 3 "People Get Diverted from Criminal Justice System Involvement"**

Within each section, bill analysis is framed around several "areas of focus." There are 12 areas of focus in total. These areas of focus are not exhaustive; instead, they represent issues of critical importance to NAMI's mission that also saw significant legislative action in 2019. In each area of focus, key trends and standout bills are identified and briefly analyzed.

Bills are organized into mini-tables within each trend area and are also listed in this bill reference resource for further review. Bills that fit more than one section or area of focus are listed in all to which they apply. Bills that were vetoed are noted with an asterisk "*" after the bill number.

Other special components of the report include "Understanding the Issue" features that provide a deeper dive on complex mental health policy issues and "Advocacy Spotlights," which showcase a NAMI State Organization's involvement with a key piece of legislation and illustrate how other advocates may replicate their success.

Methodology

This report is focused on standalone mental health legislation that was enacted or nearly enacted in calendar year 2019. The research for this report was conducted primarily using legislative tracking software (Quorum). Only bills that had reached the minimum status of "Passed Second Chamber" in 2019 were considered for analysis. A secondary source of research were NAMI State Organizations' 2019 state legislative summaries (when available). Review was limited to legislation from the 50 states and Washington, DC.

Bills that did not meet the threshold of having "Passed Second Chamber" (*i.e.*, those that did not advance far into the legislative process) were not included in this report, except where otherwise noted. State budget and appropriations bills were excluded due to the vast differences in how states fund and administer their mental health services and programs across state

INTRODUCTION

agencies and county/local entities. There are a few exceptions in which budget bills are mentioned in this report to discuss a specific provision from that bill. Finally, bills that did not meet one of the "areas of focus" for this report, or bills that were not primarily mental health-focused, were also excluded.

Note that mental health policy spans many issues, all of which are important and worthy of policymakers' attention. However, in the interest of creating an accessible, brief and usable document for advocates and other interested parties, the report's scope had to remain limited and, therefore, this report is not comprehensive of all possible issue areas and related legislation.

Even within these limits, over 600 state mental health bills were collected for consideration in this report. Upon further refinement, nearly 100 bills were included in the final report.

REPORT NAVIGATION KEY

The top right corner of each page features a set of interactive links allowing you to navigate easily to different sections of this report.

Tap a number to navigate to the beginning of each report section.

Tap the hamburger menu to navigate to the interactive Table of Contents.

STATE BILL REFERENCE LINKS

Summary tables of exemplary state bills also include links to the entire bill language.

Tap a bill button to review the entire bill online.

People Get Help Early

Growing evidence shows that when people get help early, it can reduce the long-term symptoms of their conditions. "Getting help early" means providing connections to care, identifying symptoms of a mental health condition early, and intervening with evidence-based and effective treatments as soon as possible to help an individual get well and stay well.

When people get help early, it can change their life's trajectory. Strategies to ensure people get help early include offering mental health education in schools to build awareness and acceptance of mental health conditions and symptoms. It also includes providing school-based or school-linked mental health care to make sure every school-age child can get needed mental health services and supports. But getting help early is not limited to youth and young adults. NAMI believes that all individuals — from youth through adulthood — should have access to care at the earliest signs or symptoms of a mental health condition, including reducing risk factors for suicide.

In this section, we review key trends in legislation in three areas of focus:

1. *Early Intervention*
2. *Mental Health Education*
3. *Suicide Prevention*

The legislation covered in this section is aimed at increasing the early identification, support, and treatment of mental health conditions for children and adults.

Early Intervention

Typically, a person experiencing early episodes of a mental health condition faces long delays before getting treatment that helps. However, recent research shows that early intervention and treatment dramatically impacts the course of mental illness. With effective and timely treatment, early intervention can prevent symptoms from becoming worse, helping an individual continue to stay engaged socially and in school or work. While half of mental health conditions develop by age 14, and 75% by age 24, early intervention is important at all ages — regardless of when symptoms first arise in a person's life.

What does early intervention look like?

Early invention is most often understood to mean early detection and treatment of mental health symptoms before symptoms become unmanageable. While this is true, early intervention can also include other individual and community-level strategies, such as:

- Mental health awareness promotion, education and prevention programs;

- Creating safe and supportive communities where people have options to seek help and support; and

- Reducing mental health risk factors, such as poverty, homelessness, unemployment, suicidal thoughts and access to illicit substances.

Trends in 2019 Early Intervention Legislation

Early Childhood Development

States are increasingly investing in children's early social and emotional development. These programs are focused on young children, recognizing the opportunity to identify children at risk for serious emotional disturbance (SED) and intervening early to achieve the best outcomes.

Iowa's enacted HF 690, which required the creation of a children's behavioral health system with its own unique core services and created a state board for oversight, is a highlight in early intervention policy from 2019 (read more about this effort in the Advocacy Spotlight on page 10).

1   2   3   ≡

1   PEOPLE GET HELP EARLY

Examples of 2019 Legislation Addressing Early Childhood Development

STATE	BILL NUMBER	DESCRIPTION
CO	HB 19-1120	An act that requires the Department of Education to create a mental health education resource bank and adopt education standards for mental health and suicide prevention, and allows for children 12 years and older to receive psychotherapy services without parental consent. Includes appropriations.
IA	HF 690	An act that establishes a children's behavioral health system and a children's behavioral health system state board, and requires certain children's behavioral health core services be available.
ME	LD 997	An act that requires the establishment and implementation of an early childhood consultation program to enable providers to reduce behavioral health issues in children using low-cost strategies.
NH	HB 111	An act that creates a state committee to study the effect of the opioid crisis, substance abuse disorders, and mental health and behavioral problems in New Hampshire children and students.
ND	SB 2313	An act that calls for the development of a system to provide behavioral health services, including early intervention and recovery services, to children; the provision of mental health awareness resources to schools; and the creation of a Children's cabinet to coordinate care across state government, including tribal nations.
OH	HB 12	An act that creates a comprehensive learning network to support young children and their families in facilitating behavioral development and to seek to reduce behavioral health disparities among young children.

Advocacy Spotlight

IOWA

Creating a Children's Mental Health System in Iowa

In Iowa, caring for people with mental health conditions had traditionally been the responsibility of counties, rather than the state. This approach led to huge disparities in what services families could access based on where they lived. Many hurdles contributed to Iowa's challenges, especially workforce shortages, as there are only 55 child psychiatrists in Iowa. NAMI Iowa Executive Director Peggy Huppert explained that this has meant families face three to four months-long waiting lists for services and traveling several hours to see a provider.

In 2019, NAMI Iowa and other advocates made the first step to address their lack of a coordinated children's mental health system by passing a state law (HF 690) guaranteeing the development of a statewide children's mental health system to support all Iowan families. Iowa HF 690 established a children's behavioral health system, a related board and required specific services to be available statewide.

Momentum for this change first came in 2018 when Governor Kim Reynolds (R) signed an executive order to create the Children's Mental Health Board, comprised of patient/family advocates (including NAMI Iowa), elected officials, providers, health plans and other stakeholders. Charged with creating a plan for a viable children's behavioral health system to help families no matter where they lived in the state, the Board had a plan to take to the state legislature by December.

Ultimately, that plan became HF 690, which laid out a vision for a comprehensive children's mental health system. Most significantly, the bill mandated a specific set of services for children that must be made available in every region of the state by set dates. The bill also mandated crisis services, which were virtually non-existent for children with behavioral health concerns, said Huppert.

HF 690 was passed with overwhelming support in both chambers. "We had the right group of people at the right time with the right amount of pressure to get it done," said Huppert.

NAMI Iowa Executive Director Peggy Huppert (center) pictured with Iowa Governor Kim Reynolds (left) and Lieutenant Governor Adam Gregg (right).

1   2   3   ≡

1   PEOPLE GET HELP EARLY

Advocacy Spotlight
IOWA

It is now the
law in Iowa
that we have a
system of care
for children."

While the bill had widespread support, NAMI Iowa and their partners did encounter some opposition, including concerns on a provision to require universal behavioral health screening for children. "The stigma surrounding mental health is so strong for some communities that we had parents tell us, 'I don't want my kid getting any diagnosis because it will mark them for life,'" explained Huppert.

Finding funding for the new system is the most critical roadblock to implementation, and the COVID-19 pandemic will certainly have an impact. Another challenge is to hold providers, legislators and government agencies accountable to the timeline, even amid the pandemic. Huppert believes that is NAMI's role. "We, as NAMI, have to bring up the issues that no one else will," she said.

Despite ongoing challenges, NAMI Iowa knows that the state has taken a huge step toward ensuring children and families can access life-changing care. "It is now the law in Iowa that we have a system of care for children," said Huppert. "By certain dates, services are to become available. They are not suggestions; they are mandates. I know that people like me and organizations like NAMI are going to continue to put pressure on regions and providers to make sure that those promises are fulfilled."

NAMI Iowa's Keys to Success

Looking back at the passage of HF 690, NAMI Iowa shared the following advice for other mental health advocates:

Go Big and Plan for the Long Haul
Be willing to negotiate, but only when it proves absolutely necessary and not simply to make your bill's passage more likely.

Build Relationships with Legislators
Look at your state representatives to see who has the power and influence to help you meet your goals.

Recruit Powerful Allies
Find support in your community and activate broad coalitions to help tackle issues that affect mental health.

Hold Systems Accountable
Bring the power of lived experience to the negotiating table and add oversight mechanisms into the bill language to hold key stakeholders accountable.

Early Psychosis

Early or first-episode psychosis (FEP) refers to when a person first shows signs of losing contact with reality, such as hallucinations or delusions. This episode of time is critical to connecting a person with potentially life-changing treatment. Sadly, this opportunity is often missed because the type of treatment most effective for FEP, known as coordinated specialty care (CSC), is not widely available. However, in 2019, Illinois and Washington sought to expand access to CSC with new laws aimed at addressing funding barriers for CSC.

Examples of 2019 Legislation Addressing Early Psychosis

STATE	BILL NUMBER	DESCRIPTION
IL HB 2154	An act that requires state regulated health insurance plans to provide coverage of coordinated specialty care for first episode psychosis treatment.
WA SB 5903	An act that requires the state Medicaid authority to collaborate with the University of Washington and the Washington Council on Behavioral Health to develop a statewide plan to implement and finance coordinated specialty care programs in licensed or certified community behavioral health agencies.

Understanding the Issue

Coordinated Specialty Care for First Episode Psychosis

1   2   3   ☰

1   PEOPLE GET HELP EARLY

Coordinated specialty care (CSC) for First Episode Psychosis (FEP) is a highly effective, evidence-based intervention which helps young people experiencing early psychosis reach their recovery goals. Every year, roughly 100,000 youth and young adults experience a first episode of psychosis, which can involve loss of contact with reality, such as hallucinations — seeing or hearing things that others do not — or delusions — beliefs that are not based in reality. Psychosis is often associated with schizophrenia and related mental health conditions.

Inadequate and delayed treatment can take a heavy toll on individuals and families. Schizophrenia costs the U.S. economy an estimated $155.7 billion a year in direct health care costs, unemployment and lost productivity for caregivers. Historically, treatment for psychosis has started only after crises — frequently long after the first episode of psychosis. At that stage, treatment is often limited to managing symptoms rather than promoting wellness.

The Recovery After Initial Schizophrenia Episode (RAISE) study by the National Institute of Mental Health (NIMH) showed that FEP programs delivering the CSC model help young people with psychosis get significantly better. This team-based model promotes early intervention and includes recovery-oriented psychotherapy, case management, medication management, family support and education, supported education and employment, and peer support services.

FEP programs delivering CSC are setting a new standard of care and are changing the trajectory of mental illness, including reducing the severity of symptoms, resulting in fewer hospitalizations, and helping young people stay in school longer, get back to work and stay socially connected.

Despite the strong research base, funding remains a challenge for FEP programs. In part due to NAMI's advocacy, the federal Community Mental Health Services Block Grant provides a base level of money for FEP programs in states. Unfortunately, that funding is not adequate to make programs readily available to all who need it. Medicaid plans and commercial health insurance typically do not cover the full cost of FEP programs, especially the critical component of supported education and employment, as well as outreach to the community. Because of this, additional funding is needed to sustain effective, evidenced-based FEP programs.

NAMI believes that every young person experiencing psychosis deserves to realize the promise of hope and recovery. States should consider dedicating general funds to expanding FEP programs, making CSC available to everyone who needs it. Additionally, states should explore innovative ways to ensure program sustainability by developing alternative payment models within state Medicaid programs and regulating coverage for CSC within commercial insurance plans (see IL HB 2154).

For additional resources on Coordinated Specialty Care, see:

NAMI's *First Episode Psychosis Programs: A Guide to State Expansion*
NIMH's research on Recovery After an Initial Schizophrenia Episode (RAISE)

Mental Health Education

Education is an essential strategy for removing the stigma associated with mental health conditions. The general lack of visibility and discussion around mental health in our society has contributed to children growing up with little or no understanding of what mental health is, how to identify symptoms, how to support their peers and, most importantly, how to manage their own thoughts and emotions.

Health education is a common component of many students' education experience. With depression and anxiety on the rise in youth, incorporating mental health into health education programs, or adding stand-alone mental health curricula, is critical to support youth mental health. This is why NAMI has given priority to growing mental health education in schools as a key objective in NAMI's 2020–2025 Strategic Plan.

What does mental health education look like?

Connecting youth to the right services and supports starts with teaching them how to recognize mental health challenges in themselves and others. Mental health education can teach students from an early age how to talk about mental health, how to recognize signs and symptoms of mental health challenges in themselves as well as friends and family, and where they can go for help.

Beyond mental health curricula, schools can further support students by adopting policies and training programs for staff geared toward supporting youth with mental health challenges and connecting them to services. Examples can include training school personnel on how to recognize the signs and symptoms of mental health conditions and intervene, introducing wellness programs into schools, and developing school processes for regularly notifying students and parents of available mental health resources.

Trends in 2019 Mental Health Education Legislation
Mental Health Curricula

Building up mental health education in primary and secondary schools can significantly reduce the stigma around mental illness, as well as help youth identify symptoms personally and among peers and know how to seek help. In 2019, several states required schools to incorporate mental health into their health curricula or expanded their existing mental health education requirements.

Texas's enacted SB 11 was a highlight in mental health education policy in 2019. The bill requires public school districts to add mental health and suicide prevention education to their curricula, increase school personnel's capacity to support students' mental health, and increase community-based mental health treatment for children. The law was enacted in a challenging environment that many mental

1 PEOPLE GET HELP EARLY

health advocates face in the wake of incidents of mass violence. Read more about this effort in the Advocacy Spotlight on page 16.

Examples of 2019 Legislation Addressing Mental Health Curricula

STATE	BILL NUMBER	DESCRIPTION
CO	HB 19-1120	An act that requires the Department of Education, upon request, to provide technical assistance to a school district in designing mental health curricula.
MN	HF 1	An act that encourages school districts and charter schools to provide mental health instruction for grades 4-12 and requires that the Commissioner of Education provide districts and charter schools with resources gathered by Minnesota mental health advocates every other year.
NV	SB 204	An act that requires health education courses include instruction on mental health.
NH	HB 131	An act that establishes a commission on mental health education and behavioral health and wellness programs in K-12 schools; the commission is responsible for expanding community and non-profit mental health services, developing threat assessment task forces, promoting evidence-based best practice suicide prevention information and more.
NH	SB 282	An act that requires school districts and chartered public schools to develop suicide prevention policies, provide training for school faculty on suicide prevention, establish a point of contact if a student is believed to be high risk, and educate students on the importance of healthy choices and warning signs of mental health issues.
NJ	S 2861	An act that ensures that students K-12 receive mental health education in conjunction with physical health education and that the curriculum also includes age-appropriate information on substance abuse.
TX	SB 11	An act that requires mental health and suicide prevention as part of the school health curriculum, among other changes.

Advocacy Spotlight

TEXAS

Changing School Climate with Mental Health Education

SB 11 requires that mental health be a part of students' education.

On May 18, 2018, a school shooting in Santa Fe, TX, resulted in the death of eight students and two teachers, making it the third-deadliest high school shooting in the U.S. to date. In the aftermath of such tragedies, lawmakers often turn to mental health reform, despite recent studies indicating that mental illness does not drive mass violence. Yet even in this challenging environment, NAMI Texas found success advancing student mental health while fighting stereotypes and misinformation about mental illness with Senate Bill 11 (SB 11).

During the legislative session, NAMI Texas made investing in student mental health and wellbeing a top priority. According to NAMI Texas Executive Director Greg Hansch, it was clear that "all too often, children fall through the cracks and their mental health conditions aren't addressed until it is a crisis situation." Research backs up this claim, showing that the delay from the onset of mental health symptoms to treatment is an average of 11 years.

SB 11 requires that mental health be a part of students' education and school personnel be trained in how to respond to youth experiencing mental health challenges, and it also boosts the children's mental health workforce. However, the original bill was not a "mental health" bill, it was focused on school safety, violent threats and emergencies. That changed when NAMI Texas and allied organizations succeeded in attaching several amendments to SB 11, adapted from priority bills that had died earlier in the session.

To build support for SB 11 and the need for mental health resources in schools, NAMI Texas worked with the Texas Coalition for Healthy Minds, a diverse coalition of groups dedicated to improving mental health and substance use care in Texas. NAMI Texas identified a unique role they could play in the SB 11 campaign by bringing attention to the role of parents in student mental health. NAMI Texas succeeded in getting language added to the bill that encourages schools to provide parents with mental health information and resources. To make this possible, Alissa Sughrue, Policy

Mental health advocates gather at the NAMI Texas 2019 Mental Health Capitol Day Rally.

1 2 3 ≡

1 PEOPLE GET HELP EARLY

Advocacy Spotlight
TEXAS

This provision
will help
them better
understand
what their
classmates are
going through
and how they
can help their
classmates,
friends or peers
access care."

Coordinator at NAMI Texas, explained, "We had to be aggressive about it. Not because anyone was opposed, but because groups consistently forgot about the parents in this issue."

The biggest challenge NAMI Texas had was repeatedly needing to educate legislators and their staff that mental illness does not cause violence. Attitudes started to change after a hearing on SB 11 when NAMI Texas decided to shift their messaging strategy. "Rather than talking about what does not cause violence, we decided to start talking about what is connected to violence, and that made a big difference," Sughrue explained.

Ultimately, NAMI Texas and their partners' advocacy transformed SB 11 from a bill that largely addressed the physical security of school buildings to a broader effort aimed at creating the best possible climate for students to learn and thrive. NAMI Texas is especially excited about the long-term impact of bringing mental health education into the schools. "[This policy change will] facilitate more understanding among public school students," said Hansch. "They often don't have any foundation of knowledge about mental health because it's not something they have been educated on before. So, when they see their fellow students having a hard time, they mistake it for something else and may stigmatize and bully when their classmate/peer is struggling. This provision will help them better understand what their classmates are going through and how they can help their classmates, friends or peers access care."

NAMI Texas' Keys to Success

Looking back at the passage of SB 11, NAMI Texas shared the following advice for other mental health advocates:

Fight Myths with Facts
Do not allow mental illness and violence to be tied together. Relentlessly educate decision makers about mental illness and the complexities of predicting violence.

Scout for Opportunities
Look for other avenues for legislative successes if your priority bills hit a

roadblock. NAMI Texas became involved with SB 11 later in session, but they were still able to leave their mark on the bill by inserting key priorities.

Reflect Marginalized Communities
Examine policies and language for blind spots or disproportionate consequences toward marginalized communities.

1 PEOPLE GET HELP EARLY

School Protocols and Staff Training

School personnel can be critical to identifying early symptoms in students and connecting them to care. Several bills in 2019 required schools to design and implement new policies and protocols to promote their students' mental health and wellness, as well as train school personnel on how to recognize and respond to signs of a mental health condition or crisis, including suicidal ideation.

A 2019 highlight in this area of policy was Washington's SB 5903, which requires widespread mental health supports to be available and requires trainings for staff. Specifically, the bill requires coordination and training on behavioral health for school district staff, requires the state to provide infant and early childhood mental health consultations to parents, and requires a statewide plan to develop school-based supports for students.

Examples of 2019 Legislation Addressing School Protocols and Staff Training

STATE	BILL NUMBER	DESCRIPTION
CA SB 428*	An act that requires school districts and charter schools to bi-annually notify students and parents on how to access student mental health services on campus and in the community; the bill also requires that a specific percentage of school staff receive mental and behavioral health training.
CT SB 750	An act that creates a task force to study policies and procedures for higher education institutions regarding the availability of mental health services; the task force will also analyze the way that the institution facilitates the return of students who took a leave of absence due to mental illness and evaluate the mental health training provided to faculty and staff.
IL SB 1731	An act that requires that every two years, school staff and administrators who work with students K–12 to undergo training to better identify warning signs of mental health conditions and at-risk behavior and to appropriately intervene.
IL HB 2152	An act that requires each public university to implement peer support programs utilizing student peers living with mental health conditions on campus, in addition to increasing access to clinical mental health services and requiring universities to have specific policies in place to raise mental health awareness and engage students who are in need of mental health services.
NV SB 80	An act that requires the establishment of a Handle with Care Program, which requires law enforcement officers and others to notify trained public school personnel of a child who has been exposed to a traumatic event.

* Denotes a bill that was vetoed.

1   PEOPLE GET HELP EARLY

Examples of 2019 Legislation Addressing School Protocols and Staff Training
(Continued)

STATE	BILL NUMBER	DESCRIPTION
NH	HB 131	An act that establishes a commission on mental health education and behavioral health and wellness programs in K-12 schools; the commission is responsible for expanding community and non-profit mental health services, developing threat assessment task forces, promoting evidence-based best practice suicide prevention information and more.
OR	HB 2191	An act that includes the mental or behavioral health of a student as a valid reason to be excused by a principal or teacher from school.
TX	SB 11	An act that increases teacher training on mental health and trauma-informed practices; creates a funding mechanism for schools to develop student mental health and suicide prevention strategies; requires schools to increase parental awareness and engagement on issues of mental health, suicide and substance abuse; requires the Texas Education Agency to disseminate mental health resource information to education service centers; and creates the Texas Child Mental Health Consortium.
TX	HB 19	An act that requires local mental health authorities to employ a mental health professional who would be housed at the regional education service center and serve as a resource for school districts in their region.
WA	SB 5903	An act that implements policies relating to children's mental health including, the creation of a children's mental health work group, behavioral health training for school district staff, a provision of mental health literacy and healthy relationship curriculum by the superintendent of the school district.

1   2   3   ≡

Suicide Prevention

As the 10th leading cause of death in the United States, suicide is a national public health crisis. In 2018, 10.7 million adults seriously contemplated suicide, including 3.3 million who made suicide plans and 1.4 million who made a nonfatal suicide attempt. Although suicide is rarely caused by any single factor, experiencing a mental health or substance use condition elevates a person's risk for suicide.

According to the CDC, rates of suicide have increased in nearly every state since 1999. Some demographic groups have seen sharper increases, with dramatic spikes in suicide rates for Black youth and in rural and frontier communities.

Many factors contribute to suicide among those with and without diagnosed mental health conditions. Regardless of an individual's history, suicidal ideation represents a mental health crisis that requires an early and immediate mental health response with supports like crisis counseling.

What do suicide prevention strategies look like?

Because there is no single cause of suicidal ideation, there are several policy strategies that have been effective in preventing suicide or reducing suicide attempts. First, state legislation may focus on reducing factors that increase risk of suicide, including creating suicide prevention programs that promote outreach and reduce isolation for at-risk students. Additionally, states have pursued strategies that promote resilience and coping strategies at all levels of society (individual, family and community). For example, recent legislation in Louisiana (HB 53) requires school staff to educate students on coping strategies and warning signs of mental health conditions and requires schools to identify a person in the school who can serve as a point of contact for at-risk students. Other bills have encouraged special training to help school personnel communicate with family members about these issues and direct families to appropriate resources.

Trends in 2019 Suicide Prevention Legislation

State Bodies to Study and Develop Suicide Prevention Strategies

In reaction to state-level crises, states will often pursue legislation to create a cross-functional body to study the impact of the issue and explore solutions that will work within that state given its unique make-up. Responding to the growing rates of suicide, in 2019 state policymakers pursued establishing commissions and other bodies to study the issue and develop systemic suicide prevention strategies (MI SB 228 and OR SB 707). In one case, a state sought to specifically examine the issue of suicide in Black youth (NY A6740B).

1   PEOPLE GET HELP EARLY

Examples of 2019 Legislation Addressing State Bodies to Study and Develop Suicide Prevention Strategies

STATE	BILL NUMBER	DESCRIPTION
MI	SB 228	An act that creates a suicide prevention commission within the Michigan Department of Health and Human Services and describes its duties.
NY	A6740B*	An act that establishes a suicide prevention task force to study current mental health practices and prevention models for Black youth, recommend practices to increase effectiveness, determine potential reasons for the high number of Black youth suicides, and provide a report to the governor of its findings.
OR	SB 707	An act that creates a Youth Suicide Intervention and Prevention Advisory Committee to advise the Oregon Health Authority on the development and administration of strategies to address suicide intervention and prevention for children and youth 10–24 years of age.

* Denotes a bill that was vetoed.

Suicide Prevention Training

Suicide rates for young adults are particularly high, with suicide being the second-leading cause of death for people aged 10–34 years old. As a result, state policymakers worked in 2019 to implement trainings on how to recognize and respond to the warning signs of suicide for students and school personnel in primary and secondary schools and higher education settings (HI SB 383; LA HB 53; NV AB 114; NV SB 204; NH SB 282; OR SB 52; and TN HB 1354). Lawmakers also focused on suicide prevention programs for first responders (NJ A 1028 and NV SB 483). An outlier and notable highlight in suicide prevention legislative activity was Maryland's HB 77, which decriminalized attempted suicide.

Nevada's enacted legislation, SB 204, was a high point in suicide prevention policymaking in 2019. The legislation required a multi-faceted policy for suicide prevention to be adopted by each public and private school that will include prevention procedures, outreach and training. Implementation will be supported by a provision requiring the development of a model policy for schools to follow. More broadly, the law also adds mental health into schools' health education courses.

1   2   3   ≡

1   PEOPLE GET HELP EARLY

Examples of 2019 Legislation Addressing Suicide Prevention Training

STATE	BILL NUMBER	DESCRIPTION
HI	SB 383	An act that requires the development of mandatory youth suicide awareness and prevention programs for public and charter schools' teachers and school staff.
LA	HB 53	An act that requires suicide prevention training for school employees, including awareness of risk factors, communication skills with parents, and dissemination of information on mental health resources to students and families.
MD	HB 77	An act that decriminalizes attempted suicide.
NV	AB 114	An act that requires schools to report whether or not they provide mental health or suicide prevention courses, suicide prevention training for teachers and administrators and the number of incidents of suicide or attempted suicide by students.
NV	SB 204	An act that requires suicide prevention plans to be adopted by all schools, requires plans to reach out to students who are at high risk of suicide, requires health classes to include instruction on mental health, and authorizes the denial of a license to operate a private school for failure to adhere to this legislation.
NV	SB 483	An act that extends an existing State Program for Suicide Prevention to include family members of veterans, members of the military and other persons at risk of suicide in the list of persons to whom such training must be provided. Previously, the training was limited to law enforcement, health care providers and school employees.
NH	SB 282	An act that requires school districts and chartered public schools to develop suicide prevention policies, provide training for school faculty on suicide prevention, establish a point of contact if a student is believed to be high risk, educate students on the importance of healthy choices and warning signs of mental health issues and identify a person who can serve as a point of contact for at-risk students.
NJ	A 1028	An act that requires the state to create a training curriculum to prevent suicide by law enforcement officers and requires law enforcement agencies to report incidents of suicide by a law enforcement officer to the Attorney General.

1   PEOPLE GET HELP EARLY

Examples of 2019 Legislation Addressing Suicide Prevention Training
(Continued)

STATE	BILL NUMBER	DESCRIPTION
OR	SB 52	An act that requires that each school district adopt a policy regarding student suicide prevention for students K-12; the plan must require interventions and activities that reduce risk and promote healing, including identification of school officials who will handle reports of suicide risk, a procedure by which a person may request a school district review action of a school regarding suicide risk, and methods to address the needs of high-risk groups.
TN	HB 1354	An act that requires each state higher institution develop and implement a suicide prevention plan for students and faculty and provide the plan once a semester; each state higher institution may also seek help from appropriate organizations regarding the development of suicide prevention programs.

1   PEOPLE GET HELP EARLY

OTHER AREAS OF FOCUS

People Get Help Early

Mental Health Professionals in Schools

To bolster students' access to mental health care in educational settings (primary, secondary and higher education), some states have set minimum student-to-mental health professional ratios (KY SB 1; IL HB 2152; and WA HB 1355) and encouraged partnerships with local mental health treatment providers (CA SB 75).

Foster Care System Reform

In 2019, states prepared for foster care system changes to implement both mandatory and optional components of the federal Family First Prevention Services Act (FFPSA), which was passed in 2018 with implementation ongoing. These changes focused on compliance with mandatory federal congregate care requirements and development of optional prevention services programs for children "at-risk" of entering foster care (CO HB 19-1308; MT HB 604; NH SB 14; OR SB 221; TX SB 355; TX SB 781; VT H 532; WA HB 1900; WV HB 2010).

Multi-System Youth

Another theme of 2019 state policymaking was to study the unique needs of multi-system youth (ND SB 2313) and several efforts to support youth in the juvenile justice system specifically. This included state legislation clarifying the civil rights of justice-involved youth (IL HB 2649); defining acceptable standards for holding, incarcerating and discharging juveniles (MS SB 2840); and establishing requirements for justice-involved juveniles' access to mental health treatment and other programming (IL HB 3704 and NH SB 14). Other notable bills increased resources for homeless youth (CA AB 1235) and youth that had been sex-trafficked (MS HB 571).

NOTE: *Any bills listed in the section are not included in the Bill Reference Resource. Use links for more information.*

People Get the Best Possible Care

One in five adults in the U.S. experiences a mental health condition, but less than half receive treatment. NAMI's priority that every person "get the best possible care" means that comprehensive mental health care should be the standard for everyone in our country, with access to quality treatment when and where people need it.

When people get the best possible care, they have health insurance that includes parity coverage of mental health and substance use care. They are also able to access a full continuum of culturally competent mental health services and treatment options. To do that, NAMI supports policies that expand the mental health workforce and inclusion of peers and families in decisions that impact them.

In this section, we focus on legislation in six areas of focus:

1. Medicaid and State-Regulated Health Insurance Coverage
2. Mental Health and Substance Use Parity
3. Medication Access
4. Continuum of Mental Health Services
5. Mental Health Workforce
6. Inclusive and Culturally Competent Care

The legislation covered in this section is aimed at expanding and ensuring access to effective treatment options and quality and affordable care.

Medicaid and State-Regulated Health Insurance Coverage

NAMI believes that all people with mental health conditions deserve accessible, affordable and comprehensive health care. This is critical for individuals with mental health conditions to access care for both their mental and physical health needs. There are a variety of types of insurance coverage, governed by both federal and state governments. States play a significant role in Medicaid plans, as well as fully insured health benefit plans and state employee health benefit plans (collectively referred to as "state-regulated coverage" in this report).

Medicaid is the public health insurance program for individuals with low income and is the single largest payer of mental health services in the U.S. In fact, Medicaid covers more than one in four non-elderly adults with serious mental illness. While Medicaid benefits vary from state to state, Medicaid plans usually offer more comprehensive mental health benefits than private insurers. And more people have been able to get Medicaid coverage in recent years due to the Affordable Care Act (ACA), which made Medicaid expansion possible.

State-regulated plans represent a significant portion of the private health insurance market. The most common examples of state-regulated plans include individual and small group plans, such as those available on the federal health insurance exchange (Healthcare.gov) and state-based exchanges.

What should health insurance coverage for mental health care look like?
Every health plan should include mental health benefits that are comprehensive, accessible and affordable — and covered at parity with other types of health care benefits. Mental health benefits should cover a range of mental health services spanning from outpatient to acute care, and an extensive variety of mental health professionals should be covered. Coverage should be barrier-free, meaning individuals should not have to jump through any administrative hurdles, such as work requirements, to sign up or maintain their coverage.

 Trends in 2019 Medicaid and State-Regulated Health Insurance Coverage Legislation
Medicaid Coverage
To date, 39 states (including Washington, DC) have expanded Medicaid as allowed in the ACA. Medicaid expansion has proven to be a critical source of coverage and care for persons with mental health conditions.

Sadly, most of the legislative action in 2019 on Medicaid expansion involved state legislatures pursuing only limited expansions, including some that rolled back voter-approved full Medicaid expansion, while other bills would have restricted access to

services by adding barriers such as work requirements. NAMI opposes any effort to take Medicaid coverage away from people who do not meet a work requirement. Instead, NAMI urges all states to expand Medicaid, as indicated in the ACA, to ensure more people with mental health conditions have access to essential health care services and supports.

In 2019, Tennessee sought to become the first state to condense their Medicaid funding into a block grant with HB 1280 and a subsequent waiver proposal. NAMI opposes block grants or per-capita caps in Medicaid, which impose financing limits that jeopardize coverage and services for individuals with mental health conditions. Read more about the impact of block grants and NAMI Tennessee's efforts to protect Medicaid funding in the Advocacy Spotlight on page 28.

One notable exception and positive development in Medicaid legislation in 2019 was North Dakota's SB 2012. Not only did the bill extend the state's Medicaid expansion program through July 2021, the bill expanded the number of Medicaid-covered mental health services and mental health professionals to better serve people with serious mental illness.

Example of 2019 Legislation Addressing Medicaid Coverage

STATE | BILL NUMBER	DESCRIPTION
ND SB 2012	An act that extends the existing Medicaid expansion program through July 2021; creates a community behavioral health program to provide comprehensive community-based services; and establishes a peer support specialist certification.

Advocacy Spotlight

TENNESSEE

Don't Cap Our Care: Protecting Medicaid as a Mental Health Lifeline

We have a responsibility to ensure that all individuals, regardless of income level or employment status, have access to mental health care."

Medicaid is one of the most important pathways for people to receive mental health care. Medicaid is traditionally funded with an open-ended funding formula that allows the program to easily expand to serve those in need. Yet in 2019, Tennessee became the first state in the nation to take a step toward forgoing the traditional Medicaid funding formula and implementing a block grant, putting individuals with mental health conditions and their families at risk of losing coverage and care.

After promises from the Trump Administration to provide states with greater flexibility in running their state Medicaid programs, the Tennessee legislature passed HB 1280, a bill ordering the state's Medicaid agency to seek a waiver to transform their federal Medicaid funding into a single lump-sum block grant, which would cap funds from the federal government and jeopardize care.

The resulting Medicaid waiver proposal concerned health advocates across the state (and country). NAMI Tennessee got involved in the waiver process right away, realizing they brought a unique voice to the conversation by drawing attention to the mental health-specific impact of the Medicaid block grant. "I was surprised at the lack of groups that were stepping up to talk about mental health," explained NAMI Tennessee Director of Public Policy Alisa LaPolt.

NAMI Tennessee's campaign to protect Medicaid involved sending advocates to attend public hearings on the proposed waiver and offering testimony to put a spotlight on how critical Medicaid funding is to the mental health community. NAMI Tennessee leaders were strategic with their public comments, ensuring they would be heard at the first public hearing on the waiver, when there was heavy media attention. Further, to show the broad opposition to the proposal, NAMI Tennessee mobilized NAMI Affiliates to reach their local advocates, educate them on the issue and activate them to contact policymakers.

Advocates united against the block grant have faced a tough political environment, with both the governor and state legislature leaders enthusiastically supporting the block grant proposal on the argument that, if

Advocates gather for NAMI Tennessee's 2019 Day at the Hill at the Tennessee State Capitol in Nashville.

Advocacy Spotlight
TENNESSEE

approved, it would offer flexibility and even generate savings. (At the time of this report, the waiver is still under review by the Centers for Medicare and Medicaid Services). However, nonpartisan analysis has consistently shown that Medicaid block grants equal Medicaid cuts. "The block grant program is capped at a certain dollar amount, and that is an incentive for the state to save money by cutting programs," said LaPolt.

Despite the unknown outcome, NAMI Tennessee knows that their advocacy has been effective and worthwhile. LaPolt emphasized why this Medicaid fight was so important to NAMI Tennessee: "We have a responsibility to ensure that all individuals, regardless of income level or employment status, have access to mental health care."

NAMI Tennessee's Keys to Success

Looking back at their fight to protect Medicaid, NAMI Tennessee shared the following advice for other mental health advocates:

Simpler Is Better

Simplify the issue down to its core impact so it can better resonate with both your advocates and legislators.

Consider Your Word Choices

How you talk about benefits or programs matters. Avoid using any language characterizing Medicaid as an "entitlement" or "handout." Equate Medicaid to other types of health insurance; do not say Medicaid "beneficiary" and instead say Medicaid "enrollee" or "member."

Understand Political Realities

Avoid burning bridges if a legislator happens to vote against your policy priorities. You may not have their support for every vote, but if you keep communication lines open and respectful, you can gain their support in the future.

Seek Out Experts

NAMI Tennessee reached out to NAMI's national office for technical assistance in analyzing and responding to the TN waiver proposal.

2   PEOPLE GET THE BEST POSSIBLE CARE

Patient Protections in State-Regulated Plans

The ACA made vast improvements in the availability, quality and affordability of health insurance, including the expansion of mental health as an essential health benefit. However, the ACA's future is uncertain due to a pending federal lawsuit challenging the law's constitutionality, which is expected to be decided in spring of 2021, as well as ongoing efforts to chip away at the landmark health law. In response, states have stepped in to take preemptive action to protect individuals by incorporating important ACA consumer protections into state law.

Washington's HB 1870 is particularly noteworthy as one of the more comprehensive state laws that preserves a wide range of ACA consumer protections, including those most vital to people with mental health conditions. Another bill to note is Maryland's enacted SB 28, which applies mental health and substance use parity protections to short-term limited duration health plans (STLD), a type of "junk" insurance. NAMI opposes the expansion of STLD plans and has joined a lawsuit to invalidate the federal STLD insurance plan rule. To understand the dangers of STLD plans for individuals with mental health conditions, read this factsheet.

Examples of 2019 Legislation Addressing Patient Protections in State-Regulated Plans

STATE	BILL NUMBER	DESCRIPTION
MD	SB 28	An act that requires coverage for behavioral health disorders in short-term limited duration insurance; a health benefit plan must provide benefits of the diagnosis and treatment of mental illness, emotional disorders, drug use disorders and alcohol use disorders.
NV	AB 170	An act that requires an insurer to provide certain information relating to accessing health care services to the Office of Consumer Health Assistance; requires an insurer to offer a health benefit plan regardless of health status.
VT	H 524	An act that requires minimum essential coverage based on the criteria established in federal law; requires that applicable individuals and their dependents are covered at all times.
WA	HB 1870	An act that ensures state law is consistent with federal consumer protection laws and the Affordable Care Act.

Understanding the Issue

ACA Consumer Protections

The Patient Protection and Affordable Care Act (ACA) of 2010 included consumer protections to help improve the quality and affordability of health insurance and ended many discriminatory practices. These protections have helped people with mental health conditions gain comprehensive health coverage and receive mental health services.

Before the ACA, state laws had a patchwork of protections that left large gaps in coverage, especially for people who didn't have employer-based insurance. Policies in the individual or small group insurance market covered fewer benefits and were more expensive, with few states requiring health plans to cover mental health services. Health insurers could deny or cancel health insurance because of having a mental health condition, or charge people more for their coverage. This meant that many people with preexisting conditions, such as mental health conditions or substance use disorders, could not afford private health insurance, and if they could, mental health coverage was often inadequate — if covered at all.

The ACA changed this by:

Expanding Medicaid coverage for adults with incomes up to 133% of the federal poverty level.

Mandating coverage of mental health as one of 10 Essential Health Benefits in many health plans.

Applying mental health and substance use parity protections to all new small group and individual market plans so that coverage of mental health and substance use disorder services is on par with medical and surgical benefits.

Ending health insurers' ability to cancel, limit, outright deny, or charge more for coverage of people with pre-existing health conditions, including mental illness.

Prohibiting yearly and lifetime spending caps so that people are not cut off from critical mental health services during periods of great need.

Extending family coverage up to age 26, giving young adults more coverage options at a time when many mental health conditions first appear.

Requiring coverage of a wide range of preventive services at no out-of-pocket cost.

Providing tax credits and cost sharing subsidies to make health insurance more affordable for individuals and families.

These ACA protections opened the door for many people with mental health and substance use disorders to gain health coverage. For example, before the ACA, many young people were kicked off their parents' insurance by early adulthood — often a critical time when symptoms of mental illnesses can first appear. Thanks to the ACA, young adults with mental health conditions are more likely to be insured and receive care, reducing the economic and emotional burden on these young adults and their families.

Understanding the Issue

ACA Consumer Protections

NAMI believes that all people with mental health conditions deserve accessible, affordable and comprehensive health care. At the time of this report, the ACA remains the law of the land, but legal and regulatory efforts have weakened the law and attempted to repeal it entirely. This includes efforts to expand other forms of insurance that do not have these same consumer protections, also called "junk insurance," which often do not cover mental health and can leave people with few options when they need care. NAMI continues to advocate for comprehensive mental health coverage and consumer protections at the federal level and supports efforts to strengthen state-level insurance requirements, oversight and enforcement.

For more information on how the ACA impacted health insurance for people with mental health conditions, see:

NAMI's *What the Affordable Care Act Has Meant for People with Mental Health Conditions — And What Could Be Lost*

Mental Health and Substance Use Parity

A person's health insurance plan determines what mental health services they can receive, how much those services will cost and which mental health providers they can see. Too often, health insurance covers mental health care differently than other types of medical services, creating barriers to affordable, accessible mental health care and reinforcing a stigma around mental illness and seeking mental health treatment.

Parity is the basic idea that mental health and substance use care are to be covered at the same level as care for other health conditions. In 2008, Congress passed the Mental Health Parity and Addiction Equity Act (MHPAEA), which required plans that cover mental health and substance use care to provide equitable coverage compared to coverage of medical/surgical treatment. The ACA further expanded the impact of the federal parity law by requiring most health plans to cover mental health and substance use disorder care. To build on this, states have enacted parity legislation to expand protections and/or improve compliance and enforcement of the federal law. These efforts have helped create a more level playing field to treat mental and physical health conditions alike.

What do state parity efforts look like?

While MHPAEA is federal law, its enforcement has largely been the responsibility of the states, namely state departments of insurance. Active implementation of parity requirements has been challenging for state regulators and insurers alike. Insurance data shows that the disparity in benefits between what the parity law requires versus what individuals can access is large and is only growing larger.

Fortunately, state policymakers and mental health advocates, including many NAMI State Organizations, have led the call for greater transparency and accountability of parity compliance to stop insurance discrimination against individuals with mental health conditions.

Trends in 2019 Mental Health and Substance Use Parity Legislation

A number of states in 2019 advanced or enacted legislation based on the Kennedy Forum's model parity bill, which is endorsed by NAMI and other mental health and addiction advocacy organizations. The model bill establishes reporting requirements for insurers to demonstrate how they design and apply their managed care tactics and specifies how state insurance departments can implement parity and report on their activities.

An often-overlooked element of insurance coverage related to parity is network adequacy. Ideally, insurers will have robust listings of in-network providers for

individuals to easily find the right provider. However, a recent Milliman report discovered that mental health and substance use provider networks are often inadequate, forcing people to go out-of-network. Massachusetts' enacted H 4210 helps address this problem by requiring insurers to maintain more accurate information on their networks and is a highlight in parity policy from 2019 (read more about this effort in the Advocacy Spotlight on page 35).

Examples of 2019 Legislation Addressing Mental Health and Substance Use Parity

STATE	BILL NUMBER	DESCRIPTION
CO	HB 19-1269	An act that requires full compliance with federal parity requirements in Medicaid and for certain private health plans, updates language on mental health and substance use disorders (SUD) and updates SUD coverage requirements.
DC	B22-0597	An act that requires health insurers comply with the requirements of MHPAEA; imposes annual reporting requirements on health insurers; and bars treatment limitations on the provision of benefits for mental health or substance use disorders unless certain requirements are met. *Note that DC B22-0597 passed in 2017 but was enacted in 2019.*
ME	LD 1694	An act that requires health plans to report their compliance with MHPAEA to the Bureau of Insurance and specifies how the Superintendent of Insurance can monitor and then enforce parity based on these reports.
MA	H 4210	An act that that ensures that accurate information concerning providers is properly listed for each network plan and requires that the provider directory be electronically available, in a searchable format, updated on a monthly basis and accessible to the general public.
NH	SB 272	An act that authorizes the insurance commissioner to enforce MHPAEA and requires the commissioner to examine and evaluate health insurers, health service corporations and health maintenance organizations for compliance.
NJ	A 2031	An act that requires certain insurers provide coverage for medically necessary behavioral health care services; prevents insurers from imposing less favorable benefit limitations on mental health and substance use disorder benefits; and requires the Department of Banking and Insurance to report publicly and to the legislature on parity compliance activities.
WY	HB 211	An act that mandates health insurance coverage parity for mental health and substance use disorders; the commissioner may promulgate reasonable rules which establish exemptions from this application.

2 PEOPLE GET THE BEST POSSIBLE CARE

Advocacy Spotlight

MASSACHUSETTS

Getting Rid
of Ghosts in
Massachusetts

Massachusetts has a serious ghost problem, but haunted houses aren't to blame. For NAMI members, the "ghosts" are found inside their health plan.

If you have sought out mental health care by calling up your health insurance plan's list of providers, you may have noticed that few, if any, of the providers listed are truly available. These networks — ones that appear robust on paper but, in reality, don't exist — are called "ghost" or "phantom" networks. To address this, NAMI Massachusetts fought for H 4210, a new state law aimed at eliminating ghost networks for behavioral health.

Ghost networks for mental health care are a common experience for NAMI families. "Parents would look up the list of providers to help their kids. They'd call up the 50 names listed and by the end they'd just be in tears," explained Monica Luke, Board Member for NAMI Massachusetts. Providers listed by insurers often aren't taking new patients, are no longer accepting that insurance, have closed or have the wrong contact information — all of which forces people to look outside of their network to receive care and causes families to pay more.

NAMI Massachusetts partnered with several groups, including the Children's Mental Health Campaign, the Massachusetts Mental Health Coalition and Massachusetts Association for Mental Health, to work on state legislation to eliminate ghost networks (S 2295, which was later rolled into H 4210). This broad coalition prioritized holding insurance companies accountable for the information they provide — not only which clinicians are in-network but, more importantly, which clinicians are open to new patients.

> Parents would look up the list of providers to help their kids. They'd call up the 50 names listed and by the end they'd just be in tears."

Being part of a coalition meant sharing responsibility for the legislation's progress. NAMI Massachusetts' role was to ensure that the voice of lived experience would be front-and-center during the process. That meant having members from local NAMI Affiliate organizations testify during committee hearings and also building grassroots support for the bill. NAMI Massachusetts relied on digital advocacy campaigns to activate grassroots leaders and credits those campaigns for helping to get the bill over the finish line. "When our community contacts legislators, it's much different than a provider or any other stakeholder. These services are for us," explained Luke.

"Ghost-buster" graphic from the Children's Mental Health Campaign used by coalition partners, including NAMI Massachusetts.

Advocacy Spotlight
MASSACHUSETTS

When our community contacts legislators, it's much different than a provider or any other stakeholder. These services are for us."

Additionally, NAMI Massachusetts found a natural ally with providers' associations, whose members had consistently struggled to get on insurance panels because they were reported as "full" by insurers. Of course, the experience of individuals and families painted a much different picture.

While the strength of the coalition got the legislation passed, implementation of the law has not been without challenges. Compared to other providers, mental health providers may not take as many patients because mental health care is time-intensive, and patients are seen frequently, often once a week or more. However, NAMI Massachusetts was able to collaborate with other members of the Massachusetts Mental Health Coalition on working with the Massachusetts Division of Insurance to prioritize implementation, as well as helping them determine what data needs to be collected to provide an accurate picture of behavioral health providers' availability.

Despite these challenges, Luke shared that it was easy and straightforward to educate legislators and grassroots advocates on the issue. Luke said, "Once we gave folks an example of what a ghost network was, they immediately understood, probably because they'd encountered one before in their own personal life."

NAMI Massachusetts' Keys to Success

Looking back at the passage of H 4210, NAMI Massachusetts shared the following advice for other mental health advocates:

Amplify Your Power Through Coalitions

Partner with coalitions to expand your capacity to get things done. Often, coalition leads will produce template action alerts and other helpful resources for the benefit of all coalition members, and coalitions with diverse organizations can bring unique and powerful perspectives to the table.

Seek Community Input

Take the time to speak directly with your members to better understand what issues are affecting your specific community and learn what advocacy opportunities you might have to make an impact.

Understanding the Issue

The Limits of Parity Law and How to Respond

The 2008 federal parity law was an unprecedented advancement in mental health coverage and a testament to the advocates, including many NAMI leaders, that ensured its passage. Sadly, ensuring access to comprehensive mental health care is more complicated than ensuring the enforcement of this landmark law. There are limits to where parity applies, how well it can strengthen mental health benefits and the types of insurance discrimination it can address. Fortunately, states are finding solutions to these limitations.

Occasionally, the federal parity law is misrepresented as a cure-all for fixing poor insurance coverage of mental health care. That is largely based on the misconceptions that the federal parity law:

1) applies to all health plans and

2) requires coverage of all possible mental health and substance use services.

In truth, the federal parity law only applies to some health plans. Parity does not apply to Medicare plans, small group self-insured employer-based plans or Medicaid fee-for-service plans.

Additionally, parity only comes into play for plans that have or are required to offer a mental health benefit in the first place. For those plans, the parity law requires mental health coverage that is equitable to medical/surgical health coverage but does not require complete coverage. Understanding these nuances is critical in light of new federal flexibilities that allow for the expanded sale of health plans that have fewer required benefits — including plans that lack mental health benefits altogether. In

other words, as junk insurance plans have become more common, mental health parity is at risk.

Further undermining the vision set forth in the parity law is the improper use of "medical necessity" criteria. In March 2018, a federal court found that a subsidiary of UnitedHealth Group used flawed clinical criteria to deny coverage of mental health and substance use services. The court found that they repeatedly deemed mental health and substance use disorder services not "medically necessary," despite providers' recommendations, as a strategy for denying care to enrollees and reducing costs. This type of insurance discrimination cannot be addressed by parity strategies, as care is denied too early in the insurance review process for a parity analysis to even be done.

States can help protect consumers from these harmful practices and strengthen the reach and impact of parity laws. States can prohibit, limit or aggressively regulate the sale of junk insurance plans (for example, MD SB 28 that extends parity protections to short term, limited duration plans). States can also ensure that their statutes extend parity protections to all health insurance plans within their jurisdiction (Medicaid and state-regulated plans). Finally, new strategies are emerging for addressing mental health and substance use disorder insurance discrimination based on medical necessity criteria. California's SB 855, enacted in 2020, is one such trailblazing measure that specifies medical necessity criteria must be based on generally accepted standards of care and that all medically necessary mental health services must be covered by insurance.

Medication Access

Although it may not always be a part of an individual's mental health treatment, medication can be a valuable tool in a person's recovery. Access to prescription medications is essential for many people to successfully manage their mental health condition. For individuals who take medications, one size does not fit all. Mental health medications affect people in different ways, and individuals need to be able to use a medication that works best for them.

Research has found that medication access issues for individuals with mental health conditions result in the worsening of symptoms and increased psychiatric hospitalizations and emergency department visits.

Unfortunately, many barriers often make it harder for individuals to get their prescriptions. Common barriers include step therapy (or "fail first") protocols, prior authorization requirements and preferred drug lists or formulary restrictions. These obstacles can block or delay needed treatment, as well as increase the administrative burden on providers.

What does protecting medication access look like?

Protecting medication access is about ensuring the fewest possible barriers come between individuals and the medications that they need. If barriers are in place, such as step therapy or prior authorization, states should require that it is clear how and why those processes are applied, how prescribers and patients can request an exemption from the process if needed, and that psychiatric medications be exempted from these processes as much as possible. For psychiatric medications, it's also important, regardless of what type of health plan, that formularies be as open as possible and psychiatric medications be categorically excluded from preferred drug lists, which limit patients to certain drugs within the same class.

Trends in 2019 Medication Access Legislation

Step therapy reform was the biggest legislative trend in improving access to medications for mental health conditions at the state level in 2019. Step therapy policies are especially harmful to people with mental health conditions. (Read our "Understanding the Issue" on page 40 to better understand the impact of step therapy on the mental health community and state spending.)

Reform efforts in 2019 focused on limiting the use of step therapy, establishing a clear and timely process for patients to request a step therapy exemption from their insurer, and ensuring that patients who are successfully using a specific medication are not forced to switch.

2   PEOPLE GET THE BEST POSSIBLE CARE

Oklahoma's 2019 bipartisan step therapy law (OK SB 509) was particularly effective. The legislation requires health plans to establish step therapy guidelines based on clinical practice standards, and it also requires processes for exemptions to be created for any drug subjected to step therapy protocols.

Other trends that improved medication access included establishing clear exemptions from and timelines for prior authorization processes (MD HB 751) and limiting out-of-pocket drug costs for patients with chronic conditions, including mental health conditions (NJ A 2431).

Examples of 2019 Legislation Addressing Medication Access
Note some of the bills in this table did not meet "Passed Second Chamber" threshold.

STATE	BILL NUMBER	DESCRIPTION
DE	HB 105	An act that allows patients and prescribing practitioners to have a clear, readily accessible and convenient process to request a step therapy exception determination.
KS	SB 93	An act that requires health insurance plans to consider available and recognized evidence-based and peer-reviewed clinical practice guidelines when establishing step therapy protocols; requires health insurance plans to provide any clinical review criteria applicable to a specific prescription drug covered by the plan; and requires access for patients and prescribers to a clear and readily accessible process to request an exception.
MD	HB 751	An act that requires a certain entity to allow a health care provider to indicate whether a drug is to be used to treat a certain condition; prohibits an entity from requesting a reauthorization for a repeat prescription during a specific time period; and requires a detailed explanation for denial of coverage.
NJ	A 2431	An act that requires health insurers, under certain policies or contracts that provide coverage for prescription drugs, to place limitations on covered persons' cost sharing for prescription drugs.
OK	SB 509	An act that requires insurers use clinical practice guidelines for developing step therapy protocols; requires insurers to provide a process to request a step therapy exception; and requires the step therapy exception process be posted online.
WA	HB 1879	An act that requires a prescription drug utilization management protocol be evidence-based and updated regularly; and requires that the patient and prescribing practitioner have access to a clear, readily accessible and convenient process to request an exception.

Understanding the Issue

Step Therapy

Step therapy (also known as "fail first") refers to an insurance practice that requires individuals to take a lower-cost drug before permitting them to take another, more expensive drug — regardless of what their physician or prescriber recommends. Used to cut costs, step therapy policies are applied when someone is seeking treatment for the first time, but they can also be applied when someone is already taking a pricier medication and doing well on it but switches their health insurance plan.

Step therapy policies are particularly harmful to people with mental health conditions for two reasons:

Mental health conditions are complex. Psychiatric illnesses arise from both biological and experiential factors. For example, different people with the same clinical diagnosis of "depression" may have widely different symptoms and root causes of their condition. As a result, there are no "one-size-fits-all" treatments for any mental health condition.

Psychiatric medications are not interchangeable, even within the same drug class. While psychiatric medications may have similar effectiveness as other drugs in the same drug class, they are unique in how they affect each person and their symptoms. The side effects also impact individuals differently.

NAMI members know all too well how common it is for people to spend weeks, months or even years trying to find the right antidepressant, antipsychotic or other psychiatric medication that helps to manage their symptoms without any intolerable side effects.

The costs of medication failure for people with mental health conditions are substantial. When individuals with mental illness are forced to try and fail on a certain medication simply because it's cheaper, that process can have disastrous results, including an increased chance of emergency department visits, hospitalization, homelessness, incarceration or suicide.

NAMI believes that individuals deserve access to the full array of treatment options, including access to the right medication at the right time. Due to the unique harms that step therapy poses for individuals with mental health and other complex health conditions, some states have implemented reform to limit the use of step therapy. Notably, in the over 20 states that have enacted step therapy reform legislation, none have shown any actual added costs to the state as a result of that legislation (source: State Access to Innovative Medicines Coalition Step Therapy Fiscal Impact June 2020 Fact Sheet).

Continuum of Mental Health Services

The lack of accessible services is a huge reason why 60% of people in need of mental health care never receive it. As the primary administrators of public mental health systems, state governments must figure out how to best allocate and coordinate available resources to close this treatment gap.

Fortunately, studies show that public investment in mental health services is not only effective, but a wise financial decision. For every dollar spent on community mental health services, the return on investment is many times over.

In order to meet their specific needs, individuals and families deserve choices in services, settings and providers. Yet, traditional state mental health systems and funding streams are piecemeal and fragmented, leaving huge gaps in what services are available.

What does a mental health continuum-of-care look like?

An effective mental health system for individuals and families affected by mental health conditions requires a full continuum-of-care, a term which refers to the complete range of services and supports that aid in treatment. There is no single course of mental health treatment that is appropriate for all individuals; rather there are many pathways to the successful management of mental health conditions. Read more about the distinct elements in a continuum-of-care in our "Understanding the Issue" on page 43.

Trends in 2019 Continuum of Mental Health Services Legislation

While mental health systems often have many gaps, crisis services and intensive services are especially hard to access. In 2019, lawmakers sought to fill common mental health service gaps — such as emergency services and intermediate/intensive care for mental health — by improving health coverage for those services and by defining new types of mental health facilities and services in state law.

Of particular note is Washington's HB 1394, which contains significant system changes to support individuals with intensive needs. The law creates a new provider type, Intensive Behavioral Health Facility (IBHF), a community-based residential treatment facility for individuals with behavioral health conditions who require care that cannot be met in other settings. This bill further creates Mental Health Drop-In Centers to provide individuals with voluntary, short-term non-crisis services. Finally, the bill aims to increase psychiatric treatment capacity in hospitals for individuals receiving treatment on an involuntary basis.

An additional effort in Texas required local mental health authorities to assess their capacity for providing a wide range of mental health services (TX SB 633).

Examples of 2019 Legislation Addressing Continuum of Mental Health Services
Note some of the bills in this table did not meet "Passed Second Chamber" threshold.

STATE	BILL NUMBER	DESCRIPTION
CA	AB 451	An act that requires a psychiatric unit within a general acute care hospital to provide emergency services regardless of whether the facility operates as an emergency department.
MA	H 907	An act that requires insurers to allow any individual who is engaged in a continuing course of treatment with a licensed mental health provider eligible for coverage to continue treatment with said provider through an out-of-network option and restricts additional charges that can be placed on individuals for such care.
MA	H 909	An act that provides health care coverage for emergency psychiatric services to individuals who are insured under group insurance commission benefits on a non-discriminatory basis for medically necessary programs.
NH	SB 11	An act that authorizes the Department of Health and Human Services to use general surplus funds for designated receiving facilities and voluntary inpatient psychiatric admissions; requires insurers to reimburse certain facilities for emergency room boarding.
TX	SB 633	An act that increases the capacity of local mental health authorities to provide access to services in specific counties; the Health and Human Services Commission is required to implement a provision of this Act only if the legislature appropriates money for this specific purpose.
WA	HB 1394	An act that ensures continuum of care for behavioral health patients; authorizes the Department of Health to certify/credential Intensive Behavioral Health Treatment Facilities and Mental Health Peer Respite Centers; and establishes a pilot Mental Health Drop-In Center program.

Understanding the Issue

Using NAMI's Mental Health Ecosystem to Identify Service Gaps

Mental health care does not always begin and end in the mental health system. Due to the high rate of justice system involvement for people with mental health conditions, advocates, mental health professionals and law enforcement must partner to divert people with mental illness from the criminal justice system. While many of these efforts have improved responses to people experiencing a mental health crisis, many frontline personnel continue to ask: "Divert to what?"

NAMI developed *Divert to What? Community Services that Enhance Diversion,* a Mental Health Ecosystem framework that can be used to identify the gaps in services and opportunities that can support these efforts. The Ecosystem can be used as an advocacy tool for speaking with policymakers, but it can also be effective for collaborative groups involving law enforcement, mental health professionals, advocates, and other stakeholders committed to reducing their community's dependence on the criminal justice system to respond to mental health issues. It identifies supports and services that are often necessary to help people with mental illness maintain their wellness, but it also acknowledges that every community's ecosystem will look different based on needs, the resources available to meet those needs, and the existing system available to build upon.

Services and supports in the Ecosystem are broken into four categories (*peer and family supports should be available across all categories*):

Outpatient Care is a set of services to support people experiencing symptoms of mental health conditions in getting help early, staying in the community and reducing their need for more intensive — and costly — services later. These services include screenings and assessments for mental health conditions, medications and medication management, cognitive and behavioral therapies, primary health care and treatment for co-occurring disorders.

Social Support refers to services that assist in recovery and wellness beyond just medication and cognitive therapy. Access to a safe place to live, income and a supportive community are key pillars to overall wellness. Services include transportation, income supports, housing, supported employment and education, NAMI programs, case management and intensive multidisciplinary programs.

Crisis Services include a variety of supports that provide a safe and humane response to someone experiencing a mental health crisis. With a goal to reduce the role of law enforcement and increase connections to community-based care, crisis care should include crisis respite centers, hotlines, mobile crisis units, non-law enforcement crisis transportation and mobile outreach.

Inpatient Care refers to mental health care provided in a hospital or residential setting, which can reduce the stress of daily responsibilities for a period for those who require more intensive care. In addition to providing psychiatric services, services should include programming that focuses on life skills that prepare someone to return to their community. Inpatient care includes short-term inpatient care, long-term inpatient care and competency restoration services.

For more information, visit:
nami.org/divert-to-what

1   2   3   ≡

Mental Health Workforce

Many types of professionals deliver the evidence-based cognitive, behavioral and medication therapies that are key to mental health treatment. Those professionals include (but are not limited to): psychiatrists, psychologists, nurses, physician assistants, counselors, marriage and family therapists, social workers and peer support workers.

Unfortunately, there is a severe mental health workforce shortage in the U.S. A 2016 report from the Health Resources & Services Administration (HRSA) shows that certain areas of the country have few or no mental health or substance use disorder treatment providers at all. Workforce shortages are further intensified by problems such as high turnover and job vacancy rates, a lack of specialized providers (e.g., for children or older adults), aging workers, and low salaries and service reimbursement rates in the mental health field.

What does addressing the workforce shortage look like?

To meet the increased demand for services, especially during national crises, states must invest in and support strategies to grow the workforce, train talented professionals and retain their skills within the mental health system. This can include addressing licensure rules, offering financial incentives and expanding the workforce through peer support specialists.

Trends in 2019 Mental Health Workforce Legislation

Licensure and Practice Rules

To address workforce shortages, states have bolstered their mental health workforce with changes to mental health professionals' licensure and practice rules. These changes include: making out-of-state providers available with licensure reciprocity agreements (GA HB 26; KY SB 22; ND SB 2012; and WA SB 5054); creating new licensures for mental health-related professionals (NJ A 4608 and NJ A 1604); expanding/clarifying the scope of practice of specific health professionals (NH SB 225); and enabling providers to fulfill certain staffing requirements via telehealth (MD HB 570).

2 PEOPLE GET THE BEST POSSIBLE CARE

Examples of 2019 Legislation Addressing Licensure and Practice Rules

STATE	BILL NUMBER	DESCRIPTION
GA	HB 26	An act that revises provisions relating to exceptions in licensure; requires criminal background checks for licensure; establishes and provides telepsychology; and enters an interstate compact known as the Psychology Interjurisdictional Compact.
KY	SB 22	An act that develops a streamlined process that allows physicians to become licensed in multiple states to enhance the portability of a medical license.
MD	HB 570	An act that requires regulations be adopted by authorizing outpatient behavioral health programs to satisfy any regulatory requirement that a medical director be onsite through the use of telehealth instead.
NH	SB 225	An act that expands the state's mental health workforce to include physician assistants, including providing reimbursement for their services and authorizing them to carry out involuntary emergency admissions examinations.
NJ	A 1604	An act that provides for the licensure of recreational therapists; upon payment to the board, a license may be granted to any person who is licensed in another state if the requirements are equivalent.
NJ	A 4608	An act that provides for the licensure of behavior analysts and establishes the State Board of Behavior Analyst Examiner.
ND	SB 2012	An act that requires behavioral health divisions to enter reciprocity agreements with others states to certify non-resident applicants as peer support specialists.
WA	SB 5054	An act that increases the behavioral health workforce by establishing a reciprocity program; allows providers with credentials in another state to practice without examination if standards in states are equivalent.

Financial Incentives for Workforce Recruitment

Providers report that recruiting and retaining well-trained staff is a major challenge due to low payment rates from insurers that limit the salaries they can offer potential employees. To incentivize individuals to pursue careers in mental health care and target that care to underserved populations, states have created programs that offer financial incentives, including student loan forgiveness for mental health professionals.

California's AB 565 should be noted for adding county mental health programs as an eligible "practice setting" for an existing state loan forgiveness program. Often, mental health providers are inadvertently excluded from workforce incentive programs because the settings in which they provide care are not explicitly named as eligible sites in the original program.

Examples of 2019 Legislation Addressing Financial Incentives for Workforce Recruitment
Note some of the bills in this table did not meet "Passed Second Chamber" threshold.

STATE	BILL NUMBER	DESCRIPTION
CA	AB 565	An act that establishes a program that provides financial incentives, including repayment of educational loans to a physician or surgeon who practices in medically underserved areas; establishes an appropriated account to provide funding for this program; and expands groups of persons eligible for financial incentives.
IA	HF 532	An act that requires the University of Iowa hospitals and clinics to give priority in awarding federal residency positions to residents of Iowa or individuals who earned degrees from Iowa and requires University of Iowa Carver College of Medicine to conduct a study related to workforce challenges regarding recruitment.
WA	HB 1668	An act that creates the Washington Health Corps, providing loan repayment and conditional scholarships, to support healthcare professionals who provide services in underserved communities. The Washington Health Corps includes a new Behavioral Health Loan Repayment Program (BHLRP). The BHLRP provides loan repayment for credentialed health care professionals who serve in underserved behavioral health areas.

Peer Support Training and Certification

Using peer support workers to expand the mental health workforce and improve access to care has gained attention as a promising strategy across the country. Peer support workers draw upon their personal knowledge and lived experience to provide clients with education and support, make connections to other services, and promote recovery and resiliency. Depending upon their training and certification, they may provide either mental health and/or substance use support services.

In 2019, states worked to grow peer support services by establishing training and certification programs for mental health peer specialists.

Examples of 2019 Legislation Addressing Peer Support Training and Certification

STATE	BILL NUMBER	DESCRIPTION
CA	SB 10*	An act that requires the State Department of Health Care Services to establish by July 2020 a statewide peer support specialist certification program; requires an amendment of the Medicaid state plan to include certified peer support specialists as a provider type for Medi-Cal program.
ND	SB 2012	An act that establishes peer support specialist certification.

* Denotes a bill that was vetoed.

Inclusive and Culturally Competent Care

Lived experience, culture, beliefs, sexual orientation, gender identity, values, race and language all affect how individuals experience mental health conditions. In fact, cultural differences can influence what treatments, coping mechanisms and supports work for a person with a mental health condition. Moreover, no one should be subject to practices that can cause or worsen mental health symptoms. The care and treatment a person receives should not only be evidence-based, but it should also reflect a person's culture and identity.

People with mental health conditions have always faced stigma and discrimination. More than half of individuals with a mental health condition don't receive treatment, and members of some communities, including Black, Indigenous and People of Color (BIPOC) and LGBTQI+, face even more barriers to accessing care and effective treatments. But when a person is able to access care, and that treatment incorporates cultural needs and differences, it can significantly improve outcomes.

What does providing inclusive and culturally competent care look like?
To provide effective care relevant to individuals' experiences, states should include peers and families in any efforts to reform or change mental health systems. Inclusion of peers and families is not only important at the individual treatment level, but the voices of lived experience are also crucial to inform changes to mental health systems and can help ensure that the needs of those affected by mental illness are met. States should also work to prioritize policies that tailor mental health care to the needs of unique communities and ban discredited practices that can cause further trauma.

Trends in Inclusive and Culturally Competent Care Legislation
Lived Experience Requirements for Advisory Bodies
In 2019, several states commissioned formal advisory bodies to improve the state's mental health system (such as Iowa's efforts on children's mental health, as noted on page 10 in the Early Intervention area of focus). Many of these advisory bodies specifically require the inclusion of peers and family members with lived experience of mental health conditions. These measures showcase the community-level impact of state mental health policies and provide for greater transparency and opportunity for community input on state mental health systems.

Bringing the voice of lived experience to the policymaking table is always a best practice, no matter how broad or specific the issue. Maine's LD 40 required family members to be part of a Commission tasked with revamping the entire system serving children with behavioral health conditions and developmental disabilities. Meanwhile, Oregon's SB 138 required a "consumer of mental health services" or a

"family member of a consumer" to be a part of the Mental Health Clinical Advisory Group, which advises the state on medication algorithms of psychiatric medications.

Ideally, the bodies will have multiple representatives from statewide mental health advocacy organizations that include openings for both individuals with direct lived experience and the lived experience of family members/caregivers to provide the broadest possible perspective of the mental health system from the peer and family communities.

Examples of 2019 Legislation Addressing Lived Experience Requirements for Advisory Bodies

STATE | BILL NUMBER	DESCRIPTION
CA — AB 1352	An act that establishes a mental health board to serve in an advisory role and requires the board to review local public mental health systems and advise governing bodies; encourages governing bodies to provide mental health board budget.
IA — HF 690	An act that establishes a children's behavioral health system and a children's behavioral health system state board to oversee implementation of the new system.
ME — LD 40	An act that establishes the Commission to Study Children's Mental Health to study children's mental health and state and federal laws regarding mental health; commission's report must be submitted in time for the following legislative session.
MI — SB 228	An act that creates a suicide prevention commission within the legislative council; designates responsibilities to certain state officers and entities; and allows the commission to research policy recommendations from relevant sources from other states in order to make recommendations to the governor on health policy.
OR — SB 138	An act that creates the Mental Health Clinical Advisory group which shall develop evidence-based mental health treatments and drugs; requires advisory group to report to interim committees on its program in developing algorithms for mental health drugs.

Culturally Relevant Responses

Mental health care is also more effective when it is tailored to be relevant to the culture of the people it is serving. Increasingly, there has been a state legislative focus on studying and responding to mental health concerns, particularly suicide, within the context of specific populations, including military service members and veterans (AZ HB 2488 and NV SB 483), first responders (IL HB 2766 and NJ A 1028) and African Americans (NY A 6740B*).

Examples of 2019 Legislation Addressing Culturally Relevant Responses

STATE	BILL NUMBER	DESCRIPTION
AZ	HB 2488	An act that requires the Department of Health Services to compile an annual report on veteran suicides; report must not contain any personal identifiers; Department of Veterans' Services shall submit all data, including protected health information, if deemed necessary.
IL	HB 2766	An act that creates the First Responders Suicide Task Force to help reduce risk and rates of suicide; requires Task Force to issue final report by Dec 2020 and be dissolved by end of 2021.
NV	SB 483	An act that requires the Statewide Program for Suicide Prevention to include provision of suicide prevention training for family members of veterans, at-risk military members, law enforcement and other groups; and creates public awareness for issues relating to suicide prevention.
NJ	A 1028	An act that establishes a training curriculum designed to prevent suicide by law enforcement officers; training shall be made available to each state, county and municipal law enforcement department and each campus police department; training shall be administered once every five years.
NY	A 6740B*	An act that creates a Black youth suicide prevention task force that will examine and evaluate how to improve mental health and suicide prevention for Black youth.

* Denotes a bill that was vetoed.

Banning of Discredited Practices

Members of the LGBTQI+ community have been subjected to a "treatment" known as conversation therapy, a discredited practice that attempts to alter a person's gender identity and/or sexual orientation. Research shows that conversion therapy is harmful, especially for LGBTQI+ youth, and can trigger depression, anxiety or self-destructive behavior. NAMI opposes the practice of conversation therapy and applauds the states that took action in 2019 to ban it.

Examples of 2019 Legislation Addressing Discredited Practices

STATE	BILL NUMBER	DESCRIPTION
CO	HB 19-1129	An act that prohibits a licensed psychiatric physician from engaging in conversion therapy with a patient under the age of 18; a licensee who engages in these practices is subject to disciplinary action.
HI	HB 664	An act that clarifies that the existing ban on sexual orientation change efforts applies to conversion therapy practices or treatments that seek to change an individual's sexual orientation or gender identity.
MA	H 140	An act that establishes that a health care provider shall not advertise or engage in sexual orientation or gender identity change efforts with patients less than 18 years old; health care providers who violate this act shall be subject to discipline by licensing board.
NY	A 576	An act that prohibits mental health professionals from engaging in sexual orientation change efforts with patients less than 18 years old; expands definition of professional misconduct with respect to mental health professionals.

OTHER AREAS OF FOCUS

People Get the Best Possible Care

Integration of Care

In order to improve the quality of mental health care that individuals and families receive, some states focused on increasing integration between primary and mental health care (IL SB 2085; WA SB 5432; and WA HB 1593), including through the use of behavioral health homes (OR SB 22). Integrated health care brings specialty mental health care together with primary care to better treat the whole person and improve health outcomes.

Involuntary Treatment

Regarding inpatient involuntary treatment (also known as inpatient commitment), the state of Hawaii enacted legislation to create a task force to examine existing laws and make recommendations to the legislature to reduce unnecessary emergency department admissions and improve access to the most appropriate level of care (HI HB 1013). States continue to develop policies on the use of involuntary outpatient treatment, also known as Assisted Outpatient Treatment (AOT). Building off trends from recent years, a few states expanded their commitment statutes and lowered outpatient commitment criteria (MD SB 0403; UT SB 39; and WA HB 1907).

NOTE: *Any bills listed in the section are not included in the Bill Reference Resource. Use links for more information.*

People Get Diverted from Justice System Involvement

When people are in a mental health crisis, they frequently encounter police rather than get medical attention. As a result, people with mental illness are over-represented in the criminal justice system. On any given day, approximately 44% of people incarcerated in jails and 37% of people in state and federal prisons have a history of mental illness. Jails and prisons have become America's de facto mental health providers but are often unable to provide adequate care as part of a system that is not built to provide health services. That's why NAMI prioritizes diverting people with mental health conditions from justice system involvement.

Diverting people from justice system involvement ensures that mental health crises get a mental health response. Every community should have robust crisis services for people experiencing a psychiatric emergency — allowing them to receive the help they need. Communities should also prioritize diverting people with mental health conditions to treatment and services at every opportunity — before arrest, after arrest and at all points within the justice system. For those who are already justice-involved, states should prioritize efforts to connect individuals with mental health conditions to care during and after incarceration.

In this section, we review trends in three key focus areas:

1. *Crisis Response*
2. *Diversion*
3. *Rehabilitation and Reentry*

The legislation covered in this section is aimed at providing appropriate care to people in a mental health crisis and keeping individuals connected to care by diverting them to treatment and supports rather than incarceration.

Crisis Response

Any mental health crisis requires a safe and humane response. When people in crises don't receive the care they need, they can instead end up in hospital emergency rooms, living on the streets, involved in the criminal justice system or losing their lives.

A mental health crisis should have a mental health response, ideally from a robust crisis care system. Sadly, people in a mental health crisis are often more likely to encounter police than to be connected to appropriate care, with tragic consequences. Receiving timely and appropriate crisis services can be the difference between life and death for individuals with serious mental illness, as nearly one in four people shot and killed by police officers since 2015 has had a mental health condition. Crisis care offers effective alternatives to a law enforcement-only response, including (but not limited to):

- Mobile crisis units
- Crisis hotlines
- Crisis centers
- Non-law enforcement crisis transportation

What does providing robust mental health crisis care look like?

Mental health crisis response services should be a vital part of states' broader mental health systems. While crisis services are highly localized, state policymakers can facilitate community-level changes by requiring training and collaboration for key stakeholders and by offering funding mechanisms for desperately needed crisis services.

Trends in 2019 Crisis Response Legislation

De-Escalation Training for First Responders

One strategy to help ensure that people in a mental health crisis do not end up in jail or prison is to provide training to first responders, primarily law enforcement, about the signs of mental health conditions and how to successfully de-escalate mental health crisis situations, often in the form of Crisis Intervention Team (CIT)-related training. In 2019, many states passed legislation to bolster their current mental health training requirements.

Note that beyond training, CIT and similar programs aim to not only train officers, but also forge ongoing partnerships between law enforcement, mental health treatment providers and the advocacy community (read more about this in our "Understanding the Issue" section on page 58).

Examples of 2019 Legislation Addressing De-Escalation Training Efforts for First Responders

STATE	BILL NUMBER	DESCRIPTION
NV	AB 478	An act that requires that peace officers annually complete at least 12 hours of continuing education on racial profiling, mental health and officer wellbeing.
WA	HB 1064	An act that adopts annual de-escalation training and curriculum for law enforcement officers and makes de-escalation and less lethal options required as a part of law enforcement decision making.

Crisis Services

During a mental health crisis, and often after an initial law enforcement encounter, people with mental illness are too often taken to jail simply because "there's nowhere else to go." Unfortunately, the lack of robust crisis care means there is nowhere to divert people in a mental health crisis. To address this problem, states have passed legislation to invest in building out crisis service systems that include 24/7 crisis treatment centers, crisis lines and mobile crisis outreach teams.

By setting aside funding for mental health crisis service centers and a mobile crisis unit, New Hampshire's enacted SB 11 was a 2019 highlight in mental health crisis services legislation. The law was enacted to help address significant psychiatric boarding. Read more about NAMI New Hampshire's effort to draw attention to this issue in the Advocacy Spotlight on page 56).

Examples of 2019 Legislation Addressing Crisis Services

STATE	BILL NUMBER	DESCRIPTION
MT	HB 660	An act that establishes a mobile crisis unit program; the department shall award competitive grants to local communities for establishing mobile crisis units.
NH	SB 11	An act that establishes that the Department of Health and Human Services commissioner shall solicit requests for proposals for either a fourth mobile crisis team or a second behavioral health crisis treatment center.
WI	AB 56	An act that establishes funding for mobile crisis outreach teams, regional crisis centers and crisis intervention programs.

Advocacy Spotlight

NEW HAMPSHIRE

Numbers
Don't Lie:
Addressing
Psychiatric
Boarding in
New Hampshire

[Psychiatric
boarding is]
medically,
legally, morally,
ethically, and
economically
wrong."

In New Hampshire, if someone goes to the emergency room because they are having a mental health crisis, they consistently find that the hospital has no inpatient capacity to treat them. While the hospital would normally transfer the patient to another hospital or center that specializes in mental health, there aren't enough beds statewide to accommodate the number of people in need. Patients are stuck waiting, with minimal care, in emergency rooms until a bed opens somewhere, a problem known as "psychiatric boarding."

NAMI New Hampshire has been a longtime, vocal advocate against psychiatric boarding. NAMI New Hampshire Executive Director Ken Norton has described the issue as "medically, legally, morally, ethically, and economically wrong." Through their advocacy, NAMI New Hampshire has made the issue a priority for state policymakers and successfully pressed the state to track and release data on how many people were being boarded each day.

NAMI New Hampshire and other organizations helped shape legislation, Senate Bill 11 (SB 11), to address psychiatric boarding by increasing resources for the mental health service delivery system. The legislation not only set aside funding for crisis service centers and a mobile crisis unit, but it also ensured that people who are involuntarily hospitalized receive a timely hearing. Additionally, SB 11 provided a mechanism for hospitals to be reimbursed for people who are held in emergency rooms, which NAMI New Hampshire hopes will lead to better conditions for those waiting on a bed.

NAMI New Hampshire first drew attention to this issue with a large press conference in 2013. Once the state began releasing data on how many people were being boarded, NAMI New Hampshire started posting those numbers on social media twice per week. These posts drew a lot of attention and comments, and were widely shared, which in turn garnered a lot of media attention. Norton also took this data directly to Governor Chris Sununu (R) when he took office in 2017.

SB 11 emerged in part from a 10-Year Mental Health Plan, developed by the state to increase mental health resources and quality of care. That plan came from legislation

New Hampshire Governor Chris Sununu signs SB 11 into law at NAMI New Hampshire office.

1 2 3 ≡

3 *PEOPLE GET DIVERTED FROM JUSTICE SYSTEM INVOLVEMENT*

Advocacy Spotlight
NEW HAMPSHIRE

NAMI New Hampshire helped craft in 2017 (House Bill 400, which required creation of a new mental health plan). A delay in completion of the 10-year plan resulted in numerous mental health bills being introduced, which created confusion and conflict among advocates who had been hoping that the 10-year plan would prompt the state legislature to produce a more comprehensive reform bill.

Advocates argued whether psychiatric boarding should take top priority or if, instead, they should focus on other elements of the 10-year plan. Eventually, NAMI New Hampshire and others were able to coalesce support around SB 11 by reaffirming the commitment that they would continue to fight for all elements of the 10-year plan, including and beyond SB 11.

The enactment
of SB 11 takes
an important
step forward
in realizing the
vision of the
10-year Mental
Health Plan.

The enactment of SB 11 takes an important step forward in realizing the vison of the 10-Year Mental Health Plan. Although the fight for adequate crisis resources is not over, SB 11 will help "divert people from the hospital, law enforcement and incarceration," explained Norton. He added that SB 11 was made possible by "incredible compromise, ongoing discussions and political maneuvering" by the mental health advocacy community together with legislators from both parties determined to move mental health reform forward. NAMI New Hampshire was thrilled when Governor Sununu asked if he could sign the bill at their office, and there was a big turnout of legislators, advocates, families, and people who had experienced psychiatric boarding, and media on hand as the bill was signed into law.

NAMI New Hampshire's Keys to Success
Looking back at the passage of SB 11, NAMI New Hampshire shared the following advice for other mental health advocates:

Stay on Message
Stay united with other organizations whenever possible and emphasize commitment to common goals.

Leverage the Power of Data
To increase awareness and attract media attention, use clear and convincing data to illustrate the issue at hand.

1   2   3   ≡

Understanding the Issue

3 PEOPLE GET DIVERTED FROM JUSTICE SYSTEM INVOLVEMENT

Involving Community Stakeholders and Building Partnerships for Crisis Response

People with mental illness are overrepresented in our nation's criminal justice system. A main contributor to this issue is the absence of comprehensive crisis systems and a reliance on law enforcement to address the needs of people experiencing a mental health crisis. But a mental health crisis deserves a mental health response, which is why many communities are developing crisis response systems to effectively divert people with mental illness away from the justice system and into mental health care.

Effective crisis response must work across systems to meet the needs of people experiencing a mental health crisis, so community partnerships involving a variety of stakeholders are essential when building a local crisis response system. Strong partnerships with key stakeholders involved can help gain buy-in for developing and sustaining a new system, help inform aspects of the new crisis system, and support the work of implementation and ongoing sustainability.

Some key partners might include:

Law Enforcement
Despite the importance of reducing the role of law enforcement in mental health crisis, they are currently the primary responders to mental health crises in most communities. Their knowledge of current crisis response can be essential to identifying gaps and opportunities. There also may be instances where law enforcement will need to be part of a crisis response, so getting their buy-in early is helpful.

Mental Health Providers and Local Agencies
Mental health providers can provide insights into crisis response, particularly current barriers to developing and sustaining crisis services. It is also important to have leaders from local mental or behavioral health departments involved in any efforts. New services will be part of developing a crisis response system and these groups will be important in developing, operating and coordinating those services.

Mental Health Advocates
Many advocacy groups, such as NAMI, are already engaged in advocating for alternative crisis responses. Advocates play a key role in engaging policymakers and leaders, ensuring that resources and policies are committed to sustain the crisis response system. Advocates should not only be involved in raising awareness around the problems with the current system, but also ensuring that any response meets the needs of those with mental illness who have had direct interactions with the local crisis care system.

Hospitals
People in crisis are often taken to emergency rooms for evaluation and acute care, regardless of whether the hospital offers any kind of psychiatric care or not. Including hospital executives or leaders can support coordination with other health care providers to reduce delays to care for individuals in need.

Emergency Services
Emergency medical services (EMS), firefighters and 911 call centers can all play a role in responding to a

1 2 3 ≡

*Understanding
the Issue*

3 *PEOPLE GET DIVERTED FROM JUSTICE SYSTEM INVOLVEMENT*

Involving Community Stakeholders and Building Partnerships for Crisis Response

mental health crisis. Not only can they help identify current gaps and opportunities for developing a crisis response system, but their resources might also be used in a new crisis response.

Other partners to consider include leaders from homelessness services and shelters, workforce development centers or other social services providers. While they might not be involved in an immediate crisis, the ultimate goal of robust crisis care is to help people stay in the community, and these organizations are part of ongoing care and support. Business leaders and local policymakers (such as mayors, governors, city managers or county commissioners) can also be a key to ensuring the crisis response system you are developing receives the resources it needs.

For additional resources on partnerships or building crisis response systems, see:

Chapters 1 and 2 of the CIT International guide, *Crisis Intervention Team (CIT) Programs: A best practice guide for transforming community responses to mental health crises*

SAMHSA's *National Guidelines for Behavioral Health Crisis Care: Best Practice Toolkit*

Diversion

When individuals experiencing mental health symptoms come to the attention of law enforcement, communities should have policies and programs to divert them to treatment and other services — before arrest, after arrest and at all points in the justice system.

Two million times a year, people with serious mental illness are booked into America's jails and prisons. Criminalizing mental health conditions is ineffective and costly for states and harmful to the individuals who are incarcerated, their family members and their community.

What does diversion look like?

Helping people avoid or get out of jail and into community alternatives is a top priority for NAMI. Diversion programs can help ensure that individuals are guided to mental health services and supports as an alternative to incarceration. NAMI supports a variety of approaches to diverting individuals from unnecessary incarceration into appropriate treatment, including pre-booking (police-based) diversion, post-booking (court-based) diversion, alternative sentencing programs and post-adjudication diversion (conditional release).

● ● ● *Trends in 2019 Diversion Legislation*

Mental Health Courts and Diversion Programs

Ideally, mental health diversion takes place pre-arrest or pre-booking, so individuals avoid incarceration altogether. However, post-arrest or post-booking diversion programs are the more common type of jail diversion. Mental health courts, specialized courts that give individuals suspended sentences in exchange for completion of a court-ordered treatment plan, are an example of a post-arrest diversion program. In 2019, New Hampshire and Texas enacted legislation dedicated to creating and expanding their mental health courts. Notably, Washington increased access to pre-booking diversion with SB 5444, which gives law enforcement the authority they need to divert individuals to treatment instead of arresting them.

3 *PEOPLE GET DIVERTED FROM JUSTICE SYSTEM INVOLVEMENT*

Examples of 2019 Legislation Addressing Mental Health Courts and Diversion Programs

STATE | BILL NUMBER	DESCRIPTION
NH | SB 51	An act that establishes a commission to study the expansion of the mental health court system; the commission shall submit a report of its findings on or before November 2020.
TX | HB 601	An act that clarifies procedures and reporting requirements for individuals in the criminal justice system who may have a mental illness with the aim of diverting more individuals to a mental health court or treatment program.
WA | SB 5444	An act that establishes that when a police officer has reasonable cause to believe an individual who has committed a crime suffers from a mental disorder, the police officer has the authority to and should take the individual to a crisis stabilization unit or triage facility.

Rehabilitation and Reentry

Once incarcerated, many individuals lose access to needed medications and other treatment services and end up getting worse, not better. In fact, less than half of people (45%) with a history of mental illness receive mental health treatment while held in local jails.

And individuals with a mental illness stay in jail longer than their counterparts without mental illness. They are at risk of victimization and, often, their mental health conditions can get worse.

Most of the individuals who are incarcerated are not violent criminals, and most people in jails have not even gone to trial yet, so they have not been convicted of a crime. Many others are serving short sentences for minor crimes. In addition to having inadequate access to mental health care in jail, this problem continues after individuals are released. After leaving jail, many individuals no longer have health insurance coverage and no connection to community-based health care. A criminal record often makes it hard for individuals to get a job or housing. Many individuals, especially without access to mental health services and supports, have a difficult time successfully re-entering the community and avoiding re-incarceration.

What does successful rehabilitation and reentry look like?

Individuals should experience a timely competency evaluation and restoration process to reduce the amount of time spent in jail. Additionally, when individuals are in jail or prison, they should have access to needed medication and support, be exposed to opportunities to further their education and future employment opportunities, and should not be subjected to harmful practices, such as solitary confinement.

As they approach their release date, individuals should be signed up for health coverage before release, if possible, and should get extensive help planning for their basic needs to ensure they get back on track. This should include, but is not limited to, connections to a community-based mental health treatment provider (including setting up an initial appointment), safe and stable housing, income support, food assistance, and continued support with their education and finding a job.

● ● ● *Trends in 2019 Rehabilitation and Reentry Legislation*

Competency Restoration

For any criminal trial to move forward, courts must first determine that the defendant is competent to stand trial. For people with mental illness, they can spend months waiting for a competency evaluation and even longer for competency restoration services, which typically involves psychiatric services. This creates a

1 2 3 ═══

3 PEOPLE GET DIVERTED FROM JUSTICE SYSTEM INVOLVEMENT

backlog of court cases and greatly extends the amount of time people with mental health conditions are forced to stay in jail.

Fortunately, states can take legislative action to create a timelier process for competency evaluations and restorations.

Examples of 2019 Legislation Addressing Competency Restoration

STATE	BILL NUMBER	DESCRIPTION
CO	SB 19-223	An act that enables courts to order competency evaluations be conducted on an outpatient basis or at the place the defendant is in custody; if the department conducts in-custody competency evaluations, the evaluation shall begin as soon as practicable; and evaluations shall be completed within 42 days if out-of-custody.
WA	SB 5444	An act that provides timely competency evaluations and restoration services to persons suffering from behavioral health disorders; to be eligible for outpatient competency restoration, a defendant must adhere to medication and abstain from alcohol and unprescribed drugs.

Solitary Confinement

Solitary confinement can trigger and worsen mental health symptoms and increases the risk of suicide and self-harm. Solitary confinement is particularly harmful for individuals with mental health conditions, and NAMI urges all federal, state and local corrections officials to use alternatives to solitary confinement for this population.

Recognizing the evidence on the dangers of solitary confinement, some states passed laws restricting its use in 2019.

Examples of 2019 Legislation Addressing Solitary Confinement

STATE	BILL NUMBER	DESCRIPTION
NJ	A 314	An act that declares that isolated confinement in state correctional facilities should only be used when necessary and should not be used against vulnerable populations or for time periods that foster trauma.
NM	HB 364	An act that establishes that an inmate who is younger than 18 years old or an inmate who is pregnant shall not be placed in restricted housing; an inmate with a serious mental disability shall not be placed in restricted housing; an inmate with a serious mental disability may be placed in restricted housing for no more than 48 hours if to prevent an imminent threat on the inmate or another inmate and a report must be filed.
VA	HB 1642	An act that requires the Department of Corrections to report to the General Assembly and the Governor on or before October 1 of each year certain population statistics (including mental health codes) of persons incarcerated in state correctional institutions, including certain statistics regarding offenders placed in and released from restrictive housing.
VA	SB 1777	

Health Services for Justice-Involved Populations

Strengthening access to health care for people who are incarcerated and re-entering the community helps to both improve their mental health and reduces the likelihood that they will return to jail or prison. In 2019, states took measures to improve the health of justice-involved populations, including by increasing reimbursement rates for health services provided in correctional settings (NC H 106), providing navigator services to those re-entering the community (WA SB 5444), and implementing changes to connect correctional health systems with community-based health care systems (OR SB 973). Additionally, Nevada became the fourth state to ban private prisons, citing concerns that for-profit correctional institutions can jeopardize inmates' access to health care (NV AB 183).

A notable highlight for promising policy promoting health services for justice-involved individuals is Washington's SB 5444, which created the position of Forensic Navigator. This new position is designed to help people with mental health conditions connect to services in the community with the aim of stopping the revolving door in and out of our corrections system.

Examples of 2019 Legislation Addressing Health Services for Justice-Involved Populations

STATE	BILL NUMBER	DESCRIPTION
NV	AB 183	An act that prohibits private entities from providing certain core correctional services in state prisons; services include housing, custody, medical and mental health treatment.
NC	H 106	An act that improves inmate health care reimbursement and establishes a telemedicine pilot program; requires departments to work together to enable social workers to qualify for and receive federal reimbursement related to Medicaid eligibility for inmates.
OR	SB 973	An act that establishes the Improving People's Access to Community-based Treatment, Supports and Services Program which will award grants to counties and recognized Indian tribes to establish evidence-based and tribal-based programs to provide support and services within the criminal justice system.
WA	SB 5444	An act that establishes a forensic navigator (FN) position to assist people who are referred for a competency to stand trial evaluation or who are ordered to receive outpatient competency restoration.

State Legislation Report: Trends in State Mental Health Policy

Conclusion

2019 was a very active year in state policymaking on mental health. Across the states, clear areas of progress and focus emerged. Notably, states are bringing mental health and suicide prevention into their formal education curriculums, which is a critical step forward in helping youth understand how to recognize mental health conditions and how they can find support for themselves or a loved one.

Mental health advocates also repeatedly mobilized against harmful state legislation or administrative efforts that threatened Medicaid funding for mental health services and Medicaid coverage for people with mental health conditions. At the same time, advocates were active in reforming parts of the commercial insurance markets by passing laws that mandate more active and transparent enforcement of the federal parity law.

Finally, reforming mental health crisis response was a clear priority for many states. While NAMI envisions a world in which a robust mental health crisis service system exists to support people in crisis, law enforcement officers remain the de facto response in many areas. Fortunately, states are increasingly passing legislation to create alternatives to law enforcement response, such as mobile crisis teams and crisis treatment centers.

It is worth mentioning that this report was compiled in 2020 as we experienced the outbreak of COVID-19 and a national economic downturn, making 2020 a year like no other. COVID-19 has rocked the nation's mental health with a rapid increase in the number of individuals experiencing symptoms of mental health conditions for the first time, and those with existing conditions seeing their symptoms worsen. As of this writing, the CDC reports that one-third of people in the U.S. now meet the clinical criteria for depression or anxiety.

Our nation's public health crisis goes beyond COVID-19 as we grapple with the mental health impact of not only the pandemic, but the economic crisis and recent efforts to address racial injustice. States' support of mental health will be more critical in the years to come than ever before.

NAMI's national office and NAMI State Organizations will be closely watching how states support mental health during this time and will fight to ensure that people with mental health conditions and their families have the resources they need to survive and thrive.

Help NAMI Advocate for Change on Capitol Hill

Join our advocacy network at nami.org/ TakeAction

NAMI State Organizations fight for individuals and families affected by mental illness at your statehouse and are responsible for many of the incredible policy changes described in this report.

Find your NAMI State Organization at nami.org/Local

NAVIGATING

a mental health

CRISIS

A NAMI resource guide for those experiencing
a mental health emergency

nami

INTRODUCTION

NAMI developed this guide to support people experiencing mental health crises, their friends and families by providing important, sometimes lifesaving information. This guide outlines what can contribute to a crisis, warning signs that a crisis is emerging, strategies to help de-escalate a crisis and resources that may be available for those affected. Also included is information about advocating for a person in crisis along with a sample crisis plan.

In this guide, we use the term "mental health condition" and "mental illness" interchangeably to refer to a variety of mental illnesses including, but not limited to, depressive disorders, bipolar disorder, post-traumatic stress disorder and anxiety disorders. NAMI views mental health conditions or mental illnesses as physical conditions, often requiring medical treatment just like other conditions such as diabetes or high blood pressure. Mental health conditions are physical illnesses that result when one of the many mechanisms of the brain is not adequately doing its job.

Learning that someone you love has a mental health condition can be frightening. People experiencing episodes of mental illness—and the people who care for them—need information. However, that information is not always readily available and the search for answers may require more energy and persistence than what we have available in times of crisis.

When a mental health condition is present, the potential for a crisis is never far from mind. If you are reading this guide, it is likely that you or someone you love may be experiencing symptoms of a mental health condition.

Crisis episodes related to mental illness can feel overwhelming. There is the initial shock, followed by a flood of questions.

- Why him/her?
- Why me?
- What went wrong?
- Why is this happening now?
- What did we do?
- What didn't we do?
- What can we do?

Everyone can feel overwhelmed, confused, or experience anger, grief or guilt. It's important to remember that we all do the best that we can with the information and the resources we have available to us.

Like any other health crisis, it's important to address a mental health emergency quickly and effectively. With mental health conditions, crises

Prevalence of Mental Illness in the United States

- **1 in 5 adults—43.8 million or 18.5%**—experiences mental illness in a given year
- Among the **20.2 million adults** who experienced a substance use condition, **50.5% (10.2 million adults)** had a co-occurring mental illness
- **1 in 5 youth aged 13-18 (21.4%)** experiences a severe mental health condition at some point during their life; for children aged 8-15 that estimate is 13%
- **46% of homeless adults** staying in shelters have a mental illness and/or substance use disorder
- **20% of state prisoners** and **21% of local jail prisoners** have a recent history of a mental health condition
- **70% of youth in juvenile justice systems** have at least one mental health condition
- **60% of all adults** and almost **50% of all youth ages 8-15** with a mental illness received no mental health services in the previous year
- **African-Americans and Hispanic-Americans** used mental health services at about half the rate of Caucasian-Americans in the past year and Asian Americans at about 1/3 the rate
- **50% of adults with mental illness** report experiencing symptoms prior to the age of 14; **75%** prior to the age of 24

Source: National Institute of Mental Health www.nimh.nih.gov

can be difficult to predict because often there are no warning signs. Crises can occur even when treatment plans have been followed and mental health professionals are actively involved. Unfortunately, unpredictability is the nature of mental illness.

Unlike other health emergencies, people experiencing mental health crises often don't receive instructions or materials on what to expect after the crisis. It is also possible that the first point of contact may be with law enforcement personnel instead of medical personnel since behavioral disturbances and substance use are frequently part of the difficulties associated with mental illness.

Many NAMI affiliates work closely with local law enforcement agencies to ensure that officers receive training on how to respond effectively to people experiencing crises. NAMI believes mental health crises should be addressed efficiently and effectively. At NAMI we want you to know that:

- You are not alone
- This is not your fault
- You deserve help and support
- There is support available for you

Consequences of Lack of Treatment

- Mental illness costs America $193.2 billion in lost earnings per year
- Mood disorders, including major depression, dysthymic disorder and bipolar disorder, are the third most common cause of hospitalization in the U.S. for both youth and adults aged 18–44.
- People with mental illness face an increased risk of having chronic medical conditions. Adults in the U.S. with mental illness die on average 25 years earlier than others, largely due to treatable medical conditions
- Over one-third (37%) of students with a mental health condition age 14–21 and older who are served by special education drop out—the highest dropout rate of any disability group
- Suicide is the 10th leading cause of death in the U.S., the 3rd leading cause of death for people aged 10–24 and the 2nd leading cause of death for people aged 15–24
- More than 90% of children who die by suicide have a mental health condition
- Each day an estimated 18-22 veterans die by suicide
- 2 million people with mental illness are booked into jails each year.
- Nearly 15% of men and 30% of women booked into jails have a serious mental health condition.
- Once in jail
  - At least 83% of jail inmates with a mental illness did not have access to needed treatment and as a result, their conditions get worse
  - They stay longer than their counterparts without mental illness
  - They're at risk of victimization
- After leaving jail
  - Many no longer have access to needed health care and benefits
  - A criminal record often makes it hard for people to get a job or housing
  - Many people, especially without access to mental health services and supports, wind up homeless, in emergency rooms and often re-arrested

Simply jailing people experiencing mental health crises creates huge burdens on law enforcement, corrections facilities and state and local budgets. It does not protect public safety and people who could be helped are being ignored.

Sources: National Institute of Mental Health, U.S. Department of Justice and Substance Abuse and Mental Health Services Administration

NAMI wants to help you navigate what can be an overwhelming time in your life by helping you understand what to expect.

UNDERSTANDING mental illness

Mental illnesses are medical conditions that disrupt a person's thinking, feeling, mood, daily functioning and ability to relate to others. Mental illness doesn't develop because of a person's character or intelligence. Just as diabetes is a disorder of the pancreas, a mental illness is a disorder of the brain that can make it difficult to cope with the ordinary demands of life. No one is to blame—not the person and not the family.

Currently, there are no blood tests or tissue samples that can definitively diagnose mental illnesses. Diagnoses are based on clinical observations of behavior in the person and reports from those close to the person. Symptoms vary from one person to another, and each person responds differently, which complicates getting an accurate diagnosis. The most common mental illness diagnoses include depressive disorder, bipolar disorder, schizophrenia and anxiety disorders, but there are many others.

Regardless of the diagnosis, symptoms can be similar and can overlap, especially in times of crisis. The following are some examples of symptoms that you may have noticed in yourself or your loved one.

Social Withdrawal
- ✔ Sitting and doing nothing for long periods of time
- ✔ Losing friends, unusual self-centeredness and self-absorption
- ✔ Dropping out of previously enjoyed activities
- ✔ Declining academic, work or athletic performance

Irregular Expression of Feelings
- ✔ Hostility from one who is usually pleasant and friendly
- ✔ Indifference to situations, even highly important ones
- ✔ Inability to express joy
- ✔ Laughter at inappropriate times or for no apparent reason

Mood Disturbance
- ✔ Deep sadness unrelated to recent events or circumstances
- ✔ Depression lasting longer than two weeks
- ✔ Loss of interest in activities once enjoyed
- ✔ Expressions of hopelessness
- ✔ Excessive fatigue, or an inability to fall asleep
- ✔ Pessimism; perceiving the world as gray or lifeless
- ✔ Thinking or talking about suicide

Changes in Behavior
- ✔ Hyperactivity, inactivity, or alternating between the two
- ✔ Lack of personal hygiene
- ✔ Noticeable and rapid weight loss or gain
- ✔ Involvement in automobile accidents
- ✔ Drug and alcohol abuse
- ✔ Forgetfulness and loss of personal possessions
- ✔ Moving out of home to live on the street
- ✔ Not sleeping for several nights in a row
- ✔ Bizarre behavior, e.g. skipping, staring, strange posturing, grimacing
- ✔ Unusual sensitivity to noises, light, clothing

Thought Disturbances
- ✔ Inability to concentrate
- ✔ Inability to cope with minor problems
- ✔ Irrational statements
- ✔ Use of peculiar words or language structure
- ✔ Excessive fears or suspiciousness, paranoia

Even if a person doesn't have a formal diagnosis of substance abuse, alcohol and other drugs are frequently involved in times of mental health crises.

It's important to be aware that the presence of one or more of these symptoms is not evidence that a mental illness is present. They may be a typical reaction to stress, or they may be the result of another underlying medical condition.

In fact, one of the most important parts of an initial psychiatric evaluation is a physical work up to rule out underlying physical illnesses. This is especially true when symptoms develop rapidly.

There is always reason for hope. New, more effective therapeutic interventions, support services and medications are being developed. Recovery education and peer support can help people cope with and even lessen symptoms so they don't impact daily functioning.

Co-occurring Conditions

Often mental illness is not the only thing going on in a person's life. Other conditions may also be present that further complicate the difficulties created by mental illness. This is referred to as co-occurring, co-morbid conditions or dual diagnosis—meaning that there is more than one condition causing the difficulties.

Substance use/abuse is the most common. Even if a person doesn't have a formal diagnosis of substance abuse, alcohol and other drugs are frequently involved in times of mental health crises. In addition to complicating the symptoms of mental health conditions, alcohol and other drugs can also interfere with medications that may be used to treat the conditions.

In a crisis, it's important to let health care professionals know any information that you have about everything the person is taking including supplements, homeopathic remedies, over the counter medications, prescriptions, alcohol and street drugs to help determine what role that may play in the current crisis episode. All too frequently there can be interactions between substances, including those that are legitimately prescribed.

There is effective treatment available for co-occurring conditions. Once the crisis has resolved a health care provider can help make arrangements for a referral for appropriate services.

UNDERSTANDING
mental health crises

A mental health crisis is any situation in which a person's behavior puts them at risk of hurting themselves or others and/or prevents them from being able to care for themselves or function effectively in the community. Many things can lead to a mental health crisis. Some examples of situations that can lead or contribute to a crisis include:

Home or Environmental Stressors
- Changes in relationship with others (boyfriend, girlfriend, partner, spouse)
- Losses of any kind due to death, estrangement or relocation
- Conflicts or arguments with loved ones or friends
- Trauma or exposure to violence

School or Work Stressors
- Worrying about upcoming projects or tasks
- Feeling singled out by co-workers/peers; feeling lonely
- Lack of understanding from peers, co-workers, teachers or supervisors
- Real or perceived discrimination
- Failing grades, losing a job

Other Stressors
- Being in crowds or large groups of people
- Experiencing community violence, trauma, natural disasters, terrorism
- Pending court dates
- Using or abusing drugs or alcohol
- Starting new medication or new dosage of current medication
- Treatment stops working
- Stopping medication or missing doses

Warning Signs of a Mental Health Crisis

It's important to know that warning signs are not always present when a mental health crisis is developing. Common actions that may be a clue that a mental health crisis is developing:

- Inability to perform daily tasks like bathing, brushing teeth, brushing hair, changing clothes
- Rapid mood swings, increased energy level, inability to stay still, pacing; suddenly depressed, withdrawn; suddenly happy or calm after period of depression
- Increased agitation verbal threats, violent, out-of-control behavior, destroys property

- Abusive behavior to self and others, including substance use or self-harm (cutting)
- Isolation from school, work, family, friends
- Loses touch with reality (psychosis) - unable to recognize family or friends, confused, strange ideas, thinks they're someone they're not, doesn't understand what people are saying, hears voices, sees things that aren't there
- Paranoia

It's important to be aware of how long the changes in personality or daily functioning have been occurring and how much difficulty they're causing. This level of detail can be important for the health care professional to know.

When the Crisis Involves the Risk of Suicide

Risk of suicide is a major concern for people with mental health conditions and those who love them. Encouraging someone to get help is a first step towards safety.

People who attempt suicide typically feel overwhelming emotional pain, frustration, loneliness, hopelessness, powerlessness, worthlessness, shame, guilt, rage and/or self-hatred. The social isolation so common in the lives of those with mental illness can reinforce the belief that no one cares if they live or die.

Any talk of suicide should always be taken seriously. Most people who attempt suicide have given some warning—but this isn't always the case. If someone has attempted suicide before, the risk is even greater.

Common warning signs of suicide include:

- Giving away personal possessions
- Talking as if they're saying goodbye or going away forever
- Taking steps to tie up loose ends, like organizing personal papers or paying off debts
- Making or changing a will
- Stockpiling pills or obtaining a weapon
- Preoccupation with death
- Sudden cheerfulness or calm after a period of despondency

- Dramatic changes in personality, mood and/or behavior
- Increased drug or alcohol use
- Saying things like "Nothing matters anymore," "You'll be better off without me," or "Life isn't worth living"
- Withdrawal from friends, family and normal activities
- Failed romantic relationship
- Sense of utter hopelessness and helplessness
- History of suicide attempts or other self-harming behaviors
- History of family/friend suicide or attempts

What To Do If You Suspect Someone is Thinking About Suicide

If you notice any of the above warning signs or if you're concerned someone is thinking about suicide, don't be afraid to talk to them about it. Start the conversation.

Open the conversation by sharing specific signs you've noticed, like:

"I've noticed lately that you [haven't been sleeping, aren't interested in soccer anymore, which you used to love, are posting a lot of sad song lyrics online, etc.] ..."

Then say something like:
- ✔ "Are you thinking about suicide?"
- ✔ "Do you have a plan? Do you know how you would do it?"
- ✔ "When was the last time you thought about suicide?"

If the answer is "Yes" or if you think they might be at risk of suicide, you need to seek help immediately.
- ✔ Call a therapist or psychiatrist/physician or other health care professional who has been working with the person

- ✔ Remove potential means such as weapons and medications to reduce risk
- ✔ Call the National Suicide Prevention Line at 1-800-273-8255 or call 911

Listen, express concern, reassure. Focus on being understanding, caring and nonjudgmental, saying something like:
- ✔ "You are not alone. I'm here for you"
- ✔ "I may not be able to understand exactly how you feel, but I care about you and want to help"
- ✔ "I'm concerned about you and I want you to know there is help available to get you through this"
- ✔ "You are important to me; we will get through this together"

What Not to do
- ✗ Don't promise secrecy. Say instead: "I care about you too much to keep this kind of secret. You need help and I'm here to help you get it."
- ✗ Don't debate the value of living or argue that suicide is right or wrong
- ✗ Don't ask in a way that indicates you want "No" for an answer
  - "You're not thinking about suicide, are you?"
  - "You haven't been throwing up to lose weight, have you?"
- ✗ Don't try to handle the situation alone
- ✗ Don't' try to single-handedly resolve the situation

What Not to say
- ✗ "We all go through tough times like these. You'll be fine."
- ✗ "It's all in your head. Just snap out of it."

Please remember, a suicide threat or attempt is a medical emergency requiring professional help as soon as possible.

WHAT TO DO
in a mental health crisis

When a mental health crisis occurs, friends and family are often caught off-guard, unprepared and unsure of what to do. The behaviors of a person experiencing a crisis can be unpredictable and can change dramatically without warning.

If you're worried that you or your loved one is in crisis or nearing a crisis, seek help. Make sure to assess the immediacy of the situation to help determine where to start or who to call.

- Is the person in danger of hurting themselves, others or property?
- Do you need emergency assistance?
- Do you have time to start with a phone call for guidance and support from a mental health professional?

A person experiencing a mental health crisis can't always clearly communicate their thoughts, feelings, needs or emotions. They may also find it difficult to understand what others are saying. It's important to empathize and connect with the person's feelings, stay calm and try to de-escalate the crisis. If the following suggestions don't help, seek outside assistance and resources.

Techniques that May Help De-escalate a Crisis:

- ✔ Keep your voice calm
- ✔ Avoid overreacting
- ✔ Listen to the person
- ✔ Express support and concern
- ✔ Avoid continuous eye contact
- ✔ Ask how you can help
- ✔ Keep stimulation level low
- ✔ Move slowly
- ✔ Offer options instead of trying to take control
- ✔ Avoid touching the person unless you ask permission
- ✔ Be patient
- ✔ Gently announce actions before initiating them
- ✔ Give them space, don't make them feel trapped
- ✘ Don't make judgmental comments
- ✘ Don't argue or try to reason with the person

If you can't de-escalate the crisis yourself, you can seek additional help from mental health professionals who can assess the situation and determine the level of crisis intervention required.

If you don't believe there is an immediate danger, call a psychiatrist, clinic nurse, therapist, case manager or family physician that is familiar with the person's history. This professional can help assess the situation and offer advice including obtaining an appointment or admitting the person to the hospital. If you can't reach someone and the situation is worsening, consider calling your county mental health crisis unit, crisis response team or other similar contacts.

If the situation is life-threatening or if serious property damage is occurring, don't hesitate to call 911 and ask for immediate assistance. When you call 911, tell them someone is experiencing a mental health crisis and explain the nature of the emergency, your relationship to the person in crisis and whether there are weapons involved. Ask the 911 operator to send someone trained to work with people with mental illnesses such as a Crisis Intervention Training officer, CIT for short.

CIT officers are specially trained to recognize and de-escalate situations involving people who have a mental illness. They recognize that people with mental illnesses sometimes need a specialized response, and are familiar with the community-based mental health resources they can use in a crisis. You can always ask for a CIT officer when you call 911, although they are not available in all areas.

When providing information about a person in a mental health crisis, be very specific about the behaviors you are observing. Describe what's been going on lately and right now, not what happened a year ago. Be brief and to the point.

For example, instead of saying "My sister is behaving strangely," you might say, "My sister hasn't slept in three days, hasn't eaten anything in over five days and she believes that someone is talking to her through the television."

Report any active psychotic behavior, significant changes in behaviors (such as not leaving the house, not taking showers), threats to other people and increases in manic behaviors or agitation, (such as pacing, irritability).

Once you call 911, there are two entities that may become involved—medical/first responders and law enforcement. You need to be prepared for both.

Medical Response/Emergency Department

If the situation can't be resolved on site or it's recommended by first responders or law enforcement, taking your loved one to the emergency department may be the best option. Be aware that if they are transported in a law enforcement vehicle, usual policy is to use handcuffs. This can be upsetting for everyone involved, but may be the only option you have at the time.

You may also be allowed to transport them in your vehicle, or they may be transported via ambulance. **Remember, once first responders arrive, you are not in control of these decisions.** The most important thing is to get to a medical facility for evaluation and treatment as soon as possible.

A visit to the emergency department doesn't guarantee admission. Admission criteria vary and depend on medical necessity as determined by a physician and insurance coverage.

Be prepared for an emergency department visit to be lengthy, likely several hours. Bring anything that may help the person who is in crisis stay calm, like books, music, games, etc. Some hospitals have separate psychiatric emergency units. They're typically quieter and are staffed by mental health professionals and practitioners. Check to see if there is one in your area.

Make sure to bring any relevant medical information, including the names and doses of any medications and your crisis kit, if you have one. If you don't have a crisis kit, there is a Portable Treatment Record in this guide that can help you develop one. It includes a crisis plan and a relapse plan.

Law Enforcement Response

When the law enforcement officer arrives, provide them with as much relevant and concise information about the person as you can:

- Diagnosis
- Medications

- Hospitalization history
- Previous history of violence, suicide attempts or criminal charges

If the person has no history of violent acts, be sure to point this out. Share the facts efficiently and objectively, and let the officer decide the course of action.

Remember that once 911 has been called and officers arrive on the scene, you don't control the situation. Depending on the officers involved, and your community, they may actually take the person to jail instead of an emergency room. Law enforcement officers have broad discretion in deciding when to issue a warning, make an arrest or refer for evaluation and treatment.

You can request and encourage the officers to view the situation as a mental health crisis. Be clear about what you want to have happen without disrespecting the officer's authority. But remember, once 911 is called and law enforcement officers arrive, they determine if a possible crime has occurred, and they have the power to arrest and take a person into custody. Law enforcement can, and often will, call mental health resources in your community. Nearby supports and services may assist in deciding what options are available and appropriate.

If you disagree with the officers don't argue or interfere. Once law enforcement has left, call a friend, mental health professional or advocate—like NAMI—for support and information. To find the NAMI affiliate in your area visit www.nami.org or call 1-800-950-NAMI (6264).

And if your loved one is not admitted to treatment and the situation worsens, don't be afraid to call for help again. The situation can be reassessed and your loved one may meet the criteria for hospital admission later, even though they initially did not.

Family Reactions

Feelings, reactions, and responses to mental health emergencies vary from family to family and person to person within each family. Family members may feel:

- Confusion and disorientation
- Isolation, distancing or denial
- Extreme fatigue
- Guilt based on based on the mistaken assumption that the "parents are to blame"
- Fear for the safety of the individual, the family, and society

- ◆ Anger that such an awful thing has happened to your loved one and family
- ◆ Frustration over the lack of access to services and treatment facilities
- ◆ Outrage at mental health professionals because parents, close relatives, and/or the patient wasn't listened to
- ◆ Concern that you may be judged or criticized by friends, relatives, and colleagues outside the immediate family circle
- ◆ Exhaustion from being on-call 24 hours a day, 7 days a week, 52 weeks a year
- ◆ Desire to escape the stress by leaving, or even abusing substances

If you don't feel safe at any time, leave the location immediately.

When Calling 911 for a Mental Health Emergency

Remember to:
- ✔ Remain calm
- ✔ Explain that your loved one is having a mental health crisis and is not a criminal
- ✔ Ask for a Crisis Intervention Team (CIT) officer, if available

They will ask:
- ✔ Your name
- ✔ The person's name, age, description
- ✔ The person's current location
- ✔ Whether the person has access to a weapon

Information you may need to communicate:
- ✔ Mental health history, diagnosis(es)
- ✔ Medications, current/discontinued
- ✔ Suicide attempts, current threats
- ✔ Prior violence, current threats
- ✔ Drug use
- ✔ Contributing factors (i.e. current stressors)
- ✔ What has helped in the past
- ✔ Any delusions, hallucinations, loss of touch with reality

Tips for While You Wait for Help to Arrive

If you don't feel safe at any time, leave the location immediately.

If you feel safe staying with your loved one until help arrives:
- ✔ Announce all of your actions in advance
- ✔ Use short sentences
- ✔ Be comfortable with silence
- ✔ Allow your loved one to pace/move freely
- ✔ Offer options (for example "do you want the lights off?)
- ✔ Reduce stimulation from TV, bright lights, loud noises, etc.
- ✗ Don't disagree with the person's experience

WHAT TO EXPECT
from mental health treatment

There are a variety of treatment options available for people with mental illness and the best combination of treatment and other services will be different for each person. Recommendations are made by health care professionals based on the type of illness, the severity of symptoms and the availability of services. Treatment decisions should be made by the individual in collaboration with the treatment team and their family when possible. In a crisis, the recommendation may be a hospital stay.

Voluntary admission is always preferable. The immediate outlook is brighter for the person who understands the necessity and benefit of hospitalization and is willing to participate in a treatment plan.

Private insurance may only cover a short hospitalization. Contact the insurance company to see how many hospital days are covered, both per year and per lifetime. Although federal law and the law of most states require parity insurance coverage (meaning psychiatric conditions are supposed to be covered in the same way other physical health conditions are), there are many exceptions to such coverage. Knowing what your insurance will cover before a crisis occurs can help things go smoothly if emergency care is needed. Be sure to check with your insurance company about what age coverage stops for your adult children.

Involuntary admission—commitment—may be recommended for someone who is experiencing extreme symptoms such as psychosis, being violent or suicidal or refuses the health care professional's recommendation to go to a treatment facility. If law enforcement and/or mental health professionals become involved, you may have no choice.

Getting a court order for involuntary hospitalization of an adult with mental illness is complex and varies from state to state. It's designed to balance the need to provide treatment in the least restrictive environment, with protection of the civil liberties of the person who is in crisis. When families see the rapid deterioration of a loved one, the instinct to protect them is strong. We are terrified that they

may get hurt, injure someone else, or even die. Balancing the urgent need for treatment with the person's basic civil rights can be controversial and difficult. Seeking involuntary hospitalization of a family member, without having it damage family relationships or the self-esteem of the person is challenging.

There are specific laws in each state defining the criteria for involuntary commitment to a psychiatric facility. This is a legal process that involves a judge and a hearing. Typically, the criteria include:

- Recent threats or attempts to physically harm themselves or others
- Recent inability to care for themselves—food, clothing, shelter or medical care—due to the mental illness symptoms
- Recent risk of harm to themselves or others

Emergency holds are another option in crisis situations and can be ordered by a physician (and in some states others such as law enforcement) to temporarily confine the person in a secure facility, such as a hospital. Emergency holds typically last for 72 hours—not including weekends and holidays. The purpose of the hold is to keep the person safe while deciding next steps. An emergency hold doesn't necessarily initiate the involuntary commitment process. It's a way to further assess the person while keeping them safe.

Inpatient psychiatric units are more like an Intensive Care Unit (ICU). They can be noisy and appear hectic. Unlike other areas of the hospital where patients generally stay in their room or bed, patients and staff are usually moving around the unit. People may be talking loudly or expressing intense emotions.

Being hospitalized for a mental illness is also different because of the restrictions in place to protect the person receiving treatment. These can include locked doors, clothing and gift rules, restrictive visiting hours and limits on where patients can go. Phones are located only in common areas and their use is sometimes restricted. These rules are in place to help ensure the safety of the patient and others.

Due to privacy laws and treatment schedules, family may have a difficult time reaching their loved one by phone or visiting while they're hospitalized. Many hospitals require the patient to sign a privacy release to allow family members or friends to contact them while hospitalized. When calling the main number, the receptionist will not tell you if your loved one is even in the hospital.

You can ask to be connected to the unit and depending on the hospital, your call may be transferred to the patient phone area or the nursing desk. Be polite but assertive and request that a message be taken to your loved one.

During the hospital stay, it's important that your loved one connects with people from their community who provide support and reassurance. Encourage your loved one to allow calls or visits from friends, neighbors, advocates, specific family members or their spiritual leader.

Visiting hours are often limited to make time for therapy sessions and other treatment. Check with the hospital about these times and any age restrictions. Frequently children under 15 years old may not be allowed to visit. Exceptions may be made if your loved one's children want to visit.

For the health and safety of your loved one and other patients, there are limits on what you can bring into the hospital. You may be required to let staff lock up your purse and coat. Everything brought to your loved one may be inspected,

check with the hospital for what items are allowed. You can always ask a staff member about bringing in an item you are unsure about, such as their favorite food.

Confidentiality

If you are the parent or guardian of someone younger than 18, you generally have access to medical records and input into treatment decisions. It is always preferable for your adult family member to share information with you. However, there are exceptions under federal law (HIPAA - Health Insurance Portability and Accountability Act) that permit providers to release information to you without consent. To learn more about these exceptions, see the guide HIPAA Privacy Rule and Sharing Information Related to Mental Health. You can find the document at www.hhs.gov/sites/default/files/hipaaprivacy-rule-and-sharing-info-related-to-mentalhealth.pdf.

For best results, ask your loved one to sign an authorization for release of this medical information to you during the emergency evaluation or admission process. If they refuse, ask staff to continue asking them throughout treatment in hopes that they will change their mind as their condition improves.

If a release has been signed, family members should request to attend a treatment team meeting that usually involves a social worker, nurse and psychiatrist. Ask the team for the following:

You can give the providers information about your family member, even if they have not consented to have the hospital share information with you.

- Diagnosis and what the diagnosis means
- Course of the illness and its prognosis
- Treatment plan
- Symptoms causing the most concern, what they indicate and how they're being monitored
- Medications prescribed, why these particular medicines have been selected, the dosage, the expected response and potential side effects
- If the diagnosis, medications and treatment plan have been discussed with your loved one, and the reasoning behind those decisions and if not, explain the reasoning
- Pamphlets and book recommendations that explain the illness(es) being treated
- How often you can meet with the treatment team to discuss progress
- Whom you can contact for information between meetings
- The aftercare plan once your family member has been discharged from the facility, and what to do if your loved one leaves against medical advice

At the treatment team meeting, you can describe what factors you think contributed to your loved one's crisis, any particular stressors and anything else you think might be helpful for effective treatment including challenges with adherence to treatment in the past. It's also helpful for you to suggest the most appropriate living situation after their discharge. Be honest and don't apologize if living with you isn't an option.

For more an overview of the Privacy Rule go to: www.hhs.gov/ocr/privacy/hipaa/understanding/consumers/index.html

Types of Treatment

Treatment generally takes place in one of two types of setting: outpatient or inpatient. Outpatient mental health services are provided while the person lives at home and continues their regular routines with work, school and family life. For this reason, outpatient services are considered the least restrictive form of treatment.

Inpatient means that the person is admitted to a treatment environment that requires staying overnight. It may be a hospital, a residential treatment center, or a crisis unit of some sort, but the treatment is provided while the person is on site at the treatment facility 24 hours a day. The length of stay in an inpatient setting varies, and usually depends heavily on the severity of the crisis as well as health insurance coverage.

Research has shown the most effective treatment plan involves a combination of intervention types, regardless of whether treatment takes place in an inpatient psychiatric unit or in an outpatient setting. Examples of interventions or treatment options include:

Psychosocial treatments, including certain forms of psychotherapy (often called talk-therapy) and social and vocational training, are helpful in providing support, education, and guidance for people with mental illnesses and their families.

- **Individual psychotherapy** involves regularly scheduled sessions between the person and a mental health professional. Examples include cognitive behavior therapy (CBT), dialectical behavior therapy (DBT) and interpersonal therapy.
- **Psychoeducation** involves teaching people about their mental health condition and treatment options.
- **Self-help and peer support groups** for people and families led by and for people with personal experience. These groups are comforting because participants learn that others have experiences like theirs and that they're not alone. NAMI Connection and NAMI Family Support groups are examples of peer support groups.
- **Peer recovery education** is structured instruction taught by people who have lived experience and can take place in a single session or a series. NAMI Peer-to-Peer is an example of a peer recovery education program.
- **Peer-run services** are mental health programs where the staff uses information, skills and resources they have gained in their own personal recovery to help others. Peer services are based on principles of empowerment, choice, mutual help and recovery. The goal of peer-run programs is to create a supportive place in which people can find peers who understand them, learn recovery skills and help others. Common types of peer-run programs include:

  ✔ Drop-in or peer support center such as a clubhouse program
  ✔ Peer mentoring, peer case management

- **Certified Peer Support Specialist** work alongside other health care professionals in traditional mental health programs to provide an extra level of support services to people with mental illness

Medications often help a person with mental illness to think more clearly, gain control and stabilize emotions. Although any licensed physician can prescribe medication, psychiatrists and psychiatric nurse practitioners are the most knowledgeable about psychotropic medicines (those used to treat mental illnesses). Ask the prescribing health care professional

- What to expect from the medication
- What is the therapeutic range of dosage
- What side effects are common (and not so common)
- How long it takes for the medication to start working
- How to know if the medicine is working
- What to look for that shows it is working or not
- What to do or say if taking the medication or taking it regularly is a challenge

Keep a written record of all prescribed medications, the recommended dose and how well (or poorly) each works and is tolerated. A medication that works well for one person may be ineffective or intolerable for another. If the medicine isn't working, it's important for one of you to tell the doctor so that adjustments can be made.

Pharmacists are also an excellent source of information if you have questions. Read the package inserts that come with the medicine. It's important to discuss this information and any questions with the doctor who knows the patient and is prescribing the medication(s).

In addition to their intended therapeutic effects, psychotropic medications often have side effects which vary, both among individuals and in intensity and severity. It's important to monitor both intended and unexpected side effects of medicine(s) and report these to the doctor.

It can take weeks or even months for psychotropic medications to be effective, which can be frustrating. If side effects are experienced it's important to contact the clinician that prescribed the medication immediately and discuss options. Stopping a medication without talking with the health care professional first can lead to unwanted complications including a return of symptoms.

Types of Health Care Professionals Involved in Mental Health Treatment

There are different types of health care professionals who treat mental health conditions. A combination of these professionals works as a treatment team with the person and the family to provide the best care possible. Some of the more common types of health care professionals include the following.

- **Psychiatrists** are medical doctors who specialize in psychiatry and are typically in charge of the patient's care plan.

- **Psychologists** administer diagnostic tests, conduct individual, family or group therapy sessions.

- **Psychiatric nurse practitioners** diagnose and treat mental health conditions and provide health care, including prescribing medication.

- **Physician assistants** treat illnesses, including prescribing medications.

- **Registered nurses (RN)** assess the patient's progress and provide emotional support, encouragement and health education. The RN also, administers medications and monitors the overall health of the patient.

- **Therapists** conduct individual, group, or family therapy. The therapist can be a Psychologist (Ph.D.), Licensed Clinical Social Worker (LCSW), Licensed Professional Counselor (LPC), or Marriage and Family Therapist (MFT).

- **Social workers** identify social service and therapeutic needs, help connect the patient with community resources and make referrals for services. They work directly with the patient, their family and community providers to explain treatment options and plans and identify any ongoing needs for the patient.

- **Nursing assistant/psychiatric aide/mental health worker/behavior technicians** work under the direction of psychiatrists, psychologists, nurses and social workers in inpatient settings to provide routine nursing and personal care for the patient, including eating, dressing, grooming and showering. They help ensure that the unit is safe.

- **Case managers** assist with applying for resources such as Social Security benefits and Medicaid. They're aware of housing options in their area and know how to get housing vouchers or rental assistance. They know about community programs and groups, and about job training and possible work.

- **Patient advocates** assist families to resolve or address issues regarding quality, appropriateness and coordination of care for the patient.

♦ **Occupational therapist (OT)/recreational therapists** assess the patient's ability to function independently. Assessment areas include the patient's strengths, behaviors, social skills and cognitive skills, thought processes, activities of daily living, functional abilities, work skills, goals and sensory needs. They also perform evaluations to help determine the best living situation for patients.

Complementary Health Approaches

Traditional medical and therapeutic methods have improved over the years, but they often don't completely get rid of symptoms. As a result, many people use complementary and alternative methods to help with recovery. These non-traditional treatments can be helpful but it's important to keep in mind that, unlike prescription medications, the U.S. Food and Drug Administration (FDA) does not review, regulate, monitor or approve most of them.

The National Center for Complementary and Integrative Health (NCCIH) is the main government agency for investigating non-traditional treatments for mental illness and other conditions. Complementary health approaches, the term favored by NCCIH, encompasses three areas of unconventional treatment:

♦ Complementary methods where non-traditional treatments are given in addition to standard medical procedures
♦ Alternative methods of treatment used instead of established treatment
♦ Integrative methods that combine traditional and non-traditional as part of a treatment plan

To learn more about these options visit https://nccih.nih.gov.

Remember, complementary health approaches may provide additional help but should not be considered as substitutes for traditional therapeutic treatment methods.

Creating an Effective Discharge Plan

The discharge plan includes ways you can help care for and support your loved one once they're released from a hospital or other inpatient treatment setting. Discharge plans are not always shared with family members, but don't hesitate to ask what the plan is for your loved one's care once they're released. The plan should include:

♦ Reason for admission
♦ Information on diagnosis in terms that are easy to understand

- Medications to take after discharge and the following information:
  - Purpose of medication
  - Dosage of medication
  - When to take medication
  - How to take medication
  - Possible side effects
  - Where to get medication and refills
  - Instructions about over-the-counter medications legal substances such as alcohol and nicotine as well as illegal substances considering the patient's history
- Self-care activities such as exercise and diet, physical activity level or limitations and weight monitoring
- Coping skills such as sleep hygiene, meditation or yoga
- Recovery goals, plans for work, school and social outlets
- Crisis management
  - Symptoms that should be reported to the treatment team including the urgency of the issue, whom to contact, how to contact them, and what to do in an emergency during after-clinic hours
  - Action steps and care options for when warning signs occur
- Follow-up appointments (usually within seven business days of leaving the hospital). Make sure you know:
  - When the appointment is (date and time)
  - Where the appointment is
  - Who the appointment is with
  - What the appointment is for
  - How to reschedule the appointment if necessary
- Referrals to community support services, including
  - Mental health and/or substance use disorder support groups
  - Social services available through a variety of county and nonprofit organizations including financial assistance for medications, transportation assistance, nutrition support, emergency housing and volunteer opportunities

Confirm that the medications prescribed at discharge are covered by any heath insurance plan that is in place. Discuss benefit coverage and affordability with the doctor, nurse practitioner or whoever is prescribing the medications. Any changes in medications should be clear to you and your family. It's always best for both the person and the family to be involved in the discharge process.

Everyone should understand why, how and when to take the medications and what other treatment services are planned. Each person can also help inform the treatment team about anything else that will be helpful.

Following a Crisis

A critical part of the discharge plan is an appointment with a mental health care professional, typically within seven days of being discharged. If there are other physical illness concerns, an appointment with an appropriate medical provider should also be scheduled. These appointments should be made before leaving the facility where crisis services were received.

To assist the mental health care professional at the follow-up appointments be prepared with the following information:

- Name all medications
- Purpose of the medication
- Dosage
- Side effects experienced
- Any changes in living situation, access to transportation or other previously unidentified concerns
- Difficulties obtaining or paying for medications
- Success with self-care strategies and coping skills
- Any concerns you have since discharge and how your loved one has responded
- If the crisis plan continues to meet your loved one's needs
- How other medical conditions are being managed

There is a sample Portable Treatment Record at the end of this guide that provides a format for you to use to capture this information and track it going forward. Having a system in place can help make future crises easier because you will have the critical information in a single place. It is good to periodically review the crisis plan with your loved one to be sure it's up to date.

It's important to remember that crisis services are meant to help people with symptoms of mental illness get the help they need in a safe setting. Recovery can be a process that requires ongoing care, treatment and support.

ADVOCATING
for treatment

Your loved one deserves effective and appropriate care for their mental health. However, it can be difficult to find appropriate services or even know where to start looking. Being an advocate, the person that supports and at times speaks for your loved one, is an important role to play. There are three types of advocacy related to mental health: personal advocacy, public advocacy and legislative advocacy.

Personal advocacy starts with educating yourself about available services and understanding client/patient rights. It also includes working through the challenges that may be part of accessing treatment services in your community and state.

Tips to help you in personal advocacy efforts and general communications with health care professionals are:

- Be organized
- Be objective
- Stay calm
- Be effective
- Get support

Effective communication helps ensure that you or your loved one receive appropriate treatment. Good communication involves verbal and nonverbal language and listening skills. It also involves using the language of the professionals. By communicating in a professional manner, you help ensure that there is mutual understanding.

Verbal and nonverbal communication work together to convey a message. You can improve your spoken communication by using nonverbal signals and gestures that reinforce and support what you are saying. Non-verbal techniques include:

- Use eye contact
- Concentrate on keeping a calm tone of voice
- Avoid nonverbal gestures and hand signals that can be misread
- Sit next to the most important person at the meeting
- Speak slowly and clearly

You can also develop verbal skills to show that you are listening and understand what has been said. Some of these techniques include:

- **Paraphrasing:** putting into your own words what the other person has said; do this by using fewer words and highlighting the facts
- **Reflective listening**: focusing on the feeling or emotion of what has been said; state back what you hear and see, while taking note of the nonverbal and verbal communication
- **Summarizing:** restate the important points the other person said; do this after a person has spoken for a long period of time
- **Questioning:** ask open-ended questions to clarify what has been said.
- **Using I-Statements:** begin sentences with I-statements; doing that clarifies that you're speaking from your point of view, conveys how you feel and are non-judgmental, you might say "I hear my loved one is…is that correct?"
- **Listening:** focus on what the other person is saying without letting your own thoughts and feelings interfere; be open to what others suggest since they may have a good idea that you haven't considered

Public advocacy includes speaking to organizations, faith communities, clubs, school classes or other groups about your experience with mental health conditions. Every time you write a letter to the editor, speak to someone outside your work or social circle, forward a social media post, you are doing public advocacy. These actions help reduce stigma by normalizing the public's understanding of how mental illness affects people.

Legislative advocacy is what most of us think of when we hear the word 'advocacy.' It's actually easier than it sounds. Every time you call, write, meet with or testify in front of elected representative(s) you are doing legislative advocacy. Getting involved with your local NAMI organization is a way to be involved in public and legislative advocacy efforts and make your voice heard.

Programs such as NAMI In Our Own Voice, NAMI Ending the Silence and NAMI Smarts provide an opportunity to learn to tell your story effectively.

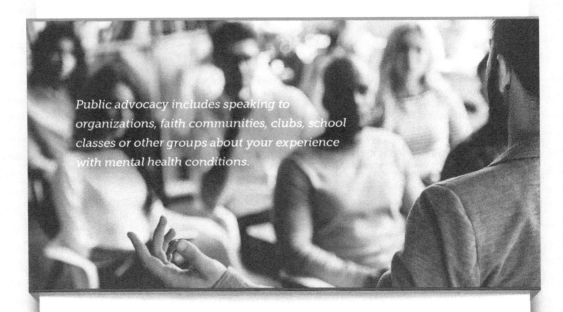

Public advocacy includes speaking to organizations, faith communities, clubs, school classes or other groups about your experience with mental health conditions.

Remember that you have the power to make a difference for yourself and your loved one!

Who to Contact with Concerns/ Grievances

If there are concerns about the care provided or other aspects of the treatment services, bring them first to the treatment facility's direct care staff. If that person is not available or the issue is not resolved, speak with the facility director, an administrator or nurse manager. If the problem is not resolved, you may want to contact the patient advocate for the organization.

For concerns that can't be resolved with the facility, contact your state's Disability Rights Services office. You can also contact the organization that certifies the facility, such as the state department of health or mental health, or the Joint Commission on Accreditation of Healthcare Organizations (JCAHO). This information should be displayed in public areas of the facility.

OTHER TYPES
of crisis situations

Searching for a Missing Loved One

Once you determine your loved one is missing, contact law enforcement immediately. Provide them with all the information you can. If the person remains missing more than three days, ask the law enforcement officials to place them on the FBI's National Crime Information Center (NCIC) list as an "endangered adult." This computer network provides information nation wide. If you make it clear to police that this is a mental health issue, they may be able to reduce the number of days it takes to file a report.

Federal law prohibits law enforcement from imposing a waiting period before accepting a missing child report. Within 2 hours of receiving a missing child report, law enforcement must add the information to the FBI's National Crime Information Center Missing Person File. You should then call the National Center for Missing and Exploited Children (CMEC) 1-800-843-5678. CMEC will provide technical and case management assistance to help ensure all available search and recovery methods are used.

When a missing person over the age 21 is located, law enforcement cannot hold the person against their will if they haven't committed a crime and are not a danger to themselves or others. In order for that to occur, medical guardianship or court order stating those actions must exist. You may ask law enforcement to let you know if when they locate your loved one, even if your loved one refuses to contact you.

Register with the National Missing and Unidentified Persons System (NamUs)

Upload information about your loved one on www.findthemissing.org. This resource will help you, law enforcement and other members of the justice community enter data about the person who is missing.

Check nearby hospitals, religious centers, homeless shelters and libraries

Although some of these places may say that they are unable to confirm if your loved one is there due to confidentiality rules, you need to know that

Facebook, Twitter, Instagram and other social media used by your loved one may provide clues to their location.

HIPAA in fact gives health care providers discretion to confirm that a loved one is there even though they may be unable to share specific information about the person's treatment.

Create a missing person poster that includes
- Two recent photos
- Name
- Hometown plus state
- Height, weight, age and features such as scars or tattoos
- Vehicle license plate number and photo of car
- Place last seen
- Phone number of who to contact if located

Check out social media or create a website

Facebook, Twitter, Instagram and other social media used by your loved one may provide clues to their location. Look at their friends' social media accounts as well.

Contact your NAMI State Organization or NAMI Affiliate

Your NAMI organization may know about local resources and places to look for your loved one. They may also be able to help share your flyers and expand the search.

Alert local media

Ask the local media to make a public announcement. The publicity may be seen by your loved one or provide information to law enforcement that may help find your loved one. Keep in mind that the media may not cover your story.

Handling the Arrest of a Family Member

Medication
If your family member requires medication, he or she should inform the jail staff. If the jail staff hasn't been informed, ask the jail's physician to contact your loved one's treatment team. You may need to contact your loved one's doctor yourself. Do this in writing and follow-up with a phone call. Your request should include:

- Your loved one's diagnosis
- The type of medication
- Contact information for the doctor
- Your contact information

Mistreatment
If your family member is being mistreated in jail, contact your state's protection and advocacy agency, which is responsible for protecting the rights of individuals with disabilities. You may also contact your state's Department of Mental Health, Legal Aid or your state's affiliate of the American Civil Liberties Union (ACLU).

Going to Court
The arrest of a family member may mean they need to appear in court. Knowing what to expect can help you provide support for your loved one and hopefully lead to the best outcome.

Working with a Public Defender Attorney
Most people charged with crimes are assigned a public defender if they can't afford a private attorney. The public defender works for your family member, not you. You can ask your loved one to sign a release that allows the attorney to share information with you.

Here is what you should do:

- **Contact the public defender.** Attorneys are often in court all day, so call early in the morning or during lunch. Leave a message or call the office and ask for an email address or text number. If you can't reach them, mail a brief summary (no more than three pages) of your loved one's medical information to the office.
- **Attend the initial hearing.** Introduce yourself to the public defender. Be brief and polite. Thank them for their time and let them know you're available to provide whatever information would be helpful.
- **Ask the attorney to consider any jail diversion or pre-trial release programs.** If you don't know about any programs, contact your NAMI Affiliate to find out if there is a jail diversion program, mental health court or other program to help defendants with mental health conditions in your community.

You may also hire a private defense attorney who has experience working with clients with mental health conditions.

Help Finding an Attorney
The NAMI HelpLine (1-800-950-NAMI (6264)) maintains a Legal Resource Service that provides you with information on legal services or refer you to an attorney from our legal directory. The directory includes attorneys who have volunteered with NAMI and are interested in working with cases relating to mental health issues. The Legal Resource Service can't provide direct legal advice, they can provide information that will help you support your loved one.

Preparing for a Court Appearance

If your loved one is released, they may still need to appear in court. If they do not want to appear in court, you can ask the attorney if there's a way that the hearing can continue without their presence. If they need to attend, here are some things you can do to make the experience easier

- Have a friend drive and drop you off at the courthouse door
- If you drive, arrive early to find parking
- Security may search bags and ask you to remove clothing like a belt or jacket; if your loved one will be upset by these procedures, ask if you can carry these items into the courthouse for them
- Bring medicine in case you are in court for several hours
- If allowed, bring snacks
- Dress nicely; this will make a good impression on the court and show that you are taking the hearing seriously

PREPARING
for a crisis

No one wants to worry about the possibility of a crisis—but sometimes it can't be avoided. It's rare that a person suddenly loses control of thoughts, feelings and behavior. General behavior changes often occur before a crisis. Examples include sleeplessness, ritualistic preoccupation with certain activities, increased suspiciousness, unpredictable outbursts, increased hostility, verbal threats, angry staring or grimacing.

Don't ignore these changes, talk with your loved one and encourage them to visit their doctor or nurse practitioner. The more symptomatic your family member becomes, the more difficult it may be to convince them to seek treatment.

If you're feeling like something isn't right, talk with your loved one and voice your concern. If necessary, take action to get services for them and support for yourself.

When a mental health crisis begins, it is likely your family member is unaware of the impact of their behavior. Auditory hallucinations, or voices, may be giving life-threatening suggestions or commands. The person believes they are hearing, seeing or feeling things that aren't there. Don't underestimate the reality and vividness of hallucinations. Accept that your loved one has an altered state of reality and don't argue with them about their experience. In extreme situations, the person may act on these sensory distortions.

If you are alone and feel safe with them, call a trusted friend, neighbor or family member to come be with you until professional help arrives. In the meantime, the following tips may be helpful:

✔ Learn all you can about the illness your family member has.

✔ Remember that other family members (siblings, grandparents, aunts and uncles...) are also affected, so keep lines of communication open by talking with each other.

✘ Avoid guilt and assigning blame to others. It's not helpful or useful to do so. The illness is no one's fault.

✔ Find out about benefits and support systems when things are going well. Don't wait until there is a crisis. Support systems should encompass both physical and mental health.

✔ Learn to recognize early warning signs of relapse, such as changes in sleeping patterns, increasing social withdrawal, inattention to hygiene, and signs of irritability.

✔ Talk to your family member, especially when they're doing well. They can usually identify such signs (and other more personal ones). Let them tell you what helps to reduce symptoms and relieve stress. A visit to a psychiatrist, case manager, therapist, support group, or friend may help prevent a full-blown relapse. The person may also need an adjustment in medication.

✘ Don't threaten; this may be interpreted as a play for power and increase fear or prompt an assault.

✘ Don't shout or raise your voice. If your loved one doesn't appear to hear or be listening to you, it's not because he or she is hard of hearing. Other voices or sensory input is likely interfering or predominating.

✘ Don't criticize or make fun of the person. It can't make matters better and may make them worse.

✘ Don't argue with other family members, particularly in your loved one's presence. This is not the time to argue over best strategies, allocate blame or prove a point. You can discuss the situation when everyone has calmed down.

✘ Don't bait the person. He or she may just act on any threats made if you do. The consequences could be tragic.

✘ Don't stand over the person. If the person is sitting down, you sit down (or stand well away from him or her). If the person is standing, keep your distance.

✘ Avoid direct, continuous eye contact or touching the person. Such contact may seem threatening.

✔ Do what your loved one wants, as long as it's reasonable and safe. Complying with reasonable requests helps them regain some sense of control.

✘ Don't block the doorway or any other exit. You don't want to give your loved one the feeling of being trapped.

Sometimes your loved one may become violent, particularly if he or she has been drinking alcohol or has taken a street drug. Substance use increases the risk of violence for anyone, not just those who have a mental illness. Clues that a person may become violent include clenched fists, a prominent blood vessel in the neck or forehead, working of the jaw, a hard and set expression to the face, and angry staring or talking. Acknowledge your own uneasiness, tell your loved one how their behavior is making you feel. Sometimes such feedback can diffuse the situation.

If you and the rest of your family have made a limit setting plan, now is the time to use it. If you haven't already warned your loved one of the consequences of certain behaviors while he or she was calm, use your judgment and past experience to decide to warn him or her, or simply go ahead with the plan.

Give your loved one plenty of physical and emotional space. Never corner a person who is agitated. This is not the time to make verbal threats or sarcastic remarks. Don't try to lecture or reason with your loved one when he or she is agitated or losing control. Find an exit and leave if you are scared or they become violent.

Get help. Having other people there, including law enforcement, may defuse the situation. Developing a plan is another way to feel more prepared when emergency situations occur.

A crisis plan is a written plan developed by the person with the mental health condition and their support team, typically family and close friends. It's designed to address symptoms and behaviors and help prepare for a crisis. Every plan is individualized, some common elements include:

♦ Person's general information
♦ Family information

♦ Behaviors present before the crisis occurs, strategies and treatments that have worked in the past, a list of what actions or people that are likely to make the situation worse, a list of what helps calm the person or reduces symptoms
♦ Current medication(s) and dosages
♦ Current diagnoses
♦ History of suicide attempts, drug use or psychosis
♦ Treatment choices/preferences
♦ Local crisis lines
♦ Addresses and contact information for nearby crisis centers or emergency rooms
♦ Mobile crisis unit information, if there is one in the area
♦ Contact information for health care professionals (phone and email)
♦ Supports - adults the person has a trusting relationship with such as neighbors, friends, family members, favorite teacher or counselor at school, people at faith communities or work acquaintants
♦ Safety plans

The crisis plan is a collaboration between the person with the mental health condition and the family. Once developed, the plan should be shared by the person with involved family, friends and professionals. It should be updated whenever there is a change in diagnosis, medication, treatment or providers. A sample crisis plan is included in the Portable Treatment Record at the end of this guide.

The more the person with the mental health condition and the family can work together to identify and understand what contributes to a crisis and what strategies helped, the more prepared you will be for a future crisis.

Helpful tips to remember:

♦ Create a safe environment by removing all weapons and sharp objects
♦ Lock up medications, both over-the-counter and prescription medications
♦ Discuss with others in the household about how to stay safe during a crisis
♦ Post the number of your county mental health crisis team
♦ Contact your local law enforcement and provide them with a copy of the crisis plan

Psychiatric Advance Directives (PAD) are legal documents that share a person's specific instructions or preferences regarding future mental health treatment. PADs are used during a psychiatric emergency if the person loses their capacity to give or withhold informed consent to treatment. PADS can also include specific consent to communicate with family members, caregivers or friends during crisis situations. The National Resource Center on Psychiatric Advance Directives (NRC-PAD, www.nrc-pad.org) provides information for person with a mental health condition, family members, clinicians and policy makers interested in PADs. State laws vary on PADs. Learn more by asking your health care provider or your attorney for information about your state. Once you, or your loved one, have developed the advance directives, share it with the health care professionals involved in the treatment plan as well as concerned family members.

NAMI resources

NAMI is the nation's largest grassroots mental health organization. NAMI provides advocacy, education, support and public awareness so that all people and families affect by mental illness can build better lives. There are NAMI organizations at the national, state and local level.

We educate.

Offered in thousands of communities across the United States through NAMI state organizations and affiliates, our education programs ensure hundreds of thousands of families, individuals, professionals, students and educators get the support and information they need.

We advocate.

NAMI shapes national public policy for people with mental illness and their families and provides volunteer leaders with the tools, resources and skills necessary to save mental health in all states.

We listen.

Our toll-free NAMI HelpLine (1-800-950-NAMI (6264)) responds to hundreds of thousands of requests each year, providing free referral, information and support.

We lead.

Public awareness events and activities, including Mental Illness Awareness Week and NAMIWalks, successfully fight stigma and encourage understanding.

To learn more about NAMI
- Visit www.nami.org
- Call the NAMI HelpLine: 800-950-NAMI (6264)
- Email the NAMI Helpline: info@nami.org Find a NAMI near you: www.nami.org/local Information about NAMI's education classes, presentation and support groups: www.nami.org/programs.

NAMI Classes

NAMI Basics is a 6-session course for taught by and for parents/caregivers of people younger than 22 years of age experiencing mental health challenges. The course is offered in Spanish as Bases y Fundamentos de NAMI in a limited number of states.

NAMI Family-to-Family is a 12-session course for taught by and for families, partners and friends of people with mental health conditions. The course is offered in Spanish as De Familia a Familia de NAMI in a limited number of states.

NAMI Homefront is a 6-session mental health course for taught by and for families, partners and friends of military Service Members and Veterans. NAMI Homefront is also available online, taught live in a virtual classroom.

NAMI Peer-to-Peer is an 8-session recovery course for taught by and for adults (18 years and older) with a mental health condition. The course is offered in Spanish as De Persona a Persona de NAMI in a limited number of states.

NAMI Provider is available as a 5-session course or a 4-hour introductory seminar for health care staff.

NAMI Presentations

NAMI Ending the Silence (ETS) is a 50-minute prevention and early intervention program that engages school-aged youth in a discussion about mental health. ETS also has presentations for school staff and parents.

NAMI In Our Own Voice is an interactive presentation that provides insight into what it's like to have a mental illness.

NAMI Support Groups

NAMI Connection is a recovery support group program facilitated by and for any adult (18 years and older) with a mental health condition.

NAMI Family Support Group is a support group facilitated by and for family members, caregivers and loved ones of individuals with mental illness.

Portable Treatment Record

Name: _____ Date of birth: _____

Emergency contacts

Name: _____ Phone: _____

Relationship: _____

Name: _____ Phone: _____

Relationship: _____

Pharmacy: _____ Phone: _____

Location: _____

Primary care physician

Name: _____ Phone: _____

Office address: _____

Psychiatrist

Name: _____ Phone: _____

Office address: _____

Other mental health professionals (therapist, case manager, psychologist, etc.)

Name: _____ Phone: _____

Type of mental health professional: _____

Office address: _____

Name: _____ Phone: _____

Type of mental health professional: _____

Office address: _____

Name: _____ Phone: _____

Medical History

Allergies to medications:

Medication	Reaction

Psychiatric medications that caused severe side effects:

Medication	Side effects	Approximate date discontinued

Major medical illnesses:

Illness	Treatment	Current status

Major medical procedures (ex: surgeries, MRI, CT scan)

Date	Procedure	Result

Current Medical Information

Diagnosis:

Date	Procedure	Who made the diagnosis

Psychiatric hospitalizations:

Date of admission	Reason for hospitalization	Name of facility	Date of discharge

Medication Record

Date prescribed	Physician	Medication	Dosage	Date discontinued

Crisis Plan

Emergency resource 1: _____

Phone: _____ Cell phone _____

Emergency resource 2: _____

Phone: _____ Cell phone: _____

Physician: _____ **Phone:** _____

If we need help from professionals, we will follow these steps (include how the children and other vulnerable family members will be taken care of):

1. _____

_____

2. _____

_____

3. _____

_____

4. _____

_____

5. _____

_____

When will we think about going to the hospital? What type of behavior would make us consider doing this?

When will we think about calling 911? What type of behavior would make us consider doing this?

Relapse Plan

The person with the mental health condition and the family should talk together and agree on the following parts of their plan:

How do we know the symptoms are returning? List signs and symptoms of relapse:

1. _____

2. _____

3. _____

When the symptoms on line 1 appear, we will:

♦ _____

♦ _____

♦ _____

When the symptoms on line 2 appear, we will:

♦ _____

♦ _____

♦ _____

When the symptoms on line 3 appear, we will:

♦ _____

♦ _____

♦ _____

When will we think about going to the hospital? What type of behavior would make us consider doing this?

When will we think about calling 911? What type of behavior would make us consider doing this?

You are NOT
ALONE

Millions of people are affected by mental illness each year. Across the country, many people just like you work, perform, create, compete, laugh, love and inspire every day.

1 in 5 U.S. adults experience mental illness

1 in 25 U.S. adults experience serious mental illness

17% of youth (6-17 years) experience a mental health disorder

12 MONTH PREVALENCE OF COMMON MENTAL ILLNESSES (ALL U.S. ADULTS)

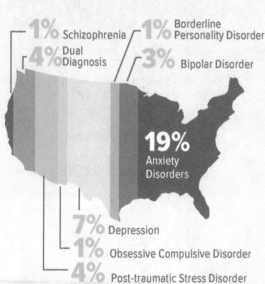

- **1%** Schizophrenia
- **4%** Dual Diagnosis
- **1%** Borderline Personality Disorder
- **3%** Bipolar Disorder
- **19%** Anxiety Disorders
- **7%** Depression
- **1%** Obsessive Compulsive Disorder
- **4%** Post-traumatic Stress Disorder

12 MONTH PREVALENCE OF ANY MENTAL ILLNESS (ALL U.S. ADULTS)

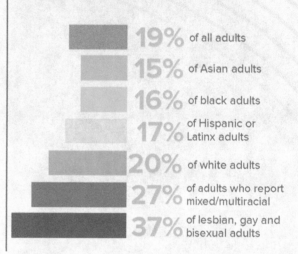

- **19%** of all adults
- **15%** of Asian adults
- **16%** of black adults
- **17%** of Hispanic or Latinx adults
- **20%** of white adults
- **27%** of adults who report mixed/multiracial
- **37%** of lesbian, gay and bisexual adults

WAYS TO REACH OUT AND GET HELP

Talk with a health care professional

Call the **NAMI** HelpLine at 800-950-NAMI (6264)

Connect with friends and family

Join a support group

Data from CDC, NIMH and other select sources. Find citations for this resource at nami.org/mhstats

NAMI HelpLine 800-950-NAMI (6264)

 NAMI

NAMICommunicate

NAMICommunicate

www.nami.org

 **nami** National Alliance on Mental Illness

Mental Health Care
MATTERS

Mental health treatment — therapy, medication, self-care — have made recovery a reality for most people experiencing mental illness. Although taking the first steps can be confusing or difficult, it's important to start exploring options.

The average delay between symptom onset and treatment is

11 YEARS

PEOPLE WHO GET TREATMENT IN A GIVEN YEAR

43% of adults with mental illness

64% of adults with serious mental illness

51% of youth (6-17) with a mental health condition

Adults with a mental health diagnosis who received treatment or counseling in the past year

25% of Asian adults

31% of black adults

32% of adults who report mixed/multiracial

33% of Hispanic or Latinx adults

49% of white adults

49% of lesbian, gay and bisexual adults

For therapy to work, you have to be open to change. I'm proud to say that I changed. **Therapy saved my life.**

– NAMI Program Leader

Data from CDC, NIMH and other select sources. Find citations for this resource at nami.org/mhstats

NAMI HelpLine
800-950-NAMI (6264)   NAMI   NAMICommunicate   NAMICommunicate   www.nami.org

nami
National Alliance on Mental Illness

The
RIPPLE EFFECT
of Mental Illness

Having a mental illness can make it challenging to live everyday life and maintain recovery. Let's look at some of the ways mental illness can impact lives — and how the impact can ripple out.

 People with serious mental illness have an increased risk for chronic disease, like diabetes or cancer

PERSON

 19% of U.S. adults with mental illness also have a substance use disorder

 Rates of cardiometabolic disease are twice as high in adults with serious mental illness

 At least **8.4 million** Americans provide care to an adult with an emotional or mental illness

FAMILY

 Caregivers spend an average of **32 hours** per week providing unpaid care

 20% of people experiencing homelessness also have a serious mental illness

COMMUNITY

 37% of people incarcerated in state and federal prison have a diagnosed mental condition

70% of youth in the juvenile justice system have at least one mental health condition

 1 in 8 of all visits to U.S. emergency departments are related to mental and substance use disorders

WORLD

 Depression is the leading cause of disability worldwide

 Depression and anxiety disorders cost the global economy **$1 trillion** each year in lost productivity

Data from CDC, NIMH and other select sources. Find citations for this resource at nami.org/mhstats

 NAMI HelpLine 800-950-NAMI (6264)   NAMI   NAMICommunicate   NAMICommunicate   www.nami.org

  nami
National Alliance on Mental Illness

Common WARNING SIGNS of Mental Illness

Diagnosing mental illness isn't a straightforward science. We can't test for it the same way we can test blood sugar levels for diabetes. Each condition has its own set of unique symptoms, though symptoms often overlap. Common signs and/or symptoms can include:

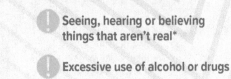

- **Feeling very sad or withdrawn for more than two weeks**
- **Trying to harm or end one's life or making plans to do so**
- **Severe, out-of-control, risk-taking behavior that causes harm to self or others**
- **Sudden overwhelming fear for no reason, sometimes with a racing heart, physical discomfort or difficulty breathing**
- **Significant weight loss or gain**

- **Seeing, hearing or believing things that aren't real***
- **Excessive use of alcohol or drugs**
- **Drastic changes in mood, behavior, personality or sleeping habits**
- **Extreme difficulty concentrating or staying still**
- **Intense worries or fears that get in the way of daily activities**

*Various communities and backgrounds might view this sign differently based on their beliefs and experiences. Some people within these communities and cultures may not interpret hearing voices as unusual.

WORRIED ABOUT YOURSELF OR SOMEONE YOU CARE ABOUT?

 If you notice any of these symptoms, it's important to ask questions

 Try to understand what they're experiencing and how their daily life is impacted

Making this connection is often the first step to getting treatment

50% of all lifetime mental illness begins by age **14**

75% by age **24**

KNOWLEDGE IS POWER

 Talk with a health care professional

 Learn more about mental illness

 Take a mental health education class

 Call the NAMI HelpLine at 800-950-NAMI (6264)

Data from CDC, NIMH and other select sources. Find citations for this resource at nami.org/mhstats

 NAMI HelpLine 800-950-NAMI (6264)   NAMI NAMICommunicate NAMICommunicate   www.nami.org

 **nami** National Alliance on Mental Illness

It's Okay to Talk About SUICIDE

Thoughts of giving up and suicide can be frightening. Not taking these kinds of thoughts seriously can have devastating outcomes.

Suicide is NOT the answer.

2nd Suicide is the 2nd leading cause of death for people ages 10-34

 The overall suicide rate has increased 35% since 1999

 Suicide is the 10th leading cause of death in the U.S.

46% of people who die by suicide have a diagnosed mental health condition

90% of people who die by suicide have experienced symptoms of a mental health condition

 If you start thinking about suicide, seek help. Call or text a crisis line or a trusted friend.

Make an appointment with a health care professional to talk about what you're thinking or how you're feeling.

HIGH RISK POPULATIONS

78% of all people who die by suicide are male **78%**

4x Lesbian, gay and bisexual youth are four times more likely to attempt suicide than straight youth

Transgender people are 12 times more likely to attempt suicide than the general population **12x**

 Suicidal thoughts are a symptom, just like any other — they can be treated, and they can improve over time.

 If you are concerned about suicide and don't know what to do, call the National Suicide Prevention Lifeline at 1-800-273-8255.

Data from CDC, NIMH and other select sources. Find citations for this resource at nami.org/mhstats

 NAMI HelpLine 800-950-NAMI (6264)   NAMI   NAMICommunicate    NAMICommunicate   www.nami.org

 **nami**
National Alliance on Mental Illness

Emergent Crisis of COVID-19 Pandemic: Mental Health Challenges and Opportunities

Amir Radfar[1], Maria M. Ferreira[2]*, Juan P. Sosa[3] and Irina Filip[4]

[1] Assistant Professor of Medical Education, University of Central Florida, Orlando, FL, United States, [2] Division of Research, Universidad Autónoma de Bucaramanga, Bucaramanga, Colombia, [3] Division of Research, Universidad Nacional de Tucuman, San Miguel de Tucumán, Argentina, [4] Department of Clinical Psychiatry, Western University of Health Sciences, Pomona, CA, United States

Mental health is a fundamental human right and is part of the well-being of society. The public health burden of mental health disorders affects people's social and economic status around the world. Coronavirus's (COVID-19) negative impact on the economy and mental health worldwide is concerning. This is a worldwide emergency, and there is an urgent need for research about this topic to prevent long-lasting adverse effects on the population. Unpreparedness and inconsistencies in guidelines, lockdowns, containment strategies, unemployment, financial losses, physical distancing, isolation, chaos, and uncertainty are among factors that lead to a rise in emotional distress, anxiety, and depression. Governments' decisions affect the socioeconomic status of a country and the psychological well-being of the people. COVID-19 pandemic exposed disparities in multiple mental health care systems by having adverse mental health effects in people with pre-existing mental health disorders and previously healthy individuals. Aggregation of concurrent or cumulative comorbid risk factors for COVID-19 disease and its psychosocial sequelae could provide invaluable information for the public health stakeholders. This review aims to address the burden and the psychosocial impact of the COVID-19 pandemic, the challenges and opportunities facing mental health systems, and proposes new strategies to improve the mental health outcomes in the post-COVID era.

Keywords: mental health services, mental health, COVID-19, pandemic, economic crisis, policy development, public health

OPEN ACCESS

Edited by:
Joanna Lai,
UNICEF United Nations International
Children's Emergency Fund,
United States

Reviewed by:
Prama Bhattacharya,
O.P. Jindal Global University, India
Migita Michael D'Cruz,
National Institute of Mental Health and
Neurosciences (NIMHANS), India

*Correspondence:
Maria M. Ferreira
mferreira@unab.edu.co

Specialty section:
This article was submitted to
Public Mental Health,
a section of the journal
Frontiers in Psychiatry

Received: 19 November 2020
Accepted: 25 June 2021
Published: 19 July 2021

Citation:
Radfar A, Ferreira MM, Sosa JP and
Filip I (2021) Emergent Crisis of
COVID-19 Pandemic: Mental Health
Challenges and Opportunities.
Front. Psychiatry 12:631008.
doi: 10.3389/fpsyt.2021.631008

INTRODUCTION

The Burden of Mental Disorders

Public Health is a fundamental human right, and governments are responsible for providing a healthy environment for the population. Mental health is part of public health and is defined by the World Health Organization (WHO) as a "state of wellbeing in which the individual realizes his or her own abilities can cope with the normal stresses of life, can work productively and fruitfully and is able to make a contribution to his or her community" (1). Public health systems are influential in providing, maintaining, shaping mental health services, and designing policies for the mentally ill and the population at risk.

The mental and addictive disorders' point prevalence worldwide in 2016 was 1,110,075,000 (16% of the world's population) (2). Mental and addictive disorders caused the loss of 162.5 million Disability-Adjusted Life Years (DALYs) and comprised 7% of all global burden of disease as measured in DALYs and 19% of all global Years Lived with Disability (YLD) in 2016 (2).

Based on the Global Burden of Disease study's findings, poor mental health and substance use disorders increased by 11% in the U.S. between 1990 and 2016 (3). Mental health issues are among the top 10 causes of premature death and disability in males and females in 2016 (3).

Additionally, it is currently one of the most expensive health care issues, affecting the health care industry, lowering productivity, and increasing costs in the U.S. economy (4). United States indicators estimate that 47.6 million adults aged 18 or older (19.1 %) had any mental illness, 11.4 million adults (23.9%) had a severe mental illness (SMI) and 3.5 million adolescents (14.4%) had a major depressive episode in 2018 (5).

There is also a geographical variation and socio-demographic status in the U.S.'s prevalence of mental health problems (6). East South-Central U.S. had the highest prevalence rate, with 14.88%, and West North-Central had the lowest rate, with 9.42% (6).

Mental disorders also affect social stability and reduce the quality of life. This leads to low educational attainment, decreases motivation and performance, impairment in personal and family functioning, discrimination, low income, increased poverty, violence, and higher mortality and suicide rates (7). The consequences of non-treatment increase the likelihood of violent and aggressive behaviors. Individuals with untreated or partially treated schizophrenia and bipolar disorder commit about 10% of all homicides in the U.S. and 33% of mass killings (8). Those with severe mental illness have 11 times increased likelihood of being victims of violence, assault, rape, or robbery (9). One-third of the homeless population is made up of individuals with an untreated mental illness (10). About 20% of jail inmates and 15% in state prisons have a severe mental illness (11). Failure to provide adequate care to patients with mental illness can turn into a social disaster.

Although the understanding of mental problems has evolved in the past decades, America's mental health system crisis has been a problem for many years. Despite all efforts made to deliver high-quality mental care, there are still gaps that need to be addressed. A 2018 survey from the National Council on Behavioral Health (NCBH) showed that 56% of patients want to access a mental healthcare provider, but many face barriers to care (12). Delivery of mental health care is determined by the financial resources available and has been a responsibility of the states, government insurances (Medicare and Medicaid), private providers (private insurance and out-of-pocket), and NGOs.

This review tries to shed light on the status of the mental health post-COVID-19 era, underscores the U.S. mental health care system's shortages, and proposes strategies and opportunities to improve mental health outcomes.

DISCUSSION

COVID-19 Pandemic and Mental Health Issues

Past tragedies have shown long-lasting consequences on mental health and could contribute to a greater prevalence of mental disorders than the pandemic itself (13). It has been reported that the rates of suicide may momentarily decrease immediately after the initial disaster period, and inversely followed by a consequent increase in suicidal behaviors (14). Vulnerable populations such as people with mental health problems incarcerated population, victims of sexual and physical violence, the bereaved, minorities such as lesbian, gay, bisexual, transgender, and queer (LGBTQ) community are especially at risk.

COVID-19 pandemic can lead to a secondary mental illness paradigm. The pandemic's burden on mental health triggered an economic crisis by posing an increased risk of suicide and long-standing emotional distress. The economic decline due to unemployment, financial worries, increased isolation and lack of support, increased strain and violence in relationships due to confinement at home, decreased contact with people from outside the home who can provide support, decreased access to mental health services are among factors contributing to the increased risk of psychological distress and suicide and highlights the need and necessities of mental health programs such as suicide prevention programs (15). A web-based survey conducted post-COVID-19 outbreak in China shows that young individuals are more prone to developing depressive and generalized anxiety disorders and lower sleep quality than older people. The study found that younger people with a higher time spent on social media and healthcare workers overthinking about the outbreak were at high risk of mental illness (16). Fear of infection, anxiety, anger, post-traumatic stress disorder, stigma, avoidant behaviors, boredom, and frustration could contribute to individuals' mental health post COVID. The hypochondriac concerns add to other psychosocial and economic stressors, limited socialization, and isolation problems (17).

As the COVID-19 pandemic brings gaps in mental health services back to attention, it raises additional concerns. Prior studies conducted during the HIN1 and SARS outbreaks emphasize the mental health burden on health professionals. Feelings of uncertainty, vulnerability, fear of death, irritability, psychological distress, restriction of social contacts, and intentional absenteeism were seen in quarantined medical staff and are anticipated to be seen during the COVID-19 pandemic (18, 19).

Mental health care gaps between the need for treatment and the available services always existed but were amplified by the COVID-19 pandemic and became a worldwide emergency.

Recent findings reveal substantial neuropsychiatric morbidities in the 6 months after COVID-19 infection. These risks were higher in, but not limited to, patients who had severe COVID-19 (20).

Some of these challenges include limited access to care, limited availability and affordability of mental health care services, lack of funding, high priced drugs, lack of psychiatric beds, insurance and policies gaps, physician shortage, unintegrated system, treatment gaps, insufficient mental health care policies, stigma, post-COVID-19 syndrome, and lack of education on mental illness (21).

MENTAL HEALTH CARE IN UNITED STATES AND ITS CHALENGES

In the United States, based on the U.S. Constitution and the U.S. federalist system, the federal and state governments are responsible for their citizens' mental health. They are responsible for developing mental health policies and setting standards that effectively allow the public and private sectors to deliver mental health care, which can influence shaping services and policies for mentally ill patients.

The federal government participates in developing laws and regulations of mental health systems and providers; they also play a role in protecting individuals' rights with mental health disorders and supporting and funding services, research, and innovation (35). On the other hand, the states' mental health system must meet specific federal government standards since they have significant power in making decisions to expand beyond what exists at the federal level and improve services, access, and protections for consumers (36).

Mental Health Financial Budget Shortages

The financing of mental health services changed dramatically over the years. The U.S. government allocated about $723 million for mental health services, $150 million for community behavioral health centers, $125 million for children's mental health services, and $133 million for school violence prevention in 2020 (37). The U.S. government's Fiscal Year 2020 budget revealed critical shortages and cutbacks for Medicaid, Medicare, and mental health research, putting at risk the quality of mental health care (22). This fund reduction created more gaps in the mental health system.

Public mental health services significantly deteriorated over the past three decades, suggesting that a fair amount of mental health care funds is lost to fraud, excess profits, or are wasted, rather than being used toward mental health care (38). With Medicare (national health insurance programs in the United States) being the largest source of funds for institutionalized patients and lacking incentives to finance a more extended inpatient stay, patients continue to be discharged from hospitals to live on the streets ending up being homeless or in jails. In addition, for the fiscal year 2021, National Tobacco Control Program, Pediatric Mental Healthcare Access grants, children's hospitals graduate medical education (CHGME) budgets either eliminated or flat-funded from previous year levels (22).

Physicians, Mental Health Care Providers Shortage and Treatment Gaps

The gaps in treatment, diagnosis, and knowledge of mental disorders are a worldwide and public health problem and priority. Common treatment barriers of the psychiatric population are lack or difficulty in accessing mental health care, physician shortage, increasing prevalence and incidence of mental disorders, lack of infrastructure and psychiatric beds, financial gaps, rising drug pricing, lack of insurance, and more.

The federal and states governments provide many supportive programs to assist individuals with mental illnesses, and it connects them with job placement services, housing, behavioral health, and housing to divert them from the criminal justice system. However, these agencies do not specifically focus on assisting individuals with serious mental illness, which has led to fragmentation among these programs due to a lack of coordination among agencies (23).

According to The Substance Abuse and Mental Health Services Administration (SAMHSA), nearly 91 million Americans live in regions with severe shortages in available mental health professionals and estimates that a minimum of 1,846 psychiatrists and 5,931 other practitioners would be necessary to fill these gaps (24). The Association of American Medical Colleges projects that the United States will see a shortage of up to 122,000 physicians by 2032, with demands exceeding supply not only in primary care but also among specialist physicians (25).

In addition, there is an increase in severe mental illnesses among young adults (18–25 years old) and adults (26–49 years old) in 2018 (39). About 46.5% of young adults and 36.3% of adults were untreated in 2018 (39).

The Government Accountability Office reported 112 federal programs supporting individuals with serious mental illness and found a lack of interagency coordination and a lack of completed program evaluations (23). The uncoordinated agencies and care delivery, the lack of monitoring and assessment of the efficacy of programs, stigma, and the failure to detect and treat mental health conditions create gaps in the mental health care system leading to failure to meet the needs of this vulnerable population. Furthermore, new policies seeking the repealing and replacement of the Patient Protection and Affordable Care Act (ACA), which were developed since creating the American Health Care Act (AHCA) in 2017, lead to new disparities and limitations in mental health care and substance abuse disorders, affecting the quality and access to mental health services.

Moreover, even though more interventions and drugs are available every year, not everyone will have access to them due to the rising costs. The drug pricing system is a highly complex process that involves manufacturers, states, wholesalers, and pharmacies. The more significant limitation of this system is that there is no direct transaction between manufacturers and patients. Instead, there are at least three transaction systems in between (manufacturer to wholesaler, wholesaler to the pharmacy, and pharmacy to the patient), leading to variations of drug pricing in the U.S.

COVID-19 pandemic has highlighted the treatment gaps in the mental health care system. Among these gaps, one can name insurance barriers, financial resources, shortages in mental and behavioral health providers, emergency rooms overload, insufficient beds to hospitalize severely mentally ill patients, uncoordinated mental health providers networks, tele-mental health implementation barriers, as well as disparities to access to care in low-income population and communities of color.

A recent report by the Center for the Study of Latino Health and Culture (CESLAC) shows Latinos and Native and black Americans are disproportionately affected by a higher rate of Covid 19 infection, hospitalization, and death (21, 40).

Emergence of New Neuropsichiatric Disorders

It has been reported that 4 weeks from the onset of COVID-19 viral illness, some post-acute residual effects, complications, or persistent symptoms affect different organs and systems of the body (26). The post-acute COVID-19 syndrome involves the neuropsychiatric system by immune dysregulation, inflammation, accumulation of memory T cells, neuronal injury, dysfunctional lymphatic drainage, microvascular thrombosis, iatrogenic effects of medications, or psychosocial impacts of COVID-19 (26).

Studies have reported that 30–40% of COVID-19 survivors presented anxiety, fatigue, psychological distress, depression, sleep abnormalities, and PTSD after the acute phase of COVID-19 (26). It is recommended that survivors of COVID-19 at high risk for post-acute COVID-19, including those with severe illness during COVID-19 acute phase, admission to ICU, advanced age, or presence of comorbidities, be given integrated outpatient care including screening for neuropsychiatric impairments, neuropsychological evaluation, and imaging studies (26).

OPPORTUNITIES TO IMPROVE MENTAL HEALTH CARE

Mental health care should concern government and public health advocates to assess and develop better policies and response programs to overcome these gaps and challenges. Policy decisions should focus on strengthening community-based care, support, building local public mental health research capacity, and easy access to treatment and health care services.

Integrating mental health care into the primary care setting could provide a more comprehensive approach to health care following the bio-psycho-social model, enabling early detection, treatment, and accessibility to psychiatric care, minimizing the stigma associated with seeking psychiatric care. The integration process needs adequate financial resources and specialized education and training for primary health care providers (27).

As an approach to address the funding shortages in different mental health sectors, a transfer of funds between different departments could provide a feasible solution (23). The federal government could efficiently address this gap and step forward in fixing the mental health system by removing the Medicaid restriction of funding the patients with mental health issues only in hospitals (28).

Strengthening acts such as the ACA can fill some gaps in the quality and coverage policies by improving access to mental health coverage and addiction treatment. ACA improved preventive care coverage, including screening for depression and alcohol misuse, autism, and behavioral assessments for children. Similarly, ACA expanded the coverage of the essential

TABLE 1 | Recommendations to improve the burden of mental illnesses in the post-COVID era (22–34).

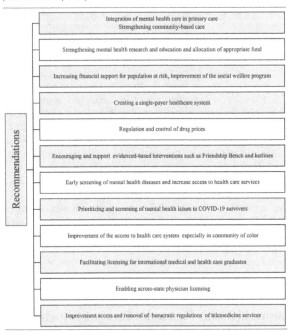

health benefits involving mental health, substance abuse, and prescription drugs.

Another important action is to increase mental care access and affordability by creating a single-payer healthcare system rather than multiple competing health insurance companies. Due to the lack of transparency and cost control, it is necessary to establish control measures to address this problem. Government and the states should address the cost control of interventions and prescription drugs available to the population (29, 30).

To address mental health during this pandemic, other resources should develop to provide responses and support. Many hotlines such as the National Suicide prevention lifeline, disaster distress helpline, crisis text line, national domestic violence hotline, and the partnership for drug-free kids' helpline can be used as immediate responses. Additionally, financial support resources should be available to relieve financial stress and address its adverse outcomes over mental health.

Evidence-based interventions, such as the Friendship Bench, consisting of a task-sharing approach and implementing a validated assessment tool delivered by trained personnel for early detection and early therapy of mental health problems, are a great way to bridge the mental health treatment gaps (31, 32). Furthermore, implementing early screening and detection of mental illness plays an essential role in improving the mental health system (26). Some actions, such as increasing access to suicide hotlines, are essential to decrease the burden of mental health problems, especially in the Post Covid 19 era.

Continuous evaluation and inter-agency coordination of social welfare programs, such as those addressing homelessness, are deemed to improve mental health and are instrumental in accomplishing the government's strategic planning goals and standards. Coordination of severe mental illness programs requires specific legislation and an appropriate leadership level to achieve successful management (23).

COVID-19 pandemic raises the concerns of a health system with a growing shortage of trained personnel. It is difficult to incentivize mental health professionals to work in areas with limited resources and state licensure regulations.

The U.S. medical graduates are not enough to face the weaknesses of a challenged mental health system. This shortage could be quickly addressed by facilitating licensing for international medical graduates, enabling across-state licensing, and increasing access to trained international medical graduates to areas of need (24, 25). Telemedicine and other digital tools can tackle the barriers in mental health care delivery, improve access, affordability, and shortages of services, especially in the post-COVID 19 era (33). Recommendations to improve the burden of mental illnesses in the post-COVID era are mention on **Table 1**.

CONCLUSION

Mental illness has been a public health problem for a long time due to its high prevalence. Public mental health services significantly deteriorated over the past three decades, suggesting that a fair amount of mental health care funds is lost to fraud, excess profits, or are wasted, rather than being used toward mental health care (38).

Delivering high-quality mental care to the U.S. population has been challenged due to the numerous gaps in the mental health care system such as treatment disparities, high drug pricing, uncoordinated systems, failure of effective policies, structural issues, workforce shortages, lack of funding, inaccessibility, and financial barriers. Addressing these gaps and challenges is more

alarming nowadays due to increasing mental health issues caused by the COVID-19 pandemic.

The mental health care system needs to evolve and be integrated with primary care. By strengthening the leadership and governance for mental health, reducing mental health stigma, assuring the provision of adequate integrated mental health and social community-based services, implementing strategies for promotion, prevention, and early detection, implementing e-health, increasing trained personnel, and strengthening the information systems, the U.S. federal government could overcome current challenges, assist the delivery of adequate mental health and social well-being to its citizens and eliminate disparities. It is important to educate health care workers to monitor and support mental health needs. Also, there is an increased need for research to assess psychological factors, understand causal mechanisms, and propose interventions to improve mental health. The findings of this manuscript could help in service planning and identification of research priorities.

AUTHOR CONTRIBUTIONS

AR made contributions to conception, design of the work, acquisition, and interpretation of the findings, has drafted the work, and substantially revised it. MF and JS contributed to data acquisition, interpretation of findings, drafted the work, and substantially revised the manuscript. IF supervised the acquisition, interpretation of findings and drafted the work, and substantially revised the manuscript. All authors approved the final submitted version, agreed to be personally accountable for its own contributions and ensures that questions related to the accuracy or integrity of any part of the work, even ones in which the author was not personally involved, are appropriately investigated, resolved, and the resolution documented in the literature, and agreed with the order of authors.

ACKNOWLEDGMENTS

The content of this manuscript has been presented (IN PART) at the (NEI CONFERENCE/CNS SPECTRUM) (21).

REFERENCES

1. World Health Organization. *Promoting Mental Health: Concepts, Emerging Evidence, Practice (Summary Report)*. Geneva: World Health Organization. (2004). Retrieved from: https://www.who.int/mental_health/evidence/en/promoting_mhh.pdf (accessed October 1, 2020).
2. Rehm J, Shield KD. Global burden of disease and the impact of mental and addictive disorders. *Curr Psychiatry.* (2019) 21:10. doi: 10.1007/s11920-019-0997-0
3. Institute for Health Metrics and Evaluation (IHME). *Infographic State Burden Mental-Health Risk Profile*. Seattle, WA: IHME, University of Washington. (2016). Retrieved from: http://www.healthdata.org/sites/default/files/files/infographics/Infographic_State_burden_Mental-Health_risk_profile_Page_1_0.png (accessed September 24, 2020).
4. Scarbrough JA. The growing importance of mental health parity. *Am J Law Med.* (2018) 44:453–74. doi: 10.1177/0098858818789432

5. Substance Abuse and Mental Health Services Administration. *Key Substance Use and Mental Health Indicators in the United States: Results From the 2018 National Survey on Drug Use and Health.* (2019). Retrieved from: https://www.samhsa.gov/data/sites/default/files/cbhsq-reports/NSDUHNationalFindingsReport2018/NSDUHNationalFindingsReport2018.pdf (accessed October 1, 2020).
6. Charara R, El Bcheraoui C, Kravitz H, Dhingra SS, Mokdad AH. Mental distress and functional health in the United States. *Prev Med.* (2016) 89:292–300. doi: 10.1016/j.ypmed.2016.06.011
7. Kohn R, Ali A, Puac-Polanco V, Figueroa C, López-Soto V, Morgan K, et al. Mental health in the Americas: an overview of the treatment gap. *Rev Panam Salud Publica.* (2018) 42:e165. doi: 10.26633/RPSP.2018.165
8. Treatment Advocacy Center. *Serious Mental Illness and Homicide.* (2016). Retrieved from: https://www.treatmentadvocacycenter.org/storage/documents/backgrounders/smi-and-homicide.pdf (accessed September 25, 2020).

9. Treatment Advocacy Center. *Victimization and Serious Mental Illness.* (2016). Retrieved from: https://www.treatmentadvocacycenter.org/evidence-and-research/learn-more-about/3630-victimization-and-serious-mental-illness (accessed October 5, 2020).

10. Treatment Advocacy Center. *Serious Mental Illness and Homelessness.* (2016). Retrieved from: https://www.treatmentadvocacycenter.org/storage/documents/backgrounders/smi-and-homelessness.pdf (accessed October 5, 2020).

11. Treatment Advocacy Center. *Serious Mental Illness Prevalence in Jails and Prisons.* (2016). Retrieved from: https://www.treatmentadvocacycenter.org/storage/documents/backgrounders/smi-in-jails-and-prisons.pdf (accessed October 10, 2020).

12. National Council for Behavioral Health. *New Study Reveals Lack of Access as Root Cause for Mental Health Crisis in America.* (2018). Retrieved from: https://www.thenationalcouncil.org/press-releases/new-study-reveals-lack-of-access-as-root-cause-for-mental-health-crisis-in-america/ (accessed 13 September 2020).

13. Ornell F, Schuch JB, Sordi AO, Kessler FH. "Pandemic fear" and COVID-19: mental health burden and strategies. *Braz J Psychiatry.* (2020) 42:232–5. doi: 10.1590/1516-4446-2020-0008

14. Kõlves K, Kõlves KE, De Leo D. Natural disasters and suicidal behaviours: a systematic literature review. *J Affect Disord.* (2013) 146:1–14. doi: 10.1016/j.jad.2012.07.037

15. Wasserman D, Iosue M, Wuestefeld A, Carli V. Adaptation of evidence-based suicide prevention strategies during and after the COVID-19 pandemic. *World Psychiatry.* (2020) 19:294–306. doi: 10.1002/wps.20801

16. Huang Y, Zhao N. Generalized anxiety disorder, depressive symptoms and sleep quality during COVID-19 outbreak in China: a web-based cross-sectional survey. *Psychiatry Res.* (2020) 288:112954. doi: 10.1016/j.psychres.2020.112954

17. Mian A, Al-Asad S, Khan, S. Mental health burden of COVID-19. *Fam Pract.* (2020) 38:cmaa100. doi: 10.1093/fampra/cmaa100

18. Goulia P, Mantas C, Dimitroula D, Mantis D, Hyphantis T. General hospital staff worries, perceived sufficiency of information and associated psychological distress during the A/H1N1 influenza pandemic. *BMC Infect Dis.* (2010) 10:322. doi: 10.1186/1471-2334-10-322

19. Chong MY, Wang WC, Hsieh WC, Lee CY, Chiu NM, Yeh WC, et al. Psychological impact of severe acute respiratory syndrome on health workers in a tertiary hospital. *Br J Psychiatry.* (2004) 185:127–33. doi: 10.1192/bjp.185.2.127

20. Taquet M, Geddes JR, Husain M, Luciano S, Harrison PJ. 6-month neurological and psychiatric outcomes in 236379 survivors of COVID-19: a retrospective cohort study using electronic health records. *Lancet Psychiatry.* (2021) 8:416–27. doi: 10.1016/S2215-0366(21)00084-5

21. Radfar A, Caceres M, Sosa J, Filip I. Overcoming the challenges of the mental health care system in United States in the aftermath of COVID-19. *CNS Spectr.* (2021) 26:176–6. doi: 10.1017/S1092852920002886

22. Canady VA. Proposed FY 2020 budget reveals critical cuts in MH supports. *Mental Health Weekly.* (2019) 29:4–5. doi: 10.1002/mhw.31819

23. United States Government Accountability Office. *Mental Health: HHS Leadership Needed to Coordinate Federal Efforts Related to Serious Mental Illness.* GAO-15-113 (2014). Retrieved from: https://www.gao.gov/products/gao-15-113 (accessed September 13, 2020).

24. National Alliance on Mental Illness. *The Doctor is Out. Continuing Disparities in Access to Mental and Physical Health Care.* (2017). Retrieved from: https://www.nami.org/Support-Education/Publications-Reports/Public-Policy-Reports/The-Doctor-is-Out/DoctorIsOut (accessed September 10, 2020).

25. Association of American Medical Colleges. *The Complexities of Physician Supply and Demand: Projections From 2017-2032.* (2020). Retrieved from: https://aamc-black.global.ssl.fastly.net/production/media/filer_public/31/13/3113ee5c-a038-4c16-89af-294a69826650/2019_update_-_the_complexities_of_physician_supply_and_demand_-_projections_from_2017-2032.pdf?utm_medium=email&utm_source=transaction (accessed October 10, 2020).

26. Nalbandian A, Sehgal K, Gupta A, Madhavan MV, McGroder C, Stevens JS, et al. Post-acute COVID-19 syndrome. *Nat Med.* (2021) 27:601–15. doi: 10.1038/s41591-021-01283-z

27. Saxena S, Funk M, Chisholm D. World health assembly adopts comprehensive mental health action plan 2013–2020. *Lancet.* (2013) 381:1970–1. doi: 10.1016/S0140-6736(13)61139-3

28. Fuller ET, Kennard SA, Esliger SD, Lamb R, Pavle J. *More Mentally Ill Persons are in Jails and Prisons Than Hospitals: A Survey of the States.* (2020). Retrieved from: http://www.treatmentadvocacycenter.org/storage/documents/final_jails_v_hospitals_study.pdf (accessed October 6, 2020).

29. Gronde TV, Uyl-de Groot CA, Pieters T. Addressing the challenge of high-priced prescription drugs in the era of precision medicine: a systematic review of drug life cycles, therapeutic drug markets and regulatory frameworks. *PLoS ONE.* (2017) 12:e0182613. doi: 10.1371/journal.pone.0182613

30. Kesselheim AS, Avorn J, Sarpatwari A. The high cost of prescription drugs in the United States: origins and prospects for reform. *JAMA.* (2016) 316:858–71. doi: 10.1001/jama.2016.11237

31. Chibanda D, Bowers T, Verhey R, Rusakaniko S, Abas M, Weiss HA, et al. The Friendship Bench programme: a cluster randomised controlled trial of a brief psychological intervention for common mental disorders delivered by lay health workers in Zimbabwe. *Int J Ment Health Syst.* (2015) 9:21. doi: 10.1186/s13033-015-0013-y

32. Chibanda D. Reducing the treatment gap for mental, neurological and substance use disorders in Africa: lessons from the Friendship Bench in Zimbabwe. *Epidemiol Psychiatr Sci.* (2017) 26:342–7. doi: 10.1017/S2045796016001128

33. Wind TR, Rijkeboer M, Andersson G, Riper H. The COVID-19 pandemic: the 'black swan' for mental health care and a turning point for e-health. *Int Interv.* (2020) 20:100317. doi: 10.1016/j.invent.2020.100317

34. Kilbourne AM, Beck K, Spaeth-Rublee B, Ramanuj P, O'Brien RW, Tomoyasu N, et al. Measuring and improving the quality of mental health care: a global perspective. *World Psychiatry.* (2018) 17:30–8. doi: 10.1002/wps.20482

35. Mental Health America. *The Federal and State Role in Mental Health.* (2020). Retrieved from: https://www.mhanational.org/issues/federal-and-state-role-mental-health (accessed October 3, 2020).

36. Zhou W, Yu Y, Yang M, Chen L, Xiao S. Policy development and challenges of global mental health: a systematic review of published studies of national-level mental health policies. *BMC Psychiatry.* (2018) 18:138. doi: 10.1186/s12888-018-1711-1

37. National Council for Behavioral Health. *President Trump Releases FY 2020 Budget Proposal.* (2019). Retrieved from: Retrieved from: https://www.thenationalcouncil.org/capitol-connector/2019/03/president-trump-releases-fy-2020-budget-proposal/ (accessed September 10, 2020).

38. OPEN MINDS Market Intelligence Report. *The U.S. Mental Health Market $225.1 Billion in Spending in 2019 an OPEN MINDS Market Intelligence Report.* (2020). Retrieved from: https://www.openminds.com/intelligence-report/the-u-s-mental-health-market-225-1-billion-in-spending-in-2019-an-open-minds-market-intelligence-report/ (accessed October 9, 2020).

39. McCance-Katz EF. *The National Survey on Drug Use and Health.* Substance Abuse and Mental Health Services Administration (2018). Retrieved from: https://www.samhsa.gov/data/sites/default/files/cbhsq-reports/Assistant-Secretary-nsduh2018_presentation.pdf (accessed October 10, 2020).

40. Martinez LE, Balderas-Medina Y MPH, Vargas-Bustamante A, Martinez CV, Santizo-Greenwood S, Hernandez S, et al. *California's Physician Shortage During COVID-19. A Policy Roadmap to Expand Access to Care.* Retrieved from: https://latino.ucla.edu/wp-content/uploads/2020/04/LPPI-CPS-COVID-19-.pdf (accessed May 22, 2021).

Conflict of Interest: The authors declare that the research was conducted in the absence of any commercial or financial relationships that could be construed as a potential conflict of interest.

Disorders by Diagnostic Category

ADHD
    Adjustment Disorders

Anxiety Disorders
    Agoraphobia
    General Anxiety Disorder
    Panic Disorder
    Phobias
    Selective Mutism
    Separation Anxiety Disorder
    Social Anxiety Disorder

Autism Spectrum Disorders
    Autism
    Asperger's Syndrome

Bipolar and Related Disorders
    Depressive Disorders
    Depression
    Dysthymic Disorder
    Major Depression
    Postpartum Depression
    Premenstrual Dysphoric Disorder

Disruptive, Impulse-Control and Conduct Disorders
    Conduct Disorder
    Intermittent Explosive Disorder
    Kleptomania
    Pathological Gambling
    Pyromania
    Trichotillomania

Dissociative Disorders
    Depersonalization Disorder
    Dissociative Amnesia
    Dissociative Fugue
    Dissociative Identity Disorder

Feeding and Eating Disorders
    Anorexia Nervosa
    Bulimia Nervosa

Gender Dysphoria

Neurocognitive Disorders
    Delirium
    Dementias
    Amnestic Disorders

Neurodevelopmental Disorders
    Attention Deficit/Hyperactivity Disorder (ADHD)
    Autism Spectrum Disorder
    Asperger's Syndrome
    Autistic Disorder
    Conduct Disorder
    Tic Disorders
    Chronic Motor or Vocal Tic Disorder
    Transient Tic Disorder
    Tourette's Syndrome

Obsessive Compulsive Disorder

Personality Disorders
    Paranoid Personality Disorder
    Schizoid Personality Disorder
    Schizotypal Personality Disorder
    Antisocial Personality Disorder
    Borderline Personality Disorder
    Narcissistic Personality Disorder
    Avoidant Personality Disorder
    Dependent Personality Disorder
    Obsessive-Compulsive Disorder

Schizophrenia Spectrum and Other Psychotic Disorders
    Brief Psychotic Disorder
    Delusional Disorders
    Schizoaffective Disorder
    Schizophrenia

Sexual Disorders
    Sexual Desire Disorders
        Hypoactive Sexual Desire Disorder (HASSD)
        Sexual Aversion Disorder (SAD)
    Sexual Arousal Disorders
        Female Sexual Arousal Disorder (FSAD)
        Male Erectile Disorder (MED)
    Orgasmic Disorders
        Female and Male Orgasmic Disorders
        Premature Ejaculation
        Delayed Ejaculation
        Erectile Dysfunction
    Sexual Pain Disorders
        Dyspareunia
        Vaginismus
    Paraphilias
        Exhibitionism
        Fetishism
        Frotteurism
        Sexual Masochism
        Sexual Sadism
        Transvestic Fetishism
        Voyeurism

Sleep-Wake Disorders
    Breathing-related Sleep Disorder
    Circadian Rhythm Sleep Disorder
    Hypersomnolence
    Insomnia
    Narcolepsy
    Nightmare Disorder
    Parasomnias
    Restless Legs Syndrome
    Substance Abuse Induced Sleep Disorder
    Sleep Apnea
    Sleep Terror Disorder

Somatic Symptom and Related Disorders
    Hypochondria
    Factitious Disorder
    Malingering Disorder
    Somatization Disorder

Substance-Related and Addictive Disorders
Substance-Related Abuse
Substance-Related Dependence

Suicide

Tic Disorders

Trauma and Stressor-Related Disorders
Post Traumatic Stress Syndrome (PTSD)
Obsessive Compulsive Disorder (OCD)

User's Guide

Below is a sample listing illustrating the kind of information that is or might be included in an Association entry, with additional fields that apply to publication and trade show listings. Each numbered item of information is described in the paragraphs on the User's Key.

1. **12345**

    2. **Association for People with Mental Illness**
    3. 29 Simmons Street
       Philadelphia, PA 15201

    4. 234-555-1111
    5. 234-555-1112
    6. 800-555-1113
    7. TDD: 234-555-1114
    8. info@association-mh.com
    9. www.association-mh.com

10. William Lancaster, Executive Director
    Monty Spitz, Marketing Manager
    Kathleen Morrison, Medical Consultant

11. Association for Mental Health is funded by the Mental Health Community Support Program. The purpose of the association is to share information about services, providers, and ways to cope with mental illnesses. Available services include referrals, professional seminars, support gourps, and a variety of publications.

12. 1 M *Members*

13. *Founded*: 1984

14. Bi-monthly

15. $59.00

16. 110,000

User's Key

1. **Record Number:** Entries are listed alphabetically within each category and numbered sequentially. The entry numbers, rather than the page numbers, are used in the indexes to refer to listings.

2. **Title:** Formal name of association or publication. Where names are completely capitalized, the listing will appear at the beginning of the section. If listing is a publication or trade show, the publisher or sponsoring organization will appear below the title.

3. **Address:** Location or permanent address of the association.

4. **Phone Number:** The listed phone number is usually for the main office of the association, but may also be for the sales, marketing, or public relations office as provided.

5. **Fax Number:** This is listed when provided by the association.

6. **Toll-Free Number:** This is listed when provided by the association.

7. **TDD:** This is listed when provided by the association. It refers to Telephone Device for the Deaf.

8. **E-mail:** This is listed when provided by the association.

9. **Web Site:** This is listed when provided by the association and is also referred to as a URL address.

10. **Key Executives:** Lists key contacts of the association, publication or sponsoring organization.

11. **Description:** This paragraph contains a brief description of the association, their purpose and services.

12. **Members:** Total number of association members.

13. **Founded:** Year association was founded.

14. **Frequency:** If listing is a publication.

15. **Subscription Price:** If listing is a publication.

16. **Circulation:** If listing is a publication.

ADHD

Introduction

Attention Deficit Hyperactivity Disorder (ADHD) is characterized by certain patterns of behavior that must be present across several settings. ADHD primarily affects children. However, some individuals continue to experience the illness into adulthood. Symptoms are categorized into two groups: hyperactivity/impulsivity and inattention. They must be present before the age of twelve. At least some of the symptoms must appear before the age of seven.

The problems caused by hyperactivity show themselves in constant movement, especially among younger children. Preschool children with hyperactivity cannot sit still, even for quiet activities that usually absorb children of the same age. They are always on the move and run rather than walk. In older children the intensity of the hyperactivity is reduced but fidgeting, getting up during meals or homework, and excessive talking continue.

Adolescents and adults experience impulsivity more than hyperactivity. They have difficulty with executive control, meaning that they may have problems with time management, prioritizing tasks, focusing, and/or impulsive spending.

Impulsivity and inattention are also present in children. They can be impatient, interrupt, make comments out of turn, grab objects from others, clown around, and cause trouble at home, in school, at work, and in social settings.

The consequences of ADHD can be severe. From a young age, people with Attention Deficit Hyperactivity Disorder tend to experience failure repeatedly, including rejection by peers, resulting in low self-esteem and sometimes more serious problems.

SYMPTOMS

1. Inattention, as compared with others at the same developmental level
• Often fails to attend to details, or makes careless mistakes in schoolwork, work or other activities;
• Often finds it difficult to maintain attention in tasks or play activities;
• Often does not seem to listen when spoken to;
• Often does not follow through on instructions and does not finish schoolwork, chores, or tasks;
• Often has difficulty organizing tasks or activities;
• Often avoids tasks that demand sustained mental effort, such as schoolwork or homework;
• Often loses things needed for tasks or activities, such as toys and school assignments;
• Often is easily distracted;
• Often is forgetful in daily activities.

2. Hyperactivity/impulsivity, as compared with others at the same developmental level
• Often fidgets with hands or feet, or squirms in chair;
• Often leaves seat in classroom or other situations where remaining seated is expected;
• Often runs or climbs about in situations in which it is inappropriate (among adolescents or adults, this may be a feeling of restlessness);
• Often has difficulty playing or handling leisure activities quietly;

• Often is on the go, moving excessively.
• Often talks excessively;
• Often blurts out answers impulsively before questions are finished;
• Often has difficulty waiting in turn;
• Often intrudes impulsively on others' games, activities or conversations.

Parts of this description may apply to all or most children at times, but behaving in this way nearly all the time wreaks havoc on the child and family. Three distinctions are made in the diagnosis:

Combined Type if symptoms of inattention, hyperactivity and impulsivity (Lists 1 and 2) are exhibited;

Predominantly Inattentive Type if six or more inattention symptoms (List 1 only) are displayed;

Predominantly Hyperactive-Impulse Type if six or more hyperactivity and impulsivity symptoms (List 2 only) are applicable.

ASSOCIATED FEATURES

Certain behaviors often go along with Attention Deficit Hyperactivity Disorder. The person is often frustrated and angry, exhibiting outbursts of temper and bossiness. To an observer, the lack of application and inability to finish tasks may look like laziness or irresponsibility. Other conditions may also be associated with the disorder, including Hyperthyroidism (an overactive thyroid). There may be a higher prevalence of anxiety, depression, and learning disorders among people with ADHD.

A careful assessment and diagnosis by a professional familiar with ADHD are absolutely essential, especially since some of the typical ADHD behaviors may resemble those of other disorders. Family, school, and other possible problems must be taken into account and addressed. This is a lifelong disorder, though sometimes attenuated in adulthood.

The diagnosis is especially difficult to establish in young children - e.g., at the toddler and preschool level - because behavior that is typical at that age is similar to the symptoms of ADHD. Children at that age may be extremely active but not develop the disorder.

PREVALENCE

ADHD occurs in various cultures. Historically, it has been more frequent in males than females, with male to female ratios at 4:1 in the general population, and 9:1 in clinic populations. However, research has shown that females tend to present with Predominantly Inattentive Type ADHD. Females are now being diagnosed at a similar rate to males.

The prevalence among school-age children is from five percent to twelve percent. ADHD can exist throughout a lifetime and, in fact, may be diagnosed in teen or adult years. There is emerging literature concerning adult ADHD, and evidence that some adults can benefit from the same treatments used for children.

TREATMENT OPTIONS

ADHD is treated using a three-tiered approach consisting of education programs (including resources and tutorial help), psychological programs (individual, group and family counseling) to help with self-esteem and stress, and medical therapy.

The person with ADHD has great need for external motivation, consistency, and structure. This should be provided by a professional who is familiar with the disorder. For a school-aged child, it is important to enlist the help of the school in designing a treatment plan which should include concrete steps aimed at developing specific competencies (e.g., handling time, sequencing, problem-solving, and social interaction).

Medication is often prescribed but should not be the only treatment. Newer preparations of medications, such as Concerta and Biphentin, offer once or twice a day dosing, so that children do not need to take medication during the school day.

Since this condition affects all members of the family, the family needs help in providing consistency and structure, and in not defining the role of the person with ADHD as the one who always gets into trouble. Treatment should be based on an understanding that ADHD is not intentional, and that punishment is not a cure.

Current treatments can have a positive impact and, in some cases, transform behaviors so that a formerly chaotic life becomes more in control.

Associations & Agencies

2   Attention Deficit Disorder Association
PO Box 7557
Wilmington, DE 19803
800-939-1019
www.add.org

Duane Gordon, President
Annette Tabor, Education Committee Chair

Provides information, support groups, publications, workshops, and networking opportunities for people with Attention Deficit Hyperactivity Disorder. Strives to improve the lives of those with ADHD.

3   Brain & Behavior Research Foundation
747 Third Avenue
33rd Floor
New York, NY 10017
646-681-4888
800-829-8289
E-mail: info@bbrfoundation.org
www.www.bbrfoundation.org

Donald M. Boardman, Treasurer
Jeffrey Borenstein, MD, President and CEO
Louis Innamorato, CPA, VP and Chief Financial Officer
Faith Rothblatt, Vice President, Development

The Brain and Behavior Research Foundation awards grants aimed at advancing scientific understandings of mental health treatments and mental disorders such as depression and schizophrenia. The Brain and Behavior Research Foundation's mission is to eliminate the suffering caused by mental illness.

Year Founded: 1987

4   Center for Mental Health Services (CMHS)
Substance Abuse and Mental Health Services
Administration
5600 Fishers Lane
Rockville, MD 20857
877-726-4727
TTY: 800-487-4889
www.samhsa.gov/about-us/who-we-are/offices-centers

Anita Everett, MD, DFAPA, Director

Promotes the treatment of mental illness and emotional disorders by increasing accessibility to mental health programs; supporting outreach, treatment, rehabilitation, and support programs and networks; and encouraging the use of scientifically-based information when treating mental disorders. CMHS provides information about mental health via a toll-free number and numerous publications. Developed for users of mental health services and their families, the general public, policy makers, providers, and the media.

Year Founded: 1992

5   Children and Adults with AD/HD (CHADD)
4221 Forbes Boulevard
Suite 270
Lanham, MD 20706
301-306-7070
E-mail: customer_service@chadd.org
www.chadd.org

Patricia M. Hudak, PCC, BCC, President
Rhonda Buckley, Interim CEO
Bob O'Malley, Secretary
Harvey Parker, Founder

National nonprofit organization serving individuals with Attention Deficit Hyperactivity Disorder (ADHD) and their families. Offers support and information for individuals, parents, teachers, professionals, and others, and advocates for the rights of people with ADHD. Available on Facebook and Twitter.

Year Founded: 1987

6   Learning Disabilities Association of America
4068 Mount Royal Boulevard
Suite 224B
Allison Park, PA 15101
412-341-1515
E-mail: info@ldaamerica.org
www.ldaamerica.org

Kevin Gailey, Chair
Cindy Cipoletti, Executive Director
Charles (CJ) Pascarella, Treasurer
Bev Johns, Secretary

Educates individuals with learning disabilities and their families through conferences, workshops, and symposiums; advocates for the rights of individuals with learning disabilities; provides support for parents; and promotes research in the assessment and prevention of learning disabilities.

Year Founded: 1964

7   NAPCSE National Association of Parents with
Children in Special Education
3642 East Sunnydale Drive
Chandler Heights, AZ 85142

800-754-4421
E-mail: contact@napcse.org
www.napcse.org

Dr. George Giuliani, President

The NAPCSE is dedicated to ensuring quality education for all children and adolescents with special needs. NAPCSE provides resources, support, and assistance to parents with children in special education.

8 National Alliance on Mental Illness
4301 Wilson Boulevard
Suite 300
Arlington, VA 22203
703-524-7600
800-950-6264
E-mail: info@nami.org
www.nami.org

Shirley J. Holloway, President
Joyce A. Campbell, First Vice President
Daniel H. Gillison, Jr., Chief Executive Officer
David Levy, Chief Financial Officer

NAMI is an organization dedicated to raising awareness on mental health and providing support and education for Americans affected by mental illness. NAMI advocates for access to services and treatment and fosters an environment of awareness and understanding for those concerned with mental health.

Year Founded: 1979

9 National Association for the Dually Diagnosed (NADD)
321 Wall Street
Kingston, NY 12401
845-331-4336
E-mail: info@thenadd.org
www.thenadd.org

Jeanne M. Farr, MA, Chief Executive Officer
Bruce Davis, President
Juanita St. Croix, Vice President
Ray Snyder, Secretary

NADD is a nonprofit organization designed to increase awareness of, and provide services for, individuals with developmental disabilities and mental illness. NADD emphasizes the importance of quality mental healthcare for people with mental health needs and offers conferences, information resources, educational programs, and training materials to professionals, parents, and organizations.

Year Founded: 1983

10 National Center for Learning Disabilities
1220 L Street NW
Suite 100
Washington, DC 20005
301-966-2234
www.ncld.org

Margi Booth, Co-Chair
Joe Zimmel, Co-Chair
Kena Mayberry, Chief Operating Officer
Kenneth Plevan, Secretary

The NCLD's mission is to ensure success for all individuals with learning disabilities in school, at work, and in life. They connect parents with resources, guidance, and support to advocate effectively for their children; deliver evidence-based tools, resources, and professional development to educators to improve student outcomes; and develop pol-

icies and engage advocates to strengthen educational rights and opportunities.

Year Founded: 1977

11 National Federation of Families for Children's Mental Health
15800 Crabbs Branch Way
Suite 300
Rockville, MD 20855
240-403-1901
E-mail: ffcmh@ffcmh.org
www.ffcmh.org

Lynda Gargan, PhD, Executive Director
Gail Cormier, Project Director
Leann Sherman, Project Coordinator

The National Federation of Families for Children's Mental Health is a national organization focused on advocating for the rights of children affected by mental health challenges, assisting family-run organizations across the nation, and ensuring that children and families concerned with mental health have access to services.

Year Founded: 1989

12 National Institute of Mental Health
6001 Executive Boulevard
Room 6200, MSC 9663
Bethesda, MD 20892-9663
866-615-6464
E-mail: nimhinfo@nih.gov
www.nimh.nih.gov

Joshua Gordon, MD, PhD, Director

The National Institute of Mental Health conducts clinical research on mental disorders and seeks to expand knowledge on mental health treatments.

13 National Mental Health Consumers' Self-Help Clearinghouse
E-mail: selfhelpclearinghouse@gmail.com
www.mhselfhelp.org

Joseph Rogers, Founder and Executive Director
Susan Rogers, Director

The Clearinghouse is a peer-run national technical assistance center focused on achieving respect and equality of opportunity for those with mental illnesses. The Clearinghouse helps with the growth of the mental health consumer movement by evaluating mental health services, advocating for mental health reform, and providing consumers with news, information, publications, and consultation services.

Year Founded: 1986

14 National Resource Center on ADHD
Children and Adults with AD/HD
4221 Forbes Boulevard
Suite 270
Lanham, MD 20706
301-306-7070
www.chadd.org/about/about-nrc/

Dr L. Eugene Arnold, MD, MEd, Resident Expert
Zuali Malsawma, NRC Director
Susan Buningh, MRE, Director of Communications

The National Resource Center, a program of CHADD, is a resource platform focused on disseminating the latest science-based information on ADHD. The NRC provides comprehensive information and program activities for children and adults with ADHD, parents, caregivers, professionals, and other members of the public.

15 PACER Center
8161 Normandale Boulevard
Bloomington, MN 55437
952-838-9000
800-537-2237
www.pacer.org

Paula F. Goldberg, Co-Founder & Executive Director

PACER provides information, training, and assistance to parents of children and young adults with all disabilities (physical, learning, cognitive, emotional, and health). Its mission is to help improve the quality of life for young people with disabilities and their families.

Year Founded: 1977

16 Sutcliffe Clinic
851 Fremont Avenue
Suite 110
Los Altos, CA 94024
650-941-1698
E-mail: info@sutcliffedbp.com
www.www.sutcliffeclinic.com

Trenna Sutcliffe, MD, MS, Medical Director

Sutcliffe Developmental & Behavioral Pediatrics is an organization that specializes in the treatment of ADHD, autism spectrum disorder, anxiety disorders, conduct disorders, learning disabilities, and more. Sutcliffe works with community services, school districs, and primary physicians, and provides family counseling.

17 The Center for Family Support
2811 Zulette Avenue
Bronx, NY 10461
718-518-1500
E-mail: svernikoff@cfsny.org
www.www.cfsny.org

Steven Vernikoff, Executive Director
Barbara Greenwald, Chief Operating Officer
Jos, Martin Jara, President
Elise Geltzer, Vice President

The Center for Family Support offers assistance to individuals with developmental and related disabilities, as well as their families, and provides support services and programs that are designed to accommodate individual needs. Offers services throughout New York City, Westchester County, Long Island, and New Jersey.

Year Founded: 1954

Periodicals & Pamphlets

18 ADDitude Magazine
ADD Warehouse
300 NW 70th Avenue
Suite 102
Plantation, FL 33317-2360
954-792-8944
800-233-9273
E-mail: sales@addwarehouse.com
www.addwarehouse.com

Harvey C Parker, Owner

Provides valuable resource information for professionals-teachers, healthcare providers, employers and others-who interact with AD/HD people everyday. *$19.97*

19 Attention Magazine
Children and Adults with AD/HD (CHADD)
4221 Forbes Boulevard
Suite 270
Lanham, MD 20706
301-306-7070
www.chadd.org

Dr L. Eugene Arnold, MD, MEd, Resident Expert
Sarah Brown, MA, NRC Program Manager
Susan Buningh, MRE, Director of Communications

A bi-monthly magazine for members of CHADD that offers practical information, clinical insights, and strategies for managing ADHD. Attention manazine also offers a digital edition subscription. *$24.00*

6 per year

20 Attention-Deficit/Hyperactivity Disorder in Children and Adolescents
Center for Mental Health Services: Knowledge Exchange Network
PO Box 42557
Washington, DC 20015-557
800-789-2647
TDD: 866-889-2647
E-mail: ken@mentalhealth.org
www.mentalhealth.samhsa.gov/publications/

This fact sheet defines attention-deficit/hyperactivity disorder, describes the warning signs, discusses types of help available, and suggests what parents or other caregivers can do.

3 pages

21 Learning Disabilities: A Multidisciplinary Journal

Richard T. Boon, author

Learning Disabilities Association of America
4068 Mount Royal Boulevard
Suite 224B
Allison Park, PA 15101
412-341-1515
E-mail: info@LDAAmerica.org
www.ldaamerica.org

Kevin Gailey, Chair
Cindy Cipoletti, Executive Director
Charles (CJ) Pascarella, Treasurer
Bev Johns, Secretary

The most current research designed for professionals in the field of LD. *$60.00*

Support Groups & Hot Lines

22 Children and Adults with AD/HD (CHADD)
4221 Forbes Boulevard
Suite 270
Lanham, MD 20706
301-306-7070
E-mail: customer_service@chadd.org
www.chadd.org

Patricia M. Hudak, PCC, BCC, President
Rhonda Buckley, Interim CEO

Bob O'Malley, Secretary
Harvey Parker, Founder

Nonprofit organization serving individuals with AD/HD and their families. Over 16,000 members in 200 local chapters throughout the United States. Chapters offer support for individuals, parents, teachers, professionals, and others. Available on Facebook and Twitter.

Video & Audio

23 ADHD & LD: Powerful Teaching Strategies & Accomodations
ADD Warehouse
300 NW 70the Avenue
Suite 102
Plantation, FL 33317-2360
954-792-8100
800-233-9273
E-mail: websales@addwarehouse.com
www.addwarehouse.com

Sandra Rief, Author

Provides instructional strategies for engaging attention and active participation, classroom management and behavioral interventions, gives academic strategies and accomodations, and collaborates teaming for success. 45 minutes. *$129.00*

24 ADHD-Inclusive Instruction & Collaborative Practices
ADD Warehouse
300 NW 70th Avenue
Suite 102
Plantation, FL 33317-2360
954-792-8100
800-233-9273
E-mail: websales@addwarehouse.com
www.addwarehouse.com

Sandra Rief, Author

Describes classroom modifications, teaching strategies, and interventions that can be used to maximize learning and ensure that all students achieve success. 38 minutes. *$99.00*

ISBN 1-887943-04-8

25 ADHD: What Can We Do?
ADD WareHouse
300 NW 70th Avenue
Suite 102
Plantation, FL 33317-2360
954-792-8100
800-233-9273
E-mail: websales@addwarehouse.com
www.addwarehouse.com

Russell A. Barkley, Author

Can serve as a companion to ADHD: What Do We Know?, this video focuses on the most effective ways to manage ADHD, both in the home and in the classroom. Scenes depict the use of behavior management at home and accommodations and interventions in the classroom which have proven to be effective in the treatment of ADHD. Thirty five minutes. *$95.00*

ISBN 0-898629-72-1

26 ADHD: What Do We Know?
ADD WareHouse
300 NW 70th Avenue
Suite 102
Plantation, FL 33317-2360
954-792-8100
800-233-9273
E-mail: websales@addwarehouse.com
www.addwarehouse.com

Russell A. Barkley, Author

This video provides an overview of the disorder and introduces the viewer to three young people who have ADHD. Discusses how ADHD affects the lives of the children and adults, causes of the disorder, associated problems, outcome in adulthood and provides vivid illustrations of how individuals with ADHD function at home, at school and on the job. Thirty five minutes. *$95.00*

ISBN 0-898629-71-3

27 Adults with Attention Deficit Disorder: ADD Isn't Just Kids Stuff
ADD WareHouse
300 NW 70th Avenue
Suite 102
Plantation, FL 33317-2360
954-792-8100
800-233-9273
E-mail: websales@addwarehouse.com
www.addwarehouse.com

Harvey C Parker, Owner

Explains this often misunderstood condition and the effects it has on one's work, home and social life. With the help of a panel of six adults, four ADD adults and two of their spouses, the book addresses the most common concerns of adults with ADD and provides information that will help families who are experiencing difficulties. 86 minutes. *$ 47.00*

28 Educating Inattentive Children
ADD WareHouse
300 NW 70th Avenue
Suite 102
Plantation, FL 33317-2360
954-792-8100
800-233-9273
E-mail: websales@addwarehouse.com
www.addwarehouse.com

Samuel Goldstein, Ph.D., Author
Michael Goldstein, M.D., Author

This two-hour video is ideal for in-service to regular and special educators concerning problems experienced by inattentive elementary and secondary students. Provides educators with information necessary to indentify and evaluate classroom problems caused by inattention and a well-defined set of practical guidelines to help educate children with ADD. *$49.00*

29 Medication for ADHD
ADD WareHouse
300 NW 70th Avenue
Suite 102
Plantation, FL 33317-2360
954-792-8100
800-233-9273
E-mail: websales@addwarehouse.com
www.addwarehouse.com

Dr. Andrew Adesman, Author

This comprehensive DVD addresses the critical questions regarding the use of medication in the treatment of ADD or ADHD. Allows those involved with ADHD to make well-informed and constructive decisions that may deeply change someone's life. *$39.95*

ISBN 1-889140-18-X

30   New Look at ADHD: Inhibition, Time and Self Control
Guilford Press
72 Spring Street
New York, NY 10012-4068
212-431-9800
800-365-7006
E-mail: info@guilford.com

Bob Matloff, President
Seymour Weingarten, Editor-in-Chief

This video provides an accessible introduction to Russell A Barkley's influential theory of the nature and origins of ADHD. The program brings to life the conceptual framework delineated in Barkley's other books. Discusses concrete ways that our new understanding of the disorder might facilitate more effective clinical interventions. This lucid, state of the art program is ideal viewing for clinicians, students and inservice trainees, parents of children with ADHD and adults with the disorder. 30 minutes. *$95.00*

ISBN 1-572304-97-9

31   Outside In: A Look at Adults with Attention Deficit Disorder
ADD Warehouse
300 NW 70th Avenue
Suite 102
Plantation, FL 33317-2360
954-792-8100
800-233-9273
E-mail: websales@addwarehouse.com
www.addwarehouse.com

Ted Kay, Director

Documentary film about adults with ADD and their journeys and the strategies they used to succeed. 29 minutes *$27.95*

32   Understanding Mental Illness
Educational Video Network
1401 19th Street
Huntsville, TX 77340
936-295-5767
800-762-0060
www.www.evndirect.com

A video to learn and understand mental illness and how it affects you. *$79.95*

ISBN 1-589501-48-9

33   Understanding and Treating the Hereditary Psychiatric Spectrum Disorders
Hope Press
10 Mill Road
Duarte, CA 91010
626-622-4978
800-209-9182
E-mail: dcomings@earthlink.net
www.hopepress.com

Books cover: ADHD, Tourette Syndrome, Obsessive-Compulsive Disorder, Conduct Disorder, Oppositional Defiant Disorder, Autism and other Hereditary Psychiatric Spectrum Disorders. *$75.00*

34   Understanding the Defiant Child
Guilford Press
72 Spring Street
New York, NY 10012-4068
212-431-9800
800-365-7006
E-mail: info@guilford.com

Bob Matloff, President
Seymour Weingarten, Editor-in-Chief

Presents information on Oppositional Defiant Disorder and Conduct Disorder with scenes of family interactions, showing the nature and causes of these disorders and what can and should be done about it. Thirty five minutes with a manual that contains more information. 30 minutes. *$95.00*

ISBN 1-572301-66-X

35   Why Won't My Child Pay Attention?
ADD WareHouse
300 NW 70th Avenue
Suite 102
Plantation, FL 33317-2360
954-792-8100
800-233-9273
E-mail: websales@addwarehouse.com
www.addwarehouse.com

Sam Goldstein, PhD, Author

Provides an easy-to-follow explanation concerning the effect ADD has on children at school, home and in the community. Provides guidelines to help parents and professionals successfully and happily manage the problems these behaviors can cause. 76 minutes. *$38.00*

Web Sites

36   www.CHADD.org
Children/Adults with Attention Deficit/Hyperactivity Disorder

37   www.LD-ADD.com
Attention Deficit Disorder and Parenting Site

38   www.aap.org
American Academy of Pediatrics Practice Guidelines on ADHD

Site serves the purpose of giving the public guidelines for diagnosing and evaluating children with possible ADHD.

39   www.add.about.com
Attention Deficit Disorder

Hundreds of sites.

40   www.add.org
Attention Deficit Disorder Association

Provides information, resources and networking to adults with ADHD and to the professionals who work with them.

41 **www.additudemag.com**
Happy Healthy Lifestyle Magazine for People with ADD

42 **www.addvance.com**
Answers to Your Questions About ADD

Provides answers to questions about ADD, ADHD for families and individuals at every stage of life from preschool through retirement years.

43 **www.adhdnews.com/Advocate.htm**
Advocating for Your Child

44 **www.adhdnews.com/sped.htm**
Special Education Rights and Responsibilities

Writing IEP's and TIEPS. Pursuing special education services.

45 **www.babycenter.com/rcindex.html**
BabyCenter

46 **www.cfsny.org**
Center for Family Support (CFS)

Devoted to providing support and assistance to individuals with developmental and related disabilities, and to the family members who care for them.

47 **www.cyberpsych.org**
CyberPsych

Hosts the American Psychoanalyists Foundation, American Association of Suicideology, Society for the Exploration of Psychotherapy Intergration, and Anxiety Disorders Association of America. Also subcategories of the anxiety disorders, as well as general information, including panic disorder, phobias, obsessive compulsive disorder (OCD), social phobia, generalized anxiety disorder, post traumatic stress disorder, and phobias of childhood. Book reviews and links to web pages sharing the topics.

48 **www.nami.org**
National Alliance on Mental Illness

From its inception in 1979, NAMI has been dedicated to improving the lives of individuals and families affected by mental illness.

49 **www.nichcy.org**
National Information Center for Children and Youth with Disabilities

Excellent information in English and Spanish.

50 **www.nimh.nih.gov/publicat/adhd.cfm**
Attention Deficit Hyperactivity Disorder

Thirty page booklet.

51 **www.oneaddplace.com**
One ADD Place

52 **www.planetpsych.com**
Planetpsych.com

Learn about disorders, their treatments and other topics in psychology. Articles are listed under the related topic areas. Ask a therapist a question for free, or view the directory of professionals in your area. If you are a therapist sign up for the directory. Current features, self-help, interactive, and newsletter archives.

53 **www.psychcentral.com**
Psych Central

Personalized one-stop index for psychology, support, and mental health issues, resources, and people on the Internet.

54 **www.store.samhsa.gov**
Substance Abuse and Mental Health Services Administration

Resources on mental disorders as well as treatment and recovery.

55 **www.thenadd.org**
National Association for the Dually Diagnosed (NADD)

An association for persons with developmental disabilities and mental health needs.

Adjustment Disorders

Introduction

The experience of stress in life is inevitable. When we are faced with significant life changes, we do our best to cope, get through it, and move on. How we cope and how long it takes to get through it vary according to the stressful situation and the resources the individual brings to it. In most situations, we respond appropriately to the stressful event or situation and show an adaptive response.

Adjustment Disorders are maladaptive reactions to a stressful event or situation. The adjustment is to a real event or situation (e.g., the end of a relationship or job loss), and the disorder signifies that the reaction is more extreme than would be warranted considering the stressor, and/or keeps the individual from functioning as usual.

SYMPTOMS

• The development of emotional or behavioral symptoms is in response to an identifiable stressor, except bereavement, within three months of the appearance of the stressor;
• The emotions or behaviors are significant either because the distress is more extreme than would normally be caused by the stressor, or because the emotions or behaviors are clearly impairing the person's social, school, or work functioning;
• If the symptoms persist for less than six months after the stressor ends, the disorder is considered acute; if symptoms persist for longer than six months, the disorder is considered to be chronic, leading to a different diagnosis, such as PTSD or Major Depressive Disorder.

Adjustment Disorders are divided into several subtypes:

• **Depressed Mood** - predominant mood is depression, with symptoms such as tearfulness, hopelessness, sadness, sleep disturbances;
• **Anxiety** - predominant symptoms are edginess, nervousness, worry, or in children, fears of separation from important attachment figures;
• **Anxiety and Depressed Mood** - chief manifestations are a combination of depression and anxiety;
• **Disturbance of Conduct** - predominant symptoms are conduct which involves either a violation of other people's rights (e.g., reckless driving, fighting), or the violation of social norms and rules;
• **Disturbance of Emotions and Conduct** - predominant manifestations are a combination of anxiety, depression, and behavioral symptoms;
• **Unspecified** - symptoms that differ from those associated with other Adjustment Disorder subtypes, such as physical problems or issues related to home, work, or social life.

ASSOCIATED FEATURES

Many commonplace events can be stressful (e.g., first day of school, changing jobs). If the stressor is an acute event (like an impending surgical procedure), the onset of the disturbance is usually immediate but may not last more than six months after the stressor ends. If the stressor or its consequences continue (such as a long-term illness), the Adjustment Disorder may also continue. Whatever the nature of the event, it caused the person to feel overwhelmed. A person may be reacting to one or many stressors; the stressor may affect one person or the whole family. The more severe the stressor, the more likely that an Adjustment Disorder will develop. If a person is already vulnerable, e.g., is suffering from a disability including a mental disorder, an Adjustment Disorder is more likely.

Symptoms that are part of a personality disorder and become worse under stress are not usually considered to be Adjustment Disorders unless they are new types of symptoms for the individual.

There are three questions to consider in diagnosing Adjustment Disorder: How out-of-proportion is the response to the stressor? How long does it go on? To what extent does it impair the person's ability to function in social, workplace, and school settings?

The emotional response may show itself in excessive worry and edginess, excessive sadness and hopelessness or a combination of these. There may also be changes in behavior in response to the stressful event or situation, with the person violating other people's rights or breaking agreed-upon rules and regulations. The emotional response and the changes in behavior persist, even after the stressful event or circumstances have ended. Finally, the response significantly affects the person's normal functioning in social, school or work settings.

Adjustment Disorders increase the risk of suicidal behavior and completed suicide, and they also complicate the course of other medical conditions (for example, patients may not take their medication, eat properly, etc).

PREVALENCE

Men and women of all ages, as well as children, can suffer from this disorder. Women are twice as likely as men to have an Adjustment Disorder, while chances are similar for boys and girls. In outpatient mental health centers, the diagnosis of Adjustment Disorder is made in five to twenty percent of patients. Adjustment Disorder is one of the most common mental disorders diagnosed in workers.

TREATMENT OPTIONS

Anyone who is experiencing one or more stressful events or circumstances, and feels overwhelmed or markedly distressed and cannot function normally, should seek help. A psychiatrist or other mental health professional should make an evaluation including a referral for physical examination if necessary. Treatment prescribed is often psychotherapy, and, depending on the circumstances, can include individual, couple, or family therapy. Medication is sometimes prescribed for a few weeks or months. In most instances long-term therapy will not be necessary, and the person can expect marked improvement within 8 to 12 sessions.

Associations & Agencies

57 Alive Alone
PO Box 182
Van Wert, OH 45891
E-mail: alivalon@bright.net
www.alivealone.org

Kay Bevington, Founder
Rodney Bevington, Founder

Alive Alone is a nonprofit organization dedicated to educating and supporting bereaved parents whose children are deceased. Alive Alone provides a self-help network and publishes bimonthly newsletters to help parents with no surviving children to find friendship and healing, resolve their grief, and work towards a positive future.

Year Founded: 1988

58   Center for Loss in Multiple Birth (CLIMB), Inc.
PO Box 190401
Anchorage, AK 99519
E-mail: climb@climb-support.org
www.climb-support.org

Jean Kollantai, Founder

A nonprofit organization focused on educating the public on the risks of multiple births and the importance of preventing the losses associated with them. CLIMB provides support for parents who are coping with the loss of one or more of their multiple birth children from conception through early childhood, and also extends assistance to twins, caregivers, families, and multiples organizations.

Year Founded: 1987

**59   Center for Mental Health Services (CMHS)
Substance Abuse and Mental Health Services
Administration**
5600 Fishers Lane
Rockville, MD 20857
240-276-1310
www.samhsa.gov/about-us/who-we-are/offices-centers

Anita Everett, MD, DFAPA, Director

Promotes the treatment of mental illness and emotional disorders by increasing accessibility to mental health programs; supporting outreach, treatment, rehabilitation, and support programs and networks; and encouraging the use of scientifically-based information when treating mental disorders. CMHS provides information about mental health via a toll-free number and numerous publications. Developed for users of mental health services and their families, the general public, policy makers, providers, and the media.

Year Founded: 1992

60   Empty Cradle
31938 Temecula Parkway
Suite A, #385
Temecula, CA 92592
619-573-6515
E-mail: info@emptycradle.org
www.emptycradle.org

Rachel Redhouse, Co-President
John Redhouse, Co-President & Treasurer
Bella Carson, Vice President
Lori Knierium, Secretary

A nonprofit peer support group for parents who have experienced the death of a baby. Focusing on parents in the San Diego and Riverside County area, Empty Cradle supports grieving families through educational resources, monthly meetings, and a network of volunteer parents seeking to offer friendship and emotional support.

Year Founded: 1982

61   First Candle
21 Locust Avenue
Suite 2B
New Canaan, CT 06840

203-966-1300
www.firstcandle.org

Alison Jacobson, Chief Executive Officer
Abby Lundy, Director, Development
Barb Himes, IBCLC, Director, Education Services

First Candle is a nonprofit organization dedicated to preventing infant death from Sudden Infant Death Syndrome (SIDS), stillbirth, miscarriage, and other Sudden Unexpected Infant Deaths (SUID). First Candle offers support for bereaved families and promotes research, education, and advocacy programs focused on helping all babies to survive.

Year Founded: 1987

**62   Grief Recovery After a Substance Passing
(GRASP)**
11819 N Deerfield Drive
Dunlap, IL 61614
302-492-7717
E-mail: administrator@grasphelp.org
www.grasphelp.org

Tamara Olt, Executive Director
Darleen Berg, Chair
Denise Cullen, Co-Founder

GRASP provides information resources, offers support, and organizes meetings and events for families or individuals who have experienced the death of a loved one as a result of substance abuse or addiction.

Year Founded: 2002

63   M.I.S.S. Foundation/Center for Loss & Trauma
PO Box 9195
Austin, TX 78766
602-279-6477
888-455-6477
E-mail: info@missfoundation.org
www.missfoundation.org

Dr. Joanne Cacciatore, PhD., Founder and Chairman
Kelli Montgomery, Executive Director

M.I.S.S. Foundation is committed to supporting those who have experienced the death of a child and using research and education to limit the number of child deaths. The Foundation offers ongoing support for families coping with the loss of a child; provides information, newsletters, referrals, support groups, and online chat room support; and participates in legislative issues, advocacy movements, and community events.

Year Founded: 1996

**64   National Association for the Dually Diagnosed
(NADD)**
321 Wall Street
Kingston, NY 12401
845-331-4336
E-mail: info@thenadd.org
www.thenadd.org

Jeanne M. Farr, MA, Chief Executive Officer
Bruce Davis, President
Juanita St. Croix, Vice President
Ray Snyder, Secretary

NADD is a nonprofit organization designed to increase awareness of, and provide services for, individuals with developmental disabilities and mental illness. NADD emphasizes the importance of quality mental healthcare for people with mental health needs and offers conferences, information resources, educational programs, and training materials to professionals, parents, and organizations.

Year Founded: 1983

65   National Mental Health Consumers' Self-Help Clearinghouse

E-mail: selfhelpclearinghouse@gmail.com
www.mhselfhelp.org

Joseph Rogers, Founder and Executive Director
Susan Rogers, Director

The Clearinghouse is a peer-run national technical assistance center focused on achieving respect and equality of opportunity for those with mental illnesses. The Clearinghouse helps with the growth of the mental health consumer movement by evaluating mental health services, advocating for mental health reform, and providing consumers with news, information, publications, and consultation services.

Year Founded: 1986

66   National Organization of Parents of Murdered Children

635 West 7th Street
Suite 104
Cincinnati, OH 45203
513-721-5683
E-mail: natlpomc@pomc.org
www.pomc.com

Connie Sheely, President
Bev Warnock, National Executive Director
Lori King, Vice President
Martha Lasher-Warner, Secretary

The organization provides ongoing support services for parents of children who were murdered, as well as other survivors, with the goal of helping them to work towards a healthy future. Monthly meetings, newsletters, and court accompaniment are also offered in many areas. This organization offers guidelines for starting local chapters. Parole Block Program and Second Opinion Services are also available.

Year Founded: 1978

67   Survivors of Loved Ones' Suicides (SOLOS)

8310 Ewing Halsell Drive
San Antonio, TX 78229
210-885-7069
E-mail: solossanantonio@gmail.com
www.solossa.org

Located in San Antonio, Texas, SOLOS organizes ongoing support group meetings for persons affected by the loss of loved ones from suicide.

Year Founded: 1987

68   The Center for Family Support

2811 Zulette Avenue
Bronx, NY 10461
718-518-1500
E-mail: svernikoff@cfsny.org
www.www.cfsny.org

Steven Vernikoff, Executive Director
Barbara Greenwald, Chief Operating Officer
Jos, Martin Jara, President
Elise Geltzer, Vice President

The Center for Family Support offers assistance to individuals with developmental and related disabilities, as well as their families, and provides support services and programs that are designed to accommodate individual needs. Offers services throughout New York City, Westchester County, Long Island, and New Jersey.

Year Founded: 1954

69   UNITE, Inc.

PO Box 298
Oxford, PA 19363
484-758-0002
E-mail: administrator@unitegriefsupport.org
www.unitegriefsupport.org

Barbara Bond-Moury, Board Chairperson
Denise Paul, Group Facilitators Director
Karen Powers, Vice President of Fundraising

A nonprofit organization committed to providing support services for those who have lost a baby from miscarriage, stillbirth, ectopic pregnancy or early infant death. UNITE, Inc. organizes grief support groups for parents and offers educational programs, training workshops, literature, referrals, and group development assistance.

Year Founded: 1975

70   Zur Institute

321 S. Main Street
#29
Sebastopol, CA 95472
833-961-1344
E-mail: info@zurinstitute.com
www.www.zurinstitute.com

Dr. Ofer Zur, Director

Provides quality online continuing education, tools, and services that enhance the ability of psychotherapists, couselors, therapists, social workers, and other health care professionals to meet the needs of those concerned with mental health.

Year Founded: 1995

Periodicals & Pamphlets

71   A Journey Together
Bereaved Parents of the USA

PO Box 622
St Peters, MO 63376
443-865-9666
800-273-8255
E-mail: jbgoodrich@sbcglobal.net
www.bereavedparentsusa.org

Richard Berman, Editor
Lee Ann Hutson, Vice President, Web Liason
Linda Fehrman, Secretary
John Goodrich, National Contact

The newsletter contains articles of interest to the bereaved about grief. It also has book reviews and information about upcoming Grief Gatherings and other support groups.

4 per year

72   Alive Alone Newsletter

PO Box 182
Van Wert, OH 45891
E-mail: alivalon@bright.net
www.alivealone.org

Kay Bevington, Founder
Rodney Bevington, Founder

The Alive Alone newsletter is published quarterly and contains articles on the topic of the loss of a child. The newsletter features articles, poems, and letters written by bereaved parents.

4 per year

73 Journal of Mental Health Research in Intellectual Disabilities (JMHRID)

Angela Hassiotis, author

321 Wall Street
Kingston, NY 12401
845-331-4336
E-mail: info@thenadd.org
www.thenadd.org

Bruce Davis, President
Jeanne M. Farr, MA, Chief Executive Officer
Juanita St. Croix, Vice President
Ray Snyder, Secretary

Quarterly publication designed to promote interest of professional and parent development with resources for individuals who have the coexistence of mental illness and developmental disabilities.

4 per year ISSN 1931-5864

Support Groups & Hot Lines

74 Bereaved Parents of the USA
PO Box 622
St Peters, MO 63376
708-748-7866
800-273-8255
E-mail: jbgoodrich@sbcglobal.net
www.bereavedparentsusa.org

Lee Ann Hutson, President
Jodi Norman, Vice President
Delain Johnson, Secretary
Bill Lagemann, Treasurer

BP/USA is a national nonprofit self-help group that offers support, understanding, compassion and hope especially to the newly bereaved, whether they are granparents, parents or siblings.

75 Compassionate Friends, Inc
1000 Jorie Boulevard
Suite 140
Oak Brook, IL 60523
630-990-0010
877-969-0010
E-mail: nationaloffice@compassionatefriends.org
www.compassionatefriends.org

Patrick O'Donnell, President
Lisa Corrao, Chief Operating Officer
Georgia Cockerham, Vice President
Alan Pederson, Interim Executive Director

Bereavement support for families grieving the death of a child of any age regardless of cause.

Year Founded: 1978

76 Friends for Survival, Inc.
PO Box 214463
Sacramento, CA 95821

916-392-0664
800-646-7322
www.friendsforsurvival.org

A national nonprofit outreach organization open to those who have lost family or friends by suicide, and also to professionals who work with those who have been touched by a suicide tragedy. Dedicated to providing a variety of peer support services that comfort those in grief, encourage healing and growth, foster the development of skills to cope with a loss and educate the entire community regarding the impact of suicide.

77 National Share Office
42 Jackson Street
Saint Charles, MO 63301-3468
636-947-6164
800-821-6819
E-mail: info@nationalshare.org
www.www.nationalshare.org

Michael Margherio, President
Gary Wellman, Vice President
Matthew Hans, Secretary
Megan Rowekamp, CPA, Treasurer

Pregnancy and infant loss support.

Year Founded: 1977

78 Rainbows
1007 Church Street
Suite 408
Evanston, IL 60201
847-952-1770
800-266-3206
E-mail: info@rainbows.org
www.rainbows.org

Anthony Taglia, Chairman
Bob Thomas, Executive Director and CEO
Burt Heatherly, CFO
Bill Olbrisch, National Community Outreach Dir.

Rainbows is an international, nonprofit organization that fosters emotional healing among children grieving a loss from a life-altering crisis. Rainbows believes that grieving youth deserve supporting, loving listeners as they struggle with their feelings. Available to participants of all races and religions. Serves as an advocate for youth who face life-altering crises.

Year Founded: 1983

79 Survivors of Loved Ones' Suicides (SOLOS)
8310 Ewing Halsell Drive
San Antonio, TX 78229
210-885-7069
E-mail: solossanantonio@gmail.com
www.solossa.org

Located in San Antonio, Texas, SOLOS organizes ongoing support group meetings for persons affected by the loss of loved ones from suicide.

Year Founded: 1987

Video & Audio

80 Effective Learning Systems, Inc.
5108 W 74th
St #390160
Minneapolis, MN 55439

239-948-1660
800-966-0443
E-mail: info@efflearn.com
www.effectivelearning.com
Robert E Griswold, President/ Founder
Deirdre M Griswold, VP

The mission of Effective Learning Systems is to develop and distribute the most effective programs- incorporating the most powerful, scientifically sound techniques- to help as many people as possible learn to use the power of their mind to achieve their goals and realize significant, positive changes in their lives. Audio tapes for self-help.

Web Sites

81 **AtHealth.Com**
At Health

Providing trustworthy online information, tools, and training that enhance the ability of practitioners to furnish high quality, personalized care to those they serve. For mental health consumers, find practitioners, treatment centers, learn about disorders and medications, news and resources.

82 **forums.grieving.com**
Death and Dying Grief Support

Information on grief and loss.

83 **www.alivealone.org**
Alive Alone

An organization for the education and charitable purposes to benefit bereaved parents, whose only child or all children are deceased, by providing a self-help network and publications to promote communication and healing, to assist in resolving their grief, and a means to reinvest their lives for a positive future.

84 **www.bereavedparentsusa.org**
Bereaved Parents of the USA (BP/USA)

Self-help group that offers support, understanding, compassion and hope especially to the newly bereaved be they bereaved parents, grandparents or siblings struggling to rebuild their lives after the death of their children, grandchildren or siblings.

85 **www.cfsny.org**
Center for Family Support (CFS)

Devoted to providing support and assistance to individuals with developmental and related disabilities, and to the family members who care for them.

86 **www.climb-support.org**
Center for Loss in Multiple Birth (CLIMB), Inc.

Support by and for parents who have experienced the death of one or more of their twins or higher multiples during pregnance, birth, in infancy, or childhood. Newsletter, information on specialized topics, pen pals, phone support.

87 **www.compassionatefriends.org**
The Compassionate Friends

Organization for those having lost a child.

88 **www.counselingforloss.com**
Counseling for Loss and Life Changes, Inc.

Offers individual and family counseling services for grieving people.

89 **www.cyberpsych.org**
CyberPsych

CyberPsych presents information about psychoanalysis, psychotherapy and topics like anxiety disorders, substance abuse, homophobia, and traumas. It hosts mental health organizations and individuals with content of interest to the public and professional communities. There is also a free therapist finder service.

90 **www.divorceasfriends.com**
Bill Ferguson's How to Divorce as Friends

Articles, Resources, and Support to help minimize conflict in divorce situations.

91 **www.divorcecentral.com**
Divorce Central

Offers helpful advice and suggestions on what to expect emotionally, and how to deal with the emotional effects of divorce.

92 **www.divorceinfo.com**
Divorce Information

Simply written and covers all the issues.

93 **www.divorcemag.com**
Divorce Magazine

The printed magazine's commercial site.

94 **www.divorcesupport.com**
Divorce Support

Covers all aspects of divorce.

95 **www.emptycradle.org**
Empty Cradle

A peer support group for parents who have experienced the loss of baby due to early pregnancy loss, stillbirth or infant death.

96 **www.firstcandle.org**
First Candle

For those who have suffered the loss of an infant through SIDS.

97 **www.friendsforsurvival.org**
Friends for Survival

Assisting anyone who has suffered the loss of a loved one through suicide death.

98 **www.grasphelp.org**
Grief Recovery After A Substance Passing

Support and advocacy group for parents who have suffered the death of a child due to substance abuse. Provides opportunity for parents to share theri greif and experiences without shame or recrimination. They will provide information and suggestions for those wanting to start a similar group elsewhere.

99 **www.griefnet.org**
GriefNet

Internet community of persons dealing with grief, death, and major loss.

100 **www.mhselfhelp.org**
National Mental Health Consumers' Self-Help Clearinghouse

Encouraging the development and growth of consumer self-help groups.

101 **www.misschildren.org**
Mothers in Sympathy and Support (MISS) Foundation

Provides immediate and ongoing support to grieving families, empowerment through community volunteerism opportunities, public policy and legislative education, and programs to reduce infant and toddler death through research and education.

102 **www.nationalshare.org**
National SHARE Office

Pregnancy and infant loss support.

103 **www.planetpsych.com**
PlanetPsych

Learn about disorders, their treatments and other topics in psychology. Articles are listed under the related topic areas. Ask a therapist a question for free, or view the directory of professionals in your area. If you are a therapist sign up for the directory. Current features, self-help, interactive, and newsletter archives.

104 **www.pomc.com**
National Organization of Parents Of Murdered Children, Inc.

Help for anyone who has suffered the loss of a murdered child.

105 **www.psychcentral.com**
Psych Central

Personalized one-stop index for psychology, support, and mental health issues, resources, and people on the Internet.

106 **www.psycom.net/depression.central.grief.html**
Grief and Bereavement

Helpful information for those grieving from the loss of a loved one.

107 **www.rainbows.org**
Rainbows

Group for grieving parents and children.

108 **www.relationshipjourney.com**
The Relationship Learning Center

Marriage and relationship counseling and information.

109 **www.safecrossingsfoundation.org**
Safe Crossings Foundation

For children facing a loved one's death.

110 **www.spig.clara.net/guidline.htm**
Shared Parenting Information Group (SPIG)

Useful information that helps to decrease the stress associated with separation.

111 **www.store.samhsa.gov**
Substance Abuse and Mental Health Services Administration

Resources on mental disorders as well as treatment and recovery.

112 **www.thenadd.org**
National Association for The Dually Diagnosed (NADD)

An association for persons with developmental disabilities and mental health needs.

113 **www.unitegriefsupport.org**
UNITE, Inc.

Grief support after miscarriage, stillbirth and infant death.

114 **www.widownet.org**
WidowNet

Online information and self-help resource for, and by, widows and widowers. Topics covered include grief, bereavement, recovery, and other information helpful to people who have suffered the death of a spouse or life partner.

Directories & Databases

115 **After School and More**
Resources for Children with Special Needs
116 E 16th Street
5th Floor
New York, NY 10003-2164
212-677-4650
www.resourcesnyc.org

Rachel Howard, Executive Director
Stephen Stern, Director , Finance and Administr
Todd Dorman, Director, Communications and Out
Helen Murphy, Director, Program and Fund Devel

The most complete directory of after school programs for children with disabilities and special needs in the metropolitan New York area focusing on weekend and holiday programs. $25.00

ISBN 0-967836-57-3

Anxiety Disorders

Introduction

Anxiety disorders make up the most common mental illnesses. They affect roughly 25 million Americans, which is about 30% of the adults in the United States. While fear and worry are normal, adaptive traits in humans, an access of nervousness or fear that impairs a person's ability to function normally often signifies an illness. Anxiety disorders often affect job or school performance and relationships. People with anxiety disorders tend to avoid stressful situations to an extreme degree. Medical help should be sought when a person cannot rid themselves of worry or their anxiety is affecting relationships and work for longer than seems appropriate to a given situation.

There are many different kinds of anxiety disorders. Several of the most prevalent are discussed in detail below. Treatment is tailored to the particular disorder and is, therefore, more effective. It is important to address the possible or likely role of discrimination and abuse, whether on the basis of race, gender identification, or other, in diagnosis and treatment.

SYMPTOMS

Generalized Anxiety Disorder
• Excessive worry and anxiety on most days for at least six months about several events or activities such as work or school performance;
• Difficulty in controlling the worry;
• The anxiety is connected with at least three of the following: restlessness/feeling on edge; being easily tired; difficulty concentrating; irritability; muscle tension; difficulty falling/staying asleep or restless sleep;
• The anxiety or physical symptoms seriously affect the person's social life, work life, or other important areas;
• The anxiety is not better explained by another mental disorder (e.g., OCD or panic disorder) or by the side effects of a substance.

Panic Disorder
• Characterized by recurring panic attacks. A panic attack is a period of intense fear in which four or more of the following symptoms escalate suddenly, reaching a peak within ten minutes, after which they diminish:
Palpitations and pounding;
Rapid heartbeat;
Sweating;
Trembling or shaking;
Shortness of breath;
Feeling of choking;
Chest pain;
Nausea;
Feeling dizzy or faint;
Feelings of unreality or detachment;
Fear of losing control or going crazy;
Fear of dying;
Numbness or tingling;
Chills or hot flashes.
• Panic attacks can often have a trigger but can occur without one as well.
• Panic attacks are often comorbid with depression or PTSD.

Agoraphobia
• Usually involves fears connected with being outside the home and alone;
• Anxiety about being in places or situations from which it is difficult or embarrassing to escape (e.g., in the middle seat of a row in a theatre) or in which help may not be immediately available (as in an airplane);
• Such situations are avoided or endured with distress and fear of having a panic attack;
• The anxiety significantly interferes with the individual's ability to participate normally in work, domestic, and/or recreational activities.

Social Anxiety Disorder
• Fear of being humiliated or embarrassed in a social situation with strangers or where other people are watching;
• Being in the situation causes intense anxiety, sometimes with panic attacks;
• Realizing that the fear is irrational;
• Unlike simple shyness, the fear leads to avoidance of important or uncomplicated social situations and interferes with the ability to function at work or with friends.

Phobias
• Persistent, unreasonable, and exaggerated fear of the presence or anticipated presence of a particular object or situation (e.g., snake, flying in an airplane, blood);
• The presence of such an object or situation triggers immediate anxiety which may result in a panic attack;
• Knowledge that the fear is exaggerated and unreasonable;
• The phobic situation is either avoided or experienced with extreme distress;
• The avoidance, fearful anticipation, and distress seriously affects the person's normal routine, work and social activities, and relationships.

Separation Anxiety Disorder
Separation Anxiety Disorder (SAD) is an anxiety disorder in which an individual experiences excessive anxiety regarding separation from home or from people to whom the individual has a strong emotional attachment. To be diagnosed with SAD, one must display at least three of the following for over six months in adults (four weeks in children):

• Recurrent excessive distress when anticipating or experiencing separation from home or from major attachment figures;
• Persistent and excessive worry about losing major attachment figures or about possible harm to them;
• Persistent and excessive worry about experiencing an untoward event that causes separation from a major attachment figure;
• Persistent reluctance or refusal to go out, away from home, to school, to work, or elsewhere because of fear of separation;
• Persistent and excessive fear of or reluctance about being along or without major attachment figures at home or in other settings;
• Persistent reluctance or refusal to sleep away from home or to go to sleep without being near a major attachment figure;
• Repeated nightmares involving the theme of separation;
• Repeated complaints of physical symptoms when separation from major attachment figures occurs or is anticipated.

ASSOCIATED FEATURES

Anxiety can be acute and intense, such as the fear of imminent death in a panic attack, or it can be experienced as chronically, such as nagging worry in Generalized Anxiety Disorder. Whatever its intensity or frequency, it persists over time. One of the hallmarks of Anxiety Disorders is that the person is unable to control the anxiety, even when he or she knows it is exaggerated and unreasonable. To other people, the person may seem edgy, irritable, to have unexpected outbursts of anger, or to be consumed by an unreasonable fear. For the anxious person, the problem takes up time and effort and becomes a major preoccupation.

In addition to the psychological effects (and entangled with them) are the physical effects, that is, a frequent or constant state of physical arousal and tension. This can lead to gastrointestinal upset, headaches, and cardiovascular disease. Using alcohol or drugs to resolve the problem is common but ineffective and dangerous. Anxiety Disorders negatively affect all aspects of lifeÄfamily, work, and friends.

PREVALENCE

Anxiety Disorders are the most common psychiatric disorders in the U.S. Anxiety Disorders are approximately twice as common in women as in men. They affect about 30% of Americans.

TREATMENT OPTIONS

It is important to have a full evaluation so that a proper diagnosis can be made. In general, people should have a primary care evaluation as part of the diagnostic process for all disorders to rule out a general medical condition that could be causing the symptoms. For example, hyperthyroidism can cause anxiety problems and can look like depression. Self-medication with alcohol, tranquilizers, or other drugs is dangerous and can lead to serious drug abuse. Treatment will vary depending on which of the Anxiety Disorders is diagnosed. Medications, psychotherapy, or both will be prescribed. Some psychotherapies that have proven helpful in certain cases are cognitive-behavioral therapies, including exposure therapy, and eye movement desensitisation reprogramming (EMDR). Benzodiazepines, or minor tranquillizers, can be useful for the acute treatment of anxiety symptoms; however, care must be taken, because these medications have addictive potential. Selective Serotonin Reuptake Inhibitors, or SSRIs, which were originally developed as antidepressants, have proven to be effective in several Anxiety Disorders and are now the mainstays of treatment. Since new drugs are frequently introduced, and already approved medications given new therapeutic indications by the USDA, it is wise to consult an expert or recent expert reference before making a treatment decision.

It is important to note that suddenly stopping an SSRI can cause rebound symptoms including sleeplessness, headaches, and irritability. Medications should be tapered under the care of a physician.

Associations & Agencies

117 A.I.M. Agoraphobics in Motion
7636 Emerson
Washington, MI 48094

248-710-5719
E-mail: aimforrecovery@gmail.com
www.aimforrecovery.com

James Fortune, President
Robert Diedrich, Vice President & Secretary
Harley Sherman, Treasurer

AIM is a nonprofit support group organization committed to the support and recovery of people with anxiety disorders, as well as their families.

Year Founded: 1983

118 Adventure Camp
Advanced Therapeutic Solutions
600 W 22nd Street
Suite 250
Oak Brook, IL 60523
630-230-6505
www.www.selectivemutismtreatment.net

Carmen M. Tumialan Lyna, PhD, Clinical Psychologist/Owner

A summer camp designed to help children with selective mutism. This exposure therapy program is designed to simulate a classroom environment, and each child is assigned a counselor for one-on-one therapy.

119 Anxiety and Depression Association of America
8701 Georgia Avenue
Suite 412
Silver Spring, MD 20910
240-485-1030
E-mail: information@adaa.org
www.adaa.org

Charles B. Nemeroff, MD, President
Susan K. Gurley, JD, Executive Director
Tanja Jovanovic, PhD, Treasurer
Sanjay Matthew, PhD, Secretary

An international nonprofit organization committed to the use of education and research to promote the prevention, treatment, and cure of anxiety, depressive, obssesive compulsive, and other trauma related disorders. ADAA's mission is to improve the lives of all people with anxiety and mood disorders.

Year Founded: 1979

120 Anxiety and Phobia Treatment Center
79 East Post Road
White Plains, NY 10601
914-286-4430
www.www.phobia-anxiety.org

Judy Lake Chess, LMSW, Coordinator
Thomas Cirolia, LCSW, Group Leader

Treatment for individuals suffering from phobias and other anxiety disorders. Specializes in the use of cognitive-behavioral therapy and exposure therapy.

Year Founded: 1971

121 Brain & Behavior Research Foundation
747 Third Avenue
33rd Floor
New York, NY 10017
646-681-4888
800-829-8289
E-mail: info@bbrfoundation.org
www.www.bbrfoundation.org

Donald M. Boardman, Treasurer
Jeffrey Borenstein, MD, President and CEO
Louis Innamorato, CPA, VP and Chief Financial Officer
Faith Rothblatt, Vice President, Development

The Brain and Behavior Research Foundation awards grants aimed at advancing scientific understandings of mental health treatments and mental disorders such as depression and schizophrenia. The Brain and Behavior Research Foundation's mission is to eliminate the suffering caused by mental illness.

Year Founded: 1987

122 Center for Mental Health Services (CMHS)
Substance Abuse and Mental Health Services
Administration
5600 Fishers Lane
Rockville, MD 20857
240-276-1310
www.samhsa.gov/about-us/who-we-are/offices-centers

Anita Everett, MD, DFAPA, Director

Promotes the treatment of mental illness and emotional disorders by increasing accessibility to mental health programs; supporting outreach, treatment, rehabilitation, and support programs and networks; and encouraging the use of scientifically-based information when treating mental disorders. CMHS provides information about mental health via a toll-free number and numerous publications. Developed for users of mental health services and their families, the general public, policy makers, providers, and the media.

Year Founded: 1992

123 Depression & Bipolar Support Alliance
55 East Jackson Boulevard
Suite 490
Chicago, IL 60604
800-826-3632
E-mail: info@dbsalliance.org
www.dbsalliance.org

Roger McIntyre, Chair
Michael Pollock, Chief Executive Officer
Maria Margaglione, Programs Director
Hannah Zeller, Program Manager

The Depression and Bipolar Support Alliance is a national organization focused on improving the lives of individuals with depression, bipolar disorder, and other mood disorders. DBSA organizes peer-led support groups; educates patients, families, professionals, and the public on mental health; and works to ensure the availability of quality care for all people.

124 Freedom From Fear
308 Seaview Avenue
Staten Island, NY 10305
718-351-1717
E-mail: help@freedomfromfear.org
www.freedomfromfear.org

Mary Guardino, Founder and Executive Director

A national nonprofit organization, the mission of Freedom From Fear is to aid and counsel individuals suffering from anxiety and depressive disorders through advocacy, education, research, and community support.

Year Founded: 1984

125 Goodwill's Community Employment Services
Goodwill Industries-Suncoast, Inc.
10596 Gandy Blvd.
St. Petersburg, FL 33702
727-523-1512
888-279-1988
TDD: 727-579-1068
www.goodwill-suncoast.org

Sandra Young, Chair
Louise Lopez, Sr. Vice Chair
Dominic Macrone, Board Secretary

The St. Petersburg headquarters serves ten counties in the state of Florida. Their mission is to help people with disabilities gain employment through training programs, employment services, and affordable housing.

Year Founded: 1954

126 Mental Health America
500 Montgomery Street
Suite 820
Alexandria, VA 22314
703-684-7722
800-969-6642
www.mentalhealthamerica.net

Schroeder Stribling, President & CEO
Sachin Doshi, Sr. Dir., Finance & Operations

Mental Health America is a community-based nonprofit organization committed to enabling the mental wellness of all Americans. MHA advocates for greater access to quality health services and seeks to educate individuals on identifying symptoms, as well as intervention and prevention.

Year Founded: 1909

127 NAPCSE National Association of Parents with
Children in Special Education
3642 East Sunnydale Drive
Chandler Heights, AZ 85142
800-754-4421
E-mail: contact@napcse.org
www.napcse.org

Dr. George Giuliani, President

The NAPCSE is dedicated to ensuring quality education for all children and adolescents with special needs. NAPCSE provides resources, support, and assistance to parents with children in special education.

128 National Alliance on Mental Illness
4301 Wilson Boulevard
Suite 300
Arlington, VA 22203
703-524-7600
800-950-6264
E-mail: info@nami.org
www.nami.org

Shirley J. Holloway, President
Joyce A. Campbell, First Vice President
Daniel H. Gillison, Jr., Chief Executive Officer
David Levy, Chief Financial Officer

NAMI is an organization dedicated to raising awareness on mental health and providing support and education for Americans affected by mental illness. NAMI advocates for access to services and treatment and fosters an environment of awareness and understanding for those concerned with mental health.

Year Founded: 1979

129 National Association for the Dually Diagnosed (NADD)
321 Wall Street
Kingston, NY 12401
845-331-4336
E-mail: info@thenadd.org
www.thenadd.org

Jeanne M. Farr, MA, Chief Executive Officer
Bruce Davis, President
Juanita St. Croix, Vice President
Ray Snyder, Secretary

NADD is a nonprofit organization designed to increase awareness of, and provide services for, individuals with developmental disabilities and mental illness. NADD emphasizes the importance of quality mental healthcare for people with mental health needs and offers conferences, information resources, educational programs, and training materials to professionals, parents, and organizations.

Year Founded: 1983

130 National Council for Behavioral Health
1400 K Street NW
Suite 400
Washington, DC 20005
E-mail: communications@thenationalcouncil.org
www.thenationalcouncil.org

Tim Swinfard, Chair
Charles Ingoglia, President and CEO
Jeannie Campbell, Executive VP and COO
Bruce Pelleu, CPA, VP, Finance & Administration

The National Council for Behavioral Health serves to unify America's behavioral health organizations. The council is dedicated to ensuring that quality mental health and addictions care is readily accessible to all Americans.

131 National Institute of Mental Health
6001 Executive Boulevard
Room 6200, MSC 9663
Bethesda, MD 20892-9663
866-615-6464
TTY: 301-443-8431
E-mail: nimhinfo@nih.gov
www.nimh.nih.gov

Joshua Gordon, MD, PhD, Director

The National Institute of Mental Health conducts clinical research on mental disorders and seeks to expand knowledge on mental health treatments.

132 National Mental Health Consumers' Self-Help Clearinghouse
E-mail: selfhelpclearinghouse@gmail.com
www.mhselfhelp.org

Joseph Rogers, Founder and Executive Director
Susan Rogers, Director

The Clearinghouse is a peer-run national technical assistance center focused on achieving respect and equality of opportunity for those with mental illnesses. The Clearinghouse helps with the growth of the mental health consumer movement by evaluating mental health services, advocating for mental health reform, and providing consumers with news, information, publications, and consultation services.

Year Founded: 1986

133 Selective Mutism Association (SMA)
E-mail: info@selectivemutism.org
www.www.selectivemutism.org

Jami Furr, PhD, President
Pamela Martis Zambriski, Treasurer
Emily Doll, MA, MS, CCC-SLP, Secretary
Lisa Kovac, PhD, BCBA, Executive Director

An organization that increases awareness and education about selective mutism. SMA supports families and professionals through an annual conference, expert chat sessions, professional training, online resources, and providing connections with research institutions.

134 Selective Mutism Research Institute
505 North Old York Road
Jenkintown, PA 19046
E-mail: Research@SelectiveMutismCenter.org
www.selectivemutismresearchinstitute.org

Dr. Elisa Shipon-Blum, President & Director

A nonprofit organization dedicated to raising better awareness, treatment, and resources for children dealing with selective mutism and other social communication anxiety.

135 Sutcliffe Clinic
851 Fremont Avenue
Suite 110
Los Altos, CA 94024
650-941-1698
E-mail: info@sutcliffedbp.com
www.www.sutcliffeclinic.com

Trenna Sutcliffe, MD, MS, Medical Director

Sutcliffe Developmental & Behavioral Pediatrics is an organization that specializes in the treatment of ADHD, autism spectrum disorder, anxiety disorders, conduct disorders, learning disabilities, and more. Sutcliffe works with community services, school districs, and primary physicians, and provides family counseling.

136 Territorial Apprehensiveness (TERRAP) Anxiety & Stress Program
755 Park Avenue
Suite 140
Huntington, NY 11743
631-549-8867
E-mail: info@anxietyandpanic.com
www.anxietyandpanic.com

Julian Herskowitz, PhD, Director

Helps to treat anxiety and stress disorders through Territorial Apprehensiveness Programs, developed by Dr. Arthur Hardy in the 1960s. The program systematically addresses the behavioral and thought processes of those suffering from stress and anxiety.

Year Founded: 1975

137 The Center for Family Support
2811 Zulette Avenue
Bronx, NY 10461
718-518-1500
E-mail: svernikoff@cfsny.org
www.www.cfsny.org

Steven Vernikoff, Executive Director
Barbara Greenwald, Chief Operating Officer
Jos, Martin Jara, President
Elise Geltzer, Vice President

The Center for Family Support offers assistance to individuals with developmental and related disabilities, as well as their families, and provides support services and programs that are designed to accommodate individual needs. Offers services throughout New York City, Westchester County, Long Island, and New Jersey.

Year Founded: 1954

138 The Children's and Adult Center for OCD and Anxiety
3138 Butler Pike
Suite 200
Plymouth Meeting, PA 19462
www.childrenscenterocdandanxiety.com

Tamar Chansky, PhD, Founder

A center comprising five private practice psychologists delivering treatment and therapy to children and adults with OCD, Separation Anxiety, and other mental health disorders. They also offer parent workshops on skills and strategies to help their child cope with anxiety.

Year Founded: 1988

139 The SMart Center: Selective Mutism, Anxiety, & Related Disorders Treatment Center
505 N Old York Road
Jenkintown Square, Lower Level
Jenkintown, PA 19046
215-887-5748
www.selectivemutismcenter.org

Dr. Elisa Shipon-Blum, President and Director
William Lavalle, PsyD, Director of Clinical Training
Jennifer Brittingham, MA, Lead Clinical Counselor

A center that provides treatment and support to children and young adults with selective mutism and other social communication issues. The SMart Center uses the evidence-based Social Communication Anxiety Treatment (S-CAT) program, and also offers products, services, and events for parents, professionals, researchers, and educators.

140 Thriving Minds
10524 E Grand River Avenue
Suite 100
Brighton, MI 48116
810-225-3417
E-mail: office@thrivingminds.info
www.www.thrivingmindsbehavioralhealth.com

Amiee Kotrba, PhD, Owner
Bryce Hella, PhD, Director, Brighton Clinic
Becky Thomson, PhD, Director, Chelsea Clinic
Katelyn Reed, MS, LLP, Director, Selective Mutism

Thriving Minds is an organization that offers therapy to people with anxiety, behavioral issues, and depression. With locations in Brighton and Chelsea, Thriving Minds uses a mix of research-based interventions, such as Cognitive Behavioral Therapy; parent coaching; and school interventions in order to help children, teens, and adults deal with their anxiety.

Periodicals & Pamphlets

141 Anxiety Disorders in Children and Adolescents
Center for Mental Health Services: Knowledge Exchange Network
1 Choke Cherry Road
Rockville, MD 20015
800-789-2647
TDD: 866-889-2647
E-mail: ken@mentalhealth.org
www.mentalhealth.samhsa.gov/

Tracy L Morris, Editor
John S March, Editor

This fact sheet defines anxiety disorders, identifies warning signs, discusses risk factors, describes types of help available, and suggests what parents or other caregivers can do.

395 pages

142 Families Can Help Children Cope with Fear, Anxiety
PO Box 42490
Washington, DC 20015
800-789-2647
TDD: 866-889-2647
www.mentalhealth.org

2 pages

143 Journal of Anxiety Disorders
Elsevier Publishing
1600 John F Kennedy Boulevard
Suite 1800
Philadelphia, PA 19103-2879
212-989-5800
800-325-4177
E-mail: custserv.ehs@elsevier.com

Deborah Beidel, Author

Interdisciplinary journal that publishes research papers dealing with all aspects of anxiety disorders for all age groups (child, adolescent, adult and geriatrics). *$195.00*

8 per year ISSN 0887-6185

144 Let's Talk Facts About Panic Disorder
American Psychiatric Publishing, Inc.
1000 Wilson Boulevard
Suite 1825
Arlington, VA 22209-3901
703-907-7322
800-368-5777
E-mail: appi@psych.org
www.appi.org

Robert E Hales MD, Editor-in-Chief
Ron McMillen, Chief Executive Officer
John McDuffie, Editorial Director

Contains an overview of the illness, its symptoms, and the illness's effect on family and friends. A biliography and list of resources make them ideal for libraries or patient education. *$29.95*

6 pages ISBN 0-890423-57-1

145 Panic Attacks
ETR Associates
4 Carbonero Way
Scotts Valley, CA 95066-4200

831-438-4060
800-321-4407
www.etr.org

David Kitchen,MBA, Chief Financial Officer
Talita Sanders,BS, Director,Human Resources
Coleen Cantwell,MPH, Director,Business Development Pl
Matt McDowell,BS, Director,Marketing

Describes causes of panic attacks, including genetics, stress, and drug use; prevention and treatment, and how to stop a panic attack in its tracks. *$16.00*

146   Real Illness: Panic Disorder
National Institute of Mental Health
6001 Executive Boulevard
Room 8184
Bethesda, MD 20892
301-443-4513
866-615-6464
TTY: 301-443-8431
E-mail: nimhinfo@nih.gov

Do you often have feelings of sudden fear that don't make sense? If so, you may have panic disorder. Read this pamplet of simple information about getting help.

9 pages

Research Centers

147   Columbia University Pediatric Anxiety and Mood Research Clinic
1051 Riverside Drive
New York, NY 10032
646-774-5793
www.childadolescentpsych.cumc.columbia.edu

Laura Mufson, PhD, Unit Chief, Children's Day Unit
Pablo Goldberg, MD, Medical Director
Anthony C. Puliafico, PhD, Consulting Psychologist
Mara Eilenberg, MSW, LCSW, Clinician

A research clinic desinged to help children with anxiety, depression, and OCD. The clinic provides evaluations, evidence-based therapy and medications, and a day-treatment program. All evaluation and treatment services are free of charge.

148   UAMS Psychiatric Research Institute
4224 Shuffield Drive
Little Rock, AR 72205
501-526-8100
E-mail: kramerteresal@uams.edu
www.www.psychiatry.uams.edu

John Fortney PhD, Director
Geoff Curran PhD, Associate Director
Keith Berner MD, Clinical Faculty

Combining research, education and clinical services into one facility, PRI offers inpatiend and outpatient services, with 40 psychiatric beds, therapy options, and specialized treatment for specific disorders, including: addictive eating, anxiety, deppressive and post-traumatic stress disorders. Research focuses on evidence-based care takes into consideration the education of future medical personnel while relying on research scientists to provide innovative forms of treatment. PRI includes the Center for Addiction Research as well as a methadone clinic.

Support Groups & Hot Lines

149   Agoraphobics Building Independent Lives
2008 Bremo Road
Suite #101
Richmond, VA 23226
804-257-5591
866-400-6428
E-mail: info@mhav.org
www.mhav.org

Joanne Whitley, President
Ali Faruk, Vice President & Public Policy C
Anne Edgerton, Executive Director
Sarah Rudden, Project Coordinator

A nonprofit organization for people dealing with anxiety and panic disorders, incorporated in the State of Virginia. It has support groups nationwide.

150   Emotions Anonymous International Service Center
PO Box 4245
St. Paul, MN 55104-0245
651-647-9712
E-mail: director@emotionsanonymous.org
www.emotionsanonymous.org

Elaine Weber Nelson, Executive Director
Scott J., President
John W., Vice President
Paul N., Treasurer

A community-based organization to provide support managing mental health difficulties. Groups meet weekly to share experiences, strength, and hope.

151   Recovery International
1415 W. 22nd Street
Tower Floor
Oak Brook, IL 60523
312-337-5661
866-221-0302
E-mail: info@recoveryinternational.org
www.www.recoveryinternational.org

Sandra K. Wilcoxon, Chief Executive Officer
Joanne Lampey, President
Nicole Cilento, Vice President
Hal Casey, Treasurer

Recovery International is an organization that uses a peer-to-peer, self-help training system developed by Abraham Low in order to help individuals with mental health issues lead more productive lives.

Year Founded: 1937

Video & Audio

152   Anxiety Disorders
American Counseling Association
PO Box 31110
Alexandria, VA 22310-9998
800-347-6647
E-mail: webmaster@counseling.org
www.counseling.org

Richard Yep, Executive Director
Dr. S. Kent Butler, President

Increase your awareness of anxiety disorders, their symptoms, and effective treatments. Learn the effect these disorders can have on life and how treatment can change the quality of life for people presently suffering from these disorders. Includes 6 audiotapes and a study guide. *$140.00*

153 DSM-IV-TR
American Psychiatric Publishing, Inc.
1000 Wilson Boulevard
Suite 1825
Arlington, VA 22209-3901
703-907-7322
800-368-5777
E-mail: appi@psych.org
www.appi.org

Cathryn A Galanter, M.D, Editor
Peter S Jensen, M.D, Editor
John McDuffie, Editorial Director

Series of three clinical programs that reveals additions and changes for mood, psychotic and anxiety disorders. Each video focuses on a different level of disorder as well as giving three 10 minute interviews. Approximately 60 minutes. *$57.00*

744 pages ISBN 0-880488-98-0

154 Dealing With Social Anxiety
Educational Video Network
1401 19th Street
Huntsville, TX 77340
936-295-5767
800-762-0060
www.www.evndirect.com

A video to learn and understand social anxiety. *$89.95*

ISBN 1-589501-48-9

155 Driving Far from Home
NewHarbinger Publications
5674 Shattuck Avenue
Oakland, CA 94609-1662
510-652-0215
800-748-6273
E-mail: customerservice@newharbinger.com
www.newharbinger.com

Edmund J. Bourne, Author

120 minute videotape that reduces fear associated with leaving the safety of your home base. *$15.95*

ISBN 1-572240-14-8

156 Effective Learning Systems, Inc.
5108 W 74th Street
#390160
Minneapolis, MN 55439
952-943-1660
800-966-0443
E-mail: info@efflearn.com
www.www.effectivelearning.com

Bob Griswold, Founder
Deirdre M Griswold, VP

Audio tapes for stress management, deep relaxation, anger control, peace of mind, insomnia, weight and smoking, self-image and self-esteem, positive thinking, health and healing. Since 1972, Effective Learning Systems has helped millions of people take charge of their lives and make positive changes.

157 Understanding Mental Illness
Educational Video Network
1401 19th Street
Huntsville, TX 77340
936-295-5767
800-762-0060
www.www.evndirect.com

A video to learn and understand mental illness and how it affects you. *$79.95*

ISBN 1-589501-48-9

158 Understanding and Treating the Hereditary Psychiatric Spectrum Disorders
Hope Press
PO Box 188
Duarte, CA 91009-188
818-303-0644
800-209-9182
E-mail: dcomings@earthlink.net
www.hopepress.com

David E Comings MD, Presenter

Learn with ten hours of audio tapes from a two day seminar given in May 1997 by David E Comings MD. Tapes cover: ADHD, Tourette Syndrome, Obsessive-Compulsive Disorder, Conduct Disorder, Oppositional Defiant Disorder, Autism and other Hereditary Psychiatric Spectrum Disorders. Eight audio tapes. *$75.00*

Web Sites

159 www.bcm.tmc.edu/civitas/caregivers.htm
Caregivers Series

Sophisticated articles describing the effects of childhood trauma on brain development and relationships.

160 www.cyberpsych.org
CyberPsych

Presents information about psychoanalysis, psychotherapy and special topics such as anxiety disorders, the problematic use of alcohol, homophobia, and the traumatic effects of racism. Explains in detail what anxiety it is how it is treated and the symptoms associated with anxiety.

161 www.goodwill-suncoast.org
Career Assessment & Planning Services

A comprehensive assessment for the developmentally disabled persons who may be unemployed or underemployed.

162 www.guidetopsychology.com
A Guide To Psychlogy & Its Practice

Free information on various types of psychology.

163 www.healthanxiety.org
Anxiety and Phobia Treatment Center

Treatment groups for individuals suffering from phobias.

164 www.healthyminds.org
Anxiety Disorders

American Psychiatric Association publication diagnostic criteria and treatment.

165 www.lexington-on-line.com
Panic Disorder

Explains development and treatment of panic disorder.

166 **www.mayoclinic.com**
Mayo Clinic

Provides information on obsessive-compulsive disorder and anxiety.

167 **www.mentalhealth.Samhsa.Gov**
Center for Mental Health Services Knowledge Exchange Network

Information about resources, technical assistance, research, training, networks and other federal clearinghouses.

168 **www.mentalhealth.com**
Internet Mental Health

On-line information and a virtual encyclopedia related to mental disorders, possible causes and treatments. News, articles, on-line diagnostic programs and related links. Designed to improve understanding, diagnosis and treatment of mental illness throughout the world. Awarded the Top Site Award and the NetPsych Cutting Edge Site Award.

169 **www.nami.org**
National Alliance on Mental Illness

From its inception in 1979, NAMI has been dedicated to improving the lives of individuals and families affected by mental illness.

170 **www.nimh.nih.gov/anxiety/anxiety/ocd**
National Institute of Health

Information on anxiety disorders and OCD.

171 **www.npadnews.com**
National Panic/Anxiety Disorder Newsletter

This resource was founded by Phil Darren who collects and collates information of recovered anxiety disorder sufferers who want to distribute some of the lessons that they learned with a view to helping others.

172 **www.panicattacks.com.au**
Anxiety Panic Hub

Information, resources and support.

173 **www.panicdisorder.about.com**
Agoraphobia: For Friends/Family

174 **www.planetpsych.com**
Planetpsych.com

Learn about disorders, their treatments and other topics in psychology. Articles are listed under the related topic areas. Ask a therapist a question for free, or view the directory of professionals in your area. If you are a therapist sign up for the directory. Current features, self-help, interactive, and newsletter archives.

175 **www.psychcentral.com**
Psych Central

Personalized one-stop index for psychology, support, and mental health issues, resources, and people on the Internet.

176 **www.selectivemutismfoundation.org**
Selective Mutism Foundation

Promotes awareness and understanding for individuals and families affected by mutism.

177 **www.selfhelpmagazine.com/articles/stress**
Meditation, Guided Fantasies, and Other Stress Reducers

Meditative and stress reduction resources for eyes, ears, minds, and hearts.

178 **www.terraphouston.com**
Territorial Apprehensiveness Programs (TERRAP)

Shirley Riff, Director

Formed to disseminate information concerning the recognition, causes and treatment of anxieties, fears and phobias.

179 **www.thenadd.org**
National Association for the Dually Diagnosed (NADD)

An association for persons with developmental disabilities and mental health needs.

Autism Spectrum Disorders

Introduction

Autism Spectrum Disorder (ASD) is a neurological condition characterized by impairment in language, communication skills, and abnormal behaviors. Previously, the disorder was broken into four separate illnesses. However, experts combined the criteria because ASD falls on a spectrum. Since this amalgamation in 2013, doctors use the criteria from all the previous disorders to place a diagnosis on a spectrum from mild to severe.

Autism Spectrum Disorder is a pervasive developmental disorder whose main symptoms are a marked lack of interest in connecting, interacting, or communicating with others. People with this disorder find it difficult or impossible to share something of interest with other people, rarely make eye contact with others, avoid physical contact, show little facial expression, and do not make friends easily (or sometimes at all). ASD is a lifelong condition associated with wide range of disabilities, often including behavior problems, such as hyperactivity, obsessive compulsive behavior, self-injury, and tics.

A person must show symptoms from early childhood. Previously, children must have shown symptoms before the age of three; however, experts found that criterion limiting. It is possible to notice the symptoms retroactively, but doctors agree it's better to diagnose early when possible. Very young children with autism show no desire for affection and cuddling, and sometimes show aversion to it.There is no socially directed smiling or facial responsiveness, and no responsiveness to the voices of parents and siblings. As a result, parents may sometimes worry that their child is deaf. Later, the child may be more willing to interact socially, but the quality of interaction is unusual, usually inappropriately intrusive with little understanding of social rules and boundaries. The autistic child seems not to have the abilities and desires that would make it possible for him or her to become a social being. Instead, the child seems locked up in an interior world which is both incomprehensible and inaccessible to parents, siblings, and others. They may display repetitive behaviors such as banging their heads. They often have obsessive interests in some field. They have great difficulty tolerating change, and exposure to new and stimulating situations.

Asperger's Syndrome (AS) is one of the four outdated diagnoses to fall under ASD. Now, it is considered a milder form of ASD where the individual lacks nonverbal communication skills and empathy, and shows extreme interest in a particular subject. There are many support groups for people with Asperger's Syndrome. There is a strong community among those with the label, and many continue to use it.

SYMPTOMS

Twin and family studies have shown a genetic predisposition to ASD. Several genes, but not one specific gene, have recently been identified as associated with autism. Some researchers have proposed that the disorder may stem from abnormalities during critical stages of fetal development, including defects in the genes that control and regulate normal brain growth and growth patterns. There is no standardized test for Autism Spectrum Disorder. Early signs that a child should be assessed include having trouble with

eye contact, others' emotions, or have trouble reacting to changes in routine. Early diagnosis and intervention can greatly improve outcomes. A comprehensive list of symptoms is below.
• Lack of nonverbal behavior (e.g., eye contact, facial expression, body postures, and gestures), which gives meaning to social interaction and social behavior;
• Difficulty in making, or failure to make, friends in age-appropriate ways;
• Lack of spontaneously seeking to share interests or achievements with others (e.g., not showing things to others, not pointing to, or bringing interesting objects to others);
• Notable lack of awareness of others. Oblivious of other children (including siblings), of their excitement, distress, or needs.
• Delay in, or lack of, spoken language development. Those who speak cannot initiate or sustain communication with others;
• Lack of spontaneous make-believe or imitative play common among young children;
• When speech does develop, it may be abnormal and monotonous;
• Repetitive use of language.
• Restricted range of interests often fixed on one subject and its facts (e.g., baseball);
• A great deal of exact repetition in play, (e.g., lining up play objects in the same way again and again);
• Resistance and distress if anything in the environment is changed, (e.g., a chair moved to a different place);
• Insistence on following certain rules and routines (e.g., walking to school by the same route each day);
• Repeated body movements (e.g., body rocking, hand clapping);
• Persistent preoccupation with details or parts of objects (e.g., buttons).
• Problems with non-verbal communication, including the restricted use of gestures, limited or inappropriate facial expressions, or a peculiar, stiff gaze;
• Clumsy and uncoordinated motor movements.

ASSOCIATED FEATURES

Autism seems to bring with it an increased risk of other disorders. Seventy-five percent of autistic children have cognitive deficits, and twenty-five percent have cognitive abilities at or above average. Twenty-five percent of individuals with autism also have seizure disorders. The development of intellectual skills is usually uneven. An autistic child may be able to read extremely early, but not be able to comprehend what he or she reads. Other symptoms include hyperactivity, short attention span, impulsivity, aggressiveness, and self-injury, such as head banging, hair pulling, and arm biting (particularly in young children). There may be unusual responses to stimuli: less than normal sensitivity to pain but extreme sensitivity to sounds or to being touched. There may be abnormalities in emotional expression, giggling or weeping for no apparent reason, and little or no emotional reaction when one would be expected. Similar abnormal responses may be shown in relation to fear; an absence of fear in response to real danger, but great fearfulness in the presence of harmless objects.

In adolescence or adulthood, people with ASD who have the capacity for insight may become depressed when they realize how seriously impaired they are. Autism Spectrum Disorder sometimes follows medical and obstetrical problems, such as encephalitis, anoxia (absence of oxygen) during birth, and prenatal infections (such as maternal rubella). The disorder is not caused by inappropriate parenting or by routine immunizations.

PREVALENCE

There are two to five cases of the disorder per 10,000 births. Rates of autism are four to five times greater among males than females. Females with ASD are more likely to be severely affected by the disorder than males. Follow-up studies suggest that only a small percentage of people with severe ASD live independent adult lives. Even the highest functioning adults continue to have problems in social interaction and communication, together with greatly restricted interests and activities. The siblings of people with the disorder are at increased risk.

After years of controversy, there is a growing consensus that the incidence and prevalence of autism spectrum disorders has increased significantly in recent years. The reason(s) for the increase are not clear.

TREATMENT OPTIONS

It is difficult or unusual to be able to mitigate all the symptoms of Autism Spectrum Disorder, but there are many intervention and education programs which help to improve functioning. It is extremely important, however, that a proper assessment and diagnosis be made. Since the disturbance in behavior is so wide ranging, this can require an array of professional skills - psychological, language development, neuropsychological, and medical. Use of multiple assessments establishes the presence or absence of other disorders, the level of intellectual functioning, together with individual strengths and weaknesses, and the child's capacity for social and personal self-sufficiency. Since the symptoms of ASD vary widely, a proper assessment is the foundation for designing and planning an individually tailored intervention program.

The autistic person may benefit from a combination of educational and behavioral interventions, which may reduce many of the behavioral disturbances, and improve the quality of life for the person and his or her family. One treatment method is applied behavior analysis (ABA), which builds on social interaction, imitation and language skills, as well as attention to social stimuli. Other treatments include speech and language therapy, occupational therapy, life skills training and psychological counseling. In some cases, medication may also be prescribed for the symptoms that sometimes co-exist with Autism Spectrum Disorder (e.g., stimulant drugs forhyperactivity, antidepressants for anxiety). There is no drug that specifically treats the neurological problems associated with ASD.

The diagnosis of Autism Spectrum Disorder can be a shattering experience for any family. The outcome of the diagnosis is open ended, uncertain, and includes a lifetime of care. Every member of the family is affected and it is vital to work with and support them.

Associations & Agencies

181 Achieve Beyond
7000 Austin Street
Suite 200
Forest Hills, NY 11375

866-696-0999
E-mail: info@achievebeyondusa.com
www.achievebeyondusa.com
Julia Sue Matuza, Chief Executive Officer

Achieve Beyond provides therapeutic and educational ser-vices to children with developmental disabilities and their families, with particular focus on children with bilingual needs. Services include special education, speech language therapy, occupational therapy, physical therapy, and behavioral management.
Year Founded: 1995

182 Asperger Autism Spectrum Education Network
PO Box 109
Oceanport, NJ 07757
732-321-0880
www.aspennj.org
Lori Shery, President and Executive Director
Rich Meleo, Vice President
Anita Finkel, Treasurer
Ann Hiller, Secretary

A nonprofit organization seeking to assist individuals with Autism Spectrum Disorders and Nonverbal Learning Dis-abilities and their families. Provides educational resources on the disorders and issues surrounding them, supports in-dividuals with ASDs and NLD in realizing their full poten-tial, and advocates for public awareness, educational programs, and medical research funding.

183 Asperger/Autism Network (AANE)
51 Water Street
Suite 206
Watertown, MA 02472
617-393-3824
E-mail: info@aane.org
www.aane.org
Brenda Dater. MSW, MPH, Executive Director
Janet Barbieri, MSW, LICSW, Director, Programs

An organization that helps people with Asperger Syndrome and related conditions live meaningful and productive lives. Provides information, offers support, and engages in advocacy while fostering awareness, respect, and accep-tance for individuals with AS and their families.
Year Founded: 1996

184 Autism Research Foundation
72 East Concord Street
Room 1010
Boston, MA 02118
E-mail: hello@theautismresearchfoundation.org
www.theautismresearchfoundation.org
Dr. Margaret L. Bauman, Founding Director

A nonprofit, tax-exempt organization dedicated to research-ing autism and related developmental disorders. Supports changing developments in the field of autism through edu-cation, social inclusion programs, and family life resources.
Year Founded: 1990

185 Autism Research Institute
4182 Adams Avenue
San Diego, CA 92116
833-281-7165
E-mail: info@autism.org
www.autism.org

Stephen M. Edelson, PhD, Executive Director

A nonprofit organization that provides information and supports research on Autism and Asperger's Syndrome.

Year Founded: 1967

186 Autism Services Inc.
40 Hazelwood Drive
Amherst, NY 14228
716-631-5777
www.friendsofasi.org

Dr. Edmund Egan, President
David Mansour, Vice President
Matthew Shriver, Treasurer
Lindsay McKenna, Secretary

An agency exclusively dedicated to providing educational programs, quality of life programs, and support services for children and adults with autism and their families.

187 Autism Society
6110 Executive Boulevard
Suite 305
Rockville, MD 20852
800-328-8476
E-mail: info@autism-society.org
www.autism-society.org

Tracey Staley, Executive Chair
Christopher Banks, President and CEO
John Dabrowski, Chief Financial Officer
Brian Roth, Vice Chair

Promotes inclusivity for individuals on the autism spectrum and their families and works towards ensuring their full participation in the community through advocacy, public awareness, education, and research related to autism. Hosts a national conference, publishes a magazine, engages in public policy activities at local, state, and federal levels, and provides information and referral services via phone and email. The Autism Society consists of a nationwide network of local chapters.

Year Founded: 1965

188 Autism Speaks
1060 State Road
2nd Floor
Princeton, NJ 08540
646-385-8500
E-mail: help@autismspeaks.org
www.autismspeaks.org

Keith Wargo, President and CEO
Joe Vanyo, Chief Operating Officer
Andy Shih, Ph.D., Interim Chief Science Officer
Stuart Spielman, Executive VP of Advocacy

Autism Speaks was founded in 2005 and serves as an organization for autism science and advocacy. Autism Speaks funds biomedical research focused on the causes, treatments, and prevention of autism; educates the public and raises awareness about autism as well as its effects on people and society; and advocates for the needs of individuals and families concerned with autism.

Year Founded: 2005

189 Brain & Behavior Research Foundation
747 Third Avenue
33rd Floor
New York, NY 10017

646-681-4888
800-829-8289
E-mail: info@bbrfoundation.org
www.www.bbrfoundation.org

Donald M. Boardman, Treasurer
Jeffrey Borenstein, MD, President and CEO
Louis Innamorato, CPA, VP and Chief Financial Officer
Faith Rothblatt, Vice President, Development

The Brain and Behavior Research Foundation awards grants aimed at advancing scientific understandings of mental health treatments and mental disorders such as depression and schizophrenia. The Brain and Behavior Research Foundation's mission is to eliminate the suffering caused by mental illness.

Year Founded: 1987

190 Brain Resources and Information Network (BRAIN)
National Institute of Neurological Disorders and Stroke
PO Box 5801
Bethesda, MD 20824
800-352-9424
www.ninds.nih.gov

Walter J. Koroshetz, MD, Director, NINDS

Federal agency focused on supporting neuroscience research and working towards reducing the burdens associated with neurological disease.

Year Founded: 1950

191 Center for Mental Health Services (CMHS)
Substance Abuse and Mental Health Services Administration
5600 Fishers Lane
Rockville, MD 20857
240-276-1310
www.samhsa.gov/about-us/who-we-are/offices-centers

Anita Everett, MD, DFAPA, Director

Promotes the treatment of mental illness and emotional disorders by increasing accessibility to mental health programs; supporting outreach, treatment, rehabilitation, and support programs and networks; and encouraging the use of scientifically-based information when treating mental disorders. CMHS provides information about mental health via a toll-free number and numerous publications. Developed for users of mental health services and their families, the general public, policy makers, providers, and the media.

Year Founded: 1992

192 Community Services for Autistic Adults and Children
8615 East Village Avenue
Montgomery Village, MD 20886
240-912-2220
E-mail: csaac@csaac.org
www.csaac.org

Eric Salzano, Executive Director
Paul Martineau, Director, Operations
Peter Donaghy, Director of Finance
Eva Muiruri, Assistant Executive Director

CSAAC provides quality services for people with autism, offers employment and early intervention programs, and operates community living residences in Montgomery

County. CSAAC seeks to help individuals with autism to realize their highest potential and to become active participants in their community.

Year Founded: 1979

193   Families for Early Autism Treatment
PO Box 255722
Sacramento, CA 95865-5722
916-303-7405
E-mail: contact.us@feat.org
www.feat.org

A nonprofit organization offering a support network for families with children who have an Autism Spectrum Disorder. Organizes meetings where families can meet and discuss autism, treatment options, and other issues surrounding the disorder.

Year Founded: 1993

194   Indiana Resource Center for Autism (IRCA)
2810 E Discovery Parkway
Bloomington, IN 47408
812-855-6508
E-mail: prattc@indiana.edu
www.iidc.indiana.edu/pages/irca

Cathy Pratt, PhD, BCBA, Center Director
Julie Deaton, Administrative Program Secretary
Catherine Davies, MEd, MSC, LMHC, Educational Consultant

The Indiana Resource Center for Autism focuses on improving the quality of life for people with autism spectrum disorders, and promotes early diagnosis of autism and effective childhood programs, employment and living options, family support and other opportunities. The Center also conducts research on the most effective methods for supporting individuals with autism, and provides consultations and disseminates information on autism for families and professionals.

195   NAPCSE National Association of Parents with Children in Special Education
3642 East Sunnydale Drive
Chandler Heights, AZ 85142
800-754-4421
E-mail: contact@napcse.org
www.napcse.org

Dr. George Giuliani, President

The NAPCSE is dedicated to ensuring quality education for all children and adolescents with special needs. NAPCSE provides resources, support, and assistance to parents with children in special education.

196   National Alliance on Mental Illness
4301 Wilson Boulevard
Suite 300
Arlington, VA 22203
703-524-7600
800-950-6264
E-mail: info@nami.org
www.nami.org

Shirley J. Holloway, President
Joyce A. Campbell, First Vice President
Daniel H. Gillison, Jr., Chief Executive Officer
David Levy, Chief Financial Officer

NAMI is an organization dedicated to raising awareness on mental health and providing support and education for Americans affected by mental illness. NAMI advocates for access to services and treatment and fosters an environment of awareness and understanding for those concerned with mental health.

Year Founded: 1979

197   National Association for the Dually Diagnosed (NADD)
321 Wall Street
Kingston, NY 12401
845-331-4336
E-mail: info@thenadd.org
www.thenadd.org

Jeanne M. Farr, MA, Chief Executive Officer
Bruce Davis, President
Juanita St. Croix, Vice President
Ray Snyder, Secretary

NADD is a nonprofit organization designed to increase awareness of, and provide services for, individuals with developmental disabilities and mental illness. NADD emphasizes the importance of quality mental healthcare for people with mental health needs and offers conferences, information resources, educational programs, and training materials to professionals, parents, and organizations.

Year Founded: 1983

198   National Autism Center
41 Pacella Park Drive
Door 2
Randolph, MA 02368
877-313-3833
www.nationalautismcenter.org

Lauren C. Solotar, PhD, ABPP, President
Michael Tobin, CPA, Chief Financial Officer
Debra Blair, MBA, CMA, CPA, Chief Operating Officer

The National Autism Center is committed to promoting evidence-based information and practices surrounding the treatment of autism spectrum disorder, and providing trustworthy resources for families and professionals.

199   National Institute of Mental Health
6001 Executive Boulevard
Room 6200, MSC 9663
Bethesda, MD 20892-9663
866-615-6464
E-mail: nimhinfo@nih.gov
www.nimh.nih.gov

Joshua Gordon, MD, PhD, Director

The National Institute of Mental Health conducts clinical research on mental disorders and seeks to expand knowledge on mental health treatments.

200   National Institute on Deafness and Other Communication Disorders
31 Center Drive
MSC 2320
Bethesda, MD 20892-2320
301-827-8183
800-241-1044
TTY: 800-241-1055
www.www.nidcd.nih.gov

Debara L. Tucci, MD, MSD, MBA, Director
Judith A. Cooper, PhD, Deputy Director
Timothy J. Wheeles, Executive Officer
Lisa Portnoy, Deputy Executive Officer

NIDCD is one of the institutes that comprise the National Institutes of Health, and is dedicated to conducting research on communication disorders through biomedical and behavioral research on hearing, balance, taste, speech, language, smell, and voice. The institute also addresses problems associated with communication impairments.

Year Founded: 1988

201 National Mental Health Consumers' Self-Help Clearinghouse
E-mail: selfhelpclearinghouse@gmail.com
www.mhselfhelp.org

Joseph Rogers, Founder and Executive Director
Susan Rogers, Director

The Clearinghouse is a peer-run national technical assistance center focused on achieving respect and equality of opportunity for those with mental illnesses. The Clearinghouse helps with the growth of the mental health consumer movement by evaluating mental health services, advocating for mental health reform, and providing consumers with news, information, publications, and consultation services.

Year Founded: 1986

202 New England Center for Children: Autism Education and Research
33 Turnpike Road
Southborough, MA 01772-2108
508-481-1015
www.necc.org

Vincent Strully, Jr., President and CEO

A nonprofit research organization dedicated to using education and technology to make a positive impact on the lives of children with autism around the world. Provides evidence-based educational services for parents and teachers and assists autistic children and their families.

Year Founded: 1975

203 Pacific Autism Center For Education (PACE)
1880 Pruneridge Avenue
Santa Clara, CA 95050
408-245-3400
E-mail: info@pacificautism.org
www.pacificautism.org

Kurt Ohlfs, Executive Director, PACE
Karen Kennan, Assistant Executive Director
Sadie Randle, School Program Director
Tom McGovern, President

PACE is a behavioral program serving children with autism. The program implements teaching methods based upon Applied Behavior Analysis, including behavior assessment, behavior consultation, ABA therapy services, and parent and community training. The school also uses PECS (Picture Exchange Communication System), TEACCH (Treatment and Education of Autistic and related Communication-Handicapped Children, and DIR/Floortime (Developmental, Individual Difference, Relationship-based Model).

Year Founded: 1995

204 Sutcliffe Clinic
851 Fremont Avenue
Suite 110
Los Altos, CA 94024

650-941-1698
E-mail: info@sutcliffedbp.com
www.www.sutcliffeclinic.com

Trenna Sutcliffe, MD, MS, Medical Director

Sutcliffe Developmental & Behavioral Pediatrics is an organization that specializes in the treatment of ADHD, autism spectrum disorder, anxiety disorders, conduct disorders, learning disabilities, and more. Sutcliffe works with community services, school districs, and primary physicians, and provides family counseling.

205 The Center for Family Support
2811 Zulette Avenue
Bronx, NY 10461
718-518-1500
E-mail: svernikoff@cfsny.org
www.www.cfsny.org

Steven Vernikoff, Executive Director
Barbara Greenwald, Chief Operating Officer
Jos, Martin Jara, President
Elise Geltzer, Vice President

The Center for Family Support offers assistance to individuals with developmental and related disabilities, as well as their families, and provides support services and programs that are designed to accommodate individual needs. Offers services throughout New York City, Westchester County, Long Island, and New Jersey.

Year Founded: 1954

Periodicals & Pamphlets

206 Autism Matters
Autism Society Ontario
1179 King Street West
Suite 004
Toronto, ON M6K 3-5
416-246-9592
800-472-7789
www.autismsociety.on.ca

Covers society activities and contains information on autism. Recurring features include news of research, a calendar of events, reports of meetings, and book reviews.
$25.00

10 pages 4 per year

207 Autism Research Review International
Autism Research Institute
4182 Adams Avenue
San Diego, CA 92116-2599
619-281-7165
www.autism.com

Stephen M Edelson, PhD, Executive Director
Jane Johnson, Managing Director
Valerie Paradiz ,PhD, Director,ARI Autistic Global Ins
Rebecca McKenney, Office Manager

Discusses current research and provides information about the causes, diagnosis, and treatment of autism and related disorders. *$18.00*

8 pages 4 per year ISSN 0893-8474

208 Autism Society News
Utah Parent Center
230 West 200 South
Suite 1101
Salt Lake City, UT 84117-4428
801-272-1067
800-468-1160
www.utahparentcenter.org

Helen Post, Executive Director

Presents news, research information, and legislative updates regarding autism. Recurring features include a calendar of events and columns titled Parent Meetings, What's On in the News, Research News, Parent Corner, Legislative Summary, and A Big Thank You!

8 pages

209 Autism Spectrum Disorders in Children and Adolescents
Center for Mental Health Services: Knowledge Exchange Network
PO Box 42490
Washington, DC 20015
800-789-2647
TDD: 866-889-2647
E-mail: ken@mentalhealth.org
www.mentalhealth.org

Lee A Wilkinson, Author

This fact sheet defines autism, describes the signs and causes, discusses types of help available, and suggests what parents or other caregivers can do.

264 pages

210 Autism in Children and Adolescents
Center for Mental Health Services: Knowledge Exchange Network
PO Box 42557
Washington, DC 20015-557
800-789-2647
TDD: 866-889-2647
E-mail: ken@mentalhealth.org

This fact sheet defines autism, describes the signs and causes, discusses types of help available, and suggests what parents or other caregivers can do.

2 pages

211 Facts About Autism
Indiana Institute on Disability and Community
1 East 33rd Street
4th Floor
New York, NY 10016
212-252-8584
800-280-7010
TTY: 812-855-9396
www.www.autismspeaks.org/

Liz Feld, President
Jennifer Bizubÿ, Chief Human Resources Officer
Alec M Elbert, Chief Strategy and Development O
Jamitha Fields, Vice President - Community Affai

Provides concise information describing autism, diagnosis, needs of the person with autism from diagnosis through adulthood. Information on the Autism Society of America chapters in Indiana are listed in the back, along with a description of the Indiana Resource Center for Autism and suggested books to look for in the local library. Also available in Spanish. *$1.00*

212 Journal of Autism and Developmental Disorders
Springer Science & Business Media
Heidelberger Plate 3
14197 Berlin
Germany,
www.springer.com

Fred R. Volkmar, Editor-in-Chief

Features research and case studies involving the entire spectrum of interventions and advances in the diagnosis and classification of disorders.

6 per year ISSN 0162-3257

213 Sex Education: Issues for the Person with Autism
Autism Society of North Carolina Bookstore
955 Woodland Street
Nashville, TN 37206
615-385-2077
866-508-4987
E-mail: support@autismtn.org
www.www.autismtn.org

Nancy Dalrympale, Author
Susan Gray, Author
Lisa Ruble, Author
Kay Walker, Director, Development

Discusses issues of sexuality and provides methods of instruction for people with autism. *$4.00*

18 pages

214 The Source Newsletter
MAAP
PO Box 524
Crown Point, IN 46308-524
219-662-1311

Story C Landis, Director
Wlater J Koroshetz, MD, Deputy Director
Caroline Lewis, Executive Officer

Newsletter from the Global Information and Support Network for More Advanced Persons with Austism and Asperger's Syndrome.

4 per year

Research Centers

215 Indiana Resource Center for Autism (IRCA)
1905 North Range Road
Bloomington, IN 47408-9801
812-855-6508
800-825-4733
TTY: 812-855-9396
E-mail: prattc@indiana.edu
www.iidc.indiana.edu/pages/irca

Cathy Pratt, PhD, BCBA, Center Director
Pamela Anderson, Outreach/Resource Specialist
Catherine Davies, MEd, MSC, LMHC, Educational Consultant

The Indiana Resource Center for Autism focuses on improving the quality of life for people with autism spectrum disorders, and promotes early diagnosis of autism and effective childhood programs, employment and living options, family support and other opportunities. The Center also conducts research on the most effective methods for supporting individuals with autism, and provides consultations and disseminates information on autism for families and professionals.

216   **TEACCH**
CB# 6305
University of NC at Chapel Hill
Chapel Hill, NC 27599
919-966-2174
E-mail: teacch@unc.edu
www.teacch.com

Dr Laura Klinger, Director
Rebecca Mabe, Assistant Director of Business a
Walter Kelly, Business Officer
Mark Klinger, Director, Research

This organization is the division for the treatment and education of autistic and related communication handicapped children.

Video & Audio

217   **Asperger's Unplugged, an Interview with Jerry Newport**
Program Development Associates
32 Court St
21st Floor
Brooklyn, NY 11201
315-452-0643
800-876-1710
E-mail: info@disabilitytraining.com
www.disabilitytraining.com

Meet the man who answered a question in the film 'Rain Man' - How much is 4,343 x 1,234? - before the autistic savant character played by Dustin Hoffman answered it. Jerry Newport discovered Asperger's Syndrome while watching 'Rain Man' and has since become an engaging speaker and self-help organizer. This inspiring interview, available on VHS or DVD, supports teachers, staff developers and people with high functioning autism. 40 minutes. *$79.95*

218   **Autism Spectrum Disorders and the SCERTS**
Program Development Associates
32 Court St
21st Floor
Brooklyn, NY 11201
315-452-0643
800-876-1710
E-mail: info@disabilitytraining.com
www.disabilitytraining.com

Early intervention for children with Autism Spectrum Disorders. Shows a model in action with higher-functioning children who require less support. 105 minutes between three tapes. *$279.00*

219   **Autism in the Classroom**
Program Development Associates
32 Court St
21st Floor
Brooklyn, NY 11201
315-452-0643
800-876-1710
E-mail: info@disabilitytraining.com
www.disabilitytraining.com

Overviews symptoms, behaviors and treatments, and interviews children with autism, along with their parents and their teachers. 16 minutes. *$69.95*

220   **Autism is a World**
Program Development Associates
32 Court St
21st Floor
Brooklyn, NY 11201
315-452-0643
800-876-1710
E-mail: info@disabilitytraining.com
www.disabilitytraining.com

Takes a look inside the life of a woman who lives with the disorder. She explains how she feels, how she relates to others, her obsession and why her behavior can be so very different. Gives teachers and professionals striving to understand Autism Spectrum Disorder a glimpse from the inside out of this developmental disability. 40 minutes & can also be ordered as a DVD with special features. *$99.95*

221   **Autism: A Strange, Silent World**
Filmakers Library
3212 Duke Street
Alexandria, VA 22314
212-808-4980
E-mail: sales@alexanderstreet.com

Sue Oscar, Manager

British educators and medical personnel offer insight into autism's characteristics and treatment approaches through the cameos of three children. 52 minutes. *$295.00*

222   **Autism: A World Apart**
Fanlight Productions
32 Court Street
21st Floor
Brooklyn, NY 11201
718-488-8900
800-876-1710
E-mail: fanlight@fanlight.com
www.fanlight.com

Karen Cunninghame, Author

In this documentary, three families show us what the textbooks and studies cannot; what it's like to live with autism day after day, raise and love children who may be withdrawn and violent and unable to make personal connections with their families. Video cassette. 29 minutes. *$199.00*

ISBN 1-572950-39-0

223   **Autism: Being Friends**
Indiana Institute on Disability and Community
Indiana University
2853 E Tenth Street
Bloomington, IN 47408-2601
812-855-9396
800-280-7010
TTY: 812-855-9396

David Mank, Executive Director

This autism awareness videotape was produced specifically for use with young children. The program portrays the abilities of the child with autism and describes ways in which peers can help the child to be a part of the everyday world. *$10.00*

224 Avoiding The Turbulance: Guiding Families of Children Diagnosed with Autism
Program Development Associates
32 Court St
21st Floor
Brooklyn, NY 11201
315-452-0643
800-876-1710
E-mail: info@disabilitytraining.com
www.disabilitytraining.com

Focuses primarily on the best strategies of early intervention. Good resources for primary care medical providers and agency professionals involved in early intervention autism programs. 12 minutes. *$79.95*

225 Breakthroughs: How to Reach Students with Autism
ADD WareHouse
300 NW 70th Avenue
Suite 102
Plantation, FL 33317-2360
954-792-8100
800-233-9273
E-mail: websales@addwarehouse.com
www.addwarehouse.com

Karen Sewell, Author

This video is designed for instructors of children with autism, K-12. The program provides a fully-loaded teacher's manual with reproducible lesson plans that will take you through an entire school year as well as an award-winning video that demonstrates the instructional and behavioral techniques recommended in the manual. Covers math, reading, fine motor, self-help, vocational, social and life skills. Features a veteran instructor who was named 'Teacher of the Year' by the Autism Society of America. *$89.00*

243 pages

226 Children and Autism: Time is Brain
Program Development Associates
PO Box 2038
Syracuse, NY 13220-2038
315-452-0643
800-543-2119
E-mail: info@disabilitytraining.com
www.disabilitytraining.com/autism

Video features Applied Behavior Analysis (ABA) as an autism treatment technique by focusing on two families raising a child with autism. Gives documentation on their interaction with therapists and behavior analysts. 28 minutes. *$99.95*

227 Dr. Tony Attwood: Asperger's Syndrome Volume 2 DVD
Program Development Associates
32 Court St
21st Floor
Brooklyn, NY 11201
315-452-0643
800-876-1710
E-mail: info@disabilitytraining.com
www.disabilitytraining.com

Following rave national reviews that autism expert Dr. Tony Attwood received for his Volume 1 introduction to Asperger's Syndrome, here's the new DVD of his latest conference presentations. Volume 2 leaps off the DVD screen with Dr. Attwood's interactive, in-depth, theory-of-mind approach to Asperger's. 180 minutes. *$109.95*

228 Going to School with Facilitated Communication
Syracuse University, Facilitated Communication Institute
370 Huntington Hall
Syracuse, NY 13244-1
315-443-9657
www.soeweb.syr.edu/thefci

Douglas Biklen, Author

A video in which students with autism and/or severe disabilities illustrate the use of facilitated communication focusing on basic principles fostering facilitated communication.

229 I'm Not Autistic on the Typewriter
Syracuse University, Facilitated Communication Institute
370 Huntington Hall
Syracuse, NY 13244-1
315-443-9657
www.soeweb.syr.edu/thefci

A video introducing facilitated communication, a method by which persons with autism express themselves.

11 pages

230 Interview with Dr. Pauline Filipek
Program Development Associates
PO Box 2038
Syracuse, NY 13220-2038
315-452-0643
800-543-2119
E-mail: info@disabilitytraining.com
www.disabilitytraining.com/autism

An interview that presents early stage developmental autism, with diagnosis and age-level comparisons, research, interventions and myths and false and future treatments. 14 minutes. *$79.95*

231 Matthew: Guidance for Parents with Autistic Children
Program Development Associates
PO Box 2038
Syracuse, NY 13220-2038
315-452-0643
800-543-2119
E-mail: info@disabilitytraining.com
www.disabilitytraining.com/autism

A resource video guide for parents of autistic children. Shows parents where they should go, who to consult and what did or did not work for Matthew and his parents. 28 minutes. *$79.95*

232 Rising Above a Diagnosis of Autism
Program Development Associates
32 Court St
21st Floor
Brooklyn, NY 11201
315-452-0643
800-876-1710
E-mail: info@disabilitytraining.com

Focuses primarily on the period when a child receives a diagnosis of Autism. Meet with others who are involved somehow with autistic children, and hear recommendations from professionals and meet children that have Autism, PDD, Asperger's Syndrome or any other forms of Austism Spectrum Disorder. 30 minutes. *$99.95*

233 Rylee's Gift - Asperger Syndrome
Program Development Associates
PO Box 2038
Syracuse, NY 13220-2038
315-452-0643
E-mail: info@disabilitytraining.com
www.disabilitytraining.com

Martha Rylee, Author

This video or DVD spotlights Rylee - through his mother, grandparents, doctor, teacher - and adults with Asperger's Syndrome. Balances views of difficult transitions and melt-down behaviors, with sensory therapy, socialization and the amazing capabilities of people with this syndrome/gift. 56 minutes. *$89.95*

234 Straight Talk About Autism with Parents and Kids
ADD WareHouse
300 NW 70th Avenue
Suite 102
Plantation, FL 33317-2360
954-792-8100
800-233-9273
E-mail: websales@addwarehouse.com
www.addwarehouse.com

Jeff Schultz, Author

These revealing videos contain intimate interviews with parents of kids with autism and the young people themselves. Topics discussed include friends and social isolation, communication difficulties, hypersensitivities, teasing, splinter skills, parent support groups and more. One video focuses on childhood issues, while the second covers adolescent issues. Two 40 minute videos. *$99.00*

235 Struggling with Life: Asperger's Syndrome
Program Development Associates
PO Box 2038
Syracuse, NY 13220-2038
315-452-0643
E-mail: info@disabilitytraining.com
www.disabilitytraining.com

ABC News correspondent Jay Schadler's report on the neurological disorder called Asperger's focuses on the telling line between intense interests and obsessions. The latter may be an early symptom of the syndrome. This closed caption video is grounded on studies by Fred Voklmar at Yale that explore compulsive fixations and unreadable facial expressions, both of which are typical of Asperger's and inhibit normal peer interactions among children. VHS or DVD. 14 minutes. *$ 69.95*

Web Sites

236 www.aane.org
Asperger's Association of New England

Working advocacy group of Massachusetts parents of adults and teens with AS who have come together with the goal of getting state funding for residential supports for adults with AS. At the present time no state agency will provide these needed supports. Interested parents and AS adults are welcome to join this working group.

237 www.ani.ac
Autism Network International

This organization is run by and for the autistic people. The best advocates for autistic people are autistic people themselves. Provides a forum for autistic people to share information, peer support, tips for coping and problem solving, as well as providing a social outlet for autistic people to explore and participate in autistic social experiences. In addition to promoting self advocacy for high-functioning autistic adults, ANI also works to improve the lives of autistic people who, whether they are too young or because they do not have the communication skills, are not able to advocate for themselves. Helps autistic people by providing information and referrals for parenting and teachers. Also strives to educate the public about autism.

238 www.aspennj.org
Asperger Syndrome Education Network (ASPEN)

Regionally-based non-profit organization headquarted in New Jersey, with 11 local chapters, providing families and those individuals affected with Asperger Syndrome, PDD-NOS, High Function Autism, and related disorders. Provides education about the issues surrounding Asperger Syndrome and other related disorders. Support in knowing that they are not alone and in helping individuals with AS achieve their maximum potential. Advocacy in areas of appropriate educational programs and placement, medical research funding, and increased public awareness and understanding.

239 www.aspergerinfo.com
Aspergers Resource Links

AspergerInfo.com offers a safe place to ask questions, share experiences, and discuss treatments relating to Asperger Syndrome.

240 www.aspergers.com
Aspergers Resource Links

Asperger's Disorder Homepage

241 www.aspergersyndrome.org
Aspergers Resource Links

Barbara Kirby, Founder

A collection of web resources on Asperger's Syndrome and related topics. Hosted by the University of Delaware.

242 www.aspiesforfreedom.com
Aspies for Freedom

Aspies for Freedom (AFF) is a web site with chat rooms, forums and information relating to Austism and Asperger's Syndrome.

243 www.autism-society.org
Autism Society of America

Promotes lifelong access and opportunities for persons within the autism spectrum and their families, to be fully included, participating members of their communities through advocacy, public awareness, education and research related to autism.

244 www.autism.org
Center for the Study of Autism (CSA)

Located in the Salem/Portland, Oregon area. Provides information about autism to parents and professionals, and conducts research on the efficacy of various therapeutic interventions. Much of our research is in collaboration with the Autism Research Institute in San Diego, California.

245 www.autismresearchinstitute.org
Autism Research Institute

Devoted to conducting research on the causes of autism and on the methods of preventing, diagnosing and treating autism and other severe behavioral disorders of childhood.

246 www.autismservicescenter.org
Autism Services Center

Makes available technical assistance in designing programs. Provides supervised apartments, group homes, respite services, independent living programs and job-coached employment.

247 www.autismspeaks.org
National Alliance for Autism Research (NAAR)

National non-profit, tax-exempt organization dedicated to finding the causes, preventions, effective treatments and, ultimately, a cure for the autism spectrum disorders. NAAR's mission is to fund, promote and support biomedical research into autism. Aims to have an aggressive and far-reaching research program. Seeks to encourage scientists outside the field of autism to apply their insights and experience to autism. Publishes a newsletter that focuses on developments in autism research. Supports brain banks and tissue consortium development.

248 www.autisticservices.com
Autistic Services

Dedicated to serving the unique lifelong needs of autistic individuals.

249 www.cfsny.org
Center for Family Support (CFS)

Devoted to providing support and assistance to individuals with developmental and related disabilities, and to the family members who care for them.

250 www.csaac.org
Community Services for Autistic Adults & Children

Enables individuals to achieve their highest potential and contribute as confident members in their community, instead of living in institutions.

251 www.cyberpsych.org
CyberPsych

Hosts the American Psychoanalyists Foundation, American Association of Suicideology, Society for the Exploration of Psychotherapy Intergration, and Anxiety Disorders Association of America. Also subcategories of the anxiety disorders, as well as general information, including panic disorder, phobias, obsessive compulsive disorder (OCD), social phobia, generalized anxiety disorder, post traumatic stress disorder, and phobias of childhood. Book reviews and links to web pages sharing the topics.

252 www.feat.org
Families for Early Autism Treatment

A non-profit organization of parents and professionals, designed to help families with children who are diagnosised with autism or pervasive developmental disorder. It offers a network of support for families. FEAT has a Lending Library, with information on autism and also offers Support Meetings on the third Wednesday of each month.

253 www.iidc.indiana.edu
Indiana Resource Center for Autism (IRCA)

Conducts outreach training and consultations, engage in research and develop and disseminate info on behalf of individuals across the autism spectrum.

254 www.ladders.org
The Autism Research Foundation

A non-profit, tax-exempt organization dedicated to researching the neurological underpinnings of autism and other related developmental brain disorders. Seeking to rapidly expand and accelerate research into the pervasive developmental disorders. To do this, time and efforts goes into investigating the neuropathology of autism in their laboratories, collecting and redistributing brain tissue to promising research groups for use by projects approved by the Tissue Resource Committee, studies frozen autistic brain tissue collected by TARF. They believe that only aggressive scientific and medical research will reveal the cure for this lifelong disorder.

255 www.maapservices.org
MAAP Services

Provides information and advice to people with Asperger Syndrome, Autism and Pervasive Developmental Disorders. Provides parents and professionals a chance to network with others to learn more within the autism spectrum.

256 www.mentalhealth.Samhsa.Gov
Center for Mental Health Services Knowledge Exchange Network

Information about resources, technical assistance, research, training, networks and other federal clearinghouses and fact sheets and materials.

257 www.mhselfhelp.org
National Mental Health Consumer's Self-Help Clearinghouse

Encourages the development and growth of consumer self-help groups.

258 www.nami.org
National Alliance on Mental Illness

From its inception in 1979, NAMI has been dedicated to improving the lives of individuals and families affected by mental illness.

259 www.necc.org
New England Center for Children

Serves students diagnosed with autism, learning disabilities, language delays, behavior disorders and related disabilities.

260 www.planetpsych.com
Planetpsych.com

Learn about disorders, their treatments and other topics in psychology. Articles are listed under the related topic areas. Ask a therapist a question for free, or view the directory of professionals in your area. If you are a therapist sign up for the directory. Current features, self-help, interactive, and newsletter archives.

261 www.resourcesnyc.org
Resources for Children with Special Needs

Gives a general introduction on autism, educational approaches, available resources, supplementary services, definitions and other related services are included.

262 www.son-rise.org
Son-Rise Autism Treatment Center of America

Training center for autism professionals and parents of autistic children. Programs focus on the design and implementation of home-based/child-centered alternatives.

263 www.thenadd.org
National Association for the Dually Diagnosed (NADD)

An association for persons with developmental disabilities and mental health needs.

264 www.wrongplanet.net
Wrong Planet

WrongPlanet.net is a web community designed for individuals with Asperger's Syndrome and other PDDs. They provide a forum where members can communicate with each other, may read or submit essays or how-to guides about various subjects, and a chatroom for communication with other Aspies.

Conferences & Meetings

265 Asperger Syndrome Education Network (ASPEN) Conference
PO Box 109
Oceanport, NJ 07757
732-321-0880
www.www.aspennj.org

Lori Shery, President and Executive Director
Rich Meleo, Vice President
Anita Finkel, Treasurer
Ann Hiller, Secretary

Annual conference.

Directories & Databases

266 After School and More
Resources for Children with Special Needs
116 E 16th Street
5th Floor
New York, NY 10003-2164
212-677-4650
www.resourcesnyc.org

Rachel Howard, Executive Director
Stephen Stern, Director , Finance and Administr
Todd Dorman, Director, Communications and Out
Helen Murphy, Director, Program and Fund Devel

The most complete directory of after school programs for children with disabilities and special needs in the metropolitan New York area focusing on weekend and holiday programs. *$15.00*

252 pages ISBN 0-967836-57-3

Bipolar and Related Disorders

Introduction

Bipolar and Related Disorders are a group of severe mental illnesses characterized by alterations between depression and manic euphoria.

The two states are not independent of each other, but part of the same illness. Individuals in the manic phase of Bipolar Disorder feel exuberant, invincible, or even immortal. They may be awake for days at a time and be able to work tirelessly; they may rush from one idea to the next, carried by a nearly uncontrollable burst of energy that leaves others bewildered and unable to keep up. (Some extraordinarily creative people, Vincent Van Gogh, for example, have had Bipolar Disorder. Whether or not the disorder makes a positive contribution to creativity is a controversial question.) In the depressed phase which follows a manic high, the patient may feel worthless, lose interest or pleasure in activities, or even be suicidal. The depressed phase of the illness mirrors a major depressive episode.

There are three forms of Bipolar Disorders: Bipolar I Disorder, Bipolar II Disorder, and Cyclothymic Disorder. Bipolar I Disorder is characterized by bouts of mania followed by depression. However, Bipolar II Disorder consists of repeated depressive episodes interspersed with hypomanic (not full blown mania) episodes. The individual with Cyclothymic Disorder has a history of at least two years of repeated episodes of elevated and depressed moods that don't meet all the criteria for mania or depression but that cause distress and/ordecreased ability to function.

A number of researchers are closing in on genetic links to the illness. Like all mental disorders, however, the relationship between genetic physiologic, psycho logical, and environmental causes is complex. Lithium was the first medication found to be effective; several other medications are now available and effective. Many patients with Bipolar Disorders need a combination of medications to address both the manic and depressive aspects of the disease. While medication is quite effective, patients also need psychotherapy as well to address issues like compliance with medication, noting early signs of relapse, dealing with friends and family and environmental life stressors.

SYMPTOMS

A **manic episode** consists of the following:

• A distinct period of abnormally and persistently elevated, expansive, or irritable mood, lasting at least one week;
• Inflated self-esteem or grandiosity; decreased need for sleep;
• More talkative than usual;
• Flight of ideas (a succession of topics with little relationship to one another) or a subjective experience that thoughts are racing;
• Distractibility;
• Increase in goal-directed activity;
• Excessive involvement in activities that have a high potential for painful consequences;
• The mood disturbances are severe enough to cause impairment in social or occupational functioning;
• The symptoms are not due to the direct physiological effects of a substance.

The **depressive phase** consists of the following:

• Depressed mood most of the day, nearly every day, as indicated by either subjective report or observation;
• Markedly diminished interest or pleasure in almost all activities most of the day;
• Significant weight loss when not dieting, or weight gain, or decrease or increase in appetite nearly every day;
• Insomnia or hypersomnia nearly every night;
• Psychomotor agitation or retardation nearly every day;
• Fatigue or loss of energy nearly every day;
• Feelings of worthlessness or excessive or inappropriate guilt nearly every day.

ASSOCIATED FEATURES

Bipolar Disorder is a severe mental illness that can cause extreme disruption to individual lives and careers, and to whole families. While manic, patients may spend all of a family's money (or borrow great sums), engage in indiscriminate sexual activity, and behave in other ways that leave lasting negative effects. Suicide is a risk factor in the illness, and an estimated ten percent to fifteen percent of individuals with Bipolar I Disorder commit suicide. Abuse of children, spouses or other family members, or other types of violence, may occur during the manic phase of the illness. Untreated mania, during which the individual gets no sleep, little or no nutrition, and expends great quantities of energy, can result in death as well.

It is important for patients with depression to be carefully screened for any manic or hypomanic symptoms so that a Bipolar Disorder can be diagnosed and the appropriate treatment prescribed. Most people with Bipolar Disorder present, or are referred, for care while in the depressive state; it is essential that any individual diagnosed with depression be carefully evaluated to rule out bipolar disorder before antidepressant medication is prescribed. Antidepressant medication alone can precipitate a manic episode in an individual with Bipolar Disorder. The cycles of mood changes tend to become more frequent, shorter, and more intense as the patient gets older.

Disturbances in work, school or social functioning are common, resulting in frequent school truancy or failure, occupational failure, divorce, or episodic antisocial behavior. A variety of other mental disorders may accompany Bipolar Disorder; these include Feeding and Eating Disorders, ADHD, Panic Disorder, Social Phobia, and Substance-Related and Addictive Disorders.

PREVALENCE

The prevalence of Bipolar Disorder varies, but it can occur in up to 2.5 percent of the community. The average onset for Bipolar Disorder is usually between 18 and 24 years, but it can develop in childhood, or as late as the forties and fifties.

TREATMENT OPTIONS

Lithium is the most commonly prescribed drug for Bipolar Disorder and is effective for stabilizing patients in the manic phase of the illness and preventing mood swings. However, compliance is a problem among patients both because of the nature of the condition (some patients may actually miss the high of their mood swings and other people often envy their enthusiasm, energy, and confidence) and because of the side effects associated with

33

the drug. These include weight gain, excessive thirst, tremors and muscle weakness. Lithium is also very toxic in overdose. Blood levels of lithium must be measured daily or weekly to begin with, and in at least six-month intervals thereafter. The disruptive nature of the condition also necessitates the use of psychotherapy and family therapy to help patients rebuild relationships, to maintain compliance with treatment and a positive attitude toward living with chronic illness, and to restore confidence and self-esteem.

Anticonvulsants/mood stabilizers, such as Valproate, Carbamazepine, Lamotrigine, Gabapentin, and Topiramate have also become first-line treatments, as have several antipsychotic medications.

Education of the family is crucial for successful treatment, as is education of patients about the disorder and treatment.

Associations & Agencies

268 Brain & Behavior Research Foundation
747 Third Avenue
33rd Floor
New York, NY 10017
646-681-4888
800-829-8289
E-mail: info@bbrfoundation.org
www.www.bbrfoundation.org

Donald M. Boardman, Treasurer
Jeffrey Borenstein, MD, President and CEO
Louis Innamorato, CPA, VP and Chief Financial Officer
Faith Rothblatt, Vice President, Development

The Brain and Behavior Research Foundation awards grants aimed at advancing scientific understandings of mental health treatments and mental disorders such as depression and schizophrenia. The Brain and Behavior Research Foundation's mission is to eliminate the suffering caused by mental illness.

Year Founded: 1987

269 Center for Mental Health Services (CMHS)
Substance Abuse and Mental Health Services
Administration
5600 Fishers Lane
Rockville, MD 20857
240-276-1310
www.samhsa.gov/about-us/who-we-are/offices-centers

Anita Everett, MD, DFAPA, Director

Promotes the treatment of mental illness and emotional disorders by increasing accessibility to mental health programs; supporting outreach, treatment, rehabilitation, and support programs and networks; and encouraging the use of scientifically-based information when treating mental disorders. CMHS provides information about mental health via a toll-free number and numerous publications. Developed for users of mental health services and their families, the general public, policy makers, providers, and the media.

Year Founded: 1992

270 Depression & Bipolar Support Alliance
55 East Jackson Boulevard
Suite 490
Chicago, IL 60604
800-826-3632
E-mail: info@dbsalliance.org
www.dbsalliance.org

Roger McIntyre, Chair
Michael Pollock, Chief Executive Officer
Maria Margaglione, Programs Director
Hannah Zeller, Program Manager

The Depression and Bipolar Support Alliance is a national organization focused on improving the lives of individuals with depression, bipolar disorder, and other mood disorders. DBSA organizes peer-led support groups; educates patients, families, professionals, and the public on mental health; and works to ensure the availability of quality care for all people.

271 Mood Disorders Center
Department of Psychiatry and Behavioral Sciences
at Johns Hopkins
600 North Wolfe Street
Baltimore, MD 21218
410-955-5212
877-666-3754
www.www.hopkinsmedicine.org/psychiatry/specialty_areas

J. Raymond DePaulo, MD, Co-Director
Kay Redfield Jamison, PhD, Co-Director
Mehdi Pirooznia, MD, Research Team
Peter Zandi, PhD, Research Team

The Mood Disorders Center at Johns Hopkins Medicine provides specialized clinical services to patients with mood disorders; conducts research on the causes of mood disorders, treatment responses, and brain function and structure; and educates patients, caregivers, and the public on mood disorders through symposia, publications, community presentations, and the Adolescent Depression Awareness Program.

272 National Alliance on Mental Illness
4301 Wilson Boulevard
Suite 300
Arlington, VA 22203
703-524-7600
800-950-6264
E-mail: info@nami.org
www.nami.org

Shirley J. Holloway, President
Joyce A. Campbell, First Vice President
Daniel H. Gillison, Jr., Chief Executive Officer
David Levy, Chief Financial Officer

NAMI is an organization dedicated to raising awareness on mental health and providing support and education for Americans affected by mental illness. NAMI advocates for access to services and treatment and fosters an environment of awareness and understanding for those concerned with mental health.

Year Founded: 1979

273 National Association for the Dually Diagnosed
(NADD)
321 Wall Street
Kingston, NY 12401
845-331-4336
E-mail: info@thenadd.org
www.thenadd.org

Jeanne M. Farr, MA, Chief Executive Officer
Bruce Davis, President
Juanita St. Croix, Vice President
Ray Snyder, Secretary

NADD is a nonprofit organization designed to increase awareness of, and provide services for, individuals with developmental disabilities and mental illness. NADD emphasizes the importance of quality mental healthcare for people with mental health needs and offers conferences, information resources, educational programs, and training materials to professionals, parents, and organizations.

Year Founded: 1983

274 National Institute of Mental Health
6001 Executive Boulevard
Room 6200, MSC 9663
Bethesda, MD 20892-9663
866-615-6464
E-mail: nimhinfo@nih.gov
www.nimh.nih.gov

Joshua Gordon, MD, PhD, Director

The National Institute of Mental Health conducts clinical research on mental disorders and seeks to expand knowledge on mental health treatments.

275 National Mental Health Consumers' Self-Help Clearinghouse
E-mail: selfhelpclearinghouse@gmail.com
www.mhselfhelp.org

Joseph Rogers, Founder and Executive Director
Susan Rogers, Director

The Clearinghouse is a peer-run national technical assistance center focused on achieving respect and equality of opportunity for those with mental illnesses. The Clearinghouse helps with the growth of the mental health consumer movement by evaluating mental health services, advocating for mental health reform, and providing consumers with news, information, publications, and consultation services.

Year Founded: 1986

276 The Balanced Mind Parent Network
Depression and Bipolar Support Alliance
55 East Jackson Boulevard
Suite 490
Chicago, IL 60604
800-826-3632
E-mail: community@dbsalliance.org
www.www.dbsalliance.org

Michael Pollock, CEO
Maria Margaglione, Programs Director

The Balanced Mind provides support, information, and assistance to families raising children with mood disorders and related conditions.

277 The Center for Family Support
2811 Zulette Avenue
Bronx, NY 10461
718-518-1500
E-mail: svernikoff@cfsny.org
www.www.cfsny.org

Steven Vernikoff, Executive Director
Barbara Greenwald, Chief Operating Officer
Jos, Martin Jara, President
Elise Geltzer, Vice President

The Center for Family Support offers assistance to individuals with developmental and related disabilities, as well as their families, and provides support services and programs that are designed to accommodate individual needs. Offers

services throughout New York City, Westchester County, Long Island, and New Jersey.
Year Founded: 1954

Periodicals & Pamphlets

278 DBSA Support Groups: An Important Step on the Road to Wellness
Depression and Bipolar Support Alliance
730 North Franklin Street
Suite 501
Chicago, IL 60654-7225
312-642-0049
800-826-3632
www.dbsalliance.org

Cheryl T Magrini,MS.Ed,MTS,PhD, Chair
Allen Doederlein, President
Cindy Specht, ExecutiveVice president
Gregory E Ostfeld, Treasurer

Support groups for people with depression or bipolar disorder to discuss the experiences, and helpful treatments.

10 pages

279 Finding Peace of Mind: Treatment Strategies for Depression and Bipolar Disorder
Depression and Bipolar Support Alliance
730 North Franklin Street
Suite 501
Chicago, IL 60654-7225
312-642-0049
800-826-3632
www.dbsalliance.org

Helps to build a good, cooperative relationship with your doctor by explaining some of the treatments for mood disorders and how they work. Also includes a guide for medication that has been frequently prescribed and new treatments that are being investigated.

20 pages

280 Getting Better Sleep: What You Need to Know
Depression and Bipolar Support Alliance
730 North Franklin Street
Suite 501
Chicago, IL 60654-7225
312-642-0049
800-826-3632
www.dbsalliance.org

Sue Bergeson, President

Describes some causes of sleep loss, and how sleep loss relates to bipolar disorder and depression. Also provides information on how to get better sleep.

281 Introduction to Depression and Bipolar Disorder
Depression and Bipolar Support Alliance
730 North Franklin Street
Suite 501
Chicago, IL 60654-7225
312-642-0049
800-826-3632
www.dbsalliance.org

Sue Bergeson, President

Quick and easy-to-read brochure describing syptoms and treatments for mood disorders.

282 McMan's Depression and Bipolar Weekly
McMan's Depression and Bipolar Web
PO Box 5093
Kendall Park, NJ 08824-5093
E-mail: mcman@mcmanweb.com
www.mcmanweb.com

John McManamy, Editor/Publisher

Online newsletter devoted to the issues of bipolar and depression disorders. There is no charge, just for you to understand different things about the disorders.

283 Mood Disorders
Center for Mental Health Services: Knowledge Exchange Network
PO Box 42490
Washington, DC 20015
800-789-2647
TDD: 866-889-2647
E-mail: ken@mentalhealth.org
www.store.samhsa.gov

This fact sheet provides basic information on the symptoms, formal diagnosis, and treatment for bipolar disorder.

3 pages

284 Myths and Facts about Depression and Bipolar Disorders
Depression and Bipolar Support Alliance
730 North Franklin Street
Suite 501
Chicago, IL 60654-7225
312-642-0049
800-826-3632
www.dbsalliance.org

Gives some myths about depression and bipolar disorder and the truths that combat them.

285 Oxcarbazepine and Bipolar Disorder: A Guide
Madison Institute of Medicine
6515 Grand Teton Plaza
Suite 100
Madison, WI 53719
608-827-2470
www.factsforhealth.org

W Jefferson James, Author
John H Greist, Author
David J Katzelnick,MD, Author

This 31 page booklet provides patients with the information they need to know about the use of oxcarbazepine in the treatment of bipolar disorder, including information about proper dosing, medication management, and possible side effects. *$5.95*

31 pages

286 Recovering Your Mental Health: a Self-Help Guide
SAMHSA'S National Mental Health Informantion Center
1 Choke Cherry Road
Rockville, MD 20857
877-726-4727
E-mail: ken@mentalhealth.org
www.mentalhealth.samhsa.gov

Mary Ellen Copeland, Author
Edward B Searle, Deputy Director

This booklet offers tips for understanding symptoms of depression and other conditions and getting help. Also details the advantages of counseling, medications available, options for professional help, relaxation techniques and paths to positive thinking.

32 pages

287 Storm In My Brain
Depression & Bi-Polar Support Alliance
730 North Franklin Street
Suite 501
Chicago, IL 60654-7225
312-642-0049
800-826-3632
www.dbsalliance.org

Sue Bergeson, President
Ingrid Deetz, Program Director

Pamphlet free on the Internet or by mail. Discusses child or adolesent Bi-Polar symptoms.

288 You've Just Been Diagnosed...What Now?
Depression and Bipolar Support Alliance
730 North Franklin Street
Suite 501
Chicago, IL 60654-7225
312-642-0049
800-826-3632
www.dbsalliance.org

Sue Bergeson, President

Pamphlet to help you understand about the disorder you have just been diagnosed with. Tells you basic facts about mood disorders and will help you work towards a diagnosis.

19 pages

Research Centers

289 Bipolar Clinic and Research Program
The Massachusetts General Hospital Bipolar Clinic & Research Program
50 Staniford Street
Suite 580
Boston, MA 02114-2540
617-726-5855
www.www.massgeneral.org

Michael Jellinek,MD, President
Laurie Ansorge Ball, Executive Director,MGH Departmen
Jerrold F Rosenbaum,MD, Chief of Psychiatry,MGH

Dedicated to providing quality clinical care, conducting clinically informative research, and educating our colleagues, patients, as well as the community.

290 Bipolar Disorders Clinic
Standford School of Medicine
401 Quarry Road
Stanford, CA 94305-5723
650-723-3305
www.bipolar.stanford.edu

Terrence A Ketter,MD, Chief,Bipolar Disorders Clinic
Shelley Hill,MS, Clinical Research Coordinator

Offers an on-going clinical treatment, manage clinical trials and neuroimaging studies, lecture and teach seminar courses at Stanford University and train residents in the School of Medicine.

291 Bipolar Research Program at University of Pennsylvania
3535 Market Street
6th Floor
Philadelphia, PA 19104-3413
215-898-4301
www.www.med.upenn.edu/psych/bipolar_research.html

Laszlo Gyulai, MD, Program Director
Chang-Gyu Hahn, MD, Ph.D., Clinical Team Member

Offers and conducts research on treatments for bipolar disorders. The program provides comprehensive care for persons with bipolar affective disorder (manic depressive illness), seasonal affective disorder, and rapid cycling bipolar disorder. Services offered for individuals who are in the ages of 18 or older include evaluations, consultations, and ongoing treatment options.

292 Epidemiology-Genetics Program in Psychiatry
John Hopkins University School of Medicine
PO Box 1997
Baltimore, MD 21203
888-289-4095
www.www.hopkinsmedicine.org

The research program is to help characterize the genetic (biochemical) developmental, and environmental components of bipolar disorder. The hope is that once scientists understand the biological causes of this disorder new medications and treatments can be developed.

293 Yale Mood Disorders Research Program
Department of Psychiatry
300 George Street
Suite 901
New Haven, CT 06511-6624
203-785-2090
www.psychiatry.yale.edu

John H Krystal, Chair
Rajita Sinha, Chief, Psychology Section

MDRP is dedicated to understanding the science of mood disorders, including bipolar disorder and depression. The MDRP brings together a multi-disciplinary group of scientists from across the Yale campus in a highly collaborative research effort. Goals of the MDRP include the identification of biological markers for mood disorders and discovery of new treatment strategies.

Support Groups & Hot Lines

294 Recovery International
1415 W. 22nd Street
Tower Floor
Oak Brook, IL 60523
312-337-5661
866-221-0302
E-mail: info@recoveryinternational.org
www.www.recoveryinternational.org

Sandra K. Wilcoxon, Chief Executive Officer
Joanne Lampey, President
Nicole Cilento, Vice President
Hal Casey, Treasurer

Recovery International is an organization that uses a peer-to-peer, self-help training system developed by Abraham Low in order to help individuals with mental health issues lead more productive lives.

Year Founded: 1937

Video & Audio

295 Anger Management-Enhanced Edition
Educational Video Network, Inc.
1401 19th Street
Huntsville, TX 77340
936-295-5767
800-762-0060
www.www.evndirect.com

Learn what causes anger and understand why our bodies react as they do when we're angry. Effective techniques for assuaging anger are discussed.

296 Bipolar Disorder: Shifting Mood Swings
Educational Training Videos
136 Granville St
Suite 200
Gahanna, OH 43230
www.educationaltrainingvideos.com

Different from the routine ups and downs of life, the symptoms of bipolar disorder are severe - even to the point of being life-threatening. In this insightful program, patients speak from their own experience about the complexities of diagnosis and the very real danger of suicide, while family members and close friends address the strain of the condition's cyclic behavior.

297 Clinical Impressions: Identifying Mental Illness
Educational Training Videos
136 Granville St
Suite 200
Gahanna, OH 43230
www.educationaltrainingvideos.com

How long can mental illness stay hidden, especially from the eyes of trained experts? This program rejoins a group of ten adults- five of them healthy and five of them with histories of mental illness- as psychiatric specialists try to spot and correctly diagnose the latter. Administering a series of collaborative and one-on-one tests, including assessments of personality type, physical self-image, and rational thinking, the panel gradually makes decisions about who suffers from depression, bipolar disorder, bulimia, and social anxiety.

298 Families Coping with Mental Illness
Mental Illness Education Project
25 West Street
Brookline Village, MA 01581
617-562-1111
800-343-5540
www.miepvideos.org

Ten family members share their experiences of having a family member with schizophrenia or bipolar disorder. Designed to provide insights and support to other families, the tape also profoundly conveys to professionals the needs of families when mental illness strikes. In two versions: a 22-minute version ideal for short classes and workshops, and a richer 43-minute version with more examples and details. Discounted price for families/consumers. *$99.95*

299 Kay Redfield Jamison: Surviving Bipolar Disorder
Educational Training Videos
136 Granville St
Suite 200
Gahanna, OH 43230
www.educationaltrainingvideos.com

Psychiatry professor and clinical psychologist Kay Redfield Jamison knows all about bipolar disorder- from the inside out. She talks frankly about her experiences with a mental illness that almost claimed her life.

300   Understanding Mental Illness
Educational Video Network, Inc.
1401 19th Street
Huntsville, TX 77340
936-295-5767
800-762-0060
www.www.evndirect.com

Contains information and classifications of mental illness. Mental illness can strike anyone, at any age. Learn about various organic and functional mental disorders as discussed and their causes and symptoms, and learn where to seek help for a variety of mental health concerns.

Web Sites

301   www.befrienders.org
Samaritans International

Support, helplines, and advice.

302   www.bpso.org
BPSO-Bipolar Significant Others

Informational site intended to provide information and support to the spouses, families, friends and other loved ones of those who suffer from bi-polar.

303   www.cfsny.org
Center for Family Support (CFS)

Devoted to providing support and assistance to individuals with developmental and related disabilities, and to the family members who care for them.

304   www.dbsalliance.org
Depression & Bi-Polar Support Alliance

Mental health news updates and local support group information.

305   www.goodwill-suncoast.org
Suncoast Residential Training Center

Group home that serves individuals diagnosed as developmentally disabled, with a secondary diagnosis of psychiatric difficulties as evidenced by problem behavior.

306   www.med.yale.edu
Yale University School of Medicine

Research center dedicated to understanding the science of mood disorders.

307   www.mentalhealth.Samhsa.Gov
Center for Mental Health Services Knowledge Exchange Network

Information about resources, technical assistance, research, training, networks, and other federal clearinghouses, fact sheets and materials.

308   www.mhselfhelp.org
National Mental Health Consumer's Self-Help Clearinghouse

Encourages the development and growth of consumer self-help groups.

309   www.miminc.org
Bipolar Disorders Treatment Information Center

Provides information on mood stabilizers other than lithium for bipolar disorders.

310   www.nami.org
National Alliance on Mental Illness

From its inception in 1979, NAMI has been dedicated to improving the lives of individuals and families affected by mental illness.

311   www.planetpsych.com
Planetpsych.com

Learn about disorders, their treatments and other topics in psychology. Articles are listed under the related topic areas. Ask a therapist a question for free, or view the directory of professionals in your area. If you are a therapist sign up for the directory. Current features, self-help, interactive, and newsletter archives.

312   www.psychcentral.com
Psych Central

Personalized one-stop index for psychology, support, and mental health issues, resources, and people on the Internet.

313   www.shpm.com
Self Help Magazine

Articles and discussion forums, resource links.

314   www.store.samhsa.gov
Substance Abuse and Mental Health Services Administration

Resources on mental disorders as well as treatment and recovery.

315   www.thenadd.org
National Association for the Dually Diagnosed (NADD)

An association for persons with developmental disabilities and mental health needs.

Depressive Disorders

Introduction

Major Depressive Disorder is an illness characterized by extreme, long-lasting feelings of sadness, despair, and worthlessness. Feelings of sadness are common to everyone, and quite natural in response to unfortunate circumstances. The death of a loved one, the end of a relationship, or other traumatic life experiences are bound to bring on the blues. However, when feelings of sadness and despair persist beyond a reasonable period, arise for no particular reason, or begin to affect a person's ability to function, help is needed.

Depression is a diagnosis made by a psychiatrist or other mental health professional to describe serious and prolonged symptoms of sadness or despair. While it is common, Major Depressive Disorder should not be taken lightly; depression can be deadly. Many people who are deeply depressed think about or actually try to commit suicide. Even a relatively mild depression, if untreated, can disrupt marriages and relationships or impede careers.

Symptoms
Depression is diagnosed when an individual experiences
1) persistent feelings of sadness or
2) loss of interest or pleasure in usual activities, in addition to five of the following symptoms for at least two weeks:
• Significant weight gain or loss unrelated to dieting;
• Inability to sleep or, conversely, sleeping too much;
• Restlessness and agitation;
• Fatigue or loss of energy;
• Feelings of worthlessness or guilt;
• Diminished ability to think or concentrate;
• Recurrent thoughts of death or suicide;
• Distress not caused by a medication or the symptoms of a medical illness.

Associated Features
Because depression can range from mild to severe, people who are depressed may exhibit a variety of behaviors. Often, people who are depressed are tearful, irritable, or brooding. Problems sleeping (either insomnia or sleeping too much) are common. People with depression may worry unnecessarily about being sick or having a disease, or they may report physical symptoms such as headaches or other pains. Depression can seriously affect people's friendships and intimate relationships.

Depression can make people worry about having a disease, but this is not a central symptom. Depression very frequently coexists with anxiety disorders. There is a genetic predisposition in some people.

Abuse of alcohol, prescription drugs, or illegal drugs is also common among people who are depressed. The most s

SYMPTOMS

erious risk associated with Depresion is the risk of suicide: people who have tried to commit suicide are especially at risk. Individuals who have another mental disorder, such as Schizophrenia, in addition to Depression are also more likely to commit suicide.

Prevalence
Every year, more than 17 million Americans suffer some type of depressive illness. Depression does not discriminate; anyone can have it. Children, adults, and the elderly are susceptible. Nevertheless, studies do indicate that women are twice as likely to have Depression as men. Depression has significant adverse effects on children's functioning and development; among adolescents, suicide is believed to be the third leading cause of death. Depression is also common among the elderly, and can be treated as an illness distinct from loneliness or sadness that may accompany old age.

Treatment Options
Depression is a medical disease and does not respond to the usual ways we have of cheering up ourselves or others. In fact, attempts to cheer depressed individuals may have the opposite and unfortunate consequence of making them feel worse, often because they are frustrated and feel guilty that others' well-meaning efforts do not help. If a person experiences the symptoms of Depression, he or she should seek treatment from a qualified professional. The vast majority of people with Depression get better when they are treated properly, and virtually everyone gets some relief from their symptoms.

A psychiatrist or other mental health professional should conduct a thorough evaluation, including an interview. A physical examination should also be done by a primary care provider. On the basis of a complete evaluation, the appropriate treatment will be prescribed. Most likely, the treatment will be medication or psychotherapy, or both. Antidepressants usually take effect within three to six weeks after treatment has begun; it is important to give medications long enough to work, and to increase dosages or change or add medications if depression does not resolve completely.

The natural (untreated) course of a depressive episode is about nine months. Therefore, treatment should be continued for at least that length of time even though the individual feels better. If treatment is discontinued prematurely, the depression is very likely to return. Depression is also a recurring disease; the risk of an episode after a first episode is 50%; after two episodes, 67%; and after three, over 90%. Therefore, some patients prefer to continue taking antidepressant medication indefinitely.

Physical exercise is beneficial for both prevention and treatment. The same is true for the evaluation and treatment of insomnia, which is often a complicating feature.

Dysthymic disorder is a form of depression. It is described as less severe than Major Depressive Disorder, but it has many similar features. The biggest difference between Dysthymic disorder and Major Depressive Disorder is that Dysthymia is chronic and lasts for two years or more while Major Depression is episodic.

Dysthymia can be treated with medication and psychotherapy as well. Psychotherapy, or talk therapy, may be used to help the patient improve the way he or she thinks about things and deals with specific life problems. Individual, family, or couple's therapy may be recommended, depending on the patient's life experiences. If the depression is not severe, treatment can take a few weeks; if the depression has been a longstanding problem, it may take much longer, but in many cases, a patient will experience improvement in 10-15 sessions. Self-help groups and patient and family education may also be of benefit to people with Dysthymia or Depression.

ASSOCIATED FEATURES

Within days to a year after giving birth, women may experience a spectrum of psychological symptoms related to both the abrupt hormonal changes and the psychological and social demands of motherhood. The mildest of these symptoms, 'baby blues,' is not a psychiatric condition. It consists of a few days of heightened emotionality starting within days after birth and resolving spontaneously. Women may become concerned when the emotionality leads to tears, but women with 'baby blues,' and their families, need only reassurance.

Postpartum depression is sometimes a continuation of depression starting during pregnancy, but can begin up to a year after a baby is born. The symptoms, which are listed below, are much the same as those of depression occurring at any other time of life. The fact that the postpartum period is almost always associated with problems with sleep, appetite, libido, energy, and concentration makes those symptoms less useful for diagnosis at this time. Two cardinal questions are: 'Are you feeling sad most of the time?' and 'Are you unable to enjoy things that you usually enjoy?' Women with postpartum depression are preoccupied with concerns about their ability to be good mothers. Unlike an average, tired new mother, the depressed woman cannot enjoy her baby. She is often guilty and reluctant to tell her family about it because she knows she is supposed to appreciate her good fortune and be happy. Severe Postpartum Depression, or Postpartum Psychosis,that causes confusion, disorientation, delusions, and hallucinations, and can cause suicide or infanticide, is a serious medical condition demanding immediate professional attention. Fortunately, there is increasing awareness and understanding of postpartum depression among the general population.

Symptoms
In addition to the symptoms of Depression:
• Preoccupation with concerns of being a good mother;
• Inability to rest while the baby is sleeping;
• Inability to enjoy her baby accompanied with feelings of guilt.

Prevalence
Very mild depression after delivery, or 'baby blues,' affects over half, perhaps up to 90% of postpartum women. Baby blues is actually not depression at all; rather it is a common condition characterized by sensitivity and emotionality, both happy and sad. Postpartum Depression affects approximately 10% of new mothers. Postpartum Psychosis is estimated to affect one in 1,000 women after they give birth. While rare, it is possible for fathers to experience postpartum depression. Couples who adopt may also be affected.

Treatment Options
Treatment for Postpartum Depression is similar to treatment for depression in general. Possible risks of medications taken during pregnancy and breastfeeding have to be weighed against the risks of leaving the depression untreated. Women who discontinue antidepressant medication because they wish to become or have become pregnant are at a very high risk of relapse.

Associations & Agencies

317 Anxiety and Depression Association of America
8701 Georgia Avenue
Suite 412
Silver Spring, MD 20910
240-485-1001
E-mail: information@adaa.org
www.adaa.org

Charles B. Nemeroff, MD, President
Susan K. Gurley, JD, Executive Director
Tanja Jovanovic, PhD, Treasurer
Sanjay Matthew, PhD, Secretary

An international nonprofit organization committed to the use of education and research to promote the prevention, treatment, and cure of anxiety, depressive, obssesive compulsive, and other trauma related disorders. ADAA's mission is to improve the lives of all people with anxiety and mood disorders.

Year Founded: 1979

318 Brain & Behavior Research Foundation
747 Third Avenue
33rd Floor
New York, NY 10017
646-681-4888
800-829-8289
E-mail: info@bbrfoundation.org
www.www.bbrfoundation.org

Donald M. Boardman, Treasurer
Jeffrey Borenstein, MD, President and CEO
Louis Innamorato, CPA, VP and Chief Financial Officer
Faith Rothblatt, Vice President, Development

The Brain and Behavior Research Foundation awards grants aimed at advancing scientific understandings of mental health treatments and mental disorders such as depression and schizophrenia. The Brain and Behavior Research Foundation's mission is to eliminate the suffering caused by mental illness.

Year Founded: 1987

319 Center for Mental Health Services (CMHS)
Substance Abuse and Mental Health Services
Administration
5600 Fishers Lane
Rockville, MD 20857
240-276-1310
www.samhsa.gov/about-us/who-we-are/offices-centers

Anita Everett, MD, DFAPA, Director

Promotes the treatment of mental illness and emotional disorders by increasing accessibility to mental health programs; supporting outreach, treatment, rehabilitation, and support programs and networks; and encouraging the use of scientifically-based information when treating mental disorders. CMHS provides information about mental health via a toll-free number and numerous publications. Developed for users of mental health services and their families, the general public, policy makers, providers, and the media.

Year Founded: 1992

320 Depression & Bipolar Support Alliance
55 East Jackson Boulevard
Suite 490
Chicago, IL 60604

800-826-3632
E-mail: info@dbsalliance.org
www.dbsalliance.org

Roger McIntyre, Chair
Michael Pollock, Chief Executive Officer
Maria Margaglione, Programs Director
Hannah Zeller, Program Manager

The Depression and Bipolar Support Alliance is a national organization focused on improving the lives of individuals with depression, bipolar disorder, and other mood disorders. DBSA organizes peer-led support groups; educates patients, families, professionals, and the public on mental health; and works to ensure the availability of quality care for all people.

321   Freedom From Fear
308 Seaview Avenue
Staten Island, NY 10305
718-351-1717
E-mail: help@freedomfromfear.org
www.freedomfromfear.org

Mary Guardino, Founder and Executive Director

A national nonprofit organization, the mission of Freedom From Fear is to aid and counsel individuals suffering from anxiety and depressive disorders through advocacy, education, research, and community support.

Year Founded: 1984

322   Mood Disorders Center
**Department of Psychiatry and Behavioral Sciences
at Johns Hopkins**
600 North Wolfe Street
Baltimore, MD 21218
410-955-5212
877-666-3754
www.www.hopkinsmedicine.org/psychiatry/specialty_areas

J. Raymond DePaulo, MD, Co-Director
Kay Redfield Jamison, PhD, Co-Director
Mehdi Pirooznia, MD, Research Team
Peter Zandi, PhD, Research Team

The Mood Disorders Center at Johns Hopkins Medicine provides specialized clinical services to patients with mood disorders; conducts research on the causes of mood disorders, treatment responses, and brain function and structure; and educates patients, caregivers, and the public on mood disorders through symposia, publications, community presentations, and the Adolescent Depression Awareness Program.

323   National Alliance on Mental Illness
4301 Wilson Boulevard
Suite 300
Arlington, VA 22203
703-524-7600
800-950-6264
E-mail: info@nami.org
www.nami.org

Shirley J. Holloway, President
Joyce A. Campbell, First Vice President
Daniel H. Gillison, Jr., Chief Executive Officer
David Levy, Chief Financial Officer

NAMI is an organization dedicated to raising awareness on mental health and providing support and education for Americans affected by mental illness. NAMI advocates for access to services and treatment and fosters an environment

of awareness and understanding for those concerned with mental health.

Year Founded: 1979

**324   National Association for the Dually Diagnosed
(NADD)**
321 Wall Street
Kingston, NY 12401
845-331-4336
E-mail: info@thenadd.org
www.thenadd.org

Jeanne M. Farr, MA, Chief Executive Officer
Bruce Davis, President
Juanita St. Croix, Vice President
Ray Snyder, Secretary

NADD is a nonprofit organization designed to increase awareness of, and provide services for, individuals with developmental disabilities and mental illness. NADD emphasizes the importance of quality mental healthcare for people with mental health needs and offers conferences, information resources, educational programs, and training materials to professionals, parents, and organizations.

Year Founded: 1983

325   National Institute of Mental Health
6001 Executive Boulevard
Room 6200, MSC 9663
Bethesda, MD 20892-9663
866-615-6464
E-mail: nimhinfo@nih.gov
www.nimh.nih.gov

Joshua Gordon, MD, PhD, Director

The National Institute of Mental Health conducts clinical research on mental disorders and seeks to expand knowledge on mental health treatments.

**326   National Mental Health Consumers' Self-Help
Clearinghouse**
E-mail: selfhelpclearinghouse@gmail.com
www.mhselfhelp.org

Joseph Rogers, Founder and Executive Director
Susan Rogers, Director

The Clearinghouse is a peer-run national technical assistance center focused on achieving respect and equality of opportunity for those with mental illnesses. The Clearinghouse helps with the growth of the mental health consumer movement by evaluating mental health services, advocating for mental health reform, and providing consumers with news, information, publications, and consultation services.

Year Founded: 1986

327   Postpartum Support International
6706 Southwest 54th Avenue
Portland, OR 97219
503-894-9453
800-944-4773
www.postpartum.net

Wendy N. Davis, PhD, Executive Director

A nonprofit organization focused on providing support for pregnant, post-loss and postpartum women across the world. Postpartum Support International seeks to raise awareness about the emotional and mental health issues that women face during pregnancy and postpartum.

Year Founded: 1987

328 Sutcliffe Clinic
851 Fremont Avenue
Suite 110
Los Altos, CA 94024
650-941-1698
E-mail: info@sutcliffedbp.com
www.www.sutcliffeclinic.com

Trenna Sutcliffe, MD, MS, Medical Director

Sutcliffe Developmental & Behavioral Pediatrics is an organization that specializes in the treatment of ADHD, autism spectrum disorder, anxiety disorders, conduct disorders, learning disabilities, and more. Sutcliffe works with community services, school districs, and primary physicians, and provides family counseling.

329 The Balanced Mind Parent Network
Depression and Bipolar Support Alliance
55 East Jackson Boulevard
Suite 490
Chicago, IL 60604
800-826-3632
E-mail: community@dbsalliance.org
www.www.dbsalliance.org

Michael Pollock, CEO
Maria Margaglione, Programs Director

The Balanced Mind provides support, information, and assistance to families raising children with mood disorders and related conditions.

330 The Center for Family Support
2811 Zulette Avenue
Bronx, NY 10461
718-518-1500
E-mail: svernikoff@cfsny.org
www.www.cfsny.org

Steven Vernikoff, Executive Director
Barbara Greenwald, Chief Operating Officer
Jos, Martin Jara, President
Elise Geltzer, Vice President

The Center for Family Support offers assistance to individuals with developmental and related disabilities, as well as their families, and provides support services and programs that are designed to accommodate individual needs. Offers services throughout New York City, Westchester County, Long Island, and New Jersey.

Year Founded: 1954

331 Thriving Minds
10524 E Grand River Avenue
Suite 100
Brighton, MI 48116
810-225-3417
E-mail: office@thrivingminds.info
www.www.thrivingmindsbehavioralhealth.com

Amiee Kotrba, PhD, Owner
Bryce Hella, PhD, Director, Brighton Clinic
Becky Thomson, PhD, Director, Chelsea Clinic
Katelyn Reed, MS, LLP, Director, Selective Mutism

Thriving Minds is an organization that offers therapy to people with anxiety, behavioral issues, and depression. With locations in Brighton and Chelsea, Thriving Minds uses a mix of research-based interventions, such as Cognitive Behavioral Therapy; parent coaching; and school interventions in order to help children, teens, and adults deal with their anxiety.

332 Coping With Unexpected Events: Depression & Trauma
Depression & BiPolar Support Alliance
730 North Franklin Street
Suite 501
Chicago, IL 60654-7225
312-642-0049
800-826-3632
E-mail: programs@dbsalliance.org
www.dbsalliance.org

Cheryl T Magrini, MS.Ed, MTS, PhD, Chair
Allen Doederlein, President
Cindy Specht, ExecutiveVice president
Gregory E Ostfeld, Treasurer

The mission of DBSA is to provide hope, help, and support to improve the lives of people living with mood disorders. DBSA pursues and accomplishes this mission through peer-based, recovery-oriented, empowering services and resources when people want them, where they want them, and how they want to receive them.

333 Coping with Mood Changes Later in Life
Depression & Bipolar Support Alliance
730 North Franklin Street
Suite 501
Chicago, IL 60654-7225
312-642-0049
800-826-3632
www.dbsalliance.org

Sue Bergeson, President

14 pages

334 Depression
National Institute of Mental Health
6001 Executive Boulevard
Room 8184
Bethesda, MD 20892-1
301-443-4513
866-615-6464
TTY: 301-443-8431
E-mail: nimhinfo@nih.gov

This brochure gives descriptions of major depression, dysthymia and bipolar disorder (manic depression). It lists symptoms, gives possible causes, tells how depression is diagnosed and discusses available treatments. This brochure provides help and hope for the depressed person, family and friends.

23 pages

335 Depression: Help On the Way
ETR Associates
4 Carbonero Way
Scotts Valley, CA 95066-4200
831-438-4060
800-321-4407
www.etr.org

David Kitchen, MBA, Chief Financial Officer
Talita Sanders, BS, Director, Human Resources
Coleen Cantwell, MPH, Director, Business Development Pl
Matt McDowell, BS, Director, Marketing

Includes symptoms of minor depression, major depression, and seasonal affective depression; treatment options and medication, and the importance of exercise and laughter. Sold in lots of 50.

336 Depression: What Every Woman Should Know
National Institute of Mental Health
6001 Executive Boulevard
Room 8184,MSC 9663
Bethesda, MD 20892-9663
301-443-4513
866-615-6464
TTY: 301-443-8431
E-mail: nimhinfo@nih.gov
www.www.nimh.nih.gov/

This booklet discusses the symptoms of depression and some of the reasons that make women so vulnerable. It also discusses the types of therapy and where to go for help.

24 pages

337 Finding Peace of Mind: Treatment Strategies for Depression and Bipolar Disorder
Depression and Bipolar Support Alliance
730 North Franklin Street
Suite 501
Chicago, IL 60654-7225
312-642-0049
800-826-3632
www.dbsalliance.org

Helps to build a good, cooperative relationship with your doctor by explaining some of the treatments for mood disorders and how they work. Also includes a guide for medication that has been frequently prescribed and new treatments that are being investigated.

20 pages

338 Getting Better Sleep: What You Need to Know
Depression and Bipolar Support Alliance
730 North Franklin Street
Suite 501
Chicago, IL 60654-7225
312-642-0049
800-826-3632
www.dbsalliance.org

Sue Bergeson, President

Describes some causes of sleep loss, and how sleep loss relates to bipolar disorder and depression. Also provides information on how to get better sleep.

339 Introduction to Depression and Bipolar Disorder
Depression and Bipolar Support Alliance
730 North Franklin Street
Suite 501
Chicago, IL 60654-7225
312-642-0049
800-826-3632
www.dbsalliance.org

Sue Bergeson, President

Quick and easy-to-read brochure describing syptoms and treatments for mood disorders.

340 Let's Talk About Depression
National Institute of Mental Health
6001 Executive Boulevard
Room 8184,MSC 9663
Bethesda, MD 20892-9663
301-443-4513
866-615-6464
TTY: 301-443-8431

E-mail: nimhinfo@nih.gov
www.www.nimh.nih.gov/

Facts about depression, and ways to get help. Target audience is teenaged youth.

341 Major Depression in Children and Adolescents
PO Box 42557
Washington, DC 20015-557
800-789-2647
TDD: 866-889-2647
E-mail: ken@mentalhealth.org
www.mentalhealth.samhsa.gov

A Kathryn Power, MEd, Director
Edward B Searle, Deputy Director

2 pages

342 McMan's Depression and Bipolar Weekly
McMan's Depression and Bipolar Web
PO Box 5093
Kendall Park, NJ 08824-5093
E-mail: mcman@mcmanweb.com
www.mcmanweb.com

John McManamy, Editor/Publisher

Online newsletter devoted to the issues of bipolar and depression disorders. There is no charge, just for you to understand different things about the disorders.

343 Men and Depression
National Institute of Mental Health
6001 Executive Boulevard
Room 8184,MSC 9663
Bethesda, MD 20892-9663
301-443-4513
866-615-6464
TTY: 301-443-8431
E-mail: nimhinfo@nih.gov
www.www.nimh.nih.gov/

Have you known a man who is grumpy, irritable, and has no sense of humor? Maybe he drinks too much or abuses drugs. Maybe he physically or verbally abuses his wife and his kids. Maybe he works all the time, or compulsively seeks thrills in high-risk behavior. Or maybe he seems isolated, withdrawn, and no longer interested in the people or activities he used to enjoy. Perhaps this man is you. Talk to a healthcare provider about how you are feeling, and ask for help.

36 pages

344 Myths and Facts about Depression and Bipolar Disorders
Depression and Bipolar Support Alliance
730 North Franklin Street
Suite 501
Chicago, IL 60654-7225
312-642-0049
800-826-3632
www.dbsalliance.org

Gives some myths about depression and bipolar disorder and the truths that combat them.

345 New Message
Emotions Anonymous
PO Box 4245
Saint Paul, MN 55104-0245

651-647-9712
E-mail: info@EmotionsAnonymous.org
www.EmotionsAnonymous.org

Features stories and articles of recovery, plus the latest news from EA International. *$8.00*

4 per year

346 Recovering Your Mental Health: a Self-Help Guide
SAMHSA'S National Mental Health Informantion Center
1 Choke Cherry Road
Rockville, MD 20857
877-726-4727
E-mail: ken@mentalhealth.org
www.mentalhealth.samhsa.gov

Mary Ellen Copeland, Author
Edward B Searle, Deputy Director

This booklet offers tips for understanding symptoms of depression and other conditions and getting help. Also details the advantages of counseling, medications available, options for professional help, relaxation techniques and paths to positive thinking.

32 pages

347 What to do When a Friend is Depressed: Guide for Students
National Institute of Mental Health
6001 Executive Boulevard
Room 8184
Bethesda, MD 20892-1
301-443-4513
866-615-6464
TTY: 301-443-8431
E-mail: nimhinfo@nih.gov
www.www.vamh.org

This brochure offers information on depression and its symptoms and suggests things a young person can do to guide a depressed friend in finding help. It is especially good for health fairs, health clinics, and school health units.

3 pages

348 You've Just Been Diagnosed...What Now?
Depression and Bipolar Support Alliance
730 North Franklin Street
Suite 501
Chicago, IL 60654-7225
312-642-0049
800-826-3632
www.dbsalliance.org

Sue Bergeson, President

Pamphlet to help you understand about the disorder you have just been diagnosed with. Tells you basic facts about mood disorders and will help you work towards a diagnosis.

19 pages

Research Centers

349 Brain & Behavior Research Foundation
747 Third Avenue
33rd Floor
New York, NY 10017

646-681-4888
800-829-8289
E-mail: info@bbrfoundation.org
www.www.bbrfoundation.org

Donald M. Boardman, Treasurer
Jeffrey Borenstein, MD, President and CEO
Louis Innamorato, CPA, VP and Chief Financial Officer
Anne Abramson, Vice President

The Brain and Behavior Research Foundation awards grants aimed at advancing scientific understandings of mental health treatments and mental disorders such as depression and schizophrenia. The Brain and Behavior Research Foundation's mission is to eliminate the suffering caused by mental illness.

Year Founded: 1987

350 UAMS Psychiatric Research Institute
University of Arkansas for Medical Sciences
4224 Shuffield Drive
Little Rock, AR 72205
501-526-8100
www.psychiatry.uams.edu

Donald R Bobbitt, President
William Bowes,MS, Vice Chancellor,Finance And CFO
Roxane A Townsend,MD, Chief Executive Officer
Christina L Clark,BA, Chief of Staff

Combining research, education and clinical services into one facility, PRI offers inpatiend and outpatient services, with 40 psychiatric beds, therapy options, and specialized treatment for specific disorders, including: addictive eating, anxiety, deppressive and post-traumatic stress disorders. Research focuses on evidence-based care takes into consideration the education of future medical personnel while relying on research scientists to provide innovative forms of treatment. PRI includes the Center for Addiction Research as well as a methadone clinic.

351 University of Texas: Mental Health Clinical Research Center
6363 Forest Park Road
7th Floor, Suite 749
Dallas, TX 75390-9121
214-648-3111
www.utsouthwestern.edu

Research activity of major and atypical depression.

352 Yale Mood Disorders Research Program
Department of Psychiatry
300 George Street
Suite 901
New Haven, CT 06511-6624
203-785-2090
www.psychiatry.yale.edu

John H Krystal, Chair
Rajita Sinha, Chief,Psychology Section

MDRP is dedicated to understanding the science of mood disorders, including bipolar disorder and depression. The MDRP brings together a multi-disciplinary group of scientists from across the Yale campus in a highly collaborative research effort. Goals of the MDRP include the identification of biological markers for mood disorders and discovery of new treatment strategies.

Support Groups & Hot Lines

353 Depressed Anonymous
PO Box 17414
Louisville, KY 40217
502-569-1989
www.depressedanon.com

Formed to provide therapeutic resources for depressed individuals of all ages. Works with the chronically depressed and those recently discharged from health facilities who were treated for depression.

354 Emotions Anonymous International Service Center
2233 University Ave W
Ste 402
Saint Paul, MN 55114-1629
651-647-9712
E-mail: info@emotionsanonymous.org
www.emotionsanonymous.org

Elaine Weber Nelson, Executive Director

A community-based organization to provide support managing mental health difficulties. Groups meet weekly to share experiences, strength, and hope.

Year Founded: 1971

355 Recovery International
1415 W. 22nd Street
Tower Floor
Oak Brook, IL 60523
312-337-5661
866-221-0302
E-mail: info@recoveryinternational.org
www.www.recoveryinternational.org

Sandra K. Wilcoxon, Chief Executive Officer
Joanne Lampey, President
Nicole Cilento, Vice President
Hal Casey, Treasurer

Recovery International is an organization that uses a peer-to-peer, self-help training system developed by Abraham Low in order to help individuals with mental health issues lead more productive lives.

Year Founded: 1937

Video & Audio

356 A Madman's Journal
Educational Training Videos
136 Granville St
Suite 200
Gahanna, OH 43230
www.educationaltrainingvideos.com

For two years, the narrator of this program went through a nightmare, feeling a self-hatred and worthlessness beyond love and redemption that he described as the concentration camp of the mind. This video presents one man's attempt to convey the ordeal of severe depression by writing a memoir about the experience.

357 Beating Depression
Educational Training Videos
136 Granville St
Suite 200
Gahanna, OH 43230
www.educationaltrainingvideos.com

This program comes to grips with depression through the experiences of five patients whose backgrounds span the socioeconomic spectrum. Three cases of chronic depression, one of which is complicated by borderline personality disorder and another by alcohol abuse, and two cases of bipolar disorder, one of which is extreme, are presented.

358 Bundle of Blues
Fanlight Productions
32 Court Street
21st Floor
Brooklyn, NY 11201
718-488-8900
800-876-1710
E-mail: info@fanlight.com
www.fanlight.com

Serena Down, Author

The stories in this thoughtful documentary represent a range of experiences from minor postpartum depression through postpartum psychosis. It stresses that PDD can happen to any new mother, but that it can be managed. 13 minutes.

359 Clinical Impressions: Identifying Mental Illness
Educational Training Videos
136 Granville St
Suite 200
Gahanna, OH 43230
www.educationaltrainingvideos.com

How long can mental illness stay hidden, especially from the eyes of trained experts? This program rejoins a group of ten adults- five of them healthy and five of them with histories of mental illness- as psychiatric specialists try to spot and correctly diagnose the latter. Administering a series of collaborative and one-on-one tests, including assessments of personality type, physical self-image, and rational thinking, the panel gradually makes decisions about who suffers from depression, bipolar disorder, bulimia, and social anxiety.

360 Coping with Depression
NewHarbinger Publications
5674 Shattuck Avenue
Oakland, CA 94609-1662
510-652-0215
800-748-6273
E-mail: customerservice@newharbinger.com
www.newharbinger.com

Matthew McKay, Owner

60 minute videotape that offers a powerful message of hope for anyone struggling with depression. *$39.95*

ISBN 1-879237-62-8

361 Coping with Stress
Educational Video Network, Inc.
1401 19th Street
Huntsville, TX 77340
936-295-5767
800-762-0060
www.www.evndirect.com

Stress affects everyone, both emotionally and physically. For some, mismanaged stress can result in substance abuse, violence, or even suicide. This program answers the question, How can a person cope with stress?

362 Covert Modeling & Covert Reinforcement
NewHarbinger Publications
5674 Shattuck Avenue
Oakland, CA 94609-1662
510-652-0215
800-748-6273
E-mail: customerservice@newharbinger.com
www.newharbinger.com

Matthew McKay, Owner

Based on the essential book of cognitive behavioral techniques for effecting change in your life, Thoughts & Feelings. Learn step-by-step protocols for controlling destructive behaviors such as anxiety, obsessional thinking, uncontrolled anger, and depression. *$ 11.95*

ISBN 0-934986-29-0

363 Dark Glasses and Kaleidoscopes: Living with Manic Depression
Depression and Bipolar Support Alliance
730 N Franklin Street
Suite 501
Chicago, IL 60654-7225
312-642-0049
800-826-3632
www.dbsalliance.org

Allen Doederlein, President
Cindy Specht, Executive Vice President
Lisa Goodale, Vice President, Peer Support Ser
Nancy Heffernan, Vice President, Finance and Admi

Dr. Kowatch speaks about the prevalence, diagnosis, comorbidity, medication treatment, and outcome of child/adolescent bipolar disorder. He addresses some of the unique traits of cild bipolar, as well as some factors that make it difficult to diagnose. He covers treatment options for both the manic and depressive phases in detail, using clinical studies as evidence. *$5.00*

364 Day for Night: Recognizing Teenage Depression
DRADA-Depression and Related Affective Disorders Association
2330 W Joppa Road
Suite 100
Lutherville, MD 21093-4614
410-583-2919
www.drada.org

Catherine Pollock, Executive Director
Sallie Mink, Director Education
Vice Preside

In an effort to help teens gain a better understanding of depression, this video was created to build awareness of the illness and, in the process, save lives. Offering an in-depth look at the signs, symptoms and treatment of teenage depression, this video includes interviews with young people who are dealing with clinical depression and bipolar disorder. Featuring their families and friends, as well as interviews with health professionals, the video's goal is to provide education, support and hope to those suffering from this debilitating yet treatable disease. *$22.50*

365 Dealing with Depression
Educational Video Network, Inc.
1401 19th Street
Huntsville, TX 77340

936-295-5767
800-762-0060
www.www.evndirect.com

As more and more young people are falling victim to depression, it is important to understand what causes it and to know how to get the help that can rid a person of this life-wrecking affliction.

366 Depression & Anxiety Management
NewHarbinger Publications
5674 Shattuck Avenue
Oakland, CA 94609-1662
510-652-0215
800-748-6273
E-mail: customerservice@newharbinger.com
www.newharbinger.com

Matthew McKay, Owner

Offers step-by-step help for identifying the thoughts that make one anxious and depressed, confronting unrealistic and distorted thinking, and replacing negative mental patterns with healthy, realistic thinking. *$11.95*

ISBN 1-879237-46-6

367 Depression: Fighting the Dragon
Fanlight Productions
32 Court Street
21st Floor
Brooklyn, NY 11201
718-488-8900
800-876-1710
E-mail: info@fanlight.com
www.fanlight.com

Sue Ridout, Author

Follows five people who have struggled for years to overcome this debilitating condition. Two of the five have family histories of the disease. Their moving personal stories are enriched by the perspectives of leading researchers, and by glimpses of the sophisticated brain-imaging technologies which now enable us to see what is happening in the human brain during depression and its treatment. *$149.00*

368 FRONTLINE: The Released
PBS
2100 Crystal Drive
Arlington, VA 22202
www.pbs.org

Will Lyman, Actor
Narrator
Miri Navasky, Director
Karen O'Connor, Director

The documentary states that of the 700,000 inmates released from American prisons each year, half of them have mental disabilities. This work focused on those with severe problems who keep entering and exiting prison. Full of good information on the challenges they face with mental illnesses; housing, employment, stigmatization, and socialization.

369 Living with Depression and Manic Depression
NewHarbinger Publications
5674 Shattuck Avenue
Oakland, CA 94609-1662
510-652-0215
800-748-6273

E-mail: customerservice@newharbinger.com
www.newharbinger.com

Matthew McKay, Owner

Describes a program based on years of research and hundreds of interviews with depressed persons. Warm, helpful, and engaging, this tape validates the feelings of people with depression while it encourages positive change. *$11.95*

ISBN 1-879237-63-6

370 Mental Disorder
Educational Training Videos
136 Granville St
Suite 200
Gahanna, OH 43230
www.educationaltrainingvideos.com

What is abnormality? Using the case studies of two young women; one who has depression, one who has an anxiety disorder; as a springboard, this program presents three psychological perspective on mental disorder.

371 No More Shame: Understanding Schizophrenia, Depression, and Addiction
Educational Training Videos
136 Granville St
Suite 200
Gahanna, OH 43230
www.educationaltrainingvideos.com

These programs examine research about the physiological, psychological, sociological, and cultural aspects of these disorders and their treatments. The goal of these programs is to explain what we do and do not know about each of these conditions, as well as to destigmatize the disorders by presenting them in the context of the same research process that is applied to all medical disorders.

372 Understanding Mental Illness
Educational Video Network, Inc.
1401 19th Street
Huntsville, TX 77340
936-295-5767
800-762-0060
www.www.evndirect.com

Contains information and classifications of mental illness. Mental illness can strike anyone, at any age. Learn about various organic and functional mental disorders as discussed and their causes and symptoms, and learn where to seek help for a variety of mental health concerns.

373 Why Isn't My Child Happy? Video Guide About Childhood Depression
ADD WareHouse
300 NW 70th Avenue
Suite 102
Plantation, FL 33317-2360
954-792-8100
800-233-9273
E-mail: websales@addwarehouse.com
www.addwarehouse.com

Sam Goldstein, PhD, Author

The first of its kind, this new video deals with childhood depression. Informative and frank about this common problem, this book offers helpful guidance for parents and professionals trying to better understand childhood depression. 110 minutes. *$55.00*

Web Sites

374 www.befrienders.org
Samaritans International

Support, helplines, and advice.

375 www.blarg.net/~charlatn/voices
Voices of Depression

Compilation of writings by people suffering from depression.

376 www.cfsny.org
Center for Family Support (CFS)

Devoted to providing support and assistance to individuals with developmental and related disabilities, and to the family members who care for them.

377 www.cyberpsych.org
CyberPsych

Hosts the American Psychoanalysts Foundation, American Association of Suicideology, Society for the Exploration of Psychotherapy Intergration, and Anxiety Disorders Association of America. Also subcategories of the anxiety disorders, as well as general information, including panic disorder, phobias, obsessive compulsive disorder (OCD), social phobia, generalized anxiety disorder, post traumatic stress disorder, and phobias of childhood. Book reviews and links to web pages sharing the topics.

378 www.dbsalliance.org
Depression & Bi-Polar Support Alliance

Mental health news updates and local support group information.

379 www.emdr.com
EMDR Institute, Inc.

Discusses EMDR-Eye Movement Desensitization and Reprocessing-as an innovative clinical treatment for trauma, including sexual abuse, domestic violence, combat, crime, and those suffering from a number of other disorders including depressions, addictions, phobias and a variety of self-esteem issues.

380 www.goodwill-suncoast.org
Suncoast Residential Training Center

Group home that serves individuals diagnosed as developmentally disabled, with a secondary diagnosis of psychiatric difficulties as evidenced by problem behavior.

381 www.ifred.org
National Foundation for Depressive Illness

Support, helplines, and advice.

382 www.klis.com/chandler/pamphlet/dep/
Jim Chandler MD

White paper on depression in children and adolesents.

383 www.manicdepressive.org
The Massachusetts General Hospital Bipolar Clinic/Research Program

Dedicated to providing quality clinical care, conducting clinically informative research, and educating colleagues, patients and the community.

384 **www.med.yale.edu**
Yale University School of Medicine

Research center dedicated to understanding the science of mood disorders.

385 **www.mentalhealth.Samhsa.Gov**
Center for Mental Health Services Knowledge Exchange Network

Information about resources, technical assistance, research, training, networks, and other federal clearinghouses, fact sheets and materials.

386 **www.mhselfhelp.org**
National Mental Health Consumer's Self-Help Clearinghouse

Encourages the development and growth of consumer self-help groups.

387 **www.nami.org**
National Alliance on Mental Illness

From its inception in 1979, NAMI has been dedicated to improving the lives of individuals and families affected by mental illness.

388 **www.nimh.nih.gov/publicat/depressionmenu.cfm**
National Institute of Mental Health

National Institute of Mental Health offers brochures organized by topic. Depression discusses symptoms, diagnosis, and treatment options.

389 **www.nimh.nih.gov/publist/964033.htm**
National Institute of Mental Health

Discusses depression in older years, symptoms, treatment, going for help.

390 **www.planetpsych.com**
Planetpsych.com

Learn about disorders, their treatments and other topics in psychology. Articles are listed under the related topic areas. Ask a therapist a question for free, or view the directory of professionals in your area. If you are a therapist sign up for the directory. Current features, self-help, interactive, and newsletter archives.

391 **www.psychcentral.com**
Psych Central

Personalized one-stop index for psychology, support, and mental health issues, resources, and people on the Internet.

392 **www.psychologyinfo.com/depression**
Psychology Information On-line: Depression

Information on diagnosis, therapy, and medication.

393 **www.psycom.net/depression.central.html**
Dr. Ivan's Depression Central

Medication-oriented site. Clearinghouse on all types of depressive disorders.

394 **www.queendom.com/selfhelp/depression/depression.html**
Queendom

Articles, information on medication and support groups.

395 **www.shpm.com**
Self Help Magazine

Articles and discussion forums, resource links.

396 **www.store.samhsa.gov**
Substance Abuse and Mental Health Services Administration

Resources on mental disorders as well as treatment and recovery.

397 **www.thebalancedmind.org/flipswitch**
Flipswitch

Educational site dedicated to helping teens, parents and teachers understand symptoms of teenage depression. Provides resources for those ready to seek help.

398 **www.thenadd.org**
National Association for the Dually Diagnosed (NADD)

An association for persons with developmental disabilities and mental health needs.

399 **www.utsouthwestern.edu**
UT Southwestern Medical Center

Research to find the corticosteroid effects on the human brain, dual-diagnosed patients, and depression in asthma patients.

400 **www.wingofmadness.com**
Wing of Madness: A Depression Guide

Accurate information, advice, support, and personal experiences.

Disruptive, Impulse-Control and Conduct Disorders

Introduction

Most people have experienced a situation in which they have angry or aggressive outbursts. As is the case with many conditions, there is a cultural element associated with aggressive interactions. This kind of behavior only becomes a disorder when the behavior is frequent, long lasting, occurs across several situations, and causes significant disruption in the person's life. Impulse Control Disorders include Kleptomania, Pyromania, Conduct Disorder, Intermittent Explosive Disorder, and Oppositional Defiance Disorder. Behaviors associated with these disorders can include physical harm to people or animals, damage to property, deceitfulness or theft, and extreme violations of rules. It is important to note that troublesome behavior can also result from adverse circumstances; the circumstances need to be fully investigated, and attempts to rectify adversity made, before an impulse control disorder is diagnosed. The diagnosis can be divided into two types, depending on the age of diagnosis: childhood-onset type and adolescent-onset type. Early diagnosis and intensive, individualized therapy is necessary to help children and adolescents with conduct disorder make a successful transition to adulthood.

SYMPTOMS

Disruptive and Impulse-Control Disorders

Kleptomania
• Recurrent failure to resist the impulse to steal objects, often objects that the individual could have paid for or does not particularly want;
• Theft is not due to anger, delusions, or hallucinations;
• Awareness that stealing is senseless and wrong;
• Feelings of depression and guilt after stealing.

Kleptomania should not be confused with thefts which are deliberate or for personal gain. Kleptomania is strongly associated with depression, anxiety disorders, and feeding and eating disorders.

Kleptomania is very rare, but is it usually kept secret, and is more common among females than males.

Behavior therapy, which focuses on changing the behavior, has had some success.

Pyromania
• Purposefully setting fires more than once;
• Increased tension before the deed;
• Fascination with and curiosity about fire;
• Pleasure or relief when setting or watching fires;
• The fire is not set for financial gain or revenge.

Pyromaniacs make complicated preparations for setting a fire, seem not to care about consequences, and may get pleasure from the destruction. Many who set fires often have symptoms of ADHD or Adjustment Disorders. It is more common among males with alcohol, learning and societal problems. Treatment is difficult, and may include anger management, problem solving, and behavior therapy.

Oppositional Defiant Disorder
• Refuses to comply with authority figures, has trouble with rules and requests;
• Loses temper easily;
• Can act spitefully.

The symptoms of ODD must be more severe than is the norm and cause problems at school/work. The person must demonstrate these behaviors with at least one person who is not their sibling at least once a week for six months or longer. For children, they must exhibit the symptoms most days for at least six months. It is important for a person to have a thorough evaluation to eliminate any other causes for their behavioral problems, such as ADHD, anxiety, depression, or abusive situations.

ODD is generally treated with cognitive behavioral therapy and training for parents and children.

Intermittent Explosive Disorder
• Recurrent instances of aggressive behavior that are
• Impulsive;
• Out of proportion to the triggering event;
• Cause feelings of guilt and remorse after aggressive behavior;

Intermittent Explosive Disorder is associated with substance abuse disorders and certain neurological disorders, but should not be confused with the aggression seen in other forms of psychiatric and organic brain disorders, such as head trauma, substance withdrawal, and borderline personality disorder. Intermittent Explosive Disorder is a rare disorder, that is more common in men than women. Symptoms usually begin to emerge between late childhood and the early 20s. Children under the age of six are not diagnosed with this disorder.

Explosive Disorder is generally treated with cognitive behavior therapy.

Conduct Disorder
• Aggression to people and animals, including bullying, fighting, using weapons, physical cruelty to people and animals, stealing, or forcing someone into sexual activity;
• Destruction of property;
• Deceitfulness and theft, including breaking and entering, lying to obtain goods/favors, or shoplifting;
• Violations of rules, including staying out past curfews, running away from home, and truancy from school.

Conduct disorder is often associated with early onset of sexual activity, drinking and smoking. The disorder leads to school disruption, problems with the police, sexually transmitted diseases, unplanned pregnancy, and injury from accidents and fights. Suicide and suicidal attempts are more common among adolescents with Conduct Disorder, probably both because they have a history of abuse and neglect and because their behavior results in adverse consequences. Individuals with Conduct Disorder appear to have little remorse for their acts, though they may learn that expressing guilt can diminish punishment; and they often show little or no empathy for the feelings, wishes, and well-being of others.

PREVALENCE

Prevalence of Conduct Disorder appears to have increased in recent years. The disorder seems to be more common in males than females. For males under 18 years of age, rates range from six percent to sixteen percent; for females, rates range from two percent to nine percent. Onset can be before the age of ten, or in adolescence.

TREATMENT OPTIONS

There is no agreement on the best way to treat conduct disorder. Approaches range from incarceration and 'tough love,' to psychotherapy (usually cognitive behavioral therapy with an emphasis on anger management techniques) and medication. This condition is stressful for family members of the affected child or adolescent; it is crucial that they are supported and involved in the treatment. It is also crucial to evaluate the possible impact of discrimination and abuse, especially with regards to racism.

Associations & Agencies

402 American Association of Children's Residential Centers

648 North Plankinton Avenue
Suite 245
Milwaukee, WI 53203
877-332-2272
E-mail: info@togetherthevoice.org
www.togetherthevoice.org

Dana K. Dorn, President
Trish Cocoros, Treasurer
Kari Sisson, Executive Director

The American Association of Children's Residential Centers is a national organization focused on providing residential therapeutic treatment for children and adolescents with behavioral health disorders.

Year Founded: 1956

403 Association for Behavioral and Cognitive Therapies

305 Seventh Avenue
16th Floor
New York, NY 10001
212-647-1890
www.abct.org

Mary Jane Eimer, CAE, Executive Director
David Teisler, CAE, Deputy Director

A multidisciplinary organization dedicated to utilizing and advancing scientific approaches in the understanding and prevention of human behavioral and cognitive problems.

Year Founded: 1966

404 Center for Mental Health Services (CMHS) Substance Abuse and Mental Health Services Administration

5600 Fishers Lane
Rockville, MD 20857
240-276-1310
www.samhsa.gov/about-us/who-we-are/offices-centers

Anita Everett, MD, DFAPA, Director

Promotes the treatment of mental illness and emotional disorders by increasing accessibility to mental health programs; supporting outreach, treatment, rehabilitation, and support programs and networks; and encouraging the use of scientifically-based information when treating mental disorders. CMHS provides information about mental health via a toll-free number and numerous publications. Developed for users of mental health services and their families, the general public, policy makers, providers, and the media.

Year Founded: 1992

405 Goodwill's Community Employment Services
Goodwill Industries-Suncoast, Inc.

10596 Gandy Blvd.
St. Petersburg, FL 33702
727-523-1512
888-279-1988
TDD: 727-579-1068
www.goodwill-suncoast.org

Sandra Young, Chair
Louise Lopez, Sr. Vice Chair
Dominic Macrone, Board Secretary

The St. Petersburg headquarters serves ten counties in the state of Florida. Their mission is to help people with disabilities gain employment through training programs, employment services, and affordable housing.

Year Founded: 1954

406 Mental Health America

500 Montgomery Street
Suite 820
Alexandria, VA 22314
703-684-7722
800-969-6642
www.mentalhealthamerica.net

Schroeder Stribling, President & CEO
Sachin Doshi, Sr. Dir., Finance & Operations

Mental Health America is a community-based nonprofit organization committed to enabling the mental wellness of all Americans. MHA advocates for greater access to quality health services and seeks to educate individuals on identifying symptoms, as well as intervention and prevention.

Year Founded: 1909

407 National Association for the Dually Diagnosed (NADD)

321 Wall Street
Kingston, NY 12401
845-331-4336
E-mail: info@thenadd.org
www.thenadd.org

Jeanne M. Farr, MA, Chief Executive Officer
Bruce Davis, President
Juanita St. Croix, Vice President
Ray Snyder, Secretary

NADD is a nonprofit organization designed to increase awareness of, and provide services for, individuals with developmental disabilities and mental illness. NADD emphasizes the importance of quality mental healthcare for people with mental health needs and offers conferences, information resources, educational programs, and training materials to professionals, parents, and organizations.

Year Founded: 1983

408 National Mental Health Consumers' Self-Help Clearinghouse

E-mail: selfhelpclearinghouse@gmail.com
www.mhselfhelp.org

Joseph Rogers, Founder and Executive Director
Susan Rogers, Director

The Clearinghouse is a peer-run national technical assistance center focused on achieving respect and equality of opportunity for those with mental illnesses. The Clearinghouse helps with the growth of the mental health consumer movement by evaluating mental health services, advocating for mental health reform, and providing consumers with news, information, publications, and consultation services.

Year Founded: 1986

409 The Balanced Mind Parent Network
Depression and Bipolar Support Alliance
55 East Jackson Boulevard
Suite 490
Chicago, IL 60604
800-826-3632
E-mail: community@dbsalliance.org
www.www.dbsalliance.org

Michael Pollock, CEO
Maria Margaglione, Programs Director

The Balanced Mind provides support, information, and assistance to families raising children with mood disorders and related conditions.

410 The Center for Family Support
2811 Zulette Avenue
Bronx, NY 10461
718-518-1500
E-mail: svernikoff@cfsny.org
www.www.cfsny.org

Steven Vernikoff, Executive Director
Barbara Greenwald, Chief Operating Officer
Jos, Martin Jara, President
Elise Geltzer, Vice President

The Center for Family Support offers assistance to individuals with developmental and related disabilities, as well as their families, and provides support services and programs that are designed to accommodate individual needs. Offers services throughout New York City, Westchester County, Long Island, and New Jersey.

Year Founded: 1954

411 The Shulman Center for Compulsive Theft,
Spending & Hoarding
PO Box 250008
Franklin, MI 48025
248-358-8508
E-mail: terrenceshulman@theshulmancenter.com
www.theshulmancenter.com

Terrence Shulman, JD, LMSW, CPC, Founder and Director

The Shulman Center provides counseling and professional services designed to help individuals with compulsive stealing, spending, and hoarding disorders. The Shulman Center supports individuals, families, companies, and communities through education, assessment, and treatment.

Year Founded: 1992

412 The TLC Foundation for Body-Focused
Repetitive Behaviors
716 Soquel Avenue
Suite A
Santa Cruz, CA 95062
831-457-1004
E-mail: info@bfrb.org
www.www.bfrb.org

The TLC Foundation, formerly The Trichotillomania Learning Center, serves to raise awareness on trichotillomania and related body-focused repetitive disorders, support research, and disseminate scientifically-based

information about trichotillomania, and offer support services for individuals and families affected by the disorders. The TLC Foundation aims to eliminate the suffering caused by trichotillomania and body-focused repetitive behaviors.

Year Founded: 1991

Periodicals & Pamphlets

413 Conduct Disorder in Children and Adolescents
PO Box 42557
Washington, DC 20015-557
800-789-2647
TDD: 866-889-2647
E-mail: ken@mentalhealth.org
www.mentalhealth.samhsa.gov

G Pirooz Shovelar, Editor
Edward B Searle, Deputy Director

414 pages

414 Mental Health Matters
E-mail: ryan@mhmatters.com
www.mental-health-matters.com

Sean Bennick, Editor

Mental Health Matters serves as a source of information about mental health issues. Provides mental health consumers, professionals, and students with resources on disorders, symptoms, treatment, and medications.

415 Mental, Emotional, and Behavior Disorders in
Children and Adolescents
SAMHSA'S National Mental Health Information
Center
PO Box 42557
Washington, DC 20015-557
800-789-2647
TDD: 866-889-2647
E-mail: ken@mentalhealth.org

A Kathryn Power, MEd, Director
Edward B Searle, Deputy Director

This fact sheet describes mental, emotional, and behavioral problems that can occur during childhood and adolescence and discusses related treatment, support services, and research.

4 pages

416 Treatment of Children with Mental Disorders
National Institute of Mental Health
6001 Executive Boulevard
Room 8184,MSC 9663
Bethesda, MD 20892-9663
301-443-4513
866-615-6464
TTY: 301-443-8431
E-mail: nimhinfo@nih.gov
www.www.nimh.nih.gov/

Francis S Collins, MD, PhD

A short booklet that contains questions and answers about therapy for children with mental disorders. Includes a chart of mental disorders and medications used.

Research Centers

417 Child & Family Center
Menninger Clinic
21545 Centre Pointe Parkway
Santa Clarita, CA 91350
661-259-9439
800-351-9058
E-mail: webmaster@menninger.edu
www.www.childfamilycenter.org/

Steven Zimmer, Board Chair
Darrellÿ Paulk, CEO
Bill Cooper, Vice Chair
Joan Aschoff, Executive Vice President of Prog

The Center's goals: to further develop emerging understanding of the impact of childhood maltreatment and abuse; to chart primary prevention strategies that will foster healthy patterns of caregiving and attachment and reduce the prevalence of maltreatment and abuse; to develop secondary prevention strategies that will promote early detection of attachment-related problems and effective interventions to avert the development of chronic and severe disorders; and to develop more effective treatment approaches for those individuals whose early attachment problems have eventuated in severe psychopathology.

Year Founded: 1976

418 Impulse Control Disorders Clinic
University of Minnesota
231 Pillsbury Drive,South East.
240 Williamson Hall
Minneapolis, MN 55455-0213
612-625-2008
800-752-1000
TTY: 612-625-9051

A group of doctors and trainees engaged in research in Impulse-Control Disorders (ICD) and Obsessive-Compulsive Disorder (OCD) and treating patients in a specialty clinic. Conducts research to elucidate pathophysiological links to the ICD and OCD and conducts clinical trials to come up with better and improved treatments for patients.

Support Groups & Hot Lines

419 Gam-Anon Family Groups International Service Office, Inc.
PO Box 307
Massapequa Park, NY 11762
718-352-1671
E-mail: gamanonoffice@gam-anon.org
www.gam-anon.org

A 12-step self-help fellowship of men and women who have been affected by the gambling problems of a loved one. Their program works through literature and meetings. At meetings individuals learn how other members applied the Gam-Anon program to find serenity and a more normal way of thinking and living.

420 Gamblers Anonymous
PO Box 17173
Los Angeles, CA 90017
626-960-3500
E-mail: isomain@gamblersanonymous.org
www.gamblersanonymous.org

Fellowship of men and women who share their experience, strength and hope with each other so that they may solve their common problem and help others recover from a gambling problem.

Year Founded: 1957

421 Kleptomaniacs Anonymous
The Shulman Center for Compulsive Theft, Spending & Hoarding
PO Box 250008
Franklin, MI 48025
248-358-8508
www.kleptomaniacsanonymous.com

Terrence Shulman,JD,LMSW, Founder/Director

Kleptomaniacs And Shoplifters Anonymous (CASA) is a unique, independent and secular weekly self-help group.

Year Founded: 1992

422 The TLC Foundation for Body-Focused Repetitive Behaviors
716 Soquel Avenue
Suite A
Santa Cruz, CA 95062
831-457-1004
E-mail: info@bfrb.org
www.www.bfrb.org

The TLC Foundation, formerly The Trichotillomania Learning Center, serves to raise awareness on trichotillomania and related body-focused repetitive disorders, support research, and disseminate scientifically-based information about trichotillomania, and offer support services for individuals and families affected by the disorders. The TLC Foundation aims to eliminate the suffering caused by trichotillomania and body-focused repetitive behaviors.

Year Founded: 1991

Video & Audio

423 A Desperate Act
Trichotillomania Learning Center
207 McPherson Street
Suite H
Santa Cruz, CA 95060-5863
831-457-1004
www.trich.org

Joanna Heitz, President
Brenda Cameron, Secretary
Deborah M. Kleinman, Treasurer
Jennifer Raikes, Executive Director

A performance artist with TTM discusses her experiences in front of a live audience.

424 Active Parenting Now
Active Parenting Publishers
1220 Kennestone Circle
Suite 130
Marrietta, GA 30066
770-429-0565
800-825-0060
E-mail: cservice@activeparenting.com

Michael Popkin, PhD, Author

A complete video-based parenting education program curriculum. Helps parents of children ages two to twelve raise responsible, courageous children. Emphasizes nonviolent discipline, conflict resolution and improved communication. With Leader's Guide, videotapes, Parent's Guide and more. Also available in Spanish. *$ 349.00*

ISBN 1-880283-89-1

425 Addictive Behavior: Drugs, Food and Relationships
Educational Video Network, Inc.
1401 19th Street
Huntsville, TX 77340
936-295-5767
800-762-0060
www.www.evndirect.com

Addiction is a serious and very real problem for many people. It can come in the forms of caffeine, heroin, food or love. Find out what makes one person more likely to develop an addiction than someone else, learn about the different types of addiction, the signs and the consequences.

426 Aggression Replacement Training Video: A Comprehensive Intervention for Aggressive Youth
Research Press
PO Box 7886
PO Box 9177
Champaign, IL 61826
217-352-3273
800-519-2707
E-mail: rp@researchpress.com
www.researchpress.com

Dr. Barry Glick, Author
Dr. John C. Gibbs, Author

This staff training video illustrates the training procedures in the Aggression Replacement Training (ART) book.It features scenes of adolescents participating in group sessions for each of ART's three interventions: Prosocial Skills, Anger Control, and Moral Reasoning. A free copy of the book accompanies the video program. *$35.95*

426 pages ISBN 0-878226-37-5

427 Anger Management-Enhanced Edition
Educational Video Network, Inc.
1401 19th Street
Huntsville, TX 77340
936-295-5767
800-762-0060
www.www.evndirect.com

Learn what causes anger and understand why our bodies react as they do when we're angry. Effective techniques for assuaging anger are discussed.

428 Clinical Impressions: Identifying Mental Illness
Educational Training Videos
136 Granville St
Suite 200
Gahanna, OH 43230
www.educationaltrainingvideos.com

How long can mental illness stay hidden, especially from the eyes of trained experts? This program rejoins a group of ten adults- five of them healthy and five of them with histories of mental illness- as psychiatric specialists try to spot and correctly diagnose the latter. Administering a series of collaborative and one-on-one tests, including assessments of personality type, physical self-image, and rational thinking, the panel gradually makes decisions about who suffers

from depression, bipolar disorder, bulimia, and social anxiety.

429 Coping with Stress
Educational Video Network, Inc.
1401 19th Street
Huntsville, TX 77340
936-295-5767
800-762-0060
www.www.evndirect.com

Stress affects everyone, both emotionally and physically. For some, mismanaged stress can result in substance abuse, violence, or even suicide. This program answers the question, How can a person cope with stress?

430 Dealing with ADHD: Attention Deficit/Hyperactivity
Educational Video Network, Inc.
1401 19th Street
Huntsville, TX 77340
936-295-5767
800-762-0060
www.www.evndirect.com

Learn about attention deficit/hyperactivity disorder and learn what factors are thought to contribute to the development of this disorder. Other disorders that commonly co-exist with ADHD will be identified. The impulsivity and risk-taking behaviors of ADHD teens will be focused upon and tips that ADHD students can use to succeed academically will be provided. Laws that require schools to make special accommodations for ADHD students will be reviewed, and viewers will learn how to contact organizations that exist to help people who are dealing with ADHD.

431 FRONTLINE: The Released
PBS
2100 Crystal Drive
Arlington, VA 22202
www.pbs.org

Will Lyman, Actor
Narrator
Miri Navasky, Director
Karen O'Connor, Director

The documentary states that of the 700,000 inmates released from American prisons each year, half of them have mental disabilities. This work focused on those with severe problems who keep entering and exiting prison. Full of good information on the challenges they face with mental illnesses; housing, employment, stigmatization, and socialization.

432 Mental Disorder
Educational Training Videos
136 Granville St
Suite 200
Gahanna, OH 43230
www.educationaltrainingvideos.com

What is abnormality? Using the case studies of two young women; one who has depression, one who has an anxiety disorder; as a springboard, this program presents three psychological perspective on mental disorder.

433 No More Shame: Understanding Schizophrenia, Depression, and Addiction
Educational Training Videos
136 Granville St
Suite 200
Gahanna, OH 43230
www.educationaltrainingvideos.com

These programs examine research about the physiological, psychological, sociological, and cultural aspects of these disorders and their treatments. The goal of these programs is to explain what we do and do not know about each of these conditions, as well as to destigmatize the disorders by presenting them in the context of the same research process that is applied to all medical disorders.

434 Obsessions: Understanding OCD
Educational Training Videos
136 Granville St
Suite 200
Gahanna, OH 43230
www.educationaltrainingvideos.com

Are compulsive hair-pulling, hand-washing, and even gambling learned behaviors or inherited diseases? Where do obsessions come from and how can they be managed so they do not dominate a person's life? This two-part series attempts to understand the roots of obsessive-compulsive disorder, or OCD, and looks at both standard and experimental treatment options.

435 Our Personal Stories
Trichotillomania Learning Center
207 McPherson Street
Suite H
Santa Cruz, CA 95060-5863
831-457-1004
www.trich.org

Joanna Heitz, President
Brenda Cameron, Secretary
Deborah M. Kleinman, Treasurer
Jennifer Raikes, Executive Director

Documentary detailing 8 womens' personal experiences with TTM. *$28.00*

436 Trichotillomania: Overview and Introduction to HRT
Trichotillomania Learning Center
207 McPherson Street
Suite H
Santa Cruz, CA 95060-5863
831-457-1004
www.trich.org

Joanna Heitz, President
Brenda Cameron, Secretary
Deborah M. Kleinman, Treasurer
Jennifer Raikes, Executive Director

A lecture on Behavior Therapy and Habit Reversal Training for TTM. *$30.00*

437 Understanding & Managing the Defiant Child
Courage to Change
1 Huntington Quadrangle
Suite: 1N03
Melville, NY 11747
800-962-1141
www.couragetochange.com

Russell A Barkley, PhD, Presenter

Understanding and Managing the Defiant Child provides a proven approach to behavior management. *$205.95*

438 Understanding Mental Illness
Educational Video Network
1401 19th Street
Huntsville, TX 77340
936-295-5767
800-762-0060
www.www.evndirect.com

Contains information and classifications of mental illness. Learn about various organic and functional mental disorders as discussed and their causes and symptoms, and learn where to seek help for a variety of mental health concerns. *$79.95*

ISBN 1-589501-48-9

439 Understanding and Treating the Hereditary Psychiatric Spectrum Disorders
Hope Press
PO Box 188
Duarte, CA 91009-188
818-303-0644
800-209-9182
E-mail: dcomings@earthlink.net
www.hopepress.com

David E Comings MD, Presenter

Learn with ten hours of audio tapes from a two day seminar given in May 1997 by David E Comings, MD. Tapes cover: ADHD, Tourette Syndrome, Obsessive-Compulsive Disorder, Conduct Disorder, Oppositional Defiant Disorder, Autism and other Hereditary Psychiatric Spectrum Disorders. Eight audio tapes. *$75.00*

Web Sites

440 www.apa.org/pubinfo/anger.html
Controlling Anger-Before It Controls You

From the American Psychological Association.

441 www.cfsny.org
Center for Family Support (CFS)

Devoted to providing support and assistance to individuals with developmental and related disabilities, and to the family members who care for them.

442 www.cyberpsych.org
CyberPsych

Presents information about psychoanalysis, psychotherapy and special topics such as anxiety disorders, the problematic use of alcohol, homophobia, and the traumatic effects of racism. Includes an archive of older site content.

443 www.members.aol.com/AngriesOut
Get Your Angries Out

Guidelines for kids, teachers, and parents.

444 www.mentalhelp.net/psyhelp/chap7
Anger and Aggression

Therapeutic approaches.

445 **www.mhselfhelp.org**
National Mental Health Consumer's Self-Help Clearinghouse

A national consumer technical assistance center, has played a major role in the development of the mental health consumer movement.

446 **www.ncwd-youth.info/node/245**
Center for Mental Health Services Knowledge Exchange Network

Information about resources, technical assistance, research, training, networks and other federal clearinghouses, fact sheets and materials.

447 **www.planetpsych.com**
PlanetPsych.com

Learn about disorders, their treatments and other topics in psychology. Articles are listed under the related topic areas. Ask a therapist a question for free, or view the directory of professionals in your area. If you are a therapist sign up for the directory. Current features, self-help, interactive, and newsletter archives.

448 **www.psychcentral.com**
Psych Central

Personalized one-stop index for psychology, support, and mental health issues, resources, and people on the Internet.

449 **www.stopbitingnails.com**
Stop Biting Nails

Online organization created for those who bite their nails. Created a product which is used to prevent nailbiting.

450 **www.store.samhsa.gov**
Substance Abuse and Mental Health Services Administration

Resources on mental disorders as well as treatment and recovery.

451 **www.thenadd.org**
National Association for the Dually Diagnosed (NADD)

An association for persons with developmental disabilities and mental health needs.

Dissociative Disorders

Introduction

Dissociative Disorders are a cluster of mental disorders, characterized by a profound problems with memory, perception, emotion, and identity. People with a dissociative disorder may abruptly take on different personalities, or undergo long periods in which they do not remember anything that happened; in some cases, individuals may embark on lengthy international travels, returning home with no recollection of where they have been or why they had gone.

Dissociative disorders are uncommon, mysterious and somewhat controversial; reports of dissociative disorders have grown more frequent in recent years and a degree of debate surrounds the validity of these reports. Some professionals say the disorders are far rarer than is reported and that these individuals are highly vulnerable to the suggestions of others.

Dissociative disorders are believed to be related in many cases to severe trauma, although the historical validity of these cases is difficult to determine. There are three types of dissociative disorders: Dissociative Amnesia, Dissociative Identity Disorder, and Depersonalization Disorder.

SYMPTOMS

Dissociative Amnesia

• One or more episodes of inability to recall important personal information, usually of a traumatic or stressful nature, that is too extensive to be explained by ordinary forgetfulness;
• The disturbance does not occur exclusively during the course of any other dissociative disorder and is not due to the direct physiological effects of a substance abuse or general medical condition;
• The symptoms cause clinically significant distress or impairment in social, occupational, or other important areas of functioning.

Dissociative Identity Disorder

• The presence of two or more distinct identities or personality states that take control of the person's behavior;
• Inability to recall important personal information, or the presence of gaps in memories about everyday events;
• The disturbance is not due to the direct physiological effects of a substance or a general medical condition, or by a cultural or spiritual practice.

Depersonalization Disorder

• Persistent or recurrent experiences of feeling detached from one's body and mental processes;
• During the depersonalization experience, reality testing remains intact;
• The depersonalization causes clinically significant distress or impairment in social, occupational, or other important areas of functioning;
• The depersonalization does not occur during the course of another dissociative disorder or as a direct physiological effect of a substance or general medical condition;
• Akin to depersonalization (feeling one is not real) is derealization, which is feeling that one's environment and/or perceptions are not real.

ASSOCIATED FEATURES

Patients with any of the dissociative disorders may be depressed, and may experience depersonalization, or a feeling of not being in their own bodies. They often experience impairment in work or interpersonal relationships, and they may practice self-mutilation or have aggressive and suicidal impulses. They may also have symptoms typical of a Mood or Personality Disorder. Individuals with Dissociative Amnesia and Dissociative Identity Disorder (sometimes known as multiple personality disorder) often report severe physical and/or sexual abuse in childhood. Individuals with Dissociative Identity Disorder may have symptoms typical of Post-Traumatic Stress Disorder, as well as Bipolar, Substance Abuse Related, Sexual, Eating, or Wake-Sleep Disorders.

PREVALENCE

The prevalence of dissociative disorders is difficult to ascertain, and subject to controversy. The recent rise in the US in reports of Dissociative Amnesia and Dissociative Identity Disorder related to traumatic childhood abuse has been very controversial. Some say these disorders are overreported, the result of suggestibility in individuals and the unreliability of childhood memories. Others say the disorders are underreported, given the propensity for children and adults to dismiss or forget abusive memories and the tendency of perpetrators to deny or obscure their abusive actions. Dissociative Identity Disorder is diagnosed three to nine times more frequently in females than in males, and Depersonalization Disorder is twice as likely to occur in women than men.

TREATMENT OPTIONS

Treatment for Dissociative Amnesia may involve supportive psychotherapy or hypnosis to help the patient recover traumatic memories. Another stage of psychotherapy may then be initiated to enable the patient to deal with the uncovered memories. Great care must be taken to avoid suggesting memories.

Treatment for Dissociative Identity Disorder may include psychotherapy, family therapy, and cognitive behavioral therapy. Therapy can be difficult because it often involves reliving trauma. Medications such as antidepressants and anti-anxiety agents may also be prescribed to treat symptoms associated with the disorder but not the disorder itself.

In some cases, Depersonalization Disorder can resolve on its own without therapy. In other cases, treatment such as hypnosis, psychodynamic psychotherapy (in which the focus is on unconscious thoughts and how they are revealed in a patient's behavior), or cognitive behavioral therapy (in which the patient learns to replace negative thoughts and behaviors with positive ones) may be used. Medications such as benzodiazepine tranquilizers, tricyclic antidepressants, and selective serotonin reuptake inhibitors (SSRIs) may also be prescribed.

Associations & Agencies

453 Center for Mental Health Services (CMHS)
Substance Abuse and Mental Health Services Administration
5600 Fishers Lane
Rockville, MD 20857
240-276-1310
www.samhsa.gov/about-us/who-we-are/offices-centers

Anita Everett, MD, DFAPA, Director

Promotes the treatment of mental illness and emotional disorders by increasing accessibility to mental health programs; supporting outreach, treatment, rehabilitation, and support programs and networks; and encouraging the use of scientifically-based information when treating mental disorders. CMHS provides information about mental health via a toll-free number and numerous publications. Developed for users of mental health services and their families, the general public, policy makers, providers, and the media.

Year Founded: 1992

454 International Society for the Study of Trauma and Dissociation
4201 Wilson Boulevard
3rd Floor
Arlington, VA 22203
844-994-7783
E-mail: info@isst-d.org
www.isst-d.org

ISSTD seeks to provide educational resources, programs, conferences, and publications on the prevalence and consequences of chronic trauma and dissociation.

455 National Association for the Dually Diagnosed (NADD)
321 Wall Street
Kingston, NY 12401
845-331-4336
E-mail: info@thenadd.org
www.thenadd.org

Jeanne M. Farr, MA, Chief Executive Officer
Bruce Davis, President
Juanita St. Croix, Vice President
Ray Snyder, Secretary

NADD is a nonprofit organization designed to increase awareness of, and provide services for, individuals with developmental disabilities and mental illness. NADD emphasizes the importance of quality mental healthcare for people with mental health needs and offers conferences, information resources, educational programs, and training materials to professionals, parents, and organizations.

Year Founded: 1983

456 National Mental Health Consumers' Self-Help Clearinghouse
E-mail: selfhelpclearinghouse@gmail.com
www.mhselfhelp.org

Joseph Rogers, Founder and Executive Director
Susan Rogers, Director

The Clearinghouse is a peer-run national technical assistance center focused on achieving respect and equality of opportunity for those with mental illnesses. The Clearinghouse helps with the growth of the mental health consumer movement by evaluating mental health services, advocating

for mental health reform, and providing consumers with news, information, publications, and consultation services.
Year Founded: 1986

457 Sidran Traumatic Stress Institute
7238 Muncaster Mill Road
Suite 376
Derwood, MD 20855
410-825-8888
E-mail: admin@sidran.org
www.sidran.org

Esther Giller, President and Director
Ruta Mazelis, Editor, The Cutting Edge/Trainer

Sidran Institute provides useful, practical information for child and adult survivors of any type of trauma, for families/friends, and for the clinical and frontline service providers who assist in their recovery. Sidran's philosophy of education through collaboration brings together great minds (providers, survivors, and loved ones) to develop comprehensive programs to address the practical, emotional, spiritual, and medical needs of trauma survivors.

Year Founded: 1986

458 The Center for Family Support
2811 Zulette Avenue
Bronx, NY 10461
718-518-1500
E-mail: svernikoff@cfsny.org
www.www.cfsny.org

Steven Vernikoff, Executive Director
Barbara Greenwald, Chief Operating Officer
Jos, Martin Jara, President
Elise Geltzer, Vice President

The Center for Family Support offers assistance to individuals with developmental and related disabilities, as well as their families, and provides support services and programs that are designed to accommodate individual needs. Offers services throughout New York City, Westchester County, Long Island, and New Jersey.
Year Founded: 1954

Video & Audio

459 Different From You
Fanlight Publications
32 Court Street
21st Floor
Brooklyn, NY 11201
718-488-8900
800-876-1710
E-mail: fanlight@fanlight.com
www.fanlight.com

Milt L. Kogan, MD, MPH, Author
Demetrio Cuzzocrea, Author

As a result of the 'deinstituionalization' of mental patients, people with mental illnesses now make up a majority of the homeless in many areas. This video explores the problem through the work of a compassionate physician who cares for mentally ill people living on the streets and in inadequate 'board and care' facilities in Los Angeles.

460 Understanding Mental Illness
Educational Video Network
1401 19th Street
Huntsville, TX 77340

936-295-5767
800-762-0060
www.www.evndirect.com

A video to learn and understand mental illness and how it affects you. *$79.95*

ISBN 1-589501-48-9

461 Understanding Personality Disorders DVD
Educational Video Network
1401 19th Street
Huntsville, TX 77340
936-295-5767
800-762-0060

Defines to adolescents what a personality disorder really is. *$89.95*

462 Understanding Self Destructive Behavior
Educational Video Network
1401 19th Street
Huntsville, TX 77340
936-295-5767
800-762-0060

helps adolescents learn how to deal with their destructive behavior due to their mental illness. *$129.95*

Web Sites

463 www.cyberpsych.org
CyberPsych

Hosts the American Psychoanalyists Foundation, American Association of Suicideology, Society for the Exploration of Psychotherapy Intergration, and Anxiety Disorders Association of America. Also subcategories of the anxiety disorders, as well as general information, including panic disorder, phobias, obsessive compulsive disorder (OCD), social phobia, generalized anxiety disorder, post traumatic stress disorder, and phobias of childhood. Book reviews and links to web pages sharing the topics.

464 www.fmsf.com
False Memory Syndrome Facts

Access to literature.

465 www.isst-D.Org
International Society for the Study of Dissociation

A non-profit, professional society that promotes research and training in the identification and treatment of dissociative disorders, provides professional and public education about dissociative states, and serves as a catalyst for international communication and cooperation among clinicians and researchers working in this field.

466 www.planetpsych.com
Planetpsych.com

Learn about disorders, their treatments and other topics in psychology. Articles are listed under the related topic areas. Ask a therapist a question for free, or view the directory of professionals in your area. If you are a therapist sign up for the directory. Current features, self-help, interactive, and newsletter archives.

467 www.psychcentral.com
Psych Central

Personalized one-stop index for psychology, support, and mental health issues, resources, and people on the Internet.

468 www.sidran.org
Trauma Resource Area

Resources and Articles on Dissociative Experiences Scale and Dissociative Identity Disorder, PsychTrauma Glossary and Traumatic Memories.

469 www.store.samhsa.gov
Substance Abuse and Mental Health Services Administration

Resources on mental disorders as well as treatment and recovery.

Feeding and Eating Disorders

Introduction

Eating is integral to human health, and for many people food is a pleasure that can be enjoyed without too much thought. However, some people experience a disturbance in their behavior, thoughts, and emotions related to eating that is severe enough to be a disorder. There are three principle eating disorders: 1) Anorexia Nervosa, 2) Bulimia Nervosa, and 3) Binge Eating Disorder. All three are similar in their underlying pathology: an obsessive concern with food, body image, and body weight.

Though there has been an increase in rates of obesity in North America, obesity in itself is not categorized as an eating disorder. It appears that human beings are hard-wired, so to speak, to eat whenever food is available, and food is ever more available and more caloric. In addition, the eating patterns and weight of pregnant women seems to result in physiologic changes in their unborn babies, who are predisposed to become obese after birth regardless of diet.

Many people believe that feeding and eating disorders are, in part, culturally determined: in the Western world, and particularly the US, a pervasive cultural preference for slimness causes many people to spend extra ordinary amounts of time, money, and energy dieting and exercising in order to stay slim. At the same time, people are flooded with media; celebrations of anorexia, and suggested strategies for remaining thin, can be easily found on the Internet, on television, and in magazines. Cultural preference is likely to exert pressure on people, especially young women, who may be genetically or psychologically predisposed to the illness. It is important to be wary of media, including the Internet, which can expose young people to counterproductive influences. Overeating is another type of eating disorder, as it reflects the paradox that, as society values thinness more and more, more and more people are obese. Feeding and Eating Disorders may do lasting physical damage; because of this, treatment must first restore a patient to a safe and healthy body weight. Treatment of the disorder is a long-term process, involving psychotherapy, family interventions and, for depressed or obsessional patients, antidepressant medication. Fortunately, most people who are appropriately treated can and do recover.

SYMPTOMS

Anorexia Nervosa:

A person must be at least fifteen percent under the normal bodyweight for their height to be diagnosed with Anorexia Nervosa. In addition to the hallmarks of Anorexia (limiting intake of food, negative body image, and an intense fear of gaining weight or becoming "fat"), signs that a person is suffering from Anorexia Nervosa are:
• In menstruating females, the absence of at least three consecutive menstrual cycles;
• Brittle hair or nails;
• Dry or yellow cast to skin;
• Drop in blood pressure;
• Lethargy or depression.

Anorexia Nervosa is associated with amenorrhea and infertility, which may lead patients to seek help from a gynecologist, who must then make the diagnosis.

Bulimia Nervosa:

• Recurrent episodes of binge eating characterized by eating more food than most people would eat during a similar period of time and under similar circumstances, often thousands of calories;
• A sense of loss of control over eating;
• Binge eating is then followed by purging: self-induced vomiting or misuse of laxatives, and excessive fasting or exercise;
• The binge eating and purging, on average, at least twice a week for three months;
• Body image is unduly influenced by body shape and weight;
• The disturbance does not occur exclusively during episodes of Anorexia Nervosa.
Because the binging behavior is often done in secret and people with Bulimia Nervosa are often of normal weight, it can be difficult to know someone is struggling with the disorder. There are some physical signs that are side-effects of purging behavior:
• A chronically inflamed or sore throat;
• A puffy face due to swollen saliva glands;
• Erosion of tooth enamel;
• Intense dehydration;
• Intestinal problems.

Binge Eating Disorder:

Binge Eating Disorder is similar to Bulimia in that a person will ingest large portions of food in short amounts of time. However, unlike those with Bulimia, people who have Binge Eating Disorder do not engage in the post-binging behaviors such as purging or extreme exercise.
To be diagnosed with Binge Eating Disorder, a person must have been binging at least once a week for over three months **and** engage in three or more of the following behaviors.
• Eat faster than normal;
• Feel out of control while eating;
• Eat until uncomfortably full;
• Eat large quantities when not physically hungry;
• Eat alone because they feel embarrassed about eating;
• Feel disgusted with oneself or guilty after eating.

ASSOCIATED FEATURES

Patients with Anorexia Nervosa may be severely depressed, and may experience insomnia, irritability, and diminished interest in sex. These features may be exacerbated if the patient is severely underweight. People with Feeding and Eating Disorders also share many of the features of Obsessive Compulsive Disorder. For instance, someone with an Eating Disorder may have an excessive interest in food; they may hoard food, or spend unusual amounts of time reading and researching about foods, recipes, and nutrition. People with Anorexia Nervosa may also exhibit a strong need to control their environment and may be socially and emotionally withdrawn. Approximately twenty to thirty percent of patients attempt suicide.

Individuals with Bulimia Nervosa are often within the normal weight range, but prior to the development of the disorder they may be overweight. Depression, Bipolar and other related disorders are common among people with bulimia. Substance abuse occurs in about one-third of individuals with bulimia.

Anxiety Disorders and fear-based illnesses are common in

those with Eating Disorders. Fear of social situations can be a precipitating factor in binging episodes.

PREVALENCE

Prevalence studies in females have found rates of 0.5 to one percent for Anorexia Nervosa. The prevalence of Anorexia Nervosa in males is approximately 0.3 percent. The prevalence of Bulimia Nervosa among adolescent females is approximately one to three percent. The rate of the disorder among males is approximately 0.5 percent.

TREATMENT OPTIONS

Because of the physical damage these disorders can do to a patient, the first step in treatment is always nutritional counseling and monitoring to restore and maintain proper body weight. In patients with Bulimia Nervosa and Binge Eating Disorder, it is crucial to interrupt the binge/purge cycle, or interrupt and stop the binge cycle, respectively.

It is critical to recognize that all Eating Disorders are, in addition to being life-threatening, extremely complex. Simply restoring the patient to an acceptable body weight is not enough. Many patients have complex and conflicting psychological issues that trigger the compulsion to binge, or the morbid fear of gaining weight. These issues need to be addressed by psychotherapy. Forms of psychotherapy that may be useful include psychodynamic psychotherapy (in which longstanding and sometimes unconscious emotional issues related to the feeding and eating disorders are explored) and cognitive behavior therapy, which aims to identify the thought patterns that trigger the disorder and to establish healthy eating habits. Recent literature suggests that psychotherapeutic approaches are often more effective than medications in the treatment of Anorexia. Family involvement in treatment is critical, and peer pressure can be used to compel patients to maintain adequate nutrition. Feeding and Eating Disorders are serious — untreated Anorexia can kill a patient — and treatment may be required over a course of many years.

Associations & Agencies

471 Brain & Behavior Research Foundation
747 Third Avenue
33rd Floor
New York, NY 10017
646-681-4888
800-829-8289
E-mail: info@bbrfoundation.org
www.www.bbrfoundation.org

Donald M. Boardman, Treasurer
Jeffrey Borenstein, MD, President and CEO
Louis Innamorato, CPA, VP and Chief Financial Officer
Faith Rothblatt, Vice President, Development

The Brain and Behavior Research Foundation awards grants aimed at advancing scientific understandings of mental health treatments and mental disorders such as depression and schizophrenia. The Brain and Behavior Research Foundation's mission is to eliminate the suffering caused by mental illness.

Year Founded: 1987

472 Center for Mental Health Services (CMHS)
Substance Abuse and Mental Health Services Administration
5600 Fishers Lane
Rockville, MD 20857
240-276-1310
www.samhsa.gov/about-us/who-we-are/offices-centers

Anita Everett, MD, DFAPA, Director

Promotes the treatment of mental illness and emotional disorders by increasing accessibility to mental health programs; supporting outreach, treatment, rehabilitation, and support programs and networks; and encouraging the use of scientifically-based information when treating mental disorders. CMHS provides information about mental health via a toll-free number and numerous publications. Developed for users of mental health services and their families, the general public, policy makers, providers, and the media.

Year Founded: 1992

473 Council on Size and Weight Discrimination (CSWD)
PO Box 305
Mount Marion, NY 12456
845-750-7710
E-mail: info@cswd.org
www.cswd.org

Miriam Berg, President
Lynn McAfee, Director of Medical Advocacy

The Council on Size and Weight Discrimination is a not-for-profit group aiming to change dominant perceptions about weight. CSWD advocates for the rights of larger people, particularly in the areas of media image, job discrimination, and medical treatment.

Year Founded: 1991

474 International Association of Eating Disorders Professionals Foundation
PO Box 1295
Pekin, IL 61555-1295
800-800-8126
E-mail: iaedpmembers@earthlink.net
www.iaedp.com

Bonnie Harken, Managing Director
Blanche Williams, Director, International Dev.
Joel Jahraus, President
Vicki Berkus, Secretary

IAEDP Foundation seeks to strengthen the level of quality among professionals who treat individuals with eating disorders. The Foundation provides training, education, and certifications; encourages professional and ethical standards; raises awareness on eating disorders; and participates in prevention efforts.

Year Founded: 1985

475 Multiservice Eating Disorders Association
1320 Centre Street
Suite 101
Newton, MA 02459
617-558-1881
888-350-4049
E-mail: info@medainc.org
www.medainc.org

Rebecca Manley, MS, Founder
Leslie Bernstein, Chair

Monika Ostroff, LICW, CEDS-S, Executive Director
Carolyn Judge, Director of Operations

MEDA is a nonprofit organization dedicated to the prevention and treatment of eating disorders and disordered eating. MEDA'S mission is to prevent the continuing spread of eating disorders through educational awareness and early detection. MEDA serves as a support network and resource for clients, loved ones, clinicians, educators and the general public.

Year Founded: 1994

476 National Alliance for Eating Disorders

4400 North Congress Avenue
Suite 100
West Palm Beach, FL 33407
866-662-1235
www.allianceforeatingdisorders.com

Judy Rifkin, Chair
Johanna Kandel, Founder and CEO
Nina Taylor, Education Manager
Joann Hendelman,PhD,RN,FAED, Clinical Director

The National Alliance for Eating Disorders (formerly The Alliance for Eating Disorders Awareness) is the leading national nonprofit organization providing referrals, education, and support for all eating disorders.

Year Founded: 2000

477 National Alliance on Mental Illness

4301 Wilson Boulevard
Suite 300
Arlington, VA 22203
703-524-7600
800-950-6264
E-mail: info@nami.org
www.nami.org

Shirley J. Holloway, President
Joyce A. Campbell, First Vice President
Daniel H. Gillison, Jr., Chief Executive Officer
David Levy, Chief Financial Officer

NAMI is an organization dedicated to raising awareness on mental health and providing support and education for Americans affected by mental illness. NAMI advocates for access to services and treatment and fosters an environment of awareness and understanding for those concerned with mental health.

Year Founded: 1979

478 National Association for the Dually Diagnosed (NADD)

321 Wall Street
Kingston, NY 12401
845-331-4336
E-mail: info@thenadd.org
www.thenadd.org

Jeanne M. Farr, MA, Chief Executive Officer
Bruce Davis, President
Juanita St. Croix, Vice President
Ray Snyder, Secretary

NADD is a nonprofit organization designed to increase awareness of, and provide services for, individuals with developmental disabilities and mental illness. NADD emphasizes the importance of quality mental healthcare for people with mental health needs and offers conferences, information resources, educational programs, and training materials to professionals, parents, and organizations.

Year Founded: 1983

479 National Association of Anorexia Nervosa and Associated Disorders (ANAD)

PO Box 409047
Chicago, IL 60640
888-375-7767
E-mail: hello@anad.org
www.anad.org

Maria Rago, President
Matt DeBoer, CFP, Treasurer
Kristen Portland, MA, Executive Director
Omri Avraham, Program Coordinator

A nonprofit organization dedicated to preventing anorexia nervosa, bulimia nervosa, binge eating disorder, and other eating disorders. ANAD serves as a clearinghouse of information with the goal of raising awareness and supports research and educational programs focused on understanding and preventing eating disorders.

Year Founded: 1976

480 National Association to Advance Fat Acceptance (NAAFA)

PO Box 61586
Las Vegas, NV 89160-1586
916-558-6880
E-mail: admin@naafa.org
www.naafa.org

Tigress Osborn, Chair
Amanda Cooper, Public Relations Director
Darliene Howell, Administrative Director

A nonprofit organization committed to defending the rights of fat people and improving their quality of life. NAAFA opposes discrimination against fat people, including discrimination in advertising, employment, fashion, medicine, insurance, social acceptance, the media, schooling, and public accommodations.

Year Founded: 1969

481 National Eating Disorders Association

3308 Preston Road
Suite 350-111
Plano, TX 10036
212-575-6200
800-931-2237
E-mail: info@nationaleatingdisorders.org
www.nationaleatingdisorders.org

Geoffrey Craddock, Chair
Elizabeth Thompson, Chief Executive Officer
Margo Lucero, Chief Development Officer
Lauren Smolar, VP, Mission & Education

NEDA offers a national information phone line, an international treatment referral directory, and a support group directory. The organization sponsors an annual conference; provides resources on eating disorders for individuals, parents, and educators; funds research; and raises awareness of eating disorders.

Year Founded: 2001

482 National Institute of Mental Health Eating Disorders Research Program

6001 Executive Boulevard
Room 7126, MSC 9632
Bethesda, MD 20892-9663

301-443-8942
866-615-6464
TTY: 301-443-8431
E-mail: mchavez1@mail.nih.gov
www.nimh.nih.gov

Mark Chavez, PhD, Program Chief

The program supports studies and research on eating disorders in areas including assessment, risk factors, and intervention development.

483 National Mental Health Consumers' Self-Help Clearinghouse
E-mail: selfhelpclearinghouse@gmail.com
www.mhselfhelp.org

Joseph Rogers, Founder and Executive Director
Susan Rogers, Director

The Clearinghouse is a peer-run national technical assistance center focused on achieving respect and equality of opportunity for those with mental illnesses. The Clearinghouse helps with the growth of the mental health consumer movement by evaluating mental health services, advocating for mental health reform, and providing consumers with news, information, publications, and consultation services.

Year Founded: 1986

484 TOPS Take Off Pounds Sensibly
4575 South 5th Street
PO Box 070360
Milwaukee, WI 53207
414-482-4620
www.tops.org

TOPS is a nonprofit network of weight loss support groups and wellness education organizations. Promotes healthy lifestyles and sensible approaches to weight management. Provides meetings, educational tools and programs based on positive reinforcement and motivation. Supports people of all ages, sizes, and shapes.

Year Founded: 1948

485 The Center for Family Support
2811 Zulette Avenue
Bronx, NY 10461
718-518-1500
www.www.cfsny.org

Steven Vernikoff, Executive Director
Barbara Greenwald, Chief Operating Officer
Jos, Martin Jara, President
Elise Geltzer, Vice President

The Center for Family Support offers assistance to individuals with developmental and related disabilities, as well as their families, and provides support services and programs that are designed to accommodate individual needs. Offers services throughout New York City, Westchester County, Long Island, and New Jersey.

Year Founded: 1954

Periodicals & Pamphlets

486 Anorexia: Am I at Risk?
ETR Associates
4 Carbonero Way
Scotts Valley, CA 95066-4200
831-438-4060
800-321-4407

E-mail: customerservice@etr.org
www.etr.org

David Kitchen, MBA, Chief Operations Officer
Laurie Searson, Publisher
Sarah Stevens, Director, Product Development
Yvonne Collins, Sales Director

Offers a clear overview of anorexia; Lists symptoms; Explains helath problems.

487 Body Image
ETR Associates
4 Carbonero Way
Scotts Valley, CA 95066-4200
831-438-4060
800-321-4407
www.etr.org

David Kitchen,MBA, Chief Financial Officer
Talita Sanders,BS, Director,Human Resources
Coleen Cantwell,MPH, Director,Business Development Pl
Matt McDowell,BS, Director,Marketing

Discusses the difference between healthy and distorted body image; the link between poor body image and low self esteem; five point list to help people check out their own body image.

488 Bulimia
ETR Associates
4 Carbonero Way
Scotts Valley, CA 95066-4200
831-438-4060
800-321-4407
E-mail: customerservice@etr.org
www.etr.org

Bonnie Graves, Author
Laurie Searson, Publisher
Sarah Stevens, Director, Product Development
Yvonne Collins, Sales Director

Includes warning signs that someone's bulimic, health consequesnces of bulimia, and how to help a friend.

489 Eating Disorder Sourcebook
Gurze Books
PO Box 2238
Carlsbad, CA 92018-2238
760-434-7533
800-756-7533
www.gurze.net

Carolyn Costin, Author
Lindsay Cohn, Co-Owner

Includes 125 books and tapes on eating disorders and related subjects for both lay and professional audiences, basic facts about eating disorders, a list of national organizations and treatment facilities. Also publishes a bimonthly newsletter for clinicians and are executive editors of Eating Disorders the Journal of Treatment and Prevention.

336 pages 1 per year

490 Eating Disorders
ETR Associates
4 Carbonero Way
Scotts Valley, CA 95066-4200
831-438-4060
800-321-4407
www.etr.org

David Kitchen,MBA, Chief Financial Officer
Talita Sanders,BS, Director,Human Resources
Coleen Cantwell,MPH, Director,Business Development Pl
Matt McDowell,BS, Director,Marketing

Includes anorexia and bulimia, eating patterns versus eating disorders, treatment and getting help.

491 Eating Disorders: Facts About Eating Disorders and the Search for Solutions
National Institute of Mental Health
6001 Executive Boulevard
Room 8184,MSC 9663
Bethesda, MD 20892-9663
301-443-4513
866-615-6464
TTY: 301-443-8431
E-mail: nimhinfo@nih.gov
www.www.nimh.nih.gov/

Francis S Collins PhD, Director

Eating is controlled by many factors, including appetite, food availability, family, peer, and cultural practices, and attempts at voluntary control. Dieting to a body weight leaner than needed for health is highly promoted by current fashion trends, sales campaigns for special foods, and in some activities and professions. Eating disorders involve serious disturbances in eating behavior, such as extreme and unhealthy reduction of food intake or severe overeating, as well as feelings of distress or extreme concern about body shape or weight. There is help, and there is every hope for recovery.

8 pages

492 Fats of Life
ETR Associates
4 Carbonero Way
Scotts Valley, CA 95066-4200
831-438-4060
800-321-4407
E-mail: customerservice@etr.org
www.etr.org

Caroline M Pond, Author
Laurei Searson, Publisher
Sarah Stevens, Director, Product Development
Yvonne Collins, Sales Director

Stresses that health, not body weight, is what's important; dispels myths about dieting; includes chart to help people determine their body mass index.

344 pages

493 Food and Feelings
ETR Associates
4 Carbonero Way
Scotts Valley, CA 95066-4200
831-438-4060
800-321-4407
E-mail: customerservice@etr.org
www.etr.org

David Kitchen, Chief Operations Officer
Laurie Searson, Publisher
Sarah Stevens, Director, Product Development
Yvonne Collins, Sales Director

Helps students recognize eating disorders; emphasizes the seriousness of eating disorders; encourages the sufferers to seek treatment.

494 Getting What You Want from Your Body Image
ETR Associates
4 Carbonero Way
Scotts Valley, CA 95066-4200
831-438-4060
800-321-4407
www.etr.org

Melinda M Mueller, Author
Laurie Searson, Publisher
Sarah Stevens, Director, Product Development
Yvonne Collins, Sales Director

Discusses topics such as the influence of the media, the truth about dieting, and body image survival tips.

8 pages

495 Restrictive Eating
ETR Associates
4 Carbonero Way
Scotts Valley, CA 95066-4200
831-438-4060
800-321-4407
E-mail: customerservice@etr.org
www.etr.org

David Kitchen, MBA, Chief Operations Officer
Laurie Searson, Publisher

Discusses the spectrum of eating patterns, signs of restrictive eating and why it is a problem, how to help a friend, and where to go for help.

496 Teen Image
ETR Associates
4 Carbonero Way
Scotts Valley, CA 95066-4200
831-438-4060
800-321-4407
E-mail: customerservice@etr.org
www.etr.org

Mary Nelson, President

Dispels unrealistic media images; offers ways to boost body image and self esteem; includes tips to maintain a good body image.

Research Centers

497 Center for the Study of Anorexia and Bulimia
1841 Broadway 4th Floor
New York, NY 10023-7603
212-333-3444
www.www.icpnyc.org/csab/

Jill M Pollack, Director
Jill E Daino, Co-Director
Tracy McClair, CSAB Program Administrator

Established as a division of the Institute for Contemporary Psychotherapy in 1979 and is the oldest non-profit eating disorders clinic in New York City. Using an eclectic approach, the professional staff and affiliates are on the cutting edge of treatment in their field. The treatment staff includes social workers, psychologists, registered nurses and nutritionists, all with special training in the treatment of eating disorders.

Year Founded: 1979

498 Obesity Research Center
St. Luke's-Roosevelt Hospital
1111 Amsterdam Ave., Babcock 10
New York, NY 10025
212-523-4161
www.www.nyorc.org/

Lee C Bollinger, President
John H Coatsworth, Provost
Robert Kasdin, Sr Executive Vice President
Nicholas B Dirks, EVP, Arts ans Sciences

Helps reduce the the incidence of obesity and related diseases through leadership in basic research, clinical research, epidemiology and public health, patient care, and public education.

499 UAMS Psychiatric Research Institute
4224 Shuffield Drive
Little Rock, AR 72205
501-526-8100
E-mail: kramerteresal@uams.edu
www.www.psychiatry.uams.edu

Dan Rahn, MD, Chancellor

Combining research, education and clinical services into one facility, PRI offers inpatiend and outpatient services, with 40 psychiatric beds, therapy options, and specialized treatment for specific disorders, including: addictive eating, anxiety, deppressive and post-traumatic stress disorders. Research focuses on evidence-based care takes into consideration the education of future medical personnel while relying on research scientists to provide innovative forms of treatment. PRI includes the Center for Addiction Research as well as a methadone clinic.

500 University of Pennsylvania Weight and Eating Disorders Program
3535 Market Street
Suite 3108
Philadelphia, PA 19104-3313
215-898-7314
www.www.med.upenn.edu/weight/

Dwight L. Evans, MD, Chair

Conducts a wide variety of studies on the causes and treatment of weight-related disorders.

Support Groups & Hot Lines

501 Food Addicts Anonymous
529 N W Prima Vista Blvd.
#301 A
Port St. Lucie, FL 34983
772-878-9657
E-mail: faawso@bellsouth.net
www.foodaddictsanonymous.org

Linda Closy, Manager

The FAA program is based on the belief that food addiction is a bio-chemical disease. We share our experience, strength, and hope with others allows us to recover from this disease.

502 Multiservice Eating Disorders Association
1320 Centre Street
Suite 101
Newton, MA 02459
617-558-1881
888-350-4049

E-mail: info@medainc.org
www.medainc.org

Rebecca Manley, MS, Founder
Leslie Bernstein, Chair
Monika Ostroff, LICW, CEDS-S, Executive Director
Carolyn Judge, Director of Operations

MEDA is a nonprofit organization dedicated to the prevention and treatment of eating disorders and disordered eating. MEDA'S mission is to prevent the continuing spread of eating disorders through educational awareness and early detection. MEDA serves as a support network and resource for clients, loved ones, clinicians, educators and the general public.

503 National Center for Overcoming Overeating
PO Box 1257
Old Chelsea Station
New York, NY 10113-1257
212-875-0442
E-mail: webmaster@overcomingovereating.com
www.overcomingovereating.com

Is an educational and training organization working to end body hatred and dieting.

504 Overeaters Anonymous General Service Office
6075 Zenith Court,NorthEast
Rio Rancho, NM 87144-6424
505-891-2664
E-mail: info@oa.org
www.oa.org

OA offers a program of recovery from compulsive eating using the Twelve Steps and Twelve Traditions of OA. It addresses physical, emotional and spiritual well-being.

Year Founded: 1960

Video & Audio

505 Eating Disorder Video
Active Parenting Publishers
1955 Vaughn Road NW
Suite 108
Kennesaw, GA 30144-7808
770-429-0565
800-825-0060
E-mail: cservice@activeparenting.com

Features compelling interviews with several young people who have suffered from anorexia nervosa, bulimia and compulsive eating. Discusses the treatments, causes and techniques for prevention with field experts. *$39.95*

ISSN Q6456

Web Sites

506 www.anred.com
Anorexia Nervosa and Related Eating Disorders

Online resource providing information about eating disorders and how to recover from them.

507 www.bulimia.us.com
Bulimia: News & Discussion Forum

Eating disorders forum with news and information about bulimia, anorexia, male and teen eating disorders; treatment, help and resources information, events and inspirational stories.

508 www.closetoyou.org/eatingdisorders
Close to You

Information about eating disorders, anorexia, bulimia, binge eating disorder, and compulsive overeating.

509 www.cyberpsych.org
CyberPsych

Hosts the American Psychoanalyists Foundation, American Association of Suicideology, Society for the Exploration of Psychotherapy Intergration, and Anxiety Disorders Association of America. Also subcategories of the anxiety disorders, as well as general information, including panic disorder, phobias, obsessive compulsive disorder (OCD), social phobia, generalized anxiety disorder, post traumatic stress disorder, and phobias of childhood. Book reviews and links to web pages sharing the topics.

510 www.edap.org
Eating Disorders Awareness and Prevention

A source of educational brochures and curriculum materials.

511 www.gurze.com
Gurze Bookstore

Hundreds of books on eating disorders.

512 www.healthyplace.com/Communities/
Peace, Love, and Hope

Click on Body Views for information on body dysmorphic disorder.

513 www.kidsource.com/nedo/
National Eating Disorders Organization

Educational materials on dynamics, causative factors and evaluating treatment options.

514 www.mentalhelp.net
Anorexia Nervosa General Information

Introductory text on Anorexia Nervosa.

515 www.mirror-mirror.org/eatdis.htm
Mirror, Mirror

Relapse prevention for eating disorders.

516 www.planetpsych.com
Planetpsych.com

Learn about disorders, their treatments and other topics in psychology. Articles are listed under the related topic areas. Ask a therapist a question for free, or view the directory of professionals in your area. If you are a therapist sign up for the directory. Current features, self-help, interactive, and newsletter archives.

517 www.psychcentral.com
Psych Central

Personalized one-stop index for psychology, support, and mental health issues, resources, and people on the Internet.

518 www.something-fishy.com
Something Fishy Music and Publishing

Continuously educating the world on eating disorders to encourage every sufferer towards recovery.

519 www.store.samhsa.gov
Substance Abuse and Mental Health Services Administration

Resources on mental disorders as well as treatment and recovery.

Gender Dysphoria

Introduction

With a wide scope of questions and confusion surrounding human sexuality and gender-explicit roles in the modern era, many children, adolescents, and adults have been perplexed by the concepts of homosexuality and cross-gender identification. Homosexuality is a matter of sexual orientation: whether one is sexually attracted to men or women. The American Psychiatric Association ceased to classify homosexuality as an illness in 1973. Gender identity, in contrast, is a matter of what gender one feels oneself to be; people with Gender Dysphoria feel that their psychological experience conflicts with the physical body with which they were born. Gender Dysphoria can have serious social and occupational repercussions.

Diagnosis of Gender Dysphoria requires two sets of criteria: (1) a heavy and persistent insistence that the individual is, or has a strong desire to be, of the opposite sex, and (2) a constant discomfort about his/her designated sex, a feeling of inappropriateness towards his/her biological designation. Typically, boys meeting critera for the disorder are predisposed to dressing as girls, drawing explicit pictures of females, playing with pre-designated feminine toys, fantasizing and role playing as females, and interacting primarily with girls. Girls who exhibit Gender Dysphoria are often mistaken for boys due to attire and hair style, and may assert that they will develop into men. For adolescents and adults, ostracism in school and the workplace is likely to occur, as is a profound inability to associate with others and poor relationships with family members and members of either sex.

There is a sharp divide among persons whose biological gender feels wrong: some insist that this is not a psychiatric disorder but rather a biological variant; others feel strongly that they have a psychiatric disorder. Some of this conviction is driven by the need to demonstrate 'medical necessity' in order for health insurance to cover hormonal or surgical interventions to make the individual look like the gender he or she feels they are.

SYMPTOMS

In boys
• A marked preoccupation with traditionally feminine activites;
• A preference for dressing as a girl;
• Attraction to stereotypical female games and toys;
• Portraying female characters in role playing;
• Assertion he is a girl;
• Insistence on sitting to urinate;
• Displaying disgust for his genitals, wishing to remove them.

In girls
• Aversion to traditional female attire;
• Shared interest in contact games;
• A preference for associating with boys;
• Refusing to urinate sitting down;
• Show little interest in playing with stereotypical female toys such as dolls;
• Assertion that she will grow a penis, not breasts;
• Identification with strong male figures.

In adolescents

• Ostracism in school and social situations;
• Social isolation, peer rejection and peer teasing;
• Significant cross-gender identification and mannerisms;
• Similar symptoms as children.

In adults
• Adoption of social roles, physical appearance, and mannerisms of opposite sex;
• Surgical and/or hormonal manipulation of biological state;
• Discomfort in being regarded by others, or functioning, as his/her designated sex;
• Cross-dressing;
• Transvestic Fetishism.

ASSOCIATED FEATURES

Those who have Gender Dysphoria are at risk of mental and physical harm resulting, not from the condition itself, but from the reactions of other people to the condition. In children, a manifestation of separation anxiety disorder, generalized anxiety disorder, and symptoms of depression may result. For adolescents, depression and suicidal thoughts or ideas, as well as actual suicide attempts can result from prolonged feelings of ostracism by peers. Relationships with either one or both parents may weaken from resentment, lack of communication, and misunderstanding; many with this condition may drop out of or avoid school due to peer teasing. For many, lives are built around attempts to decrease gender distress. They are often preoccupied with appearance. In extreme cases, males with the condition perform their own castration. Prostitution has been linked with the condition because young people who are rejected by their families and ostracized by others may resort to prostitution as the only way to support themselves, a practice which increases the risk of acquiring sexually transmitted diseases. Some people with the condition resort to substance abuse and other forms of abuse in an attempt to deal with the associated stress.

PREVALENCE

In most cases, the age of onset for Gender Dysphoria is in the pre-school years. However, it should be noted that Gender Dysphoria in childhood does not always continue into adulthood.

TREATMENT OPTIONS

Therapists who attempt to pathologize and 'cure' sexual orientation have been unsuccessful. So-called conversion therapy causes more harm than good. In contrast, some people with Gender Dysphoria decide to live as members of the opposite sex; some choose to undergo sex-change surgery.

There is some controversy about the diagnosis; some groups protest that their condition, like homosexuality, should not be classified as a mental illness.

Psychological assistance can help individuals to gain acceptance of themselves, and can teach methods of dealing with discrimination, prejudice, and violence. Supportive counseling may also help families accept the gender identity of the family member with Gender Dysphoria.

For youth with Gender Dysphoria, treatment may include hormone blockers, which suppress the physical changes of puberty, and cross-sex hormone therapy. Treatment for adults may include hormone replacement therapy and supportive counseling.

It is important that people with Gender Dysphoria receive the support and therapy that they need in order to reduce the risk of depression and emotional distress, and increase the chance of a happy, productive life. Tragically, these conditions have been politicized, with imputations that they are dangerous or sinful, resulting in efforts in some states and communities to forbid education, discussion, and tolerance.

Associations & Agencies

521   Center for Mental Health Services (CMHS)
Substance Abuse and Mental Health Services Administration
5600 Fishers Lane
Rockville, MD 20857
240-276-1310
www.samhsa.gov/about-us/who-we-are/offices-centers

Anita Everett, MD, DFAPA, Director

Promotes the treatment of mental illness and emotional disorders by increasing accessibility to mental health programs; supporting outreach, treatment, rehabilitation, and support programs and networks; and encouraging the use of scientifically-based information when treating mental disorders. CMHS provides information about mental health via a toll-free number and numerous publications. Developed for users of mental health services and their families, the general public, policy makers, providers, and the media.

Year Founded: 1992

522   CenterLink
PO Box 24490
Ft Lauderdale, FL 33307
954-765-6024
www.lgbtcenters.org

Denise Spivak, CEO
Adriana Orozco, Finance Director
Amhir Hidalgo, Development Director
Julia Landis, Director of Operations

Founded in 1994, CenterLink is a member-based coalition designed to support the growth and development of LGBT community centers across the world. The organization collaborates with other national organizations to provide key information to LGBT community centers and to advocate for the rights of the LGBT community.

Year Founded: 1994

523   Gender Diversity
6523 California Avenue SW
Suite 144
Seattle, WA 98136
833-343-6337
E-mail: info@genderdiversity.org
www.www.genderdiversity.org

Aidan Key, Founder and Executive Director

A nonprofit organization that aims to increase awareness and understanding of gender diversity in children, adolescents, and adults. Gender Diversity provides support groups for youth, adults, and families; education and training for schools and workplaces; and conferences.

524   Gender Spectrum
1271 Washington Avenue
Suite 834
San Leandro, CA 94577
E-mail: info@genderspectrum.org
www.www.genderspectrum.org

Liam Day, Interim Executive Director
Stephanie Brill, Founder and Chair
Joel Baum, Senior Director
Kim Westheimer, Director, Strategic Initiatives

An organization that provides a variety of serivces to support families, schools, professionals, and youth who are dealing with gender identity issues.

Year Founded: 2006

525   Human Rights Campaign
1640 Rhode Island Ave. N.W.
Washington, DC 20036-3278
202-628-4160
800-777-4723
TTY: 202-216-1572
E-mail: feedback@hrc.org
www.hrc.org

Joni Madson, Interim President
Jay Brown, SVP, Programs/Research/Training
Nicole Cozier, SVP, Diversity/Equity/Inclusion
Nicole Greenridge-Hoskins, SVP, General Counsel

Founded in 1980, the Human Rights Campaign is a civil rights organization that advocates for the rights of lesbian, gay, bisexual, and transgender people in the United States. HRC organizes grassroots movements, educates the public about LGBT issues, and works towards achieving a world in which lesbian, gay, bisexual, and transgender people are respected as equal and full members of society.

Year Founded: 1980

526   National Association for the Dually Diagnosed (NADD)
321 Wall Street
Kingston, NY 12401
845-331-4336
E-mail: info@thenadd.org
www.thenadd.org

Jeanne M. Farr, MA, Chief Executive Officer
Bruce Davis, President
Juanita St. Croix, Vice President
Ray Snyder, Secretary

NADD is a nonprofit organization designed to increase awareness of, and provide services for, individuals with developmental disabilities and mental illness. NADD emphasizes the importance of quality mental healthcare for people with mental health needs and offers conferences, information resources, educational programs, and training materials to professionals, parents, and organizations.

Year Founded: 1983

527   National Coalition for LGBT Health
2000 S Street Northwest
Washington, DC 20009
202-232-6749
E-mail: info@healthlgbt.org
www.healthlgbt.org

Brian Hujdich, Executive Director
Scott Bertani, Director of Advocacy

Michael Shankle, Director of Advocacy and Edu.
Matthew Prior, Dir. of Comms./Content Strategy

The National Coalition for LGBT Health is a coalition of over 70 state and national organizational advocates and health services providers dedicated to using advocacy, education, and research to improve the health of lesbian, gay, bisexual, and transgender individuals.

528 National Commission on Correctional Heath Care

1145 West Diversey Parkway
Chicago, IL 60614
773-880-1460
E-mail: info@ncchc.org
www.ncchc.org

Robert E. Morris, MD, Chair
Nancy B. White, Treasurer
Carolyn Sufrin, MD, PhD, Secretary
Joseph V. Penn, MD, CCHP-MH, Chair-Elect

The National Commission on Correctional Health Care is committed to improving the standards of health care provided for individuals in prisons, jails, and juvenile confinement facilities. The organization seeks to ensure that the needs of all correctional health patients, including gender nonconforming people and individuals with gender dysphoria, are met.

Year Founded: 1983

529 National Institute of Mental Health

6001 Executive Boulevard
Room 6200, MSC 9663
Bethesda, MD 20892-9663
866-615-6464
E-mail: nimhinfo@nih.gov
www.nimh.nih.gov

Joshua Gordon, MD, PhD, Director

The National Institute of Mental Health conducts clinical research on mental disorders and seeks to expand knowledge on mental health treatments.

530 National LGBTQ Task Force

1050 Connecticut Ave NW
Suite 65500
Washington, DC 20035
202-393-5177
www.thetaskforce.org

Candy Cox, Co-Chair
Dr. Anika Simpson, Co-Chair
Rodney McKenzie, Jr., Secretary
Colgate Darden, Treasurer

The National LGBTQ Task Force advocates for justice and equality for LGBTQ people and mobilizes activists throughout the nation to eliminate discrimination against the LGBTQ community.

Year Founded: 1973

531 National Mental Health Consumers' Self-Help Clearinghouse

E-mail: selfhelpclearinghouse@gmail.com
www.mhselfhelp.org

Joseph Rogers, Founder and Executive Director
Susan Rogers, Director

The Clearinghouse is a peer-run national technical assistance center focused on achieving respect and equality of

opportunity for those with mental illnesses. The Clearinghouse helps with the growth of the mental health consumer movement by evaluating mental health services, advocating for mental health reform, and providing consumers with news, information, publications, and consultation services.

Year Founded: 1986

532 PFLAG

1625 K Street NW
Suite 700
Washington, DC 20006
202-467-8180
E-mail: info@pflag.org
www.pflag.org

Brian K. Bond, Executive Director
Jamie Curtis, Director of Chapter Engagement
Liz Owen, Director of Communications
Maggie Ardiente, Director of Development

An organization of families and friends of LGBTQ individuals. Dedicated to offering support for people who are LGBTQ and educating the public about LGBTQ issues.

Year Founded: 1973

533 The Center for Family Support

2811 Zulette Avenue
Bronx, NY 10461
718-518-1500
E-mail: svernikoff@cfsny.org
www.www.cfsny.org

Steven Vernikoff, Executive Director
Barbara Greenwald, Chief Operating Officer
Jos, Martin Jara, President
Elise Geltzer, Vice President

The Center for Family Support offers assistance to individuals with developmental and related disabilities, as well as their families, and provides support services and programs that are designed to accommodate individual needs. Offers services throughout New York City, Westchester County, Long Island, and New Jersey.

Year Founded: 1954

534 The Lesbian, Gay, Bisexual & Transgender Community Center

208 W. 13th Street
New York, NY 10011
212-620-7310
www.gaycenter.org

Glennda Testone, Executive Director
Renee Colombo, Chief Development Officer
Edward Herrera, Chief Financial Officer
Jeffrey Klein, Chief Operations Officer

An organization that advocates for LGBT individuals to lead healthy and successful lives. The Center offers health and wellness programs, as well as recovery and family support services.

Year Founded: 1983

535 Trans Youth Equality Foundation

PO Box 201
Orono, ME 04473
207-478-4087
E-mail: contact@transyouthequality.org
www.www.transyouthequality.org

Susan Maasch, Director
Jack Montgomery, Director
Rebecca Oglesby, Director and Treasurer

A nonprofit organization that provides education, advocacy, and support for transgender, gender nonconforming, and intersex youth ages 2-18, as well as their families. TYEF runs annual youth reatreats, a podcast program, training for educational and medical professionals, and youth workshops.

536 World Professional Association for Transgender Health (WPATH)
www.www.wpath.org

Walter Pierre Bouman, MD, PhD, President
Marci Bowers, MD, President-Elect
Asa Radix, MD, PhD, MPH, Secretary
Loren Schechter, MD, Treasurer

Formerly known as the Harry Benjamin International Gender Dysphoria Association, WPATH is a nonprofit organization dedicated to transgender health. Members of WPATH engage in clinical and academic research in order to further the understanding of Gender Dysphoria and to create a high quality of care for transsexual, transgender, and gender-nonconforming individuals globally.

Periodicals & Pamphlets

537 Similarities and Differences Between Sexual Orientation and Gender Identity
PFLAG
PO Box 3313
San Luis Obispo, CA 93403
805-801-2186
E-mail: pflag.slo@gmail.com
www.pflagcentralcoastchapter.net

Moises Torreblanca, President
John Sullivan, Vice President
Val Barboza, Treasurer
Barabara Adams, Secretary

An explanation of the simialrities and differences of both a person sexual orientation and how they relate to gender.

538 The United Nations Speaks Out: Tackling Discrimination on Grounds of Sexual Orientation and Gender Identity
Unesco-Globe NY
E-mail: unescoglobe@gmail.com
www.www.unescoglobe.wordpress.com

Irina Bokova, UNESCO Director-General
Engida Getachew, Deputy Director-General, UNESCO

Support Groups & Hot Lines

539 Gender Trust
76 The Ridgeway
Astwood Bank, B96 6LX, WO
527-894-838
www.gendertrust.org.uk

Gender Trust is a listening ear, a caring support and an information centre for anyone with any question or problem concerning their gender identity, or whose loved one is struggling with gender identity issues.

540 TransYouth Family Allies
PO Box 1471
Holland, MI 49422-1471
888-462-8932
E-mail: info@imatyfa.org
www.imatyfa.org

Shannon Garcia, Founding Member, President
Lisa Gilinger, Vice President
Amy G., Founding Member, Treasurer
Kim Pearson, Founding Member, Training Direct

TYFA empowers children and families by partnering with educators, service providers and communities to develop supportive environments in which gender may be expressed and respected.

Year Founded: 2006

Web Sites

541 www.cyberpsych.org
CyberPsych

Presents information about psychoanalysis, psychotherapy and special topics such as anxiety disorders, the problematic use of alcohol, homophobia, and the traumatic effects of racism.

542 www.gidreform.wordpress.com
Gender Identity Disorder Reform Advocates

GID Reform Advocates is a group of medical professionals, researchers, scholars, members of the transgender, bisexual, lesbian and gay communities, and other individuals who are concerned with the psychiatric classification of gender diversity as mental disorder and who advocate for the reform of the diagnostic criteria surrounding gender nonconforming people. The GID Reform Weblog addresses the issues surrounding these diagnostic categories.

543 www.health.nih.gov
National Institutes of Health

Part of the U.S. Department of Health and Human Services that is the nation's medical research agency-making important medical discoveries that improve health and save lives.

544 www.healthfinder.gov
Healthfinder

Developed by the U.S. Department of Health and Human Services, a key resource for finding the best government and nonprofit health and human services information on the internet.

545 www.intelihealth.com
Aetna InteliHealth

Aetna InteliHealth's mission is to empower people with trusted solutions for healthier lives.

546 www.kidspeace.org
KidsPeace

KidsPeace is a private charity dedicated to serving the behavioral and mental health needs of children, preadolescents and teens.

547 www.mayohealth.com
Mayo Clinic Health Oasis

Their mission is to empower people to manage their health. They accomplish this by providing useful and up-to-date information and tools that reflect the expertise and standard of excellence of Mayo Clinic.

548   www.nlm.nih.gov
National Library of Medicine

The National Library of Medicine (NLM), on the campus of the National Institutes of Health in Bethesda, Maryland, is the world's largest medical library. The Library collects materials and provides information and research services in all areas of biomedicine and health care

549   www.planetpsych.com
Planet Psych

The online resource for mental health information

550   www.psychcentral.com
Psych Central

The Internet's largest and oldest independent mental health social network created and run by mental health professionals to guarantee reliable, trusted information and support communities.

551   www.store.samhsa.gov
Substance Abuse and Mental Health Services Administration

Resources on mental disorders as well as treatment and recovery.

552   www.xs4all.nl/~rosalind/cha-assr.html
Support and Information on Sex Reassignement

The purpose of this newsgroup is to provide a supportive and informative environment for people who are undergoing or who have undergone sex reassignment surgery (SRS) and for their relatives and significant others.

Conferences & Meetings

553   Religion and Gender: Identity, Conflict, and Power Conference
Feminist Studies in Religion
Harvard Divinity School
45 Francis Avenue
Cambridge, MA 02138
617-384-8046
E-mail: fsr@fsrinc.org
www.www.fsrinc.org

Dr Pushpa Iyer, Conference Chair
Quinn Van Valler-Campbell, Conference Administrator
Judith Plaskow, Founding Editor
Elisabeth Schussler Fiorenza, Founding Editor

The conference will highlight the complex relationships between religion and gender in a global context. It seeks to explore conflicts that arise at the nexus of gender and religion while simultaneously promoting spaces for empowerment that arise in these interactions.

Year Founded: 1983

Neurocognitive Disorders

Introduction

Neurocognitive disorders are a group of conditions characterized by impairments in the ability to think, reason, plan, and organize. The DSM 5 recategorized neurocognitive disorders into major and minor, with a separate section for delirium. Previously, there was a category for dementia, but the authors of the DSM 5 have renamed dementia "major neurocognitive disorder." Within this classification, there are many subtypes, such as Alzheimer's, Lewy body, and Huntington's Disease.

Delirium is a relatively short-term condition in which the level of consciousness waxes and wanes. It is common in patients after surgery or during illness, as with high fever. It resolves when the underlying problem resolves. There are three categories of causes of delirium: a general medical condition, substance-induced, and multiple causes.

Major neurocognitive disorder (dementia) is categorized by a neurocognitive decline in the patient and diminishes their ability to live independently. Areas affected by neurocognitive disorder are complex attention, executive abilities, learning/memory, language, social cognition, and visual perception. People with a neurocognitive disorder might show apathy, agitation, mood disturbance, or psychosis.

Alzheimer's is the most prevalent of the major neurocognitive disorder subtypes. It is a progressive disorder that slowly kills nerve cells in the brain. While definitive treatments are lacking, there is a prodigious amount of research on the condition. Though such hopeful breakthroughs remain distant, there is much that families and patients can do when the condition is recognized and care and support are sought early in the disorder's progression.

Since other, serious, treatable disorders can resemble Alzeimer's Disease, it is very important for individuals who are losing cognitive functions to be evaluated by a physician. Early detection of Alzheimer's Disease, with early treatment, may improve the chances for slowing the rate of decline.

Because of its prevalence, the following discusses Alzheimer's Disease.

SYMPTOMS

• Langugae disorders;
• Impaired ability to carry out motor activities despite intact motor function;
• Failure to recognize or identify objects despite intact sensory perception;
• Disturbance in executive functioning (planning, organizing, sequencing, abstracting);
• The deficits cause impairment in social or occupational functioning and represent a decline from previous level of functioning;
• The course is gradual and continuous;
• The deficits are not due to central nervous system conditions such as Parkinson's Disease, other conditions known to cause dementia, and are not substance-induced;
• The deficits do not occur during the course of delirium and are not better accounted for by severe depression or schizophrenia.

ASSOCIATED FEATURES

Alzheimer's Disease generally begins gradually, not with deficits in cognition but with a marked change in personality. For instance, a person may suddenly become given to fits of anger for no apparent reason.

Soon, however, family and acquaintances may notice that the individual begins to mix up facts, or gets lost driving to a familiar place. In the early stages, the afflicted individual may become aware of slipping cognitive functions, adding to confusion, fright, and depression. After a period, lapses in memory grow more obvious; patients with Alzheimer's are apt to repeat themselves and may forget the names of grandchildren or long-time friends. They may also be increasingly agitated and combative when family members or other caretakers try to correct them or help with accustomed tasks. The memory lapses in patients with Alzheimer's differ markedly from those in normal aging: a patient with Alzheimer's may often forget entire experiences and rarely remembers them later; the patient only grudgingly acknowledges lapses. In contrast, the individual with normal aging or depression is extremely concerned about, and may even exaggerate, the extent of memory loss. In Alzheimer's, skills deteriorate, and a patient is increasingly unable to follow directions, or care for him/herself. Eventually the disease leads to death.

PREVALENCE

An estimated one in 10 people over age 65 has Alzheimer's Disease. Other types of major neurocognitive disorder are believed to be much less common. Prevalence of the condition increases with age, particularly after age 75. Of people who have been diagnosed with Alzheimer's Disease, 81 percent are age 75 or older.

TREATMENT OPTIONS

There is no known cure or definitive treatment for Alzheimer's Disease. Newly developed drugs likely offer false hope to patients and their families, and do not offer a proven cure for Alzheimer's. Psychiatrists treating patients with Alzheimer's Disease may also be able to prescribe medications that can treat the depression and anxiety that accompanies the condition.

Researchers suggest that close to half of the cases of Alzheimer's are related to modifiable risk factors, such as smoking and cognitive and physical inactivity. A healthy lifestyle may reduce the risk of developing Alzheimer's disease.

Families are strongly encouraged to take advantage of adjunctive services including support groups, counseling and psychotherapy. There is a high incidence of depression among family members caring at home for persons with Alzheimer's Disease.

Associations & Agencies

555 Alzheimer's Association National Office
225 North Michigan Avenue
17th Floor
Chicago, IL 60601
www.alz.org

Brian Richardson, Chair
Harry Johns, Chief Executive Officer

Joanne Pike, President
Maria Carrillo, Chief Science Officer

Headquarters for Alzheimer's Association, an organization dedicated to helping all those with Alzheimer's disease and dementia, and their families. Funds Alzheimer's research, engages in Alzheimer's advocacy, and offers referrals, support groups, educational sessions, safety services, and publications.

Year Founded: 1980

556 **Alzheimer's Disease & Related Dementias**
National Institute on Aging
31 Center Drive, MSC 2292
Building 31, Room 5C27
Bethesda, MD 20892
800-438-4380
E-mail: adear@nia.nih.gov
www.nia.nih.gov/alzheimers

Richard J. Hodes, MD, Director
Patrick Shirdon, Director of Management
Luigi Ferrucci, MD, PhD, Scientific Director
Marie A. Bernard, MD, Deputy Director

The ADEAR Center provides information about Alzheimer's Disease and related disorders to health professionals, patients and their families, and the public.

Year Founded: 1990

557 **Brain Research Through Advancing Innovative Neurotechnologies (BRAIN)**
National Institute of Neurological Disorders & Stroke
PO Box 5801
Bethesda, MD 20824
800-352-9424
E-mail: braininfo@ninds.nih.gov
www.braininitiative.nih.gov

Federal agency focused on supporting neuroscience research and working towards reducing the burdens associated with neurological disease.

Year Founded: 1950

558 **BrightFocus Foundation**
22512 Gateway Center Drive
Clarksburg, MD 20871
800-437-2423
E-mail: info@brightfocus.org
www.brightfocus.org

Stacy Pagos Haller, President and CEO
Kaci Baez, VP, Integrated Marketing
Diane Bovenkamp, PhD, VP, Scientific Affairs
Michael Buckley, VP, Public Affairs

Raises awareness of Alzheimer's disease, macular degeneration, and glaucoma and supports research and programs to cure brain and eye diseases.

Year Founded: 1973

559 **Caregiver Action Network**
1150 Connecticut Avenue Northwest
Suite 501
Washington, DC 20036-3904
202-454-3970
E-mail: info@caregiveraction.org
www.caregiveraction.org

Melissa Rowley, Chair
Michael Shaughnessy, Vice Chair
Marion T.R. Watkins, Treasurer
Joff Masukawa, Secretary

Caregiver Action Network is a nonprofit organization that acts as a support and an advocate for family caregivers of individuals with chronic conditions, diabilities, diseases, or old age. CAN provides education, peer support, and resources free of charge.

Year Founded: 1993

560 **Center for Mental Health Services (CMHS)**
Substance Abuse and Mental Health Services Administration
5600 Fishers Lane
Rockville, MD 20857
240-276-1310
www.samhsa.gov/about-us/who-we-are/offices-centers

Anita Everett, MD, DFAPA, Director

Promotes the treatment of mental illness and emotional disorders by increasing accessibility to mental health programs; supporting outreach, treatment, rehabilitation, and support programs and networks; and encouraging the use of scientifically-based information when treating mental disorders. CMHS provides information about mental health via a toll-free number and numerous publications. Developed for users of mental health services and their families, the general public, policy makers, providers, and the media.

Year Founded: 1992

561 **Federation of Associations in Behavioral and Brain Sciences (FABBS)**
1200 New York Ave. NW
Suite 459
Washington, DC 20005
202-749-8419
www.fabbs.org

Philip Rubin, PhD, President
Rae Silver, PhD, Vice President
Juliane Baron, Executive Director

FABBS is a coalition of scientific societies focused on expanding scientific knowledge on the brain, mind, and behavior. FABBS educates the public and policymakers on the importance of brain, mind, and behavior sciences research; provides quality sources to federal agencies and the media; advocates for research-focused policy and legislation; and promotes exchange of information among scientific organizations.

Year Founded: 1980

562 **National Association for the Dually Diagnosed (NADD)**
321 Wall Street
Kingston, NY 12401
845-331-4336
E-mail: info@thenadd.org
www.thenadd.org

Jeanne M. Farr, MA, Chief Executive Officer
Bruce Davis, President
Juanita St. Croix, Vice President
Ray Snyder, Secretary

NADD is a nonprofit organization designed to increase awareness of, and provide services for, individuals with developmental disabilities and mental illness. NADD empha-

sizes the importance of quality mental healthcare for people with mental health needs and offers conferences, information resources, educational programs, and training materials to professionals, parents, and organizations.
Year Founded: 1983

563 National Association of Councils on Developmental Disabilities
1825 K Street Northwest
Suite 600
Washington, DC 20006
202-506-5813
E-mail: info@nacdd.org
www.nacdd.org

Donna A. Meltzer, Chief Executie Officer
Robin Troutman, Deputy Director
Erin Prangley, Director of Public Policy
Sheryl Matney, Director of Technical Assistance

A national membership association representing the 56 State and Territorial Councils on Developmental Disabilities. An organization with the purpose of promoting the programs and policies that its member councils advocate, as well as ensuring inclusion for Americans with developmental disabilities.

564 National Mental Health Consumers' Self-Help Clearinghouse
E-mail: selfhelpclearinghouse@gmail.com
www.mhselfhelp.org

Joseph Rogers, Founder and Executive Director
Susan Rogers, Director

The Clearinghouse is a peer-run national technical assistance center focused on achieving respect and equality of opportunity for those with mental illnesses. The Clearinghouse helps with the growth of the mental health consumer movement by evaluating mental health services, advocating for mental health reform, and providing consumers with news, information, publications, and consultation services.
Year Founded: 1986

565 National Niemann-Pick Disease Foundation PO Box 49
Fort Atkinson, WI 53538-0049
877-287-3672
E-mail: nnpdf@nnpdf.org
www.nnpdf.org

Justin Hopkin, MD, Board Chair
Becky McGuire, Vice Chair
Liz Heinze, Secretary
Mike Smith, Treasurer

The Foundations promotes research and offers support and funding for individuals with Niemann-Pick Disease and their support network.
Year Founded: 1993

566 The Center for Family Support
2811 Zulette Avenue
Bronx, NY 10461
718-518-1500
E-mail: svernikoff@cfsny.org
www.www.cfsny.org

Steven Vernikoff, Executive Director
Barbara Greenwald, Chief Operating Officer
Jos, Martin Jara, President
Elise Geltzer, Vice President

The Center for Family Support offers assistance to individuals with developmental and related disabilities, as well as their families, and provides support services and programs that are designed to accommodate individual needs. Offers services throughout New York City, Westchester County, Long Island, and New Jersey.
Year Founded: 1954

Periodicals & Pamphlets

567 Alzheimer's Disease Research and the American Health Assistance Foundation
American Health Assistance Foundation
22512 Gateway Center Drive
Clarksburg, MD 20871-2005
301-948-3244
800-437-2423
E-mail: info@brightfocus.org
www.www.brightfocus.org

Grace Frisone, Chairman
Stacy Pagos Haller, President and CEO
Michael H Barnett,Esq, Vice Chairman
Nicholas W Raymond, Treasurer

Provides information on treatment, medication, medical referrals.

Video & Audio

568 A Change of Character
Fanlight Productions
32 Court Street
21st Floor
Brooklyn, NY 11201
718-488-8900
800-876-1710
E-mail: fanlight@fanlight.com
www.fanlight.com

Neal Goodman, Author

Truett Allen's personality changed drastically after a series of strokes resulted in damage to the frontal lobes of his brain. this captivating video features neuroscientist Dr. Elkhonon Goldberg, author of The Executive Brain, as well as neurologist and best-selling author Dr. Oliver Sacks.

569 Effective Learning Systems
5108 W 74th
St #390160
Minneapolis, MN 55439
239-948-1660
800-966-0443
E-mail: info@efflearn.com
www.effectivelearning.com

Robert E Griswold, President
Deirdre M Griswold, VP

Audio tapes for stress management, deep relaxation, anger control, peace of mind, insomnia, weight and smoking, self-image and self-esteem, positive thinking, health and healing. Since 1972, Effective Learning Systems has helped millions of people take charge of their lives and make positive changes. Over 75 titles available, each with a money-back guarantee. Price range $12-$14.

570 Understanding Mental Illness
Educational Video Network
1401 19th Street
Huntsville, TX 77340
936-295-5767
800-762-0060
www.www.evndirect.com

A video to learn and understand mental illness and how it affects you. *$79.95*

ISBN 1-589501-48-9

Web Sites

571 www.Nia.Nih.Gov/Alzheimers
Alzheimer's Disease Education and Referral

A division of the National Institute on Aging of the National Institute of Health. Solid information and a list of federally funded centers for evaluation, referral, treatment.

572 www.aan.com
American Academy of Neurology

Provides information for both professionals and the public on neurology subjects, covering Alzheimer's and Parkinson's diseases to stroke and migraine, includes comprehensive fact sheets.

573 www.agelessdesign.com
Ageless Design

Information on age related diseases such as Alzheimer's disease.

574 www.ahaf.org/alzdis/about/adabout.htm
American Health Assistance Foundation

Alzheimer's resource for patients and caregivers.

575 www.alz.co.uk
Alzheimer's Disease International

Umbrella organization of associations that support people with dementia.

576 www.alzforum.org
Alzheimer Research Forum

Information in layman's terms, plus many references and resources listed.

577 www.alzheimersbooks.com/
Alzheimer's Disease Bookstore

578 www.alzheimersupport.Com
AlzheimerSupport.com

Information and products for people dealing with Alzheimer's Disease.

579 www.biostat.wustl.edu
Washington University - Saint Louis

Page on Alzheimer's information, from basic care to friends and family networking experiences for support.

580 www.cyberpsych.org
CyberPsych

Hosts the American Psychoanalyists Foundation, American Association of Suicideology, Society for the Exploration of Psychotherapy Intergration, and Anxiety Disorders Association of America. Also subcategories of the anxiety disorders, as well as general information, including panic disorder, phobias, obsessive compulsive disorder (OCD), social phobia, generalized anxiety disorder, post traumatic stress disorder, and phobias of childhood. Book reviews and links to web pages sharing the topics.

581 www.mayohealth.org/mayo/common/htm/
MayoClinic.com

Information for dealing with Alzheimer's Disease.

582 www.mentalhealth.com
Internet Mental Health

On-line information and a virtual encyclopedia related to mental disorders, possible causes and treatments. News, articles, on-line diagnostic programs and related links. Designed to improve understanding, diagnosis and treatment of mental illness throughout the world. Awarded the Top Site Award and the NetPsych Cutting Edge Site Award.

583 www.mindstreet.com/training.html
Cognitive Therapy: A Multimedia Learning Program

The basics of cognitive therapy are presented.

584 www.ninds.nih.gov
National Institute of Neurological Disorders & Stroke

Neuroscience updates and articles.

585 www.noah-health.org/en/bns/disorders/
alzheimer.html
Ask NOAH About: Aging and Alzheimer's Disease

Links to brochures on medical problems of the elderly.

586 www.ohioalzcenter.org/facts.html
University Memory and Aging Center

Alzheimer's disease fact page.

587 www.planetpsych.com
Planetpsych.com

Learn about disorders, their treatments and other topics in psychology. Articles are listed under the related topic areas. Ask a therapist a question for free, or view the directory of professionals in your area. If you are a therapist sign up for the directory. Current features, self-help, interactive, and newsletter archives.

588 www.psych.org/clin_res/pg_dementia.cfm
American Psychiatric Association

Practice guidelines for the treatment of patients with Alzheimer's.

589 www.psychcentral.com
Psych Central

Personalized one-stop index for psychology, support, and mental health issues, resources, and people on the Internet.

590 www.rcpsych.ac.uk/info/help/memory
Royal College of Psychiatrists

Memory and Dementia

591 **www.store.samhsa.gov**
Substance Abuse and Mental Health Services
Administration

Resources on mental disorders as well as treatment and recovery.

592 **www.zarcrom.com/users/alzheimers**
Alzheimer's Outreach

Detailed and practical information.

593 **www.zarcrom.com/users/yeartorem**
Year to Remember

A memorial site covering many aspects of Alzheimer's disease.

Neurodevelopmental Disorders

Introduction

Neurodevelopmental Disorders describe a range of brain function disorders that affect emotion, learning, ability, self control, and memory which unfold as the individual grows. Parents, other relatives, guardians, and teachers are concerned about not missing the signs of a treatable disorder while, at the same time, not subjecting a child to unnecessary and potentially stigmatizing diagnosis and treatment. Most of these disorders are now contained with the category of Autism Spectrum Disorder (see that section for specifics).

When there is publicity about a medical disorder, however, the number of diagnoses goes up. In the case of Bipolar Disorder, cases that may have been overlooked before such public awareness are being accurately diagnosed. Still, many cases are diagnosed and treated without a full evaluation. As noted in the chapter on Autism Spectrum Disorders, while awareness of the diagnosis has brought more children to diagnosis and treatment, it also seems that the actual incidence of the condition is on the rise; the reasons are still unknown.

The American Academy of Child and Adolescent Psychiatry (http://www.aacap.org/) provides accurate and useful information to help those responsible for children decide: whether a child's behavior is normal for his or her age; if a child is being adversely influenced by circumstances; what is a warning sign for mental disorder; and what constitutes a mental disorder. Warning signs of mental illness in children and youth may include self-harm, substance abuse, sudden and unexplained weight loss, difficulty focusing, drastic behavior changes, dangerous or out-of-control behavior, and drastic mood swings.

In general, a child or adolescent is evaluated not only on the basis of particular behaviors that cause concern, but also with respect to meeting the milestones expected at his or her age. A child should be increasingly able to relate to other people, both children and adults, and to learn. An untreated mental disorder can deprive a child of essential years of social and educational growth. Anyone concerned about a child should start with the child's pediatrician. A child should not be given a diagnosis or prescribed medication without a complete physical health evaluation, specialized observation, and interviews with parents, teachers, and others familiar with him or her. There is a shortage of fully qualified experts in child and adolescent mental health; it may require considerable persistence to ensure that a child receives the attention necessary, but it will be worthwhile. There should be no hesitation to obtain a second opinion. Health professionals should be able to explain why a child was or was not given a specific diagnosis, and the pros and cons of the treatment choices.

Note: Vaccinations do not cause autism, and going un-vaccinated exposes both a child to diseases that can be serious, even fatal, and all those the child comes in contact with.

Associations & Agencies

595   AHRC New York City
83 Maiden Lane
New York, NY 10038
212-780-2500
www.www.ahrcnyc.org

Raymond Ferrigno, President
Patricia A. Murphy, Esq., 1st Vice President
Cory Olicker Henkel, 2nd Vice President
Andreas Chrysostomou, Financial Secretary

AHRC New York City is an organization dedicated to helping people with intellectual and developmental disabilities build full lives. Provides support services, training programs, clinics, workshops, schools, and residential facilities to individuals with developmental and intellectual disabilities.

Year Founded: 1949

596   American Academy of Child and Adolescent Psychiatry
3615 Wisconsin Avenue Northwest
Washington, DC 20016-3007
202-966-7300
E-mail: communications@aacap.org
www.aacap.org

Warren Y.K. Ng, MD, MPH, President
Tami D. Benton, MD, President-Elect
Debra E. Koss, MD, Secretary
Neal Ryan, MD, Treasurer

Nonprofit membership-based organization comprised of child and adolescent psychiatrists committed to serving the health care needs of children and their families. The AACAP disseminates information and research findings on mental illnesses, promotes accessibility to proper treatment and services, and advances efforts in mental illness prevention.

Year Founded: 1953

597   American Academy of Pediatrics
345 Park Boulevard
Itasca, IL 60143
888-227-1770
www.aap.org

Mark Del Monte, JD, CEO/President
Christine Bork, MBA, Chief Development Officer
Vera Tait, MD, FAAP, Chief Medical Officer
John Miller, CPA, Chief Financial Officer

The American Academy of Pediatrics is an organization consisting of 66,000 pediatricians committed to ensuring the well-being, health, and safety of all infants, children, adolescents, and young adults.

Year Founded: 1930

598   American Pediatric Society
9303 New Trails Drive
Suite 350
The Woodlands, TX 77381
346-980-9707
E-mail: info@aps1888.org
www.www.aps1888.org

Mary Leonard, President
Lisa Robinson, President-Elect
Clifford Bogue, Secretary/Treasurer

Society of professionals working on pediatric health care issues, through research, advocacy, and education. The society offers conferences and a variety of publications.

Year Founded: 1888

599 Association for Children's Mental Health
6017 W. St. Joe Highway
Suite 200
Lansing, MI 48917
517-372-4016
888-226-4543
www.acmh-mi.org

Kelly Gluszewski, President
Beverly Schumer, Treasurer
Jane Shank, Executive Director
Terri Henrizi, Education Coordinator

A Michigan-based nonprofit organization serving families of children and youth with emotional, behavioral, or mental health needs. Provides information, support, resources, referrals, advocacy, and networking and leadership opportunities for youth.

Year Founded: 1989

600 Federation for Children with Special Needs (FCSN)
529 Main Street
Suite 1M3
Boston, MA 02129
617-236-7210
800-331-0688
E-mail: info@fcsn.org
www.fcsn.org

John Reichenbach, President
Pam Nourse, Executive Director
Matthew Trivella, Treasurer

The Federation for Children with Special Needs is an organization dedicated to supporting parents of children with disabilities. The Federation seeks to ensure the full participation of all people in community life, including persons with disabilities.

601 INCLUDEnyc
116 E. 16th St.
5th Floor
New York, NY 10003
212-677-4650
E-mail: info@includenyc.org
www.includenyc.org

Owen P.J. King, Chair
Ellen Miller-Wachtel, Vice President
Jamie H. Klein, Vice President
Barbara A. Glassman, Executive Director

INCLUDEnyc, formerly Resources for Children with Special Needs, is an organization dedicated to providing assistance and support to families and young people with disabilities across all five boroughs in New York City. INCLUDEnyc offers programs and services to help children with disabilities develop their skills and reach their full potential.

Year Founded: 1983

602 Lifespire
1 Whitehall Street
9th Floor
New York, NY 10004

212-741-0100
E-mail: info@lifespire.org
www.lifespire.org

Michael S. Gross, Chairman
Thomas Lydon, CEO and President
Keith Lee, Chief Financial Officer
Bonita Hinson, Chief Operating Officer

Lifespire seeks to provide support to individuals with disabilities and assist them with the development of the skills needed to become independent and contributing members of the community.

Year Founded: 1951

603 Mentally Ill Kids in Distress (MIKID)
7816 North 19th Avenue
Phoenix, AZ 85021
602-253-1240
E-mail: phoenix@mikid.org
www.mikid.org

Kathryn Hart, President
Sue Gilbertson, Founder
Jeff Kazmierczak, RN, MSN, Chief Executive Officer
Bonnie Kolakowski, MBA, Chief Financial Officer

Mentally Ill Kids in Distress provides support and assistance to families in Arizona with children and youth who are struggling with behavioral problems. MIKID seeks to improve the behavioral health and wellness of youth across Arizona. Offers information centers, assistance by phone, email or in person, support groups, educational meetings, referrals to resources, and direct support services.

Year Founded: 1987

604 NAPCSE National Association of Parents with Children in Special Education
3642 East Sunnydale Drive
Chandler Heights, AZ 85142
800-754-4421
E-mail: contact@napcse.org
www.napcse.org

Dr. George Giuliani, President

The NAPCSE is dedicated to ensuring quality education for all children and adolescents with special needs. NAPCSE provides resources, support, and assistance to parents with children in special education.

605 National Federation of Families for Children's Mental Health
15800 Crabbs Branch Way
Suite 300
Rockville, MD 20855
240-403-1901
E-mail: ffcmh@ffcmh.org
www.ffcmh.org

Lynda Gargan, PhD, Executive Director
Gail Cormier, Project Director
Leann Sherman, Project Coordinator

The National Federation of Families for Children's Mental Health is a national organization focused on advocating for the rights of children affected by mental health challenges, assisting family-run organizations across the nation, and ensuring that children and families concerned with mental health have access to services.

Year Founded: 1989

606 Parent to Parent of Omaha
Ollie Webb Center
1941 South 42nd Street
Suite 122
Omaha, NE 68105-2942
402-346-5220
www.olliewebbinc.org/parent-to-parent

Laurie Ackermann, Executive Director
David Ackermann, Education Coordinator
Tim McAreavey, President
Warren Miller, 1st Vice President

Consists of parents, professionals, and others who are interested in providing emotional and peer support to parents of children with disabilities. Offers a parent-matching program which matches new parents with parents who have had sufficient experience and training.

Year Founded: 1971

607 Parents Helping Parents
Sobrato Center for Nonprofits
1400 Parkmoor Avenue
Suite 100
San Jose, CA 95126
408-727-5775
855-727-5775
E-mail: info@php.com
www.php.com

Maria Daane, Executive Director
Mark Fishler, Development Director
Janet Nunez, Development Director
Virginia Hildebrand, Finance Director

Parents Helping Parents is a community-based organization dedicated to helping individuals with special needs realize their full potential through the provision of support services, information, training, and resources for children and adults with special needs, their families, and professionals.

Year Founded: 1976

608 Research and Training Center for Pathways to Positive Futures
Portland State University
1600 Southwest 4th Avenue
Suite 900
Portland, OR 97201
503-725-4040
E-mail: rtcpubs@pdx.edu
www.pathwaysrtc.pdx.edu

Janet Walker, Director
Nancy Koroloff, Coordinator of Research

The Research and Training Center for Pathways to Positive Futures conducts research, training, and information dissemination with the goal of improving the lives of youth and young adults with mental health needs.

Year Founded: 2009

609 Society for Pediatric Research
9303 New Trails Drive
Suite 350
The Woodlands, TX 77381
346-980-9710
E-mail: info@societyforpediatricresearch.org
www.www.societyforpediatricresearch.org

Beth A. Tarini, MD, MS, President
Kate Ackerman, MD, MBA, President-Elect
David Hunstad, MD, Strategy/Operations Officer

A society that aims to improve pediatric health by creating a network of multi-disciplinary researchers through meetings/conferences, career opportunities, and advocacy on medical system issues.

610 The Center for Family Support
2811 Zulette Avenue
Bronx, NY 10461
718-518-1500
E-mail: svernikoff@cfsny.org
www.www.cfsny.org

Steven Vernikoff, Executive Director
Barbara Greenwald, Chief Operating Officer
Jos, Martin Jara, President
Elise Geltzer, Vice President

The Center for Family Support offers assistance to individuals with developmental and related disabilities, as well as their families, and provides support services and programs that are designed to accommodate individual needs. Offers services throughout New York City, Westchester County, Long Island, and New Jersey.

Year Founded: 1954

611 Young Adult Institute and Workshop (YAI)
460 West 34th Street
11th Floor
New York, NY 10001-2382
212-273-6100
www.yai.org

George Contos, Chief Executive Officer
Kevin Carey, Chief Financial Officer
Alek Hoyos, Chief of Staff
Ravi Dahiya, Chief Program Officer

The YAI Network is an organization that serves people with intellectual and developmental disabilities. The YAI Network seeks to enhance the lives of people with disabilities by creating new opportunities for them. Provides a range of family support, employment training and placement, clinical, and residential services.

Year Founded: 1957

612 ZERO TO THREE: National Center for Infants, Toddlers, and Families
2445 M Street NW
Suite 600
Washington, DC 20037
202-638-1144
www.zerotothree.org

Brenda Jones Harden, President
Matthew Melmed, Executive Director
Walter S. Gilliam, Vice President
Eugene P. Stein, Treasurer

A national, nonprofit organization that provides information and resources on early development to parents, professionals, and policymakers. Zero To Three's mission is to improve the lives of infants and toddlers, and to promote their health and development.

Year Founded: 1977

Periodicals & Pamphlets

613 Helping Hand
Performance Resource Press
1270 Rankin Drive
Suite F
Troy, MI 48083-2843
248-588-7733
800-453-7733
www.store.amplifiedlifenetwork.com

Lyle Labardee, mS, LPC, NCC, President

A newsletter on child and adult behavioral health.

4 pages 9 per year

Research Centers

614 Child Neurology and Developmental Center
1510 Jericho Turnpike
New Hyde Park, NY 11040
516-352-2500
www.childbrain.com

Rami Grossmann, M.D.

Pediatric neurology practice of Rami Grossmann, M.D. in New York. Neurologists are highly trained to treat disorders of the nervous system. This includes diseases of the brain, spinal cord, nerves, and muscles. Common problems that Dr. Grossmann diagnoses and treats include the following: AD/HD, Autism, a form of PDD, Developmental delays, Epilepsy, Headaches, Learning difficulties, and Tic Disorders.

615 KidsHealth
The Nemours Foundation
10140 Centurion Parkway
Jacksonville, FL 32256
904-697-4100
E-mail: comments@KidsHealth.org
www.kidshealth.org

Alfred I. duPont, Nemour's Foundation Creator
Neil Izenberg, MD, Editor-in-Chief & Founder

KidsHealth is more than just the facts about health. As part of The Nemours Foundation's Center for Children's Health Media, KidsHealth also provides families with perspective, advice, and comfort about a wide range of physical, emotional, and behavioral issues that affect children and teens. The Nemours Center for Children's Health Media is a part of The Nemours Foundation, a nonprofit organization created by philanthropist Alfred I. duPont in 1936 and devoted to improving the health of children.

Year Founded: 1936

Support Groups & Hot Lines

616 Alateen and Al-Anon Family Groups
1600 Corporate Landing Parkway
Virginia Beach, VA 23454-5617
757-563-1600
888-425-2666
E-mail: wso@al-anon.org
www.al-anon.alateen.org

Mary Ann Keller, Director Members Services

Strength and hope for friends and families of problem drinkers.

617 Girls and Boys Town of New York
281 Park Avenue South
5th Floor
New York, NY 10010
212-725-4260
800-448-3000
www.www.boystown.org

Guy Cleveland, Chairman
John C. Scott, Ph.D., Board Secretary
Jennifer Armstrong, Senior Vice President of New Pro
Crystal Denunzio, Vice President of Business Devel

Crisis intervention and referrals.

Year Founded: 1990

618 Kidspeace National Centers
4085 Independence Drive
Schnecksville, PA 18078
800-257-3223
www.kidspeace.org

Mary Jane Willis, Chairman
William R Isemann, President & CEO
James Horan, Executive VP,CFO,Treasurer
Michael Slack, EVP,Business Development

Mission is to give hope, help and healing to children, families and communities. Helping people in need overcome challenges and transform their lives by providing emotional and physical healthcare and educational services in an atmosphere of teamwork, compassion and creativity.

619 National Youth Crisis Hotline
5331 Mount Alifan Drive
San Diego, CA 92111-2622
800-448-4663
www.1800hithome.com/

Information and referral for runaways, and for youth and parents with problems.

620 One Place for Special Needs
One Place for Special Needs, Ltd.
PO Box 9701
Naperville, IL 60567
E-mail: info@oneplaceforspecialneeds.com
www.oneplaceforspecialneeds.com

Dawn Villarreal, Founder

An information network and social community that allows the disability community to share resources and make connections in their own neighborhood. And a place where those who actively work with those who have disabilities can let families learn about their products, program and services.

Year Founded: 2002

621 Rainbows
1360 Hamilton Parkway
Itasca, IL 60143
847-952-1770
800-266-3206
E-mail: info@rainbows.org
www.rainbows.org

Anthony Taglia, Chair
Bob Thomas, Executive Director and CEO
Burt Heatherly, CFO

The largest international children's charity dedicated solely to helping youth successfully navigate the very difficult grief process. Every day, children are touched by emotional suffering caused by a death, divorce, deployment of a family member, incarceration of a loved one, or any of a multitude of significant event traumas including natural or manmade disasters.

Year Founded: 1983

622 SADD: Students Against Destructive Decisions
255 Main Street
Marlborough, MA 01752-5505
508-481-3568
877-723-3462
E-mail: info@sadd.org
www.sadd.org

Danna Mauch,PhD, Chairman
Penny Wells, President and CEO
Susan Scarola, Treasurer
James E Champagne, Secretary/Clerk

Providing students with the best prevention tools possible to deal with the issues of underage drinking, other drug use, risky and impaired driving, and other destructive decisions.

Year Founded: 1981

Video & Audio

623 Aggression Replacement Training Video: A Comprehensive Intervention for Aggressive Youth
Research Press
PO Box 7886
PO Box 9177
Champaign, IL 61826
217-352-3273
800-519-2707
E-mail: rp@researchpress.com
www.researchpress.com

This staff training DVD features scenes of adolescents participating in group sessions for each of ART's three interventions. Viewers will see a prosocial skills training group, an anger management session, and a moral reasoning group. *$125.00*

ISBN 0-878225-91-0

624 Anger Management-Enhanced Edition
Educational Video Network, Inc.
1401 19th Street
Huntsville, TX 77340
936-295-5767
800-762-0060
www.www.evndirect.com

Learn what causes anger and understand why our bodies react as they do when we're angry. Effective techniques for assuaging anger are discussed.

625 Are the Kids Alright?
Fanlight Productions
32 Court Street
21st Floor
Brooklyn, NY 11201
718-488-8900
800-876-1710
E-mail: orders@fanlight.com
www.fanlight.com

Karen Bernstein, Author
Ellen Spiro, Author

Filmed in courtrooms, correctional institutions, treatment centers, and family homes, this searing documentary documents the results of the tragic decline in mental health services for children and adolescents at risk.

626 Bipolar Disorder: Shifting Mood Swings
Educational Training Videos
136 Granville St
Suite 200
Gahanna, OH 43230
www.educationaltrainingvideos.com

Different from the routine ups and downs of life, the symptoms of bipolar disorder are severe - even to the point of being life-threatening. In this insightful program, patients speak from their own experience about the complexities of diagnosis and the very real danger of suicide, while family members and close friends address the strain of the condition's cyclic behavior.

627 Bipolar Focus, Bipolar Disorder Audio and Video Files: Bipolar and Children/Adolescents
Bipolar Focus
www.pendulum.org/video/videospecial.htm

Website with list of playable video and audio files on topics including: children and mental health, antipsychotics in special populations: pediatrics and adolescents, mental health in childre, parts I and II, mental health and illness in teenagers, adult minds- mental health in early adulthood, college students and mental health, and pregnancy and the mind.

628 Case Studies in Childhood Obsessive-Compulsive Disorder
Educational Training Videos
136 Granville St
Suite 200
Gahanna, OH 43230
www.educationaltrainingvideos.com

This edition of Primetime tracks the treatment of Bridget, Rocco, and Michelle as they attempt to reclaim their lives and overcome the stigma associated with the disorder. Original ABC News broadcast title: Kids Battle Obsessive-Compulsive Disorder.

629 Children: Experts on Divorce
Courage to Change
1 Huntington Quadrangle
Suite: 1N03
Melville, NY 11747
800-962-1141
www.couragetochange.com/

Dede L Pitts, CEO

This DVD should be played for divorcing parents in your waiting room or client library. Children, ages 5-17, speak of what they need from their parents, what helps and what hurts. Judges, mediators, therapists and Karl Malone also appear on camera. DVD makes parents more ready to collaborate and make agreements that will benefit their children. Have a box of tissues handy. *$34.95*

630 Chill: Straight Talk About Stress
Childs Work/Childs Play
303 Crossways Park Dr
Woodbury, NY 11797-2099

800-962-1141
E-mail: info@Childswork.com
www.Childswork.com

Encourages youth to recognize, analyze and handle the stresses in their lives. 22 minutes. *$96.95*

631 Clinical Impressions: Identifying Mental Illness
Educational Training Videos
136 Granville St
Suite 200
Gahanna, OH 43230
www.educationaltrainingvideos.com

How long can mental illness stay hidden, especially from the eyes of trained experts? This program rejoins a group of ten adults- five of them healthy and five of them with histories of mental illness- as psychiatric specialists try to spot and correctly diagnose the latter. Administering a series of collaborative and one-on-one tests, including assessments of personality type, physical self-image, and rational thinking, the panel gradually makes decisions about who suffers from depression, bipolar disorder, bulimia, and social anxiety.

632 Coping with Emotions
Educational Video Network, Inc.
1401 19th Street
Huntsville, TX 77340
936-295-5767
800-762-0060
www.www.evndirect.com

Anger, indifference, sadness, confusion and ecstatic happiness are emotions that manifest themselves frequently during the teen years. The hormones that change the body physically also have a great effect on a teenager's emotions. Discover the gamut of emotions that rule a teenager's life and what can be done to control them.

633 Coping with Stress
Educational Video Network, Inc.
1401 19th Street
Huntsville, TX 77340
936-295-5767
800-762-0060
www.www.evndirect.com

Stress affects everyone, both emotionally and physically. For some, mismanaged stress can result in substance abuse, violence, or even suicide. This program answers the question, How can a person cope with stress?

634 Dark Voices: Schizophrenia
Educational Training Videos
136 Granville St
Suite 200
Gahanna, OH 43230
www.educationaltrainingvideos.com

This program seeks to understand how schizophrenia touches the lives of patients and their family members while examining the disease's etiology and pathology. A Discovery Channel Production.

635 Dealing with ADHD: Attention Deficit/ Hyperactivity
Educational Video Network, Inc.
1401 19th Street
Huntsville, TX 77340

936-295-5767
800-762-0060
www.www.evndirect.com

Learn about attention deficit/hyperactivity disorder and learn what factors are thought to contribute to the development of this disorder. Other disorders that commonly co-exist with ADHD will be identified. The impulsivity and risk-taking behaviors of ADHD teens will be focused upon and tips that ADHD students can use to succeed academically will be provided. Laws that require schools to make special accommodations for ADHD students will be reviewed, and viewers will learn how to contact organizations that exist to help people who are dealing with ADHD.

636 Dealing with Depression
Educational Video Network, Inc.
1401 19th Street
Huntsville, TX 77340
936-295-5767
800-762-0060
www.www.evndirect.com

As more and more young people are falling victim to depression, it is important to understand what causes it and to know how to get the help that can rid a person of this life-wrecking affliction.

637 Dealing with Grief
Educational Video Network, Inc.
1401 19th Street
Huntsville, TX 77340
936-295-5767
800-762-0060
www.www.evndirect.com

Grief allows us to acknowledge and mourn our losses so we can reconcile our feelings and move forward in life. Learn how to deal with your grief and become a better person for having gone through it.

638 Dealing with Social Anxiety
Educational Video Network, Inc.
1401 19th Street
Huntsville, TX 77340
936-295-5767
800-762-0060
www.www.evndirect.com

Social anxiety is America's third-largest psychiatric disorder. It generally develops during the mid-teen years, and almost always before the age of 25. Understand what may trigger the development of anxiety and learn how it sometimes evolves into full-blown panic disorder, which is characterized by recurrent attacks of terror or fear. The consequences of social anxiety are examined and effective treatments are discussed.

639 Don't Kill Yourself: One Survivor's Message
Educational Training Videos
136 Granville St
Suite 200
Gahanna, OH 43230
www.educationaltrainingvideos.com

This is the story of a young man, David, who at 16 years of age survived a suicide attempt. Now 22, he shares the events of his life leading up to the attempt, including how low self-esteem led to drug addiction, and how the addiction encouraged the sense that life was no longer worth living.

640 **Fetal Alcohol Syndrome and Effect DVD**
Hazelden
15251 Pleasant Valley Road
PO Box 11
Center City, MN 55012-0011
651-213-4200
800-328-9000
E-mail: info@hazelden.org
www.hazelden.org

Mark Mishek, President and CEO
James A. Blaha, Vice President Finance and Admin
Ann Bray, General Counsel and Vice Preside
Sharon Birnbaum, Corporate Director of Human Reso

Excellent for women in treatment, addiction professionals, and community education programs, the video is centered on the work being done with children affected by fetal alcohol and their families. It provides a factual definition of Fetal Alcohol Syndrome and Effect, explains how children are diagnossed and, most importantly, vividly illustrates the positive prognosis possible for fetal alcohol children. Medical and educational professionals, biological and adoptive parents and siblings, and the children themselves speak in this video about FAS. *$225.00*

641 **Legacy of Childhood Trauma: Not Always Who They Seem**
Research Press
Dept 24 W
PO Box 9177
Champaign, IL 61826-9177
217-352-3273
800-519-2707
E-mail: rp@researchpress.com
www.researchpress.com

Russell Pense, VP Marketing

Focuses on the connection between so-called delinquent youth and the experience of childhood trauma such as emotional, sexual, or physical abuse. The video features the unique stories of four young adults who are survivors of childhood trauma. They candidly discuss their troubled childhood and teenage years and reveal how, with the help of caring adults, they were able to salvage their lives. The caregivers, who helped these young adults through their teenage years, are joined by other helping professionals who provide thorough discussions of diagnosis and treatment issues. They offer valuable guidelines and insights on working with adolescents who have experienced childhood trauma. *$195.00*

642 **Mental Disorder**
Educational Training Videos
136 Granville St
Suite 200
Gahanna, OH 43230
www.educationaltrainingvideos.com

What is abnormality? Using the case studies of two young women; one who has depression, one who has an anxiety disorder; as a springboard, this program presents three psychological perspective on mental disorder.

643 **Overcoming Obstacles and Self-Doubt**
Educational Video Network, Inc.
1401 19th Street
Huntsville, TX 77340
936-295-5767
800-762-0060
www.www.evndirect.com

When feelings of self-doubt are combined with the sudden appearance of an overwhelming obstacle, the situation can be emotionally crippling.

644 **Suicide among Teens**
Educational Video Network, Inc.
1401 19th Street
Huntsville, TX 77340
936-295-5767
800-762-0060
www.www.evndirect.com

Suicide devastates surviving loved ones. Find out why it should never be considered as a solution and learn how to recognize warning signs in a suicidal person.

645 **Teenage Anxiety, Depression, and Suicide**
Educational Video Network, Inc.
1401 19th Street
Huntsville, TX 77340
936-295-5767
800-762-0060
www.www.evndirect.com

This program can provide helpful insight to those in need of assistance.

646 **Understanding Mental Illness**
Educational Video Network, Inc.
1401 19th Street
Huntsville, TX 77340
936-295-5767
800-762-0060
www.www.evndirect.com

Contains information and classifications of mental illness. Mental illness can strike anyone, at any age. Learn about various organic and functional mental disorders as discussed and their causes and symptoms, and learn where to seek help for a variety of mental health concerns.

647 **Understanding Personality Disorders**
Educational Video Network, Inc.
1401 19th Street
Huntsville, TX 77340
936-295-5767
800-762-0060
www.www.evndirect.com

For many people, the onset of a psychological disorder goes undiagnosed and untreated, and, as a result, they face a constant, if not impossible, struggle to maintain good mental health. This can be especially true when individuals suffer from a personality disorder. However, with identification and understanding, crippling personality disorders can be brought out of the shadows of ignorance and into the light of treatment.

648 **Why Isn't My Child Happy? Video Guide About Childhood Depression**
ADD WareHouse
300 NW 70th Avenue
Suite 102
Plantation, FL 33317-2360
954-792-8100
800-233-9273

E-mail: sales@addwarehouse.com
www.addwarehouse.com

Sam Goldstein, PhD, Author

The first of its kind, this new video deals with childhood depression. Informative and frank about this common problem, this book offers helpful guidance for parents and professionals trying to better understand childhood depression. 110 minutes. *$55.00*

Web Sites

649 **www.Al-Anon-Alateen.org**
Al-Anon and Alateen

AA literature may serve as an introduction.

650 **www.CHADD.org**
CHADD: Children/Adults with Attention Deficit/Hyperactivity Disorder

Offers support for individuals, parents, teachers, professionals, and others.

651 **www.aacap.org**
American Academy of Child and Adolescent Psychiatry

Represents over 6,000 child and adolescent psychiatrists, brochures availible online which provide concise and up-to-date material on issues ranging from children who suffer from depression and teen suicide to stepfamily problems and child sexual abuse.

652 **www.adhdnews.com/Advocate.htm**
Advocating for Your Child

653 **www.adhdnews.com/sped.htm**
Special Education Rights and Responsibilities

Writing IEP's and TIEPS. Pursuing special education services.

654 **www.couns.uiuc.edu**
Self-Help Brochures

Address issues teens deal with.

655 **www.freedomvillageusa.com**
Freedom Village USA

Faith-based home for troubled teens.

656 **www.kidshealth.org/kid/feeling/index.html**
Dealing with Feelings

Ten readings. Examples are: Why Am I So Sad; Are You Shy; Am I Too Fat or Too Thin; and A Kid's Guide to Divorce.

657 **www.naturalchild.com/home**
Natural Child Project

Articles by experts.

658 **www.nospank.net**
Project NoSpank

Site for those against paddling in schools.

659 **www.oneplaceforspecialneeds.com**
One Place for Special Needs, Ltd.

660 **www.parentcenterhub.org**
National Dissemination Center for Children with Disabilities

The Center for Parent Information and Resources hosts many of the resources published by the National Dissemination Center for Children with Disabilities, including English and Spanish resources.

661 **www.parenthood.com**
Parenthood.Com

A leading online destination for moms, mothers-to-be, and families.

662 **www.rtckids.fmhi.usf.edu**
Research & Training Center for Children's Mental Health

The Research and Training Center for Children's Mental Health at the University of South Florida was formed to conduct research, provide training, and contribute to the improvement of services for children with emotional and behavioral disabilities and their families. The Research and Training Center was funded by the National Institute on Disability and Rehabilitation Research and the Substance Abuse and Mental Health Services Administration from 1984 to 2009. Resources available on website.

663 **www.wholefamily.com**
About Teens Now

Addresses important issues in teens lives.

664 **www2.mc.duke.edu/pcaad**
Duke University's Program in Child and Anxiety Disorders

Obsessive Compulsive Disorder

Introduction

Obsessive-Compulsive Disorder, commonly known as OCD, is characterized by uncontrollable, reoccurring thoughts and behaviours that an individual feels the strong or irresistible urge to repeat over and over. Almost everyone will have obsessive thoughts/compulsive behaviors at some point in their lives, but for people with OCD the obsessions and compulsions become so extreme that they consume a lot of time and can interfere with other aspects of life, such as work, school, and personal relationships.

Related disorders include Hoarding Disorder, trichotillomania (hair pulling), and Excoriation (skin picking).

SYMPTOMS

Obsessive-Compulsive Disorder
• Individuals with OCD have overwhelming obsessions, compulsions, or both.
Obsessions are repeated, intrusive, unwanted thoughts that cause distressing emotions such as anxiety or anguish.
A compulsion is the reaction to the obsessive thought. It can be a behavior (e.g., hand washing), or a mental act (e.g., praying), performed to alleviated distress or prevent a dreaded situation. These behaviors are generally seen as excessive and unrealistic;
• The obsessions or compulsions are time consuming (taking at least one hour of time a day) or significantly interfere with the person's normal routine, occupational or academic functioning, or usual social activities;
• The symptoms are not due to another mental illness. For example, excessive worry that is linked to General Anxiety Disorder, or patterns of behavior that are linked to Autism Spectrum Disorder.

Hoarding Disorder
• Extreme and persistent difficulty discarding items, distress when parting with items, strong urges to save items;
• Accumulation of possessions is such that rooms/spaces are not able to be used as intended.

Excoriation
• Repeated skin picking causing skin legions;
• Repeated efforts to stop or decrease skin picking without success.

Trichotillomania
• Repeated hair pulling so that hair loss is noticeable;
• Repeated effforts to stop hair pulling without success.

ASSOCIATED FEATURES

In OCD, the person is unable to control the anxiety even when he or she knows it is exaggerated and unreasonable. To other people, the person may seem edgy, irritable, to have unexpected outbursts of anger, or to be consumed by an unreasonable fear. The problem takes up time and effort and becomes a major preoccupation. The OCD affected persona can further that time and expenditure of energy in creating a ritual to manage the obsession, such as performing an action a specific number of times in a particular order.

PREVALENCE

Obsessive-Compulsive Disorder
OCD usually begins in adolescence or early adulthood, but may begin in childhood. In males the onset is earlier (between 6 and 15 years old) than for women (between 20 and 29), though it is equally common in both males and females.

Hording Disorder
Hoarding Disorder begins to present when a person is going through puberty (generally around 12-15 years of age) and their symptoms worsen as they age. People with Hoarding Disorder are likely to have a mood or anxiety disorder. The disorder causes severe problems with everyday functioning.

Excoriation and Trichotillomania
These disorders are more common in females and begin to show symptoms around puberty

TREATMENT OPTIONS

Obsessive-Compulsive Disorder
It is very important to have a full evaluation so that a proper diagnosis can be made. In general, people should have a primary care evaluation as part of the diagnostic process, so as to rule out a general medical condition that could be causing the signs and symptoms. Patients with OCD may benefit from behavioral therapy and/or a variety of medications. Particularly effective is exposure and response prevention therapy, in which a therapist carefully exposes the patient to situations that cause anxiety and provoke the obsessive-compulsive behavior. Slowly the patient learns to decrease and eventually end the ritualistic behaviors.

Hoarding Disorder
To date, there is no evidence to suggest that any pharmacotherapy works for hoarding. Therefore, behavior therapy is used with the aim to reduce the hoarded items and not acquire new ones.

Excoriation
There have been few studies to research the implications of pharmacotherapy on Excoriation. Currently, the treatment for the disorder is habit reversal therapy.

Trichotillomania
The current treatment for Trichotillomania is habit reversal therapy.

Associations & Agencies

666 Anxiety and Depression Association of America
8701 Georgia Avenue
Suite 412
Silver Spring, MD 20910
240-485-1001
E-mail: information@adaa.org
www.adaa.org

Charles B. Nemeroff, MD, President
Susan K. Gurley, JD, Executive Director
Tanja Jovanovic, PhD, Treasurer
Sanjay MatthewW, PhD, Secretary

An international nonprofit organization committed to the use of education and research to promote the prevention, treatment, and cure of anxiety, depressive, obssesive compulsive, and other trauma related disorders. ADAA's mission is to improve the lives of all people with anxiety and mood disorders.

Year Founded: 1979

667   Brain & Behavior Research Foundation
747 Third Avenue
33rd Floor
New York, NY 10017
646-681-4888
800-829-8289
E-mail: info@bbrfoundation.org
www.www.bbrfoundation.org

Donald M. Boardman, Treasurer
Jeffrey Borenstein, MD, President and CEO
Louis Innamorato, CPA, VP and Chief Financial Officer
Faith Rothblatt, Vice President, Development

The Brain and Behavior Research Foundation awards grants aimed at advancing scientific understandings of mental health treatments and mental disorders such as depression and schizophrenia. The Brain and Behavior Research Foundation's mission is to eliminate the suffering caused by mental illness.

Year Founded: 1987

668   Center for Mental Health Services (CMHS)
Substance Abuse and Mental Health Services
Administration
5600 Fishers Lane
Rockville, MD 20857
240-276-1310
www.samhsa.gov/about-us/who-we-are/offices-centers

Anita Everett, MD, DFAPA, Director

Promotes the treatment of mental illness and emotional disorders by increasing accessibility to mental health programs; supporting outreach, treatment, rehabilitation, and support programs and networks; and encouraging the use of scientifically-based information when treating mental disorders. CMHS provides information about mental health via a toll-free number and numerous publications. Developed for users of mental health services and their families, the general public, policy makers, providers, and the media.

Year Founded: 1992

669   Goodwill's Community Employment Services
Goodwill Industries-Suncoast, Inc.
10596 Gandy Blvd.
St. Petersburg, FL 33702
727-523-1512
888-279-1988
TDD: 727-579-1068
www.goodwill-suncoast.org

Sandra Young, Chair
Louise Lopez, Sr. Vice Chair
Dominic Macrone, Board Secretary

The St. Petersburg headquarters serves ten counties in the state of Florida. Their mission is to help people with disabilities gain employment through training programs, employment services, and affordable housing.

Year Founded: 1954

670   International OCD Foundation, Inc.
PO Box 961029
Boston, MA 02196
617-973-5801
E-mail: info@iocdf.org
www.iocdf.org

Susan Boaz, President
David Calusdian, Vice President
Ron Prevost, Treasurer
Denise Egan Stack, LMHC, Secretary

An organization for people with obsessive-compulsive disorder, as well as their families and friends. The Foundation aims to educate the public and professional communities about OCD and related disorders, work towards achieving increased accessibility to effective treatment, and support research into the causes and treatment methods of OCD.

Year Founded: 1986

671   Mental Health America
500 Montgomery Street
Suite 820
Alexandria, VA 22314
703-684-7722
800-969-6642
www.mentalhealthamerica.net

Schroeder Stribling, President & CEO
Sachin Doshi, Sr. Dir., Finance & Operations

Mental Health America is a community-based nonprofit organization committed to enabling the mental wellness of all Americans. MHA advocates for greater access to quality health services and seeks to educate individuals on identifying symptoms, as well as intervention and prevention.

Year Founded: 1909

672   NAPCSE National Association of Parents with
Children in Special Education
3642 East Sunnydale Drive
Chandler Heights, AZ 85142
800-754-4421
E-mail: contact@napcse.org
www.napcse.org

Dr. George Giuliani, President

The NAPCSE is dedicated to ensuring quality education for all children and adolescents with special needs. NAPCSE provides resources, support, and assistance to parents with children in special education.

673   National Alliance on Mental Illness
4301 Wilson Boulevard
Suite 300
Arlington, VA 22203
703-524-7600
800-950-6264
E-mail: info@nami.org
www.nami.org

Shirley J. Holloway, President
Joyce A. Campbell, First Vice President
Daniel H. Gillison, Jr., Chief Executive Officer
David Levy, Chief Financial Officer

NAMI is an organization dedicated to raising awareness on mental health and providing support and education for Americans affected by mental illness. NAMI advocates for access to services and treatment and fosters an environment of awareness and understanding for those concerned with mental health.

Year Founded: 1979

674 National Association for the Dually Diagnosed (NADD)
321 Wall Street
Kingston, NY 12401
845-331-4336
E-mail: info@thenadd.org
www.thenadd.org

Jeanne M. Farr, MA, Chief Executive Officer
Bruce Davis, President
Juanita St. Croix, Vice President
Ray Snyder, Secretary

NADD is a nonprofit organization designed to increase awareness of, and provide services for, individuals with developmental disabilities and mental illness. NADD emphasizes the importance of quality mental healthcare for people with mental health needs and offers conferences, information resources, educational programs, and training materials to professionals, parents, and organizations.

Year Founded: 1983

675 National Council for Behavioral Health
1400 K Street NW
Suite 400
Washington, DC 20005
E-mail: communications@thenationalcouncil.org
www.thenationalcouncil.org

Tim Swinfard, Chair
Charles Ingoglia, President and CEO
Jeannie Campbell, Executive VP and COO
Bruce Pelleu, CPA, VP, Finance & Administration

The National Council for Behavioral Health serves to unify America's behavioral health organizations. The council is dedicated to ensuring that quality mental health and addictions care is readily accessible to all Americans.

676 National Institute of Mental Health
6001 Executive Boulevard
Room 6200, MSC 9663
Bethesda, MD 20892-9663
866-615-6464
E-mail: nimhinfo@nih.gov
www.nimh.nih.gov

Joshua Gordon, MD, PhD, Director

The National Institute of Mental Health conducts clinical research on mental disorders and seeks to expand knowledge on mental health treatments.

677 Sutcliffe Clinic
851 Fremont Avenue
Suite 110
Los Altos, CA 94024
650-941-1698
E-mail: info@sutcliffedbp.com
www.www.sutcliffeclinic.com

Trenna Sutcliffe, MD, MS, Medical Director

Sutcliffe Developmental & Behavioral Pediatrics is an organization that specializes in the treatment of ADHD, autism spectrum disorder, anxiety disorders, conduct disorders, learning disabilities, and more. Sutcliffe works with community services, school districs, and primary physicians, and provides family counseling.

678 Territorial Apprehensiveness (TERRAP) Anxiety & Stress Program
755 Park Avenue
Suite 140
Huntington, NY 11743
631-549-8867
E-mail: info@anxietyandpanic.com
www.anxietyandpanic.com

Julian Herskowitz, PhD, Director

Helps to treat anxiety and stress disorders through Territorial Apprehensiveness Programs, developed by Dr. Arthur Hardy in the 1960s. The program systematically addresses the behavioral and thought processes of those suffering from stress and anxiety.

Year Founded: 1975

679 The Center for Family Support
2811 Zulette Avenue
Bronx, NY 10461
718-518-1500
E-mail: svernikoff@cfsny.org
www.www.cfsny.org

Steven Vernikoff, Executive Director
Barbara Greenwald, Chief Operating Officer
Jos, Martin Jara, President
Elise Geltzer, Vice President

The Center for Family Support offers assistance to individuals with developmental and related disabilities, as well as their families, and provides support services and programs that are designed to accommodate individual needs. Offers services throughout New York City, Westchester County, Long Island, and New Jersey.

Year Founded: 1954

680 The Children's and Adult Center for OCD and Anxiety
3138 Butler Pike
Suite 200
Plymouth Meeting, PA 19462
www.childrenscenterocdandanxiety.com

Tamar Chansky, PhD, Founder

A center comprising five private practice psychologists delivering treatment and therapy to children and adults with OCD, Separation Anxiety, and other mental health disorders. They also offer parent workshops on skills and strategies to help their child cope with anxiety.

Year Founded: 1988

Periodicals & Pamphlets

681 OCD Newsletter
18 Tremont Street
Suite 903
Boston, MA 02196
617-973-5801
E-mail: info@iocdf.org
www.ocfoundation.org

Denise Egan Stack LMHC, President
Jeff Szymanski,PhD, Executive Director
Susan B Dailey, Vice President
Michael J Stack,CFA, Treasurer

A source of news, entertainment, and inspiration to individuals with OCD, their loved ones, and to OCD professionals and researchers.

8-12 pages

Support Groups & Hot Lines

682 International OCD Foundation
18 Tremont Street
Suite 903
Boston, MA 02108
617-973-5801
E-mail: info@ocfoundation.org
www.ocfoundation.org

Denise Egan Stack LMHC, President
Susan B. Dailey, Vice President
Michael J. Stack CFA, Treasurer
Diane Davey RN, Secretary

An international not-for-profit organization made up of people with Obsessive Compulsive Disorder and related disorders, as well as their families, friends, professionals and others.

Year Founded: 1986

683 Obsessive-Compulsive Anonymous
PO Box 215
New Hyde Park, NY 11040
516-739-0662
E-mail: west24th@aol.com
www.obsessivecompulsiveanonymous.com

Is a fellowship of people who share their Experience, Strength, and Hope with each other that they may solve their common problem and help others to recover from OCD.

Video & Audio

684 Hope and Solutions for OCD
International OCD Foundation
18 Tremont Street
Suite 903
Boston, MA 02108
617-973-5801
E-mail: info@ocfoundation.org
www.ocfoundation.org

Denise Egan Stack LMHC, President
Susan B. Dailey, Vice President
Michael J. Stack CFA, Treasurer
Diane Davey RN, Secretary

Finally, a video series about obsessive compulsive disorder. With some straight forward solutions, answers, and advice for individuals who have OCD, their families, their doctors, and school personnel. The Awareness Foundation for OCD & Related Disorders had produced this highly useful, informative, and inspirational series to help guide those with OCD towards confidence, recovery, and hope. *$89.95*

685 Touching Tree
Obsessive-Compulsive Foundation
18 Tremont Street
Suite 903
Boston, MA 02108
617-973-5801
E-mail: info@ocfoundation.org
www.ocfoundation.org

Denise Egan Stack LMHC, President
Susan B. Dailey, Vice President

Michael J. Stack CFA, Treasurer
Diane Davey RN, Secretary

This video will foster awareness of early onset obsessive-compulsive disorder (OCD) and demonstrate the symptoms and current therapies that are most successful. Typical ritualistic compulsions of children and adolescents such as touching, hand washing, counting, etc. are explained. *$49.95*

Web Sites

686 www.cyberpsych.org
CyberPsych

Presents information about psychoanalysis, psychotherapy and special topics such as anxiety disorders, the problematic use of alcohol, homophobia, and the traumatic effects of racism. Explains in detail what anxiety it is how it is treated and the symptoms associated with anxiety.

687 www.guidetopsychology.com
A Guide To Psychlogy & Its Practice

Free information on various types of psychology.

688 www.mayoclinic.com
Mayo Clinic

Provides information on obsessive-compulsive disorder and anxiety.

689 www.mentalhealth.Samhsa.Gov
Center for Mental Health Services Knowledge Exchange Network

Information about resources, technical assistance, research, training, networks and other federal clearinghouses.

690 www.nami.org
National Alliance on Mental Illness

From its inception in 1979, NAMI has been dedicated to improving the lives of individuals and families affected by mental illness.

691 www.nimh.nih.gov/anxiety/anxiety/ocd
National Institute of Health

Information on anxiety disorders and OCD.

692 www.nimh.nih.gov/publicat/ocdmenu.cfm
Obsessive-Compulsive Disorder

Introductory handout with treatment recommendations.

693 www.ocdhope.com/gdlines.htm
Guidelines for Families Coping with OCD

694 www.ocfoundation.org
Obsessive-Compulsive Foundation

An international not-for-profit organization composed of people with obsessive compulsive disorder and related disorders, their families, friends, professionals and other concerned individuals.

695 www.thenadd.org
National Association for the Dually Diagnosed (NADD)

An association for persons with developmental disabilities and mental health needs.

Personality Disorders

Introduction

Personality is deeply rooted in our sense of ourselves and how others see us; it is formed from a complex intermingling of genetic factors and life experience. Everyone has personality characteristics that are likable and unlikable, attractive and unattractive, to others. By adulthood, most of us have personality traits that are difficult to change. Sometimes, these deeply rooted personality traits can get in the way of our happiness, hinder relationships, and even cause harm to ourselves or others. For example, a person may have a tendency to be deeply suspicious of other people with no good reason.

Personality Disorders, by definition, do not cause symptoms, which are experiences that are troublesome to the individual. They consist of whole sets of distorted experiences of the outside world that pervade every or nearly every aspect of a person's life, causing traits and behaviors leading to interpersonal problems which only secondarily cause distress to the individual. The problem is blamed on other people. For example, people with dependent personality disorder feel that they need more care and protection than others, not that they are inordinately demanding of care and protection. People with narcissistic personality disorder feel that others do not respect them, not that they demand more attention and admiration than others; people with paranoid personality disorder feel that others are out to trick and cheat them, not that they are inordinately suspicious; peoplewith obsessive personality disorder feel that others are sloppy, not that they are overly preoccupied with order and tidiness.

A diagnosis of a Personality Disorder should be distinguished from labeling someone as a bad or disagreeable person and not be used to stigmatize people who are simply unpopular, rebellious, or otherwise unorthodox. A Personality Disorder is not simply a personality style, but a condition that interferes with successful living. A Personality Disorder refers to an enduring pattern or experience and behavior that is inflexible, long lasting (often beginning in adolescence or early childhood) and which leads to distress and impairment. Personality disorders frequently co-exist with substance abuse, eating disorders, suicidal thinking and behavior, depression, and other mental disorders.

There are ten types of personality disorders:
• Paranoid Personality Disorder;
• Schizoid Personality Disorder;
• Schizotypal Personality Disorder;
• Antisocial Personality Disorder;
• Borderline Personality Disorder;
• Narcissistic Personality Disorder;
• Avoidant Personality Disorder;
• Dependent Personality Disorder;
• Histrionic Personality Disorder
• Obsessive-Compulsive Personality Disorder.

SYMPTOMS

A Personality Disorder is an enduring pattern of inner experience and behavior that deviates markedly from the expectations of the individual's culture:
• This pattern significantly / impacts both interpersonal and self-directed functioning;
• The person has one or more pathological personality traits (detachment, antagonism disinhibition, low emotional stability)
• The enduring pattern is inflexible and pervasive across a broad range of personal and social situations;
• The enduring pattern leads to clinically significant distress or impairment in social, occupational, or other important areas of functioning;
• The pattern is stable and of long duration and its onset can be traced back at least to adolescence or early adulthood;
• The enduring pattern is not better accounted for as a manifestation or consequence of another mental disorder;
• The enduring pattern is not due to the direct physiological effects of a substance or a general medical condition.

Antisocial Personality Disorder
• Ego-centric, goal setting for personal gain;
• Failure to honor commitments, disregard for rules;
• Inability to have a mutually intimate relationship;
• Lack of concern for the feelings of others;
• Acting impulsively;
• Deception or manipulation of others;
• Lack of remorse.

Avoidant Personality Disorder
• Low self-esteem associated with being inferior, feelings of shame or inadequacy;
• Unrrealistic standards for goal setting, unwilling to take risks;
• Sensitivity to criticism, anxiety regarding how they are perceived;
• Fear of being shamed, reluctance to befriend people;
• Avoidance of social contact and intimate relationships;
• Excessive anxiety regard social events;
• Lack of enjoyment in activities.

Borderline Personality Disorder
• Undefined self-identity/self-image;
• Unstable goals, emotions, or values;
• Inability to properly assess others' feelings or needs (generally skewing negatively);
• Frequent mood changes, intense feelings of anxiety or panic regarding uncertainty;
• Fear of rejection, frequent feelings of hopelessness
• Impulsivity in reacting to stimuli;
• Anger or frustration out of proportion to the situation.

Dependent Personality Disorder
• Exhibits an excessive need to be taken care of;
• Feelings of inadequacy, helplessness and incompetence;
• Lack of decision-making or self-motivation skills.

Narcissistic Personality Disorder
• Remarkably increased or decreased self-appraisal;
• Hypersensitivity to the reactions of others, but only in relation to the self;
• Sense of entitlement;
• Attention seeking;
• Superficial relationships.

Obsessive Compulsive Personality Disorder
• Sense of self comes from productivity/work;
• Unreasonably high expectations for self-often does not reach goals;
• Relationships valued as secondary to work;
• Workaholic tendencies;
• Inflexibility;
• Rigid perfectionism that disrupts everyday living;

• Over-criticism of self and others.

Paranoid Personality Disorder
• Unjustified mistrust and suspicion of others;
• Social isolation;
• Aggressiveness;
• Hostility.

Schizoid Personality Disorder
• Inability to relate to other people;
• Lack of emotion;
• Mechanical behavior;
• Social isolation;
• Social awkwardness;
• Lack of desire for personal interaction.

Schizotypal Personality Disorder
• Confused boundaries between self and others;
• Difficulty forming relationships;
• Mechanical, inappropriate, or stereotyped behavior;
• Detachment from emotional situations;
• Avoidance of social contact;
• Lack of desire for personal interaction.

Histrionic Personality Disorder
• Discomfort not being the center of attention;
• Use of seductive or provocative behavior;
• Emotions are shallow and shift easily but can be dramatic;
• Use of appearances to draw attention to one's self;
• Considering relationships more intimate than they are.

TREATMENT OPTIONS

Most people who suffer from a Personality Disorder do not see themselves as having psychological problems, and therefore do not seek treatment. For those who do, the most effective treatment is long-term (at least one year) psychotherapy. People with Personality Disorders generally seek treatment only because they are distressed about the behavior of those around them. It is important for a patient to find a mental health professional with expert knowledge and experience in treating personality disorders. Some therapists specialize in treating Borderline Personality Disorder. Antisocial Personality Disorder is notably difficult to treat, especially in extreme cases, when the affected individual lacks all concern for others.

Psychotherapy encourages patients to talk about their suspicions, doubts, and other personality traits that have a negative impact on their lives, and therefore helps to improve social interactions.

Psychotherapeutic treatment should include attention to family members, stressing the importance of emotional support, reassurance, explanation of the disorder, and advice on how to manage and respond to the patient. Group therapy is helpful in many situations.

Antipsychotic medication can be useful in patients with certain Personality Disorders, specifically Schizotypal and Borderline Disorders.

Associations & Agencies

697   Brain & Behavior Research Foundation
747 Third Avenue
33rd Floor
New York, NY 10017
646-681-4888
800-829-8289
E-mail: info@bbrfoundation.org
www.www.bbrfoundation.org

Donald M. Boardman, Treasurer
Jeffrey Borenstein, MD, President and CEO
Louis Innamorato, CPA, VP and Chief Financial Officer
Faith Rothblatt, Vice President, Development

The Brain and Behavior Research Foundation awards grants aimed at advancing scientific understandings of mental health treatments and mental disorders such as depression and schizophrenia. The Brain and Behavior Research Foundation's mission is to eliminate the suffering caused by mental illness.

Year Founded: 1987

698   Center for Mental Health Services (CMHS)
Substance Abuse and Mental Health Services
Administration
5600 Fishers Lane
Rockville, MD 20857
240-276-1310
www.samhsa.gov/about-us/who-we-are/offices-centers

Anita Everett, MD, DFAPA, Director

Promotes the treatment of mental illness and emotional disorders by increasing accessibility to mental health programs; supporting outreach, treatment, rehabilitation, and support programs and networks; and encouraging the use of scientifically-based information when treating mental disorders. CMHS provides information about mental health via a toll-free number and numerous publications. Developed for users of mental health services and their families, the general public, policy makers, providers, and the media.

Year Founded: 1992

699   Goodwill's Community Employment Services
Goodwill Industries-Suncoast, Inc.
10596 Gandy Blvd.
St. Petersburg, FL 33702
727-523-1512
888-279-1988
TDD: 727-579-1068
www.goodwill-suncoast.org

Sandra Young, Chair
Louise Lopez, Sr. Vice Chair
Dominic Macrone, Board Secretary

The St. Petersburg headquarters serves ten counties in the state of Florida. Their mission is to help people with disabilities gain employment through training programs, employment services, and affordable housing.

Year Founded: 1954

700   National Alliance on Mental Illness
4301 Wilson Boulevard
Suite 300
Arlington, VA 22203
703-524-7600
800-950-6264

E-mail: info@nami.org
www.nami.org

Shirley J. Holloway, President
Joyce A. Campbell, First Vice President
Daniel H. Gillison, Jr., Chief Executive Officer
David Levy, Chief Financial Officer

NAMI is an organization dedicated to raising awareness on mental health and providing support and education for Americans affected by mental illness. NAMI advocates for access to services and treatment and fosters an environment of awareness and understanding for those concerned with mental health.

Year Founded: 1979

701 National Association for the Dually Diagnosed (NADD)
321 Wall Street
Kingston, NY 12401
845-331-4336
E-mail: info@thenadd.org
www.thenadd.org

Jeanne M. Farr, MA, Chief Executive Officer
Bruce Davis, President
Juanita St. Croix, Vice President
Ray Snyder, Secretary

NADD is a nonprofit organization designed to increase awareness of, and provide services for, individuals with developmental disabilities and mental illness. NADD emphasizes the importance of quality mental healthcare for people with mental health needs and offers conferences, information resources, educational programs, and training materials to professionals, parents, and organizations.

Year Founded: 1983

702 National Institute of Mental Health
6001 Executive Boulevard
Room 6200, MSC 9663
Bethesda, MD 20892-9663
866-615-6464
E-mail: nimhinfo@nih.gov
www.nimh.nih.gov

Joshua Gordon, MD, PhD, Director

The National Institute of Mental Health conducts clinical research on mental disorders and seeks to expand knowledge on mental health treatments.

703 National Mental Health Consumers' Self-Help Clearinghouse
E-mail: selfhelpclearinghouse@gmail.com
www.mhselfhelp.org

Joseph Rogers, Founder and Executive Director
Susan Rogers, Director

The Clearinghouse is a peer-run national technical assistance center focused on achieving respect and equality of opportunity for those with mental illnesses. The Clearinghouse helps with the growth of the mental health consumer movement by evaluating mental health services, advocating for mental health reform, and providing consumers with news, information, publications, and consultation services.

Year Founded: 1986

704 TARA Association for Borderline Personality Disorder
23 Greene Street
#3
New York, NY 10013
212-966-6514
E-mail: tara4bpd@gmail.com
www.tara4bpd.org

Valerie Porr, MA, Founder and President

A not-for-profit organization promoting educational programs and research on the causes and treatment of personality disorders. TARA seeks to raise awareness on personality disorder and to eliminate the stigma attached to it.

Year Founded: 1994

705 The Center for Family Support
2811 Zulette Avenue
Bronx, NY 10461
718-518-1500
E-mail: svernikoff@cfsny.org
www.www.cfsny.org

Steven Vernikoff, Executive Director
Barbara Greenwald, Chief Operating Officer
Jos, Martin Jara, President
Elise Geltzer, Vice President

The Center for Family Support offers assistance to individuals with developmental and related disabilities, as well as their families, and provides support services and programs that are designed to accommodate individual needs. Offers services throughout New York City, Westchester County, Long Island, and New Jersey.

Year Founded: 1954

Support Groups & Hot Lines

706 Out of the FOG
www.www.outofthefog.net

Providing information and support to the family members and loved-ones of individuals who suffer from a personality disorder. A supportive, close-knit community encouraging one another through the many challenges that come with having a family member or significant other who has a personality disorder. FOG stands for Fear, Obligation, and Guilt, feelings which often result from being in a relationship with a person who suffers from a Personality Disorder.

Year Founded: 2007

707 Paranoid Personality Disorder Forum
Mental Health Matters
www.www.psychforums.com/paranoid-personality/

A helpful user to user forum for support and information about Paranoid Personality Disorders.

708 S.A.F.E. Alternatives
7115 W North Avenue
PMB 319
Oak Park, IL 60302-1002
708-366-9066
800-366-8288
E-mail: info@selfinjury.com
www.selfinjury.com

Karen Conterio, CEO & Founder
Wendy Lader, PhD, M.Ed, Clinical Director
Michelle Seliner MSW, LCSW, Chief Operating Officer
Joni Nowicki, BA, Admissions Coordinator

A world-renowned treatment program that in it's more than twenty years of operation has helped thousands of people successfully end self-injurious behavior. A treatment team of experts uses therapy, education, and support to empower clients to identify healthier ways to cope with emotional distress. The S.A.F.E. Alternatives philosophy and model of treatment focus on shifting control to the client, empowering them to make healthy choices, including the choice to not self-injure.

Year Founded: 1986

Video & Audio

709 **Anger Management-Enhanced Edition**
Educational Video Network, Inc.
1401 19th Street
Huntsville, TX 77340
936-295-5767
800-762-0060
www.www.evndirect.com

Learn what causes anger and understand why our bodies react as they do when we're angry. Effective techniques for assuaging anger are discussed.

710 **Beating Depression**
Educational Training Videos
136 Granville St
Suite 200
Gahanna, OH 43230
www.educationaltrainingvideos.com

This program comes to grips with depression through the experiences of five patients whose backgrounds span the socioeconomic spectrum. Three cases of chronic depression, one of which is complicated by borderline personality disorder and another by alcohol abuse, and two cases of bipolar disorder, one of which is extreme, are presented.

711 **Clinical Impressions: Identifying Mental Illness**
Educational Training Videos
136 Granville St
Suite 200
Gahanna, OH 43230
www.educationaltrainingvideos.com

How long can mental illness stay hidden, especially from the eyes of trained experts? This program rejoins a group of ten adults- five of them healthy and five of them with histories of mental illness- as psychiatric specialists try to spot and correctly diagnose the latter. Administering a series of collaborative and one-on-one tests, including assessments of personality type, physical self-image, and rational thinking, the panel gradually makes decisions about who suffers from depression, bipolar disorder, bulimia, and social anxiety.

712 **Dealing with Social Anxiety**
Educational Video Network, Inc.
1401 19th Street
Huntsville, TX 77340
936-295-5767
800-762-0060
www.www.evndirect.com

Social anxiety is America's third-largest psychiatric disorder. It generally develops during the mid-teen years, and almost always before the age of 25. Understand what may trigger the development of anxiety and learn how it sometimes evolves into full-blown panic disorder, which is characterized by recurrent attacks of terror or fear. The consequences of social anxiety are examined and effective treatments are discussed.

713 **FRONTLINE: The Released**
PBS
2100 Crystal Drive
Arlington, VA 22202
www.pbs.org

Will Lyman, Actor
Narrator
Miri Navasky, Director
Karen O'Connor, Director

The documentary states that of the 700,000 inmates released from American prisons each year, half of them have mental disabilities. This work focused on those with severe problems who keep entering and exiting prison. Full of good information on the challenges they face with mental illnesses; housing, employment, stigmatization, and socialization.

714 **Lost in the Mirror: Women with Multiple Personalities**
Educational Training Videos
136 Granville St
Suite 200
Gahanna, OH 43230
www.educationaltrainingvideos.com

In this program, ABC News anchors Diane Sawyer and Sam Donaldson study the causes and key signs of dissociative identity disorder and the fragmented lives of two people dealing with its effects.

715 **Mental Disorder**
Educational Training Videos
136 Granville St
Suite 200
Gahanna, OH 43230
www.educationaltrainingvideos.com

What is abnormality? Using the case studies of two young women; one who has depression, one who has an anxiety disorder; as a springboard, this program presents three psychological perspective on mental disorder.

716 **Multiple Personality Disorder: In the Shadows**
Educational Training Videos
136 Granville St
Suite 200
Gahanna, OH 43230
www.educationaltrainingvideos.com

This program shows how therapy can integrate the multiple personalities and make a patient whole again. Following two MPD patients and health care professionals, the program traces the struggles and triumphs in treating this disorder.

717 **Understanding Mental Illness**
Educational Video Network, Inc.
1401 19th Street
Huntsville, TX 77340

936-295-5767
800-762-0060
www.www.evndirect.com

Contains information and classifications of mental illness. Mental illness can strike anyone, at any age. Learn about various organic and functional mental disorders as discussed and their causes and symptoms, and learn where to seek help for a variety of mental health concerns.

718 Understanding Personality Disorders
Educational Video Network, Inc.
1401 19th Street
Huntsville, TX 77340
936-295-5767
800-762-0060
www.www.evndirect.com

For many people, the onset of a psychological disorder goes undiagnosed and untreated, and, as a result, they face a constant, if not impossible, struggle to maintain good mental health. This can be especially true when individuals suffer from a personality disorder. However, with identification and understanding, crippling personality disorders can be brought out of the shadows of ignorance and into the light of treatment.

Web Sites

719 www.cyberpsych.org
CyberPsych

Presents information about psychoanalysis, psychotherapy and special topics such as anxiety disorders, the problematic use of alcohol, homophobia, and the traumatic effects of racism

720 www.mentalhealth.com
Internet Mental Health

Offers online psychiatric diagnosis in the hope of reaching the two-thirds of individuals with mental illness who do not seek treatment.

721 www.mhsanctuary.com/borderline
Borderline Personality Disorder Sanctuary

Borderline personality disorder education, communities, support, books, and resources.

722 www.nimh.nih.gov/publicat/ocdmenu.cfm
Obsessive-Compulsive Disorder

Introductory handout with treatment recommendations.

723 www.ocdhope.com/ocd-families.php
OCD Resource Center of Florida

724 www.outofthefog.net
Out of the FOG

Information and support for those with a family member or loved one who suffers from a personality disorder.

725 www.planetpsych.com
Planetpsych.com

The online resource for mental health information.

726 www.psychcentral.com
Psych Central

The Internet's largest and oldest independent mental health social network created and run by mental health professionals to guarantee reliable, trusted information and support communities to you.

727 www.store.samhsa.gov
Substance Abuse and Mental Health Services Administration

Resources on mental disorders as well as treatment and recovery.

Schizophrenia Spectrum and Other Psychotic Disorders

Introduction

Schizophrenia is an old term meaning, approximately, 'split personality.' While the name of the diagnosis survives, the concept of split personality is outdated.

Schizophrenia is a devastating disease of the brain that severely impairs an individual's ability to think, feel, and function normally. Though not a common disorder, it is one of the most destructive, disrupting the lives of sufferers, as well as of family members and loved ones. Long misunderstood, people with Schizophrenia and their families have also borne a burden of stigma in addition to the burden of their illness.

Although family and other environmental stressors can play a role in precipitating or exacerbating episodes of illness, theories that the disease is caused by poor parenting have been discredited. Much has been learned about the disease in recent years and treatments have improved markedly.

Schizophrenia is a largely genetically determined disorder of the brain. One theory is that it is a disorder of information processing resulting from a defect in the prefrontal cortex of the brain. Because this system is defective, an individual with Schizophrenia is easily overwhelmed by the amount of information and stimuli coming from the environment. Schizophrenia causes hallucinations, which are sensory experiences in the absence of actual stimuli (hearing voices when no one is speaking), and delusions, which are bizarre beliefs (that the individual is God, that the television is conveying messages specifically aimed at the individual, that some power is removing the individual's thoughts from his or her mind). Speech may be tangential or confused. These are called 'positive symptoms.' The individual also loses some normal behaviors and experiences, engaging in little behavior or social interaction and displaying catatonic behavior and a flat or grossly inappropriate emotional state. These are called 'negative symptoms.' Schizophrenia is a chronic disease and, once diagnosed, a person often needs treatment for the rest of his or her life. However, great strides have been made in treating the disease and many individuals with schizophrenia can hold jobs, marry, parent children, and have gratifying and productive lives.

SYMPTOMS

To be diagnosed with Schizophrenia, one must have two or more of the following symptoms for a period of at least six months. Further, these symptoms must cause social and occupational dysfuction.

Positive symptoms (experiences not shared by people in society):
• Delusions or false and bizarre beliefs;
• Hallucinations.

Negative symptoms (the loss of normal behaviors):
• Withdrawing from social contact;
• Speaking less;
• Losing interest in things and the ability to enjoy them;
• Disorganized speech;
• Grossly disorganized or catatonic behavior (extremely ag-

itated or zombie-like.)

The symptoms must not be related to mood or depressive disorders, substance abuse, or general medical conditions.

ASSOCIATED FEATURES

Because their disease causes difficulty in perceiving their environment and responding to it normally, people with Schizophrenia often act strange, and have odd beliefs. Hallucinations and delusions can make a person's behavior appear bizarre to others. Anhedonia, the inability to enjoy pleasurable activities, is common in Schizophrenia, as are sleep disturbances and abnormalities of psychomotor activity. The latter may take the form of pacing, rocking, or immobility. Negative symptoms can be more disabling than positive ones. Family members often become annoyed because they think the individual is just lazy. Schizophrenia takes many forms, and there are a number of subtypes of the illness, including paranoid schizophrenia.

Individuals with untreated Schizophrenia, under the influence of hallucinations and delusions, have a slightly greater propensity for violence than the general population, but only when there is co-existing alcohol or substance abuse, which is quite common. Schizophrenia is known as a heterogenous disease, meaning that the illness takes many forms, depending on a variety of individual characteristics and circumstances. Patients who receive appropriate treatment are not more violent than the general population. In fact, individuals with schizophrenia are far more likely to be the victims of, rather than than perpetrators of, violence.

The life expectancy of people with Schizophrenia is shorter than the general population for a variety of reasons:suicide is common among people with the disease (about ten percent die from suicide) and people with Schizophrenia often receive poor medical care and have poor health.

PREVALENCE

The first episode of Schizophrenia usually occurs in teenage years, although some cases may occur in the late thirties or forties. Onset prior to puberty is rare, though cases in five-year olds have been reported. Women have a later average of onset and a better prognosis. Estimates of the prevalence of Schizophrenia vary widely around the world, but probably about one percent of the world population has the disease.

TREATMENT OPTIONS

Medications can diminish or eliminate many of the positive symptoms of Schizophrenia. Older medications, such as Haldol, are effective and inexpensive, but cause more side effects than newer medications, such as Zyprexa and Geodon. Clozapine was the first and is still one of the most effective treatments, but it causes a low incidence of a life-threatening blood disorder; therefore, people who take it must have blood tests at regular intervals. The newer medications are more effective in treating the negative, as well as the positive, symptoms.

Often, patients report that antipsychotic medications make them feel foggy, or lethargic. Antipsychotic medications can have serious side effects, including Tardive Dyskinesia, which consists of involuntary muscular movements. The newer antipsychotic medications are less sedating and have a decreased risk of causing Tardive Dyskinesia, but are associated with significant weight gain and increased risk of diabetes. There is considerable public controversy as to whether the weight gain, and risk of diabetes associated with the newer medications, along with their cost, outweigh their advantages.

Having Schizophrenia interferes with taking care of oneself and getting proper medical care in several ways; Schizophrenia often depletes financial resources so that patients cannot afford medication, nutrition, and medical care. Untreated Schizophrenia can also interfere with an individual's ability to understand signs and symptoms of medical disorders.

Compliance with medication is often a problem, and failure to continue taking medication is a major cause of relapse. For this reason, treatment should include supportive therapy, in which a psychiatrist or other mental health professional provides counseling aimed at helping the patient maintain a positive and optimistic attitude focused on staying healthy. Other forms of therapy, such as social skills training, have also found some success and may be useful in helping a person with Schizophrenia learn appropriate social and interpersonal behavior. Cognitive behavioral therapy may also be helpful in treating Schizophrenia. Peer support and support groups play a very important role in allowing people with Schizophrenia to lead successful lives.

Families of persons with Schizophrenia are often also affected by the disease and can be helped by support and advocacy groups.

It is important to note that psychotic illness does not necessarily affect all aspects of an individual's thinking. People with Schizophrenia may have bizarre beliefs or behavior in one sphere of life but be perfectly able to make decisions and function in other areas. In addition, it is crucial not to destroy an individual or family's hopes of a normal life by communicating the message that Schizophrenia is hopeless.

Associations & Agencies

729 Brain & Behavior Research Foundation
747 Third Avenue
33rd Floor
New York, NY 10017
646-681-4888
800-829-8289
E-mail: info@bbrfoundation.org
www.www.bbrfoundation.org

Donald M. Boardman, Treasurer
Jeffrey Borenstein, MD, President and CEO
Louis Innamorato, CPA, VP and Chief Financial Officer
Faith Rothblatt, Vice President, Development

The Brain and Behavior Research Foundation awards grants aimed at advancing scientific understandings of mental health treatments and mental disorders such as depression and schizophrenia. The Brain and Behavior Research Foundation's mission is to eliminate the suffering caused by mental illness.

Year Founded: 1987

730 Center for Mental Health Services (CMHS)
Substance Abuse and Mental Health Services
Administration
5600 Fishers Lane
Rockville, MD 20857
240-276-1310
www.samhsa.gov/about-us/who-we-are/offices-centers

Anita Everett, MD, DFAPA, Director

Promotes the treatment of mental illness and emotional disorders by increasing accessibility to mental health programs; supporting outreach, treatment, rehabilitation, and support programs and networks; and encouraging the use of scientifically-based information when treating mental disorders. CMHS provides information about mental health via a toll-free number and numerous publications. Developed for users of mental health services and their families, the general public, policy makers, providers, and the media.

Year Founded: 1992

731 Goodwill's Community Employment Services
Goodwill Industries-Suncoast, Inc.
10596 Gandy Blvd.
St. Petersburg, FL 33702
727-523-1512
888-279-1988
TDD: 727-579-1068
www.goodwill-suncoast.org

Sandra Young, Chair
Louise Lopez, Sr. Vice Chair
Dominic Macrone, Board Secretary

The St. Petersburg headquarters serves ten counties in the state of Florida. Their mission is to help people with disabilities gain employment through training programs, employment services, and affordable housing.

Year Founded: 1954

732 Mental Health America
500 Montgomery Street
Suite 820
Alexandria, VA 22314
703-684-7722
800-969-6642
www.mentalhealthamerica.net

Schroeder Stribling, President & CEO
Sachin Doshi, Sr. Dir., Finance & Operations

Mental Health America is a community-based nonprofit organization committed to enabling the mental wellness of all Americans. MHA advocates for greater access to quality health services and seeks to educate individuals on identifying symptoms, as well as intervention and prevention.

Year Founded: 1909

733 National Alliance on Mental Illness
4301 Wilson Boulevard
Suite 300
Arlington, VA 22203
703-524-7600
800-950-6264
E-mail: info@nami.org
www.nami.org

Shirley J. Holloway, President
Joyce A. Campbell, First Vice President
Daniel H. Gillison, Jr., Chief Executive Officer
David Levy, Chief Financial Officer

NAMI is an organization dedicated to raising awareness on mental health and providing support and education for Americans affected by mental illness. NAMI advocates for access to services and treatment and fosters an environment of awareness and understanding for those concerned with mental health.

Year Founded: 1979

734 National Association for the Dually Diagnosed (NADD)
321 Wall Street
Kingston, NY 12401
845-331-4336
E-mail: info@thenadd.org
www.thenadd.org

Jeanne M. Farr, MA, Chief Executive Officer
Bruce Davis, President
Juanita St. Croix, Vice President
Ray Snyder, Secretary

NADD is a nonprofit organization designed to increase awareness of, and provide services for, individuals with developmental disabilities and mental illness. NADD emphasizes the importance of quality mental healthcare for people with mental health needs and offers conferences, information resources, educational programs, and training materials to professionals, parents, and organizations.

Year Founded: 1983

735 National Institute of Mental Health
6001 Executive Boulevard
Room 6200, MSC 9663
Bethesda, MD 20892-9663
866-615-6464
E-mail: nimhinfo@nih.gov
www.nimh.nih.gov

Joshua Gordon, MD, PhD, Director

The National Institute of Mental Health conducts clinical research on mental disorders and seeks to expand knowledge on mental health treatments.

736 National Mental Health Consumers' Self-Help Clearinghouse
E-mail: selfhelpclearinghouse@gmail.com
www.mhselfhelp.org

Joseph Rogers, Founder and Executive Director
Susan Rogers, Director

The Clearinghouse is a peer-run national technical assistance center focused on achieving respect and equality of opportunity for those with mental illnesses. The Clearinghouse helps with the growth of the mental health consumer movement by evaluating mental health services, advocating for mental health reform, and providing consumers with news, information, publications, and consultation services.

Year Founded: 1986

737 The Center for Family Support
2811 Zulette Avenue
Bronx, NY 10461
718-518-1500
E-mail: svernikoff@cfsny.org
www.www.cfsny.org

Steven Vernikoff, Executive Director
Barbara Greenwald, Chief Operating Officer
Jos, Martin Jara, President
Elise Geltzer, Vice President

The Center for Family Support offers assistance to individuals with developmental and related disabilities, as well as their families, and provides support services and programs that are designed to accommodate individual needs. Offers services throughout New York City, Westchester County, Long Island, and New Jersey.

Year Founded: 1954

738 Schizophrenia
National Institute of Mental Health
6001 Executive Boulevard
Room 8184
Bethesda, MD 20892-1
301-443-4513
866-615-6464
TTY: 301-443-8431
E-mail: nimhinfo@nih.gov

This booklet answers many common questions about schizophrenia, one of the most chronic, severe and disabling mental disorders. Current research-based information is provided for people with schizophrenia, their family members, friends and the general public about the symptoms and diagnosis of schizophrenia, possible causes, treatments and treatment resources.

28 pages

739 Schizophrenia Research
1600 John F Kennedy Boulevard
Suite 1800
Philadelphia, PA 19103-2879
212-633-3730
800-545-2522
E-mail: usbkinfo@elsevier.com
www.elsevier.com

H.A Nasrallah, Editor-in-Chief
L.E DeLisi, Editor-in-Chief

The journal of choice for international researchers and clinicians to share their work with the global schizophrenia research community. Publishes novel papers that really contribute to understanding the biology and treatment of schizophrenic disorders; Schizophrenia Research brings together biological, clinical and psychological research in order to stimulate the synthesis of findings from all disciplines involved in improving patient outcomes in schizophrenia.

ISSN 0920-9964

Research Centers

740 Brain & Behavior Research Foundation
747 Third Avenue
33rd Floor
New York, NY 10017
646-681-4888
800-829-8289
E-mail: info@bbrfoundation.org
www.www.bbrfoundation.org

Herbert Pardes, MD, Treasuer
Jeffrey Borenstein, MD, President and CEO
Louis Innamorato, CPA, VP and Chief Financial Officer
Anne Abramson, Vice President

The Brain and Behavior Research Foundation awards grants aimed at advancing scientific understandings of mental health treatments and mental disorders such as depression and schizophrenia. The Brain and Behavior Research Foundation's mission is to eliminate the suffering caused by mental illness.

Year Founded: 1981

Support Groups & Hot Lines

741 Common Ground Sanctuary
1410 S. Telegraph
Bloomfield Hills, MI 48302
248-456-8150
800-231-1127
www.www.commongroundsanctuary.org

Tony Rothschild, President & CEO
Steve Mitchell, Board Chair
Gary Dembs, Secretary
Charles Schmidt, Treasurer

A 24-hour nonprofit agency dedicated to helping youths, adults and families in crisis. Through its crisis line and in person through various programs, Common Ground Sanctuary provides professional and compassionate service to more than 40,000 people a year, with most services provided free of charge. Mission is to provide a lifeline for individuals and families in crisis, victims of crime, persons with mental illness, people trying to cope with critical situations and runaway and homeless youth.

Year Founded: 1998

742 Family-to-Family: National Alliance on Mental Illness
4301 Wilson Boulevard
Suite 300
Arlington, VA 22203
703-524-7600
888-999-6264
E-mail: info@nami.org
www.nami.org

The NAMI Family-to-Family Education Program is a free, 12-week course for family caregivers of individuals with severe mental illnesses. The course is taught by trained family members, all instruction and course materials are free to class participants, and over 300,000 family members have graduated from this national program.

Video & Audio

743 Bonnie Tapes
Mental Illness Education Project, Inc.
25 West Street
Westborough, MA 01581
617-562-1111
www.miepvideos.org

Bonnie's account of coping with schizophrenia will be a revelation to people whose view of mental illness has been shaped by the popular media. She and her family provide an intimate view of a frequently feared, often misrepresented, and much stigmatized illness-and the human side of learning to live with a psychiatric disability.

744 Clinical Impressions: Identifying Mental Illness
Educational Training Videos
136 Granville St
Suite 200
Gahanna, OH 43230

www.educationaltrainingvideos.com

How long can mental illness stay hidden, especially from the eyes of trained experts? This program rejoins a group of ten adults- five of them healthy and five of them with histories of mental illness- as psychiatric specialists try to spot and correctly diagnose the latter. Administering a series of collaborative and one-on-one tests, including assessments of personality type, physical self-image, and rational thinking, the panel gradually makes decisions about who suffers from depression, bipolar disorder, bulimia, and social anxiety.

745 Dark Voices: Schizophrenia
Educational Training Videos
136 Granville St
Suite 200
Gahanna, OH 43230
www.educationaltrainingvideos.com

This program seeks to understand how schizophrenia touches the lives of patients and their family members while examining the disease's etiology and pathology. A Discovery Channel Production.

746 FRONTLINE: The Released
PBS
2100 Crystal Drive
Arlington, VA 22202
www.pbs.org

Will Lyman, Actor
Narrator
Miri Navasky, Director
Karen O'Connor, Director

The documentary states that of the 700,000 inmates released from American prisons each year, half of them have mental disabilities. This work focused on those with severe problems who keep entering and exiting prison. Full of good information on the challenges they face with mental illnesses; housing, employment, stigmatization, and socialization.

747 Families Coping with Mental Illness
Mental Illness Education Project
PO Box 470813
Brookline Village, MA 02447-813
617-562-1111
800-343-5540
www.miepvideos.org

Christine Ledoux, Executive Director

Designed to provide insights and support to other families, the tape also has profound messages for professionals about the needs of families when mental illness strikes. *$68.95*

748 Mental Disorder
Educational Training Videos
136 Granville St
Suite 200
Gahanna, OH 43230
www.educationaltrainingvideos.com

What is abnormality? Using the case studies of two young women; one who has depression, one who has an anxiety disorder; as a springboard, this program presents three psychological perspective on mental disorder.

749 My Name is Walter James Cross: The Reality of Schizophrenia
Educational Training Videos
136 Granville St
Suite 200
Gahanna, OH 43230
www.educationaltrainingvideos.com

Walter James Cross tried to kill himself and failed, so he decided to tell his story instead. Created by a psychiatrist who has worked for many years with schizophrenic patients, this compelling dramatic monologue presents an acurate depiction of a devastating, costly, much maligned, and misunderstood illness.

750 No More Shame: Understanding Schizophrenia, Depression, and Addiction
Educational Training Videos
136 Granville St
Suite 200
Gahanna, OH 43230
www.educationaltrainingvideos.com

These programs examine research about the physiological, psychological, sociological, and cultural aspects of these disorders and their treatments. The goal of these programs is to explain what we do and do not know about each of these conditions, as well as to destigmatize the disorders by presenting them in the context of the same research process that is applied to all medical disorders.

751 To See What I See - The Stigma of Mental Illness
Northern Lakes Community Mental Health

People served by Northern Lakes Community Mental Health have come together as Stigma Busters - creating artwork, photographs, recovery stories, media campaigns, personal testimonies, buttons, and other projects for the purpose of eliminating the stigma associated with mental illness and spreading the word that recovery is possible. This is their story.

752 Understanding Mental Illness
Educational Video Network, Inc.
1401 19th Street
Huntsville, TX 77340
936-295-5767
800-762-0060
www.www.evndirect.com

Contains information and classifications of mental illness. Mental illness can strike anyone, at any age. Learn about various organic and functional mental disorders as discussed and their causes and symptoms, and learn where to seek help for a variety of mental health concerns.

Web Sites

753 www.cyberpsych.org
CyberPsych

Presents information about psychoanalysis, psychotherapy and special topics such as anxiety disorders, the problem-atic use of alcohol, homophobia, and the traumatic effects of racism.

754 www.hopkinsmedicine.org/epigen
Epidemology-Genetics Program in Psychiatry

Research program to help characterize the genetic, developmental and environmental componenets of bipolar disorder and schizophrenia.

755 www.mentalhealth.com
Internet Mental Health

Offers online psychiatric diagnosis in the hope of reaching the two-thirds of individuals with mental illness who do not seek treatment.

756 www.naminys.org
National Alliance on Mental Illness

From its inception in 1979, NAMI has been dedicated to improving the lives of individuals and families affected by mental illness.

757 www.planetpsych.com
Planetpsych.com

The online resource for mental health information.

758 www.psychcentral.com
Psych Central

The Internet's largest and oldest independent mental health social network created and run by mental health professionals to guarantee reliable, trusted information and support communities to you.

759 www.schizophrenia.com
Schizophrenia

A non-profit community providing in-depth information, support and education related to schizophrenia, a disorder of the brain and mind.

760 www.schizophrenia.com/discuss/
Schizophrenia

On-line support for patients and families.

761 www.schizophrenia.com/newsletter/buckets/success.html
Schizophrenia

Success stories including biographical accounts, links to stories of famous people who have schizophrenia, and personal web pages.

762 www.store.samhsa.gov
Substance Abuse and Mental Health Services Administration

Resources on mental disorders as well as treatment and recovery.

Sexual Disorders

Introduction

It is not possible to know what degree of sexual interest, desire, or activity is 'normal'; at best, we have averages, not indications of the optimal state. A Sexual Disorder is diagnosed when lack of desire or activity is repeated, persists over time, and causes distress or interferes with the person's functioning in other important areas of life. Sexual Disorders are divided into four groups: Disorders of Sexual Desire; Disorders of Sexual Arousal; Orgasmic Disorders; and Disorders involving Sexual Pain. It is essential to know whether the problem is lifelong or was precipitated by a recent event, and whether it occurs only with a particular partner or in a particular situation. It is also essential not to make assumptions about sexual activity based on age, socioeconomic status, or sexual orientation.

Male Hypoactive Sexual Desire Disorder (MHSDD)
• Persistent or repeated lack of sexual fantasies and desire for sexual activities;
• The lack of sexual fantasies and desire cause marked distress or interpersonal problems

The person with a Sexual Desire Disorder commonly has a poor body image and avoids nudity. In HSDD, a person does not initiate sexual activity, or respond to the partner's initiation attempts. The disorder is often associated with the inability to achieve orgasm in women, and in the inability to achieve an erection in men. It can also be associated with other psychiatric and medical problems, including a history of sexual trauma and abuse.

SEXUAL DESIRE DISORDERS SYMPTOMS

Treatment Options
Treatment of Sexual Desire Disorders may include psychotherapy (to treat any underlying psychological problems that might be causing the symptoms) and couples counseling.

Sexual Arousal Disorder

Female Sexual Interest/Arousal Disorder (FSIAD)
• Persistent or repeated inability to attain or maintain adequate lubrication-swelling (sexual excitement) response throughout sexual activity;
• The disorder causes clear distress or interpersonal problems.

Erectile Disorder (ED)
• Persistent or repeated inability to maintain an adequate erection throughout sexual activity;
• The disorder causes clear distress or interpersonal problems.

Associated Features
While both these disorders are common, men tend to be more upset by it than women. Contributing issues include performance anxiety (especially in men), fear of failure, inadequate stimulation, and relationship conflicts. Other problems are also associated with FSIAD and ED, such as childhood sexual trauma, sexual identity concerns, religious orthodoxy, depression, lack of intimacy or trust, and power conflicts. ED is frequently associated with diabetes, peripheral nerve disorders, and hypertension, and is a side effect of a variety of medications. In addition, the medications used to treat ED are contraindicated in some medical conditions, such as heart conditions.

Prevalence
Prevalence information varies for FSIAD. Most studies report a prevalence of 13% and 24%, with a range of 6% to 28% of women. It appears that prevalence of FSIAD increases with increasing age, but also that women become less distressed by the disorder. In a study of happily married couples, about one third of women complained of difficulty in achieving or maintaining sexual excitement.

Erectile difficulties in men are estimated to be very common, affecting 20-30 million men in the US. The frequency of erectile problems increases steeply with age. In one survey, fifty-two percent of men aged 40-70 reported erectile problems, with three times as many older men reporting difficulties. The disorder is common among married, single, heterosexual, and homosexual men.

Treatment Options
In FSIAD, cognitive-behavioral psychotherapy is often recommended, including practical help such as the use of water-soluble lubricating products. Hormone treatment, such as testosterone-estrogen compounds, is sometimes helpful.

An array of treatments is available for Erectile Dysfunction, including prosthetic devices for physiological penile problems. In cases of hormonal problems, testosterone treatments have had some results. (However, the use of testosterone to treat sexual disorders in menopausal women is controversial and can have serious side effects.) Viagra has produced success for male erectile dysfunction, as have two newer medications for ED, vardenafil (Levitra) and tadalafil (Cialis).

When sexual problems are limited to a particular partner or situation, psychotherapy (individual or couple) is necessary to resolve the difficulty.

Orgasmic Disorder

Female Orgasmic Disorder/Delayed Ejaculation
• Persistent or repeated delay in, or absence of, orgasm despite a normal sexual excitement phase;
• The disorder causes clear distress or interpersonal problems.

Premature Ejaculation
• Persistent or recurring ejaculation with minimal sexual stimulation before, upon, or shortly after penetration and earlier than desired;
• The disorder causes clear distress or interpersonal problems.

Associated Features
When Female Orgasmic Disorder or Delayed Ejaculation occur only in certain situations, difficulty with desire and arousal are often also present. All of these disorders are associated with poor body image, self-esteem, or relationship problems. In Female Orgasmic Disorder or Delayed Ejaculation, medical or surgical conditions can also play a role, such as multiple sclerosis, spinal cord injury, surgical prostatectomy (males), and some medications. Premature Ejaculation is likely to be very disruptive. Some males may have had the disorder all their lives, for others it may be situational. Few illnesses or drugs are associated with PE.

Prevalence
Female Orgasmic Disorder is probably the most frequent sexual disorder among females. Among those who have sought sex therapy twenty-four percent to thirty-seven percent report the problem. In general population samples, 15.4 percent of premenopausal women report the disorder, and 34.7 percent of postmenopausal women do so. More single than married women report that they have never had an orgasm. There is no association between Female Orgasmic Disorder and race, socioeconomic status, education, or religion. Delayed Ejaculation is relatively rare; only three percent to eight percent of men seeking treatment report having the disorder, though there is a higher prevalence among homosexual males (ten to fifteen percent).

Premature Ejaculation is very common: twenty-five to forty percent of adult males report having, or having had PE.

Treatment Options
Psychotherapeutic treatments are similar to those for Sexual Desire and Sexual Arousal Disorders. In both males and females with Orgasmic Disorders there may be a lack of desire, performance anxiety, and fear of impregnation or disease. Therapy should take into account contextual and historical information concerning the onset and course of the problem. Cognitive-behavioral methods to help change the assumptions and thinking of the person have sometimes been helpful.

Genito-Pelvic Pain/Penetration Disorder
• Recurring or persistent pain with sexual intercourse in a female;
• The disorder causes clear distress or interpersonal problems.
• Persistent or recurrent involuntary spasm of the vagina that interferes with sexual intercourse;
• The disorder causes clear distress or interpersonal problems.

Associated Features
It may be associated with lack of desire or arousal. People with penetration pain tend to avoid gynecological exams, and the disorder is most often associated with psychological and interpersonal issues. Various physical factors are associated with genito-pelvic pain, such as pelvic inflammatory disease, hymenal or childbirth-related scarring, and vulvar vestibulitis. Genito-Pelvic Pain/Penetration Disorder is not a clear symptom of any physical condition, and in women it is often combined with Depression and interpersonal conflicts. Other associated psychosocial factors include religious orthodoxy, low self-esteem, poor body image, poor couple communication, and history of sexual trauma.

Prevalence
Genito-Pelvic Pain/Penetration Disorder is seen quite often in sex therapy clinics - in fifteen to seventeen percent of women coming for treatment.

Treatment Options
The most successful treatment for women with these disorders is the reinsertion of a graduated sequence of dilators in the vagina. This treatment should be done in conjunction with relaxation training, sensate focusing exercises (which help people focus on the pleasures of sex rather than the performance), and sex therapy.

General Treatment Options
It is important to know whether or not a medical or medication issue is present. However, many with these disorders do not seek treatment. Their lack of desire for sex is often combined with a lack of desire for sex therapy. Even with therapy, relapse is commonly reported. Treatments that have had some success are ones that challenge the cognitive assumptions and distortions of client(s), e.g., that sex should be perfect, that without intercourse and without both partners having an orgasm it is not real sex.

ORGASMIC DISORDER SYMPTOMS

Therapy often also includes sensate focusing in which the person is encouraged and trained to give up the role of agitated spectator to love-making in favor of participating in it. A sexual history should be part of every mental health evaluation, and patients receiving psychotropic medications should be asked about sexual side effects. Having information about sexual function before medication is prescribed will prevent pre-existing sexual problems from being confused with any that may result from medication.

PARAPHILIAS
Paraphilias are sexual disorders or perversions in which sexual intercourse is not the desired goal. Instead, the desire is to use non-human objects or non-sexual body parts for sexual activities sometimes involving the suffering of, or inflicting pain onto, non-consenting partners.

Symptoms
• Recurrent, intense, sexually arousing fantasies, urges, or behavior involving the particular perversion for at least six months;
• The fantasies, urges, or behavior cause distress and/or disruption in the person's functioning in social, work, and interpersonal areas.

There are seven Paraphilias, described below, categorized as either victimless, or as victimizing someone who has not consented to the sexual activity, with relevant associated features.

Exhibitionistic Disorder
The exposure of the genitals to a stranger or group of strangers. Sometimes the paraphiliac masturbates during exposure. The onset of this disorder usually occurs before age 18 and becomes less severe after age 40.

Fetishistic Disorder
Using non-living objects, known as fetishes, for sexual gratification. Objects commonly used by men with the disorder include women's underwear, shoes, or other articles of women's clothing. The person often masturbates while holding, rubbing, or smelling the fetish object. This disorder usually begins in adolescence; it is chronic.

Frotteuristic Disorder
Sexual arousal, and sometimes masturbation to orgasm, while rubbing against a non-consenting person. The behavior is usually planned to occur in a crowded place, such as on a bus, subway, or in a swimming pool, where detection is less likely. Frotteurism usually begins in adolescence, is most frequent between the ages of 15 and 25, then gradually declines.

Sexual Masochism Disorder
Acts of being bound, beaten, humiliated, or made to suffer in some other way in order to become sexually aroused. The behaviors can be self-inflicated or performed with a partner, and include physical bondage, blindfolding, and humiliation. Masochistic sexual fantasies are likely to have been present since childhood. The activities themselves begin at different times but are common by early adulthood; they are usually chronic. The severity of the behaviors may increase over time.

Sexual Sadism Disorder
Acts in which the person become sexually excited through the physical or psychological suffering of someone else. Some Sexual Sadists may conjure up the sadistic fantasies during sexual activity without acting on them. Others act on their sadistic urges with a consenting partner (who may be a Sexual Masochist), or act on their urges with a non-consenting partner. The behavior may involve forcing the other person to crawl, be caged or tortured. Sadistic sexual fantasies are likely to have been present in childhood. The onset of the behavior varies but most commonly occurs by early adulthood. The disorder is usually chronic, and severity tends to increase over time. When the disorder is severe or coupled with Antisocial Personality Disorder, the person is likely to seriously injure or kill his victim.

Transvestic Fetishism
Consists of arousal from clothing associated with the opposite sex. It is important to note that there is considerable controversy over this diagnosis; some people who cross dress seem to have little distress and function normally. This condition typically begins in childhood or adolescence. Often the cross dressing is not done publicly until adulthood.

Voyeurism
Peeping Tom disorder, involving the act of observing one or more unsuspecting persons (usually strangers who are naked, in the process of undressing, or engaged in sexual activity, in order for the voyeur to become sexually excited. Sexual activity with the people being observes is not usually sought. The voyeur may masturbate during the observation or later. The onset of this disorder is usually before age 15. It tends to be chronic.

Prevalence
Paraphiliacs are almost exclusively male. Very few volunteer to disclose their activities or to seek treatment. It is estimated that more have deficts in interpersonal or sexual relationships. In one study, two thirds were diagnosed with Mood Disorders and fifty percent had alcohol or drug abuse problems.

Recent studies provide evidence that the great majority of Paraphiliacs are active in more than one form of sexually perverse behavior; less than ten percent have only one form; and thirty-eight percent engage in five or more difference sexually deviant behaviors.

At the same time, the incidence and prevalence of some sexual perversions are hard to estimate, or unknown, because they are rarely reported or the people involved do not come into contact with authorities. All the Paraphilias are difficult to treat. It is important for the professional making the diagnosis to take a very careful history, and to be sensitive to the presence of other, e.g., personality,

disorders. Relapse is common.

Diagnostic techniques can be useful. Penile plethysmography measures the degree of penile erection while the individual is exposed to visual sexual stimulation. Some people are treatedin a formal Sex Offenders Program, developed for individuals arrested for and convicted of paraphilias that are crimes. Sometimes treatment occurs within the context of individual therapy where trust can be established. Other have been treated by means of conditioning techniques, e.g., where a fetish object is paired with an aversive stimulus such as a mild electric shock.

Medication is also used. Pedophilia and other Paraphilias are sometimes treated through the use of female hormones or other medications, which diminishes sexual appetite. Other medications may include serotonin reuptake inhibitors (SSRIs) and anti-androgens (agents that reduce the level of testosterone in the blood). Behavior therapy may also be used.

Treatment can be difficult because it is associated with the risk of reporting and punishment; many individuals do not have any real interest in being treated. They may deliberately deceive the professional, or deny the problem. Sex offenders are also more likely to exaggerate treatment gains, resist treatment, or end treatment prematurely.

The fact that these conditions are classified as mental disorders does not relieve individuals who violate laws of criminal responsibility.

Associations & Agencies

764 American Association of Sexuality Educators, Counselors and Therapists (AASECT)
35 E Wacker Drive
Suite 850
Chicago, IL 60601
202-449-1099
E-mail: info@aasect.org
www.www.aasect.org

Chris Fariello, Phd, MA, President
Rosalyn Dischavio, EdD, MA, President-Elect
Melissa Novak, LCSW, CST, CSTS, Secretary
Christopher Belous, PhD, LMFT, CSE, Treasurer

A nonprofit professional organization for sexuality educators, cousnelors, sex therapists, physicians, social workers, and psychologists. Members of the association advance the fields of sexual therapy, counseling, and education.
Year Founded: 1967

765 American Sexual Health Association (ASHA)
PO Box 13827
Research Triangle Park, NC 27709
919-361-8400
E-mail: info@ashasexualhealth.org
www.www.ashasexualhealth.org

Lynn Barclay, President and CEO
Deborah Arrindell, Vice President, Health Policy

A nonprofit organization that aims to foster healthy sexual behaviours. ASHA's objectives are to educate individuals with scientifically based information, collaborate with other organizations, and advocate for beneficial changes in sexual health policy.

Year Founded: 1914

766   American Society for Reproductive Medicine
1209 Montgomery Highway
Birmingham, AL 35216-2809
205-978-5000
E-mail: asrm@asrm.org
www.www.asrm.org

Marcelle I. Cedars, MD, President
Michael A. Thomas, MD, President Elect
Paula Amato, MD, MCR, Vice President
Jim P. Toner, Jr., MD, Secretary/Treasurer

A nonprofit, multidisciplinary organization composed of urologists, obstetricians/gynecologists, embryologists, mental health professionals, nurses, reproductive endocrinologists, and other reproductive health professionals. The society aims to advance the science and practice of reproductive medicine through education, research, and advocacy.

Year Founded: 1944

767   American Urological Association
1000 Corporate Boulevard
Linthicum, MD 21090
410-689-3700
866-746-4282
E-mail: aua@AUAnet.org
www.www.auanet.org

Raju Thomas, MD, FACS, FRCS, President
Edward M. Messing, MD, FACS, President-Elect
John D. Denstedt, MD, FRCSC, Secretary
Thomas F. Stringer, MD, FACS, Treasurer

An association of professionals who promote high standards of urological care, including male infertility. The Association provides support for urologists through education, funding for research, and networking/information sharing opportunities.

Year Founded: 1902

768   Center for Healthy Sex
10700 Santa Monica Boulevard
Suite 311
Los Angeles, CA 90025
310-843-9902
E-mail: info@centerforhealthysex.com
www.centerforhealthysex.com

Alexandra Katehakis, Founder and Clinical Director

A therapy center that specializes in the treatment of sexual dysfunction, sexual aversion/anorexia, sex addiction, and love addiction.

Year Founded: 2005

769   Center for Mental Health Services (CMHS)
Substance Abuse and Mental Health Services
Administration
5600 Fishers Lane
Rockville, MD 20857
240-276-1310
www.samhsa.gov/about-us/who-we-are/offices-centers

Anita Everett, MD, DFAPA, Director

Promotes the treatment of mental illness and emotional disorders by increasing accessibility to mental health programs; supporting outreach, treatment, rehabilitation, and support programs and networks; and encouraging the use of scientifically-based information when treating mental disorders. CMHS provides information about mental health via a toll-free number and numerous publications. Developed for users of mental health services and their families, the general public, policy makers, providers, and the media.

Year Founded: 1992

770   Center for Women's Health
3181 S.W. Sam Jackson Park Road
Portland, OR 97239-3098
503-494-8311
www.www.ohsu.edu/womens-health

Danny Jacobs, MD, MPH, FACS, President
David B. Jacoby, MD, Executive Vice President
Peter G. Barr-Gillespie, PhD, EVP/Chief Research Officer
Alice Cuprill-Comas, JD, EVP/General Counsel

A center dedicated to providing services in many areas of women's health, including women's sexual health.

771   International Society for the Study of Women's
Sexual Health (ISSWSH)
14305 Southcross Dr.
Suite 100
Burnsville, MN 55306
952-683-9025
952-314-8212
E-mail: info@isswsh.org
www.www.isswsh.org

Tessa Benitez, Executive Director
Bobbi Hahn, Association Manager
Vivian Gies, Meeting Director

The ISSWSH promotes communication among scholars, researchers, and practitioners about women's sexual function and sexual experience; supports high standards of ethics and professionalism in research, education, and clinical practice of women's sexuality; and provides the public with accurate information about women's sexuality and sexual health.

772   National Association for the Dually Diagnosed
(NADD)
321 Wall Street
Kingston, NY 12401
845-331-4336
E-mail: info@thenadd.org
www.thenadd.org

Jeanne M. Farr, MA, Chief Executive Officer
Bruce Davis, President
Juanita St. Croix, Vice President
Ray Snyder, Secretary

NADD is a nonprofit organization designed to increase awareness of, and provide services for, individuals with developmental disabilities and mental illness. NADD emphasizes the importance of quality mental healthcare for people with mental health needs and offers conferences, information resources, educational programs, and training materials to professionals, parents, and organizations.

Year Founded: 1983

773   National Mental Health Consumers' Self-Help
Clearinghouse
E-mail: selfhelpclearinghouse@gmail.com
www.mhselfhelp.org

Joseph Rogers, Founder and Executive Director
Susan Rogers, Director

The Clearinghouse is a peer-run national technical assistance center focused on achieving respect and equality of opportunity for those with mental illnesses. The Clearinghouse helps with the growth of the mental health consumer movement by evaluating mental health services, advocating for mental health reform, and providing consumers with news, information, publications, and consultation services.

Year Founded: 1986

774 Sexual Medicine Society of North America
14305 Southcross Drive
Suite 100
Burnsville, MN 55306
952-683-1917
E-mail: info@smsna.org
www.www.sexhealthmatters.org

David Casalod, Executive Director
Tessa Benitez, Associate Executive Director

A nonprofit professional association of physicians, researchers, nurses, and assistants who are dedicated to treating human sexual function and dysfunction.

Year Founded: 1994

775 The Center for Family Support
2811 Zulette Avenue
Bronx, NY 10461
718-518-1500
E-mail: svernikoff@cfsny.org
www.www.cfsny.org

Steven Vernikoff, Executive Director
Barbara Greenwald, Chief Operating Officer
Jos, Martin Jara, President
Elise Geltzer, Vice President

The Center for Family Support offers assistance to individuals with developmental and related disabilities, as well as their families, and provides support services and programs that are designed to accommodate individual needs. Offers services throughout New York City, Westchester County, Long Island, and New Jersey.

Year Founded: 1954

776 Urology Care Foundation
1000 Corporate Boulevard
Linthicum, MB 21090
410-689-3700
800-828-7866
E-mail: info@UrologyCareFoundation.org
www.www.urologyhealth.org

Harris M. Nagler, MD, FACS, President
Gopal H. Badlani, MD, Secretary
Thomas F. Stringer, MD, FACS, Treasurer

Associated with the American Urological Association, the Urology Care Foundation is a nonprofit organization that partners with urological health professionals, reserchers, patients, caregivers, and families to support the treatment of urological diseases such as male erectile dysfunction.

Year Founded: 1987

Video & Audio

777 Understanding Mental Illness
Educational Video Network, Inc.
1401 19th Street
Huntsville, TX 77340
936-295-5767
800-762-0060
www.www.evndirect.com

Contains information and classifications of mental illness. Mental illness can strike anyone, at any age. Learn about various organic and functional mental disorders as discussed and their causes and symptoms, and learn where to seek help for a variety of mental health concerns.

Web Sites

778 www.emdr.com
EMDR Institute

Eye Movement Desensitization and Reprocessing (EMDR) integrates elements of many effective psychotherapies in structured protocols that are designed to maximize treatment effects. These include psychodynamic, cognitive behavioral, interpersonal, experiential, and body-centered therapies.

779 www.mentalhealth.com
Internet Mental Health

Offers online psychiatric diagnosis in the hope of reaching the two-thirds of individuals with mental illness who do not seek treatment.

780 www.planetpsych.com
Planetpsych.com

Online resource for mental health information.

781 www.priory.com/sex.htm
Sexual Disorders

Diagnoses and treatments.

782 www.psychcentral.com
Psych Central

The Internet's largest and oldest independent mental health social network created and run by mental health professionals to guarantee reliable, trusted information and support communities to you.

783 www.shrinktank.com
Shrinktank

Psychology-related programs, shareware and freeware.

784 www.store.samhsa.gov
Substance Abuse and Mental Health Services Administration

Resources on mental disorders as well as treatment and recovery.

785 www.vaginismus.com
Vaginismus.com

An online resource for individuals who suffer from sexual pain. Vaginismus.com offers products, materials in a variety of languages, and a forum for people with Vaginismus to connect with each other.

Sleep-Wake Disorders

Introduction

Sleep-Wake Disorders are a group of disorders characterized by extreme distruptions in normal sleeping patterns. These include Insomnia, Hypersomnolence, Narcolepsy, Sleep Apnea, Circadian Rhythm Sleep Disorder, Substance Abuse Induced Sleep Disorder, Nightmare Disorder, Sleep Terror Disorder, Parasomnias, and Restless Legs Syndrome.

Insomnia consists of the inability to sleep, with excessive daytime sleepiness, for at least one month.

Narcolepsy is characterized by chronic, involuntary and irresistible sleep attacks; a person with the disorder can suddenly fall asleep at any time of the day and during nearly any activity, including driving a car.

Sleep Apnea is diagnosed when sleep is distrupted by an obstruction of the breathing apparatus.

Circadian Rhythm Sleep Disorder is a disruption of normal sleep patterns leading to a mismatch between the schedule required by a person's environment and his or her sleeping patterns; i.e., the individual is irresistibly sleepy when he or she is required to be awake, and awake at those times that he or she should be sleeping.

Nightmare Disorder is diagnosed when there is a repeated occurrence of frightening dreams that lead to waking.

Sleep Terror Disorder is the repeated occurrence of sleep terrors, or abrupt awakenings from sleeping with a shriek or a cry.

SYMPTOMS

This discussion addresses the disorder with the greatest prevalence: Insomnia. A diagnosis of Insomnia is made if the following criteria are met:

• Difficulty initiating or maintaining sleep or nonrestorative sleep for at least one month;
• The impairment causes clinically significant distress or impairment in social, occupational, or other important areas of functioning;
• The disturbance does not occur exclusively during the course of other sleep-related disorders;
• The disturbance is not due to another general medical or psychiatric disorder, or the direct physiological effects of a substance.

ASSOCIATED FEATURES

Individuals with Insomnia have a history of light sleeping. Interpersonal or work-related problems typically arise because of lack of sleep. Accidents and injuries may result from lack of attentiveness during waking hours, and sleep inducing, tranquillizer, or other medications may be misused or abused by people with Insomnia. Once general medical problems are ruled out, a careful sleep history will often reveal that the individual has poor sleep habits or is reacting to an adverse life situation. These problems can then be addressed with advice or psychotherapy.

PREVALENCE

Surveys indicate a one-year prevalence of Insomnia complaints in thirty percent to forty percent of adults. Insomnia becomes more prevalent with increased age, and women are more likely than men to suffer from Insomnia. Insomnia plays an important role in the onset, experience and effect of many other disorders.

TREATMENT OPTIONS

Treatment for Sleep-Wale Disorders includes an examination by a primary care physician to determine physical condition and sleeping habits, and a discussion with a somnologist, a professional trained in Sleep-Wake Disorders, or other mental health professional, to determine the individual's emotional state.

Referrals may be made to sleep clinics, which can be situated in hospitals, or sleep disorder centers in hospitals, universities or psychiatric institutions. To determine the cause of sleep disturbances, an individual in a sleep clinic or sleep disorder center may undergo interviews, psychological tests and laboratory observation. The patient will sleep in the sleep laboratory while an overnight polysomnography is conducted. In this procedure, the person is wired to electrodes that monitor the various sleep stages. Polysomnography can also determine if the individual is suffering from Sleep Apnea.

The main treatments for Insomnia are behavioral therapy and sleep medications. Behavioral methods used to help people with Insomnia may include relaxation exercises, planning a transition time for unwinding before bed, going to bed only when sleepy, getting out of bed if unable to sleep, getting up at the same time every morning, reserving the bedroom for sleeping only, avoiding daytime naps and limiting the amount of time in bed to actual sleep time. People with Insomnia are also encouraged to practise good sleep habits, such as exercising regularly, avoiding stimulants and alcohol before bedtime, and keeping the bedroom quiet and dark.

Medications that may be part of treatment for Sleep-Wake Disorders include drugs known as hypnotics, or sleeping pills, including temazepam, Ambien, Sonata, and Lunesta. Some medications are more helpful with falling, and others with staying, asleep; a new formulation of Ambien has been developed in an attempt to address both. Melatonin supplementation and over-the-counter medications that contain diphenhydramine may also help in treating Insomnia. Many cases of Insomnia will resolve with improved sleep hygiene, and treatment of pain and other remediable causes. The drug Provigil helps people with Narcolepsy to stay awake. Sleep medications can lose effectiveness if taken over extended periods; use should always be supervised by a physician.

Associations & Agencies

787 American Academy of Dental Sleep Medicine
1001 Warrenville Road
Suite 175
Lisle, IL 60532
630-686-9875
E-mail: info@aadsm.org
www.aadsm.org

Daniel Baker, PhD, NADD-CC, Immediate Past President
Bruce Davis, PhD, NADD-CC, President
Tony Thomas, LISW-S, ACSW, Treasurer
Juanita St. Croix, BSc, Vice President

The American Academy of Dental Sleep Medicine is a professional membership organization focused on raising awareness on the involvement of dentistry in sleep-related breathing disorders treatment and research. The AADSM seeks to expand research on the use of oral appliances and dental surgery in the diagnosis and treatment of sleep-related breathing disorders. The AADSM assists in the education of practitioner dentists through clinical meetings and establishes relationships with sleep centers and other professional medical groups to help drive research on sleep breathing disorders.

Year Founded: 1991

788 American Academy of Sleep Medicine

2510 North Frontage Road
Darien, IL 60561
630-737-9700
E-mail: contact@aasm.org
www.aasmnet.org

Raman Malhotra, MD, President
Steve Van Hout, Executive Director
James A. Rowley, MD, Secretary and Treasurer
Jennifer L. Martin, PhD, President-Elect

The American Academy of Sleep Medicine is a professional society committed to fostering health care, research, and education in the field of sleep medicine. Consisting of 10,000 accredited members specializing in the study, diagnosis, and treatment of sleep-related disorders, the AASM seeks to improve sleep health. The AASM also advocates for accessibility to quality sleep care, organizes educational events on sleep medicine, and produces publications on the latest research findings in the field.

Year Founded: 1975

789 International Restless Legs Syndrome Study Group

3270 19th Street NW
Suite 110
Rochester, MN 55901
507-316-0084
E-mail: secretary@irlssg.org
www.irlssg.org

Allan O'Bryan, Executive Director

A nonprofit organization of professionals aiming to advance clinical research of Restless Legs Syndrome.

790 Narcolepsy Network

PO Box 2178
Lynnwood, WA 98036
401-667-2523
888-292-6522
E-mail: info@narcolepsynetwork.org
www.narcolepsynetwork.org

Keith Harper, President
Sharon O'Shaughnessy, MA, SLP, Vice President
Paul Reynolds, Treasurer
Rajeev Sachdeva, Secretary

A nonprofit organization dedicated to providing support for individuals with narcolepsy and related sleep disorders. Narcolepsy Network offers information and resources, raises public awareness of narcolepsy, and provides services to assist and advocate for all persons with the sleep disorder.

Year Founded: 1986

791 National Alliance on Mental Illness

4301 Wilson Boulevard
Suite 300
Arlington, VA 22203
703-524-7600
800-950-6264
E-mail: info@nami.org
www.nami.org

Shirley J. Holloway, President
Joyce A. Campbell, First Vice President
Daniel H. Gillison, Jr., Chief Executive Officer
David Levy, Chief Financial Officer

NAMI is an organization dedicated to raising awareness on mental health and providing support and education for Americans affected by mental illness. NAMI advocates for access to services and treatment and fosters an environment of awareness and understanding for those concerned with mental health.

Year Founded: 1979

792 National Association for the Dually Diagnosed (NADD)

321 Wall Street
Kingston, NY 12401
845-331-4336
E-mail: info@thenadd.org
www.thenadd.org

Jeanne M. Farr, MA, Chief Executive Officer
Bruce Davis, President
Juanita St. Croix, Vice President
Ray Snyder, Secretary

NADD is a nonprofit organization designed to increase awareness of, and provide services for, individuals with developmental disabilities and mental illness. NADD emphasizes the importance of quality mental healthcare for people with mental health needs and offers conferences, information resources, educational programs, and training materials to professionals, parents, and organizations.

Year Founded: 1983

793 National Mental Health Consumers' Self-Help Clearinghouse

E-mail: selfhelpclearinghouse@gmail.com
www.mhselfhelp.org

Joseph Rogers, Founder and Executive Director
Susan Rogers, Director

The Clearinghouse is a peer-run national technical assistance center focused on achieving respect and equality of opportunity for those with mental illnesses. The Clearinghouse helps with the growth of the mental health consumer movement by evaluating mental health services, advocating for mental health reform, and providing consumers with news, information, publications, and consultation services.

Year Founded: 1986

794 Restless Legs Syndrome Foundation, Inc.

3006 Bee Caves Road
Suite D206
Austin, TX 78746

512-366-9109
E-mail: info@rls.org
www.www.rls.org

Carla Rahn Phllips, PhD, Chair
Linda R. Secretan, Secretary
Lewis Phelps, Chair Emeritus
Karla Dzienkowski, RN, BSN, Executive Director

A nonprofit organization dedicated to increasing awareness, and improving treatments and research in order to find a cure for Restless Legs Syndrome.

Year Founded: 1992

795 Sleep Foundation
1414 NE 42nd St.
Suite 400
Seattle, WA 98105
703-243-1697
www.sleepfoundation.org

Joseph M. Ojile, Chairman
Helene Emsellem, Vice Chairman
David M. Cloud, MBA, Chief Executive Officer

The National Sleep Foundation is committed to improving the health of Americans suffering from sleep problems and disorders. Through sleep education and advocacy, NSF provides patients, medical professionals, and the public with resources on sleep medicine, sleep hygiene, and sleep disorders. NSF seeks to help the public better understand the benefits of healthy sleep habits and the importance of identifying the signs of sleep problems so that they can be properly treated.

Year Founded: 1990

796 The Center for Family Support
2811 Zulette Avenue
Bronx, NY 10461
718-518-1500
E-mail: svernikoff@cfsny.org
www.www.cfsny.org

Steven Vernikoff, Executive Director
Barbara Greenwald, Chief Operating Officer
Jos, Martin Jara, President
Elise Geltzer, Vice President

The Center for Family Support offers assistance to individuals with developmental and related disabilities, as well as their families, and provides support services and programs that are designed to accommodate individual needs. Offers services throughout New York City, Westchester County, Long Island, and New Jersey.

Year Founded: 1954

797 The Johns Hopkins Center for Restless Legs Syndrome
Johns Hopkins University School of Medicine
Johns Hopkins Asthma & Allergy Center
5501 Hopkins Bayview Circle
Baltimore, MD 21224-6801
410-550-0571
410-464-6713
www.www.hopkinsmedicine.org/neurology_neurosurgery/

A reseach center dedicated to the research of Restless Legs Syndrome. The center is part of the Johns Hopkins University of Medicine, and provides dissemination of health information as well as programs related to the cause, prevention, and treatmet of RLS. The center is located in the Asthma and Allergy Center at the Johns Hopkins Bayview Campus.

798 Thriving Minds
10524 E Grand River Avenue
Suite 100
Brighton, MI 48116
810-225-3417
E-mail: office@thrivingminds.info
www.www.thrivingmindsbehavioralhealth.com

Amiee Kotrba, PhD, Owner
Bryce Hella, PhD, Director, Brighton Clinic
Becky Thomson, PhD, Director, Chelsea Clinic
Katelyn Reed, MS, LLP, Director, Selective Mutism

Thriving Minds is an organization that offers therapy to people with anxiety, behavioral issues, and depression. With locations in Brighton and Chelsea, Thriving Minds uses a mix of research-based interventions, such as Cognitive Behavioral Therapy; parent coaching; and school interventions in order to help children, teens, and adults deal with their anxiety.

Periodicals & Pamphlets

799 Narcolepsy In the Classroom
Narcolepsy Network
129 Waterwheel Lane
North Kingstown, RI 02852
401-667-2523
888-292-6522
E-mail: NarNet@narcolepsynetwork.org
www.narcolepsynetwork.org

Sara Kowalczyk, MA, MPH, President
Eveline Honig, MD, MPH, Executive Director
Mark Patterson,MD,PhD, Vice President
Louise O'Connell, Treasurer

Concerned about a sleepy student? Essential information for school nurses, administrators, special education teams, parents, teachers, and students.

800 Narcolepsy Q&A
Narcolepsy Network
129 Waterwheel Lane
North Kingstown, RI 02852
401-667-2523
888-292-6522
E-mail: NarNet@narcolepsynetwork.org
www.narcolepsynetwork.org

Sara Kowalczyk, MA, MPH, President
Eveline Honig, MD, MPH, Executive Director
Mark Patterson,MD,PhD, Vice President
Louise O'Connell, Treasurer

Common questions about narcolepsy for doctors' offices, public service buildings as well as psychiatrist offices and sleep study programs.

801 Narcolepsy and You
Narcolepsy Network
129 Waterwheel Lane
North Kingstown, RI 02852
401-667-2523
888-292-6522
E-mail: NarNet@narcolepsynetwork.org
www.narcolepsynetwork.org

Sara Kowalczyk, MA, MPH, President
Eveline Honig, MD, MPH, Executive Director
Mark Patterson,MD,PhD, Vice President
Louise O'Connell, Treasurer

This booklet provides information about narcolepsy and tips on how to live a healthy life with this often misunderstood condition.

16 pages

802 Sleep Health Journal
National Sleep Foundation
1010 North Glebe Road
Suite 420
Arlington, VA 22201
703-243-1697
www.www.sleephealthjournal.org/

Lauren Hale, PhD, Editor-in-Chief
Orfeu Buxton, PhD, Associate Editor
Michael Grandner, PhD, Associate Editor
Amy Wolfson, PhD, Associate Editor

A peer-reviewed journal that advances the sleep health of all members of society. The journal covers the topic of sleep throughout a variety of disciplines, and includes articles, reports, letters to the editor, editorials, and commentaries.

ISSN 2352-7218

803 Sleep and Breathing
American Academy of Dental Sleep Medicine
2510 North Frontage Road
Darien, IL 60561
630-737-9761
E-mail: info@aadsm.org
www.www.aadsm.org

B. Gail Demko, DMD, President
Michael Simmons,DMD, Director
Todd Morgan,DMD, Director
Leslie C Dort,DDS, Secretary/Treasurer

The official peer-reviewed journal of the AADSM, features the most recent original research in dental sleep medicine. Timely and original studies on the management of the upper airway during sleep in addition to common sleep disorders and disruptions, including sleep apnea, insomnia and shiftwork. Coverage includes patient studies and studies that emphasize the principles of physiology and pathophysiology or illustrate novel approaches to diagnosis and treatment.

4x per year

Research Centers

804 Sleep Studies
eRiver Neurology of New York, LLC
21 Fox Street
Suite 102
Poughkeepsie, NY 12601-4723
845-452-9750
www.eriverneurology.com/Sleep%20Disorders%20Lab.htm

The all-night sleep study is frequently used by sleep physicians to evaluate adult patients when they are sleeping. This laboratory tet is extremely valuable for diagnosing and treating many sleep disorders, including neurologic disorders, movement disorders and breathing disorders at night. Sleep studies are generally easy to tolerate, comfortable for

patients, and give sleep physicians the information they need to accurately diagnose and treat the sleep disorder.

805 Standford Sleep Medicine Center
450 Broadway Street, Pavilion B
2nd Floor, MC 5730
Redwood City, CA 94063
650-723-6601
www.stanfordhealthcare.org/search-results.clinics.html

Fiona Barwick, PhD, Psychologist
Mark Buchfuhrer, MD, Sleep Specialist
Clete A. Kushida, MD, PhD, Sleep Specialist
Emmanuel Mignot, MD, PhD, Sleep Specialist

A research center that deals with sleep disorders in children and adults, including Restless Leg Syndrome, Sleep Apnea, Insomnia, Narcolepsy, Parasomnias, and more. The Sleep Medicine Center has three clinics specifically for Narcolepsy, Parasomnias, and Restless Legs Syndrome.

Support Groups & Hot Lines

806 ASAA A.W.A.K.E. Network
American Sleep Apnea Association (ASAA)
6856 Eastern Avenue NW
Suite 203
Washington, DC 20012
202-293-3650
www.stanford.edu/~dement/sleeplinks.html#so

Plays a crucial role in the ASAA's educational and avocacy efforts. A.W.A.K.E. is an acronym for Alert, Well, And Keeping Energetic. A mutual-help support group for persons affected by sleep apnea, composed of more than 200 groups in 45 states. Meetings are held regularly and guest speakers are often invited to address the group. Topics may include advice on complying with CPAP therapy, legal issues affecting those with sleep apnea, weight loss, treatment options such as oral appliances, and new research findings. Baltimore, New York, California, Oakland California, and Western Pennsylvania are just a few of the many locations of A.W.A.K.E. groups.

807 Night Terrors Forum
Night Terrors Resource Center
www.www.nightterrors.org/forum.htm

David W. Richards, Site Administrator

Helping people understand that there are medical solutions and reasons for Night Terrors. Information on causes, medications, personal stories, sleep stages, and frequently asked questions about night terrors.

Year Founded: 1996

808 eHealthForum Sleep Disorder Support Forum
www.ehealthforum.com/health/sleep_disorders.html#b

A health community featuring member and doctor discussions ranging from a specific symptom to related conditions, treatment options, medication, side effects, diet, and emotional issues surrounding medical sleep conditions.

Video & Audio

809 Clinical Impressions: Identifying Mental Illness
Educational Training Videos
136 Granville St
Suite 200
Gahanna, OH 43230

www.educationaltrainingvideos.com

How long can mental illness stay hidden, especially from the eyes of trained experts? This program rejoins a group of ten adults- five of them healthy and five of them with histories of mental illness- as psychiatric specialists try to spot and correctly diagnose the latter. Administering a series of collaborative and one-on-one tests, including assessments of personality type, physical self-image, and rational thinking, the panel gradually makes decisions about who suffers from depression, bipolar disorder, bulimia, and social anxiety.

810 **Coping with Stress**
Educational Video Network, Inc.
1401 19th Street
Huntsville, TX 77340
936-295-5767
800-762-0060
www.www.evndirect.com

Stress affects everyone, both emotionally and physically. For some, mismanaged stress can result in substance abuse, violence, or even suicide. This program answers the question, How can a person cope with stress?

811 **Effective Learning Systems**
5108 W 74th
St #390160
Minneapolis, MN 55439
952-943-1660
800-966-0443
www.effectivelearning.com

Audio tapes for stress management, deep relaxation, anger control, peace of mind, insomnia, weight and smoking, self-image and self-esteem, positive thinking, health and healing. Since 1972, Effective Learning Systems has helped millions of people take charge of their lives and make positive changes. Over 75 titles available.

812 **Insomnia**
Educational Training Videos
136 Granville St
Suite 200
Gahanna, OH 43230
www.educationaltrainingvideos.com

An inability to sleep is far more than a nuisance- it's a genuine health problem. This program examines insomnia from a medical perspective, exploring the physical, emotional, and psychological aspects of the disorder. Interview with doctors who specialize in treating sleep difficulties provide historical background on the affliction, the personal and professional hazards it can present, and dietary and behavioral adjustments that can improve the quality of sleep.

813 **Mental Disorder**
Educational Training Videos
136 Granville St
Suite 200
Gahanna, OH 43230
www.educationaltrainingvideos.com

What is abnormality? Using the case studies of two young women; one who has depression, one who has an anxiety disorder; as a springboard, this program presents three psychological perspective on mental disorder.

814 **Understanding Mental Illness**
Educational Video Network, Inc.
1401 19th Street
Huntsville, TX 77340
936-295-5767
800-762-0060
www.www.evndirect.com

Contains information and classifications of mental illness. Mental illness can strike anyone, at any age. Learn about various organic and functional mental disorders as discussed and their causes and symptoms, and learn where to seek help for a variety of mental health concerns.

Web Sites

815 **ehealthforum.com/health/sleep_disorders. html#b**
eHealthForum Sleep Disorder Support Forum

A health community featuring member and doctor discussions ranging from a specific symptom to related conditions, treatment options, medication, side effects, diet, and emotional issues surrounding medical sleep conditions.

816 **www.aadsm.org**
American Academy of Dental Sleep Medicine

Promotes research on the use of oral appliances and dental surgery for the treatment of sleep disordered breathing and provides training and resources for those who work directly with patients. The organization builds bridges and forms relationships with the medical community, especially in sleep centers, and other professional groups who play an integral part of the sleep disorders treatment and research team. The AADSM also reaches out to the community at large, working toward the creation of a positive public awareness of sleep disorders and the role of the dentist in recognition and treatment of sleep breathing disorders.

817 **www.aasmnet.org**
American Academy of Sleep Medicine

A professional society that is dedicated exclusively to the medical subspecialty of sleep medicine.

818 **www.cyberpsych.org**
CyberPsych

Presents information about psychoanalysis, psychotherapy and special topics such as anxiety disorders, the problematic use of alcohol, homophobia, and the traumatic effects of racism.

819 **www.mentalhealth.com**
Internet Mental Health

Offers on-line psychiatric diagnosis in the hope of reaching the two-thirds of individuals with mental illness who do not seek treatment.

820 **www.narcolepsynetwork.org**
Narcolepsy Network
www.narcolepsynetwork.org

A non profit organization dedicated to individuals with narcolepsy and related sleep disorders. Mission is to provide services to educate, advocate, support and improve awareness of this neurological sleep disorder.

821 **www.nhlbi.nih.gov/about/ncsdr**
National Institute of Health National Center on Sleep Disorders

The Center seeks to fulfill its goal of improving the health of Americans by serving four key functions: research, training, technology transfer, and coordination.

822 **www.nightterrors.org/forum.htm**
Night Terrors Resource Center, Night Terrors Forum

Helping people understand that there are medical solutions and reasons for Night Terrors. Information on causes, medications, personal stories, sleep stages, and frequently asked questions about night terrors.

823 **www.nlm.nih.gov/medlineplus/sleepdisorders.html**
MEDLINEplus on Sleep Disorders

Compilation of links directs you to information on sleep disorders.

824 **www.planetpsych.com**
Planetpsych.com

Online resource for mental health information.

825 **www.psychcentral.com**
Psych Central

The Internet's largest and oldest independent mental health social network created and run by mental health professionals to guarantee reliable, trusted information and support communities to you.

826 **www.reggiewhitefoundation.org**
Reggie White Sleep Disorders Research & Education Foundation, Inc.

Helping provide CPAP treatment equipment to those people who might otherwise be unable to secure the needed equipment. CPAP equipment is provided to patients who qualify for the foundation's assistance and who have a current prescription for it. Co-founded by Reggie White's wife, Sara, who recognized the role of her husbands sleep disorder in cutting his life short. Started the Foundation to help people of all economic backgrounds to understand the symptoms and risks of sleep disorders.

827 **www.sdrfoundation.org**
Sleep Disorder Relief Foundation

A public non profit organization founded to: assist the underpriveleged suffering from sleep disorders by creating a network of relief, further the field of sleep medicine through organizing and funding sleep disorder researcch, and spread domestic and international awareness about the importance of sleep and the prevalence of sleep disorders.

828 **www.sleepfoundation.org**
National Sleep Foundation

Alerting the public, healthcare providers and policymakers to the live-and-death importance of adequate sleep is central to the mission of NSF. NSF is dedicated to improving the quality of life for Americans who suffer from sleep problems and disorders. This means helping the public better understand the importance of sleep and the benefits of good sleep habits, and recognizing the signs of sleep problems so that they can be properly diagnosed and treated.

829 **www.stanford.edu/~dement/sleeplinks.html#so**
ASAA A.W.A.K.E. Network

Plays a crucial role in the ASAA's educational and avocacy efforts. A.W.A.K.E. is an acronym for Alert, Well, And Keeping Energetic. A mutual-help support group for persons affected by sleep apnea, composed of more than 200 groups in 45 states. Meetings are held regularly and guest speakers are often invited to address the group. Topics may include advice on complying with CPAP therapy, legal issues affecting those with sleep apnea, weight loss, treatment options such as oral appliances, and new research findings. Baltimore, New York, California, Oakland California, and Western Pennsylvania are just a few of the many locations of A.W.A.K.E. groups.

830 **www.store.samhsa.gov**
Substance Abuse and Mental Health Services Administration

Resources on mental disorders as well as treatment and recovery.

831 **www.uic.edu/nursing/CNSHR/index.html**
Center for Narcolepsy, Sleep & Health Research

Primary goal is to conduct important basic, clinical and bio-behavioral research for improving, preserving or promoting health through good sleep. The Center also aims to continue as an important source of sleep science and health expertise for colleagues, aspiring sleep researchers, clinicians, patients and families. Researching sleep and sleep-related disorders; educating young scientists for productive careers in sleep research; and transferring technologies and knowledge developed through research into practice or into the private sector.

Somatic Symptom and Related Disorders

Introduction

The disorders in this category are characterized by multiple physical symptoms or the conviction that one is ill despite negative medical examinations and laboratory tests. Those who have a somatizing disorder persist in believing they are ill, or experience physical symptoms over long periods, and their beliefs negatively affect all areas of their functioning.

Two main types of somatizing disorders are Hypochondriasis (also known as Hypochondria), which consists of being convinced that one is ill despite evidence to the contrary, and Somatization Disorder, consisting of experiencing physical symptoms without a discernible basis.

Factitious Disorder and Malingering are also conditions in which physical symptoms are not caused by an identifiable general medical condition, but in which symptoms are deliberately and consciously produced. A malingerer deliberately complains or mimics symptoms to achieve a specific goal, such as winning a medical malpractice suit or obtaining disability insurance.

Individuals with Factitious Disorder deliberately cause significant medical conditions in themselves, for example by introducing fecal contamination intravenously, or taking insulin to the point of severe hypoglycemia. The motivations for this behavior are unclear. Once the diagnosis is suspected, and the suspicion is conveyed to the patient, these individuals nearly always flee the medical care venue and are unwillingto undergo more definitive diagnostic examinations.

SYMPTOMS

HYPOCHONDRIASIS
• Pre occupation with fears of having a serious illness based on a misinterpretation of bodily symptoms or sensations;
• The preoccupation persists in spite of medical reassurance;
• The preoccupation is a source of distress and difficulty in social, work, and other areas;
• The duration of the preoccupation is at least six months.

SOMATIZATION DISORDER
• A history beginning before age 30 and continuing over years, resulting in a search for treatment or clear difficulties in social, work, or interpersonal areas;
• Four pain symptoms related to at least four anatomical areas or functions;
• Two gastrointestinal problems other than pain, e.g. nausea, diarrhea;
• One sexual symptom other than pain, e.g. irregular menstruation, sexual disinterest, erectile dysfunction;
• One pseudoneurological symptom other than pain, e.g., weakness, double vision;
• Symptoms cannot be explained by a medical condition;
• When a medical condition exists, physical complaints and social difficulties are greater than normal.

ASSOCIATED FEATURES

The person with either of these somatizing disorders visits many doctors, but physical examinations and negative lab results neither reassure them nor resolve their symptoms. They often believe they are not getting proper respect or attention, and, indeed, they may be viewed in medical settings as troublesome. Persons with these disorders often suffer from anxiety and depression as well. Physical symptoms appearing after the somatization diagnosis is made, however, should not be dismissed completely out of hand. Sufferers can have general medical disorders at the same time as Somatizing Disorders.

The person may be treated by several doctors at once, which can lead to unwitting and possibly dangerous combinations of treatments. There may be suicide threats and attempts, and deteriorating personal relationships.

PREVALENCE

Hypochondriasis is equally common in both sexes. The age of onset is usually young adulthood. Its prevalence in the general population is estimated to be one to five percent. In general medical practice, two percent to seven percent of patients have the disorder. It is usually chronic.

Somatization Disorder was once thought to be mainly a disease of women, but occurs in both sexes. It is slightly less common among men in the general population of the US than in other countries, but not uncommon in general medical practice. It is more common among Puerto Rican and Greek men, which suggests that cultural factors influence the sex ratios. It is estimated that between 0.2 percent and two percent of the general population suffers from Somatization Disorder.

TREATMENT OPTIONS

These disorders are chronic by definition, and are difficult to manage. Repeated reassurance is not successful. The aim is to limit the extent to which the physical concerns and symptoms preoccupy an individual's thoughts and activities, and drain family, emotional, and financial resources. Individuals suffering from these disorders often resist mental health referral because they interpret it, sometimes correctly, as an indication that their symptoms are not being taken seriously. Treatment, whether by the primary care or mental health professional or both, should focus on maintaining function despite the symptoms. It is important that the psychological management and treatment is coordinated with medical treatment if possible by one physician only; one person should oversee all the medical treatment, including the psychological, so that care does not become fragmented and/or repetitive as the patient sees many different clinicians. Some individuals with Hypochondriasis respond to treatment which combines medication with intensive behavioral and cognitive techniques to manage anxiety and modify beliefs about the origin and course of physical symptoms.

People with Hypochondriasis and Somatization Disorders do not deliberately produce or falsely complain of physical symptoms; their beliefs and behaviors are engendered by psychological conflict, and often by modeling on someone who was important to them when they were growing up.

Treatment for Hypochondriasis may include psychological counseling and medication. Cognitive behavioral therapy, which gives patients techniques to manage anxiety and

109

modify beliefs about the origin and course of physical symptoms, is considered helpful in treating Hypochondriasis. Other treatments may include stress management techniques and exposure therapy (in which patients practise confronting their anxieties until they are better able to manage them). Medications such as serotonin reuptake inhibitors (SSRIs) and tricyclic antidepressants are sometimes prescribed.

Treatment of Somatization Disorder may include cognitive behavioral therapy, as well as relaxation techniques and communication skills training. Patients are also encouraged to increase their activity level. Antidepressant medications may be prescribed to help treat symptoms.

Associations & Agencies

833 Academy of Psychosomatic Medicine
4800 Hampden Ln
Ste. 200
Bethesda, MD 20814-2934
301-718-6520
E-mail: info@CLpsychiatry.org
www.apm.org

Philip Biaeler, MD, FACLP, President
Maryland Pao, MD, FACLP, President-Elect
James Vrac, CAE, Executive Director
Shannon Sperati, CAE, Deputy Executive Director

The Academy of Psychosomatic Medicine represents psychiatrists focused on improving education, medical science, and healthcare for individuals with comorbid psychiatric and general medical conditions. The Academy seeks to promote interdisciplinary education and drive research and public policy with the goal of achieving outstanding clinical care for patients with comorbid psychiatric and general medical conditions throughout the world. They also created the Foundation of the Academy of Psychosomatic Medicine, a scientific foundation supporting education and research programs.

834 Center for Mental Health Services (CMHS)
Substance Abuse and Mental Health Services
Administration
5600 Fishers Lane
Rockville, MD 20857
240-276-1310
www.samhsa.gov/about-us/who-we-are/offices-centers

Anita Everett, MD, DFAPA, Director

Promotes the treatment of mental illness and emotional disorders by increasing accessibility to mental health programs; supporting outreach, treatment, rehabilitation, and support programs and networks; and encouraging the use of scientifically-based information when treating mental disorders. CMHS provides information about mental health via a toll-free number and numerous publications. Developed for users of mental health services and their families, the general public, policy makers, providers, and the media.

Year Founded: 1992

835 Goodwill's Community Employment Services
Goodwill Industries-Suncoast, Inc.
10596 Gandy Blvd.
St. Petersburg, FL 33702
727-523-1512
888-279-1988

TDD: 727-579-1068
www.goodwill-suncoast.org

Sandra Young, Chair
Louise Lopez, Sr. Vice Chair
Dominic Macrone, Board Secretary

The St. Petersburg headquarters serves ten counties in the state of Florida. Their mission is to help people with disabilities gain employment through training programs, employment services, and affordable housing.

Year Founded: 1954

836 Institute for Contemporary Psychotherapy
33 W 60th St.
4th Floor
New York, NY 10023
212-333-3444
www.icpnyc.org

Ron Taffel, PhD, Chair
Andrea Green-Lewis, LCSW-R, Director of Operations
Fred Lipschitz, PhD, Co-Founder
Mary Labiento, Associate Director of Operations

The Institute for Contemporary Psychotherapy is a New York City-based mental health treatment and training facility. Consisting of a group of 150 licensed psychotherapists, the Institute focuses on educating the public about the issues surrounding mental health, providing post-graduate training for therapists, and offering therapy at moderate costs.

Year Founded: 1971

837 National Association for the Dually Diagnosed
(NADD)
321 Wall Street
Kingston, NY 12401
845-331-4336
E-mail: info@thenadd.org
www.thenadd.org

Jeanne M. Farr. MA, Chief Executive Officer
Robert J. Fletcher, DSW, Founder and CEO Emeritus
Carly Winnie, Director of Finance and Admin.
Kristin McGill, PhD, Research Consultant

NADD is a nonprofit organization designed to increase awareness of, and provide services for, individuals with developmental disabilities and mental illness. NADD emphasizes the importance of quality mental healthcare for people with mental health needs and offers conferences, information resources, educational programs, and training materials to professionals, parents, and organizations.

Year Founded: 1983

838 National Mental Health Consumers' Self-Help
Clearinghouse
E-mail: selfhelpclearinghouse@gmail.com
www.mhselfhelp.org

Joseph Rogers, Founder and Executive Director
Susan Rogers, Director

The Clearinghouse is a peer-run national technical assistance center focused on achieving respect and equality of opportunity for those with mental illnesses. The Clearinghouse helps with the growth of the mental health consumer movement by evaluating mental health services, advocating for mental health reform, and providing consumers with news, information, publications, and consultation services.

Year Founded: 1986

839 The Center for Family Support
2811 Zulette Avenue
Bronx, NY 10461
718-518-1500
E-mail: svernikoff@cfsny.org
www.www.cfsny.org

Steven Vernikoff, Executive Director
Barbara Greenwald, Chief Operating Officer
Jos, Martin Jara, President
Elise Geltzer, Vice President

The Center for Family Support offers assistance to individuals with developmental and related disabilities, as well as their families, and provides support services and programs that are designed to accommodate individual needs. Offers services throughout New York City, Westchester County, Long Island, and New Jersey.

Year Founded: 1954

Periodicals & Pamphlets

840 Asher Meadow Newsletter
18209 Smoke House Court
Germantown, MD 20874-2425

Asher Meadow is a wholly-owned non-profit subsidiary of American Marvels, an Internet development company that provides a newsletter for survivors of MSBP.

Video & Audio

841 Clinical Impressions: Identifying Mental Illness
Educational Training Videos
136 Granville St
Suite 200
Gahanna, OH 43230
www.educationaltrainingvideos.com

How long can mental illness stay hidden, especially from the eyes of trained experts? This program rejoins a group of ten adults- five of them healthy and five of them with histories of mental illness- as psychiatric specialists try to spot and correctly diagnose the latter. Administering a series of collaborative and one-on-one tests, including assessments of personality type, physical self-image, and rational thinking, the panel gradually makes decisions about who suffers from depression, bipolar disorder, bulimia, and social anxiety.

842 Coping with Stress
Educational Video Network, Inc.
1401 19th Street
Huntsville, TX 77340
936-295-5767
800-762-0060
www.www.evndirect.com

Stress affects everyone, both emotionally and physically. For some, mismanaged stress can result in substance abuse, violence, or even suicide. This program answers the question, How can a person cope with stress?

843 Dealing with Depression
Educational Video Network, Inc.
1401 19th Street
Huntsville, TX 77340
936-295-5767
800-762-0060
www.www.evndirect.com

As more and more young people are falling victim to depression, it is important to understand what causes it and to know how to get the help that can rid a person of this life-wrecking affliction.

844 Dealing with Social Anxiety
Educational Video Network, Inc.
1401 19th Street
Huntsville, TX 77340
936-295-5767
800-762-0060
www.www.evndirect.com

Social anxiety is America's third-largest psychiatric disorder. It generally develops during the mid-teen years, and almost always before the age of 25. Understand what may trigger the development of anxiety and learn how it sometimes evolves into full-blown panic disorder, which is characterized by recurrent attacks of terror or fear. The consequences of social anxiety are examined and effective treatments are discussed.

845 FRONTLINE: The Released
PBS
2100 Crystal Drive
Arlington, VA 22202
www.pbs.org

Will Lyman, Actor
Narrator
Miri Navasky, Director
Karen O'Connor, Director

The documentary states that of the 700,000 inmates released from American prisons each year, half of them have mental disabilities. This work focused on those with severe problems who keep entering and exiting prison. Full of good information on the challenges they face with mental illnesses; housing, employment, stigmatization, and socialization.

846 Mental Disorder
Educational Training Videos
136 Granville St
Suite 200
Gahanna, OH 43230
www.educationaltrainingvideos.com

What is abnormality? Using the case studies of two young women; one who has depression, one who has an anxiety disorder; as a springboard, this program presents three psychological perspective on mental disorder.

847 Mind-Body Problems: Psychotherapy with Psychosomatic Disorders
Jason Aronson, Inc.- Rowman Littlefield Imprint
4501 Forbes Blvd.
Suite 200
Lanham, MD 20706
301-459-3366
www.rowmanlittlefield.com

Janet Schumacher Finell, Author

The opening paper profitably links psychosomatic disorders to alexithymia, the absence or deadening of feeling, the inability to identify or express emotion.

376 pages ISBN 1-568216-54-8

848 **Neurotic, Stress-Related, and Somatoform Disorders**
Educational Training Videos
136 Granville St
Suite 200
Gahanna, OH 43230
www.educationaltrainingvideos.com

This program, filmed in the UK, discusses the following disorders and their differential diagnoses; phobic anxiety; anxiety; obsessive-compulsive disorder, from minor to acute; stress reaction and adjustment; and dissociative disorders. Sub-disorders discussed include Korsakov's syndrome; agoraphobia and social phobia; generalized anxiety and mixed-anxiety-and-depressive disorder; panic disorder; and post-traumatic stress syndrome. Patients suffering from each disorder exhibit the various symptoms in interviews conducted by psychiatrists.

849 **Somatoform Disorders: A Medicolegal Guide**
Cambridge University Press
32 Ave of the Americas
New York, NY 10013-2473
212-337-5000
E-mail: newyork@cambridge.org
www.cambridge.org

Michael Trimble, Author

This book is an in-depth, clinically oriented review of the somatoform disorders and related clinical manifestations (such as chronic fatigue syndrome) and how they appear in a medico-legal setting. The volume is aimed at clinicians and lawyers who deal with injury claims where these disorders impact much more frequently than generally recognized.

268 pages ISBN 0-521169-25-9

850 **Understanding Mental Illness**
Educational Video Network, Inc.
1401 19th Street
Huntsville, TX 77340
936-295-5767
800-762-0060
www.www.evndirect.com

Contains information and classifications of mental illness. Mental illness can strike anyone, at any age. Learn about various organic and functional mental disorders as discussed and their causes and symptoms, and learn where to seek help for a variety of mental health concerns.

Web Sites

851 **www.mbpexpert.com**
MBP Expert Services

Expert services from Louisa J Lasher, MA, provides Munchausen by Proxy maltreatment training, case consultation, technical assistance, and expert witness services in an objective manner and in the best interest of the child or children involved.

852 **www.mentalhealth.com**
Internet Mental Health

Offers online psychiatric diagnosis in the hope of reaching the two-thirds of individuals with mental illness who do not seek treatment.

853 **www.msbp.com**
Mothers Against Munchausen Syndrome by Proxy Allegations

Begun in response to the fast growing number of false allegations of Munchausen Syndrome by Proxy.

854 **www.munchausen.com**
Munchause Syndrome

Dr. Marc Feldman's Munchausen Syndrome, Malingering, Factitious Disorder, & Munchausen by Proxy page. Includes articles, related book list, personal stories and links.

855 **www.planetpsych.com**
Planetpsych.com

Online resource for mental health information

856 **www.psychcentral.com**
Psych Central

The Internet's largest and oldest independent mental health social network created and run by mental health professionals to guarantee reliable, trusted information and support communities to you.

857 **www.store.samhsa.gov**
Substance Abuse and Mental Health Services Administration

Resources on mental disorders as well as treatment and recovery.

Substance-Related and Addictive Disorders

Introduction

Substance use and addictive disorders are among the most destructive mental disorders in America today, contributing to a host of medical and social problems and to widespread individual suffering. Many substances can negatively affect the user when used in a disordered way. Substances included in Substance Use Disorder (SUD) are

• alcohol,
• opioids (oxycodone, morphine, heroin),
• tobacco,
• cannabis,
• hallucinogens (LSD, ketamine),
• inhalants (glue, gasoline),
• sedatives (Valium), and
• stimulants (cocaine, methamphetamine).

Substance Use Disorders are characterized by repeated use despite repeated adverse consequences, and by physical and psychological craving. SUDs can be treated, but successful recovery is dependent on acceptance by the patient that he or she has an illness; lack of this acceptance is often the greatest stumbling block to treatment.

Relapse is common for several reasons: lack of acceptance of the diagnosis; genetic vulnerability; and social factors. Successful treatment very often requires involvement by the patient in some form of self-help group, such as Alcoholics Anonymous or another 12-step program. The great majority of motivated individuals with these disorders can recover, but it often requires three or more separate episodes of treatment to prevent relapse and lead to recovery.

Scientific understanding of how alcohol and other substances work on the body and the brain, and the underlyingphysiology of addiction, has advanced remarkably in recent years. With the help of brain imaging and other techniques, we can now see that these disorders are associated with structural changes in the brain.

Experts now classify gambling as an Addictive Disorder. Previously associated with compulsive behavior, gambling has shown to form similar neurological pathways as substance use, but to a lesser extent.

SYMPTOMS

Substance Use:

To be diagnosed with a Substance Use Disorder, a person must have two or more of the following symptoms in the span of a year.
• Inability to fulfill fundamental obligations at work, school, or home due to substance use (e.g., repeated absences, poor work performance, family neglect);
• Hazardous use (e.g., driving or operating a machine while impaired);
• Substance-related legal problems (e.g., arrests for disorderly conduct);
• Social or interpersonal problems worsened by the effects of substance use;
• Substance is often taken in greater amounts than intended;
• A great deal of time is spent using;
• Activities are given up in order to use;
• Psychological or physical experience related to use (e.g., depression induced by cocaine or continued drinking)

• Tolerance, or a need for increased amounts of alcohol or the substance to achieve desired effect;
• Withdrawal when not using (e.g., physical and mental symptoms, such as headaches, diarrhea, shaking, anxiety and depression);
• Craving.

Gambling Disorder

Problematic gambling behavior persists for a year or more and the person experiences four or more of the following symptoms but cannot be explained by a manic episode.
• Gambling disrupts family, work, and personal activities;
• Preoccupation with gambling (often reliving past experiences or planning future wins);
• Chases losses (returns to gambling to "even the score" after losing money);
• Increasingly needs to gamble higher amounts of money to achieve the same excitement;
• Gambles when feeling anxious, guilty, helpless, or generally distressed;
• Gambling continues despite repeated efforts to stop;
• Restlessness and irritable when trying to cut back or stop gambling;
• May lose job, relationship, and career opportunities;
• Needs financial support from others.

ASSOCIATED FEATURES

Alcohol is the most used substance in Substance Use Disorder and affects all those around the user. Frequently, alcohol use occurs together with the use of other substances, and alcohol may be used to counteract the ill effects of these substances. Depression, anxiety, and sleep disorders are common in alcohol dependence.

Typically, accidents, injuries and suicide accompany alcohol dependence, and it is estimated that half of all traffic accidents involve alcoholic intoxication. Absenteeism, low work productivity and injuries on the job are often caused by alcohol dependence. Alcohol is also the most common cause of preventable birth defects, including fetal alcohol syndrome, according to the American Psychiatric Association.

Women and men tend to have different drinking patterns. Society is more tolerant of male drunkenness than of female; women tend to drink alone and in secret and are more susceptible to medical complications of alcoholism. Severe alcohol use severely damages organ systems including the brain, liver, heart, and digestive tract.

Genetics has a considerable influence on a person's propensity for substance use disorders, and such disorders are associated with significant changes in the brain. These changes underscore the fact that alcohol and substance use problems are medical diseases, not failure of character. At the same time, those suffering from these disorders have an obligation to seek and utilize treatment and to ensure that their disorders do not cause injury to others.

Many individuals with substance-related and addictive disorders take more than one substance and suffer from other mental symptoms and disorders as well. Individuals with a wide variety of mental disorders sometimes use drugs as an attempt to medicate themselves. People with Antisocial Personality Disorder often use substances, including amphetamines and cocaine. Substance-related disorders can also lead to other mental disorders. Use of the synthetic hallucinogen Ecstasy is associated with acute and paranoid psychoses, and the prolonged use of cocaine (a stimulant) can lead to paranoid psychosis with violent behavior. Substance use and the effects on an individual's employment and relationships, as well as legal difficulties, can precipitate anxiety and mood disorders. Intravenous substance use is associated with a high risk of HIV infections and other medical complications.

The recent legalization initiatives surrounding marijuana and associated chemicals have raised many questions about the short and long-term effects of the drug, including effects on behavior such as driving.

Chronic drug and alcohol use can lead to difficulty in memory and problem solving, and impaired sexual functioning.

Childhood sexual abuse is strongly associated with substance dependence and with a number of other mental symptoms and disorders.

PREVALENCE

Alcohol use is among the most prevalent mental disorders in the general population. One community study in the US found that about eight percent of the adult population had alcohol dependence and about five percent had alcohol abuse at some time in their lives. Approximately six percent had alcohol dependence or abuse during the preceding year.

There are large cultural differences in attitudes toward the use of substances. In some cultures, mood altering drugs, including alcohol, are well accepted; in others they are strictly forbidden.

Those between the ages of 18 and 24 have a high prevalence for abuse of all substances. Early adolescent drug and alcohol use is associated with a slight but significant decline in intellectual abilities. Substance related disorders are more common among males than females. The lifetime prevalence of use of any drugs (aside from alcohol) in the US is 11.9 percent; in males it is twice as high as in females.

TREATMENT OPTIONS

Substance Use

Diagnosis and treatment of substance use has improved as understanding of the physiology of addiction has advanced. But successful treatment still relies on acceptance by the patient that he or she has an illness, as well as support from other people who have gone through the same process. For this reason, medical treatment is most often successful when it is accompanied by involvement in a support group, for both the patient and family members; these may include Alcoholics Anonymous (AA) and Al-Anon, 12-step spiritual programs that have gained popularity over the years. Local groups can be found in every community and are listed in the phone book and on the Internet. Recently, similar groups have formed that do not emphasize spirituality, as these do, but rely on group support for sobriety.

There is a growing controversy over the need for people who have had an substance problem to abstain completely from alcohol for the rest of their lives, one of the central beliefs of AA. Some researchers and clinicians argue that it

is possible for some former alcoholics to resume controlled drinking. AA, in the past, has discouraged members from using psychotropic medications; this is often counterproductive. Many alcohol treatment programs have been developed with men's needs and personalities in mind. Successful programs for women are far less confrontational than men's programs and include arrangements for childcare. There is a tendency for women's alcohol and substance use disorders to be addressed punitively rather than therapeutically. Women who are pregnant and/or are mothers may be reluctant to seek treatment if they risk imprisonment and loss of child custody - outcomes that do not help them or their children.

Treatment for alcoholism has been hospital-based in the past, but has increasingly moved to the outpatient setting. There are many treatment programs that offer no professional help, and yet are reimbursed by insurance, and are not very effective. New treatment protocols and medications allow for outpatient detoxification/withdrawal in many cases. There is a considerable dispute about the need for inpatient care, which may not be covered by health insurance. Much depends upon the nature of the individual's support system. Hospital treatment is necessary for withdrawal when alcohol use has been heavy and steady. Delirium tremens, a consequence of very heavy drinking, can be fatal.

Denial of illness and ambivalence about abstinence can make treatment difficult. A patient's cravings can be overwhelmingly intense, and the individual's social circle is often composed of other substance users, making it hard for the individual to maintain relationships while becoming or remaining abstinent - the goal of treatment. A wide range of intervention may be individual's social circle is often composed of other substance users, making it hard for the individual to maintain relationships while becoming or remaining absstinent - the goal of treatment. A wide range of intervention may be needed, including a general assessment of the drug use, and evaluation of medical, social, and psychological problems. An explicit treatment plan should be worked out with the person (and partner/family/friends if appropriate) with concrete goals for which the person takes responsibility, which should include not only stopping substance use, but also dealing with associated problems concerning health, personal relationships, and work.

Another option is maintenance therapy, in which a drug is prescribed that has a slower action and is less addictive than the street drug (e.g., methadone vs. heroin). Therapy is added to help with withdrawal and other problems associated with drug use. Cognitive behavioral therapy can help with increasing the substance user's personal skills, resulting in a reduced dependency on drugs. Rehabilitation in a therapeutic community is another option.

Dropout during treatment and relapse after initial success are common, but many people do achieve lifelong cures with abstinence from further substance use.

Associations & Agencies

859 **AMERSA The Association for Medical Education and Research in Substance Abuse**
135 Lyndon Road
Cranston, RI 02905

401-230-2165
E-mail: doreen@amersa.org
www.amersa.org

Rebecca Northup, Executive Director

AMERSA is a nonprofit organization of healthcare professionals dedicated to improving education and clinical care in the management of problems related to substance abuse.

Year Founded: 1976

860 **Adult Children of Alcoholics World Service Organization, Inc.**
PO Box 811
Lakewood, CA 90714
310-534-1815
www.adultchildren.org

Adult Children of Alcoholics is a 12 Step, 12 Tradition program for adult women and men who grew up in alcoholic or otherwise dysfunctional homes, and for adults who have experienced abuse or neglect in the past. The program involves ACA members meeting with each other in a mutually respectful, safe environment and sharing their experiences, as well as applying the program's 12 Steps for recovery to their own lives.

Year Founded: 1978

861 **Alcoholics Anonymous (AA): Worldwide**
475 Riverside Drive at West 120th Street
11th Floor and 8th Floors
New York, NY 10115
212-870-3400
www.aa.org

Bill Wilson, Co-Founder
Dr. Bob Smith, Co-Founder

A fellowship of men and women around the world who share experiences, strength, and hope with each other with the goal of solving their drinking problem and helping others to recover from alcoholism.

Year Founded: 1935

862 **American Academy of Addiction Psychiatry (AAAP)**
400 Massasoit Avenue
Suite 307, 2nd Floor
East Providence, RI 02914
401-524-3076
www.aaap.org

Kathryn Cates-Wessel, Chief Executive Officer
Joe Barboza, Director of Finance
Bethany Banner, Director of Professional Dev.
Jamie Edwards, Director of Education/Training

An organization of healthcare professionals dedicated to helping those with mental health disorders. Promotes the use of evidence-based research in the assessment and treatment of substance abuse and mental disorders, as well as in public policy and clinical practice. Provides education to healthcare professionals and the public on patient care, recovery, and the safe treatment of those suffering from substance abuse disorders.

863 **American Public Human Services Association**
1300 17th St. N
Suite 340
Arlington, VA 22209-3801

202-682-0100
E-mail: memberservice@aphsa.org
www.aphsa.org

Tracy Wareing Evans, President/CEO
Ray Davidson, Chief Operating Officer
Jessica Garon, MA, Communications Director
Sherray G. Whatley, CSM, Executive Coordinator

APHSA is a nonprofit organization dedicated to improving health and human services by supporting state and local agencies, and working with partners and policymakers to drive effective policies.

Year Founded: 1930

864 **American Society of Addiction Medicine**
11400 Rockville Pike
Suite 200
Rockville, MD 20852
301-656-3920
E-mail: email@asam.org
www.asam.org

William F. Haning, III, MD, President
Brian Hurley, MD, MBA, President-Elect
Timothy Wiegand, MD, FACMT, Vice-President
Aleksandra Zgierska, MD, PhD, Secretary

ASAM's mission is to support the practice of Addiction Medicine and to improve the quality of care and treatment for people struggling with addiction.

Year Founded: 1954

865 **Brain & Behavior Research Foundation**
747 Third Avenue
33rd Floor
New York, NY 10017
646-681-4888
800-829-8289
E-mail: info@bbrfoundation.org
www.www.bbrfoundation.org

Donald M. Boardman, Treasurer
Jeffrey Borenstein, MD, President and CEO
Louis Innamorato, CPA, VP and Chief Financial Officer
Faith Rothblatt, Vice President, Development

The Brain and Behavior Research Foundation awards grants aimed at advancing scientific understandings of mental health treatments and mental disorders such as depression and schizophrenia. The Brain and Behavior Research Foundation's mission is to eliminate the suffering caused by mental illness.

Year Founded: 1987

866 **Center for Mental Health Services (CMHS)**
Substance Abuse and Mental Health Services Administration
5600 Fishers Lane
Rockville, MD 20857
240-276-1310
www.samhsa.gov/about-us/who-we-are/offices-centers

Anita Everett, MD, DFAPA, Director

Promotes the treatment of mental illness and emotional disorders by increasing accessibility to mental health programs; supporting outreach, treatment, rehabilitation, and support programs and networks; and encouraging the use of scientifically-based information when treating mental disorders. CMHS provides information about mental health via a toll-free number and numerous publications. Developed for users of mental health services and their families, the general public, policy makers, providers, and the media.

Year Founded: 1992

867 Centre for Addiction and Mental Health
1001 Queen Street West
Toronto, ON M6J 1H4,
800-463-2338
E-mail: info@camh.ca
www.camh.ca

Dr Catherine Zahn, President and CEO

The Centre for Addiction and Mental Health is a mental health and addiction teaching hospital and research centre based in Canada. CAMH seeks to support people affected by mental health and addiction issues through research, education, policy development, clinical care, and the promotion of health.

868 Community Anti-Drug Coalitions of America (CADCA)
500 Montgomery Street
4th Floor
Alexandria, VA 22314
703-706-0560
E-mail: international@cadca.org
www.cadca.org

Mary Bono, Chairman
Larry P. Cote, Esq., Vice Chairman
Gregory Puckett, Secretary
Donald K. Truslow, Treasurer

Community Anti-Drug Coalition of America is a national organization representing the interests of over 5,000 anti-drug coalitions across the United States. CADCA participates in public policy advocacy and provides community coalitions with marketing programs, technical assistance and training, and special events with the purpose of making communities safe and drug-free.

Year Founded: 1992

869 FASD United
PO Box 251
McLean, VA 22101
202-785-4585
E-mail: information@nofas.org
www.nofas.org

Tom Donaldson, President and CEO
Kathleen Tavenner Mitchell, MHS, Vice President
Andy Kachor, Communications Director
Jennifer Wisdahl, Advocacy Coordinator

Educates the public about the risks associated with alcohol use during pregnancy, including Fetal Alcohol Spectrum Disorders, which causes birth defects and developmental disabilities in children. Dedicated to preventing alcohol consumption during pregnancy and reducing the number of birth defects. Provides support for individuals and families concerned with Fetal Alcohol Spectrum Disorders.

870 Goodwill's Community Employment Services
Goodwill Industries-Suncoast, Inc.
10596 Gandy Blvd.
St. Petersburg, FL 33702
727-523-1512
888-279-1988
TDD: 727-579-1068
www.goodwill-suncoast.org

Sandra Young, Chair
Louise Lopez, Sr. Vice Chair
Dominic Macrone, Board Secretary

The St. Petersburg headquarters serves ten counties in the state of Florida. Their mission is to help people with disabilities gain employment through training programs, employment services, and affordable housing.

Year Founded: 1954

871 Grief Recovery After a Substance Passing (GRASP)
11819 N Deerfield Drive
Dunlap, IL 61614
302-492-7717
E-mail: administrator@grasphelp.org
www.grasphelp.org

Tamara Olt, Executive Director
Darleen Berg, Chair
Denise Cullen, Co-Founder

GRASP provides information resources, offers support, and organizes meetings and events for families or individuals who have experienced the death of a loved one as a result of substance abuse or addiction.

Year Founded: 2002

872 Mental Health America
500 Montgomery Street
Suite 820
Alexandria, VA 22314
703-684-7722
800-969-6642
www.mentalhealthamerica.net

Schroeder Stribling, President & CEO
Sachin Doshi, Sr. Dir., Finance & Operations

Mental Health America is a community-based nonprofit organization committed to enabling the mental wellness of all Americans. MHA advocates for greater access to quality health services and seeks to educate individuals on identifying symptoms, as well as intervention and prevention.

Year Founded: 1909

873 NAADAC, The Association for Addiction Professionals
44 Canal Center Plaza
Suite 301
Alexandria, VA 22314
703-741-7686
E-mail: naadac@naadac.org
www.naadac.org

Mita M. Johnson, EdD, LPC, MAC, President
Diane Sevening, EdD, LAC, Immediate Past President
Angela E. Maxwell, PhD, CPS, President-Elect
Susan Coyer, MA, AADC-S, Secretary

The Association for Addiction Professionals is an organization representing the professional interests of over 85,000 healthcare professionals. Members consist of addiction counselors, healthcare professionals, and educators who specialize in addiction, including the areas of education, treatment, prevention, and recovery support. Dedicated to promoting and enabling healthier individuals, families, and communities.

Year Founded: 1972

874 NAATP National Association of Addiction Treatment Providers

1120 Lincoln Street
Suite 1303
Denver, CO 80203
888-574-1008
E-mail: info@naatp.org
www.naatp.org

Robert Ferguson, Board Chair
Jay Crosson, Vice Chair
Marvin Ventrell, JD, Chief Executive Officer
Katie Strand, MS, CMP, Chief Operating Officer

NAATP ensures the availability and accessibility of high quality addiction treatment across the country through leadership, advocacy, training, and other member support services.

Year Founded: 1978

875 National Alliance on Mental Illness

4301 Wilson Boulevard
Suite 300
Arlington, VA 22203
703-524-7600
800-950-6264
E-mail: info@nami.org
www.nami.org

Shirley J. Holloway, President
Joyce A. Campbell, First Vice President
Daniel H. Gillison, Jr., Chief Executive Officer
David Levy, Chief Financial Officer

NAMI is an organization dedicated to raising awareness on mental health and providing support and education for Americans affected by mental illness. NAMI advocates for access to services and treatment and fosters an environment of awareness and understanding for those concerned with mental health.

Year Founded: 1979

876 National Association of State Alcohol/Drug Abuse Directors

1919 Pennsylvania Avenue NW
Suite M-250
Washington, DC 20006
202-293-0090
E-mail: dcoffice@nasadad.org
www.nasadad.org

Sara Goldsby, President
Jennifer Smith, Secretary
Michael Langer, Treasurer
Jared Yurow, Vice President for Treatment

The National Association of State Alcohol and Drug Abuse Directors is a private, not-for-profit organization focused on the promotion of educational and scientific materials on alcohol, drug abuse, and related fields. NASADAD seeks to support and further the development of effective alcohol and other drug abuse treatment programs in the United States.

Year Founded: 1971

877 National Coalition for the Homeless

2201 P Street Northwest
Washington, DC 20037
202-462-4822
E-mail: info@nationalhomeless.org
www.nationalhomeless.org

Barbara Anderson, Treasurer
Donald Whitehead, Executive Director
Megan Hustings, Deputy Director

The National Coalition for the Homeless is an organization serving to protect the needs of those experiencing homelessness, while striving to prevent and end homelessness. NCH promotes effective treatment, services, and programs for those struggling with homelessness as well as substance abuse problems.

Year Founded: 1982

878 National Council for Behavioral Health

1400 K Street NW
Suite 400
Washington, DC 20005
E-mail: communications@thenationalcouncil.org
www.thenationalcouncil.org

Tim Swinfard, Chair
Charles Ingoglia, President and CEO
Jeannie Campbell, Executive VP and COO
Bruce Pelleu, CPA, VP, Finance & Administration

The National Council for Behavioral Health serves to unify America's behavioral health organizations. The council is dedicated to ensuring that quality mental health and addictions care is readily accessible to all Americans.

879 National Institute on Alcohol Abuse and Alcoholism

National Institute on Health

9000 Rockville Pike
Rockville, MD 20892
301-496-4000
TDD: 301-402-9612
E-mail: niaaaweb-r@exchange.nih.gov
www.niaaa.nih.gov

Dr. George F. Koob, PhD, Director
Dr. Patricia A. Powell, Deputy Director

NIAAA seeks to reduce alcohol-related problems by conducting scientific research in a range of areas, including neuroscience, treatment, prevention, and epidemiology; working with other research institutes, federal programs, and organizations focused on the issues surrounding alcohol abuse; and disseminating information to healthcare providers, researchers, policymakers, and the public.

880 National Mental Health Consumers' Self-Help Clearinghouse

E-mail: selfhelpclearinghouse@gmail.com
www.mhselfhelp.org

Joseph Rogers, Founder and Executive Director
Susan Rogers, Director

The Clearinghouse is a peer-run national technical assistance center focused on achieving respect and equality of opportunity for those with mental illnesses. The Clearinghouse helps with the growth of the mental health consumer movement by evaluating mental health services, advocating for mental health reform, and providing consumers with news, information, publications, and consultation services.

Year Founded: 1986

881 Recovered

99 Wall Street
#1312
New York, NY 10005

E-mail: info@recovered.org
www.recovered.org

The National Council on Alcoholism and Drug Dependence is an organization of writers and editors dedicated to raising awareness on susbtance abuse.

882 Research Society on Alcoholism
7801 North Lamar Boulevard
Suite D-89
Austin, TX 78752-1038
512-454-0022
E-mail: debbyrsa@sbcglobal.net
www.rsoa.org

Michael Miles, MD, PhD, President
Lara Ray, PhD, Vice President
Bonnie Nagel, PhD, Secretary
Jessica Cronce, PhD, Treasurer

The Research Society on Alcoholism, founded in 1976, scrvcs as a forum for scientists and researchers focused on the fields of alcoholism and alcohol-related problems. The Society promotes research with the purpose of advancing treatment of alcoholism and finding potential cures.

Year Founded: 1976

883 Section for Psychiatric and Substance Abuse Services (SPSPAS)
155 North Wacker Drive
Chicago, IL 60606
312-422-3000
800-424-4301
www.www.aha.org

Richard J. Pollack, President and CEO
Michelle Hood, EVP and CEO
Stacey Hughes, EVP and Govt. Relations
Susan Gergely, EdD, SVP and Chief People Officer

A membership section that represents over 1,660 behavioral health providers and professionals who are members of the American Hospital Association (AHA). The Section applies AHA policy, advocacy, and service efforts to advance understandings of behavioral health care and to emphasize its importance.

Year Founded: 1898

884 Substance Abuse and Mental Health Services Administration (SAMHSA)
5600 Fishers Lane
Rockville, MD 20857
877-726-4727
TTY: 800-487-4889
www.www.samhsa.gov

Mary Roary, PhD, Director
Kurt John, EdD, MPA, MSF, Acting Director

SAMHSA is a public agency within the US Department of Health and Human Services focused on expanding the accessibility of information, services, and research on mental health and substance abuse. SAMHSA's mission is to reduce the impact of mental illness and substance abuse on communities across America.

Year Founded: 1992

885 The Center for Family Support
2811 Zulette Avenue
Bronx, NY 10461

718-518-1500
E-mail: svernikoff@cfsny.org
www.www.cfsny.org

Steven Vernikoff, Executive Director
Barbara Greenwald, Chief Operating Officer
Jos, Martin Jara, President
Elise Geltzer, Vice President

The Center for Family Support offers assistance to individuals with developmental and related disabilities, as well as their families, and provides support services and programs that are designed to accommodate individual needs. Offers services throughout New York City, Westchester County, Long Island, and New Jersey.

Year Founded: 1954

Periodicals & Pamphlets

886 About Alcohol
ETR Associates
4 Carbonero Way
Scotts Valley, CA 95066-4200
831-438-4060
800-321-4407
www.etr.org

David Kitchen,MBA, Chief Financial Officer
Talita Sanders,BS, Director,Human Resources
Coleen Cantwell,MPH, Director,Business Development Pl
Matt McDowell,BS, Director,Marketing

What it is, why it's dangerous, and its negative effects on the body and in prenatal development. Title #079.

887 About Crack Cocaine
ETR Associates
4 Carbonero Way
Scotts Valley, CA 95066-4200
831-438-4060
800-321-4407
E-mail: customerservice@etr.org
www.etr.org

Mary Nelson, President

Describes what crack cocaine is and why it's dangerous and lists the effects on the body. *$16.00*

888 About Drug Addiction
ETR Associates
4 Carbonero Way
Scotts Valley, CA 95066-4200
831-438-4060
800-321-4407
www.etr.org

David Kitchen,MBA, Chief Financial Officer
Talita Sanders,BS, Director,Human Resources
Coleen Cantwell,MPH, Director,Business Development Pl
Matt McDowell,BS, Director,Marketing

Includes answers to commonly asked questions about drug addiction, a 13'x 17' wall chart presents the stages of addiction and recovery, covers denial, withdrawal and relapse. *$18.00*

889 Alateen Talk
Al-Anon Family Group Headquarters
1600 Corporate Landing Parkway
Virginia Beach, VA 23454-5617
757-563-1600
888-425-2666

E-mail: wso@al-anon.org
www.al-anon.alateen.org

Alateen members from all over the world share their experience, strength, and hope through the written words of Alateen Talk. Their sharings relate to their personal lives, how their Alateen group is functioning, and ways in which to carry the Alateen message to young people who are still suffering from someone else's drinking. *$7.50*

4 pages 4 per year ISSN 1054-1411

890 Alcohol ABC's
ETR Associates
4 Carbonero Way
Scotts Valley, CA 95066-4200
831-438-4060
800-321-4407
E-mail: customerservice@etr.org
www.etr.org

PALS , Author

Presents the consequenes of drinking and explains the difference between use and abuse in a straightforward, matter-of-fact way. Title #R712.

891 Alcohol Issues Insights
Beer Marketer's Insights
49 East Maple Avenue
Suffern, NY 10901-5507
845-507-0040
E-mail: eric@beerinsights.com
www.beerinsights.com

Eric Shepard, Editor

Newsletter that provides information on the use and misuses of alcohol. Covers such topics as misrepresentation in the media, minimum age requirements, advertising bans, deterrence of drunk driving, and the effects of tax increases on alcoholic beverage consumption. *$375.00*

4 pages 12 per year ISSN 1067-3105

892 Alcohol Self-Test
ETR Associates
4 Carbonero Way
Scotts Valley, CA 95066-4200
831-438-4060
800-321-4407
www.etr.org

David Kitchen,MBA, Chief Financial Officer
Talita Sanders,BS, Director,Human Resources
Coleen Cantwell,MPH, Director,Business Development Pl
Matt McDowell,BS, Director,Marketing

Thought provoking questions include: What do I know about alcohol? How safely do I drink? When and why do I drink? Title #H259.

893 Alcohol: Incredible Facts
ETR Associates
4 Carbonero Way
Scotts Valley, CA 95066-4200
831-438-4060
800-321-4407
www.etr.org

David Kitchen,MBA, Chief Financial Officer
Talita Sanders,BS, Director,Human Resources
Coleen Cantwell,MPH, Director,Business Development Pl
Matt McDowell,BS, Director,Marketing

Strange but true facts to trigger discussion about alcohol use, social consequences, and risks involved. Title #R719.

894 Alcoholism: A Merry-Go-Round Named Denial
Hazelden
PO Box 11
Center City, MN 55012-0011
651-213-4200
800-257-7810
E-mail: info@hazelden.org
www.hazelden.org

Joseph L Kellerman, Author

Revised and expanded for today's recovering person, family, and concerned others, this classic piece defines the roles of the alcoholic and those who are close to the alcoholic. This new version includes easier-to-understand, more accessible language and expanded descriptions of The Enabler, The Victim, and The Provoker roles. Also includes a section on the disease in adolescents and seniors- increasing its value to everyone touched by substance abuse. *$3.50*

20 pages ISBN 0-894860-22-4

895 Alcoholism: A Treatable Disease
Hazelden
PO Box 11
Center City, MN 55012-0011
651-213-4200
800-257-7810
E-mail: info@hazelden.org
www.hazelden.org

A hard look at the disease of chemical dependence, the confusion and delusion that go with it, intervention and a hopeful conclusion - alcoholism is treatable. *$2.95*

20 pages ISBN 0-935908-37-4

896 American Journal on Addictions
American Academy of Addiction Psychiatry
400 Massasoit Avenue
Suite 307,2nd Floor
Easy Providence, RI 02914
401-524-3076
E-mail: aja@aaap.org
www.www.aaap.org

Ismene L Petrakis,MD, Chair,Area Director
Laurence M Westreich MD, President
Thomas R Kosten,MD, Editor-in-Chief,AJA
Shelly F Greenfield,MD,MPH, Vice President

Covers a wide variety of topics ranging from codependence to genetics, epidemiology to dual diagnostics, etiology to neuroscience, and much more. Features of the journal, all written by experts in the field, include special overview articles, clinical or basic research papers, clinical updates, and book reviews within the area of addictions.

ISSN 1055-0496

897 Binge Drinking: Am I At Risk?
ETR Associates
4 Carbonero Way
Scotts Valley, CA 95066-4200
831-438-4060
800-321-4407
www.etr.org

David Kitchen,MBA, Chief Financial Officer
Talita Sanders,BS, Director,Human Resources

Coleen Cantwell,MPH, Director,Business Development Pl
Matt McDowell,BS, Director,Marketing

Easy-to-follow checklists help students decide if they have a problem with binge drinking, make a plan, and get help. Title #R018.

898 Crossing the Thin Line: Between Social Drinking and Alcoholism
Hazelden
PO Box 11
Center City, MN 55012-0011
651-213-4200
800-257-7810
E-mail: info@hazelden.org
www.hazelden.org

Terence Williams, Author
Mark Sheets, Executive Director
Marvin Seppala MD, Chief Medical Officer
Nick Motu, Publisher, VP of Marketing

This pamphlet encourages people to look at their own drinking habits to decide if they are crossing the very thin line between social drinking and alcoholism. An excellent resource for anyone who has wondered about his or her own drinking habits. *$2.95*

20 pages ISBN 0-894860-77-1

899 Designer Drugs
ETR Associates
4 Carbonero Way
Scotts Valley, CA 95066-4200
831-438-4060
800-321-4407
E-mail: customerservice@etr.org
www.etr.org

M Foster Olive, Author

Traces the evolution of designer drugs like China White and MDMA, explains how addiction works and suggests why designer drugs are so addictive. *$16.00*

112 pages

900 Drinking Facts
ETR Associates
4 Carbonero Way
Scotts Valley, CA 95066-4200
831-438-4060
800-321-4407
www.etr.org

David Kitchen,MBA, Chief Financial Officer
Talita Sanders,BS, Director,Human Resources
Coleen Cantwell,MPH, Director,Business Development Pl
Matt McDowell,BS, Director,Marketing

Addresses changing attitudes about drinking, and examines the basic facts of alcohol. Shows how to avoid risky situations, explains about the blood alcohol levels, and offers tips for curbing consumption. Title #R843

901 Drug Dependence, Alcohol Abuse and Alcoholism
Elsevier Publishing
1600 John F Kennedy Boulevard
Suite 1800
Philadelphia, PA 19103-2879
314-872-8370
800-542-2522

E-mail: usbkinfo@elsevier.com
www.elsevier.com

Erik Engstrom, CEO

This journal aims to provide its readers with a swift, yet complete, current awareness service. Careful selection of relevent abstracts (and other bibliographic data) from the latest issues of 4,000 leading international biomedical journals. The journal covers all aspects of the abuse of drugs, alcohol and organic solvents and includes material relating to experimental pharmacology of addiction, although, in general, experimental pharmacology of narcotics is not covered.

ISSN 0925-5958

902 Drug Facts Pamphlet
ETR Associates
4 Carbonero Way
Scotts Valley, CA 95066-4200
831-438-4060
800-321-4407
www.etr.org

David Kitchen,MBA, Chief Financial Officer
Talita Sanders,BS, Director,Human Resources
Coleen Cantwell,MPH, Director,Business Development Pl
Matt McDowell,BS, Director,Marketing

Overview of 11 of the most commonly abused drugs includes: Description of drug, short-term effects and long-term effects. *$18.00*

903 Drug and Alcohol Dependence An International Journal on Biomedical an Psychosocial Approaches
Customer Support Services
1600 John F Kennedy Boulevard
Suite 1800
Philadelphia, PA 19103-2879
212-633-3730
800-654-2452
www.elsevier.com

Eric C. Strain, Editor-in-Chief
Andraya Dolbee, Editorial Office Manager

An international journal devoted to publishing original research, scholarly reviews, commentaries, and policy analyses in the area of drug, alcohol and tobacco use and dependence. Articles range from studies of the chemistry of substances of abuse, their actions at molecular and cellular sites, in vitro and in vivo investigations of their biochemical, pharacological and behavioural actions, laboratory-based and clinical research in humans, substance abuse treatment and prevention research, and studies employing methods from epidemiology, sociology, and economics.

15 per year ISSN 0376-8716

904 DrugLink
Facts and Comparisons
Red Lion Lane
Trefoil House
Hemel Hempstead, UK HP3 9-E
192-326-0733
800-223-0554
www.www.druglink.co.uk

Rosemary Farmer, Chairman
John Pins, VP of Finance

Denise Basow MD, VP, General Manager, Editor
David Del Toro, VP, General Manager

DrugLink is an eight-page newsletter that provides abstracts of drug-related articles from various journals. DrugLink allows health care professionals to stay up-to-date on hot topics without having to subscribe to multiple publications. *$52.95*

8 pages

905 Drugs: Talking With Your Teen
ETR Associates
4 Carbonero Way
Scotts Valley, CA 95066-4200
831-438-4060
800-321-4407
www.etr.org

David Kitchen,MBA, Chief Financial Officer
Talita Sanders,BS, Director,Human Resources
Coleen Cantwell,MPH, Director,Business Development Pl
Matt McDowell,BS, Director,Marketing

Suggestions for effective communication include: avoid scare tatics, clarify family rules, other alternative for drug use. *$ 16.00*

906 Getting Involved in AA
Hazelden
PO Box 11
Center City, MN 55012-0011
651-213-4200
800-328-9000
E-mail: info@hazelden.org
www.hazelden.org

Bob W, Author
Mark Sheets, Executive Director
Marvin Seppala MD, Chief Medical Officer
Nick Motu, Publisher, VP of Marketing

Shares the experiences of many members in joining AA and answers questions readers may have. The author's message is that your entry to AA can go smoothly. *$3.50*

32 pages ISBN 0-894861-36-0

907 Getting Started in AA
Hazelden
PO Box 11
Center City, MN 55012-0011
651-213-4200
800-328-9000
E-mail: info@hazelden.org
www.hazelden.org

Hamilton B, Author

The tradition and wisdom associated with the Twelve Step AA program has been captured in this comprehensive guide. Practical suggestions for staying sober; summaries of AA principles, concepts, and slogans; and a historical overview help the reader understand the spirit of the program. *$13.95*

232 pages ISBN 1-568380-91-7

908 Getting What You Want From Drinking
ETR Associates
4 Carbonero Way
Scotts Valley, CA 95066-4200
831-438-4060
800-321-4407
www.etr.org

David Kitchen,MBA, Chief Financial Officer
Talita Sanders,BS, Director,Human Resources
Coleen Cantwell,MPH, Director,Business Development Pl
Matt McDowell,BS, Director,Marketing

Practical ideas for drinking more safely, preventing hangovers, weight gain, and injuries; blood alcohol chart shows the effect of alcohol on the mind and body. Title #H220.

909 Hazelden Voice
Hazelden Foundation
PO Box 11
Center City, MN 55012-0011
612-213-4200
800-257-7810
E-mail: info@hazelden.org
www.hazelden.org

Mark Mishek, President and CEO,Hazeldon Betty
James A Blaha, VP Finance,Administration/CFO
Marvin D Seppala,MD, Chief Medical Officer
Mark Sheets, Execurive Director,Regional serv

Reports on Hazelden activities and programs, and discusses developments and issues in chemical dependency treatment and prevention. Carries notices of professional education opportunities, reviews of resources in the field, and a calendar of events.

910 I Can't Be an Alcoholic Because...
Hazelden
PO Box 11
Center City, MN 55012-0011
651-213-4200
800-328-9000
E-mail: info@hazelden.org
www.hazelden.org

David C Hancock, Author
Mark Sheets, Executive Director
Marvin Seppala MD, Chief Medical Officer
Nick Motu, Publisher, VP of Marketing

This pamphlet describes fallacies and misconceptions about alcoholism and includes facts and figures about alcohol, its use, and its abuse. Available in Spanish. *$1.95*

20 pages ISBN 0-894861-58-1

911 ICPA Reporter
ICPADD
12501 Old Columbia Pike
Silver Spring, MD 20904-6601
301-680-6719
www.www.icpa.ca

Ed Wozniak, Executive Director
Tineke De Waele, Executive Director Designee
Cassandra Johnson, Business Manager
Koert Swierstra, Office of the President

Reports on activities of the Commission worldwide, which seeks to prevent alcoholism and drug dependency. Recurring features include a calendar of events and notices of publications available.

4 pages 4 per year

912 Journal of Substance Abuse Treatment
Elsevier Publishing
1600 John F Kennedy Boulevard
Suite 1800
Philadelphia, PA 19103-2879

314-872-8370
800-545-2522
E-mail: custserv@elsevier.com
www.elsevier.com

Mark P. McGovern, Editor-in-Chief

Features original research, systematic reviews and reports on meta-analyses and, with editorial approval, special articles on the assessment and treatment of substance use and addictive disorders, including alcohol, illicit and prescription drugs, and nicotine.

ISSN 0740-5472

913 NIDA Notes
National Institute of Drug Abuse (NIDA)
6001 Executive Boulevard
Room 5213,MSC 9561
Bethesda, MD 20892-9561
301-443-1124
www.drugabuse.gov

Beverly Jackson, Manager
Beverly Jackson, Public Information Director

Covers the areas of drug abuse treatment and prevention research, epidemiology, neuroscience and behavioral research, health services research and AIDS. Seeks to report on advances in the field, identify resources, promote an exchange of information, and improve communications among clinicians, researchers, administrators, and policymakers. Recurring features include synopses of research advances and projects, NIDA news, news of legislative and regulatory developments, and announcements.

914 Real World Drinking
ETR Associates
4 Carbonero Way
Scotts Valley, CA 95066-4200
800-321-4407
E-mail: customerservice@etr.org
www.etr.org

Mary Nelson, President

Credible young people talk about benefits of not drinking and risks of drinking. Title #R746.

915 Teens and Drinking
ETR Associates
4 Carbonero Way
Scotts Valley, CA 95066-4200
800-321-4407
E-mail: customerservice@etr.org
www.etr.org

Mary Nelson, President

Includes common sense messages about drinking, binge drinking, and important things to know about drinking. Title #R717.

916 The Chalice
Calix Society
PO Box 9085
St Paul, MN 55109-9969
651-773-3117
800-398-0524
www.calixsociety.org

William J Montroy, Founder

Directed toward Catholic and non-Catholic alcoholics who are maintaining their sobriety through affiliation with and participation in Alcoholics Anonymous. Emphasizes the virtue of total abstinence, through contributed stories regarding spiritual and physical recovery. Recurring features include statistics, book announcements, and research. *$15.00*

4-6 pages 24 per year

917 The Prevention Researcher
Integrated Research Services
66 Club Road
Suite 370
Eugene, OR 97401-2464
541-683-9278
800-929-2955

Steven Ungerleider PhD, Advisory Board
Gerald Mader PhD, Advisory Board
Juan Jerry Lopez MSW, Advisory Board

A quarterly journal that provides professionals with practical, relevant research for their work with youth. Each issue features a single topic focused on successful adolescent development. Articles are written by authors who lead in their respective fields and whose research covers the latest findings on significant issues facing today's youth. *$20.00*

12-16 pages 4 per year ISSN 1086-4385

918 When Someone You Care About Abuses Drugs and Alcohol: When to Act, What to Say
Hazelden
PO Box 11
Center City, MN 55012-0011
651-213-4200
800-328-9000
E-mail: info@hazelden.org
www.hazelden.org

Mark Mishek, President and CEO,Hazeldon Betty
James A Blaha, VP Finance,Administration/CFO
Marvin D Seppala,MD, Chief Medical Officer
Mark Sheets, Execurive Director,Regional serv

Assists concerned family members and friends in determining their options for helping someone abusing alcohol and/or drugs. Addictive behavior is described, with clear guidelines for how and when to respond to the abuser's behavior. Throughout, the personal responsibility of concerned family and friends is reinforced, with suggestions for examining our motives for intervening. *$2.95*

20 pages ISBN 1-592855-29-6

919 Why Haven't I Been Able to Help?
Hazelden
15251 Pleasant Valley Road
PO Box 176
Center City, MN 55012-176
651-213-4200
800-257-7810
E-mail: customersupport@hazelden.org
www.hazelden.org

Mark Mishek, President, CEO
Mark Sheets, Executive Director
Marvin Seppala MD, Chief Medical Officer
Nick Motu, Publisher, VP of Marketing

Explains how the spouse also gets trapped by the disease, and discusses how the disease progresses within the alcoholic. Ends on a note of hope by briefly indicating how the alcoholic, the spouse, and other family members can escape the trap of alcoholism. *$2.50*

18 pages ISBN 0-935908-40-4

920 Your Brain on Drugs
Hazelden
PO Box 11
Center City, MN 55012-0011
651-213-4200
800-257-7810
E-mail: info@hazelden.org
www.www.hazelden.org

John O'Neill, L.C.D.C., Author
Carlton Erickson, Author
Nick Motu, Publisher, VP of Marketing
Marvin Seppala MD, Chief Medical Officer

This pamphlet explains the effects of alcohol and other drugs on the brain. Illustrations, activities, and exercises help to reinforce easy-to-read text. *$3.50*

32 pages ISBN 1-568389-04-3

Research Centers

921 UAMS Psychiatric Research Institute
4224 Shuffield Drive
Little Rock, AR 72205
501-526-8100
E-mail: kramerteresal@uams.edu
www.www.psychiatry.uams.edu

Combining research, education and clinical services into one facility, PRI offers inpatiend and outpatient services, with 40 psychiatric beds, therapy options, and specialized treatment for specific disorders, including: addictive eating, anxiety, deppressive and post-traumatic stress disorders. Research focuses on evidence-based care takes into consideration the education of future medical personnel while relying on research scientists to provide innovative forms of treatment. PRI includes the Center for Addiction Research as well as a methadone clinic.

Support Groups & Hot Lines

922 Adult Children of Alcoholics
PO Box 3216
Torrance, CA 90510-3216
562-595-7831
E-mail: info@adultchildren.org
www.adultchildren.org

An anonymous Twelve Step, Twelve Tradition program of women and men who grew up in an alcoholic or otherwise dysfunctional homes.

923 Al-Anon Family Group National Referral Hotline
1600 Corporate Landing Parkway
Virginia Beach, VA 23454-5617
757-563-1600
E-mail: wso@al-anon.org
www.al-anon.alateen.org

Al-Anon is a mutual support group of peers who share their experience in applying the Al-Anon principles to problems related to the effects of a problem drinker in their lives. It is not group therapy and is not led by a counselor or therapist; This support network complements and supports professional treatment.

924 Alateen and Al-Anon Family Groups
1600 Corporate Landing Parkway
Virginia Beach, VA 23454-5617
757-563-1600
888-425-2666
E-mail: wso@al-anon.org

Mary Ann Keller, Director Members Services

A fellowship of men, women, children and adult children affected by another persons drinking.

925 Alcoholics Anonymous (AA): World Services
475 Riverside Drive at West 120th Street
11th Floor
New York, NY 10115
212-870-3400
www.aa.org

For men and women who share the common problems of alcoholism.

Year Founded: 1935

926 Chemically Dependent Anonymous
PO Box 423
Severna Park, MD 21146
888-232-4673
www.www.cdaweb.org

A 12-step fellowship for anyone seeking freedom from drug and alcohol addiction. The basis of the program is abstinence from all mood-changing and mind-altering chemicals, including street-type drugs, alcohol and unnecessary medication.

927 Cocaine Anonymous
21720 S. Wilmington Ave
Suite 304
Long Beach, CA 90810-1641
310-559-5833
E-mail: cawso@ca.org
www.ca.org

Fellowship of men and women who share their experience, stength and hope with each other in hope that they may solve their common problem and help others recover from their addiction.

928 Infoline
United Way of Connecticut
1344 Silas Deane Highway
Rocky Hill, CT 06067-1350
860-571-7500
800-203-1234
TTY: 800-671-0737
www.ctunitedway.org

Richard Porth, CEO

Infoline is a free, confidential, help-by-telephone service for information, referral, and crisis intervention. Trained professionals help callers find information, discover options or deal with a crisis by locating hundreds of services in their area on many different issues, from substance abuse to elder needs to suicide to volunteering in your community. Infoline is certified by the American Association of Suicidology. Operates 24 hours a day, everyday. Multilingual caseworkers are available. For Child Care Infoline, call 1-800-505-1000.

929 Join Together Online
352 Park Avenue South
9th Floor
New York, NY 10010
212-922-1560
855-378-4373
www.www.drugfree.org/join-together

Patricia F Russo, Chairman
Stephen J Pasierb, President,CEO
Robert Caruso, CFO
Paul Healy, Chief Development Officer

Join Together is a collaboration of the Boston University School of Public Health and The Partnership at Drugfree.org, dedicated to advancing effective drug and alcohol policy, prevention and treatment.

930 MADD-Mothers Against Drunk Drivers
511 E John Carpenter Freeway
Suite 700
Irving, TX 75062-8187
877-275-6233
www.www.madd.org

Jan Withers, National President
Debbie Weir, CEO

Mission is to stop drunk driving, support the victims of this violent crime and prevent underage drinking. MADD's work has saved nearly 300,000 lives and counting.

Year Founded: 1980

931 Marijuana Anonymous
PO Box 7807
Torrance, CA 90504-9207
800-766-6779
E-mail: office@marijuana-anonymous.org
www.marijuana-anonymous.org

A fellowship of men and women who share experience, strength and hope with each other to solve common problem and help others to recover from marijuana addiction.

932 Nar-Anon Family Groups
22527 Crenshaw Blvd
Suite 200B
Torrance, CA 90505
310-534-8188
800-477-6291
www.nar-anon.org

Cathy Khaledi, Executive Director

Twelve-step program for families and friends of addicts.

933 Narcotics Anonymous
PO Box 9999
Van Nuys, CA 91409-9099
818-773-9999
www.na.org

For narcotic addicts: Peer support for recovered addicts.

934 Pathways to Promise
5400 Arsenal Street
Saint Louis, MO 63139-1403
www.pathways2promise.org

An interfaith cooperative of many faith groups, providing assistance and a resource center which offers liturgical and educational materials, program models, caring ministry with people experiencing a mental illness and their families.

935 Rational Recovery
PO Box 800
Lotus, CA 95651-800
530-621-2667
www.rational.org

Jack Trimpey, President

Exclusive, worldwide source of counseling, guidance and direct instruction on self-recovery from addiction to alcohol and other drugs through planned, permanent abstinence.

Year Founded: 1986

936 SADD: Students Against Destructive Decisions
255 Main Street
Marlborough, MA 01752-5505
508-481-3568
877-723-3462
E-mail: info@sadd.org
www.sadd.org

Danna Mauch,PhD, Chairman
Penny Wells, President and CEO
Susan Scarola, Treasurer
James E Champagne, Secretary/Clerk

SADD's mission is to provide students with the best prevention tools possible to deal with the issues of underage drinking, other drug use, risky and impaired driving, and other destructive decisions.

Year Founded: 1981

937 SMART-Self Management and Recovery Training
7304 Mentor Avenue
Suite F
Mentor, OH 44060-5463
440-951-5357
866-951-5357
E-mail: info@smartrecovery.org
www.smartrecovery.org

Shari Allwood, Executive Director

The leading self-empowering addiction recovery support group. Participants learn tools for addiction recovery based on the latest scientific research and participate in a world-wide community which includes free, self-empowering, science-based mutual help groups.

Video & Audio

938 Alcohol Abuse Dying For A Drink
Educational Video Network
1401 19th Street
Huntsville, TX 77340
936-295-5767
800-762-0060
www.www.evndirect.com

A video explaining alcohol abuse and its consequenses.
$59.95

ISBN 1-589501-48-9

939 Alcohol and Sex: Prescription for Poor Decision Making
ETR Associates
4 Carbonero Way
Scotts Valley, CA 95066-4200

831-438-4060
800-321-4407
E-mail: customerservice@etr.org
www.etr.org

Pamela Anderson, PhD, Senior Research Associate
Eric Blanke, BS, Director, Solutions
Nancy Calvin, CES, Administrative Specialist
Shannon Campe, BA, Research Associate III

Explains how alcohol use can interfere with healthy decisions about sex and intimacy, as well as describing the effects of alcohol on the brain. Also, includes information about the date rape drug, how alcohol affects relationships, and includes a Teacher Resource Book. *$139.95*

940 Alcohol and You
Educational Video Network
1401 19th Street
Huntsville, TX 77340
936-295-5767
800-762-0060
www.www.evndirect.com

A video explaining alcohol abuse and its consequenses. *$49.95*

ISBN 1-588451-32-7

941 Alcohol and the Brain
Educational Video Network
1401 19th Street
Huntsville, TX 77340
936-295-5767
800-762-0060
www.www.evndirect.com

A video explaining alcohol abuse and its consequenses. *$79.95*

ISBN 1-589501-32-7

942 Alcohol: the Substance, the Addiction, the Solution
Hazelden
15251 Pleasant Valley Road
PO Box 11
Center City, MN 55012-0011
651-213-4200
800-328-9000
E-mail: info@hazelden.org
www.hazelden.org

Mark Mishek, President and CEO
James A. Blaha, Vice President Finance and Admin
Ann Bray, General Counsel and Vice Preside
Sharon Birnbaum, Corporate Director of Human Reso

Weaves dramatic personal stories of recovery from alcoholism with essential facts about alcohol itself. Emphasizes the impact of using and abusing alcohol in conjunction with other drugs. Educates about the dangers of this legally sanctioned drug, including the myth of safer versions such as wine and beer. *$149.00*

943 Binge Drinking
ETR Associates
4 Carbonero Way
Scotts Valley, CA 95066-4200
831-438-4060
800-321-4407
E-mail: customerservice@etr.org
www.etr.org

Pamela Anderson, PhD, Senior Research Associate
Eric Blanke, BS, Director, Solutions
Nancy Calvin, CES, Administrative Specialist
Shannon Campe, BA, Research Associate III

Explains the physiological and psychological effects of alcohol, covers the warning signs for alcohol poisoning and procedures to take to save someone, and delivers a no-nonsense message about why binge drinking is dangerous. Describes the catastrophic realities that can result from party behavior, such as car crashes, falls, bad decisions and acquaintance rape. *$139.95*

944 Cocaine & Crack: Back from the Abyss
Hazelden
15251 Pleasant Valley Road
PO Box 11
Center City, MN 55012-0011
651-213-4200
800-257-7810
E-mail: info@hazelden.org
www.hazelden.org

Mark Mishek, President and CEO
James A. Blaha, Vice President Finance and Admin
Ann Bray, General Counsel and Vice Preside
Sharon Birnbaum, Corporate Director of Human Reso

Provides clients in correctional, educational, and treatment settings an understanding of the history, pharamacology, and medical impact of cocaine/crack use through personal stories of addiction and recovery. Reveals proven methods for overcoming addiction and discusses the best ways to maintain recovery. 46 minutes. *$149.00*

ISBN 1-592852-97-1

945 Cross Addiction: The Back Door to Relapse
Hazelden
15251 Pleasant Valley Road
PO Box 11
Center City, MN 55012-0011
651-213-4200
800-328-9000
E-mail: info@hazelden.org
www.hazelden.org

Mark Mishek, President and CEO
James A. Blaha, Vice President Finance and Admin
Ann Bray, General Counsel and Vice Preside
Sharon Birnbaum, Corporate Director of Human Reso

Firsthand testimony from recovering alcoholics and addicts, chemicl dependency professionals, and a medical doctor dispel the myth that there is any such thing as a safe substance for people in recovery. *$225.00*

946 Disease of Alcoholism Video
Hazelden
15251 Pleasant Valley Road
PO Box 11
Center City, MN 55012-0011
651-213-4200
800-328-9000
E-mail: info@hazelden.org
www.hazelden.org

Mark Mishek, President and CEO
James A. Blaha, Vice President Finance and Admin
Ann Bray, General Counsel and Vice Preside
Sharon Birnbaum, Corporate Director of Human Reso

This video is used daily in treatment, corporations, and schools. Dr. Ohlms discusses startling and convincing information on the genetic and physiological aspects of alcohol addiction. *$395.00*

947 Effective Learning Systems, Inc.
5108 W 74th Street
#390160
Minneapolis, MN 55439
239-948-1660
800-966-0443
www.www.effectivelearning.com

Bob Griswold, Founder
Deirdre M Griswold, VP

Audio tapes for stress management, deep relaxation, anger control, peace of mind, insomnia, weight and smoking, self-image and self-esteem, positive thinking, health and healing. Since 1972, Effective Learning Systems has helped millions of people take charge of their lives and make positive changes. Over 75 titles available, each with a money-back guarantee. Price range $12-$14.

948 Fetal Alcohol Syndrome and Effect
Hazelden
15251 Pleasant Valley Road
PO Box 11
Center City, MN 55012-0011
651-213-4200
800-328-9000
E-mail: info@hazelden.org
www.hazelden.org

Mark Mishek, President and CEO
James A. Blaha, Vice President Finance and Admin
Ann Bray, General Counsel and Vice Preside
Sharon Birnbaum, Corporate Director of Human Reso

If you're a chemical dependency counselor or work with women in pregnancy planning or self-care, this resource is filled with facts to help you better meet your clients needs. *$225.00*

949 Fetal Alcohol Syndrome and Effect, Stories of Help and Hope
Hazelden
15251 Pleasant Valley Road
PO Box 11
Center City, MN 55012-0011
651-213-4200
800-328-9000
E-mail: info@hazelden.org
www.hazelden.org

Mark Mishek, President and CEO
James A. Blaha, Vice President Finance and Admin
Ann Bray, General Counsel and Vice Preside
Sharon Birnbaum, Corporate Director of Human Reso

Provides clients with a factual defintion of the medical diagonosis of fetal alcohol syndrome and its effects, including how children are diagnosed and the positive prognosis possible for these children. *$225.00*

950 Heroin: What Am I Going To Do?
Hazelden
15251 Pleasant Valley Road
PO Box 11
Center City, MN 55012-0011
651-213-4200
800-328-9000

E-mail: info@hazelden.org
www.hazelden.org

Mark Mishek, President and CEO
James A. Blaha, Vice President Finance and Admin
Ann Bray, General Counsel and Vice Preside
Sharon Birnbaum, Corporate Director of Human Reso

Shares powerful stories and keen insights from recovering heroin addicts and the rewards of clean living. Teaches clients how to use honesty, surrender and responsibility as the power tools for a successful recovery. Deglamorizes heroin use, with a portrait of drug's inevitable degration of the mind, body and spirit. 30 minutes. *$225.00*

951 I'll Quit Tomorrow
Hazelden
15251 Pleasant Valley Road
PO Box 11
Center City, MN 55012-0011
651-213-4200
800-328-9000
E-mail: info@hazelden.org
www.hazelden.org

Mark Mishek, President and CEO
James A. Blaha, Vice President Finance and Admin
Ann Bray, General Counsel and Vice Preside
Sharon Birnbaum, Corporate Director of Human Reso

Show clients the progressive nature of alcoholism through one of the most powerful films ever made about this disease. This three-part video series and facilitator's guide use a dramatic personal story to provide a clear and thorough introduction to the disease concept of alcoholism, enabling the intervention process, treatment and the hope of healing and recovery. *$300.00*

952 Marijuana: Escape to Nowhere
Hazelden
15251 Pleasant Valley Road
PO Box 11
Center City, MN 55012-176
651-213-4200
800-328-9000
E-mail: info@hazelden.org
www.hazelden.org

Mark Mishek, President and CEO
James A. Blaha, Vice President Finance and Admin
Ann Bray, General Counsel and Vice Preside
Sharon Birnbaum, Corporate Director of Human Reso

Challenges myths about marijuana by clearly stating that marijuana is addictive and use results in physical, emotional and spiritual consequences. Explains to clients in simple language the pharmacology of today's more potent marijuana and shares the hope and healing of recovery. 30 minutes. *$225.00*

953 Medical Aspects of Chemical Dependency
Active Parenting Publishers
Hazelden
15251 Pleasant Valley Road
PO Box 11
Center City, MN 55012-0011
651-213-4200
800-328-9000
E-mail: info@hazelden.org
www.hazelden.org

Mark Mishek, President and CEO
James A. Blaha, Vice President Finance and Admin

Ann Bray, General Counsel and Vice Preside
Sharon Birnbaum, Corporate Director of Human Reso

This curriculum helps professionals educate clients in treatment and other settings about medical effects of chemical use and abuse. The program includes a video that explains body and brain changes that can occur when using alcohol or other drugs, a workbook that helps clients apply the information from the video to their own situations, a handbook that provides in-depth information on addiction, brain chemistry and the physiological effects of chemical dependency and a pamphlet that answers critical questions clients have about the medical effects of chemical dependency. Available to purchase separately. Program value packages available. *$225.00*

954 Methamphetamine: Decide to Live Prevention Video
Hazelden
15251 Pleasant Valley Road
PO Box 11
Center City, MN 55012-0011
651-213-4200
800-328-9000
E-mail: info@hazelden.org
www.hazelden.org

Mark Mishek, President and CEO
James A. Blaha, Vice President Finance and Admin
Ann Bray, General Counsel and Vice Preside
Sharon Birnbaum, Corporate Director of Human Reso

Methamphetamine: Decide to Live presents the latest information on the devastating consequences of meth addiction and the struggles and rewards of recovery. Facts, medical aspects, personal stories, and insights on the recovery process illuminate the path to healing. The video is divided into two parts and is 38 minutes long. *$225.00*

955 Prescription Drugs: Recovery from the Hidden Addiction
Hazelden
15251 Pleasant Valley Road
PO Box 11
Center City, MN 55012-0011
651-213-4200
800-328-9000
E-mail: info@hazelden.org
www.hazelden.org

Mark Mishek, President and CEO
James A. Blaha, Vice President Finance and Admin
Ann Bray, General Counsel and Vice Preside
Sharon Birnbaum, Corporate Director of Human Reso

Combines essential facts about prescription drugs with vivid personal stories of addiction and recovery. Classifies prescription medications and gives the corresponding street forms. Offers solutions to problems unique to presciption drugs, addresses the particular needs of older adults and elaborates on the dangers of cross-addiction. 31 minutes. *$225.00*

956 Reality Check: Marijuana Prevention Video
Hazelden
15251 Pleasant Valley Road
PO Box 11
Center City, MN 55012-0011
651-213-4200
800-328-9000

E-mail: info@hazelden.org
www.hazelden.org

Mark Mishek, President and CEO
James A. Blaha, Vice President Finance and Admin
Ann Bray, General Counsel and Vice Preside
Sharon Birnbaum, Corporate Director of Human Reso

This video creates a strong message for kids about the dangers of marijuana use. A combination of humor, animated graphics, testimonials and music deliver the facts on the pharmacology of marijuana and both it's short and long use consequences. Suitable for kids grades 7-12. 15 minute video. *$225.00*

957 SmokeFree TV: A Nicotine Prevention Video
Hazelden
15251 Pleasant Valley Road
PO Box 11
Center City, MN 55012-0011
651-213-4200
800-328-9000
E-mail: info@hazelden.org
www.hazelden.org

Mark Mishek, President and CEO
James A. Blaha, Vice President Finance and Admin
Ann Bray, General Counsel and Vice Preside
Sharon Birnbaum, Corporate Director of Human Reso

Key facts, consequences of use and refusal skills guide children in understanding why they should avoid nicotine. Animated graphics, stories, humor, and music appeal to young people. Pharmacology of nicotine, its consequences and ways to refuse it are also explored. 15 minute video. *$225.00*

958 Straight Talk About Substance Use and Violence
ADD WareHouse
300 NW 70th Avenue
Suite 102
Plantation, FL 33317-2360
954-792-8100
800-233-9273
E-mail: websales@addwarehouse.com
www.addwarehouse.com

Mark Mishek, President and CEO
James A. Blaha, Vice President Finance and Admin
Ann Bray, General Counsel and Vice Preside
Sharon Birnbaum, Corporate Director of Human Reso

Substance abuse and violence prevention begins with this three video program featuring the frank testimonials of 19 teens with significant chemical dependency issues who range in age from 13 to 22. In the starkest terms they discuss their most personal issues: substance abuse, sexual abuse, physical abuse, suicide attempts, violent acting out, depression, and abusive relationships. Includes 95 page discussion guide and three 30 minute videos. *$259.00*

959 What Should I Tell My Child About Drinking?
NADD-National Council on Alcoholism and Drug Dependence, Inc.
217 Broadway
Suite 712
New York, NY 10007-3128
212-269-7797
800-622-2255
www.www.ncadd.org

Greg Muth, Chairman
William H. Foster, PhD, President and Chief Executive Of
Leah Brock, Director of Affiliate Relations
Jayne Restivo, Director of Development

Offers a series of teachable moments for different age groups that provide parents a structured opportunity to discuss alcohol with their children $59.99

12 pages

Web Sites

960 www.aa.org
AA-Alcoholics Anonymous

Group sharing their experience, strength and hope with each other to recover from alcoholism.

961 www.addictionresourceguide.com
Addiction Resource Guide

A comprehensive directory of addiction treatment facilities online.

962 www.adultchildren.org
Adult Children of Alcoholics World Services Organization, Inc.

12 step and 12 tradition program for adults raised in an environment including alcohol or other dysfunctions.

963 www.al-anon.alateen.org
Al-Anon/Alateen

Program for relatives and friends of persons with alcohol problems.

964 www.alcoholism.about.com
The Alcoholism Home Page

Information about addictive drug use, behaviors, and alcoholism.

965 www.cfsny.org
Center for Family Support (CFS)

Devoted to providing support and assistance to individuals with developmental and related disabilities, and to the family members who care for them.

966 www.doitnow.org
The Do It Now Foundation

Copies of brochures on drugs, alcohol, smoking, drugs and kids, and street drugs.

967 www.drugabuse.gov
National Institute on Drug Abuse

Many publications useful for patients. Research Reports, summaries about chemicals and treatments.

968 www.drugabuse.gov/drugpages
Commonly Abused Drugs: Street Names for Drugs of Abuse

Current names, periods of detection, medical uses.

969 www.drugfree.org/join-together
Join Together

Alcohol and substance abuse information, legislative alerts, new and updates.

970 www.higheredcenter.org
National Clearinghouse for Alcohol & Drug Information

One-stop resource for information about abuse prevention and addiction treatment.

971 www.jacsweb.org
Jewish Alcoholics Chemically Dependent Persons

Ten articles dealing with denial and ignorance.

972 www.lifering.org
LifeRing

Offers nonreligious approach with links to groups.

973 www.madd.org
MADD-Mothers Against Drunk Driving

A crusade to stop alcohol consumption, and underage drinking.

974 www.mentalhealth.com
Internet Mental Health

On-line information and a virtual encyclopedia related to mental disorders, possible causes and treatments. News, articles, on-line diagnostic programs and related links. Designed to improve understanding, diagnosis and treatment of mental illness throughout the world. Awarded the Top Site Award and the NetPsych Cutting Edge Site Award.

975 www.mhselfhelp.org
National Mental Health Consumers Self-Help Clearinghouse

Encourages the development and growth of consumer self-help groups.

976 www.naadac.org
The Association for Addiction Professionals

NAADAC is the premier global organization of addiction focused professionals who enhance the health and recovery of individuals, families and communities. NAADAC's mission is to lead, unify and empower addiction focused professionals to achieve excellence through education, advocacy, knowledge, standards of practice, ethics, professional development and research.

977 www.niaaa.nih.gov
National Institute on Alcohol Abuse & Alcoholism

Supports research nationwide on alcohol abuse and alcoholism.

978 www.nofas.org
National Organization on Fetal Alcohol Syndrome

Develops and implements innovative prevention and education strategies assessing fetal alcohol syndrome.

979 www.psychcentral.com
Psych Central

Personalized one-stop index for psychology, support, and mental health issues, resources, and people on the Internet.

980 www.sadd.org
SADD-Students Against Destructive Decisions

Peer leadership organization dedicated to preventing destructive decisions.

981 **www.samhsa.gov**
Substance Abuse and Mental Health Services Administration

Provides links to government resources related to substance abuse and mental health.

982 **www.sapacap.com**
American Council on Alcohol Problems

Referrals to DWI classes and treatment centers.

983 **www.smartrecovery.org**
Self Help for Substance Abuse & Addiction

Four-Point program includes maintaining motivation, coping with urges, managing feelings and behavior, balancing momentary/enduring satisfactions.

984 **www.soulselfhelp.on.ca/coda.html**
Souls Self Help Central

Discusses self-help, mental health, issues of co-dependency.

985 **www.store.samhsa.gov**
SAMHSA's National Mental Health Info Center

Information about resources, technical assistance, research, training, networks, and other federal clearing houses, and fact sheets and materials.

986 **www.thenationalcouncil.org**
National Council for Commuity Behavioral Healthcare

A network for sharing information and provding assistance among those working in the healthcare management field.

987 **www.well.com**
Web of Addictions

Links to fact sheets from trustworthy sources.

Directories & Databases

988 **National Directory of Drug and Alcohol Abuse Treatment Programs**
SAMHSA
1 Choke Cherry Road
Rockville, MD 20857
877-SAM-SA 7
www.store.samhsa.gov

Directory of substance abuse treatment programs for use by persons seeking treatment and by professionals. Lists facility name, address, telephone number and services offered. Updated annually. Searchable on-line version on web site. CD-ROM

Suicide

Introduction

Suicide is an event, not a mental disorder, but it is the lethal consequence of some mental disorders. Suicide involves a complex interaction of psychological, neurological, medical, social, and family factors.

Most professionals distinguish at least two suicide groups: those who actually kill themselves, i.e. completed suicides; and those who attempt it, usually harming themselves, but survive. Those who succeed in killing themselves are nearly always suffering from one or more psychiatric disorders, most commonly depression, often along with alcohol or substance abuse. Some individuals plan suicide very carefully, taking steps to ensure that they will not be discovered and rescued, and they use lethal means (shooting themselves, or jumping from high places). Some act impulsively, such as reacting to a life disappointment by jumping off a nearby bridge. Some suicide attempts or gestures use means that make discovery and rescue probable, and are not likely to be lethal (e.g. taking insufficient pills). Some people make repeated suicide attempts. Unfortunately, recurrent suicidal gestures cannot be dismissed; each unsuccesful attempt increases the likelihood of a completed suicide.

ASSOCIATED FEATURES

Nine of ten suicides are associated with some form of mental disorder, especially Depression, Schizophrenia, Alcohol/Substance Abuse, Bipolar Disorder, and Anxiety Disorders. In addition, Personality Disorders have been diagnosed in one-third to one-half of people who kill themselves. These suicides often occur in younger people who live in an environment where drug and alcohol abuse, as well as violence, are common. The most common personality disorders associated with suicide are Borderline Personality Disorder, Antisocial Personality Disorder, and Narcissistic Personality Disorder. Among people with Schizophrenia, especially those suffering from Paranoid Schizophrenia, suicide is the main reason for premature death.

Drug and alcohol abuse is a risk factor for suicide. In a study among 113 young people who killed themselves in California, fifty-five percent had some kind of substance abuse problems, usually long-standing and including several different drugs. A history of trauma or abuse is also a risk factor for suicide, as is a family history of suicide, loss of a job, loss of a loved one, lack of social support, and barriers to accessible health care.

Some suicides result from insufficiently treated, severe, debilitating, or terminal physical illness. The pain, restricted function, and dread of dependence can all contribute to suicidal behavior, especially in illnesses such as Huntington's Disease, cancer, MS, spinal cord injuries and AIDS. Some or many of these risk factors are present in most completed suicides. Depression and suicide are not inevitable for people with severe general medical diagnoses. The recognition and treatment of depression, when it does occur, can prevent many suicides.

PREVALENCE

Suicide is the tenth leading cause of death in the United States and the second leading cause among 15-24 year-olds.

It is estimated that over five million people have suicidal thoughts, though there are only 30,000 deaths from it each year. This may be a serious underestimate, however, since suicide is still stigmatized and often goes unreported. Boys are more likely to complete suicide than girls, largely because they use more lethal means, such as firearms. Compared to other countries, guns are particularly common in the U.S. as a means of suicide. Children who kill themselves often have a history of antisocial behavior, and depression and suicide is more common in their families than in families in general.

More males than females commit suicide, both among adults and adolescents. Among adults, the most likely suicides are among men who are widowed, divorced, or single, who lack social support, who are unemployed, who have a diagnosed mental disorder (especially Depression), who have a physical illness, a family history of suicide, who are in psychological turmoil, who have made previous attempts, who use or abuse alcohol, and/or who have easy access to firearms. Among adolescents, the most likely suicides are married males (or unwed and pregnant females), who have suffered from parental abuse or absence, who have academic problems, Bipolar Disorder, who are substance abusers, suffer from AD/HD or epilepsy, who have conduct disorder, problems with impulse control, a family history of suicide, and/or access to firearms. Keeping guns in the home is a suicide risk for both males and females.

Elderly people (those over age 65) are more likely than any other age group to commit suicide. As in other population groups, elderly men are more likely to kill themselves than elderly women but the difference between the sexes is much bigger in this age group than in other age groups. Among all ages, the rate of suicide for men is about 20 per 100,000 and for women five per 100,000. Among the elderly, the rate for men is about 42 per 100,000 and for women about six and one-half per 100,000. Thus the great overall gender differences become even bigger among the elderly and more so as the elderly get older. The highest rate of suicide is among elderly white men, probably because their economic and social status drops severely with age, and because they may lack good social support systems and be reluctant to ask for help.

Although all the factors discussed here are risk factors, it should be kept in mind that 99.9 percent of those at risk do not commit suicide.

TREATMENT OPTIONS

Considering the risk factors, a professional must first make a careful assessment, taking all the risk factors into account, including the availabilty of weapons, pill and other lethal means, as well as whether or not the person has conveyed the intention to commit suicide, and whether the method the patient plans to use is available (one can only jump off a bridge if there is a bridge, or drive into a wall if one has access to a vehicle). Every individual who feels that life is not worth living, or who is contemplating suicide, should be asked about guns in the home and should be encouraged to remove them. The same is true for medications that are dangerous in overdose.

Someone who has no thought of death or has thoughts of death that are not connected with suicide is at a lower risk than someone who is thinking about suicide. Among those who are thinking of it, those who have not worked out the means of committing suicide are at a lower risk than those who have thought of a specific method of carrying it out.

Treatment is partly based on the level of intervention that is believed to be required. If the person is seriously depressed and is also anxious, tense and angry, and in overwhelming psychological anguish, the risk is more acute. The first priority is to ensure the safety of the client. To that end, hospitalization may be necessary.

After safety is assured, treatment is aimed at the underlying disorder. It may include psychological support, medication, and other therapies: group, art, dance/movement, music. Professional treatment should involve working with the family when possible, and other medical staff, e.g. a physician, and should include regular reassessments.

In cases of Personality Disorders, there may be anger and aggression, and the suicidal thoughts and ideas may be chronic or repetitive. This is a particular strain on professionals, patients, and family. They all must work together to understand the chronicity of the condition, and the fact that suicide cannot always be prevented. It is essential to develop a working alliance between the therapist and client, based on trust, mutual respect, and on the client's belief that the therapist genuinely cares about him/her. At the same time, the therapist must set limits on patient demands to prevent burn out.

Reassessments include getting information from other professionals involved in treating the patient, including medication with the prescribing physician, and from family members or others significant in the life of the client who should participate in planning and following up. Assessment must also include assessment of the client's ability to understand and participate in the treatment, information about his/her psychological state (hopeless, despairing, depressed) and cognitive competence.

PREVENTION

Despite our increasing knowledge about suicide, many cases occur in individuals with no psychiatric disorder, but appear to be impulsive after an unfortunate life event. Therefore, societal interventions are crucial. For example, there is ample evidence that providing barriers on bridges that are commonly used for suicide attempts drastically decreases the number of successful suicides. There is a misconception that a person who is frustrated with one method of suicide will immediately seek another. Decreasing availability of firearms is another crucial component of suicide prevention.

Associations & Agencies

990 American Association of Suicidology
1717 N Street NW
STE 1
Washington, DC 20036
202-237-2280
E-mail: info@suicidology.org
www.suicidology.org

Anthony Wood, Chair
Jacque Christmas, MPA, BSW, Secretary
Don Wright, Treasurer

The American Association of Suicidology is a nonprofit membership organization for those affected by suicide, as

well as those involved in suicide prevention and intervention. AAS aims to foster an environment of understanding and support for all those who have been affected by suicide. AAS works towards the advancement of suicide prevention programs and scientific efforts through research, education, and training, information dissemination, and support services for survivors.
Year Founded: 1968

991 Brain & Behavior Research Foundation
747 Third Avenue
33rd Floor
New York, NY 10017
646-681-4888
800-829-8289
E-mail: info@bbrfoundation.org
www.www.bbrfoundation.org

Donald M. Boardman, Treasurer
Jeffrey Borenstein, MD, President and CEO
Louis Innamorato, CPA, VP and Chief Financial Officer
Faith Rothblatt, Vice President, Development

The Brain and Behavior Research Foundation awards grants aimed at advancing scientific understandings of mental health treatments and mental disorders such as depression and schizophrenia. The Brain and Behavior Research Foundation's mission is to eliminate the suffering caused by mental illness.
Year Founded: 1987

992 Byron Peter Foundation for Hope
31 Hartfort Pike
North Scituate, RI 02857
401-647-9295

A nonprofit foundation established to honor the life of Byron Peter Harrington II, a young man who took his own life in 2001. The Foundation seeks to inspire troubled young people to attain hope for the future. The Foundation provides opportunities for at risk youth, including those struggling with depression or drug use.

993 National Alliance on Mental Illness
4301 Wilson Boulevard
Suite 300
Arlington, VA 22203
703-524-7600
800-950-6264
E-mail: info@nami.org
www.nami.org

Shirley J. Holloway, President
Joyce A. Campbell, First Vice President
Daniel H. Gillison, Jr., Chief Executive Officer
David Levy, Chief Financial Officer

NAMI is an organization dedicated to raising awareness on mental health and providing support and education for Americans affected by mental illness. NAMI advocates for access to services and treatment and fosters an environment of awareness and understanding for those concerned with mental health.
Year Founded: 1979

994 National Center for the Prevention of Youth Suicide
American Association of Suicidology
1717 N Street NW
STE 1
Washington, DC 20036
202-237-2280
E-mail: ajkulp@suicidology.org
www.suicidology.org/ncpys

Anthony Wood, Chair
Jacque Christmas, MPA, BSW, Secretary
Don Wright, Treasurer

The goal of the National Center for the Prevention of Youth Suicide is to reduce the rate of suicide attempts and deaths among youth. The National Center provides information on the warning signs of suicide, works with other organizations to help develop effective suicide prevention practices among youth caregivers, promotes better mental health and forms strategies to address suicide risk factors, and encourages youth to participate in grassroots suicide prevention movements.

Year Founded: 1968

995 National Institute of Mental Health
6001 Executive Boulevard
Room 6200, MSC 9663
Bethesda, MD 20892-9663
866-615-6464
E-mail: nimhinfo@nih.gov
www.nimh.nih.gov

Joshua Gordon, MD, PhD, Director

The National Institute of Mental Health conducts clinical research on mental disorders and seeks to expand knowledge on mental health treatments.

996 National Organization for People of Color Against Suicide (NOPCAS)
PO Box 8443
Silver Spring, MD 20910
301-529-4699
E-mail: dhb@dhbwellnessllc.com
www.nopcas.org/

Donna Barnes, PhD, Co-Founder and President
Doris Smith, Co-Founder, VP and Treasurer
Les Franklin, Co-Founder
Nicole Aandahl, Policy Advisor

NOPCAS is a national organization whose mission is to raise awareness on suicide and to promote suicide education, particularly within communities of color. NOPCAS works with minorities in suicide prevention through the production of education resources and publications for communities of color, the development of culturally appropriate training opportunities for professionals, and the promotion of community-based strategies that mobilize minority communities around suicide prevention efforts.

997 National P.O.L.I.C.E. Suicide Foundation
6039 Cypress Gardens Boulevard
#350
Winter Haven, FL 33884
863-875-2298
E-mail: redoug2001@aol.com
www.psf.org

Robert E. Douglas, Jr., Founder and Executive Director
Orlando Ramos, Board Member

Nichole Alvarez, PhD, Board Member
Luis Centeno, Board Member

A nonprofit educational foundation focused on the issue of police suicide. Provides support services and training programs on suicide awareness and prevention for police, emergency responders, and their families. Seeks to address the psychological, emotional, and spiritual needs of officers and law enforcement families affected by suicide.

Year Founded: 1997

998 Suicide Awareness Voices of Education (SAVE)
7900 Xerxes Avenue South
Suite 810
Bloomington, MN 55431
952-946-7998
www.save.org

Daniel J. Reidenberg, Psy.D., Executive Director
Linda Mars, National Outreach Network Dir.
Andrea Wendt, Business Manager
Jennifer Owens, Program Manager

Suicide Awareness Voices of Education's mission is to prevent suicide through the elimination of stigma and the organization of education programs designed to raise awareness on depression, mental illnesses, the importance of assessment, treatment and intervention, the warning signs of suicide, and community resources. SAVE also provides resources for those who have been affected by suicide.

Year Founded: 1989

999 Survivors of Loved Ones' Suicides (SOLOS)
8310 Ewing Halsell Drive
San Antonio, TX 78229
210-885-7069
E-mail: solossanantonio@gmail.com
www.solossa.org

Located in San Antonio, Texas, SOLOS organizes ongoing support group meetings for persons affected by the loss of loved ones from suicide.

Year Founded: 1987

1000 The Jason Foundation, Inc.
18 Volunteer Drive
Hendersonville, TN 37075
615-264-2323
888-881-2323
E-mail: contact@jasonfoundation.com
www.jasonfoundation.com

Clark Flatt, President
Michele Ray, Senior Vice President and CEO
Deanne Ray, Vice President and COO
Morgan Marks, National Director of Divisions

An educational organization dedicated to the awareness and prevention of youth suicide. Develops educational programs that provide young people, youth workers, educators, and parents with the knowledge and resources needed to help identify and support at-risk youth.

1001 Yellow Ribbon Suicide Prevention Program
Light for Life Foundation International
PO Box 644
Westminster, CO 80036
303-429-3530
800-273-8255

E-mail: ask4help@yellowribbon.org
www.yellowribbon.org

The Yellow Ribbon Suicide Prevention Program provides support services for survivors; promotes the participation of communities, families, and individuals in suicide prevention efforts; develops community-based programs; partners with local agencies to organize suicide prevention trainings; and gives motivational presentations to schools, youth, and adults.

Year Founded: 1994

Periodicals & Pamphlets

1002 Suicide Talk: What To Do If You Hear It
ETR Associates
4 Carbonero Way
Scotts Valley, CA 95066-4200
831-438-4060
800-321-4407
www.etr.org

David Kitchen,MBA, Chief Financial Officer
Talita Sanders,BS, Director,Human Resources
Coleen Cantwell,MPH, Director,Business Development Pl
Matt McDowell,BS, Director,Marketing

Includes suicide warning signs, how to help a friend, and ways to relieve stress. *$16.00*

1003 Suicide: Who Is at Risk?
ETR Associates
4 Carbonero Way
Scotts Valley, CA 95066-4200
831-438-4060
800-321-4407
E-mail: customerservice@etr.org
www.etr.org

Infinite Mind, Author

Includes warning signs, symptoms, and what to do. *$ 16.00*

Research Centers

1004 American Foundation for Suicide Prevention
120 Wall Street
29th Floor
New York, NY 10005
212-363-3500
888-333-2377
E-mail: info@afsp.org
www.afsp.org

Nancy Farrell,M.P.A, Chairman
Yeates Conwell,M.D, President
Maria Oquendo,M.D, Vice President
Robert Gebbia, Chief Executive Officer

AFSP has been at the forefront of a wide range of suicide prevention initiatives, each designed to reduce loss of life from suicide. AFSP is investing in groundbreaking research, new educational campaigns, innovative demonstration projects and critical policy work. Also expanding assistance to people whose lives have been affected by suicide, reaching out to offer support and offering opportunities to become involved in prevention.

Year Founded: 1987

Support Groups & Hot Lines

1005 Covenant House Nineline
461 Eighth Avenue
New York, NY 10001
212-613-0300
800-388-3888
www.nineline.org

Andrew P. Bustillo, Board Chair
Kevin Ryan, President and CEO

Nationwide crisis/suicide hotline.

Year Founded: 1972

Video & Audio

1006 A Madman's Journal
Educational Training Videos
136 Granville St
Suite 200
Gahanna, OH 43230
www.educationaltrainingvideos.com

For two years, the narrator of this program went through a nightmare, feeling a self-hatred and worthlessness beyond love and redemption that he described as the concentration camp of the mind. This video presents one man's attempt to convey the ordeal of severe depression by writing a memoir about the experience.

1007 Bipolar Disorder: Shifting Mood Swings
Educational Training Videos
136 Granville St
Suite 200
Gahanna, OH 43230
www.educationaltrainingvideos.com

Different from the routine ups and downs of life, the symptoms of bipolar disorder are severe - even to the point of being life-threatening. In this insightful program, patients speak from their own experience about the complexities of diagnosis and the very real danger of suicide, while family members and close friends address the strain of the condition's cyclic behavior.

1008 Clinical Impressions: Identifying Mental Illness
Educational Training Videos
136 Granville St
Suite 200
Gahanna, OH 43230
www.educationaltrainingvideos.com

How long can mental illness stay hidden, especially from the eyes of trained experts? This program rejoins a group of ten adults- five of them healthy and five of them with histories of mental illness- as psychiatric specialists try to spot and correctly diagnose the latter. Administering a series of collaborative and one-on-one tests, including assessments of personality type, physical self-image, and rational thinking, the panel gradually makes decisions about who suffers from depression, bipolar disorder, bulimia, and social anxiety.

1009 Coping with Stress
Educational Video Network, Inc.
1401 19th Street
Huntsville, TX 77340
936-295-5767
800-762-0060
www.www.evndirect.com

Stress affects everyone, both emotionally and physically. For some, mismanaged stress can result in substance abuse, violence, or even suicide. This program answers the question, How can a person cope with stress?

1010 Dealing with Depression
Educational Video Network, Inc.
1401 19th Street
Huntsville, TX 77340
936-295-5767
800-762-0060
www.www.evndirect.com

As more and more young people are falling victim to depression, it is important to understand what causes it and to know how to get the help that can rid a person of this life-wrecking affliction.

1011 Dealing with Grief
Educational Video Network, Inc.
1401 19th Street
Huntsville, TX 77340
936-295-5767
800-762-0060
www.www.evndirect.com

Grief allows us to acknowledge and mourn our losses so we can reconcile our feelings and move forward in life. Learn how to deal with your grief and become a better person for having gone through it.

1012 Don't Kill Yourself: One Survivor's Message
Educational Training Videos
136 Granville St
Suite 200
Gahanna, OH 43230
www.educationaltrainingvideos.com

This is the story of a young man, David, who at 16 years of age survived a suicide attempt. Now 22, he shares the events of his life leading up to the attempt, including how low self-esteem led to drug addiction, and how the addiction encouraged the sense that life was no longer worth living.

1013 FRONTLINE: The Released
PBS
2100 Crystal Drive
Arlington, VA 22202
www.pbs.org

Will Lyman, Actor
Narrator
Miri Navasky, Director
Karen O'Connor, Director

The documentary states that of the 700,000 inmates released from American prisons each year, half of them have mental disabilities. This work focused on those with severe problems who keep entering and exiting prison. Full of good information on the challenges they face with mental illnesses; housing, employment, stigmatization, and socialization.

1014 Suicide among Teens
Educational Video Network, Inc.
1401 19th Street
Huntsville, TX 77340
936-295-5767
800-762-0060
www.www.evndirect.com

Suicide devastates surviving loved ones. Find out why it should never be considered as a solution and learn how to recognize warning signs in a suicidal person.

1015 Teenage Anxiety, Depression, and Suicide
Educational Video Network, Inc.
1401 19th Street
Huntsville, TX 77340
936-295-5767
800-762-0060
www.www.evndirect.com

This program can provide helpful insight to those in need of assistance.

Web Sites

1016 www.afsp.org
American Foundation for Suicide Prevention

AFSP has been at the forefront of a wide range of suicide prevention initiatives, each designed to reduce loss of life from suicide. AFSP is investing in groundbreaking research, new educational campaigns, innovative demonstration projects and critical policy work. Also expanding assistance to people whose lives have been affected by suicide, reaching out to offer support and offering opportunities to become involved in prevention.

1017 www.break-the-silence.org
Break the Silence

A non profit organization whose basis and foundation came from first-hand knowledge and experience that inpatient safety is not always provided to those in need of protection, causing a desperate need for a watch-dog organization like Break the Silence.

1018 www.friendsforsurvival.org
Friends for Survival

Assisting anyone who has suffered the loss of a loved one through suicide death.

1019 www.griefguidance.com
Grief Guidance Inc.

A company created by Doreen Cammarata to promote intervention services for suicide survivors.

1020 www.jasonfoundation.com
The Jason Foundation, Inc.

An educational organization dedicated to the awareness and prevention of youth suicide. JFI believes that awareness and education are the first steps to prevention.

1021 www.mentalhealth.samhsa.gov
Substance Abuse & Mental Health Services Administration

Information about resources, technical assistance, research, training, networks, and other federal clearing houses, and fact sheets and materials. Information specialists refer callers to mental health resources in their communities as well as state, federal and nonprofit contacts.

1022 www.nami.org
National Alliance on Mental Illness

Nation's leading self-help organization for all those affected by severe brain disorders. Mission is to bring consumers and families with similar experiences together to share information about services, care providers, and ways to cope with the challenges of schizophrenia, manic depression, and other serious mental illnesses.

1023 www.nineline.org
Covenant House Nineline

Nationwide crisis/suicide hotline.

1024 www.nopcas.com
National Organization for People of Color Against Suicide

NOPCAS serves as the only national organization of its kind addressing the issue of suicide prevention and intervention, specifically in communities of color. Primary focus and mission is to increase suicide education and awareness. Offering unique opportunities for outreach partnerships and community education efforts directed at communities of color across the nation.

1025 www.psf.org
National P.O.L.I.C.E. Suicide Foundation

This foundation provides educational training seminars for emergency responders, primarily associated with law enforcement on the issue of police suicide. Providing police suicide awareness and prevention training programs and support services that will meet the psychological, emotional, and spiritual needs of law enforcement, on every level, and their families.

1026 www.save.org
Suicide Awareness Voices of Education (SAVE)

One of the nation's first organizations dedicated to the prevention of suicide and was a co-founding member of the National Council for Suicide Prevention. Leading national non profit organization with staff dedicated to prevent suicide. Based on the foundation and belief that suicide should no longer be considered a hidden or taboo topic and that through raising awareness and educating the public, we can SAVE lives.

1027 www.solossa.org
Survivors of Loved Ones' Suicides (SOLOS)

Organization to help provide support for the families and friends who have suffered the suicide loss of a loved one.

1028 www.store.samhsa.gov
Substance Abuse and Mental Health Services Administration

Resources on mental disorders as well as treatment and recovery.

1029 www.suicide.supportgroups.com
SupportGroups

An online support group community bringing people together around life's challenges by providing concise, up-to-date information and a meeting place for individuals, their friends and families, and professionals who offer pathways to help.

1030 www.suicidology.org
American Association of Suicidology

AAS is a membership organization for all those involved in suicide prevention and intervention, or touched by suicide. AAS is a leader in the advancement of scientific and programmatic efforts in suicide prevention through research, education and training, the development of standards and resources, and survivor support services.

1031 www.yellowribbon.org
Yellow Ribbon Suicide Prevention Program

Dedicated to preventing suicide and attempts by making suicide prevention accessible to everyone and removing barriers to help by empowering individuals and communities through leadership, awareness and education, and by collaborating and partnering with support networks to reduce stigma and help save lives.

Tic Disorders

Introduction

A tic is described as an involuntary, sudden, rapid, recurrent, non-rhythmic motor movement or vocalization. Four disorders are associated with tics: Chronic Motor or Vocal Tic Disorder, Transient Tic Disorder, Tic Disorder Not Otherwise Specified, and Tourette's Syndrome. Tourette's Syndrome is the most extreme case, consisting of multiple motor tics and one or more vocal tics, and will be the focus of this chapter. The most common initial symptom of Tourette's Syndrome is a facial tic, such as rapid eye blinking or mouth twitching. Sometimes, the first sign of the disorder is throat clearing or sniffling. The vocalizations of Tourette's Syndrome can consist of grunts, obscenities, or other words the individual otherwise would not make. They are disruptive and can be profoundly embarrassing.

SYMPTOMS

• Multiple motor, as well as one or more vocal tics have been present during the illness, not necessarily at the same time;
• The tics occur many times during a day (often in bouts) nearly every day or intermittently throughout for more than one year, and during this period there was never a tic-free period of more than three consecutive months;
• The disturbance causes clear distress or difficulties in social, work, or other areas;
• The onset is before age 18;
• The involuntary movements or vocalizations are not due to the direct effects of a substance (e.g., stimulants) or a general medication condition.

ASSOCIATED FEATURES

Between ten percent and forty percent of people with Tourette's Syndrome also have echolalia (automatically repeating words spoken by others) or echopraxia (imitating someone else's movements). Fewer than ten percent have coprolalia (the involuntary utterance of obscenities).

There seems to be a clear association between tic disorders, such as Tourette's Syndrome, and Obsessive Compulsive Disorder (OCD). As many as twenty percent to thirty percent of people with OCD report having or having had tics, and between five percent and seven percent of those with OCD also have Tourette's Syndrome. In studies of patients with Tourette's Syndrome it was found that thirty-six percent to fifty-two percent also meet the criteria for OCD. There is evidence that Tourette's Syndrome and Obsessive Compulsive Disorder share a genetic basis or some underlying pathological/physiological disturbance. The genetic evidence is further strengthened by the concordance rate in twins (i.e., the likelihood that if one member of the pair has the disorder, the other will also develop it): in identical twins, who have the same genes, the concordance is fifty-three percent, whereas in fraternal twins, who are no more closely related than other siblings, it is eight percent.

Other conditions commonly associated with Tourette's Syndrome are hyperactivity, distractibility, impulsivity, difficulty in learning, emotional disturbances, and social problems. The disorder causes social uneasiness, shame, self-consciousness, and depression. The person may be rejected by others and may develop anxiety about the tics, negatively affecting social, school, and work functioning.

In severe cases, the disorder may interfere with everyday activities like reading and writing.

PREVALENCE

Tourette's Syndrome is reported in a variety of ethnic and cultural groups. It is one and one-half to three times more common in males than females and about 10 times more prevalent in children and adolescents than in adults. Overall prevalence is estimated at between four and five people in 10,000.

While the age of onset can be as early as two years, it commonly begins during childhood or early adolescence. The median age for the development of tics is seven years. The disorder usually lasts for the life of the person, but there may be periods of remission of weeks, months, or years. The severity, frequency, and variability of the tics often diminish during adolescence and adulthood. In some cases, tics can disappear entirely by early adulthood.

TREATMENT OPTIONS

Many treatments have been tried. Children who are not bothered by their tics should not be treated with medications. Medications are reserved for those whose tics lead to symptoms which impair behavioral, physiologic, or social function. Haloperidol, an antipsychotic drug, may be used for more severe cases; it acts directly on the brain source of the tic, counteracting the overactivity, and can have a calming effect. However, it also can have unwanted side effects and can sometimes cause other movement disorders after prolonged use. SSRIs (Selective Serotonin Reuptake Inhibitors) have also been effective in some cases of Tic Disorders. Simple tics respond to benzodiazepines (tranquilizers).

Whether drug treatment is used or not, patients and their families may need counseling to deal with the disease's secondary effects (e.g., bullying at school, conflict within the family). During periods of high stress, relaxation techniques and biofeedback may be useful. Other alternative therapies like acupuncture and yoga may also be of some benefit. In many cases, comprehensive behavioral intervention for tics (CBIT) is an effective treatment. With this approach, patients are shown ways to prevent themselves from engaging in a tic so that the tic is diminished over time.

Symptoms of the disorder usually become less severe with increasing age, and many people learn to live with them.

Associations & Agencies

1033 Centers for Disease Control & Prevention
Division of Disability and Health Promotion
1600 Clifton Road
Atlanta, GA 30329-4027
800-232-4636
TTY: 888-232-6348
www.www.cdc.gov/ncbddd/disabilityandhealth/index.html

Centers for Disease Control and Prevention serves to provide health information and promote the use of science and advanced technology to protect America from disease, disability, and other health concerns. The Division of Disability and Health Promotion aims to improve the lives of individuals with disabilities through programs, surveillance, research, and policies that facilitate better healthcare.

1034 National Alliance on Mental Illness
4301 Wilson Boulevard
Suite 300
Arlington, VA 22203
703-524-7600
800-950-6264
E-mail: info@nami.org
www.nami.org

Shirley J. Holloway, President
Joyce A. Campbell, First Vice President
Daniel H. Gillison, Jr., Chief Executive Officer
David Levy, Chief Financial Officer

NAMI is an organization dedicated to raising awareness on mental health and providing support and education for Americans affected by mental illness. NAMI advocates for access to services and treatment and fosters an environment of awareness and understanding for those concerned with mental health.

Year Founded: 1979

1035 National Association for the Dually Diagnosed (NADD)
321 Wall Street
Kingston, NY 12401
845-331-4336
E-mail: info@thenadd.org
www.thenadd.org

Jeanne M. Farr, MA, Chief Executive Officer
Bruce Davis, President
Juanita St. Croix, Vice President
Ray Snyder, Secretary

NADD is a nonprofit organization designed to increase awareness of, and provide services for, individuals with developmental disabilities and mental illness. NADD emphasizes the importance of quality mental healthcare for people with mental health needs and offers conferences, information resources, educational programs, and training materials to professionals, parents, and organizations.

Year Founded: 1983

1036 National Mental Health Consumers' Self-Help Clearinghouse
E-mail: selfhelpclearinghouse@gmail.com
www.mhselfhelp.org

Joseph Rogers, Founder and Executive Director
Susan Rogers, Director

The Clearinghouse is a peer-run national technical assistance center focused on achieving respect and equality of opportunity for those with mental illnesses. The Clearinghouse helps with the growth of the mental health consumer movement by evaluating mental health services, advocating for mental health reform, and providing consumers with news, information, publications, and consultation services.

Year Founded: 1986

1037 The Center for Family Support
2811 Zulette Avenue
Bronx, NY 10461
718-518-1500
E-mail: svernikoff@cfsny.org
www.www.cfsny.org

Steven Vernikoff, Executive Director
Barbara Greenwald, Chief Operating Officer
Jos, Martin Jara, President
Elise Geltzer, Vice President

The Center for Family Support offers assistance to individuals with developmental and related disabilities, as well as their families, and provides support services and programs that are designed to accommodate individual needs. Offers services throughout New York City, Westchester County, Long Island, and New Jersey.

Year Founded: 1954

1038 Tourette Association of America
42-40 Bell Boulevard
Suite 205
Bayside, NY 11361-2874
888-486-8738
E-mail: support@tourette.org
www.tourette.org

Amanda Talty, President and CEO
Karon Williams, VP, Resource Dev. and Marketing
Sonja Mason-Vidal, MBA, VP, Finance/Administration
Diana Felner, VP, Public Policy

The Tourette Association of America is a nonprofit membership organization dedicated to raising awareness about Tourette Syndrome and tic disorders, educating professionals and the public, advancing scientific understandings about tic disorders as well as care and treatment options, and advocating for public policies and services that support the needs of those affected by tic disorders. The Tourette Association seeks to challenge stereotypes about tic disorders and promote social acceptance across the nation.

Year Founded: 1972

Research Centers

1039 Child Neurology and Developmental Center
1510 Jericho Turnpike
New Hyde Park, NY 11040
516-352-2500
www.childbrain.com

Rami Grossmann, M.D.

Pediatric neurology practice of Rami Grossmann, M.D. in New York. Neurologists are highly trained to treat disorders of the nervous system. This includes diseases of the brain, spinal cord, nerves, and muscles. Common problems that Dr. Grossmann diagnoses and treats include the following: AD/HD, Autism, a form of PDD, Developmental delays, Epilepsy, Headaches, Learning difficulties, and Tic Disorders.

1040 KidsHealth
The Nemours Foundation
10140 Centurion Parkway
Jacksonville, FL 32256
904-697-4100
E-mail: comments@KidsHealth.org
www.kidshealth.org

Alfred I. duPont, Nemour's Foundation Creator
Neil Izenberg, MD, Editor-in-Chief & Founder

KidsHealth is more than just the facts about health. As part of The Nemours Foundation's Center for Children's Health Media, KidsHealth also provides families with perspective, advice, and comfort about a wide range of physical, emotional, and behavioral issues that affect children and teens. The Nemours Center for Children's Health Media is a part of The Nemours Foundation, a nonprofit organization created by philanthropist Alfred I. duPont in 1936 and devoted to improving the health of children.

Year Founded: 1936

Support Groups & Hot Lines

1041 DailyStrength: Tourette Syndrome Support Forum
3280 Peachtree Rd
Suite 600
Atlanta, GA 30305
www.dailystrength.org

DailyStrength is a subsidiary of Sharecare, Inc., the first truly interactive healthcare ecosystem giving consumers the ability to ask, learn, and act on the questions of health. DailyStrength was created and operated by some very passionate and dedicated people that get great satisfaction knowing that this site can be a positive force for everyone who faces challenges in their lives.

Video & Audio

1042 After the Diagnosis...The Next Steps
Tourette Syndrome Association
42-40 Bell Boulevard
Suite 205
Bayside, NY 11361-2874
718-224-2999
888-486-8738
www.tsa-usa.org

Judit Ungar, President
Gary Frank, EVP
Mark Levine, VP Development
Richard Dreyfuss, Narrator

When the diagnosis is Tourette Syndrome, what do you do first? How do you sort out the complexities of the disorder? Whose advice do you follow? What steps do you take to lead a normal life? Six people with TS—as different as any six people can be—relate the sometimes difficult, but finally triumphant path each took to lead the rich, fulfilling life they now enjoy. Narrated by Academy Award-winning actor, Richard Dreyfuss, the stories are refreshing blends of poignancy, fact, and inspiration illustrating that a diagnosis of TS can be approached with confidence and hope. Includes comments by family and friends, teachers, counselors and leading medical authorities on Tourette Syndrome. A must-see for the newly diagnosed child, teen or adult. *$35.00*

1043 Clinical Counseling: Toward a Better Understanding of TS
Tourette Syndrome Association
42-40 Bell Boulevard
Suite 205
Bayside, NY 11361-2874
718-224-2999
888-486-8738
E-mail: ts@tsa-usa.org
www.tsa-usa.org

Judit Ungar, President
Gary Frank, EVP
Mark Levine, VP Development
Dylan McDermott, Narrator

Certain key issues often surface during the counseling sessions of people wwith TS and their families. These important areas of concern are explored for counselors, social workers, educators, psychologists and other allied profes-sionals. Expert clinical practitioners offer invaluable insights for those working with people affected by Tourette Syndrome. *$30.00*

1044 Clinical Impressions: Identifying Mental Illness Educational Training Videos
136 Granville St
Suite 200
Gahanna, OH 43230
www.educationaltrainingvideos.com

How long can mental illness stay hidden, especially from the eyes of trained experts? This program rejoins a group of ten adults- five of them healthy and five of them with histories of mental illness- as psychiatric specialists try to spot and correctly diagnose the latter. Administering a series of collaborative and one-on-one tests, including assessments of personality type, physical self-image, and rational thinking, the panel gradually makes decisions about who suffers from depression, bipolar disorder, bulimia, and social anxiety.

1045 Complexities of TS Treatment: Physician's Roundtable
Tourette Syndrome Association
42-40 Bell Boulevard
Suite 205
Bayside, NY 11361-2874
718-224-2999
888-486-8738
www.tsa-usa.org

Judit Ungar, President
Gary Frank, EVP
Mark Levine, VP Development

Three of the most highly regarded experts in the diagnosis and treatment of Tourette Syndrome offer insight, advice and treatment strategies to fellow physicians and other healthcare professionals. *$ 30.00*

1046 Family Life with Tourette Syndrome... Personal Stories
Tourette Syndrome Association
42-40 Bell Boulevard
Suite 205
Bayside, NY 11361-2874
718-224-2999
888-486-8738
www.tsa-usa.org

Judit Ungar, President
Gary Frank, EVP
Mark Levine, VP Development

In extended, in-depth interviews, all the people engagingly profiled in After the Diagnosis. The Next Steps, reveal the individual ways they developed to deal with TS. Each shows us that the key to leading a successful life in spite of having TS, is having a loving, supportive network of family and friends. Available in its entirety or as separate vignettes. *$50.00*

1047 Understanding and Treating the Hereditary Psychiatric Spectrum Disorders
Hope Press
PO Box 188
Duarte, CA 91009-188
818-303-0644
800-209-9182

E-mail: dcomings@earthlink.net
www.hopepress.com

David E Comings MD, Presenter

Learn with ten hours of audio tapes from a two day seminar given in May 1997 by David E Comings, MD. Tapes cover: ADHD, Tourette Syndrome, Obsessive-Compulsive Disorder, Conduct Disorder, Oppositional Defiant Disorder, Autism and other Hereditary Psychiatric Spectrum Disorders. Eight Audio tapes. *$75.00*

Web Sites

1048 www.mentalhealth.com
Internet Mental Health

Offers online psychiatric diagnosis in the hope of reaching the two-thirds of individuals with mental illness who do not seek treatment.

1049 www.planetpsych.com
Planetpsych.com

Online resource for mental health information.

1050 www.psychcentral.com
Psych Central

The Internet's largest and oldest independent mental health social network created and run by mental health professionals to guarantee reliable, trusted information and support communities to you.

1051 www.store.samhsa.gov
Substance Abuse and Mental Health Services Administration

Resources on mental disorders as well as treatment and recovery.

1052 www.tourette-syndrome.com
Tourette Syndrome

Online community devoted to children and adults with Tourette Syndrome disorder and their families, friends, teachers, and medical professionals. Provides an interactive meeting place for those interested in Tourette Syndrome or people wanting to help others who have TS.

1053 www.tourettesyndrome.net
Tourette Syndrome Plus

Parent and teacher friendly site on Tourette Syndrome, Attention Deficit Disorder, Executive Dysfunction, Obsessive Compulsive Disorder, and related conditions.

1054 www.tsa-usa.org
Tourette Syndrome Association

Web site of the association dedicated to identifying the cause, finding the cure and controlling the effects of TS.

Information Services

1055 Tourette Syndrome Plus
Leslie E. Packer, PhD
940 Lincoln Place
North Bellmore, NY 11710-1016
516-785-2653
E-mail: admin@tourettesyndrome.net
www.www.tourettesyndrome.net

Leslie E. Packer, PhD

Information on Tourette Syndrome PLUS the Associated Disorders.

Trauma and Stressor-Related Disorders

Introduction

Posttraumatic stress disorder, or PTSD, consists of the psychological and physiological symptoms that arise from experiencing, witnessing, or participating in a traumatic event. PTSD affects a significant number of individuals returning from war zones, as well as those affected by terrorism, natural disasters, and sexual assault.

Many individuals in minority groups of all kinds suffer serious, ongoing stress, which causes a variety of psychiatric disorders, including anxiety, depression, and many others.

It is possible to see the effects of PTSD in the past. During and after World War I, traumatized soldiers' symptoms of hypersensitivity, avoidance, and other characteristics of what we now call PTSD were called 'shell shock' or 'combat fatigue.'

PTSD continues to be identified with military service, but it is not limited to members of the military. It can affect adults and children exposed to terrifying and dangerous events in any circumstances: natural disasters, physical and/or sexual attacks, acts of terrorism, and accidents. By definition, the precipitating event must be outside the bounds of everyday human experience and the individual must feel helpless to protect him or herself from the event. Women appear to be more vulnerable to PTSD than men.

SYMPTOMS

PTSD symptoms occur in four categories: re-experience, avoidance, negative cognition/mood, and arousal. They are listed below.

Re-experience:
• Intense anxiety when the individual is exposed to a situation reminiscent of the event;
• Recurrent distressing flashbacks, nightmares, and/or dreams of the event;
• Acting or feeling as if the traumatic event were taking place immediately in the present. At these times, physiologic changes, such as a fast heartbeat, breathlessness, or gastrointestinal symptoms occur along with the anxiety.

Avoidance:
• Extreme avoidance of physical stimuli (e.g., people, places, conversations) associated with the trauma;
• Avoidance of distressing thoughts or memories associated with the traumatic event.

Negative Cognition/Mood:
• Diminished interest in activities;
• Distorted sense of blame (whether directed at themselves or others);
• Consistent/persistent negative feelings (e.g., cannot feel happiness);
• Desensitization of emotional response or estrangement with people they love.

Arousal:
• Aggressive or irritable behavior;
• Hypervigilance;
• Sleep disturbances;
• Reckless behavior;
• Extreme startle response.

The duration of the disturbance is more than one month, and it causes clinically significant distress or impairment. It is easy to see how any or all of these symptoms not only cause terrible distress for the individual, but also are incomprehensible and disturbing to members of the family.

ASSOCIATED FEATURES

The recognition of PTSD as a disorder has been controversial in the military. The American Psychiatric Association has acknowledged that the term 'disorder' carries negative connotations and may be a deterrent to those who need help. However, the diagnosis can be a great relief to members of the military who had no explanation extremely painful symptoms. Instead of being grateful to have survived, they are irritable and jumpy. Now that their symptoms have a name, they can seek treatment.

Increasing knowledge about PTSD has also benefited other individuals with previously unexplained symptoms, including those who had been diagnosed as having a personality disorder, specifically borderline personality disorder. For example, women who developed symptoms as a result of domestic violence had been labeled 'borderline,' which made it seem that they, rather than their abusers, were responsible for their symptoms. Under these circumstances, a loving and capable, but symptomatic, mother might have lost custody of her children to the abusive partner who was the cause of her symptoms.

If a person survives a life-threatening event, they may experience feelings of guilt, particularly if others did not survive the event. People with PTSD often avoid situations that remind them of the traumatic event, which can seriously disrupt normal life (e.g. taking detours to go to work or run errands). People with PTSD may experience a dissociative state when in threatening situations, allowing them to have no recollection afterwards. They may also experience somatic physical problems with no discernible anatomic or physiological explanation. People with PTSD may also suffer from other mental illnesses brought on by the PTSD, such as depression, OCD, or substance abuse.

PREVALENCE

Most people exposed to a particular traumatic event do not develop PTSD. Some of the vulnerability is genetic. Because we might assume that people repeatedly exposed to trauma, for example those living in war zones or other dangerous areas, would develop resistance to the resulting anxiety, it is especially important to note that the opposite is true. People who have been traumatized in the past are more likely to develop PTSD after a future traumatic event.

TREATMENT OPTIONS

There are three core therapeutic ways to treat PTSD: Cognitive Processing Therapy, Prolonged Exposure Therapy, and Group Therapy. Some antidepressant medications, including paroxetine and sertraline, can help with symptoms but are not a cure for PTSD. Non-pharmacologic treatments have been more successful.

The underlying concept is to decrease the negative symptoms the person experiences from the memories of the traumatic event. In Cognitive Processing Therapy, the individual confronts the distressing memories and thoughts. With the help of a therapist, the person works to control and modify associated negative thoughts like "I've failed." In Prolonged Exposure Therapy, however, the individual is exposed to triggering experiences in a safe space. The therapist then helps the person learn to manage and reduce the negative symptoms. Virtual Reality has been used to simulate warzones without the true threat. Group Therapy can be used in tandem with Cognitive Processing or Prolonged Exposure therapy. It draws upon peer support. People with PTSD discuss their experiences with others who understand and won't judge them.

Psychiatrists have discussed the problem with military leaders. While it is a relief to know that one's symptoms are part of a recognized illness that affects many others, and while access to treatment can require medical diagnosis, there is also stigma against having a mental illness. The President of the United States has agreed to give veterans afflicted with PTSD the same recognition of battle-related injuries, with medals of honor for example, that are given to those with more obvious bodily injuries. Members of the military continue to be concerned, sometimes with good reason, that having a psychiatric diagnosis will adversely affect their military careers. The ongoing discussions may enable us to develop a special descriptive term, other than 'disorder' for PTSD resulting from the trauma of war.

Associations & Agencies

1057 Association of Traumatic Stress Specialists
5000 Old Buncombe Road
Suite 27-11
Greenville, SC 29617
864-294-4337
E-mail: admin@atss.info
www.atss.info

Christine Dernederlanden, CBT, President
Jeff Cartwright, CTR, CWT, Vice President

An international organization that helps those suffering from trauma by offering education, training, and professional development resources.

1058 Brain & Behavior Research Foundation
747 Third Avenue
33rd Floor
New York, NY 10017
646-681-4888
800-829-8289
E-mail: info@bbrfoundation.org
www.www.bbrfoundation.org

Donald M. Boardman, Treasurer
Jeffrey Borenstein, MD, President and CEO
Louis Innamorato, CPA, VP and Chief Financial Officer
Faith Rothblatt, Vice President, Development

The Brain and Behavior Research Foundation awards grants aimed at advancing scientific understandings of mental health treatments and mental disorders such as depression and schizophrenia. The Brain and Behavior Research Foundation's mission is to eliminate the suffering caused by mental illness.

Year Founded: 1987

1059 Center for Mental Health Services (CMHS)
Substance Abuse and Mental Health Services Administration
5600 Fishers Lane
Rockville, MD 20857
240-276-1310
www.samhsa.gov/about-us/who-we-are/offices-centers

Anita Everett, MD, DFAPA, Director

Promotes the treatment of mental illness and emotional disorders by increasing accessibility to mental health programs; supporting outreach, treatment, rehabilitation, and support programs and networks; and encouraging the use of scientifically-based information when treating mental disorders. CMHS provides information about mental health via a toll-free number and numerous publications. Developed for users of mental health services and their families, the general public, policy makers, providers, and the media.

Year Founded: 1992

1060 Goodwill's Community Employment Services
Goodwill Industries-Suncoast, Inc.
10596 Gandy Blvd.
St. Petersburg, FL 33702
727-523-1512
888-279-1988
TDD: 727-579-1068
www.goodwill-suncoast.org

Sandra Young, Chair
Louise Lopez, Sr. Vice Chair
Dominic Macrone, Board Secretary

The St. Petersburg headquarters serves ten counties in the state of Florida. Their mission is to help people with disabilities gain employment through training programs, employment services, and affordable housing.

Year Founded: 1954

1061 International Critical Incident Stress Foundation
3290 Pine Orchard Lane
Suite 106
Ellicott City, MD 21042
410-750-9600
E-mail: info@icisf.org
www.icisf.org

Richard Barton, Chief Executive Officer
Victor Welzant, PsyD, Education & Training Director
Lisa Joubert, Chief Financial Officer

A nonprofit, open membership foundation committed to preventing disabling stress by providing education, training, support, and consultation services for emergency service professionals and organizations around the world.

1062 International Society for Traumatic Stress Studies
111 West Jackson Blvd.
Suite 1412
Chicago, IL 60604
847-686-2234
E-mail: info@istss.org
www.istss.org

Ananda Amstadter, PhD, President
Nicole Nugent, PhD, Vice President
Andrea J. Phelps, Treasurer
Brian N. Smith, PhD, Secretary

An organization that serves as a forum for the sharing of research, clinical strategies, public policy concerns, and other information resources on trauma throughout the world. Dedicated to discovering information and circulating knowledge about policies, programs, and services that focus on reducing traumatic stressors and their consequences.

Year Founded: 1985

1063 Mental Health America

500 Montgomery Street
Suite 820
Alexandria, VA 22314
703-684-7722
800-969-6642
www.mentalhealthamerica.net

Schroeder Stribling, President & CEO
Sachin Doshi, Sr. Dir., Finance & Operations

Mental Health America is a community-based nonprofit organization committed to enabling the mental wellness of all Americans. MHA advocates for greater access to quality health services and seeks to educate individuals on identifying symptoms, as well as intervention and prevention.

Year Founded: 1909

1064 National Alliance on Mental Illness

4301 Wilson Boulevard
Suite 300
Arlington, VA 22203
703-524-7600
800-950-6264
E-mail: info@nami.org
www.nami.org

Shirley J. Holloway, President
Joyce A. Campbell, First Vice President
Daniel H. Gillison, Jr., Chief Executive Officer
David Levy, Chief Financial Officer

NAMI is an organization dedicated to raising awareness on mental health and providing support and education for Americans affected by mental illness. NAMI advocates for access to services and treatment and fosters an environment of awareness and understanding for those concerned with mental health.

Year Founded: 1979

1065 National Association for the Dually Diagnosed (NADD)

321 Wall Street
Kingston, NY 12401
845-331-4336
E-mail: info@thenadd.org
www.thenadd.org

Jeanne M. Farr, MA, Chief Executive Officer
Bruce Davis, President
Juanita St. Croix, Vice President
Ray Snyder, Secretary

NADD is a nonprofit organization designed to increase awareness of, and provide services for, individuals with developmental disabilities and mental illness. NADD emphasizes the importance of quality mental healthcare for people with mental health needs and offers conferences, information resources, educational programs, and training materials to professionals, parents, and organizations.

Year Founded: 1983

1066 National Institute of Mental Health

6001 Executive Boulevard
Room 6200, MSC 9663
Bethesda, MD 20892-9663
866-615-6464
E-mail: nimhinfo@nih.gov
www.nimh.nih.gov

Joshua Gordon, MD, PhD, Director

The National Institute of Mental Health conducts clinical research on mental disorders and seeks to expand knowledge on mental health treatments.

1067 Sidran Traumatic Stress Institute

7238 Muncaster Mill Road
Suite 376
Derwood, MD 20855
410-825-8888
E-mail: admin@sidran.org
www.sidran.org

Esther Giller, President and Director
Ruta Mazelis, Editor, The Cutting Edge/Trainer

Sidran Institute provides useful, practical information for child and adult survivors of any type of trauma, for families/friends, and for the clinical and frontline service providers who assist in their recovery. Sidran's philosophy of education through collaboration brings together great minds (providers, survivors, and loved ones) to develop comprehensive programs to address the practical, emotional, spiritual, and medical needs of trauma survivors.

Year Founded: 1986

1068 Territorial Apprehensiveness (TERRAP) Anxiety & Stress Program

755 Park Avenue
Suite 140
Huntington, NY 11743
631-549-8867
E-mail: info@anxietyandpanic.com
www.anxietyandpanic.com

Julian Herskowitz, PhD, Director

Helps to treat anxiety and stress disorders through Territorial Apprehensiveness Programs, developed by Dr. Arthur Hardy in the 1960s. The program systematically addresses the behavioral and thought processes of those suffering from stress and anxiety.

Year Founded: 1975

1069 The Center for Family Support

2811 Zulette Avenue
Bronx, NY 10461
718-518-1500
E-mail: svernikoff@cfsny.org
www.www.cfsny.org

Steven Vernikoff, Executive Director
Barbara Greenwald, Chief Operating Officer
Jos, Martin Jara, President
Elise Geltzer, Vice President

The Center for Family Support offers assistance to individuals with developmental and related disabilities, as well as their families, and provides support services and programs that are designed to accommodate individual needs. Offers services throughout New York City, Westchester County, Long Island, and New Jersey.

Year Founded: 1954

Periodicals & Pamphlets

1070 101 Stress Busters
ETR Associates
4 Carbonero Way
Scotts Valley, CA 95066-4200
831-438-4060
800-321-4407
www.etr.org

David Kitchen,MBA, Chief Financial Officer
Talita Sanders,BS, Director,Human Resources
Coleen Cantwell,MPH, Director,Business Development Pl
Matt McDowell,BS, Director,Marketing

These 101 stress busters were written by students to help fellow students relieve stress: tell a joke, laugh out loud, beat a pillow to smitherines. *$16.00*

1071 Five Smart Steps to Less Stress
ETR Associates
4 Carbonero Way
Scotts Valley, CA 95066-4200
831-438-4060
800-321-4407
www.etr.org

David Kitchen,MBA, Chief Financial Officer
Talita Sanders,BS, Director,Human Resources
Coleen Cantwell,MPH, Director,Business Development Pl
Matt McDowell,BS, Director,Marketing

Steps to managing stress include: know what stresses you, manage your stress, take care of your body, take care of your feelings, ask for help. *$16.00*

1072 Five Ways to Stop Stress
ETR Associates
4 Carbonero Way
Scotts Valley, CA 95066-4200
831-438-4060
800-321-4407
www.etr.org

David Kitchen,MBA, Chief Financial Officer
Talita Sanders,BS, Director,Human Resources
Coleen Cantwell,MPH, Director,Business Development Pl
Matt McDowell,BS, Director,Marketing

An easy to read pamphlet that discusses how to recognize the signs of stress, explains the big and little changes that can produce stress and the different causes of stress. *$18.00*

1073 Getting What You Want From Stress
ETR Associates
4 Carbonero Way
Scotts Valley, CA 95066-4200
831-438-4060
800-321-4407
E-mail: customerservice@etr.org
www.etr.org

Mary Nelson, President

Includes signs of stress, some stress can be healthy, and when to change, when to adapt. *$18.00*

1074 Let's Talk Facts About Post-Traumatic Stress Disorder
American Psychiatric Publishing, Inc.
1000 Wilson Boulevard
Suite 1825
Arlington, VA 22209-3901

703-907-7322
800-368-5777
E-mail: appi@psych.org
www.appi.org

Robert E Hales MD, Editor-in-Chief
Ron McMillen, Chief Executive Officer
John McDuffie, Editorial Director

$12.50

8 pages ISBN 0-890423-63-6

1075 Real Illness: Post-Traumatic Stress Disorder
6001 Executive Boulevard
Room 8184
Bethesda, MD 20892
301-443-4513
866-615-6464
TTY: 301-443-8431
E-mail: nimhinfo@nih.gov

9 pages

1076 Stress
ETR Associates
4 Carbonero Way
Scotts Valley, CA 95066-4200
831-438-4060
800-321-4407
E-mail: customerservice@etr.org
www.etr.org

Mary Nelson, President

Includes common changes that cause stress, symptoms of stress, and effects on feelings, actions and physical health.

1077 Stress Incredible Facts
ETR Associates
4 Carbonero Way
Scotts Valley, CA 95066-4200
831-438-4060
800-321-4407
www.etr.org

David Kitchen,MBA, Chief Financial Officer
Talita Sanders,BS, Director,Human Resources
Coleen Cantwell,MPH, Director,Business Development Pl
Matt McDowell,BS, Director,Marketing

Strange-but-true facts to trigger discussion about how stress affects the body, how to use it and long-term risks.

1078 Stress in Hard Times
ETR Associates
4 Carbonero Way
Scotts Valley, CA 95066-4200
831-438-4060
800-321-4407
E-mail: customerservice@etr.org
www.etr.org

Mary Nelson, President

Discusses stress caused by troubling world events, describes short and long term symptoms, and suggests ways to cope. *$ 16.00*

1079 Teen Stress!
ETR Associates
4 Carbonero Way
Scotts Valley, CA 95066-4200

831-438-4060
800-321-4407
www.etr.org

David Kitchen,MBA, Chief Financial Officer
Talita Sanders,BS, Director,Human Resources
Coleen Cantwell,MPH, Director,Business Development Pl
Matt McDowell,BS, Director,Marketing

Explains what stress is, outlines the causes and effects and offers ideas for handling stress. *$16.00*

Video & Audio

1080 Anxiety Disorders
American Counseling Association
PO Box 31110
Alexandria, VA 22310-9998
800-347-6647
E-mail: webmaster@counseling.org
www.counseling.org

Richard Yep, Executive Director
Dr. S. Kent Butler, President

Increase your awareness of anxiety disorders, their symptoms, and effective treatments. Learn the effect these disorders can have on life and how treatment can change the quality of life for people presently suffering from these disorders. Includes 6 audiotapes and a study guide. *$140.00*

1081 Legacy of Childhood Trauma: Not Always Who They Seem
Research Press
Dept 12 W
PO Box 9177
Champaign, IL 61826-9177
217-352-3273
800-519-2707
E-mail: rp@researchpress.com
www.researchpress.com

This powerful video focuses on the connection between so-called delinquent youth, and the experience of childhood trauma such as emotional, sexual, or physical abuse. Four young adults, survivors of childhood trauma, candidly discuss their troubled childhood and teenage years and reveal how, with the help of caring adults, they were able to salvage their lives. They offer valuable guidelines and insights on working with adolescents who have experienced childhood trauma. *$ 195.00*

1082 Treating Trauma Disorders Effectively
Colin A Ross Institute for Psychological Trauma
1701 Gateway
Suite 349
Richardson, TX 75080-3546
972-918-9588
E-mail: rossinst@rossinst.com
www.rossinst.com

Dr Colin A Ross,MD, Founder,President
Melissa Caldwell, Manager

A training video that gives a comprehensive overview of clinical interventions with trauma patients. The video teaches advanced techniques for treating Dissociative Identity Disorder, Post Traumatic Stress Disorder, & trauma related Depression, Anxiety, Addictions, and Borderline Personality Disorder. The video's teaching modalities consist of case examples, with dramatic reenactments, and narrator discussion by Colin Ross, M.D. The teaching methods

used clearly demonstrate effective therapeutic techniques that are backed by years of experience and research. *$85.00*

Web Sites

1083 www.apa.org/practice/traumaticstress.html
American Psychological Association

Provides tips for recovering from disasters and other traumatic events.

1084 www.bcm.tmc.edu/civitas/caregivers.htm
Caregivers Series

Sophisticated articles describing the effects of childhood trauma on brain development and relationships.

1085 www.cyberpsych.org
CyberPsych

CyberPsych presents information about psychoanalysis, psychotherapy and topics like anxiety disorders, substance abuse, homophobia, and traumas. It hosts mental health organizations and individuals with content of interest to the public and professional communities. There is also a free therapist finder service.

1086 www.icisf.org
International Critical Incident Stress Foundation

A nonprofit, open membership foundation dedicated to the prevention and mitigation of disabling stress by education, training and support services for all emergency service professionals. Continuing education and training in emergency mental health services for psychologists, psychiatrists, social workers and licensed professional counselors.

1087 www.mentalhealth.com
Internet Mental Health

On-line information and a virtual encyclopedia related to mental disorders, possible causes and treatments. News, articles, on-line diagnostic programs and related links. Designed to improve understanding, diagnosis and treatment of mental illness throughout the world. Awarded the Top Site Award and the NetPsych Cutting Edge Site Award.

1088 www.ncptsd.org
National Center for PTSD

Aims to advance the clinical care and social welfare of U.S. Veterans through research, education and training on PTSD and stress-related disorders

1089 www.planetpsych.com
PlanetPsych

Learn about disorders, their treatments and other topics in psychology. Articles are listed under the related topic areas. Ask a therapist a question for free, or view the directory of professionals in your area. If you are a therapist sign up for the directory. Current features, self-help, interactive, and newsletter archives.

1090 www.psychcentral.com
Psych Central

Personalized one-stop index for psychology, support, and mental health issues, resources, and people on the Internet.

1091 www.ptsdalliance.org
Post Traumatic Stress Disorder Alliance

Website of the Post Traumatic Stress Disorder Alliance.

1092 www.sidran.org
**Sidran Institute, Traumatic Stress Education &
Advocacy**

Helps people understand, recover from, and treat traumatic
stress (including PTSD), dissociative disorders, and
co-occuring issues, such as addictions, self injury, and
suicidality.

1093 www.sidran.org/trauma.html
Trauma Resource Area

Resources and Articles on Dissociative Experiences Scale
and Dissociative Identity Disorder, PsychTrauma Glossary
and Traumatic Memories.

1094 www.store.samhsa.gov
**Substance Abuse and Mental Health Services
Administration**

Resources on mental disorders as well as treatment and recovery.

1095 www.trauma-pages.com
David Baldwin's Trauma Information Pages

Focus primarily on emotional trauma and traumatic stress,
including PTSD (Post-traumatic Stress Disorder) and dissociation, whether following individual traumatic experi-
ence(s) or a large-scale disaster.

Associations & Organizations

National

1096 Advocates for Human Potential, Inc. (AHP)
490-B Boston Post Road
Sudbury, MA 01776
978-443-0055
E-mail: cgalland@ahpnet.com
www.ahpnet.com

Neal Shifman, MA, President and CEO
Charles Galland, MD, MBA, Chief Operating Officer
David Wetherbee, MBA, Chief Information Officer
Damien Newman, CPA, MBA, Chief Financial Officer

Excels in research and evaluation; technical assistance and training; system and program development, including strategic planning and information management; and resource development and dissemination. Staff are experts in content areas critical to addressing the behavioral health needs of vulnerable populations: mental health policy and services, addictions and substance abuse, criminal justice, health care reform, housing, homelessness, population health management, veterans, and workforce development.

Year Founded: 1980

1097 American Academy of Child and Adolescent Psychiatry
3615 Wisconsin Avenue Northwest
Washington, DC 20016-3007
202-966-7300
E-mail: communications@aacap.org
www.aacap.org

Warren Y.K. Ng, MD, MPH, President
Tami D. Benton, MD, President-Elect
Debra E. Koss, MD, Secretary
Neal Ryan, MD, Treasurer

The AACAP is the leading national professional medical association dedicated to treating and improving the quality of life for children, adolescents, and families affected by these disorders. Members actively research, evaluate, diagnose, and treat psychiatric disorders and pride themselves on giving direction to and responding quickly to new developments in addressing the health care needs of children and their families. Widely distributes information in an effort to promote an understanding of mental illnesses and remove the stigma associated with them; advance efforts in prevention of mental illnesses; and assure proper treatment and access to services for children and adolescents.

Year Founded: 1953

1098 American Academy of Pediatrics
345 Park Boulevard
Itasca, IL 60143
888-227-1770
www.aap.org

Mark Del Monte, JD, CEO/President
Christine Bork, MBA, Chief Development Officer
Vera Tait, MD, FAAP, Chief Medical Officer
John Miller, CPA, Chief Financial Officer

The mission of the AAP is to attain optimal physical, mental, and social health and well-being for all infants, children, adolescents, and young adults. A professional membership organization of 67,000 primary care pediatricians, pediatric medical sub-specialists, and pediatric surgical specialists.

Year Founded: 1930

1099 American Association for Geriatric Psychiatry
6728 Old McLean Village Drive
McLean, VA 22101
703-718-6026
E-mail: main@aagponline.org
www.aagponline.org

Brent Forester, MD, DFAAGP, President
Marc E. Agronin, MD, DFAAGP, President-Elect
Elizabeth J. Santos, MD, DFAAGP, Secretary/Treasurer
Ilse Wiechers, MD, MPP, MHS, Secretary/Treasurer Elect

The only national association that has products, activities, and publications which focus exclusively on the challenges of geriatric psychiatry. Practitioners, researchers, educations, students, and the public have relied on AAGP as the key driver for progress for elderly mental health care.

Year Founded: 1978

1100 American Association on Intellectual and Developmental Disabilities (AAIDD)
8403 Colesville Road
Suite 900
Silver Spring, MD 20910
202-387-1968
www.aaidd.org

Elisa Velardo, MMHS, FAAIDD, President
Karrie Shogren, PhD, FAAIDD, President Elect
Dalun "Dan" Zhang, PhD, Vice President
Melissa DiSipio, MSA, FAAIDD, Secretary-Treasurer

AAIDD provides worldwide leadership in the field of intellectual and developmental disabilities. The oldest and largest interdisciplinary organization of professionals and citizens concerned about intellectual and developmental disabilities. AAIDD promotes progressive policies, research, and universal human rights for people with intellectual and developmental diabilities.

Year Founded: 1876

1101 American Holistic Health Association (AHHA)
PO Box 17400
Anaheim, CA 92817-7400
714-779-6152
E-mail: mail@ahha.org
www.ahha.org

Suzan V. Walter, MBA, President
Gena E. Kadar, DC, CNS, Treasurer
Mira Dessy, NE, Secretary

The leading national resource connecting people with vital solutions for reaching a higher level of wellness through a holistic approach to health and healthcare.

Year Founded: 1989

1102 American Network of Community Options and Resources (ANCOR)
1101 King Street
Suite 380
Alexandria, VA 22314
703-535-7850
E-mail: ancor@ancor.org
www.ancor.org

Heidi Mansir, President
Barbara Merrill, Chief Executive Officer
Gabrielle Sedor, Chief Operations Officer
Sean Luechtefeld, Senior Communications Director

A national trade association representing private providers of community living, employment supports, and services to individuals with disabilities. As a nonprofit organization, ANCOR continually advocates for the crucial role private providers play in enhancing and supporting the lives of people with disabilities and their families.

Year Founded: 1985

1103 American Pediatric Society

9303 New Trails Drive
Suite 350
The Woodlands, TX 77381
346-980-9707
E-mail: info@aps1888.org
www.www.aps1888.org

Mary Leonard, President
Lisa Robinson, President-Elect
Clifford Bogue, Secretary/Treasurer

Society of professionals working on pediatric health care issues, through research, advocacy, and education. The society offers conferences and a variety of publications.

Year Founded: 1888

1104 American Psychiatric Association

800 Maine Avenue Southwest
Suite 900
Washington, DC 20024
202-559-3900
888-357-7924
E-mail: apa@psych.org
www.www.psychiatry.org

Vivian B. Pender, MD, President
Rebecca W. Brendel, MD, JD, President-Elect
Sandra DeJong, MD, MSc, Secretary
Richard F. Summers, MD, Treasurer

The world's largest psychiatric organization. It is a medical specialty society representing more than 38,500 psychiatric physicians from the United States and around the world. Its member physicians work together to ensure humane care and effective treatment for all persons with mental disorders. Members are primarily medical specialists who are psychiatrists or in the process of becoming psychiatrists.

Year Founded: 1844

1105 American Psychological Association

750 First Street NE
Washington, DC 20002-4242
202-336-5500
800-374-2721
TDD: 202-336-6123
TTY: 202-336-6123
www.apa.org

Frank C. Worrell, PhD, President
Thema S. Bryant, PhD, President-Elect
Jean A. Carter, PhD, Treasurer
Kathleen S. Brown, PhD, Recording Secretary

The American Psychological Association seeks to advance psychology as a science, a profession, and as a means of promoting health, education, and human welfare. This organization of researchers, educators, clinicians, consultants, and students promotes research in psychology and the improvment of research methods; establishes high standards of ethics, conduct, and education; and disseminates psychological knowledge through professional and academic networks.

Year Founded: 1892

1106 American Speech-Language-Hearing Association

2200 Research Boulevard
Rockville, MD 20850-3289
301-269-5700
800-638-8255
TTY: 301-296-5650
www.asha.org

Judy Rudebusch Rich, EdD, President
Robert M. Augustine, PhD, President-Elect
Vicki R. Deal-Williams, MA, Chief Executive Officer
Craig E. Coleman, MA, Vice President for Planning

The professional, scientific, and credentialing association for members and affiliates who are audiologists, speech-language pathologists, and speech, language, and hearing scientists in the United States and internationally. Supports audiologists and speech-language scientists in their research and practices.

Year Founded: 1925

1107 Association for Behavioral Health and Wellness

700 12th Street NW
Suite 700
Washington, DC 20005
202-449-7660
E-mail: info@abhw.org
www.www.abhw.org

Pamela Greenberg, MPP, President and CEO
Maeghan Gilmore, MPH, Sr. Director, Government Affairs
Deepti A. Loharikar, JD, Dr. Director, Regulatory Affairs
Brian Coyne, MPA, Chairman of the Board

An association of the nation's leading behavioral health and wellness companies that manage behavioral health insurance. These companies provide an array of services related to mental health, substance use, employee assistance, disease management, and other health and wellness programs to over 200 million people in both the public and private sectors.

Year Founded: 1994

1108 Association of Mental Health Librarians (AMHL)

140 Old Orangeburg Road
Orangeburg, NY 10962
845-398-6576
E-mail: moss@nki.rfmh.org
www.mhlib.org

Len Levin, MS LIS, MA, President

A professional organization of individuals working in the field of mental health information delivery. The organization is open to libraries, library assistants, and library associates. AMHL hosts an annual conference, and provides opportunities for networking and enhancing professional skills.

1109 Attitudinal Healing International

3001 Bridgeway
Suite K-368
Sausalito, CA 94965-3100
877-244-3392
E-mail: info@ahinternational.org
www.ahinternational.org

Gerald G. Jampolsky, MD, Founder
Diane V. Cirincione-Jampolsky, Executive Director and Founder
Paige Peterson, Chief Consult/Growth & Devel.
Trish Ellis, International Comms. Coordinator

Attitudinal Healing is based on the principle that it is not other people or situations that cause individuals distress. Rather, it is their own thoughts and attitudes that are responsible. AHInternational's mission is to create, develop, and support the official home portal for Attitudinal Healing and to help facilitate the organic creation and growth of independent centers, groups, and individuals worldwide.

Year Founded: 1975

1110 Bazelon Center for Mental Health Law

1090 Vermont Avenue NW
Suite 220
Washington, DC 20005
202-467-5730
E-mail: communications@bazelon.org
www.www.bazelon.org

Holly O'Donnell, CEO
Ira Burnim, Director
Lewis Bossing, Senior Staff Attorney

National legal advocate for people with mental disabilities. Through precedent-setting litigation and in the public policy arena, the Bazelon Center works to advance and preserve the rights of people with mental illnesses and development disabilities.

Year Founded: 1972

1111 Bellefaire Jewish Children's Bureau

One Pollock Circle
22001 Fairmont Boulevard
Cleveland, OH 44118
216-932-2800
800-879-2522
E-mail: info@bellefairejcb.org
www.bellefairejcb.org

Adam G. Jacobs, PhD, President
Jeffrey Lox, LISW-S, ACSW, Executive Director
Scott Moore, CPA, Chief Financial Officer
Leigh Hall, General Counsel

Bellefaire JCB provides a variety of behavioral health, education, and prevention services for children, adolescents, and their families. Serves children, families, and young adults throughout the United States through its residential and autism treatment programs. Bellefaire JCB also meets the needs of children internationally through its Hague-accredited international adoption program.

Year Founded: 1868

1112 Best Buddies International (BBI)

100 Southeat Second Street
Suite 2200
Miami, FL 33131
800-892-8339
E-mail: Info@BestBuddies.org
www.bestbuddies.org

Anthony Kennedy Shriver, Founder, Chairman & CEO
John M. Carlin, Senior Director, Major Gifts
Jen Miller, SVP, Finance and Operations
Lisa Derx, VP, Government Relations

An international organization that has grown from one original chapter to almost 1,500 middle school, high school,

and college chapters worldwide. Best Buddies programs engage participants in each of the 50 United States, and in 50 countries around the world, to help enhance the lives of people with intellectual and developmental disabilities.

Year Founded: 1989

1113 Bethesda Lutheran Communities

600 Hoffmann Drive
Watertown, WI 53094
800-369-4636
E-mail: info@ablelight.org
www.bethesdalutherancommunities.org

Keith Jones, President and CEO
Jeff Kaczmarski, EVP and Chief Legal Officer
Dave Sneddon, Chief Operating Officer

A Christian organization whose mission is to provide homes, support, and awareness for people with intellectual and developmental disabilities.

1114 Black Mental Health Alliance for Education & Consultation, Inc.

900 East Fayette Street
Suite 22111
Baltimore, MD 21203
410-338-2642
E-mail: info@blackmentalhealth.com
www.blackmentalhealth.com

Andrea Brown, Executive Director
Richard A. Rowe, Resident Consultant
Cheryl Maxwell, Program Manager
Lynne Johnson, Program Manager

BMHA promotes appropriate mental health care, service delivery, and theoretical understanding of all the mental health programs. An organization that provides training, education, consultation, public information, support groups, and resource referrals regarding mental health and related issues. The primary mission of BMHA is to provide a forum and promote a holistic, culturally relevant approach to the development and maintenance of optimal mental health programs and services for African Americans and other people of color.

Year Founded: 1984

1115 Canadian Art Therapy Association

PO Box 658, Stn Main
Parksville, BC, V9P 2G7,
E-mail: admin@canadianarttherapy.org
www.www.canadianarttherapy.org

Amanda Gee, President
Nicole Le Bihan, Vice President
Waqas Yousafzai, Treasurer
Sharona Bookbinder, Governance

A nonprofit organization promoting art therapy in Canada. Objectives are to encourage professional growth of art therapy through the exchange and collaboration of Art Therapists; to maintain national standards of training, practice, and professional registration; to foster research and publications in art therapy; and to increase awareness of art therapy as an important mental health discipline within the community Services.

Year Founded: 1977

1116 Canadian Federation of Mental Health Nurses
7270 Woodbine Avenue
Suite 305
Markham, ON, L3R 4B9,
416-426-7229
E-mail: drosser@firststageinc.com
www.www.cfmhn.ca

Sarah Flogen, President
Stephen VanSlyke, Treasurer
Stephanie Svensson, Secretary

The CFMHN is a membership organization that provides a
voice for pssychiatric and mental health nursing in Canada.
An associate group of the Canadian Nurses' Association
(CNA), CFMHN assures the development and application
of mental health and psychiatric nursing standards, addresses mental health issues, facilitates psychiatric and
mental health nursing through professional and networking
opportunities, and examines government policy.

Year Founded: 1988

1117 Canadian Mental Health Association
Canadian Mental Health Association
250 Dundas Street West
Suite 500
Toronto, ON M5T 2Z5,
416-646-5557
E-mail: info@cmha.ca
www.cmha.ca

Margaret Eaton, National CEO
Kelly Puddister, National Executive Coordinator
Anne MacPhee, National Director, Finance/Ops.
Katherine Janson, National Director, Comms.

As a nation-wide, voluntary organization, the Canadian
Mental Health Association promotes the mental health of
all and supports the resilience and recovery of people experiencing mental illness. The CMHA accomplishes this mission through advocacy, education, research, and services.
CMHA has programs that assist with employment, housing,
early intervention for youth, peer support, recreation services for people with mental illness, stress reduction workshops, and public education campaigns for the community.
It also acts as a social advocate to encourage public action
and commitment to strengthening community mental health
services and legislation.

Year Founded: 1918

1118 Center for Mental Health Services (CMHS)
Substance Abuse and Mental Health Services
Administration
5600 Fishers Lane
Rockville, MD 20857
240-276-1310
www.samhsa.gov/about-us/who-we-are/offices-centers

Anita Everett, MD, DFAPA, Director

Promotes the treatment of mental illness and emotional disorders by increasing accessibility to mental health programs; supporting outreach, treatment, rehabilitation, and
support programs and networks; and encouraging the use of
scientifically-based information when treating mental disorders. CMHS provides information about mental health
via a toll-free number and numerous publications. Developed for users of mental health services and their families,
the general public, policy makers, providers, and the media.

Year Founded: 1992

1119 Centre for Addiction and Mental Health
1001 Queen Street West
Toronto, ON M6J 1H4,
800-463-2338
E-mail: info@camh.ca
www.camh.ca

Dr Catherine Zahn, President and CEO

CAMH is Canada's leading addiction and mental health organization, integrating specialized clinical care with innovative research, education, health promotion and policy
development. CAMH is fully affiliated with the University
of Toronto, and is a Pan American Health Organiza-
tion/World Health Organization Collaborating Centre.
CAMH combines clinical care, research, education, policy
and health promotion to transform the lives of people
affected by mental health and addiction issues.

Year Founded: 1998

1120 Child & Parent Resource Institute (CPRI)
600 Sanatorium Road
London, ON N6H 3W7,
519-858-2774
877-494-2774
TTY: 519-858-0257
E-mail: CPRI.Intake@ontario.ca

A tertiary centre that provides highly specialized voluntary
services to children and youth with multi complex, severe
behavioural disturbances and/or developmental challenges
that impacts the child/youth in all areas, i.e. home, school,
and/or community. 100% funded by the Ontario Ministry
of Children and Youth Services.

1121 Child Mind Institute
101 East 56th Street
New York, NY 10022
212-257-0481
www.childmind.org

Harold S. Koplewicz, MD, President and Medical Director
Amie Clancy, Chief Administrative Officer
Mimi Corcoran, Executive Director
Maryana Geller, Chief Financial Officer

An independant, national nonprofpit organization that helps
children and their families struggling with mental health
disorders through free resources, access to effective treatments, and the advancement of pediatric research to improve diagnosis and treatment of mental health disorders in
children.

1122 Community Access
17 Battery Place
Suite 1326
New York, NY 10004
212-780-1400
www.communityaccess.org

Stephen H. Chase, President
Dan Wurtzel, Vice President
Ramesh Shah, Treasurer
Mary Massimo, PhD, Secretary

Community Access assists people with psychiatric disabilities in making the transition from shelters and institutions
to independent living. Community Access provides safe,
affordable housing and support services, and advocates for
the rights of people to live without fear or stigma. They
provide a range of housing, job skills, employment placement, and professional support services to help break the
cycle of homelessness, institutionalization, and/or incarcer-

ation that often complicates the lives of people who have a history of mental illness. Community access creates pathways to meaningful and successful community life.

Year Founded: 1974

1123 Council for Learning Disabilities

9032 W 114th St
Overland Park, KS 66210
913-491-1011
E-mail: CLDinfo@cldinternational.org
www.www.council-for-learning-disabilities.org

Joseph Morgan, President
Margaret Flores, Vice President
Alyson Collins, Secretary
Linda Nease, Executive Director

An international organization that promotes evidence-based teaching, collaboration, research, leadership, and advocacy. CLD is comprised of professionals who represent diverse disciplines and are committed to enhancing the education and quality of life for individuals with learning disabilities and others who experience challenges in learning.

1124 Council on Quality and Leadership (CQL)

100 West Road
Suite 300
Towson, MD 21204
410-583-0060
E-mail: info@thecouncil.org
www.thecouncil.org

Mary Kay Rizzolo, President and CEO
Trina Douglas, VP, Finance and Administration
Jennifer Becher, Chair
Trina Sieling, Vice Chair

CQL offers consultation, accreditation, training, and certification services to organizations and systems that share the vision of dignity, opportunity, and community for all people. CQL provides leadership to improve the quality of life for people with disabilities, people with mental illness, and older adults.

Year Founded: 1969

1125 Emotions Anonymous International Service Center

2233 University Ave W
Ste 402
Saint Paul, MN 55114-1629
651-647-9712
E-mail: info@emotionsanonymous.org
www.emotionsanonymous.org

Elaine Weber Nelson, Executive Director

A community-based organization to provide support managing mental health difficulties. Groups meet weekly to share experiences, strength, and hope.

Year Founded: 1971

1126 Eye Movement Desensitization and Reprocessing International Association (EMDRIA)

7000 N Mo Pac Expy
Ste 200
Austin, TX 78731-3013
512-451-5200
E-mail: info@emdria.org
www.emdria.org

Wendy Byrd, LPC, LMFT, President
Kriss Jarecki, LCSWR, Secretary
Candida Condor, PsyD, LMFT, Director
Marisol Erlacher, LPC, President Elect

A professional association for EMDR practitioners seeking high standars of practice in EDMR therapy.

Year Founded: 1995

1127 Families Anonymous, Inc.

701 Lee Street
Suite 670
Des Plaines, IL 60016
847-294-5877
800-736-9805
E-mail: info@familiesanonymous.org
www.familiesanonymous.org

A-12 step fellowship for families and friends of individuals who have dealt or are dealing with mental health issues caused by drugs, alcohol, or related behavioral problems.

Year Founded: 1971

1128 Federation for Children with Special Needs (FCSN)

529 Main Street
Suite 1M3
Boston, MA 02129
617-236-7210
800-331-0688
E-mail: info@fcsn.org
www.fcsn.org

John Reichenbach, President
Pam Nourse, Executive Director/Admin.
Matthew Trivella, Treasurer

The federation provides information, support, and assistance to parents of children with disabilities, their professional partners, and their communities. Promotes the active and informed participation of parents of children with disabilities in shaping, implementing, and evaluating public policy that affects them.

Year Founded: 1974

1129 Gam-Anon Family Groups International Service Office, Inc.

PO Box 307
Massapequa Park, NY 11762
718-352-1671
E-mail: gamanonoffice@gam-anon.org
www.gam-anon.org

A 12-step self-help organization for close friends and family of compulsive gamblers.

1130 Genetic Alliance, Inc.

26400 Woodfield Road
Suite 189
Damascus, MD 20872
202-966-5557
E-mail: info@geneticalliance.org
www.geneticalliance.org

Sharon Terry, MA, CEO
Natasha Bonhomme, Chief Strategy Officer
Ruth Child, Chief Financial Officer

Genetic Alliance is the world's leading nonprofit health advocacy organization committed to transforming health through genetics and promoting an environment of openness centered on the health of individuals, families, and communities.

Year Founded: 1986

1131 Healing for Survivors
5245 E Lyell Ave
Fresno, CA 93727
559-442-3600

Jan Kister, President/Founder

A community-based non-profit organization dedicated to provideing education, counseling, resources, and a safe place for individuals and families impacted by physical, emotional and/or sexual abuse to pursue wholeness and healing.

Year Founded: 1990

1132 Hong Fook Mental Health Association
3320 Midland Avenue
Suite 201
Scarborough, ON M1V 5E6,
416-493-4242
E-mail: info@hongfook.ca
www.hongfook.ca

Ramon Tam, President
Janice Chu, Vice President
Winnie Tsang, Vice President
Eric Ngai, Treasurer

Hong Fook Mental Health Association aims to facilitate access to mental health services for people with linguistic and cultural barriers. Mental health services includes self-help programs; family initiatives; clinical services, including group psychotherapy, intake, and case management; youth programs; and prevention and promotion programs.

Year Founded: 1982

1133 Human Services Research Institute
2336 Massachusetts Avenue
Cambridge, MA 02140
617-876-0426
www.hsri.org

David Hughes, President
Sebrina Johniken, Vice President - HR & Admin.
Roy Gabriel, Secretary & Treasurer

Assists state and federal government to enhance services and support people with mental illness and people with developmental disabilities.

Year Founded: 1976

1134 Institute of Living-Anxiety Disorders Center; Center for Cognitive Behavioral Therapy
The Institute of Living/Hartford Hospital
200 Retreat Avenue
Hartford, CT 06106
860-545-7000
E-mail: ADC@hhchealth.org
www.harthosp.org/instituteofliving

Javeed Sukhera, MD, Chair of Psychiatry

The Anxiety Disorders Center provides treatment, conducts research, and educates mental health professionals on anxiety disorders. Treatment options include group therapy, cognitive behavioral therapy, and virtual reality therapy, and are offered at no cost.

Year Founded: 1822

1135 Institute on Violence, Abuse and Trauma at Alliant International University
10065 Old Grove Road
Suite 101
San Diego, CA 92131
858-527-1860
E-mail: ivat@ivatcenters.org
www.www.ivatcenters.org

Robert Geffner, PhD, President
Sandi Capuano Morrison, MA, Chief Executive Officer

IVAT strives to be a comprehensive resource, training, and research center dealing with all aspects of violence, abuse, and trauma. IVAT interfaces with Alliant International University's academic schools and centers, which provide resource support and educational training. Through a focus on collaborations with various partnering organizations, IVAT desires to bridge gaps and help improve current systems of care on a local, national, and global level.

Year Founded: 1984

1136 International Society of Psychiatric-Mental Health Nurses
2424 American Lane
Madison, WI 53704-3102
608-443-2463
E-mail: info@ispn-psych.org
www.ispn-psych.org

Cheryl Woods Giscombe, PhD, RN, President
Ukamaka M. Oruche, PhD, RN, President-Elect
Shawn Gallagher, PhD, Treasurer
Barbara Peterson, PhD, Director

The mission of ISPN is to unite and strengthen the presence and the voice of specialty psychiatric-mental health nursing while influencing health care policy to promote equitable, evidence-based and effective treatment and care for individuals, families, and communities.

Year Founded: 1999

1137 Judge Baker Children's Center
53 Parker Hill Avenue
Boston, MA 02120
617-232-8390
E-mail: info@jbcc.harvard.edu
www.jbcc.harvard.edu

Robert P. Franks, PhD, President and CEO
Christina Minassian, MBA, VP, Admin./Operations
Richard Voccio, VP, Finance

A nonprofit organization dedicated to improving the lives of children whose emotional and behavioral problems threaten to limit their potential. Integrating education, service, research, and training, the Center is the oldest child mental health organization in New England and a national leader in the field of children's mental health. Promoting the best possible mental health of children through the integration of research, intervention, training, and advocacy.

Year Founded: 1917

1138 Learning Disabilities Association of America
4068 Mount Royal Boulevard
Suite 224B
Allison Park, PA 15101
412-341-1515
E-mail: info@ldaamerica.org
www.ldaamerica.org

Kevin Gailey, Chair
Cindy Cipoletti, Executive Director
Charles (CJ) Pascarella, Treasurer
Bev Johns, Secretary

LDA's mission is to educate individuals with learning disabilities and their families through conferences, workshops, and symposiums, as well as advocate for the rights of individuals with learning disabilities and provide support for parents.

Year Founded: 1964

1139 Life Development Institute
5940 W. Union Hills Dr.
Suite D-200
Glendale, AZ 85308
623-773-1545
www.discoverldi.com

Rob Crawford, MEd, Chief Executive Officer
Veronica Lieb Crawford, MA, President

LDI is a special education school dedicated to motivating and inspiring its students to seek and experience success. Learning disability program staff and administrators are devoted to actively working with and supporting parents to help their child succeed and be independent for life.

1140 Lifespire
1 Whitehall Street
9th Floor
New York, NY 10004
212-741-0100
E-mail: info@lifespire.org
www.lifespire.org

Michael S. Gross, Chairman
Thomas Lydon, CEO and President
Keith Lee, Chief Financial Officer
Bonita Hinson, Chief Operating Officer

Lifespire seeks to provide support to individuals with disabilities and assist them with the development of the skills needed to become independent and contributing members of the community.

Year Founded: 1951

1141 Menninger Clinic
12301 Main Street
Houston, TX 77035
713-275-5400
www.www.menningerclinic.com

Robert J. Boland, MD, Senior VP and Chief of Staff
Armando E. Colombo, President and CEO
Cory Walker, DO, Chief Medical Officer
Gerald Noll, MBA, Chief Financial Officer

Menninger is a leading psychiatric hospital dedicated to treating individuals with mood, personality, anxiety, and addictive disorders; teaching mental health professionals; and advancing mental healthcare through research.

Year Founded: 1925

1142 Mental Health America
500 Montgomery Street
Suite 820
Alexandria, VA 22314
703-684-7722
800-969-6642
TTY: 800-433-5959
www.mentalhealthamerica.net

Schroeder Stribling, President & CEO
Sachin Doshi, Sr. Dir., Finance & Operations

Mental Health America is a community-based nonprofit organization committed to enabling the mental wellness of all Americans and improving treatments and services for individuals with mental health needs. Provides information about a range of disorders, including panic disorder, obsessive-compulsive disorder, post traumatic stress, generalized anxiety disorder and phobias; advocates for policies focused on advancing early intervention and prevention; and organizes education and outreach initiatives.

Year Founded: 1909

1143 Mental Health Media
25 West Street
Westborough, MA 01581
617-562-1111
www.www.mentalhealth-media.org

Mental Health Media, formerly The Mental Illness Education Project, is engaged in the production of video-based educational and support materials for the following specific populations: people with psychiatric disabilities, families, mental health professionals, special audiences, and the general public. The videos are designed to be used in hospital, clinical, and educational settings, and at home by individuals and families.

Year Founded: 1990

1144 Mental Health and Aging Network (MHAN) of the American Society on Aging (ASA)
American Society on Aging
605 Market Street
Suite 1111
San Francisco, CA 94105-2869
800-537-9728
E-mail: info@asaging.org
www.asaging.org

Michael Adams, Chair
Peter Kaldes, Esq., President and CEO
Jacki Bennett, Chief of Staff
Robert R. Lowe, Chief Operating Officer

MHAN is dedicated to improving the supportive interventions for older adults with mental health problems and their caregivers by creating a network of professionals with expertise in geriatric mental health, improving systems of care for older adults with dementia, and advocating services and programs that help older adults with mental health issues.

Year Founded: 1954

1145 Nathan S. Kline Institute for Psychiatric Research
140 Old Orangeburg Road
Orangeburg, NY 10962
845-398-5500
E-mail: webmaster@nki.rfmh.org
www.www.rfmh.org/nki

Donald C. Goff, MD, Director
Antonio Convit, MD, Deputy Director
Thomas O. O'Hara, MBA, Deputy Director/Institute Admin.
Michael Kohn, PhD, Head of Research Support

A facility of the New York State Office of Mental Health that has earned a national and international reputation for its pioneering contributions in psychiatric research, especially in the areas of psychopharmacological treatments for schizophrenia and major mood disorders, and in the application of computer technology to mental health services. A broad range of studies are conducted at NKI, including basic, clinical, and services research. All work is intended to improve care for people suffering from these complex, psychobiologically-based, severely disabling mental disorders.

Year Founded: 1952

1146 National Alliance on Mental Illness

4301 Wilson Boulevard
Suite 300
Arlington, VA 22203
703-524-7600
800-950-6264
E-mail: info@nami.org
www.nami.org

Shirley J. Holloway, President
Joyce A. Campbell, First Vice President
Daniel H. Gillison, Jr., Chief Executive Officer
David Levy, Chief Financial Officer

NAMI is an organization dedicated to raising awareness on mental health' and providing support and education for Americans affected by mental illness. NAMI advocates for access to services and treatment and fosters an environment of awareness and understanding for those concerned with mental health.

Year Founded: 1979

1147 National Association for Rural Mental Health

660 North Capital Street
Suite 400
Washington, DC 20001
202-942-4276
E-mail: info@narmh.org
www.narmh.org

Jonah Cunningham, President/CEO
Jennifer Christman, Treasurer

NARMH provides a forum for rural mental health professionals and advocates to identify and solve challenges, to work cooperatively toward improving the delivery of rural mental health services, and to promote the unique needs and concerns of rural mental health policy and practice issues. NARMH sponsors an annual conference where rural mental health professionals benefit from the sharing of knowledge and resources.

Year Founded: 1977

1148 National Association for the Dually Diagnosed (NADD)

321 Wall Street
Kingston, NY 12401
845-331-4336
E-mail: info@thenadd.org
www.thenadd.org

Bruce Davis, President
Jeanne M. Farr, MA, Chief Executive Officer
Juanita St. Croix, Vice President
Ray Snyder, Secretary

NADD is a nonprofit organization designed to increase awareness of, and provide services for, individuals with developmental disabilities and mental illness. NADD emphasizes the importance of quality mental healthcare for people with mental health needs and offers conferences, informa-

tion resources, educational programs, and training materials to professionals, parents, and organizations.

Year Founded: 1983

1149 National Association of State Mental Health Program Directors (NASMHPD)

66 Canal Center Plaza
Suite 302
Alexandria, VA 22314
703-739-9333
E-mail: brian.hepburn@nasmhpd.org
www.nasmhpd.org

Brian Hepburn, MD, Executive Director
Jay Meek, CPA, MBA, Chief Financial Officer
David Shern, PhD, Senior Public Health Advisor
Meighan Haupt, MS, Chief of Staff

The only national association to represent state mental health commissioners/directors and their agencies. A private nonprofit membership organization, NASMHPD helps set the agenda and determine the direction of state mental health agency interests across the country, including state mental health planning, service delivery, and evaluation. The association provides members with the opportunity to exchange diverse views and experiences, learning from one another in areas vital to effective public policy development and implementation. Provides a broad array of services designed to identify and respond to critical policy issues, cutting-edge consultation, training, and technical assistance.

Year Founded: 1959

1150 National Center for Learning Disabilities

1220 L Street NW
Suite 100
Washington, DC 20005
301-966-2234
www.ncld.org

Margi Booth, Co-Chair
Joe Zimmel, Co-Chair
Kena Mayberry, Chief Operating Officer
Kenneth Plevan, Secretary

The NCLD's mission is to ensure success for all individuals with learning disabilities in school, at work, and in life. They connect parents with resources, guidance, and support to advocate effectively for their children; deliver evidence-based tools, resources, and professional development to educators to improve student outcomes; and develop policies and engage advocates to strengthen educational rights and opportunities.

Year Founded: 1977

1151 National Center on Addiction and Substance Abuse (CASA) at Columbia University

633 3rd Avenue
19th Floor
New York, NY 10017-6706
212-841-5200
E-mail: contact@casacolumbia.org
www.casacolumbia.org

Joseph J. Plumeri, Executive Chair
Joseph A. Califano, Founder and Chairman Emeritus
James G. Niven, Co-Chair
Creighton Drury, President

The National Center on Addiction and Substance Abuse (CASA) at Columbia University is a science-based, multidisciplinary organization focused on transforming society's understanding of and responses to substance use and the disease of addiction. Founded by Former U.S. Secretary of Health, Education, and Welfare Joseph A. Califano, Jr., CASA remains the only national organization that assembles under one roof all of the professional skill needed to research and develop proven, effective ways to prevent and treat substance abuse and addiction to all substances - alcohol, nicotine as well as illegal, prescription, and performance enhancing drugs - in all sectors of society.

Year Founded: 1992

1152 National Council for Behavioral Health

1400 K Street NW
Suite 400
Washington, DC 20005
E-mail: communications@thenationalcouncil.org
www.thenationalcouncil.org

Tim Swinfard, Chair
Charles Ingoglia, President and CEO
Jeannie Campbell, Executive VP And COO
Bruce Pelleu, CPA, VP, Finance & Administration

The National Council for Behavioral Health serves to unify America's behavioral health organizations. The council is dedicated to ensuring that quality mental health and addictions care is readily accessible to all Americans.

1153 National Disability Rights Network, Inc.

820 1st Street, NE
Suite 740
Washington, DC 20002
202-408-9514
TTY: 220-408-9521
E-mail: info@ndrn.org
www.ndrn.org

J.J. Rico, President
Patty Anderson, Vice President
Curtis L. Decker, JD, Executive Director
Archie Jennings, Secretary

NDRN is a nonprofit membership organization for the Protection and Advocacy Systems and the Client Assistance Programs. These programs work to guard against abuse, advocate for basic rights, and ensure acocunability throughout a variety of areas for people with disabilities and mental illnesses.

Year Founded: 1982

1154 National Empowerment Center

599 Canal Street
Lawrence, MA 01840
978-685-1494
800-769-3728
E-mail: info4@power2u.org
www.power2u.org

Daniel B. Fisher, MD, PhD, Chief Executive Officer
Oryx Cohen, MPA, Chief Operating Officer
Kimberly D. Ewing, Coordinator, Emotional CPR

A consumer/survivor/expatient-run organization that is dedicated to helping people with mental health issues, trauma, and/or extreme states. Their central message revolves around recovery, empowerment, and healing.

1155 National Federation of Families for Children's Mental Health

15800 Crabbs Branch Way
Suite 300
Rockville, MD 20855
240-403-1901
E-mail: ffcmh@ffcmh.org
www.ffcmh.org

Lynda Gargan, PhD, Executive Director
Gailÿ Cormier, Project Director
Leann Sherman, Project Coordinator

The National Federation of Families for Children's Mental Health is a national organization focused on advocating for the rights of children affected by mental health challenges, assisting family-run organizations across the nation, and ensuring that children and families concerned with mental health have access to services.

Year Founded: 1989

1156 National Institute of Drug Abuse (NIDA)
Office of Science Policy & Communications, Public Information Branch

6001 Executive Boulevard
Room 5213, MSC 9561
Bethesda, MD 20892-9561
301-443-6441
E-mail: media@nida.nih.gov
www.nida.nih.gov

Dr. Nora Volkow, Director
Dr. Wilson Compton, Deputy Director
Joellen Austin, Associate Director, Management
Steven Gust, PhD, Director, International Program

NIDA is part of the National Institute of Health, and aims to advance research on the causes and consequences of drug use and addiction in order to improve public health.

1157 National Institute of Mental Health

6001 Executive Boulevard
Room 6200, MSC 9663
Bethesda, MD 20892-9663
866-615-6464
E-mail: nimhinfo@nih.gov
www.www.nimh.nih.gov

Joshua A. Gordon, MD, PhD, Director

One of 27 components of the National Institutes of Health, the Federal government's principal biomedical and behavioral research agency. The National Institute of Mental Health is an expert in mental disorders and aims to improve the treatment and recovery of mental illness through clinical research.

1158 National Institutes of Health Clinical Center

10 Center Dr
Bethesda, MD 20892
301-496-4000
E-mail: ccpressgroup@cc.nih.gov
www.clinicalcenter.nih.gov

James K. Gilman, MD, Chief Executive Officer
Pius A. Aiyelawo, FACHE, Chief Operating Officer
Daniel Lonnerdal, MS, FACHE, Executive Officer
John I. Gallin, MD, Chief Scientific Officer

The NIH Clinical Center is composed of the Warren Grant Magnuson Clinical Center and the later addition, The Mark O. Hatfield Clinical Research Center. The Center was designed with patient care facilities close to research laboratories so new findings of basic and clinical scientists can be quickly applied to the treatment of patients. Upon referral by physicians, patients are admitted to NIH clinical studies.

Year Founded: 1953

1159 National Mental Health Consumers' Self-Help Clearinghouse

E-mail: selfhelpclearinghouse@gmail.com
www.mhselfhelp.org

Joseph Rogers, Founder and Executive Director
Susan Rogers, Director

The Clearinghouse is a peer-run national technical assistance center focused on achieving respect and equality of opportunity for those with mental illnesses. The Clearinghouse helps with the growth of the mental health consumer movement by evaluating mental health services, advocating for mental health reform, and providing consumers with news, information, publications, and consultation services.

Year Founded: 1986

1160 National Network for Mental Health Inclusion Network

PO Box 1539
Station Main
St. Catharines, ON, ZZ
www.nmhin.ca

May Recollect, Indigenous Representative
Dr. Kathleen Thompson, Co-Chair, Saskatchewan
Dr. William Wai Tak Chan, Co-Chair, Winnipeg
Anita Levesque, Media/Comms. Director/Treasurer

The purpose of the NNMH is to advocate, educate, and provide expertise and resources that benefit the Canadian consumer/survivor community. The focus of the organization is to network with Candian consumer/survivors and family and friends of consumer/survivors to provide opportunities for resource sharing, information distribution, and education on issues impacting persons living with mental health issues/illness/disability.

Year Founded: 1992

1161 National Organization on Disability

77 Water Street
Suite 204
New York, NY 10005
646-505-1191
E-mail: info@nod.org
www.nod.org

Gov. Tom Ridge, Chairman
Carol Glazer, President
Luke Visconti, Vice Chairman
Laura Giovacco, Treasurer

NOD is a private, nonprofit organization that is dedicatd to helping people with disabilities live full, independent lives. NOD conducts research on disability employment issues, including the field's most widely used polls on employment trends and the quality of life for people with disabilities. They work in partnership with employers, schools, the military, service providers, researchers, and disability advocates. Current employment progrmas are benefiting high school students with disabilities, seriously injured service members returning from Iraq and Afghanistan, employers seeking to become more disability friendly, and state governments engaged in policy reform.

Year Founded: 1982

1162 National Rehabilitation Association

PO Box 150235
Alexandria, VA 22315
703-836-0850
888-258-4295
E-mail: membership@nationalrehab.org
www.www.nationalrehab.org

Lou Adams, President
Paul Barnes, President-Elect
Courtney Sweatman, Treasurer
Danielle Ami Narh, Secretary

The National Rehabilitation Association is concerned with the rights of people with disabilities. Their mission is to provide advocacy, awareness, and career advancement for professionals in the fields of rehabilitation. Members include rehab counselors; physical, speech, and occupational therapists; job trainers; consultants; independent living instructors; and other professionals involved in the advocacy of programs and services for people with disabilities.

Year Founded: 1927

1163 New Hope Foundation

80 Conover Road
Marlboro, NJ 07746
723-946-3030
800-705-4673
www.newhopeibhc.org

Tony Comerford, PhD, President and CEO
David Roden, LCSW, LCADC, Vice President and COO

A nonprofit corporation serving those in need of treatment for alcoholism, drug addiction, and compulsive gambling. Over the years, New Hope has expanded its capacity and capabilities to include specialized programming for adolescents, women, and those with co-occuring disorders. New Hope constantly strives to advance the quality of addiction treatment through ongoing professional education and participation in select research projects.

1164 Parents Helping Parents
Sobrato Center for Nonprofits

1400 Parkmoor Avenue
Suite 100
San Jose, CA 95126
408-727-5775
855-727-5775
E-mail: info@php.com
www.php.com

Maria Daane, Executive Director
Mark Fishler, Development Director
Janet Nunez, Development Director
Virginia Hildebrand, Finance Director

PHP's mission is to help children and adults with special needs receive the support and services they need to reach their full potential by providing information, training, and resources to build strong families and improve systems of care.

Year Founded: 1976

1165 Recovery International

1415 W. 22nd Street
Tower Floor
Oak Brook, IL 60523
312-337-5661
866-221-0302

E-mail: info@recoveryinternational.org
www.www.recoveryinternational.org

Sandra K. Wilcoxon, Chief Executive Officer
Joanne Lampey, President
Nicole Cilento, Vice President
Hal Casey, Treasurer

Recovery International is an organization that uses a peer-to-peer, self-help training system developed by Abraham Low in order to help individuals with mental health issues lead more productive lives.

Year Founded: 1937

1166 Sidran Traumatic Stress Institute
7238 Muncaster Mill Road
Suite 376
Derwood, MD 20855
410-825-8888
E-mail: admin@sidran.org
www.sidran.org

Esther Giller, President and Director
Ruta Mazelis, Editor, The Cutting Edge/Trainer

Sidran Institute provides useful, practical information for child and adult survivors of any type of trauma, for families/friends, and for the clinical and frontline service providers who assist in their recovery. Sidran's philosophy of education through collaboration brings together great minds (providers, survivors, and loved ones) to develop comprehensive programs to address the practical, emotional, spiritual, and medical needs of trauma survivors.

Year Founded: 1986

1167 The Arc New York
29 British American Boulevard
2nd Floor
Latham, NY 12110
518-439-8311
E-mail: Info@TheArcNY.org
www.www.thearcny.org

Dr. John Kowalczyk, President
Daniel Martindale, Senior Vice President
Rosa Rodriguez, Secretary
Steven Drobysh, Treasurer

Formerly known as NYSARC, The Arc's goal is to improve the quality of life for people with intellectual and other developmental disabilities by providing support, information, direction, and services; to have one of the best service delivery systems in the nation, including family members, self-advocates, and professionals in all matters; and to continually build training and educational opportunities into all aspects of The Arc New York.

Year Founded: 1949

1168 The Center for Family Support
2811 Zulette Avenue
Bronx, NY 10461
718-518-1500
E-mail: svernikoff@cfsny.org
www.www.cfsny.org

Steven Vernikoff, Executive Director
Barbara Greenwald, Chief Operating Officer
Jos, Martin Jara, President
Elise Geltzer, Vice President

The Center for Family Support offers assistance to individuals with developmental and related disabilities, as well as their families, and provides support services and programs that are designed to accommodate individual needs. Offers services throughout New York City, Westchester County, Long Island, and New Jersey.

Year Founded: 1954

1169 The Center for Workplace Mental Health
C/O American Psychiatric Foundation
800 Maine Avenue SW
Suite 900
Washington, DC 20024
202-559-3140
E-mail: workplacementalhealth@psych.org
www.workplacementalhealth.org

Darcy Gruttadaro, JD, Director
Emma Jellen, Associate Director
Lilia Coffin, Operations Manager
Brittany Raymond, Program Manager

The Center works with businesses to ensure that employees and their families living with mental illness, including substance use disorders, receive effective care. It does so in recognition that employers purchase healthcare for millions of American workers and their families.

1170 The SickKids Centre for Community Mental Health
440 Jarvis Street
Toronto, ON M4Y 2H4,
416-924-1164
855-944-4673
E-mail: info@sickkidscmh.ca
www.www.sickkidscmh.ca

Jeff Mainland, Chair
Christina Bartha, Executive Director
Dr. Marshall Korenblum, Medical Director
Neil Carson, Clinical Director & Site Lead

A nonprofit children's mental health centre providing mental health services to infants, children, youth, and families. Formerly known as The Hincks-Dellcrest Centre, the SickKids Center provides prevention, intervention, outpatient, and residential treatment programs; assists with the education and training of mental health clinicians and managers; conducts research and develops and evaluates new methods for treatment; and increases awareness of the issues surrounding children's mental health. CCMH seeks to eradicate the stigma about mental illness and to promote social, emotional, and behavioral health in children and families.

Year Founded: 1998

1171 The World Bank Group
1818 H Street NW
Washington, DC 20433
202-473-1000
www.www.worldbank.org

David Malpass, President
Axel van Trotsenburg, Managing Director of Operations
Anshula Kant, Chief Financial Officer
Shaolin Yang, Chief Administrative Officer

The World Bank helps develop low and middle income countries to improve peoples health and to guard against the poverty that can result from sudden illness, including mental disorders.

Year Founded: 1944

1172 Thresholds
4101 N. Ravenswood Avenue
Chicago, IL 60613
773-572-5500
E-mail: contact@thresholds.org
www.www.thresholds.org

Suzet M. McKinney, DrPH, MPH, President
Mark Ishaug, MA, Chief Executive Officer
Mike Faley, General Counsel
Mark Furlong, LCSW, Chief Operating Officer

Thresholds is an organization that serves people with severe and persistent mental illness with a range of programs designed with the individual's recovery as a goal. Strong leadership, an enduring vision, and a solid belief in the resilience and value of all individuals has made Thresholds one of the nation's most successful and respected provider of services for people with severe mental illness. Their goal is to help those with mental illness reclaim their lives through care, employment, advocacy, and housing.

Year Founded: 1959

1173 VOR
836 S. Arlington Heights Road
Suite 351
Elk Grove Village, IL 60007
E-mail: info@vor.net
www.vor.net

Harris Capps, President
Hugo Dwyer, Executive Director
Sam Friedman, 1st Vice President
Joanne St. Amand, 2nd Vice President

Through national programs, VOR achieves its mission to unite advocates, as well as educate and assist families, organizations, public officials, and individuals concerned with the quality of life and choice for persons with intellectual disabilities within a full array of residential options, including community and facility-based care. VOR is the only national organization to advocate for a full range of quality residential options and services, including own home, family home, community-based service options. VOR advocates for the right of individuals with intellectual/developmental disabilities and their right to choose what is best for them.

Year Founded: 1983

1174 World Federation for Mental Health
PO BOX 807
Occoquan, VA 22125

Nasser Loza, President

An international organization to advance the prevention of mental and emotional disorders, the proper treatment and care of those with such disorders, and the promotion of mental health. The Federation has responded to international mental health crises through its role as the only worldwide grassroots advocacy and public education organization in the mental health field. The organization's broad and diverse membership makes possible collaboration among governments and non-governmental organizations to advance the cause of mental health services, research, and policy advocacy worldwide.

Year Founded: 1948

1175 Young Adult Institute and Workshop (YAI)
460 West 34th Street
11th Floor
New York, NY 10001-2382
212-273-6100
www.yai.org

George Contos, Chief Executive Officer
Kevin Carey, Chief Financial Officer
Alek Hoyos, Chief of Staff
Ravi Dahiya, Chief Program Officer

Serves more than 20,000 people of all ages and levels of mental, developmental, and learning disabilities. Provides a full range of early intervention, preschool, family supports, employment training and placement, clinical and residential services, as well as recreation and camping services. YAI/National Intitute for People with Disabilities is also a professional organization, nationally renowned for its publications, conferences, training seminars, video training tapes, and innovative television programs.

Year Founded: 1957

1176 ZERO TO THREE: National Center for Infants, Toddlers, and Families
2445 M Street NW
Suite 600
Washington, DC 20037
202-638-1144
www.zerotothree.org

Brenda Jones Harden, President
Matthew Melmed, Executive Director
Walter S. Gilliam, Vice President
Eugene P. Stein, Treasurer

A national, nonprofit organization that provides information and resources on early development to parents, professionals, and policymakers. Zero to Three's mission is to improve the lives of infants and toddlers, and to promote their health and development. Publishes books and pamphlets on the social and emotional development of infants, toddlers, and their families. Produces the Zero to Three journal, a professional publication. Sponsors the National Training Institute, an annual professional training conference in December, and offers a fellowship program.

Year Founded: 1977

State

Alabama

1177 Horizons School
2018 15th Avenue South
Birmingham, AL 35205
205-322-6606
800-822-6242
E-mail: info@horizonsschool.org
www.horizonsschool.org

Dr. Brian Geiger, Executive Director
Don Lutomski, President/Interim Treasurer
Craig Landrum, Vice-President

The Horizons School provides a non-degree transition program designed to help students with specific learning disabilities and other mild learning problems develop the skills necessary to become independent, productive individuals. Classes teach life skills, social skills and career training. The program aims to prepare students for successful transitions to the community.

Year Founded: 1991

1178 Mental Health America in Montgomery

1116 S Hull Street
Montgomery, AL 36104
334-262-5500
E-mail: mha@mha-montgomery.org
www.mha-montgomery.org

An affiliate of Mental Health America, which is a community-based non-profit organization committed to enabling the mental wellness of all Americans. MHA advocates for greater access to quality health services and seeks to educate individuals on identifying symptoms, as well as intervention and prevention.

1179 Mental Health America of Etowah County

254 S. College Street
Gadsden, AL 35901
256-613-7279
E-mail: mhaofetowah@gmail.com
www.www.mhaofetowah.com

An affiliate of Mental Health America, which is a community-based non-profit organization committed to enabling the mental wellness of all Americans. MHA advocates for greater access to quality health services and seeks to educate individuals on identifying symptoms, as well as intervention and prevention.

1180 Mental Health Center of North Central Alabama

1316 Somerville Road Southeast
Suite 1
Decatur, AL 35601
256-355-6105
800-365-6008
www.mhcnca.org

Henry White, President
Luke Slaton, Vice President
Dianne Norwood, Secretary
Judy Thomas, Treasurer

Non-profit organization serving Lawrence, Limestone and Morgan counties. Provides treatment, education and assistance services and programs for people affected by mental health problems.

Year Founded: 1967

1181 NAMI Alabama (National Alliance on Mental Illness)

1401 I-85 Parkway
Suite A
Montgomery, AL 36106
334-396-4797
800-626-4199
E-mail: kemerson@namialabama.org
www.namialabama.org

Connie Ewing, President
Kelly Emerson, Executive Director

NAMI Alabama is a non-profit organization of local support and advocacy groups committed to improving the treatment and care available to persons diagnosed with a mental illness in Alabama. NAMI Alabama aims to enhance the quality of life for Alabamians with mental health needs.

Year Founded: 1979

1182 National Alliance on Mental Illness: Alabama

1401 I-85 Parkway
Suite A
Montgomery, AL 36106
334-396-4797
800-626-4199
www.www.namialabama.org

Connie Ewing, Chapter President
Kelly Emerson, Chapter Executive Director

Local chapter of the National Alliance on Mental Illness, an organization dedicated to raising awareness on mental health and providing support and education for Americans affected by mental illness. Mission is to help consumers and families share information about services, care providers, and ways to cope with the challenges of mental illness.

Year Founded: 1986

Alaska

1183 Alaska Association for Infant and Early Childhood Mental Health

PO Box 240331
Fairbanks, AK 99524
E-mail: alaska.aimh@gmail.com
www.akaimh.org

Nonprofit organization of parents and professionals dedicated to supporting the healthy mental, emotional and social development of infants and young children.

Year Founded: 2009

1184 National Alliance on Mental Illness: Alaska

1057 West Fireweed Lane
Suite 206
Anchorage, AK 99503
907-277-0227
E-mail: info@namianchorage.org
www.www.namianchorage.org

Jason Lessard, Chapter Executive Director

Local chapter of the National Alliance on Mental Illness, an organization dedicated to raising awareness on mental health and providing support and education for Americans affected by mental illness. Mission is to help consumers and families share information about services, care providers, and ways to cope with the challenges of mental illness.

Year Founded: 1984

Arizona

1185 Community Partners Inc.

401 N. Bonita Ave.
Tucson, AZ 85745
520-721-1887
www.communitypartnersinc.org

Rose Lopez, MBA, President and CEO
Jim Vitt, Chief Financial Officer
Sharen Northern, Chief Human Resources Officer
Dr. William Ruby, Chief Medical Officer

Formerly Community Partnership of Southern Arizona, Community Partners Inc. is an organization that offers services in behavioral health care across Arizona.

Year Founded: 2013

1186 Devereux Arizona
2025 N. 3rd Street
Suite 250
Phoenix, AZ 85004
602-283-1573
www.devereuxaz.org

Dr. Yvette Jackson, LMSW, DBH, Executive Director
Janelle Westfall, LPC, BCBA, Clinical Director
Robert "Bob" Kelly, Director of Finance
Ron Herget, PHR, SHRM-CP, People Operations Director

Nonprofit behavioral health organization providing clinical, educational and employment programs and services for individuals affected by learning, behavioral and emotional challenges.

Year Founded: 1967

1187 Mental Health America of Arizona
5110 North 40th Street
Suite 201
Phoenix, AZ 85018
602-576-4828
E-mail: mhaofarizona@gmail.com
www.mhaarizona.org

Ericka Irvin, Executive Director
Matthew Moody, MC, Board President
Francine Sumner, Board Vice Presiden
Jason Berstein, CPA, Treasurer

An affiliate of Mental Health America, the organization promotes care and treatment for people with mental illness, educates Arizonans about mental health and participates in advocacy efforts, and strives for better mental health for people in Arizona.

s pages Year Founded: 1954

1188 Mentally Ill Kids in Distress (MIKID)
7816 North 19th Avenue
Phoenix, AZ 85021
602-253-1240
E-mail: phoenix@mikid.org
www.mikid.org

Kathryn Hart, President
Sue Gilbertson, Founder
Jeff Kazmierczak, RN, MSN, Chief Executive Officer
Bonnie Kolakowski, MBA, Chief Financial Officer

Mentally Ill Kids in Distress provides support and assistance to families in Arizona with children and youth who are struggling with behavioral problems. MIKID seeks to improve the behavioral health and wellness of youth across Arizona. Offers information centers, assistance by phone, email or in person, support groups, educational meetings, referrals to resources, and direct support services.

Year Founded: 1987

1189 National Alliance on Mental Illness: Arizona
5025 E. Washington Street
Suite 112
Phoenix, AZ 85034
480-994-4407
www.www.namiarizona.org

Jim Dunn, Chapter Executive Director
Sherron Candelaria, Chapter President

Local chapter of the National Alliance on Mental Illness, an organization dedicated to raising awareness on mental health and providing support and education for Americans affected by mental illness. Mission is to help consumers and families share information about services, care providers, and ways to cope with the challenges of mental illness.

Arkansas

1190 National Alliance on Mental Illness: Arkansas
1012 Autumn Road
Suite 1
Little Rock, AR 7221
800-844-0381
E-mail: help@namiarkansas.org
www.namiarkansas.org

Chris Beckers, LPN, Chapter President
Buster Lackey, PhD, LPC, Chapter Executive Director

Local chapter of the National Alliance on Mental Illness, an organization dedicated to raising awareness on mental health and providing support and education for Americans affected by mental illness. Mission is to help consumers and families share information about services, care providers, and ways to cope with the challenges of mental illness.

California

1191 Assistance League of Los Angeles
6640 Sunset Blvd.
Los Angeles, CA 90028
323-469-1973
E-mail: info@assistanceleaguela.org
www.assistanceleaguela.org

Melanie Merians, Chief Executive Officer
Rafe Pery, Chief Financial Officer

Provides services to meet the physical and emotional needs of children and families. Focuses on helping children who live in poverty within Los Angeles communities through the development of programs designed to promote learning and improve self-esteem.

Year Founded: 1919

1192 California Association of Marriage and Family Therapists
7901 Raytheon Road
San Diego, CA 92111
858-292-2638
www.camft.org

Danah Williams, LMFT, President
Lisa Romain, PhD, LMFT, President-Elect
Peter Cellarius, LMFT, Secretary
Robin Andersen, MA, LMFT, Chief Financial Officer

Independent professional organization representing the interests of licensed marriage and family therapists. Dedicated to advancing marriage and family therapy as a mental health profession. Seeks to maintain standards of quality and ethics for the profession and to raise awareness of the profession.

88 pages 6 per year Year Founded: 2002 ISSN 1540-2770

1193 California Association of Social Rehabilitation Agencies
3350 E. 7th Street
Suite 509
Long Beach, CA 90804
562-343-2621
E-mail: casra@casra.org
www.casra.org

Chad Costello, CPRP, Executive Director
Joe Ruiz, Director, Training and Education

Aims to improve the lives of people with psychiatric disabilities by developing mental health programs and services that promote growth and recovery, addressing legislative issues surrounding mental health services, and providing educational and training opportunities that address the importance of meeting mental health needs and social rehabilitation.

Year Founded: 1989

1194 California Health Information Association

5055 E. McKinley Ave.
Fresno, CA 93727-1964
559-251-5038
E-mail: info@californiahia.org
www.californiahia.org

Larry Smith , MHA, RHIA, President
Sharon Lewis, MBA, RHIA, CHPS, CEO/Executive Director
Debi Boynton, Operations/Finance Manager

Nonprofit association that offers education, advocacy and resources for health information management professionals in California. Members contribute to the delivery of quality patient care through the management of personal health information.

Year Founded: 1949

1195 California Institute for Behavioral Health Solutions

1760 Creekside Oaks Dr.
Ste. 175
Sacramento, CA 95833
916-556-3480
E-mail: info@cibhs.org
www.cibhs.org

Percy Howard, III, LCSW, President and CEO
Rick Goscha, PhD, Sr. Vice President of Programs
Jennifer Clancy, MSW, Director of Strategy
Robert Diaz, MBA, Director of Finance

Nonprofit agency that assists professionals and agencies with improving the lives of individuals struggling with mental illness and substance use problems through training, technical assistance, research and policy development.

Year Founded: 1993

1196 California Psychological Association

1231 I Street
Suite 204
Sacramento, CA 95814
916-286-7979
E-mail: cpa@cpapsych.org
www.calpsych.org

Jo Linder-Crow, PhD, Chief Executive Officer
David Lin, PsyD, President
David Hindman, PhD, President-Elect
Mary Malik, PhD, Treasurer

Non-profit organization representing psychiatrists who specialize in the care of patients with mental and emotional disorders. The California Psychiatric Association advocates for access to quality care, educates the public about psychiatry, and provides news and information on mental health issues. CPA is area six of the American Psychiatric Association, and is composed of members of APA's five district branches in California.

Year Founded: 1948

1197 Calnet

805-660-8719
E-mail: blamb@calnetcare.com
www.calnetcare.com

A not-for-profit network serving to bring mental health and chemical dependency treatment providers together with managed care organizations for business opportunities.

Year Founded: 1983

1198 Filipino American Service Group

135 North Park View Street
Los Angeles, CA 90026
213-908-5050
E-mail: admin@fasgi.org
www.fasgi.org

Celina T. Duffy, Acting Board Chairperson
Ermelinda Abeleda, Board Treasurer
Cora Aragon Soriano, Board Secretary

Filipino American Service Group focuses on improving the physical and mental well-being of mentally ill, homeless, and/or low income individuals in Los Angeles. Provides independent health and social services. Aims to help enhance the quality of life for members of the community in Historic Filipinotown and the Greater Los Angeles area.

Year Founded: 1981

1199 Five Acres: Boys and Girls Aid Society of Los Angeles County

760 West Mountain View Street
Altadena, CA 91001
626-798-6793
800-696-6793
TDD: 626-204-1375
E-mail: wecanhelp@5acres.org
www.5acres.org

John Reith, Chairman
Rustin Mork, Vice Chair
Christianne Kerns, Vice Chair
Chanel Boutakidis, Chief Executive Officer

Serves to prevent child abuse and neglect, and connect children to safe and loving families. Develops support services and outreach programs to help treat and educate abused and neglected children, conducts research and promotes evidence-based treatment, engages in advocacy, and provides educational resources to family, professionals and the community on the prevention of child abuse and neglect.

Year Founded: 1888

1200 Health Services Agency: Behavioral Health

1430 Freedom Blvd.
Suite F
Watsonville, CA 95076
831-763-8200
800-952-2335
E-mail: hsabhserviceinfo@santacruzcounty.us
www.santacruzhealth.org

Serves to improve and protect the public health of Santa Cruz County and to ensure access to quality health care and treatment for residents. The Health Services Agency develops programs and services in mental health, as well as environmental health, public health, medical care, and substance abuse prevention and treatment. The HSA advocates for public health policy and seeks to eliminate the stigma associated with mental illness and other diseases.

1201 Mental Health America of California
PO Box 567
Sacramento, CA 95812-0567
916-557-1167
www.mhac.org

Heidi Strunk, President & CEO
Curtis Paullins, Executive Administrator

An affiliate of Mental Health America, which is a community-based non-profit organization committed to enabling the mental wellness of all Americans. MHA advocates for greater access to quality health services and seeks to educate individuals on identifying symptoms, as well as intervention and prevention.

1202 National Alliance on Mental Illness: California
425 University Avenue
Suite 200
Sacramento, CA 95825
916-567-0163
E-mail: info@namica.org
www.namica.org

Patrick Courneya, MD, Chapter President
Jessica Cruz, MPA, HS, Chapter Executive Director

Local chapter of the National Alliance on Mental Illness, an organization dedicated to raising awareness on mental health and providing support and education for Americans affected by mental illness. Mission is to help consumers and families share information about services, care providers, and ways to cope with the challenges of mental illness.

1203 National Alliance on Mental Illness: Gold Country
PO Box 1088
Angels Camp, CA 95222-1088
209-736-4264
E-mail: davispatricia0@gmail.com
www.nami.org

Local chapter of the National Alliance on Mental Illness, an organization dedicated to raising awareness on mental health and providing support and education for Americans affected by mental illness. Mission is to help consumers and families share information about services, care providers, and ways to cope with the challenges of mental illness.

1204 National Health Foundation
515 South Figueroa Street
Suite 1300
Los Angeles, CA 90071
213-538-0700
www.nationalhealthfoundation.org

Jeffrey L. Thompson, Chair
Kelly Bruno, President & CEO
Mia Arias, Chief Operating Officer
Danielle Cameron, Chief Strategy Officer

Public charity whose mission is to improve the healthcare available to underserved groups through the development, support and provision of programs that address the systemic barriers in healthcare access and delivery.

Year Founded: 1973

1205 Orange County Psychiatric Society
5000 Campus Drive
Newport Beach, CA 92660
949-250-3157
www.ocps.org

Robert Bota, MD, President
Alexis Seegan, Secretary
Larry Faziola, MD, Treasurer

Works to promote public awareness of mental health and improve care for people affected by mental illness.

1206 UCLA Department of Psychiatry & Biobehavioral Sciences
760 Westwood Plaza
Los Angeles, CA 90095
310-825-0511
www.www.semel.ucla.edu/psychiatry

Alexander Young, Interim Chair

Programs for clinical research on the causes of and treatments for psychiatric and behavioral disorders in adults and children.

1207 United Advocates for Children and Families
3133 Arden Way
Sacramento, CA 95825
916-692-8087
E-mail: info@uacf4hope.org
www.uacf4hope.org

A nonprofit organization that works on behalf of children and youth with mental, emotional, and behavioral challenges and their families.

Year Founded: 1993

Colorado

1208 CAFCA
1176 Lincoln Street
Ste. 1100
Denver, CO 80203
720-240-9516
www.voiceforcokids.org

Scott Shields, President
Rebecca Hea, PsyD, Vice President
Brandon Miller, Secretary/Treasurer
Becky Miller Updike, PhD, Executive Director

Provides agencies dedicated to helping Colorado's vulnerable children with research, education and training. The services provided by member agencies include: adoption, alcohol and drug treatment, day treatment, education, family support and preservation, foster care, group homes, independent living, kinship care, mental health treatment and counseling, pregnancy counseling, residential care at all levels, services for homeless and runaway youth, services for sexually reactive youth, sexual abuse services and transitional living.

Year Founded: 1982

1209 CHINS UP Youth and Family Services
Griffith Centers for Children
10 North Farragut Avenue
Colorado Springs, CO 80909
719-636-2122
E-mail: info@griffithcenters.org
www.griffithcenters.org

Christina Murphy, President and CEO
Tania Sossi, Chief Operating Officer
Ryan Brown, Chief Financial Officer
Lisa Lamoreaux, Director of Community Programs

A division of The Griffith Centers for Children, Chins Up is a nonprofit multi-service agency serving Colorado Springs children and adolescents with emotional or behavioral problems, as well as children who were victims of abuse. Chins Up provides community-based programs and services with the hope of healing the broken lives of children and families.

Year Founded: 1927

1210 Colorado Health Partnerships
609 1/2 Main Street
Alamosa, CO 81101
719-587-0899
www.chnpartners.com

Comprised of partnerships between ValueOptions (now Beacon Health Options) and eight community mental health centers. Provides mental health services to Medicaid eligible individuals in southern and Western Colorado.

Year Founded: 1995

1211 Federation of Families for Children's Mental Health: Colorado Chapter
7475 West Fifth Avenue
Suite 307
Lakewood, CO 80226
888-429-3369
E-mail: ian@leepetersoncpa.com
www.coloradofederation.org

Advocates for children, youth, and families affected by mental illness and aims to improve mental health programs, services, and policies in Colorado.

Year Founded: 1993

1212 Mental Health America of Colorado
1120 Lincoln Street
Suite 1606
Denver, CO 80203
720-208-2220
www.www.mentalhealthcolorado.org

Vincent Atchity, President & CEO
Moe Keller, Director of Advocacy
David McLaughlin, Vice President, Operations

An affiliate of Mental Health America, which is a community-based non-profit organization committed to enabling the mental wellness of all Americans. MHA advocates for greater access to quality health services and seeks to educate individuals on identifying symptoms, as well as intervention and prevention.

Year Founded: 1953

1213 National Alliance on Mental Illness: Colorado
3333 S Bannock Street
Suite 430
Denver, CO 80110
303-321-3104
E-mail: info@namicolorado.org
www.namicolorado.org

Local chapter of the National Alliance on Mental Illness, an organization dedicated to raising awareness on mental health and providing support and education for Americans affected by mental illness. Mission is to help consumers

and families share information about services, care providers, and ways to cope with the challenges of mental illness.

Connecticut

1214 Joshua Center Programs
Natchaug Hospital
189 Storrs Road
Mansfield Center, CT 06250
860-426-7792
www.natchaug.org

The Joshua Center Programs at Natchaug Hospital provide a range of services designed to treat children and adolescents who are struggling with emotional and behavioral problems, including mental illness, emotional trauma, and substance abuse. Intensive, structured treatment programs include group therapy, psycho-education, individual and family treatment, and medication management. Programs utilize a positive approach with the goal of maintaining recovery. Treatment programs offered with Joshua Centers include: Partial Hospital Program, Intensive Outpatient Program, and Extended Day Program. Natchaug Hospital provides Joshua Center programs at seven locations throughout Connecticut.

1215 Mental Health Connecticut (Mental Health America)
61 S Main Street
Suite 100
West Hartford, CT 06107
860-529-1970
E-mail: info@mhconn.org
www.www.mhconn.org

Luis B. Perez, LCSW, President & CEO
Jennifer A. Pulse, Chief Financial Officer
Jill M. Currier, SPHR, Chief Human Resources Officer
Remi G. Kyek, MA, MFT, Chief Experience Officer

An affiliate of Mental Health America, which is a community-based non-profit organization committed to enabling the mental wellness of all Americans. MHA advocates for greater access to quality health services and seeks to educate individuals on identifying symptoms, as well as intervention and prevention.

1216 National Alliance on Mental Illness: Connecticut
1030 New Britain Avenue
Suite 201
West Hartford, CT 06110
860-882-0236
E-mail: admin@namict.org
www.namict.org

Liz P. Taylor, Chapter Executive Director

Local chapter of the National Alliance on Mental Illness, an organization dedicated to raising awareness on mental health and providing support and education for Americans affected by mental illness. Mission is to help consumers and families share information about services, care providers, and ways to cope with the challenges of mental illness.

Year Founded: 1984

1217 Women's Support Services
13a Porter Street
Lakeville, CT 06039

860-364-1080
E-mail: info@wssdv.org
www.wssdv.org

Alexandra Lange, Co-Chair
Barbara Kahn Moller, Co-Chair
Betsey Mauro, Executive Director
Elizabeth Webb, Secretary

Support and advocacy for those affected by emotional, physical, psychological, or sexual trauma in the Northwest region of Connecticut and nearby areas in New York and Massachusetts. Raises awareness on domestic abuse and seeks to engage all members of the community in the movement to end domestic violence.

Delaware

1218 Mental Health America in Delaware

100 W 10th Street
Wilmington, DE 19801
302-654-6833
E-mail: information@mhainde.org
www.www.mhainde.org

Larence Kirby, PhD, LPCMH, President
Victoria Kim Chang, EdD, Vice-President
Sandra Rodriguez, Treasurer
Emily Vera, LCSW, Executive Director

An affiliate of Mental Health America, which is a community-based non-profit organization committed to enabling the mental wellness of all Americans. MHA advocates for greater access to quality health services and seeks to educate individuals on identifying symptoms, as well as intervention and prevention.

Year Founded: 1932

1219 National Alliance on Mental Illness: Delaware

2400 West 4th Street
Wilmington, DE 19805
302-427-0787
E-mail: namide@namide.org
www.namidelaware.org

Joshua Thomas, Chapter Executive Director/CEO

Local chapter of the National Alliance on Mental Illness, an organization dedicated to raising awareness on mental health and providing support and education for Americans affected by mental illness. Mission is to help consumers and families share information about services, care providers, and ways to cope with the challenges of mental illness.

Year Founded: 1983

1220 National Association of Social Workers: Delaware Chapter

100 West 10th Street
Suite 608
Wilmington, DE 19801
302-288-0931
www.naswde.org

Jennifer Thompson, Executive Director
Elise Marie Mora, President
Devon Vitti, Vice President
Maya Thomas, Secretary

Member organization of professional social workers serving to help with the development of its members and the practice of social work, and to assist with improving the well-being of individuals and families through work and advocacy.

District of Columbia

1221 Department of Health and Human Services/OAS

200 Independence Avenue Southwest
Washington, DC 20201
877-696-6775
www.hhs.gov

Xavier Becerra, Secretary
Andrea Palm, Deputy Secretary
McArthur Allen, Chief Administrative Law Judge

The DHHS is the United States government's principal agency for protecting the health of all Americans, providing health and human services, and supporting initiatives in medicine, public health, and social services.

1222 Mental Health America in Southeast Florida

7145 W Oakland Park Boulevard
Lauderhill, FL 33313-1012
954-746-2055
www.www.mhasefl.org

Diane Mittelstaedt, MS, Chair
Toni Powers, Esq., First Vice Chair
Paul Jaquith, LCSW, CAP, President & CEO
Janet Gerner, LCCSW, CGAC, Secretary

An affiliate of Mental Health America, which is a community-based non-profit organization committed to enabling the mental wellness of all Americans. MHA advocates for greater access to quality health services and seeks to educate individuals on identifying symptoms, as well as intervention and prevention.

Year Founded: 1957

1223 Mental Health America of East Central Florida

531 S Ridgewood Avenue
Daytona Beach, FL 32114
386-252-5785
E-mail: info@mhavolusia.org
www.mhavolusia.org

An affiliate of Mental Health America, which is a community-based non-profit organization committed to enabling the mental wellness of all Americans. MHA advocates for greater access to quality health services and seeks to educate individuals on identifying symptoms, as well as intervention and prevention.

1224 Mental Health America of Southwest Florida

2335 9th Street N Naples, FL 34103
239-261-5405
www.www.mhaswfl.org

Petra M. Jones, MPA, Executive Director
Joshua Rudnick, PA, President
Dale Klaus, PA, Vice President

An affiliate of Mental Health America, which is a community-based non-profit organization committed to enabling the mental wellness of all Americans. MHA advocates for greater access to quality health services and seeks to educate individuals on identifying symptoms, as well as intervention and prevention.

Year Founded: 1957

1225 National Alliance on Mental Illness: District of Columbia
422 8th Stree SE
2nd Floor
Washington, DC 20003
202-546-0646
888-796-4357
E-mail: namidc@namidc.org
www.www.namidc.org

Jean Harris, Chapter President

Local chapter of the National Alliance on Mental Illness, an organization dedicated to raising awareness on mental health and providing support and education for Americans affected by mental illness. Mission is to help consumers and families share information about services, care providers, and ways to cope with the challenges of mental illness.

Year Founded: 1984

Florida

1226 Family Network on Disabilities
26750 U.S. Highway 19 North
Suite 410
Clearwater, FL 33761
727-523-1130
800-825-5736
E-mail: fnd@fndusa.org
www.fndusa.org

Rich La Belle, CEO
Joseph La Belle, Director of Programs Impact
Heidi Flatt, CPA, CGMA, Director of Finance
Laura Mattson, Trust and Operations Director

Family Network on Disabilities is a grassroots organization for individuals with disabilities or special needs and their families, as well as professionals and concerned citizens. FND seeks to assist families affected by disabilities through support services and the sharing of information. FND strives to eradicate systemic barriers and to work towards inclusion and equality of people with disabilities. FND organizes a number of programs in Florida, including the Parent Education Network, Family STAR (Support, Training, Assistance, Resources), and the Youth Advocacy and Action Project.

Year Founded: 1985

1227 Federation of Families of Central Florida
National Federation of Families for Children's Mental Health
2605 Maitland Center Parkway
Suite D
Fern Park, FL 32751
407-334-8049
E-mail: info.ffcfl@gmail.com
www.ffcflinc.org

Muriel Jones, Executive Director

An affiliate of the National Federation of Families for Children's Mental Health, the Federation of Families of Central Florida serves children and youth with emotional, behavioral, and mental health challenges and their families through advocacy, support, and education.

1228 Florida Health Care Association
307 West Park Avenue
PO Box 1459
Tallahassee, FL 32301

850-224-3907
E-mail: info@fhca.org
www.fhca.org

Marco Carrasco, President
Anita Faulmann, Senior Vice President
Julie Bell-Morris, Secretary
J. Emmett Reed, CAE, CEO

FHCA is dedicated to providing the highest quality care for elderly, chronically ill, and disabled individuals in Florida.

Year Founded: 1954

1229 Mental Health America in Georgia
2250 N Druid Hills Road NE
Suite 275
Atlanta, GA 30329-3141
770-741-1481
E-mail: info@mhageorgia.org
www.mhageorgia.org

Abdul Henderson, Executive Director
Erin Clayton, Director of Programs
Lorie Summers, Director of Youth Programs
Madison Scott, Director of Development

An affiliate of Mental Health America, which is a community-based non-profit organization committed to enabling the mental wellness of all Americans. MHA advocates for greater access to quality health services and seeks to educate individuals on identifying symptoms, as well as intervention and prevention.

1230 Mental Health Association of West Florida
840 West Lakeview Avenue
Pensacola, FL 32501-1967
850-438-9879
www.mhawfl.org

Offers support services, advocacy, information and referrals for individuals and families affected by mental illness.

Year Founded: 1957

1231 National Alliance on Mental Illness: Florida
PO Box 961
Tallahassee, FL 32302
850-671-4445
E-mail: info@namiflorida.org
www.namiflorida.org

Ashley Grimes, Chapter President

Contains thirty-six affiliates in communities throughout Florida that provide education, advocacy, and support groups for individuals and families affected by mental illness. Seeks to help persons with mental health needs become productive members of the community.

Year Founded: 1984

1232 National Association of Social Workers Florida Chapter
1931 Dellwood Drive
Tallahassee, FL 32303
850-224-2400
800-352-6279
E-mail: Info.naswfl@socialworkers.org
www.naswfl.org

Billy Spivey, LCSW, ACSW, President
Tara Moser, LCSW, RPT-S, Vice President
Paula Lupton, LCSW, Secretary
Tanya Fookes, LCSW, ACSW, Treasurer

NASW Florida is a membership organization for professional social workers in Florida. NASWFL provides: continuing education, information and resources, and advocacy for employment and legislation.

Year Founded: 1955

Georgia

1233 Georgia Parent Support Network
1381 Metropolitan Parkway
Atlanta, GA 30310-4455
404-758-4500
800-832-8645
E-mail: info@gpsn.org
www.gpsn.org

Sue Smith, Chief Executive Officer
Brett Barton, Chief Operating Officer
John Zolkowski, Chief Financial Offccer

The Georgia Parent Support Network assists children with mental, emotional, and behavioral challenges and their families through support, education, and advocacy.

Year Founded: 1989

1234 Grady Health Systems: Behavioral Health Services
10 Park Place
Atlanta, GA 30303
404-616-1000
www.gradyhealth.org

Grady Behavioral Health Services focuses on the treatment of individuals with chronic and mental illnesses in Fulton and DeKalb counties and strives to offer quality, evidence-based mental health and substance abuse care for clients. Grady provides a full range of adult behavioral health services, including peer support, individual and group treatment, and medication clinics, and conducts research with the goal of advancing the treatment of clients with trauma and mental illness.

Year Founded: 1892

1235 National Alliance on Mental Illness: Georgia
4120 Presidential Pkwy
Suite 200
Atlanta, GA 30340
770-234-0855
E-mail: programs@namiga.org
www.namiga.org

Ron Koon, Chapter President
Kim H. Jones, Chapter Executive Director

Local chapter of the National Alliance on Mental Illness, an organization dedicated to raising awareness on mental health and providing support and education for Americans affected by mental illness. Mission is to help consumers and families share information about services, care providers, and ways to cope with the challenges of mental illness.

1236 Together Georgia
5456 Peachtree Blvd
Suite 521
Atlanta, GA 30341
404-572-6170
E-mail: office@togetherga.net
www.togetherga.net

Juanita Stedman, Executive Director
Claire Wood, Deputy Director

Sally Buchanan, President
Nikki Raymond, Vice President

Together Georgia, formerly the Georgia Association of Homes and Services for Children, is an organization consisting of child and family service providers dedicated to caring for children who have experienced risk and neglect. Together Georgia provides staff training and information, organizes regular meetings for members, and strives for a positive future for Georgia's children and families.

Hawaii

1237 Hawaii Families As Allies
PO Box 1971
Aiea, HI 96701
808-682-1511
E-mail: hfaa@hfaa.net
www.www.hifamilies.org

Support and outreach group for parents with children who have mental disorders.

Year Founded: 1986

1238 Mental Health America of Hawai'i
1136 Union Mall
Suite 208
Honolulu, HI 96813
808-521-1846
800-753-6879
www.mentalhealthhawaii.org

Ryan Kusumoto, President
Bryan Talisayan, Executive Director
Mestisa Gass, Program Director
Jere Medeiros, Operations Manager

An affiliate of Mental Health America, which is a community-based non-profit organization committed to enabling the mental wellness of all Americans. MHA advocates for greater access to quality health services and seeks to educate individuals on identifying symptoms, as well as intervention and prevention.

1239 National Alliance on Mental Illness: Hawaii
770 Kapiolani Boulevard
Suite 613
Honolulu, HI 96813
808-591-1297
E-mail: info@namihawaii.org
www.namihawaii.org

Anisa Wiseman, Chapter Program Director

Local chapter of the National Alliance on Mental Illness, an organization dedicated to raising awareness on mental health and providing support and education for Americans affected by mental illness. Mission is to help consumers and families share information about services, care providers, and ways to cope with the challenges of mental illness.

Idaho

1240 National Alliance on Mental Illness: Idaho
1985 E 25th Street
Idaho Falls, ID 83404
208-242-7430
E-mail: idahonami@gmail.com
www.idahonami.org

Christina Cernasnsky, Chapter President
Beth Markley, Chapter Executive Director

Local chapter of the National Alliance on Mental Illness, an organization dedicated to raising awareness on mental health and providing support and education for Americans affected by mental illness. Mission is to help consumers and families share information about services, care providers, and ways to cope with the challenges of mental illness.

Year Founded: 1991

Illinois

1241 Allendale Association
PO Box 1088
Grand Avenue & Offield Drive
Lake Villa, IL 60046
847-356-2351
www.allendale4kids.org

Jason Keeler, LCSW, President/CEO
Chris Schrantz, Senior VP, Finance/CFO
Connie Borucki, Senior VP, HR/COO
Jennifer Stiemsma, VP, Specialized Edu. Services

The Allendale Association is a private, non-profit organization committed to providing quality care, education, treatment, support, and advocacy for troubled children in need of intervention and their families.

Year Founded: 1897

1242 Baby Fold
108 East Willow Street
Normal, IL 61761
309-454-1770
www.thebabyfold.org

Dianne Schultz, President and CEO
Aimee Beam, VP, Development/Public Relations
Dr. Rob Lusk, Clinical Director
Kathy Kujawa, VP of Business Operations

The Baby Fold is an Illinois-based multi-service agency that provides residential, special education, child welfare, and family support services to children with emotional and behavioral disabilities and autism spectrum disorders, as well as at-risk children.

Year Founded: 1902

1243 Chaddock
205 South 24th Street
Quincy, IL 62301
217-222-0034
888-242-3625
www.chaddock.org

Debbie Reed, PhD, President and CEO
Matt Obert, Executive Director
Josh Carlson, Executive Director
Cory Powell, Director of Education

A faith-based, not-for-profit organization dedicated to supporting children and families and providing hope and healing. Chaddock offers educational and treatment services for children who have experienced abuse, neglect, or trauma, including child and adolescent residential treatment, independent living and group home programs, special education school, in-home intensive program, and foster care and adoption services.

Year Founded: 1853

1244 Chicago Child Care Society
5467 South University Avenue
Chicago, IL 60615

773-643-0452
E-mail: info@family-focus.org
www.cccsociety.org

Dara T Munson, MPA, Chief Executive Officer
Dottie Johnson, Chief Financial Officer
Dennis Abboud, Chairperson
Caragh DeLuca, Vice-Chairperson

Chicago Child Care Society strives to meet the needs of vulnerable children and their families through the provision of community-based education and social service programs. CCCS provides vulnerable children with services and opportunities designed to help enable their physical, mental, and social development. CCCS programs focus on a range of issues, including teen pregnancy, poverty, and inadequate child healthcare. The Chicago Child Care Society was founded in 1849 and is the oldest child welfare agency in Illinois.

Year Founded: 1849

1245 Children's Home Association of Illinois
2130 North Knoxville Avenue
Peoria, IL 61603
309-685-1047
www.chail.org

Matt George, Chief Executive Officer
Melissa Riddle, President and CFO
Cindy Hoffman, Executive Vice President
Tegan Camden, VP, Behavioral Health

Not-for-profit, multiple program and social service organization dedicated to providing community-based counseling, education and support programs for children and families in the Peoria area.

Year Founded: 1866

1246 Coalition of Illinois Counselor Organizations
PO Box 1086
Northbrook, IL 60065-1086
815-787-0515
E-mail: myimhca@gmail.com
www.cico-il.org

Daniel Stasi, Consultant

The Coalition of Illinois Counselor Organizations represents and advocates for counselors and psychologists and their clients in Illinois, with focus on government branches and agencies, relevant segments of the private sector, and mental health organizations.

1247 Family Service Association of Greater Elgin Area
1140 North McLean Boulevard
Suite 1
Elgin, IL 60123
847-695-3680
www.fsaelgin.org

Bernadette May, Executive Director
Janeth Barba, Director of Clinical Services
Tameron Keeffe, Director of Crisis Services
Nicole Eschenbach, Manager of Crisis Services

A private, non-profit agency, Family Service Association has served children, adolescents, and adults in the Greater Elgin area since 1931. The Family Service Association provides a range of counseling services and programs, including family support, outpatient therapy, school-based therapy and screening assessments.

Year Founded: 1931

1248 Human Resources Development Institute
222 South Jefferson Street
Chicago, IL 60661
312-441-9009
E-mail: info@hrdi.org
www.hrdi.org

Eugene Humphrey, Executive Director
Tammie Morris, Deputy Director
Deborah Parnell, Director Clinical Strategies

Community-based behavioral healthcare organization. Human Resources Development Institute seeks to provide quality community and behavioral health care services and programs in the areas of mental health, disabilities, alcohol and substance abuse, family services, community health, and youth prevention.

Year Founded: 1974

1249 Illinois Alcoholism and Drug Dependence Association
937 South Second Street
Springfield, IL 62704
217-528-7335
E-mail: iadda@iadda.org
www.iadda.org

Sara Howe, Chief Executive Officer

The Illinois Alcoholism and Drug Dependence Association represents over 50 substance abuse and mental health prevention and treatment agencies, as well as individual members who are interested in the field of substance abuse. IADDA advocates for sound public policies that address behavioral health issues. The goal of the IADDA is to work towards a healthier society with accessibility to mental health and addiction treatments, and reduced occurrences in substance use and mental disorders.

Year Founded: 1967

1250 Little City Foundation (LCF)
1760 W Algonquin Road
Palatine, IL 60067
847-358-5510
E-mail: info@littlecity.org
www.littlecity.org

Shawn Jeffers, Executive Director
Chris Taylor, Chief Finance/Admin. Officer
Bill Brennan, Dir. of Facilities/Maintenance

The mission of Little City Foundation is to provide quality services for children and adults with intellectual and developmental disabilities and to offer opportunities that will enable them to lead productive and fulfilling lives.

Year Founded: 1959

1251 Mental Health America of Illinois
1218 N. Grove Ave
Oak Park, IL 60302
312-368-9070
E-mail: becky@mhai.org
www.mhai.org

Ray Connor, President & Executive Director
Joseph Troiani, PhD, CADC, Vice President
Cindy Summers, Treasurer
Rebecca Ogrodny, MEd, Secretary

An affiliate of Mental Health America, which is a community-based non-profit organization committed to enabling the mental wellness of all Americans. MHA advocates for greater access to quality health services and seeks to edu-cate individuals on identifying symptoms, as well as intervention and prevention.

Year Founded: 1909

1252 Metropolitan Family Services
101 North Wacker Drive
17th Floor
Chicago, IL 60606
312-986-4000
E-mail: contactus@metrofamily.org
www.metrofamily.org

Matthew W. Walch, Chair
Amanda Amert, Vice Chair

Metropolitan Family Services provides programs and services designed to help families across Chicago, DuPage County, Evanston/Skokie and the southwest suburbs achieve stability and self-sufficiency.

Year Founded: 1857

1253 National Alliance on Mental Illness: Illinois
1010 Lake St.
Suite 200
Oak Park, IL 60301-1132
217-522-1403
800-346-4572
E-mail: nami@namiillinois.org
www.namiillinois.org

John Schladweiler, Chapter President
Andy Wade, Chapter Executive Director

Local chapter of the National Alliance on Mental Illness, an organization dedicated to raising awareness on mental health and providing support and education for Americans affected by mental illness. Mission is to help consumers and families share information about services, care providers, and ways to cope with the challenges of mental illness.

Year Founded: 1984

Indiana

1254 Indiana Resource Center for Autism (IRCA)
2810 E Discovery Parkway
Bloomington, IN 47408
812-855-6508
TTY: 812-855-9396
E-mail: prattc@indiana.edu
www.www.iidc.indiana.edu/irca/index.html

Cathy Pratt, PhD, BCBA, Center Director

The Indiana Resource Center for Autism focuses on providing communities, organizations, and families with the information and skills to support children and individuals with autism, Asperger's syndrome, and other pervasive developmental disorders. The IRCA conducts outreach training and research, disseminates information about autism spectrum disorders, and encourages communication among professionals and families concerned with autism.

1255 Mental Health America of Indiana
1431 N Delaware Street Indianapolis, IN 46202
317-638-3501
E-mail: info@mhai.net
www.mhai.net

Stephen C. McCaffrey, JD, President & CEO
David Berman, MPH, MPA, Vice President of Harm Dev.

An affiliate of Mental Health America, which is a community-based non-profit organization committed to enabling the mental wellness of all Americans. MHA advocates for greater access to quality health services and seeks to educate individuals on identifying symptoms, as well as intervention and prevention.

1256 National Alliance on Mental Illness: Indiana
921 E 86th Street
Suite 130
Indianapolis, IN 46240
317-925-9399
800-677-6442
E-mail: info@namiindiana.org
www.namiindiana.org

Linh Preston, Chapter President
Barbara Thompson, Chapter Executive Director

Local chapter of the National Alliance on Mental Illness, an organization dedicated to raising awareness on mental health and providing support and education for Americans affected by mental illness. Mission is to help consumers and families share information about services, care providers, and ways to cope with the challenges of mental illness.

Iowa

1257 Mental Health America of Dubuque County
PO Box 0283 Dubuque, IA 52004-0283
563-580-7718
E-mail: info@mhadbq.org
www.mhadbq.org

Sue Whitty, President
Heather Heins, Vice-President
Stephanie Mettille, Treasurer

An affiliate of Mental Health America, which is a community-based non-profit organization committed to enabling the mental wellness of all Americans. MHA advocates for greater access to quality health services and seeks to educate individuals on identifying symptoms, as well as intervention and prevention.

1258 National Alliance on Mental Illness: Iowa
3839 Merle Hay Road
Suite 229
Des Moines, IA 50310
515-254-0417
E-mail: info@namiiowa.org
www.namiiowa.org

Jim Romar, Chapter President
Peggy Huppert, Chapter Executive Director

Local chapter of the National Alliance on Mental Illness, an organization dedicated to raising awareness on mental health and providing support and education for Americans affected by mental illness. Mission is to help consumers and families share information about services, care providers, and ways to cope with the challenges of mental illness.

Year Founded: 1984

Kansas

1259 Keys for Networking: Kansas Parent Information & Resource Center
900 South Kansas Avenue
Suite 301
Topeka, KS 66612
785-233-8732
E-mail: info@keys.org
www.www.keys.org

A non-profit organization offering assistance to families in Kansas whose children have behavioral, educational, emotional, and substance abuse challenges. Mission is to provide parents and youth in Kansas with services, information, resources, support, education, and training.

1260 Mental Health America of South Central Kansas, Inc.
555 N Woodlawn Street
Suite 3105
Wichita, KS 67208
316-685-1821
www.www.mhasck.org

Brendan O'Bryhim, Chairman
Arnold Hudspeth, Treasurer
Charles McClellan, Secretary
Mary Jones, LCMFT, LCAC, President/CEO

An affiliate of Mental Health America, which is a community-based non-profit organization committed to enabling the mental wellness of all Americans. MHA advocates for greater access to quality health services and seeks to educate individuals on identifying symptoms, as well as intervention and prevention.

Year Founded: 1957

1261 National Alliance on Mental Illness: Kansas
1801 SW Wanamaker Road
Unit G6
Topeka, KS 66604
785-233-0755
800-539-2660
E-mail: resources@namikansas.org
www.namikansas.org

David Schmitt, Chapter President
Sherrie Vaughn, Chapter Executive Director

Local chapter of the National Alliance on Mental Illness, an organization dedicated to raising awareness on mental health and providing support and education for Americans affected by mental illness. Mission is to help consumers and families share information about services, care providers, and ways to cope with the challenges of mental illness.

Kentucky

1262 Beacon Health Options
200 State Street
Boston, MA 02109
888-204-5581
www.beaconhealthoptions.com

Glenn MacFarlane, President
Kelly Walsh, Chief of Staff to the President
Robert Flowe, Chief Financial Officer
Maureen Tarpinian, Chief Operating Officer

Beacon Health Options combines two behavioral health companies, Beacon Health Strategies and ValueOptions. Seeks to improve the quality and delivery of behavioral health care for regional health plans, employers, and federal, state and local governments. Provides behavioral health care services and programs in employee assistance and work and life support.

1263 Children's Alliance
420 Capital Avenue
Frankfort, KY 40601
502-875-3399
www.childrensallianceky.org

Michelle Sanborn, President
Melissa Muse, Director of Member Services
Kathy Adams, Director of Public Policy

Mission is to enhance the well-being of at-risk children and families in Kentucky. Engages in public policy advocacy and promotes the provision of quality and effective services to children and families.

Year Founded: 1961

1264 KY-SPIN (Kentucky Special Parent Involvement Network)
10301-B Deering Road
Louisville, KY 40272
502-937-6894
800-525-7746
E-mail: spininc@kyspin.com
www.kyspin.com

Rhonda Logsdon, Executive Director

Non-profit organization dedicated to helping individuals with disabilities and their families improve their quality of life through information, resources, programs, training opportunities, and support networks.

Year Founded: 1988

1265 Kentucky Partnership for Families and Children
600 Teton Trail
Frankfort, KY 40601
502-875-1320
800-369-0533
www.kypartnership.org

Non-profit organization focused on the needs of children and youth with behavioral health challenges and their families. Works to enhance the quality of services, effect policy changes, and educate legislators about emotional disabilities in children.

Year Founded: 1998

1266 Kentucky Psychiatric Medical Association
649 Charity Court
Suite 13
Frankfort, KY 40601
502-695-4843
www.kypsych.org

A non-profit association of physicians specializing in the treatment of mental illnesses and substance use disorders.

1267 Mental Health America of Kentucky
1588 Leestown Rd
Ste. 130 #279
Lexington, KY 40511
859-684-7778
E-mail: mhaky@mhaky.org
www.www.mhaky.org

Mary Malone, RN, BSN, MA, President
Sheila Schuster, PhD, Vice President
Kyle Melloan, JD, Treasurer
Marcie Timmerman, Executive Director

An affiliate of Mental Health America, which is a community-based non-profit organization committed to enabling the mental wellness of all Americans. MHA advocates for greater access to quality health services and seeks to educate individuals on identifying symptoms, as well as intervention and prevention.

1268 National Alliance on Mental Illness: Kentucky
201 Mechanic Street
Lexington, KY 40507
859-225-6264
888-388-4164
E-mail: namiky@namiky.org
www.namiky.org

Melony Cunningham, Chapter Executive Director

NAMI Kentucky is a non-profit, self-help organization and the state chapter of the National Alliance on Mental Illness, an organization dedicated to improving the quality of life for mentally ill individuals and reducing the stigma associated with mental illness. NAMI Kentucky focuses on providing support, education, and advocacy for people with mental illnesses and their families.

1269 National Association of Social Workers: Kentucky Chapter
3070 Lake Crest Circle
Suite 400-155
Lexington, KY 40513
859-227-6587
E-mail: brosen.naswky@socialworkers.org
www.naswky.socialworkers.org

Lauren Barks, LCSW, President
Angela Anderson, MSW, CSW, 1st Vice President
Randy Stafford, MSW, CSW, 2nd Vice President
Erin Warfel, LCSW, Secretary

Membership organization representing professional social workers across Kentucky.

Louisiana

1270 Louisiana Federation of Families for Children's Mental Health
5627 Superior Drive
Suite A-2
Baton Rouge, LA 70816
985-276-4288

A parent-run organization focused on addressing the needs of children and youth with emotional, behavioral or mental challenges and their families. Works with parents to provide resources and advocate for improved mental health care for children in Louisiana.

Year Founded: 1991

1271 Mental Health America for Greater Baton Rouge
544 Colonial Drive Baton Rouge, LA 70806
225-929-7674
www.www.mhagbr.com

Melissa Silva, Executive Director

An affiliate of Mental Health America, which is a community-based non-profit organization committed to enabling the mental wellness of all Americans. MHA advocates for greater access to quality health services and seeks to educate individuals on identifying symptoms, as well as intervention and prevention.

1272 National Alliance on Mental Illness: Louisiana
PO Box 1509
Baton Rouge, LA 70821
225-291-6262
866-851-6264

E-mail: info@namilouisiana.org
www.namilouisiana.org

Antonio P.D. Carriere, Chapter President
LaShonda Williams, Chapter Executive Director

Local chapter of the National Alliance on Mental Illness, an organization dedicated to raising awareness on mental health and providing support and education for Americans affected by mental illness. Mission is to help consumers and families share information about services, care providers, and ways to cope with the challenges of mental illness.

Year Founded: 1984

Maine

1273 National Alliance on Mental Illness: Maine
52 Water Street
Hallowell, ME 04347
800-464-5767
E-mail: info@namimaine.org
www.namimaine.org

Michael Pooler, Chapter President
Linda Schreiber, Chapter Interim Executive Dir.

Local chapter of the National Alliance on Mental Illness, an organization dedicated to raising awareness on mental health and providing support and education for Americans affected by mental illness. Mission is to help consumers and families share information about services, care providers, and ways to cope with the challenges of mental illness.

Year Founded: 1977

Maryland

1274 Community Behavioral Health Association of Maryland: CBH
18 Egges Lane
Catonsville, MD 21228-4511
410-788-1865
E-mail: info@mdcbh.org
www.mdcbh.org

Shannon Hall, Executive Director
Lori Doyle, Public Policy Director
Lauren Grimes, Assistant Director

Professional association representing the network of community behavioral health providers operating in the public and private sectors in Maryland. Strives to improve the quality of care for individuals and families with mental illness, addiction and substance use problems.

1275 Maryland Psychiatric Research Center
55 Wade Avenue
Catonsville, MD 21228-4663
410-402-7666
www.www.mprc.umaryland.edu

The Maryland Psychiatric Research Center is a research center within the University of Maryland School of Medicine. The MPRC studies the causes and treatments of schizophrenia and related disorders, and provides treatments for patients with schizophrenia.

Year Founded: 1807

1276 Mental Health Association of Maryland
1301 York Road
Suite 505
Lutherville, MD 21093

443-901-1550
E-mail: info@mhamd.org
www.www.mhamd.org

Tim Santoni, President
Beatrice Rodgers, Vice President
Henry Harbin, MD, Secretary
Randall M. Lutz, Esq., Treasurer

An affiliate of Mental Health America, which is a community-based non-profit organization committed to enabling the mental wellness of all Americans. MHA advocates for greater access to quality health services and seeks to educate individuals on identifying symptoms, as well as intervention and prevention.

1277 National Alliance on Mental Illness: Maryland
10632 Little Patuxent Parkway
Suite 454
Columbia, MD 21044
410-884-8691
E-mail: info@namimd.org
www.namimd.org

Joe Ashworth, Chapter President
Denise Evans, Chapter First Vice President
Ton Gardeniers, Chapter Treasurer
Kate Farinholt, Chapter Executive Director

Local chapter of the National Alliance on Mental Illness, an organization dedicated to raising awareness on mental health and providing support and education for Americans affected by mental illness. Mission is to help consumers and families share information about services, care providers, and ways to cope with the challenges of mental illness.

1278 National Association of Social Workers: Maryland Chapter
5750 Executive Drive
Suite 100
Baltimore, MD 21228-1700
410-788-1066
E-mail: nasw.md@verizon.net
www.nasw-md.org

Barbie Johnson-Lewis, President
Gail Martin, Vice President

The National Association of Social Workers, Maryland Chapter supports the social work profession and the professional development of social workers, and advocates for just social policies and professional social work standards.

1279 National Federation of Families for Children's Mental Health
15800 Crabbs Branch Way
Suite 300
Rockville, MD 20855
240-403-1901
E-mail: ffcmh@ffcmh.org
www.ffcmh.org

Lynda Gargan, PhD, Executive Director
Gail Cormier, Project Director
Leann Sherman, Project Coordinator

The National Federation of Families for Children's Mental Health is a national organization focused on advocating for the rights of children affected by mental health challenges, assisting family-run organizations across the nation, and ensuring that children and families concerned with mental health have access to services.

Year Founded: 1989

1280 Sheppard Pratt
6501 N Charles Street
Baltimore, MD 21204
410-938-3800
E-mail: info@sheppardpratt.org
www.www.sheppardpratt.org

Harsh K. Trivedi, MD, MBA, President & CEO
Gregory Gattman, FACHE, Vice President & COO
Jeffrey Grossi, JD, Chief of Government Relations
Thomas D. Hess, MBA, MEd, Chief of Staff

Sheppard Pratt is dedicated to improving community healthcare in Maryland by offering mental health, addiction, and special education services.

Year Founded: 1853

Massachusetts

1281 Behavioral Health Clinics and Trauma Services
Justice Resource Institute
160 Gould Street
Suite 300
Needham, MA 02494-2300
781-559-4900
www.jri.org

Andy Pond, MSW, MAT, President
Mia DeMArco, MPA, Chief Operating Officer
Bisser Dokov, MBA, Chief Financial Officer
Roody Herold, MBA, MAUML, Chief Information Officer

Provides outpatient mental health services for children and families with developmental disabilities, behavioral and emotional problems, and medical complications. Services include in-home and outpatient therapies, mentoring services, in-home behavioral support, parent and caregiver support, and education, and mental health evaluation and consultation services to juvenile courts.

Year Founded: 1973

1282 Bridgewell
10 Dearborn Road
Peabody, MA 01960
781-593-1088
E-mail: info@bridgewell.org
www.bridgewell.org

Chris Tuttle, President and CEO
Elaine White, Chief Operating Officer
Kenneth C. Halkin, MBA, Chief Financial Officer
Jeff Bickford, MBA, CSM, Chief Information Officer

Private, non-profit corporation that provides services and support for persons with developmental and psychiatric disabilities. Services offered include residential services, behavioral health services, employment training, affordable housing, transitional homeless services, and substance abuse and addiction services.

Year Founded: 1958

1283 CASCAP
231 Somerville Avenue
Somerville, MA 02143
617-492-5559
www.cascap.org

Cascap Inc. seeks to assist underserved and disadvantaged members of the community and improve their quality of life. Provides a range of clinical, residential, and educational services for disabled, impoverished, or elderly individuals.

Year Founded: 1973

1284 Depression and Bipolar Support Alliance of Boston
115 Mill Street
PO Box 102
Belmont, MA 02478
617-855-2795
E-mail: info@dbsaboston.org
www.dbsaboston.netfirms.com

Lillian Cravotta-Crouch, President
Peter Liberman, Treasurer
Mary Johnston, Secretary

DBSA-BOSTON is a non-profit organization dedicated to helping people with psychiatric illnesses lead healthy lives.

1285 Jewish Family and Children's Service
1430 Main Street
Waltham, MA 02451
781-647-5327
E-mail: info@jfcsboston.org
www.jfcsboston.org

Gail Schulman, Chief Executive Officer
Andrew Pearlstein, Board President
Elayne Weinstein, Chief Financial Officer
Karen Silverman, Chief Marketing Officer

The Jewish Family & Children's Service supports families and individuals through the provision of health care programs based upon Jewish traditions of social responsibility, compassion, and respect for all community members. JF&CS assists all persons in need of care, with particular focus on vulnerable populations such as children and adults with disabilities or mental illness, seniors, and people experiencing domestic abuse, hunger, or financial crisis.

1286 Massachusetts Association for Mental Health (MAMH)
50 Federal Street
6th Floor
Boston, MA 02110
617-742-7452
E-mail: info@mhamd.org
www.www.mamh.org

Danna Mauch, PhD, President & CEO
Robert Fleischner, JD, Senior Consultant

An affiliate of Mental Health America, which is a community-based non-profit organization committed to enabling the mental wellness of all Americans. MHA advocates for greater access to quality health services and seeks to educate individuals on identifying symptoms, as well as intervention and prevention.

Year Founded: 1913

1287 Massachusetts Behavioral Health Partnership
1000 Washington Street
Suite 310
Boston, MA 02118-5002
617-790-4000
800-495-0086
TTY: 877-509-6981
www.masspartnership.com

Sharon Hanson, Chief Executive Officer
Chad Muller, MBA, MSF, Vice President/Finance Director
Russell Kopp, CPA, MBA, Chief Financial Officer

The Massachusetts Behavioral Health Partnership provides medical and behavioral health care for MassHealth Members who select the Division's Primary Care Clinician Plan, as well as children in state custody.

Year Founded: 1996

1288 National Alliance on Mental Illness: Massachusetts

331 Montvale Avenue
2nd Floor
Woburn, MA 01801
617-580-8541
E-mail: info@namimass.org
www.namimass.org

Annabel Lane, Chapter President

Local chapter of the National Alliance on Mental Illness, an organization dedicated to raising awareness on mental health and providing support and education for Americans affected by mental illness. Mission is to help consumers and families share information about services, care providers, and ways to cope with the challenges of mental illness.

Year Founded: 1979

1289 National Association for Behavioral Healthcare (NABH)

900 17th Street NW
Suite 420
Washington, DC 20006
202-393-6700
E-mail: nabh@nabh.org
www.www.nabh.org

Matt J. Peterson, Board Chair
Shawn Coughlin, President & CEO
Jessica Zigmond, Director of Communications
Maria Merlie, Director of Operations

The National Association for Behavioral Heatlhcare (NABH) is dedicated to promoting community-based mental health and substance abuse services, advocating for public policy changes, and addressing issues surrounding mental health and addiction treatment services.

Year Founded: 1933

1290 Parent Professional Advocacy League

77 Rumford Ave
Waltham, MA 02453
866-815-8122
E-mail: info@ppal.net
www.ppal.net

Grassroots family organization providing support, education, publications, and advocacy for children with mental health needs and their families.

Michigan

1291 Association for Children's Mental Health

6017 W. St. Joe Highway
Suite 200
Lansing, MI 48917
517-372-4016
888-226-4543
www.acmh-mi.org

Kelly Gluszewski, President
Beverly Schumer, Treasurer
Jane Shank, Executive Director
Terri Henrizi, Education Coordinator

Michigan-based non-profit organization serving families of children and youth with emotional, behavioral, or mental health needs. Provides information, support, resources, referrals, advocacy, and networking and leadership opportunities for youth.

Year Founded: 1989

1292 Borgess Behavioral Health

1521 Gull Road
Kalamazoo, MI 49048
269-226-7000
www.healthcare.ascension.org

Offers patients and families a wide array of services to address their mental health concerns.

1293 Holy Cross Children's Services

1030 North River Rd.
Saginaw, MI 48609
989-696-3557
E-mail: info@hccsnet.org
www.holycrossservices.org

Holy Cross Children's Services is a private, not-for-profit child and family services provider based in Michigan. The mission of Holy Cross Children's Services is to assist children and adults in leading productive and healthy lives.

Year Founded: 1948

1294 Macomb County Community Mental Health

19800 Hall Road
Clinton Twp, MI 48038
855-996-2264
www.mccmh.net

John Kinch, Executive Director
Jim Losey, Deputy Director
Norma Josef, MD, Medical Director
Herbert Wendt, Director, Finance

Offers a range of mental health treatment and support services for individuals affected by mental illness, developmental disabilities, and substance use disorders, and seeks to advance their recovery, independence, and self-sufficiency.

1295 Mental Health Association in Michigan (MHAM)

1100 West Saginaw
Suite 1-1B
Lansing, MI 48901
517-898-3907
www.www.mha-mi.com

Marianne Huff, President and CEO
Matthew Hudkins, Operations Manager
Arlene Gorelick, MPH, Board Chair
Ben Robinson, Vice Chairperson

MHAM advocates for greater access to quality health services and seeks to educate individuals on identifying symptoms, as well as intervention and prevention.

Year Founded: 1937

1296 National Alliance on Mental Illness: Michigan

401 South Washington
Lansing, MI 48933
517-485-4049
E-mail: info@namimi.org
www.namimi.org

Steve Slayton, Chapter President

Local chapter of the National Alliance on Mental Illness, an organization dedicated to raising awareness on mental health and providing support and education for Americans affected by mental illness. Mission is to help consumers and families share information about services, care providers, and ways to cope with the challenges of mental illness.
Year Founded: 1979

1297 Southwest Solutions
5716 Michigan Avenue
Suite 3000
Detroit, MI 48210
313-481-3102
www.swsol.org

Sean de Four, President and CEO
Michelle Sherman, Chief Operating Officer
Stephanie Miller, Chair
Mark Lezotte, Vice Chair

Southwest Solutions provides human development, economic development, and community engagement programs for individuals living with mental illness. Southwest seeks to help marginalized persons build meaningful futures.
Year Founded: 1970

1298 Woodlands Behavioral Healthcare Network
960 M-60 East
Cassopolis, MI 49031
269-445-2451
800-323-0335
www.woodlandsbhn.org

Tim Smith, Executive Director
Provides community behavioral health services.

Minnesota

1299 Mental Health America Minnesota
2233 University Avenue W
Suite 200
St. Paul, MN 55114
651-493-6634
800-862-1799
E-mail: info@mentalhealthmn.org
www.www.mentalhealthmn.org

Shannah Mulvihill, MA, CFRE, Executive Director
Bethany Gladhill, Business Manager
Holly Raab, Program Manager
Patrick Rhone, President

An affiliate of Mental Health America, which is a community-based non-profit organization committed to enabling the mental wellness of all Americans. MHA advocates for greater access to quality health services and seeks to educate individuals on identifying symptoms, as well as intervention and prevention.
Year Founded: 1939

1300 NASW Minnesota Chapter
PO Box 44323
Eden Prairie, MN 55344
651-293-1935
888-293-6279
E-mail: admin.naswmn@socialworkers.org
www.naswmn.socialworkers.org

Jenn Hamrick Vander Woude, President
Angelo Flowers, President-Elect
Dr. Karen Goodenough, Executive Director

NASW-MN is the state chapter of the National Association of Social Workers, a membership organization representing the interests of professional social workers. The mission of NASW-MN is to advance and promote the profession of social work, support the professional growth of its members, and advocate for clients through the promotion of social policies.

1301 National Alliance on Mental Illness: Minnesota
1919 University Avenue W
Suite 400
Saint Paul, MN 55104
651-645-2948
888-626-4435
E-mail: namihelps@namimn.org
www.namimn.org

Mariah C. Ownes, Chapter President
Sue Abderholden, Chapter Executive Director

Local chapter of the National Alliance on Mental Illness, an organization dedicated to raising awareness on mental health and providing support and education for Americans affected by mental illness. Mission is to help consumers and families share information about services, care providers, and ways to cope with the challenges of mental illness.
Year Founded: 1976

1302 North American Training Institute (NATI)
314 West Superior Street
Suite 508
Duluth, MN 55802
218-722-1503
888-989-9234
E-mail: info@nati.org
www.nati.org

The North American Training Institute is a not-for-profit organization based in Minnesota. NATI's mission is to promote research and professional training about gambling addiction. NATI provides resources and services for individuals at risk of developing a gambling addiction, particularly adolescents.
Year Founded: 1988

1303 PACER Center
8161 Normandale Boulevard
Bloomington, MN 55437
952-838-9000
800-537-2237
www.pacer.org

Paula F. Goldberg, Co-Founder & Executive Director

PACER provides information, training, and assistance to parents of children and young adults with all disabilities (physical, learning, cognitive, emotional, and health). Its mission is to help improve the quality of life for young people with disabilities and their families.
Year Founded: 1977

Mississippi

1304 Mental Health Association of South Mississippi (Mental Health America)
4803 Harrison Circle Gulfport, MS 39507
228-864-6274
E-mail: info@msmentalhealth.org
www.www.msmentalhealth.org

Eric Oliver, President
Liz Hoop, Vice President
Kay Daneault, Executive Director
Kimberly Barta, Director of Programs

An affiliate of Mental Health America, which is a community-based non-profit organization committed to enabling the mental wellness of all Americans. MHA advocates for greater access to quality health services and seeks to educate individuals on identifying symptoms, as well as intervention and prevention.

1305 National Alliance on Mental Illness: Mississippi
2618 Southerland Street
Suite 100
Jackson, MS 39216
601-899-9058
800-357-0388
E-mail: stateoffice@namims.org
www.namims.org

Mary Harrington, Chapter President
Sitaniel Johnson Wimbley, Chapter Executive Director

Local chapter of the National Alliance on Mental Illness, an organization dedicated to raising awareness on mental health and providing support and education for Americans affected by mental illness. Mission is to help consumers and families share information about services, care providers, and ways to cope with the challenges of mental illness.

Year Founded: 1989

Missouri

1306 Depressive and Bipolar Support Alliance (DBSA)
55 E Jackson Blvd
Suite 490
Chicago, IL 60604
800-826-3632
E-mail: info@dbsalliance.org
www.dbsalliance.org

Michael Pollock, Chief Executive Officer
John Quinn, Chief Financial Officer

The Depression and Bipolar Support Alliance is the leading patient-directed national organization focusing on the most prevalent mental illnesses. The organization fosters an environment of understanding about the impact and management of these life threatening illnesses by providing up-to-date, scientifically based tools and information written in language the general public can understand.

Year Founded: 1985

1307 Mental Health America of Eastern Missouri
1905 S Grand Boulevard St. Louis, MO 63104
314-773-1399
www.www.mha-em.org

Suzanne King, President & CEO
Brittany Graham, LCSW, Chief Program Officer
LaDonna Haley, Chief Administrative Officer

An affiliate of Mental Health America, which is a community-based non-profit organization committed to enabling the mental wellness of all Americans. MHA advocates for greater access to quality health services and seeks to educate individuals on identifying symptoms, as well as intervention and prevention.

1308 Missouri Behavioral Health Council (MBHC)
221 Metro Drive
Jefferson City, MO 65109
573-634-4626
www.www.mobhc.org

Brent McGinty, President and CEO
Rachelle Glavin, VP of Clinical Initiatives
Chelsea Hughes, Director of Administration
Mark Shwartz, Director of Govt. Affairs

The Missouri Coalition for Community Behavioral Healthcare seeks to improve access to mental health services for all residents of Missouri.

Year Founded: 1963

1309 Missouri Institute of Mental Health
4633 World Parkway Circle
St. Louis, MO 63134-3115
314-516-8400
E-mail: info@mimh.edu
www.mimh.edu

The Missouri Institute of Mental Health is a health services research organization providing professional training, research, program evaluation, policy development, and community outreach to the Missouri Department of Mental Health, as well as state agencies, service provider agencies, and other organizations and individuals pursuing information on mental health and related issues.

Year Founded: 1962

1310 National Alliance on Mental Illness: Missouri
3405 West Truman Boulevard
Suite 102
Jefferson City, MO 65109
573-634-7727
800-374-2138
E-mail: info@namimissouri.org
www.namimissouri.org

Debora Biggs, Chapter President
Gena Terlizzi, Chapter Executive Director

Local chapter of the National Alliance on Mental Illness, an organization dedicated to raising awareness on mental health and providing support and education for Americans affected by mental illness. Mission is to help consumers and families share information about services, care providers, and ways to cope with the challenges of mental illness.

Year Founded: 1985

Montana

1311 Mental Health America of Montana
PO Box 88
Bozeman, MT 59771
406-587-7774
E-mail: genea@mhaofmt.org
www.www.mhaofmt.org

Dan Aune, President
Casey Cote, Treasurer

An affiliate of Mental Health America, which is a community-based non-profit organization committed to enabling the mental wellness of all Americans. MHA advocates for greater access to quality health services and seeks to educate individuals on identifying symptoms, as well as intervention and prevention.

Year Founded: 1948

1312 National Alliance on Mental Illness: Montana
1331 Helena Ave
Helena, MT 59601
406-443-7871
E-mail: colleen@namimt.org
www.namimt.org

Matt Kuntz, Chapter Executive Director

Local chapter of the National Alliance on Mental Illness, an organization dedicated to raising awareness on mental health and providing support and education for Americans affected by mental illness. Mission is to help consumers and families share information about services, care providers, and ways to cope with the challenges of mental illness.

Nebraska

1313 Mental Health America of Nebraska
1645 N Street
Suite A
Lincoln, NE 68508
402-441-4371
E-mail: info@mha-ne.org
www.www.mha-ne.org

Kent Mattson, Chair
Nichole Bogen, Vice Chair
Vanessa Emlich, Secretary
Kasey Parker, Executive Director

An affiliate of Mental Health America, which is a community-based non-profit organization committed to enabling the mental wellness of all Americans. MHA advocates for greater access to quality health services and seeks to educate individuals on identifying symptoms, as well as intervention and prevention.

Year Founded: 2001

1314 Mutual of Omaha's Health and Wellness Programs
833-719-1003
www.mutualofomaha.com

James T. Blackledge, Chairman/Chief Executive Officer
Jason Coyle, Chief Internal Auditor
Nancy Crawford, General Counsel
Tracy DeWald, Chief Risk Officer

Mutual of Omaha's Health and Wellness Programs provide assistance and professional support in a variety of areas including family concerns; depression/anxiety; gambling and other addictions; parenting issues; drug/alcohol abuse; grief issues and life changes.

Year Founded: 1910

1315 National Alliance on Mental Illness: Nebraska
6001 Dodge St
CEC 219
Omaha, NE 68182-0305
402-345-8101
800-950-6264
www.naminebraska.org

Keneth McCartney, Chapter President
Carrin Meadows, Chapter Interim Executive Dir.
Nancy Kelley, Chapter Vice President
Angie Schindler-Berg, Chapter Secretary

Local chapter of the National Alliance on Mental Illness, an organization dedicated to raising awareness on mental health and providing support and education for Americans affected by mental illness. Mission is to help consumers and families share information about services, care providers, and ways to cope with the challenges of mental illness.

1316 National Association of Social Workers: Nebraska Chapter
650 'J' Street
Suite 14
Lincoln, NE 68508
402-477-7344
www.naswne.socialworkers.org

Andrea Phillips, LCSW, LMHP, President
Jessica Kroeker, Vice President
Kate McDougall, LCSW,LIMHP, Secretary
Terry Werner, Executive Director

NASW-NE is an affiliate of the National Association of Social Workers, a membership organization representing professional social workers.

Year Founded: 1955

1317 Nebraska Department of Health and Human Services
301 Centennial Mall South
Lincoln, NE 68509
402-471-3121
800-833-7352
www.dhhs.ne.gov

Danette R. Smith, Chief Executive Officer
Larry Kahl, Chief Operating Officer
Bo Botelho, General Counsel

Mission is to assure the public that health-related practices provided by individuals, facilities and programs are safe, of acceptable quality, and that the cost of expanded services is justified by the need.

1318 Nebraska Family Support Network
3568 Dodge Street
Suite 2
Omaha, NE 68131
402-345-0791
E-mail: info@nefamilysupport.org
www.nefamilysupportnetwork.org

A family-goverened organization dedicated to providing mental health and social services in Nebraska.

1319 Parent to Parent of Omaha
Ollie Webb Center
1941 South 42nd Street
Suite 122
Omaha, NE 68105-2942
402-346-5220
www.olliewebbinc.org/parent-to-parent

Laurie Ackermann, Executive Director
David Ackermann, Education Coordinator
Tim McAreavey, President
Warren Miller, 1st Vice President

Consists of parents, professionals, and others who are interested in providing emotional and peer support to parents of children with disabilities. Offers a parent-matching program which matches new parents wih parents who have had sufficient experience and training. Publications: The Gazette, newsletter, published 6 times a year. Also has chapters in Arizona and limited other states.

Year Founded: 1971

Nevada

1320 National Alliance on Mental Illness: Nevada
100 N. Arlington Ave
Suite 360
Reno, NV 89501
775-440-5600
E-mail: info@naminevada.org
www.naminevada.org

Steve Shell, Chapter President
Tom McCourt, Chapter Vice President
Kat Miller, Chapter Secretary
Bob Seale, Chapter Treasurer

Local chapter of the National Alliance on Mental Illness, an organization dedicated to raising awareness on mental health and providing support and education for Americans affected by mental illness. Mission is to help consumers and families share information about services, care providers, and ways to cope with the challenges of mental illness.

1321 Nevada Principals' Executive Program
7211 W. Charleston Blvd.
Las Vegas, NV 89117
702-388-8899
800-216-5188
E-mail: pepinfo@nvpep.org
www.nvpep.org

Bryce Loveland, Chairperson
Kelly Wooldridge, Vice Chairperson
Rita Varney, Treasurer
Retta Dermody, Secretary

To strengthen and renew the knowledge, skills, and beliefs of public school leaders so that they might help improve the conditions for teaching and learning in schools and school districts.

Year Founded: 1995

New Hampshire

1322 Monadnock Family Services (MFS)
64 Main Street
Suite 201
Keene, NH 03431
603-357-4400
www.mfs.org

Brian Donovan, Chair
John Round, Treasurer
Aaron Moody, Secretary
Sharman Howe, Assistant Secretary

A nonprofit community mental health agency serving the mental health needs of children, youth and adults through counseling, support services, and programs in parent education, family support, youth development, and substance abuse prevention and treatment.

Year Founded: 1905

1323 National Alliance on Mental Illness: New Hampshire
85 North State Street
Concord, NH 03301
603-225-5359
800-242-6264
E-mail: info@naminh.org
www.naminh.org

Susan L. Stearns, Chapter Executive Director

Local chapter of the National Alliance on Mental Illness, an organization dedicated to raising awareness on mental health and providing support and education for Americans affected by mental illness. Mission is to help consumers and families share information about services, care providers, and ways to cope with the challenges of mental illness.

Year Founded: 1982

New Jersey

1324 Advocates for Children of New Jersey
35 Halsey Street
2nd Floor
Newark, NJ 07102
973-643-3876
E-mail: advocates@acnj.org
www.acnj.org

Cecilia Zalkind, President and CEO
Mary Coogan, Vice President

Advocates for Children of New Jersey is a statewide non-profit organization focused on advocating for the rights of children. ACNJ operates on behalf of children and families by collaborating with local, state and federal leaders to enact law and policy changes that will benefit the children of New Jersey. The mission of ACNJ is to raise awareness and to serve the needs of children through research, policy and strategic communications. ACNJ seeks to help children lead healthy, safe and educated lives so that they can become productive members of New Jersey's communities. ACNJ operates a children's legal resource center that serves to provide information on children and legal issues for parents, children, service providers, educators, attorneys and others.

Year Founded: 1847

1325 Disability Rights New Jersey
210 S Broad Street
3rd Floor
Trenton, NJ 08608
609-292-9742
800-922-7233
TTY: 609-633-7106
E-mail: advocate@drnj.org
www.disabilityrightsnj.org

Gwen Orlowski, Executive Director
Ken Boyden, Director of Development
Michael Brower, Legal Director
Cathy Coryat, Chief Financial Officer

Legal and non legal advocacy, information and referral, technical assistance and training, outreach and education in support of the human, civil, and legal rights of people with disabilities in New Jersey.

Year Founded: 1994

1326 Jewish Family Service of Atlantic and Cape May Counties
607 North Jerome Avenue
Margate, NJ 08402-1527
609-822-1108
www.jfsatlantic.org

Joel Caplan, PhD, President
Matthew Simpson, Vice President
Melissa Rosenblum, Esq., Vice President
Andrea Steinberg, LCSW, Chief Executive Officer

Multi-service family counseling agency committed to strengthening and preserving individual, family, and community well-being while following Jewish philosophy and values.

Year Founded: 1930

1327 Mental Health Association in New Jersey
673 Morris Avenue
Suite 100
Springfield, NJ 07081
973-571-4001
www.www.mhanj.org

An affiliate of Mental Health America, which is a community-based non-profit organization committed to enabling the mental wellness of all Americans. MHA advocates for greater access to quality health services and seeks to educate individuals on identifying symptoms, as well as intervention and prevention.

1328 National Alliance on Mental Illness: New Jersey
1562 Route 130
Brunswick, NJ 08902
866-626-4664
E-mail: info@naminj.org
www.naminj.org

Mark T. Williams, Chapter President
Meredith Masin Blount, Chapter Executive Director

Local chapter of the National Alliance on Mental Illness, an organization dedicated to raising awareness on mental health and providing support and education for Americans affected by mental illness. Mission is to help consumers and families share information about services, care providers, and ways to cope with the challenges of mental illness.

Year Founded: 1985

1329 New Jersey Association of Mental Health and Addiction Agencies
3635 Quakerbridge Road
Suite 35
Mercerville, NJ 08619
609-838-5488
E-mail: info@njamhaa.org
www.njamhaa.org

Susan Loughery, MBA, Chair
Jacques Hryshko, MS, LPC, Vice Chair
Anthony Comerford, PhD, Treasurer
Debra L. Wentz, PhD, President and CEO

The New Jersey Association of Mental Health and Addiction Agencies represents mental healthcare and substance use treatment providers serving New Jersey residents affected by mental illness or addictions and their families.

Year Founded: 1951

1330 New Jersey Psychiatric Association
208 Lenox Ave
#198
Westfield, NJ 07090
908-588-3540
E-mail: info@njpsychiatry.org
www.www.njpsychiatry.org

Ramond solhkhah, MD, President
Stephen Mateka, DO, President-Elect
Lauren Kaplan-Sagal, MD, Vice President
Kenan Osmanovic, MD, Secretary/Treasuer

A professional organization of about 100 physicians qualified by training and experience in the treatment of mental illness.

Year Founded: 1935

New Mexico

1331 National Alliance on Mental Illness: New Mexico
3900 Osuna Road NE
Albuquerque, NM 87109
505-260-0154
E-mail: info@naminewmexico.org
www.naminewmexico.org

Alicia Blasingame, Chapter Interim President
Gabrielle Dietrich, Chapter Interim Executive Dir.

Local chapter of the National Alliance on Mental Illness, an organization dedicated to raising awareness on mental health and providing support and education for Americans affected by mental illness. Mission is to help consumers and families share information about services, care providers, and ways to cope with the challenges of mental illness.

New York

1332 AspireHope NY, Inc.
25 W Steuben Street
Bath, NY 14810-1511
607-776-2164
E-mail: flpninc25@flpn.org
www.flpn.org

A parent-governed organization dedicated to adults and adolescents with emotional, behavioral, and mental disorders. Formerly the Finger Lakes Parent Network.

Year Founded: 1990

1333 Compeer
1179 Kenmore Avenue
Buffalo, NY 14217
716-883-3331
800-836-0475
E-mail: info@compeer.org
www.compeer.org

Ellen Daly, Chair
Michael Bogucki, Vice President
Gretchen Kelly, Secretary
Cheri Alvarez, Interim CEO

Nonprofit mental wellness organization. Develops a model program that matches volunteers and mentors with children and adults with mental health needs. Seeks to improve the quality of life for individuals and families with mental health challenges through support and inclusion.

Year Founded: 1973

1334 Families Together in New York State
737 Madison Avenue
Albany, NY 12208
518-432-0333
888-326-8644
E-mail: info@ftnys.org
www.ftnys.org

Paige Pierce, Chief Executive Officer
Geraldine Burton, President
Lynn Rogers, Vice President
Robin Nelson, Treasurer

Non-profit, parent-run organization that serves families of children and youth affected by social, emotional, and behavioral challenges through advocacy, information, referrals, public awareness, education, and training.

1335 Healthcare Association of New York State
1 Empire Drive
Rensselaer, NY 12144
518-431-7600
www.hanys.org

Bea Grause, RN, JD, President
Courtney Burke, COO/Chief Innovation Officer
Sandi Toll, General Counsel
Amy Nickson, Interim SVP, State Policy

Statewide healthcare association serving as the primary advocate for more than 550 non-profit and public hospitals, health systems, long-term care, home care, hospice, and other health care organizations throughout New York State.

1336 Mental Health America in New York State, Inc.
194 Washington Avenue
Suite 415
Albany, NY 12210
518-434-0439
E-mail: info@mhanys.org
www.mhanys.org

William T. Gettman, Jr. MPA, Chair of the Board
Keith Leahey, MSW, Vice-Chair/Secretary
James L. Stone, Treasurer
Glenn Liebman, CEO

An affiliate of Mental Health America, which is a community-based non-profit organization committed to enabling the mental wellness of all Americans. MHA advocates for greater access to quality health services and seeks to educate individuals on identifying symptoms, as well as intervention and prevention.

1337 Mental Health Association in Orange County Inc
73 James P. Kelly Way
Middletown, NY 10940
845-342-2400
E-mail: mha@mhaorangeny.com
www.mhaorangeny.com

Robert Gaydos, President
Elizabeth Franqui, Vice President
Angela Jo Henze, Executive Director
Neil J. Meyer, Treasurer

Seeks to promote the positive mental health and emotional well-being of Orange County residents, working towards reducing the stigma of mental illness, developmental disabilities, and providing support to victims of sexual assault and other crimes.

1338 National Alliance on Mental Illness: New York State
150 Broadway
Suite 406
Menands, NY 12204
518-462-2000
E-mail: info@naminys.org
www.naminys.org

Wendy Burch, Chapter Executive Director
Matthew Shapiro, Chapter Associate Director

Local chapter of the National Alliance on Mental Illness, an organization dedicated to raising awareness on mental health and providing support and education for Americans affected by mental illness. Mission is to help consumers and families share information about services, care providers, and ways to cope with the challenges of mental illness.

1339 National Association of Social Workers New York State Chapter
188 Washington Avenue
Albany, NY 12210
518-463-4741
E-mail: info.naswnys@socialworkers.org
www.naswnys.org

Michael Cappiello, LCSW-R, President
Victoria Rizzo, PhD, LCSW-R, President Elect
Nikita Banks, LMSW, VP and Chair of Diversity
Samantha Fletcher, PhD, MSW, Executive Director

The National Association of Social Workers is a membership association representing professional social workers. NASW New York State advocates for public policies that address health, welfare, and education issues involving individuals and families, continues the education of its members through workshops and seminars, and maintains professional standards within social work practice.

Year Founded: 1955

1340 New York Association of Psychiatric Rehabilitation Services
194 Washington Avenue
Suite 400
Albany, NY 12210
518-436-0008
www.nyaprs.org

Harvey Rosenthal, Chief Executive Officer
Len Statham, Chief Operating Officer

New York Association of Psychiatric Rehabilitation Services (NYAPRS) is a statewide coalition of New Yorkers who receive or provide mental health services. NYAPRS is committed to improving the quality and availability of services for individuals with psychiatric disabilities. NYAPRS promotes mental health recovery and rehabilitation and works to fight the discrimination that persons with psychiatric disabilities face both within the mental health system and in the larger community.

Year Founded: 1981

1341 Northeast Business Group on Health
80 Pine St.
29th Floor
New York, NY 10005
212-252-7440
E-mail: nebgh@nebgh.org
www.nebgh.org

Candice Sherman, CEO
Courtney Wilson-Myers, Vice President, Operations
Amy Tippett-Strangler, Senior Vice President
Jeanette Fuente, Director, Programs

The Northeast Business Group on Health is a not-for-profit coalition of providers, insurers, and organizations in New York, New Jersey, Connecticut and Massachusetts. The mission of NEBGH is to promote a value-based health care system by improving health care delivery and contributing to health care decisions.

1342 State University of New York at Stony Brook
Department of Psychiatry and Behavioral Health
Health Sciences Tower
T10-020
Stony Brook, NY 11794-8101
631-216-8527
E-mail: marc.halterman@stonybrookmedicine.edu
www.renaissance.stonybrookmedicine.edu/psychiatry/

Marc Halterman, MD, PhD, Interim Chairperson
Jeanete Buonora, Department Administrator

Conducts clinical and translational psychiatry research and
provides clinical services.

Year Founded: 1971

North Carolina

1343 Autism Society of North Carolina
5121 Kingdom Way
Suite 100
Raleigh, NC 27607
800-442-2762
E-mail: info@autismsociety-nc.org
www.autismsociety-nc.org

Chris Whitfield, Chair
Ron Howrigon, Vice Chair
Kristin Selby, 2nd Vice Chair
Tracey Sheriff, Chief Executive Officer

Committed to providing support for individuals within the
autism spectrum and their families through advocacy, training and education, and residential, recreational, vocational,
and community-based services.

Year Founded: 1970

1344 Mental Health America of Central Carolinas,
Inc.
3701 Latrobe Drive
Suite 140
Charlotte, NC 28211
704-365-3454
E-mail: mha@mhacentralcarolinas.org
www.mhaofcc.org

Heather McCullough, President
John Cheek, President-Elect
Timothy P. Beyer, CFA, Treasurer
Tiffany Morgan, Secretary

An affiliate of Mental Health America, which is a community-based non-profit organization committed to enabling
the mental wellness of all Americans. MHA advocates for
greater access to quality health services and seeks to educate individuals on identifying symptoms, as well as
intervention and prevention.

Year Founded: 1933

1345 National Alliance on Mental Illness: North
Carolina
309 West Millbrook Road
Suite 121
Raleigh, NC 27609
919-788-0801
800-451-9682
E-mail: mail@naminc.org
www.naminc.org

Judy Jenkins, Chapter President
Garry Crites, Chapter Executive Director

Local chapter of the National Alliance on Mental Illness,
an organization dedicated to raising awareness on mental
health and providing support and education for Americans
affected by mental illness. Mission is to help consumers
and families share information about services, care providers, and ways to cope with the challenges of mental illness.

1346 National Association of Social Workers: North
Carolina Chapter
412 Morson Street
PO Box 27582
Raleigh, NC 27601
919-828-9650
www.naswnc.org

Valerie Arendt, MSW, MPP, Executive Director
Hope Venetta, Director of Professional Dev.
Kristen Carter, Operations Manager
Seth Maid, MSW, Director of Membership & Comm.

NASW North Carolina is a state chapter of the National
Association of Social Workers, a membership organization
serving to promote and protect social workers and the social work profession. NASW aims to help improve the
well-being of families and individuals through work and
advocacy.

Year Founded: 1955

1347 North Carolina Mental Health Consumers'
Organization
916 Richardson Drive
Raleigh, NC 27603
919-819-6024

The North Carolina Mental Health Consumers' Organization is a non-profit organization providing support for individuals in North Carolina with mental illness through
advocacy, resources, and education.

Year Founded: 1989

North Dakota

1348 Mental Health America of North Dakota
PO Box 4106
Bismarck, ND 58502-4106
701-255-3692
www.mhand.org

Carlotta McCleary, Executive Director
Tom Regan, President
Marcia Hettich, Vice President
Siobhan Deppa, Secretary

An affiliate of Mental Health America, which is a community-based non-profit organization committed to enabling
the mental wellness of all Americans. MHA advocates for
greater access to quality health services and seeks to educate individuals on identifying symptoms, as well as
intervention and prevention.

Year Founded: 1952

1349 National Alliance on Mental Illness: North
Dakota ND
E-mail: naminorthdakota@gmail.com
www.nami.org

Local chapter of the National Alliance on Mental Illness,
an organization dedicated to raising awareness on mental
health and providing support and education for Americans
affected by mental illness. Mission is to help consumers
and families share information about services, care provid-

ers, and ways to cope with the challenges of mental illness. This organization is run soley by volunteers. Please allow for time for them to respond to emails.

1350 National Association of Social Workers: North Dakota Chapter
1120 College Drive, Suite 100
PO Box 1775
Bismarck, ND 58503
800-742-4089
E-mail: info.naswnd@socialworkers.org
www.naswnd.socialworkers.org

Alison Traynor, MPH, LSW, President
BevAnn Walth, Vice President
Amy Phillips, Secretary
Chapter Staff, Executive Director

NASW North Dakota is the state chapter of the National Association of Social Workers, an organization representing professional social workers. NASWND promotes the profession of social work and advocates for access to services for all.

1351 North Dakota Federation of Families for Children's Mental Health
523 N. 4th St.
Bismarck, ND 58501
701-222-3310
877-822-6287
E-mail: cmccleary@ndffcmh.com
www.ndffcmh.org

Carlotta McCleary, Executive Director
Robin Hoger, Executive Assistant

The North Dakota Federation of Families for Children's Mental Health is an advocacy organization working to meet the needs of children and youth with emotional, behavioral and mental challenges and their families.

Year Founded: 1994

Ohio

1352 Allwell Behavioral Health Services
2845 Bell Street
Zanesville, OH 43701
740-454-9766
E-mail: info@allwell.org
www.allwell.org

James McDonald, President and CEO
Daniel Carpenetti, Chief Operating Officer
Robert Montgomery, Chief Clinical Officer
Sue Ellen Foraker, Chief Financial Officer

Six County Inc. is a private not-for-profit community mental health service provider operating in Coshocton, Guernsey, Morgan, Muskingum, Noble and Perry counties. Provides traditional treatment services and specialized services. Counseling and support services include outpatient counseling services, medication management, 24-hour crisis intervention, employee assistance, residential services, and peer support.

1353 Mental Health America of Ohio
2323 W Fifth Avenue
Suite 160
Columbus, OH 43204
614-221-1441
E-mail: info@mhaohio.org
www.mhaohio.org

Kenton Beachy, MA, MPA, Executive Director
Tonya Fulwider, Associate Director

An affiliate of Mental Health America, which is a community-based non-profit organization committed to enabling the mental wellness of all Americans. MHA advocates for greater access to quality health services and seeks to educate individuals on identifying symptoms, as well as intervention and prevention.

Year Founded: 1956

1354 National Alliance on Mental Illness: Ohio
1225 Dublin Road
Suite 125
Columbus, OH 43215
614-224-2700
800-686-2646
E-mail: namiohio@namiohio.org
www.namiohio.org

Judge Joyce Campbell, Chapter President
Lovell Custard, Chapter First Vice President
Tom Standish, Chapter Treasurer
Janet Polzer, Chapter Secretary

Local chapter of the National Alliance on Mental Illness, an organization dedicated to raising awareness on mental health and providing support and education for Americans affected by mental illness. Mission is to help consumers and families share information about services, care providers, and ways to cope with the challenges of mental illness.

Year Founded: 1982

1355 National Association of Social Workers: Ohio Chapter
400 West Wilson Bridge Road
Suite 103
Worthington, OH 43085
614-461-4484
E-mail: info@naswoh.org
www.naswoh.org

Tiffany Lombardo, President
Chant, Meadows, Vice President
Bridget Branning, Secretary
Danielle Smith, MSW, MA, LSW, Executive Director

NASW Ohio represents the interests of professional social workers in Ohio. The mission of NASW Ohio is to strengthen the profession of social work, maintain social work professional standards, and advocate for equitable social policies.

1356 Ohio Children's Alliance
2600 Corporate Exchange Drive
Suite 180
Columbus, OH 43231
614-461-0014
www.www.ohiochildrensalliance.org

Mark M. Mecum, Chief Executive Officer
Karen Hill, COO/CFO
Sarah LaTourette, Chief Advocacy Officer
John Banchy, President

The Ohio Children's Alliance is an association of child and family service providers in Ohio. The mission of the association is to strengthen the quality of services for children, young adults, and families in Ohio through efforts in policy advocacy, as well as support of member agencies. Formerly known as the Ohio Association of Child Caring Agencies.

Year Founded: 1973

1357 Ohio Council of Behavioral Health & Family Services Providers
17 S. High Street
Suite 799
Columbus, OH 43215
614-228-0747
www.theohiocouncil.org

Teresa Lampl, Chief Executive Officer
Jeff O'Neil, President
Paul Bolino, Vice President
Joe Shorokey, Secretary/Treasurer

A trade association representing Ohio-based organizations that provide alcohol and drug addiction treatment, mental health, behavioral healthcare and family services to their communities.

Year Founded: 1979

1358 Ohio Department of Mental Health & Addiction Services
30 East Broad Street
36th Floor
Columbus, OH 43215-3430
614-466-2596
E-mail: questions@mha.ohio.gov
www.mha.ohio.gov

Lori Criss, Director
Austin Criss, Chief Fiscal Officer (CFO)

State agency responsible for the oversight and funding of public mental health programs and services.

1359 Planned Lifetime Assistance Network of Northeast Ohio
Jewish Family Service Association of Cleveland
29125 Chagrin Blvd
Peper Pike, OH 44122
216-292-3999
E-mail: info@jfsa-cleveland.org
www.jfsa-cleveland.org

Renny Wolfson, Board Chair
Shari Perlmuter, Vice Chair
Michael Guggenheim, Treasurer
Allan Goldner, Secretary

PLAN is a membership organization that provides help and support for individuals living with mental illness, cognitive disabilities, and autism spectrum disorder and their families. PLAN seeks to help people achieve emotional and cognitive development through the provision of social and wellness programs, work and volunteer opportunities, and family advocacy.

Year Founded: 1989

1360 Positive Education Program
3100 Euclid Avenue
Cleveland, OH 44115-2508
216-361-4400
E-mail: info@pepcleve.org
www.pepcleve.org

Habeebah R. Grimes, Chief Executive Officer
Noreen Kilbane, Chief Administrative Officer
Christine Fowler-Mack, Secretary
Dr. Keith Lockyer, Treasurer

The Positive Education Program (PEP) is a non-profit agency serving to help troubled children and youth develop skills to learn and grow successfully.

Year Founded: 1971

Oklahoma

1361 MHA (Mental Health America) of Oklahoma
5330 E 31st Street
Suite 1000
Tulsa, OK 74135
918-585-1213
E-mail: info@mhaok.org
www.mhaok.org

Terri L. White, MSW, Chief Executive Officer
Gregory A. Shinn, MSW, Chief Housing Officer
Mark A. Davis, LCSW, Chief Programs Officer
Jessica Phillips, CPA, Chief Financial Officer

An affiliate of Mental Health America, which is a community-based non-profit organization committed to enabling the mental wellness of all Americans. MHA advocates for greater access to quality health services and seeks to educate individuals on identifying symptoms, as well as intervention and prevention.

1362 National Alliance on Mental Illness: Oklahoma
3812 North Santa Fe Avenue
Suite 305
Oklahoma City, OK 73118
405-601-8283
800-583-1264
E-mail: info@namioklahoma.org
www.namioklahoma.org

Kelly Willingham, Chapter President
Lorna Palmer, Chapter Executive Director

Local chapter of the National Alliance on Mental Illness, an organization dedicated to raising awareness on mental health and providing support and education for Americans affected by mental illness. Mission is to help consumers and families share information about services, care providers, and ways to cope with the challenges of mental illness.

Year Founded: 1985

Oregon

1363 National Alliance on Mental Illness: Oregon
4701 Southeast 24th Avenue
Suite E
Portland, OR 97202
503-230-8009
800-343-6264
E-mail: namioregon@namior.org
www.namior.org

Chris Bouneff, Chapter Executive Director
Michelle Madison, Chatper Outreach Manager
Peter Link, Chapter Programs Manager

Local chapter of the National Alliance on Mental Illness, an organization dedicated to raising awareness on mental health and providing support and education for Americans affected by mental illness. Mission is to help consumers and families share information about services, care providers, and ways to cope with the challenges of mental illness.

1364 Oregon Family Support Network
7110 SW Fir Loop
Suite 160
Tigard, OR 97223
503-430-0917
www.ofsn.org

Mitchell Barrington, President
Mary Buzzell, Secretary
Steve Hufford, Treasurer
Sandy Bumpus, Executive Director

A non-profit organization working to help families with children and youth affected by mental or behavioral disorders and to represent families and youth in local and state policy making. Provides advocacy, support, education and services.

Year Founded: 1991

1365 Oregon Psychiatric Physicians Association

5434 River Rd N #371
Keizer, OR 97303
E-mail: info@oregonpsychiatric.org
www.www.oregonpsychiatricphysicians.org

Patrick Sieng, Executive Director
Jennifer Boverman, Membership/Program Coordinator

The Oregon Psychiatric Physicians Association is an organization of medical doctors in Oregon specializing in psychiatry. The OPPA works to ensure the effective treatment of individuals with mental disorders through public education, advocacy, and the provision of resources.

Year Founded: 1966

Pennsylvania

1366 American Anorexia & Bulimia Association of Philadelphia

www.aabaphila.org

The American Anorexia and Bulimia Association of Philadelphia is a non-profit organization serving individuals with eating disorders and their families. Its purpose is to aid in the education and prevention of eating disorders. AABA provides support, resources, and advocacy to assist in the treatment and recovery process.

1367 Health Federation of Philadelphia

123 S. Broad Street
Suite 650
Philadelphia, PA 19109
215-567-8001
www.healthfederation.org

Mary Kargbo, Board Chair
Natalie Levkovich, Executive Director
Scott McNeal, Board Secretary/Treasurer

A non-profit membership organization of community health centers in Southeastern Pennsylvania. The Health Federation of Philadelphia seeks to improve the availability and quality of health care services for underserved families and people.

Year Founded: 1983

1368 Mental Health America in Pennsylvania

922 N 3rd Street
Harrisburg, PA 17102
717-346-0549
866-578-3659
E-mail: info@mhapa.org
www.mhapa.org

Alex J. Hazzouri, President/Acting Treasurer
Laurie Barnett Levine, Secretary

An affiliate of Mental Health America, which is a community-based non-profit organization committed to enabling the mental wellness of all Americans. MHA advocates for greater access to quality health services and seeks to educate individuals on identifying symptoms, as well as intervention and prevention.

1369 Mental Health Association of Southeastern Pennsylvania (MHASP)

1211 Chestnut Street
Suite 1100
Philadelphia, PA 19107
215-751-1800
800-688-4226
www.mhasp.org

The Mental Health Association of Southeastern Pennsylvania (MHASP) is a nonprofit corporation that seeks to transform mental health services to better meet the needs of individuals with mental illnesses and their families. MHASP addresses mental health issues through advocacy, support, training and education, information and referral, and technical assistance. MHASP's mission is to create opportunities for recovery for individuals with mental health challenges. MHASP offers services in Bucks, Chester, Delaware, Montgomery and Philadelphia counties.

Year Founded: 1951

1370 National Alliance on Mental Illness: Keystone Pennsylvania

105 Braunlich Drive
McKnight Plaza, Suite 200
Pittsburgh, PA 15237
412-366-3788
888-264-7972
E-mail: info@namikeystonepa.org
www.namikeystonepa.org

Charma D Dudley, PhD, FPPR, President
Kathy Testoni, Vice President
Mim Schwartz, Secretary
Michelle Hottenstein, Treasurer

Local chapter of the National Alliance on Mental Illness, an organization dedicated to raising awareness on mental health and providing support and education for Americans affected by mental illness. Mission is to help consumers and families share information about services, care providers, and ways to cope with the challenges of mental illness.

1371 Pennsylvania Psychiatric Society

550M Ritchie Highway
#271
Severna Park, MD 21146
800-422-2900
410-544-4640
E-mail: info@papsych.org
www.papsych.org

A district branch of the American Psychiatric Association, the PPS is a non-profit association comprising of 1,800 physicians who specialize in psychiatry. The Pennsylvania Psychiatric Society represents the interests of the psychiatric profession and their patients, and seeks to ensure the provision of high quality psychiatric services through education, advocacy, and the maintenance of ethical standards.

1372 University of Pittsburgh Medical Center

200 Lothrop Street
Pittsburgh, PA 15213-2582

412-647-8762
800-533-8762
www.upmc.com

The University of Pittsburgh Medical Center is a health care provider and insurer focused on developing new models of patient-centered care. Its mission is to engage in clinical research, education and innovation to ensure excellence in patient care.

Rhode Island

1373 MHA (Mental Health America) of Rhode Island
345 Blackstone Boulevard
Sawyer Building, Room 310
Providence, RI 02906
401-726-2285
E-mail: info@mhari.org
www.mhari.org

Laurie-Marie Pisciotta, Executive Director
Clement Cicilline, MS, President
Julia Steiny, Vice President
Robert Andrade, Treasurer

An affiliate of Mental Health America, which is a community-based non-profit organization committed to enabling the mental wellness of all Americans. MHA advocates for greater access to quality health services and seeks to educate individuals on identifying symptoms, as well as intervention and prevention.

1374 National Alliance on Mental Illness: Rhode Island
154 Waterman Street
Suite 5B
Providence, RI 02906-3116
401-331-3060
E-mail: info@namirhodeisland.org
www.namirhodeisland.org

Stephen Duryea, Chapter President
Beth Lamarre, Chapter Executive Director

Local chapter of the National Alliance on Mental Illness, an organization dedicated to raising awareness on mental health and providing support and education for Americans affected by mental illness. Mission is to help consumers and families share information about services, care providers, and ways to cope with the challenges of mental illness.

Year Founded: 1983

1375 Parent Support Network of Rhode Island
535 Centerville Road
Suite 202
Warwick, RI 02886
401-467-6855
800-483-8844
www.psnri.org

Bevon Bovell, Board President
George McDonough, Vice President
Lisa Conlan Lewis, CPRS, Executive Director
Gene Cavielere, Treasurer

Non-profit organization of families providing support for families with children and youth who have, or are at risk for, behavioral, emotional, or mental health problems. Parent Support Network promotes mental health and well-being with the goal of strengthening families. Parent Support Network provides advocacy, training, support services, and education, and works to raise public awareness on children

and behavioral health. Parent Support Network works on behalf of children and families and aims to ensure access to effective services for all.

South Carolina

1376 Federation of Families of South Carolina
810 Dutch Square Boulevard
Suite 486
Columbia, SC 29210
803-772-5210
866-779-0402
E-mail: Info@fedfamsc.org
www.fedfamsc.org

Nonprofit organization providing assistance and support for families of children with emotional, behavioral, or psychiatric disorders. The Federation offers support networks, educational materials, publications, conferences, workshops, and other activities. The goal of the Federation of Families of South Carolina is to meet the needs of children and youth with emotional, behavioral, and mental disorders and their families, and assist them in building productive lives.

1377 MHA (Mental Health America) South Carolina
1823 Gadsden Street
Columbia, SC 29201
803-779-5363
www.mha-sc.org

Joy Jay, Executive Director
Andrew Frankle, Clinical Director
Jean Ann Lambert, Community Resource Director
Darlene Riggins, Housing Coordinator

Mental Health America of South Carolina is an affiliate of Mental Health America, a national mental health advocacy organization. MHASC focuses on educating the public about mental illness, advocating for adequate mental health care and sound mental health practices, and organizing conferences designed to address the issues surrounding mental health.

Year Founded: 1954

1378 National Alliance on Mental Illness: South Carolina
1735 St. Julian Place
Suite 300
Columbia, SC 29204
800-788-5131
E-mail: namisc@namisc.org
www.namisc.org

Jim Hayes, MD, Chapter President
Bill Lindsey, Chapter Executive Director
Corinne Matthews, Office Manager
Sharyn Pittman, Program Coordinator

Local chapter of the National Alliance on Mental Illness, an organization dedicated to raising awareness on mental health and providing support and education for Americans affected by mental illness. Mission is to help consumers and families share information about services, care providers, and ways to cope with the challenges of mental illness.

Year Founded: 1986

South Dakota

1379 National Alliance on Mental Illness: South Dakota
1601 E 69th Street
Suite 210
Sioux Falls, SD 57108
605-271-1871
800-551-2531
E-mail: namisd@midconetwork.com
www.namisouthdakota.org

Sheri Nelson, Chapter Executive Director
Christie Lueth, Chapter President
Michi Hittle, Chapter Treasurer
Jon Pochop, Chapter Vice-President

Local chapter of the National Alliance on Mental Illness, an organization dedicated to raising awareness on mental health and providing support and education for Americans affected by mental illness. Mission is to help consumers and families share information about services, care providers, and ways to cope with the challenges of mental illness.

Year Founded: 1987

Tennessee

1380 MHA (Mental Health America) of East Tennessee, Inc.
9050 Executive Park Drive
Suite 104-A
Knoxville, TN 37923
865-584-9125
877-642-3866
www.mhaet.com

Ben Harrington, MA Ed, CEO
Leah Bevins, Finance/Operations Director
Brina Terrell, Marketing Director
Emily Scheuneman, President

An affiliate of Mental Health America, which is a community-based non-profit organization committed to enabling the mental wellness of all Americans. MHA advocates for greater access to quality health services and seeks to educate individuals on identifying symptoms, as well as intervention and prevention.

Year Founded: 1948

1381 Memphis Business Group on Health
4728 Spottswood Ave
#376
Memphis, TN 38117
901-767-9585
www.memphisbusinessgroup.org

Cristie Upshaw Travis, Chief Executive Officer
Janis M Slivinski, Administrative Assistant

Memphis Business Group on Health is a coalition of member employers seeking to manage health benefits, implement wellness programs and promote a healthy workforce.

Year Founded: 1985

1382 National Alliance on Mental Illness: Tennessee
1101 Kermit Drive
Suite 605
Nashville, TN 37217
615-361-6608
800-467-3589
E-mail: info@namitn.org
www.namitn.org

Jeff Fladen, Chapter Executive Director
Roger Stewart, Chapter Deputy Director
Susan Ezzell, Chapter Finance Coordinator

Local chapter of the National Alliance on Mental Illness, an organization dedicated to raising awareness on mental health and providing support and education for Americans affected by mental illness. Mission is to help consumers and families share information about services, care providers, and ways to cope with the challenges of mental illness.

Year Founded: 1984

1383 Tennessee Association of Mental Health Organization
PO Box 1274
Brentwood, TN 37024
615-244-2220
800-568-2642
E-mail: tamho@tamho.org
www.tamho.org

Ellyn Wilbur, Executive Director
Alysia Smith Knight, Director of Policy and Advocacy
Teresa S. Fuqua, Director of Member Services
Laura B. Jean, Director of Admin. Services

State wide trade association representing primarily community mental health centers, community-owned corporations that have historically served the needs of the mentally ill and chemically dependent citizens of Tennessee regardless of their ability to pay.

Year Founded: 1958

1384 Tennessee Mental Health Consumers' Association
3931 Gallatin Pike
Nashville, TN 37216
615-250-1176
888-539-0393
E-mail: info@tmhca-tn.org
www.tmhca-tn.org

Anthony Fox, President/CEO
Paul Turney, President
Charles McClain, Vice President
Suzie McBroom, Secretary/Treasurer

A not for profit organization whose members are mental health consumers and other individuals and groups who support our mission. TMHCA recognizes our members as individuals whose life experiences and dreams for the future are invaluable in the structuring of ourplans and policies.

Year Founded: 1983

1385 Tennessee Voices for Children
500 Professional Park Dr.
Goodlettsville, TN 37202
615-269-7751
800-670-9882
www.tnvoices.org

Rikki Harris, Chief Executive Officer
Brian Taylor, Vice President of Finance/IT
Willie M. Voss, Chief Operating Officer
Mark McFerran, Chief Development Officer

Speaks out as active advocates for the emotional and behavioral well-being of children and their families. A non-profit organization of families, professionals, business and community leaders, and government representatives committed to improving and expanding services related to the emotional and behavioral well-being of children.

Year Founded: 1990

1386 Vanderbilt University: John F Kennedy Center for Research on Human Development

110 Magnolia Circle
Peabody College
Nashville, TN 37203
615-322-8240
TDD: 615-343-2958
E-mail: kc@vanderbilt.edu
www.kc.vanderbilt.edu

Research and research training related to disorders of thinking, learning, perception, communication, mood and emotion caused by disruption of typical development. Available services include behavior analysis clinic, referrals, lectures and conferences, and a free quarterly newsletter.

Year Founded: 1965

Texas

1387 Children's Mental Health Partnership

1210 San Antonio Street
Suite 200
Austin, TX 78701
512-454-3706
E-mail: mhainfo@mhatexas.org
www.mhatexas.org

A coalition of human services providers, parents, educators and juvenile court professionals who care about the special mental health needs of Austin area youth and families.

Year Founded: 1935

1388 Jewish Family Service of Dallas

The Edna Zale Building
5402 Arapaho Road
Dallas, TX 75248
972-437-9950
E-mail: info@jfsdallas.org
www.jfsdallas.org

Cathy Barker, Chief Executive Officer
Steven Brown, Chief Financial Officer
Deizel Sarte, Chief Operations Officer
Lindsay Stengle, Secretary

A nonsectarian mental health and social services association dedicated to improving healthcare for the Greater Dallas community.

Year Founded: 1911

1389 Jewish Family Service of San Antonio

12500 NW Military Hwy
#250
San Antonio, TX 78231
210-302-6920
E-mail: info@jfs-sa.org
www.www.jfs-sa.org

Jennifer Regnier, Chief Executive Officer
Ray Rodriguez, Director of Finance
Ryan Curran, LPC-s, Clinical Director
Carrie Douglas, President

The Jewish Family Services of San Antonio (JFS) is a nonsectarian association dedicated to improving community healthcare in San Antonio and the surrounding area.

1390 Mental Health America of Greater Dallas

624 North Good-Latimer Expy
Suite 200
Dallas, TX 75204
214-871-2420
www.mhadallas.org

Bonnie Cook, MAS, Executive Director
Angela D. Owen, MA, Community Outreach Coordinator
Meaghan Reed, Public Policy Director
Tracy Curts, Chair

An affiliate of Mental Health America, which is a community-based non-profit organization committed to enabling the mental wellness of all Americans. MHA advocates for greater access to quality health services and seeks to educate individuals on identifying symptoms, as well as intervention and prevention.

Year Founded: 1955

1391 Mental Health America of Greater Houston, Inc.

2211 Norfolk
Suite 810
Houston, TX 77098
713-523-8963
E-mail: info@mhahouston.org
www.mhahouston.org

Renae Vania Tomczak, MBA, President & CEO
Anne Eldredge, Vice President & CFO
Alejandra Posada, MEd, Chief Operating Officer
Angela Synek, Chief Development Officer

An affiliate of Mental Health America, which is a community-based non-profit organization committed to enabling the mental wellness of all Americans. MHA advocates for greater access to quality health services and seeks to educate individuals on identifying symptoms, as well as intervention and prevention.

Year Founded: 1954

1392 Mental Health America of Southeast Texas

700 North Street
Suite 95
Beaumont, TX 77701
409-550-0134
www.mhasetx.org

Vernice Monroe, President
Shelley Tortorice, Vice President
Toni Mulvaney, Secretary
Bree Babineaux, Executive Director

An affiliate of Mental Health America, which is a community-based non-profit organization committed to enabling the mental wellness of all Americans. MHA advocates for greater access to quality health services and seeks to educate individuals on identifying symptoms, as well as intervention and prevention.

Year Founded: 1942

1393 National Alliance on Mental Illness: Texas

Austin State Hospital Campus
Bulding 781, Room 428
Austin, TX 78703
512-693-2000
E-mail: officemanager@namitexas.org
www.namitexas.org

Andrew Horner, Chapter President
Greg Hansch, Chapter Executive Director

Local chapter of the National Alliance on Mental Illness, an organization dedicated to raising awareness on mental health and providing support and education for Americans affected by mental illness. Mission is to help consumers and families share information about services, care providers, and ways to cope with the challenges of mental illness.

Year Founded: 1984

1394 Texas Counseling Association (TCA)

1204 San Antonio
Suite 201
Austin, TX 78701-1870
512-472-3403
E-mail: info@txca.org
www.txca.org

Adrian Warren, President
Elsa Leggett, President-Elect
Cyndi Mattews, Secretary
Jan Friese, Executive Director

The Texas Counseling Association is dedicated to providing leadership, advocacy and education to promote the growth and development of the counseling profession and those that are served.

1395 Texas Psychological Association

PO Box 163236
Austin, TX 78716
888-872-3435
E-mail: admin@texaspsyc.org
www.texaspsyc.org

Brian Stagner, PhD, Director of Professional Affairs
Angie Guy, MPA, Operations/Convention Director
Dena Goldstein, Marketing/Communications Manager

Dedicated to advancing psychology as a profession in Texas through improved research and high standards of professional education and ethics.

Year Founded: 1947

1396 Texas Society of Psychiatric Physicians

401 W 15th Street
Suite 675
Austin, TX 78701
512-478-0605
E-mail: TxPsychiatry@aol.com
www.www.txpsych.org/tspp/

Michael Arambula, MD, PharmD, President
Karen Dineen Wagner, MD, PhD, President-Elect
Lynda Parker, MD, Secretary-Treasurer

A nonprofit organization dedicated to advancing the science of psychiatry, psychiatric facilities, and mental health awareness in Texas.

Year Founded: 1956

1397 re:MIND

PO Box 27607
Houston, TX 77227
713-600-1131
E-mail: info@remindsupport.org
www.www.emindsupport.org

Walter O'Donnell, Chair
Don Condon, Secretary
Philip Rodriguez, Treasurer
Jennifer Leal, Executive Director

re:Mind provides free and confidential peer support groups for individuals living with, and family and friends affected by, depression and bipolar disorders.

Utah

1398 Healthwise of Utah

3110 State Office Building
Suite 30270
Salt Lake City, UT 84114
801-538-3800
800-439-3805
www.insurance.utah.gov

Todd E. Kiser, Insurance Commissioner

1399 National Alliance on Mental Illness: Utah

1600 West 2200 South
Suite 202
West Valley City, UT 84119
801-323-9900
E-mail: education@namiut.org
www.namiut.org

Amanda Rapacz, Chapter President
Rob Wesemann, Chapter Executive Director

Local chapter of the National Alliance on Mental Illness, an organization dedicated to raising awareness on mental health and providing support and education for Americans affected by mental illness. Mission is to help consumers and families share information about services, care providers, and ways to cope with the challenges of mental illness.

Year Founded: 1988

1400 Utah Parent Center

5296 S Commerce Drive
Suite 302
Murray, UT 84107
801-272-1051
800-468-1160
E-mail: info@utahparentcenter.org
www.utahparentcenter.org

Joey Hanna, Executive Director
Esperanza Reyes, Associate Director

The Utah Parent Center is a statewide nonprofit organization founded in 1984 to provide training, information, referral and assistance to parents of children and youth with all disabilities: physical, mental, learning and emotional. Staff at the center are primarily parents of children and youth with disabilities who carry out the philosophy of Parents Helping Parents.

1401 Utah Psychiatric Association

310 E 4500 Sth
Suite 500
Salt Lake City, UT 84107-4250
801-747-3500
E-mail: paige@utahmed.org
www.utah.psychiatry.org

Christian Df Agricola, MD, President
Brent M. Kious, MD, PhD, President-Elect
Steven G. Sugden, MD, MPH, Secretary

The Utah Psychiatric Association aims to improve the science of psychiatry through improved research methods, training, and practice in the State of Utah. The UPA is a Distrcit Branch of the American Psychiatric Society.

Year Founded: 1962

Vermont

1402 National Alliance on Mental Illness: Vermont
600 Blair Park
Suite 301
Williston, VT 05495
802-876-7949
800-639-6480
E-mail: info@namivt.org
www.namivt.org

Sara Moran, Chapter President
Laurie Emerson, Chapter Executive Director
Amy Perry, Chapter Program Director

Local chapter of the National Alliance on Mental Illness, an organization dedicated to raising awareness on mental health and providing support and education for Americans affected by mental illness. Mission is to help consumers and families share information about services, care providers, and ways to cope with the challenges of mental illness.

Year Founded: 1983

1403 Vermont Association for Mental Health & Addiction Recovery
100 State Street
Suite 352
Montpellier, VT 05602
802-223-6263
E-mail: info@vamhar.org
www.vamhar.org

Peter Espenshade, President
Danielle Sessler, VP, Communications/Innovation
Melissa Story, Chief Operating Officer
Trista Ringer, Camp Daybreak Director

Advocates for greater access to quality health services and seeks to educate individuals on identifying symptoms, as well as intervention and prevention.

Year Founded: 1939

1404 Vermont Federation of Families for Children's Mental Health
600 Blair Park Road
PO Box 1577
Williston, VT 05495
800-639-6071
E-mail: vffcmh@vffcmh.org
www.vffcmh.org

John Pierce, President
Gladys Konstantin, Secretary
Sandi Yandow, Executive Director

Supports families with children who are experiencing emotional, behavioral, or mental health challenges.

Virginia

1405 Garnett Day Treatment Center
75 Crystal Run Road
Middletown, NY 10941
845-333-7800
www.garnethealth.org

Ulrick Vieux, DO, Psychiatry
Shajiuddin Mohammed, MD, Psychiatry
Manouchehr Lavian, MD, Psychiatry

The Garnett Day Treatment Center offers counseling services for children, adolescents, and adults to treat their behavioral, emotional, and mental health needs.

1406 Mental Health America of Virginia
2008 Bremo Road
Suite 101
Richmond, VA 23226
804-257-5591
E-mail: info@mhav.org
www.mhav.org

Bruce Cruser, Executive Director
Rev. Arcelia Jackson, President
Stephanie Barker, Vice President
Jeannette Doree, Secretary

An affiliate of Mental Health America, which is a community-based non-profit organization committed to enabling the mental wellness of all Americans. MHA advocates for greater access to quality health services and seeks to educate individuals on identifying symptoms, as well as intervention and prevention.

Year Founded: 1937

1407 National Alliance on Mental Illness
4301 Wilson Blvd.
Suite 300
Arlington, VA 22203
703-524-7600
888-950-9264
E-mail: info@nami.org
www.nami.org

Shirley J. Holloway, President
Joyce A. Campbell, First Vice President
Daniel H. Gillison, Jr., Chief Executive Officer
Ken Duckworth, Chief Medical Officer

Dedicated to the elimination of mental illnesses and to the improvement of the quality of life for all individuals and families affected by mental illness.

Year Founded: 1979

1408 National Alliance on Mental Illness: Virginia
PO Box 8260
Richmond, VA 23226-0260
804-285-8264
E-mail: info@namivirginia.org
www.namivirginia.org

Sandy Mottesheard, Chapter President
Kathy Harkey, Chapter Executive Director
Deborah Michael, Chapter Director of Finance
Mary Beth Walsh, Acting Director of Programs

Local chapter of the National Alliance on Mental Illness, an organization dedicated to raising awareness on mental health and providing support and education for Americans affected by mental illness. Mission is to help consumers and families share information about services, care providers, and ways to cope with the challenges of mental illness.al illness.

Year Founded: 1984

1409 Parent Resource Center
Division of Special Education And Student Services
Virginia Department of Education
P O Box 2120
Richmond, VA 23218-2120

804-371-7421
800-422-2083
www.www.doe.virginia.gov/special_ed/parents/
Patricia I. Wright, Superintendent of Public Instruc

Washington

1410 A Common Voice
Hope Center, Lakewood Boys/Girls Club
10402 Kline Street SW
Lakewood, WA 98499
253-537-2145
E-mail: acvsherry@msn.com
www.acommonvoice.org

Marge Critchlow, Director
Sharon Lyons, Assistant Director

A parent driven, nonprofit organization funded by Washington State Mental Health. Their goal is to provide support, technical assistance, and to bring Pierce County parents together who have experience raising children with complex needs, facilitaing partnership between communities, systems, familes, and schools.

Year Founded: 1995

1411 Children's Alliance
113 Cherry St.
P.O. 87190
Seattle, WA 98104-2205
206-324-0340
E-mail: action@childrensalliance.org
www.childrensalliance.org

Stephan Blanford, Executive Director
Adam Hyla E. Holdorf, Deputy Director
Gail Wilder, Finance Director
Charles Adkins, Health Policy Director

Washington's statewide child advocacy organization.

Year Founded: 1983

1412 Mental Health & Spirituality Support Group
Nami Eastside-Family Resource Center
16307 NE 83rd Street
Suite 203
Redmond, WA 98052
425-885-6264
E-mail: info@nami-eastside.org
www.nami-eastside.org

Donna Lurie, President
Ethan Seracka, Vice President
Margaret Andersen, Secretary
Bob Krulish, Treasurer

Nation's leading self-help organization for all those affected by severe brain disorders. Mission is to bring consumers and families with similar experiences together to share information about services, care providers, and ways to cope with the challenges of schizophrenia, manic depression, and other serious mental illnesses.

1413 National Alliance on Mental Illness Washington Coast
PO Box 153
Aberdeen, WA 98520-0041
260-783-4288
E-mail: office@namiwa.org
www.nami-wacoast.org

Local chapter of the National Alliance on Mental Illness, an organization dedicated to raising awareness on mental health and providing support and education for Americans affected by mental illness. Mission is to help consumers and families share information about services, care providers, and ways to cope with the challenges of mental illness.

1414 National Alliance on Mental Illness: Washington
1107 45th Street
Suite 330
Seattle, WA 98105
206-783-4288
E-mail: office@namiwa.org
www.www.namiwa.org

Alice Nichols, Chapter Acting President
Lauren B. Simonds, Chapter Executive Director/CEO

Local chapter of the National Alliance on Mental Illness, an organization dedicated to raising awareness on mental health and providing support and education for Americans affected by mental illness. Mission is to help consumers and families share information about services, care providers, and ways to cope with the challenges of mental illness.

Year Founded: 1979

1415 National Alliance on Mental Illness: Pierce County
PO Box 111923
Tacoma, WA 98411
253-677-6629
E-mail: info@namipierce.org
www.namipierce.org

Lovey Offerle, Chapter President
Patricia Kurz, Chapter Vice President
Lennie Lee, Chapter Secretary
Leah Merritt, Chapter Treasurer

Local chapter of the National Alliance on Mental Illness, an organization dedicated to raising awareness on mental health and providing support and education for Americans affected by mental illness. Mission is to help consumers and families share information about services, care providers, and ways to cope with the challenges of mental illness.

1416 North Suffolk Mental Health Association
301 Broadway
Chelsea, MA 02150
617-889-4860
www.northsuffolk.org

Kurt Aemmer, Quality Specialist
Annette Calder, Executive Assistant
Julie de Losada, Quality Specialist Coordinator
Shari Downing, Accounting Specialist

It is the purpose of the North Suffolk Mental Health Association to ensure the provision of quality mental health services for children and families in under-served communities.

Year Founded: 1959

1417 Nueva Esperanza Counseling Center
720 W Court Street
Suite 8
Pasco, WA 99301-4178
509-545-6506

Maria A Morcuende

1418 Sharing & Caring for Consumers, Families Alliance for the Mentally Ill
NAMI-Eastside Family Resource Center
16315 NE 87th Street
Suite B-11
Redmond, WA 98052-3537
425-885-6264
E-mail: info@nami-eastside.org
www.nami-eastside.org/

Paul Beatty, Co - President
Manka Dhingra, Co - President
Shari Shovlin, Vice President
Michael C.Maloney, Secretary

Nation's leading self-help organization for all those affected by severe brain disorders. Mission is to bring consumers and families with similar experiences together to share information about services, care providers, and ways to cope with the challenges of schizophrenia, manic depression, and other serious mental illnesses.

1419 South King County Alliance for the Mentally Ill
515 West Harrison Street
Suite 215
Kent, WA 98032-4403
253-854-6264
E-mail: info@namiskc.org
www.namiskc.org

Marsha Williams, President
Dan Hamilton, Vice President
Paul Sjoholm, Treasurer

Nation's leading self-help organization for all those affected by severe brain disorders. Mission is to bring consumers and families with similar experiences together to share information about services, care providers, and ways to cope with the challenges of schizophrenia, manic depression, and other serious mental illnesses.

Year Founded: 1985

1420 Spanish Support Group Alliance for the Mentally Ill
NAMI-Eastside
2601 Elliott Avenue
Suite 4143
Seattle, WA 98121-1399
425-747-7892
www.nami-eastside.org/

Paul Beatty, Co - President
Manka Dhingra, Co - President
Shari Shovlin, Vice President
Michael C.Maloney, Secretary

Nation's leading self-help organization for all those affected by severe brain disorders. Mission is to bring consumers and families with similar experiences together to share information about services, care providers, and ways to cope with the challenges of schizophrenia, manic depression, and other serious mental illnesses.

1421 Spokane Mental Health
107 South Division Street
Spokane, WA 99202-1510
509-838-4651
www.fbhwa.org

David Panken, CEO
Jennifer Allen, UC Coordinator

Since 1970, Spokane Mental Health, a not-for-profit organization, has served children, families, adults and elders throughout Spokane County. Our professional staff provides quality treatment and rehabilitation for those with mental illness and co-occurring disorders. These services include crisis response services; individual, family and group therapy; case management and support; vocational rehabilitation; psychiatric and psychological services; medication management and consumer education. We tailor services to the unique needs and strengths of each person seeking care.

1422 Washington Advocates for the Mentally Ill
NAMI Eastside Family Resource Center
16315 NE 87th Street
Suite B-11
Redmond, WA 98052-3537
425-885-6264
800-782-9264
E-mail: info@nami-eastside.org
www.nami-eastside.org/

Paul Beatty, Co - President
Manka Dhingra, Co - President
Shari Shovlin, Vice President
Michael C.Maloney, Secretary

Nation's leading self-help organization for all those affected by severe brain disorders. Mission is to bring consumers and families with similar experiences together to share information about services, care providers, and ways to cope with the challenges of schizophrenia, manic depression, and other serious mental illnesses.

1423 Washington Institute for Mental Illness Research and Training
Washington State University, Spokane
PO Box 1495
Spokane, WA 99210-1495
509-358-7514
www.spokane.wsu.edu/research&service/

Michael Hendrix, Director
Sandie Kruse, Training Coordinator

Governmental organization focusing on mental illness research.

1424 Washington State Psychological Association
2525 E 29th Ave
Ste 10B #368
Spokane, WA 99223
206-547-4220
E-mail: wspa@wapsych.org
www.wapsych.org

Marvo Reguindin, Executive Director
Samantha Slaughter, Psy.D., Director of Professional Affairs

To support, promote and advance the science, education and practice of psychology in the public interest.

Year Founded: 1947

West Virginia

1425 CAMC Health System, Inc.
PO Box 1547
Suite 108
Charleston, WV 25326
304-388-5432
www.www.camc.org

David L. Ramsey, President/CEO
Glenn Crotty Jr., MD, Executive Vice President/COO
Jeff Sandene, Executive Vice President/CFO

A nonprofit organization committed to improving the mental wellness of patients in Charleston. Includes over 8,000 medical leaders, including more than 700 physicians.

Year Founded: 1972

1426 Mountain State Parent Child and Adolescent Contacts

2351 Garfield Avenue
Parkersburg, WV 26101
304-428-0365
800-244-5385
E-mail: DonnaMoss@msp-can.org
www.www.msp-can.org

A private non-profit, family-run organization that improves outcomes for children with serious emotional disorders and their families.

1427 National Alliance on Mental Illness: West Virginia

The state organization of NAMI in West Virginia is currently being rebuilt. If you would like to help in this effort, contact fieldcapacity@nami.org.There are local NAMI chapters within the state of West Virginal.

Wisconsin

1428 Mental Health America of Wisconsin

600 W Virginia Street
Suite 502
Milwaukee, WI 53204
414-276-3122
866-948-6483
E-mail: info@mhawisconsin.org
www.mhawisconsin.org

Martina Gollin-Graves, President/CEO

An affiliate of Mental Health America, which is a community-based non-profit organization committed to enabling the mental wellness of all Americans. MHA advocates for greater access to quality health services and seeks to educate individuals on identifying symptoms, as well as intervention and prevention.

Year Founded: 1935

1429 National Alliance on Mental Illness: Wisconsin

4233 West Beltline Highway
Madison, WI 53711
608-268-6000
800-236-2988
E-mail: nami@namiwisconsin.org
www.namiwisconsin.org

Sita Diehl, Chapter President
Mary Kay Battaglia, Chapter Executive Director
Kelly Armstrong, Vice President
James Weber, Treasurer

Local chapter of the National Alliance on Mental Illness, an organization dedicated to raising awareness on mental health and providing support and education for Americans affected by mental illness. Mission is to help consumers and families share information about services, care providers, and ways to cope with the challenges of mental illness.

Year Founded: 1977

1430 Wisconsin Association of Family & Children's Agencies (WAFCA)

16 N. Carroll St.
#750
Madison, WI 53703
608-257-5939
E-mail: info@wafca.org
www.wafca.org

Kathy Markeland, Executive Director
Emily Coddington, Associate Director
Scott Strong, Chairperson
Mechele Pitt Shipman, Vice-Chairperson

WAFCA represents over 50 child and family-serving agencies that advocate for federal and state policies that improve the lives of families and children.

Year Founded: 1980

1431 Wisconsin Family Ties

16 N Carroll Street
Suite 230
Madison, WI 53703
608-267-6800
800-422-7145
E-mail: info@wifamilyties.org
www.wifamilyties.org

Ashlee Glowacki, President
Hasmig Tempesta, Vice President
Heidi Lehman, Secretary
Michael Witkovsky, Treasurer

Wisconsin's largest parent-governed association dedicated to improving mental healthcare for children.

Wyoming

1432 Central Wyoming Behavioral Health at Lander Valley

1320 Bishop Randall Drive
Lander, WY 82520-3939
307-332-4420
800-788-9446
www.landerhospital.com/patientservices.htm

Rebecca K Smith

1433 National Alliance on Mental Illness: Wyoming

PO Box 1883
Casper, WY 82602
307-265-2573
E-mail: namiwyominginfo@gmail.com
www.namiwyoming.org

Roy C. Walworth, Chapter President
Donna Sedey, Chapter Vice President
Becky Foster, Chapter Treasurer

Local chapter of the National Alliance on Mental Illness, an organization dedicated to raising awareness on mental health and providing support and education for Americans affected by mental illness. Mission is to help consumers and families share information about services, care providers, and ways to cope with the challenges of mental illness.

Year Founded: 1979

1434 Uplift

109 E 17th Street
Suite 211
Cheyenne, WY 82001

307-432-4055
800-492-3199
E-mail: info@upliftwy.org
www.upliftwy.org

Michelle C. Heinen, Executive Director
Erin Fausset, Family Support Specialist

Wyoming Chapter of the Federation of Familes for Children's Mental Health. Providing support, education, advocacy, information and referral for parents and professionals focusing on emotional, behavioral and learning needs of children and youth.

Year Founded: 1990

Government Agencies

Federal

1435 Administration for Children and Families
330 C Street SW
Washington, DC 20201
www.www.acf.hhs.gov

Jennifer Cannistra, Acting Assistant Secretary
Larry Handerhan, Chief of Staff
Ben Goldhaber, Deputy Asst. Secretary, Admin.
Lila Lee, Acting Deputy Asst. Secretary

The Administration for Children and Families is responsible for federal programs that promotes the economic and social well-being of families, children, individuals, and communities.

Year Founded: 1991

1436 Administration on Aging
Administration for Community Living
330 C Street SW
Washington, DC 20201
202-401-4634
www.acl.gov/about-acl/administration-aging

Alison Barkoff, Acting Admin./Asst. Secretary
Kelly Cronin, Deputy Administrator
Vicki Gottlich, Dir., Center for Policy
Rick Nicholls, Chief of Staff

One of the nation's largest providers of home and community-based care for older persons and their caregivers. The mission is to promote the dignity and independence of older people, and help society prepare for an aging population. The Administration on Aging is part of the Administration for Community Living.

1437 Administration on Intellectual and Developmental Disabilities
Administration for Community Living
330 C Street SW
Washington, DC 20201
202-401-4634
www.www.acl.gov

Alison Barkoff, Acting Admin./Asst. Secretary
Kelly Cronin, Deputy Administrator
Vicki Gottlich, Dir., Center for Policy
Ricki Nicholls, Chief of Staff

AIDD ensures that people with disabilities are able to live without abuse, neglect, or expoitation, as well as supports their efforts to live full, independent lives. AIDD forms networks throughout each state, made up of State Councils; State Protection and Advocacy Systems; and University Centers. AIDD is a part of the Administration for Community Living, and runs the President's Committee on Intellectual Disabilities.

1438 Agency for Healthcare Research and Quality
Office of Communications and Knowledge Transfer
5600 Fishers Lane
7th Floor
Rockville, MD 20857
301-427-1364
www.www.ahrq.gov

Robert "Bob" Otto Valdez, PhD, MHSA, Director
David Meyers, MD, Deputy Director

The Agency provides policymakers and other health care leaders with information needed to make critical health care decisions.

1439 Association of Maternal and Child Health Programs (AMCHP)
1825 K Street
Suite 250
Washington, DC 20006-1202
202-775-0436
E-mail: info@amchp.org
www.www.amchp.org

Manda Hall, MD, President
Belinda Pettiford, MPH, President-Elect
Terrance E. Moore, MA, Chief Executive Officer
Caroline Stampfel, MPH, Chief Strategy & Program Officer

A national nonprofit organization representing state public health workers. AMCHP provides leadership to assure the health and well-being of women of reproductive age, children, youth, including those with special health care needs, and their families.

Year Founded: 1950

1440 Center for Behavioral Health Statistics and Quality
Substance Abuse and Mental Health Services Administration
5600 Fishers Lane
Rockville, MD 20857
240-276-1310
www.samhsa.gov

Anita Everett, MD, DFAPA, Director

The Center for Behavioral Health Statistics Quality, formerly the Office of Applied Studies, provides the latest national data on behavioral health statistics. The center also collaborates with Federal agencies to develop national health statistics policy, and promotes research in behavioral health data systems.

Year Founded: 1992

1441 Center for Mental Health Services Homeless Programs Branch
Substance Abuse and Mental Health Services Administration
5600 Fishers Lane
Rockville, MD 20857
240-276-1310
877-726-4727
TTY: 800-487-4889
www.samhsa.gov/about-us/who-we-are/offices-centers

Anita Everett, MD, DFAPA, Director

A Federal agency concerned with the prevention and treatment of mental illness and the promotion of mental health. Homeless Programs Branch administers a variety of programs and activities. Provides professional leadership for collaborative intergovernmental initiatives designed to assist persons with mental illnesses who are homeless. Also supports a contract for the National Resource Center on Homelessness and Mental Illness.

Year Founded: 1992

1442 Center for Substance Abuse Treatment
Substance Abuse Mental Health Services
Administration
5600 Fishers Lane
Rockville, MD 20857
240-276-1310
www.samhsa.gov/about-us/who-we-are/offices-centers

Anita Everett, MD, DFAPA, Director

CSAT promotes the quality and availability of community based substance abuse treatment services for individuals and families who need them. CSAT works with State and community based groups to improve and expand existing subsance abuse treatment services under the Substance Abuse Prevention and Treatment Block Grant Program.

Year Founded: 1992

1443 Centers for Disease Control & Prevention
1600 Clifton Road
Atlanta, GA 30329
800-232-4636
TTY: 888-232-6348
E-mail: cdcinfo@cdc.gov
www.cdc.gov

The CDC protects the health and safety of people at home and abroad, provides credible information to enhance health decisions, and promotes health through strong partnership. The CDC serves as the national focus for developing and applying disease prevention and control, environmental health, and health promotion in education activities designed to improve the health of the people of the United States.

1444 DC Department of Behavioral Health
Government of the District of Columbia
64 New York Avenue, NE
3rd Floor
Washington, DC 20002
202-673-2200
TTY: 202-673-7500
E-mail: dbh@dc.gov
www.dbh.dc.gov

Barbara J. Bazron, PhD, Director

The goal of the Department of Behavioral Health is to develop, support, and oversee a comprehensive, community-based, consumer driven, culturally competent, quality mental health system. This system should be responsive and accessible to children, youths, adults, and their families. It should leverage continuous positive change through its ability to learn and to partner. It should also ensure that mental health providers are accountable to consumers and offer services that promote recovery from mental illness.

1445 Equal Employment Opportunity Commission
131 M Street NE
Washington, DC 20507
800-669-4000
TTY: 800-669-6820
E-mail: info@eeoc.gov
www.www.eeoc.gov

The EEOC is dedicated to eradicating workplace discrimination. They enforce federal laws that make it illegal to discriminate against an employee/job applicant based on race, religion, color, sex, age, or disability.

Year Founded: 1965

1446 Health Care For All (HCFA)
One Federal Street
5th Floor
Boston, MA 02110
617-350-7279
800-272-4232
TTY: 617-350-0974
www.www.hcfama.org

Amy Rosenthal, Executive Director
Kerwin Amo, Policy & Project Coordinator
Lorraine Anyango, Health Justice Organizer
Suzanne Curry, Behavioral Health Policy Dir.

HCFA is dedicated to working with state, federal, and local administrations to improve the health care system so that everyone in Massachusstts has affordable and comprehensive health coverage.

1447 Health and Human Services Office of Assistant
Secretary for Planning & Evaluation
200 Independence Avenue SW
Room 415F
Washington, DC 20201
202-690-7858
E-mail: osaspeinfo@hhs.gov
www.aspe.hhs.gov

Rebecca Haffajee, Acting Assistant Secretary
Tisamarie Sherry, Deputy Assistant Secretary
Gavin Kennedy, Associate Deputy Asst. Secretary
Erin Bagalman, Behavioral Health Policy Dir.

ASPE is the principal advisor to the Secretary of the U.S. Department of Health and Human Services on policy development, and is responsible for major activities in policy coordination, legislation development, strategic planning, policy research, evaluation, and economic analysis.

Year Founded: 1972

1448 NIH Office of Science Policy
6707 Rockledge Drive
Suite 750
Bethesda, MD 20892
301-496-9838
E-mail: SciencePolicy@mail.nih.gov
www.osp.od.nih.gov

Lyric Jorgenson, PhD, Acting Associate Director
Jessica Tucker, PhD, Acting Deputy Director

Advises the NIH Director on science policy issues affecting the medical research community; participates in the development of new policy and program initiatives; monitors and coordinates agency planning and evaluation activities; plans and implements a comprehensive science education program and develops and implements NIH policies and procedures for the safe conduct of recombinant DNA and other biotechnology activities.

1449 National Association of Community Health
Centers
7501 Wisconsin Avenue
Suite 1100W
Bethesda, MD 20814
301-347-0400
www.nachc.com

Michael A. Holmes, Chair of the Board
Paloma Hernandez, Chair-Elect
Blake Hall, Secretary
John Santistevan, Treasurer

NACHC, is a national advocacy organization for community-based health centers, as well as for persons who are uninsured. NACHC conducts research and informs public and private sectors on the value of community health centers on the health care system, and also provides training to health centers.

Year Founded: 1971

1450 National Center for HIV, STD and TB Prevention
Centers For Disease Control and Prevention
1600 Clifton Road
Atlanta, GA 30329-4027
800-232-4636
TTY: 888-232-6348
E-mail: cdcinfo@cdc.gov
www.www.cdc.gov/nchhstp/default.htm

CDC's mission is to collaborate to create the expertise, information, and tools that people and communities need to protect their health - through health promotion, prevention of disease, injury and disability, and prepaedness for new health threats and diseases. The National Center aims to eradicate HIV/AIDS, STDs, and TB.

1451 National Institute of Drug Abuse (NIDA)
6001 Executive Boulevard
Room 5213, MSC 9561
Bethesda, MD 20892-9561
301-443-6441
E-mail: media@nida.nih.gov
www.nida.nih.gov

Nora D. Volkow, MD, Director
Wilson M. Compton, MD, MPE, Deputy Director
Joellen Austin, MPAff, MSM, Associate Director, Management

NIDA covers the areas of drug abuse treatment and prevention research, epidemiology, neuroscience and behavioral research, health services research, and AIDS. NIDA seeks to report on advances in the field, identify resources, promote an exchange of information, and improve communications among clinicians, researchers, administrators, and policymakers. Recurring features include synopses of research advances and projects, NIDA news, news of legislative and regulatory developments, and announcements.

1452 National Institute of Mental Health: Psychotic Disorders Research Program
6001 Executive Boulevard
Room 7122, MSC 9625
Bethesda, MD 20892-9625
866-615-6464
E-mail: sarah.morris@nih.gov
www.www.nimh.nih.gov

Sarah E. Morris, PhD, Program Chief

A program that supports research into psychotic disorders. The goals of the program are to uncover information on the origin, onset, causes, and outcome of psychotic disorders, so that there may be better prevention and treatment put in place.

1453 National Institute of Mental Health: Geriatr ics and Aging Processes Research Branch
6001 Executive Boulevard
Room 7113, MSC 9637
Bethesda, MD 20892

301-443-1369
866-615-6464
E-mail: je180t@nih.gov
www.www.nimh.nih.gov

Jovier D. Evans, PhD, Branch Chief

The Geriatrics and Aging Processes Research Branch supports programs and research into mental disorders that occur later in life, such as Alzheimer's. This branch also looks into the relationship between aging and mental disorders, as well as the treatment and prevention of aging-related disorders.

1454 National Institute of Mental Health: Office of Science Policy, Planning, and Communications
6001 Executive Boulevard
Room 6189
Bethesda, MD 20892
866-615-6464
E-mail: meredith.fox@nih.gov
www.www.nimh.nih.gov

Meredith A. Fox, PhD, Director
Julie L. Mason, PhD, Deputy Director

The Office of Science Policy, Planning, and Communications plans and directs efforts for science program planning, research training and coordination, and technology and information transfer. The Office is also responsible for the Institute's information dissemination, media relations, and internal communications.

1455 National Institute on Alcohol Abuse and Alcoholism
National Institute on Health
9000 Rockville Pike
Rockville, MD 20892
301-496-4000
TDD: 301-402-9612
E-mail: niaaaweb-r@exchange.nih.gov
www.niaaa.nih.gov

Dr. George F. Koob, PhD, Director
Dr. Patricia A. Powell, Deputy Director

NIAAA's vision is to increase the understanding of normal and abnormal biological functions and behavior relating to alcohol use; to improve the diagnosis, prevention, and treatment of alcohol use disorders; and to enhance the quality of health care.

1456 National Institute on Drug Abuse: Division of Neuroscience and Behavior
301 North Stonestreet Ave
3WFN MSC 6018
Bethesda, MD 20892
301-443-1887
www.drugabuse.gov

Rita Valentino, PhD, Director
Roger Little, PhD, Deputy Director
John Satterlee, PhD, Health Scientist Administrator

The Division of Neuroscience and Behavior addresses the problem on drug use and addiction by supporting clinical biomedical neuroscience and behavioral research.

1457 National Institute on Drug Abuse: Office of Science Policy and Communications
301 North Stonestreet Ave
3WFN MSC 6024
Bethesda, MD 20892

301-443-1124
www.drugabuse.gov

Jennifer Hobin, PhD, Director
Carole Andrews, Lead Program Analyst
Holly Buchanan, Staff Assistant
Michelle Rankin, PhD, Health Science Admin.

The Office of Science Policy and Communications (OSPC) carries out a wide variety of functions in support of the Director, NIDA, and on behalf of the Institute. OSPC is made up of the Office of the Director and three branches, the Digital Communications Branch, the Public Information and Liaison Branch, and the Science Policy Branch.

1458 National Institutes of Mental Health: Office on AIDS
National Institutes of Health
6001 Executive Boulevard
Room 6105, MSC 9615
Bethesda, MD 20892-9619
301-443-2781
866-615-6464
E-mail: drausch@mail.nih.gov
www.www.nimh.nih.gov

Dianne M. Rausch, PhD, Director

The Office on AIDS supports biomedical and behvaioral research in order to develop a better understanding of HIV, which leads to better diagnosis, treatment, and prevention of HIV/AIDS. The Office also collaborates with other NIH components, Federal agencies, and health organizations to identify AIDS-related needs.

1459 National Library of Medicine
National Institutes of Health
8600 Rockville Pike
Bethesda, MD 20894
301-594-5983
888-346-3656
www.www.nlm.nih.gov

Dr. Patricia Flatley Brennan, Director
Jerry Sheehan, Deputy Director
Kathy Cravedi, Director, Communications

The National Library of Medicine (NLM), on the campus of the National Institutes of Health in Bethesda, Maryland, is the world's largest medical library. The Library collects materials and provides information and research services in all areas of biomedicine and health care.

Year Founded: 1836

1460 Office of Disease Prevention & Health Promotion
US Department of Health and Human Services
1101 Wootton Parkway
Suite 420
Rockville, MD 20852
240-453-8281
www.health.gov

Paul Reed, MD, Director

The Office of Disease Prevention and Health Promotion works to strengthen the disease prevention and health promotion priorities of the Department within the collaborative framework of the HHS agencies. ODPHP is part of the HHS, under the Office of the Assistant Secretary for Health.

Year Founded: 1976

1461 Office of National Drug Control Policy
www.www.whitehouse.gov/ondcp/

The Office of National Drug Control Policy is a component of the Executive Office of the President. The director acts as the principal advisor to the president on drug control activities, and the ONDCP coordinates the activities of 16 federal departments and agencies. The ONDCP also produces an annual publication, the National Drug Control Strategy, which outlines the efforts to reduce drug abuse.

1462 President's Committee for People with Intellectual Disabilities
US DHHS, Administration for Children & Families
330 C Street SW
Washington, DC 20201
www.www.acf.hhs.gov

Jennifer Cannistra, Acting Assistant Secretary
Larry Handerhan, Chief of Staff
Ben Goldhaber, Deputy Asst. Secretary, Admin.
Lila Lee, Acting Deptuy Asst. Secretary

The Committee acts in an advisory capacity to the President and the Secretary of Health and Human Services on matters relating to programs and services for persons with intellectual disabilities. It has adopted several national goals in order to better recognize and uphold the right of all people with intellectual disabilities to enjoy a quality of life that promotes independence, self-determination and participation as productive members of society.

1463 Presidential Commission on Employment of the Disabled
Frances Perkins Building
200 Constitution Avenue NW
Washington, DC 20210
866-633-7365
www.dol.gov/odep

Thomas E. Perez, Secretary of Labor
Rhonda Basha, Chief of Staff
Dylan Orr, Special Assistant/Advisor

The Office of Disability Employment Policy (ODEP) was authorized by Congress in the Department of Labor's FY 2001 appropriation. Recognizing the need for a national policy to ensure that people with disabilities are fully integrated into the 21 st Century workforce, the Secretary of Labor Elaine L. Chao delegated authority and assigned responsibility to the Assistant Secretary for Disability Employment Policy. ODEP is a sub-cabinet level policy agency in the Department of Labor.

1464 Protection and Advocacy Program for the Mentally Ill
US Department of Health and Human Services
5600 Fishers Lane
Rockville, MD 20857
877-726-4727
www.www.samhsa.gov/paimi-program

Charissa Pallas, Director of Communications
Neeraj Gandotra, MD, Chief Medical Officer
Anita Everett, MD, DFAPA, Director of Mental Health Svcs.
Sonia Chessen, Chief of Staff

Federal formula grant program to protect and advocate the rights of people with mental illnesses who are in residential facilities and to investigate abuse and neglect in such facilities.

1465 Public Health Foundation
1300 L Street NW
Suite 800
Washington, DC 20005
202-218-4400
E-mail: info@phf.org
www.phf.org

Ron Bialek, President
Sue Madden, Chief Operating Officer
Valerie Usher, Chief Financial Officer

A high-performing public health system that protects and promotes health in every community by improving public health infrastructure and performance through innovative solutions and measurable results.

1466 Substance Abuse and Mental Health Services Administration
1 Choke Cherry Road
Rockville, MD 20857
800-662-4357
TTY: 800-487-4889
E-mail: SAMHSAInfo@samhsa.hhs.gov
www.samhsa.gov

Tom Coderre, Acting Deputy Asst. Secretary
Sonia Chessen, Chief of Staff
Trina Dutta, Senior Advisor
Gary M. Blau, PhD, Senior Advisor

SAMHSA's mission is to reduce the impact of substance abuse and mental illness on America's communities. The Agency was established by Congress to target effectively substance abuse and mental health services to the people most in need and to translate research in these areas more effectively and more rapidly into the general health care system. SAMHSA has demonstrated that prevention works, treatment is effective, and people recover from mental and substance use disorders. Behavioral health services improve health statuse and reduce health care costs to society. The Agency's programs are carried out through: the Center for Mental Health Services (CMHS); The Centers for Substance Abuse Prevention and Treatment (CSAP/T); and the Office of Applied Studies.

Year Founded: 1992

1467 The Alcohol Policy Information System (APIS) National Institute on Alcohol Abuse and Alcoholism
National Institute of Health
9000 Rockville Pike
Rockville, MD 20892
301-496-4000
TDD: 301-402-9612
E-mail: niaaaweb-r@exchange.nih.gov
www.alcoholpolicy.niaaa.nih.gov

Dr. George F. Koob, Director, NIAAA
Dr. Patricia A. Powell, Deputy Director, NIAAA

The Alcohol Policy Information System (APIS) is an online resource that provides detailed information on a wide variety of alcohol-related policies in the United States at both State and Federal levels. It features compilations and analyses of alcohol-related statutes and regulations. Designed primarily as a tool for researchers, APIS simplifies the process of ascertaining the state of the law for studies on the effects and effectiveness of alcohol-related policies.

1468 US Department of Health and Human Services: Office of Women's Health (OWH)
200 Independence Avenue SW
SW Room 712E
Washington, DC 20201
202-690-7650
www.www.womenshealth.gov

Dr. Dorothy Fink, Deputy Assistant Secretary
Adrienne Smith, PhD, MS, CHES, Dir.,
Policy/Performancer Mngmt.
Richelle West Marshall, Deputy Dir., Operations/Mngmt.

The Office on Women's Health (OWH) was established in 1991 within the U.S. Department of Health and Human Services. OWH coordinates the efforts of all the HHS agencies and offices involved in women's health. OWH works to improve the health and well-being of women and girls in the United States through its innovative programs, by educating health professionals, and motivating behavior change in consumers through the dissemination of health information.

Year Founded: 1991

State

Alabama

1469 Alabama Department of Human Resources
50 N. Ripley St.
Montgomery, AL 36104
334-242-1310
www.www.dhr.alabama.gov

Governor Kay Ivey, Chairperson
Wayne Sellers, Vice Chair
Leslie D. Sanders, Secretary

Member of the National Leadership Council. The mission of the Alabama Department of Human Resources is to partner with communities to promote family stability and provide for the safety and self-sufficiency of vulnerable Alabamians.

Year Founded: 1935

1470 Alabama Department of Mental Health
100 North Union Street
PO Box 301410
Montgomery, AL 36130
334-242-3454
800-367-0955
E-mail: Alabama.DMH@mh.alabama.gov
www.mh.alabama.gov

Lynn T. Beshear, Commissioner
Kimberly G. Boswell, Associate Commissioner

State agency charged with providing services to citizens with mental illness, developmental disabilities and substance abuse disorders.

1471 Alabama Department of Public Health
201 Monroe Street
Montgomery, AL 36104
334-206-5300
800-252-1818
www.www.alabamapublichealth.gov

Scott Harris, MD, MPH, State Health Officer
Mary G. McIntyre, MD, MPH, Chief Medical Officer
Michele B. Jones, MD, Chief of Staff
Brian Hale, JD, General Counsel

Provides public health related information about the State of Alabama.

1472 Alabama Disabilities Advocacy Program
Tuscaloosa, AL 35487
205-348-6010
E-mail: adap@adap.ua.edu
www.adap.ua.edu

James A. Tucker, Director
Nancy E. Anderson, Associate Director
Alexandra Abernathy, Legal Assistant
Angie Allen, Senior Case Advocate

Federally mandated, statewide, Protection and Advocacy system serving eligible individuals with disabilities in Alabama. ADAP's five programs are: Protection and Advocacy for Persons with Developmental Disabilities, Protection and Advocacy for Individuals with Mental Illness, Protection and Advocacy of Individual Rights, Protection and Advocacy for Assistive Technology and Protection and Advocacy for Beneficiaries of Social Security.

Alaska

1473 Alaska Council on Emergency Medical Services
www.dhss.alaska.gov

The mission of the Emergency Medical Services program in Alaska is to reduce both the human suffering and economic loss to society resulting from premature death and disability due to injuries and sudden illness.

1474 Alaska Department of Health & Social Services
3601 C Street
Suite 902
Anchorage, AK 99503
907-269-7800
www.dhss.alaska.gov

Adam Crum, Commissioner

The mission of the Alaska Department of Health and Social Services is to promote and protect the health and well being of Alaskans.

1475 Alaska Department of Mental and Social
Services: Division of Behavioral Health
3601 C Street
Ste 934
Anchorage, AK 99503
907-269-4804
E-mail: gennifer.moreau-johnson@alaska.gov
www.dhss.alaska.gov

Gennifer Moreau-Johnson, Director
Farina Brown, Deputy Director

The mission of the Division of Behavioral Health is to manage an integrated and comprehensive behavioral health system based on sound policy, effective practices and partnerships.

1476 Alaska Mental Health Board
PO Box 110608
Juneau, AK 99811-0608
907-465-8920
888-464-8920
www.dhss.alaska.gov/amhb/Pages/default.aspx

Bev Schoonover, Executive Director
Teri Tibbett, Advocacy Coordinator

Planning and advocacy body for public mental health services. The board works to ensure that Alaska's mental health program is integrated and comprehensive. It recommends operating and capital budgets for the program. The Governor appoints twelve - sixteen members to the board. At least half the members must be consumers of mental health services or family members. Two members are mental health service providers and one an attorney.

1477 Mental Health Association in Alaska
4045 Lake Otis Parkway
Suite 209
Anchorage, AK 99508
907-563-0880
www.alaska.net/~mhaa/

Virginia L. Hostman, M.S., Chairman
Janet McGillivary, M.Ed., President & CEO
William F. Hostman, B.A., Assistant to the CEO

The MHAA is a Division of the National Mental Health Association. It advocates for the improvement of mental health services in the State of Alaska.

Year Founded: 1953

Arizona

1478 Arizona Department of Health Services
150 North 18th Avenue
Phoenix, AZ 85007
602-542-1025
www.www.azdhs.gov

Promotes and protects the health of Arizona's children and adults. Its mission is to set the standard for personal and community health through direct care, science, public policy, and leadership.

Year Founded: 1979

1479 Arizona Department of Health Services:
Behavioral Health Services
150 N. 18th Avenue
Phoenix, AZ 85007
602-542-1025

Administers Arizona's publicly funded behavioral health service system for individuals, families and communities.

Year Founded: 1986

1480 Northern Arizona Regional Behavioral Health
Authority
616 N. Beaver Street
Flagstaff, AZ 86001
928-233-8667
E-mail: info@narbha.org
www.narbha.org

Mary Jo Gregory, RN, MS, President and CEO
Nathan Jones, JD, CHC, General Counsel
Michael Kuzmin, MPA, Chief Financial Officer
Jon Perez, PhD, Chief Program Officer

The Northern Arizona Regional Behavioral Health Authority's (NARBHA) mission is to provide solutions that improve the health and healthcare experience of diverse communities. We serve individuals and families across northern Arizona who are eligible for State and federally-funded behavioral health services.

Year Founded: 1967

Arkansas

1481 Arkansas Department of Human Services
Donaghey Plaza
PO Box 1437
Little Rock, AR 72203
501-682-1001
TDD: 501-682-8820
www.humanservices.arkansas.gov

The Arkansas Department of Human Services provides Medicaid, mental health and substance abuse resources.

Year Founded: 1977

1482 Arkansas Division of Children & Family Services
700 Main Street
P O Box 1437 Slot S 560
Little Rock, AR 72203-1437
501-682-8770
TDD: 501-682-1442
www.humanservices.arkansas.gov/about-dhs/dcfs

Mischa Martin, Director
Leslie Sebren, Deputy Director
Rachel Tiffee, Asst. Dir., Mental Health Svcs.
Tiffany Wright, Asst. Dir., Community Svcs.

The Arkansas Division of Children's Services is a member of the National Leadership Council and provides information and resources on adoption, daycare and child abuse prevention.

1483 Arkansas Division on Youth Services
700 Main Street
Slot 450
Little Rock, AR 72203
502-682-8654
www.humanservices.arkansas.gov

Michael Crump, Director
Glenn Holt, Deputy Director

The Division of Youth Services (DYS) provides in a manner consistent with public safety, a system of high quality programs to address the needs of the juveniles who come in contact with, or are at risk of coming into contact with the juvenile justice system.

1484 Mental Health Council of Arkansas
500 Woodlane St.
Suite 136S
Little Rock, AR 72201
501-372-7062
E-mail: mhca@mhca.org
www.mhca.org

Dianne S. Skaggs, LCSW, Executive Director

The Mental Health Council of Arkansas is a non-profit organization governed by a board of directors with a representative from each of the 13 participating community mental health centers and their affiliates. The MHCA assists its members to achieve the goal of community based treatment which focuses on the whole person with emphasis on physical, mental and emotional wellness and promotes the comprehensive diagnostic, treatment, and wrap around services provided by the private non-profit community mental health centers of Arkansas. The MHCA is dedicated to improving the overall health and well-being of the citizens and communities of Arkansas.

California

1485 California Department of Corrections and Rehabilitation
916-324-7308
www.www.cdcr.ca.gov

Kathleen Allison, Secretary

Our mission is founded on delivering a balance of quality and cost-effective health care in a safe, secure correctional setting.

1486 California Department of Education: California Healthy Kids Resource Center
209-468-9103
800-676-1443
E-mail: nhana@sjcoe.net
www.californiahealthykids.net

The California Healthy Kids Resource Center was established to assist schools in promoting health literacy. Health literacy is the capacity of an individual to obtain, interpret, and understand basic health information and services and the competence to use such information and services in ways that are health enhancing.

1487 California Hispanic Commission on Alcohol Drug Abuse
1901 Royal Oaks Drive
Suite 101
Sacramento, CA 95815
916-443-5473
www.chcada.org

James Hernandez, Executive Director

Services can consist of developing Latino-based agencies, program management, consultation related to proposal development, Board of Directors training, program planning, and information dissemination. Populations or groups served include Latino alcohol and drug service agencies, groups and/or individuals planning to initiate services to Latinos, other AOD agencies with a commitment to serve the Latino community, and County Alcohol and Drug Program offices.

Year Founded: 1975

1488 California Institute for Behavioral Health Solutions (CIBHS)
1760 Creekside Oaks Dr.
Ste. 175
Sacramento, CA 95833
916-556-3480
E-mail: info@cibhs.org
www.www.cibhs.org

Percy Howard, III, LCSW, President and CEO
Rick Goscha, PhD, Sr. VP, Programs
Victor Kogler, VP, Substance Use and Disorders
Jennifer Clancy, MSW, Director of Strategy

CIBHS is a behavioral health consultancy working with mental health organizations on policy development, training, and research.

Colorado

1489 Colorado Department of Health Care Policy and Financing
1570 Grant Street
Denver, CO 80203-1818

303-866-2993
www.www.colorado.gov/hcpf?

Kim Bimestefer, Executive Director
Tom Massey, Deputy Executive Director
Bettina Schneider, Chief Financial Officer

The Department of Health Care Policy and Financing manages the Colorado Medicaid Community Mental Health Services program. the program provides mental health care to medicaid clients in Colorado, through Behavioral Health Organization contracts.

1490 Colorado Department of Human Services (CDHS)

1575 Sherman St.
Denver, CO 80203
303-866-5700
www.www.colorado.gov

Michelle Barnes, Executive Director
Clint Woodruff, Chief Financial Officer
Katie McLoughlin, Chief Legal Officer
Ren,e Marquardt, MD, Chief Medical Officer

CDHS oversees the state's 64 county departments of social/human services, the state's public mental health system, Colorado's system of services for people with developmental disabilities, the state's juvenile corrections system and all state and veterans' nursing homes, through more than 5,000 employees and thousands of community-based service providers. Colorado is a state-supervised, county-administered system for the traditional social services, including programs such as public assistance and child welfare services.

1491 El Paso County Human Services

1675 W. Garden of the Gods
1st Floor
Colorado Springs, CO 80907
719-636-0000
www.humanservices.elpasoco.com

The mission of the El Paso County Department of Human Services is to strengthen families, assure safety, promote self-sufficiency, eliminate poverty, and improve the quality of life in our community. They aim to keep families together and help them to become self sufficient and enable them to work closely with community organizations to stretch the safety net they provide even further.

1492 MINDSOURCE

1575 Sherman Street
10th Floor
Denver, CO 80203
720-591-6793
www.mindsourcecolorado.org

James E. Graham, PhD, DC, FACRM, Board Member
Jennifer Coker, Board Member
Jason Kacmarski, Board Member
Angie Goodger, Board Member

MINDSOURCE strives to support all people in Colorado with traumatic brain injury through services, research and education. Formerly known as the Colorado Brain Injury Program.

Connecticut

1493 Connecticut Department of Mental Health and Addiction Services

410 Capitol Avenue
P O Box 341431
Hartford, CT 06134
860-418-7000
800-446-7348
TDD: 860-418-6707
www.portal.ct.gov/dmhas

The mission of the Department of Mental Health and Addiction Services is to improve the quality of life of the people of Connecticut by providing an integrated network of comprehensive, effective and efficient mental health and addiction services that foster self-sufficiency, dignity and respect.

1494 Connecticut Department of Children and Families

505 Hudson Street
Hartford, CT 06106
860-550-6300
E-mail: commissioner.dcf@ct.gov
www.portal.ct.gov/dcf

The mission of the Department of Children and Families is to protect children, improve child and family well-being and support and preserve families. These efforts are accomplished by respecting and working within individual cultures and communities in Connecticut, and in partnership with others. Member of the National Leadership Council

Delaware

1495 Delaware Department of Health & Social Services

1901 North Dupont Highway
Main Building
New Castle, DE 19720
800-372-2022
www.dhss.delaware.gov

The mission of the Delaware Department of Health and Social Services is to improve the quality of life for Delaware's citizens by promoting health and well-being, fostering self-sufficiency, and protecting vulnerable populations.

1496 Delaware Division of Family Services

1825 Faulkland Road
Wilmington, DE 19805-1195
302-663-2665
E-mail: info.dscyf@state.de.us
www.kids.delaware.gov

Trenee Parker, Director
Susan Murray, Deputy Director

The Division of Family Services is mandated by law to investigate complaints about child abuse and neglect. Since 1875, state agencies have been balancing the children's right of safety and the parent's right to choose what is good for the family. The Adoption and Safe Families Act of 1997 clearly puts the focus on the protection, safety and permanency plan of children as the first priority. Services provided are child oriented and family focused.

Year Founded: 1983

District of Columbia

1497 DC Commission on Mental Health Services
64 New York Avenue, NE
4th Floor
Washington, DC 20002
202-673-2200
TTY: 202-673-7500
E-mail: dbh@dc.gov
www.dmh.dc.gov

Regulates the District's mental health system for adults, children and youth, and their families, and provides mental health services directly through the Community Service Agency (for community-based consumers of mental health services) and St. Elizabeths Hospital.

1498 DC Department of Human Services
64 New York Avenue NE
6th Floor
Washington, DC 20002
202-671-4200
E-mail: dhs@dc.gov
www.dhs.dc.gov/dhs

Laura Green Zeilinger, Director
Tania Mortensen, Chief Operating Officer
David Ross, Chief of Staff
Monica Brown, General Counsel

The Department of Human Services provides protection, intervention and social services to meet the needs of vulnerable adults and families to help reduce risk and promote self-sufficiency.

1499 Health & Medicine Counsel of Washington DDNC Digestive Disease National Coalition
50 F St NW
Suite 730
Washington, DC 20001
202-544-7497
www.ddnc.org

Ceciel Rooker, Chairperson
Bryan Green, MD, President
Cathy Griffith, Vice Chairperson
James Hobley, MD, Vice President

The Digestive Disease National Coalition (DDNC) is an advocacy organization comprised of the major national voluntary and professional societies concerned with digestive diseases. The DDNC focuses on improving public policy related to digestive diseases and increasing public awareness with respect to the many diseases of the digestive system. Based in Washington, D.C.

Year Founded: 1978

Florida

1500 Florida Department Health and Human Services: Substance Abuse Program
www.www.myflfamilies.com/service-programs/samh/

The Substance Abuse Program Office is dedicated to the development of a comprehensive system of prevention, emergency/detoxification, and treatment services for individuals and families at risk of or affected by substance abuse; to promote their safety, well-being, and self-sufficiency.

1501 Florida Department of Children and Families
2415 North Monroe Street
Suite 400
Tallahassee, FL 32303-4190

850-487-1111
www.www.myflfamilies.com

Provides rules, regulations, monitoring of fifteen district mental health program offices and mental health providers throughout the state.

1502 Florida Department of Health and Human Services Tallahassee, FL
850-245-4444
www.www.floridahealth.gov

The mission of the Florida Department of Health and Human Services is to promote and protect the health and safety of all people in Florida through the delivery of quality public health services and the promotion of health care standards.

Year Founded: 1996

1503 Florida Department of Mental Health and Rehabilitative Services
Department of Children and Families
2415 North Monroe Street
Suite 400
Tallahassee, FL 32303-4190
850-487-1111
www.www.myflfamilies.com

The Mental Health Program Office is committed to focusing its resources to meet the needs of people who cannot otherwise access mental health care.

1504 Florida Medicaid State Plan
2727 Mahan Drive
Tallahassee, FL 32308
850-412-3630
850-922-6484
www.ahca.myflorida.com

Cody L. Farrill, Chief of Staff
Josefina M. Tamayo, General Counsel
William H. Roberts, Deputy General Counsel
Mary Clemmons-Haire, Asst. to Deputy General Counsel

Provides information about the Medicare plans, benefits and how to enroll in them. Medicaid is the state and federal partnership that provides health coverage for selected categories of people with low incomes. Its purpose is to improve the health of people who might otherwise go without medical care for themselves and their children. Florida implemented the Medicaid program on January 1, 1970, to provide medical services to indigent people. Over the years, the Florida Legislature has authorized Medicaid reimbursement for additional services. A major expansion occurred in 1989, when the United States Congress mandated that states provide all Medicaid services allowable under the Social Security Act to children under the age of 21.

Georgia

1505 Georgia Department of Behavioral Health and Developmental Disabilities (DBHDD)
2 Peachtree Street NW
24th Floor
Atlanta, GA 30303
404-657-2252
www.dbhdd.georgia.gov

Judy Fitzgerald, Commissioner

Provides treatment and support services to people with mental illnesses and addictive diseases, and support to people with developmental disabilities. DBHDD serves people of all ages with the most severe and likely to be long-term conditions. The division also funds evidenced-based prevention services aimed at reducing substance abuse and related problems.

1506 Georgia Department of Human Resources
60 Executive Park South, NE
Atlanta, GA 30329
404-679-4940
www.dca.state.ga.us

Christopher Nunn, Commissioner
David Whisnant, Chief Operating Officer
Stephanie Green, Chief Financial Officer

Provides programs that control the spread of disease, enable older people to live at home longer, prevent children from developing lifelong disabilities, train single parents to find and hold jobs, and help people with mental or physical disabilities live and work in their communities.

Hawaii

1507 Hawaii Department of Health
808-586-4400
www.health.hawaii.gov

Elizabeth A. Char, MD, Director of Health
Cathy Ross, MPH, MBA, Deputy Director
Danette Wong Tomiyasu, MBA, Deputy Dir., Health Resources
Kathleen Ho, JD, LLM, Deputy Dir., Env. Health

The mission of the Department of Health is to protect and improve the health and environment for all people in Hawaii.

Idaho

1508 Department of Health and Welfare: Medicaid & Health Division
208-334-5747
877-456-1233
E-mail: MyBenefits@dhw.idaho.gov
www.healthandwelfare.idaho.gov

Dave Jeppesen, Director
Juliet Charron, Division of Medicaid

Mission is to improve mental health services for Idahoans through healthcare coverage.

1509 Idaho Department of Health & Welfare
877-456-1233
E-mail: MyBenefits@dhw.idaho.gov
www.healthandwelfare.idaho.gov

Dave Jeppesen, Director
Miren Unsworth, Deputy Director
Lisa Hettinger, Deputy Director

Dedicated to improving health programs and services to Idahoans.
Year Founded: 1974

1510 Idaho Department of Health and Welfare: Children and Families
208-334-5700
www.healthandwelfare.idaho.gov

Cameron Gilliland, Administrator

Mission is to improve child care programs and services offered to families in Idaho.

1511 Idaho Maternal and Child Health (MCH)
PO Box 83720
Boise, ID 83720-3
208-334-5962
E-mail: IdahoMCH@dhw.idaho.gov
www.healthandwelfare.idaho.gov

The MCH program is dedicated to improving healthcare services and support offered to mothers and children, including families with special healthcare needs.

Illinois

1512 Illinois Alcoholism and Drug Dependency Association
937 S 2nd Street
Springfield, IL 62704
217-528-7335
E-mail: iadda@iadda.org
www.iadda.org

Sara Howe, Chief Executive Officer

The IADD Association works hard to educate the general public about the disease of addiction, sharing the message that addiction can be prevented. It can be treated and people can recover from it. It is done through comprehensive media campaigns, community forums, town hall meetings, and letter writing efforts.

1513 Illinois Department of Alcoholism and Substance Abuse
800-843-6154
TTY: 866-324-5553
www.www.dhs.state.il.us

DASA consists of three operational Bureau's designed to reflect our mission and planning goals and objectives. Primary responsibilities are to develop, maintain, monitor and evaluate a statewide treatment delivery system designed to provide screening, assessment, customer-treatment matching, referral, intervention, treatment and continuing care services for indigents alcohol and drug abuse and dependency problems. These services are provided by numerous community-based substance abuse treatment organizations contracted by DASA according to the needs of various communities and populations.
Year Founded: 1997

1514 Illinois Department of Children and Family Services
217-524-2029
800-232-3798
www.www2.illinois.gov/dcfs/Pages/default.aspx

The Illinois Department of Children and Family Services provides child welfare services in Illinois. It is also the nation's largest state child welfare agency to earn accreditation from the Council on Accreditation for Children and Family Services (COA). The Department's organization includes the Divisions of Child Protection, Placement Permanency, Field Operations, Guardian & Advocacy, Clinical Practice & Professional Development, Service Intervention, Budget & Finance, Planning & Performance Management, and Communications.

1515 Illinois Department of Health and Human Services
800-843-6154
TTY: 866-324-5553
www.www.dhs.state.il.us/page.aspx

DHS serves Illinois citizens through seven main programs: Welfare programs, including temporary assistance for needy families, Food Stamps, and child care; Alcoholism and substance abuse treatment and prevention services; Developmental disabilities; Health services for pregnant women and mothers, infants, children, and adolescents; Prevention services for domestic violence and at-risk youth; Mental health and Rehabilitation services.

Year Founded: 1997

1516 Illinois Department of Healthcare and Family Services
201 S Grand Avenue E
Springfield, IL 62763
217-782-1200
www.www2.illinois.gov/hfs

Theresa Eagleson, Director
Ben Winick, Chief of Staff
Jenny Aguirre, Assistant Director
Steffanie Garrett, Office of General Counsel

The Illinois Department of Healthcare and Family Services, formerly the Department of Public Aid, is the state agency dedicated to improving the lives of Illinois' families through health care coverage, child support enforcement and energy assistance.

1517 Illinois Department of Mental Health 2nd Floor Springfield, IL 62765
800-843-6154
TDD: 866-324-5553
TTY: 312-814-5050
www.dhs.state.il.us/mhdd/dd/

Michelle R B Saddler, Secretary
Grace Hong Duffin, Chief of Staff

Our mission is to provide a full array of quality, outcome-based, person-and community-centered services and supports for individuals with developmental disabilities and their families in Illinois.

1518 Illinois Department of Public Health: Division of Food, Drugs and Dairies/FDD
525-535 West Jefferson Street
Springfield, IL 62761
217-782-4977
TTY: 800-547-0466
www.www.idph.state.il.us

Ngozi O. Ezike, MD, Director

The mission of the Illinois Department of Public Health is to promote the health of the people of Illinois through the prevention and control of disease and injury.

Indiana

1519 Indiana Department of Public Welfare Division of Family Independence: Food Stamps/Medicaid/Training
Family and Social Services Administration
402 W Washington Street
PO Box 7083
Indianapolis, IN 46207

800-403-0864
www.in.gov/fssa

Dan Rusyniak, MD, Secretary
Michael Gargano, Deputy Secretary/Chief of Staff
Paul Bowling, Chief Financial Officer
Cate Marshall, Executive Assistant

The mission of the Division of Family Independence is to strengthenfamilies and children through temporary assistance to needy families, food stamps, housing, child care, foster care, adoption, energy assistance, homeless services, and job programs.

1520 Indiana Family and Social Services Administration: Division of Mental Health
402 W Washington Street
PO Box 7083
Indianapolis, IN 46207
800-901-1133
www.www.in.gov/fssa/dmha/2688.htm

Dan Rusyniak, MD, Secretary
Michael Gargano, Deputy Secretary/Chief of Staff
Paul Bowling, Chief Financial Officer
Cate Marshall, Executive Assistant

The mission of the Indiana Family and Social Services Administration Division of Mental Health is to strengthening families and children through temporary assistance to needy families, food stamps, housing, child care, foster care, adoption, energy assistance, homeless services, and job programs.

1521 Indiana Family and Social Services Administration
402 W Washington Street
PO Box 7083
Indianapolis, IN 46207
800-403-0864
www.in.gov/fssa

Dan Rusyniak, MD, Secretary
Michael Gargano, Deputy Secretary/Chief of Staff
Paul Bowling, Chief Financial Officer
Cate Marshall, Executive Assistant

The mission of the Indiana Department of Family and Social Services is to strengthen families and children through temporary assistance to needy families, food stamps, housing, child care, foster care, adoption, energy assistance, homeless services, and job programs.

1522 The Indiana Consortium for Mental Health Services Research (ICMHSR)
Institute for Social Research Indiana University
1022 East Third Street
Bloomington, IN 47401-3779
812-855-3841
E-mail: acapshew@indiana.edu
www.indiana.edu/~icmhsr/

Bernice A Pescosolido Ph.D, Director, Indiana Consortium for
Alex Capshew, Administrative Operations Manage
Jack K. Martin, Director, Karl F. Schuessler Ins
Mary Hannah, Production & Dissemination Manag

The Indiana Consortium for Mental Health Services Research (ICMHSR) focuses on developing high quality scholarly and applied research projects on mental health and related services for people with severe mental disorders. A major commitment of the ICMHSR is to use research to foster public awareness and improve public policy and decision-making regarding these devastating illnesses.

Iowa

1523 Iowa Department of Human Services
800-972-2017
E-mail: contactdhs@dhs.state.ia.us
www.dhs.state.ia.us

Kelly Kennedy Garcia, Director

The Mission of the Iowa Department of Human Services is to help individuals and families achieve safe, stable, self-sufficient, and healthy lives, thereby contributing to the economic growth of the state. We do this by keeping a customer focus, striving for excellence, sound stewardship of state resources, maximizing the use of federal funding and leveraging opportunities, and by working with our public and private partners to achieve results.

Year Founded: 1937

1524 Iowa Department of Human Services: Division of Mental Health & Disability Services
1305 E. Walnut Street
Des Moines, IA 50319
515-229-2945
E-mail: wdephil@dhs.state.ia.us
www.dhs.iowa.gov

Wendy DePhillips, Contact

The Mental Health and Disability Services Commission is the state policy-making body for the provision of services to persons with mental illness, intellectual disabilities or other developmental disabilities, or brain injury.

1525 Iowa Department of Public Health
321 E. 12th Street
Des Moines, IA 50319-0075
515-281-7689
TTY: 800-735-2942
www.idph.iowa.gov

Kelly Garcia, Department Director
Sarah Reisetter, Deputy Director
Jerilyn Oshel, Division Director

Under the direction of the director, the Iowa Department of Public Health exercises general supervision of the state's public health; promotes public hygiene and sanitation; does health promotion activities, prepares for and responds to bioemergency situations; and, unless otherwise provided, enforces laws on public health.

1526 Iowa Department of Public Health: Division of Substance Abuse
321 E. 12th Street
Des Moines, IA 50319-0075
515-281-7689
TTY: 800-735-2942
www.idph.iowa.gov/substance-abuse

DeAnn Decker, Bureau Chief

The Office of Substance Abuse Prevention/Staff of the Office of Substance Abuse Prevention provides the following services: technical assistance to individuals, groups, and contracted agencies and organizations; coordinate and collaborate with multiple state agencies and organizations for assessment, planning, and implementation of statewide prevention initiatives; and coordinate, train, and monitor funding to local community-based organizations for alcohol, tobacco, and other drug prevention services.

Kansas

1527 Kansas Council on Developmental Disabilities: Rehabilitation Services
900 SW Jackson
Room 569
Topeka, KS 66612-1570
785-296-2608
877-431-4604
E-mail: kcdd@kcdd.org
www.www.dcf.ks.gov

Steve Gieber, Executive Director
Craig Knutson, Policy Analyst
Jeff Schroeder, Public Policy Coordinator
Charline Cobbs, Senior Administrative Assistant

Established as an umbrella agency to oversee social services and state institutions in Kansas.

Year Founded: 1973

Kentucky

1528 Kentucky Cabinet for Health and Family Services: Division of Behavioral Health (DBH)
275 East Main St. 4W-F
Frankfort, KY 40601
502-564-4527
www.dbhdid.ky.gov/dbh

Administers state and federally funded mental health and substance abuse treatment services throughout Kentucky.

1529 Kentucky Cabinet for Health and Human Services
275 E. Main St.
Frankfort, KY 40621
800-372-2973
TTY: 800-627-4702
www.chfs.ky.gov

The goal of the Cabinet for Health and Family Services is to provide the finest health care possible for people in our state facilities; To provide the best preventative services through our public health programs; To provide the most outstanding service for our families and children; To protect and prevent the abuse of children, elders and people with disabilities and To build quality programs across-the-board; and by doing all of these things.

1530 Kentucky Justice Cabinet: Department of Juvenile Justice
1025 Capital Center Drive
Frankfort, KY 40601
502-573-2044
www.djj.ky.gov

Vicki Reed, Commissioner

The Kentucky Department of Juvenile Justice's mission is to improve public safety by providing balanced and comprehensive services that hold youth accountable, and to provide the opportunity for youth to develop into productive, responsible citizens.

Louisiana

1531 Louisiana Commission on Law Enforcement and Administration (LCLE)
602 N 5th St.
Baton Rouge, LA 70802
225-342-1500
www.www.lcle.state.la.us

Jim Craft, Executive Director
Hope Davis, Human Resources
Lisa Dreher, Administrative Assistant
Verna Hamilton, Executive Staff Officer

Lastest news and information on LCLE programs, resources, job openings, and general agency information on a monthly basis and for an in-depth review of our criminal justice programs.

1532 Louisiana Department of Health: Office of Behavioral Health
628 N. 4th Street
Baton Rouge, LA 70802
225-342-9500
www.www.dhh.louisiana.gov

Karen Stubbs, Assistant Secretary
James Hussey, MD, Medical Director
Amanda Joyner, Deputy Assistant Secretary
Robyn McDermott, Deputy Assistant Secretary

The mission of the Office of Mental Health (OMH) is to perform the functions of the state which provide or lead to treatment, rehabilitation and follow-up care for individuals in Louisiana with mental and emotional disorders. OMH administers and/or monitors community-based services, public or private, to assure active quality care in the most cost-effective manner in the least restrictive environment for all persons with mental and emotional disorders.

Maine

1533 Maine Department Health and Human Services Children's Behavioral Health Services
109 Capitol Street
11 State House Station
Augusta, ME 04333
207-287-3707
www.maine.gov/dhhs/ocfs

Dr. Adrienne Carmack, Medical Director
Elissa Wynne, Associate Director

Children's Behavioral Health Services (CBHS), a branch of the Department of Health and Human Services (DHHS) has a long tradition of advocacy for children with special needs. Once known as the Bureau of Children's with Special Needs (BCSN), this part of the Department became known as Children's Services in 1995. In a continuing effort to meet the diverse and growing needs of Maine families, Children's Behavioral Health Services (CBHS) is going through a further transition. Most services formerly provided directly through the Department are now delivered through contracted community agencies.

1534 Maine Office of Substance Abuse: Information and Resource Center
295 Water Street
Suite 200
Augusta, ME 04330
207-621-8118
800-499-0027
TTY: 800-606-0215
www.www.masap.org

Pat Kimball, President
Peter McCorison, Vice President
Ruth E. Blauer, Executive Director
Catherine Ryder, Secretary

Provides Maine's citizens with alcohol, tobacco and other drug information, resources and research for prevention, education and treatment.

Maryland

1535 Centers for Medicare and Medicaid Services: Office of Financial Management/OFM
7500 Security Boulevard
Baltimore, MD 21244
800-633-4227
TTY: 877-486-2048
www.www.cms.gov

Chiquita Brooks-LaSure, Administrator
Jonathan Blum, Principal Deputy Admin./COO
Erin Richardson, Chief of Staff
Karen Jackson, Deputy Chief Operating Officer

OFM has overall reponsibility for the fiscal integrity of CMS' programs.

1536 Maryland Alcohol and Drug Abuse Administration
55 Wade Avenue
Catonsville, MD 21228
410-402-8600
TTY: 410-528-2258

The Alcohol and Drug Abuse Administration (ADAA) is the single state agency responsible for the provision, coordination, and regulation of the statewide network of substance abuse prevention, intervention and treatment services. It serves as the initial point of contact for technical assistance and regulatory interpretation for all Maryland Department of Health and Mental Hygiene (DHMH) prevention and certified treatment programs.

1537 Maryland Department of Health
201 W. Preston Street
Baltimore, MD 21201
410-767-6500
877-463-3464
www.dhmh.maryland.gov

Provides information on a variety of services including mental health and substance abuse, health plans and providers, nutrition and maternal care, environmental health and developmental disabilities.

Massachusetts

1538 Massachusetts Department of Mental Health
25 Staniford Street
11th Floor
Boston, MA 02114
617-626-8000
877-382-1609
E-mail: dmhinfo@dmh.state.ma.us
www.www.mass.gov/dmh

The Massachusetts Department of Mental Health provides clinical, rehabilitative and supportive services for adults with serious mental illness, and children and adolescents with serious mental illness or serious emotional disturbance.

1539 Massachusetts Department of Public Health

1000 Washington Street
Suite 310
Boston, MA 02118-5002
617-790-4000
800-495-0086
TTY: 877-509-6981
www.masspartnership.com

Sharon Hanson, Chief Executive Officer
Chad Muller, MBA, MSF, Vice President/Finance Director
Russell Kopp, CPA, MBA, Chief Financial Officer

Our mission, to serve all the people in the Commonwealth, particularly the under served, and to promote healthy people, healthy families, healthy communities and healthy environments through compassionate care, education and prevention. Your health is our concern.

Year Founded: 1996

1540 Massachusetts Department of Public Health: Bureau of Substance Abuse Services

1000 Washington Street
Suite 310
Boston, MA 02118-5002
617-790-4000
800-495-0086
TTY: 877-509-6981
www.masspartnership.com

Sharon Hanson, Chief Executive Officer
Chad Muller, MBA, MSF, Vice President/Finance Director
Russell Kopp, CPA, MBA, Chief Financial Officer

The Bureau of Substance Abuse Services oversees the substance abuse prevention and treatment services in the Commonwealth. Responsibilities include: licensing programs and counselors; funding and monitoring prevention and treatment services; providing access to treatment for the indigent and uninsured; developing and implementing policies and programs; and, tracking substance abuse trends in the state.

Year Founded: 1996

1541 Massachusetts Department of Transitional Assistance

Massachusetts Department of Health and Human Services
2201 Washington St.
Roxbury, MA 02119
617-989-2200
www.mass.gov/dta/

Amy Kershaw, Commissioner

The mission of the Department of Transitional Assistance is to serve the Commonwealth's most vulnerable families and individuals with dignity and respect, ensuring those eligible for our services have access to those services in an accurate, timely and culturally sensitive manner and in a way that promotes client's independence and long term self-sufficiency.

1542 Massachusetts Executive Office of Public Safety and Security

1 Ashburton Place
Suite 2133
Boston, MA 02108
617-727-7775
TTY: 617-727-6618
E-mail: eopsinfo@state.ma.us
www.www.mass.gov/eopss/

Plans and manages public safety efforts by supporting, supervising and providing planning and guidance to a variety of state agencies.

Michigan

1543 Michigan Department of Community Health

Department of Mental Health
333 S. Grand Ave
PO Box 30195
Lansing, MI 48909
517-373-3740
800-649-3777
E-mail: mccurtisj@michigan.gov
www.michigan.gov/mdch/

Provides information on drug control and substance abuse treatment policies.

1544 Michigan Department of Human Services

235 S Grand Ave
PO Box 30037
Lansing, MI 48909-7537
517-373-2305
TTY: 517-373-8071
www.michigan.gov/dhs/

The Department of Human Services (DHS) is Michigan's public assistance, child and family welfare agency. DHS directs the operations of public assistance and service programs through a network of over 100 county department of human service offices around the state.

1545 National Council on Alcoholism and Drug Dependence: Greater Detroit Area

2400 East McNichols
Detroit, MI 48212
313-868-1340
www.ncadd-detroit.org

Benjamin A. Jones, President & CEO
Mary Duncan, Board Chair
Hon. Martha G. Scott, Treasurer
James H. Boyce, Secretary

The National Council on Alcoholism and Drug Dependence-Greater Detroit Area is a non-profit agency committed to improving mental health through substance abuse prevention, education, training, treatment and advocacy.

Minnesota

1546 Lakes Center for Youth & Families

20 Lake Street North
Suite 103
Forest Lake, MN 55025
651-464-3685
www.www.lc4yf.org

Linda Madsen, PhD, Executive Director
Jenna Jones, Assistant Executive Director
James D. Schoppenhorst, Chair
Richard R. Peterson, Chair-Elect

Provides enrichment programs and intervention support to youth and families.

Year Founded: 1976

1547 Minnesota Department of Human Services
PO Box 64977
Saint Paul, MN 55164-0977
651-431-2460
www.mn.gov/dhs/

Jodi Harpstead, Commissioner
Nikki Farago, Deputy Commissioner
Charles E. Johnson, Deputy Commissioner
Stacy Twite, Chief of Staff

The Minnesota Department of Human Services helps people meet their basic needs by providing or administering health care coverage, economic assistance, and a variety of services for children, people with disabilities and older Minnesotans.

1548 Minnesota Department of Human Services: Chemical Health Divison
PO Box 64977
Saint Paul, MN 55164-0977
651-431-2460
E-mail: YourOpinionMatters.DHS@state.mn.us
www.mn.gov/dhs/

Jodi Harpstead, Commissioner
Nikki Farago, Deputy Commissioner
Charles E. Johnson, Deputy Commissioner
Stacy Twite, Chief of Staff

The Chemical Health Division is the state alcohol and drug authority responsible for defining a statewide response to drug and alcohol abuse. This includes providing basic information on chemical health. It also includes planning a broad-based community service system, evaluating the effectiveness of various chemical dependency services, and funding innovative programs to promote reduction of alcohol and other drug problems and their effects on individuals, families and society.

Mississippi

1549 Mississippi Alcohol Safety Education Program
1 Research Blvd
Suite 103
Starkville, MS 39762
662-325-7127
www.www.ssrc.msstate.edu

Emile Creel, Communications Coordinator
Jennifer Flannagan, Business Manager
Lori Stubbs, Office Associate

MASEP is the statewide program for first-time offenders convicted of driving under the influence of alcohol or another substance which has impaired one's ability to operate a motor vehicle.

1550 Mississippi Department of Human Services
200 South Lamar St.
Jackson, MS 39201
601-359-4500
800-948-3020
www.www.mdhs.ms.gov

Robert G. Anderson, Executive Director

The mission of the Department of Human Services is to provide services for people in need by optimizing all available resources to sustain the family unit and to encourage traditional family values thereby promoting self-sufficiency and personal responsibility for all Mississippians.

1551 Mississippi Department of Mental Health: Division of Alcohol and Drug Abuse
239 N Lamar Street
1101 Robert E Lee Building
Jackson, MS 39201
601-359-1288
877-210-8513
TDD: 601-359-6230
www.www.dmh.ms.gov

Dr. Jim Herzog, Chair
Sampat Shivangi, M.D., Vice Chair

The Division of Alcohol and Drug Abuse Services is responsible for establishing, maintaining, monitoring and evaluating a statewide system of alcohol and drug abuse services, including prevention, treatment and rehabilitation. The division has designed a system of services for alcohol and drug abuse prevention and treatment reflecting its philosophy that alcohol and drug abuse is a treatable and preventable illness.

1552 Mississippi Department of Mental Health
239 N Lamar Street
1101 Robert E Lee Building
Jackson, MS 39201
601-359-1288
877-210-8513
TDD: 601-359-6230
www.www.dmh.ms.gov

Dr. Jim Herzog, Chair
Sampat Shivangi, M.D., Vice Chair

Dedicated to the improvement and implementation of services to meet the needs of individuals with developmental disabilities.

1553 Mississippi Department of Mental Health: Division of Medicaid
239 N Lamar Street
1101 Robert E Lee Building
Jackson, MS 39201
601-359-1288
877-210-8513
TDD: 601-359-6230
www.www.dmh.ms.gov

Dr. Jim Herzog, Chair
Sampat Shivangi, M.D., Vice Chair

Medicaid is a national health care program. It helps pay for medical services for low-income people. For those eligible for full Medicaid services, Medicaid is paid to providers of health care. Providers are doctors, hospitals and pharmacists who take Medicaid. We strive to provide financial assistance for the provision of quality health services to our beneficiaries with professionalism, integrity, compassion and commitment. We are advocates for, and accountable to the people we serve.

1554 Mississippi Department of Rehabilitation Services: Office of Vocational Rehabilitation (OVR)
1281 Highway 51
PO Box 1698
Madison, MS 39110
800-443-1000
www.mdrs.ms.gov/VocationalRehab/Pages/default.aspx

Lavonda Hart, Director

The Office of Vocational Rehabilitation (OVR) provides services designed to improve economic opportunities for individuals with physical and mental disabilities through employment. Work related services are individualized and may include but are not limited to: counseling, job development, job training, job placement, supported employment, transition services and employability skills training program. OVR has a network of 17 community rehabilitation centers (Allied Enterprises) located throughout the state, which provide vocational assessment, job training and actual work experience for individuals with disabilities. Thousands of Mississippians are successfully employed each year through the teamwork at OVR.

Missouri

1555 Missouri Department Health & Senior Services

912 Wildwood
PO Box 570
Jefferson City, MO 65102
573-751-6400
E-mail: info@health.mo.gov
www.health.mo.gov

Paul F. Nickelson, Acting Director
Debbie Mebruer, Executive Assistant
Dr. Laura Naught, Deputy Director

The Missouri Department of Health and Senior Services provides information on a variety of topics including senior services and health, current news and public notices, laws and regulations, and statistical reports.

1556 Missouri Department of Mental Health

1706 E Elm Street
Jefferson City, MO 65101
573-751-4122
800-364-9687
E-mail: dbhmail@dmh.mo.gov
www.dmh.mo.gov

State law provides three principal missions for the department: (1) the prevention of mental disorders, developmental disabilities, substance abuse, and compulsive gambling; (2) the treatment, habilitation, and rehabilitation of Missourians who have those conditions; and (3) the improvement of public understanding and attitudes about mental disorders, developmental disabilities, substance abuse, and compulsive gambling.

1557 Missouri Department of Mental Health: Behavioral Health - Substance Use and Mental Illness

1706 East Elm Street
Jefferson City, MO 65101
573-751-4122
800-364-9687
E-mail: dbhmail@dmh.mo.gov
www.dmh.mo.gov/behavioral-health

Valerie Huhn, Director
Heidi DiBiaso, Administrative Assistant

The Division provides funding for prevention, outpatient, residential, and detoxification services to community-based programs that work with communities to develop and implement comprehensive coordinated plans. The Division provides technical assistance to these agencies and operates a certification program that sets standards for treatment programs, qualified professionals, and alcohol and drug related educational programs.

1558 Missouri Department of Public Safety

1101 Riverside Drive
PO Box 749
Jefferson City, MO 65102
573-751-4905
E-mail: dpsinfo@dps.mo.gov
www.www.dps.mo.gov

Sandy Karsten, Director
Kevin Bond, Deputy Director
Kylie Dickneite, Homeland Security Director
Nathan Weinert, General Counsel

The Office of the Director is the Department of Public Safety's central administrative unit. Our office administers federal and state funds in grants for juvenile justice, victims' assistance, law enforcement, and narcotics control. Other programs in the Director's Office provide support services and resources to assist local law enforcement agencies and to promote crime prevention.

1559 Missouri Department of Social Services

PO Box 1537
Jefferson City, MO 65102-1527
573-751-4815
TDD: 800-735-2966
www.dss.mo.gov

Robert Knodell, Acting Director
Jennifer Tidball, Chief Operating Officer
Patrick Luebbering, Chief Financial Officer
Caitlin Whaley, Director, Legislation & Comms.

Dedicated to keeping families together, preventing abuse and neglect, and encouraging self-sufficiency and independence.

1560 Missouri Department of Social Services: MO HealthNet Division

615 Howerton Court
P O Box 6500
Jefferson City, MO 65102-6500
573-751-3425
800-735-2966
www.dss.mo.gov/mhd/

The purpose of the MO HealthNet Program is to provide mental health care services for low income and vulnerable citizens of the State of Missouri. The agency assures quality health care through development of service delivery systems, standards setting and enforcement, and education of providers and recipients.

Year Founded: 1965

1561 Missouri Division of Developmental Disabilities

573-751-4054
800-207-9329
E-mail: ddmail@dmh.mo.gov
www.dmh.mo.gov/dd

Jessica Bax, Division Director
Julia LePage, Director, Community Supports
April Maxwell, Director, State-Operated Program

The Division of Developmental Disabilities (DD) serves a population that has developmental disabilities such as intellectual disabilities, cerebral palsy, head injuries, autism, epilepsy, and certain learning disabilities. Its mission is to improve lives of individuals with developmental disabilities through supports and services that foster self-determination.

Year Founded: 1974

Montana

1562 Montana Department of Health and Human Services: Child & Family Services Division
PO Box 8005
Helena, MT 59604-8005
406-841-2400
866-820-5437
www.dphhs.mt.gov/cfsd/

The Child and Family Services Division (CFSD) is a part of the Montana Department of Public Health and Human Services. Its mission is to keep Montana's children safe and families strong. The division provides state and federally mandated protective services to children who are abused, neglected, or abandoned. This includes receiving and investigating reports of child abuse and neglect, working to prevent domestic violence, helping families to stay together or reunite, and finding placements in foster or adoptive homes.

1563 Montana Department of Human & Community Services
PO Box 4210
Helena, MT 59604
406-444-5622
TTY: 406-444-1421
www.dphhs.mt.gov

Adam Meier, Director
Charles Brereton, Chief of Staff
Morgan Taylor, Chief Policy Officer
Kim Aiken, Chief Financial Officer

The mission of the Montana Department of Human & Community Services is to promote job preparation and work as a means to help needy families become self-sufficient.

Year Founded: 1887

1564 Montana Department of Public Health & Human Services: Addictive and Mental Disorders Division
100 N Park
Suite 300
Helena, MT 59601-4168
406-444-3964
www.dphhs.mt.gov

Adam Meier, Director
Charles Brereton, Chief of Staff
Morgan Taylor, Chief Policy Officer
Kim Aiken, Chief Financial Officer

The mission of the Addictive and Mental Disorders Division (AMDD) of the Montana Department of Public Health and Human Services is to implement and improve an appropriate statewide system of prevention, treatment, care, and rehabilitation for Montanans with mental disorders or addictions to drugs or alcohol.

1565 Montana Department of Public Health and Human Services: Disability Employment & Transitions Division
Disability Services Division
111 North Last Chance Gulch
Suite 4C
Helena, MT 59601-4520

406-444-2590
877-296-1197
www.dphhs.mt.gov

Cathy Murphy, Program Support Supervisor
Lisa Nehl, Eligibility Specialist

The mission of the Disability Employment and Transitions Division is to provide services that help Montanans with disabilities to live, work and fully participate in their communities.

Nebraska

1566 Nebraska Department of Health and Human Services (NHHS)
301 Centennial Mall South
Lincoln, NE 68509
402-471-3121
800-833-7352
www.dhhs.ne.gov

Danette R. Smith, Chief Executive Officer
Larry Kahl, Chief Operating Officer
Bo Botelho, General Counsel

The mission of the NHHS is to help people live better lives through effective health and human services.

1567 Nebraska Health & Human Services: Medicaid and Long-Term Care
301 Centennial Mall South
Lincoln, NE 68509
402-471-3121
TDD: 800-833-7352
www.hhs.state.ne.us

Kevin Bagley, Director

The Finance and Support agency aligns human resources, financial resources, and information needs for the Nebraska Health and Human Services System and is the designated Title XIX (Medicaid) agency responsible for provider enrollment activities.

1568 Nebraska Health and Human Services Division: Department of Mental Health
301 Centennial Mall South
Lincoln, NE 68509
402-471-3121
TDD: 800-833-7352
www.dhhs.ne.gov/Pages/Behavioral-Health.aspx

Sheri Dawson, Director

Mental health services are designed for individuals and their families who have a serious and persistent mental illness that can create lifetime disabilities, and in some cases make the individuals dangerous to themselves or others. Services are also designed for people experiencing acute, serious mental illnesses, which in some cases may cause a life threatening event such as suicide attempts. In addition, services are provided for children and to their families.

1569 Nebraska Mental Health Centers
4545 South 86th Street
Lincoln, NE 68526-9227
402-483-6990
888-210-8064
www.www.nmhc-clinics.com

Jill Zlome McPherson, MA, CEO and Executive Director
Lisa Logsden, Psy.D., Internship Training Director
Alexandra Munet, Psy.D., Psychologist

We are a primary mental health care center that is truly committed to being of service to the Lincoln/Lancaster community and Greater Nebraska.

Nevada

1570 Nevada Department of Health and Human Services
4126 Technology Way
#100
Carson City, NV 89706
775-684-4000
www.dhhs.nv.gov

Richard Whitley, Director
Deborah A. Hassett, Deputy Director, Admin. Svcs.
Stacey Johnson, Deputy Director, Fiscal Svcs.
Marla McDade Williams, Deputy Director, Programs

The Department of Health and Human Services (DHHS) promotes the health and well-being of Nevadans through the delivery or facilitation of essential services to ensure families are strengthened, public health is protected, and individuals achieve their highest level of self-sufficiency.

1571 Nevada Division of Mental Health & Developmental Services
4150 Technology Way
Carson City, NV 89706
775-684-4200
www.mhds.state.nv.us

Lisa Sherych, Administrator
Debi Reynolds, Deputy Adminstrator
Jo Malay, Deputy Administrator
Julia Peek, MHA, CPM, Deputy Administrator

The Nevada Division of Mental Health provides a full array of clinical services to over 24,000 consumers each year. Services include: crisis intervention, hospital care, medication clinic, outpatient counseling, residential support and other mental health services targeted to individuals with serious mental illness.

1572 Nevada Employment Training & Rehabilitation Department
500 E. Third Street
Carson City, NV 89713
775-684-3849
TTY: 775-687-5353
E-mail: detradmn@detr.nv.gov
www.nvdetr.org

The Department of Employment, Training and Rehabilitation (DETR) is comprised of four divisions with numerous bureaus programs, and services housed in offices throughout Nevada to provide citizens the state's premier source of employment, training, and rehabilitative programs.

1573 Northern Nevada Adult Mental Health Services
4150 Technology Way
Carson City, NV 89706
775-684-4200
www.mhds.state.nv.us

Lisa Sherych, Administrator
Debi Reynolds, Deputy Administrator
Jo Malay, Deputy Administrator
Julia Peek, MHA, CPM, Deputy Administrator

The mission of Northern Nevada Adult Mental Health Services is to provide psychiatric treatment and rehabilitation

services in the least restrictive setting to support personal recovery and enhance quality of life.

1574 Southern Nevada Adult Mental Health Services
6161 W Charleston Boulevard
Las Vegas, NV 89146
702-486-6000
www.dpbh.nv.gov

Lisa Sherych, Administrator
Debi Reynolds, Deputy Administrator
Jo Malay, Deputy Administrator
Julia Peek, MHA, CPM, Deputy Administrator

State operated community mental health center. Provides inpatient and outpatient psychiatric services.

New Hampshire

1575 New Hampshire Department of Health & Human Services: Bureau of Community Health Services
129 Pleasant Street
Concord, NH 03301-3852
603-271-6200
800-322-9191
TDD: 800-735-2964
www.www.dhhs.state.nh.us/dphs/bchs/index.htm

The Bureau of Community Health Services oversees grants to community-based agencies for medical and preventive health services, sets policy, provides technical assistance and education, and carries out quality assurance activities in its programmatic areas of expertise.

1576 New Hampshire Department of Health and Human Services: Bureau of Developmental Services
129 Pleasant Street
Concord, NH 03301-3852
603-271-5034
www.www.dhhs.state.nh.us/dcbcs/bds

The NH developmental services system offers its consumers with developmental disabilities and acquired brain disorders a wide range of supports and services within their own communities. BDS is comprised of a main office in Concord and 12 designated non-profit and specialized service agencies that represent specific geographic regions of NH; the community agencies are commonly referred to as Area Agencies. All direct services and supports to individuals and families are provided in accordance with contractual agreements between BDS and the Area Agencies.

1577 New Hampshire Department of Health and Human Services: Bureau of Behavioral Health
129 Pleasant Street
Concord, NH 03301-3852
603-271-5007
www.www.dhhs.state.nh.us/dcbcs/bbh/index.htm

The Bureau of Behavioral Health (BBH) seeks to promote respect, recovery, and full community inclusion for adults, including older adults, who experience a mental illness and children with an emotional disturbance. By law and rule, BBH is mandated to ensure the provision of efficient and effective services to those citizens who are most severely and persistently disabled by mental, emotional, and behavioral dysfunction. To this end, BBH has apportioned the entire state into community mental health regions. Each of the ten regions has a BBH contracted Community Mental

Health Center and many regions have Peer Support Agencies.

New Jersey

1578 Juvenile Justice Commission
1001 Spruce Street
Suite 202
Trenton, NJ 08638-3957
609-292-1400
E-mail: commission@njjjc.org
www.www.nj.gov/lps/jjc/index.html

Christopher Edwards, Executive Asst. Attorney General
Jonathan Garelick, Chief of Staff
Jeremy Feigenbaum, State Solicitor
Stephan Finkel, Director of Legislative Affairs

The Juvenile Justice Commission (JJC) has three primary responsibilities: the care and custody of juvenile offenders committed to the agency by the courts, the support of local efforts to plan for and provide services to at-risk and court-involved youth through County Youth Services Commissions and the state Incentive Program, and the supervision of youth on aftercare/parole.

Year Founded: 1995

1579 New Jersey Department of Human Services
Capital Place One
PO Box 700
222 S Warren Street
Trenton, NJ 08608-2306
609-292-3717
www.www.state.nj.us/humanservices/

Sarah Adelman, Commissioner
Andrea Katz, Esq, Chief of Staff
Elisa Neira, Deputy Commissioner

The New Jersey Department of Human Services (DHS) is the state's social services agency, serving more than one million of New Jersey 's most vulnerable citizens, or about one of every eight New Jersey residents. Through the work of DHS and its 13 major divisions, individuals and families in need are able to keep their lives on track, their families together, a roof over their heads, and their health protected. Human Services offers individuals and families the breathing room they need in order to find permanent solutions to otherwise daunting problems.

1580 New Jersey Division of Mental Health Services
5 Commerce Way
PO Box 362
Hamilton, NJ 08625-0362
800-382-6717
www.www.state.nj.us/humanservices/dmhas/home/

Sarah Adelman, Commissioner
Andrea Katz, Esq, Chief of Staff
Elisa Neira, Deputy Commissioner

The Division of Mental Health Services (DMHS) serves adults with serious and persistent mental illnesses. Central to the Division's mission is the fact that these individuals are entitled to dignified and meaningful lives. Services are available to anyone in the state who feels they need help with a mental health problem.

New Mexico

1581 New Mexico Behavioral Health Collaborative
E-mail: deborah.fickling@state.nm.us
www.newmexico.networkofcare.org/mh/index.aspx

At the heart of the Collaborative's vision is the expectation that the lives of individuals with mental illness and substance use disorders (customers) will improve, that customers and family members will have an equal voice in the decisions that affect them and their loved ones, and that those most affected by mental illness and substance abuse can recover to lead full, meaningful lives within their communities. To achieve this will require a paradigm shift not only within the service delivery culture but also within the existing customer/family member networks.

1582 New Mexico Department of Health
1190 S St. Francis Drive
PO Box 26110
Santa Fe, NM 87505
www.nmhealth.org

The mission of the New Mexico Department of Health is to promote health and sound health policy, prevent disease and disability, improve health services systems and assure that essential public health functions and safety net services are available to New Mexicans.

1583 New Mexico Department of Human Services
PO Box 2348
Santa Fe, NM 87504-2348
800-283-4465
E-mail: eckert@state.nm.us
www.www.hsd.state.nm.us

David R. Scrase, MD, Secretary

The Department strives to provide New Mexicans access to support and services so that they may move toward self-sufficiency.

1584 New Mexico Health & Environment
Department
1190 St. Francis Drive
Suite N4050
Santa Fe, NM 87505
800-219-6157
www.nmenv.state.nm.us

Main goal is to provide the highest quality of life throughout New Mexico by promoting a safe, clean and productive environment.

1585 New Mexico Kids, Parents and Families Office
of Child Development: Children, Youth and
Families Department
1634 University Blvd NE
Albuquerque, NM 88102
800-691-9067
E-mail: resourceandreferral@unm.edu
www.www.newmexicokids.org

The Children, Youth and Families Department Office of Child Development (OCD) works collaboratively with the State Department of Education, Department of Health, Department of Labor and higher education and community programs to establish a five-year plan for Early Care, Education and Family Support Professional Development. The New Mexico Professional Development Initiative supports OCD's legislative mandate to articulate and implement training and licensure requirements for individuals working in all recognized settings with children from birth to age eight.

New York

1586 New York State Office of Mental Health
44 Holland Avenue
Albany, NY 12229
800-597-8481
www.www.omh.ny.gov

Ann Marie T. Sullivan, MD, Commissioner
Thomas Smith, MD, Chief Medical Offcer

Promoting the mental health of all New Yorkers with a particular focus on providing hope and recovery for adults with serious mental illness and children with serious emotional disturbances.

North Carolina

1587 North Carolina Addictions Specialist Professional Practice Board
PO Box 10126
Raleigh, NC 27605
919-832-0975
www.www.ncsappb.org

Barden Culbreth, Executive Director
Katie Gilmore, Associate Executive Director
Marcie Murfin, Customer Support Lead
Donna Strickland, Education & Training Specialist

Provides guidelines for the certification of professionals in the substance abuse field of human services.

Year Founded: 1984

1588 North Carolina Division of Mental Health
2001 Mail Service Center
Raleigh, NC 27699-2000
984-236-5000
800-662-7030
www.www.ncdhhs.gov/mhddsas/

Deepa Avula, Contact

North Carolina will provide people with, or at risk of, mental illness, developmental disabilities and substance problems and their families the necessary prevention, intervention, treatment, services and supports they need to live successfully in communities of their choice.

1589 North Carolina Division of Social Services
2001 Mail Service Center
Raleigh, NC 27699-2000
919-527-6335
800-662-7030
www.www.ncdhhs.gov/dss/

Kody Kinsley, Secretary of Health/Human Svcs.
Robert W. Kindsvatter, Chief Financial Officer
Victor Armstrong, Chief Health Equity Officer
Susan Osborne, Contact

The North Carolina Dept of Health and Human Services, in collaboration with its partners, protects the health and safety of all North Carolinians and provides essential human services.

North Dakota

1590 North Dakota Department of Human Services: Behavioral Health Division
600 E. Boulevard Ave.
Dept. 325
Bismarck, ND 58505-0325

701-328-8920
800-755-2719
E-mail: dhsbhd@nd.gov
www.nd.gov/dhs/services/mentalhealth

Christopher Jones, Executive Director

Provides leadership for the planning, development and oversight of a system of care for children, adults and families with severe emotional disorders, mental illness and/or substance abuse issues. Mental health and substance abuse services are delivered through eight Regional Human Services Centers and the North Dakota State Hospital in Jamestown.

Ohio

1591 Ohio Department of Mental Health
30 East Broad Street
8th Floor
Columbus, OH 43215-3430
614-466-2596
TTY: 614-752-9696
E-mail: questions@mha.ohio.gov
www.www.mha.ohio.gov

Lori Criss, Director
Alisa Clark, Asst. Dir., Community Planning
Angelika McClelland, Chief Communications Officer
Jonathan Baker, Administration Chief of Staff

Ensures high quality mental health care is available to all Ohioans, particularly individuals with severe mental illness.

Oklahoma

1592 Oklahoma Department of Human Services
2400 North Lincoln Blvd
Oklahoma City, OK 73105
405-521-2779
877-751-2972

The mission of the Oklahoma Department of Human Services is to help individuals and families in need help themselves lead safer, healthier, more independent and productive lives.

1593 Oklahoma Department of Mental Health and Substance Abuse Service (ODMHSAS)
2000 N. Classen Blvd.
Suite 2-600
Oklahoma City, OK 73106
405-248-9200
TDD: 405-522-3851
www.www.ok.gov

State agency responsible for mental health, substance abuse, and domestic violence and sexual assault services.

1594 Oklahoma Healthcare Authority
4345 N. Lincoln Blvd.
Oklahoma City, OK 73105
405-522-7300
www.www.okhca.org

Provides health and medical policy information to Medicaid consumers and providers, administers SoonerCare and other health related programs.

Year Founded: 1993

1595 Oklahoma Mental Health Consumer Council
3200 NW 48th
Suite 102
Oklahoma City, OK 73112
405-604-6975
888-424-1305
E-mail: selfhelpclearinghouse@gmail.com
www.omhcc.org

Joseph Rogers, Founder & Executive Director
Susan Rogers, Director

Supports individuals with mental health conditions by connecting them with self-help and advocacy resources. Affiliated with the Temple University Collaborative on Community Inclusion.

Year Founded: 1986

1596 Oklahoma Office of Juvenile Affairs
3812 North Santa Fe
Suite 400
Oklahoma City, OK 73118
405-530-2800
E-mail: info@oja.ok.gov
www.ok.gov/oja/

Rachel Canuso Holt, Executive Director

State agency charged with delivery of programs and services to delinquent youth. Services include delinquency prevention, diversion, counseling in both community and secure residential programs. OJA provides counseling services with counselors, social workers and psychologists, as well as contracted service providers.

Year Founded: 1995

Oregon

1597 Marion County Health Department
555 Court St NE
Suite 5232
Salem, OR 97301
503-588-5212
E-mail: commissioners@co.marion.or.us
www.co.marion.or.us

Kevin Cameron, County Commissioner
Danielle Bethell, County Commissioner
Colm Willis, County Commissioner
Jan Fritz, Chief Administrative Officer

The Marion County Health Department fosters wellness, monitors health trends, and responds to community health needs.

1598 Oregon Department of Human Resources: Division of Health Services
800 NE Oregon Street
Portland, OR 97232-2162
971-673-1555
TTY: 971-673-0372
www.oregonindependentcontractors.com

Stephanie Hoskins, Chief Executive Officer
Jerry Waybrant, Deputy Asst Director
Sandy Dugan, Operations Support Manager

Health Services administers low-income medical programs, and mental health and substance abuse services. It provides public health services such as monitoring drinking-water quality and communicable-disease outbreaks, inspecting restaurants and promoting healthy behaviors.

1599 Oregon Health Policy and Research: Policy and Analytics Division
500 Summer Street
NE, E-20
Salem, OR 97301-1097
503-947-2340
www.www.oregon.gov/oha/hpa/pages/index.aspx

Facilitates collaborative health services and research and policy analysis on issues affecting the Oregon Health Plan population and works to effectively communicate timely, quality results of health services research and analysis in the interest of informing health policy.

Pennsylvania

1600 Pennsylvania Department of Human Services: Office of Mental Health and Substance Abuse Services
717-705-8395
www.dhs.pa.gov

The Office provides individuals with opportunities for growth, recovery and inclusion, and culturally competent services and supports.

Rhode Island

1601 Rhode Island Council on Alcoholism and Other Drug Dependence
500 Prospect Street
Suite 202
Pawtucket, RI 02860
401-725-0410

The Rhode Island Council on Alcoholism and Other Drug Dependence is a private, non-profit corporation whose mission is to help individuals, youth and families who are troubled with alcohol, tobacco and other drug dependence.

Year Founded: 1969

1602 Rhode Island Department of Behavioral Healthcare, Developmental Disabilities and Hospitals
14 Harrington Road
Cranston, RI 02920
401-462-3421
E-mail: Kevin.Savage@bhddh.ri.gov
www.www.bhddh.ri.gov

Kevin Savage, Director
Heather Mincey, Assistant Director
Brenda DuHamel, Associate Dir., Admin. Services
Tracy Levesque, Clinical Administrator

The department's mission is to serve individuals who live with mental illness, substance use disorder and/or a developmental disability by maintaining a system of high quality, safe, affordable and coordinated care across the spectrum of behavioral health care services.

1603 Rhode Island Division of Substance Abuse
3 Capitol Hill
Providence, RI 02908
401-222-5960
www.health.ri.gov/addiction/

James McDonald, MD, MPH, Interim Director

Responsible for planning, coordinating and administering a comprehensive statewide system of substance abuse, treatment and prevention activities. Develops, supports and advocates for high quality, accessible, comprehensive and clinically appropriate substance abuse prevention and treatment services in order to decrease the negative effects of alcohol, tobacco and other drug use in Rhode Island, and improve the overall behavioral health of Rhode Islanders.

South Carolina

1604 South Carolina Department of Alcohol and Other Drug Abuse Services (DAODAS)
1801 Main Street
4th Floor
Columbia, SC 29201
803-896-5555
www.www.daodas.state.sc.us

Sara Goldbsy, Director

DAODAS is the cabinet-level department responsible for ensuring the availability of comprehensive alcohol and other drug abuse services for the citizens of South Carolina.

Year Founded: 1957

1605 South Carolina Department of Mental Health
Office of Administration
PO Box 485
Columbia, SC 29202
803-898-8581
TTY: 800-647-2066
www.www.scdmh.net

Kenneth Rogers, MD, State Director

The administrative offices of the South Carolina Department of Mental Health are located in Columbia and provide support services including long-range planning, performance and clinical standards, evaluation and quality assurance, personnel management, communications, information resource management, legal counsel, financial, and procurement. In addition, the central office administers services for the hearing impaired; children, adolescents and their families; people with developmental disabilities; those needing alcohol and drug treatment; the elderly; and patients who need long-term care.

1606 South Carolina Department of Social Services
1535 Confederate Avenue Extension
Columbia, SC 29201-1915
803-898-7601
www.dss.sc.gov

Michael Leach, State Director
Susan Roben, Chief Financial Officer
Don Grant, Deputy State Director
Kelly Cordell, Director, Adult Advocacy

The mission of the South Carolina Department of Social Services is to ensure the safety and health of children and adults who cannot protect themselves, and to assist those in need of food assistance and temporary financial assistance while transitioning into employment.

South Dakota

1607 South Dakota Department of Social Services Office of Medical Services
700 Governors Drive
Pierre, SD 57501
605-773-3165
E-mail: Medical@STATE.SD.US
www.www.dss.sd.gov

Laurie Gill, Cabinet Secretary
Brenda Tidball-Zeltinger, Deputy Secretary
Jason Simmons, Chief Financial Officer

The South Dakota Office of Medical Services covers medical care provided to low income people who meet eligibility standards either under Medicaid (Title XIX) or the Children's Health Insurance Program (CHIP). These programs are financed jointly by state and federal government and are managed by the SD Department of Social Services.

1608 South Dakota Human Services Center
700 Governors Drive
Pierre, SD 57501
605-773-3165
www.dss.sd.gov/behavioralhealth/hsc/services.aspx

Laurie Gill, Cabinet Secretary
Brenda Tidball-Zeltinger, Deputy Secretary
Jason Simmons, Chief Financial Officer

To provide persons who are mentally ill or chemically dependent with effective, individualized professional treatment that enables them to achieve their highest level of personal independence in the most therapeutic environment.

Tennessee

1609 Bureau of TennCare: State of Tennessee
310 Great Circle Road
Nashville, TN 37243
800-342-3145
E-mail: Tenn.Care@tn.gov
www.www.tn.gov/tenncare.html

Stephen Smith, Deputy Commissioner

On January 1, 1994, Tennessee began a new health care reform program called TennCare. This program, which required no new taxes, essentially replaced the Medicaid program in Tennessee. TennCare was designed as a managed care model. It extended coverage to uninsured and uninsurable persons who were not eligible for Medicaid.

Year Founded: 1994

1610 Council for Alcohol & Drug Abuse Services (CADAS)
207 Spears Avenue
Chattanooga, TN 37405
423-756-7644
877-282-2327
E-mail: info@cadas.org
www.cadas.org

Paul Fuchcar MEd, EdD, Executive Director

The CADAS mission is to deliver the highest quality treatment, prevention, and educational services to the chemically dependent, their families, and the community at large.

Year Founded: 1964

1611 Memphis Alcohol and Drug Council
4918 William Arnold Rd
Memphis, TN 38117
844-787-5862

Provides referrals, alcohol and other drug prevention, intervention and treatment services. Also, regional and county school prevention coordination, and a clearinghouse for Shelby County including national data search and materials distribution.

1612 Middle Tennessee Mental Health Institute
221 Stewarts Ferry Pike
Nashville, TN 37214
615-902-7400
www.state.tn.us

Joyce Kovacs, CEO

TDMHDD aims to provide quality mental health care to patients, serving 18 counties in Middle Tennessee, and offering 4 long-term care units, 3 short-term care units, and 207 psychiatric beds.

Year Founded: 1995

1613 Tennessee Commission on Children and Youth
502 Deaderick St.
9th Floor
Nashville, TN 37243
615-741-2633
E-mail: tccy.info@tn.gov
www.www.tennessee.gov/tccy/

Richard Kennedy, Executive Director

Advocates for children and youth through legislative reforms in Tennessee.

1614 Tennessee Department of Health
710 James Robertson Parkway
Andrew Johnson Tower
Nashville, TN 37243
615-741-3111
E-mail: tn.health@tn.gov
www.www.tn.gov

Lisa Percey, MD, MBA, FAAP, Commissioner

Provides information on a wide variety of topics including community services, health maintenance organizations, immunizations and alcohol and drug services.

1615 Tennessee Department of Human Services
505 Deaderick Street
Nashville, TN 37243-1403
615-313-4700
www.www.tn.gov

Clarence H. Carter, Commissioner

Provides information about available programs and services, such as family assistance and child support, community programs, and rehabilitation services.

Texas

1616 Texas Department of Family and Protective Services
4900 N. Lamar Blvd.
Austin, TX 78751
512-438-4800
www.www.dfps.state.tx.us

Jaime Masters, Commissioner

The mission of the Texas Department of Family and Protective Services (DFPS) is to protect the unprotected children, elderly, and people with disabilities from abuse, neglect, and exploitation.

Year Founded: 2004

1617 The Harris Center for Mental Health and IDD
9401 Southwest Freeway
Houston, TX 77074

713-970-7000
866-970-4770
www.www.theharriscenter.org

Shaukat Zakaria, Chairperson of the Board
Wayne Young, MBA, LPC, FACHE, Chief Executive Officer

The center provides high quality, efficient, and cost effective services to persons with mental disabilities, so that they may live with dignity as fully functioning, participating and contributing members of the community, regardless of their ability to pay.

Utah

1618 Utah Department of Health
PO Box 141010
Salt Lake City, UT 84114-1010
801-538-6003
www.health.utah.gov

Nathan Checketts, Executive Director
Emma Chacon, Interim Dir., Health Financing
Navina Forsythe, Dir., Health Data/Informatics
Sarah Wollsey, MD, Dir., Family Health/Preparedness

Oversees and regulates health care services for children, seniors, the mentally ill, substance abusers, and all residents of Utah.

1619 Utah Department of Health: Health Care Financing
288 North 1460 West
Salt Lake City, UT 84116
801-538-6155
www.medicaid.utah.gov

Provides information and assistance on Utah Medicaid programs including eligibility and additional contact information.

1620 Utah Department of Human Services
195 N. 1950 W.
Salt Lake City, UT 84116
801-538-4171
800-662-3722
E-mail: dhsinfo@utah.gov
www.dhs.utah.gov

Tracy S. Gruber, Executive Director
Nate Checketts, Deputy Director
David Litvack, Deputy Director
Nate Winters, Assistant Deputy Director

Provides services for the elderly, substance abusers, and people wih disabilities.

1621 Utah Department of Human Services: Division of Substance Abuse And Mental Health
195 North 1950 West
Salt Lake City, UT 84116
801-538-3939
801-520-2777
E-mail: dsamh@utah.gov
www.www.dsamh.utah.gov

The Utah State Division of Substance Abuse and Mental Health Division is the agency responsible for ensuring that substance abuse and mental health prevention and treatment services are available statewide. The Division also acts as a resource by providing general information, research, and statistics to the public regarding substances of abuse and mental health services.

Virginia

1622 Virginia Department of Behavioral Health and Developmental Services (DBHDS)
PO Box 1797
Richmond, VA 23218-1797
804-786-3921
TDD: 804-371-8977
www.dbhds.virginia.gov

Nelson Smith, Commissioner
Cort Kirkley, Deputy Commissioner, Admin Svcs.
Robert Hobbelman, Chief Information Oficer

The Virginia Department of Behavioral Health and Developmental Services is a mental health and substance abuse services system working to improve the quality of treatment and prevention services for individuals and families whose lives are affected by mental illness, intellectual disabilities, or substance abuse disorders.

1623 Virginia Department of Medical Assistance Services
600 East Broad Street
Richmond, VA 23219
www.www.dmas.virginia.gov

DMAS is the agency that administers Medicaid and the State Childrens Health Insurance Program (CHIP) in the State of Virginia.

1624 Virginia Department of Social Services (VDSS)
801 E. Main Street
Richmond, VA 23219-2901
804-726-7000
800-552-3431
TDD: 800-828-1120
TTY: 800-828-1120
E-mail: citizen.services@dss.virginia.gov
www.dss.virginia.gov

Social services system providing programs, services and benefits designed to ensure the health and well-being of citizens, families and communities.

1625 Virginia Office of the Secretary of Health and Human Resources
1111 East Broad Street
Richmond, VA 23219
804-786-7765
E-mail: healthandhumanresources@governor.virginia.gov
www.hhr.virginia.gov

The Secretary of Health and Human Resources oversees the state agencies that provide services to the people of Virginia, including individuals with disabilities, low-income working families, children, the aging community, and caregivers.

West Virginia

1626 West Virginia Bureau for Behavioral Health
West Virginia Department of Health and Human Resources
350 Capitol Street
Room 350
Charleston, WV 25301
304-358-0627
www.dhhr.wv.gov/bbh/Pages/default.aspx

Cynthia E. Beane, Commissioner
Becky Manning, Deputy Commissioner, Finance
Sarah Young, Deputy Commissioner, Operations
Frederick S. Lewis, Deputy Commissioner, Plan Mngmt.

The mission of the Bureau for Behavioral Health and Health Facilities is to help individuals with mental illness, intellectual and developmental disabilities, and substance abuse disorders realize their full potential and build positive and meaningful futures. The Bureau provides support for families and communities, and assists with the improvement of services in West Virginia.

1627 West Virginia Department of Health & Human Resources (DHHR)
One Davis Square
Suite 100 East
Charleston, WV 25301
304-558-0684
E-mail: DHHRSecretary@wv.gov
www.dhhr.wv.gov

The DHHR consists of five bureaus that serve to promote the health and well-being of the citizens of West Virginia.

1628 West Virginia Department of Welfare Bureau for Children and Families
West Virginia Department of Health and Human Resources
350 Capitol Street
Room 730
Charleston, WV 25301
304-558-0628
www.dhhr.wv.gov/bcf/

Jeffrey M. Pack, Commissioner

The Bureau for Children and Families works to provide a service system for individuals and families in West Virginia. The Bureau's mission is to ensure the well-being of West Virginia's children, families and adults, and to help them improve their quality of life.

Wisconsin

1629 Journey Mental Health Center, Inc.
25 Kessel Court
Suite 105
Madison, WI 53711
608-280-2700
www.journeymhc.org

James Christiansen, Chair
Tanya Lettman-Shue, President and CEO
Connie Walker, Secretary
Howard Gesbeck, Treasurer

The Journey Mental Health Center is a nonprofit agency and outpatient mental health and substance abuse treatment clinic serving to assist Southern Wisconsin residents with mental illnesses and substance use disorders. The Journey Mental Health Center seeks to improve the lives of the people of Southern Wisconsin through the provision of behavioral health programs and services.

1630 University of Wisconsin Population Health Institute
610 Walnut Street
575 WARF
Madison, WI 53726

608-263-6294
E-mail: uwphi@med.wisc.edu
www.uwphi.pophealth.wisc.edu/programs/

Sheri Johnson, PhD, Director
Wajiha Akhtar, Assistant Director
Sara Lindberg, Evaluation Research Director

The University of Wisconsin Population Health Institute, within the University of Wisconsin-Madison School of Medicine and Public Health, works to improve health and well-being for all people. The Institute strives to address an array of problems related to health; build partnerships between researchers and private and public policy makers; and contribute to the development of programs and policies designed to advance the population's health and well-being.

Year Founded: 1984

1631 Wisconsin Department of Health and Family Services

1 West Wilson Street
Madison, WI 53703
608-266-1865
TTY: 800-947-3529
www.dhs.wisconsin.gov

The Wisconsin Department of Health and Family Services administers services to clients in the areas of public health, mental health, substance abuse, medical assistance, aging, and disability. The mission of the Department of Health Services is to advance the health and safety of the people of Wisconsin.

Wyoming

1632 Wyoming Department of Family Services

2300 Capitol Avenue
Hathaway Building, 3rd Floor
Cheyenne, WY 82002
307-777-7564
800-457-3659
E-mail: dfs-directorsoffice@wyo.gov
www.dfsweb.wyo.gov

The Wyoming Department of Family Services is an agency dedicated to advancing the well-being and safety of families in Wyoming. The DFS serves to connect people in Wyoming with child and family resources, programs and services in order to help build healthy and self-sufficient families.

Professional & Support Services

Support Groups & Hot Lines

1633 Midwest Center for Personal/Family Developme Midwest Center for Personal/Family Development
2550 University Avenue West
Suite 435-South
Saint Paul, MN
651-647-1900
E-mail: tquesnell@hmr.net
www.mentalhealthinc.com

Tim Quesneil, Administrator
Kari Droubic, Manager

Accreditation & Quality Assurance

1634 American Board of Examiners in Clinical Social Work
241 Humphrey Street
Shetland Park
Marblehead, MA 01945
781-639-5270
800-694-5285
www.www.abecsw.org

Bob Booth, CEO
Robert Booth, Executive Director
Michael Brooks MSW BCD, Business Development, Policy Dir

Clinical Social Work certifying and standard setting organization. ABE's no cost online and CD ROM directories (both searchable/sortable) are sources used by the healthcare industry nationwide for network development and referrals. They contain verified information about the education, training, experience and practice specialties of over 11,000 Board Certified Diplomates in Clinical Social Work (BCD). Visit our website for the directory, employment resources, continuing education and other services.

1635 American Board of Examiners of Clinical Social Work Regional Offices
645 Broadway
Suite C
Sonoma, CA 95476
707-938-5833
888-279-9378
www.abecsw.org

Yvette Colon,PhD,BCD, President
Robert Booth, Executive Director
Carolyn Messner,DSW,BCD, Vice President
Bob Booth, Chief Executive Officer

Sets national practice standards, issues an advance-practice credential, and publishes reference information about its board-certified clinicians.

Year Founded: 1987

1636 Brain Imaging Handbook
WW Norton & Company
500 5th Avenue
New York, NY 10110-54
212-354-5500
800-233-4830
E-mail: npb@wwnorton.com
www.books.wwnorton.com/

J. Douglas Bremner, Author

The past 10 years have seen an explosion in the use of brain imaging technologies to aid treatment of medical as well as mental health conditions. MRI, CT scans, and PET scans are now common. This book is the first quick reference to these technologies, rich in illustrations and including discussions of which techniques are best used in particular instances of care.

224 pages

1637 CARF International
6951 East Southpoint Road
Tucson, AZ 85756-9407
520-325-1044
888-281-6531
TTY: 888-281-6531
www.carf.org

Brian J. Boon, Ph.D., President/CEO
Cindy L. Johnson, CPA, Chief Resource Officer

CARF assists organizations to improve the quality of their services, to demonstrate value, and to meet internationally recognized organizational and practice standards.

Year Founded: 1966

1638 Cenaps Corporation
13194 Spring Hill Drive
Spring Hill, FL 34609
352-596-8000
E-mail: info@cenaps.com
www.cenaps.com

Tresa Watson, Business Manager

CENAPS is an acronym for the Center for Applied Sciences. They are a private training firm committed to providing advanced clinical skills training for the addiction and behavioral health fields.

1639 CompHealth Credentialing
6440 South Millrock Drive
Suite 175
Salt Lake City, UT 84121
801-930-3000
800-453-3030
E-mail: info@comphealth.com
www.comphealth.com

Assists in analyzing the total costs involved in credentialing verifications, including some items frequently overlooked; assesses and/or develops a provider application to meet accreditation standards; can assess current credentialing files; can assist in developing policy and procedures for the verification process.

1640 Consumer Satisfaction Team
1210 Stanbridge Street
Suite 600
Norristown, PA 19401-5300
610-270-3685
www.cstmont.com

Sue Soriano, President
Tim Tunner, Vice President
Molly Frantz, Treasurer
Dr Romani George, Secretary

The central role of CST is to provide the Montgomery County Office of MH/MR/DD with information about satisfaction with the mental health services that adults are receiving and make recommendations for change.

1641 Council on Social Work Education
333 John Carlyle Street
Suite 400
Alexandria, VA 22314
703-683-8080
E-mail: info@cswe.org
www.cswe.org

Darl Spence Coffey, PhD, MSW, President
Patrick Dunne, Vice President, Comms./Marketing
Tanya Smith Brice, PhD, MSW, Vice President, Education
Arminn H. Leopold, Vice President, Finance and CFO

A national association that preserves and enhances the quality of social work education for the purpose of promoting the goals of individual and community well being and social justice. Pursues this mission through setting and maintaining policy and program standards, accrediting bachelors and masters degree programs in social work, promoting research and faculty development, and advocating for social work education.

Year Founded: 1952

1642 Healtheast Behavioral Care
559 Capitol Boulevard
Saint Paul, MN 55103-2101
651-232-2228
www.healtheast.org

Robert Beck, President/CEO
Robert D. Gill, VP Finance/CFO
Robert J. Beck, VP Medical Affairs

Assessment and referral for: Psychiatric, Inpatient, Chemical Dependancy.

1643 Joint Commission on Accreditation of Healthcare Organizations
1 Renaissance Boulevard
Oakbrook Terrace, IL 60181-4294
630-792-5000
E-mail: customerservice@jcaho.org
www.jointcommission.org

Mark Chassin, President
Mark Angood, VP/Chief Patient Safety Officer

The Joint Commission evaluates and accredits nearly 20,000 health care organizations and programs in the United States. An independent, not-for-profit organization, the Joint Commission is the nation's predominant standards-setting and accrediting body in health care. The Joint Commission has developed state-of-the-art, professionally-based standards and evaluated the compliance of health care organizations against these benchmarks.

Year Founded: 1951

1644 Lanstat Incorporated
4663 Mason Street
Port Townsend, WA 98368
425-334-3124
800-672-3166
E-mail: info@lanstat.com
www.lanstat.com

Landon Kimbrough, President
Sherry Kimbrough, VP/Co-Founder

Provides quality technical assistance to behavioral health treatment agencies nationwide, including tribal and goverment agencies.

1645 Med Advantage
11301 Corporate Boulevard
Suite 300
Orlando, FL 32817-1445
407-282-5131
E-mail: info@med-advantage.com
www.www.med-advantage.com

John Witty, Owner

Fully accredited by URAC and certified in all 11 elements by NCQA, Med Advantage is one of the oldest credentials verification organizations in the country. Over the past eight years, they have developed sophisticated computer systems and one of the largest data warehouses of medical providers in the nation, containing information on over 900,000 healthcare providers. Their system is continually updated from primary source data required to meet the standards of the URAC, NCQA and JCAHO.

1646 Mertech
PO Box 787
Norwell, MA 02061-787
781-659-0701
888-794-7447
E-mail: kwoodman@mertech.org
www.mertech.org

John Kopacz, Founder

A business development organization that specializes in helping clients capitalize on business opportunities in an efficient and effective manner to meet their goals and objectives. They have three business units: Mertech Health Care Consultants, Mertech Personal Health Improvement Program and Managed Care Information Systems.

1647 National Board for Certified Counselors
3 Terrace Way
Greensboro, NC 27403-3670
336-547-0607
E-mail: nbcc@nbcc.org
www.nbcc.org

Joseph D. Wehrman, Chairman
Thomas Clawson, President/CEO
Brandon Hunt, Vice Chair
Kylie P. Dotson-Blake, Secretary

National voluntary certification board for counselors. Certified counselors have met minimum criteria. Referral lists can be provided to consumers.

Year Founded: 1982

1648 National Register of Health Service Providers in Psychology
1200 New York Ave NW
Ste 800
Washington, DC 20005
202-783-7663
www.nationalregister.org

Raymond A. Follen, President/Chairman
Glenace E. Edwall, Vice President/Vice-Chair
Erica H. Wise, Secretary
William A. Hancur, Treasurer

Nonprofit credentialing organization for psychologists; evaluates education, training, and experience of licensed psychologists. Committed to advancing psychology as a profession and improving the delivery of health services to the public.

Year Founded: 1974

1649 SUPRA Management
2424 Edenborn Avenue
Suite 660
Metairie, LA 70001-6465
504-837-5557

Associations

1650 Academy of Psychosomatic Medicine
4800 Hampden Ln
Ste. 200
Bethesda, MD 20814-2934
301-718-6520
E-mail: info@CLpsychiatry.org
www.apm.org

Philip Bialer, MD, FACLP, President
Maryland Pao, MD, FACLP, President-Elect
James Vrac, CAE, Executive Director
Shannon Sperati, CAE, Deputy Executive Director

Represents psychiatrists dedicated to the advancement of medical science, education, and healthcare for persons with comorbid psychiatric and general medical conditions and provides national and international leadership in the furtherance of those goals.

1651 Agency for Healthcare Research and Quality
Office of Communications and Knowledge Transfer
5600 Fishers Lane
7th Floor
Rockville, MD 20857
301-427-1364
www.www.ahrq.gov

Robert "Bob" Otto Valdez, PhD, MHSA, Director
David Meyers, MD, Deputy Director

The Agency for Healthcare Research and Quality's (AHRQ) mission is to improve the quality, safety, efficiency, and effectiveness of health care for all Americans. Information from AHRQ's research helps people make more informed decisions and improve the quality of healthcare services.

1652 Alliance for Strong Families and Communities
1825 K St. N.W.
Suite 600
Washington, DC 20006
800-221-3726
E-mail: pgoldberg@alliance1.org
www.www.alliance1.org

Jody Levison-Johnson, President and CEO
Jim Carr, Chief Financial Officer
Ruby Goyal-Carkeek, Sr. VP, Programs and Services
Lenore Schell, Sr. VP, Operations

National membership association representing nonprofit child and family-serving organizations. Its mission is to strengthen members' capacity to serve and advocate for children, families and communities.

1653 American Academy of Addiction Psychiatry (AAAP)
400 Massasoit Avenue
Suite 307, 2nd Floor
East Providence, RI 02914
401-524-3076
www.aaap.org

Kathryn Cates-Wessel, Executive Director
Joe Barboza, Director of Finance
Bethany Banner, Director of Professional Dev.
Jamie Edwards, Director of Education/Training

Professional membership organization with approximately 1,000 members in the United States and around the world. The membership consists of psychiatrists who work with addiction in their practices, faculty at various academic institutions.

1654 American Academy of Child and Adolescent Psychiatry
3615 Wisconsin Avenue Northwest
Washington, DC 20016-3007
202-966-7300
E-mail: communications@aacap.org
www.aacap.org

Warren Y.K. Ng, MD, MPH, President
Tami D. Benton, MD, President-Elect
Debra E. Koss, MD, Secretary
Neal Ryan, MD, Treasurer

Provides information on childhood psychiatric disorders.

Year Founded: 1953

1655 American Academy of Clinical Psychiatrists
7 Century Drive
Suite 301
Parsippany, NJ 07054
920-395-2330
E-mail: clinicalpsychiatrists@gmail.com
www.aacp.com

Henry A. Nasrallah, MD, President
Carol S. North, MD, MPE, Medical Director
Donald W. Black, MD, Secretary/Treasurer/Editor
Jeff Bauer, Editor

Practicing board-eligible or board-certified psychiatrists. Promotes the scientific practice of psychiatric medicine. Conducts educational and teaching research. Publications: Annals of Clinical Psychiatry, quarterly journal. Current Psychiatry, website.

Year Founded: 1975

1656 American Academy of Psychiatry and the Law (AAPL)
One Regency Drive
PO Box 30
Bloomfield, CT 06002
860-242-5450
800-331-1389
E-mail: office@aapl.org
www.aapl.org

Susan Hatters Friedman, MD, President
James Knoll, MD, President-Elect
Karen Rosenbaum, MD, Vice President
Britta Ostermeyer, MD, Vice President

Seeks to exchange ideas and experience in areas where psychiatry and the law overlap and develop standards of practice in the relationship of psychiatry to the law and encourage the development of training programs for psychiatrists in this area. Publications: Journal of the American Academy of Psychiatry and the Law, quarterly. Scholarly articles on forensic psychiatry. Newsletter of the American Academy of Psychiatry and Law, quarterly. Membership Directory, annual.

Year Founded: 1969

1657 American Academy of Psychoanalysis and Dynamic Psychiatry (AAPDPP)
One Regency Drive
PO Box 30
Bloomfield, CT 06002
888-691-8281
E-mail: info@aapdp.org
www.aapsa.org

Joanna E. Chambers, MD, President
Jacquelyn T. Coleman, CAE, Executive Director

Founded to provide an open forum for psychoanalysts to discuss relevant and responsible views of human behavior and to exchange ideas with colleagues and other social behavioral scientists. Aims to develop better communication among psychoanalysts and psychodynamic psychiatrists in other disiplines in science and the humanities. Meetings of the Academy provide a forum for inquiry into the phenomena of individual and interpersonal behavior. Advocates an acceptance of all relevant and responsible psychoanalytic views of human behavior, rather than adherence to one particular doctrine.

Year Founded: 1956

1658 American Association for Marriage and Family Therapy
112 South Alfred St.
Suite 300
Alexandria, VA 22314
703-838-9808
E-mail: central@aamft.org
www.memberservices.aamft.org

The professional association for the field of marriage and family therapy. They represent the professional interests of more than 23,000 marriage and family therapists throughout the United States, Canada and abroad. They facilitate research, theory development and education; develop standards for graduate education and training, clinical supervision, professional ethics and the clinical practice of marriage and family therapy; and host an annual national training conference each fall as well as a week-long series of continuing education institutes in the summer.

1659 American Association for Technology in Psychiatry
E-mail: aatp@techpsych.org
www.www.techpsych.org/new2/

Formerly the Psychiatric Society for Informatics. A nonprofit association representing mental health professionals. Dedicated to advancing the field of psychiatry through research, education opporunities, and networking sessions. Special features for members include annual meetings and access to the organization's online, peer-reviewed journal (ATTP eJournal).

Year Founded: 1995

1660 American Association of Community Psychiatrists (AACP)
www.www.communitypsychiatry.org

Altha Stewart, President
Peter Chien, Vice President
Ann Hackman, Secretary
Rob Cotes, Treasurer

The mission of AACP is to inspire, empower and equip Community Psychiatrists to promote and provide quality care and to integrate practice with policies that improve the well being of individuals and communities.

1661 American Association of Chairs of Departments of Psychiatry (AACDP)
PO Box 570218
Dallas, TX 75357-0218
972-613-0985
E-mail: psychiatrychairs@gmail.com
www.aacdp.org

Jair C. Soares, MD, PhD, President
Erika Saunders, MD, President-Elect
Stephen Scheinthal, DO, Secretary/Treasurer
Petros Levounis, MD, MA, Councilor

Represents the leaders of departments of psychiatry in all the medical schools in the United States and Canada. Committed to promotion of excellence in psychiatric education, research and clinical care. Advocate for health policy to create appropriate and affordable psychiatric care for all.

1662 American Association of Directors of Psychiatric Residency Training
PO Box 30618
Indianapolis, IN 46230
317-407-1173
E-mail: exec@aadprt.org
www.aadprt.org

Mike Travis, MD, President
Sallie DeGolia, MD, MPH, President-Elect
Randy Welton, MD, Secretary
Erick Hung, MD, Treasurer

To better meet the nation's mental healthcare needs, the mission of the American Association of Directors of Psychiatric Residency Training is to promote excellence in education and training of future psychiatrists.

Year Founded: 1970

1663 American Association of Geriatric Psychiatry
6728 Old McLean Village Drive
McLean, VA 22101
703-718-6026
E-mail: main@aagponline.org
www.aagponline.org

Brent Forester, MD, DFAAGP, President
Marc E. Agronin, MD, DFAAGP, President-Elect
Elizabeth J. Santos, MD, DFAAGP, Secretary/Treasurer
Ilse Wiechers, MD, MPP, MHS, Secretary/Treasurer Elect

Members are psychiatrists interested in promoting better mental health care for the elderly.

Year Founded: 1978

1664 American Association of Healthcare Consultants
www.www.consultprism.com/aahc.htm

Mission is to serve as the preeminent credentialing, professional, and practice development organization for the healthcare consulting profession; to advance the knowledge, quality, and standards of practice for consulting to management in the healthcare industry; and to enhance the understanding and image of the healthcare consulting profession and Member Firms among its various publics.

Year Founded: 1949

1665 American Association of Homes and Services for the Aging

2519 Connecticut Avenue NW
Washington, DC 20008-1520
202-783-2242
E-mail: info@aahsa.org

An association committed to advancing the vision of healthy, affordable, ethical long term care for America. The association represents not-for-profit nursing homes, continuing care facilities and community care retirement facilities and community service organizations.

1666 American Association of Pastoral Counselors

2233 S Presidents Dr.
Suite F
Salt Lake City, UT 84120
800-626-2633
E-mail: info@aapc.org
www.aapc.org

Colleen Gianastasio, MHS, CPC, President
Rhonda Buckholtz, CPC, CDEO, President-Elect
Stephanie Thebarge, CPC, CPB, Member Relations Officer

Organized to promote and support the ministry of pastoral counseling within religious communities and the field of mental health in the United States and Canada.

Year Founded: 1963

1667 American Association of Pharmaceutical Scientists

2107 Wilson Boulevard
Suite 700
Arlington, VA 22201-3042
703-243-2800
E-mail: membership@aaps.org
www.aaps.org

Tina Morris, Executive Director
Joy Davis, Managing Director

The American Association of Pharmaceutical Scientists will be the premier organization of all scientists dedicated to the discovery, development and manufacture of pharmaceutical products and therapies through advances in science and technology.

1668 American Association of Retired Persons

888-687-2277
TTY: 877-434-7598
www.aarp.org

Jo Ann Jenkins, Chef Executive Officer
Martha M. Boudreau, Chief Comms./Marketing Officer
Kevin Donnellan, EVP/Chief of Staff
Scott Frisch, EVP/Chief of Operating Officer

AARP is a non profit membership organization of persons 50 and older dedicated to addressing their needs and interests.

1669 American Association on Intellectual and Developmental Disabilities (AAIDD)

8403 Colesville Road
Suite 900
Silver Spring, MD 20910
202-387-1968
www.aaidd.org

Elisa Velardo, MMHS, FAAIDD, President
Karrie Shogren, PhD, FAAIDD, President Elect
Dalun "Dan" Zhang, PhD, Vice President
Melissa DiSipio, MSA, FAAIDD, Secretary-Treasurer

AAIDD provides worldwide leadership in the field of intellectual and developmental disabilities. The oldest and largest interdisciplinary organization of professionals and citizens concerned about intellectual and developmental disabilities. AAIDD promotes progressive policies, research, and universal human rights for people with intellectual and developmental diabilities.

Year Founded: 1876

1670 American Board of Professional Psychology (ABPP)

600 Market Street
Suite G3
Chapel Hill, NC 27516
919-537-8031
www.abpp.org

Brenda J. Spiegler, PhD, ABPP, President
David R. Cox, PhD, ABPP, Executive Officer

The mission is to increase consumer protection through the examination and certification of psychologists who demonstrate competence in approved specialty areas in professional psychology

Year Founded: 1947

1671 American Board of Psychiatry and Neurology, Inc.

7 Parkway N
Deerfield, IL 60015
847-229-6500
www.abpn.com

Larry R. Faulkner, M.D., President/CEO

ABPN is a nonprofit organization that promotes excellence in the practice of psychiatry and neurology through lifelong certification including compentency testing processes.

Year Founded: 1934

1672 American College Health Association

8455 Colesville Road
Suite 740
Silver Spring, MD 20910
410-859-1500
E-mail: contact@acha.org
www.acha.org

Jessica D. Higgs, MD, FAAFP, President
Darren Aaron, MSHA, NREMT, Vice President
James Wilkinson, MA, CAE, Chief Executive Officer
Cheryl Hug-English, MD, MPH, President-Elect

Principal advocate and leadership organization for college and university health. Provides advocacy, education, communications, products and services as well as promotes research and culturally competent practices to enhance its members' ability to advance the health of all students and the campus community.

Year Founded: 1920

1673 American College of Health Care Administrators (ACHCA)
1101 Connecticut Avenue, NW
Suite 450
Washington, DC 20036
800-561-3148
www.achca.org

Bob Lane, CNHA, FACHCA, President and CEO

A non-profit professional membership association which provides superior educataional programming, professional certification, and career development opportunities for its members.

Year Founded: 1962

1674 American College of Healthcare Executives
300 S. Riverside Plaza
Suite 1900
Chicago, IL 60606-6698
312-424-2800
E-mail: contact@ache.org
www.ache.org

Anthony A. Armada, FACHE, Chair
Delvecchio S. Finley, FACHE, Chair-Elect
Deborah J. Bowen, FACHE, CAE, President and CEO

International professional society of over 48,000 healthcare executives. ACHE is known for its prestigious credentialing and educational programs. ACHE is also known for its journal, Journal of Healthcare Management, and magazine, Healthcare Executive, as well as ground-breaking research and career development programs. Through its efforts, ACHE works toward its goal of improving the health status of society by advancing healthcare management excellence.

1675 American College of Psychiatrists
11 E. Wacker Drive
Suite 1440
Chicago, IL 60601
312-938-8840
www.acpsych.org

Larry R. Faulkner, President
Eugene V. Beresin, President-Elect
Barbara S. Schneidman, Secretary-General
Carol A. Bernstein, Treasurer

Nonprofit honorary association of psychiatrists who, through excellence in their chosen fields, have been recognized for thier significant contributions to the profession. The society's goal is to promote and support the highest standards in psychiatry through education, research and clinical practice.

Year Founded: 1963

1676 American College of Psychoanalysts (ACPA)
www.apsa.org

Norman A. Clemens, President

Honorary, scientific and professional organization for physician psycholanalysts. Goal is to contribute to the leadership and support high standards in the practice of psychoanalysis, and understanding the relationship between mind and brain.

1677 American Counseling Association
PO Box 31110
Alexandria, VA 22310-9998
800-347-6647
E-mail: webmaster@counseling.org
www.counseling.org

Richard Yep, Executive Director
Dr. S. Kent Butler, President

ACA serves professional counselors in the US and abroad. Provides a variety of programs and services that support the personal, professional and program development goals of its members. ACA works to provide quality services to the variety of clients who use their services in college, community agencies, in mental health, rehabilitation and related settings. Offers a large catalog of books, manuals and programs for the professional counselor.

Year Founded: 1952

1678 American Geriatrics Society
40 Fulton Street
Suite 809
New York, NY 10038
212-308-1414
E-mail: info@americangeriatrics.org
www.www.americangeriatrics.org

Peter Hollmann, MD, AGSF, President
Nancy E. Lundebjerg, Chief Executive Officer
Mark Supiano, MD, AGSF, Treasurer
Donna Fick, PhD, GCNS-BC, Secretary

Nationwide, nonprofit association of geriatric health care professionals, research scientists and other concerned individuals dedicated to improving the health, independence and quality of life for all older people. Pivotal force in shaping attitudes, policies and practices regarding health care for older people.

Year Founded: 1942

1679 American Group Psychotherapy Association
355 Lexington Avenue
15th Floor
New York, NY 10017
212-297-2190
E-mail: info@agpa.org
www.agpa.org

Dr. Molyn Leszcz, MD, FRCPC, CGP, President
Angela Moore Stephens, CAE, Chief Executive Officer
Katarina Cooke, MA, CAE, Professional Development Dir.
Diane C. Feirman, CAE, Public Affairs Senior Dir.

Interdisciplinary community that has been enhancing practice, theory and research of group therapy for over 50 years. Provides support to enhance your work as a mental health care professional, or your life as a member of a therapeutic group.

Year Founded: 1942

1680 American Health Care Association
1201 L Street NW
Washington, DC 20005
202-842-4444
www.www.ahcancal.org

Mark Parkinson, President and CEO

Nonprofit federation of affiliated state health organizations, together representing over 14,000 nonprofit and for profit assisted living, nursing facility, developmentally disabled and subacute care providers that care for more than 1.5 million elderly and disabled individuals nationally. AHCA represents the long term care community at large — to government, business leaders and the general public. It also serves as a force for change within the long term care field, providing information, education, and administrative tools that enhance quality at every level.

1681 American Health Information Management Association

233 N Michigan Avenue
21st Floor
Chicago, IL 60601-5809
312-233-1100
E-mail: info@ahima.org
www.ahima.org

Tim J. Keough, MPA, RHIA, President and Chair
Wylecia Wiggs Harris, PhD, CAE, Chief Executive Officer

Dynamic professional association that represents health information management professionals who work throughout the healthcare industry. Health information management professionals serve the health care industry and the public by managing, analyzing and utilizing data vital for patient care and making it accessible to healthcare providers when it is needed most.

1682 American Humane Association

1400 16th Street NW
Suite 360
Washington, DC 20036
800-227-4645
E-mail: info@americanhumane.org
www.americanhumane.org

Robin R. Ganzert, PhD, President and CEO
Jack Hubbard, Senior Vice President and COO
Stephanie Carmody, Esq., SVP and Chief Compliance Officer
Clifford Rose, Interim Chief Financial Officer

Leader in developing programs, policies and services to prevent the abuse and neglect of children, while strengthening families and communities and enhancing social service systems.

Year Founded: 1877

1683 American Medical Association

330 N. Wabash Ave.
Suite 39300
Chicago, IL 60611-5885
312-464-4782
www.ama-assn.org

James L. Madara, MD, CEO & EVP, Pathology
Todd Askew, SVP, Advocacy
Toni Canda, SVP, HR & Corporate Services
Thomas J. Easley, SVP, Publishing & Mission Ops.

Speaks out in issues important to patients and the nation's health. AMA policy on such issues is decided through its democratic policy making process, in the AMA House of Delegates, which meets twice a year. The House is comprised of physician delegates representing every state; nearly 100 national medical specialty societies, federal service agents, including the Surgeon General of the US; and 6 sections representing hospital and clinic staffs, resident physicians, medical students, young physicians, medical schools and international medical graduates. The AMA's envisioned future is to be a part of the professional life of every physician and an essential force for progress in improving the nation's health.

Year Founded: 1847

1684 American Medical Directors Association (AMDA) - The Society for Post-Acute and Long-Term Care Medicine

10500 Little Patuxent Parkway
Suite 210
Columbia, MD 21044
410-740-9743
800-876-2632
E-mail: info@paltc.org
www.paltc.org

Suzanne M. Gillespie, MD, RD, CMD, President
Rajeev Kumar, MD, FACP, CMD, Vice-President
Swati Gaur, MD, MBA, CMD, Treasurer
Christopher E. Laxton, CAE, Executive Director

Professional association of medical directors and physicians practicing in the long-term care continuum, dedicated to excellence in patient care by providing education, advocacy and professional development.

Year Founded: 1977

1685 American Medical Group Association

One Prince Street
Alexandria, VA 22314-3318
703-838-0033
www.amga.org

Jerry Penso, MD, MBA, President and CEO
Ryan A. O'Connor, MBA, CAE, Chief Operating Officer
Clyde L. Morris, Jr., CPA, Chief Financial Officer
Grace Emerson Terrell, MD, Chair

The American Medical Group Association (AMGA) is a 501(c)(6) trade association representing medical groups, health systems and other organized systems of care, including some of the nation's largest, most prestigious integrated delivery systems. AMGA is a leading voice in advocating for efficient, team-based, and accountable care. AMGA members encompass all models of organized systmes of care in the healthcare industry. More than 150,000 physicians practice in AMGA member organizations, providing healthcare services for 120 million patients (approximately 1 in 3 Americans). AMGA's mission is to support its members in enhancing population health and care for patients through integrated systems of care.

Year Founded: 1950

1686 American Medical Informatics Association

143 Rollins Avenue
#2248
Rockville, MD 20847
301-657-1291
www.amia.org

Gretchen Purcell Jackson, MD, Chair
Neil Sarkar, PhD, MLIS, Treasurer
Philip Payne, PhD, FACMI, Secretary
Amanda Hanova, MSM, LSSGB, SVP, Operations

Nonprofit membership organization of individuals, institutions and corporations dedicated to developing and using information technologies to improve health care. Represents over 5,600 members.

Year Founded: 1988

1687 American Mental Health Counselors Association (AMHCA)
107 S. West St.
Suite 779
Alexandria, VA 22314
703-548-6002
E-mail: vmoore@amhca.org
www.amhca.org

Melissa McSherpard, Dir. of Ops./Finance/Membership
Whitney Meyerhoeffer, Chief Strategic Officer
Rebecca Woodson, Director of Events

Professional counselors employed in mental health services and students. Aims to deliver quality mental health services to children, youth, adults, families and organizations and to improve the availability and quality of services through licensure and certification, training standards and consumer advocacy. Publishes an Advocate Newsletter, Journal of Mental Health Counseling, quarterly, Mental Health Brights, brochures. Annual National Conference.
Year Founded: 1976

1688 American Neuropsychiatric Association
PO Box 97
Abilene, KS 67410-1707
E-mail: anpaoffice@gmail.com
www.www.anpaonline.org

Kaloyan Tanev, MD, FANPA, President
David Arciniegas, MD, FANPA, President Elect
C. Edward Coffey, MD, FANPA, Treasurer

An association of professionals in neuropsychiatry and clinical neurosciences. Their mission is to promote neuroscience for the benefit of people. They work together in a collegial fashion to provide a forum for learning and provide excellent, scientific and compassionate care. They hold their annual scientific meeting in the early spring.
Year Founded: 1988

1689 American Nurses Association
8515 Georgia Avenue
Suite 400
Silver Spring, MD 20910-3492
800-284-2378
E-mail: customerservice@ana.org
www.nursingworld.org

Kelly Bouthillet, DNP, APRN, Chair
Delanor Manson, MA, BSN, RN, Vice Chair
Carole Stacy, MSN, MA, RN, Member at Large

A full-service professional organization representing the nation's 2.7 million registered nurses through its 54 constituent members associations. The ANA advances the nursing profession by fostering high standards of nursing practice, promoting the economic and general welfare of nurses in the workplace, projecting a positive and realistic view of nursing, and by lobbying the Congress and regulatory agencies on health care issues affecting nurses and the public.

1690 American Osteopathic Associatio
142 E. Ontario St.
Suite 200
Chicago, IL 60611-2864
312-202-8000
E-mail: acn-aconp@msn.com
www.osteopathic.org

Joseph Giaimo, DO, President
Ernest Gelb, DO, President-Elect
Kevin Klauer, DO, EJD, CEO

Purpose is to promote the art and science of osteopathic medicine in the fields of neurology and psychiatry; to maintain and further elevate the highest standards of proficiency and training among osteopathic neurologists and psychiatrists; to stimulate original research and investigation in neurology and psychiatry; and to collect and disseminate the results of such work for the benefit of the members of the college, the public, the profession at large, and the ultimate benefit of all humanity.

1691 American Pharmacists Association
2215 Constitution Avenue NW
Washington, DC 20037
202-628-4410
800-237-2742
E-mail: infocenter@aphanet.org
www.pharmacist.com

Scott Knoer, EVP and CEO
Rafael Saenz, Chief of Staff
Sandra Leal, President
Greg Fox, Treasurer

National professional society of pharmacists, formerly the American Pharmaceutical Association. Our members include practicing pharmacists, pharmaceutical students, pharmacy scientists, pharmacy technicians, and others interested in advancing the profession. Provides professional information and education for pharmacists and advocates for improved health of the American public through the provision of comprehensive pharmaceutical care.
Year Founded: 1852

1692 American Psychiatric Association
800 Maine Avenue Southwest
Suite 900
Washington, DC 20024
202-559-3900
888-357-7924
E-mail: apa@psych.org
www.www.psychiatry.org

Vivian B. Pender, MD, President
Rebecca W. Brendel, MD , JD, President-Elect
Sandra DeJong, MD, MSc, Secretary
Richard F. Summers, MD, Treasurer

The American Psychiatric Association is a medical specialty society comprised of over 38,500 members who work together to ensure appropriate care and effective treatment for all persons with mental disorders, including developmental disabilities and substance-related disorders.
Year Founded: 1844

1693 American Psychiatric Nurses Association
3141 Fairview Park Drive
Suite 625
Falls Church, VA 22042
571-533-1919
855-863-2762
E-mail: inform@apna.org
www.apna.org

Leslie G. Oleck, President
Evelyn J. Perkins, Secretary
Kristen Kichefski, Treasurer
Lisa Deffenbaugh Nguyen, Executive Director

Provides leadership to promote the psychiatric-mental health nursing profession, improve mental health care for culturally diverse individuals, families, groups and communities and shape health policy for the delivery of mental health services.

1694 American Psychoanalytic Association (APsaA)
309 E 49th Street
New York, NY 10017
212-752-0450
E-mail: info@apsa.com
www.apsa.org

Tom Newman, Executive Director
Tina Faison, Administrative Assistant to Exec
Carolyn Gatto, Scientific Program/Meetings Dir.
Taylor Beidler, Meetings Coordinator

Professional Membership Organization with approximately 3,500 members nationwide, with 38 Affiliate Societies and 34 Training Institutes. Seeks to establish and maintain standards for the training of psychoanalysts and for the practice of psychoanalysis, fosters the integration of psychoanalysis with other disciplines (psychiatry, psychology, social work), and encourages research. Publications include: Journal of the Psychoanalyst (JAPA), American Psychoanalyst, a quarterly newsletter; Ethics Case Book; and Roster. Twice a year the organization sponsors scientific meetings and exhibits.

Year Founded: 1911

1695 American Psychologial Association: Division of Family Psychology
750 First St., NE
Washington, DC 20002-4242
202-336-6013
E-mail: webmaster@apa.org
www.apa.org

Frank C. Worrell, PhD, President
Arthur C. Evans Jr., PhD, CEO & EVP
Kathleen S. Brown, PhD, Recording Secretary
Jean A. Carter, PhD, Treasurer

A division of the American Psychological Association. Psychologists intersted in research, teaching, evaluation, and public interest initiatives in family psychology. Seeks to promote human welfare through the development, dissemination, and application of knowledge about the dynamics, structure, and functioning of the family. Conducts research and specialized education programs.

1696 American Psychological Association
750 First Street NE
Washington, DC 20002-4242
202-336-5500
800-374-2721
TDD: 202-336-6123
TTY: 202-336-6123
www.apa.org

Frank C. Worrell, PhD, President
Thema S. Bryant, PhD, President-Elect
Jean A. Carter, PhD, Treasurer
Kathleen S. Brown, PhD, Recording Secretary

The American Psychological Association seeks to advance psychology as a science, a profession, and as a means of promoting health, education, and human welfare. This organization of researchers, educators, clinicians, consultants, and students promotes research in psychology and the improvment of research methods; establishes high stan-

dards of ethics, conduct, and education; and disseminates psychological knowledge through professional and academic networks.

Year Founded: 1892

1697 American Psychological Association: Applied Experimental and Engineering Psychology
750 First Street NE
Washington, DC 20002-4242
202-336-6013
www.apa.org

Frank C. Worrell, PhD, President

A division of the American Psychological Association. Individuals whose principal fields of study, research, or work are within the area of applied experimental and engineering psychology. Promotes research on psychological factors in the design and use of environments and systems within which human beings work and live.

1698 American Psychological Association: Society for the Psychology of Religion and Spirituality
Doctoral Program in Clinical Psychology
750 First Street NE
Washington, DC 20002-4242
202-336-6013
E-mail: division@apa.org
www.www.apa.org/about/division/div36.aspx

Caroline Behe, Executive Director

A division of the American Psychological Association. Seeks to encourage and accelerate research, theory, and practice in the psychology of religion and related areas. Facilitates the dissemination of data on religious and allied issues and on the integration of these data with current psychological research, theory and practice.

1699 American Psychology-Law Society (AP-LS)
AP-LS Central Office
750 First Street NE
Washington, DC 20002-4242
www.ap-ls.org

A division of the American Psychological Association. It is an interdisciplinary organization devoted to the scholarship, practice and public service in psychology and law. Their goals include advancing the contributions of psychology to the understanding of law and legal institutions through basic and applied research; promoting the education of psychologists in matters of law and education of legal personnel in matters of psychology.

Year Founded: 1968

1700 American Psychosomatic Society
6728 Old McLean Village Drive
McLean, VA 22101
703-718-6038
E-mail: info@psychosomatic.org
www.psychosomatic.org

Gail Ironson, MD, President
Ten, T. Lewis, PhD, President-Elect
Tara Gruenewald, PhD, MPH, Secretary-Treasurer
Laura E. Degnon, CAE, Executive Director

A worldwide community of scholars and clinicians dedicated to the scientific understanding of the interaction of mind, brain, body and social context in promoting health and contributing to the pathogenesis, course and treatment of disease. Holds an annual meeting in a different location each year.

Year Founded: 1942

1701 American Society for Adolescent Psychiatry (ASAP)

PO Box 570218
Dallas, TX 75357-218
972-613-0985
www.adolpsych.org

Frances Bell, Executive Director
Mohan Nair, President

Psychiatrists concerned with the behavior of adolescents. Provides for the exchange of psychiatric knowledge, encourages the development of adequate standards and training facilities and stimulates research in the psychopathology and treatment of adolescents. Publications: Adolescent Psychiatry, annual journal. American Society for Adolescent Psychiatry Newsletter, quarterly. ASAP Membership Directory, biennial. Journal of Youth and Adolescence, bimonthly. Annual conference. Workshops.

Year Founded: 1967

1702 American Society for Clinical Pharmacology & Therapeutics

528 N Washington Street
Alexandria, VA 22314
703-836-6981
E-mail: members@ascpt.org
www.ascpt.org

Over 2,300 professionals whose primary interest is to promote and advance the science of human pharmacology and theraputics. Most of the members are physicians or other doctoral scientists. Other members are pharmacists, nurses, research coordinators, fellows in training and other professionals.

Year Founded: 1900

1703 American Society of Addiction Medicine

11400 Rockville Pike
Suite 200
Rockville, MD 20852
301-656-3920
E-mail: email@asam.org
www.asam.org

William F. Haning, III, MD, President
Brian Hurley, MD, MBA, President-Elect
Timothy Wiegand, MD, FACMT, Vice-President
Aleksandra Zgierska, MD, PhD, Secretary

Increase access to and improve the quality of addictions treatment. Educate physicians, medical and osteopathic, and the public.

Year Founded: 1954

1704 American Society of Consultant Pharmacists

1240 N. Pitt St.
Suite 300
Alexandria, VA 22314
703-739-1300
800-355-2727
E-mail: info@ascp.com
www.ascp.com

Chad Worz, CEO & Executive Director
Kevin Fearon, Chairman of the Board

Hedva Barenholtz Levy, President
Rolf Schrader, Secretary & Treasurer

International professional association that provides leadership, education, advocacy and resources to advance the practice of senior care pharmacy. Consultant pharmacists specializing in senior care pharmacy practice are essential participants in the health care system, ensuring that their patients medications are the most appropriate, effective, the safest possible and are used correctly. They identify, resolve and prevent medication related problems that may interfere with the goals of therapy.

Year Founded: 1969

1705 American Society of Group Psychotherapy & Psychodrama

PO Box 1654
Merchantville, NJ 08109-9998
609-737-8500
E-mail: asgpp@asgpp.org
www.asgpp.org

Daniela Simmons, PhD, TEP, President

Fosters national and international cooperation among all concerned with the theory and practice of psychodrama, sociometry, and group psychotherapy. Promotes research and fruitful application and publication of the findings. Maintains a code of professional standards.

Year Founded: 1942

1706 American Society of Health System Pharmacists

E-mail: Custserv@ashp.org
www.ashp.org

Linda S. Tyler, PharmD, FASHP
Paul W. Abramowitz, CEO
Christine M. Jolowksy, Treasurer

Thirty thousand member national professional association that represents pharmacists who practice in hospitals, health maintenance organizations, long-term care facilities, ambulatory care, home care and other components of health care systems. ASHP helps people make the best use of their medications, advances and supports the professional practice of pharmacists in hospitals and health systems and serves as their collective voice on issues related to medication use and public health.

Year Founded: 1942

1707 American Society on Aging

605 Market Street
Suite 1111
San Francisco, CA 94105-2869
800-537-9728
E-mail: info@asaging.org
www.asaging.org

Michael Adams, Chair
Peter Kaldes, Esq., President and CEO
Jacki Bennett, Chief of Staff
Robert R. Lowe, Chief Operating Officer

Nonprofit organization committed to enhancing the knowledge and skills of those working with older adults and their families. They produce educational programs, publications, conferences and workshops.

Year Founded: 1954

1708 Annie E Casey Foundation
701 St. Paul Street
Baltimore, MD 21202
410-547-6600
www.aecf.org

Leslie Boissiere, Vice President, External Affairs
Kimberley Brown, Vice President, Human Resources
Patrice Cromwell, VP, Center for Economic Opp.
Sandra Gasca-Gonzalez, VP, Center for Systems Innov.

Working to build better futures for disadvantaged children and their families in the US. The primary mission of the Foundation is to foster policies, human service reforms and community supports that more effectively meet the needs of today's vulnerable children and families.

Year Founded: 1948

1709 Association for Academic Psychiatry (AAP)
17W728 Butterfield Road #114
Oakbrook Terrace, IL 60181
770-222-2265
E-mail: lhedrick@academicpsychiatry.org
www.academicpsychiatry.org

Lewis P. Krain, MD, President
Iljie Fitzgerald, MD, Vice President
Jesse Markman, MD, Secretary and Treasurer

Focuses on education in psychiatry at every level from beginning of medical school through lifelong learning for psychiatrists and other physicians. It seeks to help psychiatrists who are interested in careers in academic psychiatry develop the skills and knowledge in teaching, research and career development that they must have to succeed. The Association provides a forum for members to exchange ideas on teaching techniques, curriculum, and other issues to work together to solve problems. It works with other professional organizations on mutual interests and objectives through committee liaison and collaborative programs.

1710 Association for Ambulatory Behavioral Healthcare
757-673-3741
E-mail: info@aabh.org
www.www.aabh.org

James Rosser, President
Larry Meikel, Treasurer
Jill Stanley Nagy, Secretary
Stephen Michael, DrPH, Executive Director

Powerful forum for people engaged in providing mental health services. Promoting the evolution of flexible models of responsive cost-effective ambulatory behavioral healthcare.

1711 Association for Applied Psychophysiology & Biofeedback
10200 W 44th Avenue
Suite 304
Wheat Ridge, CO 80033-2840
303-422-8436
800-477-8892
E-mail: info@aapb.org
www.www.aapb.org

David Stumph, Executive Director
Monta Greenfield, Associate Director

Their purpose is to advance the development, dissemination, and utilization of knowledge about applied psychophysiology and biofeedback to improve health and the quality of life through research, education and practice.

Year Founded: 1969

1712 Association for Behavior Analysis International
550 W. Centre Avenue
Portage, MI 49024
269-492-9310
E-mail: mail@abainternational.org
www.abainternational.org

Ruth Anne Rehfeldt, President

Their purpose is to develop, enhance and support the growth and vitality of behavior analysis through research, education and practice. Represents over 7,000 members.

Year Founded: 1974

1713 Association for Behavioral and Cognitive Therapies
305 Seventh Avenue
16th Floor
New York, NY 10001
212-647-1890
www.abct.org

Mary Jane Eimer, CAE, Executive Director
David Teisler, CAE, Deputy Director

A multidisciplinary organization dedicated to utilizing and advancing scientific approaches in the understanding and prevention of human behavioral and cognitive problems.

Year Founded: 1966

1714 Association for Birth Psychology
PO Box 25582
Colorado Springs, CO 80936
720-490-5612
E-mail: consultant@birthpsychology.com
www.birthpsychology.com

Raylene Phillips, MD, MA, FAAP, Board President
Lynn Korst, Board Vice President
Barbara Hotelling, MSN, FACCE, Board Secretary
Zachary Tucker, MPS, CFRE, Board Chief Financial Officer

Obstetricians, pediatricians, midwives, nurses, psychotherapists, psychologists, counselors, social workers, sociologists, and others interested in birth psychology, a developing discipline concerned with the experience of birth and the correlation between the birth process and personality development. Seeks to promote communication among professionals in the field; encourage commentary, research and theory from different points of view; establish birth psychology as an autonomous science of human behavior; develop guidelines and give direction to the field. Annual conference, regional meetings, workshops.

1715 Association for Child Psychoanalysis (ACP)
1964 Rahncliff Court
#22123
Eagan, NM 55122
612-643-1807
866-534-7555
E-mail: childanalysis65@gmail.com
www.childanalysis.org

Thomas Barrett, President
Daniel Prezant, PhD, Secretary
Mali Mann, MD, Treasurer
Susan Sherkow, MD, President-Elect

An international not-for-profit organization in which all members are highly trained child and adolescent psychoanalysts. Provides a forum for the interchange of ideas and clinical experience in order to advance the psychological treatment and understanding of children and adolescents and their families.

1716 Association for Hospital Medical Education
109 Brush Creek Road
Irwin, PA 15642
724-864-7321
E-mail: info@ahme.org
www.ahme.org

Wilhelmine Wiese-Rometsch, MD, President and Board Chair
Kimball Mohn, MD, Executive Director
Caroline Diez, BA, C-TAGME, Secretary
Jill Herrin, MBA, C-TAGME, Treasurer

National, nonprofit professional association involved in the continuum of medical education — undergraduate, graduate, and continuing medical education. More than 600 members represent hundreds of teaching hospitals, academic medical centers and consortia nationwide. Promotes improvement in medical education to meet health care needs, serves as a forum and resource for medical education information, advocates the value of medical education in health care.

Year Founded: 1956

1717 Association for Humanistic Psychology
14B Beach Road
PO Box 1190
Tiburon, CA 94920
512-441-8988
801-362-6033
E-mail: info@ahpweb.org
www.ahpweb.org

Carroy U. Ferguson, PhD, Co-President

Enhances the quality of human experience and to advance the evolution of human consciousness.

Year Founded: 1961

1718 Association for Pre- & Perinatal Psychology and Health
PO Box 25582
Colorado Springs, CO 80936
720-490-5612
E-mail: consultant@birthpsychology.com
www.birthpsychology.com

Raylene Phillips, MD, MA, FAAP, Board President
Lynn Korst, Board Vice President
Barbara Hotelling, MSN, FACCE, Board Secretary
Zachary Tucker, MPS, CFRE, Board Chief Financial Officer

Forum for individuals from diverse backgrounds and disciplines interested in psychological dimensions of prenatal and perinatal experiences. Typically, this includes childbirth educators, birth assistants, doulas, midwives, obstetricians, nurses, social workers, perinatologists, pediatricians, psychologists, counselors researchers and teachers at all levels. Quarterly journal published.

Year Founded: 1983

1719 Association for Psychoanalytic Medicine (APM)
www.www.theapmnewyork.org

Jules Kerman, MD, President
Andreas Kraebber, MD, President-Elect
Susan Scheftel, PhD, Chair of Programming
Diana Moga, MD, Treasurer

A non-profit organization that is a component society of both the American Psychoanalytic Association and the International Psychoanalytic Association.

Year Founded: 1942

1720 Association for Psychological Science (APS)
1800 Massachusetts Ave NW
Suite 402
Washington, DC 20036
202-293-9300
www.psychologicalscience.org

Robert Gropp, CEO/Executive Director
Aime Ballard-Wood, COO/Deputy Director

The APS (previously the American Psychological Society) is a nonprofit organization dedicated to the advancement of scientific psychology and its representation at the national and international levels. The Association's mission is to promote, protect, and advance the interests of scientifically oriented psychology in research, application, teaching and the improvement of human welfare.

Year Founded: 1988

1721 Association for Psychological Type International
PO Box 4538
Itasca, IL 60143
E-mail: apti.contactus@gmail.com
www.aptinternational.org

Tim Beggs, President
Julie Wright, Director, Membership Experience
Michael Gaden, Director, Technology
M. Eileen Brown, Director, Marketing

Individuals involved in organizational development, religion, management, education and counseling, and who are interested in psychological type, the Myers-Briggs Type Indicator, and the works of Carl G Jung. Purpose is to share ideas related to the uses of MBTI and the application of personality type theory in any area; promotes research, development, and education in the field. Sponsors seminars, conferences, and training sessions on the use of psychological type.

Year Founded: 1979

1722 Association for Women in Psychology
Florida International University
DM 212
University Park
Miami, FL 33199-1
305-348-2408
E-mail: awp@fiu.edu
www.awpsych.org

Tiffany O'Shaughnessy, Collective Coordinator
Celina Whitmore, Website/Comms. Coordinator
Mindy J. Erchull, Treasurer

Nonprofit scientific and educational organization committed to encouraging feminist psychological research, theory and activism. They are an organization with a history of affirming and celebrating differences, deepening challenges, and experiencing growth as feminists.

Year Founded: 1969

1723 Association for the Advancement of Psychology
PO Box 38129
Colorado Springs, CO 80937-8129
800-869-6595
www.AAPNet.org

Stephen M. Pfeiffer, PhD, Executive Director
Karen Rivard, Administrative Director

Promotes the interests of all psychologists before public
and governmental bodies. AAP's fundamental mission is
the support of candidates for the US Congress who are
sympathetic to psychology's concerns, through electioneer-
ing activities.

Year Founded: 1974

1724 Association of Black Psychologists
7119 Allentown Road
Suite 203
Ft. Washington, DC 20744
301-449-3082
E-mail: abpsi@abpsi.org
www.abpsi.org

Donell Barnett, PhD, President
Shawn Jones, PhD, MHS, LCP, Secretary
Rachel Gaiter, MBA, Treasurer

Members are professional psychologists and others in associated disciplines. Aims to: enhance the psychological
well-being of black people in America; define mental
health in consonance with newly established psychological
concepts and standards, develop policies for local, state,
and national decision making that have impact on the mental health of the black community; support established
black sister organizations and aid in the development of
new, independent black institutions to enhance the psychological educational, cultural, and economic situation. Offers
training and information on AIDS. Conducts seminars,
workshops and research. Periodic conference, annual
convention.

Year Founded: 1968

1725 Association of Certified Biblical Counselors
5401 N. Oak Trafficway
Kansas City, MO 64118
816-282-2836
E-mail: info@biblicalcounseling.com
www.biblicalcounseling.com

Dale Johnson, Executive Director
Rhenn Cherry, Director of Finances
Stuart Scott, Director, Membership Services
Ethan Gentry, Communications Coordinator

ACBC is a fellowship of Christian counselors and laymen
who have banded together to promote excellence in biblical
counseling. Formerly known as the National Association of
Nouthetic Counselors.

Year Founded: 1975

1726 Association of Children's Residential Centers
648 N. Plankinton Ave.
Suite 425
Milwaukee, WI 53203
877-332-2272
E-mail: info@togetherthevoice.org
www.togetherthevoice.org

Dana K. Dorn, Board President
Trish Cocoros, Treasurer

Jennifer Ryan, Secretary
Kari Sisson, Executive Director

The Association of Children's Residential Centers is a national organization focused on providing residential therapeutic treatment for children and adolescents with
behavioral health disorders.

Year Founded: 1956

1727 Association of State and Provincial Psychology Boards
PO Box 849
Tyrone, GA 30290
678-216-1175
www.asppb.org

Alan Slusky, PhD, CPsych, President
Herbert L. Stewart, PhD, President Elect
Cindy Olvey, PsyD, Secretary-Treasurer
Mariann Burnetti-Atwell, PsyD, Chief Executive Officer

ASPPB is the association of psychology licensing boards in
the United States and Canada. They create the Examination
for Professional Practice in Psychology which is used in licensing boards to assess candidates for licensure and certification. They also publish training materials for training
programs and for students preparing to enter the profession.

Year Founded: 1961

1728 Association of the Advancement of Gestalt Therapy
PO Box 42221
Portland, OR 97242
971-238-2248
E-mail: admin@iaagt.org
www.aagt.org

Eduardo Rubio Ram¡rez, President
Maryanne Nicholls, President Elect/Vice President
Deirdre Foley, Secretary
Jing Luo, Treasurer

Inclusive, nonprofit organization committed to the advancement of theory, philosophy, practice and research in
Gestalt Therapy and its various applications. This includes
but is not limited to personal growth, mental health, education, organization and systems development, political and
social development and change, and the fine and performing arts. Their international member base includes psychiatrists, psychologists, social workers, teachers, academics,
artists, writers, organizational consultants, political and
social analysts, activists and students.

1729 Bazelon Center for Mental Health Law
1090 Vermont Avenue NW
Suite 220
Washington, DC 20005
202-467-5730
E-mail: communications@bazelon.org
www.www.bazelon.org

Holly O'Donnell, CEO
Ira Burnim, Director
Lewis Bossing, Senior Staff Attorney

National legal advocate for people with mental disabilities.
Through precedent-setting litigation and in the public policy arena, the Bazelon Center works to advance and preserve the rights of people with mental illnesses and
development disabilities.

Year Founded: 1972

1730 Behavioral Health Systems
2 Metroplex Drive
Suite 500
Birmingham, AL 35209-6827
800-245-1150
www.behavioralhealthsystems.com

Deborah L. Stephens, Founder, Chairman & CEO
Kyle Strange, LCSW, EVP & Chief Clinical Officer
William M Patterson, M.D., Medical Director
Willis C. Estis, Ed.D., LPC, Clinical Consultant

Provides behavioral health services to business and industry which are high quality and state of the art, cost effective and accountable, uniformly accessible over a broad geographic area and care continuum, and managed within a least restrictive treatment approach.

Year Founded: 1989

1731 CG Jung Foundation for Analytical Psychology
28 E 39th Street
New York, NY 10016-2587
212-697-6430
E-mail: info@cgjungny.org
www.www.cgjungny.org

Jane Selinske, President
Joanne Bruno, Vice President
Rollin Bush, Treasurer
Harmar Brereton, Secretary

Analysts who follow the precepts of Carl G Jung, a Swiss psychologist, and any other persons interested in analytical psychology. Sponsors public lectures, films, continuing education, courses and professional seminars. Operates book service which provides publications on analytical psychology and related topics, and lectures on audio cassettes. Publishes journal, Quadrant.

Year Founded: 1962

1732 California Psychological Association
1231 I Street
Suite 204
Sacramento, CA 95814
916-286-7979
E-mail: cpa@cpapsych.org
www.cpapsych.org

David Lin, PsyD, President
David Hindman, PhD, President-Elect
Mary Malik, PhD, Treasurer
Jo Linder-Crow, PhD, Chief Executive Officer

A non-profit professional association for licensed psychologists and others affiliated with the delivery of psychological services.

Year Founded: 1948

1733 Center for Applications of Psychological Type
203 NE 1st Street
Gainesville, FL 32601
E-mail: customerservice@capt.org
www.capt.org

Nonprofit organization founded to conduct research and develop applications of the Myers-Briggs Type Indicator for the constructive use of differences. The MBTI is based on CG Jung's theory of psychological types. CAPT provides training for users of the MBTI and the Murphy-Meisgeier Type Indicator for Children, publishes and distributes books and resource materials, and maintains the Isabel Briggs Myers memorial library and the MBTI Bibliography. The MBTI is used in counseling individuals and families, to understand differences in learning styles, and for improving leadership and teamwork in organizations.

Year Founded: 1975

1734 Children's Health Council
650 Clark Way
Palo Alto, CA 94304
650-326-5530
E-mail: careteam@chconline.org
www.chconline.org

Pardis Khosravi, PsyD, Clinical Director
Rosalie Whitlock, PhD, Chief Executive Officer
Terry Boyle, CPA, Chief Financial Officer & COO
Ramsey Khasho, PsyD, Chief Clinical Officer

Working to make a measurable difference in the lives of children who face severe or complex behavioral and developmental challenges by providing interdisciplinary educational, assessment and treatment services and professional training.

1735 Christian Association for Psychological Studies
PO Box 365
Batavia, IL 60510-0365
630-639-9478
E-mail: info@caps.net
www.caps.net

William C. Buhrow, Jr., Psy.D., President
Gwen White Psy.D., Chair
Jim Sells, Ph.D., Treasurer
Virginia Holeman, Ph.D., Secretary

Psychologists, marriage and family therapists, social workers, educators, physicians, nurses, ministers, researchers, pastoral counselors, and rehabilitation workers and others professionally engaged in the fields of psychology, counseling, psychiatry, pastoring and related areas. Association is based upon a genuine commitment to superior clinical, pastoral and scientific enterprise in the theoretical and applied social sciences and theology, assuming persons in helping professions will be guided to professional and personal growth and a greater contribution to others in this way.

Year Founded: 1956

1736 Clinical Social Work Association
PO Box 10
Garrisonville, VA 22463
202-599-8443
www.www.clinicalsocialworkassociation.org

Kendra C. Roberson, PhD, LCSW, President
Danny Gellersen, LISCW, Vice President
Pete Navratil, LCSW-R, Treasurer
C.J. Sorenson, LCSW, Secretary

A membership association formed for the purpose of promoting the highest standards of professional education and clinical practice. Each society is active with legislative advocacy and lobbying efforts for adequate and appropriate mental health services and coverage at their state and national levels of government.

1737 Commission on Accreditation of Rehabilitation Facilities (CARF International)
6951ÿEast Southpoint Road
Tucson, AZ 85756-9407

520-325-1044
888-281-6531
TTY: 888-281-6531
www.carf.org

Brian J. Boon, Ph.D., President/CEO
Cindy L. Johnson, CPA, Chief Resource Officer

Promotes the quality, value and optimal outcomes through a consultative accreditation process that centers on enhancing the lives of the people served.

Year Founded: 1966

1738 Commonwealth Fund
1 East 75th Street
New York, NY 10021
212-606-3800
E-mail: info@cmwf.org
www.www.commonwealthfund.org

David Blumenthal, President
Kathleen Regan, EVP and Chief Operating Officer
Melinda K. Abram, EVP, Programs

Private foundation that supports independent research on health and social issues and make grants to improve health care practice and policy.

Year Founded: 1918

1739 Community Anti-Drug Coalitions of America (CADCA)
500 Montgomery Street
4th Floor
Alexandria, VA 22314
703-706-0560
E-mail: info@cadca.org
www.cadca.org

Mary Bono, Chairman
Larry P. Cote, Esq., Vice Chairman
Gregory Puckett, Secretary
Donald K. Truslow, Treasurer

With more than five thousand members across the country, CADCA is working to build and strengthen the capacity of community coalitions to create safe, healthy, and drug free communities. CADCA supports its members with technical assistance and training, public policy, media and marketing, conferences and special events.

Year Founded: 1992

1740 Corporate Counseling Associates
475 Park Avenue South
Fifth Floor
New York, NY 10016-6901
212-686-6827
800-833-8707
E-mail: info@corporatecounseling.com
www.www.ccainc.com

Robert Levy, Founder
John Levy, Esq., President
Georgia Critsimilios, LCSW, Senior Vice President
Russell Correa, EdM, Vice President

Customized, integrated workplace solutions designed to enhance business performance by enriching employee productivity.

Year Founded: 1984

1741 Council on Social Work Education
333 John Carlyle Street
Suite 400
Alexandria, VA 22314
703-683-8080
E-mail: info@cswe.org
www.cswe.org

Darla Spence Coffey, PhD, MSW, President and CEO
Patrick Dunne, Vice President, Comms./Marketing
Tanya Smith Brice, PhD, MSW, Vice President, Education
Arminn H. Leopold, Vice President, Finance and CFO

A national association that preserves and enhances the quality of social work education for the purpose of promoting the goals of individual and community well being and social justice. Pursues this mission through setting and maintaining policy and program standards, accrediting bachelors and masters degree programs in social work, promoting research and faculty development, and advocating for social work education.

Year Founded: 1952

1742 Developmental Disabilities Nurses Association (DDNA)
1501 South Loop 288
Suite 104 - 381
Denton, TX 76205
800-888-6733
www.ddna.org

S. Diane Moore, BSN, RN, CDDN, Executive Director
Judy Stych, DNP, RN, CDDN, President
Deb Maloy, RN, CDDN, President-Elect
Chris Helfrich, RN, CDDN, First Vice President

National nonprofit professional association for nurses working with individuals with developmental disabilities. Publishes a quarterly newsletter.

Year Founded: 1992

1743 Division of Independent Practice of the American Psychological Association (APADIP)
2400 Post Road
Warwick, RI 02886
401-732-2400
E-mail: div42apa@cox.net
www.division42.org

Peter Oppenheimer, PhD, President
Robin McLeod, PhD, President-Elect
Derek Phillips, PsyD, MSCP, Secretary
Gerald Koocher, PhD, ABPP, Treasurer

Members of the American Psychological Association engaged in independent practice. Works to ensure that the needs and concerns of independent psychology practitioners are considered by the APA. Gathers and disseminates information on legislation affecting the practice of psychology, managed care, and other developments in the health care industries, office management, malpractice risk and insurance, hospital management. Offers continuing professional and educational programs. Semiannual convention, with board meeting.

1744 Employee Assistance Professionals Association, Inc.
EAPA Exchange
4350 North Fairfax Drive
Suite 740
Arlington, VA 22203

703-387-1000
www.eapassn.org

Kristin Rantala, CEAP, President
Daniel Boissonneault, CEAP, President Elect
Patrick Williams, CEAP, Secretary/Treasurer
Julie Fabsik-Swarts, MS, Chief Executive Officer

International association of approximately 5,000 members who are primarily employee assistance professionals as well as individuals in related fields such as human resources, chemical dependency treatment, mental health treatment, managed behavioral health care, counseling and benefits administration. Hosts annual EAP conference.

Year Founded: 1971

1745 Employee Assistance Society of North America
Arlington, VA 22314
703-370-7435

International group of professional leaders with competencies in such specialties as workplace and family wellness, employee benefits and organizational development. Maintains accreditation program, membership services and professional training opportunities, promotes high standards of employee assistance programs.

Year Founded: 1985

1746 Gerontoligical Society of America
1220 L Street NW
Suite 901
Washington, DC 20005-1503
202-842-1275
E-mail: geron@geron.org
www.geron.org

James Appleby, CEO
Patricia M. D'Antonio, VP, Policy/Professional Affairs
Jim Evans, VP, Operations/CFO
Judie Lieu, VP, Publishing/Prof. Resources

Nonprofit professional organization with over 5,000 members in the field of aging. GSA provides researchers, educators, practitioners and policy makers with opportunities to understand, advance, integrate and use basic and applied research on aging to improve the quality of life as one ages.

Year Founded: 1945

1747 Gorski-Cenaps Corporation Training & Consultation
13001 Spring Hill Drive
Spring Hill, FL 34609-5064
352-596-8000
E-mail: tresa@cenaps.com
www.cenaps.com

Roland Williams, MA, LAADC, CEO and Director of Training
Tresa Watson, MBA, COO and CFO
Lisa Hilko, MPA, Chief Information Officer

Cenaps provides advanced clinical skills training for the addiction behavioral health and mental health fields. Their focus is recovery and relapse prevention.

1748 Group for the Advancement of Psychiatry
PO Box 570218
Dallas, TX 75357-0218
972-613-5532
E-mail: exec@ourgap.org
www.ourgap.org

Lawrence Gross, President
Barbara Long, President Elect
Robert Roca, Secretary
Calvin Sumner, Treasurer

An organization of nationally respected psychiatrists dedicated to shaping psychiatric thinking, public programs and clinical practice in mental health. Meets twice a year at the Renaissance Westchester Hotel in White Plains, NY.

Year Founded: 1946

1749 Institute of HeartMath
14700 W Park Avenue
Boulder Creek, CA 95006
800-711-6221
E-mail: info@heartmath.org
www.heartmath.org

Sarah Childre, President and CEO
Rollin McCraty, Ph.D., EVP and Director of Research
Brian Kabaker, CFO and Director of Sales
Katherine Floriano, Chairwoman

Nonprofit research and education on stress, emotional physiology and heart-brain interactions. Purpose is to reduce stress, school violence, improve mental and emotional attitudes, promote harmony within facilities and communities, improve academic performance and improve workplace health and performance. Research facility provides psychometric assessments for both individual and organizational assessment as well as autonomic assessments for physiological assessment and diagnostic purposes. Education initiative currently developing curriculum for rehabilitation of incarcerated teen felons in drug and alcohol recovery program.

Year Founded: 1991

1750 Institute on Psychiatric Services: American Psychiatric Association
1000 Wilson Boulevard
Suite 1825
Arlington, VA 22209-3924
888-357-7924
E-mail: apa@psych.org
www.psych.org

Vivian B. Pender, M.D., President
Rebecca W. Brendel, M.D., J.D., President-Elect
Sandra DeJong, M.D., M.Sc., Secretary
Richard F. Summers, M.D., Treasurer

Open to employees of all psychiatric and related health and educational facilities. Includes lectures by experts in the field and workshops and accredited courses on problems, programs and trends. Offers on-site Job Bank, which lists opportunities for mental health professionals. Organized scientific exhibits. Publications: Psychiatric Services, monthly journal. Annual Institute on Psychiatric Services conference and exhibits in October, Chicago, IL.

1751 International Center for the Study of Psychiatry And Psychology (ISCPP)
1036 Park Avenue
Suite 1B
New York, NY 10028-971
212-861-7400
E-mail: djriccio@aol.com
www.icspp.org

Nonprofit research and educational network whose focus is the critical study of the mental health movement. ICSPP is completely independent and their funding consists solely of individual membership dues. Fosters prevention and treatment of mental and emotional disorders. Promotes alternatives to administering psychiatric drugs to children.

1752 International Society for Developmental Psychobiology

297 Kinderkamack Road
Suite 348
Oradell, NJ 07649
800-216-1050
www.isdp.org

Megan R. Gunnar, President
Tania K. Roth, President-Elect
Manon Ranger, Secretary
Kevin Bath, Treasurer

Members are research scientists in the field of developmental psychobiology and biology and psychology students. Promotes research in the field of developmental psychobiology, the study of the brain and brain behavior throughout the life span and in relation to other biological proccesses. Stimulates communication and interaction among scientists in the field. Provides the editorship for the journal, Development Psychobiology. Bestows awards. Compiles statistics. Annual conference.

1753 International Society of Political Psychology
Moynihan Institute of Global Affairs
PO Box 1213
Columbus, NC 28722
828-894-5422
E-mail: info@ispp.org
www.ispp.org

Severine Bennett, CMP, PMP, Executive Director
Tereza Capelos, President
Roberto Gonz lez, President-Elect

Facilitates communication across disciplinary, geographic and political boundaries among scholars, concerned individuals in government and public posts, the communication media and elsewhere who have a scientific interest in the relationship between politics and psychological processes. ISPP seeks to advance the quality of scholarship in political psychology and to increase the usefulness of work in political psychology.

1754 International Transactional Analysis Association (ITAA)
2843 Hopyard Road
Suite 155
Pleasanton, CA 94588
925-600-8110
E-mail: info@itaaworld.org
www.www.itaaworld.org

Chitra Ravi, President
John Oates, Treasurer
Rema Giridhar, Secretary
Michelle Thom,, Vice President, Development

A non-profit educational organization with members in over 65 countries. Its purpose is to advance the theory, methods and principles of transactional analysis.

1755 Jean Piaget Society: Society for the Study of Knowledge and Development (JPSSSKD)
Department Of Psychology
Clark University
950 Main St
Worcester, MA 01610-1400
508-793-7250
E-mail: webmaster@piaget.org
www.piaget.org

David Witherington, President
Chris Lalonde, VP, Information Technology
Elizabeth Pufall Jones, VP, Communications & Publicity
Tom Bidell, Treasurer

Scholars, teachers, and researchers interested in exploring the nature of the developmental construction of human knowledge. Purpose is to further research on knowledge and development, especially in relation to the work of Jean Piaget, a Swiss developmentalist noted for his work in child psychology, the study of human development, and the origin and growth of human knowledge. Conducts small meetings and programs.

Year Founded: 1970

1756 Med Advantage
12001 Science Dr
#115
Orlando, FL 32826
407-410-3775
E-mail: info@med-advantage.com
www.verisys.com

John P. Benson, Co-Founder and Chairman
Charlie Falcone, Chief Executive Officer
Eric Gwynn, Chief Operating Officer
Kymberly Eide, President

Fully accredited by URAC and certified in all 11 elements by NCQA, Med Advantage is one of the oldest credentials verification organizations in the country. Over the past eight years, they have developed sophisticated computer systems and one of the largest data warehouses of medical providers in the nation, containing information on over 900,000 healthcare providers. Their system is continually updated from primary source data required to meet the standards of the URAC, NCQA and JCAHO.

1757 Medical Group Management Association
124 Inverness Terrace East
Englewood, CO 80112-5306
877-275-6462
E-mail: service@mgma.com
www.mgma.com

Karen Marcelo, BSN, MBA, Board Chair
Jeffrey W. Smith, CPA, CGMA, MBA, Vice Chair
Eric D. Crockett, MBA, FACMPE, Finance/Audit Chair

The national membership association providing information networking and professional development for the individuals who manage and lead medical group practices.

Year Founded: 1926

1758 Mental Health America
500 Montgomery Street
Suite 820
Alexandria, VA 22314
703-684-7722
800-969-6642
www.www.mhanational.org

Schroeder Stribling, President and CEO
Taylor Adams, Dir., Workplace Mental Health
Stuart Allen, Chief Marketing Officer
Mary Giliberti, J.D., Chief Public Policy Officer

A community-based nonprofit organization committed to enabling the mental wellness of all Americans. MHA advocates for greater access to quality health services and seeks to educate individuals on identifying symptoms, as well as intervention and prevention initiatives.

Year Founded: 1909

1759 Mental Health Corporations of America

1876 Eider Court
Suite A
Tallahassee, FL 32308
850-942-4900
www.mhca.com

Dale Shreve, MSW, President & CEO
Lonnie Parizek, Dir., Comms. & Membership
Gena Matthews, MPA, CMP, Dir., Conference Services
Frank Collins, Direcor, Information Technology

Membership in MHCA is by invitation only. It is the organization's intent to include in its network only the highest quality behavioral healthcare organizations in the country. Their alliance is designed to strengthen members' competitive position, enhance their leadership capabilities and facilitate their strategic networking opportunities.

1760 Mental Health Materials Center (MHMC)

PO Box 304
Bronxville, NY 10708-304
914-337-6596

Alex Sareyan, President

Professionals of mental health and health education, seeking to stimulate the development of wider, more effective channels of communication between health educators and the public. Provides consulting services to nonprofit organizations on the implementation of their publishing operations in areas related to mental health and health. Publications: Study on Suicide Training Manual. Survival Manual for Medical Students. Books, booklets and pamphlets. Annual Meeting in New York City.

1761 National Academy of Neuropsychology (NAN)

7555 E Hampden Ave
Suite 420
Denver, CO 80231
303-691-3694
E-mail: office@nanonline.org
www.nanonline.org

Beth Co. Arredondo, Ph.D., President
John J. Randolph, Ph.D., President-Elect
Karin JM McCoy, Ph.D., Treasurer
Heidi Rossetti, Ph.D., Secretary

Clinical neuropsychologists and others interested in brain-behavior relationships. Works to preserve and advance knowledge regarding the assessment and remediation of neuropsychological disorders. Promotes the development of neuropsychology as a science and profession; develops standard of practice and training guidelines for the field; fosters communication between members, represents the professional interests of members, serves as an information resource, facilitates the exchange of information among related organizations. Offers continuing education programs, conducts research. Currently represents over 3,000 members.

Year Founded: 1975

1762 National Association For Children's Behavioral Health

1025 Connecticut Avenue NW
Suite 1012
Washington, DC 20036-5417
202-857-9735
www.www.nacbh.org

Charlene Hoobler, President
Michele Madley, Vice President/President-Elect
Tricia Delano, Secretary
David Napier, Treasurer

To promote the availability and delivery of appropriate and relevant services to children and adolescents with, or at risk of, serious emotional disturbances and their families. Advocate for the full array of mental health and related services necessary, the development and use of assessment and outcome tools based on functional as well as clinical indicators, and the elimination of categorial funding barriers.

1763 National Association for the Advancement of Psychoanalysis
NAAP News, E-Bulletin

850 7th Ave
Suite 800
New York, NY 10019
212-741-0515
E-mail: NAAP@NAAP.org
www.naap.org

Patricia Bratt, President

Certified psychoanalysts disseminating psychoanalytic principles to the medical-psychiatric profession and the general community. Conducts scientific meetings. Supports research programs, sponsors public educational lectures. Publications: NAAP News, Quarterly; Registry of Psychoanalysts, Annual, E-Bulletin, Online Publication.

Year Founded: 1972

1764 National Association of Addiction Treatment Providers

1120 Lincoln Street
Suite 1303
Denver, CO 80203
888-574-1008
E-mail: info@naatp.org
www.naatp.org

Robert Ferguson, Board Chair
Jay Crosson, Vice Chair
Marvin Ventrell, JD, Chief Executive Officer
Katie Strand, MS, CMP, Chief Operating Officer

The mission of the National Association of Addiction Treatment Providers (NAATP) is to promote, assist and enhance the delivery of ethical, effective, research-based treatment for alcoholism and other drug addictions. Provides members and the public with accurate, responsible information and other resources related to the treatment of these diseases, advocates for increased access to and availability of quality treatment for those who suffer from alcoholism and other drug addictions; works in partnership with other organizations and individuals that share NAATP's mission and goals.

Year Founded: 1978

1765 National Association of Community Health Centers

7501 Wisconsin Avenue
Suite 1100W
Bethesda, MD 20814
301-347-0400
www.nachc.com

Michael A. Holmes, Chair of the Board
Paloma Hernandez, Chair-Elect
Blake Hall, Secretary
John Santistevan, Treasurer

A nonprofit organization whose mission is to enhance and expand access to quality, community-responsive health care for America's medically underserved and uninsured. A major source for information, data, research, and advocacy on key issues affecting community-based health centers and the delivery of health care. Provides education, training, technical assistance, and leadership development to health center staff, boards, and others to promote excellence and cost-effectiveness in health delivery practice and community board governance. Builds partnerships and linkages that stimulate public and private sector investment in the delivery of quality health care services to medically underserved communities.

Year Founded: 1971

1766 National Association of Psychiatric Health Systems

900 17th Street NW
Suite 420
Washington, DC 20006
202-393-6700
E-mail: nabh@nabh.org
www.naphs.org

Matt J. Peterson, Board Chair
Harsh K. Trivedi, MD, MBA, Board Chair-Elect
Eric H. Paul, Secretary
Frank A. Ghinassi, PhD, ABPP, Treasurer

Advocates for behavioral health and represents provider systems that are committed to the delivery of responsive, accountable, and clinically effective treatment and prevention programs for children, adolescents, adults and older adults with mental and substance abuse disorders.

Year Founded: 1933

1767 National Association of School Psychologists (NASP)

4340 East West Highway
Suite 402
Bethesda, MD 20814
301-657-0270
www.nasponline.org

Laurie Klose, President
Celeste Malone, President-Elect
Karen Apgar, Secretary
Misty Lay, Treasurer

School psychologists who serve the mental health and educational needs of all children and youth. Encourages and provides opportunites for professional growth of individual members. Informs the public on the issues and practice of school psychology, and advances the standards of the profession. Operates national school psychologist certification system. Sponsers children's services.

1768 National Association of Social Workers

750 First Street NE
Suite 700
Washington, DC 20002
800-472-4089
E-mail: membership@socialworkers.org
www.socialworkers.org

Angelo McClain, Chief Executive Officer
Sue Jashinsky, Chief Administrative Officer
Anna Mangum, Deputy Director, Programs
Gail Woods Waller, Deputy Dir., Membership/Comms.

Works to enhance the professional growth and development of its members, to create and maintain professional standards, and to advance sound social policies.

1769 National Association of State Mental Health Program Directors (NASMHPD)

66 Canal Center Plaza
Suite 302
Alexandria, VA 22314
703-739-9333
E-mail: brian.hepburn@nasmhpd.org
www.nasmhpd.org

Brian Hepburn, MD, Executive Director
Jay Meek, CPA, MBA, Chief Financial Officer
David Shern, PhD, Senior Public Health Advisor
Meighan Haupt, MS, Chief of Staff

The only national association to represent state mental health commissioners/directors and their agencies. A private nonprofit membership organization, NASMHPD helps set the agenda and determine the direction of state mental health agency interests across the country, including state mental health planning, service delivery, and evaluation. The association provides members with the opportunity to exchange diverse views and experiences, learning from one another in areas vital to effective public policy development and implementation.

Year Founded: 1959

1770 National Business Coalition Forum on Health (NBCH)

1015 18th Street NW
Suite 730
Washington, DC 20036
202-775-9300
www.www.nbch.org

Michael Thompson, President and CEO
Margaret Rehayem, Vice President
Maria Cornjeo, Director of Operations
Karlene Lucas, RRT, MBA, Director of Dev./Program Mngmt.

A national, non-profit membership organization of employer-based coalitions. Dedicated to value-based purchasing of health care services through the collective action of public and private purchasers. NCBH seeks to accelerate the nations progress towards safe, efficient, high quality health care and the improved health status of the American population.

1771 National Coalition for the Homeless

2201 P Street Northwest
Washington, DC 20037
202-462-4822
E-mail: info@nationalhomeless.org
www.nationalhomeless.org

Barbara Anderson, Treasurer
Donald Whitehead, Executive Director
Megan Hustings, Deputy Director

The National Coalition for the Homeless is an organization serving to protect the needs of those experiencing homelessness, while striving to prevent and end homelessness. NCH promotes effective treatment, services, and programs for those struggling with homelessness as well as substance abuse problems.

Year Founded: 1982

1772 National Committee for Quality Assurance

1100 13th Street NW
Suite 1000
Washington, DC 20005
202-955-3500
www.ncqa.org

Margaret E. O'Kane, President
Tom Fluegel, Chief Operating Officer
Eric Schneider, MD, M.Sc., EVP, Quality Measurement
Mary Barton, VP, Performance Measurement

A non-profit organization whose mission is to improve health care quality everywhere and to transform health care quality through measurement, transparency and accountability.

1773 National Community Action Partnership (NCAP)

1020 19th Street, NW
Suite 700
Washington, DC 20036
202-265-7546
E-mail: info@communityactionpartnership.com
www.communityactionpartnership.com

Denise Harlow, CCAP, NCRT, Chief Executive Officer
Dalitso S. Sulamoyo, CCAP, Chair
Dreama Padgett, CCAP, Treasurer
Peter Kilde, CCAP, Secretary

The national organization representing the interests of the 1,000 Community Action Agencies working to fight poverty at the local level.

Year Founded: 1971

1774 National Council of Juvenile and Family Court Judges

PO Box 8970
Reno, NV 89507
775-507-4777
E-mail: contactus@ncjfcj.org
www.ncjfcj.org

Joey Orduna Hastings, Chief Executive Officer
Trudy Dulong, Finance Director
Tammy Rianda, MJM, Director, HR/Internal Ops.
Helen Bolstad, Director, Communications

Mission is to improve courts and systems practice and raise awareness of the core issues that touch the lives of many of our nation's childrens and families.

Year Founded: 1937

1775 National Council on Aging

251 17th Street South
Suite 500
Arlington, VA 22202

202-479-1200
E-mail: info@ncoa.org
www.ncoa.org

Ramsey Alwin, President and CEO
Alfreda Davis, Chief of Staff
Karen Davis, Chief Dev./Marketing Officer
Donna Whitt, Chief Financial Officer

NCOA is a nonprofit service and advocacy organization. NCOA is a ntional voice for millions of older adults, especially those that are vulnerable and disadvantaged and the community organizations that serve them. It brings together non profit organizations, businesses, and government to develop creative solutions that improve the lives of older adults.

Year Founded: 1950

1776 National Nurses United

8455 Colesville Rd
Suite 1100
Silver Spring, MD 20190
240-235-2000
E-mail: info@nationalnursesunited.org
www.nationalnursesunited.org

Deborah Burger, Co-President
Zenei Triunfo-Cortez, Co-President
Jean Ross, Co-President

Purpose is to help enhance the personal development as well as economic well being of its members. They provide services and benefits meaningful to the unique demands of the nursing professional.

Year Founded: 2009

1777 National Pharmaceutical Council

1717 Pennsylvania Ave., NW
Suite 800
Washington, DC 20006
202-827-2100
E-mail: info@npcnow.com
www.www.npcnow.org

John M. O'Brien, PharmD, MPH, President and CEO
Sharon Phares, PhD, MPH, Chief Scientific Officer
Michael Ciarametaro, MBA, Vice President, Research
Kathryn A. Gleason, Chief Operating Officer/SVP

NPC sponsors a variety of research and education projects aimed at demonstrating that the appropriate use of pharmaceuticals improves both patient treatment outcomes and the cost effective delivery of overall health care services.

Year Founded: 1953

1778 National Psychological Association for Psychoanalysis (NPAP)

40 West 13th Street
New York, NY 10011-7802
212-924-7440
E-mail: info@npap.org
www.npap.org

Jennifer Knobe, Administrative Director
Dana Holloman, Office Administrator
Thomas S. Taylor, President
Cristin Conneely, Secretary

Professional society for practicing psychoanalysts. Conducts training program leading to certification in psychoanalysis. Offers information and private referral service for the public. Operates speakers' bureau. Publications: National Psychological Association for Psychoanalysis-Bulletin, biennial. National Psychological Association for Psychoanalysis-News and Reviews, semiannual. Psychoanalytic Review, bimonthly journal.

Year Founded: 1948

1779 National Register of Health Service Providers in Psychology

1200 New York Avenue NW
Suite 800
Washington, DC 20005
202-783-7663
www.nationalregister.org

Beth N. Rom-Rymer, PhD, President/Chair
Morgan T. Sammons, PhD, ABPP, Chief Executive Officer
Andrew P. Boucher, Chief Operating Officer
Peter H. Marcus, PsyD, Treasurer

Psychologists who are licensed or certified by a state/provincial board of examiners of psychology and who have met council criteria as health service providers in psychology.

Year Founded: 1974

1780 National Treatment Alternative for Safe Communities

700 S. Clinton St.
Chicago, IL 60607
855-827-2444
E-mail: information@tasc-il.org
www.tasc-il.org

Jason Hutton, Chair
DeAnna E. Jones, Vice Chair
Andreason Brown, Secretary/Treasurer
Roy H. Fesmire, MAS, CPA, Vice President/CFO

TASC is a not-for-profit organization that provides behavioral health recovery management services for individuals with substance abuse and mental health disorders. They provide direct services, design model programs and build collaborative networks between public systems and community-based human service providers. TASC's purpose is to see that under-served populations gain access to the services they need for health and self-sufficiency, while also ensuring that public and private resources are used most efficiently.

Year Founded: 1976

1781 North American Society of Adlerian Psychology (NASAP)

NASAP
429 E. Dupont Road
Suite 276
Fort Wayne, IN 46825
260-267-8807
www.alfredadler.org

Tim Hartshorne, President
Hallie Williams, Sr., Vice President
Elaine Carey, Secretary
LeAnn Heimer, Treasurer

NASAP is a professional organization for couselors, educators, psychologists, parent educators, business professionals, researchers and others who are interested in Adler's Individual Psychology. Membership includes journals, newsletters, conferences and training.

Year Founded: 1952

1782 Pharmaceutical Care Management Association

325 7th Street NW
Suite 900
Washington, DC 20004
202-756-5700
E-mail: info@pcmanet.org
www.pcmanet.org

JC Scott, President and CEO
Mike Baldyga, Director, Strategic Comms.
Angela Banks, Vice President, Policy
Kristin Bass, Chief Policy Officer

A national association representing Pharmacy Benefit Managers. They are dedicated to enhancing the proven tools and techniques that PBMs have pioneered in the marketplace and working to lower the cost of prescription drugs for more than 200 million Americans.

1783 Physicians for a National Health Program

29 E. Madison St.
Ste. 1412
Chicago, IL 60602
312-782-6006
E-mail: info@pnhp.org
www.pnhp.org

Susan Rogers, MD, FACP, President
Adam Gaffney, MD, MPH, Secretary
Claudia M Fegan, MD, CHCQM, FACP, Treasurer
Ken Snyder, Executive Director

A single issue organization advocating a universal, comprehensive Single-Payer National Health Program.

Year Founded: 1987

1784 Professional Risk Management Services (PRMS)

The Psychiatrists' Program
4300 Wilson Boulevard
Suite 700
Arlington, VA 22203
800-245-3333
E-mail: TheProgram@prms.com
www.www.prms.com

Jean Clark Bates, RN, BSN, MPPM, Diretor, Claims
Donna Vanderpool, MBA, JD, Director, Risk Management
Danielle Bolger, Director, Marketing
Megan Jones, MBA, ARM, AIS, Director, Operations

PRMS, Inc. specializes in medical professional liability insurance programs and claims and risk management services - on a bundled and unbundled basis for individual healthcare providers, group practices, facilities, associations, and organizations.

Year Founded: 1986

1785 Psychiatric Rehabilitation Association (PRA)

212 E. LaSalle Ave
Suite 220
South Bend, IN 46617
312-878-9797
E-mail: info@psychrehabassociation.org
www.psychrehabassociation.org

Steve Miccio, Chair
Beth Boersma, MSW, CPRP, Vice Chair
Nicole Pashka, MS, CRC, CPRP, Treasurer/Secretary

The PRA, formerly USPRA, is an organization of psychosocial rehabilitation agencies, practitioners, and interested organizations and individuals dedicated to promoting, supporting and strengthening community-oriented rehabilitation services and resources for persons with psychiatric disabilities.

Year Founded: 1975

1786 Psychohistory Forum
627 Dakota Trail
Franklin Lakes, NJ 07417
201-891-7486
E-mail: cliospsycheeditor@gmail.com
www.cliospsyche.org

Dr. Paul H. Elovitz, PhD, Editor-in-Chief

Psychologists, psychiatrists, psychotherapists, social workers, historians, psychohistorians and others having a scholarly interest in the integration of depth psychology and history. Aids individuals in psychohistorical research. Holds lecture series. Publications: Clio's Psyche: Understanding the Why of Current Events and History, quarterly journal. Immigrant Experience: Personal Narrative and Psychological Analysis, monograph. Periodic Meeting.

Year Founded: 1994

1787 Psychonomic Society
8735 W. Higgins Road
Suite 300
Chicago, IL 60631
847-375-3696
E-mail: info@psychonomic.org
www.psychonomic.org

Louis Shomette, Executive Director
Tiffany Aurora, Dir., Membership/Marketing/Comm.
Stephanie Dylkiewicz, CMP, DES, Director, Meetings

Persons qualified to conduct and supervise scientific research in psychology or allied sciences; members must hold a PhD degree or its equivalent and must have published significant research other than doctoral dissertation. Promotes the communication of scientific research in psychology and allied sciences.

Year Founded: 1959

1788 Rapid Psychler Press
2014 Holland Ave
Suite 374
Port Huron, MI 48060
888-779-2453
E-mail: rapid@psychler.com
www.psychler.com

David Robinson, Publisher

Produces books and presentation media for educating mental health professionals. Products cover a wide range of learning needs. Where possible, humor is incorporated as an educational aid to enhance learning and retention.

1789 Risk and Insurance Management Society (RIMS)
228 Park Ave S
PMB 23312
New York, NY 10003-1502
212-286-9292
www.rims.org

Patrick Sterling, President
Jennifer Santiago, Vice President
Mary Roth, Chief Executive Officer
Annette Homan, Chief Operating Officer

Not-for-profit organization dedicated to improving the global risk management community through professional development, education sessions, and networking opportunities. Represents over 3,500 members.

Year Founded: 1950

1790 Screening for Mental Health
500 Montgomery Street
Suite 820
Alexandria, VA 22314
703-684-7722
800-969-6642
E-mail: smhinfo@mentalhealthscreening.org
www.screening.mhanational.org

Schorder Stribling, President/CEO
Taylor Adams, Dir., Workplace Mental Health
Sachin Doshi, Sr. Dir., Finance/Operations
Jessica Kennedy, Chief Strategy/Finance Officer

Nonprofit organization devoted to assisting people with undiagnosed, untreated mental illness connect with local treatment resources via national screening programs for depression, anxiety, eating disorders and alcohol problems.

1791 Sigmund Freud Archives (SFA)
16 Channing Place
c/o Harold P Blum, MD
Cambridge, MA 02138
516-621-6850
E-mail: aok@kris.org
www.www.freudarchives.org

Jennifer Stuart, Ph.D., President
Louis Rose, Ph.D., Executive Director
Nellie L. Thompson, Ph.D., Secretary
W. Craig Tomlinson, Ph.D., Treasurer

Psychoanalysts interested in the preservation and collection of scientific and personal writings of Sigmund Freud. Assists in research on Freud's life and work and the evolution of psychoanalytic thought. Collects and classifies all documents, papers, publications, personal correspondence and historical data written by, to, and on Freud. Transmits all materials collected to the Library of Congress. Annual meeting in New York City.

Year Founded: 1951

1792 Society for Pediatric Psychology (SPP)
www.www.apadivisions.org/division-54/index.aspx

Dedicated to research and practice addressing the relationship between children's physical, cognitive, social, and emotional functioning and their physical well-being, including maintenance of health, promotion of positive health behaviors, and treatment of chronic and serious medical conditions. A division of the APA. Newsletter: Progress Notes (published six times per year).

1793 Society for Personality Assessment
6109H Arlington Boulevard
Falls Church, VA 22044
703-534-4772
www.personality.org

Joni L. Mihura, PhD, ABAP, Professor
Anita L. Boss, President-Elect
Paul Anthony Arbisi, Treasurer
Jaime Anderson, Secretary

International professional trade association for psychologists, behavioral scientists, anthropologists, and psychiatrists. Promotes the study, research development and application of personality assessment.

1794 Society for Psychophysiological Research
2424 American Lane
Madison, WI 53704-3102
608-443-2470
E-mail: homeoffice@scmhr.org
www.scmhr.org

Fadia Hoyek, CCE, CME, President
Elin Ayala, Vice President
Sarikhi Chaffin, CLHRP, Vice President
Christian Karavolas, CLS, Vice President

The Society for Psychophysiological Research is an international scientific society. The purpose of the society is to foster research on the interrelationship between physiological and phychological aspects of behavior.

Year Founded: 1960

1795 Society for Women's Health Research (SWHR)
1025 Connecticut Avenue NW
Suite 1104
Washington, DC 20036
202-223-8224
E-mail: info@swhr.org
www.www.womenshealthresearch.org

Shontelle Dodson, PharmD, Board Chair
Kathryn G. Schubert, MPP, CAE, President and CEO
Gretta Stone, Secretary and Treasurer
Yonas G. Fsahaye, MBA, Chief Financial Officer

The nation's only not-for-profit organization whose sole mission is to improve the health of women through research. The SWHR advocates increased funding for research on women's health, encourages the study of sex differences that may affect the prevention, diagnosis and treatment of disease, and promotes the inclusion of women in medical research studies.

Year Founded: 1990

1796 Society for the Advancement of Social Psychology (SASP)
630 Convention Tower
Buffalo, NY 14202
301-405-5921
E-mail: info@sesp.org
www.sesp.org

Steve Stroessner, Executive Officer
David Amodio, President
Lora Park, Vice President

Social psychologists and students in social psychology. Advances social psychology as a profession by facilitating communication among social psychologists and improving dissemination and utilization of social psychological knowledge. Annual meeting every October.

1797 Society for the Psychological Study of Social Issues (SPSSI)
700 7th St E
Washington, DC 20003
202-675-6956
877-310-7778
E-mail: spssi@spssi.org
www.www.spssi.org

Linda Silka, President
Abigail Stewart, President Elect

Alaina Brenick, Secretary-Treasurer
Anila Balkissoon, Executive Director

An international group of over 3,500 psychologists, allied scientists, students, and others who share a common interest in research on the psychological aspects of important social issues. The Society seeks to bring theory and practice into focus on human problems of the group, the community, and nations as well as the increasingly important problems that have no national boundaries.

Year Founded: 1936

1798 Society of Behavioral Medicine
555 East Wells Street
Suite 1100
Milwaukee, WI 53202-3823
414-918-3156
E-mail: info@sbm.org
www.sbm.org

Lindsay Bullock, CAE, Executive Director
Elizbeth Rehorst, Development Coordinator
Irene Stephenson, Administrative Coordinator

A non-profit organization is a scientific forum for over 3,000 behavioral and biomedical researchers and clinicians to study the interactions of behavior, physiological and biochemical states, and morbidity and mortality. SBM provides an interactive network for education and collaboration on common research, clinical and public policy concerns related to prevention, diagnosis and treatment, rehabilitation, and health promotion.

Year Founded: 1978

1799 Society of Multivariate Experimental Psychology (SMEP)
University of Virginia
102 Gilmer Hall
Department of Psychology
Charlottesville, VA 22903
804-924-0656
www.smep.org

Lesa Hoffman, President-Elect
Niels Waller, President
Jonathan Templin, Coordinator Officer
Mijke Rhemtulla, Financial Officer

An organization of researchers interested in multivariate quantitative methods and their application to substantive problems in psychology. Membership is limited to 65 regular active members. SMEP oversees the publication of a research journal which publishes research articles on multivariate methodology and its use in psychological research.

Year Founded: 1960

1800 Society of Teachers of Family Medicine
11400 Tomahawk Creek Parkway
Leawood, KS 66211
800-274-7928
E-mail: stfmoffice@stfm.org
www.stfm.org

Aaron Michelfelder, MD, President
Linda Myerholtz, PhD, President-Elect
Byron Jasper, MD, MPH, Treasurer
Stacy Brungardt, CAE, Executive Director and CEO

Multidisciplinary, medical organization that offers numerous faculty development opportunities for individuals involved in family medicine education. STFM publishes a monthly journal, hosts a web site, distributes books, coordinates CME conferences devoted to family medicine teaching and research and other activities designed to improve teaching skills of family medicine educators.

Year Founded: 1967

1801 Washington Association for Marriage and Family Therapy (WAMFT)
1300 W. Nickerson St.
#128
Seattle, WA 98119
206-450-8931
E-mail: wamft@wamft.org
www.www.wamft.org

Michelle Finley, PhD, LMFT, President
Anthony Pennant, President-Elect
Theresa Winther, Secretary
Michele Sullivan, Treasurer

An Independent Affiliate of the American Association for Marriage and Family Therapy (AAMFT). Offers networking and educational opportunities to Washington members, and aims to advance the field of marriage and family therapy through training opportunities.

1802 Wellness Councils of America
17002 Marcy St.
Suite 140
Omaha, NE 68118
402-827-3590
E-mail: wellworkplace@welcoa.org
www.welcoa.org

Sarah Martin, MS, Chief Executive Officer
Maggie Gough, Chief Operating Officer
Sandie Jack, Controller
Brittany Ruzicka, Executive Creative Director

A national non-profit membership organization dedicated to promoting healthier life styles for all Americans, especially through health promotion initiatives at the worksite. They publish a number of source books, a monthly newsletter, an extensive line of brochures and conducts numerous training seminars.

Year Founded: 1987

1803 WorldatWork
14040 N Northsight Boulevard
Scottsdale, AZ 85260-3627
877-951-9191
480-951-9191
E-mail: customerrelations@worldatwork.org
www.worldatwork.org

A not-for-profit professional association dedicated to knowledge leadership in compensation, benefits and total rewards. Focuses on human resources disciplines associated with attracting, retaining and motivating employees. Provides education programs, a monthly magazine, online information resources, surveys, publications, conferences, research and networking opportunities.

Year Founded: 1955

Conferences & Meetings

1804 AAIDD Annual Meeting
501 3rd Street NW
Suite 200
Washington, DC 20001

202-387-1968
800-424-3688
E-mail: anam@aaidd.org
www.aaidd.org

Margaret A. Nygren, EdD, Executive Director & CEO
Danielle Webber, MSW, Manager
Kathleen McLane, Director
Paul D. Aitken,CPA, Director

AAIDD promotes progressive policies, sound research, effective practices and universal human rights for people with intellectual and developmental disabilities.

1 per year

1805 AMA's Annual Medical Communications Conference
American Medical Association
330 N. Wabash Ave.
Suite 39300
Chicago, IL 60611-5885
312-464-4782
www.ama-assn.org

James L. Madara, MD, CEO & EVP, Pathology
Todd ÿ Askew, SVP, Advocacy
Toni Canada, SVP, HR & Corporate Services
Thomas J. Easley, SVP, Publishing

Provides hands-on communications training and hear from top-level medical communicators, government leaders and national journalists

Year Founded: 1847

1806 ASHA Annual Convention
American Speech-Language-Hearing Association
2200 Research Blvd
Rockville, MD 20850-3289
301-269-5700
800-638-8255
TTY: 301-296-5650
E-mail: convention@asha.org
www.asha.org

Judy Rudebusch Rich, EdD, President
Robert M. Augustine, PhD, President-Elect
Vicki R. Deal-Williams, MA, Chief Executive Officer
Craig E. Coleman, MA, Vice President for Planning

ASHA is the professional, scientific and credentialing association for 140,000 members and affiliates who are audiologists, speech-language pathologists and speech, language and hearing scientists.

1 per year Year Founded: 1925

1807 American Academy of Child and Adolescent Psychiatry (AACAP): Annual Meeting
3615 Wisconsin Avenue Northwest
Washington, DC 20016-3007
202-966-7300
E-mail: communications@aacap.org
www.www.aacap.org

Warren Y.K. Ng, MD, MPH, President
Tami D. Benton, MD, President-Elect
Debra E. Koss, MD, Secretary
Neal Ryan, MD, Treasurer

Professional society of physicians who have completed an additional five years of stimulate and advance medical contributions to the knowledge and treatment of psychiatric illnesses of children and adolescents. Annual meeting.

1808 American Academy of Psychiatry and the Law (AAPL) Annual Conference
American Academy of Psychiatry and the Law
One Regency Drive
PO Box 30
Bloomfield, CT 06002
860-242-5450
800-331-1389
E-mail: office@aapl.org
www.aapl.org

Susan Hatters Friedman, MD, President
James Knoll, MD, President-Elect
Karen Rosenbaum, MD, Vice President
Britta Ostermeyer, MD, Vice President

The American Academy of Psychiatry & Law's 53rd Annual Meeting will take place on October 27-30, 2022 at the Sherton New Orleans Hotel.

Year Founded: 1969

1809 American Academy of Psychoanalysis Preliminary Meeting
American Academy of Psychoanalysis and Dynamic Psychiatry
One Regency Drive
PO Box 30
Bloomfield, CT 06002-30
888-691-8281
E-mail: info@aapdp.org
www.aapdp.org

Michaelÿ Blumenfield, M.D., President
Jacquelyn T Coleman CAE, Executive Director
Carol Filiaci, Secretary

Annual meeting, Toronto, Canada.

Year Founded: 1956

1810 American Association of Children's Residential Center Annual Conference
American Association of Children's Residential Centers
11700 W Lake Park Drive
Milwaukee, WI 53224-3021
877-332-2272
E-mail: kbehling@alliance1.org

Christopher Bellonci, M.D., President
William Powers, MHA, MPA, Chief Executive Officer
Joseph Whalen, Executive Director
Laurah Currey, Treasurer

Funded by the Mental Health Community Support Program. The purpose of the association is to share information about services, providers and ways to cope with mental illnesses. Available services include referrals, professional seminars, support groups and a variety of publications.

1811 American Association of Geriatric Psychiatry Annual Meetings
7910 Woodmont Avenue
Suite 1050
Bethesda, MD 20814-3004
301-654-7850
E-mail: main@aagponline.org
www.aagponline.org

David C.ÿ Steffens, MD, MHS, President
Christine M. deVries, CEO/Executive Vice President
Denise Disqueÿÿ, Office Manager/Executive Assista
Kateÿ McDuffieÿÿ, Director, Communications & Marke

Annual Meeting: March, Puerto Rico
Year Founded: 1978

1812 American Association on Intellectual and Developmental Disabilities Annual Meeting
501 3rd Street NW
Suite 200
Washington, DC 20001
202-387-1968
800-424-3688
E-mail: anam@aaidd.org
www.aaidd.org

Margaret A. Nygren, EdD, Executive Director & CEO
Danielle Webber, MSW, Manager
Kathleen McLane, Director
Paul D. Aitken,CPA, Director

Provides the opportunity of networking with old friends and colleagues, and is a wonderful opportunity to welcome students and new disability professionals to our Association. *$445.00*

1813 American Board of Disability Analysts Annual Conference
770 Broadway
New York, NY 10003
212-206-4400
E-mail: americanbd@aol.com
www.www.aol.com

Tim Armstrong, Chairman and Chief Executive Off
Curtis Brown, Executive Vice President and Chi
Karen Dykstra, Executive Vice President and Chi

Year Founded: 1985

1814 American College of Health Care Administrators (ACHCA) Annual Convocation & Exposition
1321 Duke Street
Suite 400
Alexandria, VA 22314
202-536-5120
www.achca.org

Mariannaÿ Kern Grachek, MSN, CNH, President & CEOÿ
Beckyÿ Reisingerÿ, Director, Membership and Busines
Whitneyÿ O'Donnell, Coordinator, Member Services
Chelseaÿ Whitman-Rush, Coordinator, Member and Chapter

A non-profit professional membership association which provides superior educataional programming, professional certification, and career development opportunities for its members.

Year Founded: 1966

1815 American College of Psychiatrists Annual Meeting
11 E. Wacker Drive
Suite 1440
Chicago, IL 60601
312-938-8840
www.acpsych.org

Larry R. Faulkner, President
Eugene V. Beresin, President-Elect
Barbara S. Schneidman, Secretary-General
Carol A. Bernstein, Treasurer

241

Nonprofit honorary association of psychiatrists who, through excellence in their chosen fields, have been recognized for their significant contributions to the profession. The society's goal is to promote and support the highest standards in psychiatry through education, research and clinical practice. Annual Meeting in February.

Year Founded: 1963

1816 American Group Psychotherapy Association Virtual Annual Meeting
American Group Psychotherapy Association
355 Lexington Avenue
15th Floor
New York, NY 10017
212-297-2190
877-668-2472
E-mail: info@agpa.org
www.agpa.org

Dr. Molyn Leszcz, MD, FRCPC, CGP, President
Angela Moore Stephens, CAE, Chief Executive Officer
Katarina Cooke, MA, CAE, Professional Development Dir.
Diane C. Feirman, CAE, Public Affairs Senior Dir.

AGPA Connect is a virtual conference for mental health workers and students held annually from February to March.

Year Founded: 1942

1817 American Health Care Association Annual Convention & Expo
1201 L Street NW
Washington, DC 20005-4046
202-842-4444
E-mail: teyet@ahca.org
www.www.ahcancal.org

Mark Parkinson, President and CEO

Exhibits and educational workshops from the nonprofit federation of affiliated state health organizations, together representing over 14,000 nonprofit and for profit assisted living, nursing facility, developmentally disabled and sub-acute care providers that care for more than 1.5 million elderly and disabled individuals nationally. AHCA represents the long term care community at large — to government, business leaders and the general public. It also serves as a force for change within the long term care field, providing information, education, and administrative tools that enhance quality at every level.

1818 American Health Information Management Association Annual Exhibition and Conference
233 N Michigan Avenue
21st Floor
Chicago, IL 60601-5809
312-233-1100
E-mail: info@ahima.org
www.ahima.org

Tim J. Keough, MPA, RHIA, President and Chair
Wylecia Wiggs Harris, PhD, CAE, Chief Executive Officer

AHIMA is offered in-person in Columbus, Ohio (October 9-12) and virtually in November. Offers networking opportunities and education sessions to healthcare professionals.

1819 American Society of Addiction Medicine
American Society of Addiction Medicine
11400 Rockville Pike
Suite 200
Rockville, MD 20852
301-656-3920
E-mail: email@asam.org
www.asam.org

William F. Haning, III, MD, President
Brian Hurley, MD, MBA, President-Elect
Timothy Wiegand, MD, FACMT, Vice-President
Aleksandra Zgierska, MD, PhD, Secretary

Goal is to present the most up-to-date information in the addictions field. to attain this goal, program sessions will focus on the latest developments in research and treatment issues and will tanslate them into clinically useful knowledge. Through a mix of symposia, courses, workshops, didactic lectures, and paper and poster presentations based on submitted abstracts, participants will have an opportunity to interact with experts in their field.

Year Founded: 1954

1820 Association for Child Psychoanalysis (ACP) Annual Meeting
1964 Rahncliff Court
#22123
Eagan, MN 55122
612-643-1807
866-534-7555
E-mail: childanalysis65@gmail.com
www.childanalysis.org

Thomas Barrett, President
Daniel Prezant, PhD, Secretary
Mali Mann, MD, Treasurer
Susan Sherkow, MD, President-Elect

An international not-for-profit organization in which all members are highly trained child and adolescent psychoanalysts. Provides a forum for the interchange of ideas and clinical experience in order to advance the psychological treatment and understanding of children and adolescents and their families.

1821 Association of Black Psychologists Annual Convention
7119 Allentown Road
Suite 203
Ft. Washington, MD 20744
301-449-3082
E-mail: abpsi@abpsi.org
www.abpsi.org

Donell Barnett, PhD, President
Shawn Jones, PhD, MHS, LCP, Secretary
Rachel Gaiter, MBA, Treasurer

Feature presentations, exhibits and workshops held over a four day period focusing on the unique concerns of Black professionals.

1822 California Psychological Association's Annual Convention
1231 I Street
Suite 204
Sacramento, CA 95814-2933
916-286-7979
E-mail: membership@cpapsych.org
www.cpapsych.org

Robert deMayo, PhD, ABPP, President
Stephen Pfeiffer, PhD, President-Elect
Jo Linder-Crow, Ph.D., CEO
Betsy Levine-Proctor, PhD, Treasurer / Chair - Finance Comm

Poster sessions, roundtable discussions, CE sessions, ethics discussions and featured speakers. *$680.00*

1823 Georgia Psychological Society Annual Conference
2200 Century Parkway
Suite 660
Atlanta, GA 30345
404-634-6272

Jennifer Stapel-Wax, President
Steven Perlow, PhD, President Elect
Mary Gresham, Vice President
Dr. Chuck Talor, Conference, Newsletter's and Jou

Proposals for symposia, papers, posters and workshops on topics in all areas of psychology are invited. Proposals should not exceed 500 words, and each proposal must include a summary that is no longer than 50 words.

1824 NADD Annual Conference & Exhibit Show
National Association for the Dually Diagnosed
321 Wall Street
Kingston, NY 12401
845-331-4336
E-mail: info@thenadd.org
www.thenadd.org

Jeanne M. Farr, MA, Chief Executive Officer
Bruce Davis, President
Juanita St. Croix, Vice President
Ray Snyder, Secretary

1825 National Alliance on Mental Illness
4301 Wilson Boulevard
Suite 300
Arlington, VA 22203
703-524-7600
800-950-6264
E-mail: info@nami.org
www.nami.org

Shirley J. Holloway, President
Joyrce A. Campbell, First Vice President
Daniel H. Gillison, Jr., Chief Executive Officer
Ken Duckworth, Chief Medical Officer

NAMI is an organization dedicated to raising awareness on mental health and providing support and education for Americans affected by mental illness. NAMI advocates for access to services and treatment and fosters an environment of awareness and understanding for those concerned with mental health.

Year Founded: 1979

1826 National Multicultural Conference and Summit
Brakins Consulting & Psychological Svs
13805 60th Avenue North
Phymouth, MN 55446-3583
www.multiculturalsummit.com

Debra Kawahara, Lead Coordinator
Michael Mobley, Programming Coordinator
Julii Green, Keynote Coordinator
Roberta Nutt, Awards Coordinator

The mission is to convene students, practitioners, and scholars in psychology and related fields to inform and inspire multicultural research and practice.

1827 New England Educational Institute
New England Educational Institute
449 Pittsfield Road
Suite 201
Lenox, MA 01240
413-499-1489
E-mail: learn@neei.org
www.neei.org

Designed to meet the educational needs of physicians (psychiatrists, family practitioners, general practitioners), psychologists, nurse practitioners, physician assistants, nurses and other health care professionals. Each half-day will provide practical and clinically relevant information for day-to-day problems. Morning lectures will be followed by panel discussions.

1828 Traumatic Incident Reduction Workshop
E-Productivity-Services.Net
Division of 21st Century Enterprises
13 NW Barry Rd PMB 214
Kansas City, MO 64155-2728
816-468-4945
www.espn.net

Frank A Gerbode, Subject Developer
Marian Volkman, President
John Durkin, Vice President
Robert H Moore, Board Member

Defines the Conditioned Response Phenomena, establishes a safe environment, analyzes and applies the Unblocking technique to resolve issues relating to emotionally charged persons, places, things and situations, and analyzes and applies Traumatic Incident Reduction (TIR) to resolve known and unknown past traumatic experiences and the unwanted feelings, emotions, sensations, attitutdes and pain associated with them.

1829 YAI/National Institute for People with Disabilities
460 W 34th Street
New York, NY 10001-2382
212-273-6100
866-292-4546
TDD: 212-290-2787
www.yai.org

Bridget Waldron, L.C.S.W., Senior Vice President, Quality E
Marco Damiani, M.A., Executive Vice President, Innova
Paul Smoller, M.A., Executive Vice President, Talent
Kelly Burke-Quinn, Vice President, Business Analysi

Annual conference "Advancing Services Across the Life Span in Intellectual and Developmental Disabilities". A major forum for the exchange of ideas and the introduction of new models and strategies that have a positive impact in the field.

Periodicals & Pamphlets

1830 AACP Newsletter
American Association of Community Psychiatrists (AACP)
www.www.communitypsychiatry.org

Dr. Isabel Norian, Editor

A triannual publication featuring news in the field of psychiatry.

19 pages 3 per year

1831 AAMI Newsletter
Arizona Alliance for the Mentally Ill (NAMI Arizona)
2210 N 7th Street
Phoenix, AZ 85006-1604
602-244-8166
800-626-5022
www.namiaz.org

Diane McVicker, President
Cheryl Weiner, Educutive Director

Provides support, education, research, and advocacy for individuals and families affected by mental illness. Reports on legislative updates, conventions, psychiatry/psychological practices, and activities of the alliance. Newsletter with membership. *$10.00*

8 pages 4 per year

1832 AAPL Newsletter
American Academy of Psychiatry and the Law
One Regency Drive
PO Box 30
Bloomfield, CT 06002
860-242-5450
800-331-1389
E-mail: office@aapl.org
www.aapl.org

Joseph R. Simpson, MD, PhD, Editor

Scholarly articles on psychiatry.

3 per year

1833 APA Monitor
American Psychological Association
750 1st Street NE
Washington, DC 20002-4242
202-336-5500
800-374-2721
TDD: 202-336-6123
TTY: 202-336-6123
www.apa.org

Nadine J. Kaslow, Ph.D., President
Barry S. Anton, Ph.D., President-Elect
Donald N. Bersoff, PhD, JD, Past President
Norman B Anderson, Ph.D., CEO, EVP

Magazine of the American Psychological Association.

12 per year ISSN 1529-4978

1834 ASAP Newsletter
American Society for Adolescent Psychiatry
PO Box 570218
Dallas, TX 75357-218
972-613-0985
www.adolpsych.org

Mohan Nair, President
Gregg Dwyer, President
Sheldon Glass, President-Elect
Gregory P. Barclay, VP

Contains articles about adolescent psychiatry and society news. Recurring features include news of research, a calendar of events, and book reviews. *$10.00*

16-20 pages 4 per year

1835 Advocate: Autism Society of America
Autism Society of America
4340 East-West Hwy
Suite 350
Bethesda, MD 20814-3067
301-657-0881
800-328-8476
E-mail: sbadesch@autism-society.org
www.autism-society.org

Scott Badesch, President, CEO
Jennifer Repella, VP, Programs
John Dabrowski, CFO
Rose Jochum, Director, Programs

Reports news and information of national significance for individuals, families, and professionals dealing with autism. Recurring features include personal features and profiles, research summaries, government updates, book reviews, statistics, news of research, and a calendar of events.

32-36 pages 6 per year ISSN 0047-9101

1836 Alcohol & Drug Abuse Weekly
John Wiley & Sons
111 River Street
Hoboken, NJ 07030-5774
201-748-6000
www.wiley.com

Stephen M. Smith, President, CEO
MJ O'Leary, SVP, Human Resources
Edward J. Melando, SVP, Corporate Controller
Gary M. Rinck, SVP, General Counsel

48-issue subsrciption offers significant news and analysis of federal and state policy developments. A resource for directors of addiction treatment centers, managed care executives, federal and state policy makers and healthcare consultants. Topics include the latest findings in treatment and prevention; funding and survival issues for providers; the impact of state and federal policy on treatment and prevention; working under managed care; and co-occurring disorders.

8 pages 48 per year ISSN 1042-1394

1837 Alliance E-News
Alliance for Strong Families and Communities
1825 K St. N.W.
Suite 600
Washington, DC 20006
800-221-3726
E-mail: pgoldberg@alliance1.org
www.www.alliance1.org

Jody Levison-Johnson, President and CEO
Jim Carr, Chief Financial Officer
Ruby Goyal-Carkeek, Sr. VP, Programs and Services
Lenore Schell, Sr. VP, Operations

Biweekly e-newsletter providing members with accurate and up-to-date information on current legislation, funding opportunities, public policy, and resources like webinars and conferences.

1838 Alliance Policy Radar
Alliance for Strong Families and Communities
1825 K St. N.W.
Suite 600
Washington, DC 20006
800-221-3726
E-mail: pgoldberg@alliance1.org
www.www.alliance1.org

Jody Levison-Johnson, President and CEO
Jim Carr, Chief Financial Officer
Ruby Goyal-Carkeek, Sr. VP, Programs and Services
Lenore Schell, Sr. VP, Operations

Biweekly policy roundup featuring commentary on the Aliiance's federal public policy agenda, issues the Alliance is advocating on Capitol Hill, and summaries of how proposed bills will affect member organizations and the people they serve.

1839 American Academy of Child and Adolescent Psychiatry
AACAP
3615 Wisconsin Avenue Northwest
Washington, DC 20016-3007
202-966-7300
E-mail: communications@aacap.org
www.aacap.org

Warren Y.K. Ng, MD, MPH, President
Rob Grant, Managing Editor
Reilly Polka, Production Editor

The American Academy of Child and Adolescent Psychiatry, (AACAP) publishes a newsletter which focuses events within the Academy, child and adolescent psychiatrists, and AACAP members.

20 pages 4 per year

1840 American Institute for Preventive Medicine
American Institute for Preventive Medicine Press
30445 Northwestern Highway
Suite 350
Farmington Hills, MI 48334-3107
248-539-1800
800-345-2476
www.healthylife.com

Don R Powell, Ph.D., President, CEO
Sue Jackson, VP
Elaine Frank, M.Ed., R.D., VP
Jeanette Karwan, Director, Product Development

AIPM is an internationally renowned developer and provider of wellness programs and publications that address both mental and physical health issues. It works with over 11,500 corporations, hospitals, MCOs, universities, and goverment agencies to reduce health care costs, lower absenteeism, and improve productivity. The Institute has a number of publications that address mental health issues, including stress management, depression, self - esteem, and EAP issues.

1841 Behavioral Health Management
3800 Lakeside Avenue
Suite 201
Cleveland, OH 44114
216-391-9100
E-mail: info@vendomegrp.com
www.behavioral.net

Richard Peck, Editorial Director
Douglas J Edwards, Managing Editor, Publisher
Kathi Homenick, Director
Judi Zeng, Traffic Manager

Informs decision makers in managed behavioral healthcare organizations, provider groups, and treatment centers of the ever-changing demands of their field. The magazine publishes analyses, editorials, and organizations case studies to give readers the information they need for best practices in a challenging marketplace.

1842 Biology of Sex Differences
Society for Women's Health Research (SWHR)
1025 Connecticut Avenue NW
Suite 601
Washington, DC 20036-5447
202-466-6069
www.bsd-journal.com

Phyllis Greenberger, MSW, President
Mary V. Hornig, VP Finance & Operations
Arthur Arnold, Univ. CA, Editor

Biology of Sex Differences considers manuscripts on all aspects of the effect of sex on biology and disease. It is an online, open access, peer-reviewed journal published in conjunction with BioMed Central.

1843 Brown University: Child & Adolescent Psychopharmacology Update
John Wiley & Sons
111 River Street
Hoboken, NJ 07030-5774
201-748-6000
www.wiley.com

Stephen M. Smith, President, CEO
MJ O'Leary, SVP, Human Resources
Edward J. Melando, SVP, Corporate Controller
Gary M. Rinck, SVP, General Counsel

Monthly newsletter that gives information on children and adolescent's unique psychotropic medication needs. Delivers updates on new drugs, their uses, typical doses, side effects and interactions, examines generic vs. name brand drugs, reports on new research and new indications for existing medications. Each issue also includes case studies, references for future reading, industry news notes, abstracts of current research and a patient psychotropic medication handout. *$ 190.00*

12 per year ISSN 1527-8395

1844 Brown University: Digest of Addiction Theory and Application (DATA)
John Wiley & Sons
111 River Street
Hoboken, NJ 07030-5774
201-748-6000
www.wiley.com

Stephen M. Smith, President, CEO
MJ O'Leary, SVP, Human Resources
Edward J. Melando, SVP, Corporate Controller
Gary M. Rinck, SVP, General Counsel

Monthly synopsis of critical research developments in the treatment and prevention of alcoholism and drug abuse, including dozens of research abstracts chosen from over 75 medical journals. *$129.00*

8 pages 12 per year ISSN 1040-6328

1845 Brown University: Geriatric Psychopharmacology Update
John Wiley & Sons
111 River Street
Hoboken, NJ 07030-5774
201-748-6000
www.wiley.com

Stephen M. Smith, President, CEO
MJ O'Leary, SVP, Human Resources
Edward J. Melando, SVP, Corporate Controller
Gary M. Rinck, SVP, General Counsel

This monthly report is an easy way to keep up to date on the newest breakthroughs in geriatric medicine that have an impact on psychiatric practice. *$190.00*

12 per year ISSN 1529-2584

1846 Brown University: Psychopharmacology Update
John Wiley & Sons
111 River Street
Hoboken, NJ 07030-5774
201-748-6000
www.wiley.com

Stephen M. Smith, President, CEO
MJ O'Leary, SVP, Human Resources
Edward J. Melando, SVP, Corporate Controller
Gary M. Rinck, SVP, General Counsel

Each issue examines the pros and cons of specific drugs, drug-drug interactions, side effects, street drugs, warning signs, case reports and more. *$199.00*

12 per year ISSN 1608-5308

1847 Bulletin of Menninger Clinic
Guilford Press
72 Spring Street
New York, NY 10012-4068
212-431-9800
800-288-3950

Bob Matloff, President

Valuable, practical information for clinicans. Recent topical issues have focused on rekindling the psychodynamic vision, treatment of different clinical populations with panic disorder, and treatment of complicated personality disorders in an era of managed care. All in an integrated, psychodynamic approach. *$75.00*

ISSN 0025-9284

1848 Bulletin of Psychological Type
Association for Psychological Type
2415 Westwood Ave.
Suite B
Richmond, VA 23230
804-523-2907
800-847-9943
www.aptinternational.org

Jane Kise, President
Susan Nash, President
Linda Berens, Past President
Maryanne DiMarzo, President-Elect

Provides information on regional, national, and international events to keep professionals up-to-date in the study and application of psychological type theory and the Myers-Briggs Type Indicator. Contains announcements of training workshops; international, national, and regional

conferences; and awards, along with articles on issues directly related to type theory.

1849 Capitation Report
National Health Information
PO Box 15429
Atlanta, GA 30333-429
404-607-9500
800-597-6300
www.nhionline.net

NHI publishes specialized, targeted information for health care executives on a variety of topics from capitation to disease management.

1850 Clinical Psychiatry News
International Medical News Group
5635 Fishers Lane
Suite 6100
Rockville, MD 20852-1886
240-221-4500
E-mail: aimhoff@frontlinemedcom.com

Stephen Stoneburn, Chairman
Alan J. Imhoff, President, CEO, Medical News Div
JoAnn Wahl, President, Custom Solutions
Marcy Holeton, President, CEO, Clinical Content

A leading independent newspaper for the Psychiatrist.

1851 Couples Therapy in Managed Care
Haworth Press
10 Alice Street
Binghamton, NY 13904-1503
607-722-5857
800-429-6784
www.haworthpress.com

Provides social workers, psychologists and counselors with an overview of the negative effects of the managed care industry on the quality of marital health care.

ISBN 7-890078-86-6

1852 Current Directions in Psychological Science
Association for Psychological Science
1800 Massachusetts Ave NW
Suite 402
Washington, DC 20036
202-293-9300
www.psychologicalscience.org

Robert Gropp, CEO/Executive Director
Aime Ballard-Wood, COO/Deputy Director

Current Directions publishes reviews by leading experts covering all of scientific psychology and its applications. Each issue features a diverse mix of reports on various topics such as language, memory and cognition, development, the neural basis of behavior and emotions, various aspects of psychopathology, and theory of mind. The articles keep readers apprised of important developments across subfields. The articles are also written to be accessible to non-experts, making them suited for classroom teaching supplements.

ISSN 0963-7214

1853 Development & Psychopathology
Cambridge University Press
40 W 20th Street
New York, NY 10011-4211

212-924-3900
www.cup.org

This multidisciplinary journal is devoted to the publication of original, empirical, theoretical and review papers which address the interrelationship of normal and pathological development in adults and children. It is intended to serve and intergrate the emerging field of developmental psychopathology which strives to understand patterns of adaptation and maladaptation throughout the lifespan. This journal is of vital interest to psychologists, psychiatrists, social scientists, neuroscientists, pediatricians and researchers. *$66.00*

4 per year ISSN 0954-5794

1854 EAPA Exchange
Employee Assistance Professionals Association
4350 North Fairfax Drive
Suite 740
Arlington, VA 22203
703-387-1000
E-mail: admanager@eapassn.org
www.www.eapassn.org

Steven Haught, President
Lucy Henry, President-Elect
Pam Ruster, Treasurer, Secretary
John Maynard, CEO

1855 ETR Associates
Health Education, Research, Training Curriculum
4 Carbonero Way
Scotts Valley, CA 95066-4200
831-438-4060
800-321-4407
www.etr.org

John Henry Ledwith, National Sales Director
Pamela Anderson, PhD, Senior Reasearch Associate
Eric Blanke, BS, Director, Solutions
Erin Cassidy-Eagle, PhD, Director, Research

Publishes a complete line of innovative materials covering the full spectrum of health education topics, including maternal/child health, HIV/STD prevention, risk and injury prevention, self esteem, fitness and nutrition, college health, and wellness education, engaging in both extensive training and research endeavors and a comprehensive K-12 health curriculum.

1856 Elsevier
Customer Support Department
1600 John F Kennedy Boulevard
Suite 1800
Philadelphia, PA 19103-2879
212-633-3730
888-437-4636
E-mail: newsroom@elsevier.com
www.elsevier.com

Youngsuk (Y.S.) Chi, Chairman
Mark Seeley, SVP, General Counsel
David Ruth, SVP, Global Communications
Adriaan Roosen, EVP, Operations
ISSN 0165-3806

1857 Employee Benefits Journal
International Foundation of Employee Benefit Plans
18700 W. Bluemound Rd.
PO Box 69
Brookfield, WI 53045
414-786-6700
888-334-3327
E-mail: marybr@ifebp.org
www.ifebp.org

Kenneth R. Boyd, President, Chairman
Richard Lyall, Past President
Thomas T. Holsman, President-Elect
Regina C. Reardon, Treasurer

Contains articles on all aspects of employee benefits and related topics. *$70.00*

32-48 pages 4 per year ISSN 0361-4050

1858 Exceptional Parent
416 Main Street
Johnstown, PA 15901
814-361-3860
www.eparent.com

Joseph M Valenzano, Jr., President,Publisher, CEO
James McGinnis, VP of Operations, CEO
Rick Rader, MD, Editor-in-Chief
Hamilton Maher, Director of Circulation & Busine

Magazine for parents and professionals involved in the care and development of children and young adults with special needs, including physical disabilities, developmental disabilities, autism, epilepsy, learning disabilities, hearing/vision impairments, emotional problems, and chronic illnesses. *$36.00*

12 per year

1859 Focal Point: Research, Policy and Practice in Children's Mental Health
Regional Research Institue-Portland State University
PO Box 751
Portland, OR 97207-0751
503-725-3000
800-547-8887
E-mail: rtcpubs@pdx.edu

Janet Walker, Editor

Features information on research, interventions, organizations, strategies, and conferences to aid families that have children with emotional, mental, and/or behavioral disorders.

24 pages

1860 From the Couch
Behavioral Health Record Section-AMRA
919 N Michigan Avenue
Suite 1400
Chicago, IL 60611-1692
312-787-2672

From the couch, the newsletter for the Behavioral Health Record section of the American Medical Record Association, covers aspects of the medical records industry that pertain to mental health records.

4 per year

1861 General Hospital Psychiatry: Psychiatry, Medicine and Primary Care
Elsevier
1600 John F Kennedy Boulevard
Suite 1800
Philadelphia, PA 19103-2879
314-447-8070
888-615-4500
E-mail: newsroom@elsevier.com
www.elsevier.com

Youngsuk (Y.S.) Chi, Chairman
Mark Seeley, SVP, General Counsel
David Ruth, SVP, Global Communications
Adriaan Roosen, EVP, Operations

Journal that explores the linkages and interfaces between psychiatry, medicine and primary care. As a peer-reviewed journal, it provides a forum for communication among professionals with clinical, academic and research interests in psychiatry's essential function in the mainstream of medicine. *$195.00*

84 pages 6 per year ISSN 01638343

1862 Geriatrics
Advanstar Communications
7500 Old Oak Boulevard
Cleveland, OH 44130-3343
440-243-8100

David Briemer, Sales Manager
Rich Ehrlich, Associate Publisher

Peer-reviewed clinical journal for primary care physicians who care for patients age 50 and older.

100 pages 12 per year

1863 Group Practice Journal
Amerian Medical Group Association
One Prince Street
Alexandria, VA 22314-3318
703-838-0033
www.amga.org

Jerry Penso, MD, MBA, President and CEO
Ryan A. O'Connor, MBA, CAE, Chief Operating Officer
Clyde L. Morris, Jr., CPA, Chief Financial Officer
Grace Emerson Terrell, MD, Chair

Penned by healthcare professionals, articles in the Group Practice Journal give a view from the trenches of modern medicine on a wide variety of topics, including innovative disease management and clinical best practices. Readers look to the publication to learn strategies and solutions from peers in the profession, healthcare thought leaders, and industry experts.

1864 Harvard Mental Health Letter
Harvard Health Publications
10 Shattuck Street
2nf Floor
Boston, MA 02115-6030
617-432-4714
E-mail: mental_health@hms.harvard.edu
www.www.health.harvard.edu

Anthony Komaroff, Owner

Delivers information on current thinking and debate on mental health issues that concern professionals and layment a like. In the ever-changing and complex field of mental health care, the newsletter has become a trusted source for psychiatrists, psychologists, social workers and therapists of all kinds. *$59.00*

8 pages 12 per year ISSN 08843783

1865 Harvard Review of Psychiatry
Taylor and Francis
01650 Toebben Drive
Independence, KY 41051
800-634-7064

An authoritative source for scholarly reviews and perspectives on important topics in psychiatry. Founded by the Harvard Medical School's Department of Psychiatry, the Harvard Review of Psychiatry features review papares that summarize and synthesize the key literature in a scholarly and clinically relevant manner. *$185.00*

6 per year

1866 Health & Social Work
National Association of Social Workers
750 1st Street NE
Suite 700
Washington, DC 20002-4241
202-408-8600
E-mail: press@naswdc.org
www.naswpress.org

Elvira Craig De Silva, President
Cheryl Y. Bradley, Publisher
Sharon Fletcher, Publications Marketing Manager
Kiera White, Marketing Coordinator

Articles cover research, policy, specialized servies, quality assurance, inservice training and other topics that affect the delivery of health care services. *$125.00*

1867 Health Data Management
Faulkner & Gray
11 Penn Plaza
New York, NY 10001-2006
212-967-7000
www.www.healthdatamanagement.com

Gary Baldwin, Editorial Director
Greg Gillespie, Editor-in-Chief
Joe Goedert, News Editor

1868 Healthcare Executive
American College of Healthcare Executives
300 S. Riverside Plaza
Suite 1900
Chicago, IL 60606-6698
312-424-0023
E-mail: he-editor@ache.org
www.ache.org

Anthony A. Armada, FACHE, Chair
Delvecchio S. Finley, FACHE, Chair-Elect
Deborah J. Bowen, FACHE, CAE, President and CEO

Published six times a year, Healthcare Executive magazine features latest news and commentaries from experts in the healthcare industry. *$70.00*

4 per year ISSN 0748-8157

1869 International Drug Therapy Newsletter
Lippincott Williams & Wilkins
351 W Camden Street
Baltimore, MD 21201-2436
410-528-4000
800-882-0483

E-mail: korourke@lww.com
www.lww.com

J Arnold Anthony, Operations

Newsletter that focuses on psychotropic drugs, discussing individual drugs, their effectiveness, and history. Examines illnesses and the drugs used to treat them, studies done on various drugs, their chemical make-up, and new developments and changes in drugs. *$149.00*

8 pages ISSN 0020-6571

1870 International Journal of Neuropsychopharmacology
Cambridge University Press
40 W 20th Street
New York, NY 10011-4211
212-924-3900
www.cup.org

1871 International Journal of Aging and Human Developments
Baywood Publishing Company
26 Austin Avenue
Box 337
Amityville, NY 11701-3052
631-691-1270
800-638-7819
www.baywood.com

Stuart Cohen, Owner

$218.00

8 per year ISSN 0091-4150

1872 International Journal of Health Services
Baywood Publishing Company
26 Austin Avenue
Box 337
Amityville, NY 11701-3052
631-691-1270
800-638-7819
www.baywood.com

Stuart Cohen, Owner

$160.00

4 per year

1873 International Journal of Psychiatry in Medicine
Baywood Publishing Company
26 Austin Avenue
Box 337
Amityville, NY 11701-3052
631-691-1270
800-638-7819
www.baywood.com

Stuart Cohen, Owner

$160.00

4 per year ISSN 0091274

1874 Journal of AHIMA
American Health Information Management Association
233 N Michigan Avenue
21st Floor
Chicago, IL 60601-5809
312-233-1100
E-mail: info@ahima.org
www.ahima.org

Tim J. Keough, MPA, RHIA, President and Chair
Wylecia Wiggs Harris, PhD, CAE, Chief Executive Officer

Monthly magazine with articles, news and event annoucements from the nonprofit federation of affiliated state health organizations, representing nonprofit and for profit assisted living, nursing facility, developmentally disabled and subacute care providers that care for more than 1.5 million elderly and disabled individuals nationally.

1875 Journal of American Medical Information Association (JAMIA)
American Medical Informatics Association
143 Rollins Avenue
#2248
Rockville, MD 20847
301-657-1291
www.www.amia.org

Suzanne Bakken, Editor-in-Chief

Peer-reviewed journal for biomedical and health professionals. Publishes clinical research to help readers stay informed of industry news.

1876 Journal of Drug Education
Baywood Publishing Company
26 Austin Avenue
Box 337
Amityville, NY 11701-3052
631-691-2048
800-638-7819
www.baywood.com

Stuart Cohen, Owner

$160.00

4 per year

1877 Journal of Education Psychology
American Psychological Association
750 1st Street NE
Washington, DC 20002-4242
202-336-5500
800-374-2721
TDD: 202-336-6123
TTY: 202-336-6123
E-mail: order@apa.org
www.apa.org

Nadine J. Kaslow, Ph.D., President
Barry S. Anton, Ph.D., President-Elect
Donald N. Bersoff, PhD, JD, Past President
Norman B Anderson, Ph.D., CEO, EVP

$102.00

4 per year ISSN 0022-0663

1878 Journal of Emotional and Behavioral Disorders
Pro-Ed Publications
8700 Shoal Creek Boulevard
Austin, TX 78757-6897
512-451-3246
800-897-3202
E-mail: info@proedinc.com

Donald D Hammill, Owner

An international, multidisciplinary journal featuring articles on research, practice and theory related to individuals with emotional and behavioral disorders and to the professionals who serve them. Presents topics of interest to individuals representing a wide range of disciplines including corrections, psychiatry, mental health, counseling, rehabilitation, education, and psychology. *$39.00*

64 pages 4 per year ISSN 1063-4266

1879 Journal of Intellectual & Development Disability
Taylor & Francis Publishing
711 3rd Avenue
8th Floor
New York, NY 10017
212-216-7800
800-634-7064
E-mail: orders@taylorandfrancis.com
www.taylorandfrancis.com

1880 Journal of Neuropsychiatry and Clinical Neurosciences
American Neuropsychiatric Association
700 Ackerman Road
Suite 625
Columbus, OH 43202-4505
614-447-2077
E-mail: anpa@osu.edu

Sandy Bornstein, Executive Director
C. Edward Coffey, Treasurer

Official publication of the organization and a benefit of membership. Our mission is to apply neuroscience for the benefit of people. Three core values have been identified for the association: advancing knowledge of brain-behavior relationships, providing a forum for learning, and promoting excellent, scientific and compassionate health care.

1881 Journal of Personality Assessment (JPA)
Society for Personality Assessment
6109H Arlington Boulevard
Falls Church, VA 22044
703-534-4772
www.personality.org

Martin Sellbom, Editor
Nicole M. Cain, Associate Editor
Joye Anestis, Associate Editor
Robert Latzman, Associate Editor

Publishes articles dealing with the development, evaluation, refinement and application of personality assessment methods.

102 pages ISSN 0022-3891

1882 Journal of Positive Behavior Interventions
Pro-Ed Publications
8700 Shoal Creek Boulevard
Austin, TX 78757-6897
512-451-3246
800-897-3202
E-mail: info@proedinc.com

Donald D Hammill, Owner

Deals with principles of positive behavioral support in school, home, and community settings for people with challenges in behavioral adaptation. *$39.00*

64 pages 4 per year ISSN 1098-3007

1883 Journal of Practical Psychiatry
Williams & Wilkins
351 W Camden Street
Baltimore, MD 21201-2436

410-528-4000
800-882-0483
E-mail: korourke@lww.com
www.lww.com

J Arnold Anthony, Operations

8 pages

1884 Journal of Professional Counseling: Practice, Theory & Research
Texas Counseling Association (TCA)
1204 San Antonio
Suite 201
Austin, TX 78701-1870
512-472-3403
800-580-8144
E-mail: jan@txca.org
www.txca.org

Jan Friese, Executive Director

The Texas Counseling Association is dedicated to providing leadership, advocacy and education to promote the growth and development of the counseling profession and those that are served. *$150.00*

50 pages 2 per year

1885 Journal of the American Academy of Child & Adolescent Psychiatry (JAACAP)
American Academy of Child and Adolescent Psychiatry
3615 Wisconsin Avenue NW
Washington, DC 20016-3007
202-966-7300
E-mail: communications@aacap.org
www.www.aacap.org

Warren Y.K. Ng, MD, MPH, President

Journal focusing on today's psychiatric research and treatment of the child and adolescent. *$175.00*

36-64 pages 12 per year ISSN 0890-8567

1886 Journal of the American Psychiatric Nurses Association
Sage Publications
2455 Teller Road
Thousand Oaks, CA 91320-2234
805-499-0721
800-818-7243
E-mail: journals@sagepub.com
www.sagepub.com

Blaise R Simqu, CEO, President
Tracey A Ozmina, EVP, COO
Chris Hickok, SVP, CFO
Phil Denvir, Global Chief Information Officer

Official Journal of the American Psychiatric Nurses Association *$128.00*

ISSN 1078-3903

1887 Journal of the American Psychoanalytic Association
Analytic Press
101 W Street
Hillsdale, NJ 07642-1421
201-358-9477
800-926-6579
www.analyticpress.com

Paul E Stepansky PhD, Managing Director
John Kerr PhD, Sr Editor

JAPA is one of the preeminent psychoanalytic journals. Recognized for the quality of its clinical and theoretical contributions, JAPA is now a major publication source for scientists and humanists whose work elaborates, applies, critiques or impinges on psychoanalysis. Topics include child psychoanalysis and the effectiveness of the intensive treatment of children, boundary violations, problems of memory and false memory syndrome, the concept of working through, the scientific status of psychoanalysis and the relevance or irrevance of infant observation for adult analysis. *$115.00*

300 pages 4 per year ISSN 0003-0651

1888 Journal of the International Neuropsychological Society
Cambridge University Press
40 W 20th Street
New York, NY 10011-4211
212-924-3900
www.cup.org

1889 Mayo Clinic Health Letter
Mayo Clinic
200 1st Street SW
Rochester, MN 55905-2
507-284-2511
E-mail: healthletter@mayo.edu
www.mayoclinic.org

Marilyn Carlson Nelson, Chairman
John H Noseworthy, M.D., President, CEO
Shirley A. Weis, VP, CAO
William C. Rupp, M.D., VP

Helping our subscribers achieve healthier lives by providing useful, easy to understand health information that is timely and of broad interest.

ISSN 0741-6245

1890 Mental & Physical Disability Law Reporter
American Bar Association
1050 Connecticut Ave. N.W.
Suite 400
Washington, DC 20036
202-662-1000
800-285-2221
TTY: 202-662-1012
E-mail: CMPDL@abanet.org
www.abanet.org

James R. Silkenat, President
Robert M. Carlson, Chair, House of Delegates
William C. Hubbard, President-Elect
Lucian T. Pera, Treasurer

Contains bylined articles and summaries of federal and state court opinions and legislative developments addressing persons with mental and physical disabilities.

6 per year ISSN 0883-7902

1891 Mental Health Law Reporter
Business Publishers Inc.
2222 Sedwick Drive
Suite 101
Durham, NC 27713

301-587-6300
800-223-8720
www.bpinews.com

Nancy Biglin, Director Marketing

Summary of court cases pertaining to mental health professionals. *$273.00*

12 per year ISSN 0741-5141

1892 Mental Health Report
Business Publishers Inc.
2222 Sedwick Drive
Suite 101
Durham, NC 27713
301-587-6300
800-223-8720
www.bpinews.com

Nancy Biglin, Director Marketing

Independent, inside Washington coverage of mental health administration, legislation and regulation, state policy plus research and trends. *$396.00*

26 per year ISSN 0191-6750

1893 Mentally Disabled and the Law
William S. Hein & Co.
2350 North Forest Rd.
Getzville, NY 14068
716-882-2600
800-828-7571
E-mail: mail@wshein.com
www.wshein.com

William Hein, Chairman
Kevin Marmion, President
Daniel Rosati, SVP
Dick Spinelli, EVP

Offers information on treatment rights, the provider-patient relationship, and the rights of mentally disabled persons in the community. *$80.00*

1894 NAAP Newsletter
National Association for Advancement of Psychoanalysis
850 7th Ave
Suite 800
New York, NY 10019
212-741-0515
E-mail: NAAP@NAAP.org
www.naap.org

Patricia Bratt, President

Members: 1400 Institute Members: 40 *$24.00*

16 pages 4x per year

1895 NAMI Advocate
National Alliance on Mental Illness
4301 Wilson Boulevard
Suite 300
Arlington, VA 22203
703-524-7600
800-950-6264
E-mail: info@nami.org
www.nami.org

Shirley J. Holloway, President
Joyce A. Campbell, First Vice President
Daniel H. Gillison, Jr., Chief Executive Officer
David Levy, Chief Financial Officer

Magazine that provides information on latest research, treatment, and medications for brain disorders. Reviews status major policy and legislation at federal, state, and local levels. Recurring features include interviews, news of research, news of educational opportunities, book reviews, politics, legal issues, and columns titled President's Column, Ask the Doctor, and News You Can Use. Included as NAMI membership benefit.

24-28 pages 24 per year

1896 NASW News
National Association of Social Works
750 1st Street NE
Suite 700
Washington, DC 20002-4241
202-408-8600
E-mail: press@naswdc.org
www.naswpress.org

Elvira Craig De Silva, President
Cheryl Y. Bradley, Publisher
Sharon Fletcher, Publications Marketing Manager
Kiera White, Marketing Coordinator

1897 Newsletter of the American Psychoanalytic Association
Analytic Press
101 W Street
Hillsdale, NJ 07642-1421
201-358-9477
800-926-6579
www.analyticpress.com

Paul E Stepansky PhD, Managing Director
John Kerr PhD, Sr Editor

A scholarly and clinical resource for all analytic practitioners and students of the field. Articles and essays focused on contemporary social, political and cultural forces as they relate to the practice of psychoanalysis, regular interviews with leading proponents of analysis, essays and reminiscences that chart the evolution of anlaysis in America. The newsletter publishes articles that are rarely if ever found in the journal literature. Sample copies available. *$29.50*

4 per year

1898 North American Society of Adlerian Psychology Newsletter
NASAP
429 E. Dupont Road
#276
Fort Wayne, IN 46825
260-267-8807
E-mail: nasap@msn.com
www.alfredadler.org

Richard Watts, President
Susan Belangee, VP
Steven J. Stein, Past-President
Susan Burak, Treasurer

Relates news and events of the North American Society of Alderian Psychology and regional news of affiliated associations. Recurring features include lists of courses and workshops offered by affiliated associations, reviews of new publications in the field, professional employment opportunities, a calendar of events, and a column titled President's Message. *$20.00*

8 pages 24 per year ISSN 0889-9428

1899 ORTHO Update
American Orthopsychiatric Association
PO Box 202798
Denver, CO 80220
720-708-0187
E-mail: amerortho@aol.com
www.www.aoatoday.com

Mary I. Armstrong, MSW, PhD, President
Deborah Klein Walker, EdD, President-Elect
Donald Wertlieb, PhD, Past President
John Sargent, MD, Treasurer

Intended for members of the Association, who are concerned with the early signs of mental and behavioral disorder and preventive psychiatry. Provides news notes and feature articles on the trends, issues and events that concern mental health, as well as Association news.

6-16 pages 3 per year

1900 Open Minds
Behavioral Health Industry News
163 York Street
Gettysburg, PA 17325-1933
717-334-1329
877-350-6463
E-mail: info@openminds.com
www.openminds.com

Monica Oss, Owner
Casey A. Miller, VP, Administration
Aida Porras, Senior Associate
Jim Jenkins, Senior Associate

Provides information on marketing, financial, and legal trends in the delivery of mental health and chemical dependency benefits and services. Recurring features include interviews, news of research, a calendar of events, job listings, book reviews, notices of publications available, and industry statistics. *$185.00*

12 pages 12 per year ISSN 1043-3880

1901 OpenMinds
Open Minds
163 York Street
Gettysburg, PA 17325-1933
717-334-1329
877-350-6463
E-mail: info@openminds.com
www.openminds.com

Monica Oss, Owner
Casey A. Miller, VP, Administration
Aida Porras, Senior Associate
Jim Jenkins, Senior Associate

Provides information on marketing, financial, and legal trends in the delivery of mental health and chemical dependency benefits and services. Recurring features include interviews, news of research, a calendar of events, job listings, book reviews, notices of publications available, and industry statistics. *$185.00*

12 pages 12 per year ISSN 1043-3880

1902 Perspective on Psychological Science
Association for Psychological Science
1800 Massachusetts Ave NW
Suite 402
Washington, DC 20036
202-293-9300
www.psychologicalscience.org

Robert Gropp, CEO/Executive Director
Aime Ballard-Wood, COO/Deputy Director

Perspectives publishes an eclectic mix of provocative reports and articles, including board integrative reviews, overviews of research programs, meta-analysis, theoretical statements, book reviews, and articles on topics such as the philosophy of science, opnion pieces about major issues in the field, autobiographical reflections of senior members in the field, and the occasional humorous essay and sketch.

6 per year ISSN 1745-6916

1903 Professional Counselor
3201 SW 15th Street
Deerfield Beach, FL 33442-8157
954-360-0909
800-851-9100
E-mail: Gary.Seidler@usjt.com
www.professionalcounselor.com

Robert Ackerman, Editor
Gary Seidler, Executive Consulting Editor
Leah Honarbakhsh, Associate Editor
Lorrie Keip, Director of Continuing Education

The number one publication serving the addictions and mental health fields.

1904 Provider Magazine
American Health Care Association
1201 L Street NW
Washington, DC 20005-4046
202-842-4444
888-656-6669
E-mail: sales@ahca.org
www.www.providermagazine.com

Bruse Yarwood, President
Bill Myers, Senior Editor
Meg LaPorte, Managing Editor
Joanne Erickson, Editor in Chief

Of interest to the professionals who work for the nearly 12,000 nonprofit and for profit assisted living, nursing facility, developmentally disabled and subacute care providers that care for more than 1.5 million elderly and disabled individuals nationally. Provides information, education, and administrative tools that enhance quality at every level.

1905 PsycINFO News
American Psychological Association
750 1st Street NE
Washington, DC 20002-4242
202-336-5500
800-374-2721
TDD: 202-336-6123
TTY: 202-336-6123
E-mail: psycinfo@apa.org
www.apa.org

Nadine J. Kaslow, Ph.D., President
Barry S. Anton, Ph.D., President-Elect
Donald N. Bersoff, PhD, JD, Past President
Norman B Anderson, Ph.D., CEO, EVP

Free newsletter that keeps you up to date on enhancements to PsycINFO products.

4 per year

1906 PsycSCAN Series
American Psychological Association
750 1st Street NE
Washington, DC 20002-4242
202-336-5500
800-374-2721
TDD: 202-336-6123
TTY: 202-336-6123
E-mail: psycinfo@apa.org
www.apa.org

Nadine J. Kaslow, Ph.D., President
Barry S. Anton, Ph.D., President-Elect
Donald N. Bersoff, PhD, JD, Past President
Norman B Anderson, Ph.D., CEO, EVP

Quarterly current awareness print publications in the fields of clinical, developmental, and applied psychology, as well as learning disorders and behavior analysis and therapy. Contains relevant citations and abstracts from the PsycINFO database. PyscScan: Psychopharmacology is an electronic only publication.

4 per year

1907 Psych Discourse
The Association of Black Psychologists
7119 Allentown Road
Suite 203
Ft. Washington, MD 20744
301-449-3082
E-mail: abpsi@abpsi.org
www.abpsi.org

Donell Barnett, PhD, President
Shawn Jones, PhD, MHS, LCP, Secretary
Rachel Gaiter, MBA, Treasurer

Publishes news of the Association. Recurring features include editorials, news of research, letters to the editor, a calendar of events, and columns titled Social Actions, Chapter News, Publications, and Members in the News.
$110.00

32-64 pages 12 per year ISSN 1091-4781

1908 Psychiatric News
American Psychiatric Publishing, Inc.
1000 Wilson Boulevard
Suite 1825
Arlington, VA 22209-3901
703-907-7322
800-368-5777
E-mail: appi@psych.org
www.appi.org

Saul Levin, M.D., M.P.A., CEO, Medical Director
Ron McMillen, Chief Executive Officer
Robert E Hales, M.D., M.B.A., Editor-in-Chief
Rebecca D. Rinehart, Publisher

Psychiatric News is the official newspaper for the American Psychiatric Association. It is published twice a month and mailed to all APA members as a member benefit as well as to about 2,000 subscribers.

1909 Psychiatric Times
Continuing Medical Education
806 Plaza Three
Jersey City, NJ 07311-1112
949-250-1008
800-993-2632
www.psychiatrictimes.com

John L. Schwartz MD, Founder and Editor Emeritus
Ronald Pies, MD, Editor Emeritus
James L. Knoll, MD, Editor in Chief
George I. Papakostas, M.D., Director, Treatment-Resistant De

Allows you to earn CME credit every month with a clinical article, as well as keeping you up to date on the current news in the field. *$54.95*

12 per year

1910 Psychiatry Drug Alerts
MJ Powers & Company
65 Madison Avenue
Ssite 220
Morristown, NJ 07960-7354
973-889-5398
800-875-0058
E-mail: psych@alertpubs.com

Evelyn Powers, Owner

Discusses drugs used in the psychiatric field, including side effects and risks. *$63.00*

8 pages 12 per year ISSN 0894-4873

1911 Psychiatry Research
Customer Support Department
PO Box 945
New York, NY 10159-945
212-633-3730
888-437-4636
www.elsevier.nl/locate/psychres

ISSN 0165-1781

1912 Psychodynamic Psychiatry
American Academy of Psychoanalysis and Dynamic Psychiatry
One Regency Drive
PO Box 30
Bloomfield, CT 06002
888-691-8281
E-mail: info@aapdp.org
www.aapsa.org

Joanna E. Chambers, MD, President
Jacquelyn T. Coleman, CAE, Executive Director

Psychodynamic Psychiatry is an indexed, peer-reviewed journal which publishes psychoanalytic theory and research on a quarterly basis. Offers academic scholars articles, reviews, case reports, and manuscripts. Available online and in print.

4 per year

1913 Psychological Abstracts
PsycINFO/American Psychological Association
750 1st Street NE
Washington, DC 20002-4242
202-336-5500
800-374-2721
TDD: 202-336-6123
TTY: 202-336-6123
E-mail: psycinfo@apa.org
www.apa.org

Nadine J. Kaslow, Ph.D., President
Barry S. Anton, Ph.D., President-Elect
Donald N. Bersoff, PhD, JD, Past President
Norman B Anderson, Ph.D., CEO, EVP

Print index containing citations and abstracts for journal articles, books, and book chapters in psychology and related disciplines. Annual indexes.

12 per year

1914 Psychological Assessment Resources INC
16130 North Florida Avenue
Lutz, FL 33549
813-449-4065
800-331-8378
www.www4.parinc.com

R. Bob Smith III, PhD, Chairman, CEO
Cathy Smith, VP, Community Relations

1915 Psychological Science
Association for Psychological Science
1800 Massachusetts Ave NW
Suite 402
Washington, DC 20036
202-293-9300
www.psychologicalscience.org

Robert Gropp, CEO/Executive Director
Aime Ballard-Wood, COO/Deputy Director

The flagship journal of the APS, it publishes cutting edge research articles, short reports, and research reports spanning the entire spectrum of the science of psychology. The Journal is the source for the latest findings in cognitive, social, developmental and health psychology, as well as behavioral neuroscience and biopsychology.

12 per year ISSN 0956-7976

1916 Psychological Science Agenda
American Psychological Association
750 1st Street NE
Washington, DC 20002-4242
202-336-5500
800-374-2721
TDD: 202-336-6123
TTY: 202-336-6123
E-mail: psycinfo@apa.org

Nadine J. Kaslow, Ph.D., President
Barry S. Anton, Ph.D., President-Elect
Donald N. Bersoff, PhD, JD, Past President
Norman B Anderson, Ph.D., CEO, EVP

This newsletter disseminates information on scientific psychology, including news on activities of the Association and congressional and federal advocacy efforts of the Directorate. Recurring features include reports of meetings, news of research, notices of publications available, interviews, and the columns titled Science Directorate News, On Behalf of Science, Science Briefs, Announcements, and Funding Opportunities.

16-20 pages 6 per year ISSN 1040-404X

1917 Psychological Science in the Public Interest
Association for Psychological Science
Massachusetts Ave NW
Suite 402
Washington, DC 20036
202-293-9300
www.psychologicalscience.org

Robert Gropp, CEO/Executive Director
Aime Ballard-Wood, COO/Deputy Director

PSPI is a unique journal featuring comprehensive and compelling views of issues that are of direct relevance to the general public. Reviews are written by teams of award-winning specialists representing a range of viewpoints, and are intended to assess the current state-of-the-science with regard to the topic.

3 per year ISSN 1529-1006

1918 Psychology Teacher Network Education Directorate
American Psychological Association
750 1st Street NE
Washington, DC 20002-4242
202-336-5500
800-374-2721
TDD: 202-336-6123
TTY: 202-336-6123
E-mail: psycinfo@apa.org
www.apa.org

Nadine J. Kaslow, Ph.D., President
Barry S. Anton, Ph.D., President-Elect
Donald N. Bersoff, PhD, JD, Past President
Norman B Anderson, Ph.D., CEO, EVP

Provides descriptions of experiments and demonstrations aimed at introducing topics as a basis for classroom lectures or discussion. Recurring features include news and announcements of courses, workshops, funding sources, and meetings; reviews of teaching aids; and reports of innovative programs or curricula occurring in schools, interviews and brief reports from prominent psychologists.
$15.00

16 pages 5 per year

1919 Psychophysiology
Cambridge University Press
40 W 20th Street
New York, NY 10011-4211
212-924-3900
www.cup.org

1920 Psychosomatic Medicine
American Psychosomatic Society
6728 Old McLean Village Drive
McLean, VA 22101-3906
703-556-9222
E-mail: info@psychosomatic.org
www.psychosomatic.org

William Lovallo, President
Karen L. Weihs, M.D., President
Mustafa al'Absi, Ph.D., President-Elect
George K. Degnon, CAE, Executive Director

News and event annoucements, examines the scientific understanding of the interrelationships among biological, psychological, social and behavioral factors in human health and disease, and the integration of the fields of science that separately examine each.

1921 Psychotherapy Bulletin
American Psychological Association
750 First Street NE
Washington, DC 20002-4242
202-336-5500
800-374-2721
TDD: 202-336-6123
TTY: 202-336-6123
E-mail: psycinfo@apa.org
www.apa.org

Nadine J. Kaslow, Ph.D., President
Barry S. Anton, Ph.D., President-Elect
Donald N. Bersoff, PhD, JD, Past President
Norman B Anderson, Ph.D., CEO, EVP

Recurring features include letters to the editor, news of research, reports of meetings, news of educational opportunities, committee reports, legislative issues, and columns titled Washington Scene, Finance, Marketing, Professional Liability, Medical Psychology Update, and Substance Abuse. *$8.00*

50 pages 4 per year

1922 Psychotherapy Finances
Managed Care Strategies & Psychotherapy Finances
14255 U.S. Highway 1
Suite 286
Juno Beach, FL 33408-1612
561-624-1155
800-869-8450
www.www.psyfin.com

John Klein, Editor
John Nelander, Managing Editor
Anne Marie Church, Marketing Director
Herbert E. Klein, Publisher

1923 Research and Training for Children's Mental Health-Update
University of South Florida
13301 Bruce B Downs Boulevard
Florida Mental Health Institute
Tampa, FL 33612-3807
813-974-4565

Services and research on children with emotional disorders.

2 per year

1924 Rural Mental Health Journal
NARMH
25 Massachusetts Ave NW
Suite 500
Washington, DC 20001
202-942-4276
E-mail: info@narmh.org
www.narmh.org

Jerry Parker, President
Paul Mackie, President-Elect
Linda Werlein, Past-President
David Weden, Treasurer

Provides a information for rural mental health professionals and advocates.

4 per year

1925 Smooth Sailing
Depression and Related Affective Disorders Association
600 N Wolfe Street
John Hopkins Hospital Meyer 3-181
Baltimore, MD 21287-5
www.med.jhu.edu/drada/

Outreach to students and parents through schools.

4 per year

1926 Social Work
NASW Press
750 1st Street NE
Suite 700
Washington, DC 20002-4241
202-408-8600
E-mail: press@naswdc.org
www.naswpress.org

Elvira Craig De Silva, President
Cheryl Y. Bradley, Publisher
Sharon Fletcher, Publications Marketing Manager
Kiera White, Marketing Coordinator

1927 Social Work Abstracts
NASW Press
750 1st Street NE
Suite 700
Washington, DC 20002-4241
202-408-8600
E-mail: press@naswdc.org
www.naswpress.org

Elvira Craig De Silva, President
Cheryl Y. Bradley, Publisher
Sharon Fletcher, Publications Marketing Manager
Kiera White, Marketing Coordinator

1928 Social Work Research
NASW Press
750 1st Street NE
Suite 700
Washington, DC 20002-4241
202-408-8600
E-mail: press@naswdc.org
www.naswpress.org

Elvira Craig De Silva, President
Cheryl Y. Bradley, Publisher
Sharon Fletcher, Publications Marketing Manager
Kiera White, Marketing Coordinator

1929 Social Work in Education
NASW Press
750 1st Street NE
Suite 700
Washington, DC 20002-4241
202-408-8600
E-mail: press@naswdc.org
www.naswpress.org

Elvira Craig De Silva, President
Cheryl Y. Bradley, Publisher
Sharon Fletcher, Publications Marketing Manager
Kiera White, Marketing Coordinator

1930 Society for Adolescent Psychiatry Newsletter
PO Box 570218
Dallas, TX 75357-218
972-613-0985
www.adolpsych.org

Mohan Nair, President
Gregg Dwyer, President
Sheldon Glass, President Elect
Gregory P. Barclay, VP

Puts psychiatrists in touch with an informed cross-section of the profession from all over North America. Dedicated to education development and advocacy of adolescents and the adolescent psychiatric field.

1931 The Bulletin
American Society of Psychoanalytic Physicians
13528 Wisteria Drive
Germantown, MD 20874-1049
301-540-3197

Christine Cotter, Executive Director

The Bulletin of the American Society of Psychoanalustic Physicians is a professional publication containing articles by members, meeting speakers and other professionals in addition to newes about the society. Papers are accepted based on a peer review process.

15 pages 1 per year

1932 World Federation for Mental Health Newsletter
World Federation for Mental Health
PO Box 807
Occoquania, VA 22125
703-838-7525
www.wfmh.com

George Christodoulou, President, Greece
Deborah Wan, Hong Kong, Immediate Past President
Gabriel Ivbijaro, President Elect, U.K.
Gwen Dixon, Office Administrator

World-wide mental health reports. Education and advocacy on mental health issues. Working to protect the human rights of those defined as mentally ill.

8 pages 1 per year

Testing & Evaluation

1933 Assessment of Neuropsychiatry and Mental Health Services
American Psychiatric Publishing, Inc.
1000 Wilson Boulevard
Suite 1825
Arlington, VA 22209-3901
703-907-7322
800-368-5777
E-mail: appi@psych.org
www.appi.org

Ron McMillen, Chief Executive Officer
Robert E. Hales MD, M.B.A, Editor-in-Chief
John McDuffie, Editorial Director, Associate Pu
Rebecca D. Rinehart, Publisher

Examines the importance of an integrated approach to neuropsychiatric conditions and looks at ways to overcome the difficulties in assessing medical disorders in psychiatric populations. Addresses neuropsychiatric disorders and their costs and implications on policy. $94.00

448 pages Year Founded: 1999 ISBN 0-880487-30-5

1934 Attention-Deficit/Hyperactivity Disorder Test: a Method for Identifying Individuals with ADHD
Pro.Ed
8700 Shoal Creek Boulevard
Austin, TX 78757-6897
512-451-3246
800-897-3202
E-mail: general@proedinc.com
www.www.proedinc.com

Donald D Hammill, Owner

An effective instrument for identifying and evaluating attention - deficit disorders in persons ages three to twenty-three. Designed for use in schools and clinics, the test is easily completed by teachers, parents and others who are knowledgeable about the referred individual. *$110.00*

Year Founded: 1995

1935 Behavioral and Emotional Rating Scale
Pro.Ed
8700 Shoal Creek Boulevard
Austin, TX 78757-6897
512-451-3246
800-897-3202
E-mail: general@proedinc.com
www.www.proedinc.com

Donald D Hammill, Owner

Helps to measure the personal strengths of children ages five through eighteen. Contains 52 items that measure five aspects of a child's strength: interpersonal strength, involvement with family, intrapersonal strength, school functioning, and affective strength. Provides overall strength score and five subtest scores. Identifies individual behavioral and emotional strengths of children, the areas in which individual strengths need to be developed, and the goals for individual treatment plans. *$165.00*

Year Founded: 1998

1936 Childhood History Form for Attention Disorders
A.D.D. Warehouse
300 NW 70th Avenue
Suite 102
Plantation, FL 33317-2360
954-792-8100
800-233-9273
E-mail: websales@addwarehouse.com
www.addwarehouse.com

Harvey C Parker, Owner

This form is completed by parents prior to a history taking session. It is designed to be used in conjunction with standardized assessment questionaires utilized in the evaluation of attention disorders. 25 per package. *$45.00*

10 pages

1937 Children's Depression Inventory
A.D.D. Warehouse
300 NW 70th Avenue
Suite 102
Plantation, FL 33317-2360
954-792-8100
800-233-9273
E-mail: websales@addwarehouse.com
www.addwarehouse.com

Harvey C Parker, Owner

A self-report, symptom-oriented scale which requires at least a first grade reading level and was designed for school-aged children and adolescents. The CDI has 27 items, each of which consists of three choices. Quickscore form scoring make the inventories easy and economical to administer. The profile contains the following five factors plus a total score normed according to age and sex: negative mood, interpersonal problems, ineffectiveness, anhedonia and negative self-esteem. Contains ten items and provides a general indication of depressive symptoms. *$148.00*

1938 Clinical Interview of the Adolescent: From Assessment and Formulation to Treatment Planning
Charles C Thomas Publisher Ltd.
2600 S 1st Street
Springfield, IL 62704-4730
217-789-8980
800-258-8980
E-mail: books@ccthomas.com
www.ccthomas.com

Michael P Thomas, President

This book addresses the process of interviewing troubled and psychologically disturbed adolescents who are seen in hospital settings, schools, courts, clinics, and residential facilities. Interviews with adolescents, younger children or adults should follow a logical, sequential and integrated procedure, accomplishing diagnostic closure and the development of a treatment formulation. The nine chapters cover the theoretical and developmental concerns of adolescence; the initial referral; meeting with parents; the therapist; getting acquainted; getting to the heart of the matter; making order out of disorder; the reasons and rationale for the behavior problems. *$59.95*

234 pages Year Founded: 1997 ISBN 0-398067-79-1

1939 Concise Guide to Assessment and Management of Violent Patients
American Psychiatric Publishing, Inc.
1000 Wilson Boulevard
Suite 1825
Arlington, VA 22209-3901
703-907-7322
800-368-5777
E-mail: appi@psych.org
www.appi.org

Ron McMillen, Chief Executive Officer
Robert E. Hales MD, M.B.A, Editor-in-Chief
John McDuffie, Editorial Director, Associate Pu
Rebecca D. Rinehart, Publisher

Written by an expert on violence, this edition provides current information on psychopharmacology, safety of clinicians and how to deal with threats of violence to the clinician. *$32.95*

180 pages Year Founded: 1996 ISBN 0-880483-44-X

1940 Conducting Insanity Evaluations
Guilford Press
72 Spring Street
New York, NY 10012-4068
212-431-9800
800-365-7006
E-mail: info@guilford.com
www.www.guilford.com

Bob Matloff, President
Seymour Weingarten, Editor-in-Chief

Great resource for both psychologists and lawyers. Covers legal standards and their applications to clinical work. Mental health professionals who evaluate defendants or consult to courts on criminal matters will find this a useful resource. *$50.00*

342 pages Year Founded: 2000 ISBN 1-572305-21-5

1941 Conners' Rating Scales
Pro.Ed
8700 Shoal Creek Boulevard
Austin, TX 78757-6897
512-451-3246
800-897-3202
E-mail: general@proedinc.com
www.www.proedinc.com

Donald D Hammill, Owner

Conner's Rating Scales are a result of 30 years of research on childhood and adolescent psychopathology and problem behavior. This revision adds a number of enhancements to a set of measures that has long been the standard instruments for the measurement of attention-deficit/hyperactivity disorder in children and adolescents. *$153.00*

Year Founded: 1997

1942 Depression and Anxiety in Youth Scale
Pro.Ed
8700 Shoal Creek Boulevard
Austin, TX 78757-6897
512-451-3246
800-897-3202
E-mail: general@proedinc.com
www.www.proedinc.com

Donald D Hammill, Owner

A unique battery of three norm-referenced scales useful in identifying major depressive disorder and overanxious disorders in children and adolescents. *$150.00*

Year Founded: 1994

1943 Diagnosis and Treatment of Multiple Personality Disorder
Guilford Press
72 Spring Street
New York, NY 10012-4068
212-431-9800
800-365-7006
E-mail: info@guilford.com
www.www.guilford.com

Bob Matloff, President
Seymour Weingarten, Editor-in-Chief

Comprehensive and integrated approach to a complex psychotherapeutic process. From first interview to crisis management to final post-integrative treatment each step is systematically reviewed, with detailed instructions on specific diagnostic and therapeutic techniques and examples of clinical applications. Specially geared to the needs of therapists, novice or expert alike, struggling with their first MPD case. *$48.00*

351 pages Year Founded: 1989 ISBN 0-898621-77-1

1944 Diagnosis and Treatment of Sociopaths and Clients with Sociopathic Traits
NewHarbinger Publications
5674 Shattuck Avenue
Oakland, CA 94609-1662
510-652-0215
800-748-6273
E-mail: customerservice@newharbinger.com
www.newharbinger.com

Matthew McKay, Owner

This text presents a full course of treatment, with special attention to safety issues and other concerns for different client populations in a range of treatment settings. *$49.95*

208 pages Year Founded: 1996 ISBN 1-572240-47-4

1945 Draw a Person: Screening Procedure for Emotional Disturbance
Pro.Ed
8700 Shoal Creek Boulevard
Austin, TX 78757-6897
512-451-3246
800-897-3202
E-mail: general@proedinc.com
www.www.proedinc.com

Donald D Hammill, Owner

Helps identify children and adolescents ages six through seventeen who have emotional problems and require further evaluation. *$140.00*

Year Founded: 1991

1946 Handbook of Psychological Assessment
John Wiley & Sons
111 River Street
Hoboken, NJ 07030-5774
201-748-6000
www.wiley.com

Stephen M. Smith, President, CEO
MJ O'Leary, SVP, Human Resources
Edward J. Melando, SVP, Corporate Controller
Gary M. Rinck, SVP, General Counsel

Classic, revised and new psychological tests are all considered for validity and overall reliability in the light of current clinical thought and scientific development. The new edition has expanded coverage of neuropsychological assessment and reports on assessment and treatment planning in the age of managed care. *$95.00*

862 pages Year Founded: 1997 ISBN 0-471419-79-6

1947 Harvard Medical School Guide to Suicide Assessment and Intervention
Jossey-Bass Publishers
989 Market Street
San Francisco, CA 94103-1708
415-433-1740
www.leadertoleader.org

Debra Hunter, President

The definitive guide for helping mental health professionals determine the risk for suicide and appropriate treatment strategies for suicidal or at-risk patients. *$85.00*

736 pages ISBN 0-787943-03-7

1948 Health Watch
28 Maple Avenue
Medford, MA 02155-7118
781-395-5515
800-643-2757
www.healthwatch.cc

Bill Govostes, Owner

On site performer of preventative health screening services and disease risk management programming. Specializing in point of care testing, we perform fast and accurate health screening tests and services to assist in indentifying participant's risk for developing future disease.

Year Founded: 1987

1949 Scale for Assessing Emotional Disturbance
Pro.Ed
8700 Shoal Creek Boulevard
Austin, TX 78757-6897
512-451-3246
800-897-3202
E-mail: general@proedinc.com
www.www. proedinc.com

Donald D Hammill, Owner

Helps you identify children and adolescents who qualify for the federal special education category Emotional Disturbance. *$100.00*

Year Founded: 1998

1950 Screening for Brain Dysfunction in Psychiatric Patients
Charles C Thomas Publisher Ltd.
2600 S 1st Street
Springfield, IL 62704-4730
217-789-8980
800-258-8980
E-mail: books@ccthomas.com
www.ccthomas.com

Michael P Thomas, President

This book presents how medical diseases can be misdiagnosed as psychiatric disorders and how clinicians without extensive training in the neurosciences can do a competent job of screening psychiatric clients for possible brain disorders. The research cited in this book, dating back to the 1890's, establishes beyond a doubt that such misdiagnoses are more common than most clinicians would guess. This book focuses on one type of medical condition that is likely to be misdiagnosed: brain injuries and illnesses. *$36.95*

148 pages Year Founded: 1998 ISBN 0-398069-21-2

1951 Sexual Dysfunction: Guide for Assessment and Treatment
Guilford Press
72 Spring Street
New York, NY 10012-4068
212-431-9800
800-365-7006
E-mail: info@guilford.com
www.www.guilford.com

Bob Matloff, President
Seymour Weingarten, Editor-in-Chief

Designed as a succinct guide to contemporary sex therapy, this book provides an empirically based overview of the most common sexual dysfunctions and a step-by-step manual for their assessment and treatment. Provides a biopsychosocial model of sexual function and dysfunction and describes the authors' general approach to management of sexual difficulties. *$25.00*

212 pages Year Founded: 1991 ISBN 0-898622-07-7

1952 Social-Emotional Dimension Scale
Pro.Ed
8700 Shoal Creek Boulevard
Austin, TX 78757-6897
512-451-3246
800-897-3202
E-mail: general@proedinc.com
www.www.proedinc.com

Donald D Hammill, Owner

A rating scale for teachers, counselors, and psychologists to screen age 5 1/2 through 18 1/2 who are at risk for conduct disorders, behavior problems, or emotional disturbance. It assesses physical/fear reaction, depressive reaction, avoidance of peer interaction, avoidance of teacher interaction, aggressive interaction, and inappropriate behaviors. *$149.00*

Year Founded: 1986

1953 Statutes & Rules For Governing the Practice of Clinical Social Work, Marriage & Family Therapy, And Mental Health Counseling in Florida

Charlene Proeger, Terry Proeger, author

Professional Resource Press
PO Box 3197
Sarasota, FL 34230-3197
941-343-9601
800-443-3364
E-mail: cs@prpress.com
www.prpress.com

The state of Florida requires social workers to have taken a course specific to the statutes and laws in Florida. This book accompnies that a three-hour course offered by Charlene Proeger, PhD and Terry S. Proeger, PhD. *$34.95*

376 pages Year Founded: 1998 ISBN 1-568870-27-2

1954 Test Collection at ETS
Educational Testing Service
660 Rosedale Road
Princeton, NJ 08541-1
609-921-9000
www.www.ets.org

Kurt M Landgraf, CEO

Provides 1,200 plus tests available in microfiche or downloadable for reaserch.

Training & Recruitment

1955 Ackerman Institute for the Family
936 Broadway
2nd Floor
New York, NY 10010
212-879-4900
E-mail: ackerman@ackerman.org
www.ackerman.org

Lois Braverman, LCSW, President, CEO
Marcia Sheinberg, LCSW, Director of Training and Clinica
Martha E. Edwards, PhD, Director of the Center for the D
Peter Fraenkel, PhD, Director of the Center for Work

A not-for-profit agency devoted to the treatment and study of families and to the training of family therapists. One of the first training institutions in the United States committed to promoting family functioning and family mental health, Acker is dedicated to helping all families at all stages of family life.

1956 Alfred Adler Institute (AAI)
372 Central Park West
New York, NY 10025
212-254-1048
E-mail: director@alfredadler-ny.org
www.www.aai-ny.org

Ellen Mendel, M.Ed., M.S., M, President, Chair of the Board
Brock Hotaling, BSc, Executive Director
Fredrica Levinson, M.A., C.R.C., Dean of Students
Ellen Mendel, M.Ed., M.S., M, Director, Admissions

Offers training in psychotherapy and analysis to psychiatrists, psychologists, social workers, teachers, clergymen and other related professional persons. Conducts three-year program to provide an understanding of the dynamics of personality and interpersonal relationships and to teach therapeutic methods and techniques. Presents the theory of Individual Psychology as formulated by Alfred Adler. Publications: Journal of Individual Psychology, quarterly. Annual meeting. Semi-annual seminar.

1957 Alliance Behavioral Care: University of Cincinnati Psychiatric Services

222 Piedmont Avenue
Suite 8800
Cincinnati, OH 45219-4231
513-475-8622
800-926-8862
www.alliancebehavioral.com

A regional managed behavioral healthcare organization committed to continuously improving the resources and programs that serve their members and providers. Their goal is to provide resources that improve the well-being of those they serve and to integrate the behavioral healthcare within the overall healthcare systems.

1958 Alliant International University

Los Angeles Campus
1000 South Fremont Avenue, Unit 5
Alhambra, CA 91803-8835
626-270-3300
866-825-5426
TDD: 800-585-5087
E-mail: admissions@alliant.edu
www.alliant.edu

Geoffrey Cox PhD, President

Offers industry-specific training to mid-management and supervisory personnel employed in behavioral healthcare organizations.

1959 Alton Ochsner Medical Foundation, Psychiatry Residency

1514 Jefferson Highway
New Orleans, LA 70121-2429
504-842-3000
E-mail: gme@ochsner.org

Doris Ratcliff, Manager

1960 American Academy of Child and Adolescent Psychiatry

3615 Wisconsin Avenue Northwest
Washington, DC 20016-3007
202-966-7300
E-mail: communications@aacap.org
www.aacap.org

Warren Y.K. Ng, MD, MPH, President
Tami D. Benton, MD, President-Elect
Debra E. Koss, MD, Secretary
Neal Ryan, MD, Treasurer

A nonprofit membership based organization composed of over 7,500 child and adolescent psychiatrists and other interested physicians. Promotes mentally healthy children, adolescents, and families through research, training, advocacy, prevention, comprehensive diagnosis and treatment, peer support, and collaboration.

Year Founded: 1953

1961 American College of Healthcare Executives

300 S. Riverside Plaza
Suite 1900
Chicago, IL 60606-6698
312-424-2800
E-mail: contact@ache.org
www.ache.org

Anthony A. . Armada, FACHE, Chair
Delvecchio S. Finley, FACHE, Chair-Elect
Deborah J. Bowen, FACHE, CAE, President and CEO

International professional society of over 48,000 healthcare executives. ACHE is known for its prestigious credentialing and educational programs. ACHE is also known for its journal, Journal of Healthcare Management, and magazine, Healthcare Executive, as well as groundbreaking research and career development programs. Through its efforts, ACHE works toward its goal of improving the health status of society by advancing healthcare management excellence.

1962 American College of Legal Medicine

1100 E Woodfield Road
Suite 350
Schaumburg, IL 60173-5125
847-969-0283
E-mail: info@aclm.org
www.aclm.org

Thomas R. McLean, MD, MS, JD, FC, President-Elect
Victoria Green, MD, JD, MBA, MH, Past President
Daniel L. Orr, II, DDS PhD JD MD, Treasurer
Charles W. Hinnant, Jr., MD, JD,, Secretary

The mission of ACWHP is to advance women-centered healthcare.

1963 Andrus Children's Center
Julia Dyckman Andrus Memorial

1156 N Broadway
Yonkers, NY 10701-1108
914-965-3700

Tecla Critelli, President/CEO

Vision is to 'give opportunity to youth.' A private, non-profit community agency that provides assessment, treatment, education and preventive services for children and their families in residential, day and other restorative programs. Mission is to serve families, without regard to background or financial status, who have or are at risk for developing behavioral health problems. A highly qualified and caring staff uses established techniques and innovative programs to accomplish these purposes.

1964 Asian Pacific Development Center for Human Development

1537 Alton Street
Aurora, CO 80010
303-923-2920
E-mail: info@apdc.org
www.apdc.org

Harry Budisidharta, Executive Director
Eri Asano, Clinic Director
Rattana Rode, Office Manager

A community-based non-profit organization that serves the needs of a growing population of Asian American and Pacific Islander residents throughout Colorado. APDC operates a licensed Community Mental Health Clinic and a multicultural Interpreters Bank.

Year Founded: 1980

1965 Behavioral Healthcare Center

464 Commonwealth Street
#147
Belmont, MA 02478
617-393-3935
E-mail: cberney@mah.harvard.edu
www.academicpsychiatry.org

Carole Berney, Administrative Director
Joan Anzia, President

A behavioral health facility providing consultation in psychiatry, psychopharmacology and psychotherapy to primary care physicians and their patients.

1966 Behavioral Medicine and Biofeedback Consultants

150 SW 12th Avenue
Suite 207
Pompano Beach, FL 33069-3238
954-202-6200
www.behavioralmedicine.com

Gary S Traub, Owner, Director

1967 Bowling Green University Psychology Department

Bowling Green State University
Bowling Green, OH 43403-0001
419-372-2531
www.www.bgsu.edu

Sherideen S. Stoll, VP, Finance and Administration,
Steve Krakoff, Associate VP, Capital Planning a
John Ellinger, Chief Information Officer
Bradley Leigh, Executive Director, Business Ope

1968 Brandeis University/Heller School

415 South Street
Waltham, MA 02453-2700
781-736-2000
www.brandeis.edu

Fred M. Lawrence, President
David A. Bunis, Senior Vice President, Chief of
Marianne Cwalina, Senior Vice President for Financ
Ellen de Graffenreid, Senior Vice President for Commun

1969 Brandeis University: Schneider Institute for Health Policy

Brandeis University
415 South Street, Mailstop 035
Waltham, MA 02454-9110
781-736-3900
E-mail: colnon@brandeis.edu
www.sihp.brandeis.edu

Stanley S Wallack, Ph.D., Executive Director

Committed to developing an objective, university-based entity capable of providing research assistance to the Federal government on the major problems it faced in financing and delivering care to the elderly, disabled and poor. Our role has always been to solve complex health care problems, and to link research studies to policy change.

1970 Breining Institute College for the Advanced Study of Addictive Disorders

8894 Greenback Lane
Orangevale, CA 95662-4019
916-987-0662
E-mail: college@breining.edu
www.breininginstitute.net

Kathy Breining, Administrator

The mission of Breining Institute faculty and staff is to ensure a consistent standard of higher education, training, testing and certification of professionals working in the field of addictions.

Year Founded: 1986

1971 California Institute of Behavioral Sciences

701 Welch Road
Suite #B 203
Palo Alto, CA 94304-1705
650-325-1501
E-mail: info@ecibs.net
www.www.ecibs.net

Sanjay Jasuja, Medical Director

Provides the following services for children, adolescents, adults and families on national and international level: Objective testing and comprehensive treatment for ADHD/ADD, depression, manic depressive disorder or Bipolar disorder, anxiety disorders, including obsessive compulsive disorder, panic attacks, phobias, post-traumatic stress disorder, Tourette's syndrome, stuttering, psychopharmacology, stress and anger control, violence and workplace issues, learning and behavior problems, and parenting support groups.

1972 Cambridge Hospital: Department of Psychiatry

1493 Cambridge Street
Cambridge, MA 02139-1047
617-665-1000
E-mail: webmaster@challiance.org
www.www.challiance.org

Jay Burke, MD, MPH, Chairman, Chief of Psychiatry
Joy Curtis, SVP, Human Resources
Elizabeth Cadigan, RN, MSN, Senior Vice President, Patient C
Judith Klickstein, SVP, Information Technology and

1973 Center for Health Policy Studies

10440 Little Patuxent Parkway
10th Floor
Columbia, MD 21044-3561
410-715-9400

1974 College of Health and Human Services: SE Missouri State

901 S National Ave
Springfield, MO 65897-27
417-836-5000
www.missouristate.edu

Dr.Frank Einhellig, Provost
Dr.Chris Craig, Associate Provost, Faculty & Aca
Dr.Rachelle Darabi, Associate Provost for Student De
Dr.Joye Norris, Associate Provost for Access and

1975 College of Southern Idaho

315 Falls Avenue
PO Box 1238
Twin Falls, ID 83303-1238

208-732-6221
800-680-0274
E-mail: info@csi.edu
www.csi.edu

Jerry Beck, President
Dr.Jeff Fox, President
Jerry Gee, Executive VP/CAO
Dr.Todd Schwarz, EVP, CAO

Addiction Studies

1976 Colonial Services Board
1657 Merrimac Trail
Williamsburg, VA 23185-5624
757-220-3200
TDD: 757-253-4377
www.colonialcsb.org

David Coe, Executive Director
Keith German, Director, Administrative Service
Dan Longo, Director, Behavioural Services
Nancy Shackleford, Director, Human Resources

MR and substance abuse

1977 Daniel and Yeager Healthcare Staffing Solutions
6767 Old Madison Pike
Suite 690
Huntsville, AL 35806-2198
256-551-1070
800-955-1919
E-mail: info@dystaffing.com
www.dystaffing.com

Mark Kingsley, VP
Susie Brown, COO
Mike Williams, CFO
Hans Edenfield, Director, Human Resources

Setting the standard for excellence in health care staffing.

1978 Dartmouth Univerisity: Department of Psychiatry
Dartmouth-Hitchcock Medical School
One Medical Center Drive
Lebanon, NH 03756
603-650-7075
www.geiselmed.dartmouth.edu/psych

1979 East Carolina University Department of Psychiatric Medicine
600 Moye Boulevard
Room 4E-98
Greenville, NC 27834-4300
252-744-4440

Joseph B Webster

1980 Emory University School of Medicine, Psychology and Behavior
1440 Clifton Road NE
Atlanta, GA 30322-1053
404-727-5630

1981 Emory University: Psychological Center
36 Eagle Row
Room 270
Atlanta, GA 30322-1122
404-727-7438
www.psychology.emory.edu

Harold Gouzoules, Ph.D., Department Chair
Nancy Feng, Research Financial Analyst
Kelly Yates, Program Coordinator
Kate Coblin, Assistant Program Director

Nonprofit community clinic providing low cost counseling and psychological testing services for children and adults.

1982 Fletcher Allen Health Care
111 Colchester Avenue
Burlington, VT 05401-1416
802-847-0000
800-358-1144

Fletcher Allen Health Care is both a community hospital and, in partnership with the University of Vermont, the state's academic health center. Their mission is to improve the health of the people in the communities they serve by integrating patient care, education and research in a caring environment.

1983 Genesis Learning Center (Devereux)
430 Allied Drive
Nashville, TN 37211-3304
615-832-4222
E-mail: admin@genesislearn.org
www.genesislearn.org

Terance Adams, Executive Director
Chuck Goon, PHR, Human Resource Director

1984 George Washington University
2121 Eye Street, NW
Washington, DC 20052-1
202-994-1000
www.www.gwu.edu

Steven Knapp, President
Steve R. Lerman, Provost, EVP, Academic Affairs
Beth Nolan, SVP, General Counsel
Louis H. Katz, EVP, Treasurer

1985 Haymarket Center, Professional Development
932 W Washington
Chicago, IL 60607-2217
312-226-7984
E-mail: info@hcenter.org
www.hcenter.org

Raymond F. Soucek, President
Donald E. Musil, Executive VP
Dan Lustig, VP, Clinical Services
Leo C. Miller, VP, Support Services

Drug and alcohol treatment programs.

1986 Heartshare Human Services
12 Metro Tech Center
29th Floor
Brooklyn, NY 11201-3858
718-422-4200
E-mail: info@heartshare.org
www.heartshare.org

Ralph A. Subbiondo, Chairman
William R. Guarinello, MS, President/ Ceo
Mia Higgins, Executive VP, Operations, Genera
Evelyn Alvarez, SVP, Developmental Disabilities

A nonprofit human services agency dedicated to improving the lives of people in need of special services and support.

1987 Hillcrest Utica Psychiatric Services
1120 S Utica Street
South Physician Bldg Suite 1000
Tulsa, OK 74104-4012
918-579-8000
www.helmerichwomenscenter.com

Steve Dobbs, CEO

1988 Institute for Behavioral Healthcare
PO Box 5710
Santa Rosa, CA 95402
650-851-8411
800-258-8411
E-mail: staff@iahb.org
www.iahb.org

Gerry Piaget, Ph.D., President
Joan Piaget, Executive Director
Jen Dames, Director, Operations

Non-profit educational organization that is a fully accredited sponsor of continuing education and continuing medical education for mental health, chemical dependency, and substance abuse treatment providers in the United States and Canada. Mission is to provide high-quality training to healthcare professionals as well as to companies and individuals with healthcare-related interests.

1989 Jacobs Institute of Women's Health
950 New Hampshire Avenue
NW, 2nd Floor
Washington, DC 20052
202-994-4184
E-mail: whieditor@gwu.edu
www.jiwh.org

Richard Mauery, MS, MPH, Managing Staff Director
Susan Wood, PhD, Executive Director
Chloe E. Bird, PhD, Editor In Chief
Carol Weisman, PhD, Associate Editor

Working to improve health care for women through research, dialogue and information dissemination. Mission is to identify and study women's health care issues involving the interaction of medical and social systems; facilitate informed dialogue and foster awareness among consumers and providers alike; and promote problem resolution, interdisciplinary coordination and information dissemination at the regional, national and international levels.

1990 John A Burns School of Medicine Department of Psychiatry
651 Ilalo Street
Medical Education Building
Honolulu, HI 96813-2409
808-692-0899
E-mail: inip@hawaii.edu
www.jabsom.hawaii.edu

Naleen Andrade, Chair
Jerris Hedges, MD, MS, MMM, Dean and Professor of Medicine
Nancy Foster, CFO
A. Roy Magnusson, MD, Associate Dean, Clinical Affairs

Medical School Programs and Residency Programs, general, geriatric, addictive and, child and adolescent.

1991 Langley Porter Psych Institute at UCSF Parnassus Campus
401 Parnassus Avenue
San Francisco, CA 94143-2211
415-476-7500
www.psych.ucsf.edu/lpphc.aspx

Alissa M Peterson
Sam Hawgood, MBBS, Interim Chancellor

1992 Laurelwood Hospital and Counseling Centers
35900 Euclid Avenue
Willoughby, OH 44094-4648
440-953-3000
800-438-4673
www.www.windsorlaurelwood.com

Farshid Afsarifard, Administrator
Leonard Barley, M.D., MBA, Chief Medical Officer
Theodore Parran, M.D., Director, Addiction Medicine
Noah Miller, M.D., Director, Child and Adolescent S

Full-service behavioral healthcare system-(comprehensive outpatient and inpatient services).

1993 Life Science Associates
1 Fenimore Road
Bayport, NY 11705-2115
631-472-2111
www.lifesciassoc.home.pipeline.com

Joann Mandriota, President
Frank Mandriota, Vice President

Publishes over fifty computer programs for individuals impaired by head trauma and stroke. Also programs for personal memory care, GSSS (Get sharp stay sharp)

1994 Locumtenens.com
2655 Northwinds Parkway
Alpharetta, GA 30009
800-930-0748
E-mail: customerservice@locumtenens.com
www.locumtenens.com

Shane Jackson, President, COO
Kevin Thill, SVP, Psychiatry
Chris Franklin, EVP
Katie Thill, EVP

Specializing in temporary and permanant placcmcnt of psychiatrists. Physicians tell us where and when they want to work and locumtenens.com will find a jop that fits those needs.

1995 MCG Telemedicine Center
1120 15th Street
Augusta, GA 30912-6
706-721-2231

Daniel W. Rahn, President
Ricardo Azziz, MD, MPH, MBA, President / Ceo
Susan L. Barcus, FAHP, SVP, Advancement, Chief Developm
David L. Brond, MBA, MHA, SVP, Communications and Marketin

1996 MCW Department of Psychiatry and Behavioral Medicine
8701 Watertown Plank Road
Milwaukee, WI 53226-3548
414-955-8296
E-mail: webmaster@mcw.edu
www.www.mcw.edu

John R. Raymond, Sr., President, CEO
Joseph E. Kerschner, MD, Deean, EVP
G. Allen Bolton, Jr., SVP, COO

1997 Market Research Alliance
1109 Spring St
Suite 704
Silver Spring, MD 20910-4032
301-588-8732
www.mr-twg.com

Frank Black Jr., Partner,President
John Marty, Managing Director
Nick Campbell, Member
Tom Bergan, Member

1998 Marsh Foundation
1229 Lincoln Highway
PO Box 150
Van Wert, OH 45891-150
419-238-1695
E-mail: marshfound@embarqmail.com
www.marshfoundation.org

Jeff Grothouse, Executive Secretary/Treasurer
Kim Mullins, P.C.C., Executive Director
Kathleen Davis, L.S.W., Director, Residential Services
Sherry Grone, Activities Coordinator

Nonprofit center serving children and families with special emphasis in juvenile sex offender population. Services include individual therapy, group therapy, case management and diagnostic assessment.

1999 Medical College of Georgia
1120 15th Street
Augusta, GA 30912-5563
706-721-0211

Daniel W. Rahn, President
Ricardo Azziz, MD, MPH, MBA, President / Ceo
Susan L. Barcus, FAHP, SVP, Advancement, Chief Developm
David L. Brond, MBA, MHA, SVP, Communications and Marketin

The mission of the Medical College of Georgia is to improve health and resuce the burden of illness in society by discovering, disseminating, and applying knowledge of human health and disease.

2000 Medical College of Ohio
3000 Arlington Avenue
Toledo, OH 43614-2595
419-383-4000
800-321-8383
E-mail: utmc.webmaster@utoledo.edu
www.utmc.utoledo.edu

Mission is to improve the human condition through the creation, dissemination and application of knowledge using wisdom and compassion as our guides.

2001 Medical College of Pennsylvania
3300 Henry Avenue
Philadelphia, PA 19129-1191
215-842-6000

A tertiary care educational facility that reaches out to a regional referral base for select specialty services while continuing to offer primary and secondary service to the residents of its immediate community.

2002 Medical College of Wisconsin
8701 Watertown Plank Road
Milwaukee, WI 53226-3548

414-955-8296
E-mail: webmaster@mcw.edu
www.mcw.edu

John R. Raymond, Sr., President, CEO
Joseph E. Kerschner, MD, Deean, EVP
G. Allen Bolton, Jr., SVP, COO
Douglas R. Campbell, Finance Executive

2003 Medical Doctor Associates
145 Technology Parkway NW
Norcross, GA 30092-2913
770-246-9191
800-780-3500
www.mdainc.com

Ken Shumard, President
Mike Pretiger, Cfo

Committed to providing the most complete staffing services available to the healthcare industry. The family of services offered by Medical Doctor Associates includes Locum Tenens, Contract, and Permanent Placement staffing for physicians, allied health and rehabilitation staffing, and credentials verification and licensing services.

2004 Medical University of South Carolina Institute of Psychiatry, Psychiatry Access Center
104 Colcock Hall
MSC - 003
Charleston, SC 29425-100
843-792-5050
800-296-0269
www.academicdepartments.musc.edu/musc/

Mark S. Sothmann, Ph.D., Interim President, VP, Academic
Lisa Montgomery, EVP, Finance and Operations
Patrick J. Wamsley, CPA, CFO
Stewart Mixon, COO

2005 Meharry Medical College
1005-David B Todd Boulevard
Nashville, TN 37208-3501
615-327-6000
E-mail: admissions@mmc.edu
www.mmc.edu

A. Cherrie Epps, Ph.D., President, CEO
Saletta Holloway, MSP, SVP, Borad of Trustees Relations
Robert Poole, B.A., SVP, Institutional Advancement
Ivanetta Davis Samuels, J.D., SVP, General Counsel and Corpora

2006 Menninger Clinic
12301 Main Street
Houston, TX 77035
713-275-5400
www.www.menningerclinic.com

Robert J. Boland, MD, Senior VP and Chief of Staff
Armando E. Colombo, President and CEO
Cory Walker, DO, Chief Medical Officer
Gerald Noll, MBA, Chief Financial Officer

Menninger is a leading psychiatric hospital dedicated to treating individuals with mood, personality, anxiety, and addictive disorders; teaching mental health professionals; and advancing mental healthcare through research.

Year Founded: 1925

2007 Nathan S Kline Institute for Psychiatric Research
140 Old Orangeburg Road
Orangeburg, NY 10962
845-398-5500
E-mail: webmaster@nki.rfmh.org
www.www.rfmh.org/nki

Donald C. Goff, MD, Director
Antonio Convit, MD, Deputy Director
Thomas O. O'Hara, MBA, Deputy Director/Institute Admin.
Michael Kohn, PhD, Head of Research Support

Research programs in Alzheimers disease, analytical psychopharmacology, basic and clinical neuroimaging, cellular and molecular neurobiology, clinical trial data management, co-occuring disorders and many other mental health studies.

2008 National Association of Alcholism and Drug Abuse Counselors
1001 N. Fairfax Street
Suite 201
Alexandria, VA 22314-1535
703-741-7686
800-548-0497
E-mail: naadac@naadac.org
www.naadac.org

Robert C. Richards, MA, NCAC II,, President
Kirk Bowden, PhD, MAC, LISA, President Elect
Cynthia Moreno Tuohy, NCAC II,, Executive Director
Autumn Kramer, Director, Operations

NAADAC is the only professional membership organization that serves counselors who specialize in addiction treatment. With 14,000 members and 47 state affiliates representing more than 80,000 addiction counselors, it is the nation's largest network of alcoholism and drug abuse treatment professionals. Among the organization's national certifacation programs are the National Certified Addiction Counselor and the Masters Addiction Counselor designations.

2009 National Association of School Psychologists
4340 E West Highway
Suite 402
Bethesda, MD 20814
301-657-0270
www.nasponline.org

Laurie Klose, President
Celeste Malone, President-Elect
Karen Apgar, Secretary
Misty Lay, Treasurer

2010 New York University Behavioral Health Programs
530 1st Avenue
Suite 7D (at 30th Street)
New York, NY 10016-6402
212-263-7419
www.www.med.nyu.edu/nyubhp/

David Ginsberg, Director
Robert Cancro, MDÿ, Professor of Psychiatry and Chai
Norman Sussman, MD, Clinical Professor of Psychiatry
Virginia Sadock, MDÿ, Clinical Professor of Psychiatry

Outpatient psychiatry group for Tisch Hospital at NYU Medical Center. Our multidisciplinary team of licensed psychiatrists and social workers offers you the most up-to-date and scientifically validated treatments.

2011 Northeastern Ohio Universities College of Medicine
4209 State Route 44
PO Box 95
Rootstown, OH 44272-95
800-686-2511

Jay A. Gershen, D.D.S., Ph.D., President
John R. Wray, Vice President, Administration a
Daniel Blain, Vice President, Advancement, Pre
Michael A. Wolff, J.D., Senior Development Officer

Mission is to graduate qualified physicians who are passionate about serving their communities. All of our graduates, regardless of specialty, have a solid background in community and public health. NEOUCOM strives to improve the quality of health care throughout northeast Ohio by instilling in each graduate the desire to serve the public and the highest ideals of the medical profession.

2012 Northwestern University Medical School Feinberg School of Medicine
420 East Superior Street
Chicago, IL 60611-3128
312-503-8194
E-mail: clinpsych@northwestern.edu
www.www.feinberg.northwestern.edu

Eric G. Neilson, MD, Dean, VP - Medical Affairs
Eva Erskine, Manager
Jim Baker, Ph.D., Science in Medicine Element Co-C
John X. Thomas, Ph.D., Teamwork & Leadership Thread Cha

The Mental Health Services and Policy Program is a multidisciplinary research/educational program on the development and implementation of outcomes management technology.

2013 Ochester Psychological Service
1924 Copper Oaks Circle
Blue Springs, MO 64015-8300
816-224-6500

Jeffery L Miller PhD, Psychologist/Owner

Offers a full range of outpatient mental health services including individuals, couples and family therapy. Offers psychological testing and evaluation. Adults, adolescents and children served.

2014 PRIMA ADD Corp.
12160 N. Abrams Rd
Suite 615
Dallas, TX 75243-4547
972-386-8599
E-mail: robinbinnig@gmail.com
www.primaadd.com; drbinnig.wordpress.com

Robin Binnig, PhD, Owner

Prima ADD Corp specializes in the diagnosis and treatment of Attention-Deficit/Hyperactivity Disorder (ADHD). We treat children and adults. Services include: psychological assessment (including intellectual, achievement and pesonality testing), counseling, coaching and consultation. We also carry books and CD's concerning ADHD.

2015 Parent Child Center
2001 W Blue Heron Blvd
Riviera Beach, FL 33404-5003
561-841-3500
800-955-8770
TTY: 800-955-8771
www.www.gocpg.org

Patrick Mc Namara, President, CEO
Laura Barry, Vice Presidentÿof Community Serv
Pamela Figoras, Vice President of Child & Family
Laura Morse, Vice Presidentÿof Development

2016 Penn State Hershey Medical Center
500 University Drive
Hershey, PA 17033-2390
717-531-6955
800-731-3032
TTY: 717-531-4395

Harold L Paz, M.D., M.S., CEO, SVP, Dean
Jeff Miller, M.D., Associate Dean for Administratio
Lisa Abbott, M.B.A., S.P.H., Associate Vice President for Hum
Sean Young, Chief Marketing Officer

2017 Pepperdine University Graduate School of Education and Psychology
6100 Center Drive
Los Angeles, CA 90045-9200
310-506-4000
800-347-4849

Andrew Benton, President

Offers graduate degree programs designed to prepare psychologists, marriage and family therapists, and mental health practitioners. Many programs accommodate a full-time work schedule with evening and weekend classes available in a trimester schedule. The average class size is 15. There are five educational centers in southern California and three community counseling clinics available to the surrounding community.

2018 Portland University Regional Research Institute for Human Services
1600 Sw 4th Ave
Suite 900
Portland, OR 97201-5521
503-725-4040
www.rri.pdx.edu

Tom Keller, Interim Director
Diane Yatchmenoff, Ph.D., Associate Director
Jennifer Williams, Assistant to the Director

2019 Postgraduate Center for Mental Health
71 W 23rd St
New York, NY 10010-4102
212-576-4168
E-mail: crichards@pgcmh.org
www.pgcmh.org

Jacob Barak, Ph.D., MBA, President, CEO
Marcia B. Holman, L.C.S.W., VP for Ambulatory Operations
Harold Moss, L.M.S.W., MA, VP for Residential Operations
John McMasters, Executive Assistant

Information on mental health.

2020 Pressley Ridge
5500 Corporate Drive
Suite 400
Pittsburgh, PA 15237
412-872-9400

Susanna L. Cole, MA, President, CEO
Laurah Currey, MA, LPC, LSW, Chief Operating Officer
Douglas A. Mullins, CPA, CFO
Edward J. Yongo, MBA, Chief Development and External R

Founded in 1832. Provides an array of social services, special education programs, and mental health services for troubled children and their families in Delaware, Maryland, Ohio, Pennsylvania, Virginia, Washngton, DC and West Virginia as well as worldwide.

2021 PsychTemps
2404 Auburn Avenue
Cincinnati, OH 45219-2735
513-651-9500
888-651-8367
E-mail: info@psychpros.com
www.psychtemps.com

Holly Dorna MA LPCC, President/CEO
Timberline Knolls, HR Director
Lauren Kofod, M.D., Member
Paul J. Schwartz, M.D., Member

Specialized recruiting and staffing company that fills temporary, permanent, and temp-to-hire job placement for the behavioral healthcare field.

2022 Psychiatric Associates
2216 W Alto Road
Kokomo, IN 46902
765-453-9338

2023 Psychological Center
135 Oakland Street
Pasadena, CA 91101
626-584-5500

Winston Gooden, Manager

2024 QuadraMed Corporation
12110 Sunset Hills Road
Suite 600
Reston, VA 20190-5852
703-709-2300
800-393-0278
www.quadramed.com

Daniel Desaulniers, CA, President, Harris Quebec Public
Jim Dowling, Executive Vice President, Enterp
Sandi Williams, Executive Vice President, Clinic
Duncan W James, CEO

2025 Skills Unlimited
2060 Ocean Ave
Suite 3
Ronkonkoma, NY 11779-6533
631-580-5319
E-mail: success@skillsunlimited.org
www.skillsunlimited.org

Jeffrey Koppelson, Program Director
Richard Kassnove, Executive Director

SUCCESS provides rehabilitative services to indivduals who are recovering from mental illness. In addition to offering clinical treatment, SUCCESS has a schedule of classes and other services that help to identify and achieve personally meaningful goals in the areas of employment, housing, education, health and socialization. Transportation is generally available free of charge. The program is open Monday through Saturday and has ectended hours two evenings per week.

2026 Southern Illinois University School of Medicine: Department of Psychiatry
PO Box 19620
Springfield, IL 62794-9620
217-545-8000
www.siumed.edu

Stephen M Soltys MD, Pfr/Chair Dpt. of Psychiatry
Philip Pan MD, Division Chief
Connie Poole, Associate Dean for Information R
Klamen Debra, MD, MHPE, Associate Dean for Education and

2027 Southern Illinois University School of Medicine SIU School of Medicine
PO Box 19620
Springfield, IL 62794-9620
217-545-8000
www.siumed.edu

Stephen M Soltys MD, Pfr/Chair Dpt. of Psychiatry
Philip Pan MD, Division Chief
Connie Poole, Associate Dean for Information R
Klamen Debra, MD, MHPE, Associate Dean for Education and

Provides high quality clinical treatment,outstanding teaching and solid efforts in research and community service.

2028 Specialzed Alternatives for Family and Youth (SAFY)
10100 Elida Road
Delphos, OH 45833-9056
419-695-8010
800-532-7239
www.safy.org

Scott Spangler, MSW, President, CEO
Jim Sherman, MA, LPC, SVP, Administrative Services
John Hollenkamp, CPA, VP, Contracts and Procurement
Marc Bloomingdale, M.S., VP, Operations

SAFY's mission is to foster an environment that possibly impacts the lives of youth and their families, whether they are with us an hour or a lifetime.

2029 St. Frnacis Medical Psych-Med Association
2616 Wilmington Road
New Castle, PA 16105-1504
724-652-2323

2030 St. Louis Behavioral Medicine Institute
1129 Macklind Avenue
Saint Louis, MO 63110-1440
314-289-9411
877-245-2688
www.slbmi.com

Ronald B. Margolis, Ph.D., President, CEO
Debbie Milfelt, Manager
Geeta Aatre-Prashar, Psy.D., Psychologist
Gelene Adkins, Ph.D., Psychologist

Offers exceptional quality, result-focused treatment. Have remained true to our commitment of providing excellence in clinical care and customer service. We offer comprehensive treatment plans to meet the individual needs of chil-

dren, adolescents, adults, older adults, and their families suffering from emotional and behavioral problems.

2031 Stonington Institute
75 Swantown Hill Road
N Stonington, CT 06359-1022
860-535-1010
800-832-1022
E-mail: andrea.keeney@uhsinc.com
www.stoningtoninstitute.com

William A. Aniskovich, M.A., J.D., CEO
Jerome M Schnitt, M.D., Medical Director
Georganna Georgie Koppermann, Director, Business Development a
Andrea Keeney, Director of Admissions

2032 Topeka Institute for Psychoanalysis
PO Box 829
Topeka, KS 66601-829
800-288-3950

A training facility for health care professionals, the Topeka Institute for Psychoanalysis has the tripartite mission of promoting research to expand the knowledge base in its field of expertise; providing didactic education and clinical supervision to trainees; and caring for patients in need of its services through a low-fee clinic.

2033 UCLA Neuropsychiatric Institute and Hospital
760 Westwood Plaza
Los Angeles, CA 90095
310-825-0291
www.www.semel.ucla.edu

Peter Whybrow, Director
Fawzy Fawzy, Associate Director
Mark Wheeler, Media Relations
Alan Han, Director of Development

Multidisciplinary institute of human neurosciences, and is unifying focus of scholarly activity at UCLA in this area. Scientific advances recent decades have shown the value in approaches that cut across traditional academic departments, and which emphasize interdisciplinary collaborations.

2034 UCLA School of Nursing
PO Box 951702
Los Angeles, CA 90095-1702
310-825-3109
E-mail: sonsaff@sonnet.ucla.edu
www.nursing.ucla.edu

Courtney H. Lyder, ND, ScD(Hon), F, Professor, Dean
Rene Dennis, Director Development
Rhonda Flenoy-Younger, Director of Recruitment, Outreac
Mark Covin, Recruitment and Admissions Coord

2035 UCSF Department of Psychiatry, Cultural Competence
3 Regent Street
Livingston, NJ 07039
973-436-5000
973-436-5004
www.reprogenetics.com

Santiago Munne, Founder, Director
Jacques Cohen, Laboratory Director, Embryologis
Kelly Ketterson, Director of Operations
Pere Colls, Laboratory Director

2036 USC School of Medicine
Health Sciences Campuses
Name/Department USC
Los Angeles, CA 90089-1
323-442-1100
www.usc.edu/schools/medicine/

2037 Ulster County Department of Health and Mental Health
239 Golden Hill Lane
Kingston, NY 12401
845-340-4110
www.ulstercountyny.gov/health/health-mental-health

Dr. Carol Smith, Commissioner
Tara McDonald, Deputy Commissioner

Responsible for planning, funding and monitoring of community mental health, developmental disability and alcohol and substance abuse services in Ulster County.

2038 Union County Psychiatric Clinic
117 Roosevelt Avenue
Plainfield, NJ 07060-1331
908-756-6870
www.www.ucpcbhc.org

Rosalind Hunt Doctor, President
Gerard Kiely, VP
Richard L. Rodgers, MSW, LCSW, Executive Director
Joseph Daniel, MA, LPC, Associate Executive Director

2039 University Behavioral Healthcare
671 Hoes Lane
Piscataway, NJ 08855
732-235-5900
800-969-5300
www.ubhc.rutgers.edu

Christopher Kosseff, President

2040 University of California Davis Psychiatry and Behavioral Sciences Department
2315 Stockton Boulevard
Sacramento, CA 95817-2201
916-734-2011

Offers opportunities for students and faculty for clinical and research applications in all aspects of psychiatry and behavioral sciences.

2041 University of Cincinnati College of Medical Department of Psychiatry
260 Stelson Street
Suite 3200
Cincinnati, OH 45221
513-558-7700
E-mail: uchealthnews@uc.edu
www.www.psychiatry.uc.edu

Stephen M. Strakowski, MD, Chair
Charles Collins, MD, Senior Vice Chair and Director o
Paul Keck, MD, Executive Vice Chair
Henry A. Nasrallah, MD, Vice Chair of Education and Trai

Researches eating disorders, bipolar disorder, and chemical dependency.

2042 University of Colorado Health Sciences Center
1250 14th Street
Denver, CO 80217

303-556-2400
877-472-2586
www.www.ucdenver.edu/pages/ucdwelcomepage.aspx
John C Slocumb

2043 University of Connecticut Health Center
263 Farmington Avenue
Farmington, CT 06030-1
860-679-2000
TDD: 860-679-2242
www.www.uchc.edu

Susan Herbst, President
Frank M. Torti, M.D., M.P.H., Executive VP for health affairs
Elizabeth Bolt, Vice President, Human Resources
Marianne Dess-Santoro, VP, Ambulatory Care

2044 University of Iowa Hospital
200 Hawkins Drive
Iowa City, IA 52242-1007
319-356-1616
800-777-8442
TDD: 319-356-4999
E-mail: uihc-webcomments@uiowa.edu
www.www.uihealthcare.org

Kenneth P. Kates, CEO
Kenneth L. Fisher, CFO
Ann Williamson, PhD, RN, Chief Nursing Officer
Theresa Brennan, MD, Chief Medical Officer

2045 University of Kansas Medical Center
3901 Rainbow Boulevard
Kansas City, KS 66160-1
913-588-5000
TDD: 913-588-7963
E-mail: kusmw@kumc.edu
www.www.kumc.edu

Douglas A. Girod, M.D., Executive Vice Chancellor
Barbara Atkinson, Executive Vice Chancellor
Tim Caboni, Vice Chancellor for Public Affai
David Vranicar, M.B.A., Vice Chancellor for Finance/CFO

An integral and unique component of the University of Kansas and the Kansas Board of Regents system, is composed of the School of Medicine, the School of Nursing, the School of Allied Health, the University of Kansas Hospital, and a Graduate School. KU Medical Center is a complex institution whose basic functions include research, education, patient care, and community service involving multiple constituencies at state and national levels.

2046 University of Kansas School of Medicine
3901 Rainbow Boulevard
Kansas City, KS 66160-1
913-588-5000
TDD: 913-588-7963
E-mail: kusmw@kumc.edu
www.kumc.edu

Douglas A. Girod, M.D., Executive Vice Chancellor
Barbara Atkinson, Executive Vice Chancellor
Tim Caboni, Vice Chancellor for Public Affai
David Vranicar, M.B.A., Vice Chancellor for Finance/CFO

2047 University of Louisville School of Medicine
Abell Administration Center
323 E. Chestnut Street
Louisville, KY 40202

502-562-3000
E-mail: meddean@louisville.edu
www.louisville.edu/medicine

Dean Ganzel, Dean
Wes Allison

Mission is to be a vital component in the University of Louisville's quest to become a premier, nationally recognized metropolitan research university, to excel in the education of physicians and scientists for careers in teching, research, patient care and community service, and to bring the fundamental discoveries of our basic and clinical scientists to the bedside.

2048 University of Maryland Medical Systems

22 S. Greene Street
Baltimore, MD 21201-1023
410-328-2132
800-492-5538
TDD: 800-735-2258
www.umm.edu

Robert A. Chrencik, MBA, CPA, President, CEO
Henry J. Franey, MBA, EVP, CFO
Megan M. Arthur, SVP, General Counsel
Janice J. Eisele, SVP, Development

2049 University of Maryland School of Medicine

655 West Baltimore Street
Baltimore, MD 21201-1509
410-706-3681
E-mail: webmaster@som.umaryland.edu
www.medschool.umaryland.edu

Nancy Ryan Lowitt, Dean/Vp Medical Affairs
E. Albert Reece, MD, PhD, MBA, Dean, VP of Medical Affairs
Richard Pierson III, MD, Senior Associate Dean for Academ
Milford M. Foxwell, Jr., MD, Associate Dean for Admissions

Dedicated to providing excellence in biomedical education, basic and clinical research, quality patient care and service to improve the health of the citizens of Maryland and beyond.

2050 University of Massachusetts Medical Center

55 Lake Avenue N
Worcester, MA 01655-1
508-856-8989
www.www.umassmed.edu

Terence R. Flotte, MD, Dean of School of Medicine, Prov
Michael F. Collins, MD, FACP, Senior Vice President for the He
Mariann M. Manno, MD, Interim Associate Dean for Admis
Aaron Lazare, Administrator

Mission is to serve the people of the commonwealth through national distinction in health sciences, education, research, public service and clinical care.

2051 University of Michigan

500 S. State Street
Ann Arbor, MI 48109
734-764-1817
E-mail: info@umich.edu
www.www.umich.edu

Mary Sue Coleman, President
Martha Pollack, Provost

Sally J. Churchill, VP, Secretary
Jerry A. May, VP, Development

2052 University of Minnesota Fairview Health Systems

2450 Riverside Ave
Minneapolis, MN 55454-1450
612-273-2229
TTY: 612-672-7300
www.fairview.org

Gordon Alexander, President
Rulon F. Stacey, PhD, FACHE, President, CEO
Daniel K. Anderson, President of Fairview Community
Daniel Fromm, SVP, CFO

Mission is to improve the health of the communities we serve. We commit our skills and resources to the benefit of the whole person by providing the finest in healthcare, while addressing the physical, emotional and spiritual needs of individuals and their families. Pledge to support the research and education efforts of our partner, the University of Minnesota, and its tradition of excellence.

2053 University of North Carolina School of Social Work

Behavioral Healthcare Resource Institute
301 Pittsboro Street
Cb # 3550
Chapel Hill, NC 27599-1
919-843-3018
E-mail: bhrinstitute@listserv.unc.edu

2054 University of Pennsylvania Health System

399 S 34th Street
Suite 2002 Penn Tower
Philadelphia, PA 19104-4316
215-662-6995
800-789-PENN

2055 University of South Florida Research Center for Children's Mental Health

13301 Bruce B Downs Boulevard
Tampa, FL 33612-3807
813-974-4565

Robert M. Friedman, Ph.D., Center Director
Albert Duchnowski, Ph.D., Deputy Director
Krista Kutash, Ph.D., Deputy Director
Mary Armstrong, PhD, Center Staff

The center conducts research, synthesized and shared existingknowledge, provided training and consultation, and served as a resource for other researchers, policy makers, administrators in the public system, and organizations representing parents, consumers, advocates, professional societies and practitioners.

2056 University of Texas Medical Branch Managed Care

301 University Boulevard
Galveston, TX 77555-5302
409-772-1506
800-917-8906
E-mail: public.affairs@utmb.edu
www.utmb.edu

David L. Callender, MD, MBA, FA, President
Danny O. Jacobs, MD, MPH, EVP, Provost, Dean
Carolee Carrie King, JD, SVP, General Counsel
David W. Niesel, PhD, VP, Dean

2057 University of Utah Neuropsychiatric
501 Chipeta Way
Salt Lake City, UT 84108-1222
801-583-2500
E-mail: sarah.latta@hsc.utah.edu
www.healthcare.utah.edu/uni

Kristin Fontaine, Manager

Located in the University's Research Park, is a full service 90-bed psychiatric hospital providing mental health and substance abuse treatment. Services include inpatient, day treatment, intensive outpatient, and ooutpatient services for children, adolescents and adults. Confidential assessments, referrals, and intervention education are available.

2058 Wake Forest University
1834 Wake Forest Road
Winston Salem, NC 27106
336-758-5000
www.wfu.edu

Nathan O. Hatch, President
Rogan Kersh, Provost
Hof Milam, SVP of Finance and Administratio
James J. Dunn, VP, Chief Investment Officer

2059 West Jefferson Medical Center
1101 Medical Center Boulevard
Marrero, LA 70072-3191
504-347-5511
www.wjmc.org

A Gary Muller, CEO

Not-for-profit community hospital on the West Bank of Jefferson Parish. Continues to strengthen its community base while maintaining its mission and values. Dedicated to considerate and respectful quality healthcare, the institution welcomes patient, family, and visitor feedback regarding programs, services, and community needs.

2060 Western Psychiatric Institute and Clinic
3811 Ohara Street
Pittsburgh, PA 15213-2597
412-624-2100
877-624-4100
www.www.upmc.com

Rizwan Parvez

A national leader in the diagnosis, management, and treatment of mental health and addictive disorders. Providing the most comprehensive range of behavioral health services available today, but also shaping tomorrow's behavioral health care through clinical innovation, research, and education.

2061 Wordsworth
3905 Ford Road
Philadelphia, PA 19131-2824
215-643-5400
800-769-0088
E-mail: info@wordsworth.org
www.www.wordsworth.org

Debra Lacks, President, CEO
Amir Malek, CFO
Andrew Gross, Executive Director of Community
Jennifer Nickels, Executive Director of Residentia

The mission of Wordsworth, a not-for-profit institution, is to provide quality education, treatment and care to children and families with special needs.

Year Founded: 1952

Video & Audio

2062 Asperger's Diagnostic Assessment with Dr. Tony Attwood
Program Development Associates PO Box 2038
Syracuse, NY 13220-2038
315-452-0643
E-mail: info@disabilitytraining.com
www.disabilitytraining.com

New from acclaimed autism expert Dr. Tony Attwood, this 4-hour DVD set with program guide offers diagnostic characteristics of Asperger's Syndrome in children and adults, patient interviews and impacts on girls. An essential guide for Child Psychologists, Special Ed teachers and Parents. *$129.95*

2063 Cognitive Behavioral Assessment
NewHarbinger Publications
5674 Shattuck Avenue
Oakland, CA 94609-1662
510-652-0215
800-748-6273
E-mail: customerservice@newharbinger.com
www.newharbinger.com

Matthew McKay, Owner

A videotape that guides three clients through PAC (Problem, Antecedents, Consequences) method of cognitive behavioral assessment. *$49.95*

ISBN 1-572243-15-5

2064 Couples and Infertility - Moving Beyond Loss
Guilford Press
72 Spring Street
New York, NY 10012-4068
212-431-9800
800-365-7006
E-mail: info@guilford.com
www.www.guilford.com

Bob Matloff, President
Seymour Weingarten, Editor-in-Chief

A VHS video explores the biological and resulting psychological and social issues of infertility. *$95.00*

ISBN 1-572302-86-0

2065 Educating Clients about the Cognitive Model
NewHarbinger Publications
5674 Shattuck Avenue
Oakland, CA 94609-1662
510-652-0215
800-748-6273
E-mail: customerservice@newharbinger.com
www.newharbinger.com

Matthew McKay, Owner

Videotape that helps three clients understand their symptoms as they work toward developing a working contract to begin cognitive restructing. *$49.95*

ISBN 1-572243-19-8

2066 Gender Differences in Depression: Marital Therapy Approach
Guilford Press
72 Spring Street
New York, NY 10012-4068
212-431-9800
800-365-7006
E-mail: info@guilford.com
www.www.guilford.com

Bob Matloff, President
Seymour Weingarten, Editor-in-Chief

Male-female treatment team is shown working with a markedly depressed couple to improve communication and sense of well being in their marriage. *$85.50*

ISBN 1-572302-87-9

2067 Group Work for Eating Disorders and Food Issues
American Counseling Association
PO Box 31110
Alexandria, VA 22310-9998
800-347-6647
E-mail: webmaster@counseling.org
www.counseling.org

Richard Yep, Executive Director
Dr. S. Kent Butler, President

A plan for working with high school and college age females who are at risk for eating disorders. This video provides a method for identifying at-risk clients, a session-by-session desciption of the group, exercises and information on additional resources. *$89.95*

ISSN 79801

2068 Help This Kid's Driving Me Crazy - the Young Child with Attention Deficit Disorder
Pro-Ed Publications
8700 Shoal Creek Boulevard
Austin, TX 78757-6897
512-451-3246
800-897-3202
E-mail: general@proedinc.com
www.www.proedinc.com

Donald D Hammill, Owner

This videotape provides information about the behavior and special needs of young children with ADD and offers suggestions on fostering appropriate behaviors. *$89.00*

2069 I Love You Like Crazy: Being a Parent with Mental Illness
Mental Illness Education Project
25 West Street
Westborough, MA Westb-roug
617-562-1111
800-343-5540
www.miepvideos.org

Christine Ledoux, Executive Director

In this videotape, eight mothers and fathers who have mental illness discuss the challenges they face as parents. Most of these parents have faced enormous obstacles from homelessness, addictions, legal difficulties and hospitalizations, yet have maintained a positive and loving relationship with their children. The tape introduces issues of work, fear, stigma, relationships with children and the rest of the fam-

ily, with professionals, and with the community at large. Discounted price for families/consumers. *$79.95*

2070 Inner Health Incorporated
Christopher Alsten, PhD
1260 Lincoln Avenue
San Diego, CA 92103-2322
619-299-7273
800-283-4679
E-mail: sleepenhancement@aol.com

Provides a series of prerecorded therapeutic audio programs for anxiety, insomnia and chemical dependency, both for adults and children. Developed over a 15 year period by a practicing psychiatrist and recording engineer they employ state-of-the-art 3-D sound technologies and the latest relaxation and psychological techniques (but no stimulants). Clients include: US Air Force, US Navy, National Institute of Health, National Institute of Aging and various psychiatric and chemical dependency facilities and companies with shiftworkers.

2071 Know Your Rights: Mental Health Private Practice & the Law
American Counseling Association
PO Box 31110
Alexandria, VA 22310-9998
800-347-6647
E-mail: webmaster@counseling.org
www.counseling.org

Richard Yep, Executive Director
Dr. S. Kent Butler, President

Forum is lead by national experts, offers answers to important questions and provides invaluable information for every practitioner. Helps to orientate practitioners on the legally permissible boundaries, legal liabilities that are seldom known and how to respond in the face of legal action. *$145.00*

ISSN 79062

2072 Life Is Hard: Audio Guide to Healing Emotional Pain
Impact Publishers
PO Box 6016
Atascadero, CA 93423-6016
805-466-5917
800-246-7228
E-mail: info@impactpublishers.com
www.impactpublishers.com

In a very warm and highly personal style, psychologist Preston offers listeners powerful advice — realistic, practical, effective, on dealing with the emotional pain life often inflicts upon us. *$11.95*

ISBN 0-915166-99-2

2073 Life Passage in the Face of Death, Vol II: Psychological Engagement of the Physically Ill Patient
American Psychiatric Publishing, Inc.
1000 Wilson Boulevard
Suite 1825
Arlington, VA 22209-3901
703-907-7322
800-368-5777
E-mail: appi@psych.org
www.appi.org

Ron McMillen, Chief Executive Officer
Robert E. Hales MD, M.B.A, Editor-in-Chief
John McDuffie, Editorial Director
Rebecca D. Rinehart, Publisher

Ongoing explanation of therapy from a recognized expert. Valuable to clinicians and students alike.

2074 Life Passage in the Face of Death, Volume I: A Brief Psychotherapy
American Psychiatric Publishing, Inc.
1000 Wilson Boulevard
Suite 1825
Arlington, VA 22209-3901
703-907-7322
800-368-5777
E-mail: appi@psych.org
www.appi.org

Ron McMillen, Chief Executive Officer
Robert E. Hales MD, M.B.A, Editor-in-Chief
John McDuffie, Editorial Director, Associate Pu
Rebecca D. Rinehart, Publisher

A senior psychoanalyst demonstrates the extraordinary impact of a very brief dynamic psychotherapy on a patient in a time of crisis — the terminal illness and death of a spouse. We not only meet the patient and observe the therapy, but our understanding is guided by the therapist's ongoing explanation of the process. He vividly illustrates concepts such as transference, clarification, interpretation, insight, denial, isolation and above all the relevance of understanding the past for changing the present. This unique opportunity to see a psychotherapy as it is conducted will be of immense value for all mental health clinicians and trainees.

2075 Medical Aspects of Chemical Dependency The Neurobiology of Addiction
Hazelden
15251 Pleasant Valley Road
PO Box 176
Center City, MN 55012-176
651-213-4200
800-257-7810
E-mail: info@hazelden.org
www.hazelden.org

Mark Mishek, President, CEO of Hazelden Betty
Nick Motu, VP of Marketing and Communicatio
William C. Moyers, VP of Foundation Relations
James A. Blaha, VP of Finance and Administration

This interactive curriculum helps professionals educate clients in treatment and other settings about medical effects of chemical use and abuse. The program includes a video that explains body and brain changes that can occur when using alcohol or other drugs, a workbook that helps clients apply the information from the video to their own situations, a handbook that provides in-depth information on addiction, brain chemistry and the physiological effects of chemical dependency and a pamphlet that answers critical questions clients have about the medical effects of chemical dependency. Total price of $244.70, available to purchase separately. Program value packages available for $395.00, with 25 workbooks, two handbooks, two video and 25 pamphlets. *$225.00*

ISBN 1-568389-87-6

2076 Mental Health Media
25 West Street
Westborough, MA 01581
617-562-1111
www.www.mentalhealth-media.org

Mental Health Media, formerly The Mental Illness Education Project, is engaged in the production of video-based educational and support materials for the following specific populations: people with psychiatric disabilities, families, mental health professionals, special audiences, and the general public. The videos are designed to be used in hospital, clinical, and educational settings, and at home by individuals and families.

2077 Physicians Living with Depression
American Psychiatric Publishing, Inc.
1000 Wilson Boulevard
Suite 1825
Arlington, VA 22209-3901
703-907-7322
800-368-5777
E-mail: appi@psych.org
www.appi.org

Ron McMillen, Chief Executive Officer
Robert E. Hales MD, M.B.A, Editor-in-Chief
John McDuffie, Editorial Director, Associate Pu
Rebecca D. Rinehart, Publisher

Designed to help doctors see the signs of depression in their fellow physicians and to alert psychiatrists to the severity of the illness in their physician patients, the tape contains two fifteen-minute interviews, one with an emergency physician and one with a pediatrician. *$25.00*

ISBN 0-890422-78-8

2078 Rational Emotive Therapy
Research Press
PO Box 7886
Champaign, IL 61826-9177
217-352-3273
800-519-2707
E-mail: rp@researchpress.com
www.researchpress.com

Robert W. Parkinson, Founder
Dennis Wiziecki, Marketing
Dr Albert Ellis, Author
Arnold Goldstein, Author

This video illustrates the basic concepts of Rational Emotive Therapy (RET). It includes demonstrations of RET procedures, informative discussions and unstaged counseling sessions. Viewers will see Albert Ellis and his colleagues help clients overcome such problems as guilt, social anxiety, and jealousy. Also, Dr. Ellis shares his perspectives on the evolution of RET. *$195.00*

2079 Solutions Step by Step - Substance Abuse Treatment Videotape
WW Norton & Company
500 5th Avenue
New York, NY 10110-54
212-354-2907
E-mail: admalmud@wwnorton.com

Drake McFeely, CEO

Quick tips, questions and examples focusing on successes that can be experienced helping substance abusers help themselves. *$100.00*

ISSN 70260-X

2080 Testing Automatic Thoughts with Thought Records
NewHarbinger Publications
5674 Shattuck Avenue
Oakland, CA 94609-1662
510-652-0215
800-748-6273
E-mail: customerservice@newharbinger.com
www.newharbinger.com

Matthew McKay, Owner

Videotape that helps a client explore the hot thoughts that contribute to depression. *$49.95*

ISBN 1-572243-17-1

Web Sites

2081 Current Psychiatry
American Academy of Clinical Psychiatrists
7 Century Drive
Suite 301
Parsippany, NJ 07054
920-395-2330
www.aacp.com

Jeff Bauer, Editor
Sathya Achia Abraham, Senior Editor
Jason Orzst, Assistant Editor
Kim Leman, Editorial Assistant

Informs members of of news and events. Includes peer-reviewed publications for psychiatric practioners, live educational events, and digital programs.

2082 www.42online.org
Psychologists In Independent Practice - American Psych Assn (APADIP)
E-mail: div42apa@cox.net
www.42online.org

Members of the American Psychological Association engaged in independent practice. Works to ensure that the needs and concerns of independent psychology practitioners are considered by the APA. Gathers and disseminates information on legislation affecting the practice of psychology, managed care, and other developments in the health care industries, office management, malpractice risk and insurance, hospital management. Offers continuing professional and educational programs. Semiannual convention, with board meeting.

2083 www.aacap.org Psychiatry
American Academy of Child and Adolescent Psychiatry
3615 Wisconsin Avenue NW
Washington, DC 20016-3007
202-966-7300
E-mail: communications@aacap.org
www.aacap.org

Warren Y.K. Ng, MD, MPH, President
Tami D. Benton, MD, President-Elect
Debra E. Koss, MD, Secretary
Neal Ryan, MD, Treasurer

Represents over 10,000 adolescent psychiatrists, brochures availible online which provide concise and up-to-date material on issues ranging from children who suffer from depression and teen suicide to stepfamily problems and child sexual abuse.

2084 www.aan.com
American Academy of Neurology
201 Chicago Avenue
Minneapolis, MN 55415
612-928-6000
800-879-1960
E-mail: memberservices@aan.com
www.www.aan.com

Timothy A. Pedley, MD, FAAN, President
Catherine M. Rydell, CAE, Executive Director, CEO

Provides information for both professionals and the public on neurology subjects, covering Alzheimer's and Parkinson's diseases to stroke and migraine, includes comprehensive fact sheets.

2085 www.aapb.org
Association for Applied Psychophysiology and Biofeedback
10200 W 44th Avenue
Suite 304
Wheat Ridge, CO 80033-2840
303-422-8436
800-477-8892
E-mail: info@aapb.org
www.www.aapb.org

David Stumph, Executive Director
Monta Greenfield, Associate Director

Represents clinicians interested in psychopsysiology or biofeedback, offers links to their mission statement, membership information, research, FAQ about biofeedback, conference listings, and links.

Year Founded: 1969

2086 www.abecsw.org
American Board of Examiners in Clinical Social Work
241 Humphrey Street
Marblehead, MA 01945
781-639-5270
800-694-5285
www.www.abecsw.org

Bob Booth, CEO
Robert Booth, Executive Director
Michael Brooks, MSW, BCD, Director of Policy and Business
Kathleen Bodoni, Credentials Manager

Information about the American Board of Examiners, credentialing, and ethics.

2087 www.about.com
About.Com
Network of comprehensive Web sites for over 600 mental health topics.

2088 www.abpsi.org
American Association of Black Psychologists
7119 Allentown Road
Suite 203
Ft. Washington, MD 20744
301-449-3082
E-mail: abpsi@abpsi.org
www.abpsi.org

Donell Barnett, PhD, President
Shawn Jones, PhD, MHS, LCP, Secretary
Rachel Gaiter, MBA, Treasurer

Includes information about the Association's history and objectives, contact and member information, upcoming events, and publications of interest.

2089 www.ama-assn.org
American Medical Association
330 N. Wabash Ave.
Chicago, IL 60611-5885
312-464-4782
www.www.ama-assn.org

James L. Madara, MD, CEO & EVP, Pathology
Tod Askew, SVP, Advocacy
Toni Canda, SVP, HR & Corporate Services
Thomas J. Easley, SVP, Publishing & Mission Ops.

Offers a wide range of medical information and links, full-text abstracts of each journal's current and past articles.

2090 www.apa.org
American Psychological Association
750 First St. NE
Washington, DC 20002-4242
202-336-5500
800-374-2721
TDD: 202-336-6123
TTY: 202-336-6123
E-mail: psycinfo@apa.org
www.www.apa.org

Nadine J. Kaslow, Ph.D., President
Barry S. Anton, Ph.D., President-Elect
Donald N. Bersoff, PhD, JD, Past President
Norman B Anderson, Ph.D., CEO, EVP

Information about journals, press releases, professional and consumer information related to the psychological profession; resources include ethical principles and guidelines, science advocacy, awards and funding programs, testing and assessment information, other on-line and real world resources.

2091 www.apna.org
American Psychiatric Nurses Association
3141 Fairview Park Drive
Suite 625
Falls Church, VA 22042
571-533-1919
855-863-2762
E-mail: inform@apna.org
www.www.apna.org

Leslie G. Oleck, President
Evelyn J. Perkins, Secretary
Kristen Kichefski, Treasurer
Lisa Deffenbaugh Nguyen, MS, Executive Director

Includes membership information, contact information, organizational information, announcements and related links.

2092 www.appi.org
American Psychiatric Publishing Inc
1000 Wilson Boulevard
Suite 1825
Arlington, VA 22209-3901
703-907-7322
800-368-5777
E-mail: appi@psych.org
www.www.appi.org

Ron McMillen, Chief Executive Officer
Robert E. Hales MD, M.B.A, Editor-in-Chief
John McDuffie, Editorial Director, Associate Pu
Rebecca D. Rinehart, Publisher

Informational site about mental disorders, 'Lets Talk Facts' brochure series.

2093 www.apsa.org
American Psychoanalytic Asssociation
309 East 49th Street
New York, NY 10017
212-752-0450
E-mail: info@apsa.org
www.www.apsa.org

Tom Newman, Executive Director

Includes searchable bibliographic database containing books, reviews and articles of a psychoanalytical orientation, links and member information.

2094 www.askdrlloyd.wordpress.com
Ask Dr Lloyd
www.www.askdrlloyd.wordpress.com

Helps individuals understand mental illnesses and addictions, what treatments and services have been proven scientifically effective, how to manage yourself or help your loved one, and how to beat a mental health system.

2095 www.assc.caltech.edu
Association for the Scientific Study of Consciousness
The Associates of the California Institu
1200 East California Boulevard
Pasadena, CA 91125
626-395-3919
E-mail: caltechassociates@caltech.edu
www.associates.caltech.edu

Catherine Reeves, Executive Director
Paula R. Elliott, Associate Director
Jerri Price-Gaines, Associate Director
Nicola Wilkins-Miller, Assistant Director

Electronic journal dedicated to interdisciplinary exploration on the nature of consciousness and its relationship to the brain, congnitive science, philosophy, psychology, physics, neuroscience, and artificial intelligence.

2096 www.blarg.net/~charlatn/voices
Compilation of Writings by People Suffering from Depression

2097 www.bpso.org
BPSO-Bipolar Significant Others
www.www.bpso.org

2098 www.bpso.org/nomania.htm
How to Avoid a Manic Episode

2099 www.cape.org
Cape Cod Institute
Professional Learning Network, LLC
270 Greenwich Avenue
Greenwich, CT 06830
203-422-0535
888-394-9293
E-mail: institute@cape.org
www.www.cape.org

Offers symposia every summer for keeping mental health professionals up-to-date on the latest developments in psychology, treatment, psychiatry, and mental health, outlines available workshops, links and other relevant information.

2100 www.chadd.org
CHADD
4221 Forbes Boulevard
Suite 270
Lanham, MD 20706
301-306-7070
www.www.chadd.org

Patricia M. Hudak, PCC, BCC, President
Rhonda Buckley, Interim CEO
Bob O'Malley, Secretary
Harvey Parker, Founder

National non-profit organization representing children and adults with attention deficit/hyperactivity disorder (AD/HD).

2101 www.cnn.com/Health
CNN Health Section
www.www.cnn.com/Health

Updated with health and mental health-related stories three to four times weekly.

2102 www.compuserve.com
IQuest/Knowledge Index
www.www.compuserve.com

On-line research and database information provider.

2103 www.counselingforloss.com
Counseling for Loss and Life Changes
420 West Main Street
Kent, OH 44240
E-mail: jbissler@counselingforwellness.com
www.www.counselingforloss.com

Jane Vair Bissler, Ph.D., Counselor, Teacher, Writer

Look under articles for reprints of writings and links.

2104 www.cyberpsych.org
CyberPsych
www.www.cyberpsych.org

Hosts the American Psychoanalysts Foundation, American Association of Suicideology, Society for the Exploration of Psychotherapy Intergration, and Anxiety Disorders Association of America. Also subcategories of the anxiety disorders, as well as general information, including panic disorder, phobias, obsessive compulsive disorder (OCD), social phobia, generalized anxiety disorder, post traumatic stress disorder, and phobias of childhood. Book reviews and links to web pages sharing the topics.

2105 www.goaskalice.columbia.edu
GoAskAlice/Healthwise Columbia University
www.www.goaskalice.columbia.edu

Oriented toward students, information on sexuality, sexual health, general health, alcohol and other drugs, fitness and nutrition, emotional wellbeing and relationships.

2106 www.grieftalk.com/help1.html
Grief Journey
800-TAL-

Short readings for clients.

2107 www.healthgate.com/
HealthGate
770-754-4513
www.www.healthgate.com

Max Shapiro, M.D., Doctor
Judith Dennis, M.D., Doctor
Richard Dukes, M.D., Doctor
Steven Richman, M.D., Doctor

On-line reference and database information service, $.75/record.

2108 www.healthtouch.com
Healthtouch Online
3500 Westgate Drive
Suite 504
Durham, NC 27707
919-490-4656
www.www.healthtouchnc.com

Anya Adams, Referral Practitioners
Petra Gustin, Referral Practitioners
Ruth Hamilton, Referral Practitioners
Mara Bishop, Referral Practitioners

Healthtouch Online is a resource that brings together valuable information from trusted health organizations.

2109 www.healthy.net
HealthWorld Online
www.www.healthy.net

Consumer-oriented articles on a wide range of health and mental health topics, including: Welcome Center, QuickN'Dex, Site Search, Free Medline, Health Conditions, Alternative Medicine, Referral Network, Health Columns, Global Calendar, Discussion, Cybrarian, Professional Center, Free Newsletter, Opportunities, Healthy Travel, Homepage, Library, University, Marketplace, Health Clinic, Wellness Center, Fitness Center, News Room, Association Network, Public Health, Self Care Central, and Nutrition Center.

2110 www.helix.com
GlaxoSmithKline
5 Crescent Drive
Philadelphia, PA 19112
888-825-5249
www.gsk.com

Roger Connor, President, Global Manufacturing
Deirdre Connelly, President, North America Pharmac
Abbas Hussain, President, Europe, Japan and EMA
Bill Louv, SVP, Core Business Services

Helix is an Education, Learning and Information exchange. Developed especially for healthcare practitioners by GlaxoSmithKline, HELIX is a premire source of on-line education and professional resources on a range of therapeutic and practice-management issues.

2111 www.human-nature.com/odmh
On-line Dictonary of Mental Health

Global information resource and research tool. It is compiled by Internet mental health resource users for Internet mental health resource users, and covers all the disciplines contributing to our understanding of mental health.

2112 www.infotrieve.com
Infotrieve Medline Services Provider
20 Westport Road
PO Box 7102
Wilton, CT 06897
203-423-2130
E-mail: marketing@infotrieve.com
www.www.infotrieve.com

Kenneth J. Benvenuto, President, CEO
Richard H. Dick Weaver, SVP
Donna Pouliot, VP, Sales
Eileen Green, VP, Finance

Infotrieve is a library services company offering full-service document delivery, databases on the web and a variety of tools to simplify the process of identifying, retrieving and paying for published literature.

2113 www.intelihealth.com
InteliHealth

2114 www.krinfo.com
DataStar/Dialog

Information provider: reference and databases.

2115 www.lollie.com/blue/suicide.html
Comprehensive Approach to Suicide Prevention
E-mail: LollieDotCom@gmail.com

Readings for anyone contemplating suicide.

2116 www.mayohealth.org/mayo
Mayo Clinic Health Oasis Library
4500 San Pablo Road
Jacksonville, FL 32224
904-953-2000
www.www.mayoclinic.org

John H. Noseworthy, M.D., President
Andy Abril, M.D., Rheumatology, Medical Staff
Michael Albus, M.D., Emergency Medicine
Francisco Alvarez, M.D., Pulmonary Medicine

Healthcare library and resources.

2117 www.med.nyu.edu/Psych/index.html
NYU Department of Psychiatry

General mental health information, screening tests, reference desk, continuing educations in psychiatry program, interactive testing in psychiatry, augmentation of antidepressants, NYU Psychoanalytic Institute, Psychology Internship Program, Internet Mental Health Resources links.

2118 www.medscape.com
WebMD Health Professional Network
825 Eighth Avenue
11th Floor
New York, NY 10019
212-301-6700
E-mail: FirstInitialLastName@webmd.net
www.www.medscape.com

Steven L. Zatz M.D., President
Michael B. Glick, EVP, Co-General Counsel
David J. Schlanger, CEO
Peter Anevski, CFO

Oriented toward physicians and medical topics, but also carries information relevant to the field of psychology and mental health.

2119 www.members.aol.com/dswgriff
Now Is Not Forever: A Survival Guide

Print out a no-suicide contract, do problem solving, and other exercises.

2120 www.mentalhealth.com/p20-grp.html
Manic-Depressive Illness

Click on Bipolar and then arrow down to Booklets.

2121 www.mentalhealth.com/story
How to Help a Person with Depression

Valuable family education.

2122 www.mentalhealthamerica.net
Mental Health America
2000 N. Beauregard Street
6th Floor
Alexandria, VA 22311
703-684-7722
800-969-6642
www.www.mentalhealthamerica.net

David L. Shern, Ph.D., Interim President, CEO
Mike Turner, VP, Development
Dianne Felton, Chief Operating Officer
Julio Abreu, Senior Director of Public Policy

Mental Health America is the nation's largest and oldest community-based network dedicated to helping all Americans live mentally healthier lives. With more than 300 affiliates across the country, Mental Health America touches the lives of millions - advocating for changes in policy; educating the public and providing critical information; & delivering urgently needed programs and services.

2123 www.metanoia.org/suicide/
If You Are Thinking about Suicide...Read This First
www.www.metanoia.org/suicide

Excellent suggestions, information and links for the suicidal.

2124 www.mhsource.com
CME Mental Health InfoSource

Mental health information and education, fully accredited for all medical specialties.

2125 www.mhsource.com/
CME Psychiatric Time

Select articles published online from the Psychiatric Times, topics relevant to all mental health professionals.

2126 www.mindfreedom.org
Support Coalition Human Rights & Psychiatry Home Page
454 Willamette, PO Box 11284
Suite 216
Eugene, OR 97440-3484
541-345-9106
877-MAD-PRID
www.www.mindfreedom.org

Celia Brown, Board President
Thomas E. Wittick, MFI Member
Mary Maddock, Founder, MindFreedom Ireland
Al Galves, PhD, Psychologist, Mental Health Cons

Support Coalition is an independent alliance of several dozen grassroots groups in the USA, Canada, Europe, New Zealand; has used protests, publications, letter-writing, e-mail, workshops, Dendron News, the arts and performances. Led by psychiatric survivors, and open to the public, membership is open to anyone who supports its mission and goals.

2127 www.mirror-mirror.org/eatdis.htm
Mirror, Mirror

Relapse prevention for eating disorders.

2128 www.naphs.org
National Association of Psychiatric Health Systems
900 17th Street NW
Suite 420
Washington, DC 20006
202-393-6700
E-mail: nabh@nabh.org
www.naphs.org

Matt J. Peterson, Board Chair
Harsh K. Trivedi, MD, MBA, Board Chair-Elect
Eric H. Paul, Secretary
Frank A. Ghinassi, PhD, ABPP, Treasurer

The NAPHS advocates for behavioral health and represents provider systems that are committed to the delivery of responsive, accountable and clinically effective prevention, treatment and care for children, adolescents and adults with mental and substance use disorders.

2129 www.naswdc.org/
National Associaton of Social Workers
750 First Street, NE
Suite 700
Washington, DC 20002-4241
202-408-8600
800-742-4089
E-mail: press@naswdc.org
www.www.naswdc.org/

Jeane W. Anastas, PhD, LMSW, President
Darrell P. Wheeler, PhD, ACSW, MP, President-Elect
E. Jane Middleton, DSW, MSW, VP
Mary L. McCarthy, PhD, LMSW, Treasurer

Central resource for clinical social workers, includes information about the federation, a conference and workshop calender, information on how to subscribe to social worker mailing lists, legislative and news updates, links to state agencies and social work societies, and publications.

2130 www.ndmda.org/justmood.htm
Just a Mood...or Something Else

A brochure for teens.

2131 www.nimh.nih.gov
National Institute of Mental Health (NIMH)
6001 Executive Boulevard
Room 6200, MSC 9663
Bethesda, MD 20892-9663
866-615-6464
TTY: 866-415-8051
E-mail: nimhinfo@nih.gov
www.www.nimh.nih.gov

The National Institute of Mental Health conducts clinical research on mental disorders and seeks to expand knowledge on mental health treatments.

2132 www.nmha.org
National Mental Health Association
2000 N. Beauregard Street
6th Floor
Alexandria, VA 22311
703-684-7722
800-969-6642
www.www.mentalhealthamerica.net

David L. Shern, Ph.D., Interim President, CEO
Mike Turner, VP, Development
Dianne Felton, Chief Operating Officer
Julio Abreu, Senior Director of Public Policy

Dedicated to promoting mental health, preventing mental disorders and achieving victory over mental illness through advocacy, education, research and service. NMHA's collaboration with the National GAINS Center for People with Co-Occuring Disorders in the Justice System has produced the Justice for Juveniles Initiative. This program battles to reform the juvenile justice system so that the inmates mental needs are addressed. Envisions a just, humane and healthy society in which all people are accorded respect, dignity and the opportunity to achieve their full potential free from stigma and prejudice.

2133 www.oclc.org
EPIC
6565 Kilgour Place
Dublin, OH 43017-3395
614-764-6000
800-848-5878
E-mail: oclc@oclc.org
www.www.oclc.org

Skip Prichard, President, CEO
Rick Schwieterman, EVP, CFO, Treasurer
Bruce Crocco, VP, Library Services for the Ame
Lorcan Dempsey, VP, OCLC Research and Chief Stra

On-line reference and database information provider, $40/hour (plus connection fees) and $.75/record.

2134 www.oznet.ksu.edu/library/famlf2/
Family Life Library
24 Umberger Hall
Kansas State University
Manhattan, KS 66506-3402
785-532-5830
E-mail: orderpub@k-state.edu
www.www.oznet.ksu.edu/library/famlf2/

2135 www.pace-custody.org
Professional Academy of Custody Evaluators
Furlong, PA 18925
800-633-7223
www.pace411.com

Dr. Barry Bricklin, Ph.D., Chair, Founding Member
Dr. Gail Elliot, Ph.D., Vice Chair, Founding Member
John J. Hare, Jr., Treasurer, Secretary

Nonprofit corporation and membership organization to acknowledge and strengthen the professionally prepared comprehensive custody evaluation; psychologicals legal knowledge base, assessment procedures, courtroom testimony, provides continuing education courses, conferences, conventions and seminars.

2136 www.paperchase.com
PaperChase
PO Box 54
Hood, VA 22723
781-325-6086
800-722-2075
E-mail: support@paperchase.com
www.www.paperchase.com

Searches may be conducted through a browsable list of topics, search engine recognizes queries made in natural language.

2137 www.parenthoodweb.com
Blended Families

Resolving conflicts.

2138 www.planetpsych.com
Planetpsych.com
www.www.planetpsych.com

Learn about disorders, their treatments and other topics in psychology. Articles are listed under the related topic areas. Ask a therapist a question for free, or view the directory of professionals in your area. If you are a therapist sign up for the directory. Current features, self-help, interactive, and newsletter archives.

2139 www.positive-way.com/step.htm
Stepfamily Information
www.www.positive-way.com/step.htm

Introduction and tips for stepfathers, stepmothers and re-married parents.

2140 www.psych.org
American Psychiatric Association
1000 Wilson Boulevard
Suite 1825
Arlington, VA 22209-3901
703-907-7322
800-368-5777
E-mail: appi@psych.org
www.www.psych.org

Ron McMillen, Chief Executive Officer
Robert E. Hales MD, M.B.A, Editor-in-Chief
John McDuffie, Editorial Director
Rebecca D. Rinehart, Publisher

A medical specialty society recognized world-wide. Its 40,500 US and international physicians specializing in the diagnosis and treatment of mental and emotional illness and substance use disorders.

384 pages Year Founded: 1993

2141 www.psychcentral.com
Psych Central
www.psychcentral.com

Personalized one-stop index for psychology, support, and mental health issues, resources, and people on the Internet.

2142 www.psychcrawler.com
American Psychological Association
750 1st Street NE
Washington, DC 20002-4242
202-336-5500
800-374-2721
TDD: 202-336-6123
TTY: 202-336-6123

E-mail: psycinfo@apa.org
www.psycnet.apa.org

Nadine J. Kaslow, Ph.D., President
Barry S. Anton, Ph.D., President-Elect
Donald N. Bersoff, PhD, JD, Past President
Norman B Anderson, Ph.D., CEO, EVP

Indexing the web for the links in psychology.

16 pages

2143 www.psychology.com/therapy.htm
Therapist Directory
800-935-3277
www.therapist.psychology.com

Therapists listed geographically plus answers to frequently asked questions.

2144 www.psycom.net/depression.central.html
Dr. Ivan's Depression Central

Medication-oriented site.

2145 www.recovery-inc.com
Recovery

Describes the organizations approach.

2146 www.reutershealth.com
Reuters Health

Relevant and useful clinical information on mental disorders, news briefs updated daily.

2147 www.save.org
SA/VE - Suicide Awareness/Voices of Education
7900 Xerxes Avenue South
Suite 810
Bloomington, MN 55431
952-946-7998
www.www.save.org

Daniel J. Reidenberg, PSY.D.,ÿFA, Executive Director
Francene Young Rolstad, Business Manager
Linda Mars, Events Coordinator
Jennifer Owens, Program Coordinator

Suicide Awareness Voices of Education's mission is to prevent suicide through the elimination of stigma and the organization of education programs designed to raise awareness on depression, mental illnesses, the importance of assessment, treatment and intervention, the warning signs of suicide, and community resources. SAVE also provides resources for those who have been affected by suicide.

2148 www.schizophrenia.com
Schizophrenia.com
E-mail: szwebmaster@yahoo.com
www.www.schizophrenia.com

Brian Chiko, BSc, Executive Director
J. Megginson Hollister, PhD, Editor
Erin Hawkes, MSc, Writer/Contributor
Marvin Ross, Science Writer - Freelance

Offers basic and in-depth information, discussion and chat.

2149 www.schizophrenia.com/ami
Alliance for the Mentally Ill
E-mail: szwebmaster@yahoo.com
www.www.schizophrenia.com

Brian Chiko, BSc, Executive Director
J. Megginson Hollister, PhD, Editor
Erin Hawkes, MSc, Writer/Contributor
Marvin Ross, Science Writer - Freelance

Information on mental disorders, reducing the stigmatization of them in our society today, and how you can be more active in your local community. Includes articles, press information, media kits, mental disorder diagnostic and treatment information, coping issues, advocacy guides and announcements.

2150 www.schizophrenia.com/newsletter
Schizophrenia.com

Comprehensive psychoeducational site on schizophrenia.

2151 www.shpm.com
Self-Help and Psychology Magazine

General psychology and self-help magazine online, offers informative articles on general well being and psychology topics. Features Author of the Month, Breaking News Stories of the Month, Most Popular Pages, What's Hot, Departments, and Soundoff (articles and opinion page). This online compendium of hundreds of readers and professionals.

2152 www.shpm.com/articles/depress
Placebo Effect Accounts for Fifty Percent of Improvement

2153 www.siop.org
Society for Industrial and Organizational Psychology
440 E Poe Rd
Suite 101
Bowling Green, OH 43402
419-353-0032
E-mail: SIOP@siop.org
www.www.siop.org

Tammy Allen, President
David Nershi, Executive Director
Linda Lentz, Administrative Services Director
Larry Nader, IT Manager

Home to the Industrial-Organizational Pyschologist newsletter, links and resources, member information, contact information for doctoral and master's level program in I/O psychology, and announcements of various events and conferences.

2154 www.stepfamily.org/tensteps.htm
Ten Steps for Steps
310 West 85th St.
Suite 1B
New York, NY 10024
212-877-3244
E-mail: Stepfamily@aol.com
www.www.stepfamily.org

Jeannette Lofas, PhD, LCSW, President

Guidelines for stepfamilies.

2155 www.stepfamilyinfo.org/sitemap.htm
Stepfamily in Formation
310 West 85th St.
Suite 1B
New York, NY 10024

212-877-3244
E-mail: Stepfamily@aol.com
www.www. stepfamily.org

Jeannette Lofas, PhD, LCSW, President

2156 www.usatoday.com
USA Today

'Mental Health' category includes news and in-depth reports.

2157 www.webmd.com
WebMD

Kristy Hammam, SVP, Programming and Content Str
Michael W. Smith, MD, Chief Medical Editor
Brunilda Nazario, MD, Lead Medical Editor
Hansa Bhargava, MD, Medical Editor

2158 www.wingofmadness.com
Wing of Madness: A Depression Guide

Accurate information, advice, support, and personal experiences.

Workbooks & Manuals

2159 Activities for Adolescents in Therapy
Charles C Thomas Publisher Ltd.
2600 S 1st Street
Springfield, IL 62704-4730
217-789-8980
800-258-8980
E-mail: books@ccthomas.com
www.ccthomas.com

Michael P Thomas, President
Susan T. Dennison, Author
Connie M. Knight, Author
Richar J. Laban, Author

In this practical resource manual, professionals will find more than 100 therapeutic group activities for use in counseling troubled adolescents. This new edition provides specifics on establishing an effective group program while, at the same time, outlining therapeutic activities that can be used in each phase of a therapy group. Step-by-step instructions have been provided for setting up, planning and facilitating adolescent groups with social and emotional problems. The interventions provided have been designed specifically for initial, middle and termination phases of group. $39.95 *$46.95*

264 pages ISBN 0-398068-07-0

2160 Activities for Children in Therapy: Guide for Planning and Facilitating Therapy with Troubled Children
Charles C Thomas Publisher Ltd.
2600 S 1st Street
Springfield, IL 62704-4730
217-789-8980
800-258-8980
E-mail: books@ccthomas.com
www.ccthomas.com

Michael P Thomas, President
Susan T. Dennison, Author
Connie M. Knight, Author
Richar J. Laban, Author

Provides the mental health professional with a wide variety of age-appropriate activities which are simultaneously fun and therapeutic for the five-to-twelve-year-old troubled child. Activities have been designed as enjoyable games in the context of therapy. Provides a comprehensive listing of books with other therapeutic intervention ideas, bibliotherapy materials, assessment scales for evaluating youngsters, and a sample child assessment for individual therapy. For professionals who provide counseling to children, such as social workers, psychologists, guidance counselors, speech/language pathologists, and art therapists. *$52.95*

302 pages ISBN 0-398069-71-9

2161 Chemical Dependency Treatment Planning Handbook
Charles C Thomas Publisher Ltd.
2600 S 1st Street
Springfield, IL 62704-4730
217-789-8980
800-258-8980
E-mail: books@ccthomas.com
www.ccthomas.com

Michael P Thomas, President
Richar J. Laban, Author
Connie M. Knight, Author
Susan T. Dennison, Author

Provides the entry-level clinician with a broad data base of treatment planning illustrations from which unpretentious treatment plans for the chemically dependent client can be generated. They are simple, largely measurable, and purposefully, with language that is cognizant of comprehension and learning needs of clients. It will be of interest to drug and alcohol counselors. *$39.95*

174 pages ISBN 0-398067-76-7

2162 Clinical Manual of Supportive Psychotherapy
American Psychiatric Publishing, Inc.
1000 Wilson Boulevard
Suite 1825
Arlington, VA 22209-3901
703-907-7322
800-368-5777
E-mail: appi@psych.org
www.appi.org

Ron McMillen, Chief Executive Officer
Robert E. Hales MD, M.B.A, Editor-in-Chief
John McDuffie, Editorial Director, Associate Pu
Rebecca D. Rinehart, Publisher

New approaches and ideas for your practice. *$101.00*

384 pages ISBN 0-880484-03-9

2163 Concise Guide to Laboratory and Diagnostic Testing in Psychiatry
American Psychiatric Publishing, Inc.
1000 Wilson Boulevard
Suite 1825
Arlington, VA 22209-3901
703-907-7322
800-368-5777
E-mail: appi@psych.org
www.appi.org

Ron McMillen, Chief Executive Officer
Robert E. Hales MD, M.B.A, Editor-in-Chief

John McDuffie, Editorial Director, Associate Pu
Rebecca D. Rinehart, Publisher

Basic strategies for applying laboratory testing and evaluation. *$19.50*

176 pages ISBN 0-880483-33-4

2164 Creating and Implementing Your Strategic Plan: Workbook for Public and Nonprofit Organizations
John Wiley & Sons
111 River Street
Hoboken, NJ 07030-5774
201-748-6000
www.wiley.com

Stephen M. Smith, President, CEO
MJ O'Leary, SVP, Human Resources
Edward J. Melando, SVP, Corporate Controller
Gary M. Rinck, SVP, General Counsel

Step-by-step workbook to conducting strategic planning in public and nonprofit organizations. *$30.00*

ISBN 0-787967-54-8

2165 Emotion-Focused Therapy
Professional Resource Press
PO Box 3197
Sarasota, FL 34230-3197
941-343-9601
800-443-3364
E-mail: cs@prpress.com
www.prpress.com

Laurie Girsch, Managing Editor

This book is a guide to Emotion-Focused Therapy (EFT). It gives an overview of the role of emotions in everyday life, the nature of emtions, and the importance of the therapists' own emtional awareness. *$13.95*

96 pages ISBN 0-943158-33-8

2166 Handbook for the Study of Mental Health
Cambridge University Press
40 W 20th Street
New York, NY 10011-4211
212-924-3900

Offers the first comprehensive presentation of the sociology of mental health illness, including original, contemporary contributions by experts in the relevant aspects of the field. Divided into three sections, the chapters cover the general perspectives in the field, the social determinants of mental health and current policy areas affecting mental health services. Designed for classroom use in sociology, social work, human relations, human services and psychology. With its useful definitions, overview of the historical, social and institutional frameworks for understanding mental health and illness, and nontechnical style, the text is suitable for advanced undergraduate or lower level graduate students. *$90.00*

694 pages ISBN 0-521561-33-7

2167 Handbook of Clinical Psychopharmacology for Therapists
NewHarbinger Publications
5674 Shattuck Avenue
Oakland, CA 94609-1662
510-652-0215
800-748-6273

E-mail: customerservice@newharbinger.com
www.newharbinger.com

Matthew McKay, Owner

This newly revised classic includes updates on new medications, and expanded quick reference section, and new material on bipolar illness, the treatment of psychosis, and the effect of severe trauma. *$55.95*

264 pages ISBN 1-572240-94-6

2168 Handbook of Constructive Therapies
John Wiley & Sons
111 River Street
Hoboken, NJ 07030-5774
201-748-6000
www.wiley.com

Stephen M. Smith, President, CEO
MJ O'Leary, SVP, Human Resources
Edward J. Melando, SVP, Corporate Controller
Gary M. Rinck, SVP, General Counsel

Learn techniques that focus on the strengths and resources of your clients and look to where they want to go rather than where they have been. *$64.00*

ISBN 0-787940-44-5

2169 Handbook of Counseling Psychology
John Wiley & Sons
111 River Street
Hoboken, NJ 07030-5774
201-748-6000
www.wiley.com

Stephen M. Smith, President, CEO
MJ O'Leary, SVP, Human Resources
Edward J. Melando, SVP, Corporate Controller
Gary M. Rinck, SVP, General Counsel

Provides a cross-disciplinary survey of the entire field and offers analysis of important areas of counseling psychology activity. the book elaborates on future directions for research, highlighting suggestions that may advance knowledge and stimulate further inquiry. Specific advice is presented from the literature in counseling psychology and related disciplines to help improve one's counseling practice. *$ 120.00*

ISBN 0-471254-58-4

2170 Handbook of Managed Behavioral Healthcare
John Wiley & Sons
111 River Street
Hoboken, NJ 07030-5774
201-748-6000
www.wiley.com

Stephen M. Smith, President, CEO
MJ O'Leary, SVP, Human Resources
Edward J. Melando, SVP, Corporate Controller
Gary M. Rinck, SVP, General Counsel

A comprehensive curriculum to understanding managed care. *$43.00*

ISBN 0-787941-53-0

2171 Handbook of Medical Psychiatry
Mosby
11830 Westline Industrial Drive
Saint Louis, MO 63146-3318
314-872-8370
800-325-4177

This large-format handbook covers almost every psychiatric, neurologic and general medical condition capable of causing disturbances in thought, feeling, or behavior and includes almost every psychopharmacologic agent available in America today. *$61.95*

544 pages ISBN 0-323029-11-6

2172 Handbook of Psychiatric Education and Faculty Development
American Psychiatric Publishing, Inc.
1000 Wilson Boulevard
Suite 1825
Arlington, VA 22209-3901
703-907-7322
800-368-5777
E-mail: appi@psych.org
www.www.appi.org

Saul Levin, M.D., M.P.A., CEO and Medical Director
Jerald Kay, M.D., Co-Editor
Edward K. Silberman, M.D., Co-Editor
Linda Pessar, M.D., Co-Editor

Putting education to work in the real world. *$68.50*

680 pages ISBN 0-880487-80-1

2173 Handbook of Psychiatric Practice in the Juvenile Court
American Psychiatric Publishing, Inc.
1000 Wilson Boulevard
Suite 1825
Arlington, VA 22209-3901
703-907-7322
800-368-5777
E-mail: appi@psych.org
www.www.appi.org

Robert E Hales M.D., M.B.A., Editor-in-Chief
Saul Levin, M.D., M.P.A., CEO and Medical Director
John McDuffie, Associate Publisher, Acquisition
Rebecca D. Rinehart, Publisher

How your practice can work with the court system, so your patients can get the help they need. *$27.95*

212 pages ISBN 0-890422-33-8

2174 Living Skills Recovery Workbook
Elsevier Science
PO Box 28430
Saint Louis, MO 63146-930
314-453-7010
800-545-2522
www.store.elsevier.com

Katie Hennessy, Medical Promotions Coordinator

Provides clinicians with the tools necessary to help patients with dual diagnoses acquire basic living skills. Focusing on stress management, time management, activities of daily living, and social skills training, each living skill is taught in relation to how it aids in recovery and relapse prevention for each patient's individual lifestyle and pattern of addiction.

224 pages ISBN 0-750671-18-1

2175 On the Client's Path: A Manual for the Practice of Brief Solution - Focused Therapy
NewHarbinger Publications
5674 Shattuck Avenue
Oakland, CA 94609-1662

510-652-0215
800-748-6273
E-mail: customerservice@newharbinger.com
www.newharbinger.com

Matthew McKay, Owner

Provides everything you need to master the solution - focused model. *$49.95*

157 pages ISBN 1-572240-21-0

2176 Relaxation & Stress Reduction Workbook
NewHarbinger Publications
5674 Shattuck Avenue
Oakland, CA 94609-1662
510-652-0215
800-748-6273
E-mail: customerservice@newharbinger.com
www.newharbinger.com

Matthew McKay, Owner

Details effective stress reduction methods such as breathing exercises, meditation, visualization, and time management. Widely reccomended by therapists, nurses, and physicians throughout the US, this fourth edition has been substantially revised and updated to reflect current research. Line drawings and charts. *$19.95*

276 pages ISBN 1-879237-82-2

2177 Skills Training Manual for Treating Borderline Personality Disorder, Companion Workbook
Guilford Press
72 Spring Street
New York, NY 10012-4068
212-431-9800
800-365-7006
E-mail: info@guilford.com
www.www.guilford.com

Bob Matloff, President
Seymour Weingarten, Editor-in-Chief

A vital component in Dr. Linehan's comprehensive treatment program, this step-by-step manual details precisely how to implement the skills training procedures and includes practical pointers on when to use the other treatment strategies described. It includes useful, clear-cut handouts that may be readily photocopied. *$27.95*

180 pages ISBN 0-898620-34-1

2178 Step Workbook for Adolescent Chemical Dependency Recovery
American Psychiatric Publishing, Inc.
1000 Wilson Boulevard
Suite 1825
Arlington, VA 22209-3901
703-907-7322
800-368-5777
E-mail: appi@psych.org
www.appi.org

Ron McMillen, Chief Executive Officer
Robert E. Hales MD, M.B.A, Editor-in-Chief
John McDuffie, Editorial Director, Associate Pu
Rebecca D. Rinehart, Publisher

Strategies for younger patients in your practice. *$ 62.00*

72 pages ISBN 0-882103-00-9

2179 Stress Owner's Manual: Meaning, Balance and Health in Your Life
Impact Publishers
PO Box 6016
Atascadero, CA 93423-6016
805-466-5917
800-246-7228
E-mail: info@impactpublishers.com
www.impactpublishers.com

Offers specific solutions: maps, checklists and rating scales to help you assess your life; dozens of stress buffer activities to help you deal with stress on the spot; life-changing strategies to prepare you for a lifetime of effective stress management. *$15.95*

224 pages ISBN 1-886230-54-4

2180 The Comprehensive Directory
Resources For Children with Special Needs
116 E 16th Street
5th Floor
New York, NY 10003-2164
212-677-4650
www.resourcesnyc.org

Rachel Howard, Executive Director
Stephen Stern, Director , Finance and Administr
Todd Dorman, Director, Communications and Out
Helen Murphy, Director, Program and Fund Devel

The directory for everyone who needs to find services for children with disabilities and special needs. Designed for parents, caregivers and professionals, it includes more than 2,500 agencies providing more than 4,000 services and programs. *$30.00*

1200 pages ISBN 0-967836-51-4

2181 Therapist's Workbook
John Wiley & Sons
111 River Street
Hoboken, NJ 07030-5774
201-748-6000
www.wiley.com

Stephen M. Smith, President, CEO
MJ O'Leary, SVP, Human Resources
Edward J. Melando, SVP, Corporate Controller
Gary M. Rinck, SVP, General Counsel

This workbook nourishes and challenges counselors, guiding them on a journey of self-reflection and renewal. *$35.00*

ISBN 0-787945-23-4

2182 Treating Alcohol Dependence: a Coping Skills Training Guide
Guilford Press
72 Spring Street
New York, NY 10012-4068
212-431-9800
800-365-7006
E-mail: info@guilford.com
www.www.guilford.com

Bob Matloff, President
Seymour Weingarten, Editor-in-Chief

Treatment program based on a cognitive-social learning theory of alcohol abuse. Presents a straight-forward treatment strategy that copes with how to stop drinking and provides the training skills to make it possible. *$21.95*

240 pages ISBN 0-898622-15-8

Directories & Databases

2183 AAHP/Dorland Directory of Health Plans
Dorland Health
1500 Walnut Street
Suite 1000
Philadelphia, PA 19102-3512
215-875-1212
855-CAL- DH1
www.dorlandhealth.com

Carol Brault, VP
Yolanda Matthews, Product Manager
Anne Llewellyn, Editor in Chief
Richard Scott, Managing Editor

Paperback, published yearly. *$215.00*

2184 American Academy of Child and Adolescent
Psychiatry - Membership Directory
3615 Wisconsin Avenue NW
Washington, DC 20016-3007
202-966-7300
E-mail: membership@aacap.org
www.aacap.org

Warren Y.K. Ng, MD, MPH, President
Tami D. Benton, MD, President-Elect
Debra E. Koss, MD, Secretary
Neal Ryan, MD, Treasurer

$30.00

179 pages 2 per year

2185 American Network of Community Options and
Resources-Directory of Members
ANCOR
1101 King Street
Suite 380
Alexandria, VA 22314-2962
703-535-7850
E-mail: ancor@ancor.org
www.ancor.org

Barbara Merrill, VP, Public Policy
Renee L Pietrangelo, CEO
Katherine Berland, Director, Government Relations
Tony Yu, Director, Web and I.T.

Covers 650 agencies serving people with developmental disabilities. *$25.00*

179 pages 1 per year

2186 American Psychiatric Association-Membership
Directory
Harris Publishing
2500 Westchester Avenue
Suite 400
Purchase, NY 10577-2515
800-326-6600

$59.95

816 pages

2187 American Psychoanalytic Association - Roster
American Psychological Association
750 1st Street NE
Washington, DC 20002-4242

202-336-5500
800-374-2721
TDD: 202-336-6123
TTY: 202-336-6123
E-mail: webmaster@apa.org
www.apa.org

Nadine J. Kaslow, Ph.D., President
Barry S. Anton, Ph.D., President-Elect
Donald N. Bersoff, PhD, JD, Past President
Norman B Anderson, Ph.D., CEO, EVP

$40.00

194 pages

2188 Association for Advancement of Behavior
Therapy: Membership Directory
305 Seventh Avenue
16th Floor
New York, NY 10001
212-647-1890
www.www.abct.org

Mary Jane Eimer, Executive Director

Covers over 4,500 psychologists, psychiatrists, social workers and other interested in behavior therapy. *$50.00*

240 pages 2 per year

2189 At Health
488 Woody Road
Rogersville, MO 65742
417-241-0553
888-284-3258
E-mail: support@athealth.com
www.athealth.com

Andy Michaels, President
Jill Michaels, Vice President

Providing trustworthy online information, tools, and training that enhance the ability of practitioners to furnish high quality, personalized care to those they serve. For the meantl health consumer, find practitioners, treatment center, learn about disorders and conditions, and about medications being used, news and resources.

2190 CARF International
Rehabilitation Accreditation Commission
6951ÿEast Southpoint Road
Tucson, AZ 85756-9407
520-325-1044
888-281-6531
TTY: 888-281-6531
www.carf.org

Brian J. Boon, Ph.D., President/CEO
Cindy L. Johnson, CPA, Chief Rersource Officer

Covers approx. 3,000 thousand organizations in 7,000 locations offering more than 1,800 hundred medical rehabilitation, behavioral health, and employment and community support services that have been accredited by CARF. *$100.00*

200 pages 1 per year

2191 Case Management Resource Guide
Dorland Health
1500 Walnut Street
Suite 1000
Philadelphia, PA 19102-3512

215-875-1212
855-CAL- DH1
www.dorlandhealth.com

Carol Brault, VP
Yolanda Matthews, Product Manager
Anne Llewellyn, Editor in Chief
Richard Scott, Managing Editor

In four volumes, over 110,000 health care facilities and support services are listed, including homecare, rehabilitation, psychiatric and addiction treatment programs, hospices, adult day care and burn and cancer centers.

5,200 pages 1 per year ISBN 1-880874-84-9

2192 Case Manager Database
Dorland Health
1500 Walnut Street
Suite 1000
Philadelphia, PA 19102-3512
215-875-1212
855-CAL- DH1
www.dorlandhealth.com

Carol Brault, VP
Yolanda Matthews, Product Manager
Anne Llewellyn, Editor in Chief
Richard Scott, Managing Editor

Largest database of information on case managers in US, especially of case managers who work for health plans and health insurers. Covers over 15,000 case managers and includes detailed data such as work setting and clinical specialty, which can be used to carefully target marketing communications. $2500 for full database, other prices available.

2193 Complete Directory for People with Disabilities
Grey House Publishing
4919 Route 22
PO Box 56
Amenia, NY 12501
518-789-8700
800-562-2139
E-mail: books@greyhouse.com
www.greyhouse.com

Richard Gottlieb, President
Leslie Mackenzie, Publisher

This one-stop annual resource provides immediate access to the latest products and services available for people with disabilities, such as Periodicals & Books, Assistive Devices, Employment & Education Programs, Camps and Travel Groups. *$165.00*

1200 pages ISBN 1-592370-07-1

2194 Complete Learning Disabilities Directory
Grey House Publishing
4919 Route 22
PO Box 56
Amenia, NY 12501
518-789-8700
800-562-2139
E-mail: books@greyhouse.com
www.greyhouse.com

Richard Gottlieb, President
Leslie Mackenzie, Publisher

This annual resource includes information about Associations & Organizations, Schools, Colleges & Testing Materi-

als, Government Agencies, Legal Resources and much more. *$195.00*

745 pages ISBN 1-930956-79-7

2195 Complete Mental Health Directory
Grey House Publishing
4919 Route 22
PO Box 56
Amenia, NY 12501
518-789-8700
800-562-2139
E-mail: books@greyhouse.com
www.greyhouse.com

Richard Gottlieb, President
Leslie Mackenzie, Publisher

This bi-annual directory offers understandable descriptions of 25 Mental Health Disorders as well as detailed information on Associations, Media, Support Groups and Mental Health Facilities. *$ 165.00*

800 pages ISBN 1-592370-46-2

2196 DSM-IV Psychotic Disorders: New Diagnostic Issue
American Psychiatric Publishing, Inc.
1000 Wilson Boulevard
Suite 1825
Arlington, VA 22209-3901
703-907-7322
800-368-5777
E-mail: appi@psych.org
www.appi.org

Ron McMillen, Chief Executive Officer
Robert E. Hales MD, M.B.A, Editor-in-Chief
John McDuffie, Editorial Director, Associate Pu
Rebecca D. Rinehart, Publisher

Updates on clinical findings. *$39.95*

2197 Detwiler's Directory of Health and Medical Resources
Dorland Health
1500 Walnut Street
Suite 1000
Philadelphia, PA 19102-3512
215-875-1212
855-CAL- DH1
www.dorlandhealth.com

Carol Brault, VP
Yolanda Matthews, Product Manager
Anne Llewellyn, Editor in Chief
Richard Scott, Managing Editor

An invaluable guide to healthcare information sources. This directory lists information on over 2,000 sources of information on the medical and healthcare industry. *$195.00*

1 per year ISBN 1-880874-57-1

2198 Directory for People with Chronic Illness
Grey House Publishing
4919 Route 22
PO Box 56
Amenia, NY 12501
518-789-8700
800-562-2139
E-mail: books@greyhouse.com
www.greyhouse.com

Richard Gottlieb, President
Leslie Mackenzie, Publisher

This bi-annual resource provides a comprehensive overview of the support services and information resources available for people diagnosed with a chronic illness. Includes 12,000 entries. *$165.00*

1200 pages ISBN 1-592370-81-0

2199 Directory of Developmental Disabilities Services
Nebraska Health and Human Services System
PO Box 94728
Department of Services
Lincoln, NE 68509-4728
402-471-2851
800-833-7352

Covers agencies and organizations that provide developmental disability services and programs in Nebraska.

28 pages

2200 Directory of Health Care Professionals
Dorland Health
1500 Walnut Street
Suite 1000
Philadelphia, PA 19102-3512
215-875-1212
855-CAL- DH1
E-mail: customer@decisionhealth.com
www.dorlandhealth.com

Carol Brault, VP
Yolanda Matthews, Product Manager
Anne Llewellyn, Editor in Chief
Richard Scott, Managing Editor

Helps you easily locate the key personnel and facilities you want by hospital name, system head-quarters, or job title. Valuable for locating industry professionals, recruiting, networking, and prospecting for industry business. *$299.00*

1 per year ISBN 1-573721-40-9

2201 Directory of Hospital Personnel
Grey House Publishing
4919 Route 22
PO Box 56
Amenia, NY 12501
518-789-8700
800-562-2139
E-mail: books@greyhouse.com
www.greyhouse.com

Richard Gottlieb, President
Leslie Mackenzie, Publisher

Best annual resource for researching or marketing a product or service to the hospital industry. Includes 6,000 hospitals and over 80,000 key contacts. *$275.00*

2400 pages ISBN 1-592370-26-8

2202 Directory of Physician Groups and Networks
Dorland Health
1500 Walnut Street
Suite 1000
Philadelphia, PA 19102-3512
215-875-1212
855-CAL- DH1
www.dorlandhealth.com

Carol Brault, VP
Yolanda Matthews, Product Manager

Anne Llewellyn, Editor in Chief
Richard Scott, Managing Editor

Reference tool with over 4,000 entries covering IPAs, PHOs, large medical group practices with 20 or more physicians, MSOs and PPMCs. Paperback, published yearly. *$345.00*

ISBN 1-880874-50-4

2203 Dorland's Medical Directory
Dorland Health
1500 Walnut Street
Suite 1000
Philadelphia, PA 19102-3512
215-875-1212
855-CAL- DH1
www.dorlandhealth.com

Carol Brault, VP
Yolanda Matthews, Product Manager
Anne Llewellyn, Editor in Chief
Richard Scott, Managing Editor

Contains expanded coverage of healthcare facilities with profiles of 616 group practices, 661 hospitals and 750 rehabilitation, subacute, hospice and long term care facilities. *$699.00*

1 per year ISBN 1-880874-82-2

2204 Drug Information Handbook for Psychiatry
Lexicomp Inc.
1100 Terex Road
Hudson, OH 44236-4438
330-650-6506
800-837-5394
www.lexi.com

Steven Kerscher, Owner
Arvind Subramanian, President, CEO, Wolters Kluwer H
Cheri Palmer, Vice President of Commercial Pro
John Pins, Vice President, Finance, Clinica

Written specifically for mental health professionals. Addresses the fact that mental health patients may be taking additional medication for the treatment of another medical condition in combination with their psychtropic agents. With that in mind, this book contains information on all drugs, not just the psychotropic agents. Specific fields of information contained within the drug monograph include Effects on Mental Status and Effects on Psychiatric Treatment. *$38.75*

1 per year ISBN 1-591951-14-3

2205 HMO & PPO Database & Directory
Dorland Health
1500 Walnut Street
Suite 1000
Philadelphia, PA 19102-3512
215-875-1212
855-CAL- DH1
www.dorlandhealth.com

Carol Brault, VP
Yolanda Matthews, Product Manager
Anne Llewellyn, Editor in Chief
Richard Scott, Managing Editor

Delivers comprehensive and current information on senior-level individuals at virtually all US HMOs and PPOs at an affordable price. *$400.00*

2206 HMO/PPO Directory
Grey House Publishing
4919 Route 22
PO Box 56
Amenia, NY 12501
518-789-8700
800-562-2139
E-mail: books@greyhouse.com
www.greyhouse.com

Richard Gottlieb, President
Leslie Mackenzie, Publisher

This annual resource provides detailed information about health maintenance organizations and preferred provider organizations nationwide. *$275.00*

500 pages ISBN 1-592370-22-5

2207 Medical & Healthcare Marketplace Guide Directory
Dorland Health
1500 Walnut Street
Suite 1000
Philadelphia, PA 19102-3512
215-875-1212
855-CAL- DH1
www.dorlandhealth.com

Carol Brault, VP
Yolanda Matthews, Product Manager
Anne Llewellyn, Editor in Chief
Richard Scott, Managing Editor

Contains valuable data on pharmaceutical, medical advice, and clinical and non-clinical healthcare service companies worldwide. *$499.00*

2208 Medical Psychoterapist and Disability Analysts
Americel Board of Medical Psychoterapists & Psychodiagnosticians
4525 Harding Pike
Nashville, TN 37205
615-327-2984
E-mail: americanbd@aol.com

Official newsletter of the American Board of Medical Psychoterapists and Psychodiagnosticians.

2209 Mental Health Directory
Office of Consumer, Family & Public Information
5600 Fishers Lane, Room 15-99
Center For Mental Health Services
Rockville, MD 20857-1
301-443-2792

Covers hospitals, treatment centers, outpatient clinics, day/night facilities, residential treatment centers for emotionally disturbed children, residential supportive programs such as halfway houses, and mental health centers offering mental health assistance. *$23.00*

468 pages

2210 National Association of Psychiatric Health Systems: Membership Directory
900 17th Street, NW
Suite 420
Washington, DC 20006
202-393-6700
E-mail: naphs@naphs.org
www.naphs.org

Mark J. Covall, President, CEO, Executive Direct
Carole Szpak, Director Communications and Oper
Nancy Trenti, JD, Director, Congressional Affairs
Kathleen McCann, RN, PhD, Director, Quality and Regulatory

Contact information of professional groups working to coordinate a full spectrum of treatment services, including inpatient, residential, partial hospitalization and outpatient programs as well as prevention and management services. *$32.10*

48 pages 1 per year

2211 National Register of Health Service Providers in Psychology
1200 New York Avenue NW
Suite 800
Washington, DC 20005-3873
202-783-7663
E-mail: andrew@nationalregister.org
www.nationalregister.org

Greg Hurley, Vice President/Vice-Chair
Judy E Hall, CEO
Andrew P. Boucher, Assistant Director
Julia Bernstein, Membership Coordinator

Psychologists who are licensed or certified by a state/provincial board of examiners of psychology and who have met council criteria as health service providers in psychology.

2212 National Registry of Psychoanalysts
National Association for the Advancement of Psychoanalysis
850 7th Ave
Suite 800
New York, NY 10019
212-741-0515
E-mail: NAAP@NAAP.org
www.naap.org

Patricia Bratt, President

NAAP provides information to the public on psychoanalysis. Publishes quarterly NAAP News, annual Registry of Psychoanalysts. *$ 15.00*

175 pages

2213 Palliative Care & End of Life Issues
Jackson P. Rainer, author

Professional Resource Press
PO Box 3197
Sarasota, FL 34230-3197
941-343-9601
800-443-3364
E-mail: cs@prpress.com
www.prpress.com

Provides a guide to end-of-life practicalities, such as the living will, healthcare power of attorney, and informed consent. *$ 64.95*

524 pages

2214 Patient Guide to Mental Health Issues: Desk Chart
Lexicomp Inc.
1100 Terex Road
Hudson, OH 44236-4438

330-650-6506
800-837-5394
www.lexi.com

Steven Kerscher, Owner
Arvind Subramanian, President, CEO, Wolters Kluwer H
Cheri Palmer, Vice President of Commercial Pro
John Pins, Vice President, Finance, Clinica

Designed specifically for healthcare professionals dealing with mental health patients. Combines eight of our popular Patient Chart titles into one, convienient desktop presentation. This will assist in explaining the most common mental health issue to your patients on a level that they will understand. *$38.75*

1 per year ISBN 1-591950-54-6

2215 PsycINFO Database
PsycINFO, American Psychological Association
750 1st Street NE
Washington, DC 20002-4242
202-336-5500
800-374-2721
TDD: 202-336-6123
TTY: 202-336-6123
E-mail: psycinfo@apa.org
www.apa.org

Nadine J. Kaslow, Ph.D., President
Barry S. Anton, Ph.D., President-Elect
Donald N. Bersoff, PhD, JD, Past President
Norman B Anderson, Ph.D., CEO, EVP

PsycINFO is a database that contains citations and summaries of journal articles, book chapters, books, dissertations and technical reports in the field of psychology and the psychological aspects of related disciplines, such as medicine, psychiatry, nursing, sociology, education, pharmacology, physiology, linguistics, anthropology, business and law. Journal coverage, spanning 1887 to present, includes international material from 1,800 periodicals written in over 30 languages. Current chapter and book coverage includes worldwide English language material published from 1987 to present. Over 75,000 references are added annually through weekly updates.

52 per year

2216 Rating Scales in Mental Health
Lexicomp Inc.
1100 Terex Road
Hudson, OH 44236-4438
330-650-6506
800-837-5394
www.lexi.com

Steven Kerscher, Owner
Arvind Subramanian, President, CEO, Wolters Kluwer H

Cheri Palmer, Vice President of Commercial Pro
John Pins, Vice President, Finance, Clinica

Ideal for clinicians as well as administrators, this title provides an overview of over 100 recommended rating scales for mental health assessment. This book is also a great tool to assist mental healthcare professionals determine the appropriate psychiatric rating scale when assessing their clients. *$38.75*

1 per year ISBN 1-591950-52-X

2217 Roster: Centers for the Developmentally Disabled
Nebraska Department of Health and Human Services
301 Centennial Mall S
Lincoln, NE 68508-2529
402-471-3121
800-254-4202
TDD: 070-119-99
www.dhhs.ne.gov

Joann Erickson RN, Program Manager

Covers approximately 160 licensed facilities in Nebraska for the developmentally disabled.

40 pages 1 per year

2218 Roster: Health Clinics
Nebraska Department of Health and Human Services
301 Centennial Mall S
Lincoln, NE 68508-2529
402-471-3121
800-254-4202
www.dhhs.ne.gov

Joann Erickson RN, Section Administrator

Covers approximately 90 licensed health clinic facilities in Nebraska.

11 pages 1 per year

2219 Roster: Substance Abuse Treatment Centers
Nebraska Department of Health and Human Services
301 Centennial Mall S
Lincoln, NE 68508-2529
402-471-3121
800-254-4202
www.dhhs.ne.gov

Joann Erickson RN, Program Manager

Covers approximately 56 licensed substance abuse treatment centers in Nebraska.

12 pages 1 per year

Publishers

2220 ABC-CLIO
88 Post Road West
Westport, CT 06880-4208
203-226-3571
E-mail: webmaster@greenwood.com
www.www.abc-clio.com/

Wayne Smith, President

Publisher of reference titles, academic and general interest books, texts, books for librarians and other profesionals, and electronic resources.

2221 Active Parenting Publishers
1220 Kennestone Circle
Suite 130
Marietta, GA 30066-6022
770-429-0565
800-825-0060
E-mail: cservice@activeparenting.com
www.ActiveParenting.com

Michael H Popkin,PhD, Founder and President
Gabrielle Tingley, Art Director,Marketing Departmen
Melody Popkin, Manager of Christian Resources
Cathie Jordet, Accounting Manager,Finance Depar

Delivers quality education programs for parents, children and teachers to schools, hospitals, social service organizations, churches and corporate market. Innovator in the educational market.

Year Founded: 1980

2222 American Psychiatric Publishing (APPI)
1000 Wilson Boulevard
Suite 1825
Arlington, VA 22209-3924
703-907-7322
800-368-5777
E-mail: appi@psych.org
www.appi.org

Saul Levin, M.D., M.P.A, CEO and Medical Director
Robert E Hales, M.D., M.B.A, Editor-in-Chief, Books
RebeccaÿD Rinehart, Publisher
John McDuffie, Editorial Director

Publisher of books, journals, and multi-media on psychiatry, mental healths and behavioral science. Offers authoratative, up-to-date and affordable information geared toward psychiatrists, other mental health professionals, psychiatric residents, medical students and the general public.

2223 Analytic Press
10 Industrial Avenue
Mahwah, NJ 07430-2253
201-258-2200

Publishes works of substance and originality that constitute genuine contributions to their respective disciplines and professions.

2224 Brookes Publishing
PO Box 10624
Baltimore, MD 21285-0624
410-337-9580
800-638-3775
E-mail: custserv@brookespublishing.com
www.brookespublishing.com

Jeffrey D. Brookes, President
Melissa A. Behm, Vice President
George Stamathis, Vice President

Publishes highly respected resources in early childhood, early interventions, inclusive and special education, developmental disabilities, learning disabilities, communication and language, behavior, and mental health

Year Founded: 1978

2225 Brookline Books/Lumen Editions
34 University Road
Brookline, MA 02445-4533
617-734-6772

Publishes books on learning disabilities, study skills, self-advocacy for the disabled, early childhood intervention, and more, in readable language that reaches beyond the academic community.

2226 Brunner-Routledge Mental Health
270 Madison Avenue
New York, NY 10016-601
212-695-6599
800-634-7064

Maura May, Publisher

The Routledge imprint publishes books and journals on clinical psychology, psychiatry, psychoanalysis, analytical psychology, psychotherapy, counseling, mental health and other professional subjects.

2227 Bull Publishing Company
PO Box 1377
Boulder, CO 80306-1377
303-545-6350
800-676-2855
E-mail: jim.bullpubco@comcast.net

Emily Sewell, Vice President of Operations
Claire Cameron, Director of Marketing

Publisher of books focused on addressing the growing need for sound health information and good advice.

2228 Cambridge University Press
32 Avenue of the Americas
New York, NY 10013-2473
212-337-5000
www.www.cambridge.org

Printing and publishing house that is an integral part of the University and has similar charitable objectives in advancing knowledge, education, learning and research.

2229 Castal Harlan
150 East 58th Street
New York, NY 10155
212-644-8600
800-775-1800
E-mail: info@castleharlan.com
www.www.castleharlan.com

Leonard M Harlan, Chairman of the Executive Commun
John K Castle, Chairman,CEO
Howard D Morgan, Co-President
William M Pruellage, Co-President

Provides quality information and entertainment services. Worldwide distributor of books, videos, music and games in all disciplines.

Year Founded: 1987

2230 Charles C Thomas Publishers
2600 South First Street
Springfield, IL 62704
217-789-8980
800-258-8980
E-mail: books@ccthomas.com
www.ccthomas.com

Producing a strong list of specialty titles and textbooks in
the biomedical sciences. Also very active in producing
books for the behavioral sciences, education and special
education, speech language and hearing, as well as rehabilitation and long-term care. One of the largest producers of
books in all areas of criminal justice and law enforcement.

Year Founded: 1927

2231 Crossroad Publishing
831 Chestnut Ridge Rd
Spring Valley, NY 10977-6356
212-868-1801
www.cpcbooks.com

Publishes words of thoughtfulness and hope. A leading independent publishing house.

2232 EBSCO Publishing
10 Estes Street
Ipswich, MA 01938-2106
978-356-6500
800-653-2726
www.www.ebsco.com/

Timothy S Collins, President
Daniel Boutchie, Inside Sales Representative
Jeffery Greaves, Inside Sales Representative

EBSCO Publishing offers electronic access to a variety of
health data: full text databases containing aggregate journals, access to publishers' electronic journals, and the
citational databases produced by the American Psychiatric
Association to name just a few. Offers a free,
nonobligation, on-line trial.

2233 Family Experiences Productions
PO Box 5879
Austin, TX 78763-5879
512-494-0338
E-mail: todd@fepi.com
www.fepi.com

R Geyer, Executive Producer

Consumers Health videos; available individually, or in
large volume (private branded) for health providers to give
to patients, professionals, staff. Postpartum Emotions,
Parenting Preschoolers, Facing Death (5-tape series) and
teen grief English and Spanish.

ISSN 1-930772-00-9

2234 Franklin Electronic Publishers
3 Terri Lane
Suite 6
Burlington, NJ 08016-4907
609-386-2500
800-266-5626
www.franklin.com

Barry J Lipsky, CEO

Publishes materials for healthcare.

2235 Free Spirit Publishing
217 Fifth Avenue North
Suite 200
Minneapolis, MN 55401-1299
612-338-2068
866-703-7322
www.freespirit.com

Judy Galbraith, Founder

Publisher of learning tools that support young people's social and emotional health. Known for unique understanding
of what young adults want and need to know to navigate
life successfully.

Year Founded: 1983

2236 Grey House Publishing
4919 Route 22
PO Box 56
Amenia, NY 12501
518-789-8700
800-562-2139
E-mail: books@greyhouse.com
www.greyhouse.com

Richard Gottlieb, President

Publishes over 100 titles including reference directories in
the areas of business, education, health, statistics and demographics, as well as educational encyclopedias and business handbooks. All titles offer detailed information in
well-organized formats. Many titles available online.

Year Founded: 1981

2237 Guilford Publications
72 Spring Street
New York, NY 10012-4068
212-431-9800
800-365-7006
E-mail: info@guilford.com
www.www.guilford.com/

Bob Matloff, President

Publisher of books, periodicals, software and audiovisual
programs in mental health, education, and the social
sciences.

Year Founded: 1973

2238 Gurze Books
5145 B Avenida Encinas
Carlsbad, CA 92008
760-434-7533
800-756-7533
www.www.gurzebooks.com

Lindsay Cohn, Co-Owner
Leigh Cohn, Co-Owner

Publishing company that specializes in resources and education on eating disorders. Offers high quality materials on
understanding and overcoming eating disorders of all
kinds.

Year Founded: 1980

2239 Harper Collins Publishers
10 East 53rd Street
New York, NY 10022-5299
212-207-7000
E-mail: feedback2@harpercollins.com
www.harpercollins.com

Brian Murray, President and CEO
Susan Katz, President/publisher,Harper Colli
Chantal Restivo-Alessi, Chief Digital Officer
Larry Nevins, Executive Vice Preisdent,Operati

A subsidiary of News Corporation, Harper Collins produces literary and commercial fiction, business books, children's books, cookbooks, mystery, romance, reference, religious, healthcare and spiritual books.

Year Founded: 1817

2240 Harvard University Press
79 Garden Street
Cambridge, MA 02138-1400
617-495-2600
800-405-1619
E-mail: contact_hup@harvard.edu
www.www.hup.harvard.edu

William Sisler, President

Publishes material on varied topics including healthcare.

Year Founded: 1913

2241 Hazelden
PO Box 11
Center City, MN 55012-0011
651-213-4200
800-257-7810
E-mail: info@hazelden.org
www.hazelden.org

Mark Mishek, President and CEO,Hazeldon Betty
James A Blaha, VP Finance,Administration/CFO
Marvin D Seppala,MD, Chief Medical Officer
Mark Sheets, Execurive Director,Regional serv

A nonprofit organization that helps people transform their lives by providing the highest quality treatment and continuing care services, education, research, and publishing products available today.

Year Founded: 1949

2242 Health Communications
3201 SouthWest 15th Street
Deerfield Beach, FL 33442-8157
954-360-0909
800-441-5569

Peter Vegso, CEO

Original publisher of informational pamphlets for the recovery community; publishes inspriation, soul/spirituality, relationships, recovery/healing, women's issues and self-help material.

Year Founded: 1977

2243 High Tide Press
Ste 2N
2081 Calistoga Dr
New Lenox, IL 60451-4833
815-206-2054
800-469-9461
www.www.hightidepress.com/

Art Dykstra, Executive Director
Steve Baker, Director

Provides high quality books, training materials and seminars to people working in the field of human services. Seek to provide the best resources in developmental, mental and learning disabilities, as well as psychology, leadership and management.

2244 Hogrefe Publishing
38 Chauncy Street
Suite 485
Boston, MA 02111
866-823-4726
www.www.hogrefe.com

Publisher of journals and books of all different variety titles including healthcare.

2245 Hope Press
110 Mill Run
Monrovia, CA 91016-1658
626-303-0644
800-321-4039
www.hopepress.com

Specializes in the publication of books on Tourette Syndrome, Attention Deficit Hyperactivity Disorder (ADHD, ADD), Conduct Disorder, Oppositional Defiant Disorder and other psychological, psychiatric and behavioral problems.

2246 Hyperion Books
237 Park Avenue
New York, NY 10017
www.hyperionbooks.com

Publishes general-interest fiction and nonfiction books for adults including healthcare titles. Includes the Miramax, ESPN Books, ABC Daytime Press, Hyperion East and Hyperion Audiobooks.

2247 Icarus Films
32 Court Street
21st Floor
Brooklyn, NY 11201
718-488-8900
800-937-4113
E-mail: info@fanlight.com
www.www.icarusfilms.com

Distributor of innovative film and video works on the social issues of our time, with a special focus on healthcare, mental health, profesional ethics, aging and gerontology, disabilites, the workplace, and gender and family issues.

Year Founded: 1978

2248 Impact Publishers
PO Box 6016
Atascadero, CA 93423-6016
805-466-5917
800-246-7228
E-mail: info@impactpublishers.com
www.impactpublishers.com

Produces a select list of psychology and self improvement books and audio-tapes for adults, children, families, organizations, and communities. Written by highly respected psychologists and other human service professionals.

Year Founded: 1970

2249 Jerome M Sattler Publisher
PO Box 1060
La Mesa, CA 91944-1060
619-460-3667
888-815-2898
E-mail: sattlerpublisher@sbcglobal.net
www.sattlerpublisher.com

Publishes books that represent the cutting edge of clinical assessment of children and families. Designed for students in training as well as for practitioners ans clinicians.

2250 John Wiley & Sons

111 River Street
Hoboken, NJ 07030-5774
201-748-6000
www.wiley.com

Peter B Wiley, Chairman of the Board
Stephen M Smith, President and Chief Executive Of
John Kritzmacher, Executive Vice President and CFO
Ellis E Cousens, Executive Vice President and COO

A global publisher of print and electronic products, specializing in scientific, technical, and medical books and journals professional and consumer books and subscription services; also textbooks and other educational materials for undergraduate and graduate students as well as lifelong learners.

2251 John Wiley & Sons, Inc.

111 River Street
Hoboken, NJ 07030-5774
201-748-6000
www.wiley.com

Peter B Wiley, Chairman of the Board
Stephen M Smith, President and Chief Executive Of
John Kritzmacher, Executive Vice President and CFO
Ellis E Cousens, Executive Vice President and COO

Jossey-Bass publishes books, periodicals, and other media to inform and inspire those interested in developing themselves, their organizations and their communities. The publications feature the work of some of the world's best-known authors in leadership, business, education, religion and spirituality, parenting, nonprofit, public health and health administration, conflict resolution and relationships.

2252 Johns Hopkins University Press

2715 North Charles Street
Baltimore, MD 21218-4363
410-516-6900
E-mail: webmaster@jhupress.jhu.edu
www.www.press.jhu.edu/

William Brody, President

Publishes 58 scholarly periodicals and more than 200 new books each year. A leading online provider of scholarly journals, bringing more than 250 periodicals to the desktops of 9 million students, scholars, and others worldwide.

Year Founded: 1878

2253 Lexington Books

4501 Forbes Boulevard
Suite 200
Lanham, MD 20706-4346
301-459-3366
800-462-6420
E-mail: pzline@rowman.com
www.lexingtonbooks.com

Julie E. Kirsch, Vice President/Publisher
Jonathan Raeder, Senior Marketing manager
Kelly Quarrington, Publicity and Advertising

Publisher of specialized new work by established and emerging scholars, including material for the healthcare community.

2254 Lippincott Williams & Wilkins

351 West Camden Street
Baltimore, MD 21201
410-528-4000

Gordon Macomber, CEO

Publishes specialized publications and software for physicians, nurses, students and specialized clinicians. Products include drug guides, medical journals, nursing journals, medical textbooks and medical pda software.

Year Founded: 1998

2255 Love Publishing

9101 East Kenyon Avenue
Suite 2200
Denver, CO 80237-1854
303-221-7333
www.lovepublishing.com

Stan Love, Owner

Publishes books that offer therapy options to children of all ages, adults, and adolescents.

Year Founded: 1968

2256 Mason Crest Publishers

450 Parkway Drive
Suite D
Broomall, PA 19008-4017
610-543-6200
866-627-2665
www.masoncrest.com

Dan Hilferty, President
Louis Cohen, Principal And Creative Director
Michelle Luke, International Rights and Marketi
Becki Stewart, Business Development

Publishes core-related materials for grades K-12. Current catalog includes many titles for health care and mental health curriculums.

2257 New Harbinger Publications

5674 Shattuck Avenue
Oakland, CA 94609-1662
510-652-0215
800-748-6273
E-mail: customerservice@newharbinger.com
www.newharbinger.com

Matthew McKay, Owner
Patrick Fanning, Co-Founder

Publisher of self-help books that teach the reader skills they could use to significantly improve the quality of their lives.

Year Founded: 1973

2258 New World Library

14 Pamaron Way
Nopvato, CA 94949-6215
415-884-2100
800-972-6657
www.newworldlibrary.com

Marc Allen, CEO

Publishes books and audios that inspire and challenge us to improve the quality of our lives and our world.

2259 New York University Press

838 Broadway
3rd Floor
New York, NY 10003-4812

212-998-2575
800-996-6987
E-mail: nyupressinfo@nyu.edu
www.www.nyupress.org

Ellen Chodosh, Director
Eric Zinner, Associate Director
Mary Beth Jarrad, Marketing and Sales Director
Laura Bisberg, Buisness/Finance Director

Publishes approximately 100 new books each year, and enjoys a backlist of over 1500 titles that includes health care and academic materials.

Year Founded: 1916

2260 Omnigraphics
155 West Congress
Suite 200
Detroit, MI 48226
313-961-1340
800-234-1340
E-mail: contact@omnigraphics.com
www.omnigraphics.com

Fred Ruffner, Co-Founder
Peter Ruffner, Co-Founder

Quality reference resources for libraries and schools.

Year Founded: 1985

2261 Oxford University Press
2001 Evans Road
Cary, NC 27513-2010
919-677-0977
800-445-9714
E-mail: custserv.us@oup.com
www.www.global.oup.com/

Publishes works that further Oxford University's objective of excellence in research, scholarship, and education, including titles in the health care and mental health field.

Year Founded: 1896

2262 Penguin Group
345 Hudson Street
New York, NY 10014-4592
212-366-2372
E-mail: librariansden@us.penguingroup.com
www.www.penguin.com/

John Makinson, Chairman and Chief Executive
Coram Williams, Chief Financial Officer
David Shanks, Chief Executive Officer
Susan Petersen Kennedy, President

Publishes under a wide range of prominent imprints and trademarks, among them Berkeley Books, Dutton, Grosset & Dunlap, New American Library, Penguin, Philomel, G.P. Putnam's Sons, Riverhead Books, Viking and Frederick Warne. Includes a variety of titles in health care and mental health subjects.

2263 Perseus Books Group
210 American Drive
Jackson, TN 38301
731-423-1973
800-343-4499
www.www.perseusbooksgroup.com/

Chris Wagner, VP

Titles include science, public issues, military history, modern maternity, health care and mental health.

2264 Princeton University Press
41 William Street
Princeton, NJ 08540-5223
609-883-1759
800-777-4726
www.www.press.princeton.edu/

Peter Dougherty, Director
Martha Camp, Administrative Assistant to the
Patrick Carroll, Associate Director and Controlle
Brigitta van Rheinberg, Assistant Director, Editor in Ch

Independent publisher with close connection to Princeton Unviersity. Fundamental mission is to disseminate through books, journals, and electronic media, with both academia and society at large on a variety of social issues, including health care and mental health.

2265 Pro-Ed Publications
8700 Shoal Creek Blvd
Austin, TX 78757-6897
512-451-3246
800-897-3202
E-mail: feedback@proedinc.com
www.www.proedinc.com/

Donald D Hammill, Owner

Leading publisher of nationally standardized tests, resource and reference texts, curricular and therapy materials, and professional journals covering: speech, language and hearing; psychology and counseling; special education including developmental disabilities, rehabilitation, and gifted education; early childhood intervention; and occupational and physical therapy.

2266 Professional Resource Exchange, Inc.
Professional Resource Press
PO Box 3197
Sarasota, FL 34230-3197
941-343-9601
800-443-3364
E-mail: cs@prpress.com
www.prpress.com

Laurie Girsch, Managing Editor
Jeff Klosterman, President

Publishers of Applied Resources for Mental Health Professionals, including Assessment Instruments and Forensic Psychology materials. Professional Resource Exchange, Inc. (Professional Resource Press) is approved by the APA to offer continuing education (CE) credits. We offer affordable, home-study CE Programs for Psychologists, Marriage & Family Therapists (LMFT), Mental Health Counselors (LMHC), Clinical Social Workers (LCSW), and School Psychologists in Florida and all other states that accept APA-approved CE sponsors.

Year Founded: 1980

2267 Rapid Psychler Press
2014 Holland Avenue
Suite 374
Port Huron, MI 48060-1994
888-779-2453
E-mail: rapid@psychler.com
www.psychler.com

Produces textbooks and presentation graphics for use in mental health education (mainly psychiatry). Products are thoroughly researched and clinically oriented. Designed by students, instructors and clinicians.

2268 Research Press Publishers
PO Box-7886
Champaign, IL 61826
217-352-3273
800-519-2707
E-mail: rp@researchpress.com
www.researchpress.com

Publishes books and videos in school counseling, special education, psychology, counseling and therapy, parenting, death and dying, and developmental disabilities.

Year Founded: 1968

2269 Riverside Publishing
3800 Golf Road
Suite 200
Rolling Meadows, IL 60008
630-467-7000
800-323-9540
E-mail: RPC_Customer_Service@hmhco.com
www.riverpub.com

Dedicated to providing society with the finest professional testing products and services available. Division of Houghton Mifflin Company.

Year Founded: 1979

2270 Rowman & Littlefield
4501 Forbes Boulevard
Suite 200
Lanham, MD 20706-4346
301-459-3366
800-462-6420
E-mail: pzline@rowman.com
www.www.rowman.com

Oliver Gadsby, President and Publisher
Karen Allman, Vice President, Marketing/Sales
Jared Hughes, Senior Marketing Manager
Lindsey Reinstrom, Marketing Manager

Publisher of entertaining and informative books for general readers, as well as academic works by established and emerging scholars, in the areas of Health, Fitness, Sexuality, and Psychology.

2271 Sage Publications
2455 Teller Road
Thousand Oaks, CA 91320-2234
805-499-0721
800-818-7243
E-mail: info@sagepub.com
www.sagepub.com

Sara Miller McCune, Founder,Chairman,Publisher
Blaise R Simqu, President and Chief Exeutive Off
Chris Hickok, Senior VP and Chief Financial Of
Tracey A Ozmina, Executive VP and Chief Operating

An independent international publisher of journals, books, and electronic media, known for commitment to quality and innovation in scholarly, educational and professional markets.

2272 Sidran Traumatic Stress Institute
7238 Muncaster Mill Road
Suite 376
Derwood, MD 20855
410-825-8888
E-mail: admin@sidran.org
www.sidran.org

Esther Giller, President and Director
Ruta Mazelis, Editor, The Cutting Edge/Trainer

Sidran Institute is a leader in traumatic stress education and advocacy. Devoted to helping people who have experienced traumatic life events by publishing books and educational materials on traumatic stress and dissociative conditions.

Year Founded: 1986

2273 Simon & Schuster
1230 Avenue of the Americas
New York, NY 10020
212-698-7000
www.simonandschuster.com

Carolyn Reidy, President and Chief Executive Of
Dennis Ealau, Executive VP,Operations and Chie
Elinor Hirschhorn, Executive VP,Chief Digital Offic
Adam Rothberg, Sr VP,Director of Corporate Comm

Leader in the field of general interest publishing, providing consumers worldwide with a diverse range of quality books and multimedia products across a wide variety of genres and formats, including health care and mental health.

Year Founded: 1924

2274 Springer Science and Business Media
233 Spring Street
New York, NY 10013-1578
212-460-1500
E-mail: service-ny@springer.com
www.www.springer.com/

William Curtis, President
Martin Mos, COO

Develops, manages and disseminates knowledge through books, journals and the internet in a variety of subjects, including health care and mental health.

2275 St. Martin's Press
175 Fifth Avenue
New York, NY 10010
212-674-5151
E-mail: permissions@stmartins.com
www.us.macmillan.com

John Sargent, CEO

Publishes 700 titles a year, including those titles in a variety of health care and mental health subjects.

2276 Taylor & Francis Group
711 3rd Avenue
8th Floor
New York, NY 10017
212-216-7800
800-634-7064
E-mail: beverley.acreman@tandf.co.uk
www.taylorandfrancis.com

Kevin Bradley, CEO

Publishes more than 1000 journals and 1800 new books each year with a books backlist in excess of 20,000 specialty titles. Providers of quality information and knowledge that enable our customers to perform their jobs efficiently, continue their education, and help contribute to the advancement of their chosen markets.

Year Founded: 1936

2277 Therapeutic Resources
PO Box 16814
Cleveland, OH 44116-814
888-331-7114
E-mail: contactus@therapeuticresources.com
www.therapeuticresources.com

Publishers of a variety of titles including ADD/ADHD, Alzheimer/Dimentia, Anger Management, Autism/PDD, Bereavement/Adjustment Disorders, Substance Abuse and more.

2278 Underwood Books
PO Box 1919
Nevada City, CA 95959-1919
800-788-3123
www.underwoodbooks.com

A publisher specializing in fantasy art, science fiction, and self-help/health related titles.

2279 University of California Press
155 Grand Avenue
Suite 400
Oakland, CA 94612-3758
510-883-8232
www.ucpress.edu

Alison Mudditty, Director

Distinguished university press that enriches lives around the world by advancing scholarships in the humanities, social sciences, and natural sciences.

2280 University of Chicago Press
1427 East 60th Street
Chicago, IL 60637-2902
773-702-7700
E-mail: marketing@press.uchicago.edu
www.www.press.uchicago.edu/

Holds an obligation to disseminate scholarship of the highest standard and to publish serious works that promote education, foster public understanding, and enrich cultural life.

Year Founded: 1891

2281 University of Minnesota Press
111 Third Avenue South
Suite 290
Minneapolis, MN 55401-2520
612-627-1970
E-mail: ump@umn.edu
www.upress.umn.edu

Douglas Armato, Director,Administrative
Susan Doerr, Operations Manager,Administrativ
Daniel Oschner, Production Manager
John Henderson, IT Manager

Publisher of groundbreaking work in social and cultural thought, critical theory, race and ethnic studies, urbanism, feminist criticism, and media studies.

Year Founded: 1925

2282 WW Norton
500 Fifth Avenue
New York, NY 10110
212-354-5500
800-233-4830
www.www.wwnorton.com

Drake McFeely, CEO

Publishing house owned by its employees, and publishes books in fiction, nonfiction, poetry, college, cookbooks, art, and professional subjects, including health care and mental health.

2283 Woodbine House
6510 Bells Mill Road
Bethesda, MD 20817-1636
301-897-3570
800-843-7323
E-mail: info@woodbinehouse.com
www.woodbinehouse.com

Irv Shapell, Owner

Publishes special needs books for parents, children, teachers and professionals.

Year Founded: 1985

Facilities

State

Alabama

2284 Taylor Hardin Secure Medical Facility
100 North Union Street
Montgomery, AL 36130-1410
334-242-3454
800-367-0955
E-mail: webmaster@mh.alabama.gov
www.mh.alabama.gov

Michelle Vilamaa, Staff Development Coordinator
Ella White, Staff Development Administrative

Alaska

2285 Alaska Psychiatric Institute
3700 Piper Street
Anchorage, AK 99508-4677
907-269-7100
www.dhss.alaska.gov/dbh/Pages/api/default.aspx

Ronald Adler, CEO
R Duane Hopson MD, Medical Director

In partnership with individuals, their families and the community, natural network and providers, API's Alaska Recovery Center provides therapeutic services which assist individuals to achieve a personal level of satisfaction and success in their recovery.

Arizona

2286 Arizona State Hospital
2500 East Van Buren
Phoenix, AZ 85008-6079
602-244-1331
www.www.azdhs.gov/azsh

John C Cooper, CEO
M Megan Mitscher LMSW, Admissions & Tribal Liaison

The Arizona State Hospital provides specialized psychiatric services to support people in achieving mental health recovery in a safe and respectful environment.

Year Founded: 1887

Arkansas

2287 Arkansas State Hospital
305 South Palm Street
Little Rock, AR 72205
501-686-9000
www.humanservices.arkansas.gov/dbhs/Pages/ArStateHosp
i

Steven Henson, Interim Administrator
Steven Domon, MD, Medical Director
April Coe-Hout, MD, Clinical Director
Hillary Hunt, Internship Training Director

The Arkansas State Hospital is a psychiatric inpatient treatment facility for those with mental or emotional disorders which includes 90 beds for acute psychiatric admission; a 60-bed forensic treatment services program which offers assistance to circuit courts throughout the state; a 16-bed adolescent treatment program for youth 13-18; and a program for juvenile sex offenders.

2288 Center for Outcomes and Evidence
Agency for Healthcare Research and Quality
540 Gaither Road
Suite 2000
Rockville, MD 20850
301-427-1104
www.ahrq.gov

Richard Kronick, Ph.D., Director
Boyce Ginieczki, Ph.D., Acting Deputy Director

Formerly the Center for Outcomes and Effectiveness Research. Conducts and supports research and assessment of health care practices, technologies, processes, and systems.

2289 UAMS Psychiatric Research Institute
4301 West Markham
Suite 605
Little Rock, AR 72205
501-660-7559
E-mail: kramerteresal@uams.edu
www.uams.edu

Combining research, education and clinical services into one facility, PRI offers inpatiend and outpatient services, with 40 psychiatric beds, therapy options, and specialized treatment for specific disorders, including: addictive eating, anxiety, deppressive and post-traumatic stress disorders. Research focuses on evidence-based care takes into consideration the education of future medical personnel while relying on research scientists to provide innovative forms of treatment. PRI includes the Center for Addiction Research as well as a methadone clinic.

California

2290 ANKA Behavioral Health
1875 Willow Pass Road
Suite 300
Concord, CA 94520-2527
925-825-4700
E-mail: info@ankabhi.org
www.www.ankabhi.org

Naja W. Boyd, PsyD, Chief Operating Officer
Chris Withrow, Chief Executive Officer
Nzinga Harrison, Chief Medical Officer
Yolanda Braxton, PsyD, VP of Business Development

Offers comprehensive services and programs designed to promote a client's overall wellness and to attain an enhanced quality of life.

2291 Atascadero State Hospital
10333 El Camino Real
Atascadero, CA 93422-5808
805-468-2009
E-mail: craig.dacus@ash.dsh.ca.gov
www.dsh.ca.gov

Craig Dacus, Public Information Officer
Joyce Ladwig, Human Resources Department

A maximum security forensic hosptial, providing inpatient forensic services for adult males who are court committed throughout the State of California. The staff members of Atascadero State Hospital (ASH) proudly serve the people of the State of California by providing protection for the community, expert evaluations for the courts, and state-of-the-science psychiatric recovery services for individuals referred to us from across the state.

Year Founded: 1954

2292 Campobello Chemical Dependency Treatment Services
3250 Guerneville Road
Santa Rosa, CA 95401-4030
707-579-4066
800-806-1833
www.campobello.org

Jim Cody, Executive Director
Kathy Leigh Willis, Executive Director

Innovative chemical dependency treatment center with the belief in the 12 step self-help programs of Alcoholics Anonymous, Narcotics Anonymous and Al-Anon for friends and family.

2293 Changing Echoes
7632 Pool Station Road
Angels Camp, CA 95222-9620
209-785-3666
800-633-7066
www.changingechoes.com

J R Maughan, Executive Director

Established as a social model chemical dependency facility with the intent to render high-quality treatment for afford- able prices to men and women who suffer from the disease of addiction.

Year Founded: 1989

2294 Department of Mental Health Vacaville Psychiatric Program
1600 California Drive
PO Box 2297
Vacaville, CA 95696-2297
707-449-6504
www.dsh.ca.gov

Victor Brewer, Executive Director

The mission of Vacaville Psychiatric Program is to provide quality mental health evaluation and treatment to in- mate-patients. This is accomplished in a safe and therapeu- tic environment, and as part of a continuum of care.

2295 Exodus Recovery Center
9808 Venice Blvd.
Suite 700
Culver City, CA 90232
310-945-3350
800-829-3923
E-mail: lezlie@exodusrecovery.com
www.exodusrecoveryinc.com

Luana Murphy, MBA, President /Chief Executive Offic
LeeAnn Skorohod, CHC - CCEP, Senior Vice President of Operati
Lezlie Murch, MA, LPCC, Senior Vice President of Program
Grace Lee, MBA, Vice President of Finance

Mission is that we believe that chemically dependent men and women can achieve freedom from the bondage of drugs and alcohol. Teaching patients and their families that the devastation of addiction can be overcome. Produce per- sonal action plans that can produce a lifetime of recovery.

2296 Family Service Agency
123 W Gutierrez Street
Santa Barbara, CA 93101-3424

805-965-1001
E-mail: hr@fsacares.org
www.fsacares.org

Robin Doell Sawaske, Co-President
Terri Suniga, Co-President
Lisa Brabo, Ph.D., Executive Director
Denise Cicourel, MAOM, Director of Administration

A non-profit human service agency whose programs help people help themselves. FSA services prevent family breakdown, intervene effectively where problems are known to exist and help individuals and families build on existing strengt

Year Founded: 1899

2297 Fremont Hospital
Psychiatric Solutions
39001 Sundale Drive
Fremont, CA 94538-2005
510-796-1100
www.fremonthospital.com

Joey A Jacobs, President/CEO/Chairman

A private, modern 96-bed behavioral healthcare facility that provides services to adolescents (ages 12-17) and adults.

2298 Life Steps Pasos de Vida
1431 Pomeroy Road
Arroyo Grande, CA 93420-5943
805-481-2505
800-530-5433
www.lifestepsfoundation.org

Sue Horowitz, President
Virginia Franco, Founder/CEO
Allen C Haile, Secretary

Develops innovative programs that target underserved pop- ulations. Goal is to help participants develop healthy life- styles free of alcohol and drugs.

2299 Lincoln Child Center
4368 Lincoln Avenue
Oakland, CA 94602-2529
510-531-3111
www.lincolncc.org

Diana Netherton, Chairman
Christine Stoner-Mertz, President/CEO
Peggy Padilla, Chief Administrative Officer
Allison Becwar, Chief Program Officer

Enables vulnerable and emotionally troubled children and their families to lead independent and fulfilling live

2300 Mental Health Association of Orange County
822 Town & Country Road
Orange, CA 92868
714-547-7559
www.mhaoc.org

Dedicated to improving the quality of life of Orange County residents impacted by mental illness through direct service, advocacy, education and information dissemination.

Year Founded: 1958

2301 Metropolitan State Hospital
11401 Bloomfield Avenue
Norwalk, CA 90650-2015

562-863-7011
TDD: 562-863-1743
www.dsh.ca.gov

Sharon Smith Nevins, Executive Director

The mission of Metropolitan State Hospital is to work in partnership with individuals to assist in their recovery by using rehabilitation services as their tool, thus preparing clients for community living.

Year Founded: 1915

2302 Napa State Hospital

2100 Napa-Vallejo Highway
Napa, CA 94558-6293
707-253-5000
TDD: 707-253-5768
E-mail: nshcontact@dmhnsh.state.ca.us
www.dsh.ca.gov

Jennifer Marshall CTRS, RTC, Chief, Rehabilitation Therapy

Napa State Hospital provides treatment and support to adults with serious mental illness, and assists each individual in achieving his/her highest potential for independence and quality of life, leading to recovery and integrating safely and successfully into society.

2303 New Life Recovery Centers

782 Park Avenue
Suite 1
San Jose, CA 95126-4800
408-297-1182
866-894-6572
www.newliferecoverycenters.com

Kevin Richardson, President
Gary Ruble, Founder

Strives to provide our clients with the very best services available. We value our employees as our greatest asset, while collectively and continuously working to adopt and implement the latest and most effective medical, clinical, and social model treatment modalities.

Year Founded: 2004

2304 Northridge Hospital Medical Center

18300 Roscoe Boulevard
Northridge, CA 91328
818-885-8500
www.northridgehospital.org

Mike Wall, President, CEO

Northridge Hospital Medical Center offers a comprehensive Behavioral Health program for both adults and adolescents. Founded in 1955.

2305 PacifiCare Behavioral Health PO Box 31053 Laguna Hills, CA 92654-1053

800-999-9585

Richard J Kelliher PsyD, Clinical Director

Provides behavioral health services to children, adolescents, adults, and seniors.

2306 Patton State Hospital
California Department of Mental Health

3102 E Highland Avenue
Patton, CA 92369
909-425-7000
TDD: 909-862-5730

E-mail: cbarrett@dmhpsh.state.ca.us
www.dsh.ca.gov

Harry Oreol, Executive Director
Nitin Kulkarni, Medical Director
Angela Fiore, Forensic Services Manager
Nancy Verela, Director, Human Resources

Patton State Hospital's mission is to empower forensic and civilly committed individuals to recover from mental illness utilizing Recovery principles and evidenced based practices within a safe, structured, and secure environment.

2307 Phoenix Programs Inc

90 E. Leslie Lane
Columbia, MO 65202-1535
573-442-3830
www.www.phoenixprogramsinc.org

Nelly Roach, President
Brock Bukowsky, Vice President/Treasurer
Deborah Beste, Executive Director
Rhiannon Pearson, Chief Financial Officer

Offers an array of services and programs designed to promote overall wellness while making it possible for all to obtain a higher quality of life.

2308 Presbyterian Intercommunity Hospital Mental Health Center

12401 Washington Boulevard
Whittier, CA 90602-1006
562-698-0811
TDD: 562-696-9267
TTY: 562-696-9267
www.www.pihhealth.org

Kenton Woods, Chair
Rich Atwood, Vice Chair
Efrain Aceves, Secretary
Jane Dicus, Treasurer

Offers an inpatient program for those with a variety of mental disorders.

Year Founded: 1959

2309 Twin Town Treatment Centers

4388 E Katella Avenue
Los Alamitos, CA 90720-3565
562-596-0050
www.twintowntreatmentcenters.com

David Lisonbee, President, CEO
Tiran Davidi-Durian, CFO
Ted Williams, MD, ASAM, Medical Director
Debbie Muehl, CATC II, Supervising Counselor

Mission is to introduce new solutions for people who find that chemically induced coping no longer works.

Colorado

2310 Centennial Mental Health Center

211 W Main Street
Sterling, CO 80751-3168
970-522-4392
E-mail: webmaster@centennialmhc.org
www.centennialmhc.org

Daniel D Hammond, Manager

A non-profit organization dedicated to providing the highest quality comprehensive mental health services to the rural communities of northeastern Colorado.

2311 Colorado Mental Health Institute at Fort Logan
3520 West Oxford Avenue
Denver, CO 80236-3108
303-866-7066
www.colorado.gov

Keith Lagrenade, CEO

The mission of the Colorado Mental Health Institute at Fort Logan is to provide the highest quality mental health services to persons of all ages with complex, serious and persistent mental illness within the resources available.

2312 Colorado Mental Health Institute at Pueblo
1600 West 24th Street
Pueblo, CO 81003-1411
303-866-5700

John De Quardo, Administrator

Provides quality mental health services focused on sustaining hope and promoting recovery.

2313 Emily Griffith Center
1724 Gilpin Street
Denver, CO 80218
303-237-6865
www.www.griffithcenters.org

Howard Shiffman, CEO
Beth Miller, Deputy Director/COO
John Smrcka, Program Director

Provides troubled children the environment and opportunities to become healthy, participating and productive members of society.

Connecticut

2314 Daytop Residential Services Division
425 Grant Street
Bridgeport, CT 06610-3222
203-337-9943

David Parachini, Chairperson
Janet Ryan, Vice Chairperson
Peter Loomis, Treasurer
Jay Broderick, Secretary

Long-term substance abuse treatment facility based on the Therapeutic Community model. Combines current research and treatment methods with traditional therapeutic community concepts.

Year Founded: 1970

2315 Jewish Family Service
733 Summer Street
Suite 602
Stamford, CT 06901-1035
203-921-4161
www.www.ctjfs.org/

Michael Alexanderÿ, President
Matt Greenberg, CEO
Iris Morrison, Associate Executive Director
Saul Cohen, Vice President

Offers a wide range of innovative programs designed to address contemporary problems and issues through counseling and therapy, crisis intervention, Jewish Family Life Education, Depression, Aging and senior mental health, Obsessions and compulsions.

Year Founded: 1978

2316 Klingberg Family Centers
370 Linwood Street
New Britain, CT 06052-1998
860-832-5504
www.klingberg.org

Lynne V. Roe, Director of Intake

To uphold, preserve and restore families in a therapeutic environment, valuing the absolute worth of every child, while adhering to the highest ethical principles in accordance with our Judaeo-Christian heritage.

2317 McCall Foundation
58 High Street
PO Box 806
Torrington, CT 06790-806
860-496-2100
www.www.mccall-foundation.org

D'Arcy Lovetere, President
Roxanne Bachand, Vice President
Marie Wallace, Secretary/Treasurer

Provides outpatient, partial hospital, intensive outpatient, residential, parenting and prevention programs for substance abusers and/or their family members; and helps to reduce area substance abuse in the local community. Funding is provided by the United Way.

2318 Mountainside Treatment Center
187 South Canaan Road
Route 7
Canaan, CT 06018-717
860-824-1397
800-762-5433
E-mail: admissions@mountainside.org
www.mountainside.org

Maureen O'Neill Biggs, LPC, LA, Clinical Director
Brittanie Decker, Continuing Care Case Manager
Bruce Dechert, LADC, ICADC, Director, Family Wellness
Susan Watso, CAC, Extended Care Counselor

Program is based on strategies and principles that promote healing and enhance the quality of life. Through the utilization of Motivational Interviewing, Directional Therapy, Gender-Specific Groups, the 12-Step Principles and Adventure Based Initiatives, individuals qwill encounter, confront and experience the challenges of recovery.

Year Founded: 1998

2319 Silver Hill Hospital
208 Valley Road
New Canaan, CT 06840-3899
203-966-1380
800-899-4455
www.silverhillhospital.org

Siguard Ackerman, President and Medical Director
Elizabeth Moore, Chief Operating Officer
Ruurd Leegstra, JD, CPA, Chief Financial Officer
Missy Fallon, Chief Development Officer

A nationally recognized, independent, not-for-profit psychiatric hospital that is focused exclusively on providing patients the best possible treatment of psychiatric illnesses and substance use disorders, in the best possible environment.

Year Founded: 1931

2320 Yale University School of Medicine: Child Study Center
230 S Frontage Road
New Haven, CT 06519-1124
203-785-2540
www.www.childstudycenter.yale.edu/index.aspx

Fred R Volkmar, MD, Director

Provides a comprehensive range of in-depth diagnostic and treatment services for children with psychiatric and developmental disorders. These services include specialized developmental evaluations for children ages zero-four, and psychological and psychiatric evaluations for children 5-18. Individualized treatment plans following evaluation make use for a range of theraputic interventions, including psychotherapy, group therapy, family therapy, psycho-pharmacological treatment, parent counseling, consultation and service planning. Immediate access for children needing to be seen within 24 hours and walk-in service is also available.

Florida

2321 Archways-A Bridge To A Brighter Future
919 NE 13th Street
Fort Lauderdale, FL 33304-2009
954-763-2030
E-mail: intake@archways.org
www.archways.org

Andrea Katz, CEO

A not-for-profit, privately-governed organization whose mission is to provide quality comprehensive behavioral health care to individuals and families who are in need of improving their quality of life.

2322 Fairwinds Treatment Center
1569 South Fort Harrison
Clearwater, FL 33756-2004
727-449-0300
800-226-0300
E-mail: fairwinds@fairwindstreatment.com
www.fairwindstreatment.com

Jess Loven, Clinical Director, CAP
Thomas H Lewis, Clinical Director

As a dually licensed psychiatric and substance abuse center, reaches far beyond standard treatment to offer medical services for substance abuse, eating disorders, and emotional/mental health issues.

2323 First Step of Sarasota
4579 Northgate Court
Sarasota, FL 34234
941-366-5333
800-266-6866
E-mail: gethelp@fsos.org
www.www.fsos.org/

Richard Carlson, Chair
Peter Abbott, Vice Chair
Elizabeth LaBoone, Secretary

Provides high quality, affordable substance abuse treatment and recovery programs on Florida's Gulf Coast. Offers a variety of programs including a medical detox, residential and outpatient services for adolescents, adults and families.

Year Founded: 1967

2324 Florida State Hospital
1317 Winewood Blvd.
Building 1, Room 202
Tallahassee, FL 32399-0700
850-487-1111
www.www.myflfamilies.com

Diane James, Administrator

FSH provides person-centered treatment and rehabilitations in order to propel the client toward their personal recovery and to prepare for roles and environments that have personal and social value.

Year Founded: 1876

2325 Gateway Community Services
555 Stockton Street
Jacksonville, FL 32204-2597
904-387-4661
E-mail: info@gatewaycommunity.com
www.gatewaycommunity.com

Candace Hodgkins, Ph.D., LMHC, President/Chief Executive Office
Laura Dale, CFO
Randy Jennings, Sr VP Operations
Dr. Yvonne Kennedy, Senior Vice President of Profess

Provides a full continuum of care that delivers effective treatment and rehabilitation services to individuals suffering from alcoholism, substance abuse and related mental health problems.

2326 Genesis House Recovery Residence
4865 40th Way South
Lake Worth, FL 33461-5301
561-439-4070
800-737-0933
E-mail: info@genesishouse.net
www.genesishouse.net

James Dodge, Founder/CEO
Kathryn Shafer, Clinical Director

Works closely with both local and out of state courts. Provides the suffering person with a safe, secure, professional environment to glean the care, answers and support they so desperately need in their lives.

2327 Manatee Glens
391 6th Avenue W
Bradenton, FL 34205-8820
941-782-4299
E-mail: Sondra.Guffey@manateeglens.org
www.www.manateeglens.org/

Paul M Duck, Chair
Mary Ruiz, CEO/President
Deborah Kostroun, COO
Thomas P Nolan, Vice Chair

Helps families in crisis with mental health and addictions services and supports the community through prevention and recovery.

2328 New Horizons of the Treasure Coast
4500 W Midway Road
Ft Pierce, FL 34981-4823
772-468-5600
888-468-5600
www.nhtcinc.org

John Wolsiefer, Chairman
Garry Wilson, Vice Chair

Robert Zomok, Treasurer
Patricia Austin-Novak, Secretary

To improve the quality of life in the community through the provision of accessible, person-centered behavioral health resources.

Year Founded: 1958

2329 North Florida Evaluation and Treatment Center

1200 NE 55th Boulevard
Gainesville, FL 32641-2759
352-375-8484
www.www.dcf.state.fl.us/facilities/nfetc/

William Baxter, Administrator

Dedicated to serving you while fulfilling our responsibilities for safety, security and a positive, caring environment.

Year Founded: 1976

2330 North Star Centre

9033 Glades Road
Boca Raton, FL 33434-3939
561-361-0500
E-mail: inquiry@northstar-centre.com
www.northstar-centre.com

Ira Kaufman, Executive Director
Randi Katz, Administrative Assistant

A uniquely comprehensive facility dedicated to restoring your sense of emotional and physical well being.

2331 Northeast Florida State Hospital

7487 South State Road 121
MacClenny, FL 32063-5480
904-259-6211

Joe Infantino, Administrator
Rufus Johnson, Evening Administrator

To provide comprehensive mental health treatment services to ensure a timely transition to the community.

Year Founded: 1959

2332 Renaissance Manor

509 Berry Street
Punta Gordaÿ, FL 33950
941-916-9621
www.www.renaissancemanor.org/

Heather Eller, Administrator

Community based assisted living facility with a limited mental health license, specializes in serving adults with neuro-biological disorders and mood disorders along with other special mental health needs. Our not-for-profit organization is a program designed to encourage positive mental health while meeting the various interest of our residents.

2333 Seminole Community Mental Health Center

237 Fernwood Blvd
Fern Park, FL 32730-2116
407-831-2411

Jim Berko, Manager

A private, nonprofit organization whose goal is to provide comprehensive, biopsychosocial rehabilitation programming in the areas of mental health and substance abuse.

2334 Starting Place

351 North State Road 7
Suite 200
Plantation, FL 33317
954-327-4060

Dr. Tammy Tucker, Chair
Marsha L. Currant, M.S.W,, CEO

Improves the lives through education, treatment and support services related to substance abuse, mental illness and co-occurring disorders

2335 The Transition House

3800 5th Street
St Cloud, FL 34769
407-892-5700
www.thetransitionhouse.org

Thomas Griffin, PhD, Chief Executive Officer
Jennifer R. Dellasanta, ICADC, CAP, Chief Operating Officer
Jeffrey Wainwright, Director of Work Release Program
Brett ms D'Aoust, MSW, CAP, Executive Director of Correction

The adress above is the men's house. The address for the women's house is: 505 N Clyde Street Kissimmee, FL 34741. All other information is the same. Mission is to provide a milieu of comprehensive educational, health, prevention and human services to Central Florida's most disenfranchised populations.

Year Founded: 1993

Georgia

2336 Central State Hospital

620 Broad Street
Milledgeville, GA 31062-7525
478-445-4128
www.dbhdd.georgia.gov

Dan Howell, Regional Hospital Administrator
Kay Brooks, Chief Nurse Executive
Lee Ann Molini, Director of Nursing

2337 Georgia Regional Hospital at Atlanta

Two Peachtree Street, N.W.
24th Floor
Atlanta, GA 30303
404-657-2252
www.dbhdd.georgia.gov

Susan Trueblood, CEO
Gwen Skinner, Director

Located on 174 Acres in DeKalb County, Georgia Regional Hospital/Atlanta operates 366 licensed, accredited inpatient beds in five major program areas: Adult Mental Health, Adolescent Mental Health, Child Mental Health, Forensic Services, and Developmental Disabilities. In addition, GRH/Atlanta also offers inpatient and outpatient Dental Services and an Outpatient Forensic Evaluation Program for juveniles and adults. Finally, GRH/Atlanta operates the Fulton County Collaborative Crisis Service System which provides mobile crisis and residential services to adults experiencing mental health problems in Fulton County.

2338 Georgia Regional Hospital at Augusta

3405 Mike Padgett Highwayÿ
Augusta, GA 30906-3897
706-792-7000

Ben Waker EdD, Contact

2339 Georgia Regional Hospital at Savannah
1915 Eisenhower Drive
Savannah, GA 31406
912-356-2011
www.www.garegionalsavannah.com/

Douglas Osborne, Contact

2340 Southwestern State Hospital
400 Pinetree Boulevard
PO Box 1378
Thomasville, GA 31792-1378
229-227-2850

Hillary Hooyou, Manager

Provides extensive behavioral healthcare services in community and hospital settings, including: residential MRDD services; inpatient, residential and case management psychiatric services; and residential care for dual-diagnosed persons.

2341 West Central Georgia Regional Hospital
3000 Schatulga Road
Columbus, GA 31907
706-568-5000
E-mail: wcgrh@dhr.state.ga.us
www.dbhdd.georgia.gov/

Mission is to treat customers with respect and dignity while providing comprehensive, person-centered behavioral healthcare.

Year Founded: 1974

Idaho

2342 Children of Hope Family Hospital
PO Box 1829
Boise, ID 83701-1829
208-703-8688
www.childofhope.org

Rev Anthony R Harper PhD, Founder
Craig Hardesty, M.B.A., Treasurer
Penny Nygaard, Secretary

Illinois

2343 Advocate Ravenswood Hospital Medical Center
3075 Highland Parkway Suite 600
Downers Grove, IL 60515
630-572-9393
www.advocatehealth.com

Kelly Jo Golson, CMO, Public Affairs & Marketing
Linda Williger, Manager, Public Affairs & Market
Vincent Pierri, Manager, Public Affairs & Market
Sarah Scroggins, Coordinator, Public Affairs & Ma

Provides a comprehensive array of services for inpatient (Adult, Adolescent, Substance Abuse), Partial Hospital, Intensive Outpatient, Psychological Rehabilitation, Emergency-Crisis, Assertive Community Outreach, Case Management, Program for Deaf and Hard of Hearing at multiple sites on the Northside of Chicago.

2344 Alexian Brothers Bonaventure House
825 W Wellington Avenue
Chicago, IL 60657-9249

773-327-9921
www.www.alexianbrothershousing.org/

Bart Winters, CEO
Marty Hansen, Director Programs/Services

Offers adult men and women with HIV/AIDS-who are homeless or at-risk for homelessness- a chance to rebuild and reclaim their lives. Bonaventure House has a wide array of on-site supportive services-case management, occupational therapy, recovery, and spiritual care-most residents are able to return to independent life in the community within a 24-month period.

2345 Alton Mental Health Center
4500 College Avenue
Alton, IL 62002-5099
618-474-3273
www.illinois.gov

Susan Shobe, Administrator

2346 Andrew McFarland Mental Health Center
901 Southwind Road
Springfield, IL 62703-5125
217-786-6900

Karen Schweighart, Administrator

2347 Delta Center
1400 Commercial Avenue
Cairo, IL 62914-1978
618-734-3626
TTY: 618-734-1350
www.deltacenter.org

Lisa Tolbert, Executive Director

A non-profit mental health center, substance abuse counseling facility, and also provides various community services to Alexander and Pulaski County, Illinois

2348 FHN Family Counseling Center
421 W Exchange Street
Freeport, IL 61032-4008
815-599-6900
www.www.fhn.org/

Lisa Mahoney, VP

2349 Habilitative Systems
415 S Kilpatrick Avenue
Chicago, IL 60644-4958
773-854-1680
TDD: 773-854-8364
E-mail: hsi@habilitative.org
www.www.habilitative.org

Donald Dew, President
Joyce Wade, VP Finance
Karen Barbee-Dixon, EdD, COO

To provide integrated human services to children, adults, families, and persons with disabling conditions that help them to achieve their highest level of self-sufficiency

Year Founded: 1978

2350 John R Day and Associates
3716 W Brighton Avenue
Peoria, IL 61615-2938
309-692-7755
www.christianpsychological.org

John R Day, Partner

Year Founded: 1974

2351 Keys To Recovery
100 North River Road
Des Plaines, IL 60016-1209
847-298-9355
www.www.reshealth.org

Philip Kolski, Director
Debra Ayanian, Nurse Manager

A leading Alcoholism and Drug Treatment Center in the
Midwest, providing innovative and effective Alcoholism
and Drug Treatment.

2352 MacNeal Hospital
3249 S. Oak Park Avenue
Berwyn, IL 60402
708-783-9100
888-622-6325
TTY: 708-783-3058
www.www.macneal.com/

Randall K Mc Givney, Program Director
Davis Yang, Center Director
John Gong, Clinical Faculty
Edward C Foley MD, Director Of Research

The MacNeal Family Practice Residency Program was one
of the first family practice programs in the country and the
first in Illinois. We have continue a progressive tradition in
all aspects of our curriculum. Our program is at the forefront of contemporary family medicine offering diverse academic and clinical opportunites and building on the
innovative ideas of our residents.

2353 McHenry County Mental Health Board
620 Dakota Street
Crystal Lake, IL 60012-3732
815-455-2828
www.mc708.org

To Provide leadership and ensure the prevention and treatment of mental illness, developmental disabilities and
chemical abuse by coordinating, developing and contract-
ing for quality services for all citizens of McHenry County,
Illinois. This is not a provider organization.

2354 Pfeiffer Treatment Center and Health Research Institute
3S 721 West Ave
Warrenville, IL 60555-4039
630-505-0300
866-504-6076
E-mail: info@hriptc.org
www.hriptc.org

Scott Filer, MPH, Executive Director
Allen Lewis MD, Medical Director
William Walsh, PhD, Research/Found Dir/Co-Founder

A not-for-profit, outpatient medical facility for children,
teens and adults seeking a biochemical assessment and
treatment for their symptons caused by a biochemical im-
balance, or to support health and promote wellness. PTC
physician precribes individualized program of vitamins,
minerals, and amino acids to address the patient's unique
biochemical needs. Common conditions: anxiety, ADHA,
autism spectrum disorder, post traumatic stress syndrome,
depression, bipolar disorder, schozophrenia and
Alzheimer's disease.

2355 Riveredge Hospital
8311 W Roosevelt
Forest Park, IL 60130-2500
708-771-7000
www.riveredgehospital.com

Carey Carlock, CEO
Lucyna Puszkarska, MD, Medical Director
Sheila Orr, JD, RN, Chief Nursing Officer and Chief
Ginny Trainor, LCSW, CADC, Director of Business
Development

Striving to foster an environment that demonstrates compassion and caring with timely and effective communication through comprehensive behavioral health care services
of clinical excellence.

2356 Sonia Shankman Orthogenic School
1365 E 60th Street
Chicago, IL 60637-2890
773-702-1203
www.orthogenicschool.uchicago.edu

Henry J Roth PhD, Executive Director

A coeducational residential treatment program for children
and adolescents in need of support for emotional issues
which cause the student to act in disruptive ways and experience unfulfilling social and educational experiences

Year Founded: 1915

2357 Stepping Stones Recovery Center
1621 Theodore Street
Joliet, IL 60435-1958
815-744-4555
E-mail: info@steppingstonestreatment.com
www.steppingstonestreatment.com

Pat Fera, President
Pete McLenighan, Executive Director

Dedicated to providing effective treatment for persons suffering from the illness of addiction to alcohol and/or other
drugs, even if these persons are unable to pay for the cost
of such services.

2358 Way Back Inn-Grateful House
1915 W Roosevelt Road
Braodview, IL 60155-2925
708-344-3301
www.waybackinn.org

Frank Lieggi, Executive Director
Anita Pindiur, Clinical Director

Provides a high level clinical treatment program specializing in addressing the needs of men and women suffering
from both chemical dependence (Alcohol and Drugs) and
also Gambling Dependence.

2359 Wells Center
1300 Lincoln Avenue
Jacksonville, IL 62650-4007
217-243-1871
TDD: 217-243-0470

Bruce Carter, Executive Director

Mission has been to improve the health and welfare of individuals and families affected by the ause of alcohol and
other substances and by mental health issues. Dedicates its
efforts to providing levels of care and support services in
settings approval to the individual needs of the patient.

Year Founded: 1974

2360 White Oaks Companies of Illinois
130 Richard Pryor Place
Peoria, IL 61605-2484
309-671-8960
800-475-0257
www.whiteoaks.com

Non profit agency offering comprehensive, state-of-the-art chemical dependency services, individually designed for each client.

Indiana

2361 Community Hospital Anderson
1515 N Madison Avenue
Anderson, IN 46011-3457
765-298-4242
www.www.communityanderson.com

Beth Tharp, President/CEO

The mission of Community Hospital is to serve the medical, health and human service needs to the people in Anderson-Madison County and contiguous counties with compassion dignity, repect and excellence. Service, although focused on injury, illness and disease will also embrace prevention, education and alternative systems of health care delivery.
Year Founded: 1962

2362 Crossroad: Fort Wayne's Children's Home
2525 Lake Avenue
Fort Wayne, IN 46805-5457
260-484-4153
800-976-2306
www.crossroad-fwch.org

Patrick T Houlihan, Chair
Randall J. Rider, President/CEO
Kyle Zanker, Chief Development Officer
Beth McNeal, Director of Human Resources

A not-for-profit treatment center for emotionally troubled youth.
Year Founded: 1883

2363 Hamilton Center
620 Eighth Avenue
Terre Haute, IN 47804-2771
812-231-8200
800-742-0787
E-mail: HumanResources@hamiltoncenter.org
www.www.hamiltoncenter.org/

Gaylan Good, CEO
Richard Pittelkow, Vice President
Cary Sparks, Treasurer
Virginia Gilman, Secretary

Provides the full continuum of psychological health and addiction services to children, adolescents, adults and families.

2364 Parkview Hospital Rehabilitation Center
2200 Randilla Drive
Ft. Wayne, IN 46805-4638
260-373-4000
888-480-5151
www.parkview.com

Sue Ehinger, CEO

31 bed inpatient rehabilitation unit serving a wide variety of diagnoses. CARF accredited for both comprehensive and

B1 programs. Outpatient services are offered at several sites throughout the community.
Year Founded: 1995

2365 Richmond State Hospital
498 NW 18th Street
Richmond, IN 47374-2851
765-966-0511
www.richmondstatehospital.org

Jeff Butler, Superintendent
Terresa Bradburn, Human Resources Director
David Shelford, Assistant Superintendent
Josh Nolan, Clinical Director

A public behavioral health facility operated by the State of Indiana that provides psychiatric and chemical dependency treatment to citizens on a state wide basis.

Iowa

2366 Cherokee Mental Health Institute
1251 W Cedar Loop
Cherokee, IA 51012-1599
712-225-6927
E-mail: rmoller@dhs.state.ia.us
www.www.dhs.state.ia.us/Consumers/Facilities/Cherokee.

Tony Morris, Manager

2367 Four Seasons Counseling Clinic
2015 West Bay Drive
Muscatine, IA 52761-2228
563-263-3869
www.www.fourseasonscounselingclinic.com/

Ruth Evans, Owner

2368 Independence Mental Health Institute
2277 Iowa Avenue
Independence, IA 50644-9215
319-334-2583
E-mail: tmain@dhs.state.ia.us
www.www.dhs.state.ia.us/Consumers/Facilities/Independe

Bhasker Dave, Manager

2369 Mount Pleasant Mental Health Institute
1200 E Washington Street
Mount Pleasant, IA 52641-1898
319-385-7231
E-mail: karla.sandoval@iowa.gov
www.www.dhs.state.ia.us/Consumers/Facilities/MtPleasan

Karla Sandoval, Contact

Kansas

2370 Prairie View
1901 E First Street
Newton, KS 67114-5010
316-284-6400
800-362-0180
E-mail: info@pvi.org
www.www.prairieview.org/

Dee Donatelli-Reber, Chair
Jessie Kaye, President and CEO
Gary Fast, MD, Medical Director
Dorothy Nickel Friesen, Secretary

A behavioral and mental health facility which consists of the main campus in Newton that consists of outpatient services, a 38-bed inpatient hospital and various other divisions of our organization. Also maintain outpatient offices in Hutchinson, KS; Marion, KS; McPherson, KS; along with two outpatient offices in Wichita, KS.

Year Founded: 1954

2371 Via Christi Research
1100 N St. Francis Street
Suite 300
Wichita, KS 67214-2871
316-291-4774
800-362-0070

Joe Carrithers, Manager
Joe Carrithers, PhD, Research Operations Director

Provide people with mental health conditions such as depression, suicidal thoughts, schizophrenia or dementia have a unique set of needs. They receive highly skilled, compassionate treatment.

Kentucky

2372 Eastern State Hospital
1351 Newtown Pike
Building 1
Lexington, KY 40511-1277
859-253-1686
www.bluegrass.org

Carolyn Siegel, Chair
David E. Hanna, Interim President & CEO
Dee Werline, Vice President Administration &
Dana Royse, Chief Financial Officer

2373 Our Lady of Bellefonte Hospital
St. Christopher Drive
Ashland, KY 41101
606-833-3333
866-910-6524
www.careyoucantrust.com

Tim O'Toole, Manager

Louisiana

2374 Medical Center of LA: Mental Health Services
1532 Tulane Avenue
New Orleans, LA 70112-2860
504-903-3000

Genaro F Arriola Jr, Contact

2375 New Orleans Adolescent Hospital
210 State Street
New Orleans, LA 70118
504-897-3400
www.dhh.louisiana.gov

Provides a fully integrated hospital and community based continuum of mental health services for children and adolescents, with serious emotional and behavioral problems, residing in Louisiana.

2376 River Oaks Hospital
1525 River Oaks Road W
New Orleans, LA 70123-2199
504-734-1740
800-366-1740
www.www.riveroakshospital.com/

Evelyn Nolting, CEO

A private psychiatric facility for adults, adolescents and children.

2377 Southeast Louisiana Hospital
23515 Highway 190
PO Box 3850
Mandeville, LA 70470-3850
985-626-6300
www.dhh.louisiana.gov

Patricia Gonzalez, Facility Director

Maine

2378 Dorthea Dix Psychiatric Center
656 State Street
PO Box 926
Bangor, ME 04402-926
207-941-4000
TTY: 888-774-5290
www.www.maine.gov/dhhs

N Lawrence Ventura, Contact

DDPC is a 100 bed psychiatric hospital serving two-thirds of the State's geographic area that provides services for people with severe mental illness.

2379 Good Will-Hinckley Homes for Boys and Girls
PO Box 159
Hinckley, ME 04944
207-238-4000
E-mail: info@gwh.org
www.gwh.org

Jack Moore, Chairman
Glenn Cummings, Ed.D, President and Executive Director
Robert Moody, Vice President of Operations
Valerie Cote, Human Resource Generalist

Provides a home for the reception and support of needy boys and girls who are in needs maintaining and operates a school for them; attends to the physical, industrial, moral and spiritual development of those who shall be placed in its care.

2380 Riverview Psychiatric Center
250 Arsenal Street
11 State House Station
Augusta, ME 04333-0011
207-624-3900
888-261-6684
www.maine.gov/dhhs/riverview/index.shtml

Mary Louise McEwen, Superintendent
William Nelson MD, Medical Director
Lauret Grommett RN, Director of Nursing

Acute care psychiatric hospital owned and operated by the state of Maine.

2381 Spring Harbor Hospital
123 Andover Road
Westbrook, ME 04092-3850
207-761-2200
866-857-6644
www.www.springharbor.org/

Tracy Hawkins, Chair
Dennis King, Chief Executive Officer
Nancy Hasenfus, M.D., Vice Chair
Anna H Wells, Secretary

Southern Maine's premier provider of inpatient services for individuals who experience acute mental illness or dual disorders issues.

Maryland

2382 Clifton T Perkins Hospital Center

One Renaissance Boulevard
8450 Dorsey Run Road
Oakbrook Terrace, IL 60181
410-724-3000
800-994-6610
E-mail: complaint@jcaho.org
www.dhmh.maryland.gov

Sheilah Davenport, JD,MS,RN, CEO
Muhammed M Ajanah MD, Clinical Director
Steve Mason, COO

CTPHC is a maximum security facility. The mission of the facilty is to perform timely pretrial evaluations of defendants referred by the judicial circuit of Maryland, provide quality assessment of and treatment for all patients, and provide maximum security custody of patients to ensure public safety.

2383 Eastern Shore Hospital Center

PO Box 800
Cambridge, MD 21613
410-221-2300
888-216-8110
www.dhmh.maryland.gov/eshc/SitePages/Home.aspx

Mary K Noren, Contact

2384 John L. Gildner Regional Institute for Children and Adolescents

201 West Preston Street
Baltimore, MD 21201
410-767-6500
877-463-3464
www.dhmh.state.md.us/jlgrica/

Thomas E. Pukalski, CEO
Claudette Bernstein, Medical Director
Debra K. VanHorn, Director of Comm. Res. & Dev.

John L. Gildner Regional Institute for Children and Adolescents (JLG-RICA) is a community-based, public residential, clinical, and educational facility serving children and adolescents with severe emotional disabilities. The program is designed to provide residential and day treatment for students in grades 5-12. JLG-RICA's goal is to successfully return its students to an appropriate family, community, and academic or vocational setting that will lead to happy and successful lives.

2385 Kennedy Krieger Institute

707 North Broadway
Baltimore, MD 21205-1888
443-923-9200
800-873-3377
TTY: 443-923-2645
E-mail: info@kennedykrieger.org
www.www.kennedykrieger.org/

Gary W Goldstein, CEO

Dedicated to improving the lives of children and adolescents with pediatric developmental disabilities through patient care, special education, research, and professional training.

Year Founded: 1937

2386 RICA: Southern Maryland

9400 Surratts Road
Cheltenham, MD 20623
301-372-1840
www.pgcps.org/~rica/

Mary Sheperd, Contact

2387 Sheppard Pratt at Ellicott City

4100 College Avenue
PO Box 0836
Ellicott City, MD 21041-836
443-364-5500
800-883-3322
www.taylorhealth.com

To provide personal, high quality mental health services for your family, by our family of health care professionals.

Year Founded: 1939

2388 Spring Grove Hospital Center

55 Wade Avenue
Catonsville, MD 21228
410-402-6000
www.www.springgrove.com/

Patrick Sokas, Contact

2389 Springfield Hospital Center

6655 Sykesville Road
Sykesville, MD 21784-7966
410-795-2100
800-333-7564
www.dhmh.state.md.us

Paula Langmead, CEO
Janice Bowen, COO
Jonathan Book, Clinical Director

A regional psychiatric hospital operated by the State of Maryland, Department of Health and Mental Hygiene, Mental Hygiene Administration.

Year Founded: 1894

Massachusetts

2390 Arbour-Fuller Hospital

200 May Street
S Attleboro, MA 02703-5520
508-761-8500
800-828-3934
TTY: 800-974-6006
www.www.arbourhealth.com

Robert Mansfield, CEO
Frank Kahr MD, Medical Director
Judith Merel, Director Marketing

Psychiatric hospital providing services to adults, adolescents and adults with developmental disabilities.

2391 Baldpate Hospital

83 Baldpate Road
Georgetown, MA 01833-2303
978-352-2131
www.www.detoxma.com/

Lucille M Batal, President

2392 Concord Family and Adolescent Services
A Division of Justice Resource Institute, Inc
160 Gould Street
Suite 300
Needham, MA 02494-2300
781-559-4900
www.jri.org

Arden O'Connor, Chairperson
Andy Pond, MSW, MAT, President
Gregory Canfield, MSW, Executive Vice President
Deborah Reuman, MBA, Chief Financial Officer

Provides professional residential schools, group home, residence for homeless teens, alternative, therapeutic high school, education and parenting programs for children, adults and families throughouth Massachusetts.

2393 First Connections and Healthy Families
A Division of Justice Resource Institute, Inc
160 Gould Street
Suite 300
Needham, MA 02494-2300
781-559-4900
www.jri.org

Arden O'Connor, Chairperson
Andy Pond, MSW, MAT, President
Gregory Canfield, MSW, Executive Vice President
Deborah Reuman, MBA, Chief Financial Officer

First Conneections provides resources, education and support to families with children birth through age three. First Connections is dedicated to providing quality, comprehensive parenting support services to a diverse communities seeking resources to compliment and enrich their parenting experience.

2394 Grip Project
A Division of Justice Resource Institute, Inc
319 Wilder St
Suite 433
Lowell, MA 01852-1926
978-452-4522
www.jri.org

Cindy Powers, Program Director

A by teens, for teens young people's program with residential services as a foundation. Grip serves young people, ages 16-20, who are homeless or aging out of foster-care/group homes and are committed to being independent. There is a separate residence for young women and men, both located in Lowell, MA.

2395 Littleton Group Home
A Division of Justice Resource Institute, Inc
22 King Street
Littleton, MA 01460-1519
978-952-6809
www.jri.org

Timothy Considine, Program Director

Prepares young men, ages 13-18 for independent living by helping them to live respectful, dignified and increasingly responsible lives. The young men participate in after school activities and have daily access to the community.

2396 Meadowridge Pelham Academy
A Division of Justice Resource Institute, Inc
160 Gould Street
Suite 300
Needham, MA 02494-2300
781-559-4900
www.jri.org

Arden O'Connor, Chairperson
Andy Pond, MSW, MAT, President
Gregory Canfield, MSW, Executive Vice President
Deborah Reuman, MBA, Chief Financial Officer

A residential treatment program that focuses on the special challenges of adolescent girls with emotional and behavioral difficulties.The students, between the ages of 12-22, have typically experienced trauma and poor functioning in their personal, educational and/or family life.

2397 Meadowridge Walden Street School
A Division of Justice Resource Institute, Inc
160 Gould Street
Suite 300
Needham, MA 02494-2300
781-559-4900
www.jri.org

Arden O'Connor, Chairperson
Andy Pond, MSW, MAT, President
Gregory Canfield, MSW, Executive Vice President
Deborah Reuman, MBA, Chief Financial Officer

A residential school program that focuses on the challenges and special needs of adolescent females age 12-22 whom are coping with educational, emotional and behavioral difficulties.

2398 Sleep Disorders Unit of Beth Israel Hospital
330 Brookline Avenue
Boston, MA 02215-5400
617-667-7000
www.bidmc.org/

Jean K Matheson MD, Contact

Provides testing and treatment for those with sleep disorders and offers educational workshops, plus support for their families.

2399 The Home for Little Wanderers
271 Huntington Avenue
Boston, MA 02115-4554
617-267-3700
888-466-3321
www.thehome.org

Joan Wallace-Benjamin, President/CEO
Michael L. Pearis, Executive Vice President and Chi
Meredith Bryan, Vice President for Development a
Thomas L. Durling, Vice President for Finance

To ensure the healthy, emotional, mental and social development of children at risk, their families and communities.

Year Founded: 1799

2400 Victor School
A Division of Justice Resource Institute, Inc
160 Gould Street
Suite 300
Needham, MA 02494-2300
781-559-4900
www.jri.org

Arden O'Connor, Chairperson
Andy Pond, MSW, MAT, President
Gregory Canfield, MSW, Executive Vice President
Deborah Reuman, MBA, Chief Financial Officer

A private, co-ed, therapeutic day school for students in grades 8-12 with a school philosophy that children learn when they can. Provides innovative and specialized educational and emotional support and treatment.

2401 Windhorse Integrative Mental Health
211 North Street
Suite 1
Northampton, MA 01060-2386
413-586-0207
877-844-8181
E-mail: admissions@windhorseimh.org
www.windhorseimh.org

Eric Friedland-Kays, MA, Admissions Manager
Jeff Bliss MSW, Director, Admissions/Marketing
Sara Watters MA, LMHC, Director, Clinical Operations

Windhorse is a nonprofit treatment and education organization with a whole person approach to recovery from serious psychiatric distress. Services are tailored in close communication with each client and their family.

Year Founded: 1981

Michigan

2402 Hawthorn Center
234 West Baraga Avenue
Marquette, MI 49855
906-228-2850
www.michigan.gov

Shobhana Joshi, Executive Director

To provide high quality inpatient mental health services to emotionally disturbed children and adolescents.

2403 Samaritan Counseling Center
29887 W Eleventh Mile Road
Farmington Hills, MI 48336
248-474-4701
E-mail: info@samaritancounselingmichigan.com
www.samaritancounselingmichigan.com

Robert A. Martin, Executive Director
Sara Kirsten, B.A., Administrative Manager

Provides professional therapeutic counseling and educational services to all God's people seeking wholeness through emotional and spiritual growth.

Minnesota

2404 River City Mental Health Clinic
1360 Energy Park Drive
Suite 340
Saint Paul, MN 55108
651-646-8985
www.rivercityclinic.com

Doug Jensen, Owner

Psychotherapy and assessment for all ages.

Mississippi

2405 East Mississippi State Hospital
PO Box 4128, W Station
Meridian, MS 39304-4128

601-482-6186
www.www.emsh.state.ms.us

Charles Carlisle, Director

To provide a continuum of behavioral health and long term care services for adults and adolescents in a caring, compassionate environment in which ethical principles guide decision making and resources are used responsibly and creatively.

Year Founded: 1882

2406 Mississippi State Hospital
PO Box 157-A
Whitfield, MS 39193-157
601-351-8018
E-mail: info@msh.state.ms.us
www.msh.state.ms.us

Facilitates improvement in the quality of life for Mississippians who are in need of psychiatric, chemical dependency or nursing home survices by rehabilitating to the least restrictive environment utilizing a reange of psychiatric and medical services that reflect the accepted standard of care and are in compliance with statutory and regulatory guidlelines.

2407 North Mississippi State Hospital
1937 Briar Ridge Road
Tupelo, MS 38804-5963
662-690-4200
TDD: 662-690-4239
E-mail: info@nmsh.state.ms.us

Paul Callens, Executive Director

2408 South Mississippi State Hospital
823 Highway 589
Purvis, MS 39475-4194
601-794-0100
www.www.smsh.state.ms.us

Wynona Winfield, Executive Director

Provides the highest quality acute psychiatric care for adults who live in southern Mississippi

Missouri

2409 Northwest Missouri Psychiatric Rehabilitation Center
3505 Frederick Avenue
Saint Joseph, MO 64506-2914
816-387-2300
www.mo.gov

Mary Attebury, Manager

Inpatient care for long-term psychiatric/adult.

2410 Southeast Missouri Mental Health Center
1010 W Columbia Street
Farmington, MO 63640-2902
573-218-6792
E-mail: cynthia.forsythe@dmh.mo.gov
www.www.dmh.mo.gov/smmhc/

Karen Adams, CEO

People shall receive services focusing on strenghts and promoting opportunities beyond the limitations of mental illness.

Nebraska

2411 Norfolk Regional Center
1700 N Victory Road
PO Box 1209
Norfolk, NE 68702-1209
402-370-3400
www.dhhs.ne.gov

William Gibson, CEO
TyLynne Bauer, Facility Operating Officer

A progressive 120-bed state psychiatric hospital providing specialized psychiatric care to adults.

Nevada

2412 Behavioral Health Options: Sierra Health Services
2724 N Tenaya Way
Las Vegas, NV 89128-424
877-393-6094

Anthony M Marlon, Chairman/CEO

to manage behavioral health services in the private and public sectors on a national basis, creating value for our customers, including brokers, employers, members, providers and shareholders

2413 Northern Nevada Adult Mental Health Services
480 Galletti Way
Sparks, NV 89431-5564
775-688-2001

David Rosin MD, Contact

2414 Southern Nevada Adult Mental Health Services
6161 W Charleston Boulevard
Las Vegas, NV 89146-1148
702-486-6000
www.mhds.state.nv.us

Anuranjan Bist, Contact

New Hampshire

2415 Hampstead Hospital
218 E Road
Hamptead, NH 03841-5303
603-329-5311

Phillip Kubiak, Chief Executive Officer
Cynthia Gove, Chief Operating Officer
Scott Ranks, Director Support Services
Lisa Ryan, Human Resources Coordinator

Provides a full range of psychiatric and chemical dependency services for children, adolescents, adults and the elderly.

2416 New Hampshire State Hospital
29 Pleasant Street
Concord, NH 03301-3852
603-271-5300

Chester G Batchelder, CEO

A state operated, publicly funded hospital providing a range of specialized psychiatric services. NHH advocates for and provides services that support an individual's recovery.

New Jersey

2417 Ancora Psychiatric Hospital
301 Spring Garden Road
Hammonton, NJ 08037

609-561-1700
www.www.state.nj.us

John M. Lubitsky, CEO

Provides quality comprehensive psychiatric, medical and rehabilitative services that encourage maximun patient independence and movement towards community reintegration with an enviroment that is safe and caring.

2418 Ann Klein Forensic Center
Sullivan Way
PO Box 7717
W Trenton, NJ 08628-717
609-633-0900
www.www.state.nj.us/humanservices/dmhs/oshm/akfc/

Glenn Ferguson, Ph.D., CEO

A 200-bed psychiatric hospital serving a unique population that requires a secured environment. The facility provides care and treatment to individuals suffering from mental illness who are also within the legal system.

2419 Greystone Park Psychiatric Hospital
59 Koch Avenue
Morris Plains, NJ 07950
973-538-1800
www.www.state.nj.us/humanservices/dmhs/oshm/gpph/

Janet Monroe, CEO

A 550 bed psychiattric hospital.

New Mexico

2420 Life Transition Therapy
110 Delgado Street
Santa Fe, NM 87501-2781
505-982-4183
800-547-2574
E-mail: therapy@lifetransitiontherapy.com
www.www.lifetransitiontherapy.com

Ralph Steele, Founder
Ralph Steele, Founder

To eliminate the fear, ignorance and conditioning that fuel racism and social injustice within the individual as well as in relationships, families, communities, and the world at large.

2421 Sequoyah Adolescent Treatment Center
3405 W Pan American Freeway NE
Albuquerque, NM 87107-4786
505-222-0355
www.nmsatc.org

Henry Gardner, Manager

A 36 bed residential treatment center whose purpose is to provide care, treatment, and reintegration into society for adolescents who are violent or who have a history of violence and have a mental disorder and who are amenable to treatment.

New York

2422 Arms Acres
75 Seminary Hill Road
Carmel, NY 10512-1921
845-225-3400
888-227-4641
www.www.armsacres.com

Frederick R Hesse, CEO
Sultan Niazi, CFO
Michele Saari, Health Information Management

A private health care system providing high quality, cost-effective care to those suffering from alcoholism and chemical dependency and to the many whose lives are affected by the diseases of addiction.

2423 Berkshire Farm Center and Services for Youth
13640 State Route 22
Canaan, NY 12029-3506
518-781-4567
E-mail: info@berkshirefarm.org
www.berkshirefarm.org

Mr. Robert A Kandel, Board Chairman
Timothy Giacchetta, President and CEO
Mr. Charles Mott, Chairman Emeritus

Mission is to strengthen children and their families so they can lives safely, independently and productively within their home communities.

2424 Bronx Psychiatric Center
1500 Waters Place
Bronx, NY 10461-2796
718-931-0600
www.www.omh.ny.gov

Pamela Turner, Executive Director
Joseph Battaglia, MD, Clinical Director
Roy Thomas, Deputy Director

A 360 bed facility that has three impatient services and a comprehensive outpatient program.

2425 Brooklyn Children's Center
1819 Bergen Street
Brooklyn, NY 11233-4513
718-221-4500
www.www.omh.ny.gov

Provides high quality comprehensive individualized mental health treatment services to serious emotionally disturbed children and adolescents in Brooklyn, and to continuously strive to improve the quality of those services.

2426 BryLin Behavioral Health System
1263 Delaware Avenue
Buffalo, NY 14209-2497
716-886-8200
800-727-9546
E-mail: info@brylin.com
www.brylin.com

Eric D. Pleskow, President and CEO
E. Paul Hettich, Senior Vice President and CFO

Founded in 1955. Provides inpatient psychiatric services for children, adolescents, adults and geriatric patients. Outpatient substance abuse services for adolescents and adults. Outpatient mental health services for adults.

2427 Buffalo Psychiatric Center
400 Forest Avenue
Buffalo, NY 14213-1298
716-885-2261
www.www.omh.ny.gov

Kimberly Karalus, Chief of Outpatient Services
Nancy Johnson, Director of Residential Services

Provides psychiatric quality inpatient, outpatient, residential, vocational, and wellness services to adults with serious mental illnesses

2428 Capital District Psychiatric Center
75 New Scotland Avenue
Albany, NY 12208-3474
518-549-6000
www.www.omh.ny.gov

Lewis Campbell, CEO

Provides inpatient psychiatric treatment and rehabilitation to patients who have been diagnosed with serious and persistenet mental illnesses and for whom brief or short-term treatment in a community hospital mental health unit has been unable to provide sympton stability.

2429 Central New York Psychiatric Center
9005 Old River Road
PO Box 300
Marcy, NY 13403
315-765-3600
www.www.omh.ny.gov

A comprehensive mental health service delivery system providing a full range of care and treatment to persons incarcerated in the New York State and county correctional system.

2430 Cornerstone of Rhinebeck
500 Milan Hollow Road
Rhinebeck, NY 12572-2970
845-266-3481
800-266-4410
E-mail: admin@cornerstoneny.com
www.cornerstoneny.com

Eileen Mc Curdy, Senior VP

Provides inpatient chemical dependency treatment and offers a comprehensive range of inpatient and outpatient treatment services for alcohol and substance abuse.

Year Founded: 1974

2431 Creedmoor Psychiatric Center
79-25 Winchester Boulevard
Queens Village, NY 11427-2128
718-464-7500
www.www.omh.ny.gov

William Fisher, MD, Clinical Director
Susan Chin, Deputy Director
John Holmes, Deputy Director
Renee Anderson, Chief Nursing Officer

Provides a continuum of inpatient, outpatient and related psychiatric services with inpatient hospitalization at the main campus and five outpatient sites in the boroughs of Queens.

2432 Elmira Psychiatric Center
100 Washington Street
Elmira, NY 14901-2898
607-737-4711
www.www.omh.ny.gov

Mark Stephany, Manager

Provides a wide array of comprehensive psychiatric services.

2433 Freedom Ranch
Freedom Village USA
5275 Rt. 14, PO Box 24
Lakemont, NY 14857-24
607-243-8126
800-842-8679
E-mail: 77pastor@fvusa.com
www.freedomvillageusa.com

Dr Fletcher Brothers, Founder

An extension of Freedom Village, Freedom Ranch offers a residential program for men 21 and older with substance abuse and emotional problems. Freedom Ranch is a faith-based program seeking to help men become productive members of society.

Year Founded: 1948

2434 Freedom Village USA
Freedom Village USA
5275 Rt. 14, PO Box 24
Lakemont, NY 14857-24
607-243-8126
800-842-8679
E-mail: 77pastor@fvusa.com
www.freedomvillageusa.com

Dr Fletcher Brothers, Founder

A not-for-profit residential campus for troubled teens. Offers a faith-based approach to teenagers in crisis or at risk. Students are required to make a voluntary one-year commitment to the program. Freedom Village has an 80% success rate with troubled teenagers.

2435 Gift of Life Home
Freedom Village USA
5275 Rt. 14, PO Box 24
Lakemont, NY 14857-24
607-243-8126
800-842-8679
E-mail: 77pastor@fvusa.com
www.freedomvillageusa.com

Dr Fletcher Brothers, Founder

An affiliate program of Freedom Village, USA, a residential program for troubled teenagers, the Gift of Life Home offers pregnant girls a safe haven, a place of refuge, where they can come and have their baby while transforming their life as well. Freedom Village is a faith-based alternative to other residential placements.

2436 Greater Binghamton Health Center
425 Robinson Street
Binghamton, NY 13904-1775
607-724-1391
www.www.omh.ny.gov

Pamela Vredenburgh, Manager

Provides comprehensive outpatient and inpatient services for adults and children who are seriously mentally ill.

2437 Hope House
573 Livingston Ave.
Albany, NY 12206
518-482-4673
www.hopehouseinc.org

Kevin M. Connally, Executive Director
Catherine Dowdell, Executive Assistant
Lynda Tymeson, Director of Program Services
Courtney Lerman, Quality Assurance Manager

Started helping the community in need of education, intervention and treatment for the persons affected by substance abuse.

2438 Hutchings Psychiatric Center
620 Madison Street
Syracuse, NY 13210-2338
315-426-3600
www.www.omh.ny.gov

Colleen Sawyer, Executive Director

A comprehensive, community-based mental health facility providing an integrated network of inpatient and outpatient services for children and adults residing in the Central New York Region.

2439 Kingsboro Psychiatric Center
681 Clarkson Avenue
Brooklyn, NY 11203-2199
718-221-7700
www.www.omh.ny.gov

Mark Lerman, Manager

Provides competent compassionate psychiatric care to people with serious mental illness with a purpose of reintegrating them to the community.

2440 Kirby Forensic Psychiatric Center
600 E 125th Street
New York, NY 10035-6000
646-672-5800
www.www.omh.ny.gov

Steve Rabinowitz, Manager

A maximum security hospital of the New York State Office of Mental Health that provides secure treatment and evaluation for the forensic patients and courts of New York City and Long Island.

Year Founded: 1985

2441 Manhattan Psychiatric Center
600 E 125th Street
New York, NY 10035-6000
646-672-6767
www.www.omh.ny.gov

Steve Rabinowitz, Manager

Offers inpatient and outpatient treatment for adults with mental illness.

2442 Mid-Hudson Forensic Psychiatric Center
2834 Route 17-M
New Hampton, NY 10958
845-374-8700
www.www.omh.ny.gov

Barbara Daria, Manager

A secure adult psychiatric center that provides a comprehensive program of evaluation, treatment, and rehabilitation for patients admitted by court order.

2443 Mohawk Valley Psychiatric Center
1400 Noyes at York
Utica, NY 13502
315-738-3800
www.www.omh.ny.gov

Sarah Rudes, CEO

Provides quality, individualized psychiatric treatment and rehabilitation services that promote recovery.

2444 Nathan S. Kline Institute for Psychiatric Research
140 Old Orangeburg Road
Orangeburg, NY 10962
845-398-5500
E-mail: webmaster@nki.rfmh.org
www.www.rfmh.org/nki

Donald C. Goff, MD, Director
Antonio Convit, MD, Deputy Director
Thomas O. O'Hara, MBA, Deputy Director/Insitute Admin.
Michael Kohn, PhD, Head of Research Support

A facility of the New York State Office of Mental Health that has earned a national and international reputation for its pioneering contributions in psychiatric research, especially in the areas of psychopharmacological treatments for schizophrenia and major mood disorders, and in the application of computer technology to mental health services. A broad range of studies are conducted at NKI, including basic, clinical, and services research. All work is intended to improve care for people suffering from these complex, psychobiologically-based, severely disabling mental disorders.
Year Founded: 1952

2445 New York Psychiatric Institute
1051 Riverside Drive
New York, NY 10032-1098
212-543-6283
www.www.nyspi.org/

Jeffrey Lieberman, MD, Chairman
Anke Ehrhardt, PhD, Vice Chair for Academic Affairs
Avalon Lance, MHA, Vice Chair for Administration an
Harold A. Pincus, MD, Vice Chair for Strategic Initiat

2446 Odyssey House
120 Wall Street
New York, NY 10005
212-361-1600
E-mail: info@odysseyhouseinc.org
www.odysseyhouseinc.org

Peter Provet, President & Chief Executive Offi
John Tavolacci, Executive Vice President & Chief
Durga Vallabhaneni, Senior Vice President & Chief Fi
Isobelle Surface, Senior Vice President & Director

Develops innovative treatment models to ensure that our systems take into account current research, utilizing what works most effectively to help these individuals overcome their difficulties and build a stable, producitve, drug-free life.
Year Founded: 1967

2447 Pahl Transitional Apartments
559-565 Sixth Avenue
Troy, NY 12182-2620
518-237-9891
www.pahlinc.org

Michael Kennedy, Clinical Director

A 9-12 month residential, chemical dependency treatment facility for males ages 16-25. The goal for the residents is to learn the skills necessary for long-term recovery and independent living.

2448 Phoenix House
164 West 74th Street
New York, NY 10023-2301

646-505-2000
www.phoenixhouse.org

Alan Hargrove, Program Director
Brian Gillam, Managing Director
Christine Balzano, Program Director
Dan Boylan, Program Director

Reclaims disordered lives, encourages individual responsibility, positive behavior, and personal growth, also strengthens families and communities, and safeguards public health. Also, promotes a drug-free society through prevention, treatment, education and training, research, and advocacy.

2449 Pilgrim Psychiatric Center
998 Crooked Hill Road
West Brentwood, NY 11717-1019
631-761-3500
www.www.omh.ny.gov

Dean Wienstock, Manager

Provides excellent, integrated care in evaluation, treatment, crisis intervention, rehabilitation, support, and self help/empowerment service to individuals with serious psychiatric illness.

2450 Queens Children's Psychiatric Center
74-03 Commonwealth Boulevard
Bellerose, NY 11426-1839
718-264-4500
www.www.omh.ny.gov

Keith Little, Executive Director

Serves seriously emotionally disturbed children and adolescents from the ages of 5 through 18 in a range of programs including Inpatient hospitalization, outpatient clinic treatment, intensive case management, homemaker services and community education and consultation services.

2451 Rochester Psychiatric Center
1111 Elmwood Avenue
Rochester, NY 14620-3090
585-241-1200
TTY: 585-241-1982
www.www.omh.ny.gov

Elizabeth Suhre, R.N., B.S., MBA, Executive Director and Director
Philip Griffin, Director for Quality Improvement
Laurence Guttmacher, M.D., Clinical Director
Christopher Kirisits, R.N., M.S.N., Chief Nursing Officer

Provides quality comprehensive treatment and rehabilitation services to people with psychiatric disabilities working toward recovery.

2452 Rockland Children's Psychiatric Center
2 First Avenue
Orangeburg, NY 10962
845-359-7400
800-597-8481
www.www.omh.ny.gov

Josefina M Moneda

A psychiatric hospital exclusively for children and adolescents

2453 Rockland Psychiatric Center
140 Old Orangeburg Road
Orangeburg, NY 10962

845-359-1000
www.www.omh.ny.gov
Provides treatment, rehabilitation, and support to adults 18 and older with severe and complex mental illness.

2454 Sagamore Children's Psychiatric Center
197 Half Hollow Road
Dix Hills, NY 11746-5859
631-370-1700
www.www.omh.ny.gov

Dennis Dubey, Executive Director

Programs for youngsters and their families include inpatient hospitalization, day hospitalization, day treatment, outpatient clinic treatment, mobile mental health team crisis services, information and referral, and community consultation and training.

2455 Samaritan Village
138-02 Queens Blvd
Briarwood, NY 11435-2647
718-206-2000
800-532-4357
www.samaritanvillage.org

Tino Hernandez, President/CEO
Douglas Apple, Executive Vice President and Chi
John Iammatteo, Senior Vice President for Financ
Sheila Greene, Vice President of Communications

Mission is to eliminate the devastating impact of substance abuse on individuals, families and communities by helping addicted men and women take responsibility for their own recovery.

2456 South Beach Psychiatric Center
777 Seaview Avenue
Staten Island, NY 10305-3409
718-667-2300
www.www.omh.ny.gov

Rosanne Gaylor, MD, Executive Director
Rosanne Gaylor, MD, Director, Clinical Services
Doreen Piazza, R.N.C., MS, Director, Nursing
Titus Mathew, BE, Deputy Director, Administration

Provides intermediate level inpatient services to persons living in western Brooklyn, southern Staten Island, and Manhattan south of 42nd street.

2457 St. Lawrence Psychiatric Center
1 Chimney Point Drive
Ogdensburg, NY 13669-2291
315-541-2001
www.www.omh.ny.gov

Sam Bastien, Executive Director

2458 Veritas Villa
5 Ridgeview Road
Kerhonkson, NY 12446-1555
845-626-3555

Joseph Stoeckeler, CEO

Inpatient rehabilitation and wellness center

Year Founded: 1957

2459 Western New York Children's Psychiatric Center
1010 E & W Road
W Seneca, NY 14224-3698

716-677-7000
www.www.omh.ny.gov

Deborah Shiffner, Manager

Provides high quality, comprehensive behavioral health care services to seriously emotionally disturbed children and adolescents, and to partner with their families throughout the continuum of care.

North Carolina

2460 Broughton Hospital
1000 S Sterling Street
Morganton, NC 28655-3999
828-433-2111
www.www.ncdhhs.gov/dsohf/broughton/

Dr Art Robarge, Interim Hospital Director/CEO

2461 Central Regional Hospital
803 Biggs Drive
Raleigh, NC 27699
919-575-7100
www.www.ncdhhs.gov/dsohf

Dale C. Armstrong, MBA, FACHE, Director
Laura White, Team Leader, Hospitals
Carol Donin, Team Leader, Developmental Cente
Wendi McDaniel, Team Leader, Facility Advocates

Formed by the merger of Dorothea Dix Hospital and John Umstead Hospital. Services include adult psychiatric services, clinical research services, child and adolescent services, medical services, and geropsychiatric services.

2462 Cherry Hospital
201 Stevens Mill Road
Goldsboro, NC 27530-1057
919-731-3411
www.www.ncdhhs.gov

J. Luckey Welsh, Jr., CEO
Nathaniel Carmichael, COO
Jim Mayo, MD, Clinical Director
Scott Mann, MD, Medical Director

North Dakota

2463 North Dakota State Hospital
2605 Circle Drive
Jamestown, ND 58401-6905
701-253-3650
TTY: 701-253-3880
www.nd.gov

Alex Schweitzer, CEO

Ohio

2464 Central Behavioral Healthcare
5965 Renaissance Place
Toledo, OH 43623-4728
419-882-5678
E-mail: info@cbhpsych.com
www.cbhpsych.com

Dennis W. Kogut, PhD, Owner

Provides patients with a broad range of high-quality behavioral healthcare in a professional and personal matter.

Year Founded: 1986

2465 Heartland Behavioral Healthcare
3000 Erie Street S
Massillon, OH 44646-7976
330-833-3135
800-783-9301
TDD: 330-832-9991
www.mha.ohio.gov

Jeffrey L. Sims, CEO
Dr. Emmanuel Nwajei, Chief Clinical Officer
Michael Waggoner, Nurse Executive
John Stocker, Client Rights Specialist

2466 Northcoast Behavioral Healthcare System
PO Box 678003
1756 Sagamore Road
Northfield, OH 44067
330-467-7131
TDD: 330-467-5522
www.www.mha.ohio.gov

Doug Kern, Chief Executive Officer
Michael Emerick, Nurse Executive
Muhammad Momen, M.D., Lead Chief Clinical Officer (CCO
Joi Chapman, Client Rights Specialist

2467 Northcoast Behavioral Healthcare System
PO Box 678003
1756 Sagamore Road
Northfield, OH 44067
330-467-7131
TDD: 330-467-5522
www.www.mha.ohio.gov

Doug Kern, Chief Executive Officer
Michael Emerick, Nurse Executive
Muhammad Momen, M.D., Lead Chief Clinical Officer (CCO
Joi Chapman, Client Rights Specialist

2468 Twin Valley Behavioral Healthcare
Columbus Campus, 2200 W Broad Street
Columbus, OH 43223
614-752-0333
877-301-8824
TDD: 614-274-7137
www.www.mha.ohio.gov

Veronica Lofton, CEO
Dr. Alan Freeland, Chief Clinical Officer (CCO)
David Blahnik, Chief Operations Officer
Susan Cross, Client Rights Specialist

State operated BHD serving severley mentally ill adults in partnership with the community.

Oklahoma

2469 Griffin Memorial Hospital
900 E Main Street
PO Box 151
Norman, OK 73070-151
405-573-6623
www.www.ok.gov

Don Bowen, Contact

2470 Oklahoma Forensic Center
PO Box 69
Vinita, OK 74301-0069

918-256-7841
www.www.ok.gov/
William Burkett, Contact

2471 Willow Crest Hospital
130 A Street Southwest
Miami, OK 74354-6800
918-542-1836
www.willowcresthospital.com
Anne Anthony, CEO

Oregon

2472 Blue Mountain Recovery Center
2600 Westgate
Pendleton, OR 97801-9604
541-276-0810
www.www.oregon.gov
Kerry Kelly, Contact

2473 Oregon State Hospital: Portland
1121 NE 2nd Avenue
Portland, OR 97232-2043
503-731-8620
www.www.oregon.gov
Nena Strickland, Executive Director
Year Founded: 1883

2474 Oregon State Hospital: Salem
2600 Center Street NE
Salem, OR 97301-2682
503-945-2800
www.www.oregon.gov
Pam Dickinson, Manager
Year Founded: 1883

2475 Riverside Center
671 Sw Main
PO Box 2259
Winston, OR 97496-2259
541-679-6129
www.riversidecenter.org

2476 St. Mary's Home for Boys
16535 SW Tualatin Valley Highway
Beaverton, OR 97006-5143
503-649-5651
E-mail: reception@stmaryshomeforboys.org
www.www.stmaryshomeforboys.org
Francis Maher, Executive Director

Founded in 1889 as an orphanage for abandoned and wayward children, today St. Mary's is a private, non-profit organization that offers comprehensive residential, day treatment and mental health services to at-risk boys between the ages of 10 and 17 who are emotionally disturbed and/or disruptive behavior disordered.
Year Founded: 1889

Pennsylvania

2477 MHNet
9606 N. Mopac Expressway
Stonebridge Plaza 1, Suite 600
Austin, TX 78759

888-646-6889
E-mail: edwynl@integra-ease.com
www.www.mhnet.com

Wesley J Brockhoeft, PhD, President/CEO
Peter Harris, MD, Corporate Medical Director
Robert Wilson, CFO
Richard T Wright, SVP Business Development

MHNet is an outgrowth of the Center for Individual and Family Counseling, a multi-disciplinary outpatient treatment clinic with a full spectrum behavioral health organization with national service delivery capability.

Year Founded: 1981

2478 Renfrew Center Foundation
475 Spring Lane
Philadelphia, PA 19128-3918
215-482-5353
E-mail: foundation@renfrew.org
www.renfrewcenter.com

Sam Menaged, President

A tax-exempt, nonprofit organization advancing the education, prevention, research, and treatment of eating disorders.

Year Founded: 1985

2479 Torrance State Hospital
PO Box 111
Torrance, PA 15779-111
724-459-4406
www.www.dpw.state.pa.us

Lyle Gardner, Director

2480 Warren State Hospital
33 Main Drive
N Warren, PA 16365-5099
814-726-4219
www.www.dpw.state.pa.us

Charlotte M. Uber, LSW, Chief Executive Officer
Nancy Saullo, HR Director
Susan Cramer, Admissions Coordinator

2481 Wernersville State Hospital
PO Box 300
Wernersville, PA 19565-300
610-678-3411

Andrea Kepler, Chief Executive Officer
Year Founded: 1891

Rhode Island

2482 Butler Hospital
345 Blackstone Boulevard
Providence, RI 02906-4829
401-455-6200
E-mail: info@butler.org
www.butler.org

Patricia Recupero, President

Rhode Island's only private, nonprofit psychiatric and substance abuse hospital for adults, adolescents, children and seniors.

Year Founded: 1844

2483 Gateway Healthcare
249 Roosevelt Avenue
Suite 205
Pawtucket, RI 02860-2134
401-724-8400
www.gatewayhealth.org

Richard Leclerc, President
Scott W DiChristofero, VP Finance
Stephen Chabot MD, Medical Director
Carolyn Kyle, Senior Vice President of Strateg

To promote resiliency and to assist people in their recovery from mental health, substance abuse, and behavioral and emotional disorder

2484 Groden Center
86 Mount Hope Avenue
Providence, RI 02906-1648
401-274-6310
E-mail: grodencenter@grodencenter.org
www.grodencenter.org

June Groden, President

Groden Center has been providing day and residential treatment and educational services to children and youth who have developmental and behavioral difficulties and their families. By providing a broad range of individualized services in the most normal and least restrictive settings possible, children and youth learn skills that will help them engage in typical experiences and interact more successfully with others. Education and treatment take place in Groden Center classrooms, in the student's homes, and in the community with every effort made to maintain typical family and peer relationships. Call or visit our web site for more information about the Center and the publications and materials we have available.

Year Founded: 1976

South Carolina

2485 CM Tucker Jr Nursing Care Center
2200 Harden Street
Columbia, SC 29203-7107
803-737-5300
www.www.state.sc.us

Laura W. Hughes, RN, BSN, MPH, Facility Director

Provides excellence in resident care in an environment of concern and compassion that is respectful to others, adaptive to change and accountable for outcome.

Year Founded: 1970

2486 Columbia Counseling Center
900 St. Andrews Road
Columbia, SC 29210-5816
803-731-4708
www.columbiacounselingcenter.com

Darrel G Shaver, President

2487 Earle E Morris Jr Alcohol & Drug Treatment Center
610 Faison Drive
Columbia, SC 29203-3218
803-935-7200
www.scdmh.org

George Mc Connell, Manager

Provides effective treatment of chemical dependence through comprehensive evaluation, safe detoxification, and state-of-the-art treatment servies.

2488 G Werber Bryan Psychiatric Hospital
220 Faison Drive
Columbia, SC 29203-3210
803-935-5761
www.www.state.sc.us

Versie Bellamy RN, MN, Deputy Director
Kimberly B. Rudd, MD, Medical Director
Algie Bryant, RN, MSN, Director of Performance Improvem
Mesa Foard, Director of Information Technolo

A 277 bed short term intensive care facility that serves adult and geriatric patients ages 16 years and older. Provides therapeutic services in a warm and nurturing environment for individuals in crisis.

2489 Patrick B Harris Psychiatric Hospital
130 Highway 252
PO Box 2907
Anderson, SC 29622-2907
864-231-2600

John Fletcher, CEO

Provides intensive, short-term, psychiatric diagnostic and treatment services on a 24 hour, emergency voluntary and involuntary basis.

2490 South Carolina State Hospital
2414 Bull Street
Columbia, SC 29202
803-898-8581
www.www.state.sc.us

John H. Magill, State Director

Psychiatric hospital

Year Founded: 1995

2491 William S Hall Psychiatric Institute
1800 Colonial Drive
PO Box 202
Columbia, SC 29203
803-898-1662
www.www.state.sc.us

Angela Forand, Ph.D.,, Program Director
Dr. Phyllis Bryant-Mobley, Medical Director
Natasha Davis, RN (Interim), Director of Nursing Services

South Dakota

2492 South Dakota Human Services Center
700 Governors Drive
Pierre, SD 57501
605-773-3165
www.dss.sd.gov/behavioralhealth/hsc/services.aspx

Laurie Gill, Cabinet Secretary
Brenda Tidball-Zeltinger, Deputy Secretary
Jason Simmons, Chief Financial Officer

To provide persons who are mentally ill or chemically dependent with effective, individualized professional treatment that enables them to achieve their highest level of personal independence in the most therapeutic environment.

Tennessee

2493 Cherokee Health Systems
2018 Weestern Avenue
Knoxville, TN 37921-5718
865-934-6734
www.cherokeehealth.com

Tracey Trench, Manager

Uses an integrated model to provide behavioral health and primary care services in a community-based setting.

Year Founded: 1960

2494 Lakeshore Mental Health Institute
5908 Lyons View Drive
Knoxville, TN 37919-7598
865-584-1561
www.www.tn.gov/

Richard L Thomas, CEO

2495 Memphis Mental Health Institute
951 Court Avenue
Memphis, TN 38103-2813
901-577-1800
www.www.tn.gov

Lisa A. Daniel, CEO
Tammy D. Ali-Carr, Psychiatric Hosp. Asst. Supt.
Lori Minor, Nurse Executive
Scott Baymiller, MD, Clinical Director

55 bed acute adult psychiatric facility operated by the State of Tennessee Department of Mental Health & Substance Abuse Services.

2496 Middle Tennessee Mental Health Institute
221 Stewarts Ferry Pike
Nashville, TN 37214-3325
615-902-7400
www.tennessee.gov

Candance Gilligan, Manager

2497 Moccasin Bend Mental Health Institute
100 Moccasin Bend Road
Chattanooga, TN 37405
423-265-2271
www.tennessee.gov

William Ventress, CEO

2498 Western Mental Health Institute
11100 U.S. Highway 64
Bolivar, TN 38008
731-228-2000
www.www.tn.gov/

Roger Pursley, Chief Officer

2499 Woodridge Hospital
403 State of Franklin Road
Johnson City, TN 37604-6034
423-928-7111
800-346-8899
www.msha.com

Kim Moore, Manager
Kim Cudebec, Clinical Director

Texas

2500 Austin State Hospital
4110 Guadalupe Street
Austin, TX 78751-4223

512-452-0381
www.www.dshs.state.tx.us
Carl Schock, CEO

Provides adult psychiatric services, specialty adult services and child and adolescent psychiatric services.

2501 Big Spring State Hospital
1901 N Highway 87
Big Spring, TX 79720-283
432-267-8216
www.www.dshs.state.tx.us

Ed Mougon, CEO

A 195-bed psychiatric hospital that provides hospitalization for people 18 years of age and older with psychiatric illnesses in a 57-county area in West Texas and the Texas Panhandle.

Year Founded: 1938

2502 Choices Adolescent Treatment Center
4521 Karnack Hwy
Marshall, TX 75670
903-938-4455
800-638-0880
E-mail: choices@sydcom.net
www.choicestreatment.com

C G Bowman, CEO

Choices residential treatment program focuses on adolescents which abuse substances and addresses related psychiatric disorders.

2503 Dallas Metrocare Services
1380 Riverbend Drive
Dallas, TX 75247
214-743-1200
877-283-2121
E-mail: metrocare@metrocareservices.org
www.metrocareservices.org

Julia P. Noble, Chair
Jill Martinez, Vice Chair
Judy N. Myers, Secretary

North Texas' leading nonprofit dedicated to helping people with mental illness, developmental disabilities, and severe emotional problems live healthier lives. Provides a comprehensive array of individually-tailored services to help the people we serve toward meaningful and satisfying lives.

Year Founded: 1967

2504 El Paso Psychiatric Center
4615 Alameda Avenue
El Paso, TX 79905-2702
915-532-2202
E-mail: zulema.carrillo@dshs.state.tx.us
www.dshs.state.tx.us

Zulema C. Carrillo, Superintendent
Raul Luna, Chief Nurse Executive
Amber Bechtel, Quality Oversight Director
David Osterhout, Assistant Superintendent

A 74-bed psychiatric hospital that provides hospitalization to the citizens of far West Texas.

2505 Green Oaks Behavioral Healthcare Service
7808 Clodus Fields Drive
Dallas, TX 75251-2206

972-991-9504
800-866-6554
www.greenoakspsych.com

Committed to developing and emulating the latest, most effective clinical practices always, and, in all things, to promote dignity, holding compassion and respect for patients and their families as the absolute standard.

2506 Homeward Bound, Inc.
5300 University Hills Boulevard
Dallas, TX 75241
214-941-3500
E-mail: ddenton@homewardboundinc.org
www.homewardboundinc.org

Jesse Oliver, Board Chair
Douglas W. Denton, MA, LCDC, LCCA, Executive Director
Nancy Pryor, Director of Grants Management
Sonny Gaither, Information Systems

Offers chemical dependence treatment for the indigent population anad those referred by the criminal justice system, local hospitals and private practitioners.

Year Founded: 1980

2507 Jewish Family and Children's Services
12500 NW Military Highway
Suite 250
San Antonio, TX 78231-1871
210-302-6920
www.jfs-sa.org

Ilene Kramer, President
Marion Bernstein, 1st Vice-President
Scott McLean, 2nd Vice-President
David Scotch, Treasurer

To strengthen community values, promote human dignity and enhance self-sufficiency of individuals and families through social, psychological, health educaitonal and financial support programs.

Year Founded: 1974

2508 Kerrville State Hospital
721 Thompson Drive
Kerrville, TX 78028-5199
830-896-2211
www.www.dshs.state.tx.us

Linda Highsmith, President

provides care for persons with major mental illnesses who need the safety, structure, and resources of an in-patient setting

2509 La Hacienda Treatment Center Hunt, TX 78024
800-749-6160
E-mail: info@lahacienda.com
www.lahacienda.com

Provides treatment for alcoholism and other chemical dependencies

Year Founded: 1972

2510 Laurel Ridge Treatment Center
17720 Corporate Woods Drive
San Antonio, TX 78259-3500
210-491-9400
800-624-7975
www.laurelridgetc.com

Dan Thomas, CEO

A psychiatric hospital offering a comprehensive continuum of behavioral healthcare services including acute programs for children, adolescents and adults and residential treatment for children and adolescents.

2511 New Horizons Ranch and Center

PO Box 549
Goldthwaite, TX 76844-549
915-938-5518
www.newhorizonsinc.com

Gary Webb, President
Mark Horn, Vice President
JB Morgan, Secretary
Michael Redden, Executive Director

To provide an environment where children, families and staff are able to heal and grow through caring relationships and unconditional love and acceptance.

Year Founded: 1971

2512 North Texas State Hospital: Vernon Campus

4730 College Drive
Vernon, TX 76384-4009
940-552-9901
E-mail: jamese.smith@dshs.state.tx.us
www.dshs.state.tx.us

James E Smith, Superintendent
Bill Lowery, Financial Officer
Kim Hays, Assistant to Financial Officer
Sheila Sidlauskas, Director, Quality Management

2513 North Texas State Hospital: Wichita Falls Campus

6515 Lake Road
Wichita Falls, TX 76308-5419
940-692-1220
E-mail: jamese.smith@dshs.state.tx.us
www.www.dshs.state.tx.us

Jim Smith, Administrator

1917 pages

2514 Rio Grande State Center

1401 South Rangerville
Harlingen, TX 78552-7638
956-364-8000
www.www.dshs.texas.gov

The only public provider south of San Antonio, Texas that offers healthcare, inpatient mental health services and long-term services for individuals with intellectual and developmental disabilities.

1956 pages

2515 Rusk State Hospital

805 North Dickinson Drive
Rusk, TX 75785
903-683-3421
www.www.dshs.state.tx.us

Brenda Slaton, Superintendent
Michelle Foster, Assistant Superintendent
Frances L. Long, Financial Officer
Joe Bates, M.D., Clinical Director

An inpatient hospital providing psychiatric treatment and care for citizens primarily from the East Texas region.

2516 San Antonio State Hospital

6711 South New Braunfels
Suite 100
San Antonio, TX 78223-3006
210-532-8811
E-mail: robert.arizpe@dshs.state.tx.us
www.dshs.state.tx.us

Bob Arizpe, Superintendent
Valerie Kroll, Assistant to Superintendent
Jessica Gutierrez-Rodriguez, Assistant Superintendent
Glenda Armstrong Huff, Assistant Superintendent

Provides intensive inpatient diagnostic, treatment, rehabilitative, and referral servious for seriously mentally ill persons from South Texas regardless of their financial status.

2517 Shades of Hope Treatment Center

402-A Mulberry Street
Buffalo Gap, TX 79508
800-588-4673
www.shadesofhope.com

Tennie McCarty, Founder/CEO
Carrie Willey, PhD, LPC, Clinical Director
Camela Balcomb, Executive Director
Becky Forrest, Admission Coordinator

A residential and outpatient all-addictions treatment center specializing in the intensive treatment of eating disorders.

2518 Starlite Recovery Center

230 Mesa Verde Drive East
PO Box 317
Center Point, TX 78010-317
866-220-1626
E-mail: info@starliterecovery.com
www.starliterecovery.com

Amy J. Swetnam, LPC, LCDC, CE, Executive Director
Bryan M. Davis, D.O., MSPH, Medical Director
Shannon Malish, LMSW, Director of Counseling Services
Nancy Kneupper, L.V.N., Director of Nursing

Provides the highest quality of care in a cost-effective manner, insuring that our valued clients receive treatment that will allow them to return to a productive way of life.

2519 Terrell State Hospital

1200 East Brin
Terrell, TX 75160-2938
972-563-6452
www.www.dshs.state.tx.us

Dorothy Floyd, Ph.D., Superintendent
Nancy Drake, Assistant to Superintendent
Mike Verseckes, Financial Officer
Judy Tanner, Assistant to Financial Officer

A 316 bed, Joint Commission accredited and Medicare certified, psychiatric inpatient hospital, that is responsible for providing services for individuals with mental illnesses residing within a 19 county, 12,052 square mile service region, with a population of over 3 million.

2520 Waco Center for Youth

3501 N 19th Street
Waco, TX 76708-2097
254-756-2171
www.dshs.state.tx.us

Eddie Greenfield, Executive Director

A psychiatric residential treatment facility that serves teen-agers, ages 13 through 17, with emotional difficulties and/or behavioral problems.

Utah

2521 Copper Hills Youth Center
5899 Rivendell Drive
West Jordan, UT 84081-6500
801-561-3377
800-776-7116
www.www.copperhillsyouthcenter.com

Phil Sheridan, CEO
Daren Woolstenhulme, CFO
Rebekah Schuler, Director of Clinical Services
Dave Anderton, Director of Risk Management

Residential treatment center for boys and girls ages 12-17. Mental health and substance abuse treatment. Also specialized programs for Autism and sexual misconduct

2522 Utah State Hospital
1300 E Center Street
Provo, UT 84606-3554
801-344-4400
E-mail: jgierisch@utah.gov

Mark I Payne, Manager

provides excellent care in a safe and respectful environment to promote hope and quality of life for individuals with mental illness

1885 pages

Vermont

2523 Brattleboro Retreat
Anna Marsh Lane
PO Box 803
Brattleboro, VT 05302-803
802-257-7785
www.www.brattlebororetreat.org

Robert E Simpson Jr, President/CEO
John E. Blaha, MBA, Senior Vice President & Chief Fi
Peter Albert, LICSW, Senior Vice President of Governm
Frederick Engstrom, MD, Chief Medical Officer

A not-for-profit health services organization which, above all else, is committed to assisting individuals to improve their health and functioning.

2524 Spring Lake Ranch Therapeutic Community
1169 Spring Lake Road
Cuttingville, VT 05738-4418
802-492-3322
E-mail: info@springlakeranch.org
www.springlakeranch.org

Rachel Stark, Admissions
Ed Oechslie, Executive Director

Offers an alternative therapeutic treatment program for adults with mental illness and/or substance abuse. Our work program and community life help residents grow and recover in the beautiful Green Mountains of Vermont. Our goal is to help people move from hospitalization or period of crisis to an independent life.

Year Founded: 1932

Virginia

2525 Catawba Hospital
5525 Catawba Hospital Drive
Catawba, VA 24070-0200
540-375-4200
800-451-5544
www.www.catawba.dmhmrsas.virginia.gov/

Jack Wood, CEO

To support the continuous process of recovery by providing quality psychiatric services to those individuals entrusted to our care

1909 pages

2526 Central State Hospital
26317 West Washington Street
PO Box 4030
Petersburg, VA 23803-30
804-524-7000

to provide state of the art mental health care and treatment to forensic and civilly committed patients in need of a structured, secure environment. The major components of the hospital's mission include Evaluation, Treatment, Protection, and Disposition

2527 Commonwealth Center for Children & Adolescents
PO Box 4000
Staunton, VA 24402-4000
540-332-2100

William J Tuell, Contact

CCCA is an acute care mental health facility for minors under the age of 18 years, operated by the State of Virginia, Department of Behavioral Health and Developmental Services.

Year Founded: 1996

2528 Dominion Hospital
2960 Sleepy Hollow Road
Falls Church, VA 22044-2082
703-536-2000
E-mail: Dominion.DLCares@HCAHealthcare.com
www.dominionhospital.com

Trula Minton, CEO

Offers individuals and families hope and help. Treats children, adolescents and adults who suffer from debilitating disorders such as anxiety, panic, depression, delusions, eating disorders, schizophrenia, school refusal, and self-injurious behavior.

2529 Eastern State Hospital
4601 Ironbound Road
Williamsburg, VA 23188-2652
757-253-5161
E-mail: eshinfo@dshs.wa.gov
www.www.esh.dbhds.virginia.gov

David M. Lyon, Director

2530 Northern Virginia Mental Health Institute
3302 Gallows Road
Falls Church, VA 22042-3398
703-207-7100

Jim Newton, Facility Director

Actively promoting recovery of individuals with serious mental illness through the use of safe, efficient, and effective treatment

2531 Piedmont Geriatric Hospital
5001 East Patrick Henry Highway
PO Box 427
Burkeville, VA 23922-427
434-767-4401
TDD: 434-767-4454

Stephen Herrick, Director

A 135-bed psychiatric hospital that provides recovery based MH services to enable the elderly to thrive in the community.

2532 Southern Virginia Mental Health Institute
382 Taylor Drive
Danville, VA 24541-4096
434-799-6220
E-mail: naomi.gibson@dbhds.virginia.gov

David Lyon, Manager

To be an inpatient mental health service provider within our Regional Service Area that responds to the patient's and area needs.

2533 Southwestern Virginia Mental Health Institute
340 Bagley Circle
Marion, VA 24354-3126
276-783-1200
TDD: 276-783-1365

Cynthia Mc Clure, CEO

2534 Western State Hospital
1301 Richmond Avenue
PO Box 2500
Staunton, VA 24402-2500
540-332-8000
TDD: 540-332-8000
www.www.wsh.dbhds.virginia.gov

Jack W Barber, Hospital Director

Year Founded: 1825

Washington

2535 Child Study & Treatment Center
2142 10th Ave West.
Seattle, WA 98119
206-298-9641
800-283-8639
E-mail: ContactCLIP@CLIPadministration.org
www.clipadministration.org

Rick Mehlman, CEO

Treats children from age 5 to 17 who can not be served in less restrictive setting within the community.

2536 Eastern State Hospital
4601 Ironbound Road
PO Box 800 Mail Stop B 32-23
Williamsburg, VA 23188-2652
757-253-5161
E-mail: eshinfo@dshs.wa.gov
www.www.esh.dbhds.virginia.gov

David M. Lyon, Director

Eastern State Hospital is a key partner in assisting adults with psychiatric illness in their recovery through expert inpatient treatment whenever needs exceed community resources.

2537 Ryther Child Center
2400 NE 95th Street
Seattle, WA 98115-2499
206-525-5050
TDD: 800-883-6388
www.ryther.org

Lee Grogg, Executive Director

Offers and develops safe places and opportunities for children, youth and families to heal and grow so that they can reach their highest potential.

West Virginia

2538 Highland Hospital
300 56th Street SE
Charleston, WV 25304-2361
304-926-1600
800-250-3806
www.highlandhosp.com

James H. Dissen, Chairman

Our mission is to identify and respond to mental health needs, and promote physical, social emotional and intellectual well-being.

2539 Mildred Mitchell-Bateman Hospital
1530 Norway Avenue
PO Box 448
Huntington, WV 25709-448
304-525-7801
800-644-9318
E-mail: MMBHospital@wv.gov
www.www.batemanhospital.org

Roy Frasher, Volunteer Services Director

Provides inpatient psychiatric treatment for the adult citizens of southern West Virginia.

2540 Weirton Medical Center
601 Colliers Way
Weirton, WV 26062-5091
304-797-6000
www.weirtonmedical.com

Joseph Endrich, CEO

Weirton Medical Center is a 238 bed, non-profit, acute-care, general community hospital located in the city of Weirton in Brooke County, West Virginia. Weirton Medical Center offers health care services to the residents of West Virginia, Ohio and Pennsylvania.

2541 William R Sharpe, Jr Hospital
936 Sharpe Hospital Road
Weston, WV 26452-8550
304-269-1210
www.www.dhhr.wv.gov

D. Parker Haddix, CEO

1994 pages

Wisconsin

2542 Bellin Psychiatric Center
744 South Webster Avenue
PO Box 23400
Green Bay, WI 54305-3400
920-433-3500
www.bellin.org/psych

Year Founded: 1907

2543 Mendota Mental Health Institute
301 Troy Drive
Madison, WI 53704-1599
608-301-1000
TDD: 888-241-9442
TTY: 888-241-9442
www.www.dhs.wisconsin.gov

A psychiatric hospital operated by the Wisconsin Department of Health and Family Services, Division of Disability and Elder Services, specializes in serving patients with complex psychiatric conditions, often combined with certain problem behaviors.

1860 pages

2544 Wheaton Franciscan Healthcare: Elmbrook Memorial
19333 W North Avenue
Brookfield, WI 53045-4132
262-785-2000
www.www.mywheaton.org/elmbrook-memorial

2545 Winnebago Mental Health Institute
1300 South Drive
PO Box 9
Winnebago, WI 54985-9
920-235-4910
TDD: 888-241-9438

Winnebago Mental Health Institute (WMHI) serves as a specialized component in a community-based mental health delivery system.

Wyoming

2546 Wyoming State Hospital
831 Highway 150 South
Evanston, WY 82930-5340
307-789-3464

William L Matchinski, Manager

A center for treatment, rehabilitation and recovery.

Clinical Management

Management Companies

2547 ABE American Board of Examiners in Clinical Social Work
27 Congress Street Suite 501
Shetland Park
Salem, MA 01970-5577
978-825-9311
800-694-5285

Robert Booth, CEO
Robert Booth, Executive Director
Leonard Hill MSW BCD, Vice President

The American Board of Examiners in Clinical Social Work (ABE) sets national practice standards, issues an advanced-practice credential, and publishes reference information about its board-certified clinicians

2548 Academy of Managed Care Providers
1945 Palo Verde Avenue
Suite 202
Long Beach, CA 90815-3445
562-682-3559
800-297-2627
www.academymcp.org

Dr. John Russell, President
William Adams, Ph.D., Advisory Board Member
Brad Bangerter, Advisory Board Member
Ellen Betts, Ph.D., Advisory Board Member

National organization of clinicans and MCO professionals. Provides many services to members including continuing education, diplomate certification, notification of panel openings and practice opportunities, newsletter, group health insurance and many other benefits.

2549 Action Healthcare Management
6245 N. 24th Parkway
Suite 112
Phoenix, AZ 85016-2029
602-265-0681
800-433-6915
www.actionhealthcare.com

Jean Rice, President

Action Healthcare Management has been an independent healthcare management company offering a full range of services that can be tailored to meet your organization's needs-from pre-certification and utilization review, management of high risk pregnancy and workers' compensation cases, to cases involving serious illness, catastrophic injury and cases requiring transplants. AHM works within your budget to assure provision of quality, affordable healthcare, negotiation of provider agreements and cost containment in the structuring of quality utilization management plans. In today's complicated healthcare system, Action Healthcare Management is a partner to both your organization and your insured. We're by your side, every step of the way.

2550 Adanta Group-Behavioral Health Services
130 Southern School Road
Somerset, KY 42501-3152
606-679-4782
TDD: 800-633-5599
TTY: 800-633-5599

E-mail: klworley@adanta.org
www.adanta.org

Jamie Burton, CEO

Adanta is composed of three major divisions which include Human Development Services, Clinical Services and the Regional Prevention Center. While each division is responsible for providing separate and distinct services, each relies on the expertise and resources available within the overall corporation. The three major divisions are made up of many smaller specialized areas, each of which include many professionals, staff and support personnel who take great pride in the quality of their work. Their professional skills, combined with time, energy and caring, have yielded and continue to yield positive results and many success stories across the region.

2551 Adult Learning Systems
1954 S Industrial Highway
Suite A
Ann Arbor, MI 48104-8601
734-668-7447

Sherri Turner, Contact

2552 Alcohol Justice
24 Belvedere Street
San Rafael, CA 94901
415-456-5692
www.alcoholjustice.org

Bruce Lee Livingston, Executive Director
Michael Scippa, Public Affairs Director
Sarah M. Mart, MS, MPH, Director of Research
Karen Kuhn, Administrative Director

2553 Aldrich and Cox
3075 Southwestern Boulevard
Suite 202
Orchard Park, NY 14127-1287
716-675-6300
www.aldrichandcox.com

Herbert C. Cox, Chairman
Charles H. Cox, President
James B. Hood, Jr, Exec. VP/ Secretary
Daniel C. Buser, J.D., CPCU, EVP

Aldrich and Cox provides independent, fee-based Risk Management, Insurance and Employee Benefit Consulting services to a wide range of clientele.

2554 Alliance Behavioral Care
PO Box 19947
Cincinnati, OH 45219-947
513-475-8622
800-926-8862
www.alliancebehavioral.com

Allen Daniels, CEO

Alliance Behavioral Care is a regional managed behavioral healthcare organization located in Cincinnati, Ohio. They are committed to continuously improving the resources and programs that serve their members and providers. Their goal is to provide resources that improve the well-being of those they serve and to integrate the behavioral healthcare within the overall healthcare systems.

2555 Allina Hospitals & Clinics Behavioral Health Services
2925 Chicago Avenue
Minneapolis, MN 55407-1321
612-775-5000
800-877-7878
www.www.allinahealth.org

Penny Ann Wheeler, MD, President, Chief Clinical Office
Duncan P. Gallagher, EVP, Administration, CFO
Christine Bent, SVP, Clinical Service Lines
Kenneth Paulus, CEO

Provides clinically and geographically integrated care delivery. Innovative programs and services across comprehensive continuum of care. Practicing guideline development, outcomes data and quality managment programs to enhance care delivery.

2556 American Managed Behavioral Healthcare Association
1325 G Street, NW
Suite 500
Washington, DC 20005
202-449-7660
E-mail: info@abhw.org
www.www.abhw.org

Pamela Greenberg, MPP, President/CEO
Rebecca Murow Klein, Associate Director, Government A
Tim Murphy, President, CEO, Beacon Health St
Larry Tallman, President, MHN
Year Founded: 1994

2557 Analysis Group
111 Huntington Avenue
Tenth Floor
Boston, MA 02199
617-425-8000
E-mail: agweb@analysisgroup.com
www.analysisgroup.com

Martha Samuelson, President/CEO
Bruce F Deal, Managing Principal
Stephen Cacciola, VP
Brian Ellman, VP

Provides economic, financial, and business strategy consulting to law firms, corporations and government agencies
Year Founded: 1981

2558 Aon Consulting Group
200 East Randolph Street
14th Floor
Chicago, IL 60601-6408
312-381-2738
www.aon.com

Mike Bungert, Chariman, AON Benfield
Gregory C Case, President, CEO
Laurel Meissner, SVP, Global Controller
Christa Davies, EVP, CFO

Aon Corporation is a leading provider of risk management services, insurance and reinsurance brokerage, human capital and management consulting, and specialty insurance underwriting.

2559 Arthur S Shorr and Associates
98 Golden Eye Lane
Port Monmouth, NJ 07758
818-225-7055
800-530-5728
E-mail: expert@hospitalexperts.com

Arthur S Shorr, MBA, FACHE, Owner
Nancy Daniels, Senior Consultant-Principal
Tom Bojko, MD, MS, JD, Managing Partner
Debra Petracca, MBA, Executive Director

Consultants to health care providers.

2560 Associated Counseling Services
8 Roberta Drive
Dartmouth, MA 02748-2020
508-992-9376

Douglas Riley, Owner

2561 Barbanell Associates
3629 Sacramento Street
San Francisco, CA 94118-1731
415-929-1155

Harriet Barbanell, Owner

2562 Barry Associates
6807 Knotty Pine Drive
PO Box 3069
Chapel Hill, NC 27515-3069
919-490-8474
www.barry-online.com

John S Barry MSW MBA, President

Provides technical assistance services to behavioral health and social service organizations in the areas of performance measurement, survey research, program evaluation, compensation system design and other selected human resource management areas.

2563 Behavioral Health Care
155 Inverness Drive West
Suite 201
Englewood, CO 80112-1411
720-490-4400
877-349-7379
TTY: 855-364-1799
www.www.bhicares.org

Julie Holtz, Chief Executive Officer
Joe Pastor M.D., Medical Director

BHI is committed to excellence in mental health service delivery. They strive to promote recovery by focusing on the unique needs, strengths and hopes of consumers and families.

2564 Behavioral Health Care Consultants
12 Windham Lane
Beverly, MA 01915-1568
978-921-5968
www.bhcconsult.com

Michael L Katzenstein, President
Robert A. DeNoble, Staff
Lincoln Williams, Staff

2565 Behavioral Health Management Group
1025 Main Street
Suite 708
Wheeling, WV 26003-2726
304-232-7232
E-mail: user655349@aol.com

William R Coburn, Practice Manager

They offer a wide range of services for men, women, adolescents, and children. The professional staff specializes in mental and emotional disorders, marital and family counseling, group therapy, vocational counseling, alcohol and substance abuse, academic adjustment counseling, psychological testing, biofeedback, and hypnotherapy.

2566 Behavioral Health Services
2925 Chicago Avenue
Minneapolis, MN 55407-1321
612-775-5000
800-877-7878
www.allina.com

Penny Ann Wheeler, MD, President, Chief Clinical Office
Duncan P. Gallagher, EVP, Administration, CFO
Christine Bent, SVP, Clinical Service Lines
Kenneth Paulus, CEO

Provides clinically and geographically integrated delivery system, innovative programs and services across comprehensive continuum of care, practice guidelines development, outcomes data and quality management programs to enhance care delivery systems.

2567 Behavioral Health Systems
2 Metroplex Drive
Suite 500
Birmingham, AL 35209-6827
800-245-1150
www.behavioralhealthsystems.com

Deborah L. Stephens, Founder, Chairman & CEO
Kyle Strange, LCSW, EVP & Chief Clinical Officer
William M. Patterson, M.D., Medical Director
Willis C. Estis, Ed.D., LPC, Clinical Consultant

Provides managed psychiatric and substance abuse and drug testing services to more than 20,000 employees nationally through a network of 7,600 providers.

Year Founded: 1989

2568 Broward County Health Care Services
115 S Andrews Avenue
Room 302
Fort Lauderdale, FL 33301
954-357-6551
TTY: 800-995-8711
E-mail: civilcitation@broward.org
www.broward.org/healthcare

Bertha Henry, County Administrator
Joni Armstrong Coffey, County Attorney
Evan Lukic, CPA, County Auditor

The Health Care Section of the Community Partnership Division provide mental health, primary health care, and special health care services, as well as funding, Mahogany Project, and the Ryan White Part A Program offices.

2569 Brown Consulting
121 N Erie Street
Toledo, OH 43604-5915
419-241-8547
800-495-6786
E-mail: info@danbrownconsulting.com
www.danbrownconsulting.com

Daniel C Brown, Owner, President
Rhonda Willhight, VP, Operations
Ross Calvin, VP, Consulting
David Galbraith, CFO

Provides a full range of consulting services to behavioral healthcare providers. Has relationships with national, regional and state behavioral healthcare organizations.

Year Founded: 1987

2570 CBCA
10900 Hampshire Avenue S
Bloomington, MN 55438-2384
952-829-3500
800-824-3882
www.cbca.com

Mary Dixon, Senior VP

Provides total health plan management including 24 hours a day, seven days a week patient access and demand management, care management, behavioral health care management, disease management and disability workers' compensation management, all supported by QualityFIRST clinical decision guidelines. These services are electronically integrated with HRM's national provider networks and electronic claims management. HRM's clients include HMOs, hospital systems, insurance and self-insured plans, workers' compensation and disability plans and Medicare/Medicaid plans throughout the US, Canada and New Zealand.

2571 CIGNA Behavioral Care
11095 Viking Drive
Suite 350
Eden Prairie, MN 55344-7234
952-996-2000
800-334-8925

Keith Dixon, CEO

Provides behavioral care benefit management, EAPs, and work/life programs to consumers through health plans offered by large U.S. employers, national and regional HMOs, Taft-Hartley trusts and disability insurers.

Year Founded: 1974

2572 Cameron and Associates
6100 Lake Forrest Drive
Suite 550
Atlanta, GA 30328-3889
404-843-3399
800-334-6014

William Cameron, Owner

Assists troubled employees and their dependents in resolving personal problems in order to provide their employer a level of acceptable job performance and efficiency, and to provide a safe working environment for all employees.

2573 Carewise
1501 4th Avenue
Suite 700
Seattle, WA 98101-3624
206-749-1100
800-755-2136

Rishabh Mehrotra, President/CEO
John McCarty, Executive Vice President/CFO

2574 Casey Family Services
127 Church Street
New Haven, CT 06510-2001
203-401-6900
E-mail: info@caseyfamilyservices.org
www.caseyfamilyservices.org

Raymond L Torres, Executive Director
Michael Brennan, Co-Chairman
Year Founded: 1976

2575 Center for the Advancement of Health
2000 Florida Avenue NW
Suite 210
Washington, DC 20009-1231
202-387-2829
www.cfah.org

Jessie C. Gruman, PhD, President, Founder
David Torresen, VP, Finance and Operations
Dorothy Jeffres, MBA.MSW, MA, Executive Director
Goldie Pyka, Communications Manager

2576 Century Financial Services
23 Maiden Lane
PO Box 98
North Haven, CT 06473
203-239-6364
www.www.centuryfinancialservices.com

William Giovanni, Sr., Director, Operations
Kim Colapietro, Director
William J. Giovanni, Jr., Director, Marketing and Sales
Donella Fields, Collection Manager

2577 Children's Home of the Wyoming Conference, Quality Improvement
1182 Chenango Street
Binghamton, NY 13901-1696
607-772-6904
800-772-6904
www.chowc.org

Robert K. Chip Houser, President and CEO
Maria Cali, VP, Education
Patricia Giglio, CFO/Chief Admin. Officer
Ann M. MacLaren, CFO

Works with social services, court systems, school systems for children who are at risk, have trouble in the home, or have been abused or abandoned.

2578 ChoiceCare
655 Eden Park Drive, Suite 400
Grand Baldwin Building
Cincinnati, OH 45202-6039
513-241-1400
800-543-7158
www.choicecare.com

2579 College Health IPA
5665 Plaza Drive
Suite 400
Cypress, CA 90630
562-467-5555
800-779-3825
TTY: 800-735-2929
E-mail: info@chipa.com
www.chipa.com

Randy Davis, President/CEO
Kevin Gardiner, VP Of Financial Operations
Brian Wheelan, Executive Vice President for Cor
Dale Seamans, Director, Corporate Communicatio

Culturally sensitive mental health referral service.

2580 College of Dupage
425 Fawell Boulevard
Glen Ellyn, IL 60137-6599
630-942-2800
www.cod.edu

Sunil Chand, President
Robert L. Breuder, President
Thomas J. Glaser, SVP, Administration, Treasurer
Joseph Collins, EVP

2581 College of Southern Idaho
315 Falls Avenue
PO Box 1238
Twin Falls, ID 83303-1238
208-732-6221
800-680-0274
E-mail: info@csi.edu
www.csi.edu

Jerry Beck, President
Dr. Jeff Fox, President
Jerry Gee, Executive VP/CAO
Mike Mason, VP, Administration

2582 Columbia Hospital M/H Services
2201 45th Street
W Palm Beach, FL 33407-2095
561-842-6141
www.columbiahospital.com

Valerie Jackson, CEO
Dana C. Oaks, CEO
Brenda Logan, CNO
Oon Soo Ung, CFO

250-bed acute-care facility with dedicated psychiatry, emergency psychiatry, geriatric psychiatry, inpatient and outpatient psychiatry, and partial day psychiatry units and programs.

2583 ComPsych
455 N City Front Plaza Drive
NBC Tower
Chicago, IL 60611-5322
312-595-4000
800-755-3050
E-mail: mpaskell@compsych.com
www.compsych.com

Richard A Chaifetz, Chairman, CEO

Worlwide leader in guidance resources, including employee assistance programs, managed behavioral health, work-life, legal, financial, and personal convenience services. ComPsych provides services worldwide covering millions of individuals. Clients range from Fortune 100 to smaller public and private concerns, government entities, health plans and Taft-Hartley groups. Guidance Resources transforms traditionally separate services into a seamless integration of information, resources and creative solutions that address personal life challenges and improve workplace productivity and performance.

2584 Comprehensive Care Corporation
3405 W. Martin Luther King Jr. Blvd
Suite 101
Tampa, FL 33607
813-288-4808

John M Hill, CEO
Robert Landis, Chairman/CFO/Treasurer

Offers a flexible system of services to provide comprehensive, compassionate and cost-effective mental health and substance abuse services to managed care organizations both public and private. CompCare is committed to providing state-of-the-art comprehensive care management services for all levels and phases of behavioral health care.

2585 Consecra Housing Network
1900 Spring Road
Suite 300
Oak Brook, IL 60523-1480
630-766-3570

Tim Rhodes, President/CEO
Susan Sinderson, Vice President
Dave Opitz, Director of Business Development

Provides therapy services in Spanish for children, families and couples. Offers substance abuse treatment and educational groups for men who batter in English and Spanish. Provides comprehensive services to Latina victims of domestic violence and their children in Spanish.

2586 Corphealth
1300 Summit Avenue
6th Floor
Fort Worth, TX 76102-4414
817-333-6400
800-240-8388

Patrick Gotcher II, President/CEO
Brae Jacobson, COO
Michael Baker, CFO

2587 Corporate Health Systems
15153 Technology Drive
Suite B
Eden Prairie, MN 55344-2221
952-939-0911
www.corphealthsys.com

Bob Hanalon, President

Benefits consulting firm to partner with clients to find the most flexible and comprehensive benefits packages for their investments.

2588 Counseling Associates
106 Milford Street
Suite 501B
Salisbury, MD 21804
410-546-1692
888-546-1692

Anne Bass Kinlaw, MSW, LCSW, President
Janet Brown, Manager
Joan Guzi, LCPC, Staff
Carol Ireland, LCSW-C, Staff

Provides therapeutic counseling to help individuals lead productive and fulfilled lives.

2589 Counseling Corner
2116 Merrick Avenue
Suite 3008A
Merrick, NY 11566
917-670-6262

Cari Sans, Founder And Director
Shari D. Siegel, Counsellor

2590 Covenant Home Healthcare
3615 19th Street
Lubbock, TX 79410-1209

806-725-2328
806-725-0000
www.covenanthealth.org

Melinda Clark, CEO

Provides quality home care to patients when hospitalization may be unneccessary, or when the length of stay may be shorter than expected.

2591 Coventry Health Care of Iowa
211 Lake Drive
Newark, DE 19702-3320
302-283-6500
800-752-7242

Al Redmen, CEO

2592 Creative Health Concepts
One Grand Central Place
Suite 2022
New York, NY 10165-2017
212-697-7207
www.creativegroupny.com

Harry F. Blair, Vice Chairman
Ira N. Gottlieb, President/CEO
Sharon S. Adair, SVP
Dan Pfeiffer, SVP

2593 Cypruss Communications
430 Myrtle Ave
Suite A
Fort Lee, NJ 07024-3913
201-735-7730
800-750-5231
E-mail: peterm@cypruss.com
www.cypruss.com

Peter Miller, VP/CFO

2594 Deloitte and Touche LLP Management Consulting
1700 Market Street
Philadelphia, PA 19103-3984
215-246-2300
www.www.deloitte.com/view/en_US/us/index.htm

Sharon Allen, Chairman
Barry Salzberg, CEO
Punit Renjen, Chairman of the Board, Deloitte
Joe Echevarria, CEO, Deloitte LLP

2595 DeltaMetrics
600 Public Ledger Building
150 S Independence Mall West
Philadelphia, PA 19106-3475
215-399-0988
800-238-2433
www.deltametrics.com

Jack Durell, M.D., President/CEO
John Cacciola, Ph.D., Senior Vice President, Scientifi
Paul Keller, VP, Business Development
Kathleen Geary, Director, Operations

National research, evaluation, and consulting organization dedicated to the improvement of substance abuse and other behavioral health care treatment.

2596 Diversified Group Administrators
6345 Flank Drive
PO Box 6250
Harrisburg, PA 17112-250
717-652-8040
800-877-6490

James Hoellman, Contact

2597 Dorenfest Group
455 N Cityfront Plaza Drive
NBC Tower Suite 2725
Chicago, IL 60611-5555
312-464-3000
E-mail: info@dorenfest.com
www.www.dorenfest.com

Sheldon Dorenfest, CEO
Xiao Liu, Manager, Consulting Services
Wei-Tih Cheng, Strategic Advisor
Michael Cohen, Strategic Advisor

2598 Dougherty Management Associates Health Strategies
9 Meriam Street
Suite 4
Lexington, MA 02420-5312
781-863-8003
800-817-7802
E-mail: mail@dmahealth.com
www.dmahealth.com

Richard H. Dougherty, Ph.D., CEO, Owner
Wendy Holt, M.P.P., Principal
D. Russell Lyman, Ph.D., Senior Associate
Lisa Feldman Braude, Ph.D., Senior Associate

Providing the public and private sectors with superior management consulting services to improve healthcare delivery systems and manage complex organizational change.

2599 Dupage County Health Department
111 North County Farm Road
Wheaton, IL 60187-3988
630-682-7400
TDD: 630-932-1447
www.dupagehealth.org

Linda A. Kurzawa, President
Dr. Lanny F. Wilson, VP
Maureen Mc Hugh, Executive Director
Scott J. Cross, Secretary

2600 Echo Management Group
15 Washington Street
PO Box 2150
Conway, NH 03818-2150
603-447-8600
800-635-8209
E-mail: info@echoman.com
www.echoman.com

John Raden, CEO

Provides financial, clinical, and administrative software applications for behavioral health and social service agencies; comprehensive, fully-intergrated Human Service Information System is a powerful management tool that enables agencies to successfully operate their organizations within the stringent guidelines of managed care mandates. Provides implementation planning, training, support and systems consulting services.

2601 Elon Homes for Children
1717 Sharon Road West
Charlotte, NC 28210
704-369-2500
www.elonhomes.org

Dr Frederick Grosse, President/CEO
Andrea Rollins, VP, Administration
Rose Cooper, VP, Institutional Performance
Jane Grosse, VP, Institutional Advancement

Provides over 1,000 children and families a year in North Carolina an excellent opportunity for safe haven, life skills and education

Year Founded: 1907

2602 Employee Assistance Professionals
1234 Summer Street
Stamford, CT 06905-5558
203-977-2446

2603 Employee Benefit Specialists
PO Box 11657
Pleasanton, CA 94588
888-327-2770
800-229-7683
www.www.ebsbenefits.com

Alan Curtis, Chairman/CEO
Curtis Fankhouser, President

2604 Employee Network
1040 Vestal Parkway E
Vestal, NY 13850-2354
607-754-1043
800-364-4748
www.eniweb.com

Gene Raymondi, Owner, Founder, CEO
Towhee V. Shupka, President, COO

2605 Entropy Limited
345 South Great Road
Lincoln, MA 01773-4303
781-259-8901
E-mail: clientservices@entropylimited.com
www.entropylimited.com

Ron Christensen, Owner

Uses pattern recognition, statistics, and computer simulation to track past behavior, see current behavior and predict future behavior. Used by insuranch companies and the healthcare industry.

2606 Essi Systems
70 Otis Street
San Francisco, CA 94103-1236
415-252-8224
800-252-3774
E-mail: essi@essisystems.com
www.sesystems.com

Esther Orioli, CEO
Karen Trocki, Research Director

2607 Ethos Consulting
3219 E Camelback Road
Suite 515
Phoenix, AZ 85018-2307
480-296-3801
E-mail: conrad@ethosconsulting.com
www.ethosconsulting.com

Conrad E Prusak, President, Co-Founder
Julie Prusak, CEO, Co-Founder

2608 FCS
1711 Ashley Circle
Suite 6
Bowling Green, KY 42104-5801
502-782-9152
800-783-9152
E-mail: admin@fcspsy.com
www.fcspsy.com

Bob Toth, President, CEO
Brian Browning, VP Of Client Services
Dale Taylor, VP, Client Services
Jason Honshell, VP, Client Services

2609 Findley, Davies and Company
One SeaGate
Suite 2050
Toledo, OH 43604-1525
419-255-1360
www.findleydavies.com

Marc Stockwell, VP, Market Leader

2610 First Consulting Group
1160 West Swedesford Road
Building One, Suite 200
Berwyn, PA 19312
800-345-7672
www.csc.com

Larry Ferguson, CEO
Thomas Watford, COO/CFO

Around the world and across the healthcare spectrum, First Consulting Group is transforming healthcare with better information for better decisions.

2611 Fowler Healthcare Affiliates
2000 Riveredge Parkway
Suite 920
Atlanta, GA 30328-4600
770-635-8758
800-784-9829

Frances J Fowler, Owner, President
Denese Estep, Senior Consultant
Elizabeth Forro, Director
Joanne Judge, Legal Consultant

Developed innovative solutions for managing cost of high cost patients.

2612 GMR Group
755 Business Center Drive
Suite 250
Horsham, PA 19044-3491
215-653-7401
www.gmrgroup.com

Barron J Ginnetti, CEO
Thomas Bishop, Vice President/COO

Provides strategic and tactical solutions to the marketing and sales challenges their clients face in the managed healthcare environment.

2613 Garner Consulting
630 North Rosemead Blvd
Suite 300
Pasadena, CA 91107-2138

626-351-2300
www.garnerconsulting.com

Gerti Reagan Garner, GBA, FL, President
John C. Garner, CEBS, CLU, CFC, CEO
Carl Isaacs, Principal
Zaven K. Kazazian, JD, CBC, Principal

Provides innovative consultation, which produces immediate, bottom line results and long term value.

2614 Gaynor and Associates
100 Whitney Avenue
New Haven, CT 06510-1265
203-865-0865
E-mail: mlg110@columbia.edu

Mark Gaynor LCSW, Principal

Clinical social work provider, EAP services, and clinical practice. Specialty weight management
Year Founded: 1980

2615 Geauga Board of Mental Health, Alcohol and Drug Addiction Services
13244 Ravenna Road
Chardon, OH 44024-9012
440-285-2282
800-750-0750
E-mail: mhrs@geauga.org
www.geauga.org

Jim Adams, Executive Director, CEO
Beth Matthews, Associate Director
Jim Mausser, Finance Manager
Sandy Cohn, Information Coordinator

2616 Glazer Medical Solutions
PO Box 121
Beach Plum Lane
Menemsha, MA 02552
508-645-9635
E-mail: glazermedicalsol@aol.com
www.glazmedsol.com

William M. Glazer, M.D., President/Founder

Glazer Medical Solutions is a national medical education consortium that has facilitated a comprehensive matrix of medical education services since 1994.

2617 HCA Healthcare
1 Park Plaza
Nashville, TN 37203-6527
615-344-9551
www.hcahealthcare.com

Richard M. Bracken, Chairman
Samuel N. Hazen, VP, Operations
R. Milton Johnson, President, CEO
David G. Anderson, SVP, Finance and Treasurer

2618 HPN Worldwide
119 W Vallette Street
Elmhurst, IL 60126-4419
630-941-9030
E-mail: info@hpn.com
www.hpn.com

Bob Gorsky, PhD, Owner
Rick Suray, Staff
Ben Gorsky, Staff
Jennifer Toreja, Staff
Year Founded: 1983

2619 HSP Verified
National Register of Health Service Psychologists
1200 New York Avenue NW
Suite 800
Washington, DC 20005-3893
202-783-7663
www.nationalregister.org

Judy E Hall, CEO
Andrew P. Boucher, Assistant Director
Julia Bernstein, Membership Coordinator
Katie Huppi, Finance and Administration Coord

Offers comprehensive, innovative credential verification services designed to help you find that precious time. It relieves health care providers and management of tedious administrative activities-leaving time and resources to focus on quality health care. Provides valuable information and cultivates alliances between cutting edge health care organizations/plans and qualified health care providers.

2620 Hays Group
1133 20th Street NW
Suite 450
Washington, DC 20036-3452
202-263-4000
E-mail: info@hayscompanies.com

2621 Health Alliance Plan
2850 W Grand Boulevard
Detroit, MI 48202-2692
313-872-8100
800-422-4641
TDD: 800-649-3777
E-mail: msweb1@hap.org
www.www.hap.org

James Connelly, President, CEO
Ronald Berry, Senior Vice President/CFO
Christopher Pike, SVP, COO
Mary Ann Tournoux, SVP, Chief Marketing Officer

2622 Health Capital Consultants
1143 Olivette Executive Pkwy
Saint Louis, MO 63132-3205
314-994-7641
800-394-8258
E-mail: solutions@healthcapital.com
www.healthcapital.com

Robert James Cimasi, MHA, ASA, President, CEO
Todd Zigrang, MBA, MHA, ASA, President
Matthew J. Wagner, MBA, VP
John R. Chwarzinski, MSF, MAE, VP

2623 Health Decisions
409 Plymouth Road
Suite 220
Plymouth, MI 48170-1834
734-451-2230
www.healthdecisions.com

Si Nahra, PhD, Owner, President
Judy L. Mardigian, CEO
Michael Falis, Senior Software Engineer
Tina Pelland, MA, Audit Practice Leader

2624 Health Management Associates
5811 Pelican Bay Boulevard
Suite 500
Naples, FL 34108-2711

239-598-3131

Gary D Newsome, President, CFO
Kelly E Curry, Chief Financial Officer
Kerry Gillespie, EVP, Operations Finance

2625 HealthPartners
2701 University Avenue SE
Minneapolis, MN 55414-3233
952-967-7992
TTY: 612-627-3584

Mary Brainerd, President/CEO

2626 Healthwise
2601 N Bogus Basin Road
Boise, ID 83702-909
208-345-1161
800-706-9646
www.healthwise.org

Donald W Kemper, MPH, Founder, CEO
Jim Giuffre, MPH, President/COO
Molly Mettler, MSW, SVP
Karen Baker, MHS, SVP

2627 Healthy Companies
2101 Wilson Boulevard
Suite 1002
Arlington, VA 22201-3048
703-351-9901
www.healthycompanies.com

Robert Rosen, Owner, Chairman, CEO
Jim Mathews, Vice Chairman
Tony Rutigliano, President
Eric Sass, COO

2628 HeartMath
14700 W Park Avenue
Boulder Creek, CA 95006
800-711-6221
E-mail: info@heartmath.org
www.heartmath.org

Sarah Childre, President and CEO
Rollin McCraty, Ph.D., EVP and Director of Research
Brian Kabaker, CFO and Director of Sales
Katherine Floriano, Chairwoman

HeartMath's Freze-Framer Interactive Learning System is an innovative approach to stress relief based on learning to change the heart rhythm pattern and create physiological coherence in the body. The Freeze-Framer has been widely used with clients to help them develop internal awareness, self-recognition and emotional management skills. Clients can learn to prevent stress by becoming aware of when the stress response starts and stopping it in the moment and taking a more active role in preventing stress, managing the emotions associated with stress, creating better health and improving performance.

2629 Helms & Company
1 Pillsbury Street
Suite 200
Concord, NH 03301-3556
603-225-6633
E-mail: info@helmsco.com
www.helmsco.com

J Michael Degnan, President, Co-Founder
Deborah J. White, Senior Consultant, Principal

Susan A. Cambria, Associate
Jeffrey G. White, Associate

They are a New Hampshire based behavioral health management company offering managed behavioral healthcare services, community service programs, and employee assistance programs for health care insurers, members, employers and their employees.

2630 Horizon Behavioral Services

2941 South Lake Vista Drive
Lewisville, TX 75067-3801
972-420-8300
800-931-4646

Mike Saul, President

Provider of national managed care, utilization management and employee assistance programs. Horizon will work in collaboration with HMOs, insurance companies, employers and hospitals to develop seamless, cost-effective managed care services including practitioner panel formation, information system development, utilization management services, EAPs, outcomes measurement systems and sales and marketing functions.

2631 Horizon Mental Health Management

2941 South Lake Vista Drive
Lewisville, TX 75067-3801
972-420-8300
800-931-4646

Johan Smith, VP

Inpatient, outpatient, partial hospitalization and home health psychiatric programs.

2632 Human Behavior Associates

1350 Hayes Street
Suite B-100
Benicia, CA 94510
707-747-0117
800-937-7770
E-mail: corporate@callhba.com
www.callhba.com

James Wallace PhD, President
Yolanda Calderon, Operations Manager

National provider of emploee assistance programs, managed behavioral healthcare services, critical incident stress management services, conflict management, organizational consultation, and substance abuse professional services. Maintains a network of 6500 licensed mental health care providers and 650 hospitals and treatment centers nationwide.

2633 Human Services Research Institute

2336 Massachusetts Avenue
Cambridge, MA 02140
617-876-0426
www.hsri.org

David Hughes, President
Sebrina Johniken, Vice President - HR & Admin.
Roy Gabriel, Secretary & Treasurer

Assists state and federal government to enhance services and support people with mental illness and people with developmental disabilities.

2634 Insurance Management Institute

6 Stafford Court
Mount Holly, NJ 08060-3281

609-267-8998
E-mail: TIMInstitute@aol.com

Michael C Hill, Management Consultant/Author

2635 Interface EAP

10370 Richmond Avenue
Suite 1100
Houston, TX 77042
713-781-3364
800-324-4327
E-mail: info@ieap.com
www.ieap.com

Fred Newman, CEO
Tina Pace, CFO

2636 Interlink Health Services

4660 Belknap Court
Suite 209
Hillsboro, OR 97124
503-640-2000
800-599-9119
E-mail: administration@interlinkhealth.com
www.interlinkhealth.com

John M. Van Dyke, CEO
Sherrie Simmons, Director of Operations
Jill Miller, Assistant Vice President-Facilit
Elizabeth Grafton, Claims Director

2637 Intermountain Healthcare

36 S State Street
Salt Lake City, UT 84111
801-442-2000
E-mail: contactus@imail.org
www.intermountainhealthcare.org

Charles W. Sorenson, MD, President, CEO
Laura S. Kaiser, Executive Vice President & COO
Greg Poulsen, Senior Vice President & CSO
Bert Zimmerli, Executive Vice President & CFO

2638 Jeri Davis International

PO Box 770534
Memphis, TN 38177-534
901-763-0696
E-mail: jeri@jeridavis.com
www.jeridavis.com

Jeri Davis, Founder/President

2639 KAI Research, Inc.

11300 Rockville Pike
Suite 500
Rockville, MD 20852
301-770-2730
www.kai-research.com

Selma C. Kunitz, Ph D., President
Rene Kozloff, Executive Vice President
Patti Shugarts, Chief Operating Officer

2640 Lake Regional Health System

54 Hospital Drive
Osage Beach, MO 65065
573-348-8000
www.lakeregional.com

Michael E. Henze, CEO
Kevin McRoberts, SVP Of Operations
David Halsell, SVP of Financial Services, CFO
Joe Butts, SVP of Facility Services

2641 Lifespan
600 Frederick Street
Santa Cruz, CA 95062
831-469-4900
www.lifespancare.com

Pamela Goodman, President
Becky Peters, CEO
Saundie Isaak, Executive Director
Ute Howland, Lifespan Care Manager

Comprehensive care management for adults who need care.

Year Founded: 1983

2642 MCW Department of Psychiatry and Behavioral Medicine
8701 Watertown Plank Road
Milwaukee, WI 53226
414-955-8990

John R. Raymond, Sr., MD, President/CEO
Joseph Kerschner, MD, Dean/Executive Vice President
G. Allen Bolton, Jr., MPH, MBA, Senior Vice President & COO

2643 MHN
2370 Kerner Blvd.
San Rafael, CA 94901
415-491-7200
800-327-2133
TDD: 800-735-2929
E-mail: mhnfeedback@mhn.com
www.mhn.com

Steven Sell, President/CEO
Juanell Hefner, COO

Provides high-quality, cost-effective behavioral health care services to the public sector.

2644 MHNet Behavioral Health
9606 N MoPac Expressway
Stonebridge Plaza I, Suite 600
Austin, TX 78759
888-646-6889
www.mhnet.com

Wesley Brockhoeft, President/CEO
Robert Wilson, CFO

Health care management and solutions company providing employee assistance programs (EAP), work life programs, managed behavioral health care and consulting services.

2645 Magellan Health Service
6950 Columbia Gateway Drive
Columbia, MD 21046-3308
410-953-1000
800-458-2740
www.magellanhealth.com

Barry M. Smith, Chairman / Chief Executive Offic
Jonathan N. Rubin, Chief Financial Officer
Gary D. Anderson, Chief Information Officer

Provides members with high quality, clinically appropriate, affordable health care which is tailored to each individual's needs.

2646 Managed Care Concepts
PO Box 812032
Boca Raton, FL 33481-2032
561-750-2240
800-899-3926

E-mail: info@theemployeeassistanceprogram.com
www.theemployeeassistanceprogram.com

Beth Harrell, Corporate Contacts Director

Provides comprehensive EAP services to large and small companies in the United States and parts of Canada. Also provides child/elder care referrals, drug free workplace program services, consultation and training services.

2647 Maniaci Insurance Services
500 Silver Spur Road
Suite 121
Palos Verdes, CA 90275
310-541-4824
866-541-4824
E-mail: mail@maniaciinsurance.com
www.maniaciinsurance.com

Dan Maniaci, Owner
Dan Maniaci, President
Kristy Maniaci, Director Of Operations

2648 McGladery
801 Nicollet Avenue
Suite 1100
Minneapolis, MN 55402
952-835-9930
800-274-3978
www.mcgladrey.com

Joe Adams, Managing Partner and Chief Execu
Mike Kirley, Chief Operating Officer
Doug Opheim, Chief Finance Officer
Bruce Jorth, Chief Risk Officer

2649 McKesson Technology Solutions
5995 Windwrad Parkway
Alphretta, GA 30005
404-338-6000

Patrick J. Blake, Executive Vice President and Gro
Jim Pesce, President, Enterprise Informatio
Patrick Leonard, President, McKesson Business Per
Emad Rizk, MD, President, McKesson Health Solut

2650 Mercer Consulting
200 Clarendon Street
Boston, MA 02116-5026
617-424-3930

M. Michele Burns, Chairman/CEO
Tom Elliott, Chief Operating Officer

2651 Midwst Center for Personal/Family Development
2550 University Avenue W
Suite 435-South
Saint Paul, MN 55114
651-647-1900
www.mentalhealthinc.com

Tim Quesnell, Administrator
Kari Droubic, Manager

2652 Mihalik Group
1300 W Belmont
Suite 500
Chicago, IL 60657
773-929-4276
www.themihalikgroup.com

Gary J. Mihalik, President and CEO
Melinda Orlando, Senior VP Operations
Michael Alcenius, VP, Accreditation Services
Cathie Abrahamsen, Senior Consultant

2653 Milliman, Inc
1301 Fifth Avenue
Suite 3800
Seattle, WA 98101-2646
206-624-7940
E-mail: more.info@milliman.com
www.milliman.com

Jeremy Engdahl-Johnson, Media inquiries

Assist plans and payors in measuring and analyzing their healthcare costs arising from behavioral health conditions, identifying specific value opportunities, and designing innovative ways to obtain increased quality and value from behavioral health care delivery.

Year Founded: 1947

2654 Murphy-Harpst Children's Centers
740 Fletcher Street
Cedartown, GA 30125
770-748-1500
www.murphyharpst.org

Charles Troutman, Chief Executive Officer
Emily Saltino, Vice President Development
Shirley Richardson, Chief Financial Officer
Tia McKnight, Director of Compliance

2655 NASW-NC
412 Morson Street
Raleigh, NC 27601
919-828-9650
E-mail: membership@naswdc.org

Kathy Boyd, Executive Director
Valerie Arendt, Associate Executive Director
Kay Castillo, Director of Advocacy, Policy & L
Kristen Carter, Office Manager

2656 National Empowerment Center
599 Canal Street
Lawrence, MA 01840
978-685-1494
800-769-3728
E-mail: info4@power2u.org
www.power2u.org

Daniel B. Fisher, MD, PhD, Chief Executive Officer
Oryx Cohen, MPA, Chief Operating Officer
Kimberly D. Ewing, Coordinator, Emotional CPR

A consumer/survivor/expatient-run organization that is dedicated to helping people with mental health issues, trauma, and/or extreme states. Their central message revolves around recovery, empowerment, and healing.

2657 Oher and Associates
10 Tanglewild Plaza
Suite 100
Chappaqua, NY 10514
917-880-6969
E-mail: joher@oher.net
www.oherandassociates.com

Jim Oher, Founder
Joel Mausner, PhD, Associate
Sheryl Spanier, Associate
Janet Taylor MD, MPH, Associate

2658 Optimum Care Corporation
30011 Ivy Glenn Drive
Suite 219
Laguna Niguel, CA 92677-5018
949-495-1100
www.optimumcare.net

Edward A Johnson, CEO

2659 Options Health Care
240 Corporate Boulevard
Norfolk, VA 23502-4900
757-393-0859
www.valueoptions.com

Barbara B Hill, CEO
Michele Alfano, Chief Operating Officer

Specializes in creating innovative services for a full range of at-risk and administrative services only benefits, including behavioral health programs, customized provider and facility networks, utilization and case management, EAPs and youth services.

2660 PMHCC
123 S Broad Street
23rd Floor
Philadelphia, PA 19109-1029
215-546-0300
www.pmhcc.org

Bernard Borislow, Executive Director
Jay Centifanti, Treasurer

2661 PRO Behavioral Health
7600 E Eastman Avenue
Ste. 500
Denver, CO 80231-4375
303-695-8007
888-687-6755

Martin Dubin, Senior Vice President
Theodore Wirecki, Chair

A managed behavioral health care company dedicated to containing psychiatric and substance abuse costs while providing high-quality health care. Owned and operated by mental health care professionals, PRO has exclusive, multi-year contracts with HMOs and insurers on both coasts and in the Rocky Mountain region.

2662 PSIMED Corporation
725 Town & Country
Suite 200
Orange, CA 92868-4723
714-689-1544

Suzanne Beals, Contact

2663 Paris International Corporation
185 Great Neck Rd
Ste. 305
Great Neck, NY 11021-3352
516-487-2630
www.parisint.com

Stuart A. Paris, CIMA, AIF, Founder and President
Robert Testa, Vice President
Michael Paris, AIF
Mark Zigman, Investment Adviser Representativ

2664 Pearson
5601 Green Valley Drive
Bloomington, MN 55437-1187

952-681-3000
800-627-7271
E-mail: pearsonassessments@pearson.com

Robert Whelan, President and Chief Executive Of
Gary Gates, PhD, Senior Vice President, Global Bu
Corey Hoesley, Vice President, Global Operation
Doug Kennedy, Senior Vice President, Finance a

pearson is a publisher of assessment tools and instructional materials in the special needs behavior management, speech, language, and mental health markets. Among their numerous products are the MMPI-2, million inventories, BASC-2, BASC monitor for ADHD, vineland adaptive behavior scales(vineland II) and the Peabody picture vocabulary test (PPVT-4).

2665 Persoma Management
2540 Monroeville Blvd
Monroeville, PA 15146-2329
412-823-5155
www.persoma.com

James Long, President
Richard Heil Jr., Staff Member

2666 Perspectives
20 N Clark Street
Suite 2650
Chicago, IL 60602-5104
312-558-5318
800-866-7556
E-mail: info@perspectivesltd.com
www.perspectivesltd.com

Bernard S. Dyme, President & CEO, Principal
Terry Cahill, Vice President of Sales and Mark
Christopher Kunze, Chief Operations Officer
Maureen Dorgan-Clemens, Vice President of
Organizational

2667 Philadelphia Health Management
260 South Broad Street
18th Floor
Philadelphia, PA 19102-5085
215-985-2500
www.www.phmc.org

Richard J Cohen, President and Chief Executive Of
Wayne Pendleton, Chief Operating Officer
Marino Puliti, Chief Financial Officer
Tine Hansen-Turton, Chief Strategy Officer

2668 Pinal Gila Behavioral Health Association
2066 W Apache Trail
Suite 116
Apache Junction, AZ 85120-3733
480-982-1317
800-982-1317
www.pgbha.org

Sandie Smith, President
Bryan Chambers, Vice President

2669 Porter Novelli
7 World Trade Center
250 Greenwich Street, 36th floor
New York, NY 10007
212-601-8000
www.porternovelli.com

Karen van Bergen, Chief Executive Officer, Senior
Brad MacAfee, President, North America, Senior

John Orme, Senior Partner, President, Asia-
Karen Ovseyevitz, President, Latin America, Senior

2670 Practice Management Resource Group
1564-A Fitzgerald Dr.
#246
Pinole, CA 94564
708-623-8202
E-mail: info@medicalpmrg.com
www.medicalpmrg.com

Ron Rosenberg, President/Founder
Curt Hill, Chief Executive Officer
Donna Connolly, Vice President of Operations

2671 Preferred Mental Health Management
401 E. Douglas
Suite 505
Wichita, KS 67202-3411
316-262-0444
800-819-9571
www.pmhm.com

Courtney Ruthven, Owner

Offers managed care services and EAP services.

Year Founded: 1987

2672 ProMetrics CAREeval
480 American Avenue
King of Prussia, PA 19406-4060
610-265-6344
E-mail: admin@prometrics.com
www.prometrics.com

Marc Duey, Owner

A joint venture formed by Father Flanagan's Home (Boys Town), Susquehanna Pathfinders and ProMetrics Consulting. These organizations combine years of experience as service providers and technical resource developers. Provides innovative ways to collect, store and analyze service outcome data to improve the effectiveness of your services.

2673 ProMetrics Consulting & Susquehanna PathFinders
480 American Avenue
King of Prussia, PA 19406-4060
610-265-6344
E-mail: admin@prometrics.com
www.prometrics.com

Marc Duey, Owner

2674 Professional Risk Management Services
1401 Wilson Boulevard
Suite 700
Arlington, VA 22209-2434
703-907-3800
800-245-3333
www.prmsva.com

Martin Tracy, CEO
Joseph Detorie, Executive Vice President/CFO

2675 PsycHealth
PO Box 5312
Evanston, IL 60204-5312
847-864-4961
800-753-5456
www.psychealthltd.com

Janet O'Brien, Manager

Specialists providing mental health services, managed care and referrals.

Year Founded: 1989

2676 Public Consulting Group
148 State Street
10th Floor
Boston, MA 02109-2589
617-426-2026
800-210-6113
E-mail: info@publicconsultinggroup.com
www.www.publicconsultinggroup.com

Dan Heaney, Chief Financial Officer
Dina Wolfman Baker, Director of Marketing and Commun
Debra V. Clark, Corporate Facilities Director
Grant Blair, Director PCG Education

Year Founded: 1986

2677 Pyrce Healthcare Group
7325 Greenfield Street
River Forest, IL 60305-1256
708-383-7700
E-mail: phg@pyrcehealthcare.com
www.www.pyrcehealthcare.com

Janice M Pyrce, President/Founder

A national consulting firm, founded in 1990, with a focus on behavioral health. The firm specializes in strategic planning, market research, integrated delivery systems, business development, retreat facilitation and management/organizational development. PHG offers significant depth of resources, with direct involvement of experienced senior staff. Clients include hospitals, healthcare systems, academic medical centers, human service agencies, physician/allied practices, professional/trade associations and investor groups. The firm has over 200 organizations with locations in over 40 states.

2678 Quinco Behavioral Health Systems
720 North Marr Road
Columbus, IN 47201-6660
812-314-3400
800-266-2341
E-mail: webmaster@centerstone.org
www.centerstone.org

Robert Williams, CEO

Nonprofit mental health care provider serving south central Indiana. 24 hour crisis line and full continuum of mental health services.

2679 Schafer Consulting
602 Hemlock Road
Coraopolis, PA 15108-9140
724-695-0652
E-mail: ask@schaferconsulting.com
www.schaferconsulting.com

Steve Schafer, Owner

2680 Seelig and Company: Child Welfare and Behavioral Healthcare
140 E 45th Street
19th Floor
New York, NY 10017-7143
212-655-3500
E-mail: rmm@msf-law.com
www.meisterseelig.com

Mark J Seelig, President
Mercedes Medina, Operations Manager
Elizabeth Roe, Billing Manager
Yvette Pena, HR Manager

Year Founded: 1994

2681 Specialized Therapy Associates
83 Summit Avenue
Hackensack, NJ 07601-1262
201-488-6678
E-mail: Information@SpecializedTherapy.com
www.specializedtherapy.com

Dr.Vanessa Gourdine, PsyD, MSN, P, Director
Dr. Cynthia Orosy, Clinical Director
Polina Levit, LPC, Assistant Director
Rick Rothman, MSW, LCSW, Assistant Director

2682 Suburban Research Associates
107 Chesley Drive
Unit 4
Media, PA 19063-1760
610-891-7200
www.suburbanresearch.com

Nikki Thomas, Marketing Director
Maureen O'Donnell, Sr. Clinical Research Coordnator
Brett Brashers, Clinical Research Coordnator
Ashley Tegler, Clinical Research Coordnator

2683 Supportive Systems
25 Beachway Drive
Suite C
Indianapolis, IN 46224-8506
317-788-4111
800-660-6645

Pam Ruster, Owner

2684 The Kennion Group Inc
800 Corporate Parkway
Suite 100
Birmingham, AL 35242-2942
205-972-0110
866-241-1682
www.kennion.com

W. Hal Shepherd, President/CEO

2685 The Lewin Group
3130 Fairview Park Drive
Suite 500
Falls Church, VA 22042-4517
703-269-5500
877-227-5042
www.lewin.com

Lisa Chimento, CEO
Ann Osborn, Vice President
Robert Page, Vice President
Linda Shields, Vice President

The Lewin Group is a national health care and human service policy, research, and consulting firm with more than 40 years' experience delivering objective analyses and strategic counsel to federal, state, and local governments foundations, associations, hospitals and health systems providers and health plans.

Year Founded: 1970

2686 Towers Perrin Integrated Heatlh Systems Consulting
335 Madison Avenue
New York, NY 10017-4605
212-309-3400
www.towersperrin.com

John Haley, Chief Executive Officer
Julie Gebauer, Managing Director, Talent and Re
Tricia Guinn, Managing Director, Risk and Fina
Gene Wickes, Managing Director, Benefits

Managed behavorial health care consultants specializing in strategy and operations, clinical effectiveness, actuarial and reimbursement and human resources for both the provider and the payer sides.

2687 Traumatic Incident Reduction Newsletter
Traumatic Incident Reduction Association
5145 Pontiac Trail
Ann Arbor, MI 48105-9279
734-761-6268
800-499-2751
E-mail: info@tir.org

Victor Volkam, Author

Traumatic Incident Reduction is a brief, person-sentered treatment for the affects of trauma and loss. This newsletter offers part of the larger subject of Applied Metapsychology, which addresses relationship, self-esteem and well-being issues of all sorts, including traumatic stress. Additional web site for TIR: www.tir.org.

16 pages 2 per year

2688 United Behavioral Health
425 Market Street
27th Floor
San Francisco, CA 94105-2406
415-547-5000
800-888-2998
www.unitedbehavioralhealth.com

Larry Renfro, CEO
Paul Bleicher, MD, PhD, Chief Executive Officer, Optum L
Stan Dennis, Executive Vice President, Physic
Karen Erickson, Executive Vice President, Chief

2689 University of North Carolina School of Social Work, Behavioral Healthcare
Tate-Turner-Kuralt Building
325 Pittsboro Street Cb#3550
Chapel Hill, NC 27599-3155
919-962-1225
E-mail: ssw@unc.edu
www.http://ssw.unc.edu

Year Founded: 1920

2690 ValueOptions Jacksonville
10199 Southside Blvd
Building 100 Suite 300
Jacksonville, FL 32256-757
800-700-8646
www.valueoptions.com

Heyward R. Donigan, President and Chief Executive Of
Douglas Thompson, M.S., M.B.A., Executive Vice President and Chi
Kyle A. Raffaniello, Executive Vice President and Chi
Dan Risku, J.D., Executive Vice President and Gen

2691 ValueOptions Norfolk
240 Corporate Blvd
Norfolk, VA 23502-4900
757-459-5100
www.valueoptions.com

Heyward R. Donigan, President and Chief Executive Of
Douglas Thompson, M.S., M.B.A., Executive Vice President and Chi
Kyle A. Raffaniello, Executive Vice President and Chi
Dan Risku, J.D., Executive Vice President and Gen

Designs and operates innovative administrative and full-risk services for a wide range of behavioral health and chemical dependency programs, Medicaid, child welfare and other human services, and Employee Assistance Programs. Develops collaborative relationships with government agencies, community providers, consumer groups, health plans, insurers, and others to foster a deeper understanding of the needs of the various populations they serve. Develops child welfare programs based upon the principles of managed care.

2692 Vedder Price
222 North LaSalle Street
Chicago, IL 60601-1003
312-609-7500
www.vedderprice.com

Michael A. Nemeroff, President and CEO
Robert J. Stucker, Chairman
Dean N. Gerber, Vice Chair
Douglas M. Hambleton, Operating Shareholder

2693 VeriCare
4715 Viewridge Avenue
Suite 110
San Diego, CA 92123
858-454-3610
800-257-8715
www.vericare.com

Cindy Watson, President/CEO
Bennett O. Voit, Chief Financial Officer
Cammile C. Bird, Vice President, Sales and Market
Karim S. Chalhoub, Executive VP of Revenue and Syst

2694 VeriTrak
179 Niblick Road
Suite 149
Paso Robles, CA 93446-4845
800-370-2440
E-mail: support@veritrak.com
www.veritrak.com

2695 Webman Associates
4 Brattle Street
Cambridge, MA 02138-3714
617-864-6769
www.webmanassociates.com

Dorothy Webman, Owner

2696 WellPoint Behavioral Health
9655 Graniteridge Drive
Sixth Floor
San Diego, CA 92123-2674
858-571-8100
800-728-9498

Lori Wright, Manager

2697 ADL Data Systems
9 Skyline Drive
Hawthorne, NY 10532-2100
914-591-1800
www.adldata.com

David Pollack, President
Aaron S. Weg, Software Development
Ulysses Fleming, Accounting Solutions
Dorothy Dreiher, Clinical Solutions

The most comprehensive software solution for MH/MRDD and the continuum of care. 38 modules to choose from. Designed to meet all financial, clinical, and administrative needs. For organizations requiring greater flexiblity and processing power. Ask about new Windows-based products utilizing the latest in technology, including bar coding, scanning, etc.

Year Founded: 1977

2698 AHMAC
4600 Linden Ave.
Mechanicsburg, PA 17055
717-730-7189

CareManager is a microcomputer based system targeted at small to medium sized HMOs, PPOs and PHOs as well as vertical markets such as Medicaid and managed mental health. Easily customized to meet the needs and requirements of the client.

Year Founded: 1983

2699 Accumedic Computer Systems
11 Grace Avenue
Suite 401
Great Neck, NY 11021-2427
516-466-6800
800-765-9300
E-mail: info@accumedic.com
www.accumedic.com

Mark Kollenscher, President
John Teubner, Vice President

AccudMed EHR, is fully ONC certified. We know the complexities you encounter in your financial and clinical program management. Now you can focus on your mission of improving quality treatment.

2700 Agilent Technologies
5301 Stevens Creek Blvd
Santa Clara, CA 95051-7201
408-345-8886
877-424-4536
www.agilent.com

William P. (Sullivan, President and Chief Executive Of
Ron Nersesian, Executive Vice President
Henrik Ancher-Jensen, Senior Vice President
Rick Burdsall, Senior Vice President

Clinical measurement and diagnostic solutions for healthcare organizations.

2701 American Medical Software
1180 South State
Route 157
Edwardsville, IL 62025-236
618-692-1300
800-423-8836

E-mail: sales@americanmedical.com
www.americanmedical.com

Practice management software for billing, electronic claims, appointments and electronic medical records.

2702 American Psychiatric Press Reference Library CD-ROM
American Psychiatric Publishing, Inc.
1000 Wilson Boulevard
Suite 1825
Arlington, VA 22209-3901
703-907-7322
800-368-5777
E-mail: appi@psych.org
www.appi.org

Robert E Hales, M.D., M.B.A., Editor-in-Chief
Saul Levin, M.D., M.P.A., CEO and Medical Director
Laura W. Roberts, M.D., Deputy Editor
John W. Barnhill, M.D., Associate Editor

$395.00
Year Founded: 1998

2703 Aries Systems Corporation
200 Sutton Street
North Andover, MA 01845-1656
978-975-7570
E-mail: marketing@edmgr.com
www.www.editorialmanager.com

Lyndon Holmes, President

Provides technical innovations that empower all of the participants in the knowledge retrieval chain: publishers, database developers, librarians.

2704 Askesis Development Group
One Chatham Center
112 Washington Place, Suite 300
Pittsburgh, PA 15219-3458
412-803-2400
E-mail: info@askesis.com
www.askesis.com

Sharon Hicks, President and Chief Executive Of
Bob Teitt, Vice President of Technology and
Beth Rotto, Vice President, Finance and Oper
Nicholas Carosella, MD, Physician Advisor

Askesis Development Group's PsychConsult is a complete informatics solution for behavioral health organizations: inpatient or outpatient behavioral health facilities, managed care organizations, and provider networks. PsychConsult is Windows NT based, and Y2K compliant. ADG development is guided by the PsychConsult Consortium, a collaborative effort of leading institutions in behavioral health.

2705 BOSS Inc
2639 N Downer Avenue
Suite 9
Milwaukee, WI 53211
414-967-9689
800-964-4789
E-mail: bmiller@healthcareboss.com
www.healthcareboss.com

Bob Miller, President

Practice management software that is easy to use and is in more than 29,000 practices nationally. Outcome management software products for social workers and hospitals.
$1499.00

Year Founded: 1986

2706 Beaver Creek Software
525 SW 6th Street
Corvallis, OR 97333-4323
541-752-5039
800-895-3344
www.www.beaverlog.com

Peter Gysegem, Owner

'The THERAPIST' practice management and billing software for Windows operating systems comes in Pro and EZ versions. The EZ version is powerful yet simple to use and is tailored to needs of smaller offices. The Pro version is designed to handle the complex needs of busy practices. Use Pro to create HIPAA compliant electronic insurance claims. Both versions let you have an unlimited number of providers at no additional cost. *$249.00*

Year Founded: 1989

2707 Behavioral Health Advisor
McKesson Clinical Reference Systems
One Post Street
San Francisco, CA 94104
415-983-8300
800-782-1334
E-mail: consumerproducts@mckesson.com
www.mckesson.com

The Behavioral Health Advisor software program provides consumer health information for more than 600 topics covering pediatric and adult mental illness, disorders and behavioral problems. Includes behavioral health topics from the American Academy of Child and Adolescent Psychiatry. Many Spanish translations available. *$4.75*

Year Founded: 1998

2708 Behaviordata
20863 Stevens Creek Boulevard
Suite 580
Cupertino, CA 95014-2154
408-342-0600
800-627-2673
www.behaviordat.com

Diana Everstine, President
Dr David Nichols, Contact

2709 Bottomline Technologies
325 Corporate Drive
Portsmouth, NH 03801
603-436-0700
800-243-2528
E-mail: info@bottomline.com
www.www.bottomline.com

Robert A. Eberle, President and Chief Executive Of
Kevin M. Donovan, Chief Financial Officer
Karen Brieger, Vice President, Human Resources
Eric Campbell, Senior Vice President, Strategic

Provides software solutions that enable organizations to achieve unprecedented speed, accuracy, functionality and quality in their document processes such as procure-to-pay, order-to-case, manufacturing and healthcare.

Year Founded: 1981

2710 Bull HN Information Systems
285 Billerica Road
Chelmsford, MA 01824

978-294-6000
www.www.bull.us

David W Bradbury, President

Provides solutions and services to key markets, including the public sector, finance, manufacturing, and telecommunications.

2711 CSI Software
3333 Richmond
2nd Floor
Houston, TX 77098-3007
713-942-7779
800-247-3431
E-mail: sales@csisoftwareusa.com
www.csisoftwareusa.com

Frank Mc Duff, VP

CSI Software designs software for the membership industry utilizing the most sophisticated software technologies, coupled with unsurpassed and experience and support.

2712 Center for Health Policy Studies
214 Massachusetts Ave NE
Washington, DC 20002-4999
202-546-4400
E-mail: info@heritage.org
www.heritage.org

Thomas A. Saunders III, Chairman
Richard M. Scaife, Vice Chairman
J. Frederic Rench, Secretary
David S. Addington, Group Vice President, Research

2713 Ceridian Corporation
3311 E Old Shackopee Road
Minneapolis, MN 55425-1640
952-548-5000
800-729-7655
www.ceridian.com

Stuart C. Harvey, Jr., Chairman
David Ossip, Chief Executive Officer
Dave MacKay, President
Lois M. Martin, Executive Vice President and Chi

A computer services and manufacturing company.

Year Founded: 1957

2714 Cincom Systems
55 Merchant Street
Cincinnati, OH 45246-3761
513-612-2769
800-224-6266
E-mail: info@cincom.com
www.www.cincom.com

Thomas M Nies, Founder and CEO

Cincom provides software and service solutions that help our clients create, manage and grow relationships with their customers through adaptive e-business information systems.

2715 Client Management Information System
WilData Systems Group
255 Bradenton Avenue
Dublin, OH 43017-2546
614-734-4719
800-860-4222
E-mail: cmis@wildatainc.com

A total Electronic Health Records (EHR) solution for behavioral health care organization like mental health centers, substance abuse providers, human service organizations, and family service agencies. Become 100% paperless by using CMIS in-house or by accessing our web based version called e-CMIS to minimize the up front capital expenditure and ongoing maintenance costs.

2716 CliniSphere version 2.0
Facts and Comparisons
77 Westport Plaza
Suite 450
Saint Louis, MO 63146-3125
317-735-5300
800-223-0554
www.factsandcomparisons.com

Arvind Subramanian, President & CEO
John Pins, Vice President, Finance
Denise Basow, MD, Vice President, General Manager
David A. Del Toro, Vice President and General Manag

Access to all information in a clinical drug reference library, by drug, disease, side-effects; thousands of drugs (prescription, OTC, investigational) all included; contains information from Drug Facts and Comparisons, most definitive and comprehensive source for comparative drug information.

2717 Clinical Nutrition Center
7555 E Hampden Avenue
Suite 301
Denver, CO 80231-4834
303-750-9454
www.clinicalnutritioncenter.com

Ethan Lazarus, M.D., President
Heather Thomas, P.A. -C., Physician Assistant

Our programs are based on the latest development in the field of nutrition, weight loss and weight control, behavior modification.

2718 CoCENTRIX
540 North Tamiami Trail
Sarasota, FL 34236-4823
941-306-4951
www.unicaresys.com

May Ahdab, Ph.D., Chief Executive Officer/Co-Found
Leigh Orlov, President/Co-Founder
Neal Tilghman, Senior Vice President, Product M
Jason Ochipa, CPA, Chief Financial Officer

UNI/CARE's mission is to offer enterprise-based solutions designed to improve clinical recovery outcomes, standardize workflows and maximize revenue cycles within a technical environment, fostering collaboration and informed decision-making. Pro-Filer is a .NETcentric Human Service Enterprise (HSE) platform designed to support the requirements of data processing and use by healthcare organizations providing an array of clinical services. It's viable in a single organization or across a consortium, offering users customized workflows, best practice guides, revenue management tools, and the ability to concurrently meet clinical and financial compliance standards.

Year Founded: 1981

2719 Computer Transition Services
3223 S Loop
Suite 556
Lubbock, TX 79423
806-793-8961
800-687-2874
www.www.ctsinet.com

David Baucum, Owner

Improve the life and business success of clients by providing integrated solutions and professional services to meet their technological and organizational needs.

2720 Cornucopia Software
PO Box 6111
Albany, CA 94706-111
510-528-7000
E-mail: supportstaff@practicemagic.com
www.practicemagic.com

Providers of Practice MAGIC, the billing and practice management software that counts for your psychotherapy practice.

2721 Creative Solutions Unlimited
203 Gilman Street
PO Box 550
Sheffield, IA 50475-550
641-892-4466
800-253-7697
E-mail: mkoch@csumail.com
www.creativesolutionsunlimited.com

Martha Koch, Vp

Reliable, comprehensive, intuitive, fully-integrated clinical software able to manage MDS 2.0 electronic submission, RUGs/PPS, triggers, Quick RAP's, survey reports, QI's, assessments, care plans, Quick Plans, physician orders, CQI, census, and hundreds of reports. Creative Solutions Unlimited provides outstanding toll-free support, training, updates, user groups, newsletters, and continuing education.

Year Founded: 1988

2722 DB Consultants
1259 Cedar Crest Blvd.
Suite 328
Allentown, PA 18103
610-820-0440
www.dbconsultants.com

AS/PC includes electronic claims submission. Healtcare professionals rely on AS/PC every day to help them provide quality care.

Year Founded: 1980

2723 DST Output
2600 Sw Blvd
Kansas City, MO 64108-2349
816-221-1234
800-441-7587

Steven J Towle, CEO
Frank Delfer, CTO
Jim Reinert, EVP Business Development

Providing a customer communications solution offering myriad benefits to healthcare payor organizations, including the ability to manage both inbound and outbound communications; ensure document control and content compliance; integrate data from portal entry; distribute data, information, and material to the right place and audience with integrity.

337

2724 DeltaMetrics
600 Public Ledger Building
150 South Independence Mall West
Philadelphia, PA 19106-3475
215-399-0988
www.deltametrics.com

Jack Durell, MD, President/CEO
John Cacciola, Ph.D., Senior Vice President & Scientif
Richard Weiss, Ph.D., Director of Research and Evaluat
Kathleen Geary, Director of Operations

DeltaMetrics is now assisting treatment agencies to design
and implement programs of Continuous Quality Improvement (CQI) within their systems of care.

2725 Docu Trac
20140 Scholar Drive
Suite 218
Hagerstown, MD 21742-6575
301-766-4130
800-850-8510
E-mail: sales@quicdoc.com
www.www.docutracinc.com

Arnie Schuster, Owner

Offering Quic Doc clinical documentation software, a comprehensive software system designed specifically for behavioral healthcare providers.

Year Founded: 1993

2726 DocuMed
3518 West Liberty Road
Ann Arbor, MI 48103-9013
734-930-9053
800-321-5595
E-mail: info@documed.com
www.www.documed.com

DocuMed 2002 is a comprehensive system for automated
documentation of physician/patient encounters in ambulatory settings for solo practitioners or multiple physician
groups.

Year Founded: 1988

2727 E Services Group
5115 Pegasus Court
Suite N
Frederick, MD 21704
301-698-1901

Dave Walsh, Owner

Our primary focus is on finding that perfect marriage of
savvy business logic and technologies so that our
healthcare IT applications solve the real world business
problems of our clients.

2728 EAP Technology Systems
PO Box 1650
Yreka, CA 96097-1650
800-755-6965
www.eaptechnology.com

Tom Amaral, Ph.D., Founder/President & CEO/Board Me
Roland Alden, Technology Development Director
Bob Watson, Business Strategy Advisor/Board
Wayne Larocque, Business Development/Capital Rai

Provider of technologies that automate work flow and enhance the business value of Employee Assistance
Programs.

2729 Echo Group
519 17th Street
Suite 400
Oakland, CA 94612-3461
603-447-8600
800-635-8209
E-mail: info@echoman.com
www.echoman.com

David Allen, Manager

Echo Group has been helping behavioral healthcare organizations to succeed in their missions of healing.

2730 Electronic Healthcare Systems
Ehs One Metroplex Drive
Suite 500
Birmingham, AL 35209
205-871-1031
888-879-7302
www.ehsmed.com

EHS develops and markets system solutions to a select
group of physicians who are leading the way to clinical excellence and practice efficiency trhough automation.

Year Founded: 1995

2731 Entre Technology Services
1501 14th St W
#201
Billings, MT 59102
406-256-5700
www.entremt.com

Mike Keene, Owner
Ben McClintock, Network Administrator
Veronica Smith, Partner Relations and Customer S
Mike Niles, Senior Systems Engineer

Software applications and website development; off site
backup solutions and disaster recovery; managed services;
product sales; seminar room and classroom rental; and
computer training.

Year Founded: 1984

2732 Experior Corporation
5710 Coventry Lane
Fort Wayne, IN 46804-7141
260-432-2020
800-595-2020
E-mail: sales@experior.com
www.experior.com

J. Richard Presser, President & CEO

Experior provides Innovative Information systems to practice management and ASC marketplace. Out products, SurgeOn and EMS provide scheduling, case costing and
billing.

Year Founded: 1978

2733 Family Services of Delaware County
600 North Olive Street
Media, PA 19063-2418
610-566-7540
www.fcsdc.org

Tracy Segal, Director Development

The Where to Turn Database is the most comprehensive
listing of Non-Profit Human Service programs in the Delaware County area, the Young Resources Database is a con-
densed version of the above.

2734 First Data Bank
701 Gateway Blvd.
Suite 600
South San Francisco, CA 94080
650-827-4564
800-633-3453
E-mail: cs@fdbhealth.com
www.firstdatabank.com

Donald M Nielsen, CEO

Provides thousands of drug knowledge base implementations ranging from pharmacy dispensing and claims processing to emerging applications including computerized physician order entry (CPOE), electronic health records (EHR), e-Prescribing and electronic medication administration records (EMAR).

2735 Gelbart and Associates
423 S Pacific Coast Highway
Suite 102
Redondo Beach, CA 90277-3731
310-792-1823
www.www.gelbartandassociates.com

Robert Cutrow, Contact

Comprehensive Psychological and Psychiatric services for individuals, families, couples and groups, treating: anxiety, depression, relationship conflicts and medication management.

2736 Genelco Software Solutions
325 McDonnell Boulevard
Hazelwood, MO 63042-2513
800-548-2040
E-mail: info@genelco.com

Offers its flagship software systems in an ASP financial model. An ASP arrangement allows an organization to maintain control over operations without maintaining the software onsite.

2737 HSA-Mental Health
1080 Emeline Avenue
Santa Cruz, CA 95060-1966
831-454-4000
TDD: 831-454-2123
www.santacruzhealth.org

Exists to protect and improve the health of the people in Santa Cruz County. Provides programs in environmental health, public health, medical care, substance abuse prevention and treatment, and mental health. Clients are entitled to information on the costs of care and their options for getting health insurance coverage through a variety of programs.

2738 Habilitation Software
204 N Sterling Street
Morganton, NC 28655-3345
828-438-9455
E-mail: info@habsoft.com
www.habsoft.com

Randy Herson, President

Personal Planning System, Windows-based computer program which assists agencies serving people with developmental disabilities with the tasks of person-centered planning; tracks outcomes, services and supports, assists with assesments and quarterly reviews, and maintains a customizable library of training programs. Also includes a census system for agencies which must maintain an exact midnight census, as well as an Accident/Incident system.

2739 Hanover Insurance
440 Lincoln Street
Worcester, MA 01653-0002
508-855-1000
800-853-0456
www.www.hanover.com

Frederick H Eppinger Jr, President and Chief Executive Of
Bruce Bartell, Chief Underwriting Officer - Cha
Mark R. Desrochers, Senior Vice President, President
David Greenfield, Executive Vice President and Chi

Offers hospice programs, rehabilitation groups and mental health services.

2740 Health Probe
5693 Bear Wallow Road
Suite 100
Morgantown, IN 46160-9315
765-346-3332
www.healthprobe.com

EMR created to eliminate the need for paper with electronic medical records.

2741 HealthLine Systems
17085 Camino San Bernardo
San Diego, CA 92127-5709
858-673-1700
800-733-8737
www.healthlinesystems.com

Dan Littrell, CEO

Provide peerless information management solutions and services that maximize the quality and delivery of healthcare.

2742 HealthSoft
PO Box 536489
Orlando, FL 32853-6489
407-648-4857
407-648-4857
E-mail: admin@healthsoftonline.com

CD - ROM and web based software for professionals on mental health nursing and developmental disabilities nursing.

2743 Healthline Systems
17085 Camino San Bernardo
San Diego, CA 92127-5709
858-673-1700
800-254-7347
E-mail: sales@healthlinesystems.com

Dan Littrell, CEO

Provider of Document Management and Physician Credentialing software solutions.

2744 Healthport
120 Bluegrass Valley Parkway
Alpharetta, GA 30005-2204
770-360-1700
800-367-1500
www.healthport.com

Michael J. Labedz, President and Chief Executive Of
Brian M. Grazzini, Chief Financial Officer

Matt Rohs, Vice President and General Manag
Bill Matits, Senior Vice President of Sales

Develops and sells Companion EMR, an electronic medical record system that eliminates paperwork, improves accuracy of information, provides instant access to patient and clinical information, and helps cuts costs while increasing revenue.

2745 Hogan Assessment Systems
2622 East 21st Street
Tulsa, OK 74114-1768
918-293-2300
800-756-0632
www.info.hoganassessments.com

Robert Hogan, President
Aaron Tracy, Chief Operating Officer
Rodney Warrentfeltz, Ph.D., Managing Partner
Ryan Ross, VP of Global Alliances

Focuses on five dimensions of personality including emotional stability, extroversion, likeability, conscientiousness and the degree to which a person needs stimulation.

2746 IBM Global Healthcare Industry
404 Wyman Street
Waltham, MA 02451-1212
781-895-2911
E-mail: tgaffin@us.ibm.com
www.ibm.com/industries/healthcare

IBM has been strategically involved in assisting the healthcare industry in addressing numerous IT challenges. IBM provides clients and partners with the industry's broadest portfolio of technology, services, skills, and insight.

2747 InfoMC
101 W Elm Street
Suite G10
Conshohocken, PA 19428-2075
484-530-0100
E-mail: info@infomc.com
www.infomc.com

JJ Farook, Chairman & CEO
Donald Gravlin, EVP Product Startegy & COO
Rick Jackson, SVP Global Wellness Solutions
Susan Norris, Senior Vice Presodent of Clinica

Develops software solutions for Managed Care organizations, EAP/Work-Life organizations, and Health and Human Services agencies.

Year Founded: 1994

2748 Informix Software
IBM Corporation
1 New Orchard Road
Armonk, NY 10504-1722
914-499-1900
800-426-4968
TTY: 800-426-3383
E-mail: ews@us.ibm.com
www.ibm.com/software

IBM Informix® software includes a comprehensive array of high-performance, stand-alone and integration tools that enable efficient application and Web development, information integration , and database administration.

2749 Inhealth Record Systems
5076 Winters Chapel Road
Atlanta, GA 30360-1832
770-396-4994
800-477-7374
E-mail: sales@inhealth.us
www.inhealthrecords.com

Sue Kay, President

Provides variety of record keeping system products for health care practices and organizations.

Year Founded: 1979

2750 Innovative Data Solutions
386 Newberry Drive
Suite 100
Elk Grove Village, IL 60007-2778
847-923-1926
www.idsincp.com

Mark Parianos, President/CEO

Provide effective web based and software solutions for business, small offices and fortune 500 clients.

Year Founded: 1991

2751 Integrated Business Services
736 N Western Ave
125
Lake Forest, IL 60045-1820
847-735-1690
800-451-5478
E-mail: info@medbase200.com
www.www.medbase200.com

Sam Tartamella, Manager

A medical research and information marketing firm providing access to highly selectable medical databases.

Year Founded: 1982

2752 Keane Care
8383 158th Avenue NE
Suite 100
Redmond, WA 98052-3846
425-869-9000
800-426-2675
E-mail: kim_A_Allen@keane.com

Thomas Weitzel, Executive
Jim Ingalls, Director Sales

Develops, markets, and supports a range of clinical and financial software.

Year Founded: 1969

2753 MEDCOM Information Systems
2117 Stonington Avenue
Hoffman Estates, IL 60169-2016
847-885-1553
800-213-2161
E-mail: medcom@emirj.com
www.emirj.com

John Holub, President

Provides a wide variety of products and services to the independent physician clinic as well as the hospital and private clinical laboratories.

Year Founded: 1991

2754 MEDecision
601 Lee Road
Chesterbrook Corporate Center
Wayne, PA 19087-5607
610-540-0202
E-mail: salesinfo@medecision.com
www.medecision.com

Scott A Storrer, CEO

Providing managed care organizations with powerful and
flexible care management solutions. MEDecision's tools
help managed care organizations improve care management
processes and align more closely with their members and
providers to improve the quality and cost outcomes of
healthcare.

Year Founded: 1988

2755 McKesson HBOC
2700 Snelling Ave N
Roseville, MN 55113-1719
651-697-5900

Chris Bauleke, VP

Our products and services are designed to meet the information needs of all participants in the integrated health
system.

2756 MedPLus
4690 Parkway Drive
Mason, OH 45040-8172
513-229-5500
800-444-6235
www.www.questdiagnostics.com

Richard A Mahoney, President
Thomas R Wagner, CTO
Philip S Present, II, COO

Developer and integrator of clinical connectivity and data
management solutions for health care organizations and
clinicians.

Year Founded: 1991

2757 Medai
Millenia Park One
4901 Vineland Rd Suite 450
Orlando, FL 32811-7192
321-281-4480
866-422-5156
www.www.medai.com

Steve Epstein, Owner
Diane Lee, EVP/Co Founder
Swati Abbott, President

Provides solutions for the improvement of healthcare delivery. Utilizing cutting-edge technology, payers are able to
predict patients at risk, identify cost drivers for their
high-risk population, predict future health plan costs, evaluate patient patterns over time, and improve outcomes.

Year Founded: 1992

2758 Medcomp Software
PO Box 16687
Golden, CO 80402-6010
303-277-0772
www.medcompsoftware.com

Developing and designing case management systems for a
wide variety of applications.

Year Founded: 1995

2759 Medi-Span
8425 Woodfield Crossing Boulevard
Suite 490
Indianapolis, IN 46240-7300
317-735-5300
855-539-7686
E-mail: medispan-support@wolterskluwer.com
www.medi-span.com

Arvind Subramanian, President & CEO, Wolters Kluwer
John Pins, Vice President, Finance, Clinica
Denise Basow, MD, Vice President, General Manager
David A. Del Toro, Vice President and General Manag

Medi-Span offers a complete line of drug databases, including clinical decision support and disease suite modules, application programming interfaces, and stand-alone PC
products.

2760 Medical Records Institute
425 Boylston Street
4th Floor
Boston, MA 02116-3315
617-964-3923
www.medrecinst.com

Peter Waegemann, CEO

Promote and enhance the journey towards electronic health
records, e-health, mobile health, mental health assessment,
and related applications of information technologies (IT).

Year Founded: 1983

2761 Medix Systems Consultants
236 E 161st Place
Suite D
S Holland, IL 60473-3374
708-331-1271
E-mail: sales@imsci.com
www.imsci.com

Systems integration and development company committed
to client/server multi vendor(open systems) solutions for a
diverse vertical market ranging from education and
healthcare.

Year Founded: 1987

2762 Mental Health Connections
21 Blossom Street
Lexington, MA 02421-8103
617-510-1318
www.mhc.com

Robert Patterson, MD, Founder/Principal

Developer of medical management software for physicians
and research scientists. Their primary product is desigend
to identify drug interactions based on the mainstream of
drug metabolism research.

Year Founded: 1983

2763 Mental Health Outcomes
2941 S Lake Vista Drive
Ste. 100
Lewisville, TX 75067-3801
800-266-4440
E-mail: johan.smith@horizonhealth.com
www.mho-inc.net

Johan Smith, VP Operations/Development

Designs and implements custom outcome measurement
systems specifically for behavioral helath programs

through its CQI Outcomes Measurement System. This system provides information for a wide range of patient and treatment focused variables for child, adolesent, adult, geriatric and substance abuse programs in the inpatient, partial hospital, residential treatment and outpatient settings.

Year Founded: 1994

2764 Micro Design International
40 Cain Dr.
Brentwood, NY 11717
631-273-4200
800-228-0891
www.mdi.com

Martin Legat, President

Provides optical (CD/DVD/MO) storage solutions through innovative achivements, easy-to-use data access, and exceptional service and support.

Year Founded: 1978

2765 Micro Office Systems
3825 Severn Road
Cleveland, OH 44118-1910
216-297-1240
E-mail: info@micro-officesystems.com
www.www.micro-officesystems.com

Norman Efroymson, Chief Executive Officer
Yosef Gold, Manger, PCG Product Group
Michael Post, Integration Solutions/ Chief Sof
Daniel Ostroff, Manager, Data Conversions

Year Founded: 1985

2766 Micromedex
6200 S Syracuse Way
Suite 300
Greenwood Village, CO 80111-4705
303-486-6444
800-525-9083
www.micromedex.com

Roy Martin, Executive Vice President and Chi
Tina Moen, PharmD, Chief Clinical Officer
Jill Sutton, Senior Vice President of Solutio
Brandy O'Connor, Vice President, Sales

A comprehensive suite of alerts, answers, protocols, and interventions directly addresses clinicians need for evidence-based information. This vital information is used to support patient care and improve outcomes.

Year Founded: 1974

2767 Misys Health Care Systems
8529 Six Forks Road
Forum IV
Raleigh, NC 27615-2963
800-877-5678
www.www.allscripts.com

Paul M. Black, Chief Executive Officer and Pres
Rick Poulton, Chief Financial Officer
Dennis Olis, Senior Vice President, Operation
Brian Farley, SVP and General Counsel

Develops and supports software and services for physicians and caregivers.

2768 MphasiS(BPO)
5353 N 16th Street
Suite 400
Phoenix, AZ 85016-3228

602-604-3100
888-604-3100
E-mail: selse@eldocomp.com
www.eldocomp.com

Sally Else, President
Len Miller, Chief Operating Officer
David J Hawkes, Executive Vice President
Hossein Abdollahi, Senior Vice President of Profess

Focused on financial services, logistics and technology verticals and spans across architecture, application development and integration, application management and business process outsourcing, including the operation of large scale customer contact centers.

2769 National Families in Action
PO Box 133136
Atlanta, GA 30333-3136
404-248-9676
E-mail: nfia@nationalfamilies.org
www.nationalfamilies.org

William F. Carter, Chairman of the Board
Sue Rusche, President and Chief Executive Of
Carol S. Reeder, Treasurer
Paula C. Kemp, Secretary

An interactive database of ever-changing names of drugs that people use and abuse for illnesses.

Year Founded: 1977

2770 NetMeeting
Microsoft Corporation
Customer Advocate Center
One Microsoft Way
Redmond, WA 98052-8300
425-882-8080
800-642-7676
www.microsoft.com

Steve Ballmer, CEO

NetMeeting delivers a complete Internet conferencing solution for all Window users with multi-point data conferencing, text chat, whiteboard, and file transfer, as well as point-to-point audio and video.

2771 Netsmart Technologies
570 Metro Place N
Dublin, OH 43017-5317
614-764-0143
800-434-2642
www.ntst.com

Kevin Scalia, Executive Vice President, Corpor
Michael Valentine, Chief Executive Officer
Frances Loshin-Turso, Senior Vice President, Child & F
Doug Abel, Executive Vice President, Soluti

Offers information systems for mental health, behavioral and public health organizations.

2772 Northwest Analytical
111 SW 5th Avenue
Suite 800
Portland, OR 97204-3606
503-224-7727
888-692-7638
E-mail: nwa@nwasoft.com
www.nwasoft.com

Bob Ward, Chief Executive Officer
Jim Petrusich, Vice President of Sales

T. Olin Nichols, Chief Financial Officer
Louis K. Halvorsen, Chief Technology Officer

Provides comprehensive SPC software tools meeting technically stringent mental health industry requirements.

Year Founded: 1980

2773 OPTAIO-Optimizing Practice Through Assessment, Intervention and Outcome
Harcourt Assessment/PsychCorp
19500 Bulverde Road
San Antonio, TX 78259-3701
210-339-5000
800-622-3231

Mike Cook, Executive

Provides the clinical information necessary for proactive decision making.

2774 Oracle
4150 Network Circle
Santa Clara, CA 95054-1778
650-960-1300
800-633-0925
www.oracle.com

Gregory M Papadopoulos, Executive VP

Provider of healthcare software.

Year Founded: 1982

2775 Oracle Corporation
500 Oracle Parkway
Redwood Shores, CA 94065-1675
650-506-7000
800-392-2999
www.oracle.com

Lawrence J Ellison, Chief Executive Officer
Safra A. Catz, President and Chief Financial Of
Mark Hurd, President
Dorian Daley, Senior Vice President, General C

PeopleSoft provides a range of applications from traditional human resources, payroll and benefits to financials.

Year Founded: 1977

2776 Orion Healthcare Technology
18047 Oak Street
Omaha, NE 68130
402-341-8880
800-324-7966
E-mail: info@orionhealthcare.com
www.myaccucare.com

Bill Allan, Owner

Orion provides technology solutions to meet the ever changing needs of the healthcare industry. To accomodate the behavioral health field, Orion developed the AccuCare software system, a highly integrated and adaptive approach to the clinical practice environment. AccuCare enables clinicians to quickly realize value, effiency and standardization without disrupting their primary focus to provide excellence in health care.

2777 Parrot Software
PO Box 250755
W Bloomfield, MI 48325-755
248-788-3223
800-727-7681

E-mail: support@parrotsoftware.com
www.parrotsoftware.com

Provide 60 different software programs for the remediation of speech, cognitive, language, attention, and memory deficits seen in individuals who have suffered aphasia from stroke or head injury.

Year Founded: 1981

2778 Psychological Assessment Resources
16204 North Florida Avenue
Lutz, FL 33549-8119
813-449-4065
800-331-8378
www.www4.parinc.com

Robert Smith Iii, President

This program produces normative-based interpretive hypotheses based on your client's scores. It produces a profile of T scores, a listing of the associated raw and percentile scores, and interpretive hypotheses for each scale. Although this program is not designed to produce a finished clinical report, it allows you to integrate BRS and SRI data with other sources of information about your client. The report can be generated as a text file for editing.

Year Founded: 1978

2779 Psychological Software Services
3304 W 75th St
Indianapolis, IN 46268
317-257-9672
E-mail: nsc@netdirect.net

Comprehensive and easy-to-use multimedia cognitive rehabilitation software. Packages include 64 computerized therapy tasks with modifiable parameters that will accommodate most requirements. Exercises extend from simple attention and executive skills, through multiple modalities of visuospatial and memory skills. For clinical and educational use with head injury, stroke, LD/ADD and other brain compromises. Price range: $260-$2,500.

Year Founded: 1984

2780 QuadraMed Corporation
12110 Sunset Hills Road
Suite 600
Reston, VA 20190-5852
703-709-2300
800-393-0278
www.quadramed.com

Daniel Desaulniers, CA, President, Harris Quebec Public
Jim Dowling, EVP, Enterprise Self-Service Sol
David L. Puckett, EVP, Revenue Cycle & Enterprise
Vicki Wheatley, EVP, Enterprise Master Person In

2781 RCF Information Systems
4200 Colonel Glenn Highway
Suite 100
Beavercreek, OH 45431-1670
937-427-5680
E-mail: administrator@rcfinfo.com
www.rcfinfo.com

Roger Harris, President

Healthcare software.

2782 Raintree Systems
28765 Single Oak Drive
Suite 200
Temecula, CA 92590
951-252-9400
800-333-1033
www.raintreeinc.com

Richard Welty, President/CTO

Provides practice management software for commerical, not-for-profit, government healthcare providers, rehabilitation facilities, and social service agencies.

Year Founded: 1983

2783 SPSS
233 S Wacker Drive
11th Floor
Chicago, IL 60606-6306
312-651-3000
800-543-2185
www.spss.com

Jack Noonan, CEO

Worldwide provider of predictive analytics software and solutions.

Year Founded: 1968

2784 Saner Software
4198 13th ST NW
Garrison, ND 58540
630-762-9440
E-mail: sales@sanersoftware.com
www.sanersoftware.com

John Parkinson, Owner

Develops health practice management software.

Year Founded: 1988

2785 Sanford Health
PO Box M.C
Fargo, ND 58122-1
701-234-2000
800-437-4010
www.www.sanfordhealth.org

Roger Gilbertson, CEO
Craig Hewitt, CIO

MeritCare is able to track your employees' health trends due to a new software program called Occusource.

2786 Stephens Systems Services
267 5th Avenue
Suite 812
New York, NY 10016-7506
212-545-7788
www.stephenssystems.com

Mike Stephens, Owner

Provides healthcare software.

2787 SumTime Software®
1152 Galvez Ct. SE
Los Lunas, NM 87031
505-990-8356
888-821-0771

Is the practice management solution for health care professionals. We offer the most comprehensive cmeans for preparing billing statements and tracking payments and maintaining records.

2788 SunGard Pentamation
3 West Broad Street
Bethlehem, PA 18018-6799
610-691-3616
866-905-8989

Provides secure and reliable K-12 student information systems, special education management, financial and human resource management software to school districts.

Year Founded: 1992

2789 Synergistic Office Solutions (SOS Software)
17445 E Apshawa Road
Clermont, FL 34715-9049
352-242-9100
E-mail: sales@sosoft.com
www.sosoft.com

Seth R Krieger, PhD, President

Produce patient management software for behavioral health service providers, including billing, scheduling and clinical records.

Year Founded: 1985

2790 Thomson ResearchSoft
1500 Spring Garden Street, Fourth Floor
Philadelphia, PA 19130
215-823-6600
800-722-1227
www.scientific.thomsonrueters.com

Software for wherever research is performed worldwide including all leading academic, corporate and government institutions, healthcare.

2791 TriZetto Group
9655 Maroon Circle
Englewood, CO 80112
949-718-4940
800-569-1222
E-mail: salesinfo@trizetto.com
www.trizetto.com

R. Andrew Eckert, CEO
Jude Dieterman, President/COO
Douglas E. Barnett, Chief Financial Officer
John Schaefer, Senior Vice President, Chief Leg

Focuses on the business of healthcare and offers a broad portfolio of technology products and services.

Year Founded: 1997

2792 Turbo-Doc EMR
6480 Pentz Rd.
Suite A
Paradise, CA 95969
530-877-8650
800-977-4868
www.turbodoc.net

Lyle B Hunt, CEO

An electronic medical record system designed to assist physicians and other health care workers in completing medical record tasks.

2793 Vann Data Services
1801 Dunn Avenue
Daytona Beach, FL 32114-1250
386-310-1702
E-mail: sales@vanndata.com
www.vanndata.com

Janice Huffstickler, President
Healthcare practice software.
Year Founded: 1978

2794 Velocity Healthcare Informatics
8441 Wayzata Boulevard
Suite 105
Minneapolis, MN 55426-1349
800-844-5648

Ellen B White, President/CEO

Provides outcomes management system.

2795 VersaForm Systems Corporation
2505 Carmel Ave
Suite 210
Brewster, NY 10509
800-448-6975
www.versaform.com

Electronic medical records and practice management.

2796 Virtual Software Systems
PO Box 815
Bethel Park, PA 15102-815
412-835-9417
E-mail: sales@vss3.com
www.vss3.com

Thomas Palmquist, Contact

Easy to use practice management, billing, and scheduling software. *$3500.00*

Information Services

2797 3m Health Information Systems
575 West Murray Boulevard
Salt Lake City, UT 84123-4611
801-265-4400
800-367-2447
www.solutions.3m.com

George W Buckley, CEO

2798 Accumedic Computer Systems
11 Grace Avenue
Suite 401
Great Neck, NY 11021-2427
516-466-6800
800-765-9300
E-mail: info@accumedic.com

Mark Kollenscher, President

Practice management solutions for mental health facilities: scheduling, billing, EMR, HIPAA.
Year Founded: 1977

2799 American Institute for Preventive Medicine
30445 Northwestern Highway
Suite 350
Farmington Hills, MI 48334-3107
248-539-1800
800-345-2476
E-mail: aipm@healthylife.com
www.healthylife.com

Don R. Powell, Ph.D., President and CEO
Year Founded: 1983

2800 American Nurses Foundation: National Communications
8515 Georgia Avenue
Suite 400
Silver Spring, MD 20910-3492
800-284-2378
E-mail: customerservice@ana.org
www.nursingworld.org

Kelly Bouthillet, DNP, APRN, Chair
Delanor Manson, MA, BSN, RN, Vice Chair
Carole Stacy, MSN, MA, RN, Member at Large

2801 Arbour Health System-Human Resource Institute Hospital
227 Babcock Street
Brookline, MA 02446-6773
617-731-3200
www.www.arbourhealth.com

Gary Gilberti, CEO

2802 Arservices, Limited
5904 Richmond Highway
Suite 550
Alexandria, VA 22303
703-820-9000
E-mail: info@arslimited.com

Jerry (Jay) McCargo, President & CEO
Robert Mortis, Chief Operating Officer
Kevin Batchelor, Chief Financial Officer

2803 Association for Ambulatory Behavioral Healthcare
757-673-3741
E-mail: info@aabh.org
www.www.aabh.org

James Rosser, President
Larry Meikel, Treasurer
Jill Stanley Nagy, Secretary
Stephen Michael, DrPH, Executive Director

Forum for people engaged in providing mental health services. Promotes the evolution of flexible models of responsive cost-effective ambulatory behavioral healthcare.

2804 Behavioral Intervention Planning: Completing a Functional Behavioral Assessment and Developing a Behavioral Intervention Plan
Pro-Ed Publications
8700 Shoal Creek Boulevard
Austin, TX 78757-6897
512-451-3246
800-897-3202
E-mail: general@proedinc.com
www.www.proedinc.com

Donald D Hammill, Owner

Provides school personnel with all tools necessary to complete a functional behavioral assessment, determine whether a behavior is related to the disability of the student, and develop a behavioral intervention plan. *$22.00*

2805 Breining Institute College for the Advanced Study of Addictive Disorders
8894 Greenback Lane
Orangevale, CA 95662-4019

916-987-0662
E-mail: Suggestions@Breining.edu
www.breininginstitute.net

Kathy Breining, Administrator

2806 Brief Therapy Institute of Denver

7800 S. Elati Street
Suite 230
Littleton, CO 80120
303-426-8757
E-mail: tayers@btid.com
www.btid.com

Marne Wine, Therapist

Our form of psychotherapy emphasizes goals, active participation between therapist and client, client strengths, resources, resiliencies and accountability of the therapy process.

2807 Buckley Productions

238 E Blithedale Avenue
Mill Valley, CA 94941-2083
415-383-2009
877-508-3979
E-mail: buckleypro@aol.com

Richard Buckley, Owner

Alcohol and drug education handbooks, videos, and web-based products for safety sensitive employers, supervisors and employees who are covered by the Department of Transportaion rules. We provide training materials for Substance Abuse Professional (SAPs) and urine collectors.

2808 CareCounsel

101 Lucas Valley Road
Suite 360
San Rafael, CA 94903
415-472-2366
888-227-3334
E-mail: staff@carecounsel.com
www.carecounsel.com

Lawrence N. Gelb, Founder, President & CEO

2809 Catholic Community Services of Western Washington

100 23rd Avenue S
Seattle, WA 98144-2302
206-328-5696
E-mail: info@ccsww.org
www.ccsww.org

Michael Reichert, President

2810 Center for Creative Living

2635 Walnut St
Denver, CO 80205
303-893-0552
E-mail: cclro@aol.com
www.centerforcreativeliving.com

Diane Braun, Owner

2811 Central Washington Comprehensive M/H

PO Box 959
402 S 4th Ave
Yakima, WA 98902-3546
509-575-4200
800-572-8122

Rick Weaver, CEO

2812 Child Welfare Information Gateway

1250 Maryland Avenue, SW
8th Floor
Washington, DC 20024-2141
703-385-7565
800-394-3366
E-mail: info@childwelfare.gov
www.childwelfare.gov

The clearinghouse serves as a facilitator of information and knowledge exchange; the Children's Bureau and its training and technical assistant network; the child abuse and neglect, child welfare, and adoption communities; and allied agencies and professions.

2813 Cirrus Technology

403 Chris Drive
Building 4 Suite H
Huntsville, AL 35802
256-539-2241
www.cirrusti.com

Jerry T Harris, President/CEO
Larry Waller, Vice President Finance
Judy Dunivant, Accounting Manager
Machisa Gaither, Humnan Resources

2814 Community Solutions

9015 Murray Avenue
Suite 100
Gilroy, CA 90520
408-842-7138
E-mail: cs@communitysolutions.org
www.communitysolutions.org

Greg Sellers, Chair
Janie Mardesich, Vice Chair
Nancy Miller, Secretary
Mike Thompson, Treasurer

2815 Consumer Health Information Corporation

8000 Wespark Drive
Suite 120
McLean, VA 22102-3661
703-734-0650
www.consumer-health.com

Dorothy L Smith, President

Specialists in development of evidence-based patient education programs that increase patient safety & patient adherence.

Year Founded: 1983

2816 Control-O-Fax Corporation

3070 W Airline Highway
Waterloo, IA 50703-9591
319-234-4651
800-553-0070
www.controlofax.com

Ken Weber, Manager

2817 DCC/The Dependent Care Connection

500 Nyla Farms
Westport, CT 06880-6270
203-226-2680

2818 Dean Foundation for Health, Research and Education

2711 Allen Boulevard
Suite 300
Middleton, WI 53562-2287
608-250-1393
800-576-8773
www.www.deancare.com

Todd Burchill, Vice President of Strategy, Comm
Carolyn J Ogland, Vice President of Medical Affair
Steve R Caldwell, Vice President of Finance
W Gehren Rall, Vice President of Finance

The Dean Foundation is the non-profit research and education entity of DHS. The Foundation currently encompasses Dean's Educational Services Department, supports community service and health education projects, funds research grants, and conducts its own ancillary research including several outcomes management studies and computer-assisted, voice-activated programs for behavioral medicine.

2819 Dorland Healthcare Information

PO Box 25128
Salt Lake City, UT 84125-128
800-784-2332
www.dorlandhealth.com

Carol Brault, Vice President
Yolanda Matthews, Product Manager
David J DeJulio, Account Executive
Anne Llewellyn, Editor in Chief

2820 FOCUS: Family Oriented Counseling Services

PO Box 921
1435 Hauck Drive
Rolla, MO 65401-2586
573-364-7551
800-356-5395
www.rollanet.org

2821 Federation of Families for Children's Mental Health

9605 Medical Center Drive
Suite 280
Rockville, MD 20850-6390
240-403-1901
E-mail: ffcmh@ffcmh.org
www.ffcmh.org

Sandra Spencer, Executive Director
Lizette Albright, Finance Director
Lynda Gargan, Senior Managing Director
Barbara Huff, Social Marketing

National family-run organization dedicated exclusively to children and adolesents with mental health needs and their families. Our voice speaks through our work in policy, training and technical assistance programs. Publishes a quarterly newsletter and sponsors an annual conference and exhibits.

2822 HSA-Mental Health

1080 Emeline Avenue
Santa Cruz, CA 95060-1966
831-454-4000
TDD: 831-454-2123
www.santacruzhealth.org

Exists to protect and improve the health of the people in Santa Cruz County. Provides programs in environmental health, public health, medical care, substance abuse prevention and treatment, and mental health. Clients are entitled to information on the costs of care and their options for getting health insurance coverage through a variety of programs.

2823 Hagar and Associates

164 W Hospitality Lane
San Bernardino, CA 92408-3316
903-583-7202
www.hagarandassociates.com

Dennis Hagar, Owner
Matt Hager, Owner

Provides clients with data, from national databases, of outcomes, patient demographics, and benchmark data. Can provide technology and/or automated data connection. Provides support in objective outcomes measurement.

2824 Healthcheck

3954 Youngfield Street
Wheat Ridge, CO 80033-3865
916-556-1880

2825 INMED/MotherNet America

20110 Ashbook Place
Suite 260
Ashburn, VA 20147
703-729-4951
www.inmed.org

Paul c Bosland, Chairman
James R Rutherford, Treasurer
Wendy balter, Secretary
Linda Pfieffer, President

2826 Information Access Technology

1100 E 6600 S
Suite 300
Salt Lake City, UT 84121-7411
801-265-8800
800-574-8801
www.iat-cti.com

David H Rudd, CEO

2827 Lad Lake

PO Box 158
W350 S1401 Waterville Rd
Dousman, WI 53118-9020
262-965-2131
www.ladlake.org

Phil Zweig, President
Hon. Derek Mosley, Vice President
Sara Walker, Treasurer
john Mikkelson, Secretary

2828 Lanstat Incorporated

4663 Mason Street
Port Townsend, WA 98368
425-377-2540
800-672-3166
E-mail: info@lanstat.com
www.lanstat.com

Landon Kimbrough, President
Sherry Kimbrough, VP/Co-Founder

Provides quality technical assistance to behavioral health treatment agencies nationwide, including tribal and government agencies.

2829 Liberty Healthcare Management Group
401 E City Avenue
Suite 820
Bala Cynwyd, PA 19004
610-688-800
800-331-7122
E-mail: liberty@libertyhealth.com
www.www.libertyhealthcare.com

Liberty provides individualized programs and a continuum of services for psychiatric and substance abuse treatment at our centers located throughout the Northeast, Oklahoma and Florida. Liberty's commitment to medical excellence within an environment of results-oriented care is evident in our outstanding record of clinical success.

2830 Managed Care Local Market Overviews
Dorland Health
PO Box 25128
Salt Lake City, UT 84125-128
800-784-2332

Carol Brault, Vice President
Yolanada Mathews, Product Manager
David DeJulio, Account Executive
Anne Llewellyn, Editor in Chief

Delivers valuable intelligence on local health and managed care marekts. Each of these 71 reports describes key market participants and competitive environment in one US market, including information on: local trends in events, key players, alliances among MCOs and providers, legislative developments, regulatory development, statistics on Managed Penetration. *$475.00*

2831 Manisses Communication Group
Manisses Communications Group
208 Governor Street
Providence, RI 02906-3246
401-831-6020
www.manisses.com

Fraser Lang, President/Publisher
Paul Newman, Director Of Sales

2832 Medical Data Research
5225 Wiley Post Way
Suite 500
Salt Lake City, UT 84116-2825
801-536-1110

Karen Beckstead, Contact

2833 Medipay
521 SW 11th Avenue
Suite 200
Portland, OR 97205-2620
503-227-6491

2834 Meridian Resource Corporation
1401 Enclave Parkway
Suite 300
Houston, TX 77077-2054
281-597-7000

Paul Ching, CEO

2835 Microsoft Corporation
1 Microsoft Way
Redmond, WA 98052-8300
425-882-8080
800-642-7676
www.microsoft.com
Steve Ballmer, CEO

2836 NASW West Virginia Chapter
750 First Street
Suite 700
Washinton, DC 20002-4241
304-345-6279
800-227-3590
E-mail: naswwv@aol.com
www.naswpress.org
Sam Hickman, Executive Director

2837 National Council on Alcoholism and Drug Dependence
217 Broadway
Suite 712
New York, NY 10007
212-269-7797
800-622-2255
www.ncadd.org

Andrew N. Pucher, President and CEO
Leah Brock, Director of Affiliate Relations
Jill Price, Director of Administration
Paul Warren, Executive Assistant

2838 National Families in Action
PO Box 133136
Atlanta, GA 30333-3136
404-248-9676
E-mail: nfia@nationalfamilies.org
www.nationalfamilies.org

William F Carter, Chairman
Sue Rusche, President/Chief Executive Office
Carol S Reeder, Treasurer
Paula C Kemp, Secretary

2839 North Bay Center for Behavioral Medicine
1100 Trancas Street
Suite 244
Napa, CA 94558-2960
707-255-7786
www.behavioralmed.org

Frank Lucchetti, Psychologist

Represents comprehensive assessment and a balanced schedule of medical and/or psychological treatments for individuals with disabilities needing relief from chronic pain, disabling conditions and stress related to depression, anxiety, and unhealthy work, community or family conditions.

2840 On-Line Information Services
PO Box 1489
Winterville, NC 28590-1489
252-758-4141
800-765-8268
TDD: 866-630-6400
www.onlineinfoservices.com

2841 Open Minds
Behavioral Health Industry News
163 York Street
Gettysburg, PA 17325-1933
717-334-0538
877-350-6463

E-mail: openminds@openminds.com
www.openminds.com

Provides information on marketing, financial, and legal trends in the delivery of mental health and chemical dependency benefits and services. Recurring features include interviews, news of research, a calendar of events, job listings, book reviews, notices of publications available, and industry statistics. *$185.00*

12 pages 12 per year ISSN 1043-3880

2842 Optum
Mail Route MN010-S203
6300 Olson Memorial Highway
Golden Valley, MN 55427-4946
763-595-3200
800-788-4863

David Elton, Senior VP

A market leader in providing comprehensive information, education and support services that enhance quality of life through improved health and well-being. Through multiple access points-the telephone, audio tapes, print materials, in-person consultations and the Internet-Optum helps participants address daily living concerns, make appropriate health care decisions, and become more effective managers of their own health and well-being.

2843 Our Town Family Center
4131 E 5th Street
Tucson, AZ 85711
520-323-1706

Sue Eggleston, Executive Director

A general social services agency which focuses on serving children, youth, and their families. We offer low or no cost assistance with counseling, prevention, services for homeless youth and runaways (their families too) mediation, services for at risk youth, residential programs, parent mentoring, and much more. Our Town has made a conscious decision to keep its services focused in Pima County, in order to better serve our community. We are nonprofit, and funded by United Way, private donations, and grants with the state, county and city.

2844 Ovid Online
Ovid Technologies
333 7th Avenue
New York, NY 10001-5004
212-563-3006
800-950-2035
E-mail: sales@ovid.com
www.ovid.com

Karen Abramson, CEO

Online reference and database information provider. $.50/record

2845 Patient Medical Records
901 Tahoka Road
Brownfield, TX 79316-3817
806-637-2556
800-285-7627

2846 Penelope Price
4281 MacDuff Pl
Dublin, OH 43016-9510
614-793-0165

2847 Physicians' ONLINE
560 White Plains Road
Tarrytown, NY 10591-5113
914-333-5800

2848 Quadramed
12110 Sunset Hills Road
Suite 600
Reston, VA 20190-5852
703-709-2300
800-393-0278
www.quadramed.com

Duncan W James, CEO

2849 SilverPlatter Information
100 River Ridge Drive
Suite 200
Norwood, MA 02062-5041
781-769-2599
www.www.silverplatter.info

2850 Stress Management Research Associates
10609-B Grant Road
Houston, TX 77070-4462
281-890-6395
E-mail: relax@stresscontrol.com
www.stresscontrol.com

Edward Charlesworth, Contact

2851 Supervised Lifestyles
2505 Carmel Ave
Suite 210
Brewster, NY 10509-1122
845-279-5639
888-822-7348

2852 Technical Support Systems
775 E 3300 S
Suite 1
Salt Lake City, UT 84106-4078
801-484-1283
www.tssutah.com

Harry Heightman, Manager
Year Founded: 1984

2853 Traumatic Incident Reduction Association
5145 Pontiac Trail
Ann Arbor, MI 48105-9279
734-761-6268
800-499-2751
E-mail: info@tir.org
www.tir.org

Marian Volkman, President
Margaret Nelson, Vice-President
Frank A Gerbode, Developer of the Subject

Traumatic Incident Reduction is a brief, person-sentered treatmetn for the affects of all sorts of trauma and loss. It is part of the larger subject of Applied Metapsychology, which addresses relationship, self-esteem and well-being issues of all sorts, including traumatic stress. Additional web site for TIR: www.tirbook.com

2854 UNISYS Corporation
8008 Westpark Drive
McLean, VA 22102-3109

703-847-2412
www.www.unisys.com

J Edward Coleman, Charman
Quincy Allen, Chuef Marketing And Strategy Off
Dominick Cavuoto, President
Janet B Haugen, Chief Financial Officer

2855 Virginia Beach Community Service Board
289 Independence Blvd
#138
Virginia Beach, VA 23462-5492
757-437-6150

2856 Well Mind Association
1201 Western Ave
Seattle, WA 98101-2936
206-728-9770
800-556-5829
www.speakeasy.net

Well Mind Association distributes information on current
research and promotes alternative therapies for mental illness and related disorders. WMA believes that physical
conditions and treatable biochemical imbalances are the
causes of many mental, emotional and behavioral
problems.

Pharmaceutical Companies

Manufacturers A-Z

2857 Abbott Laboratories
100 Abbott Park Road
Abbott Park, IL 60064-3500
847-937-6100
www.abbott.com

Miles D White, Chief Executive Officer
Wallace C Abbot, Founder

Founded in 1890. Manufactures the following psychological drugs: Cylert, Desoxyn, Depakote, Nembutal, Placidyl, Prosom, Tranxene.

2858 Actavis
400 Interpace Parkway
Parsippany, NJ 07054
862-261-7000
www.www.watson.com

Paul M Bisaro, CEO

Manufactures the following medications: Ferrlecit, Quasense, Androderm, Nicotine Polacrilex Gum USP, Trelstar, Oxycodone and Acetaminophen Tablets USP, Oxytrol.

2859 Astra Zeneca Pharmaceuticals
1800 Concord Pike
PO Box 15437
Wilmington, DE 19850-5437
302-886-3000
www.astrazeneca-us.com

David Brennan, Executive Director, CEO
Simon Lowth, Chief Financial Officer
Tony Zook, EVP, Global Commercial
Martin McKay, President

Full range of products in six therapeutic areas; gastrointestinal, oncology, anesthesia, cardiovascular, central nervous system and respiratory.

2860 Bristol-Myers Squibb
345 Park Avenue
New York, NY 10154-28
212-546-4000
www.bms.com

Lamberto Andreotti, Chief Executive Officer
Charles Bancroft, EVP, Chief Financial Officer
Brian Daniels MD, Senior Vice President
Sandra Leung, General Counsel, Corp Secretary

Manufactures the following psychological drugs: Avapro, Enfamil, Abilify, Provachol, and Serzone.

2861 Cephalon
41 Moores Road
Frazer, PA 19355-1113
610-344-0200
E-mail: humanresources@cephalon.com
www.cephalon.com

Frank Baldino Jr, CEO
Frank Baldino, Chairman/CEO

Manufactures the following pharmaceuticals: Provigil, Amrix, Fentora, Vivitrol, Trisenox, Nuvigil.

2862 Edgemont Pharmaceuticals, LLC
1250 Capital of Texas
Site 400
Austin, TX 78746
512-550-8555
888-594-4332
www.edgemontpharma.com

Douglas A Saltel, President & CEO

Manufactures Fluoxetine 60 mg tablets

2863 Eli Lilly and Company
Lilly Corporate Center
Indianapolis, IN 46285
317-276-2000
www.lilly.com

John C Lechleiter, Chairman, President & CEO
Ralph Alvarez, Executive Chairman
Katherine Baicker, Professor of Health Economics
Sir Winfried Bischoff, Chairman

Manufactures the following psychological drugs: Prozac, Ceclor, Zyprexa, Cialis, Strattera, and Symbyax.

2864 Forest Laboratories
909 Third Avenue
New York, NY 10022-4748
212-421-7850
800-947-5227
www.frx.com

Howard Solomon, Chairman, CEO

Manufactures the following psychological drugs: Lexapro, Benicar, Campral, Celexa, Namenda, Tiazac, and Viibryd.

2865 GlaxoSmithKline
5 Moore Drive
PO Box 13398
Research Triangle Park, NC 27709-3398
888-825-5249
www.gsk.com

JP Garnier, CEO

Manufactures the following psychological drugs: Lamictal, Paxil, Parnate, Zyban.

2866 Janssen
1125 Trenton-Harbourton Road
PO Box 200
Titusville, NJ 08560-1002
609-730-2000
800-526-7736
www.janssen.com

Timothy Cost, Senior VP Corporate Affairs

Janssen markets prescription medications for the treatment of schizophrenia and bipolar disorder. Medications include: Invega and Risperdal.

2867 Jazz Pharmaceuticals plc
3180 Porter Drive
Palo Alto, CA 94304
650-496-3777
www.jazzpharma.com

Bruce C Cozadd, Chairman & CEO
Robert M Myers, President
Matthew Young, SVP & Chief Financial Officer
Russell J Cox, Executive Vice President & Chief

Manufactures the following medications: Xyrem, Prialt, FazaClo, LuvoxCR

2868 Johnson & Johnson
One Johnson & Johnson Plaza
New Brunswick, NJ 08933-1
732-524-0400
www.jnj.com

William C Weldon, CEO

Manufactures the following: Concerta, Haldol, Reminyl, Daktarin, Ertaczo, Levaquin.

2869 King Pharmaceuticals
132 Windsor Road
Tenafly, NJ 07670
423-989-8000
800-776-7637
www.king-pharma.com

Brian A Markison, CEO
David Robinson, Senior Dir. Corporate Affairs

Manufactures some of the following medications: Sonata, Corgard, Cytomel, Humatin, Levoxyl, Procanbid, and Septra.

2870 Mallinckrodt
675 McDonnell Boulevard
St. Louis, MO 63042-2379
314-654-2000
www.www.mallinckrodt.com

Mark Trudeau, President & CEO
Matthew Harbaugh, Senior Vice President & CFO
Peter Edwards, Senior Vice President & General
Dr. Frank Scholz, Senior Vice President, Global Op

Manufactures the following psychological drugs: Dexedrine, Methylin, Anafranil and Restoril for insomnia.

2871 Merck & Co.
One Merck Drive
PO Box 100
Whitehouse Station, NJ 08889-0100
908-423-1000
www.merck.com

Kenenth C Frazier, Chair, President & CEO
Willie A Deese, EVP & President
Leslie A Brun, Chairman & CEO

Manufactures the following drugs: Remeron™ and Saphris

2872 Mylan
1000 Mylan Blvd
Canonsburg, PA 15317
724-514-1800
www.mylan.com

Robert J Coury, Chairman & CEO
Heather Bresch, Chief Executive Officer
Rajiv Malik, President
John D Sheehan, Chief Financial Officer

Manufactures the following psychological drugs: Ativan, BuSpar, Clonopin, Tranxene, Valium, Xanax, Xanax XR

2873 Novartis
400 Technology Square
Cambridge, MA 02139-3545
617-871-8000
www.novartis.com

Joerg Reinhardt, Chairman
Ulrich Lehner, Vice Chairman
Enrico Vanni, Vice Chairman
Joseph Jimenez, Chief Executive Officer

Manufactures the following products: Diovan, Glivec, Lamisil, Zometa, Focalin and more.

2874 Noven Pharmaceuticals
Empire State Building
350 Fifth Avenue, 37th Floor
New York, NY 10118
212-682-4420
www.www.noven.com

Kazuhide Nakatomi, Chairman
Takehiko Noda, Vice Chairman
Jeffrey F Eisenberg, Director

Manufactures the following mood disorder drugs: Daytrana, Stravzor, Pexeva, Lithobid

2875 Ortho-McNeil Pharmaceutical
1125 Trenton Harbourton Road
PO Box 200
Titusville, NJ 08560-1002
800-526-7736
www.www.janssenpharmaceuticalsinc.com

Manufactures the following: Elmiron, Modicon, Ortho-Novum, and Terazol 3.

2876 Pfizer
235 E 42nd Street
New York, NY 10017-5703
212-573-2323
800-879-3477
www.pfizer.com

Ian C Read, Chairman & CEO
Frank D Amello, Executive VP & CFO
Rady Johnson, Executive VP & Chief Compliance
Doug Lankler, Executive VP, General Councel

Manufactures the following psychological drugs: Geodon, Halcion, Navane, Navane IM, Neurontin, Reboxetine, Relpax, Sinequan, Vistaril, Xanax, Zoloft.

2877 Purdue
1 Stamford Forum
201 Tresser Boulevard
Stamford, CT 06901-3431
203-588-8000
800-877-5666
www.purduepharma.com

Mark Timney, President & CEO
Stuart D Baker, EVP, Counsel to Board
Edward B Mahony, EVP & CFO
David Long, Senior Vice President

Manufactures the following drugs: Betadine, Betasept, Butrans, Colace, Dilaudid, Dilaudid-HP, Intermezzo, MS Contin Tablets, Oxycontin, OxyIR, Peri-Colace, Ryzolt, Senokot, SenokotXTRA, Slow-Mag

2878 Roxane Laboratories
1809 Wilson Road
PO Box 16532
Columbus, OH 43216-6532
614-276-4000
800-962-8364
www.www.roxane.com

Manufactures detoxification medication: Dolophine.

2879 Sanofi-Aventis
55 Corporate Drive
Bridgewater, NJ 08807-1265
908-981-5000
800-981-2491
www.www.sanofi.us

Thomas Zerzan, President
Gregory Irace, Senior Vice President
David Meeker, Chief Executive Officer

Manufacturer of medication for cardiovascular disease, thrombosis, oncology, diabetes, central nervous system, internal medicine, and vaccines. Medication includes Wellbutrin, Wellbutrin SR, and Wellbutrin XL.

2880 Sepracor Pharmaceuticals
84 Waterford Drive
Marlborough, MA 01752-7010
508-481-6700
800-586-3782
www.www.sunovion.com

Hiroshi Nomura, Vice Chair, EVP, CFO
Anthony Loebel, MD, EVP and Chief Medical Officer
Albert P Parker, EVP, General Councel & Corporate
Richard Russell, EVP and Chief Commercial Officer

Manufactures sleep disorder drug Lunesta,as well as other medications Xopenex, and Brovana.

2881 Shire Richwood
5 Riverwalk
City West Business Campus
Dublin, PA 19087-5649
484-595-8800
www.www.shire.com

Matthew Emmens, Chairman
Flemming Ornskov, Chief Executive Officer
James Bowling, Interim Financial Officer

Manufactures the following psychological drugs: Adderall, DextroStat.

2882 Solvay Pharmaceuticals
901 Sawyer Road
Marietta, GA 30062-2250
770-578-9000
www.www.solvay.com

Jean-Pierre Clamadieu, Chairman & CEO
Karim Hajjar, Chief Fianancial Officer
Michael Defourny, General Manager Communications

Manufactures the following psychological drugs: Klonopin, Lithobid, Lithonate.

2883 Sunovion Pharmaceuticals
84 Waterford Drive
Marlborough, MA 01752
508-481-6700
888-394-7377
E-mail: info@sunovion.com
www.sunovion.com

Hiroshi Nomura, Vice Chair, EVP, CFO
Anthony Loebel, MD, EVP and Chief Medical Officer
Albert P Parker, EVP, General Councel & Corporate
Richard Russell, EVP and Chief Commercial Officer

Manufactures the following drugs: Lunesta, Latuda

2884 Synthon Pharmaceuticals
9000 Development Drive
PO Box 110487
Research Triangle, NC 27709-5487
919-493-6006
E-mail: info@synthon.com
www.www.synthon.com

Develops, produces and sells high quality alternatives to innovative medicines. Our products are marketed at the earliest possible opportunity and we sell them at competitive prices.

2885 Takeda Pharmaceuticals North America
One Takeda Parkway
Deerfield, IL 60015-5713
224-554-6500
877-582-5332
E-mail: openpayments@takeda.com
www.www.takeda.us

Shinji Honda, CEO

Manufacturer of Rozerem, Duetact, Amitiza, and Actos.

2886 Valeant Pharmaceuticals International
2150 St. Elzear Blvd.
West Laval
Quebec, CA H7l4A
514-744-6792
800-361-1448
www.valeant.com

J Michael Pearson, Chairman & CEO
G. Mason Morfit, Partner
Dr. Pavel Mirovsky, President & General Manager
Fred Hasan, Partnr & Managing Director

Develops, manufactures and markets pharmaceutical products primarily in the areas of neurology, dermatology and infectious disease.

2887 Validus Pharmaceuticals
119 Cherry Hill Road
Suite 310
Parsippany, NJ 07054
973-265-2777
www.validuspharma.com

James R Hunter, President
Lee Rios, Chief Operating Officer
Richard Post, Vice President - Sales and Marke

Manufactures the following psychological drugs: Marplan, Equetro.

2888 Warner Chilcott
400 Interpace Parkway
Parsippany, NJ 07054
862-261-7488
800-521-8813

Manufactures Sarafem

Drugs A-Z

2889 Abilify
Generic: aripiprazole

Used in the treatment of psychotic disorders and bipolar disorder. This product is manufactured by Bristol-Myers Squibb and Otsuka. See manufacturers section for company information.

2890 Adderall/Adderall XR
Generic: amphetamine/dextroamphetamine

Used to manage anxiety disorders and some cases of attention deficit hyperactivity disorder. This product is manufactured by Shire Richwood. See Manufacturers section for company information.

2891 Antabuse
Generic: disulfiram

Used in the treatment of alcohol and substance abuse. This product is manufactured by Wyeth-Ayers. See Manufacturers section for company information.

2892 Aricept
Generic: donepezil

Used in the treatment of Alzheimer's disease. This product is manufactured by Eisai. See Manufacturers section for company information.

2893 Asenapine
Generic: saphris

Sublingual tablets used in the treatment for schizophreina. Manufactured by Schering-Plough. See Manufacturers section for company information.

2894 Ativan
Generic: lorazepam

Used in the treatment of anxiety and as a preanesthetic medication in adults. This product is manufactured by Wyeth. See Manufacturers section for company information.

2895 Celexa
Generic: citalopram

Used in the treatment of depression. This product is manufactured by Forest Laboratories. See Manufacturers section for company information.

2896 Clozaril
Generic: clozapine

Used in the treatment of severe schizophrenia, and also sold as Clozaril and Fazaclo. This product is manufactured by Novartis. See Manufacturers section for company information.

2897 Cymbalta
Generic: dulozetine

Used in the treatment of depression. Manufactured by Eli Lilly and Company. See Manufacturers section for company information.

2898 Daytrana
Generic: methyphenidate transdermal system

Used in the treatment of ADHD in children 6-17 years old. This product is manufactured by Noven Pharmaceuticals. See Manufacturers section for company information.

2899 Depakote
Generic: valproic acid

Used in the treatment of manic episodes associated with bipolar disorder and mania, and also sold as Depakene. This product is manufactured by Abbott Laboratories. See Manufacturers section for company information.

2900 Desoxyn
Generic: methamphetamine

Used in the treatment of attention deficit hyperactivity disorder. This product is manufactured by Abbott Laboratories. See Manufacturers section for company information.

2901 Desyrel
Generic: trazodone hcl

Used in the treatment of major depressive disorder. This product is manufactured by Labopharm Europe Limited. See manufacturers section for company information.

2902 Dexedrine
Generic: dextroamphetamine

Used in the treatment of attention deficit hyperactivity disorder, and also sold as DextroState, Focalin (by Novartis), Metadate, and Methylin. This product is manufactured by Mallinckrodt. See Manufacturers section for company information.

2903 Effexor
Generic: venlafazine

Used in the treatment of depression and generalized anxiety disorder. This product is manufactured by Wyeth-Ayerst Laboratories. See Manufacturers section for company information.

2904 Elavil
Generic: amitryptiline

Used in the treatment of depression, also sold as Limbitrol (by Valeant). This product is manufactured by Astra Zeneca Pharmaceuticals. See Manufacturers section for company information.

2905 Emsam
Generic: selegiline

Used in the treatment of major depressive disorder. This product is manufactured by Bristol-Myers Squibb. See manufacturers section for company information.

2906 Eskalith
Generic: lithium

Used in the treatment of bipolar disorder. This product is manufactured by GlaxoSmithKline. See Manufacturers section for company information.

2907 Exelon
Generic: rivastigmine

Used in the treatment of Alzheimer's disease. This product is manufactured by Novartis. See Manufacturers section for company information.

2908 FazaClo
Generic: clozapine, USP

Used in the treatment of Schizophrenia. This product is manufactured by Jazz Pharmaceuticals plc. See Manufacturers section for company information.

2909 Fluoxetine Tablets, 60 mg

Used in the treatment of Major Depressive Disorder, Obsessive Compulsive Disorder in adults and pediatrics and Bulimia Nervosa and Panic Disorder is adults. This product is manufactured by Edgemont Pharmaceuticals. See Manufacturers section for company information.

2910 Focalin/Focalin XR
Generic: dexmethylphenidate

Used in the treatment of attention deficit hyperactivity disorder. This product is manufactured by Novartis. See Manufacturers section for company information.

2911 Haldol
Generic: haloperidol

Used in the treatment of Schizophrenia. This product is manufactured by Johnson & Johnson. See manufacturers section for company information.

2912 Intermezzo
Generic: zolpidem

Used in the treatment of insomnia. This product is manufactured by Purdue/Transcept. See Manufacturers section for company information.

2913 Invega
Generic: paliperidone

Used in the treatment of Schizophrenia. This product is manufactured by Janssen. See manufacturers section for company information.

2914 Klonopin
Generic: clonazepam

Used in the treatment of panic attacks/anxiety. This product is manufactured by Hoffman-La Roche. See Manufacturers section for company information.

2915 Lamictal
Generic: lamotrigine

Used in the treatment of bipolar disorder. This product is manufactured by GlaxoSmithKline. See Manufacturers section for company information.

2916 Latuda
Generic: lurasidone hcl

Used in the treatment of schizophrenia. This product is manufactured by Sunovion. See manufacturers section for company information.

2917 Lexapro
Generic: escitalopram

Used in the treatment of depression. This product is manufactured by Forest Laboratories. See Manufacturers section for company information.

2918 Lithobid
Generic: lithium carbonate

Used in the treatment of bipolar disorder and depression. This product is manufactured by Noven Pharmaceuticals. See Manufacturers section for company information.

2919 Lunesta
Generic: eszopiclone

Used in the treatment of insomnia. This product is manufactured by Sunovion Pharmaceuticals. See Manufacturers section for company information.

2920 Namenda
Generic: memantine

Used in the treatment of dementia. This product is manufactured by Forest Pharmaceuticals. See Manufacturers section for company information.

2921 Neurontin
Generic: gabapentin

Used in the treatment of seizures and neuropathic pais. This product is manufactured by Pfizer. See Manufacturers section for company information.

2922 Niravam
Generic: alprazolam

Used in the treatment of anxiety. This product is manufactured by Jazz Pharmaceuticals plc. See Manufacturers section for company information.

2923 Parnate
Generic: tranylcypromine

Used to help manage depression. This product is manufactured by GlaxoSmithKline. See Manufacturers section for company information.

2924 Paxil
Generic: paroxetine hcl

Used in the treatment of depression, and anxiety disorders. This product is manufactured by GlaxoSmithKline. Sold also as Pexeva by Synthon. See Manufacturers section for company information.

2925 Pexeva
Generic: paroxetine mesylate

Used in the treatment of depression, and anxiety disorders. This product is manufactured by Noven Pharmaceuticals. See Manufacturers section for company information.

2926 Pristiq
Generic: Desvenlafaxine

Used in the treatment of depression. Manufacturered by Pfizer. See Manufacturers section for company information.

2927 Prozac
Generic: fluozetine

Used in the treatment of depression and anxiety disorders. This product is manufactured by Eli Lilly and Company. See Manufacturers section for company information.

2928 Relpax
Generic: eletriptan

Used in the treatment of migraines. This product is manufactured by Pfizer. See Manufacturers section for company information.

2929 Remeron
Generic: mirtazapine

Used in the treatment of suicidality and depression. This product is manufactured by Merck & Co. See Manufacturers section for company information.

2930 Restoril
Generic: temazepam

Used in the treatment of insomnia. This product is manufactured by Mallinckrodt Pharmaceuticals Group. See manufacturers section for company information.

2931 Risperdal
Generic: risperidone

Used in the treatment of schizophrenia and other mental illnesses such as psychosis. This product is manufactured by Janssen. See Manufacturers section for company information.

2932 Ritalin
Generic: methylphenidate

Used in the treatment of attention deficit hyperactivity disorders and in some forms of narcolepsy. This product is manufactured by Novartis. See Manufacturers section for company information.

2933 Rozerem
Generic: ramelteon

Used in the treatment of insomnia. This product is manufactured by Takeda Pharmaceuticals. See Manufacturers section for company information.

2934 Saphris
Generic: asenapine

Used in the treatment of Schizophrenia and Bipolar Mania. This product is manufactured by Merck & Co. See Manufacturers section for company information.

2935 Sarafem
Generic: fluoxetine

Used in the treatment of premenstrual dysphoric disorder. This product is manufactured by Warner Chilcott. See Manufacturers section for company information.

2936 Stavzor
Generic: valproic acid

Used in the treatment of bipolar disorder. This product is manufactured by Noven Pharmaceuticals. See Manufacturers section for company information.

2937 Strattera
Generic: atomoxetine

Used in the treatment of attention deficit disorder. This product is manufactured by Eli Lilly & Company. See Manufacturers section for company information.

2938 Valium
Generic: diazepam

Used in the treatment of anxiety. This product is manufactured by Hoffman-La Roche. See Manufacturers section for company information.

2939 Viibryd
Generic: vilazodone HCl

Used in the treatment of depression. This product is manufactured by Forest Pharmacueticals. See manufacturers section for company information.

2940 Vyvanse
Generic: lixdexamfetamine

Used in the treatment of attention deficit hyperactivity disorder. This product is manufactured by Shire Richwood. See Manufacturers section for company information.

2941 Wellbutrin, Wellbutrin SR, Wellbutrin XL
Generic: bupropion

Used in the treatment of depression. This product is manufactured by Sanofi-Aventis. See Manufacturers section for company information.

2942 Xanax
Generic: alprazolam

Used in the treatment of anxiety. This product is manufactured by Pfizer. See Manufacturers section for company information.

2943 Xyrem
Generic: sodium oxybate

Used in the treatment of narcolepsy. This product is manufactured by Jazz Pharmaceuticals. See Manufacturers section for company information.

2944 Zoloft
Generic: sertraline

Used in the treatment of depression and anxiety disorders. This product is manufactured by Pfizer. See Manufacturers section for company information.

2945 Zyban
Generic: bupropion

Used in the treatment of depression. This product is manufactured by GlaxoSmithKline. See Manufacturers section for company information.

Obsessive Compulsive Disorder

Personality Disorders

Professional & Support Services

D

DailyStrength: Tourette Syndrome Support Forum, 1041
Dallas Metrocare Services, 2503
Daniel and Yeager Healthcare Staffing Solutions, 1977
Dark Glasses and Kaleidoscopes: Living with Manic Depression, 363
Dark Voices: Schizophrenia, 634, 745
Dartmouth Univerisity: Department of Psychiatry, 1978
DataStar/Dialog, 2114
David Baldwin's Trauma Information Pages, 1095
Day for Night: Recognizing Teenage Depression, 364
Daytop Residential Services Division, 2314
Daytrana, 2898
DB Consultants, 2722
DBSA Support Groups: An Important Step on the Road to Wellness, 278
DC Commission on Mental Health Services, 1497
DC Department of Behavioral Health, 1444
DC Department of Human Services, 1498
DCC/The Dependent Care Connection, 2817
Dealing with ADHD: Attention Deficit/ Hyperactivity, 430, 635
Dealing with Depression, 365, 636, 843, 1010
Dealing with Feelings, 656
Dealing with Grief, 637, 1011
Dealing With Social Anxiety, 154
Dealing with Social Anxiety, 638, 712, 844
Dean Foundation for Health, Research and Education, 2818
Death and Dying Grief Support, 82
Delaware Department of Health & Social Services, 1495
Delaware Division of Family Services, 1496
Deloitte and Touche LLP Management Consulting, 2594
Delta Center, 2347
DeltaMetrics, 2595, 2724
Depakote, 2899
Department of Children and Families, 1503
Department of Health and Human Services/OAS, 1221
Department of Health and Welfare: Medicaid & Health Division, 1508
Department of Mental Health, 1543
Department of Mental Health Vacaville Psychiatric Program, 2294
Department of Psychiatry, 293, 352
Department of Psychiatry and Behavioral Health, 1342
Department of Psychiatry and Behavioral Sciences at Johns Hopkins, 271, 322
Department Of Psychology, 1755
Depressed Anonymous, 353
Depression, 334
Depression & Anxiety Management, 366
Depression & Bi-Polar Support Alliance, 287, 304, 378
Depression & BiPolar Support Alliance, 332
Depression & Bipolar Support Alliance, 123, 270, 320, 333
Depression and Anxiety in Youth Scale, 1942
Depression and Bipolar Support Alliance, 276, 278, 279, 280, 281, 284, 288, 329, 337, 338, 339, 344, 348, 363, 409
Depression and Bipolar Support Alliance of Boston, 1284
Depression and Related Affective Disorders Association, 1925
Depression: Fighting the Dragon, 367
Depression: Help On the Way, 335
Depression: What Every Woman Should Know, 336
Depressive and Bipolar Support Alliance (DBSA), 1306
Designer Drugs, 899
Desoxyn, 2900
A Desperate Act, 423

Desyrel, 2901
Detwiler's Directory of Health and Medical Resources, 2197
Development & Psychopathology, 1853
Developmental Disabilities Nurses Association (DDNA), 1742
Devereux Arizona, 1186
Dexedrine, 2902
Diagnosis and Treatment of Multiple Personality Disorder, 1943
Diagnosis and Treatment of Sociopaths and Clients with Sociopathic Traits, 1944
Different From You, 459
Directory for People with Chronic Illness, 2198
Directory of Developmental Disabilities Services, 2199
Directory of Health Care Professionals, 2200
Directory of Hospital Personnel, 2201
Directory of Physician Groups and Networks, 2202
Disability Rights New Jersey, 1325
Disability Services Division, 1565
Disease of Alcoholism Video, 946
Diversified Group Administrators, 2596
Division of Disability and Health Promotion, 1033
Division of Independent Practice of the American Psychological Association (APADIP), 1743
A Division of Justice Resource Institute, Inc, 2392, 2393, 2394, 2395, 2396, 2397, 2400
Division of Special Education And Student Services, 1409
Divorce Central, 91
Divorce Information, 92
Divorce Magazine, 93
Divorce Support, 94
The Do It Now Foundation, 966
Doctoral Program in Clinical Psychology, 1698
Docu Trac, 2725
DocuMed, 2726
Dominion Hospital, 2528
Don't Kill Yourself: One Survivor's Message, 639, 1012
Dorenfest Group, 2597
Dorland Health, 2183, 2191, 2192, 2197, 2200, 2202, 2203, 2205, 2207, 2830
Dorland Healthcare Information, 2819
Dorland's Medical Directory, 2203
Dorthea Dix Psychiatric Center, 2378
Dougherty Management Associates Health Strategies, 2598
Dr. Ivan's Depression Central, 393, 2144
Dr. Tony Attwood: Asperger's Syndrome Volume 2 DVD, 227
DRADA-Depression and Related Affective Disorders Association, 364
Draw a Person: Screening Procedure for Emotional Disturbance, 1945
Drinking Facts, 900
Driving Far from Home, 155
Drug and Alcohol Dependence An International Journal on Biomedical an Psychosocial Approaches, 903
Drug Dependence, Alcohol Abuse and Alcoholism, 901
Drug Facts Pamphlet, 902
Drug Information Handbook for Psychiatry, 2204
DrugLink, 904
Drugs: Talking With Your Teen, 905
DSM-IV Psychotic Disorders: New Diagnostic Issue, 2196
DSM-IV-TR, 153
DST Output, 2723
Duke University's Program in Child and Anxiety Disorders, 664
Dupage County Health Department, 2599

E

E Services Group, 2727
E-Productivity-Services.Net, 1828
EAP Technology Systems, 2728
EAPA Exchange, 1854, 1744

Earle E Morris Jr Alcohol & Drug Treatment Center, 2487
East Carolina University Department of Psychiatric Medicine, 1979
East Mississippi State Hospital, 2405
Eastern Shore Hospital Center, 2383
Eastern State Hospital, 2372, 2529, 2536
Eating Disorder Sourcebook, 489
Eating Disorder Video, 505
Eating Disorders, 490
Eating Disorders Awareness and Prevention, 510
Eating Disorders: Facts About Eating Disorders and the Search for Solutions, 491
EBSCO Publishing, 2232
Echo Group, 2729
Echo Management Group, 2600
Edgemont Pharmaceuticals, LLC, 2862
Educating Clients about the Cognitive Model, 2065
Educating Inattentive Children, 28
Educational Testing Service, 1954
Educational Training Videos, 296, 297, 299, 356, 357, 359, 370, 371, 428, 432, 433, 434, 626, 628, 631, 634, 639, 642, 710, 711, 714
Educational Video Network, 32, 154, 157, 438, 460, 461, 462, 570, 938, 940, 941
Educational Video Network, Inc., 295, 300, 361, 365, 372, 425, 427, 429, 430, 624, 632, 633, 635, 636, 637, 638, 643, 644, 645, 646, 647
Effective Learning Systems, 569, 811
Effective Learning Systems, Inc., 80, 156, 947
Effexor, 2903
eHealthForum Sleep Disorder Support Forum, 808, 815
ehealthforum.com/health/sleep_disorders. html#b, 815
El Paso County Human Services, 1491
El Paso Psychiatric Center, 2504
Elavil, 2904
Electronic Healthcare Systems, 2730
Eli Lilly and Company, 2863
Elmira Psychiatric Center, 2432
Elon Homes for Children, 2601
Elsevier, 1856, 1861
Elsevier Publishing, 143, 901, 912
Elsevier Science, 2174
EMDR Institute, 778
EMDR Institute, Inc., 379
Emily Griffith Center, 2313
Emory University School of Medicine, Psychology and Behavior, 1980
Emory University: Psychological Center, 1981
Emotion-Focused Therapy, 2165
Emotions Anonymous, 345
Emotions Anonymous International Service Center, 150, 354, 1125
Employee Assistance Professionals, 2602
Employee Assistance Professionals Association, 1854
Employee Assistance Professionals Association, Inc., 1744
Employee Assistance Society of North America, 1745
Employee Benefit Specialists, 2603
Employee Benefits Journal, 1857
Employee Network, 2604
Empty Cradle, 60, 95
Emsam, 2905
Entre Technology Services, 2731
Entropy Limited, 2605
EPIC, 2133
Epidemiology-Genetics Program in Psychiatry, 292
Epidemology-Genetics Program in Psychiatry, 754
Equal Employment Opportunity Commission, 1445
eRiver Neurology of New York, LLC, 804
Eskalith, 2906
Essi Systems, 2606
Ethos Consulting, 2607
ETR Associates, 1855, 145, 335, 486, 487, 488, 490, 492, 493, 494, 495, 496, 886, 887, 888, 890, 892, 893, 897, 899, 900
Exceptional Parent, 1858
Exelon, 2907

Rational Recovery, 935
RCF Information Systems, 2781
re:MIND, 1397
Real Illness: Panic Disorder, 146
Real Illness: Post-Traumatic Stress Disorder, 1075
Real World Drinking, 914
Reality Check: Marijuana Prevention Video, 956
Recovered, 881
Recovering Your Mental Health: a Self-Help
    Guide, 286, 346
Recovery, 2145
Recovery International, 151, 294, 355, 1165
Reggie White Sleep Disorders Research &
    Education Foundation, Inc., 826
Regional Research Institue-Portland State
    University, 1859
Rehabilitation Accreditation Commission, 2190
The Relationship Learning Center, 108
Relaxation & Stress Reduction Workbook, 2176
Religion and Gender: Identity, Conflict, and Power
    Conference, 553
Relpax, 2928
Remeron, 2929
Renaissance Manor, 2332
Renfrew Center Foundation, 2478
Research & Training Center for Children's Mental
    Health, 662
Research and Training Center for Pathways to
    Positive Futures, 608
Research and Training for Children's Mental
    Health-Update, 1923
Research Press, 426, 623, 641, 1081, 2078
Research Press Publishers, 2268
Research Society on Alcoholism, 882
Resources For Children with Special Needs, 2180
Resources for Children with Special Needs, 115,
    261, 266
Restless Legs Syndrome Foundation, Inc., 794
Restoril, 2930
Restrictive Eating, 495
Reuters Health, 2146
Rhode Island Council on Alcoholism and Other
    Drug Dependence, 1601
Rhode Island Department of Behavioral
    Healthcare, Developmental Disabilities and
    Hospitals, 1602
Rhode Island Division of Substance Abuse, 1603
RICA: Southern Maryland, 2386
Richmond State Hospital, 2365
Rio Grande State Center, 2514
Rising Above a Diagnosis of Autism, 232
Risk and Insurance Management Society (RIMS),
    1789
Risperdal, 2931
Ritalin, 2932
River City Mental Health Clinic, 2404
River Oaks Hospital, 2376
Riveredge Hospital, 2355
Riverside Center, 2475
Riverside Publishing, 2269
Riverview Psychiatric Center, 2380
Rochester Psychiatric Center, 2451
Rockland Children's Psychiatric Center, 2452
Rockland Psychiatric Center, 2453
Roster: Centers for the Developmentally Disabled,
    2217
Roster: Health Clinics, 2218
Roster: Substance Abuse Treatment Centers, 2219
Rowman & Littlefield, 2270
Roxane Laboratories, 2878
Royal College of Psychiatrists, 590
Rozerem, 2933
Rural Mental Health Journal, 1924
Rusk State Hospital, 2515
Rylee's Gift - Asperger Syndrome, 233
Ryther Child Center, 2537

S

S.A.F.E. Alternatives, 708
SA/VE - Suicide Awareness/Voices of Education,
    2147

SADD-Students Against Destructive Decisions,
    980
SADD: Students Against Destructive Decisions,
    622, 936
Safe Crossings Foundation, 109
Sagamore Children's Psychiatric Center, 2454
Sage Publications, 2271, 1886
Samaritan Counseling Center, 2403
Samaritan Village, 2455
Samaritans International, 301, 374
SAMHSA, 988
SAMHSA's National Mental Health Info Center,
    985
SAMHSA'S National Mental Health Informantion
    Center, 286, 346
SAMHSA'S National Mental Health Information
    Center, 415
San Antonio State Hospital, 2516
Saner Software, 2784
Sanford Health, 2785
Sanofi-Aventis, 2879
Saphris, 2934
Sarafem, 2935
Scale for Assessing Emotional Disturbance, 1949
Schafer Consulting, 2679
Schizophrenia, 738, 759, 760, 761
Schizophrenia Research, 739
Schizophrenia.com, 2148, 2150
Screening for Brain Dysfunction in Psychiatric
    Patients, 1950
Screening for Mental Health, 1790
Section for Psychiatric and Substance Abuse
    Services (SPSPAS), 883
Seelig and Company: Child Welfare and
    Behavioral Healthcare, 2680
Selective Mutism Association (SMA), 133
Selective Mutism Foundation, 176
Selective Mutism Research Institute, 134
Self Help for Substance Abuse & Addiction, 983
Self Help Magazine, 313, 395
Self-Help and Psychology Magazine, 2151
Self-Help Brochures, 654
Seminole Community Mental Health Center, 2333
Sepracor Pharmaceuticals, 2880
Sequoyah Adolescent Treatment Center, 2421
Sex Education: Issues for the Person with Autism,
    213
Sexual Disorders, 781
Sexual Dysfunction: Guide for Assessment and
    Treatment, 1951
Sexual Medicine Society of North America, 774
Shades of Hope Treatment Center, 2517
Shared Parenting Information Group (SPIG), 110
Sharing & Caring for Consumers, Families
    Alliance for the Mentally Ill, 1418
Sheppard Pratt, 1280
Sheppard Pratt at Ellicott City, 2387
Shire Richwood, 2881
Shrinktank, 783
The Shulman Center for Compulsive Theft,
    Spending & Hoarding, 411, 421
The SickKids Centre for Community Mental
    Health, 1170
Sidran Institute, Traumatic Stress Education &
    Advocacy, 1092
Sidran Traumatic Stress Institute, 457, 1067, 1166,
    2272
Sigmund Freud Archives (SFA), 1791
Silver Hill Hospital, 2319
SilverPlatter Information, 2849
Similarities and Differences Between Sexual
    Orientation and Gender Identity, 537
Simon & Schuster, 2273
SIU School of Medicine, 2027
Skills Training Manual for Treating Borderline
    Personality Disorder, Companion Workbook,
    2177
Skills Unlimited, 2025
Sleep and Breathing, 803
Sleep Disorder Relief Foundation, 827
Sleep Disorders Unit of Beth Israel Hospital, 2398
Sleep Foundation, 795

Sleep Health Journal, 802
Sleep Studies, 804
The SMart Center: Selective Mutism, Anxiety, &
    Related Disorders Treatment Center, 139
SMART-Self Management and Recovery Training,
    937
SmokeFree TV: A Nicotine Prevention Video, 957
Smooth Sailing, 1925
Sobrato Center for Nonprofits, 607, 1164
Social Work, 1926
Social Work Abstracts, 1927
Social Work in Education, 1929
Social Work Research, 1928
Social-Emotional Dimension Scale, 1952
Society for Adolescent Psychiatry Newsletter, 1930
Society for Industrial and Organizational
    Psychology, 2153
Society for Pediatric Psychology (SPP), 1792
Society for Pediatric Research, 609
Society for Personality Assessment, 1793, 1881
Society for Psychophysiological Research, 1794
Society for the Advancement of Social Psychology
    (SASP), 1796
Society for the Psychological Study of Social
    Issues (SPSSI), 1797
Society for Women's Health Research (SWHR),
    1795, 1842
Society of Behavioral Medicine, 1798
Society of Multivariate Experimental Psychology
    (SMEP), 1799
Society of Teachers of Family Medicine, 1800
Solutions Step by Step - Substance Abuse
    Treatment Videotape, 2079
Solvay Pharmaceuticals, 2882
Somatoform Disorders: A Medicolegal Guide, 849
Something Fishy Music and Publishing, 518
Son-Rise Autism Treatment Center of America,
    262
Sonia Shankman Orthogenic School, 2356
Souls Self Help Central, 984
The Source Newsletter, 214
South Beach Psychiatric Center, 2456
South Carolina Department of Alcohol and Other
    Drug Abuse Services (DAODAS), 1604
South Carolina Department of Mental Health, 1605
South Carolina Department of Social Services,
    1606
South Carolina State Hospital, 2490
South Dakota Department of Social Services Office
    of Medical Services, 1607
South Dakota Human Services Center, 1608, 2492
South King County Alliance for the Mentally Ill,
    1419
South Mississippi State Hospital, 2408
Southeast Louisiana Hospital, 2377
Southeast Missouri Mental Health Center, 2410
Southern Illinois University School of Medicine,
    2027
Southern Illinois University School of Medicine:
    Department of Psychiatry, 2026
Southern Nevada Adult Mental Health Services,
    1574, 2414
Southern Virginia Mental Health Institute, 2532
Southwest Solutions, 1297
Southwestern State Hospital, 2340
Southwestern Virginia Mental Health Institute,
    2533
Spanish Support Group Alliance for the Mentally
    Ill, 1420
Special Education Rights and Responsibilities, 44,
    653
Specialized Therapy Associates, 2681
Specialzed Alternatives for Family and Youth
    (SAFY), 2028
Spokane Mental Health, 1421
Spring Grove Hospital Center, 2388
Spring Harbor Hospital, 2381
Spring Lake Ranch Therapeutic Community, 2524
Springer Science & Business Media, 212
Springer Science and Business Media, 2274
Springfield Hospital Center, 2389
SPSS, 2783

X

Y

Z

Massachusetts

Michigan

Minnesota

Mississippi

Mississippi Department of Mental Health: Division of Alcohol and Drug Abuse, 1551
Mississippi Department of Mental Health, 1552
Mississippi Department of Mental Health: Division of Medicaid, 1553
Mississippi Department of Rehabilitation Services: Office of Vocational Rehabilitation (OVR), 1554

Missouri

Association of Certified Biblical Counselors, 1725
Bereaved Parents of the USA, 74
CliniSphere version 2.0, 2716
College of Health and Human Services: SE Missouri State, 1974
DST Output, 2723
Genelco Software Solutions, 2736
Health Capital Consultants, 2622
Lake Regional Health System, 2640
Mallinckrodt, 2870
Mental Health America of Eastern Missouri, 1307
Missouri Behavioral Health Council (MBHC), 1308
Missouri Department Health & Senior Services, 1555
Missouri Department of Mental Health, 1556
Missouri Department of Mental Health: Behavioral Health - Substance Use and Mental Illness, 1557
Missouri Department of Public Safety, 1558
Missouri Department of Social Services, 1559
Missouri Department of Social Services: MO HealthNet Division, 1560
Missouri Institute of Mental Health, 1309
National Share Office, 77
Ochester Psychological Service, 2013
Pathways to Promise, 934
St. Louis Behavioral Medicine Institute, 2030
Traumatic Incident Reduction Workshop, 1828

Montana

Entre Technology Services, 2731
Mental Health America of Montana, 1311
Montana Department of Health and Human Services: Child & Family Services Division, 1562
Montana Department of Human & Community Services, 1563
Montana Department of Public Health & Human Services: Addictive and Mental Disorders Division, 1564
Montana Department of Public Health and Human Services: Disability Employment & Transitions Division, 1565
National Alliance on Mental Illness: Montana, 1312

Nebraska

Mental Health America of Nebraska, 1313
Nebraska Department of Health and Human Services (NHHS), 1317, 1566
Nebraska Family Support Network, 1318
Nebraska Health & Human Services: Medicaid and Long-Term Care, 1567
Nebraska Health and Human Services Division: Department of Mental Health, 1568
Nebraska Mental Health Centers, 1569
Orion Healthcare Technology, 2776
Parent to Parent of Omaha, 606, 1319
Wellness Councils of America, 1802

Nevada

National Alliance on Mental Illness: Nevada, 1320
National Association to Advance Fat Acceptance (NAAFA), 480
National Council of Juvenile and Family Court Judges, 1774
Nevada Department of Health and Human Services, 1570

Nevada Division of Mental Health & Developmental Services, 1571
Nevada Employment Training & Rehabilitation Department, 1572
Nevada Principals' Executive Program, 1321
Northern Nevada Adult Mental Health Services, 1573
Southern Nevada Adult Mental Health Services, 1574

New Hampshire

Bottomline Technologies, 2709
Dartmouth Univerisity: Department of Psychiatry, 1978
Echo Management Group, 2600
Helms & Company, 2629
Monadnock Family Services (MFS), 1322
New Hampshire Department of Health & Human Services: Bureau of Community Health Services, 1575
New Hampshire Department of Health and Human Services: Bureau of Developmental Services, 1576
New Hampshire Department of Health and Human Services: Bureau of Behavioral Health, 1577

New Jersey

Actavis, 2858
Advocates for Children of New Jersey, 1324
American Academy of Clinical Psychiatrists, 1655
American Society of Group Psychotherapy & Psychodrama, 1705
Arthur S Shorr and Associates, 2559
Asperger Autism Spectrum Education Network, 182
Autism Speaks, 188
Cypruss Communications, 2593
Disability Rights New Jersey, 1325
Insurance Management Institute, 2634
International Society for Developmental Psychobiology, 1752
Janssen, 2866
Jewish Family Service of Atlantic and Cape May Counties, 1326
Johnson & Johnson, 2868
Juvenile Justice Commission, 1578
King Pharmaceuticals, 2869
Mental Health Association in New Jersey, 1327
Merck & Co., 2871
New Hope Foundation, 1163
New Jersey Association of Mental Health and Addiction Agencies, 1329
New Jersey Department of Human Services, 1579
New Jersey Division of Mental Health Services, 1580
New Jersey Psychiatric Association, 1330
Ortho-McNeil Pharmaceutical, 2875
Psychohistory Forum, 1786
Sanofi-Aventis, 2879
Specialized Therapy Associates, 2681
UCSF Department of Psychiatry, Cultural Competence, 2035
Union County Psychiatric Clinic, 2038
University Behavioral Healthcare, 2039
Validus Pharmaceuticals, 2887
Warner Chilcott, 2888

New Mexico

National Alliance on Mental Illness: New Mexico, 1323, 1328, 1331, 1331
New Mexico Department of Health, 1582
New Mexico Department of Human Services, 1583
New Mexico Health & Environment Department, 1584
New Mexico Kids, Parents and Families Office of Child Development: Children, Youth and Families Department, 1585
Overeaters Anonymous General Service Office, 504

SumTime Software®, 2787

New York

ADL Data Systems, 2697
AHRC New York City, 595
Accumedic Computer Systems, 2699
Achieve Beyond, 181
Ackerman Institute for the Family, 1955
Alcoholics Anonymous (AA): World Services, 925
Alcoholics Anonymous (AA): Worldwide, 861
Aldrich and Cox, 2553
Alfred Adler Institute (AAI), 1956
American Board of Disability Analysts Annual Conference, 1813
American Foundation for Suicide Prevention, 1004
American Geriatrics Society, 1678
American Group Psychotherapy Association Virtual Annual Meeting, 1679, 1816
American Psychoanalytic Association (APsaA), 1694
Andrus Children's Center, 1963
Anxiety and Phobia Treatment Center, 120
AspireHope NY, Inc., 1332
Association for Behavioral and Cognitive Therapies, 403, 1713
Association of Mental Health Librarians (AMHL), 1108
Autism Services Inc., 186
Brain & Behavior Research Foundation, 121, 189, 268, 268, 318, 349, 471, 667, 697, 729, 740, 865, 991, 1058
Brain Imaging Handbook, 1636
Bristol-Myers Squibb, 2860
CG Jung Foundation for Analytical Psychology, 1731
Center for the Study of Anorexia and Bulimia, 497
Child Mind Institute, 1121
Child Neurology and Developmental Center, 614, 1039
Children's Home of the Wyoming Conference, Quality Improvement, 2577
Columbia University Pediatric Anxiety and Mood Research Clinic, 147
Commonwealth Fund, 1738
Community Access, 1122
Compeer, 1333
Corporate Counseling Associates, 1740
Council on Size and Weight Discrimination (CSWD), 473
Counseling Corner, 2589
Covenant House Nineline, 1005
Creative Health Concepts, 2592
Employee Network, 2604
Families Together in New York State, 1334
Forest Laboratories, 2864
Freedom From Fear, 124, 321
Gam-Anon Family Groups International Service Office, Inc., 419, 1129
Garnett Day Treatment Center, 1405
Girls and Boys Town of New York, 617
Healthcare Association of New York State, 1335
Heartshare Human Services, 1986
INCLUDEnyc, 601
Informix Software, 2748
Institute for Contemporary Psychotherapy, 836
International Center for the Study of Psychiatry And Psychology (ISCPP), 1751
Join Together Online, 929
Life Science Associates, 1993
Lifespire, 602, 1140
Mental Health America in New York State, Inc., 1336
Mental Health Association in Orange County Inc, 1337
Mental Health Materials Center (MHMC), 1760
Micro Design International, 2764
NADD Annual Conference & Exhibit Show, 1824
Nathan S Kline Institute for Psychiatric Research, 2007
Nathan S. Kline Institute for Psychiatric Research, 1145

AMERSA The Association for Medical Education and Research in Substance Abuse, 859
American Academy of Addiction Psychiatry (AAAP), 862, 1653
Byron Peter Foundation for Hope, 992
Division of Independent Practice of the American Psychological Association (APADIP), 1743
MHA (Mental Health America) of Rhode Island, 1373
Parent Support Network of Rhode Island, 1375
Rhode Island Council on Alcoholism and Other Drug Dependence, 1601
Rhode Island Department of Behavioral Healthcare, Developmental Disabilities and Hospitals, 1602
Rhode Island Division of Substance Abuse, 1603

South Carolina

Association of Traumatic Stress Specialists, 1057
Federation of Families of South Carolina, 1376
MHA (Mental Health America) South Carolina, 1377
Medical University of South Carolina Institute of Psychiatry, Psychiatry Access Center, 2004
South Carolina Department of Alcohol and Other Drug Abuse Services (DAODAS), 1604
South Carolina Department of Mental Health, 1605
South Carolina Department of Social Services, 1606

South Dakota

South Dakota Department of Social Services Office of Medical Services, 1607
South Dakota Human Services Center, 1608

Tennessee

Bureau of TennCare: State of Tennessee, 1609
Council for Alcohol & Drug Abuse Services (CADAS), 1610
Genesis Learning Center (Devereux), 1983
HCA Healthcare, 2617
Jeri Davis International, 2638
MHA (Mental Health America) of East Tennessee, Inc., 1380
Meharry Medical College, 2005
Memphis Alcohol and Drug Council, 1611
Memphis Business Group on Health, 1381
Middle Tennessee Mental Health Institute, 1612
Tennessee Association of Mental Health Organization, 1383
Tennessee Commission on Children and Youth, 1613
Tennessee Department of Health, 1614
Tennessee Department of Human Services, 1615
Tennessee Mental Health Consumers' Association, 1384
Tennessee Voices for Children, 1385
The Jason Foundation, Inc., 1000
Vanderbilt University: John F Kennedy Center for Research on Human Development, 1386

Texas

American Association of Chairs of Departments of Psychiatry (AACDP), 1661
American Pediatric Society, 598, 1103
American Society for Adolescent Psychiatry (ASAP), 1701
CSI Software, 2711
Children's Mental Health Partnership, 1387
Computer Transition Services, 2719
Corphealth, 2586
Covenant Home Healthcare, 2590
Developmental Disabilities Nurses Association (DDNA), 1742
Edgemont Pharmaceuticals, LLC, 2862
Eye Movement Desensitization and Reprocessing International Association (EMDRIA), 1126

Group for the Advancement of Psychiatry, 1748
Horizon Behavioral Services, 2630
Horizon Mental Health Management, 2631
Interface EAP, 2635
Jewish Family Service of Dallas, 1388
Jewish Family Service of San Antonio, 1389
M.I.S.S. Foundation/Center for Loss & Trauma, 63
MADD-Mothers Against Drunk Drivers, 930
MHNet Behavioral Health, 2644
Menninger Clinic, 1141, 2006
Mental Health America of Greater Dallas, 1390
Mental Health America of Greater Houston, Inc., 1391
Mental Health America of Southeast Texas, 1392
Mental Health Outcomes, 2763
National Alliance on Mental Illness: Texas, 1393
National Eating Disorders Association, 481
OPTAIO-Optimizing Practice Through Assessment, Intervention and Outcome, 2773
PRIMA ADD Corp., 2014
Research Society on Alcoholism, 882
Restless Legs Syndrome Foundation, Inc., 794
Society for Pediatric Research, 609
Survivors of Loved Ones' Suicides (SOLOS), 67, 79, 999
Texas Counseling Association (TCA), 1394
Texas Department of Family and Protective Services, 1616
Texas Psychological Association, 1395
Texas Society of Psychiatric Physicians, 1396
The Harris Center for Mental Health and IDD, 1617
University of Texas Medical Branch Managed Care, 2056
University of Texas: Mental Health Clinical Research Center, 351
re:MIND, 1397

Utah

American Association of Pastoral Counselors, 1666
CompHealth Credentialing, 1639
Healthwise of Utah, 1398
Intermountain Healthcare, 2637
National Alliance on Mental Illness: Utah, 1399
University of Utah Neuropsychiatric, 2057
Utah Department of Health, 1618
Utah Department of Health: Health Care Financing, 1619
Utah Department of Human Services, 1620
Utah Department of Human Services: Division of Substance Abuse And Mental Health, 1621
Utah Parent Center, 1400
Utah Psychiatric Association, 1401

Vermont

Fletcher Allen Health Care, 1982
National Alliance on Mental Illness: Vermont, 1402
Vermont Association for Mental Health & Addiction Recovery, 1403
Vermont Federation of Families for Children's Mental Health, 1404

Virginia

Agoraphobics Building Independent Lives, 149
Al-Anon Family Group National Referral Hotline, 923
Alateen and Al-Anon Family Groups, 616, 924
American Association for Geriatric Psychiatry, 1099
American Association for Marriage and Family Therapy, 1658
American Association of Geriatric Psychiatry, 1663
American Association of Pharmaceutical Scientists, 1667
American College of Health Care Administrators (ACHCA) Annual Convocation & Exposition, 1673, 1814

American Counseling Association, 1677
American Medical Group Association, 1685
American Mental Health Counselors Association (AMHCA), 1687
American Network of Community Options and Resources (ANCOR), 1102
American Psychiatric Nurses Association, 1693
American Psychiatric Press Reference Library CD-ROM, 2702
American Psychosomatic Society, 1700
American Public Human Services Association, 863
American Society for Clinical Pharmacology & Therapeutics, 1702
American Society of Consultant Pharmacists, 1704
Clinical Social Work Association, 1736
Colonial Services Board, 1976
Community Anti-Drug Coalitions of America (CADCA), 868, 1739
Council on Social Work Education, 1641, 1741
Employee Assistance Professionals Association, Inc., 2602, 1744
Employee Assistance Society of North America, 1745
FASD United, 869
Family-to-Family: National Alliance on Mental Illness, 742
Healthy Companies, 2627
Institute on Psychiatric Services: American Psychiatric Association, 1750
Mental Health America, 126, 406, 671, 671, 732, 872, 1063, 1142, 1758
Mental Health America of Virginia, 1406
NAADAC, The Association for Addiction Professionals, 873
National Alliance on Mental Illness, 128, 196, 272, 272, 323, 477, 673, 700, 733, 791, 875, 993, 1034, 1064, 1146, 1407, 1413
National Association of Alcholism and Drug Abuse Counselors, 2008
National Association of State Mental Health Program Directors (NASMHPD), 1149, 1769
National Council on Aging, 1775
National Rehabilitation Association, 1162
Options Health Care, 2659
Parent Resource Center, 1409
Professional Risk Management Services, 2674
Professional Risk Management Services (PRMS), 1784
QuadraMed Corporation, 2780, 2024
Screening for Mental Health, 1790
Society for Personality Assessment, 1793
Society of Multivariate Experimental Psychology (SMEP), 1799
The Lewin Group, 2685
ValueOptions Norfolk, 2691
Virginia Department of Behavioral Health and Developmental Services (DBHDS), 1622
Virginia Department of Medical Assistance Services, 1623
Virginia Department of Social Services (VDSS), 1624
Virginia Office of the Secretary of Health and Human Resources, 1625
World Federation for Mental Health, 1174

Washington

A Common Voice, 1410
Carewise, 2573
Children's Alliance, 1263, 1411
Gender Diversity, 523
Keane Care, 2752
Lanstat Incorporated, 1644
Mental Health & Spirituality Support Group, 1412
Milliman, Inc, 2653
Narcolepsy Network, 790
National Alliance on Mental Illness: Pierce County, 1415
NetMeeting, 2770
Nueva Esperanza Counseling Center, 1417
Sharing & Caring for Consumers, Families Alliance for the Mentally Ill, 1418

Drugs A-Z, by Brand Name

Abilify
Generic: aripiprazole
Manufacturer: Bristol-Myers Squibb
Used in the treatment of psychotic disorders
and bipolar disorder

Adderall/Adderall XR
Generic: amphetamine/dextroamphetamine
Manufacturer: Shire US, Inc.
Used to manage anxiety disorders and some
cases of attention deficit hyperactivity
disorder

Ambien
Generic: zolpidem
Manufacturer: Sanofi-Aventis
Used to treat insomnia

Anafranil
Generic: clomipramine hydrochloride
Manufacturer: Mallinckrodt, Inc.
Used to treat obsessive-compulsive disorder
(OCD)

Antabuse
Generic: disulfiram
Manufacturer: Odyssey Pharmaceuticals,
Inc.
Used in the treatment of alcohol and
substance abuse

Aricept
Generic: donepezil
Manufacturer: Pfizer, Inc.
Used in the treatment of Alzheimer's disease

Ativan
Generic: lorazepam
Manufacturer: Wyeth-Ayerst Laboratories
Used in the treatment of anxiety and as a
preanesthetic medication in adults

BuSpar
Generic: buspirone
Manufacturer: Bristol-Myers Squibb
Used to treat anxiety

Butrans
Generic: buprenorphine
Manufacturer: Purdue
Used to treat pain as well as addiction to
narcotic pain relievers

Campral
Generic: acamprosate calcium
Manufacturer: Forest Laboratories, Inc.
Used to reduce the desire to drink alcohol
Celexa
Generic: citalopram
Manufacturer: Forest Laboratories, Inc.
Used in the treatment of depression

Clozaril
Generic: clozapine
Manufacturer: Novartis
Used in the treatment of severe
schizophrenia

Cylert
Generic: pemoline
Manufacturer: Abbott Laboratories
Used to treat attention-deficit hyperactivity
disorder (ADHD) and narcolepsy

Cymbalta
Generic: duloxetine
Manufacturer: Eli Lilly and Company
Used in the treatment of depression

Daytrana
Generic: methylphenidate transdermal
Manufacturer: Noven Pharmaceuticals
Used in the treatment of ADHD in children
6-17 years old

Depakote
Generic: valproic acid
Manufacturer: Abbott Laboratories
Used in the treatment of manic episodes
associated with bipolar disorder and mania

Desoxyn
Generic: methamphetamine hydrochloride
Manufacturer: Abbott Laboratories
Used in the treatment of attention deficit
hyperactivity disorder

Desyrel
Generic: trazodone hydrochloride
Manufacturer: Bristol-Myers Squibb
Used in the treatment of major depressive
disorder

Dexedrine, DextroStat
Generic: dextroamphetamine
Manufacturer: Mallinckrodt, Inc.
Used in the treatment of attention deficit
hyperactivity disorder and narcolepsy

Dolophine
Generic: methadone
Manufacturer: Eli Lilly and Company
May be used to treat or control withdrawal
symptoms in patients being treated for
narcotic drug addiction

Edronax
Generic: reboxetine
Manufacturer: Pfizer, Inc.
Used to treat depression

Effexor
Generic: venlafaxine
Manufacturer: Wyeth-Ayerst Laboratories
Used in the treatment of depression and
generalized anxiety disorder

Elavil
Generic: amitriptyline
Manufacturer: Astra Zeneca
Pharmaceuticals
Used in the treatment of depression

Emsam
Generic: selegiline
Manufacturer: Bristol-Myers Squibb
Used in the treatment of major depressive
disorder

Equetro
Generic: carbamazepine
Manufacturer: Validus Pharmaceuticals
LLC
Used to treat seizures, nerve pain, and
bipolar disorder

Eskalith
Generic: lithium
Manufacturer: GlaxoSmithKline
Used in the treatment of bipolar disorder

Exelon
Generic: rivastigmine
Manufacturer: Novartis
Used in the treatment of Alzheimer's disease

Fanapt
Generic: iloperidone
Manufacturer: Novartis
Used to treat schizophrenia

FazaClo
Generic: clozapine
Manufacturer: Jazz Pharmaceuticals plc
Used in the treatment of Schizophrenia

Focalin/Focalin XR
Generic: dexmethylphenidate
Manufacturer: Novartis
Used in the treatment of attention deficit
hyperactivity disorder

Geodone
Generic: ziprasidone
Manufacturer: Pfizer, Inc.
Antipsychotic drug to treat schizophrenia
and bipolar disorder

Halcion
Generic: triazolam
Manufacturer: Pfizer, Inc.
Used to treat insomnia

Haldol
Generic: haloperidol
Manufacturer: Johnson & Johnson
Used in the treatment of Schizophrenia

Intermezzo
Generic: zolpidem
Manufacturer: Purdue
Used in the treatment of insomnia

Invega
Generic: paliperidone
Manufacturer: Janssen
Used in the treatment of Schizophrenia

Kapvay
Generic: clonidine hcl
Manufacturer: Concordia Pharmaceuticals
Inc.
Used to treat attention deficit hyperactivity
disorder (ADHD), and can also be used to
help with withdrawal symptoms from

narcotic drugs, and to help people quit smoking

Klonopin
Generic: clonazepam
Manufacturer: Roche
Used to treat seizures, panic disorder, and anxiety

Lamictal
Generic: lamotrigine
Manufacturer: GlaxoSmithKline
Used in the treatment of bipolar disorder

Latuda
Generic: lurasidone hcl
Manufacturer: Sunovion Pharmaceuticals
Used in the treatment of schizophrenia

Lexapro
Generic: escitalopram
Manufacturer: Forest Laboratories, Inc.
Used in the treatment of depression

Librium
Generic: chlordiazepoxide hcl
Manufacturer: ICN Pharmaceuticals, Inc.
Used to treat anxiety and acute alcohol withdrawal

Lithobid, Lithonate
Generic: lithium carbonate
Manufacturer: Solvay Pharmaceuticals Inc.
Used in the treatment of bipolar disorder and depression

Lunesta
Generic: eszopiclone
Manufacturer: Sunovion Pharmaceuticals
Used in the treatment of insomnia

LuvoxCR
Generic: fluvoxamine maleate
Manufacturer: Jazz Pharmaceuticals plc
Used to treat obsessive-compulsive disorder (OCD)

Marplan
Generic: isocarboxazid
Manufacturer: Validus Pharmaceuticals LLC
Used to treat depression

Methylin
Generic: methylphenidate
Manufacturer: Mallinckrodt, Inc.
Used to treat ADHD and narcolepsy

Namenda
Generic: memantine
Manufacturer: Forest Laboratories, Inc.
Used in the treatment of dementia

Navane
Generic: thiothixene
Manufacturer: Pfizer, Inc.
Used to treat schizophrenia

Nembutal
Generic: pentobarbital
Manufacturer: Lundbeck
Used to treat tension, anxiety, nervousness, insomnia, epilepsy and other seizures

Neurontin
Generic: gabapentin
Manufacturer: Pfizer, Inc.
Used in the treatment of seizures and neuropathic pain

Niravam
Generic: alprazolam
Manufacturer: Jazz Pharmaceuticals plc
Used in the treatment of anxiety and panic disorder

Norpramin
Generic: desipramine hcl
Manufacturer: Sanofi-Aventis
Used to treat depression

Nuvigil
Generic: armodafinil
Manufacturer: Teva Pharmaceutical Industries Ltd.
Used to treat sleepiness from narcolepsy, sleep apnea, or night shift work

Orap
Generic: pimozide
Manufacturer: Teva Pharmaceutical Industries Ltd.
Used to reduce uncontrolled movements (motor tics) or outbursts of words/sounds (vocal tics) caused by Tourette syndrome

Parnate
Generic: tranylcypromine
Manufacturer: GlaxoSmithKline
Used to help manage depression

Paxil
Generic: paroxetine hcl
Manufacturer: GlaxoSmithKline
Used in the treatment of depression, and anxiety disorders

Pexeva
Generic: paroxetine mesylate
Manufacturer: Noven Pharmaceuticals
Used in the treatment of depression, and anxiety disorders

Pristiq
Generic: desvenlafaxine
Manufacturer: Pfizer, Inc.
Used in the treatment of depression

Prolixin
Generic: fluphenazine hcl
Manufacturer: Bristol-Myers Squibb
Used to treat schizophrenia

Prosom
Generic: estasolam
Manufacturer: Abbott Laboratories
Used to treat insomnia

Provigil
Generic: modafinil
Manufacturer: Teva Pharmaceutical Industries Ltd.
Used to treat narcolepsy, sleep apnea, and shift work sleep disorder

Prozac
Generic: fluoxetine
Manufacturer: Eli Lilly and Company
Used in the treatment of depression and anxiety disorders

Remeron
Generic: mirtazapine
Manufacturer: Merck & Co
Used in the treatment of suicidality and depression

Reminyl
Generic: galantamine
Manufacturer: Shire US, Inc.

Used to treat mild to moderate confusion (dementia) related to Alzheimer's disease

Restoril
Generic: temazepam
Manufacturer: Mallinckrodt
Used in the treatment of insomnia

Risperdal
Generic: risperidone
Manufacturer: Janssen
Used in the treatment of schizophrenia and other mental illnesses such as psychosis

Ritalin
Generic: methylphenidate
Manufacturer: Novartis
Used in the treatment of attention deficit hyperactivity disorders and in some forms of narcolepsy

Rozerem
Generic: ramelteon
Manufacturer: Takeda Pharmaceuticals
Used in the treatment of insomnia

Saphris
Generic: asenapine
Manufacturer: Merck & Co
Used in the treatment of Schizophrenia and Bipolar Mania

Sarafem
Generic: fluoxetine
Manufacturer: Eli Lilly and Company
It can treat depression, obsessive-compulsive disorder (OCD), bulimia nervosa, and panic disorder

Serzone
Generic: nefazodone hydrochloride
Manufacturer: Bristol-Myers Squibb
Used to treat depression

Sinequan
Generic: doxepin
Manufacturer: Pfizer, Inc.
Used to treat depression, anxiety, and sleep disorders

Stavzor
Generic: valproic acid
Manufacturer: Bristol-Myers Squibb

Used to treat seizures and bipolar disorder. It can also help prevent migraine headaches.

Strattera
Generic: atomoxetine
Manufacturer: Eli Lilly & Company
Used in the treatment of attention deficit disorder

Symbyax
Generic: fluoxetine/olanzapine
Manufacturer: Eli Lilly & Company
Used to treat depression

Tranxene
Generic: clorazepate dipotassium
Manufacturer: Recordati Rare Diseases, Inc.
Used to treat anxiety, acute alcohol withdrawal, and seizures

Valium
Generic: diazepam
Manufacturer: Roche
Used in the treatment of anxiety

Viibryd
Generic: vilazodone hydrochloride
Manufacturer: Forest Laboratories, Inc.
Used in the treatment of depression

Vistaril
Generic: hydroxyzine
Manufacturer: Pfizer, Inc.
Used as a sedative to treat anxiety and tension and to treat allergic skin reactions

Vivitrol
Generic: naltrexone
Manufacturer: Alkermes, plc
Used to help prevent relapses into alcohol or drug abuse

Vyvanse
Generic: lisdexamfetamine
Manufacturer: Shire US, Inc.
Used in the treatment of attention deficit hyperactivity disorder

Wellbutrin, Wellbutrin SR, Wellbutrin XL
Generic: bupropion
Manufacturer: Sanofi-Aventis
Used in the treatment of depression
Xanax, Xanax XR
Generic: alprazolam

Manufacturer: Pfizer, Inc.
Used in the treatment of anxiety

Xyrem
Generic: sodium oxybate
Manufacturer: Jazz Pharmaceuticals plc
Used in the treatment of narcolepsy

Zoloft
Generic: sertraline
Manufacturer: Pfizer, Inc.
Used in the treatment of depression and anxiety disorders

Zyban
Generic: bupropion
Manufacturer: GlaxoSmithKline
Used in the treatment of depression

Zyprexa
Generic: olanzapine
Manufacturer: Eli Lilly & Company
Used to treat mental disorders, including schizophrenia and bipolar disorder

Opinions Throughout History

Opinions Throughout History: Church & State
Opinions Throughout History: The Death Penalty
Opinions Throughout History: Diseases & Epidemics
Opinions Throughout History: Drug Use & Abuse
Opinions Throughout History: The Environment
Opinions Throughout History: Free Speech & Censorship
Opinions Throughout History: Gender: Roles & Rights
Opinions Throughout History: Globalization
Opinions Throughout History: Guns in America
Opinions Throughout History: Immigration
Opinions Throughout History: Law Enforcement in America
Opinions Throughout History: National Security vs. Civil & Privacy
   Rights
Opinions Throughout History: Presidential Authority
Opinions Throughout History: Robotics & Artificial Intelligence
Opinions Throughout History: Social Media Issues
Opinions Throughout History: Voters' Rights
Opinions Throughout History: War & the Military
Opinions Throughout History: Workers Rights & Wages

This is Who We Were

This is Who We Were: Colonial America (1492-1775)
This is Who We Were: 1880-1899
This is Who We Were: In the 1900s
This is Who We Were: In the 1910s
This is Who We Were: In the 1920s
This is Who We Were: A Companion to the 1940 Census
This is Who We Were: In the 1940s (1940-1949)
This is Who We Were: In the 1950s
This is Who We Were: In the 1960s
This is Who We Were: In the 1970s
This is Who We Were: In the 1980s
This is Who We Were: In the 1990s
This is Who We Were: In the 2000s
This is Who We Were: In the 2010s

Working Americans

Working Americans—Vol. 1: The Working Class
Working Americans—Vol. 2: The Middle Class
Working Americans—Vol. 3: The Upper Class
Working Americans—Vol. 4: Children
Working Americans—Vol. 5: At War
Working Americans—Vol. 6: Working Women
Working Americans—Vol. 7: Social Movements
Working Americans—Vol. 8: Immigrants
Working Americans—Vol. 9: Revolutionary War to the Civil War
Working Americans—Vol. 10: Sports & Recreation
Working Americans—Vol. 11: Inventors & Entrepreneurs
Working Americans—Vol. 12: Our History through Music
Working Americans—Vol. 13: Education & Educators
Working Americans—Vol. 14: African Americans
Working Americans—Vol. 15: Politics & Politicians
Working Americans—Vol. 16: Farming & Ranching
Working Americans—Vol. 17: Teens in America
Working Americans—Vol. 18: Health Care Workers

Grey House Health & Wellness Guides

The Autism Spectrum Handbook & Resource Guide
Autoimmune Disorders Handbook & Resource Guide
Cardiovascular Disease Handbook & Resource Guide
Dementia Handbook & Resource Guide
Diabetes Handbook & Resource Guide
Nutrition, Obesity & Eating Disorders Handbook & Resource Guide

Consumer Health

Complete Mental Health Resource Guide
Complete Resource Guide for Pediatric Disorders
Complete Resource Guide for People with Chronic Illness
Complete Resource Guide for People with Disabilities
Older Americans Information Resource
Parenting: Styles & Strategies

Education

Complete Learning Disabilities Resource Guide
Educators Resource Guide
The Comparative Guide to Elem. & Secondary Schools
Special Education: A Reference Book for Policy & Curriculum
   Development

General Reference

American Environmental Leaders
Constitutional Amendments
Encyclopedia of African-American Writing
Encyclopedia of Invasions & Conquests
Encyclopedia of Prisoners of War & Internment
Encyclopedia of the Continental Congresses
Encyclopedia of the United States Cabinet
Encyclopedia of War Journalism
The Environmental Debate
Financial Literacy Starter Kit
From Suffrage to the Senate
The Gun Debate: Gun Rights & Gun Control in the U.S.
Historical Warrior Peoples & Modern Fighting Groups
Human Rights and the United States
Political Corruption in America
Privacy Rights in the Digital Age
The Religious Right and American Politics
Speakers of the House of Representatives, 1789-2021
US Land & Natural Resources Policy
The Value of a Dollar 1600-1865 Colonial to Civil War
The Value of a Dollar 1860-2019

Business Information

Business Information Resources
The Complete Broadcasting Industry Guide: Television, Radio, Cable
   & Streaming
Directory of Mail Order Catalogs
Environmental Resource Handbook
Food & Beverage Market Place
The Grey House Guide to Homeland Security Resources
The Grey House Performing Arts Industry Guide
Guide to Healthcare Group Purchasing Organizations
Guide to U.S. HMOs and PPOs
Guide to Venture Capital & Private Equity Firms
Hudson's Washington News Media Contacts Guide
New York State Directory
Sports Market Place

2022 Title List

Visit www.GreyHouse.com for Product Information, Table of Contents, and Sample Pages.

Statistics & Demographics

America's Top-Rated Cities
America's Top-Rated Smaller Cities
The Comparative Guide to American Suburbs
Profiles of America
Profiles of California
Profiles of Florida
Profiles of Illinois
Profiles of Indiana
Profiles of Massachusetts
Profiles of Michigan
Profiles of New Jersey
Profiles of New York
Profiles of North Carolina & South Carolina
Profiles of Ohio
Profiles of Pennsylvania
Profiles of Texas
Profiles of Virginia
Profiles of Wisconsin

Canadian Resources

Associations Canada
Canadian Almanac & Directory
Canadian Environmental Resource Guide
Canadian Parliamentary Guide
Canadian Venture Capital & Private Equity Firms
Canadian Who's Who
Cannabis Canada
Careers & Employment Canada
Financial Post: Directory of Directors
Financial Services Canada
FP Bonds: Corporate
FP Bonds: Government
FP Equities: Preferreds & Derivatives
FP Survey: Industrials
FP Survey: Mines & Energy
FP Survey: Predecessor & Defunct
Health Guide Canada
Libraries Canada

Weiss Financial Ratings

Financial Literacy Basics
Financial Literacy: How to Become an Investor
Financial Literacy: Planning for the Future
Weiss Ratings Consumer Guides
Weiss Ratings Guide to Banks
Weiss Ratings Guide to Credit Unions
Weiss Ratings Guide to Health Insurers
Weiss Ratings Guide to Life & Annuity Insurers
Weiss Ratings Guide to Property & Casualty Insurers
Weiss Ratings Investment Research Guide to Bond & Money Market
   Mutual Funds
Weiss Ratings Investment Research Guide to Exchange-Traded Func
Weiss Ratings Investment Research Guide to Stock Mutual Funds
Weiss Ratings Investment Research Guide to Stocks

Books in Print Series

American Book Publishing Record® Annual
American Book Publishing Record® Monthly
Books In Print®
Books In Print® Supplement
Books Out Loud™
Bowker's Complete Video Directory™
Children's Books In Print®
El-Hi Textbooks & Serials In Print®
Forthcoming Books®
Law Books & Serials In Print™
Medical & Health Care Books In Print™
Publishers, Distributors & Wholesalers of the US™
Subject Guide to Books In Print®
Subject Guide to Children's Books In Print®

ALEM
PRESS

2022 *Title List*

Visit www.SalemPress.com for Product Information, Table of Contents, and Sample Pages.

SALEM
PRESS

LITERATURE
Critical Insights: Authors

Louisa May Alcott
Sherman Alexie
Isabel Allende
Maya Angelou
Isaac Asimov
Margaret Atwood
Jane Austen
James Baldwin
Saul Bellow
Roberto Bolano
Ray Bradbury
The Brontë Sisters
Gwendolyn Brooks
Albert Camus
Raymond Carver
Willa Cather
Geoffrey Chaucer
John Cheever
Joseph Conrad
Charles Dickens
Emily Dickinson
Frederick Douglass
T. S. Eliot
George Eliot
Harlan Ellison
Louise Erdrich
William Faulkner
F. Scott Fitzgerald
Gustave Flaubert
Horton Foote
Benjamin Franklin
Robert Frost
Neil Gaiman
Gabriel Garcia Marquez
Thomas Hardy
Nathaniel Hawthorne
Robert A. Heinlein
Lillian Hellman
Ernest Hemingway
Langston Hughes
Zora Neale Hurston
Henry James
Thomas Jefferson
James Joyce
Jamaica Kincaid
Stephen King
Martin Luther King, Jr.
Barbara Kingsolver
Abraham Lincoln
Mario Vargas Llosa
Jack London
James McBride
Cormac McCarthy
Herman Melville
Arthur Miller
Toni Morrison
Alice Munro
Tim O'Brien
Flannery O'Connor
Eugene O'Neill
George Orwell
Sylvia Plath
Edgar Allan Poe

Philip Roth
Salman Rushdie
J.D. Salinger
Mary Shelley
John Steinbeck
Amy Tan
Leo Tolstoy
Mark Twain
John Updike
Kurt Vonnegut
Alice Walker
David Foster Wallace
Edith Wharton
Walt Whitman
Oscar Wilde
Tennessee Williams
Virginia Woolf
Richard Wright
Malcolm X

Critical Insights: Works

Absalom, Absalom!
Adventures of Huckleberry Finn
Adventures of Tom Sawyer
Aeneid
All Quiet on the Western Front
Animal Farm
Anna Karenina
The Awakening
The Bell Jar
Beloved
Billy Budd, Sailor
The Book Thief
Brave New World
The Canterbury Tales
Catch-22
The Catcher in the Rye
The Color Purple
The Crucible
Death of a Salesman
The Diary of a Young Girl
Dracula
Fahrenheit 451
The Grapes of Wrath
Great Expectations
The Great Gatsby
Hamlet
The Handmaid's Tale
Harry Potter Series
Heart of Darkness
The Hobbit
The House on Mango Street
How the Garcia Girls Lost Their Accents
The Hunger Games Trilogy
I Know Why the Caged Bird Sings
In Cold Blood
The Inferno
Invisible Man
Jane Eyre
The Joy Luck Club
Julius Caesar
King Lear
The Kite Runner
Life of Pi
Little Women

Lolita
Lord of the Flies
The Lord of the Rings
Macbeth
The Metamorphosis
Midnight's Children
A Midsummer Night's Dream
Moby-Dick
Mrs. Dalloway
Nineteen Eighty-Four
The Odyssey
Of Mice and Men
The Old Man and the Sea
On the Road
One Flew Over the Cuckoo's Nest
One Hundred Years of Solitude
Othello
The Outsiders
Paradise Lost
The Pearl
The Poetry of Baudelaire
The Poetry of Edgar Allan Poe
A Portrait of the Artist as a Young Man
Pride and Prejudice
The Red Badge of Courage
Romeo and Juliet
The Scarlet Letter
Short Fiction of Flannery O'Connor
Slaughterhouse-Five
The Sound and the Fury
A Streetcar Named Desire
The Sun Also Rises
A Tale of Two Cities
The Tales of Edgar Allan Poe
Their Eyes Were Watching God
Things Fall Apart
To Kill a Mockingbird
War and Peace
The Woman Warrior

Critical Insights: Themes

The American Comic Book
American Creative Non-Fiction
The American Dream
American Multicultural Identity
American Road Literature
American Short Story
American Sports Fiction
The American Thriller
American Writers in Exile
Censored & Banned Literature
Civil Rights Literature, Past & Present
Coming of Age
Conspiracies
Contemporary Canadian Fiction
Contemporary Immigrant Short Fiction
Contemporary Latin American Fiction
Contemporary Speculative Fiction
Crime and Detective Fiction
Crisis of Faith
Cultural Encounters
Dystopia
Family
The Fantastic
Feminism

SALEM PRESS

2022 Title List

Visit www.SalemPress.com for Product Information, Table of Contents, and Sample Pages.

Flash Fiction
Gender, Sex and Sexuality
Good & Evil
The Graphic Novel
Greed
Harlem Renaissance
The Hero's Quest
Historical Fiction
Holocaust Literature
The Immigrant Experience
Inequality
LGBTQ Literature
Literature in Times of Crisis
Literature of Protest
Love
Magical Realism
Midwestern Literature
Modern Japanese Literature
Nature & the Environment
Paranoia, Fear & Alienation
Patriotism
Political Fiction
Postcolonial Literature
Pulp Fiction of the '20s and '30s
Rebellion
Russia's Golden Age
Satire
The Slave Narrative
Social Justice and American Literature
Southern Gothic Literature
Southwestern Literature
Survival
Technology & Humanity
Truth & Lies
Violence in Literature
Virginia Woolf & 20th Century Women Writers
War

Critical Insights: Film
Bonnie & Clyde
Casablanca
Alfred Hitchcock
Stanley Kubrick

Critical Approaches to Literature
Critical Approaches to Literature: Feminist
Critical Approaches to Literature: Moral
Critical Approaches to Literature: Multicultural
Critical Approaches to Literature: Psychological

Critical Surveys of Literature
Critical Survey of American Literature
Critical Survey of Drama
Critical Survey of Graphic Novels: Heroes & Superheroes
Critical Survey of Graphic Novels: History, Theme, and Technique
Critical Survey of Graphic Novels: Independents & Underground Classics
Critical Survey of Graphic Novels: Manga
Critical Survey of Long Fiction
Critical Survey of Mystery and Detective Fiction
Critical Survey of Mythology & Folklore: Gods & Goddesses
Critical Survey of Mythology & Folklore: Heroes and Heroines
Critical Survey of Mythology & Folklore: Love, Sexuality, and Desir
Critical Survey of Mythology & Folklore: World Mythology
Critical Survey of Poetry
Critical Survey of Poetry: Contemporary Poets
Critical Survey of Science Fiction & Fantasy Literature
Critical Survey of Shakespeare's Plays
Critical Survey of Shakespeare's Sonnets
Critical Survey of Short Fiction
Critical Survey of World Literature
Critical Survey of Young Adult Literature

Cyclopedia of Literary Characters & Place
Cyclopedia of Literary Characters
Cyclopedia of Literary Places

Introduction to Literary Context
American Poetry of the 20th Century
American Post-Modernist Novels
American Short Fiction
English Literature
Plays
World Literature

Magill's Literary Annual
Magill's Literary Annual, 2022
Magill's Literary Annual, 2021
Magill's Literary Annual, 2020
Magill's Literary Annual (Backlist Issues 2019-1977)

Masterplots
Masterplots, Fourth Edition
Masterplots, 2010-2018 Supplement

Notable Writers
Notable African American Writers
Notable American Women Writers
Notable Mystery & Detective Fiction Writers
Notable Writers of the American West & the Native American Experience
Novels into Film: Adaptations & Interpretation
Recommended Reading: 600 Classics Reviewed

2022 Title List

Visit www.SalemPress.com for Product Information, Table of Contents, and Sample Pages.

HISTORY

The Decades

The 1910s in America
The Twenties in America
The Thirties in America
The Forties in America
The Fifties in America
The Sixties in America
The Seventies in America
The Eighties in America
The Nineties in America
The 2000s in America
The 2010s in America

Defining Documents in American History

Defining Documents: The 1900s
Defining Documents: The 1910s
Defining Documents: The 1920s
Defining Documents: The 1930s
Defining Documents: The 1950s
Defining Documents: The 1960s
Defining Documents: The 1970s
Defining Documents: The 1980s
Defining Documents: American Citizenship
Defining Documents: The American Economy
Defining Documents: The American Revolution
Defining Documents: The American West
Defining Documents: Business Ethics
Defining Documents: Capital Punishment
Defining Documents: Civil Rights
Defining Documents: Civil War
Defining Documents: The Constitution
Defining Documents: The Cold War
Defining Documents: Dissent & Protest
Defining Documents: Domestic Terrorism
Defining Documents: Drug Policy
Defining Documents: The Emergence of Modern America
Defining Documents: Environment & Conservation
Defining Documents: Espionage & Intrigue
Defining Documents: Exploration and Colonial America
Defining Documents: The First Amendment
Defining Documents: The Free Press
Defining Documents: The Great Depression
Defining Documents: The Great Migration
Defining Documents: The Gun Debate
Defining Documents: Immigration & Immigrant Communities
Defining Documents: The Legacy of 9/11
Defining Documents: LGBTQ+
Defining Documents: Manifest Destiny and the New Nation
Defining Documents: Native Americans
Defining Documents: Political Campaigns, Candidates & Discourse
Defining Documents: Postwar 1940s
Defining Documents: Prison Reform
Defining Documents: Secrets, Leaks & Scandals
Defining Documents: Slavery
Defining Documents: Supreme Court Decisions
Defining Documents: Reconstruction Era
Defining Documents: The Vietnam War
Defining Documents: U.S. Involvement in the Middle East
Defining Documents: World War I
Defining Documents: World War II

Defining Documents in World History

Defining Documents: The 17th Century
Defining Documents: The 18th Century
Defining Documents: The 19th Century
Defining Documents: The 20th Century (1900-1950)
Defining Documents: The Ancient World
Defining Documents: Asia
Defining Documents: Genocide & the Holocaust
Defining Documents: Nationalism & Populism
Defining Documents: Pandemics, Plagues & Public Health
Defining Documents: Renaissance & Early Modern Era
Defining Documents: The Middle Ages
Defining Documents: The Middle East
Defining Documents: Women's Rights

Great Events from History

Great Events from History: The Ancient World
Great Events from History: The Middle Ages
Great Events from History: The Renaissance & Early Modern Era
Great Events from History: The 17th Century
Great Events from History: The 18th Century
Great Events from History: The 19th Century
Great Events from History: The 20th Century, 1901-1940
Great Events from History: The 20th Century, 1941-1970
Great Events from History: The 20th Century, 1971-2000
Great Events from History: Modern Scandals
Great Events from History: African American History
Great Events from History: The 21st Century, 2000-2016
Great Events from History: LGBTQ Events
Great Events from History: Human Rights
Great Events from History: Women's History

Great Lives from History

Computer Technology Innovators
Fashion Innovators
Great Athletes
Great Athletes of the Twenty-First Century
Great Lives from History: African Americans
Great Lives from History: American Heroes
Great Lives from History: American Women
Great Lives from History: Asian and Pacific Islander Americans
Great Lives from History: Inventors & Inventions
Great Lives from History: Jewish Americans
Great Lives from History: Latinos
Great Lives from History: Scientists and Science
Great Lives from History: The 17th Century
Great Lives from History: The 18th Century
Great Lives from History: The 19th Century
Great Lives from History: The 20th Century
Great Lives from History: The 21st Century, 2000-2017
Great Lives from History: The Ancient World
Great Lives from History: The Incredibly Wealthy
Great Lives from History: The Middle Ages
Great Lives from History: The Renaissance & Early Modern Era
Human Rights Innovators
Internet Innovators
Music Innovators
Musicians and Composers of the 20th Century
World Political Innovators

2022 Title List

Visit www.SalemPress.com for Product Information, Table of Contents, and Sample Pages.

History & Government

American First Ladies
American Presidents
The 50 States
The Ancient World: Extraordinary People in Extraordinary Societies
The Bill of Rights
The Criminal Justice System
The U.S. Supreme Court

SOCIAL SCIENCES

Civil Rights Movements: Past & Present
Countries, Peoples and Cultures
Countries: Their Wars & Conflicts: A World Survey
Education Today: Issues, Policies & Practices
Encyclopedia of American Immigration
Ethics: Questions & Morality of Human Actions
Issues in U.S. Immigration
Principles of Sociology: Group Relationships & Behavior
Principles of Sociology: Personal Relationships & Behavior
Principles of Sociology: Societal Issues & Behavior
Racial & Ethnic Relations in America
World Geography

HEALTH

Addictions, Substance Abuse & Alcoholism
Adolescent Health & Wellness
Aging
Cancer
Community & Family Health Issues
Integrative, Alternative & Complementary Medicine
Genetics and Inherited Conditions
Infectious Diseases and Conditions
Magill's Medical Guide
Nutrition
Parenting: Styles & Strategies
Psychology & Behavioral Health
Women's Health

Principles of Health

Principles of Health: Allergies & Immune Disorders
Principles of Health: Anxiety & Stress
Principles of Health: Depression
Principles of Health: Diabetes
Principles of Health: Nursing
Principles of Health: Obesity
Principles of Health: Pain Management
Principles of Health: Prescription Drug Abuse

SCIENCE

Ancient Creatures
Applied Science
Applied Science: Engineering & Mathematics
Applied Science: Science & Medicine
Applied Science: Technology
Biomes and Ecosystems
Earth Science: Earth Materials and Resources
Earth Science: Earth's Surface and History
Earth Science: Earth's Weather, Water and Atmosphere
Earth Science: Physics and Chemistry of the Earth
Encyclopedia of Climate Change
Encyclopedia of Energy
Encyclopedia of Environmental Issues
Encyclopedia of Global Resources
Encyclopedia of Mathematics and Society
Forensic Science
Notable Natural Disasters
The Solar System
USA in Space

Principles of Science

Principles of Anatomy
Principles of Astronomy
Principles of Behavioral Science
Principles of Biology
Principles of Biotechnology
Principles of Botany
Principles of Chemistry
Principles of Climatology
Principles of Computer-aided Design
Principles of Information Technology
Principles of Computer Science
Principles of Ecology
Principles of Energy
Principles of Fire Science
Principles of Geology
Principles of Marine Science
Principles of Mathematics
Principles of Microbiology
Principles of Modern Agriculture
Principles of Pharmacology
Principles of Physical Science
Principles of Physics
Principles of Programming & Coding
Principles of Robotics & Artificial Intelligence
Principles of Scientific Research
Principles of Sports Medicine & Kinesiology
Principles of Sustainability
Principles of Zoology

Grey House Publishing | Salem Press | H.W. Wilson | 4919 Route, 22 PO Box 56, Amenia NY 12501-0056

2022 Title List

Visit www.SalemPress.com for Product Information, Table of Contents, and Sample Pages.

CAREERS

- Careers: Paths to Entrepreneurship
- Careers in Artificial Intelligence
- Careers in the Arts: Fine, Performing & Visual
- Careers in the Automotive Industry
- Careers in Biology
- Careers in Building Construction
- Careers in Business
- Careers in Chemistry
- Careers in Communications & Media
- Careers in Education & Training
- Careers in Engineering
- Careers in Environment & Conservation
- Careers in Financial Services
- Careers in Forensic Science
- Careers in Gaming
- Careers in Green Energy
- Careers in Healthcare
- Careers in Hospitality & Tourism
- Careers in Human Services
- Careers in Information Technology
- Careers in Law, Criminal Justice & Emergency Services
- Careers in the Music Industry
- Careers in Manufacturing & Production
- Careers in Nursing
- Careers in Physics
- Careers in Protective Services
- Careers in Psychology & Behavioral Health
- Careers in Public Administration
- Careers in Sales, Insurance & Real Estate
- Careers in Science & Engineering
- Careers in Social Media
- Careers in Sports & Fitness
- Careers in Sports Medicine & Training
- Careers in Technical Services & Equipment Repair
- Careers in Transportation
- Careers in Writing & Editing
- Careers Outdoors
- Careers Overseas
- Careers Working with Infants & Children
- Careers Working with Animals

BUSINESS

- Principles of Business: Accounting
- Principles of Business: Economics
- Principles of Business: Entrepreneurship
- Principles of Business: Finance
- Principles of Business: Globalization
- Principles of Business: Leadership
- Principles of Business: Management
- Principles of Business: Marketing

2022 Title List

Visit www.HWWilsonInPrint.com for Product Information, Table of Contents, and Sample Pages.

Core Collections

Children's Core Collection
Fiction Core Collection
Graphic Novels Core Collection
Middle & Junior High School Core
Public Library Core Collection: Nonfiction
Senior High Core Collection
Young Adult Fiction Core Collection

The Reference Shelf

Affordable Housing
Aging in America
Alternative Facts, Post-Truth and the Information War
The American Dream
Artificial Intelligence
The Business of Food
Campaign Trends & Election Law
College Sports
Democracy Evolving
The Digital Age
Embracing New Paradigms in Education
Food Insecurity & Hunger in the United States
Future of U.S. Economic Relations: Mexico, Cuba, & Venezuela
Global Climate Change
Guns in America
Hate Crimes
Immigration
Income Inequality
Internet Abuses & Privacy Rights
Internet Law
LGBTQ in the 21st Century
Marijuana Reform
Mental Health Awareness
National Debate Topic 2014/2015: The Ocean
National Debate Topic 2015/2016: Surveillance
National Debate Topic 2016/2017: US/China Relations
National Debate Topic 2017/2018: Education Reform
National Debate Topic 2018/2019: Immigration
National Debate Topic 2019/2021: Arms Sales
National Debate Topic 2020/2021: Criminal Justice Reform
National Debate Topic 2021/2022: Water Resources
National Debate Topic 2022/2023
New Frontiers in Space
Policing in 2020
Pollution
Prescription Drug Abuse
Propaganda and Misinformation
Racial Tension in a Postracial Age
Reality Television
Representative American Speeches, Annual Editions
Rethinking Work
Revisiting Gender
The South China Sea Conflict
Sports in America
The Supreme Court
The Transformation of American Cities
The Two Koreas
UFOs
Vaccinations
Voters' Rights
Whistleblowers

Current Biography

Current Biography Cumulative Index 1946-2021
Current Biography Monthly Magazine
Current Biography Yearbook

Readers' Guide to Periodical Literature

Abridged Readers' Guide to Periodical Literature
Readers' Guide to Periodical Literature

Indexes

Index to Legal Periodicals & Books
Short Story Index
Book Review Digest

Sears List

Sears List of Subject Headings
Sears: Lista de Encabezamientos de Materia

History

American Game Changers: Invention, Innovation & Transformation
American Reformers
Speeches of the American Presidents

Facts About Series

Facts About the 20th Century
Facts About American Immigration
Facts About China
Facts About the Presidents
Facts About the World's Languages

Nobel Prize Winners

Nobel Prize Winners: 1901-1986
Nobel Prize Winners: 1987-1991
Nobel Prize Winners: 1992-1996
Nobel Prize Winners: 1997-2001
Nobel Prize Winners: 2002-2018

Famous First Facts

Famous First Facts
Famous First Facts About American Politics
Famous First Facts About Sports
Famous First Facts About the Environment
Famous First Facts: International Edition

American Book of Days

The American Book of Days
The International Book of Days

Grey House Publishing | Salem Press | H.W. Wilson | 4919 Route, 22 PO Box 56, Amenia NY 12501-0056